P9-CEK-123

Bob Hyldburg

TOTAL PATRIOTS

The Definitive Encyclopedia
of the World-Class Franchise

TRIUMPH
BOOKS

To the Holy Spirit for giving me the patience and the passion to finish this labor of love.

To my wonderful wife and best friend, Millie Ridge Hyldburg. Her willingness to sacrifice our time together over many countless nights and weekends allowed me to maintain my intense focus to complete this insane quest for perfection. She was tremendously encouraging, supportive, and loving. Thank you, my dearest love.

This book is available in quantity at special discounts for your group or organization. For further information, contact:

Triumph Books
542 South Dearborn Street
Suite 750
Chicago, Illinois 60605
(312) 939-3330
Fax (312) 663-3557
www.triumphbooks.com

Printed in the U.S.A.
ISBN: 978-1-60078-099-8
Design by Patricia Frey
Photos courtesy of the *Boston Globe* and the author

Contents

Foreword

As we all know, the New England Patriots Football Club has a long and colorful history filled with memorable players, coaches, owners, and most of all, memorable moments for faithful fans. I was fortunate to be among the original Patriots players in 1960, and I have been privileged to maintain a relationship with the Patriots either as a player, a coach, a newsman, or as a radio broadcaster ever since. I have witnessed a lot of Patriots history but have never been able to sit down and see all of it so meticulously detailed in one single book.

Now Bob Hyldburg has completed the most comprehensive compilation of Patriots statistics ever assembled in one volume. It is an amazingly detailed accounting of every Patriots regular season and playoff game, recalling all the most significant touchdowns, field goals, extra points, fumbles, interceptions, safeties, and other memorable moments in Patriots history. You name it—you will find it in this book.

Total Patriots also contains detailed statistical and interesting personal information on every player who has ever worn the red, white, and blue of the Pats. Not only is every imaginable Patriots historical statistic presented, but the book is also filled with entertaining vintage photos and illustrations—including rare original Patriots program covers and other long-forgotten Patriots-related material.

Many different games, from horseshoes to professional baseball, have been called "a game of inches." Bob Hyldburg clearly made the case that football is not just a game measured in first downs, but that it too reflects the precision of a game where a measurement as small as an inch can mean the difference between victory and defeat.

Baseball has long been known as a game where statistics, batting averages, and every other conceivable measurement of team and player performance are of interest and importance to its fans. Recognizing that football, too, is a game of great and often subtle detail, Bob Hyldburg has assembled a book that illustrates the same kind of specificity long associated with baseball for Patriots football fans. Hyldburg has created a book for football "fanatics" to savor and help them recall the most memorable moments in Patriots history in amazing detail. It is sure to be a book that every Patriots fan will enjoy and go back to time and time again to recall a special season, game, player, or play. It is a trivia aficionado's dream, and a volume that is sure to be the definitive source when settling a friendly football dispute or two!

—Gino Cappelletti

Acknowledgments

Much appreciation to Richard Johnson for allowing me to review the articles and archives of the New England Sports Museum.

Regards to Ron Hobson for introducing me to legendary football researcher and editor extraordinare Pete Palmer. Observing Pete's work ethic and professional approach while we researched many of these obscure facts was truly educational and sustained my hopes of completing this Tetris puzzle.

The insight I gained while reminiscing about the old days of the Boston Patriots with former employee Jack Grinold, former director of public relations Jack Nicholson, former radio announcer Fred Cusick, former assistant coaches Tom Yewcic and Gino Cappelletti, and former team trainer Bill Bates was very enlightening. It helped me gain perspective on life in the early days of the New England Patriots.

A great deal of gratitude is due Stacey James, the vice president of media relations for the New England Patriots, and his staff including Casey O'Connell, their director of media relations. Thanks for the encouragement and support from the Patriots Alumni Club Coordinator, Donna Spigarolo. I am very thankful to the many people who contributed to the material presented in the Patriots annual media guides.

Thanks to Kyle Psaty and his article about my journey in *Fray* magazine.

I was inspired by the recognition of the value of my research by such professionals as ESPN's *Mike and Mike in the Morning, The Mike Felger Show, The Russ Francis Show, The Drive* on 1320-AM with David DiLorenzo, *Sporting News Radio* with Kevin Koffman and Phil Castinetti, and WDEV Radio in Burlington, Vermont, with Jeff Fuller.

I certainly appreciated the on-air publicity from the WTKK *Sports Huddle* radio show with Eddie Andelman regarding the Pro Football Hall of Fame credentials that I presented on behalf of Gino Cappelletti. It was exciting sharing my statistics on the Pro Football Hall of Fame career of Andre Tippett with WEEI Sports Radio host Mike Adams.

I recognize the excellent and enthusiastic editing efforts by Neal Biron and Father Dave Meskell.

Kudos to Phil Castinetti, Roger Muir, Andy Bedard, Bill Hedin, and the late Norm Resha, as they allowed me to interview their guests as they signed autographs during card shows.

I truly value my new friendship with Patriots Hall of Famer Gino Cappelletti and am extremely grateful that he wrote the foreword for this book. I applaud the superb writing talents of Ben Cafardo and his creative contributions in the Player Profiles and Postseason Stories chapters.

I salute the value of the work performed by Lisa Tuite and her staff at the *Boston Globe* for researching and scanning the hundreds of action pictures.

My gratitude for the professional expertise of Adam Motin, Don Gulbrandsen, Tom Bast, Karen O'Brien and the staff of Triumph Books and for their having faith in my dream.

Thanks for the support and encouragement that I have always received from my dad, my mom, Jean Fisher, and my sisters, Darlene, Sherry, and Bonnie. Thank you to my extended family of cousins, in-laws, and my TKE fraternity brothers.

Introduction

As a lifelong fan of the Patriots, I have always enjoyed reliving the positive memorable moments of their games with my friends and family. After a discussion with my friend, Rick Brenna, in July 1995, I became frustrated at the lack of availability of certain historical facts about the Patriots. About a week later, I decided to fulfill my curiosity and conduct my own research regarding the team's entire history.

My former colleague, Linda Mae Cusick, recommended that I contact her friend and former star running back of the Boston Patriots, Ron Burton. He was the first player drafted by the Boston Patriots and the first player that I interviewed for this book.

Just a few years later, I became aware that Ron had been diagnosed with a rare disease and become deathly ill. At that time I had collected a substantial amount of information on the careers of many Boston Patriots players. Upon hearing this news, I presented his son, Steve, who is a sports anchor and reporter for WBZ-TV in Boston, a detailed breakdown of the numerous accomplishments of Ron's professional football career.

Steve had always wished that he could break down his father's five-year career with the Patriots. With Ron in the intensive-care unit of the hospital, they had the opportunity to accomplish that dream. Ron struggled but somehow found the strength to rise above his debilitating pain and relive some of these moments with his son. While Steve was reading my notes, his dad asked him, "Who did this?" and "Why did he do this?" My answer is that I believe that it is an honor, privilege, and an obligation to provide this material to every fan of the Patriots.

Many hours were spent reviewing the archives of the New England Sports Museum and microfilm at various local libraries. Thanks to the cooperation and assistance of the Patriots Media Relations Department, I was able to review the play-by-play description of *every* play of *every* Patriots game at my leisure.

Former Patriots beat reporter Ron Hobson introduced me to former Patriots chief statistician Ed Brickley and current football statistician and editor Pete Palmer. Two other former Patriots employees who assisted me during my quest were Jack Grinold, who was the third person hired by the Boston Patriots, and Jack Nicholson, who was the director of public relations for the Boston Patriots for a few seasons.

Bill Tierney Jr. introduced me to (the late) legendary reporter Will McDonough. Will was fascinated by the amount of material I was assembling and inspired me to continue my labor of love until it was complete.

Certainly the length of time that it has taken me to complete this book has been challenging for my wife. When I shared my story with Ron "Jaws" Jaworski and John "Hog" Hannah, they both responded with the same question: "Do you have a life?" (My wife and I celebrated our 19th wedding anniversary a few months ago.)

Thanks to Phil Castinetti, I was able to interview many former Boston Patriots legends, including Gino Cappelletti, Nick Buoniconti, Houston Antwine, Tom Addison, Larry Eisenhauer, Larry Garron, and their former team trainer, Bill Bates.

I've had the pleasure of meeting many former and current players, including Tom Brady, Russ Francis, "Babe" Parilli, Brent Williams, Mosi Tatupu, John Smith, Pete Brock, Tedy Bruschi, Tim Fox, Steve Grogan, Ronnie Lippett, Steve Nelson, Garin Veris, Steve King, Raymond Clayborn, Fred Smerlas, Mike Haynes, and

Andre Tippett. I conversed with Clayton Weishuhn and ESPN's Chris Berman at the celebration party of Andre Tippett's induction to the Pro Football Hall of Fame in Canton, Ohio.

Boston Globe writer Nick Cafardo identified me as one of the more creative historians of the Patriots. I was one of the intrepid archivists who helped Charlie Pierce on his story about Bob Gladieux for his book about Tom Brady, *Moving the Chains.*

Stacey James, the vice president of media relations for the New England Patriots, granted me the access to review the team's archives. While doing some research at Gillette Stadium in 2004, Stacey offered me a part-time job with the NFL. I've been working for the NFL at every Patriots home game since the 2005 season.

This book would not be complete without the contributions from Ben Cafardo and the fantastic pictures from the *Boston Globe.*

TOTAL PATRIOTS

Down Through the Seasons

The American Football League announced on 11-16-59 that it had awarded the eighth and final franchise to William H. Sullivan Jr. Ron Burton was drafted with the first pick on 11-22-59. Mike Holovak, the team's first employee, was hired as the director of player personnel. He also worked as an assistant coach and then became the second head coach.

Jack Grinold, the third employee, was given the task of running a fan contest to help choose the team's name. Through the different media outlets, people were asked to submit an appropriate name for this new team. Local high school kids were then asked to write an essay as to which of the top three names submitted would best represent this new football team from Boston. The winning name, the Boston Patriots, was announced, and the uniform colors were established as red, white, and blue on 02-20-60.

Walt Pingree designed the first team logo. It was a tri-corner hat similar to what a colonial minuteman wore. This logo was only used during the 1960 season. Phil Bissell, a cartoonist from the *Boston Globe*, drew a picture of a Patriots player snapping the ball, and team owner Billy Sullivan liked this image so much that it was used for everything related to promoting and merchandising the team. The "Pat Patriot" logo was used for the 1961 season and lasted until the end of the 1992 season. The team displayed their new logo, a silhouette of a man's face wearing a streamlined minuteman hat on 03-31-93. The uniform colors were also changed to blue, silver, red, and white.

The Patriots opened training camp at the University of Massachusetts on 07-08-60. In the first American Football League exhibition game, the Boston Patriots defeated the Buffalo Bills 30–7 at War Memorial Stadium. Boston Patriots defensive end Bob Dee scored the first points in the AFL when he recovered a fumble in the end zone for a touchdown.

1960
Record 5–9; Fourth place in the AFL Eastern Division
The WEEI Radio 590 AM Radio announcers were Bob "Potsie" Gallagher and Fred Cusick

The Patriots lost the first game to the Denver Broncos 13–10, and then defeated the New York Titans 28–24 at the Polo Grounds. In the first victory, the Patriots scored the game-winning touchdown on the last play of the game because of a mishandled snap by the Titans punter, Rick Sapienza. All he had to do was catch the snap and run out the clock. Unfortunately, he dropped it. The loose ball was recovered by Chuck Shonta, who took it 54 yards for the touchdown. Later in the inaugural season, the Patriots won three in a row by defeating the Oakland Raiders 34–28, New York Titans 38–21, and Dallas Texans 42–14. The team finished its season losing the last four games and had a record of 5–9. Lou Saban was the head coach.

* * *

The Play of the Year was made by Bob Dee. Dee used his body to protect a young boy who was running toward the field for a ball that was fumbled into the end zone on the game's last play in a 45–16 loss to the Chargers at BU Field on 10-28-60. The problem was

The Boston Patriots Team Leaders in 1960
Offensive Team
Butch Songin tossed 22 TD passes
Jim Colclough had nine TD receptions
Dick Christy had four rushing TDs
Defensive/Special Teams
Gino Cappelletti and Harry Jacobs had four interceptions
Chuck Shonta returned a fumble 54 yards for a TD
Jack Rudolph recovered four fumbles
Harry Jacobs had four sacks
Memorable Statistic of the Year
Gino Cappelletti intercepted three passes and ran for a two-point conversion in the same game.

Gino Cappelletti

that the play had not been whistled dead. Dee smothered the kid before several large linemen and a running back fell on the ball. Chargers running back Don Rodgers recovered the ball in the end zone for the Chargers, and the Patriots defense piled on top of him for a safety. The boy was not hurt thanks to the quick reaction of the former U.S. Marine and Boston Patriots defensive end.

The Game of the Year was played against the Los Angeles Chargers at the Los Angeles Memorial Coliseum on 10-08-60.

Gino Cappelletti kicked a 23-yard field goal to cap an 11-play drive on the Patriots' first offensive series. Patriots linebacker Jack Rudolph recovered a fumble by Don Norton on the ensuing kickoff, and that turnover helped set up the Patriots' first touchdown. Ron Burton ran for a four-yard touchdown, and Cappelletti tossed a pass to Jim Crawford for the two-point conversion.

The Patriots held the Chargers on their first offensive series and forced Paul Maguire to punt. Butch Songin tossed a 19-yard touchdown pass to Jim Colclough on the Patriots' second series of downs. Billy Wells caught a pass from Butch Songin and rambled for a 78-yard gain to the 5-yard line. "Cowboy" Jim Crawford bulled through the line for a one-yard touchdown for the Patriots.

Patriots linebacker Harry Jacobs returned an interception of Jack Kemp 12 yards that helped set up the next touchdown scored by the Patriots. On first down, Butch Songin's pass that was intended for Jim Colclough hit the goal post and went incomplete. On second down, Patriots running back Dick Christy ran for a seven-yard gain. On third down, Wells ran up the middle for a one-yard touchdown.

Cappelletti kicked a 33-yard field goal later in the game to complete the scoring on the day.

The Chargers quarterback, Bobby Clatterbuck, was sacked twice. Kemp was sacked once and was intercepted by Clyde Washington in the end zone very late in the game to secure the 35–0 shutout of the Chargers. The Los Angeles Chargers recovered from this embarrassing regular season defeat, but ultimately lost to the Houston Oilers 24–16 in the 1960 AFL Championship Game.

1961

Record 9-4-1; Second place in the AFL Eastern Division
The WEEI 590 AM Radio announcers were Bob Gallagher and Fred Cusick

Mike Holovak replaced Lou Saban as the Boston Patriots' head coach after the fifth game of the 1961 AFL season.

To open the 1961 season, the Patriots lost a tough game, 21–20, to the New York Titans at BU Field. They came back strong with a 45–17 trouncing of the Denver Broncos and then squeaked out a 23–21 win over Buffalo. Later in the season, they tied the Houston Oilers 31–31. Team owner Billy Sullivan rescheduled their first game against the Buffalo Bills because of a hurricane's "potential threat." The hurricane never arrived, but the Patriots blew away the Buffalo Bills, 52–21, in the game that was played two days later on 10-22-61. They beat the Dallas Texans twice within a six-day span and finished the season with four straight victories. In the last game of this season, the defense held the Chargers to only two total yards rushing in the 41–0 shutout of San Diego on 12-17-61.

* * *

Larry Garron was responsible for the 1961 Play of the Year. He galloped 85 yards for a touchdown in the 55–21 rout of the Buffalo Bills at BU Field on 10-22-61. This is still the longest run from scrimmage by a Patriots player in a regular season game.

The Unforgettable Moment of the Year was made by a fan. This person was on the field in the end zone and disrupted a potential two-yard, game-tying touchdown pass on the last play of the game in the Patriots' 28–21 win over the Dallas Texans at BU Field on 11-03-61. Some 5,000 people were sold standing-room-only tickets, and the excess crowd had surrounded the field. With very little time on the clock, Texans receiver Chris Burford caught a 40-yard pass to bring the ball to the 2-yard line. Many of the fans standing along the sidelines rushed the field thinking that the game was over. The officials decided that the Texans could have one more

> **1961 Boston Patriots Team Leaders**
> *Offensive Team*
> Butch Songin threw 14 TD passes
> Jim Colclough had nine TD receptions
> Billy Lott and Babe Parilli had five TD runs
>
> *Defensive/Special Teams*
> Don Webb had five INTs, returned two for TDs
> Larry Garron and Ron Burton had kickoff returns for TDs
> Don Webb returned two fumbles for a TD
> LeRoy Moore recovered a blocked punt for a TD
> Bob Dee recovered five fumbles
> Rommie Loudd had eight sacks
>
> **Memorable Statistics of the Year**
> Gino Cappelletti led both leagues with 147 points scored.
> The Boston Patriots had seven AFL All-Star players in
>   1961.

play. One fan decided to stay on the field, however. Burford ran a slant pattern and was open, but this "man in the trenchcoat" cut in front of Burford and probably prevented the pass completion. When asked about the play after the game, Gino Cappelletti thought that the pass was overthrown and would have gone incomplete.

The Game of the Year was their 18–17 victory over the Dallas Texans at the Cotton Bowl on 10-29-61. Rommie Loudd sacked Randy Duncan to stop the Texans' first drive of the game. On the next Texans series, Don Webb hit Johnny Robinson after his reception for a loss of one yard and forced him to fumble. Webb then recovered and returned the fumble 49 yards for a touchdown.

Fred Bruney knocked out Abner Hayes, but the Texans moved down the field and Ben Agajanian kicked a 25-yard field goal.

Bob Dee and Loudd combined to sack quarterback Randy Duncan, forcing the Texans to attempt a long field goal that was short. Jim Crawford, who was attempting a half back option pass, was then intercepted by Dave Webster, which gave the ball back to the Texans. Ben Agajanian attempted a field goal, but it was no good.

Jerry Mays blocked a punt by Tom Yewcic and Ed Keely recovered the loose ball that helped set up the Texans' first touchdown. Cotton Davidson tossed a 10-yard touchdown pass to Max Boydston.

Patriots linebacker Loudd sacked Cotton Davidson forcing another long field-goal attempt that Ben Agajanian missed.

Davidson moved the Texans down the field and completed a 24-yard touchdown pass to Burford to take a 17–7 lead with 4:44 left.

The Patriots responded as Ron Burton took a pass by Butch Songin 45 yards before he was tackled by Smokey Stover and Dave Grayson. Jim Colclough ran a flanker reverse for a 16-yard gain and then Butch Songin tossed a four-yard touchdown pass to Joe Johnson. From the extra point kicking formation, holder Babe Parilli took the snap and ran it in for a two-point conversion.

Davidson misfired on a third-and-nine play allowing the Patriots to get the ball back with 1:36 left in the game. Songin completed an 18-yard pass to Cappelletti. Babe Parilli then completed an 11-yard pass to Cappelletti. (The Patriots alternated quarterbacks on successive plays throughout the 1961 season.) On the final play of the game, Cappelletti kicked a game-winning 24-yard field goal to defeat the Dallas Texans 18–17. Note: After the 1963 season, the Dallas Texans moved to Kansas City and became the Kansas City Chiefs.

1962

Record 9–4–1; Second place in the AFL Eastern Division
The WEEI 590 AM Radio announcers were Bob Gallagher and Fred Cusick

As in 1961, the 1962 team finished 9–4–1 but did not make the playoffs. The Patriots defeated the Houston Oilers 34–21 at Harvard Stadium on 09-16-62, destroyed the Denver Broncos 41–16 at BU Field on 09-21-62, crushed the Titans 43–14 at the Polo Grounds, and lost to the Dallas Texans at BU Field. The team beat the Chargers and Raiders in successive weeks and then tied with the Buffalo Bills on the road. The Patriots beat Denver in Denver but lost to Houston in Houston. The team finished strong and defeated the Bills, NY Titans, and Chargers but was shutout by the Oakland Raiders 20–0 in the season's last game.

* * *

The Play of the Year was made by Ron Burton. Burton returned a missed field goal by Gene Mingo 91 yards for a touchdown in the 33–29 victory over the Denver Broncos on 11-11-62. This is the only time that a Patriots player has returned a missed field goal for a touchdown.

The Game of the Year was played against the Houston Oilers at Harvard Stadium on 09-16-62. The Patriots defeated the two-time AFL champion Houston Oilers 34–21.

The game started off with some sloppy play as there was an unnecessary roughness penalty on the Patriots

---

1962 Boston Patriots Team Leaders
Offensive Team
Babe Parilli tossed 18 TD passes
Jim Colclough had 10 TD receptions
Five players each had two rushing TDs

Defensive/Special Teams
Ross O'Hanley, Dick Felt, and Tom Addison had five interceptions
Tom Addison, Ron Hall, and Fred Bruney took a pass for a TD
Larry Garron returned a kickoff 95 yards for a TD
Bob Dee and Rommie Loudd recovered two fumbles
Larry Eisenhauer had 5.5 sacks

The Memorable Statistics of the Year
Ron Burton returned a missed field goal 91 yards for a touchdown.
The Boston Patriots had six AFL All-Star players in 1962.

---

during the opening kickoff. The Oilers moved the ball on their first drive, but George Blanda missed a field-goal attempt. Gino Cappelletti returned the favor when he missed his first field-goal attempt.

Babe Parilli (15)

Charley Hennigan scored the first touchdown of the game with his 78-yard touchdown reception from Blanda. Larry Garron evened the score with his 63-yard touchdown reception from Babe Parilli on the last play of the first quarter. Three plays later, Hennigan scored on a 49-yard touchdown pass from Blanda. Not to be outdone, Garron took the next kickoff 36 yards and Ron Burton dashed 59 yards for a touchdown.

Ross O'Hanley stopped the next Oilers drive with his 16-yard interception return of a George Blanda pass. Babe Parilli moved the Patriots down the field. On third-and-goal, Jim Colclough made a diving catch of a five-yard pass from Babe Parilli for the touchdown.

The Oilers responded on the next series as Blanda tossed a 40-yard touchdown pass to Bob McLeod to tie the score at 21–21. Parilli moved the Patriots into Houston territory by completing passes of 12 yards and 17 yards to Tony Romeo. Gino Cappelletti then kicked a 46-yard field goal on the last play of the first half.

In the third quarter, the Oiler's long drive stalled. Blanda's tough angle 10-yard field-goal attempt was no good as it went wide left.

Garron's 28-yard run helped set up a 20-yard field goal by Cappelletti.

Two interceptions by the Patriots kept the Oilers off the scoreboard for the rest of the game. Fred Bruney returned an interception of Blanda 21 yards from his own 12-yard line to stop a Houston drive. Another pass by Blanda was batted in the air by Tom Addison and intercepted by Dick Felt, who returned it 17 yards to halt another Houston drive.

Parilli put the game away when he faked going inside on third-and-2 and took it outside for a 32-yard touchdown. Gino Cappelletti kicked the point after touchdown for the final point scored in the game. Blanda was intercepted once again by Patriots defensive back Dick Felt in the end zone for a touchback. Parilli ran for a three-yard gain on the next play to end the game.

1963

Record 7–6–1; Tied for first place in the AFL Eastern Division
The WEEI 590 AM Radio announcers were Bob Gallagher and Fred Cusick

The Boston Patriots defeated the New York Jets, formerly known as the New York Titans, 38–14 in the home opening game at Boston College Alumni Stadium on 09-08-63. The Patriots played the rest of their home games at Fenway Park in 1963. The Patriots defeated the Oakland Raiders twice by the same score of 20–14, beat Denver 40–21 at Fenway Park, lost to the Bills in Buffalo, and smoked Houston 45–3 at Fenway Park. San Diego beat the Patriots 7–6 at Fenway Park, and the Kansas City Chiefs tied the Patriots 24–24 at Fenway Park the next week. The Buffalo Bills came to Fenway Park and lost to the Patriots 17–7, and the Patriots defeated the Oilers 46–28 on the road in Houston. The team was in every game until they were smoked, 35–3, by the Chiefs in the last game of the year. The Patriots tied for first place in the division and made the playoffs for the first time.

The Patriots defeated the Buffalo Bills 26–8 at War Memorial Stadium for the AFL Eastern Division Championship. Ron Burton was allowed to play in this

> **1963 Boston Patriots Team Leaders**
> *Offensive Team*
> Babe Parilli tossed 13 TD passes
> Art Graham had five TD receptions
> Harry Crump and Babe Parilli had five TD runs
>
> *Defensive/Special Teams*
> Bob Suci had seven interceptions, returning two for TDs
> Jim Lee Hunt returned an interception 78 yards for a TD
> Nick Buoniconti returned a fumble seven yards for a TD
> Nick Buoniconti and Bob Dee recovered three fumbles
> Larry Eisenhauer had nine sacks
>
> **Memorable Statistics of the Year**
> Gino Cappelletti led both leagues with 113 points scored.
> The Boston Patriots had 11 AFL All-Star players in 1963.

playoff game even though he missed the entire regular season due to a back surgery. Burton caught the first pass by a Patriots player in a playoff game. The Boston Patriots were crushed by the San Diego Chargers 51–10 in the 1963 AFL Championship Game at Balboa Stadium on 01-05-64.

* * *

The Play of the Year was made by Jim Lee "Earthquake" Hunt. Hunt returned an interception 78 yards for a touchdown in the fourth quarter in a 45–3 rout of the Houston Oilers at Fenway Park on 11-01-63.

The Game of the Year was played against the Oakland Raiders at Fenway Park on 10-11-63. This was the Patriots' first regular season game ever played at Fenway Park. The Patriots stopped the Raiders, forcing them to punt on their fourth play of the game. Gino Cappelletti kicked a 37-yard field goal on the fifth play of the first drive.

The Patriots defense loved to blitz. Announcer Bob Gallagher would often exclaim, "Katie bar the door!" when the Patriots were in the process of sacking the quarterback.

Patriots linebacker Nick Buoniconti sacked Tom Flores, forcing the Raiders to punt again. Ross O'Hanley returned a Flores pass 61 yards to halt another Raiders drive. On first-and-goal from the 6-yard line, Babe Parilli was intercepted in the end zone for a touchback. The Raiders defense held.

Tom Addison

Jim McMillin took his second interception of Parilli 47 yards for a touchdown to put the Raiders up by the score of 7–3.

Patriots defensive back Ross O'Hanley intercepted a pass by Tom Flores on the Patriots 5-yard line and was able to return it seven yards to the 12-yard line. The Patriots were not able to move the ball and had to punt. (Tom Addison stole the ball from Flores and took it 26 yards for a touchdown, but penalties on both sides voided the play). Cotton Davidson replaced Flores and he scored on an 11-yard run in the third quarter.

The Patriots came back strong and scored the final 17 points in the game. Jim Colclough made a diving catch of a 44-yard pass on the 12-yard line, got up, and scampered in untouched for a 56-yard touchdown reception.

Patriots defensive end Larry Eisenhauer then strip-sacked Flores and returned the fumble seven yards to help set up a 32-yard field goal by Cappelletti.

Patriots defensive back Ross O'Hanley returned a fumble by Bo Roberson six yards to get the ball back for the offensive team. On the first play of the fourth quarter, quarterback Babe Parilli rolled out of the pocket and found Tom Neumann in the end zone for a 15-yard touchdown.

Patriots safety Chuck Shonta intercepted a long pass by Flores on the Patriots 8-yard line, and the Patriots were able to run out the clock in the 20–14 victory over the Oakland Raiders.

1964
Record 10–3–1; Second place in the AFL Eastern Division
The WEEI 590 AM Radio announcers were Bob Gallagher and Fred Cusick

In 1964, the Patriots won 10 regular season games. They won their first four games of the season beating the Raiders, Chargers, Jets, and Broncos. They lost their first game of the season to the Chargers and then tied the Raiders 43–43. (This is the highest combined scoring game in team history). They defeated the Kansas City Chiefs at Fenway Park but then lost to the Jets at Shea Stadium. They went on a five-game winning streak as they defeated the Oilers by one point, the Bills by eight points, the Broncos by five points, the Oilers by 17, and then the Chiefs by seven points. The Patriots lost to the Buffalo Bills 24–14, during a huge snow storm that delayed the start of the game by an hour, in the last game of the year. Their loss to the Bills eliminated them from the playoffs. The Buffalo Bills went on to win AFL Championship Game over the San Diego Chargers.

* * *

The Play of the Year was made by Gino Cappelletti. He kicked a 41-yard field goal to defeat the Houston Oilers 25–24 at Fenway Park on 11-06-64. Babe Parilli, who, on the previous play, ran out of bounds after a 10-yard run leaving just one second on the clock, called it, "The greatest clutch kick I have ever seen."

The Game of the Year was played on Friday night against the Houston Oilers at Fenway Park on 11-06-64. Quarterback Babe Parilli had eight carries for 96 yards and two touchdowns, and Art Graham had eight receptions for 167 yards.

Patriots running back J.D. Garrett fumbled the opening kickoff and Houston capitalized just a few

> **1964 Boston Patriots Team Leaders**
> *Offensive Team*
> Babe Parilli tossed 31 TD passes
> G. Cappelletti and L. Garron caught seven TDs
> Ron Burton had three rushing TDs
>
> *Defensive/Special Teams*
> Ron Hall had 11 interceptions
> Ross O'Hanley returned an interception 47 yards for a TD
> Larry Eisenhauer recovered four fumbles
> Larry Eisenhauer recorded 7.5 sacks
>
> **Memorable Statistics of the Year**
> Gino Cappelletti led both leagues with 155 points scored.
> The Boston Patriots had nine AFL All-Star players in 1964.

plays later. Charley Tolar scored on a two-yard run for a touchdown. Garrett returned the next kickoff 27 yards, and Parilli led the Patriots on a 16-play touchdown drive. Parilli had a 19-yard run on a bootleg play during this impressive drive, and on third-and-goal he took it in himself for a one-yard touchdown run.

George Blanda led the Oilers back into Patriots territory and on fourth-and-2 they tried a fake field goal pass. Holder Don Trull took the direct snap but only completed a one-yard pass that gave the Patriots back the ball. Parilli directed the Patriots on an 11-play drive that concluded with a 25-yard field goal by Gino Cappelletti.

On the Patriots' last possession of the first half, Barilli had another 19-yard run from scrimmage, and Cappelletti hit a 33-yard field goal with six seconds left to take a 13–7 lead.

The second half kickoff by Patriots lineman Bob Yates hit the goal post, giving the ball to the Oilers on their 20-yard line. On the first play of the second half, Houston Oilers tight end Willie Frazier caught an 80-yard touchdown pass from Blanda.

The next time Houston had the ball on offense they moved into Patriots territory only to have Blanda miss a 23-yard field goal. Patriots linebacker Nick Buoniconti stopped the Oilers on the next possession as he returned an interception of Blanda 26 yards from his own 18-yard line. The Oilers defense held, and the Patriots punted.

Blanda continued his air attack and threw a 38-yard touchdown pass to wide receiver Charley Frazier, giving the Oilers a 21–16 lead. Parilli was just as determined to lead his team to victory. He had another 19-yard run, and later in the drive rolled around his right side for a five-yard touchdown to give his team a two-point cushion. Parilli's two-point pass to Jim Crawford fell incomplete.

With limited time left in the game, Blanda was able to move his team into field-goal position. Blanda then kicked a 10-yard field goal with 32 seconds left to put the Oilers up by one point.

Not to be outdone, Parilli completed a 14-yard pass to Tony Romeo and then a 22-yard pass to Cappelletti. Parilli was flushed from the pocket and dashed for 10 yards before running out of bounds with one second on the clock. Cappelletti then kicked the game-winning 42-yard field goal on the game's last play to defeat the Houston Oilers 25–24. Cappelletti was awarded the game ball.

1965

Record 4–8–2; Third place in the AFL Eastern Division
The WEEI 590 AM Radio announcers were Bob Gallagher and Ned Martin

A tough year for the Patriots; the team lost its first five games of the 1965 season. The team tied the 1964 AFL runner-up San Diego Chargers 13–13 at Fenway Park and two weeks later soundly defeated the Chargers 22–6 in San Diego. They tied the Kansas City Chiefs 10–10 and then finished the season with three consecutive victories on their way to a 4–8–2 record. Cappelletti set an AFL record by scoring 28 points in the 42–14 rout of the Houston Oilers at Fenway Park in the last game of the 1965 season.

* * *

The Play of the Year was made by Patriots defensive back Ron Hall. He blocked a 28-yard field-goal attempt by Tommy Brooker with 26 seconds left in the 10–10 tie with the Kansas City Chiefs at Fenway Park on 11-21-65.

The Game of the Year was played against the New York Jets at Shea Stadium on 11-28-65. Ron Burton led the Patriots with 29 yards rushing. Linebacker Mike Dukes returned the opening kickoff by Jim Turner nine yards. The Patriots were not able to move the ball and were forced to punt. Joe Namath fumbled the snap on the Jets' first offensive play, and Dukes recovered the loose ball. After a 25-yard reception by Jim Whalen, Gino Cappelletti kicked a 33-yard field goal.

The Jets moved the ball down to the Patriots 7-yard line but were only able to get three points as Turner

1965 Boston Patriots Team Leaders
Offensive Team
Babe Parilli tossed 18 TD passes
Gino Cappelletti caught nine TDs
Jim Nance ran for five TDs

Defensive/Special Teams
Nick Buoniconti and Ron Hall had three interceptions
Jack Rudolph recovered three fumbles
Larry Eisenhauer recorded 9.5 sacks

Memorable Statistics of the Year
Gino Cappelletti set the AFL record by scoring 28 points in a regular season game.
The Boston Patriots had four AFL All-Star players in 1965.

kicked a 14-yard field goal. On the Jets' next possession, Joe Namath took them all the way to the end zone as he tossed a 50-yard touchdown pass to wide receiver Bake Turner.

Parilli led the Patriots on a 14-play drive to start the third quarter that resulted in a 53-yard field goal by Cappelletti. Namath was sacked by Charley Long and Mike Dukes for a loss of 13 yards. Namath was then sacked by Houston Antwine and Jim Lee Hunt for a loss of 14 yards, and the Jets were forced to punt.

The Patriots took possession after a fair catch at midfield. Parilli had a seven-yard run and then was replaced by Eddie Wilson. Eddie moved the Patriots into the red zone of the Jets and then tossed an eight-yard touchdown pass to Jim Colclough.

Ross O'Hanley intercepted Namath on the Jets' next series of downs, and that turnover led to another score by the Patriots. Parilli was back in the game, and he completed a 27-yard touchdown pass to Jim Colclough, giving his team a 20–10 lead at the end of the third quarter.

Not to be outdone, Namath marched his team down the field, and Matt Snell ran it in for a five-yard touchdown. After a punt by the Patriots, Namath completed two long passes to Don Maynard of 35 and 32 yards. Patriots defensive back Jay Cunningham then made a nice play breaking up a Namath pass intended for Bake Turner at the goal line. Namath did complete a 10-yard pass to Turner on third-and-11 though, and

the Jets had to settle for an 11-yard field goal from Jim Turner.

Parilli was intercepted by Willie West, and the Jets took advantage of this turnover when Turner kicked a 26-yard field goal.

Larry Garron had a 35-yard return on the ensuing kickoff. Big plays from Jim Colclough, who had an 18-yard reception, and Cappelletti, who had a 34-yard reception, moved the Patriots into scoring territory. On second-and-goal, Ron Burton ran for a seven-yard gain. After an incomplete pass on third-and-goal, Parilli tossed a two-yard touchdown pass to Patriots tight end Tony Romeo with 54 seconds to go in the game.

Jack Rudolph recovered the fumbled kickoff return by Dainard Paulson, giving the Patriots the ball back. After four runs without a first down, the Jets regained possession but were not able to score, and the Patriots defeated the New York Jets 27–23.

1966

Record 8–4–2; Second place in the AFL Eastern Division
The WBZ 1030 AM Radio announcers were Bob Starr and Gil Santos

The Patriots bounced back to an 8–4–2 record in 1966. They were shut out by the Chargers in San Diego to open the season. The Patriots defeated the Broncos in Denver, lost to the Chiefs at Fenway Park, tied the New York Jets at Fenway Park, and beat the Bills in Buffalo. Home victories over the Chargers and Raiders had them at 4–2–1 midway through the season. The team lost at home to the Broncos, defeated the Oilers at Fenway Park, and tied the Chiefs 27–27 at Municipal Stadium. The Patriots beat the Dolphins in Miami, had a huge victory over the Bills at Fenway Park, and crushed the Oilers in Houston. Had they defeated Joe Namath and the New York Jets at Shea Stadium in the last game of the season they would have made the playoffs and might have been in the first Super Bowl.

* * *

The Play of the Year was a made by Jim Nance. He dashed 65 yards for a touchdown in the 14–3 victory over the Buffalo Bills in "The Game" at Fenway Park on 12-04-66.

The Game of the Year was played against the Buffalo Bills at Fenway Park on 12-04-66. Defensive Tackle John "Jumbo" Mangum returned the opening kickoff by Booth Lusteg eight yards, but the Patriots failed to get a first down and had to punt.

1966 Boston Patriots Team Leaders
Offensive Team
Babe Parilli tossed 20 TD passes
Gino Cappelletti caught six TDs
Jim Nance ran for 11 TDs

Defensive/Special Teams
Ron Hall and Tom Hennessey had six interceptions
Jim Lee Hunt returned a fumble five yards for a TD
Bob Dee recovered three fumbles
Jim Lee Hunt recorded nine sacks

Memorable Statistics of the Year
Jim Nance led both leagues with 1,458 yards rushing, averaging more than 100 yards per game.
The Boston Patriots had 11 AFL All-Star players in 1966.

Jack Kemp moved the Bills to the Patriots' 13-yard line on their first series before Tom Hennessey intercepted one of Kemp's passes in the end zone for a touchback. The Patriots were forced to punt again, and Patriots safety Chuck Shonta prevented a Bills touchdown as he tackled Bobby Burnett after his 48-yard reception on the Patriots 8-yard line. The Bills had to settle for an 11-yard field goal by Booth Lusteg.

Jim Nance (35)

On third-and-2 from the Patriots' 35-yard line, Jim Nance broke through the Bills defense and dashed 65 yards for a touchdown. His run through the Bills defensive line made the cover of *Sports Illustrated* magazine. In the third quarter, Babe Parilli completed a 37-yard pass to Art Graham, and Joe Bellino caught a 20-yard pass on his back at the 5-yard line. Babe Parilli rolled to the right and ran it in to make the score 14–3.

Patriots linebacker Jim Fraser intercepted a pass by Kemp to stop the Bills. Patriots defensive end Larry Eisenhauer sacked Kemp to stop another drive by the Bills. Lonnie Farmer recovered a fumble by Daryle Lamonica to halt them once again. Jim Lee Hunt sacked Lamonica on successive plays, and his second sack forced Lamonica to fumble. Jim "Earthquake" Hunt recovered the fumble, but the Patriots could not take advantage of this turnover as a 41-yard field-goal attempt by Gino Cappelletti was blocked by Ron "The Dancing Bear" McDole.

The Bills moved the ball to the Patriots 1-yard line, but Allen Smith was stopped for no gain on the last play of the game. Head coach Mike Holovak presented the game ball to defensive back Don Webb.

1967

Record 3–10–1; Last place in the AFL Eastern Division
The WBZ 1030 AM Radio announcers were Bob Starr and Gil Santos

After a respectable campaign in 1966, the Patriots had a tough year in 1967 and fell to a 3–10–1 record. New England was the first AFL team to shut out Buffalo and did so convincingly with a 23–0 score at War Memorial Stadium on 09-24-67. The Patriots destroyed the Miami Dolphins 41–10 at Boston College Alumni Stadium and defeated the Houston Oilers 18–7 at Fenway Park on 11-05-67. The Patriots had to play a home game in San Diego because the Boston Red Sox were playing at Fenway Park in the 1967 World Series.

* * *

The Play of the Year was the last touchdown pass thrown by Boston Patriots quarterback Babe Parilli. He tossed a 19-yard touchdown pass to Bob Cappadona in the 41–32 loss to the Miami Dolphins at the Orange Bowl on 12-17-67.

The Game of the Year was played against the Miami Dolphins at Boston College Alumni Stadium on 10-15-67. This was the first trip to Boston for the Miami Dolphins. Miami had to punt after its first possession, but Leroy Mitchell fumbled on his punt return and

1967 Boston Patriots Team Leaders
Offensive Team
Babe Parilli tossed 19 TDs
Jim Whalen had five TD receptions
Jim Nance ran for seven TDs

Defensive/Special Teams
Nick Buoniconti and Don Webb had four interceptions
John Charles and Jay Cunningham returned a pass for a TD
J.D. Garrett recovered a blocked punt for a TD
Ed Philpott recovered three fumbles
Houston Antwine recorded six sacks

Memorable Statistics of the Year
Jim Whalen is the only player to have three touchdown receptions in a college game and a pro game at BC Stadium. Whalen had three touchdowns for Boston College in the win over BU and three for the Patriots in the win over Miami.
The Boston Patriots had seven AFL All-Star players in 1967.

Miami regained control. Rick Norton was sacked by Bob Dee, and Ed Philpott and the Dolphins had to settle for a 34-yard field goal by Gene Mingo.

Parilli completed a 30-yard pass to Jim Nance and then tossed a 17-yard touchdown pass to Larry Garron for the Patriots' first touchdown. In the second quarter, Babe tossed another touchdown pass to Garron, who took it 41 yards for the score.

Patriots defensive back Don Webb recovered a fumble by Joe Auer, and three plays later Jim Whalen caught a nine-yard touchdown pass from Parilli. Patriots linebacker Nick Buoniconti recovered a fumble by Jack Clancy, and after a two-yard run by Jim Nance and a 25-yard reception by Jim Whalen, Parilli threw another nine-yard touchdown pass to tight end Whalen.

Dick Westmoreland intercepted a Parilli pass on the Patriots' first series of the third quarter. Just two plays later, however, Don Webb returned an interception of Rick Norton 41 yards. On the next play, Jim Whalen hauled in a 41-yard touchdown pass from Parilli for his third touchdown reception in the game.

Miami came back after a roughing the punter penalty on the Patriots, and Rick Norton tossed a 29-yard touchdown pass to Joe Auer. In the fourth quarter, Dolphins linebacker John Bramlett blocked a field-goal attempt by Gino Cappelletti. The Patriots gave it right back when John Huarte's only pass attempt was intercepted by Bob Petrella.

The Patriots defense scored the final touchdown of the day. Patriots defensive back Jay Cunningham returned a pass by Norton 54 yards for a touchdown. Patriots linebacker Ray Ilg strip-sacked Rick Norton on fourth-and-goal with about one minute left in the game to end the final scoring opportunity for the Dolphins. The final score was 41–10.

1968

Record 4–10; Fourth place in the AFL Eastern Division
The WBZ 1030 AM Radio announcers were Bob Starr and Gil Santos

The last year that the Patriots played at Fenway Park was 1968. New England started off the season with a 16–7 win at Buffalo and then lost to the New York Jets 47–31 in a home game that was played at Legion Field in Birmingham, Alabama. The Patriots had to play in Alabama because they could not get a field in the Boston area. The Patriots were able to beat the Broncos in Denver and won home games against the Bills and Bengals to finish the season with a record of 4–10.

* * *

The Moment of the Year was during the halftime ceremony in the game against the Houston Oilers at Fenway Park on 10-13-68. The fans celebrated "Dee Day" as Bob Dee had his No. 89 retired by the Patriots. Bob was the first AFL player to have his uniform number retired.

The Play of the Year was made by Houston Antwine. Antwine sacked Dan Darragh for a loss of 10 yards, thereby forcing a long field goal that was short, near the end of the first half, in the 16–7 win over the Buffalo Bills on 09-08-68. Antwine sacked Darragh two other times and was named the AFL Defensive Player of the Week in this victory over the Bills.

The Game of the Year was played against the Denver Broncos at Bears Stadium on 09-29-68. On the second play of the game a misplayed lateral by Patriots quarterback Mike Taliaferro was recovered by Dave

> **1968 Boston Patriots Team Leaders**
> *Offensive Team*
> Tom Sherman threw 12 TD passes
> Jim Whalen had seven TD receptions
> Jim Nance had four rushing TDs
>
> *Defensive/Special Teams*
> Leroy Mitchell had seven interceptions
> Mel Witt returned an interception four yards for a TD
> Willie Porter recovered six fumbles
> Houston Antwine recorded 7.5 sacks
> Ed Philpott took a fumbled pitch 10 yards for a TD
>
> **Memorable Statistics of the Year**
> Bob Scarpitto is the only player who has caught a touchdown pass and punted for the Patriots in the same season.
> The Boston Patriots had five AFL All-Star players in 1968.

Costa, and that helped set up the Broncos first score. Patriots linebacker Ed Philpott sacked Jim LeClair on the Broncos second play, and Denver settled for a 27-yard field goal by Bobby Howfield.

On the Broncos next set of downs Patriots defensive back Leroy Mitchell intercepted a pass by Jim Leclair, giving the ball to the Patriots on Denver's side of the field. After a 20-yard completion to Jim Colclough,

Taliaferro tossed a 14-yard touchdown pass to Jim Whalen to put the Patriots ahead 7–3.

However, Denver moved right down the field and Fran Lynch scored on a one-yard touchdown run.

The Patriots defense put tremendous pressure on the Broncos passing attack. The Patriots sacked Leclair on successive plays, forcing a punt. Ed Philpott's sack set the Broncos back nine yards. Antwine strip-sacked Leclair, for a loss of seven, but the fumble was recovered by Denver's center Larry Kamiski.

Aaron Marsh kept a Patriots drive alive when he recovered a fumble by his teammate Gene Thomas. The Patriots' drive stalled and Gino Cappelletti kicked a 22-yard field goal to tie the game 10–10.

With 52 seconds left in the first half, linebacker Nick Buoniconti sacked Leclair for a loss of nine yards. With 32 seconds left in the first half, Bobby Howfield's 43-yard field-goal attempt was no good. The key halftime statistic: Jim Leclair had three completions and was sacked five times.

Patriots punter Bob Scarpitto boomed an 87-yard punt that Floyd Little mishandled and fumbled on the one-foot line. Willie Porter recovered the fumble, setting up an easy score for the Patriots. After an unsuccessful quarterback sneak by Taliaferro, Larry Garron took it in for a one-yard touchdown.

Bob Scarpitto's next punt was blocked by Paul Smith and rolled out of bounds on the Patriots 16-yard line. On the next play, Leclair was chased from the pocket, and his pass was intercepted by Patriots linebacker Ed Philpott.

Marlin Briscoe replaced Leclair as the Broncos quarterback and led his team down the field, but Bobby Howfield missed a 24-yard field-goal attempt.

Taliaferro then led his team on a 14-play drive that was aided tremendously by a third-down completion for 24 yards to Jim Whalen. On fourth-and-goal, from about six inches out, Gino Cappelletti kicked a tough angle seven-yard field goal. Because the goal post was on the goal line and not in the back of the end zone, as they are now, this wide-angle field-goal attempt was one of the most difficult in his career.

Marlin Briscoe moved the Broncos back into Patriots territory, and he scored on a 12-yard touchdown run with 1:50 left, cutting Boston's lead to only three points. Denver held the Patriots and had one more chance to score. Briscoe completed a 21-yard pass to Bill van Heusen and ran for 19 yards, but time ran out and the Patriots were victorious 20–17. Whalen had four receptions, all on third-down plays, and was awarded the game ball.

1969

Record 4–10; Tied for third place in the Eastern Division of the AFL
Clive Rush was the new head coach of the Boston Patriots
The WBZ 1030 AM Radio announcers were Bob Starr and Gil Santos

The Boston Patriots home games were played at Boston College Alumni Stadium. The Patriots lost the first seven games but then won four of the five games played during November. The Houston Oilers were shut out 23–0 on 11-02-69, and the Patriots then defeated the Bengals, Bills, and Dolphins during the last three weeks of November.

* * *

The Play of the Year was made by defensive back Daryl Johnson. Johnson tackled running back Jess Phillips in the end zone for a safety in the 25–14 win over the Bengals at Riverfront Stadium on 11-16-69.

The Game of the Year was played against the Buffalo Bills at Boston College Alumni Stadium on 11-23-69.

On the game's first play, Patriots linebacker Ed Philpott had an 11-yard return of an interception of Bills quarterback Jack Kemp. On the Patriots first offensive play of the game, Mike Taliaferro completed a

---

1969 Boston Patriots Team Leaders
Offensive Team
Mike Taliaferro tossed 19 TDs
Charley Frazier had seven TD receptions
Jim Nance ran for six TDs

Defensive/Special Teams
Larry Carwell, John Charles, and Ed Philpott had four
    interceptions
John Charles returned an interception 25 yards for a TD
Jim Cheyunski recovered three fumbles
Daryl Johnson returned a fumble 32 yards for a TD
Houston Antwine recorded five sacks

Memorable Statistics of the Year
Daryl Johnson is the only Patriots player to record a
    safety and intercept a pass in the same game.
The Boston Patriots had six AFL All-Star players in 1969.

34-yard touchdown pass to Charley Frazier. This was the first time the Patriots scored a touchdown on the first offensive play of a game.

Kemp marched his team down the field. A 40-yard reception by Haven Moses put the ball on the Patriots 1-yard line. Wayne Patrick scored on a one-yard run to tie the score. Mike Taliaferro answered with a seven-play drive that ended with his 24-yard touchdown pass to Charley Frazier to put the Patriots up by seven points again.

Linebacker Ed Philpott returned his second interception of Kemp 16 yards, from his own 9-yard line, to stop another scoring chance by the Bills. The Patriots did not take advantage of this turnover as Gino Cappelletti missed a 49-yard field-goal attempt.

Carl Garrett set up the Patriots next score with his 41-yard punt return. Ron Sellers hauled in a 35-yard touchdown pass from Mike Taliaferro, giving the Patriots a 14-point lead. The Bills came right back with a score of their own. Kemp completed a 52-yard touchdown pass to Haven Moses, and the Bills were back in the game.

Carl Garrett had a 63-yard return on the ensuing kickoff, but the Patriots offense stalled and had to punt. Larry Carwell came to the rescue as he returned an interception of Kemp for 39 yards. Bills defensive back John Pitts then intercepted a pass by Taliaferro in the end zone for a touchback, and the half ended with the Patriots up 21–14.

The Bills took advantage of an interference penalty on the Patriots and moved down to the Patriots 2-yard line. On fourth-and-goal, Kemp tossed a two-yard touchdown pass to Haven Moses to tie.

Jim Nance was a key factor in the Patriots' next offensive drive. He had a 27-yard reception to get the Patriots in scoring range. On second-and-goal, from the 2-yard line, Jim bulled his way in for a touchdown. The Patriots were up by seven points again.

Buffalo was able to move the ball down the field against the Patriots until they reached the 2-yard line. Patriots defensive back Don Webb stopped O.J. Simpson, on fourth-and-goal from the 2, and the Patriots regained possession. After a skirmish on the field over a controversial nonpenalty call by the officials, Jon Morris and Bob Taratek were ejected from the game. On the next play from scrimmage Cappelletti missed a 30-yard field goal.

John Charles intercepted a Kemp pass, but the Patriots were forced to punt. The Bills could not move

Carl Garrett

the ball, and Kemp's desperation pass on fourth-and-17 was deflected on another nice play by John Charles.

Carl Garrett then dashed 44 yards for the game clinching touchdown with about two minutes left in the game. Carl "The Road Runner" Garrett had a great game, accounting for 200 total yards. He had 96 yards rushing along with a 63-yard kickoff return and a 41-yard punt return.

1970

Record 2–12; Last place in the Eastern Division in the last season of the AFL
The WBZ 1030 AM Radio announcers were Bob Starr and Gil Santos

The Patriots beat the Miami Dolphins 27–14 on opening day at Harvard Stadium, and Joe Kapp led them to a 14–10 win over the Bills in Buffalo in the 11th week of the season for their other victory. John Mazur replaced Clive Rush as the Patriots' head coach after the seventh game of the season. Both coaches finished with 1–6 records that year.

* * *

The Moment of the Year was the "Fire in the Bleachers." Before the exhibition game against the Washington Redskins, the recently painted bleacher seats at Boston College Alumni Stadium caught fire and a huge smoke cloud engulfed the stadium.

The Game of the Year was played against the Miami Dolphins at Harvard Stadium on 09-20-70. Bob Gladieux made the tackle of Jake Scott on the opening kickoff. What was so remarkable about the tackle was that he had no idea that he would be in uniform playing for the Patriots even an hour before the game started. He was a spectator who was requested over the loudspeaker "To report to the Patriots locker room" just before the game was about to start. Gladieux made another special team tackle of Scott later in the same game.

Bob Griese led his team on a 12-play drive that culminated with his five-yard touchdown run. The Patriots answered with a 41-yard field goal by Gino Cappelletti. Jake Scott intercepted a pass by Mike Taliaferro, and Jim Kiick ran for a five-yard touchdown, giving the Dolphins the lead for the last time.

Daryl Johnson had a nine-yard interception return of a Bob Griese pass, giving the Patriots good field position. Carl Garrett ran it in for a 10-yard touchdown. Jim Lee Hunt recovered a fumble by Larry Csonka on the

---

1970 Boston Patriots Team Leaders
Offensive Team
Mike Taliaferro tossed four TDs
Ron Sellers had four TD receptions
Jim Nance ran for seven TDs

Defensive/Special Teams
Daryl Johnson had two interceptions
Ed Philpott recovered three fumbles
Ron Berger recorded nine sacks

Memorable Statistic of the Year
Offensive center Jon Morris was their only AFL All-Star
    player.

Patriots 13-yard line. After a 12-yard run by Jim Nance, Jim then scored on a one-yard touchdown run to give the Patriots an unrelinquished 17–14 lead.

The Dolphins were allowed to keep possession of the ball after a roughing the kicker penalty on the Patriots, but John Williamson's interception of a pass by Griese gave the Patriots the ball. Once again the Patriots scored after causing a turnover. With 17 seconds left in the half, Gino Cappelletti kicked a 22-yard field goal.

Mike Taliaferro tossed a 24-yard touchdown pass to Ron Sellers to complete the scoring in the fourth quarter. The Patriots defense kept the pressure on the Dolphins passing game as Jim Cheyunski, John Bramlett, Jim Lee Hunt, and Ike Lassiter had sacks, and Ron "The Whopper" Berger, who had three sacks on the day, was named the NFL Defensive Player of the Week.

1971

Record 6–8; Third place in the AFC Eastern Division
The WBZ 1030 AM Radio announcers were Gil Santos and John Carlson

The newly named New England Patriots defeated the Oakland Raiders 20–6 in Jim Plunkett's first NFL regular season game. The Patriots shut out the Jets, beat the Houston Oilers, and were victorious over the Buffalo Bills and the Miami Dolphins during the season. To the dismay of General Manager Upton Bell, the Patriots defeated the Baltimore Colts 21–17 in the

last game of the season, which allowed John Mazur to keep his head coaching position.

* * *

The Play of the Year was made by Jim Plunkett and Randy Vataha. Vataha scampered 88 yards on his pass reception from Plunkett, in the fourth quarter, to defeat the reigning world champion Baltimore Colts 21–17 at Memorial Stadium on 12-19-71.

The Game of the Year was played against the Miami Dolphins at Schaefer Stadium on 12-05-71. Julius Adams was named the NFL Defensive Player of the Week. The Patriots crowd celebrated "Gino Cappelletti Day" during the halftime ceremonies. The 10-year All-Time Patriots Anniversary Team was also announced.

Mercury Morris took the opening kickoff from Charlie Gogolak 94 yards for a touchdown. On the Patriots' first possession of the game Jim Plunkett had eight consecutive passing attempts, leading the Patriots to the 9-yard line of the Dolphins. Jim Nance broke through the line and ran for a nine-yard touchdown to tie the score 7–7.

Hubert Ginn fumbled on his kickoff return, after being hit by Patriots defensive end Bill Atessis, and Randy Edmunds recovered it for the Patriots. On the next play Jim Plunkett tossed a 26-yard touchdown pass to Randy Vataha.

Ginn fumbled the next kickoff again, after being hit by Don Webb, and Bob Gladieux recovered it for the Patriots. Charlie Gogolak kicked a 37-yard field goal, giving the Patriots a 10-point lead.

Bob Griese moved the Dolphins into Patriots territory and Garo Yepremian kicked a 26-yard field goal, keeping the Dolphins in the game.

Don Webb recovered Larry Csonka's fumble on the Dolphins next possession, giving the Patriots another chance to score before the first half ended. Patriots lineman Mike Montler recovered a fumble by Plunkett,

> ### 1971 New England Patriots Team Leaders
> *Offensive Team*
> Jim Plunkett tossed 19 TD passes
> Randy Vataha had nine TD receptions
> Jim Nance had five rushing TDs
>
> *Defensive/Special Teams*
> Larry Carwell had five interceptions
> Larry Carwell and John Outlaw returned a pass for a TD
> Jack Maitland recovered three fumbles
> Roland Moss returned a blocked punt 10 yards for a TD
> Steve Kiner recorded 6.5 sacks
>
> ### Memorable Statistic of the Year
> Jim Plunkett was the first NFL quarterback to play every offensive play during his rookie year.

allowing the Patriots to continue their drive, and Gogolak kicked a 35-yard field goal with 40 seconds left in the half.

Dolphin punter Larry Seiple ran 14 yards on a fake punt, for a first down, and Garo Yepremian kicked a 30-yard field goal to open the third quarter. The Patriots responded with a touchdown strike from Plunkett to Vataha. On this drive, Randy had two big receptions. He grabbed a 14-yard pass and continued on for a 51-yard reception, and then later he made a leaping 25-yard touchdown reception, to put the Patriots up by 14 points.

Patriots defensive back Larry Carwell returned an interception of Griese 53 yards for a touchdown, putting the game out of reach for the Dolphins.

Miami was able to move down to the Patriots 9-yard line before a series of defensive stops prevented the Dolphins from scoring again. On first-and-goal from the 9-yard line, linebacker Steve Kiner stopped Morris after a gain of five yards. On second-and-goal from the 4, linebacker Jim Cheyunski stuffed Jim Kiick on the 1-yard line. On third-and-goal, Jim Cheyunski smashed Jim Kiick again on the ½-yard line. On fourth-and-goal, linebacker Ed Weisacosky jammed Larry Csonka for no gain.

On the Dolphins' last possession, Patriots defensive back John Outlaw returned his interception of George Mira 29 yards from his own 1-yard line. An over exuberant fan was arrested on the field as time expired in this 34–13 rout of the Miami Dolphins.

Left to right: Randy Vataha and Jim Plunkett

1972

Record 3–11; Last place in the AFC Eastern Division
The WBZ 1030 AM Radio announcers were Gil Santos and Gino Cappelletti

The Patriots had a tough time in 1972. The team beat the Falcons 21–20 and the Redskins 24–23 in consecutive games. In December the Patriots beat the New Orleans Saints 17–10, as Reggie Rucker had two touchdown receptions within one minute of each other for the final win of the season. John Mazur was fired after getting shut out 52–0 by the Dolphins in Don Shula's 100th NFL career win as a head coach. Phil Bengston was 1–4 as the head coach of the Patriots for the team's final five regular season games.

* * *

The Moment of the Year occurred during the *Monday Night Football* halftime show during the team's 24–17 loss to the Baltimore Colts at Schaefer Stadium on 11-06-72. "Jumpin" Joe Gerlach jumped from a hot air balloon, which was hovering over the 50-yard line, onto an air mattress. Just as he landed a cannon was shot creating a loud booming noise. After a few seconds Joe rose up and waved to the cheering crowd. This was the Patriots first *Monday Night Football* game.

The Play of the Year was made by Larry Carwell. Larry blocked a 51-yard field-goal attempt by Horst Mulmann and returned it 45 yards for a touchdown.

The Game of the Year was played against the Atlanta Falcons at Schaefer Stadium on 09-24-72. On the Patriots' second series of offensive plays, Pat Studstill punted from his own end zone. The Falcons' second drive started on the Patriots 38-yard line and even without getting a first down were able to score via a 38-yard field goal by Bill Bell. The Falcons first drive of the second quarter ended when Bill Bell kicked a 21-yard field goal.

With two minutes to go in the first half, Jim Plunkett hit Bob Windsor for 12 yards and then for 14 yards. After two incomplete passes, he tossed a 17-yard pass to John Ashton to bring the Patriots to the Falcons 4-yard line with 53 seconds left. Ashton ran it in from four yards out for the touchdown.

After a 25-yard kickoff return by Dave Hampton, a six-yard pass reception by Art Malone, and a 43-yard pass reception by Hampton, Bill Bell attempted a 32-yard field goal. Ron Bolton rushed in from the side and blocked this field-goal attempt, and the Patriots clung to a one-point lead at the break.

Mike "Superfoot" Walker kicked off to the Falcons to start the second half. Bob Berry marched his team

---

1972 New England Patriots Team Leaders
Offensive Team
Jim Plunkett tossed eight TD passes
Reggie Rucker had three TD receptions
Carl Garrett ran for five TDs

Defensive/Special Teams
Honor Jackson had four interceptions
Ron Acks recovered four fumbles
Julius Adams recorded four sacks

Memorable Statistic of the Year
Larry Carwell is the only Patriots player who has
    blocked a field-goal attempt and returned it for a
    touchdown.

---

down the field, and Art Malone scored on a one-yard touchdown run to give the Falcons the lead.

After a Patriots punt the Falcons had successive runs of nine yards, 19 yards, and 24 yards to move down to the Patriots 4-yard line. Dave Hampton scored on a one-yard touchdown run to put the Falcons up by 13 points.

The Patriots then moved the ball 83 yards on 12 plays to get back into the game. Carl Garrett caught an 11-yard pass from Plunkett, on third-and-6, allowing the Patriots offense to stay on the field. WR Randy Vataha hauled in a 37-yard touchdown pass from Jim Plunkett to cut the Atlanta deficit to six points.

The Patriots defense forced the Falcons to punt and took possession at the Patriots 22-yard line with 10:52 left. Plunkett then took the team on a 78-yard, nine-play drive that included a 40-yard pass play to Reggie Rucker, and Carl Garrett ran it in from 12 yards out for a touchdown. Mike Walker kicked the extra point for the game's final point.

The Falcons had one more chance to win the game as they had the ball first-and-10 on the Patriots 11-yard line with 1:25 left. Patriots linebacker Jim Cheyunski stopped Art Malone after a five-yard gain. Defensive lineman Rick Cash stopped Dave Hampton after a two-yard gain and defensive end Dennis Wirgowski stopped Hampton after a two-yard gain. Bill Bell's 10-yard field-goal attempt went wide left and the Patriots held on for the one-point victory.

1973

Record 5–9; Third place in the AFC Eastern Division
The WBZ 1030 AM Radio announcers were Gil Santos and Gino Cappelletti

Chuck Fairbanks was hired as the new head coach of the Patriots. The team lost its first three games but was victorious over the Baltimore Colts at Schaefer Stadium on 10-07-73. Two weeks later the Patriots beat the Chicago Bears 13–10 at Soldier Field. Jim Plunkett had the best game in his career with the Patriots when the team defeated the Green Bay Packers 33–24 at Schaefer Stadium. The Patriots went on to shut out the Oilers 32–0 at the Astrodome and defeated the San Diego Chargers 30–14 at Schaefer for a nice three-game winning streak. The team only scored 13 points in each of its final two road games, losing to the Bills and the Colts.

* * *

The Play of the Year was made by "Mini' Mack Herron. Mack returned a kickoff by Ray Wersching 92 yards for a touchdown in the 30–14 victory over the San Diego Chargers at Schaefer Stadium on 12-02-73.

The Game of the Year was played against the Green Bay Packers at Schaefer Stadium on 11-18-73. Jim Plunkett was the NFL Offensive Player of the Week.

Jerry Tagge led the Packers' first drive to a touchdown as John Brockington swept over the left side for a four-yard score. Darryl Stingley had a 29-yard kickoff return to give the Patriots good field position. Patriots running back Bob McCall fumbled, however, on the Patriots' first offensive play, and the Packers scored again. Perry Williams ran over the right side for a four-yard touchdown.

On the Patriots' first drive of the second quarter, they finally scored. Stingley made a diving reception of a 14-yard pass from Jim Plunkett and then caught a 17-yard pass from Plunkett to get to the Packers 11-yard line. After two incomplete passes, Jeff White kicked a 19-yard field goal to put the Patriots on the scoreboard.

The next time the Patriots had the ball, Jim Plunkett moved the team into field-goal range again. Jeff White's 21-yard field-goal attempt deflected in off the goal post for another three points.

Patriots defensive back Ron Bolton stopped a Green Bay drive when he intercepted a 12-yard pass by Jerry Tagge in the end zone for a touchback. With just over two minutes left in the half, Plunkett engineered a 14-play drive. Darryl Stingley had a 19-yard reception, and Jeff White kicked a 26-yard field goal with 17 seconds left in the half.

1973 New England Patriots Team Leaders
Offensive Team
Jim Plunkett tossed 13 TD passes
Bob Windsor had four TD receptions
Jim Plunkett ran for five TDs

Defensive/Special Teams
Ron Bolton had six interceptions
Five Patriots players recovered two fumbles
Mack Herron returned a kickoff 92 yards for a TD
Julius Adams recorded eight sacks

Memorable Statistics of the Year
Randy Vataha had the Patriots longest non-special team fumble advancement for a touchdown.
Randy advanced a fumble by running back Mack Herron 46 yards for a touchdown in the 24–16 win on 10-07-73.

Mack Herron

Jeff White's squibbed kickoff gave the Packers decent field position with almost no time left on the clock. After an 18-yard reception by Barry Smith and a 15-yard penalty on the Patriots, Chester Marcol kicked a 33-yard field goal on the last play of the half.

On the second play of the third quarter, Ken Ellis returned an interception of Jim Plunkett 47 yards for a touchdown, giving the Packers a 15-point lead. The Packers would not score again.

Plunkett connected with Randy Vataha for a 32-yard gain. On fourth-and-2, Plunkett then tossed a 28-yard touchdown pass to Bob Windsor to get the Patriots back in the game.

After the Packers missed a 20-yard field-goal attempt, Plunkett took the Patriots down the field for another score. Darryl Stingley started this drive with an end around run for 18 yards. Mack Herron had a 29-yard pass reception, and Bob Windsor had a 17-yard reception, on third down and 5, to keep the drive alive. Jeff White kicked an 18-yard field goal to cut the Green Bay lead to five points.

On the first play of the Patriots' next possession, Plunkett tossed a 37-yard pass to Reggie Rucker, who took it an additional 26 yards for a 63-yard touchdown that gave the Patriots a lead for the first time in this game.

Patriots defensive lineman Ray "Sugar Bear" Hamilton recovered a fumble by Perry Williams on the Packers' next offensive play, and Plunkett led them to another touchdown. Rucker had a 22-yard reception, and Herron ran for three yards before Plunkett ran it in for a two-yard touchdown. Jeff White kicked the extra point for the final points scored in the game.

Plunkett ran for a touchdown and was 18–32 for 348 yards and tossed two touchdown passes. The Patriots scored the final 24 points in this 33–24 win over Green Bay.

1974

Record 7–7; Tied for third place in the AFC Eastern Division
The WBZ 1030 AM Radio announcers were Gil Santos and Gino Cappelletti

In 1974 the Patriots won two more games than the previous year finishing 7–7. The team won its first five games, beating the Dolphins, Giants, Rams, Colts, and Jets. The Patriots then lost six out of the next seven games. The team salvaged a 17–14 win over the Vikings before losing three consecutive games. Its first three-game losing streak was broken up by defeating the Baltimore Colts 27–17 at Memorial Stadium. The Patriots ended the season by losing the final three games to the Raiders, Steelers, and Dolphins.

* * *

The Play of the Year was made by Bob Windsor. He caught a pass on the Vikings 1-yard line and then twisted and bulled ahead for the game-winning touchdown. Windsor severely injured his knee in the process of scoring the touchdown on the last play in the 17–14 victory over the Minnesota Vikings on 10-27-74.

The Game of the Year was played against the Minnesota Vikings at Metropolitan Stadium in Bloomington, Minnesota, on 10-27-74. Mini-Mack Herron had 30 yards rushing, 51 yards receiving, 55 kickoff return yards, and 59 punt return yards.

Jim Plunkett took the Patriots on a 10-play drive that ended with a 37-yard field goal by John Smith. The key plays on this drive were a 19-yard pass completion by Plunkett to Herron, on third-and-3, and a 24-yard run on a draw play by Sam Cunningham.

1974 New England Patriots Team Leaders
Offensive Team
Jim Plunkett tossed 19 TD passes
Mack Herron had five TD receptions
Mack Herron ran for seven TDs
John Hannah fell on a fumble for a TD

Defensive/Special Teams
Ron Bolton had seven interceptions
Bob Geddes and John Sanders returned a pass for a TD
Ray Hamilton and Jack Mildren recovered two fumbles
Julius Adams recorded eight sacks

Memorable Statistic of the Year
Mini-Mack Herron set the NFL record with 2,444 combined yards from scrimmage and return yards in a year.

The Vikings' first series ended on a forced punt, and Fred Cox missed a 43-yard field-goal attempt on the second set of downs. Patriots linebacker George Webster sacked Fran Tarkenton for a loss of 16 yards forcing the Vikings to punt.

Plunkett marched the Patriots down the field in six plays to start the second quarter.

The Patriots had three plays of more than 20 yards each in this drive. Sam Cunningham had a 20-yard run on pitch-out sweep right, Herron caught a 21-yard pass, and Jim Plunkett tossed a 21-yard touchdown pass to Steve Schubert.

Both teams punted to each other twice before the Vikings were able to get a couple of first downs. With two minutes left in the half, Fran Tarkenton was intercepted by Bolton on the Patriots 1-yard line. The Vikings did get the ball back and once again marched down the field. Ron Bolton made a nice play breaking up a pass by Tarkenton on the goal line with 19 seconds left. The 34-yard field-goal attempt by Fred Cox, with nine seconds left in the half, was no good as it went wide left.

Patriots defensive back Jack Mildren intercepted a Tarkenton pass on the Patriots 4-yard line to stop the Vikings on their first drive of the third quarter. Bolton intercepted a pass by Tarkenton on the Patriots 1-yard line to stop the last drive of the Vikings in the third quarter.

Minnesota took advantage of a fumble by Patriots running back John Tarver on the 3-yard line. Two plays later, Chuck Foreman smashed through the line for a two-yard touchdown. The Vikings got the ball right back as Herron fumbled the ensuing kickoff but did not take advantage of this turnover as Jim Lash fumbled, after his 25-yard pass reception, out of the end zone for a touchback.

With 1:45 left, Tarkenton completed a 38-yard pass to Jim Gilliam, giving the Vikings great field position. A 33-yard pass interference penalty on the Patriots put the ball on the 3-yard line, and Tarkenton ran a bootleg over the left side for the touchdown. A ruckus ensued on the field after this play, and Tarkenton and Ron Bolton were both ejected from the game for unsportsmanlike conduct.

With 1:21 left, Plunkett took the Patriots 84 yards for the game-winning score. On third-and-1, from the Patriots 35-yard line, Plunkett connected on a 55-yard pass to Randy Vataha. With eight seconds left, from the 10-yard line, Plunkett tossed a nine-yard pass to Bob Windsor, who managed to take it in for the game winning touchdown, severely injuring his knee in the process. After a few penalties, John Smith kicked the extra point from 29 yards out.

1975

Record 3–11; Tied for fourth place in the AFC Eastern Division
The WBZ 1030 AM Radio announcers were Gil Santos and Gino Cappelletti

The Patriots fell back to 3–11 in 1975. The team defeated the Baltimore Colts and San Francisco 49ers in consecutive weeks and midway through the season won three out of four games. The third and final victory of the season was on November 9, when the Patriots defeated the Chargers in San Diego.

* * *

The Play of the Year came in the fourth quarter of a 34–31 loss to the Dallas Cowboys at Schaefer Stadium on 11-16-75. It was a five-yard touchdown pass by Jim Plunkett to Darryl Stingley. This was Plunkett's second touchdown pass to Stingley in the fourth quarter and it came with just 1:28 left in the game. It was to be the last touchdown pass Plunkett would ever throw for the New England Patriots. On April 5, 1976, he was traded to the San Francisco 49ers for three first-round draft picks and one second-round draft pick.

The Game of the Year was played against the San Francisco 49ers at Schaefer Stadium on 10-26-75. The Patriots forced the 49ers to punt after three offensive plays, and Plunkett moved the team into field-goal position on the Patriots' first drive. John Smith booted a 44-yard field goal for the first points scored in the game.

1975 New England Patriots Team Leaders
Offensive Team
Steve Grogan tossed 11 TD passes
Randy Vataha had six TD receptions
Sam Cunningham ran for six TDs

Defensive/Special Teams
Ron Bolton had five interceptions
Bob Howard returned an interception 44 yards for a TD
Allen Carter returned a kickoff 99 yards for a TD
Ray Hamilton returned a fumble 23 yards for a TD
John Sanders recovered four fumbles
Tony "Mac the Sack" McGee had nine sacks

Memorable Statistic of the Year
Allen Carter became the first Patriots player to return the opening kickoff for a touchdown.

On the Patriots' last drive in the first quarter, Plunkett put them in field-goal position again, but John Smith's 41-yard field-goal attempt was blocked. Smith recovered the loose ball and ran for a one-yard gain before he was tackled.

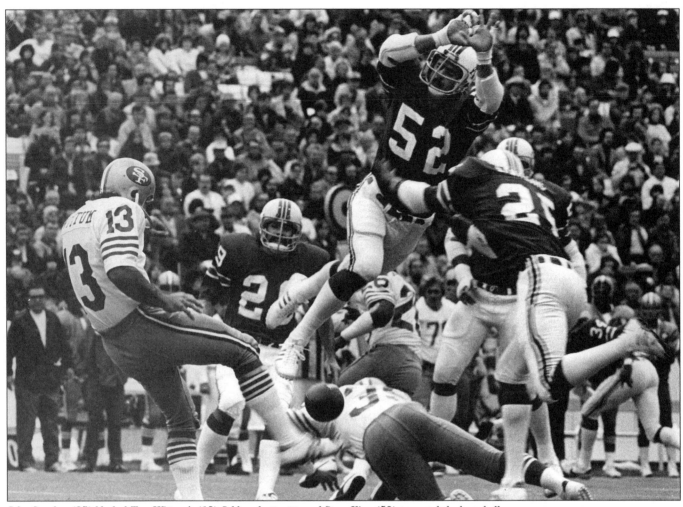

John Sanders (25) blocked Tom Wittum's (13) field-goal attempt, and Steve King (52) recovered the loose ball.

Norm Snead marched his team into field-goal position as well, but Steve Mike-Mayer's 47-yard field-goal attempt failed.

Steve Grogan took the controls for the Patriots first drive of the second quarter. He marched down to the 49ers 13-yard line, but Sam Cunningham lost five yards on a fourth-down play, and San Francisco took over on its 19-yard line.

Steve Grogan mixed up their passing and running attack and moved the team down to the 49ers 11-yard line. Sam Cunningham took a pitch over the right side for an 11-yard touchdown. With 24 seconds left, Patriots defensive back John Sanders blocked a punt by Tom Wittum, and Steve King recovered it for the Patriots on the 49ers 6-yard line. After a delay-of-game penalty on the Patriots, Grogan tossed an 11-yard touchdown pass to Andy Johnson.

On the first play of the third quarter, 49ers defensive back Ralph McGill returned a fumble by Andy Johnson 14 yards for a touchdown. When the 49ers got the ball back after Mike Patrick's punt went out of the end zone for a touchback, quarterback Norm Snead was able to move them into Patriots territory. The momentum was short lived as George Webster forced Delvin Williams to fumble after his six-yard reception, and Sam Hunt recovered the ball for the Patriots.

The next time the 49ers had the ball they advanced it to the Patriots 10-yard line but had to settle for a 28-yard field goal by Mike-Mayer. The 49ers defense held and forced the Patriots to punt, but Manfred Moore gave it right back when he fumbled on his punt return. The Patriots took full advantage of this fumble recovery by Leon McQuay. Patriots wide receiver Randy Vataha caught a seven-yard touchdown pass from Steve Grogan, putting them up by 14 points. Interceptions by Ron Bolton and Bob Howard abruptly halted two more 49ers drives.

With 56 seconds left, Snead connected on a 24-yard touchdown pass to Mike Holmes, and Steve Mike-Mayer kicked the extra point for the game's final point. Andy Johnson sealed the 24–16 victory over the 49ers by recovering an onside kick by Mike-Mayer.

1976

Record 11–3; Tied for first place in the AFC Eastern Division
The WBZ 1030 AM Radio announcers were Gil Santos and Gino Cappelletti

The 1976 team exploded to an 11–3 record, and many believe it was one of the Patriots best teams. Huge wins over the Dolphins, Steelers, Raiders, Jets, and Bills occurred during the first half of the season. After losing to the Miami Dolphins, the Patriots reeled off six straight victories and won the division. New England beat the Bills again and defeated the Colts in Baltimore and the Jets in New York. The Patriots smoked the Broncos and Saints at Schaefer Stadium and whipped up on the winless Buccaneers at Tampa Bay in the last regular season game. Ultimately the team lost to the Oakland Raiders 24–21 in the AFC Divisional Playoff Game at the Oakland Coliseum.

* * *

The Play of the Year was made by Mike Haynes. He returned a punt by Marv Bateman 89 yards for a touchdown, in the 20–10 win over the Buffalo Bills on 11-07-76. This was the first punt to be returned for a touchdown by a Patriots player in a regular season game. It is still the longest punt return in the team's history. (As a side note, Haynes had almost returned a punt for a touchdown in an exhibition game against the Browns earlier in the year, but he celebrated just a bit too early and fumbled on the 5-yard line. Darryl Stingley came to his rescue, picked it up, and took it in for the touchdown.)

The Game of the Year was played against the Oakland Raiders at Schaefer Stadium on 10-03-76.

Left to right: Steve Grogan and Pete Brock

1976 New England Patriots Team Leaders
Offensive Team
Steve Grogan tossed 18 TD passes
Darryl Stingley had four TD receptions
Andy Johnson caught four TD passes
Steve Grogan ran for 12 TDs
Steve Grogan advanced a fumble for a TD

Defensive/Special Teams
Mike Haynes had eight interceptions
Prentice McCray returned two passes for a TD in the same game
Sam Hunt returned an interception 68 yards for a TD
Mike Haynes returned two punts for a TD
Tim Fox recovered four fumbles
Tony McGee recorded 9.5 sacks

Memorable Statistics of the Year
Steve Grogan set the NFL record with 12 rushing touchdowns in a regular season by a quarterback.
The New England Patriots had four AFC Pro Bowl players.

Patriots linebacker Steve King caused Clarence Davis to fumble on the Raiders' second play of the game, and Steve Zabel recovered it for the Patriots. During the seventh consecutive running play, Andy Johnson ran around the right side for a 10-yard touchdown.

Ken Stabler marched his team to the Patriots 12-yard line, and it looked like the Raiders would soon tie the score. Tim Fox and Sam Hunt teamed up to smack Mark van Eeghen, forcing him to fumble, and Steve Zabel recovered his second fumble of the game. The Patriots took advantage of this turnover. Cunningham gained 19 yards on a screen pass, and Stingley ran for 21 yards on a wide receiver reverse. Steve Grogan tossed a 21-yard pass to Stingley for the touchdown.

Midway through the second quarter Stabler tossed a 15-yard touchdown pass to Fred Biletnikoff, but the Patriots were not fazed. With 2:45 to go Grogan moved the Patriots down to the Raiders 16-yard line and then completed a 16-yard touchdown pass to former Broncos quarterback Marlin Briscoe. Not to be denied, Stabler completed three straight passes, and Fred "Suitcase" Steinfort kicked a 44-yard field goal with six seconds left in the half to bring the score to 21–10.

Doug Beaudoin fumbled the opening kickoff of the second half, but Patriots offensive lineman Pete Brock recovered it and the Patriots maintained possession. Grogan moved his team down to the Raiders 15-yard line with the help of a 41-yard completion to Cunningham. On third-and-6, Stingley made a diving catch of a 15-yard touchdown pass from Grogan, to put the Patriots up by 18 points.

On the ensuing possession, the Raiders were then able to move the ball to the Patriots 6-yard line, but after two Raider penalties Tony "Mac the Sack" McGee strip-sacked Stabler, and Ray Hamilton recovered the loose ball for the Patriots. Steve Grogan again took the Patriots to pay dirt. The Patriots had two big plays on this drive. Johnson had a 22-yard run, and Stingley gained 27 yards on a wide receiver reverse. Grogan ran over the right side for a two-yard touchdown.

Stabler took the Raiders on an eight-play drive before he was intercepted by Prentice McCray on the goal line. Prentice returned the interception 88 yards, but a clipping penalty on the return brought the ball back to the Raiders 47-yard line, resulting in a return of only 53 yards.

Grogan called his own number a couple of times on the Patriots' next possession. Grogan ran for 30 yards on a quarterback draw. On third-and-2, he rolled over the right side for a 10-yard touchdown on the second play of the fourth quarter.

Mike Rae replaced Ken Stabler as quarterback for the Raiders. Tony McGee welcomed him to the game by sacking Rae, for a loss of 10 yards, forcing the Raiders to punt. Jess Phillips was the star of the Patriots' next drive. Phillips ran for four yards, caught an 18-yard pass, ran for no gain, and then rumbled 11 yards over the right side for a touchdown.

With about seven minutes left, Rae marched the Raiders to the 1-yard line before taking it in himself for a one-yard touchdown. The final score was Patriots 48 Raiders 17.

The Patriots had 296 yards rushing and 192 yards passing. Sam Cunningham had a career-best 195 yards from scrimmage. Stingley had 48 yards rushing.

1977

Record 9–5; Third place in the AFC Eastern Division
The WBZ 1030 AM Radio announcers were Gil Santos and Gino Cappelletti

The Patriots had another solid year, going 9–5 in 1977, beating the Chiefs on opening day and having successive three-point losses to the Browns (in overtime) and Jets. The Patriots shut out the Seahawks at Schaefer, beat the Chargers in San Diego, and defeated the Colts and Jets at Schaefer Stadium. The team lost to the Bills at home and lost to the Dolphins on the road. Four of the team's last five games were won by defeating the Bills, Eagles, Falcons, and Dolphins. The Colts win in Baltimore knocked them out of the playoffs in the last game of the season. The Colts were the AFC Eastern Champions.

* * *

The Play of the Year was recorded in the game against the San Diego Chargers on 10-16-77. Bill Munson was strip-sacked by Ray Hamilton, and the loose ball was recovered by Tony McGee on the Chargers 6-yard line, with four minutes left, in the 24–20 victory over the San Diego Chargers. Two plays later Steve Grogan tossed a four-yard touchdown pass to Don Hasselbeck, giving the Patriots an 11-point lead. Munson connected on a 16-yard touchdown pass to Charlie Joiner in the final seconds, but the Patriots prevailed because of this key defensive play.

1977 New England Patriots Team Leaders
Offensive Team
Steve Grogan tossed 17 TDs
Darryl Stingley had five TD receptions
Don Calhoun had four rushing TDs
Sam Cunningham had four rushing TDs

Defensive/Special Teams
Mike Haynes had five interceptions
Raymond Clayborn returned three kickoffs for a TD
Ray Hamilton recovered two fumbles
Tony McGee recorded 12 sacks

Memorable Statistics of the Year
Steve Grogan is the only player who attempted every
     pass attempt in a regular season for the Patriots.
Russ Francis and Mike Haynes represented the New
     England Patriots in the Pro Bowl.

The Game of the Year was played against the Kansas City Chiefs at Schaefer Stadium on 09-18-77. Patriots wide receiver Darryl Stingley had a big game on his 26th birthday as he scampered for a 34-yard touchdown and caught a 26-yard touchdown pass.

Gary Barbaro intercepted Steve Grogan on the second play of the game, but the Chiefs' drive stalled when Mike Livingston was sacked for a nine-yard loss by Julius Adams. Jim Lynch intercepted Grogan on the second play of the Patriots' second drive. MacArthur Lane scored on a one-yard touchdown run, on third-and-goal, for the first points scored in the game.

About two minutes later, Livingston connected on a 49-yard pass to Henry Marshall. Tony Reed put the Chiefs up by 14 points as he ran over the left side for a 10-yard touchdown just five minutes into the game.

On third-and-10, Grogan completed a 22-yard pass to Russ Francis for a first down, and he tossed a 10-yard pass to Sam Cunningham for another first down. On third-and-½ yard, Stingley ran a wide receiver reverse over the left side for a stunning 34-yard touchdown.

The teams traded punts and then fumble recoveries. Patriots linebacker Pete Barnes strip-sacked Livingston, and Steve Zabel recovered the fumble, but just five plays later Bill Andrews recovered a fumble by Patriots running back Don Calhoun.

Patriots safety Tim Fox strip-sacked Livingston on a safety blitz, and Pete Barnes returned the loose ball 11 yards, giving the Patriots the ball on the Chiefs 42-yard line. Four plays later Steve Grogan connected on a 21-yard touchdown pass to Darryl Stingley to tie.

Patriots designated pass rusher Tony "Mac the Sac" McGee sacked Livingston for a loss of eight yards, forcing Kansas City to punt on its first possession of the second half. Patriots defensive end Greg "Too Strong" Boyd sacked Mike Livingston for a nine-yard loss, forcing the Chiefs to punt. Stanley Morgan called for a fair catch on his 41-yard line, and the Patriots took advantage of this field position. Grogan ran over the left side for a gain of 12, Steve Burks had a 20-yard reception, and Don Calhoun's 11-yard run put the ball on the Chiefs 11-yard line. Jess Phillips ran through the right side of his offensive line for an 11-yard touchdown.

The Chiefs were able to mount a substantial drive of 76 yards in 13 plays. They moved to the Patriots 4-yard line, but Julius Adams stopped Tony Reed for no gain, on third-and-2, and Jan Stenerud kicked a 22-yard field goal.

Sam Cunningham

Cunningham's apparent 43-yard run for a touchdown was nullified by two penalties on Francis for illegal motion and a personal foul infraction. Francis was ejected from the game.

The Chiefs had one last shot with just over two minutes to go. On third-and-7, Tim Fox recorded his second sack of the day, resulting in a loss of 10 yards. Steve Nelson forced Livingston to throw an incomplete pass on fourth-and-17, and the Patriots had the ball with 1:25 left.

Don Calhoun ran for six yards, on third-and-5, and the Patriots were able to run out the clock and defeat the Kansas City Chiefs, 21–17.

1978

Record 11–5; First place in the AFC Eastern Division
The WBZ 1030 AM Radio announcers were Gil Santos and Gino Cappelletti

On 08-12-78, Darryl Stingley was paralyzed after being hit by Jack "The Assassin" Tatum in an exhibition game against the Oakland Raiders. He never was able to walk again and spent the rest of his life in a wheelchair.

After winning only one of the first three games, the Patriots then went on a seven-game winning streak starting with the 21–14 win over the Raiders in Oakland on 09-24-78. The Patriots beat the Chargers and the Eagles at Schaefer Stadium. The team beat the Bengals at Riverfront Stadium and combined to score 88 points in home wins over the Dolphins and the Jets. New England was victorious over the Bills in Buffalo but then lost to the Houston Oilers in front of the home crowd at Schaefer Stadium. The Patriots went to New York and beat the Jets and then routed the Colts in Baltimore. Dallas won by seven at Texas Stadium, but the Patriots played a strong game with a two-point win over the Bills at Schaefer. A 20-point loss to the Dolphins at the Orange Bowl ended the last game of the regular season.

Head coach Chuck Fairbanks was suspended before the Patriots' first home playoff game, as he had just agreed to become the head coach at the University of Colorado. Ron Erhardt and Hank Bullough took over as co-head coaches for their 31–14 home playoff game loss to the Houston Oilers.

* * *

The Moment of the Year occurred on 10-01-78. During the halftime ceremony of the game against the San Diego Chargers, fans voted to keep the Pat Patriot logo. The Pat Patriot logo remained on the uniforms until 1993.

The Play of the Year was made by Russ Francis. Francis caught a 25-yard touchdown pass, to end the first half, in the 21–14 win over the Oakland Raiders at the Oakland Coliseum on 09-24-78.

The Game of the Year was played against the Buffalo Bills at Schaefer Stadium on 12-10-78 in 28-degree weather with light snow and wind gusts up to 23 mph.

Tom Dempsey's opening kickoff was taken at the 14-yard line and returned to the 35-yard line by Raymond Clayborn. The Patriots ran the ball the first 12 plays, down to the Bills 14-yard line, before Andy Johnson was stopped for only one yard on fourth-and-2.

> **1978 New England Patriots Team Leaders**
> *Offensive Team*
> Steve Grogan threw 15 TD passes
> Harold Jackson had six TD receptions
> Horace Ivory ran for 11 TDs
>
> *Defensive/Special Teams*
> Mike Haynes had six interceptions, returning one for a TD
> Steve Nelson recovered four fumbles
> Tony McGee recorded 12 sacks
>
> **Memorable Statistics of the Year**
> The Patriots set the NFL record with 3,165 yards rushing in a season. Four players each ran for more than 500 yards.
> The New England Patriots had five AFC Pro Bowl players.

Steve King made a nice play breaking up a third-and-6 pass play, and the Bills were not able to get a first down on the team's first possession. After a 27-yard punt with no return New England had the ball on its own 44-yard line.

The Patriots continued to run the ball and when Steve Grogan ran a quarterback sneak for a one-yard gain, on fourth-and-½, it looked as though the Patriots might score. Unfortunately a pitch back by Grogan was fumbled out-of-bounds for a 16-yard loss and then Horace Ivory fumbled after a four-yard reception, and Randy McClanahan recovered the ball for Buffalo.

Mike Haynes got the ball back for the Patriots as he picked off a pass by Joe Ferguson, but Ivory fumbled it again after his two-yard run. Bills defensive back Charles Romes recovered the fumble.

On the last play of the first quarter, on a fourth down and one play, Bills running back Terry Miller gained six yards for a first down. Roland Hooks scored the first points of the day with a 28-yard sweep right play for a touchdown. Tom Dempsey kicked the extra point.

Raymond Clayborn had a nifty 39-yard kickoff return to give New England decent field position on its 41-yard line. Twice during this drive they went for it on fourth down. On fourth-and-½ yard, Grogan had a quarterback sneak for a one-yard gain. On fourth-and-½, Sam Cunningham dove over the line for a two-yard gain, for another first down. On the 14th play of this drive, Cunningham drove over the left side for a four-yard touchdown. David Posey kicked the extra point.

Both teams traded punts, but the Patriots punt by Jerrel Wilson went only 11 yards because of a deep rush by Mike Franckowiak. The Bills seized the moment as Tom Dempsey kicked a 26-yard field goal on the last play of the first half.

Both teams traded punts before the Bills were able to move into Patriots territory. Terry Miller ran through the left side for a 32-yard touchdown, and the Patriots were down by 10 points.

Horace Ivory took the short kickoff by Dempsey 26 yards to midfield, and the Patriots had great field position. After a two-yard run by Horace Ivory, Steve connected on a 19-yard pass to Don Westbrook that took it to the Bills 4-yard line. Steve called his own number and rolled over the right side for the four-yard touchdown.

The Bills were not able to gain a first down, and Rusty Jackson punted the ball to Stanley Morgan. The Patriots were able to get four first downs, but David Posey missed a 42-yard field-goal attempt and the Bills got the ball back.

Tony McGee strip-sacked Joe Ferguson, and Ray Hamilton recovered it for the Patriots. On the very next play Patriots running back Horace Ivory, who had fumbled twice earlier in the game, redeemed himself by dashing 20 yards for a touchdown.

Joe Ferguson took the Bills 68 yards in eight plays for a touchdown. A key play was a 25-yard completion to Reuben Gant on third-and-7. Frank Lewis hauled in a 21-yard touchdown pass from Ferguson to give the Bills the lead once again.

With about five minutes to go, the Patriots started from their own 17-yard line. Grogan ran for 23 yards. Stanley Morgan had a 52-yard reception, and in just five plays the Patriots had first-and-goal to go on the Bills 5-yard line. Cunningham took it three yards to the 2-yard line, and on second-and-goal from the 2 Cunningham tried to dive over the line for the touchdown. Shane Nelson had other ideas and forced Cunningham to fumble, and Tom Graham recovered the fumble for the Bills on the 2-yard line. The Bills defense held.

Mike Haynes had one of the many plays of the game as he stopped Terry Miller just short of the first-down marker on third-and-6. Punter Rusty Jackson was forced out of the end zone by Patriots defensive back Tim Fox for a two-point safety.

Stanley Morgan had a 17-yard return on the free kick after the safety. Grogan completed two passes to

Russ Francis (81)

Horace Ivory for a first down, ran for five yards, and then hit Cunningham for nine yards and another first down. Cunningham then broke through the middle for a 14-yard gain to the Bills 7-yard line. After an incomplete pass and a short run of three yards, David Posey kicked a 21-yard field goal with 11 seconds left.

Mike Haynes tackled Keith Moody after his 30-yard kickoff return to end the game. Fans stormed the field to celebrate the first time the Patriots won the AFC Eastern Division.

1979

Record 9–7; Second place in the AFC Eastern Division
The WBZ 1030 AM Radio announcers were Gil Santos and Jon Morris

The new head coach of the Patriots, Ron Erhardt, was hired. The Patriots lost in overtime on *Monday Night Football*, to the Steelers at Schaefer Stadium, in the season's opening game. Wheelchair-bound former wide receiver Darryl Stingley received two huge ovations from the home crowd. The next week Stingley's inspiration was channeled to smoke the New York Jets 56–3. The Patriots went on the road to beat the Bengals and then came home and hung on for a six-point win over the Chargers. Green Bay won at Lambeau Field, but then the Patriots went on a three-game winning streak by defeating the Lions, Bears, and Dolphins. Two of the team's next three road games were lost before scoring 50 points against the Colts at Schaefer Stadium. The Patriots came back to earth after losing the next three games. In the final game of the season the Vikings were beaten 27–23.

* * *

The Play of the Year was made by linebacker Steve Nelson. He intercepted a pass by Dan Fouts, on the Patriots 2-yard line late in the fourth quarter, to preserve a 27–21 win over the San Diego Chargers at Schaefer Stadium on 09-23-79.

The Game of the Year was played against the New York Jets at Schaefer Stadium on 09-09-79. The Patriots recorded nine sacks, had three interceptions, and had 597 yards of total offense in the team's biggest margin of victory.

Steve Nelson

1979 New England Patriots Team Leaders
Offensive Team
Steve Grogan tossed 28 TD passes
Stanley Morgan had 12 TD receptions
Don Calhoun ran for five TDs
Sam Cunningham ran for five TDs

Defensive/Special Teams
Raymond Clayborn had five interceptions
Mike Hawkins returned an interception for a TD
Rick Sanford returned a blocked punt for a TD
Stanley Morgan returned a punt 80 yards for a TD
Mike Haynes and Rick Sanford recovered three fumbles
Tony McGee recorded 10.5 sacks

Memorable Statistics of the Year
This is the only time that three Patriot players completed 100% of their passing attempts in a season.
The New England Patriots had three AFC Pro Bowl players.

Every pass that Harold Jackson caught in this game resulted in a touchdown. He caught a 49-yard touchdown pass in the first quarter, a 44-yard touchdown pass in the second quarter, and a 28-yard touchdown pass in the third quarter. Stanley Morgan also had three receptions for over 100 yards, but he only caught two touchdown passes. Morgan connected on a 37-yard touchdown pass from Steve Grogan in the first quarter and hauled in a 50-yard touchdown pass from Grogan in the second quarter. The score was 35–3 at the half.

Grogan completed 13 passes for 315 yards and five touchdowns. The Patriots set a team record with six touchdown passes. In the fourth quarter, Tom Owen tossed the sixth touchdown pass of the day with a 14-yard pass to Don Westbrook. Mike Hawkins recorded four sacks, and Julius Adams and Ray Hamilton each contributed two sacks. Raymond Clayborn, Ray Costict, and Prentice McCray had interceptions. Andy Johnson and Allan "Smiley" Clark each had a short yardage rushing touchdown. John Smith set the team record by kicking eight extra points.

1980

Record 10–6; Second place in the AFC Eastern Division
The WEEI 590 AM Radio announcers were John Carlson and Jon Morris

The Patriots went 10–6 but did not make the playoffs in 1980. After beating the Browns and losing to the Falcons, the Patriots won five games in a row. New England beat the Jets twice, the Colts twice, split with Buffalo and Miami, and defeated the Seahawks, Broncos, and the Saints. John Smith scored 129 points and was the only regular kicker to be successful on every extra-point attempt (51–51) during the season.

* * *

Steve Nelson, John Zamberlin, and Mike Haynes were involved in the Play of the Year. Steve Nelson blocked a 49-yard field-goal attempt by Pat Leahy. John Zamberlin picked up the loose ball and lateraled it to Mike Haynes, who took it 65 yards for a touchdown, in the 21–11 win over the New York Jets at Shea Stadium on 10-05-80.

The Game of the Year was played against the Seattle Seahawks at the Kingdome on 09-21-80. The Patriots won the toss and elected to receive but were unable to get a first down. Mike Hubach, who also kicked off for the Patriots, punted it to the Seahawks 24-yard line.

Jim Zorn fumbled the exchange on the team's second play of the game. Patriots linebacker Steve Nelson recovered the loose ball on the Seahawks 24-yard line, putting the Patriots in fantastic field goal position. On third-and-goal from the 8-yard line, Steve Grogan ran over the left side but gained only seven yards. John Smith scored the first points of the game with a 19-yard field goal.

Herman Weaver and Mike Hubach each had short punts with no return, and Seattle started its third drive on its own 43-yard line. Steve Largent hauled in a 22-yard pass, Zorn ran for a 10-yard gain, and with just a few plays was in business. Mike Hawkins stopped Dan Doornink short of a first down, on third-and-11, and Efren Herrera kicked a 33-yard field goal with 37 seconds left in the first quarter.

Zorn hit on a couple of big third-down plays to put Seattle in favorable position to score. He completed a 10-yard pass to Sam McCullum on third-and-9. Jim tossed a 20-yard pass to Largent on third-and-10. Zorn then connected on a 20-yard touchdown pass to Largent for the first touchdown of the day.

Just 12 seconds later, Grogan connected on a 68-yard touchdown pass to Stanley Morgan. John Smith kicked the extra point.

1980 New England Patriots Team Leaders
Offensive Team
Steve Grogan tossed 18 TD passes
Russ Francis had eight TD receptions
Don Calhoun ran for nine TDs

Defensive/Special Teams
Raymond Clayborn had five interceptions
Rod Shoate returned an interception 42 yards for a TD
Horace Ivory returned a kickoff 98 yards for a TD
Roland James returned a punt 75 yards for a TD
Allan Clark and Rick Sanford each returned a fumble for a TD
Mike Haynes and Rick Sanford recovered two fumbles
Julius Adams recorded nine sacks

Memorable Statistics of the Year
Rick Sanford and Allan Clark each returned a fumbled kickoff return for a touchdown in the same game. Rick scored his touchdown just 11 seconds after John Smith kicked a 35-yard field goal. Allan's touchdown was scored 12 seconds after Don Calhoun had run three yards for a touchdown.
The New England Patriots had seven AFC Pro Bowl players.

Julius Adams sacked Zorn for an eight-yard loss, on third-and-12, and Herman Weaver was forced to punt again. Don Calhoun ran over left tackle for a 14-yard gain before he fumbled, but Morgan picked it up and advanced it another three yards. On third-and-12, Steve Grogan connected on a 40-yard touchdown pass to Morgan.

Roland James almost intercepted a pass by the Seahawks punter Herman Weaver, but it went incomplete. Grogan was not as fortunate, as one of his passes was intercepted by Dave Brown in the end zone for a touchback.

Zorn took only 1:16 off the clock on the team's next scoring drive. He tossed a 10-yard pass to John Sawyer, a 22-yard pass to Steve Largent, and Jim Jodat dashed 26 yards over the left guard to put the ball on the Patriots 22-yard line. Zorn then completed a 22-yard pass in the right corner of the end zone to Sam McCullum for the touchdown.

With 1:13 left in the half, New England started from its own 34-yard line. On third-and-1 from the Patriots 43-yard line, Grogan gained seven yards on a quarterback sneak. Grogan completed three consecutive passes to move to the Seahawks 13-yard line. With two seconds left in the half, John Smith calmly kicked a 30-yard field goal.

The second time that the Patriots had the ball in the third quarter they put another seven points on the scoreboard. Vagas Ferguson and Russ Francis made a few big plays during this drive. Ferguson had three carries for 21 yards, and Francis caught a 19-yard pass on third-and-4 and grabbed a 10-yard pass on second-and-9, along the way. On third-and-3, Horace Ivory ran up the middle for a 20-yard touchdown. John Smith kicked the extra point.

Seattle came right back. Zorn scrambled for an 18-yard gain. Sherman Smith ran over the right side for a 23-yard gain. Largent hauled in a 31-yard touchdown pass from Zorn, and just like that it was only a three-point game.

Back came the Patriots. Don Calhoun rumbled for 17 yards. Harold Jackson hauled in a 40-yard pass from Steve Grogan. On third-and-9 from the 11-yard line, Grogan's pass to Francis in the right-hand corner of the end zone went incomplete. John Smith came to the rescue and kicked a 29-yard field goal.

Zorn was bound and determined to lead his team to victory. Zorn connected on a 40-yard pass to Steve Raible and moved his team in five plays to the Patriots 21-yard line. Sam McCullum caught his second touchdown pass, this one from 21 yards out, from Zorn, putting Seattle up by the score of 31–30.

Steve Grogan then methodically took his team on a 12 play, 68-yard drive, which took 5:53 off the clock, for the game-winning touchdown. Don Calhoun had four carries for 27 yards, and Vagas Ferguson had three carries for 15 yards. On fourth-and-1, Mosi Tatupu bulled ahead for a one-yard gain and the first down. The only pass that Grogan threw on this drive was the game-winning, 16-yard touchdown to Don Hasselbeck.

Patriots cornerback Raymond Clayborn intercepted a pass by Zorn with just over two minutes left to seal a 37–31 victory. The Patriots were able to run out the clock thanks to Ferguson, who ran for a first down twice on third-down plays.

1981

Record 2–14; Tied for fourth place in the AFC Eastern Division
The WEEI 590 AM Radio announcers were John Carlson and Jon Morris

The Patriots began the season with a one-point loss to the Colts and ended the season with a two-point loss to the same team. New England won every game in which at least 30 points was scored. Unfortunately, this only happened twice. The Patriots lost six games by four points or less and lost 12 games by 10 points or less.

* * *

The Play of the Year was made by Andy Johnson as he threw a 66-yard touchdown pass, on a fake wide receiver reverse pass option, to Stanley Morgan in the 33–17 win over the Kansas City Chiefs at Schaefer Stadium on 10-04-81. Johnson went on to throw three more halfback option touchdown passes during this season.

The Game of the Year was played against the Houston Oilers at Schaefer Stadium on 10-18-81. The Patriots scored the final 31 points in the 38–10 victory over the Oilers.

The Patriots won the toss, and Johnson returned a squibbed kickoff 19 yards to the Patriots 39-yard line. On third-and-4, Steve Grogan hit Harold Jackson for nine yards. On third-and-8, Ken Kennard was guilty of roughing the passer, and the Patriots had another first

> **1981 New England Patriots Team Leaders**
> *Offensive Team*
> Steve Grogan threw seven TDs
> Stanley Morgan had six TD receptions
> Don Hasselbeck had six TD receptions
> Tony Collins ran for seven TDs
>
> *Defensive/Special Teams*
> Tim Fox and Rick Sanford had three interceptions
> Rick Sanford recovered four fumbles
> Tony McGee recorded 5.5 sacks
>
> **Memorable Statistics of the Year**
> Matt Cavanaugh, Steve Grogan, Tom Owen, Andy Johnson, Harold Jackson, and Tony Collins attempted at least one pass.
> John Hannah was the team's only Pro Bowl player.

down. On third-and-9, Johnson took an option from Grogan, rolled right, and tossed a 28-yard halfback option pass to a wide open Morgan in the end zone for a touchdown.

Houston gained one yard on its first three plays and had to punt. Morgan returned Cliff Parsley's punt 26 yards before he ran into his teammate Bob Golic. Gregg Bingham forced Hasselbeck to fumble, after his three-yard reception, and the loose ball was recovered by Ken Kennard. Houston did not take advantage of this turnover and had to punt again.

Mike Stensrud recovered a fumble by Mosi Tatupu, and Houston had the ball on its 26-yard line with 14:18 left in the first half. Ken Stabler went on a 74-yard drive in 15 plays, tossing a nine-yard touchdown pass to Dave Casper, to tie the score at 7–7.

The Patriots moved down the field to the Oilers 15-yard line, but John Smith's 32-yard field-goal attempt went wide right. Tony Fritsch kicked a 42-yard field goal, with 19 seconds left in the half, to give the Oilers a three-point lead at the break.

Tim Fox returned an interception of Stabler 20 yards, on the fourth play of the third quarter, and the Patriots were back in business. On the very next play, Grogan lofted a 42-yard pass to Stanley Morgan for a touchdown.

Patriots linebacker Bob Golic made the tackle on the 25-yard kickoff return by Willie Tullis. Tony McGee stopped Earl Campbell after a three-yard gain. Ray Hamilton stopped Earl Campbell after a two-yard gain. Tony McGee dropped Adger Armstrong for a two-yard loss, and the Oilers were forced to punt.

The Patriots had first-and-goal on the Oilers 4-yard line but could not put it in the end zone. On first down Don Calhoun was stopped for no gain. A halfback option pass by Tony Collins went incomplete, and Steve Grogan's rollout pass on third down also went incomplete. John Smith salvaged the drive by kicking a 21-yard field goal.

Patriots linebacker Rod Shoate intercepted a pass by Stabler, but then he fumbled, and Mike Renfro recovered it for the Oilers. On third-and-10, Stabler completed only a five-yard pass to Mike Renfro, and the Oilers had to punt.

Tony Collins dashed for a 19-yard run. Morgan made a leaping reception that was good for another 19 yards. On third-and-2 from the Oilers 12-yard line, Calhoun went over the right side for a first down. Grogan then tossed a 10-yard touchdown pass to Andy Johnson.

On the second play of the fourth quarter, Patriots linebacker John Zamberlin intercepted a pass by Stabler on his 22-yard line and returned it 11 yards. The Patriots did not get a first down, and Ken Hartley came on the field to punt.

Patriots cornerback Keith Lee, who was replacing Mike Haynes in the starting lineup because Haynes had a collapsed lung, intercepted a pass by Stabler. Four plays later Mosi Tatupu dashed 43 yards to the Oilers 15-yard line. Ferguson went over the left side for a 15-yard touchdown.

Keith Lee made a couple of nice defensive plays. He deflected a pass that was intended for Ken Burrough, on third-and-4, and then tackled Burrough after his two-yard reception, on fourth-and-4. (Keith Lee was awarded the game ball in his first game as a starting cornerback for the Patriots.)

Don Calhoun busted through the line for a 19-yard gain. On third-and-3, Grogan called his own number and ran a naked reverse over the right side for a 24-yard touchdown and the final score of the day.

Patriots defensive lineman Ray Hamilton batted down a pass by Ken Stabler on the last play of the 38–10 rout of the Houston Oilers.

1982

Record 5–4; This season was interrupted by a players' strike that lasted eight weeks
Seventh place in the AFC; The Patriots lost to the Miami Dolphins in the first round playoff game
The WEEI 590 AM Radio announcers were John Carlson and Jon Morris

The Patriots beat the Baltimore Colts 24–13 at Memorial Stadium to open the season, lost to the New York Jets before the strike, and then lost to the Cleveland Browns after the strike was settled. After beating the Houston Oilers and losing to the Chicago Bears, the Patriots shut out the Dolphins and the Seahawks in consecutive weeks. The team lost to the Steelers in Pittsburgh but defeated the Buffalo Bills, 30–19, at Schaefer Stadium to qualify for the playoffs. The Patriots subsequently lost to the Miami Dolphins 28–13 at the Orange Bowl in the first round playoff game.

* * *

The Moment of the Year was made by work-released parolee Mark Henderson. Mark drove a John Deere tractor on the field and plowed a path for John Smith during a snowstorm in the 3–0 shutout of the Miami Dolphins on 12-12-82. Actually, he made the kick even harder for John Smith because he made the surface smoother and John had a tough time keeping his plant foot down before booting the 33-yard field goal.

Mosi Tatupu helped set up the game-winning field goal with a 26-yard run. His run was the longest play from scrimmage in the game. An earlier field-goal attempt by John Smith deflected off the helmet of Patriots lineman Bob Cryder and went wide right.

Patriots linebacker Don Blackmon intercepted a David Woodley pass on his 10-yard line, with 37 seconds left, and Roland James had intercepted a Woodley pass on his 10-yard line, on the game's last play.

The Game of the Year was played against the Buffalo Bills at Schaefer Stadium on 01-02-83. (Whichever team won this game made the playoffs.)

The Bills received the opening kickoff before going three and out. Greg Cater's 27-yard punt went out of bounds at the Patriots 47-yard line. The Patriots' first play was a 15-yard completion to Don Hasselbeck. Tony Collins had two runs for a first down, but the drive ended, and John Smith kicked 42-yard field goal.

Steve Freeman had a 12-yard return of a Steve Grogan pass that tipped off the fingers of Patriots receiver Morris Bradshaw. Joe Ferguson then completed a 17-yard pass and a 32-yard pass to Frank Lewis, and the Bills were on the Patriots 14-yard line. Joe Cribbs took it up the middle for a 14-yard touchdown.

Ferguson completed five consecutive passes, in 55 seconds, for the team's second touchdown. Frank Lewis had a 16-yard reception. Mark Brammer had a 12-yard reception and a six-yard reception, and Roosevelt Leaks

Don Hasselbeck

1982 New England Patriots Team Leaders
Offensive Team
Steve Grogan tossed seven TD passes
Stanley Morgan had three TD receptions
Tony Collins ran for a TD
Steve Grogan ran for a TD
Robert Weathers ran for a TD

Defensive/Special Teams
Mike Haynes had four interceptions
Rick Sanford returned an interception 99 yards for a TD
Don Blackmon recovered two fumble
Don Blackmon recorded 4.5 sacks
Ricky Smith returned a kickoff 98 yards for a TD

Memorable Statistics of the Year
The only time that the Patriots recorded a safety even though the quarterback was tackled on the 2-yard line.
George Crump sacked Archie Manning on the two yard line in the 29–21 win over Houston on 11-18-82.
John Hannah and Mike Haynes represented the New England Patriots in the Pro Bowl.

---

caught a 10-yard pass. Jerry Butler finished it off with his 22-yard touchdown reception. The snap on the extra point was mishandled, and Patriots defensive back Ricky Smith was there to make the tackle.

With 57 seconds left in the half, Steve Grogan led his team down the field to a touchdown. On third-and-1, Mark van Eeghen ran over the left side for a four-yard gain and a first down. Stanley Morgan hauled in a 45-yard pass to bring the ball to the Bills 11-yard line with 26 seconds left. Steve Grogan lofted an 11-yard touchdown pass to Morris Bradshaw with 11 seconds left. The Patriots trailed by only three points at halftime.

The Patriots took the second-half kickoff and marched right down the field for a touchdown. Lin Dawson caught an 11-yard pass, and Mark van Eeghen ran for nine yards and seven yards on consecutive plays. On his seven-yard run he was tackled by Jim Haslett and Fred Smerlas. Grogan completed a nine-yard pass to Morgan, and then on a roll out right he tossed a 33-yard touchdown pass to Ken Toler. John Smith was wide right on his extra-point attempt.

Joe Cribbs caught a 31-yard pass from Joe Ferguson that helped set up a 46-yard field goal by Efren Herrera. The game was now tied 16–16.

The Patriots went on an 11-play drive that had three first downs but ended with a punt. The key play was a 15-yard loss on a pass completion across the field to

Don Hasselbeck and a subsequent five-yard penalty for delay of game, on third-and-8, from the Bills 12-yard line. Rich Camarillo's 31-yard punt was downed at the 1-yard line by Paul Dombroski.

The Bills had two successful runs on third-and-short, but a Joe Ferguson pass tipped off the hands of Roosevelt Leaks to Patriots cornerback Mike Haynes. Haynes returned this interception 26 yards to the Bills 12-yard line.

Mark van Eeghen ran it to the 5-yard line and then to the 4-yard line. On third-and-2 from the 4-yard line, Tony Collins took it to the 1-yard line. On first-and-goal from the 1, Tony Collins ran over the right side for the touchdown.

Cribbs had the longest run of the day of 48 yards and the Bills were on the march again. Steve Nelson and Ken Sims combined to stop Cribbs short, on third-and-1 from the 8-yard line, and Efren Herrera came on to kick a 25-yard field goal.

Grogan took his team 74 yards in just over five minutes for the final score of the game. A key play was a 24-yard completion to Stanley Morgan. The only third down play in this drive resulted in a touchdown. On third-and-goal from the 2-yard line, Grogan lofted a pass to Hasselbeck in the left-hand corner of the end zone for the touchdown.

The Bills went three and out and punted. The Patriots ran the last 6:12 off the clock with 11 consecutive running plays, getting four first downs, to defeat the Bills 30–19.

1983

Record 8–8; Tied for second place in the AFC Eastern Division
The WEEI 590 AM Radio announcers were John Carlson and Jon Morris

The Patriots lost two, won two, lost two, won two, lost one, won two, lost two, won two, and then lost the last game of the season to finish 8–8.

The Patriots had numerous chances to win the first game of the season but missed an extra point and two field-goal attempts, which allowed Baltimore to tie the score on the last play in regulation resulting in a 29–23 overtime loss. The Patriots scored 21 points in the fourth quarter in a 34–24 loss to the Miami Dolphins in the second game of the season. Tony Collins had a team record 212 yards rushing, and Andre Tippett stopped the Jets three times inside the 7-yard line in the 23–13 win over New York on 09-18-83.

The Patriots sacked Cliff Stoudt five times and intercepted him three times in the 28–23 win over Pittsburgh on 09-25-83. Joe Montana tossed a touchdown pass to former Patriots tight end Russ Francis in the 33–13 win over the Patriots. Mike Pagel tossed a 68-yard touchdown pass to Curtis Dickey to defeat the Patriots 12–7. The Patriots scored the final 27 points in the 37–21 win over the San Diego Chargers on 10-16-83.

Roland James intercepted Joe Ferguson three times in the third quarter of the 31–0 shutout of the Buffalo Bills on 10-23-83. The Patriots had five turnovers in the 24–13 loss to the Falcons. The Patriots defense had 14 pass deflections and four interceptions in the 21–7 victory over the Bills. Ken Sims stopped Woody Bennett on fourth-and-goal from the 1-yard line, and Pete Brock tore the cartilage in his knee but played the entire

1983 New England Patriots Team Leaders
Offensive Team
Steve Grogan threw 15 TD passes
Derrick Ramsey had six TD receptions
Tony Collins ran for 10 TDs
Defensive/Special Teams
Rick Sanford had seven interceptions
Clayton Weishuhn returned a lateral 27 yards for a TD
Roland James recovered four fumbles
Andre Tippett recorded 8.5 sacks
Memorable Statistics of the Year
The only time that a Patriots linebacker, who intercepted a pass, lateraled to another linebacker, who then took the ball in for a touchdown.
Steve Nelson pitched it to Clayton Weishuhn, who took it for the touchdown, in the 28–23 win on 09-25-83.
The New England Patriots had five AFC Pro Bowl players in 1983.

game in the 17–6 win over the Dolphins on 11-13-83. Steve Grogan broke his leg in the 30-0 loss to the Cleveland Browns on 11-20-83.

The Patriots only had 208 yards of total offense in the 26–3 loss to the New York Jets at Shea Stadium. Mosi Tatupu had 128 yards rushing in the sleet and snowy conditions, and Tony Collins ran for a three-yard touchdown in the 7–0 shutout of the Saints on 12-04-83.

Tatupu ran for three touchdowns in the 21–7 win over the LA Rams at Anaheim Stadium.

Seattle clinched a wild card playoff spot by defeating the Patriots 24–6 in the last regular season game.

* * *

The Play of the Year was made by Andre Tippett who ripped the ball from Eric Dickerson in the 21–7 win over the Los Angeles Rams on 12-11-83.

The Game of the Year was played against the Pittsburgh Steelers at Three Rivers Stadium on 09-25-83. The Steelers took the opening kickoff and marched 71 yards in 15 plays, for the first score of the game. Cliff Stoudt tossed a three-yard touchdown pass, on third-and-goal, to Calvin Sweeney, and Gary Anderson kicked the extra point to put the Steelers up 7–0.

Mosi Tatupu

The Patriots were unable to get a first down on the team's first drive, but the defense scored to tie the game. Steve Nelson intercepted a pass intended for tight end Bennie Cunningham and returned it six yards. Before falling to the ground, he lateraled it to Clayton Weishuhn and Weishuhn, found the open area and took it all the way for a 27-yard touchdown. This is the first time that two linebackers of the Patriots combined to score a touchdown in a regular season game.

Cliff Stoudt took the Steelers on another long drive of 77 yards, in 17 plays, to the Patriots three-yard line. The Patriots defense held its ground as it forced an incomplete pass on third down. Gary Anderson booted a 20-yard field goal.

Robin Cole sacked Steve Grogan for a loss of seven yards, and the Patriots could not get a first down. Rick Sanford came to the rescue as he was able to return a pass by Stoudt five yards, giving New England possession of the football on its own 47-yard line. Grogan completed a 31-yard pass to Derrick Ramsey that brought the ball to the Steelers 15-yard line. On third-and-6, Grogan couldn't find a receiver open, so he ran the necessary six yards for the first down. After a one-yard run by Tony Collins, Grogan tossed a four-yard touchdown pass to Derrick Ramsey.

With 1:52 left in the half, Cliff Stoudt took the Steelers down the field for another score. He tossed a nine-yard completion to Franco Harris, an 11-yard completion to Franco Harris, and an eight-yard completion to Calvin Sweeney. On third-and-3, Franco Harris ran for six yards. Later in the drive on another third-and-3 play, Cliff Stoudt tossed a 17-yard pass to Gregg Garrity for a first down. With six seconds left in the half, Gary Anderson kicked a 34-yard field goal.

Ricky Smith returned the second half kickoff to the 20-yard line. Five minutes and 26 seconds later Tony Collins ran over the right side for a four-yard touchdown. A key play in the drive was a 32-yard reception by Stephen Starring. The Patriots did not have a third down play in this nine-play, 80-yard drive.

Both teams traded punts twice before the next turnover. Mel Blount returned a pass by Grogan 10 yards and the Steelers got the ball to their own 31-yard line. Stoudt completed three consecutive passes good for a combined 53 yards. This drive stalled on the Patriots 10-yard line, and Gary Anderson kicked a 28-yard field goal.

After a 61-yard punt by Rich Camarillo and a 22-yard return by Paul Skansi, the Steelers had the ball on their own 35-yard line. A 13-yard reception by Gregg Garrity and a 25-yard reception by Franco Harris led to great field position with about five minutes left in the game. Clayton Weishuhn tackled Harris for a one-yard loss, but Cliff Stoudt connected on a 26-yard touchdown pass to Walter Abercrombie, putting the Steelers back on top by two points.

Ricky Smith returned the kickoff to the 24-yard line, and with just over four minutes to go the Patriots had to score. Mosi Tatupu ran up the middle for two yards. On second-and-8, Grogan connected on a 76-yard touchdown pass to Stephen Starring, and the Patriots had a five-point lead.

John Smith's booming kickoff was downed in the end zone for a touchback. Patriots defensive back Rick Sanford intercepted Cliff Stoudt, and the Patriots were able to take some time off the clock. Camarillo's punt went into the end zone for a touchback, so with just over two minutes left the Steelers had one more shot.

Stoudt completed a five-yard pass to Walter Abercrombie and an 11-yard pass to Franco Harris before he was sacked by Don Blackmon for a six-yard loss. Another completion to Bennie Cunningham was good for 15 yards. On third-and-1, Harris ran for seven yards into Patriots territory. With 1:40 left the Patriots defense rose to the occasion. Doug Rogers sacked Stoudt for a 15-yard loss, and Clayton Weishuhn pressured Stoudt to run for only a one-yard gain on fourth-and-20.

Grogan knelt down for the final two plays in this encouraging road victory over the Steelers. Rick Sanford had 11 tackles and two interceptions. Weishuhn had 13 tackles and scored a touchdown. Tim Golden replaced Steve Nelson, who fractured a thumb late in the first half, and had 16 tackles. Andre Tippett, Lester Williams, Marshall Harris, Don Blackmon, and Doug Rogers each recorded a sack.

1984

Record 9–7; Second place in the AFC Eastern Division
The WEEI 590 AM Radio announcers were John Carlson and Jon Morris

Raymond Berry replaced Ron Meyer as the head coach of the Patriots after the eighth game of the 1984 season. The Patriots were 5–3 at the time.

The Patriots started the season beating the Buffalo Bills on the road but then lost to the Dolphins in Miami. The Patriots had the biggest comeback in team history beating the Seattle Seahawks 38–23 after being down 23–0 at Sullivan Stadium on 09-16-84. The Jets, Browns, and Bengals were defeated in consecutive weeks before the Patriots lost to the Dolphins again. Three of the first four games that Raymond Berry coached were won, but then the team lost three out of four to end the season with a 9–7 record.

The Play of the Year was made by Raymond Clayborn. He returned a pass by Paul McDonald 85 yards on the last play to preserve a 17–16 victory over the Cleveland Browns at Cleveland Stadium on 10-07-84.

* * *

The Game of the Year was played against the Seattle Seahawks at Sullivan Stadium on 09-16-84.

Seattle won the toss and chose to receive but were not able to get a first down and were forced to punt. Irving Fryar had a 55-yard punt return to the Seahawks 10-yard line. Unfortunately, Steve Grogan was strip-sacked by Joe Nash and Jeff Bryant, with Bryant recovering the fumble. Norm Johnson kicked a 42-yard field goal 11 plays later.

1984 New England Patriots Team Leaders

Offensive Team
Tony Eason threw 23 TD passes
Derrick Ramsey had seven TD receptions
Tony Collins and Tony Eason had five TD runs

Defensive/Special Teams
Raymond Clayborn and Ronnie Lippett had three interceptions
Cedric Jones recovered a fumble in the end zone for a TD
Roland James recovered two fumbles
Andre Tippett recorded 18.5 sacks

Memorable Statistics of the Year
Andre Tippett set the team record with 18.5 sacks. He sacked John Elway, Joe Ferguson, Dave Krieg, Pat Ryan, Paul McDonald, Matt Kofler, Art Schlichter, Danny White, Neil Lomax, and Joe Pisarcik.
The New England Patriots had four AFC Pro Bowl players in 1984.

The Patriots could not get a first down, and Luke Prestridge's 42-yard punt gave Seattle possession on its 30-yard line. On the fifth play of this drive Seattle quarterback Dave Krieg tossed a 41-yard touchdown pass to Daryl Turner. Norm Johnson missed the extra point.

Paul Johns returned the fourth punt by Luke Prestridge 47 yards for a touchdown, and Kenny Easley returned a Steve Grogan pass 25 yards for a touchdown within one minute of each other. With about six minutes to go in the second quarter, Tony Eason replaced Grogan as the Patriots quarterback. The score was Seattle 23 New England 0.

With two minutes left in the half, the Patriots had the ball on the Seahawks 44-yard line. Eason hit Derrick Ramsey for 12 yards. Eason hit Stephen Starring for 14 yards, but with 50 seconds left Eason was called for intentional grounding, bringing the ball back to the Seahawks 25-yard line. On third-and-20, with 43 seconds left in the half and under heavy pressure, Eason took off through the middle of the open field and dashed 25 yards for a touchdown.

Mosi Tatupu made the tackle on the ensuing kickoff and Dave Kreig took a knee to end the first half.

The Patriots received the kickoff to start the third quarter. Thanks to a 43-yard pass interference penalty on the Seahawks, the Patriots had the ball first-and-goal from the 4-yard line. Tatupu ran up the middle for two yards, and then Eason tossed a two-yard pass to Derrick Ramsey for the touchdown.

The Patriots defense started putting more pressure on Seattle as they stopped them from getting a first down on three consecutive possessions. Dave Krieg had a third down pass tipped incomplete on their first drive, he had a third down pass broken up on their second drive, and on third-and-10 his pass went off the intended receiver's hands. Seattle was finally able to get

its first first down in the third quarter when Eric Lane ran for a one-yard gain. Krieg then hit Steve Largent for a 16-yard gain. On the last play of the third quarter, Andre Tippett took control and sacked Dave Krieg for a 15-yard loss, on third-and-3, forcing Seattle to punt once again.

Eason took the Patriots on a 15 play, 65-yard drive, which ended in a 32-yard field goal by Tony Franklin. The Patriots had come back from being down 23–0 and now the score was 24–23. Even though it was only a one point game, the Patriots clearly had all the momentum.

On the Seahawks' first offensive play of the fourth quarter, Steve Nelson strip-sacked Dave Krieg, and Lester Williams recovered the fumble. Two plays later Mosi Tatupu ran over the right side for a 10-yard touchdown.

Patriots defensive back Paul Dombroski returned a pass by Dave Krieg 23 yards to stop a Seattle drive, and the Patriots took advantage of this turnover. Tony Collins and Stephen Starring then combined on one of the more interesting plays of the game. Collins ran for a five-yard gain over his left side but was hit and fumbled forward. Teammate Starring picked up the loose ball about 10 yards downfield and advanced it another eight yards. Three plays later Tony Eason tossed a 15-yard touchdown pass to Irving Fryar.

Rick Sanford picked off a Kreig pass with 1:11 left in the game, and Eason knelt down for the final two plays in the 38–23 comeback win over the Seahawks. This is the largest deficit the Patriots have overcome to win a regular season game.

1985

Record 11–5; Tied for second place in the AFC Eastern Division
They won three road games in the playoffs and went on to play in Super Bowl XX
The WEEI 590 AM Radio announcers were John Carlson and Jon Morris

The Patriots won the home opening game against the Packers but then lost on the road to the Bears. The Bills were beaten in Buffalo, but New England lost to the Los Angeles Raiders at Sullivan Stadium. The Browns beat the Patriots by four points in Cleveland, and then the Patriots went on a six-game winning streak. Victories over the Bills, Jets, Buccaneers, Dolphins, Colts, and Seahawks propelled them into playoff contention. After losing to the Jets on the road in overtime, the Patriots won three of their last four to make the playoffs as a wild card team.

* * *

The Play of the Year was made by Robert Weathers. He ran 42 yards for a touchdown on fourth down with

about two minutes to go to defeat the Cincinnati Bengals 34–23 at Sullivan Stadium on 12-22-85. With this victory the Patriots qualified for the playoffs.

The unforgettable Moment of the Year was when the fans carried the goal posts out of the stadium and down Route 1 after their playoff-clinching victory over the Bengals on 12-22-85.

The regular season Game of the Year was played against the New York Jets at Sullivan Stadium on 10-20-85.

The Jets won the toss, and Andre Tippett made the tackle of Kirk Springs on his 21-yard return of the opening kickoff. The Jets could not get a first down, and Dave Jennings punted the ball to Irving Fryar.

Rich Camarillo was forced to punt the ball back to the Jets. On third-and-6, Ken O'Brien was sacked by Patriots linebacker Andre Tippett for a nine-yard loss. Dave Jennings had to punt again for the Jets.

The Patriots went three and out, and Rich Camarillo's 48-yard punt was returned 40 yards by Kirk Springs. Patriots special team star Jim Bowman made the tackle. Raymond Clayborn stopped the Jets' drive when he intercepted an O'Brien pass in the end zone for a touchback.

Steve Grogan took the Patriots on a 13-play, 78-yard drive. The key play was 30-yard pass interference call on the Jets, on third-and-10 from the Patriots 48-yard line. On third-and-3 from the Jets 15-yard line, Lin Dawson also caught a 10-yard pass. The Patriots had a great opportunity but could not get into the end zone, so Tony Franklin kicked a 19-yard field goal.

Ronnie Lippett stopped the Jets when he recovered a fumble by wide receiver JoJo Townsell on the Jets 37-yard line. The Patriots went backward rather than forward with a run for a two-yard loss followed by a fumble recovery for an eight-yard loss. Camarillo hit a 42-yard punt that went out-of-bounds at the Jets 5-yard line.

O'Brien hit Mickey Shuler for a 28-yard gain, and the Jets methodically moved down the field. Ken O'Brien had a one-yard quarterback sneak on fourth down, but Julius Adams batted away a third down pass and Pat Leahy kicked a 53-yard field goal.

The Patriots came right back and moved 53 yards in 11 plays before Tony Franklin kicked a 44-yard field

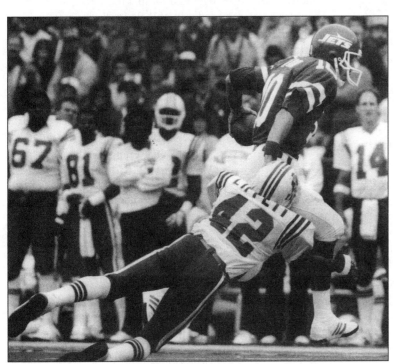

Ronnie Lippett

1985 New England Patriots Team Leaders
Offensive Team
Tony Eason tossed 11 TD passes
Irving Fryar had seven TD receptions
Craig James ran for five TDs
Irving Fryar ran for a TD

Defensive/Special Teams
Fred Marion had seven interceptions
Raymond Clayborn returned an interception for a TD
Irving Fryar returned two punts for a TD
Cedric Jones and Johnny Rembert returned a fumble for a TD
Andre Tippett returned a fumble for a TD
Don Blackmon recorded two safeties
Fred Marion and Steve Nelson recovered three fumbles
Johnny Rembert and Andre Tippett recovered three fumbles
Andre Tippett recorded 16.5 sacks

Memorable Statistics of the Year
Irving Fryar is the only Patriots player to run for a touchdown, return a punt for a touchdown, and catch a touchdown pass in the same season.
The New England Patriots had eight AFC Pro Bowl players in 1985.

---

goal. Grogan was intercepted on the last play of the half with the score Patriots 6 Jets 3.

Both teams traded punts, but Dave Jennings' punt was downed on the Patriots 5-yard line. The Patriots could not get a first down, and Camarillo was forced to punt from his own end zone. New York took possession of the ball on its 48-yard line and moved down the field. Pat Leahy put more points on the board for the Jets with his 52-yard field goal.

Roland James forced Tony Paige to fumble, after his reception in the right flat, and Patriots defensive lineman Garin Veris recovered the loose ball. Craig James, Tony Collins, and Mosi Tatupu shared the rushing duties as the Patriots had 10 consecutive running plays in this drive. On third-and-11, Grogan connected with Irving Fryar for a 36-yard touchdown.

O'Brien answered the call when he completed a 49-yard pass to Wesley Walker, putting the ball on the Patriots 2-yard line. Tony Paige ran up the middle for a two-yard touchdown, and Pat Leahy kicked the extra point to tie the score.

Stephen Starring returned the ensuing kickoff 34 yards. On the Patriots third play of this drive, Steve Grogan connected on a 47-yard pass play over the middle to Stanley Morgan. On first-and-goal from the 6-yard line, Craig James ran for three yards. Grogan then ran a bootleg over the left side for a three-yard, game-winning touchdown with just over three minutes left to play.

The Jets had one more chance, but the Patriots defense rose to the occasion. Andre Tippett sacked O'Brien for a five-yard loss. On fourth-and-11, O'Brien tossed a 12-yard pass to Walker for a first down. With about one minute left, O'Brien was hit by Andre Tippett, on third-and-10, and his pass went incomplete. On fourth-and-10, Garin Veris sacked O'Brien for a seven-yard loss to end the game.

Grogan took a knee on the final four plays, and the Patriots had defeated the New York Jets 20–13.

1986

Record 11–5; First place in the AFC Eastern Division
The Patriots lost to the Denver Broncos in the playoffs
The WEEI 590 AM Radio announcers were John Carlson and Jon Morris

The Patriots were 3–3 through the first six games. They had decisive wins over the Colts, Jets, and Dolphins. After losing to the Jets at Sullivan Stadium they went on a seven-game winning streak. The streak began with a 34–0 shutout of the Steelers and ended with a 21–20 stunning comeback over the Saints. The Patriots lost to the Bengals and the 49ers in the last two regular season home games. In the last regular season game, and for the first time in 20 years, the Patriots defeated the Miami Dolphins at the Orange Bowl to win the AFC Eastern Division title.

* * *

The Play of the Year was made by Irving Fryar. Fryar caught a 25-yard Hail Mary touchdown pass, which was tipped by Stanley Morgan, on the final play to defeat the Los Angeles Rams 30–28 at Anaheim Stadium on 11-16-86.

The Game of the Year was played against the Miami Dolphins at the Orange Bowl on 12-22-86. Patriots superstar linebacker Andre Tippett set the tone for this game as he forced Lorenzo Hampton to fumble on the Dolphins' eighth play of the game. Tony Eason was sacked by Brian Sochia on the Patriots' third play of the game, and Rich Camarillo booted a 64-yard punt, returning the ball to the Dolphins.

On third-and-4, Dan Marino only completed a three-yard pass, so Reggie Roby punted it back to the Patriots.

On third-and-5, Eason completed a seven-yard pass to Greg Baty for a first down. On third-and-9, Eason tossed a nine-yard pass to Tony Collins for another first down. On fourth-and-1, Mosi Tatupu ran up the middle for two yards to keep the drive alive on the Dolphins 29-yard line. Three plays later Eason connected on a

1986 New England Patriots Team Leaders
Offensive Team
Tony Eason threw 19 TD passes
Stanley Morgan had 10 TD receptions
Craig James ran for four TDs

Defensive/Special Teams
Ronnie Lippett had eight interceptions
Fred Marion returned an interception 37 yards for a TD
Rod McSwain returned a blocked punt for a TD
Mosi Tatupu returned a blocked punt for a TD
Irving Fryar returned a punt 59 yards for a TD
Johnny Rembert recovered a fumble for a TD
Brent Williams returned a fumble 21 yards for a TD
Brent Williams recovered four fumbles
Garin Veris recorded 11 sacks

Memorable Statistics of the Year
The only Patriots defensive lineman to return a fumble for the game-winning touchdown in a regular season game Brent Williams returned a fumble, forced by Garin Veris, 21 yards for a touchdown in the 21–20 win on 11-30-86. The Patriots set a team record of two total yards rushing in this victorious game.
The New England Patriots had five AFC Pro Bowl players in 1986.

22-yard touchdown pass to Morgan. Tony Franklin kicked the extra point.

Patriots linebacker Ed Reynolds tackled Reggie Roby, who was not able to punt the ball, and the Patriots had great field position on the Dolphins 35-yard line. Greg Hawthorne recovered a fumble by his teammate Reggie Dupard, allowing the Patriots to maintain possession. Tony Franklin kicked a 47-yard field goal.

Franklin's kickoff was fumbled by Larry Lee, and Steve Doig recovered it for the Patriots. The Patriots gave it right back, as William Judson forced Craig James to fumble, and Mark Brown returned the fumble 10 yards. Marino hit Mark Clayton for 18 yards, and Hampton dashed for another 18 yards and suddenly Miami was on the move. Fuad Reveiz kicked a 42-yard field goal to put the Dolphins on the scoreboard.

Roland James returned a Marino pass 21 yards, and the Patriots had good field position again. Steve Grogan entered the game, and his first pass was knocked down by Bob Brudzinski. His second attempt was broken up by Renya Thompson, but his third passing attempt, on third-and-10, was completed to Stanley Morgan for 18 yards. Grogan was then sacked for a loss of six yards by Mark Brown. John Offerdahl broke up another pass, but Tony Franklin was able to kick a 44-yard field goal to put the Patriots up by 10 points.

Marino completed six passes for 54 yards, and Clayton ran for 11 yards on a reverse, and in just three minutes the Dolphins scored a touchdown. On third-and-goal from the 1-yard line, Marino tossed a one-yard touchdown pass to Bruce Hardy. The score at halftime was Patriots 13 Dolphins 10.

Grogan connected on three passes, good for 42 yards, but Franklin missed a 39-yard field-goal attempt to start the third quarter.

Lorenzo Hampton dashed for a 47-yard gain, and Mark Duper caught a 13-yard pass to bring the ball to the Patriots 4-yard line. Garin Veris stopped Hampton for no gain. On second-and-goal, Marino overthrew a pass to Bruce Hardy. On third-and-goal, Ernest Gibson broke up a pass intended for James Pruit. Fuad Reveiz tied the game with a 21-yard field goal.

Glenn Blackwood returned a long pass by Steve Grogan seven yards, and Patriots wide receiver Irving Fryar made the tackle. Three plays later, Dan Marino connected on a 32-yard touchdown pass to Mark Clayton. In just 54 seconds the Dolphins took the lead 20–13.

Grogan completed four passes, good for 55 yards, including one for 32 yards to Irving Fryar, and the Patriots were on the move again. On third-and-1 from the Dolphins 7-yard line, Grogan ran over the right side for the touchdown.

The Dolphins started the fourth quarter with the ball on the Patriots 40-yard line. Three plays later Clayton was in the end zone. Marino tossed a 19-yard pass to Ron Davenport, a two-yard pass to Dan Johnson, and then a 19-yard touchdown pass to Clayton.

This was the last time the Dolphins scored in this game.

Grogan completed a 20-yard pass to Stanley Morgan and a 22-yard pass to Tony Collins to get the Patriots into Dolphins territory. On third-and-2, Collins gained five yards, and the Patriots could not be stopped. Collins caught a 12-yard touchdown pass from Steve Grogan, and the score was again tied.

On fourth-and-4, Marino pooch punted the ball to the Patriots 14-yard line. Morgan was in the end zone for the Patriots 12 plays and 86 yards later. The Patriots were successful on all three of their third down plays in the game-winning drive.

On third-and-1, Mosi Tatupu gained two yards. On third-and-3, Morgan caught a 13-yard pass. On third-and-4, Craig James gained just a bit more than four yards for the first down. Morgan hauled in the game-winning 30-yard touchdown pass from Grogan with 54 seconds left in the game.

With 44 seconds left in the game, Rod McSwain returned a Marino pass three yards to seal the victory. Grogan took the last three snaps to his knee, allowing the Patriots to win the AFC Eastern Division title.

1987

Record 8–7; Tied for second place in the AFC Eastern Division
The WHDH 850 AM Radio announcers were Curt Gowdy and Jon Morris

In the strike-shortened season, the Patriots beat the Dolphins at Sullivan Stadium on opening day and then lost on the road to the Jets. A game against the Redskins was canceled because of the player's strike. Replacement players were recruited and played in the first three games in October. The Patriots won two of these three strike-replacement games. On October 25, the NFL players came back to play. The Patriots lost to the Indianapolis Colts at the Hoosier Dome. The Patriots bounced back with a three-point win over the LA Raiders but then lost to the Giants and the Cowboys in overtime. They shut out the Colts but then lost to the Eagles in overtime. Once again they lost to the Broncos in Denver but then finished strong, winning their last three games against division opponents.

* * *

The Play of the Year was made by Stanley Morgan. Morgan caught a 40-yard pass, while being defended by former Patriots cornerback Mike Haynes, with 46 seconds left, which helped set up a game-winning 29-yard field goal with five seconds left to defeat the Los Angeles Raiders 26–23 at Sullivan Stadium on 11-01-87.

The Game of the Year was played against the Indianapolis Colts at Sullivan Stadium on 11-22-87. Jim Bowman, who suffered a mild concussion during the game, made eight tackles, had two interceptions, and a fumble recovery.

Tom Ramsey completed an 18-yard pass to Stanley Morgan on the first play of the game. The Patriots offense stalled after that, and Rich Camarillo punted to the Colts.

Patriots defensive back Jim Bowman recorded four consecutive tackles, and linebacker Johnny Rembert stopped Albert Bentley on third down, and then the Colts punted.

The teams traded missing field-goal attempts. Dean Biasucci was wide right on his 46-yard field-goal attempt, and Tony Franklin was also wide right on his 37-yard field-goal attempt.

Reggie Dupard had runs of five, six, and six yards again before Robert Perryman busted up the middle for a gain of 48 yards. Two plays later, Tom Ramsey tossed an eight-yard slant pass to Irving Fryar for a touchdown.

Raymond Clayborn stopped Framingham High School and BU graduate Bill Brooks one yard short of the first down, and Rohn Stark was forced to punt. Rich Camarillo punted the ball back because the Patriots could not move the ball either.

Brent Williams stuffed Eric Dickerson for no gain, on third-and-1, and the Patriots defense jammed George Wonsley for no gain on fourth down. The Patriots failed on a fourth down play as well, and the Colts took over on downs.

Andre Tippett sacked Gary Hogeboom for a nine-yard loss, and Irving Fryar's 23-yard punt return gave the Patriots great field position to start their next drive. Tom Ramsey's 23-yard completion to Stanley Morgan help set up a 34-yard field goal by Tony Franklin. The score was 10–0 at the end of the first half.

Rich Camarillo's punt went out of bounds at the Colts 12-yard line. They were not able to get a first down, and Rohn Stark was called in to punt. Patriots special team lineman Willie Scott broke through the line and blocked the punt. Willie recovered and took the loose ball three yards for the touchdown.

1987 New England Patriots Team Leaders
Offensive Team
Steve Grogan tossed 10 TD passes
Irving Fryar had five TD receptions
Tony Collins ran for three TDs
Reggie Dupard ran for three TDs

Defensive/Special Teams
Fred Marion had four interceptions
Ronnie Lippett returned two interceptions for a TD
Raymond Clayborn returned a blocked field goal for a TD
Willie Scott returned a blocked punt for a TD
Andre Tippett returned a fumble 29 yards for a TD
Andre Tippett recovered three fumbles
Andre Tippett recorded 12.5 sacks

Memorable Statistics of the Year
Steve Grogan is the only Patriots player to throw four touchdown passes and run for a touchdown in the same game.
Steve tossed four touchdown passes and ran for a touchdown in the 42–20 victory over the New York Jets on 12-13-87.
Stanley Morgan and Andre Tippett represented the Patriots in the 1987 Pro Bowl.

Irving Fryar

Andre Tippett sacked Hogeboom, for a loss of 10 yards, and the Colts had to punt. The Patriots could not get a first down, and they punted as well.

Jim Bowman was back in the game after a minor head injury and picked off a Hogeboom pass. The Patriots did not take advantage of this turnover and punted again. Steve Nelson forced Eric Dickerson to fumble, and Jim Bowman was there to recover it. Tony Franklin missed a 37-yard field-goal attempt.

Ronnie Lippett took the matter of scoring into his own hands as he returned a Gary Hogeboom pass 45 yards for a touchdown. Ernest Gibson picked off a Hogeboom pass in the end zone for a touchback, keeping the shutout alive.

After 10 straight rushing plays by the Patriots, Rich Camarillo punted the ball to the Colts 15-yard line. Jack Trudeau took control for the Colts and marched up to the Patriots 13-yard line. Rod McSwain deflected a fourth down pass, and the Patriots took over on downs. The Patriots ran three running plays and then punted.

Jim Bowman had a three-yard return of a fourth down pass by Trudeau, and the Patriots secured the shutout. After three rushing plays the Patriots punted. Bowman made the tackle on George Wonsley's 16-yard reception, on the last play of their 24–0 shutout of the Indianapolis Colts.

1988

Record 9–7; Tied for second place in the AFC Eastern Division
The WHDH 850 AM Radio announcers were Dale Arnold and Gino Cappelletti

The Patriots started the season with a 28–3 rout of the Jets but then lost their next three games. Doug Flutie came off the bench and led them to a comeback win over the Colts. Flutie then started in nine straight games. The Patriots won six of these nine games with Flutie at the helm. Tony Eason was the Patriots quarterback in the first victorious overtime game. On 12-11-88, in -15 degrees below zero wild-chill weather conditions, the Patriots finally won an overtime game defeating the Tampa Bay Buccaneers 10–7. Denver defeated the Patriots at Mile High Stadium in the season's last game.

* * *

The Play of the Year was made by Patriots quarterback Doug Flutie. Doug ran a naked 13-yard bootleg play for a touchdown, with 29 seconds left, to defeat the Indianapolis Colts 21–17 at Sullivan Stadium on 10-02-88. According to Patriots radio announcer Dale Arnold, the place (crowd) went "icky balookey." Doug was the AFC Offensive Player of the Week.

The Game of the Year was played against the Chicago Bears at Sullivan Stadium on 10-30-88. The Bears finished the season with a 12–4 record.

Kevin Butler's opening kickoff went into the end zone for a touchback. The Patriots' first play of the game would set the tone for the entire game. Doug Flutie floated an 80-yard touchdown pass to Irving Fryar on the game's first offensive play. Jason Staurovsky's extra point was blocked by Dan Hampton.

Jim Bowman forced a fumble on the ensuing kickoff, but Maurice Douglass recovered it for the Bears. Seven plays later Ronnie Lippett picked off a

---

1988 New England Patriots Team Leaders
Offensive Team
Doug Flutie threw eight TD passes
Irving Fryar had five TD receptions
Robert Perryman ran for six TDs
John Stephens fell on a fumble for a TD

Defensive/Special Teams
Ray Clayborn, Fred Marion and Roland James had four interceptions
Sammy Martin returned a kickoff 95 yards for a TD
Johnny Rembert recovered three fumbles
Andre Tippett recorded eight sacks

Memorable Statistics of the Year
The only Patriots player who almost scored a touchdown on his birthday was Robert Perryman.
Robert Perryman fumbled into the end zone and John Stephens recovered it for the TD on 10-16-88.
Johnny Rembert, John Stephens, and Andre Tippett represented the Patriots in the 1988 Pro Bowl.

---

pass by Jim McMahon on the Patriots 1-yard line and the Patriots had the ball back.

Richard Dent forced John Stephens to fumble, and Al Harris recovered the loose ball for the Bears. On third-and-2, Matt Suhey ran five yards for a first down. McMahon ran up the middle for a one-yard touchdown and Kevin Butler kicked the extra point. The Bears did not score again.

On the second play of the second quarter, Flutie rolled to the left side of the field and then tossed a two-yard touchdown pass to Lin Dawson. The Patriots second drive of the second quarter resulted in a forced punt, but Jeff Feagles' punt was mishandled by Wendell Davis, and Darryl Homes recovered it for the Patriots. On fourth-and-1 from the 4-yard line, Doug Flutie rolled to the right side of the field and tossed another touchdown pass to Lin Dawson.

Mosi Tatupu forced another fumbled punt return by Wendell Davis, and Marvin Allen recovered the fumble for the Patriots. The Patriots did not take advantage of this turnover, and the punt by Feagles went into the end zone for a touchback.

Mike Tomczak threw an incomplete pass, on fourth-and-3, on the Bears first drive in the third quarter. Tomczak threw an incomplete pass on fourth-and-8 on the Bears' second drive of the third quarter. Bryan Wagner punted for the Bears on the third drive of the third quarter.

The Patriots ran seven consecutive times before Flutie misfired on third-and-2. Jason Staurovsky kicked a 35-yard field goal near the end of the third quarter.

With the score 23–7, Flutie took the Patriots on a 15-play drive that took 10:54 off the clock. Flutie's only pass attempt was on the final play of the drive. On third-and-9, Flutie tossed a 26-yard touchdown pass to Stanley Morgan for the game's final touchdown. Staurovsky kicked the extra point for the final point scored in the game. Every Patriots player who caught a pass also caught a touchdown pass. Flutie only completed six passes but four were for touchdowns.

1989

Record 5–11; Fourth place in the AFC Eastern Division
The WHDH 850 AM Radio announcers were Dale Arnold and Gino Cappelletti

The Patriots defeated the New York Jets by three points, the Oilers by 10 points, the Colts by three points in overtime, the Bills by nine points, and the Colts by six points for five victories. The Patriots lost three games in a row after the team's first victory and lost three games in a row to end the season. Raymond Berry was fired at the season's end.

* * *

The Play of the Year was made by Maurice Hurst. He returned a pass by Jim Kelly on the first play of the fourth quarter 16 yards for a touchdown, making the score 30–24, in the eventual 33–24 win over the Buffalo Bills at Sullivan Stadium on 11-19-89.

The Game of the Year was played against the Indianapolis Colts at the Hoosier Dome on 10-29-89. On the second play of the game, from the Colts 9-yard line, Jack Trudeau completed a pass to Bill Brooks, who took it to midfield and then lateraled it to Andre Rison, who took it to the Patriots 20-yard line, for a 71-yard play. Trudeau fumbled the snap on the next play, and linebacker Vincent Brown recovered it for the Patriots.

On the Patriots first offensive play of the game, Steve Grogan connected with Stanley Morgan for a 50-yard pass play. Greg Davis came in and kicked a 47-yard field goal with just one minute gone in the game.

Trudeau connected on consecutive 13-yard passes to Clarence Verdin, and the Colts were on the Patriots' side of the field. On third-and-10 from the Patriots 22-yard line, Jack Trudeau connected with Rison for a touchdown.

1989 New England Patriots Team Leaders
Offensive Team
Steve Grogan threw nine TD passes
Cedric Jones had six TD receptions
John Stephens ran for seven TDs

Defensive/Special Teams
Maurice Hurst had five interceptions, returning one for a TD
Vincent Brown and Brent Williams recovered two fumbles
Brent Williams recorded eight sacks

Memorable Statistics of the Year
The only Patriots player to score the game-winning points on his birthday was Greg Davis.
Davis kicked an overtime game-winning, 51-yard field goal to defeat the Colts 23–20 on 10-20-89.
Johnny Rembert was the only player to represent the Patriots in the 1989 Pro Bowl.

With about four minutes left in the first quarter, Trudeau completed a 24-yard pass to Rison, and the Colts were back in Patriots territory. The Colt's drive stalled on the Patriots 15-yard line, and Dean Biasucci kicked a 32-yard field goal.

On the Colts' first play of the second quarter, Johnny Rembert caused Rison to fumble, and Fred Marion recovered it for the Patriots. On third-and-12, Grogan was sacked for a loss of 10 yards, and Jeff Feagles punted it back to the Colts.

On the 13th play of the Patriots' next drive, Davis missed a 38-yard field-goal attempt. Neither team was able to move the ball for the rest of the second quarter, so the score at the half was Colts 10 Patriots 3.

About midway through the third quarter Grogan led his team down the field for the game-tying touchdown. Grogan completed four passes for 44 yards, including an eight-yard touchdown pass to Cedric Jones.

Greg Davis kicked a 48-yard field goal on the sixth play of the fourth quarter, and the Patriots had a three-point lead. Jack Trudeau completed a seven-yard touchdown pass to Mark Boyer, and the Colts had a

four-point lead. Grogan completed six consecutive passes, and John Stephens ran up the middle for a one-yard touchdown to get the lead up to three points.

Biasucci kicked a 39-yard field goal with 55 seconds left in regulation.

Greg Davis missed a 46-yard field goal with just three seconds left in regulation.

On the Patriots' second possession in overtime, Grogan completed a 28-yard pass to Sammy Martin. Robert Perryman ran for a first down on second-and-2, twice. Davis redeemed his earlier miss by kicking a 51-yard field goal, on his 24th birthday, to beat the Indianapolis Colts 23–20 in overtime.

1990

Record 1–15; Last place in the AFC Eastern Division
The WHDH 850 AM Radio announcers were Dale Arnold and Gino Cappelletti

Rod Rust was hired as the new head coach of the New England Patriots. This was the only season he acted as the team's head coach. The Patriots' only victory was against the Indianapolis Colts.

* * *

The Play of the Year was made by Garin Veris and Brent Williams. Veris strip-sacked Dave Krieg, and Williams returned the loose ball 45 yards for a touchdown in a 33–20 loss to the Seattle Seahawks at Foxboro Stadium on 10-07-90.

The Game of the Year was the 16–14 victory over the Indianapolis Colts at the Hoosier Dome on 09-16-90.

Maurice Hurst intercepted a pass by Jeff George in the end zone for a touchback to stop the Colts on the team's first drive of the game. The Patriots were unable to move the ball and had to punt. Albert Bentley ended a 13-play drive by the Colts with a one-yard touchdown run, on fourth-and-goal, for the first points scored in the game.

After trading punts, the Patriots were able to move the ball under the leadership of Steve Grogan. Grogan completed a 13-yard pass and a 16-yard pass to Irving Fryar before tossing a 27-yard touchdown pass to Hart Lee Dykes.

Maurice Hurst intercepted another pass by Jeff George, this time on his 19-yard line, to stop the Colts. Irving Fryar caught a 17-yard pass, and John Stephens took a Grogan pass 23 yards to help set up a field-goal attempt by Jason Staurovsky. Unfortunately, his 49-yard field goal attempt was wide left with nine seconds left in the first half.

1990 New England Patriots Team Leaders
Offensive Team
Marc Wilson threw six TD passes
Marv Cook had five TD receptions
John Stephens ran for two TDs

Defensive/Special Teams
Maurice Hurst, Ronnie Lippett, and Fred Marion had four
   interceptions
Brent Williams returned a fumble 45 yards for a TD
Ronnie Lippett and Fred Marion recovered four fumbles
Brent Williams recorded six sacks

Memorable Statistics of the Year
Maurice Hurt blocked a punt by Dan Stryzinski even
   though the Patriots only had 10 men on the field.
Offensive tackle Bruce Armstrong represented the New
   England Patriots in the 1990 Pro Bowl.

Patriots offensive lineman Bruce Armstrong tackled Jeff Herrod on his interception return of Grogan on the Patriots' first drive of the third quarter. Ronnie Lippett got the ball right back for the Patriots as he intercepted George on the Colts' fourth play of the third quarter. After a 12-play drive by the Patriots, Staurovsky kicked a 39-yard field goal.

Patriots defensive back Roland James forced Albert Bentley to fumble, and Ray Agnew recovered it for the Patriots. The Patriots took advantage of this turnover as Staurovsky ended the drive by kicking a 27-yard field goal.

Fred Marion had a 16-yard interception return of a George pass, that was tipped by Hurst, to set up another score for the Patriots. Staurovsky then kicked a 25-yard field goal.

On the first play after their kickoff return, Colts quarterback Jeff George connected on a 68-yard touchdown pass to Bill Brooks. This narrowed the score to 16–14.

With just over two minutes left, Ronnie Lippett recovered the onside kick by Dean Biasucci. Stephens ran for a first down on third-and-2, and the Patriots were able to run out the clock and record the team's only victory during the 1990 regular season.

1991

Record 6–10; Fourth place in the AFC Eastern Division
The WBZ 1030 AM Radio announcers were Gil Santos and Gino Cappelletti

Dick MacPherson was hired as the Patriots' new head coach. The team was victorious on the road against the Colts in the season's opening game. The following week the Patriots were shut out by the Cleveland Browns in the home opening game at Foxboro Stadium. New England only scored six points in a road game loss to the Steelers but scored 24 points to win over the Oilers at Foxboro. The Patriots only scored 10 points in consecutive losses to the Cardinals and the Dolphins. Hugh Millen led the team to an exciting 26–23 overtime victory over the Vikings at Foxboro in the season's seventh game. Then the Patriots lost four games in a row. In the 12th game of the season the Patriots snuck by the Bills by three points, only to score just three points the following week in a loss to the Broncos in Denver. Another thrilling overtime win at Foxboro was over the Colts. The Bengals defeated the Patriots in front of the home crowd in the season's last game.

* * *

The Play of the Year was made by Jason Staurovsky. On the last play of the first overtime, Staurovsky kicked a 42-yard field goal to defeat the Minnesota Vikings 26–23 at Foxboro Stadium on 10-20-91.

The Game of the Year was played against the Indianapolis Colts at Foxboro Stadium on 12-08-91. Tight end Ben Coates had minus-6 yards rushing, and Hugh Millen had 330 yards passing. Patriots nose tackle Fred Smerlas had two tackles of Eric Dickerson, both for a loss of one yard.

After the Colts were forced to punt on their opening drive, the Patriots took 13 plays and drove into Colts territory on their opening possession. Greg McMurtry caught a 25-yard pass from Hugh Millen to help set up a 24-yard field goal by Charlie Baumann.

Both teams punted three times before the Colts were able get in the Patriots red zone. Jeff George tossed a 13-yard touchdown pass to Jessie Hester for the Colts' first touchdown.

1991 New England Patriots Team Leaders
Offensive Team
Hugh Millen tossed nine TD passes
Marv Cook had three TD receptions
Irving Fryar had three TD receptions
Leonard Russell had four rushing TDs
Freddie Childress fell on a fumble for a TD

Defensive/Special Teams
Maurice Hurst had three interceptions
Jon Vaughn returned a kickoff 99 yards for a TD
Andre Tippett recovered three fumbles
Andre Tippett recorded 8.5 sacks

Memorable Statistics of the Year
This is the only year that the Patriots had a game-winning touchdown reception to win a regulation and an overtime game.
Greg McMurty caught a 34-yard touchdown pass to beat Houston 24–20, and Michael Timpson beat the Colts in OT on 12-08-91.
Bruce Armstrong and Marv Cook were AFC Pro Bowl players for the Patriots in 1991.

Chip Banks strip-sacked Hugh Millen, and Tony Siragusa returned the fumble to his 1-yard line, and the Colts were again in great position to score. Eric Dickerson punched it in for a one-yard touchdown, and the Colts were up 14–3.

The Colts forced another turnover as John Baylor had a 13-yard return of a pass that was thrown by Millen. Jeff George completed a 46-yard pass to Bill Brooks, on the first play of the fourth quarter, that helped set up a 40-yard field goal by Dean Biasucci.

Millen completed a 49-yard pass to Marv Cook and a 22 yard pass to Greg McMurtry to bring the Patriots to the Colts 1-yard line. John Stephens punched it in for a

one-yard touchdown to get the Patriots back in the ball game.

Both teams punted three times again before the Patriots took over on their 49-yard line with 1:05 left in the game. Hugh Millen ran for a 14-yard gain, Cook had a 19-yard reception, and Michael Timpson took it to the Colts 2-yard line after his 26-yard reception. With nine seconds left, Hugh Millen tossed a two-yard touchdown pass to Ben Coates to tie the game and force overtime.

The Colts had the ball twice and had to punt both times in the overtime period. The Patriots started the team's second drive on their own 47-yard line. On third-and-2, Millen tossed a 45-yard, game-winning touchdown pass to Michael Timpson to defeat the Colts 23–17 in overtime at Foxboro Stadium.

1992
Record 2–14; Last place in the AFC Eastern Division
The WBZ 1030 AM Radio announcers were Gil Santos and Gino Cappelletti

Scott Zolak was the starting quarterback for the Patriots' two victories in 1992. Scott was the AFC Offensive Player of the Week in the 37–34 overtime win against the Indianapolis Colts at the Hoosier Dome. The following week Zolak led the team to a 24–3 rout of the New York Jets at Foxboro Stadium.

* * *

The Play of the Year was made by Chris Singleton. Chris returned a pass by Jeff George, which was tipped by Patriots linebacker Vincent Brown, 82 yards for a touchdown in the 37–34 overtime win vs. the Indianapolis Colts at the Hoosier Dome on 11-15-92.

The Game of the Year was played against the Indianapolis Colts at the Hoosier Dome on 11-15-92.

Dean Biasucci's opening kickoff went into the end zone for a touchback. Colts defensive lineman Tony Siragusa tackled John Stephens after his three-yard run. On second down, Jon Vaughn was stopped for no gain. John Baylor sacked Scott Zolak, on a safety blitz, for a 10-yard loss on the third play of the game. Clarence

Verdin returned the 43-yard punt by Shawn McCarthy 53 yards for a touchdown.

The Patriots went three and out again. This time Verdin only had a 15-yard return of a 55-yard punt by McCarthy.

On the Colts' first offensive play of the game, Patriots defensive back David Pool intercepted Jeff George and returned it 41 yards for a touchdown. Just four minutes into the game, both teams had scored a touchdown.

The Colts were able to get two first downs, but George threw an incomplete pass on third down, and they were forced to punt. Just three plays later Colts defensive lineman Jon Hand forced John Stephens to fumble, and Scott Redecic recovered for the Colts. Reggie Langhorne caught a 29-yard pass, bringing the ball to the Patriots 1-yard line. On third-and-goal, George tossed a 1-yard pass to Rodney Culver for the touchdown.

Scott Zolak maneuvered his team down the field for the game-tying touchdown. He tossed a 10-yard pass to Michael Timpson and completed an 11-yard pass to Irving Fryar. On third-and-6, he connected with Fryar for a 16-yard gain. Jon Vaughn then broke through the middle of the line, for a 30-yard gain, taking it to the Colts 2-yard line. Zolak lofted a two-yard touchdown pass to Ben Coates to tie the score 14–14.

George took his team on a nine-play drive, to the Patriots 18-yard line, but Dean Biasucci was wide right on a 35-yard field-goal attempt.

Colts defensive back Chris Goode returned a pass by Scott Zolak 47 yards to the Patriots 15-yard line, but Dean Biasucci was wide left on a 42-yard field-goal attempt.

On third-and-5, Stephens gained six yards. On third-and-1, later in the drive, Kevin Turner was stopped for no gain, and the Patriots had to punt.

Mike Prior called for a fair catch on a 40-yard punt by Shawn McCarthy, and Indianapolis took over on its own 15-yard line. Anthony Johnson advanced a pass by George 38 yards, and the Colts were in Patriots territory with just one play. With two minutes left in the first half, Jeff George completed a 10-yard pass to Reggie Langhorne and a 14-yard pass to Anthony Johnson. On third-and-10, with 1:04 left, Jeff George tossed a 23-yard touchdown pass to Kerry Cash.

Defensive lineman Marion Hobby returned the short kickoff by Dean Biasucci 11 yards to the Colts 33-yard line. Stephens ran for a gain of two yards to the 35-yard line. On third-and-eight with 23 seconds left, Scott connected on a 23-yard pass that Greg McMurty took all the way to the end zone for a 65-yard touchdown. Charlie Baumann kicked the extra point to tie the score 21–21 at the end of the first half.

1992 New England Patriots Team Leaders

Offensive Team

Hugh Millen tossed eight TD passes
Irving Fryar had four TD receptions
Leonard Russell ran for two TDs
John Stephens ran for two TDs

Defensive/Special Teams

Jerome Henderson and Maurice Hurst had three interceptions
David Pool returned an interception 41 yards for a TD
Chris Singleton returned an interception 82 yards for a TD
Vincent Brown returned an interception 49 yards for a TD
Jon Vaughn returned a kickoff 100 yards for a TD
Vincent Brown and Kevin Turner recovered two fumbles
Vincent Brown returned a fumble 25 yards for a TD
Tim Goad returned a fumble 19 yards for a TD
Andre Tippett recorded seven sacks

Memorable Statistics of the Year

Hugh Millen set the team record by completing 13 consecutive passes in a regular season game.
Tight end Marv Cook was the Patriots only Pro Bowl player in 1992.

On the Colts' first drive of the third quarter, George had two big completions. George completed a 22-yard pass to Anthony Johnson and a 26-yard pass to Reggie Langhorne. Dean Biasucci put three points on the board for the Colts with a 48-yard field goal.

On the Colts' second drive of the third quarter, Johnson and Reggie Langhorne continued to make big plays. Johnson caught a 13-yard pass and a 33-yard pass on consecutive plays, and then Landhorne had a 14-yard reception, putting the ball on the Patriots 1-yard line. On the first play of the fourth quarter, Rodney Culver ran over the left guard for the one-yard touchdown.

The Patriots' next possession started from the team's own 6-yard line. The Patriots were not able get a first down, and Shawn McCarthy was forced to punt from his own end zone.

After a 33-yard reception by Johnson, the Colts had first-and-goal from the Patriots 6-yard line but did not score.

Patriots linebacker Vincent Brown deflected a George pass, and Chris Singleton caught the errant pass and rumbled 82 yards for a touchdown. Just like that the Patriots were back in the game.

Patriots special team player Kevin Turner forced a fumble by Ashley Ambrose, on the ensuing kickoff, and

Todd Collins recovered the loose ball for the Patriots. Charlie Baumann kicked a 36-yard field goal and the score was tied 31–31.

Back came the Colts. George completed a 26-yard pass and a 13-yard pass on consecutive plays to Bill Brooks. On third-and-14, Johnson's 10-yard reception was four yards short of the first down marker. Biasucci came on the field and kicked a 33-yard field goal.

With 1:39 left in the fourth quarter, the Patriots had the ball on the team's own 6-yard line, down by three points. Zolak tossed a 25-yard pass to Timpson. With 44 seconds left in regulation play, Zolak hit Michael Timpson for another 19 yards. With 23 seconds to go in regulation, Zolak connected with Fryar for 16 yards. Fryar then hauled in a 13-yard pass from Zolak and left just two seconds on the clock for Baumann, who kicked a 44-yard field goal to send the game into overtime.

On the third play of overtime, Patriots defensive back Jerome Henderson intercepted George. Henderson returned this interception nine yards to the Colts 29-yard line. On third-and-6, Zolak tossed a 24-yard pass to Vaughn, who took it to the Colts 1-yard line. On first-and-goal from the 1, Baumann kicked an 18-yard field goal to defeat the Indianapolis Colts 37–34 in overtime.

1993

Record 5–11; Fourth place in the AFC Eastern Division
The WBZ 1030 AM Radio announcers were Gil Santos and Gino Cappelletti

Bill Parcells was hired as the new head coach of the New England Patriots. The Patriots then went on to lose the season's first four games. After the bye week the Patriots defeated the Phoenix Cardinals 23–21 and then proceeded to lose another seven games in a row. The Patriots beat the Browns, Bengals, Colts, and Dolphins in the last four games of the regular season, giving the team hope for the 1994 season.

* * *

The Play of the Year was made by Kevin Turner. Turner caught a 13-yard pass from Scott Secules and then lateraled it to Leonard Russell. Russell took the lateral and rumbled 69 yards to the Cardinals 2-yard line. Scott Secules then tossed a two-yard touchdown to Ben Coates for the game-winning touchdown, with just under four minutes left, in the 23–21 comeback win over the Phoenix Cardinals at Sun Devil Stadium on 10-10-93.

The Game of the Year was played against the Miami Dolphins at Foxboro Stadium on 01-02-94. Drew Bledsoe almost led the team in yards rushing as he had one less yard rushing than running back Russell, who had 28.

Miami won the toss, and O.J. McDuffie returned the opening kickoff 35 yards. On third-and-2, Terry Kirby was successful on a three-yard run. Later on this same drive, on fourth-and-1, Mark Higgs was stopped by linebackers Todd Collins and Andre Tippett for no gain, on the Patriots 35-yard line.

Kevin Turner caught an 11-yard pass from Bledsoe. Corey Croom caught a 14-yard pass from Bledsoe. Turner kept the drive alive with a three-yard run on

1993 New England Patriots Team Leaders
Offensive Team
Drew Bledsoe tossed 15 TD passes
Ben Coates had eight TD receptions
Leonard Russell ran for seven TDs

Defensive/Special Teams
Maurice Hurst had four interceptions
Andre Tippett recovered four fumbles
Chris Slade recorded nine sacks

Memorable Statistics of the Year
The only Patriots quarterback to throw a game-winning touchdown pass to beat the Phoenix Cardinals was Scott Secules.
Secules tossed a two-yard touchdown pass to Ben Coates to beat the Phoenix Cardinals 23–21 on 10-10-93.

third-and-1. The Patriots' drive stalled on the Dolphins 13-yard line, so Matt Bahr kicked a 31-yard field goal.

Dolphins quarterback Scott Mitchell moved his team into potential field-goal territory. He hit Keith Jackson for 14 yards, Tony Martin for 24 yards, and Terry Kirby for 14 yards. On third-and-9 from the Patriots 25-yard line, he was sacked by Brent Williams and Andre Tippett for a seven-yard loss, and Dale Hatcher had to punt.

Bledsoe took his team on a 16-play, 89-yard drive, which resulted in a touchdown.

The Patriots went 3–3 on third down plays in this drive. On third-and-8, Vincent Brisby caught a 12-yard pass from Bledsoe for a first down. On another third-and-8 play, Bledsoe took off up the middle for a 12-yard gain. This was the longest run by Patriots player in this game. On third-and-goal from the 11-yard line, Bledsoe tossed an 11-yard pass to Ben Coates for the touchdown.

Mitchell then took his team on a 10-play, 71-yard drive, which resulted in a touchdown. Dolphins wide receiver Irving Fryar started it off with a 16-yard reception from Scott Mitchell. Mark Higgs had runs of eight and 19 yards, and Fryar had another reception for six yards. A 10-yard pass to Mark Ingram put the ball on the Patriots 6-yard line with just two minutes left in the half. On second-and-goal from the 5, Mark Higgs went over his left tackle for the touchdown. Both quarterbacks completed nine passes for 96 yards in the first half.

Bledsoe fumbled on the third play of the third quarter, on his 16-yard line, and Jarvis Williams recovered the loose ball for the Dolphins. Four plays later

Drew Bledsoe

Pete Stoyanovich kicked a 29-yard field goal for the Dolphins.

The Patriots were determined to win their last game of this season. Drew took his team into Dolphins territory with the sole mission of scoring a touchdown. He completed three passes to his running backs, tossed a 16-yard pass to Coates, and then ran up the middle for 12 yards. Bledsoe fired an 11-yard pass, on the only third down play in this drive, to Vincent Brisby for the touchdown.

Miami took its first timeout with 40 seconds left in the third quarter. The Dolphins had a fourth-and-2 situation on the Patriots 45-yard line. Scott Mitchell threw an incomplete pass, and the Patriots took over on downs.

After the Patriots lost four yards on the first play of the team's next possession, and Bledsoe threw two incomplete passes, they had to punt. Darrell Malone blocked a punt by Mike Saxon, and the Dolphins were in business. Higgs ran for two yards. Keith Byars caught an 8-yard pass. Irving Fryar caught a 19-yard pass. Higgs ran for two yards again, and the Dolphins had first-and-goal from the 9-yard line. Tippett forced Mitchell to throw the pass away. Keith Byars' halfback option pass was thrown away. On third-and-9, Mitchell fired a nine-yard pass to Mark Ingram for a touchdown.

Coates had the big play on the Patriots' next possession. Coates broke two tackles and rumbled 42 yards before being pushed out of bounds on a pass reception from Bledsoe. On third-and-4, Chuck Klingbeil and Mike Golic combined to stop Leonard Russell after a one-yard gain, forcing the Patriots to attempt a field goal. Matt Bahr kicked a 37-yard field goal to retake the lead.

Even though Tippett sacked Mitchell for a 10-yard loss, to record his 100th and final career sack, the Dolphins were able to drive down the field and score another touchdown. Former Patriots tight end Greg Baty caught a 26-yard pass from Scott Mitchell, and three plays later Terry Kirby ran over the right side for a 15-yard touchdown.

The Patriots were trailing by four points with 3:40 left in regulation. Drew then completed 7-of-9 passes for 68 yards in the 10-play, 75-yard drive, in two minutes and 26 seconds. On third-and-4, Kevin Turner caught a five-yard pass for a first down. On third-and-3, Corey Croom ran up the middle for seven yards for another first down. With 1:17 left in the fourth quarter, Coates caught an 11-yard touchdown pass from Bledsoe.

Miami took over on its own 34-yard line. Mark Ingram had a 15-yard reception. McDuffie had an 18-yard reception. On third-and-6, with 32 seconds left in regulation, Mitchell completed a 23-yard pass to Ingram. With 14 seconds left, Patriots linebacker Vincent Brown batted away a pass that was intended for Irving Fryar. Stoyanovich kicked a 24-yard field goal with nine seconds left to force overtime.

On the Dolphins' third play in overtime, Patriots linebacker Chris Slade strip-sacked Mitchell, but Bert Weidner recovered the loose ball for the Dolphins. Ricky Harris returned the punt by Dale Hatcher six yards, giving the Patriots the ball on the team's own 35-yard line.

On the Patriots third play in overtime, Dolphins defensive back J.B. Brown returned a Bledsoe pass three yards, but the Patriots defense held. After three incomplete passes, Dale Hatcher was forced to punt again.

Ricky Harris returned the 37-yard punt 18 yards, giving the Patriots excellent field position. On second-and-10, Bledsoe tossed a 10-yard pass to Vincent Brisby, but Dolphins defensive back Stephen Braggs forced Vincent to fumble. Patriots running back Leonard Russell picked up the loose ball and advanced it another 22 yards to the Dolphins 36-yard line. Bledsoe then connected on a 36-yard touchdown pass to Timpson to defeat the Dolphins 33–27 in overtime. The Dolphins finished the season 9–7 and did not make the playoffs because of this loss to the Patriots.

1994

Record 10–6; Second place in the AFC Eastern Division
The Patriots lost to the Cleveland Browns 20–13 in the Wild Card playoff game.
The WBZ 1030 AM Radio announcers were Gil Santos and Gino Cappelletti

Drew Bledsoe threw for 801 yards and seven touchdowns and the Patriots scored 35 points each time in the first two games, but lost both. The team recovered to beat the Bengals, Lions, and Packers in successive weeks. The Patriots then lost four games in a row. Bledsoe completed 45 of his 70 passing attempts without throwing an interception and led his team to a 26–20 comeback overtime win against the Minnesota Vikings. Although trailing 20–3 at halftime, the Patriots never lost another game in the 1994 regular season. New England beat the Chargers, Colts, Jets, Colts, Bills, and the Bears and finished the season with a seven-game winning streak only to lose the AFC wild card playoff pame to the Cleveland Browns.

* * *

The Play of the Year was made by Drew Bledsoe. Bledsoe tossed a 14-yard touchdown pass to Kevin Turner to defeat the Minnesota Vikings 26-20 in overtime at Foxboro Stadium on 11-13-94.

The Game of the Year was played against the Minnesota Vikings at Foxboro Stadium on 11-13-94.

The Vikings won the toss, went down the field, and scored a touchdown in just 10 plays. Vikings running back Terry Allen ran up the middle for a two-yard touchdown.

Warren Moon took them on another 10-play scoring drive on their second possession of the game. Fuad Reveiz kicked a 40-yard field goal.

1994 New England Patriots Team Leaders
Offensive Team
Drew Bledsoe tossed 25 TD passes
Ben Coates had seven TD receptions
Marion Butts ran for eight touchdowns

Defensive/Special Teams
Maurice Hurst had seven interceptions
Ricky Reynolds returned an interception 11 yards for a TD
Ricky Reynolds returned a fumble 25 yards for a TD
Myron Guyton and Ricky Reynolds recovered three fumbles
Aaron Jones recovered three fumbles
Chris Slade recorded 9.5 sacks

Memorable Statistics of the Year
The only Patriots running back with an overtime, game-winning touchdown reception was Kevin Turner.
Kevin Turner caught a 14-yard touchdown pass from Drew Bledsoe to defeat the Vikings 26–20 in overtime on 11-13-94.
Bruce Armstrong, Drew Bledsoe, and Ben Coates represented the Patriots in the Pro Bowl.

On the Vikings second possession of the second quarter, Warren Moon completed two passes for 97 yards and one touchdown. Jake Reed had a 32-yard reception. On third-and-11, Qadry Ismail hauled in a

65-yard touchdown pass, to put the Vikings up 16–0. Reveiz kicked the extra point to make it 17–0. With 1:02 left in the first half, Reveiz added to the lead when he kicked a 33-yard field goal to make the score 20–0.

Leroy Thompson returned the ensuing kickoff 25 yards to the Patriots 32-yard line. There were 58 seconds left in the first half. Bledsoe completed a six-yard pass and then a nine-yard pass to Leroy Thompson, and then the team took its first time out. Bledsoe tossed a 20-yard pass to Michael Timpson, and then the team called its second time out. Bledsoe fired a 13-yard pass to Vincent Brisby, then spiked the ball. There were 10 seconds left in the half, and the ball was on the Vikings 20-yard line. Bledsoe took a shot at the end zone, but it went incomplete. Matt Bahr kicked a 38-yard field goal on the last play of the half. Warren Moon had 234 yards passing, and Bledsoe had just 73 yards passing in the first half.

The Patriots took the second half kickoff and in just six plays were in the end zone.

Bledsoe tossed a 31-yard touchdown pass to Ray Crittenden and Bahr kicked the extra point. The Patriots had the only other chance to score in the third quarter but Bahr missed wide left on a 39-yard field-goal attempt.

With 5:05 left in regulation, the Patriots trailed by 10 points. Bledsoe completed six consecutive passes and then four more passes in a row, and the Patriots were in the end zone again. On third-and-6, Bledsoe

fired a nine-yard pass to John Burke. His next three completions were to Ray Crittenden for eight yards, to Michael Timpson for 22 yards, and to Leroy Thompson for five yards and the touchdown. Bahr kicked the extra point.

On third-and-2, Patriots defensive back Maurice Hurst broke up a pass intended for Ismail, and Minnesota was forced to punt with two minutes left in the fourth quarter.

Bledsoe completed five consecutive passes to move the ball to the Vikings 5-yard line with 27 seconds left. After three incomplete passes, Bahr kicked a 23-yard field goal with 18 seconds left, to force overtime.

The Patriots won the toss and Leroy Thompson returned the kickoff 27 yards to the Patriots 33-yard line. Drew completed five consecutive passes to move the ball to the Vikings 25-yard line. Marion Butts ran for an eight-yard gain. On second-and-2, Butts bulled ahead for one yard. On third-and-1, Bledsoe went up the middle for a gain of two yards and a first down. Kevin Turner then grabbed a 14-yard touchdown pass from Bledsoe to defeat the Minnesota Vikings 26–20 in overtime.

Drew Bledsoe was the AFC Offensive Player of the Week as he was 45–70 for 426 yards and three touchdowns. He set the NFL record for the most completions and the most attempts in a regular season game and also had the most passing attempts without throwing an interception in a game.

1995

Record was 6–10; Fourth place in the AFC Eastern Division
The WBCN 104.1 FM Radio announcers were Gil Santos and Gino Cappelletti

The Patriots had a tough 1995 season. The team had three games in which it only scored three points. The Patriots defeated the Browns 17–14 to open the season and then lost five games in a row. New England bounced back to beat the Bills and then lost to the Panthers by three in overtime. The Patriots had a decent middle season as they won road games against the Jets and Dolphins, but then lost to the Colts at home. The team whipped the Bills in Buffalo and then lost a home game to the Saints. The Patriots beat the Jets by three in the last home game and then lost to the Steelers and the Colts to finish 6–10.

* * *

The Play of the Year was made by Troy Brown. He advanced a fumbled kickoff return by his teammate Dave Meggett 75 yards for a touchdown during the

31–28 win over the New York Jets at Foxboro Stadium on 12-10-95.

The Game of the Year was played against the Buffalo Bills at Rich Stadium on 11-26-95.

Buffalo won the toss and scored on its first possession of the game. Its first third down play was unsuccessful, so Steve Christie kicked a 51-yard field goal to finish off an eight-play drive.

Drew Bledsoe was intercepted by Bills linebacker Bryce Paup in the end zone for a touchback. On the very next play, Patriots defensive back Myron Guyton returned a Jim Kelly pass 23 yards, and the Patriots had the ball back on the Bills 15-yard line. They were unable to move the ball, so Matt Bahr kicked a 29-yard field goal to tie the score.

After a 27-yard punt by Chris Mohr, the Patriots offensive stars combined to make some big plays for the team. Curtis Martin had four carries for 20 yards, and Drew Bledsoe completed four passes for 41 yards. Ben Coates snared a six-yard touchdown pass from Bledsoe.

Patriots cornerback Ty Law returned a pass by Jim Kelly 11 yards, but the Patriots could not get a first down, and Bryan Wagner had to punt.

Kelly hit Bill Brooks for 21 yards to start the Bills drive and then connected on a 32-yard touchdown to finish it. Troy Barnett blocked the extra-point attempt by Steve Christie, leaving the Patriots up 10–9.

With 1:55 left in the half, Steve Tasker returned the Patriots' punt 17 yards. With this good field position, Christie kicked a 48-yard field goal for the Bills.

With 46 seconds left in the half, Bills linebacker Cornelius Bennett returned a Bledsoe pass 69 yards for a touchdown. The Bills led 19–10 at the break.

The Patriots took the second half kickoff and with the help of long completions by Bledsoe were able to score three points. Vincent Brisby caught a 22-yard pass, and Curtis Martin dashed 21 yards with a pass reception in the flat. Matt Bahr kicked a 43-yard field goal to finish the drive.

The Bills answered the Patriots with a scoring drive. Thurman Thomas ran up the middle for a one-yard touchdown to cap off a 13-play, 67-yard drive. Thomas was stopped on his attempt to run up the middle for a two-point conversion, and the Bills did not score the rest of the game.

On the first play of the fourth quarter, Ben Coates caught a four-yard touchdown pass from Bledsoe. Matt Bahr kicked the extra point, and now the Patriots were only down by five points.

With 5:25 left in the game, Curtis Martin ran for nine yards and then for 11 yards. The Patriots were on the move. Sam Gash caught a six-yard pass, ran up the middle for nine yards, and then caught a seven-yard pass. On third-and-2, Martin ran for six yards and a first

down. With two minutes left in the game, Bledsoe completed a 16-yard pass to Brisby. With 1:28 left in the game, Bledsoe fired a 15-yard pass to Ben Coates for a touchdown. Bledsoe tossed a pass to Martin for the two-point conversion. The Patriots had a three-point lead.

Willie McGinest forced Kelly to throw earlier than he wanted to, and Chris Slade came up with an interception. He returned the interception 27 yards for a touchdown. Todd Collins came into the game as the Bills new quarterback and completed three passes for 36 yards, and the game was over. The final score was Patriots 35 Bills 25.

1995 New England Patriots Team Leaders
Offensive Team
Drew Bledsoe tossed 13 TD passes
Ben Coates had six TD receptions
Curtis Martin ran for 14 TDs

Defensive/Special Teams
Vincent Brown had four interceptions
Chris Slade returned a fumble 27 yards for a TD
Troy Brown advanced fumbled kickoff return 75 yds for a TD
Terry Ray recovered two fumbles
Ted Johnson and Chris Slade recovered two fumbles
Willie McGinest recorded 11 sacks

Memorable Statistics of the Year
The only Patriots offensive lineman to advance an airborne fumble was Max Lane
Max Lane took the airborne fumble by Troy Brown 30 yards in the game against the Chiefs on 10-15-95.
Bruce Armstrong, Drew Bledsoe, and Curtis Martin represented the Patriots in the 1995 Pro Bowl.

1996

Record 11–5; First place in the AFC Eastern Division
The Patriots lost to the Green Bay Packers in the Super Bowl
The WBCN 104.1 FM Radio announcers were Gil Santos and Gino Cappelletti

The Patriots lost to both the Dolphins and the Bills on the road in the first two games of the season. New England crushed the Cardinals 31–0 in the first home game of the season and then beat the Jaguars by three in overtime at Foxboro Stadium. After the bye week, the Patriots won a wild game 46–38 over the Ravens in Baltimore. The Redskins stymied the Patriots in Foxboro again, but then the Patriots went on a four-

game Eastern Division winning streak. The Colts, Bills, Dolphins, and Jets were defeated. Denver smoked the Patriots in Foxboro, but the team recovered to beat the Colts, Chargers, and Jets in successive weeks. Dallas squeaked by with a six-point win, but the Patriots had a huge comeback victory on the road over the Giants in the last game of the season and finished first in the division.

* * *

The Play of the Year was made by Ben Coates, who caught a 13-yard touchdown pass from Drew Bledsoe to defeat the New York Giants 23–22 at Giants Stadium on 12-12-96.

The Game of the Year was played against the Buffalo Bills at Foxboro Stadium on 10-27-96. The Bills finished one game behind the Patriots with a record of 10–6. Bledsoe completed at least three passes to seven different receivers.

Patriots offensive lineman Mike Gisler returned the opening kickoff nine yards. On third-and-7, Shawn Jefferson caught a 22-yard pass. On fourth-and-1, Curtis Martin was stopped for no gain, and the Bills took over on downs. The Bills could not get past midfield on their first series and were forced to punt it back to the Patriots.

With four minutes left in the first quarter, the Patriots started the first scoring drive from their own 20-yard line. To start things off, Keith Byars caught a 13-yard pass, and Terry Glenn hauled in a 23-yard pass from Drew Bledsoe. Shawn Jefferson was pushed out of bounds after his 42-yard reception took him to the Bills 2-yard line. After a five-yard penalty and a three-yard run by Curtis Martin, Bledsoe tossed a four-yard pass to Martin for a touchdown. Adam Vinatieri kicked the extra point.

On the Patriots' first drive of the second quarter, Terry Glenn's 28-yard reception helped set up a field-goal attempt by Vinatieri. He booted a 40-yard field goal to put the Patriots up by 10 points.

With just over five minutes left in the first half, Bledsoe marched his team to another score. On third-and-2, Sam Gash caught a 12-yard pass. On third-and-1, Bledsoe snuck up the middle for the one-yard first down. On third-and-2, Curtis Martin ran for three yards. With two seconds left in the half, Vinatieri kicked a 32-yard field goal.

Defensive back Jeff Burris forced Martin to fumble on the Patriots' first play of the third quarter, and Phil Hansen recovered the loose ball for the Bills. The ball was on the Patriots 34-yard line. On fourth-and-1, Darick Holmes made the key play on this drive as he ran for a two-yard gain to the Patriots 16-yard line. On third-and-8, Kelly threw an incomplete pass and Steve Christie kicked a 33-yard field goal to put points on the board for the Bills.

On the Bills next set of downs Kelly completed a 33-yard pass to Andre Reed to get in the Patriots territory. Thomas ran for a 16-yard gain, and the Bills had first-and-goal on the Patriots 9-yard line. On third-and-6, Jim Kelly tossed a six-yard touchdown pass to Holmes. Steve Christie kicked the extra point.

1996 New England Patriots Team Leaders

Offensive Team

Drew Bledsoe tossed 27 TDs
Ben Coates had nine TD receptions
Curtis Martin ran for 14 TDs
Max Lane recovered three fumbles

Defensive/Special Teams

Willie Clay had four interceptions
Ty Law returned an interception 38 yards for a TD
Willie McGinest returned an interception 46 yards for a TD
Willie McGinest recovered a fumble for a TD
Corwin Brown returned a fumble 42 yards for a TD
Dave Meggett returned a punt 60 yards for a TD
Tedy Bruschi returned a blocked punt for a TD
Willie McGinest recorded 9.5 sacks

Memorable Statistics of the Year

The only Patriots defensive lineman to return an interception for the game-winning touchdown was Willie McGinest.
McGinest took a Jim Kelly pass 46 yards for the game-winning touchdown in the 28–25 win on 10-27-96.
The New England Patriots had six Pro Bowl players in 1996.

The Patriots went three and out. Tom Tupa's 51-yard punt was downed on the 1-yard line by Patriots special team star Larry Whigham. Just two plays later, Patriots defensive lineman Mike Jones forced Kelly to ground the ball for a safety.

On fourth-and-1, Martin lost one yard, failing to get the first down, so the Bills took over on downs on their 28-yard line. On fourth-and-1, Thurman Thomas ran for two yards, to the Patriots 35-yard line. Reed caught a 22-yard pass, and just a few plays later the Bills had first-and-goal on the Patriots 1-yard line. On fourth-and-goal, from the 1-yard line, Thomas broke through for the touchdown. Holmes ran over left guard for a two-point conversion.

The Patriots had a 10-play drive that ended when Vinatieri missed a 54-yard field-goal attempt. The Bills could not get a first down and punted the ball back to the Patriots.

With 2:47 left in the game, the Patriots trailed by three points and had the ball on the team's own 16-yard line. On third-and-1, Martin ran for a three-yard gain. Dave Meggett caught a 26-yard pass for the second first down on this drive. Troy Brown hauled in a 27-yard pass for another first down, and the Patriots had the ball on the Bills 19-yard line with two minutes left. On third-and-1, Martin ran over the left side for a 10-yard touchdown. Vinatieri was wide left on his extra-point attempt.

With 51 seconds left in the game, defensive end Willie McGinest picked off a pass by Kelly and returned it 46 yards for a touchdown. This is the only game that the only interception by a Patriots player was returned by a defensive lineman for a touchdown. Vinatieri successfully kicked the extra point.

The Patriots were hit with a 15-yard unsportsman-like penalty, and Eric Moulds returned the next kickoff 25 yards to the Patriots 48-yard line. On the next play, Kelly connected on a 48-yard touchdown pass to Reed. Steve Christie kicked the extra point.

Keith Byars recovered the onside kick, and Bledsoe knelt twice to end the game. The Patriots defeated the Buffalo Bills 28–25.

1997

Record 10–6; First place in the AFC Eastern Division
The WBCN 104.1 FM Radio announcers were Gil Santos and Gino Cappelletti

Pete Carroll was hired as the new head coach of the New England Patriots. The Patriots started the season with a bang, smoking the Chargers and the Colts by a combined score of 72–13. New England beat the Jets by three in overtime and then crushed the Bears by 28 points. After the bye week, Denver brought the team back to earth as the Patriots lost to the Broncos by 21 points. After the Patriots beat the Bills by 27 points, the team went on to lose four of the next five games. The Patriots finished the season winning four of the last five games and finished in first place in AFC Eastern Division. New England beat Miami twice in the last five games and defeated them again in the first round of the playoffs.

The Moment of the Year was during the halftime ceremony of the game against the Green Bay Packers at Foxboro Stadium on 10-27-97. Mike Haynes was honored for his induction in the Pro Football Hall of Fame by the home crowd and his former team.

* * *

The Play of the Year was made by Jimmy Hitchcock. He returned an interception of Dan Marino 100 yards for a touchdown, with 27 seconds left in the first half, in the 27-24 victory over the Miami Dolphins at Foxboro Stadium on 11-23-97.

The Game of the Year was played against the Buffalo Bills at Rich Stadium on 11-09-97. The Buffalo Bills were defeated 31–10.

Steve Christie kicked a 23-yard field goal with about one minute left in the first quarter for the first points scored in the game. Derrick "Flying" Cullors took the ensuing kickoff 86 yards for a touchdown. With about one minute gone in the second quarter, Adam Vinatieri kicked a 42-yard field goal.

Two plays later Ty Law picked off a pass by Alex Van Pelt, but the Patriots did not put any points on the

1997 New England Patriots Team Leaders
Offensive Team
Drew Bledsoe tossed 28 TD passes
Ben Coates had eight TD receptions
Curtis Martin ran for four TDs

Defensive/Special Teams
Willie Clay had six interceptions
Willie Clay and Jimmy Hitchcock each returned a pass for a TD
Chris Slade and Larry Whigham each returned a pass for a TD
Derrick "Flying" Cullors returned a kickoff 86 yards for a TD
Willie McGinest recovered three fumbles
Chris Slade recorded nine sacks

Memorable Statistics of the Year
The only Patriots player to block a field-goal attempt with less than 30 seconds left to force overtime was Mike Jones.
Mike blocked a 29-yard field-goal attempt, with 16 ticks left in regulation, during the 27–24 OT win against the Jets on 09-14-97.
The New England Patriots had five Pro Bowl Players in 1997.

board. Drew Bledsoe was sacked by Bryce Paup, for a loss of 13 yards, and Vinatieri missed a 42-yard field goal.

On the Patriots' third drive of the second quarter, Curtis Martin ran over right tackle for a gain of 32 yards. Terry Glenn caught a 40-yard pass from Bledsoe, and the Patriots had the ball on the Bills 6-yard line. On first-and-goal, Bledsoe lofted a 6-yard pass to Ben Coates for the touchdown.

Willie Clay picked off a pass by Alex Van Pelt, and the Patriots had the ball back. Vinatieri's 45-yard field-goal attempt hit the right upright and deflected outside rather than inside.

Tom Tupa pinned the Bills on their 7-yard line after his 39-yard punt went out of bounds. Five plays later, Chris Slade tipped a pass by Bills quarterback Todd Collins to himself and walked into the end zone for a one-yard touchdown. So far in the game the Patriots had a special team touchdown, an offensive reception for a touchdown, and a defensive return for a touchdown.

With just less than one minute left in the third quarter, Bills running back Antowain Smith ran up the middle for a one-yard touchdown. The Bills had scored the first rushing touchdown in the game.

Troy Brown caught a 50-yard pass from Bledsoe, and the Patriots had the ball on the Bills 8-yard line. On third-and-goal from the 1-yard line, Martin finally completed the scoring cycle. He ran for a one-yard touchdown.

This is the only regular season game that the Patriots scored via a kickoff return, an interception return, a pass reception, a run from scrimmage, and by kicking a field goal and at least one extra point.

1998

Record 9–7; Fourth place in the AFC Eastern Division
The Patriots lost to the Jacksonville Jaguars 25–10 in the Wild Card playoff game
The WBCN 104.1 FM Radio announcers were Gil Santos and Gino Cappelletti

The Patriots started the season losing to the Broncos in Denver but then won four in a row. Two division games in a row were lost to the Jets and the Dolphins, before New England defeated the Colts for the second time. The Patriots were crushed by the Falcons and then lost on the road to the Bills. Making a move for a playoff run, the Patriots won three in a row by beating the Dolphins by three, the Bills by four, and the Steelers by 14. St. Louis won by 14, but then New England came back and beat Steve Young and Jerry Rice's 49ers by three. The first place New York Jets smoked the Patriots by 21 points in the last regular season game.

* * *

The Play of the Year was made by Drew Bledsoe. Bledsoe, with a broken finger, fired a 25-yard, game-winning touchdown pass to Shawn Jefferson with 34 seconds left, to win 26–23 over the Miami Dolphins at Foxboro Stadium on 11-23-98.

The Game of the Year was played against the Buffalo Bills at Foxboro Stadium on 11-29-98. Bledsoe, who played with a broken index finger, was the NFL Player of the Week for the second consecutive week.

Bills defensive back Thomas Smith picked off a pass by Bledsoe on the Patriots' fourth play of the game, but it did not cost the Patriots. Steve Christie was wide left on his 35-yard field-goal attempt. At the end of the first quarter there was no score.

On the Patriots' first drive of the second quarter, Bledsoe completed a 33-yard pass to Terry Glenn to move into Bills territory. On third-and-goal from the

1998 New England Patriots Team Leaders
Offensive Team
Drew Bledsoe threw 20 TD passes
Ben Coates had six TD receptions
Robert Edwards ran for nine TDs
Bruce Armstrong recovered three fumbles

Defensive/Special Teams
Ty Law had nine interceptions, returning one 59 yards for a TD
Lawyer Milloy returned an interception 30 yards for a TD
Henry Thomas returned an interception 24 yards for a TD
Henry Thomas recorded 6.5 sacks

Memorable Statistics of the Year
Robert Edwards was the first NFL rookie to score in his first six NFL regular season games.
Ben Coates, Ty Law, and Lawyer Milloy represented the New England Patriots in the 1998 Pro Bowl.

2-yard line, Drew fired a 2-yard pass to Robert Edwards for a touchdown.

On the Patriots' second drive of the second quarter, Bledsoe moved his team down to the Bills 12-yard line before the team scored again. On third-and-6 from the 12-yard line, Bledsoe fired a 12-yard pass to Derrick Cullors for the touchdown.

Doug Flutie and Antowain Smith, along with a 26-yard penalty on Chris Canty, allowed the Bills to move into scoring position. Flutie completed two passes for a total of 11 yards, and Antowain Smith had four carries for 23 yards to get to the Patriots 16-yard line. Christie kicked a 34-yard field goal for the Buffalo Bills.

With 18 seconds left in the first half, Flutie connected on a 55-yard pass to Kevin Williams. Christie kicked a 26-yard field goal on the last play of the first half. The Patriots only had 13 yards rushing but had an eight-point cushion at the break.

On the Bills' second play of the third quarter, Eric Moulds caught an 84-yard touchdown pass from Flutie. A two-point pass by Doug Flutie to Eric Moulds went incomplete.

Patriots defensive lineman Chris Sullivan had a nine-yard kickoff return, and the Patriots were on the move. On third-and-5, Terry Glenn caught a nine-yard pass. On fourth-and-1, Robert Edwards ran for five yards to keep the drive alive. Vinatieri kicked a 44-yard field goal to finish the scoring drive.

Flutie completed a 23-yard pass to Andre Reed and a 17-yard pass to Eric Moulds, and the Bills were on the march again. Doug Flutie ran around the left side for 10 yards, taking the ball to the Patriots 8-yard line. On fourth-and-goal from the 4-yard line, Christie kicked a 22-yard field goal.

On the Bills' next drive there were seven penalty flags. The Patriots had four penalties, for 34 yards, that resulted in three first downs for the Bills. Flutie tossed a four-yard pass to Andre Reed for the touchdown. Flutie attempted another pass to Eric Moulds for a two-point conversion, but it was incomplete.

Bledsoe moved his team into field goal range, but Vinatieri's 47-yard field-goal attempt was no good. With 1:52 left the Patriots got the ball back. Bledsoe tossed an 11-yard pass to Ben Coates. Derrick Cullors caught a nine-yard pass. Terry Glenn caught an eight-yard pass. Coates caught a 12-yard pass. On fourth-and-9, with 11 seconds left, Bledsoe hit Shawn Jefferson for 10 yards. Jefferson was able to run out of bounds to stop the clock.

With six seconds left, Bledsoe threw to Glenn in the end zone. Henry Jones was called for pass interference, and the Patriots had the ball on the Bills 1-yard line with no time left on the clock. Bledsoe fired a 1-yard pass to Ben Coates for the touchdown. The Bills protested the pass interference call and the entire team walked off the field and went to the locker room. With nobody on the other side of the line of scrimmage, Vinatieri ran over the right side for the two-point conversion.

The Patriots went 82 yards in 10 plays, in under two minutes, with the aid of two penalties on the Bills, for the game-winning score in the 25–21 win over Buffalo.

1999

Record 8–8; Fourth place in the AFC Eastern Division
The WBCN 104.1 FM Radio announcers were Gil Santos and Gino Cappelletti

New England won its first four games of the season, as it did in 1997, but then lost a two-point game to the Chiefs and a one-point game to the Dolphins. The Patriots defeated the Broncos by one point and destroyed the Cardinals by 24 points. The team hit the bye week with a record of 6–2. The Patriots averaged almost 24 points per game in the first half of the season, but only 13.5 points in the second half. New England lost three division games in a row before beating the Cowboys at Foxboro Stadium. The Patriots faded quickly, losing three in a row again before crushing the Ravens by 17 points in the final game of the year.

* * *

The Play of the Year was made by Chad Eaton. Eaton returned a fumble by Tony Banks, who was strip-sacked by Ted Johnson, 23 yards for a touchdown in the 20–3 rout of the Baltimore Ravens at Foxboro Stadium on 01-02-00.

The Game of the Year was played against the Indianapolis Colts at Foxboro Stadium on 09-19-99.

Peyton Manning hit Marvin Harrison for a 42-yard touchdown on the Colts' second possession of the game. With 37 seconds left in the first quarter, Peyton Manning tossed a 10-yard touchdown pass to Harrison and the score was 14–0.

Jason Belser forced Kevin Faulk to fumble on the first play of the second quarter, and Cornelius Bennett recovered the loose ball for the Colts. Five plays later Edgerrin James ran up the middle for a one-yard touchdown. Now the score was 21–0.

Chris Carter returned a Manning pass eight yards, to the Colts 27-yard line, and the Patriots were in business. Three plays later the team was in the end zone. Drew Bledsoe tossed an 11-yard pass to Shawn Jefferson for the touchdown. Adam Vinatieri kicked the extra point to make it 21–7.

Marvin Harrison was back in the end zone 12 plays and 79 yards later. Harrison caught his third touchdown

Chad Eaton (90) with head coach Pete Carroll

pass from Manning, and with 48 seconds left in the first half, the score was 28–7.

About halfway through the third quarter the Patriots started to move the ball. Bledsoe took his team on a 10-play, 81-yard drive that resulted in a touchdown for the Patriots. Terry Allen caught an eight-yard pass, on third-and-goal, from the 8-yard line, for the touchdown.

Ty Law forced and recovered a fumble by Marcus Pollard, and the Patriots had the ball on their own 42-yard line with just one minute gone in the fourth quarter. Seven plays later, a 24-yard reception by Terry Glenn brought the ball to the Colts 3-yard line. Bledsoe fired a three-yard pass to Ben Coates for the touchdown, and the Patriots were only down by seven points.

The Colts went three and out, and New England took over on its own 22-yard line with about eight minutes left in the game. Glenn caught a 19-yard pass.

Troy Brown caught a 14-yard pass, and Terry Allen dashed for a 21-yard gain, and with nine plays the Patriots had moved to the Colts 10-yard line. Coates caught his second touchdown pass of the game, and the Patriots had tied the score 28–28.

Tedy Bruschi forced Edgerrin James to fumble, and Brandon Mitchell recovered the loose ball on the Colts 37-yard line. With 2:32 left in the game, Bledsoe marched his team down the field to victory. Rod Rutledge caught a seven-yard pass. Terry Allen ran for 13 yards. Vinatieri kicked a game-winning 26-yard field goal with 35 seconds left in the game. Chris Carter returned a Manning pass five yards with 12 seconds left in the game to seal the 31–28 victory over the Colts.

2000

Record 5–11; Fifth place in the Eastern Division
The WBCN 104.1 FM Radio announcers were Gil Santos and Gino Cappelletti

Bill Belichick was the new head coach of the New England Patriots. The Patriots lost the first four regular season games. New England beat the Broncos in Denver for its first win of the season. The Colts were defeated the following week, but then New England lost four in a row again. The last six games were split by beating the Bengals, Chiefs, and Bills in overtime and losing to the Lions, Bears, and Dolphins.

* * *

The Play of the Year was made by Michael Bishop. Bishop tossed a 44-yard touchdown pass to Tony Simmons on the last play of the first half, in the 24–16 win over the Indianapolis Colts at Foxboro Stadium on 10-08-00.

The Game of the Year was played against the Denver Broncos at Mile High Stadium on 10-01-00. The Patriots won for the first time in 32 years at Denver.

Brian Griese was strip-sacked by Willie McGinest on the fourth play of the game, and McGinest recovered the loose ball on the Broncos 29-yard line. Terry Glenn grabbed a 14-yard pass from Drew Bledsoe on the Patriots' first offensive play, and just two plays later the Patriots hit pay dirt. On third-and-6 from the Broncos 11-yard line, Troy Brown caught an 11-yard touchdown pass from Bledsoe. Adam Vinatieri kicked the extra point.

The Broncos could not get a first down and were forced to punt. Troy Brown had a 12-yard punt return and New England started its second drive on its own 24-yard line. Bledsoe tossed another 14-yard pass to Terry Glenn. Chris Calloway had a 13-yard reception, and then Troy Brown scored another touchdown. Bledsoe connected on a 44-yard touchdown pass to Brown, and just seven minutes into the game the Patriots led 14-0.

Joe Nedney put the Broncos on the scoreboard with a 20-yard field goal in the second quarter. With 31 seconds to go in the first half, J.R. Redmond caught a 12-yard touchdown pass from Bledsoe. Vinatieri kicked the extra point.

Bledsoe was intercepted by Terrell Buckley on the second play of the third quarter, but the Patriots defense held, and the turnover was not costly. The Broncos had first-and-goal on the Patriots 10-yard line but did not score. On second-and-3 from the 3-yard line, Ted Johnson stopped Mike Anderson for a gain of only one yard. Chris Slade pushed Howard Griffith out of bounds after a one-yard reception, and Johnson defended on an incomplete pass by Brian Griese on fourth-and-goal from the 1-yard line.

New england advanced the ball to its own 26-yard line before punting it back to Denver. The Broncos punted back to the Patriots, and Troy Brown called for a fair catch on his own 9-yard line. Bledsoe was sacked twice, bringing the ball to the Patriots 1-yard line. Punter Lee Johnson took the snap, and rather than punting from his own end zone he ran out-of-bounds for a safety.

Broncos returnman Deltha O'Neal took the free kick from Lee Johnson and returned it 87 yards for a touchdown. Nedney kicked the extra point. The Broncos had scored nine points in just 10 seconds.

Kevin Faulk returned the ensuing kickoff from two yards deep to the Broncos 23-yard line. Bledsoe led his team to the end zone again. Kevin Faulk ran for a four-yard gain on third-and-1 to get a first down. Troy Brown hauled in a 39-yard pass from Bledsoe for another first down. Glenn caught a nine-yard pass from Bledsoe for a touchdown. Vinatieri kicked the extra point.

2000 New England Patriots Team Leaders
Offensive Team
Drew Bledsoe tossed 17 TDs
Terry Glenn had six TD receptions
Kevin Faulk had four rushing TDs

Defensive/Special Teams
Ty Law, Tebucky Jones, and Lawyer Milloy had two interceptions
Ted Johnson recovered three fumbles
Troy Brown returned a punt 66 yards for a TD
Willie McGinest and Greg Spires had six sacks

Memorable Statistics of the Year
Tom Brady completed his first NFL pass to Rod Rutledge for a gain of six yards on 11-23-00.
The Patriots did not have a Pro Bowl player in 2000.

Tebucky Jones

Tebucky Jones intercepted Griese to stop the Broncos early in the fourth quarter. Joe Nedney missed a 43-yard field-goal attempt midway through the fourth quarter, foiling any chance of a Broncos comeback.

With 1:56 left in the game, Travis McGriff hauled in a 43-yard touchdown pass from Griese. Griese connected with Ed McCaffrey for a two-point conversion.

Eric Bjornson fell on the onside kick attempt by Nedney, and the game was over. Bledsoe knelt for the final three plays of the 28–19 win over the Denver Broncos. Bledsoe was the AFC Offensive Player of the Week as he completed 18 passes for 271 yards and four touchdowns.

2001

Record 11–5; First place in the AFC Eastern Division
The Patriots defeated the St. Louis Rams 20–17 in the Super Bowl
The WBCN 104.1 FM Radio announcers were Gil Santos and Peter Brock
for the first eight games, then Gil Santos and Gino Cappelletti

The season started very ominously. The Patriots lost the opening game to the Bengals in Cincinnati and then lost at home to the New York Jets. Drew Bledsoe was severely injured when he was hit by Mo Lewis and did not play again in the regular season. Tom Brady took over as starting quarterback and led the Patriots to big wins over the Colts, Chargers in overtime, and Colts again. New England lost to Denver at Denver but then had wins over the Falcons and the Bills. The St. Louis Rams defeated the Patriots in Foxboro, but then the Patriots won the last nine games, including three playoff games, and of course the Super Bowl.

* * *

The Play of the Year was made by David Patten, who tossed a 60-yard touchdown pass to Troy Brown in the 38–17 rout of the Indianapolis Colts at the RCA Dome on 10-21-01. Patten ran for a 29-yard touchdown, hauled in a team record 91-yard touchdown pass, and caught a six-yard touchdown pass. He was named the NFL Player of the Week.

The Game of the Year was played against the San Diego Chargers at Foxboro Stadium on 10-14-01. The Patriots defeated the Chargers 29–26 in overtime.

The Patriots won the toss and elected to receive. Kevin Faulk returned the opening kickoff 32 yards, and Tom Brady completed his first pass as a starting quarterback of two yards to David Patten. Brady completed four of eight passes for 38 yards and moved his team to the Chargers 8-yard line. Adam Vinatieri kicked as 26-yard field goal to finish the 13-play drive.

Doug Flutie took his Chargers team to the Patriots 1-yard line. On third-and-1 from the 1-yard line, Patriots linebackers Bryan Cox and Roman Phifer tackled LaDainian Tomlinson for a two-yard loss. Wade Richey kicked a 21-yard field goal on the last play of the first quarter to tie the score at 3–3.

2001 New England Patriots Team Leaders
Offensive Team
Tom Brady threw 18 TD passes
Troy Brown had five TD receptions
Antowain Smith ran for 12 TDs

Defensive/Special Teams
Otis Smith had five interceptions, returning two for a TD
Ty Law returned two interceptions for a TD
Terrell Buckley returned a pass 52 yards for a TD
Troy Brown returned two punts for a TD
Roman Phifer and Otis Smith recovered two fumbles
Bobby Hamilton had seven sacks

Memorable Statistics of the Year
The only Patriots player who has thrown a touchdown pass, caught two touchdown passes, and ran for a touchdown in a game was David Patten.
David Patten was the NFL Player of the Week in the 38–17 rout of the Indianapolis Colts on 10-21-01.
Tom Brady, Troy Brown, Ty Law, and Lawyer Milloy were Pro Bowl players.

Richey missed a 36-yard field-goal attempt on the Chargers' first drive of the second quarter. On third-and-1 from the Chargers 30-yard line, Tom Brady tossed a seven-yard pass to linebacker/running back Bryan Cox for a first down. Two plays later Brady connected on a 21-yard touchdown pass to Terry Glenn. Vinatieri's extra-point attempt went wide left.

Flutie completed four consecutive passes, good for 54 yards, and the Chargers were on the move. With 44 seconds left in the half, Wade Richey kicked a 27-yard field goal.

Brady connected on a 23-yard pass to Troy Brown and a 21-yard pass to Glenn, and the Patriots had a scoring chance with six seconds left. Vinatieri's 44-yard field-goal attempt went wide left on the last play of the half.

Patriots linebacker Roman Phifer forced LaDainian Tomlinson to fumble on the second play of the third quarter, and Bryan Cox returned the loose ball nine yards for the Patriots. Brady fumbled on two consecutive plays, but the Patriots recovered both fumbles and then punted.

Curtis Conway hauled in a 56-yard pass and then a 19-yard pass from Flutie, and the ball was on the Patriots 1-yard line. LaDainian Tomlinson went over his left guard for the touchdown.

The Patriots answered right back. Brady took his team to the Chargers 1-yard line before Antowain Smith ran up the middle for a one-yard touchdown.

On the Chargers' first drive of the fourth quarter, Flutie led his team to the end zone once again. He tossed a three-yard touchdown pass to Steve Heiden and the Chargers had a three-point lead, 19–16. Darren Bennett failed in his attempt to run over the left side for a two-point conversion.

Derrick Harris forced punter Lee Johnson to fumble, and he returned the loose ball six yards for a touchdown. Wade Richey kicked the extra point, and San Diego was up by 10 points with 8:48 left in regulation.

Brady methodically moved his team down the field on a 15-play drive that ended with a 23-yard field goal by Vinatieri. Antowain Smith ran for five yards on fourth-and-2, and Kevin Faulk caught a 12-yard pass from Brady to keep the drive alive.

Bryan Cox and Willie McGinest stopped Tomlinson for no gain, on third-and-1, and the Chargers were forced to punt with 2:24 left in regulation.

Troy Brown's only punt return of the game was for 40 yards, and with 2:10 left in regulation New England had the ball on its own 40-yard line. Brown actually returned the ball to midfield, but there was a 10-yard holding penalty on the return.

Brady completed a 12-yard pass to Brown and a few plays later tossed a 16-yard pass to Brown. David Patten then had a 26-yard reception, moving the ball to the Chargers 3-yard line. With 40 seconds left in regulation Brady hit Jermaine Wiggins for a three-yard touchdown. Vinatieri kicked the extra point to tie the game.

Tomlinson ran for 14 yards, Flutie completed a 24-yard pass to Curtis Conway, and the Chargers had a chance for a long field goal. Wade Richey's 59-yard field-goal attempt on the last play of the fourth quarter was short.

David Patten

Ronny Jenkins returned Vinatieri's overtime kickoff 39 yards, but the Chargers went three and out and had to punt.

A 37-yard pass interference call on the Chargers put the ball on the Chargers 40-yard line, and the Patriots had great field position. Brady completed an eight-yard pass to David Patten. On third-and-5, Kevin Faulk caught a nine-yard pass from Brady, and three plays later Vinatieri kicked the game-winning, 44-yard field goal to defeat the San Diego Chargers 29–26 in overtime.

2002

Record 9–7; Second place in the AFC Eastern Division
The WBCN 104.1 FM Radio announcers were Gil Santos and Gino Cappelletti

The Patriots smoked the Steelers 30–14 in the opening game and the first regular season game ever played at Gillette Stadium. New England crushed the Jets by 37 points and beat the Chiefs in overtime by three before losing to the Chargers by seven in San Diego. Then the Patriots lost to Miami, Green Bay, and Denver. New England won two consecutive road games, smashing the Bills by 31 and squeaking by the Bears by three points. The Raiders defeated the Patriots on the team's first attempt after losing to the Patriots in the 2001 play-offs. The Patriots won four of the last six games but missed the playoffs.

* * *

The Play of the Year was made by Tom Brady. Brady tossed a game-winning, 20-yard touchdown pass to David Patten, with 28 seconds left, to defeat the Chicago Bears 33–30 at Memorial Stadium on 11-10-02.

The Game of the Year was played on Monday Night against the Pittsburgh Steelers at Gillette Stadium on 09-09-02. The Patriots defeated the Pittsburgh Steelers to advance to the Super Bowl in 2001.

Patriots defensive back Terrell Buckley returned a pass by Kordell Stewart six yards, on the third play of the game, but the Patriots could not get a first down and had to punt. On the very next play, Mike Varbel picked off a pass by Stewart. Four plays and three penalties later the Patriots were in the end zone. Tom Brady tossed a four-yard pass to Christian Fauria for the touchdown. Adam Vinatieri kicked the extra point.

After a 23-yard pass interference penalty on Ty Law, the Steelers were able to move into Patriots territory and eventually to the end zone. Kordell Stewart tossed a 13-yard pass to Hines Ward for a touchdown. Todd Peterson kicked the extra point.

After another pass interference penalty on Law, this was only a 14-yard penalty, the Steelers were on the Patriots 1-yard line. The Steelers then had a false start penalty, which brought them back to the 6-yard line. On first down and goal from the 6, Tedy Bruschi sacked Stewart for a loss of one yard. Stewart threw an incomplete pass on second down. After a six-yard run by Chris Fuamatu-Ma'afala took it to the 1-yard line, the Steelers were called for a 15-yard unsportsmanlike penalty. Another false start by the Steelers offensive line put them back another five yards, and then Todd Peterson missed a 39-yard field goal.

2002 New England Patriots Team Leaders
Offensive Team
Tom Brady threw an NFL best 28 TDs
Christian Fauria had seven TD receptions
Antowain Smith ran for six TDs

Defensive/Special Teams
Terrell Buckley and Ty Law had four interceptions
Victor Green returned a pass 90 yards for a TD
Tedy Bruschi returned two interceptions for a TD
Kevin Faulk returned two kickoffs for a TD
Tebucky Jones returned a fumble 24 yards for a TD
Victor Green recovered three fumbles
Willie McGinest and Richard Seymour had 5.5 sacks

Memorable Statistics of the Year
Tebucky Jones is the only Patriots defensive back to strip-sack the quarterback and return the fumble for a touchdown.
Tebucky strip-sacked Vinny Testaverde and took the fumble 24 yards for a touchdown in the 44–7 rout on 09-15-02.
The New England Patriots had six Pro Bowl players in 2002.

Tom Brady moved his team down the field, completing six of eight passes for 44 yards. Adam Vinatieri finished the scoring drive by kicking a 45-yard field goal. The score was 10-7 at the end of the first half.

Deion Branch had a 22-yard return of the second half kickoff, and just four plays later the Patriots were in the end zone. David Patten was forced out-of-bounds after his 37-yard reception, and Donald Hayes hauled in a 40-yard pass from Brady for the touchdown.

Two plays later the Patriots had the ball back. Victor Green forced Jerome Bettis to fumble, and the loose ball was recovered by Green on the Steelers 49-yard line.

It took the Patriots just nine plays to reach the end zone again. Brady connected on a 22-yard touchdown pass to Branch, and Vinatieri kicked the extra point to put the Patriots up by 17 points.

Terrell Buckley lost two yards on his interception of a pass that was thrown by Stewart. Once again the Patriots had the ball on the Steelers 49-yard line. Antowain Smith had the big play on this drive, running for a 25-yard gain to the Steelers 9-yard line. After a run for a one-yard loss and two incomplete passes, Vinatieri kicked a 28-yard field goal to put the Patriots up by 20 points. Vinatieri also kicked a 27-yard field goal in the fourth quarter.

With 2:55 left in the game, Stewart took his team to the end zone.

Stewart completed three consecutive passes, two across midfield before the two minute warning.

Antwaan Randle El caught a 27-yard pass from Stewart, on fourth-and-5, to get to the Patriots 7-yard line. With four seconds left, on fourth-and-1, Stewart went up the middle for the touchdown. On the final play, Todd Peterson kicked the extra point in the Patriots' 30–14 victory over the Pittsburgh Steelers.

2003

Record 14–2; First place in the AFC Eastern Division
The Patriots defeated the Carolina Panthers 32–29 in the Super Bowl
The WBCN 104.1 FM Radio announcers were Gil Santos and Gino Cappelletti

The Patriots were shut out 31–0 by the Buffalo Bills at Ralph Wilson Stadium to open the regular season. Then New England crushed the Eagles by 21 points in Philadelphia and were victorious in the home opening game against the Jets. The Patriots lost to the Redskins, for the sixth time in a row, before going on a 12-game-winning streak to finish the regular season with the best record in the NFL.

* * *

The Play of the Year was made by Troy Brown. Brown caught an 82-yard touchdown pass from Tom Brady to defeat the Miami Dolphins 19–13 in overtime at Pro Player Stadium on 10-19-03. Jay Fiedler was chased from the pocket by Tedy Bruschi and was intercepted by Tyrone Poole just before this touchdown reception by Brown.

The Game of the Year was played against the Indianapolis Colts at the RCA Dome on 11-30-03. Bethel Johnson was the AFC Special Teams Player of the Week.

Bethel Johnson mishandled but maintained possession of the opening kickoff. The Patriots got three first downs, and Adam Vinatieri put three points on the scoreboard with his 43-yard field goal.

Mike Vrabel strip-sacked Peyton Manning, and Dan Klecko recovered the loose ball for the Patriots. Klecko returned the fumble four yards to the Colts 36-yard line. On third-and-5, Brady hit Kevin Faulk for a 16-yard gain, and three plays later the Patriots were in the end zone. Mike Cloud ran over the left side for a four-yard touchdown, and Vinatieri kicked the extra point.

On the seventh play of the second quarter, Brady connected with Dedric Ward for another touchdown. On third-and-7 from the Colts 31-yard line, Dedric Ward hauled in a 31-yard touchdown. Vinatieri's extra point made it 17–0.

2003 New England Patriots Team Leaders
Offensive Team
Tom Brady tossed 23 TD passes
David Givens had six TD receptions
Mike Cloud ran for five TDs
Bethel Johnson recovered two fumbles

Defensive/Special Teams
Ty Law and Tyrone Poole had six interceptions
Tedy Bruschi returned two passes for a TD
Ty Law returned an interception 65 yards for a TD
Asante Samuel returned a pass 55 yards for a TD
Bethel Johnson returned a kickoff 92 yards for a TD
Matt Chatham returned a fumble 30 yards for a TD
Matt Chatham and Willie McGinest recovered two fumbles
Mike Vrabel recorded 9.5 sacks

Memorable Statistics of the Year
The only Patriots player to return two kickoffs for at least 65 yards in the same regular season game was Bethel Johnson.
Johnson returned one 92 yards for a touchdown to end the half and returned one 65 yards to set up the final touchdown on 11-30-03.
Ty Law, Willie McGinest, and Richard Seymour were Pro Bowl players in 2003.

Thanks to a running into the punter penalty on the Patriots, the Colts were able to get into field-goal range for Mike Vanderjagt. He kicked a 40-yard field goal for the Colts' first points of the day.

With 19 seconds left in the first half, Manning tossed an eight-yard touchdown pass to Marcus Pollard. Vanderjagt kicked the extra point.

Troy Brown

Nick Harper returned his interception of Brady three yards to the Colts 26-yard line, and on the next play the Colts scored another touchdown. Manning tossed a 26-yard touchdown pass to Marvin Harrison. Vanderjagt kicked the extra point with 20 seconds left in the third quarter.

The Colts were the first team to score in the fourth quarter. Troy Walters grabbed a six-yard touchdown pass from Manning. Less than two minutes later however, the Patriots were in the end zone. Deion Branch caught a 13-yard touchdown pass from Brady, and with Vinatieri's extra point the Patriots were up by seven points again.

Marcus Washington forced Kevin Faulk to fumble, and Raheem Brock recovered the loose ball for the Colts. With 3:45 left in the game and the ball on the Patriots 11-yard line, the Colts were in prime condition to tie the game. After three consecutive incomplete passes by Manning, Vanderjagt kicked a 29-yard field goal.

The Patriots were unable to move the ball and were forced to punt. When the Colts took over on the Patriots 48-yard line with 2:57 left, there was one more chance. With 59 seconds left they had first-and-goal on the Patriots 9-yard line. Edgerrin James ran for seven yards to the 2-yard line. With 40 seconds left, Tedy Bruschi and Mike Vrabel stopped Edgerrin after a one-yard gain. On second down, Tedy Bruschi and Rodney Harrison stopped James for no gain. Manning threw an incomplete pass on third down. Willie McGinest halted James for a loss of one yard, on fourth-and-goal, with 14 seconds left in the thrilling 38–34 win over the Colts. Brady took the snap to his knees on the game's last play.

With 12 seconds left in the first half, Johnson took the kickoff on his own 8-yard line and returned it 92 yards for a touchdown. Vinatieri kicked the extra point for the final play of the first half.

On the Patriots' first series of the third quarter, Brady marched his team down the field for another touchdown. Ward caught a 19-yard pass on third-and-14 from Brady to keep the drive alive. Mike Cloud ran over the left side for a one-yard touchdown on the 11th play of this drive. Vinatieri added the extra point.

Tyrone Poole had a seven-yard return on his interception of Manning, but Donald Strickland had a 24-yard return of his interception of Brady. Peyton took the Colts on a nine-play 44-yard drive for a touchdown. Reggie Wayne caught a 13-yard touchdown pass from Manning, and Vanderjagt kicked the extra point.

2004

Record 14–2; First place in the AFC Eastern Division
The Patriots defeated the Philadelphia Eagles 24–21 in the Super Bowl
The WBCN 104.1 FM Radio announcers were Gil Santos and Gino Cappelletti

New England opened the season with six wins, extending its streak to 18 consecutive regular season victories. (21 consecutive wins, including the playoffs)

The Patriots lost to the Pittsburgh Steelers at Heinz Field on Halloween. Another six-game-winning streak ended when they lost to the Dolphins in Miami. The Patriots were victorious in the last two regular season games and swept through the playoffs, again winning the Super Bowl.

* * *

The Play of the Year was made by Richard Seymour. He returned a fumble by Drew Bledsoe, which was forced by Tedy Bruschi 68 yards for a touchdown in the 31–17 win over the Buffalo Bills at Ralph Wilson Stadium on 10-03-04.

The Game of the Year was played against the Cleveland Browns at Cleveland Stadium on 12-05-04. The Patriots had a kickoff return for a touchdown, a rushing touchdown, a defensive fumble return for a touchdown, and a passing touchdown. It is the only time that they accomplished all of these feats in the same game.

Bethel Johnson returned the opening kickoff 93 yards for a touchdown. Adam Vinatieri kicked the extra point.

Gerard Warren forced Corey Dillon to fumble, and the loose ball was recovered by Alvin McKinley. Just two plays later Rodney Harrison picked off a pass by Luke McCown, and the Patriots had the ball back. Dillon finished the Patriots 12-play, 95-yard drive with a four-yard touchdown run over the left side. Vinatieri kicked the extra point.

Defensive back Troy Brown tackled Dennis Northcutt three yards short of the first down marker, on fourth-and-5, and New England took over on downs on its own 29-yard line. Corey Dillon completed a 10-play, 72-yard drive with a one-yard touchdown run over the right guard. Vinatieri kicked the extra point.

Patrick Pass ran for only one yard on fourth-and-3, and the Browns took over on downs at the team's own 30-yard line. The Browns were in the end zone 11 plays later. McCown had three big pass completions along the way. He completed a 17-yard pass to William Green, on third-and-13, and a 25-yard pass to Dennis Northcutt, taking it the Patriots 12-yard line. On third-and-14, McCowan connected on a 16-yard touchdown pass to Antonio Bryant. Phil Dawson kicked the extra point.

On the third play of the third quarter, Richard Seymour forced William Green to fumble.

Randall Gay recovered and returned the fumble 41 yards for a touchdown. Vinatieri kicked the extra point.

2004 New England Patriots Team Leaders
Offensive Team
Tom Brady threw 28 TDs
Daniel Graham had seven TD receptions
Corey Dillon had 12 rushing TDs
Corey Dillon ran for 1,635 yards

Defensive/Special Teams
Eugene Wilson had four interceptions
Asante Samuel returned a pass 34 yards for a TD
Bethel Johnson returned a kickoff 93 yards for a TD
Richard Seymour returned a fumble 68 yards for a TD
Randall Gay returned a fumble 41 yards for a TD
Jarvis Green recovered three fumbles, including one for a TD
Willie McGinest recorded 9.5 sacks

Memorable Statistics of the Year
Troy Brown became the only Patriots player to catch a touchdown pass from a quarterback, running back, wide receiver, and a kicker.
Troy caught a touchdown pass from Dave Meggett in '97, David Patten in '01, and Adam Vinatieri in 2004.
Tom Brady, Tedy Bruschi, Larry Izzo, Richard Seymour, and Adam Vinatieri were Pro Bowl players.

Richard Seymour, Drew Bledsoe on the ground

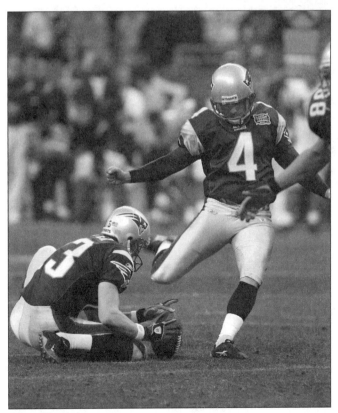

Adam Vinatieri

On the Patriots' next possession, Kevin Faulk had a 20-yard run, David Patten caught a 13-yard pass, Daniel Graham caught a 14-yard pass, and Patrick Pass had a 17-yard reception. Faulk ran over the left side for a 10-yard touchdown. Vinatieri kicked the extra point.

Vinatieri's kickoff went into the end zone for a touchback, and Cleveland took over on its own 20-yard line. Dexter Reid forced Steve Heiden to fumble after his 12-yard reception, and Eugene Wilson recovered the fumble for the Patriots. The Patriots were in the end zone four plays later. Patten hauled in a 44-yard touchdown pass from Brady for the final Patriots touch-

down of the day. Vinatieri kicked the extra point for the Patriots' final point scored in this game. The Patriots scored on special teams, on defense, and both on the ground and in the air on offense.

With just over 10 minutes left in the game, Antonio Bryant caught a 40-yard touchdown pass from McCown. Steve Heiden caught a pass from Luke McCown for a two-point conversion to make the score 42–15.

Troy Brown picked off a pass by McCown, and the Patriots were able to bring the clock all the way down to 21 seconds before they turned the ball over on downs to the Browns.

2005

Record 10–6; First place in the AFC Eastern Division
The Patriots lost to the Denver Broncos 27–13 in the Divisional playoff game
The WBCN 104.1 FM Radio announcers were Gil Santos and Gino Cappelletti

The Patriots had an up and down year in 2005. New England won and then lost each week of the first eight weeks of the season. The Patriots finally won two games in a row before losing to the Chiefs in the 11th contest. The team had a minor streak of winning four in row before losing their last game of the season to the Miami Dolphins.

* * *

The Play of the Year was Doug Flutie's drop-kicked extra point in the 28–26 loss to the Miami Dolphins at Gillette Stadium on 01-01-06. The last time an NFL player had a successful drop kick in a regular season game was in 1941.

The Game of the Year was played against the Pittsburgh Steelers at Heinz Field on 09-25-05.

The Steelers won the toss but were stopped after three plays and punted. Tim Dwight returned the punt by Chris Gardocki 19 yards, and the Patriots had the ball on the Steelers 46-yard line. seven plays later Corey Dillon was in the end zone.

Ben Roethlisberger tossed an 85-yard touchdown pass to Hines Ward, and in just one play the score was tied 7–7.

Antwaan Randle El had a 17-yard punt return, and Pittsburgh started its third drive on the Patriots 49-yard line. The drive stalled in the red zone, and Jeff Reed came on and kicked a 33-yard field goal.

Larry Foote recovered a fumble by Kevin Faulk, but the Steelers gave it right back two plays later. Antwaan Randle El caught a 49-yard pass and attempted to lateral the ball to Hines Ward, but the ball went astray.

2005 New England Patriots Team Leaders
Offensive Team
Tom Brady tossed 26 TD passes
Deion Branch had five TD receptions
Mike Vrabel had three TD receptions
Corey Dillon ran for 12 TDs

Defensive/Special Teams
Ellis Hobbs and Asante Samuel had three interceptions
James Sanders returned a tipped pass 39 yards for a TD
Mike Vrabel returned a pass 24 yards for a TD
Ellis Hobbs recovered two fumbles
Rosevelt Colvin recorded seven sacks

Memorable Statistics of the Year
This is the only regular season that 12 different receivers caught at least one touchdown pass for the Patriots. Tom Ashworth, Deion Branch, Troy Brown, Andre'Davis, Corey Dillon, David Givens, Tim Dwight, Christian Fauria, Daniel Graham, Bethel Johnson, Mike Vrabel, and Benjamin Watson had a touchdown reception.
Tom Brady and Richard Seymour represented the New England Patriots in the 2005 Pro Bowl.

Eugene Wilson recovered the loose ball on the Patriots 11-yard line. The Patriots could not get a first down and punted.

With 2:42 left in the first half, New England had the ball on its own 42-yard line because Jeff Reed had missed a 52-yard field-goal attempt. Tom Brady brought his team to the Steelers 3-yard line but was intercepted with 41 seconds left by Chris Hope at the Steelers 4-yard line. Ben Roethlisberger knelt for the final play of the first half.

Adam Vinatieri missed on a 53-yard field-goal attempt on the Patriots' first series of downs in the third quarter, and Kevin Faulk fumbled ending the second series. The Steelers took advantage of the fumble by Faulk as Jeff Reed kicked a 24-yard field goal.

Tim Dwight's 28-yard punt return helped set up a 48-yard field goal by Adam Vinatieri with 19 seconds left in the third quarter.

Brady completed five passes for 76 yards, taking his team to the Steelers 7-yard line on the Patriots' first series of the fourth quarter. David Givens' 30-yard reception, on third-and-2, was the key play on this drive. Corey Dillon went over the right side for a seven-yard touchdown. Vinatieri kicked the extra point.

Brady completed four passes for 54 yards, taking his team into Vinatieri's field-goal range. Vinatieri did his job, kicking a 35-yard field goal putting his team up by seven points.

Ricardo Colclough returned the ensuing kickoff 44 yards, and Pittsburgh had the ball on its own 49-yard line with 3:10 left. With 1:25 left Ben Roethlisberger connected on a four-yard touchdown pass to Hines Ward. Jeff Reed kicked the extra point to tie the game.

Mike Vrabel (left)

Ellis Hobbs had a 34-yard return on the kickoff, and New England had the ball on its own 38-yard line with 1:14 left in the game. Kevin Faulk had a 17-yard reception.

Brady connected with Patrick Pass for 14 yards. Givens' six-yard reception took the ball to the Steelers 35-yard line. With five seconds left in the game, Vinatieri kicked a 43-yard field goal to defeat the Steelers 23–20.

2006

Record 12–4; First place in the AFC Eastern Division
The Patriots lost to the Indianapolis Colts 38–34 in the AFC Championship Game
The WBCN 104.1 FM Radio announcers were Gil Santos and Gino Cappelletti

The Patriots won two close games, over the Bills and the Jets, to start the season. Denver won at Gillette Stadium, and then the Patriots went on a four-game-winning streak. The Colts and the Jets won in successive weeks. New England shut out the Green Bay Packers 35–0 and then beat the Bears and the Lions. Miami shut out the Patriots 21–0 at Dolphin Stadium on 12-10-06. The Patriots destroyed the Texans, barely beat the Jaguars, and then crushed the Titans to end the regular season.

* * *

The Play of the Year was made by defensive lineman Ty Warren. Warren sacked J.P. Losman for a safety to score the last points in the 19–17 victory over the Buffalo Bills at Gillette Stadium on 09-10-06.

The Game of the Year was played against the Chicago Bears at Gillette Stadium on 11-26-06.

The Patriots went three and out after winning the opening toss and punted the ball to the Bears. Asante Samuel intercepted a pass by Rex Grossman on the Bears third play of the game.

Charles Tillman returned a pass by Tom Brady five yards, and Chicago got the ball back on its own 6-yard line. Richard Seymour stopped the scoring drive by blocking a 45-yard field-goal attempt by Robbie Gould 16 plays later.

Lance Briggs forced Laurence Maroney to fumble, and Briggs recovered the loose ball. Rex Grossman fumbled the snap, and Seymour recovered the fumble on the Patriots 8-yard line, halting another Bears drive.

Brady took his team on an 11-yard play, 92-yard drive that ended with a one-yard touchdown run by Laurence Maroney. They were two key plays in this drive. Kevin Faulk caught a seven-yard pass, on third-and-4, and Daniel Graham had a 25-yard reception.

The Bears came right back with a scoring drive. Mushin Muhammad caught a 14-yard pass from Rex Grossman, on third-and-10, and Thomas Jones ran for a one-yard first down, on third-and-1, to keep the potential scoring drive going. Robbie Gould kicked a 46-yard field goal to put the Bears on the scoreboard. With six seconds left in the half, Stephen Gostkowski kicked a 52-yard field goal.

Asante Samuel returned his interception of Rex Grossman 27 yards, from his own 7-yard line, to stop the Bears in the red zone once again. The Patriots gave it right back to the Bears as Charles Tillman returned his interception of Tom Brady three yards, to the Bears 47-yard line.

After a 45-yard pass interference penalty was called on the Patriots, Cedric Benson ran for a two-yard touchdown. Robbie Gould kicked the extra point to tie the game.

Tom Brady marched his team down the field on an 11-play, 73-yard scoring drive. Benjamin Watson caught a 40-yard pass, on third-and-3, to get into Bears territory. On third-and-9, from the Bears 25-yard line, Brady faked Brian Urlacher out of his shoes for an 11-yard gain. Five plays later, the Patriots were in the end zone. Brady tossed a two-yard touchdown pass to Benjamin Watson. Stephen Gostkowski kicked the extra point.

Thomas Jones ran for two first downs, and the Patriots had a 30-yard pass interference penalty that allowed the Bears to get into field-goal range. Robbie Gould kicked a 32-yard field goal for the final points scored in the game.

With two minutes left in the game Alex Brown recovered a fumble by Corey Dillon on the Bears 22-yard line. Asante Samuel came to the rescue for the Patriots as he intercepted Rex Grossman for the third time in the game. Brady knelt for the final three plays in the 17–13 win over the Bears. The Chicago Bears would lose to the Indianapolis Colts in the Super Bowl later in the year.

2006 New England Patriots Team Leaders
Offensive Team
Tom Brady tossed 24 TD passes
Troy Brown caught four TD receptions
Reche Caldwell had four TD receptions
Corey Dillon ran for 13 TDs
Dan Koppen recovered three fumbles

Defensive/Special Teams
Asante Samuel had 10 interceptions
Ellis Hobbs returned a kickoff 93 yards for a TD
Rosevelt Colvin recorded 8.5 sacks

Memorable Statistics of the Year
This is the only year that the Patriots had three players punt at least 10 times during the regular season.
Josh Miller punted 43 times, Ken Walter punted 16 times, and Todd Sauerbrun punted 10 times.
Matt Light and Richard Seymour represented the Patriots in the 2006 Pro Bowl.

Tom Brady

2007

Record 16–0; First place in the AFC Eastern Division
The WBCN Radio announcers were Gil Santos and Gino Cappelletti

The Patriots became the only NFL team to win 16 regular season games in the same year. New England defeated six playoff-bound teams by a combined score of 234 to 116 and were victorious in five late-night games. The Patriots set the NFL record for the most touchdowns and the most points scored in a regular season.

* * *

The Play of the Year was made by both Tom Brady and Randy Moss. Moss, who on the previous play dropped a long pass, hauled in a 65-yard touchdown pass from Brady in the 38–35 win over the New York Giants on 12-29-07. This was the 50th touchdown pass by Brady and the 23rd touchdown reception by Moss (both NFL single-season records) in the 2007 regular season.

The Game of the Year could be the four-point win over the Colts or the three-point win over the Ravens, but in my opinion it is the record-setting 16th regular season win. The Patriots defeated the New York Giants 38–35 at Giants Stadium on 12-29-07. Tom Brady was the AFC Offensive Player of the Week. It was the Patriots 19th consecutive regular season win over two seasons.

On the second offensive play of the game, Plaxico Burress hauled in a 52-yard pass from Eli Manning, putting them on the Patriots 18-yard line. Five plays later, Brandon Jacobs put the Giants on the score-

---

2007 New England Patriots Team Leaders
Offensive Team
Tom Brady set an NFL record with 50 TD passes
Randy Moss had an NFL record 23 TD receptions
Laurence Maroney ran for six TDs

Defensive/Special Teams
Asante Samuel had six interceptions
Adalius Thomas returned a pass 65 yards for a TD
Asante Samuel returned a pass 40 yards for a TD
Eugene Wilson returned a pass five yards for a TD
Ellis Hobbs took a kickoff an NFL record 108 yards
Willie Andrews returned a kickoff 77 yards for a TD
Randall Gay returned a fumble 15 yards for a TD
Rosevelt Colin returned a fumble 11 yards for a TD
Ellis Hobbs returned a fumble 35 yards for a TD
Ty Warren recovered three fumbles
Mike Vrabel recorded 12.5 sacks

Memorable Statistics of the Year
Tom Brady threw 50 touchdown passes and was only intercepted eight times.
The New England Patriots had eight AFC All Pro players.

---

board with a seven-yard touchdown reception. On the Patriots' first drive of the game Stephen Gostkowski put three points on the scoreboard with a 37-yard field goal.

On the first play of the second quarter, Randy Moss tied Jerry Rice's NFL record with his 22nd touchdown reception. Domenik Hixon took the ensuing kickoff 74 yards for a touchdown. The Patriots answered with two more field goals by Stephen Gostkowski, but, with only 13 seconds left in the half, Kevin Boss caught a three-yard touchdown pass from Eli Manning.

On the Giants' first drive of the second half Plaxico Burress caught a 19-yard touchdown pass from Manning. Lawrence Tynes kicked the extra point, and the Giants were up by 12 points midway through the third quarter.

Even though the Patriots had come back to defeat Dallas, Indy, Philly, and Baltimore earlier in the year, this was the largest deficit the team had faced so late in a game. Tom Brady took his team

Laurence Maroney

on a 73-yard drive that culminated when Laurence Maroney dashed six yards for a touchdown.

The Patriots defense kept the pressure on the Giants. Adalius Thomas sacked Eli Manning for a loss of 14 yards. On third-and-22, Junior Seau, Brandon Meriweather, and Rodney Harrison combined to stop Brandon Jacobs short of a first down. On the Giants' next series of downs, Asante Samuel and Jarvis Green stopped the Giants on a third-and-long play.

On second-and-10 from the Patriots 35-yard line, Tom Brady misfired on a long pass that was intended for Randy Moss. On third-and-10 New England tried it again. This time Moss hauled in the 65-yard tochdown pass. This reception set two NFL records. It was the 50th touchdown pass thrown by Brady and the 23rd touch-down reception by Moss in the 2007 regular season. Laurence Maroney ran over the left guard for the two-point conversion.

With about 10 minutes left in the game Ellis Hobbs intercepted Eli Manning on the Patriots 48-yard line. Nine plays later, Laurence Maroney ran for a five-yard touchdown.

Manning took his team on an 11-play, 68-yard drive for the final points scored in the game. With 1:08 left, Plaxico Burress caught a three-yard touchdown pass from Manning.

Mike Vrabel recovered the onside kick by Lawrence Tynes. Brady took three snaps, and the Patriots had run the table. New England defeated the New York Giants 38–35 and finished the regular season 16–0.

2008

Record 11–5; Second place in the AFC Eastern Division
The WBCN Radio announcers were Gil Santos and Gino Cappelletti

The Patriots lost their most valuable player, quarterback Tom Brady, on the Patriots 16th offensive play of the season. Matt Cassel took over the quarterback position and led the team to an 11–5 record. New England beat the Jets in New Jersey, won in San Francisco, destroyed Denver on *Monday Night Football*, and won home games against the Rams and the Bills. The Patriots crushed the Dolphins in Miami and won the last four regular season games.

* * *

The Play of the Year was made by Adalius Thomas. He spun Brett Favre around numerous times for a 20-yard loss in the Patriots 19–10 victory over the New York Jets at the Meadowlands on 09-14-08.

The Game of the Year was the 48–28 rout of the Miami Dolphins at Dolphin Stadium on 11-23-08. For the second consecutive week Matt Cassel threw for more than 400 yards and tossed three touchdown passes. Randy Moss had eight receptions for 125 yards and three touchdowns, and Wes Welker had eight receptions for 120 yards in this victory.

Stephen Gostkowski started the scoring with a 30-yard field goal to end the Patriots' first drive of the game. Dolphins free safety Renaldo Hill returned a pass that was juggled by Randy Moss and tipped up in the air by Jason Allen. Four plays later the Dolphins were in the end zone. Chad Pennington tossed a three-yard pass to Greg Camarillo to take a 7–3 lead.

On the first play of the second quarter, Matt Cassel scored on an eight-yard run up the middle. The Patriots

---

2008 New England Patriots Team Leaders
Offensive Team
Matt Cassel threw 21 TD passes
Randy Moss had 11 TD receptions
Sammy Morris ran for seven TDs

Defensive/Special Teams
Brandon Meriweather had four interceptions
Ellis Hobbs returned a kickoff 95 yards for a TD
Richard Seymour had eight sacks
Gary Guyton recovered two fumbles

Memorable Statistics of the Year
Matt Cassel became the first NFL quarterback with 400+ yards passing and 60+ yards rushing in the same game.
Stephen Gostkowski and Wes Welker were the two Pro Bowl players for the Patriots in 2008.

---

had taken the lead back from Miami. Former Dolphins running back Sammy Morris fumbled, and Miami was able to take advantage of this second turnover by the Patriots. Chad Pennington went on a 13-play drive that ended with his seven-yard run over the left side for a touchdown.

Less than three minutes later Cassel completed a 25-yard touchdown pass to Moss. After trading punts, Mike Vrabel sacked Chad Pennington on the last play of the first half with the Patriots leading 17–14.

Ted Ginn Jr. hauled in a 46-yard pass from Pennington, and the Dolphins were in prime position to score again. Six plays later, Casey Cramer caught a two-yard touchdown pass from Chad Pennington. The Dolphins were up by four points again.

Matt Cassel marched his team down the field, on an 11-play, 78-yard drive to another score. On third-and-10 from the Dolphins 39-yard line, Randy Moss caught a 15-yard pass from Cassel. Two plays later, Moss grabbed an eight-yard touchdown pass from Cassel. The Patriots never looked back.

Wes Welker's 64-yard reception helped set up the Patriots' next score. Kevin Faulk finished off the drive with a 21-yard run up the middle for a touchdown.

On third-and-3 from the Patriots 49-yard line, Davone Bess dashed down the sideline for a 36-yard reception, and the Dolphins were not done yet. Ricky Williams made a nice diving 13-yard touchdown reception on the next play, and the Patriots lead was down to just three points.

On third-and-10 from the Patriots 42-yard line, Jabar Gaffney caught a 23-yard pass from Cassel and just two plays later the Patriots had another seven points. Moss caught a 29-yard touchdown for his third touchdown reception in the game.

Brandon Meriweather then intercepted an overthrown pass by Pennington, and the game was essentially over. After Gostkowski's 30-yard field goal went through the uprights, linemen Channing Crowder and Matt Light got tangled up. Crowder lost his helmet, and Light got off a few punches to Crowder's head. Both men were ejected for fighting.

On fourth-and-10 from the Dolphins 44-yard line, with just over four minutes left in the game, Pennington threw an incomplete pass. The Patriots took over and marched down the field. Ben Jarvus Green-Ellis scored on a one-yard touchdown run, on

Randy Moss

fourth-and-goal, with 40 seconds left in the game. New England had avenged its 25-point September home loss to the Dolphins at Gillette with this 20-point win over Miami on 11-23-08.

Player Profiles

2

"Ju Ju" Julius Adams
#85, Defensive Lineman

Julius Adams

Julius Adams was chosen from Texas Southern by the New England Patriots with the No. 27 pick in the 1971 College Football Draft. Adams shared duties with Houston Antwine as the right defensive tackle and was occasionally used as a roving linebacker during his rookie season in 1971. Julius "the Jewel" Adams was named the NFL Defensive Player of the Week as he led the Patriots defense in the 34-13 rout of the Miami Dolphins on 12-05-71. He played on the left side of the defensive line in the 4-3 defensive alignment in 1972. In 1973, he was used at the right defensive tackle position. Julius utilized his speed and quickness and played on the outside as the defensive end from both the left and right side in 1974. In 1975, he played on the right side of the defensive line in the 4-3 defensive alignment.

Adams finally settled into one position and played as the right defensive end during the 1976–87 seasons. Adams led the team in sacks during the 1972–74 seasons and again in 1980.

Adams was a force on the defensive line and recorded 80.5 sacks. His favorite overall target was New York Jets quarterback Richard Todd, who he tackled for a loss six times. His favorite target in one game was Steve Bartkowski, who he sacked four times in the Patriots 16–10 win over the Atlanta Falcons on 12-04-77. Ken Stabler was on his radar sack screen as well, as Adams nailed him three times in the Patriots Playoff Game loss to the Oakland Raiders in 1976.

Adams had 12 regular season games in which he recorded at least two sacks. The Pro Football Hall of Fame quarterbacks who have been brought down while attempting to pass by Julius Adams are Terry Bradshaw, Dan Fouts, Bob Griese, Ken Stabler, Roger Staubach, Joe Namath, Len Dawson, Dan Marino, and Joe Montana. Some of the NFC quaterbacks who have been sacked by Adams include Bobby Avellini, Lynn Dickey, Bobby Douglass, Roman Gabriel, Jim McMahon, Joe Pisarcik, Joe Theismann, and Roger Staubach. The most obscure player that Adams sacked was Dolphins WR Mark Clayton, who he tackled for a 7-yard loss in the Patriots' 17–13 win over Miami on 11-03-85. The other quarterbacks he sacked include James Harris, Bill Nelson, Joe Ferguson, Al Woodhall, Norm Snead, Marty Domres, Steve Ramsey, Mike Livingston, Jim Zorn, Don Strock, Vince Ferragamo, David Woodley, Mike Pagel, and Art Schlichter.

Adams was also a force on special teams. He blocked an extra-point attempt in the 29–28 loss to the Buffalo Bills on 11-03-74. His huge hands blocked a 37-yard field-goal attempt by Pat Leahy in the 30–27 loss to the New York Jets on 10-02-77. In the 3–0 shutout of the Miami Dolphins, the "Snow Plow" Game, he blocked a 45-yard field-goal attempt by Uwe von Schamann. Adams was awarded one of the game balls for his overall defensive play and his block of a 42-yard field-goal attempt by Raul Allegre in the fourth quarter of the 16–10 win over the Indianapolis Colts on 12-16-84.

Adams was alert and nimble as he recovered fumbles by Dennis Shaw, Bob Griese, Joe Ferguson, Jon Keyworth, Lynn Dickey, Curt Warner, and recovered his strip sack of Archie Manning. He returned a fumble by Joe Ferguson 12 yards in the 23–6 win over the Detroit Lions on 12-08-85.

An obscure fact about Julius Adams is that he wore uniform No. 69 for two games during the 1987 season. Adams was recognized as an AFC Pro Bowl defensive end in 1980. He played in 206 regular season games and in five playoff games during the 1971–85 and 1987 seasons. Only Bruce Armstrong has played in more regular season games for the Patriots than Julius Adams.

Tom Addison
#53, Linebacker

Addison was instrumental in the formation of a player's union in the American Football League. He was known as "Big T" and "Plugger." He had a notable and productive career, producing 15 sacks, 16 interceptions, and recovering four fumbles for the Boston Patriots.

Some of Addison's most memorable moments came in games against the Houston Oilers. He sacked Jacky Lee twice in a game in 1960. He sacked and intercepted George Blanda during the 1962 season. He intercepted and sacked Jacky Lee and sacked George Blanda in 1963. In 1964, he intercepted a pass by Houston Oilers quarterback George Blanda. The Boston Patriots had an aggressive and frequently blitzing defense. Addison's favorite quarterback target to sack was Jacky Lee, whom he nailed 5.5 times.

Addison recorded a sack and an interception in the same game five times. He had multiple sacks in a game twice in his career. In various games against the Denver Broncos he blocked an extra point by Gene Mingo, sacked Jacky Lee, Frank Trupicka, George Shaw, John McCormick, and Mickey Slaughter, and intercepted George Herring and Mickey Slaughter.

In the longtime rivalry the Patriots have had against the Raiders, Addison has sacked Tom Flores and intercepted Tom Flores and Cotton Davidson. The other quarterbacks he sacked in a regular season game include Abner Hayes, Jack Kemp, Len Dawson, John Hadl, Warren Rabb, and Tobin Rote.

Addison has recorded a sack and an interception in the same game four times in his career. In the Patriots 24–20 win over the San Diego Chargers in 1962, Addison had one sack and two interceptions. Addison had 2.5 sacks in the Patriots' 46–28 win over the Houston Oilers on 12-08-63. Among his 16 interceptions that were returned for 103 yards was his 12-yard return for a touchdown of a pass by Lee Grosscup in the 43–14 rout of the New York Titans at the Polo Grounds on 10-06-62.

Tom Addison

Addison played in 106 regular season games and in two playoff games for the Boston Patriots during the 1960-67 AFL seasons. Addison recovered a fumble by Jack Kemp in the 26–8 AFL Divisional Playoff Game victory over the Buffalo Bills on 12-28-63. Addison was recognized as an AFL All-Star linebacker from 1960–64. Addison has been inducted in the South Carolina Hall of Fame.

Houston Antwine
#65, Defensive Tackle

Antwine was acquired in a trade for a third-round draft pick with the Houston Oilers on 10-09-61. He played for both the Boston Patriots and the New England Patriots.

He initially played as an offensive guard but was moved to defensive tackle and went on to be one of the best defensive tackles in the American Football League. Antwine was an AFL All-Star defensive tackle for six straight seasons from 1963–68. He led the Patriots in sacks for three straight years during the 1967–69 seasons. Antwine recovered fumbles by Paul Lowe, Darrell Lester, Bert Coan, and Dennis Shaw.

Antwine was awarded the game ball for his performance in the 26–10 win over the New York Jets at Boston College Alumni Stadium on 09-27-64. Antwine was the AFL Defensive Player of the Week, as he had three sacks of Dan Darragh in the 16–7 victory over the Buffalo Bills at War Memorial Stadium on 09-08-68. He had a career high 10 tackles in the 33–14 win over the Cincinnati Bengals at Fenway Park on 12-01-68.

The Pro Football Hall of Fame quarterbacks who have been sacked by Houston Antwine are George Blanda, Joe Namath, Len Dawson, Bob Griese, Fran Tarkenton, and Johnny Unitas. He had four games with at least two sacks.

His favorite quarterback target to sack was Bob Griese, whom he sacked 4.5 times. Houston played in 142 regular season games and in two playoff games for the Patriots during the 1961–71 seasons.

Houston Antwine

Bruce Armstrong "Army"
#78, Offensive Left Tackle

Bruce Armstrong played with spirit, determination, and force—sheer force. He was a leader on the New England Patriots offensive line due to his unparalleled blocking abilities. As Drew Bledsoe constructed his legacy as a quarterback, he was fortunate to have the luxury of Bruce Armstrong's protection.

Armstrong is one of the best players to have ever played his position. "Army," as he was called, played college football at the University of Louisville and became the No. 23 pick in the 1987 College Football Draft. The former college Most Outstanding Lineman created a stellar college legacy, and the anticipation for his arrival to the National Football League was immense.

Bruce Armstrong is as much a New England Patriot as anyone who has had the honor of donning the uniform. In fact, he is the most prolific Patriot of all time as he played in a franchise-record 212 regular season games during his 14-year career with the team. In addition to the regular season, Armstrong competed in seven playoff games wearing the red and blue.

The Best of Bruce Armstrong: The Highlights
- Recovered nine fumbles and made nine tackles.
- Recovered three fumbles by Drew Bledsoe and fumbles by Marc Wilson, John Stephens, Hugh Millen, Sam Gash, Robert Edwards, and Terry Allen.
- Advanced a fumble by Marc Wilson four yards in the Patriots' 17–10 loss to Miami on 10-18-90.

The superstar offensive tackle made the Pro Bowl consistently, appearing in the game in 1990, 1991, 1994, 1995, 1996, and 1997. His total of six Pro Bowls is second in Patriots franchise history to the legendary John Hannah.

Although Bruce Armstrong's physical ability was awe-inspiring and second to none, he played with heart and soul as much as with his ability. In 1993 "Army" won the honorable Ed Block Courage Award. Furthermore, he was a natural leader with a unique ability to draw inspiration from his teammates. He was named Patriots captain during the 1996 and 1998 seasons.

His No. 78 uniform has been retired by the team, and "Army" was recognized for his contributions to the franchise when he was inducted into the New England Patriots Hall of Fame on September 30, 2001. Bruce Armstrong is an offensive tackle for the ages.

Bruce Armstrong

Joe Bellino
#27, Running Back

Joe "The Jet" Bellino won the Heisman Trophy and the Maxwell Award in 1960 and was a 19th round pick in the 1961 College Draft from the Naval Academy. Joe served in the U.S. Navy before playing for the Boston Patriots in 1965. Joe is the only Patriot running back who has won the Heisman Trophy. (The Patriot running backs who have received votes for the Heisman Trophy are Ron Burton, who finished tenth in the voting in 1959; Keith Byars, who finished second to Doug Flutie in 1984; Vagas Ferguson, who was fifth in 1979; and Blair Thomas, who was tenth in 1989.) Bellino was inducted into the Orange Bowl Hall of Honor for his performance in the 1961 Orange Bowl.

Bellino caught a 15-yard pass from former Heisman Trophy winner John Huarte in the Patriots 38–14 rout of the Houston Oilers on 12-11-66. This is the only time that two former Heisman Trophy winners touched the ball on the same play for the Patriots in a regular season game.

Bellino caught a deflected pass on his back to continue a drive that resulted in a touchdown in the 14–3 win over the Buffalo Bills in "The Game" at Fenway Park on 12-04-66. Joe had the Patriots' longest kickoff return in 1966 of 43 yards and caught a 25-yard touchdown pass in the 20–10 win over the Buffalo Bills at War Memorial Stadium on 10-08-66. Bellino had 30 carries, 11 receptions, 43 kickoff returns, and 19 punt returns in 35 games for the Boston Patriots during the 1965–67 seasons.

Joe graduated from Winchester, Massachusetts High School and was inducted in the College Football Hall of Fame on 12-06-77.

Joe Bellino

Drew Bledsoe
#11, Quarterback

Drew Bledsoe's arrival in Foxboro could not have come at a better time. The franchise was in the midst of a difficult stretch in its history, and the popularity of the sport in New England had dwindled. The organization was in need of a player to turn its fortunes around, and in 1993 it got just that. The Patriots chose Bledsoe with the first overall pick in the '93 College Football Draft out of Washington State University. At WSU, Drew was a stud on the field. He finished eighth in the Heisman Trophy voting in 1992 and was named the Most Valuable Player of the Copper Bowl the same year. To say his arrival in Foxboro was anticipated was an understatement, and Drew did not disappoint.

The 6'6" laser-armed quarterback could throw a deep ball like nobody's business. Throughout the 1990s he racked up yards, found pay dirt, and smashed franchise records as one of the biggest stars in the National Football League. He was a Pro Bowl quarterback in 1994, 1996, and 1997. In many ways, 1994 was Bledsoe's breakout year. Not only was he was voted to his first Pro Bowl, but it was the year that hosted some of his most defining performances, including his brilliantly orchestrated come-from-behind overtime win against the Minnesota Vikings. On September 4, 1994, he set the team passing record with 421 yards in a 39–35 loss to the Miami Dolphins.

During the 1996 season, No. 11 led the Patriots on a tear through the American Football Conference playoffs, culminating in a Super Bowl birth against the Green Bay Packers—the first appearance for the Patriots in the big game in more than a decade. On September 23, 2001, Bledsoe suffered internal bleeding after being tackled on the sideline by New York Jets linebacker Mo Lewis. That moment changed the course of Bledsoe's Patriots career.

Bledsoe carried himself with class and dignity during the highly publicized Brady vs. Bledsoe "controversy." After head coach Bill Belichick decided to stick with the momentum the team had captured with Tom Brady at the helm, Bledsoe was a true teammate, offering guidance and assistance to a young Brady whenever necessary. During the memorable 2001 postseason run, Bledsoe's number was called in the AFC Championship Game, as he stepped in for an injured Brady. Bledsoe threw a touchdown pass to David Patten and led the

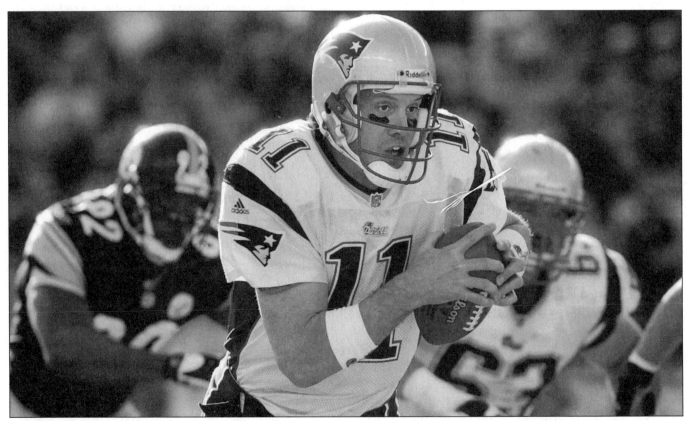

Drew Bledsoe

The Best of Drew Bledsoe: The Highlights

- Became the youngest NFL quarterback with 10,000 career passing yards in the 31–28 victory over the New York Jets on 12-10-95.
- AFC Offensive Player of the Week when he tossed two touchdown passes and led his team to a game-winning field goal in the Patriots' 17–16 victory over the Green Bay Packers on 10-02-94.
- AFC Offensive Player of the Week as he attempted an NFL-record 70 passes without throwing an interception, completing 45 of them for 426 yards, in the Patriots' 26–20 comeback overtime win vs. the Vikings on 11-13-94.
- Bledsoe threw four touchdown passes and two two-point conversion passes and was the AFC Offensive Player of the Week in the Patriots' 46–38 win over the Ravens on 10-06-96.
- NFL Player of the Week as he fractured his right index finger in the fourth quarter but led the team on a 15-play, 80-yard drive to defeat the Dolphins 26–23 in a *Monday Night Football* game played on 11-23-98. Bledsoe threw for 423 yards and tossed a 25-yard touchdown pass to Shawn Jefferson with 29 seconds left in the game.
- Named NFL Player of the Week as he tossed four touchdown passes in the Patriots' 45–7 rout of the Chargers on 12-01-96.
- AFC Offensive Player of the Week as he threw for 423 yards and two touchdowns in the 26–23 win over Miami on 11-23-98.
- NFL Player of the Week as he threw three touchdown passes, including the game winner on the final play of the 25–21 win over the Buffalo Bills on 11-29-98.
- His uniform No. 11 jersey was donated to the NFL Hall of Fame when he was the first to be named the NFL Player of the Week in consecutive weeks.
- AFC Offensive Player of the Week as he threw four touchdown passes and led his team to the game-winning field goal in the 31–28 win over the Colts on 09-19-99.
- AFC Offensive Player of the Week as he threw four touchdown passes in the 28–19 win over the Broncos on 10-01-00.
- Tossed a touchdown pass with broken finger with 26 seconds left to defeat Miami 26–23 on 11-23-98.
- Tossed four touchdown passes including an overtime game-winning 36-yard touchdown pass to Michael Timpson in the Patriots' 33–7 win vs. the Dolphins and knocked Miami out of the Playoffs on 01-02-94.
- Threw a 14-yard touchdown pass to Jimmy Smith in the 1998 Pro Bowl.
- Was 4-for-4 for 62 yards in leading the Patriots to a game-winning 27-yard field goal by Adam Vinatieri on the last play of the Patriots 30–27 win over the New Orleans Saints at the Superdome on 10-04-98.
- Was 11-for-13 for 115 yards and tossed the game-winning two-yard touchdown pass to Keith Byars in the fourth quarter of the 31–27 win over the New York Jets at the Meadowlands on 11-10-96.
- His longest run was for 25 yards in the Patriots' 13–10 overtime loss to the Buffalo Bills on 12-26-99.
- Threw six touchdown passes in the playoffs and replaced Tom Brady and threw a touchdown pass to David Patten in the Patriots' 2001 AFC Championship Game win over the Pittsburgh Steelers.
- Member of the 2001 championship team.

team to victory, ensuring a spot in Super Bowl XXVI against St. Louis. While Bledsoe's Patriots tenure ended in controversy, his impact on this franchise cannot be debated and will not be forgotten.

The star quarterback threw for 29,657 yards and 166 touchdowns in 126 regular season games as a New England Patriot. In 1999, he won the Ed Block Courage Award. Drew Bledsoe deserves credit as the player who restored faith in the New England Patriots franchise. He became one of the most popular players in team history throughout the 1990s and left the organization with class. He went on to play for the Buffalo Bills and the Dallas Cowboys, enjoying reasonable success in both destinations.

Tom Brady
#12, Quarterback

From backup quarterback to the front page of *GQ*, his star has shined to a level previously unseen in Foxboro. He's not just a star; he's an American original. Today, Tom Brady is a legend, an icon, and one of the few athletes that have truly transcended the sport. His story is so famous that it almost seems repetitive to go back and reminisce about how it all started.

He backed up Brian Griese at the University of Michigan and then he backed up Drew Bledsoe in New England. Tom Brady's meteoric rise to superstardom could have never been predicted. Sure, coaches along the way always said Tom had something special. He had a knowledge and understanding of the game on a deeper level that separated him from his peers. However, what he needed was an opportunity. One fateful day in the fall of 2001, he got it.

When Bledsoe, the Pats' former franchise quarterback, was mauled and almost killed by Mo Lewis, Brady's number was called. The rest, as they say, is history. What's amazing is just how much history has been made.

From the moment No. 12 took the reins of the offense, he captured the hearts and minds of not only New Englanders but of football fans across the globe. During the Patriots' initial Super Bowl run in 2001, Brady's accomplishments were downplayed. The experts said he only "managed" the game and simply had to leave the game up to the superb Patriots defense. However, as the Pats continued winning, and Brady continued to perform in the clutch, it became apparent that all that talk was just talk.

Tom Brady has led the New England Patriots to three Super Bowl championships in 2001, 2003, and 2004. In the process, he captured two Super Bowl Most Valuable Player Awards. During the Patriots' 2002 campaign, Brady led the NFL in touchdown passes. Fast forward to 2007 when he led the Patriots on a historic offensive romp through the National Football League en route to a record-breaking 16–0 mark. In addition, he won his first regular-season Most Valuable Player Award after passing for a mind-boggling 50 touchdowns, breaking the record set just three years earlier by his chief rival, Peyton Manning. Six of his 50 touchdowns came in the October 21 game in Miami where he lit up his division rival en route to a 49–28 victory and a 158.3 quarterback rating. The number one beneficiary

Tom Brady

The Best of Tom Brady: The Highlights
- NFL Offensive Player of the Year for 2007.
- AFC Offensive Player of the Week on 10-14-01.
- NFL Player of the Week as he threw four touchdown passes in the Patriots' 34–17 win over the Saints on 11-25-01.
- AFC Offensive Player of the Week on 09-09-02.
- AFC Offensive Player of the Week in the Patriots' 38–7 rout of the Buffalo Bills on 11-03-02.
- AFC Offensive Player of the Week in the 30–26 win over the Denver Broncos on 11-03-03.
- AFC Offensive Player of the Week as he tossed four touchdown passes in the first half of the 31–0 shutout of the Buffalo Bills on 12-27-03.
- AFC Offensive Player of the Week as he had 350 yards passing and three touchdowns in the 31–28 win over Atlanta on 10-09-05.
- Threw two touchdowns in the fourth quarter, including one to David Patten with 21 seconds left, in the 33–30 win over the Chicago Bears on 11-10-02.
- Member of the 2001, 2003, and 2004 championship teams.

of Brady's 2007 wizardry was Randy Moss, who caught 23 of Brady's 50 touchdown passes, breaking Jerry Rice's previous record of 22.

No. 12 has mastered his position. Some of his defining characteristics include his calmness under pressure, his ability to read any defense and make changes on the spot, and his knack for finding the open man. Brady's favorite receiver is the open one, and he hits him most every time. His accuracy was never more evident than in the 2008 Divisional Playoff Game against Jacksonville when he completed 26-of-28 passes, breaking the single-game playoff record for best completion percentage—92.9 percent. He also has demonstrated an unparalleled ability to avoid the sack. He knows exactly how long to hold the ball and exactly when to release it. His footwork in the pocket is extraordinary and did not come naturally. It is a true testament to his hard work and dedication in practice.

Let's go down the list. Championships? Check. Supermodel wife? Check. 16–0 undefeated season? Check. Defining playoff moments? Check. Brady is cooler than the other side of the pillow under pressure, and his knack for performing in the clutch has been seen time and time again. In both Super Bowl XXXVI and XXXVIII he led scintillating two-minute drills, setting up Adam Vinatieri's game-winning, last-second field goals. In the famous AFC Divisional Playoff Game against Oakland in 2001 he fought through the blizzard conditions in one of the grittiest, gutsiest performances in NFL history. Brady ran for his first career rushing touchdown and passed for more than 350 yards en route to the momentous "Snow Bowl" victory.

Despite his success, nobody crowned Tom Brady king. He had to build his reputation and continuously beat his critics over the head with accomplishment after accomplishment before he received his proper due. Super Bowl after Super Bowl, Tom Brady has crushed his contemporaries. His only competition now: the heroes, legends, and warriors of football's past. Today, Tom Brady is the Joe Montana of his era, but it is for the next generation to decide who the next Tom Brady will be.

"Just" Pete Brock
#58, Offensive Lineman

Brock was chosen from Colorado with the No. 12 pick by the New England Patriots in the 1976 College Football Draft. (This draft pick was acquired by the Patriots in exchange for trading Jim Plunkett to the 49ers)

Brock played a multitude of positions and acquired the nickname "Mr. Versatility" when he played left tackle, long snapper, tight end, and wingback on the same drive during the Patriots 27–7 victory over the Chicago Bears at Soldier Field on 10-14-79.

Brock was given the nickname "Deep Threat" because he caught a six-yard touchdown pass in the 38–24 victory over the New York Jets on 11-21-76. Upon delivering the play from the sidelines, Brock told Steve Grogan in the huddle that the name of the play was "222 to me" rather than "222 Tight End Delay."

Brock tore the cartilage in his knee but played the entire game and was awarded the game ball in the 17–6 win over the Miami Dolphins on 11-13-83. He played against his brother, Stan, in the Patriots' 38–27 win over the New Orleans Saints on 12-21-80. Brock recovered fumbles by Doug Beaudoin, Horace Ivory, Matt Cavanaugh, and two fumbles by Steve Grogan. Brock recovered a fumble by Tony Eason in the 22–17 playoff game loss to the Denver Broncos on 01-04-87.

Brock was the starting right guard in two games, the starting left guard in three games, the starting left tackle in six games, and the starting center in 78 regular season games and in six playoff games. Brock played in 154 regular season games and in eight playoff games during the 1976–87 seasons. Brock won the Ed Block Courage Award in 1985.

Pete Brock

Troy "Mr. Patriot" Brown
#80, Special Teams, Defensive Back, and Wide Receiver

Troy Brown was chosen from Marshall University with the No. 198 pick by the New England Patriots in the 1993 College Football Draft.

Brown is the team leader in career punt returns and career punt return yards and had the most career punts returned for a touchdown. Brown returned a punt by Mark Royals 66 yards for a touchdown in the 21–16 loss to Tampa Bay on 09-03-00. He returned a punt by Chris Gardocki 85 yards for a touchdown in the 27–16 win over the Browns on 12-09-01. Brown returned a punt by Todd Sauerbrun 61 yards for a touchdown in the 38–6 rout of the Panthers on 01-06-02. Brown also returned a punt by Josh Miller 55 yards for a touchdown in the 24–17 AFC Championship Game victory over the Pittsburgh Steelers at Heinz Field on 01-27-02.

Troy Brown

Brown has been a key contributor on special teams as he advanced a fumbled kickoff return by Dave Meggett 75 yards for a touchdown in the 31–28 win over the New York Jets on 12-10-96. Brown caught a nine-yard touchdown pass and recovered an onside kick by Mike Hollis in the 26–20 win over the Jacksonville Jaguars on 12-07-97.

Brown was recognized as the AFC Special Team Player of the Month as he returned a punt for a touchdown and had 175 punt return yards in December 2001. Brown picked up a blocked field goal and took it 11 yards before pitching it back to Antwan Harris, who took it in for a touchdown in the 24–17 AFC Championship Game win over the Pittsburgh Steelers on 01-27-02.

Brown is the ultimate team player and filled in admirably when the Patriots secondary was felled by injuries. He returned a pass by Drew Bledsoe 17 yards in the 29–6 rout of the Buffalo Bills on 11-14-04. Brown picked off a pass that was thrown by Luke McCown in the 42–15 rout of the Browns on 12-05-04, and he returned a Jon Kitna pass five yards in the 35–28 win over the Bengals on 12-12-04.

Brown led the Patriots with 33 yards rushing in the 21–16 loss to Tampa Bay on 09-03-00. He caught a pass for a two-point conversion for the last points scored in the 33–30 win over the Chicago Bears on 11-10-02. Brown also caught a pass for a two-point conversion in the 28–21 win over the Detroit Lions on 12-03-06.

Who can forget his 13-yard reception—on his back, for a first down, on third-and-13—in the 23–22 comeback win over the New York Giants at Giants Stadium on 12-21-96? How about his 82-yard game-winning touchdown reception from Tom Brady in overtime to defeat the Miami Dolphins 19–13 at Pro Player Stadium on 10-19-03?

The obscure fact about "Mr. Patriot" Troy Brown was that he wore No. 86 during the 1994 regular season. Brown was recognized as an AFC Pro Bowl wide receiver in 2001. He is a member of the 2001, 2003, and 2004 championship teams. Troy Brown won the Ed Block Courage Award in 1998.

"Fearless" Fred Bruney
#33, Defensive Back and Special Teams

Fred Bruney is an Ohio State Buckeye who played defensive back and was the holder for kicker Gino Cappelletti during the 1960–62 AFL seasons. Bruney had a pass interception in three consecutive games in 1960. He returned a pass by Tom Flores 17 yards in the 29–6 rout of the Bills on 11-04-60. Bruney returned a pass from the goal line 18 yards in the 38–21 win over the New York Titans on 11-11-60. He picked off a pass by Cotton Davidson in the 42–14 rout of the Dallas Texans on 11-18-60.

Bruney returned eight interceptions for 125 yards and one touchdown. Bruney intercepted both Jack Kemp and Hunter Enis in the 41–0 shutout of the San Diego Chargers on 12-17-61. He returned a pass by George Blanda 20 yards in the 34–21 loss to the Houston Oilers at Harvard on 09-16-62. Bruney took a George Shaw pass 33 yards for a touchdown in the 41–16 rout of the Denver Broncos on 09-21-62. He returned a pass by Lee Grosscup 17 yards in the 43–14 rout of the New York Titans at the Polo Grounds on 10-06-62.

Bruney had 30 punt returns for 148 yards and had a 20-yard kickoff return and a 19-yard punt return in the 28–24 victory over the New York Titans at the Polo Grounds on 09-16-60. He also attempted an onside kick in the 28–24 win over the New York Titans at the Polo Grounds on 09-16-60.

Bruney recovered a fumble by Jack Rudolph in the 35–0 shutout of the Los Angeles Chargers on 10-08-60. He recovered a fumble by Johnny Robinson in the 42–14 rout of the Dallas Texans on 11-18-60. Bruney recovered a fumble by Charley Hennigan in the 37–21 loss to the Houston Oilers on 12-18-60. His only sack was of Frank Tripucka in the 41–16 rout of the Denver Broncos on 09-21-62.

Bruney played in 40 regular season games for the Boston Patriots and was recognized as an AFL All-Star defensive back in 1961 and 1962. He was a coach of the defensive backfield for the Boston Patriots during the 1962–63 seasons and would go on to be the only undefeated NFL head coach. Fred Bruney was the head coach for the Philadelphia Eagles in the 37–35 win over the Detroit Lions on 12-22-85.

Tedy Bruschi
#54, Linebacker

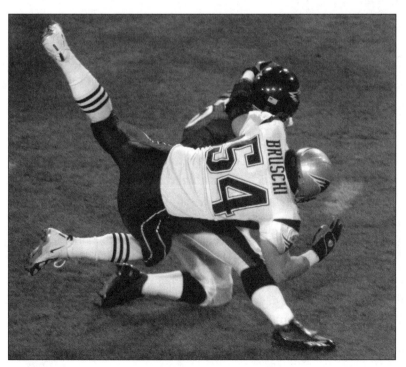

Tedy Bruschi

One of the qualities that has defined the New England Patriots in the 21st century is the number of so-called "character guys" on the roster. No player in the National Football League has more character than Tedy Bruschi. Bruschi has long been making an impact on the football field. At the University of Arizona he became college football's all-time sack leader and was named the Defensive Most Valuable Player for his efforts in the 1994 Fiesta Bowl. Not too shabby.

He was the 86th pick in the 1996 College Football Draft, and he entered the league with high expectations. Suffice it to say; he has met them all with flying colors. He plays with as much heart and soul as he does speed and power and is a true leader on and off the field. His hard work, intensity, and positive attitude have been representative of the way the Patriots play the game.

Bruschi has played an irreplaceable role in the Patriots' three Super Bowl championships. This was never more evident than in Super Bowl XXXIX against the Philadelphia Eagles. Bruschi recorded six tackles in the game and was a thorn in Philly quarterback Donavan McNabb's side. He sacked McNabb and intercepted a pass late in the fourth quarter to help preserve the 24–21 Patriots lead, thus ensuring the victory. The star linebacker made his one and only Pro Bowl appearance after Super Bowl XXXIX, and it's safe to say he had reached the pinnacle of his career. However, just a few days later he would be in for the scare of his life.

In a terrifying moment for his family and friends, as well as his countless fans, Tedy Bruschi suffered a stroke. The show of support from fans during his subsequent recovery was overwhelming. Many people felt his playing days were over, and it almost came to that. However, in a true nod to his perseverance and determination, Bruschi returned during the 2005 season. He wanted to leave the game on his terms and worked harder than ever to get back to the level needed to compete in the NFL.

Bruschi's return during Week 6 of the 2005 season was as emotional a moment as football fans have ever seen in Foxboro. Bruschi wasted little time erasing any doubt that he was ready to return. He was more expressive than ever as he flew all over the field and recorded 10 tackles in the Patriots' 21–16 win over Buffalo. Poetically, Bruschi was named AFC Defensive Player of the Week in a game that many people thought he'd never play again. He would go on to be a Co-Comeback Player of the Year. Furthermore, he won the Ed Block Courage Award in 2005 for the second time in his career; the first came in 2000.

Anybody who has followed Tedy Bruschi and the Patriots knows that Bruschi can draw emotion from the crowd. He was the AFC Defensive Player of the Week during a Patriots 12–0 shutout of the Miami Dolphins in Foxboro on December 7, 2003. In one of the most photographed games in recent history, Bruschi returned a Jay Fielder pass for a touchdown, dropped to his knees in the end zone, and pumped his fists. In an unforgettable moment, the 68,000-plus fans at Gillette started throwing snow in the air, and Bruschi celebrated right along with them. That is the kind of emotion the man evokes.

Tedy Bruschi is one of the most beloved New England Patriots of all time. A true superstar, Bruschi's presence on the defensive side can never be disputed, nor should it ever be overlooked. Simply put, Tedy Bruschi plays football the way the game was meant to be played.

The Best of Tedy Bruschi: The Highlights

- AFC Defensive Player of the Week as he returned a Donovan McNabb pass 18 yards for a touchdown in the Patriots' 31–10 rout of the Eagles on 09-14-03.
- AFC Defensive Player of the Week as he had two sacks and forced a fumble that was returned for a touchdown in the Patriots' 31–17 win over Buffalo on 10-03-04.
- Had 15 tackles and was named the AFC Defensive Player of the Week in the 21–7 win over San Francisco on 01-02-05
- Bruschi intercepted a tipped pass with 15 seconds left to secure the Patriots' 24–17 win over the Jets on 09-17-06.
- Returned a punt that was blocked by Larry Whigham four yards for a touchdown in the Patriots' 46–38 win over the Baltimore Ravens on 10-06-96.
- Returned a kickoff 11 yards and a pass interception 48 yards for a touchdown in the Patriots' 27–20 loss to the Raiders on 11-17-02. He is the only Patriots linebacker with a kickoff return and an interception return for a touchdown in the same regular season game.
- Returned a pass by Joey Harrington 27 yards for a touchdown in the Patriots' 20–12 win over Detroit on Thanksgiving Day on 11-28-02.
- Strip-sacked Kyle Boller, and Jarvis Green fell on the fumble in the end zone for a touchdown in the Patriots' 24–3 rout of the Ravens on 11-28-04.
- Tipped a pass by J.P. Losman, that was returned 39 yards for a touchdown by James Sanders in the Patriots' 35–7 rout of the Buffalo Bills on 12-11-05.
- Returned a pass by Chad Pennington three yards on the Jets' second play from scrimmage in the Patriots' 21–16 victory over the New York Jets at the Meadowlands on 12-20-03.
- Has returned six kickoffs for 47 yards, and his longest regular season return was for 11 yards on 11-17-02.
- Returned four consecutive pass interceptions for touchdowns.
- Returned a kickoff 15 yards in the Patriots' 20–3 playoff rout of the Indianapolis Colts on 01-16-05.
- Member of the 2001, 2003, and 2004 championship teams.

Nick Buoniconti
#85, Linebacker

Buoniconti was also known as "All World," "Hydrant," and "Skip." He was an offensive guard from Notre Dame who was picked in the 13th round in the 1962 College Draft. (He graduated from Springfield Cathederal High School in Springfield, Massachusetts.)

He was an aggressive, big hitting middle linebacker for the Boston Patriots during the 1962-68 AFL seasons. On 03-24-69 Buoniconti was traded to the Miami Dolphins for Kim Hammond and John Bramlett. He almost retired after his trade to the Dolphins because he was a lawyer from Suffolk University.

Patriots linebacker Nick Buoniconti recorded sacks of Pro Football Hall of Fame quarterbacks George Blanda, Len Dawson, and Joe Namath. He recorded a sack and an interception in the same game four times. He had at least two sacks in a game twice and at least two interceptions in a game three times. Buoniconti intercepted passes by Pro Football Hall of Fame quarterbacks George Blanda and Len Dawson, and he blocked a field-goal attempt by George Blanda as well.

Buoniconti is the only Patriots linebacker to return a punt.

Buoniconti recorded two blocked field goals and an extra-point attempt while playing for the Boston Patriots. He was recognized as the AFL Defensive Player of the Week twice. He led the defense and tackled Roy Hopkins in the end zone for a safety in the 18–7 win over the Oilers at Fenway Park on 11-05-67. Buoniconti was the AFL Defensive Player of the Week, as he had three interceptions in the 23–6 victory over the Buffalo Bills at Fenway Park on 10-20-68.

Buoniconti had a sack, returned an interception of Cotton Davidson 13 yards, and took a pass by Tom Flores three yards with about two minutes left to preserve the 20–14 win over the Oakland Raiders on 09-22-63. He returned an interception of John Hadl 41 yards in the 35–17 rout of the San Diego Chargers at Fenway Park on 09-24-65. Buoniconti intercepted Tom Flores twice in the 23–0 shutout of the Buffalo Bills on 09-24-67. (It was the first time that the Buffalo Bills had been shut out.) Buoniconti is the only Patriots linebacker to have three interceptions in a game, as he robbed quarterback Dan Darragh three times in the 23–6 victory over the Buffalo Bills at Fenway Park on 10-20-68. He was the second AFL linebacker to record three interceptions in a regular season game.

He returned a fumble 12 yards for a touchdown in the 1965 AFL All-Star Game. Buoniconti received the most votes for the 1967 AFL All-Star Game and was an AFL All-Star linebacker for the Boston Patriots from 1963–67.

Buoniconti led the Patriots defense that held the Chiefs, Jets, Bills, and Chargers to less than 80 yards rushing in consecutive games in 1966. He had 10 unassisted tackles in the 24–21 win over the Raiders at Fenway Park on 10-30-66. Buoniconti was the middle linebacker for the Patriots in the only regular season game that they recorded 10 sacks.

Buoniconti was a member of the 1972 and 1973 championship Miami Dolphins teams. Nick has been inducted in the Florida Sports Hall of Fame, the Patriots Hall of Fame, and the Pro Football Hall of Fame.

Nick Buoniconti

Ron Burton
#22, Running Back/Returner

From Northwestern University, Burton was the first overall draft choice of the Boston Patriots in 1960. He was an All-American running back at Northwestern and finished tenth in the voting for the 1959 Heisman Trophy. On 12-04-90, Ron Burton was inducted in the College Football Hall of Fame.

Burton was the first Patriots player to run for a first down on a fourth-down play in the 13–0 loss to the Buffalo Bills at BU Field on 09-23-60. He was the first Patriots player to rush for 100 yards in a game as he had 127 yards rushing, including his career longest run of 77 yards, in the 31–24 loss to the Denver Broncos on 10-23-60. Burton was the first Patriots player to run for a touchdown on a fourth-down play. Burton was the first Patriots player to have a run from scrimmage of at least 70 yards and have a punt return of at least 60 yards. He was the first Patriots player with a pass reception in a playoff game. Burton is the only Patriots player who has returned a missed field goal for a touchdown.

Burton returned a kickoff 91 yards for the game-winning touchdown in the infamous 28–21 win over the Dallas Texans on 11-03-61. (In this game the potential game-tying touchdown pass was deflected by a fan was on the field on the last play of the game. Cotton Davidson was moving the Texans down the field and threw a pass to a wide-open Chris Burford in the end zone as time was expiring. A man who was standing on the edge of the field, along with a few hundred other people, ran onto the field and interfered on the play, and the Patriots won the game. Thousands of fans then stormed the field to celebrate this Patriots victory. The Dallas Texans head coach Hank Stram, who had his own crew filming the game, protested the egregious error to the league office to no avail.

Because he was such a versatile player other teams coveted the services of Ron Burton but Team Owner Billy Sullivan did not want to trade him.

Burton had his career longest reception of 73 yards for a touchdown in the 13–13 tie with the San Diego Chargers at Fenway Park on 10-17-65. He had a career best 97 yards receiving in the 21–10 victory over the Buffalo Bills at BU Field on 11-23-62. He had four touchdown receptions of at least 50 yards. Burton had a 69-yard touchdown reception in consecutive games during the 1962 AFL season.

Ron Burton was a tremendous special teams return man as he averaged 16 yards per punt return in 1961 and led the AFL with 21 punt returns in 1962. Burton returned a missed field goal 91 yards for the game-winning touchdown in the 33–29 win over the Denver Broncos on 11-11-62. He had the longest kickoff return (91 yards for a touchdown) by a Patriots player in a regular season game played at BU Field.

Burton led the Patriots with 1,009 total yards from scrimmage and led the team with 1,369 total yards rushing, receiving, and returning during the 1962 season. He did not play during the 1963 regular season due to back surgery but led the Boston Patriots with seven receptions in the playoffs. The Patriots had to appeal to the league to allow him to play in the playoffs.

For his career totals he had 1,536 yards rushing and nine touchdowns; 1,205 yards receiving and eight touchdowns; 1,119 yards returning kickoffs and one touchdown; and 389 yards returning punts. Burton is the only Patriots player to return a missed field-goal attempt for a touchdown. He played in 69 regular season games and in two playoff games for the Boston Patriots from 1960–65.

Burton bought land in Hubbardston, Massachusetts, to set up his Ron Burton Training Village. This village holds free summer camps for disadvantaged inner city youths.

Ron Burton

Gino Cappelletti "Duke"
#20, Receiver/Kicker

Gino Cappelletti is a New England Patriots original. His game was revolutionary and innovative, and his dedication to the team, even today, is admirable. His presence in the Patriots' organization spans across five decades, giving millions of fans the opportunity to know and recognize Cappelletti in the many facets of his career in New England. However, let's start at the beginning.

Cappelletti played for the Boston Patriots from 1960–70. During the course of the decade, he amassed a stunning 1,130 total points—155 of which came in 1964 as a wide receiver and a field goal kicker. It was a record that stood until 2005 when Adam Vinatieri finally eclipsed it. There was nobody in football that could score with the ball like Cappelletti in the 1960s. He is the most prolific scorer in the history of the American Football League, and he outperformed his peers on a regular basis. Cappelletti led the AFL in scoring on five occasions. On October 10, 1964, Cappelletti broke the record for most field goals made without a miss in a single game. His six three-pointers helped the Pats wallop Denver 39–10. It is no wonder "Duke" is a member of the 1960s All-Patriots team.

Gino Cappelletti is the conscience of the New England Patriots. His presence in the organization is

The Best of Gino Cappelletti: The Highlights

- AFL Player of the Year in 1964.
- Finished second to George Blanda for the AFL Player of the Year in 1961.
- He was the second AFL defensive back to record three interceptions in a regular season game.
- Second AFL player to record three interceptions in a regular season game.
- Averaged 9.5 points per game over a six-year period when the Patriots record was 47–29–8.
- Scored at least 20 points in a game eight times.
- Only professional football player to average 7.5 points per game over a career of at least 10 years.
- Holds the AFL record with 1,100 points scored.
- Held the AFL/NFL record for the most field goals kicked in a game (without a miss) for 32 years.
- Cappelletti caught a 52-yard touchdown pass, kicked a 35-yard field goal, and kicked six extra points in the Patriots' 45–17 rout of the Broncos on 09-16-61.
- Caught four passes for 129 yards, including one for 51 yards in the Patriots' 26–8 AFL Eastern Division playoff game win over the Buffalo Bills at War Memorial Stadium on 12-28-63.
- Kicked a 33-yard field goal with six seconds left in the half and a game-winning 41-yard field goal to defeat the Houston Oilers, 25–24, at Fenway Park on 11-06-64. Cappelletti was awarded the game ball and Babe Parilli remarked that Cappelletti's game-winning field goal was the greatest clutch kick he had ever seen.
- Selected as a member of the All-AFL 10-year anniversary team in 1971.
- Only player to account for at least 34% of his team's total points scored in a season for eight consecutive seasons.
- Cappelletti scored 24 points in the Patriots' 36–28 win over the Bills at War Memorial Stadium on 11-15-64.
- Accounted for 21 points in the Patriots' five-point win over the 1963 AFL champion San Diego Chargers on 09-20-64.
- Scored 24 points in the Patriots' eight-point win over the eventual 1964 AFL champion Buffalo Bills on 11-15-64.
- Caught two touchdown passes and kicked four extra points in the Patriots' 28–20 win over Denver on 12-12-65.
- Set the AFL record by scoring 28 points in the Patriots' 42–14 rout of the Houston Oilers at Fenway Park on 12-18-65. Cappelletti caught two touchdown passes and kicked four field goals and four extra points.
- Booted a sharp angled field goal from close range for the game-winning points late in the 20–17 victory over the Denver Broncos on 09-29-68.
- Cappelletti caught a 19-yard touchdown pass in the Patriots' 27–17 loss to the San Diego Chargers at Fenway Park on 11-10-68 and became the first AFL player to score 1,000 points in the league. The football was donated to the NFL Hall of Fame in recognition of this event.

enduring and cherished by all true fans of the team. In his era, he had no equal. A five-time AFL All-Star and the Most Valuable Player in 1964, Cappelletti was as timely as he was talented, and he gained a reputation as a clutch performer. No better example of his ability to perform under pressure exists than in 1964 when he kicked the game-winning field goal in New England's 25–24 victory over the Houston Oilers at Fenway Park. His "Grand Opera" partner Babe Parilli remarked that it was the greatest clutch kick he had ever witnessed.

The final game of his playing career occurred on December 20, 1970. At the game's conclusion, he was one of only three players who partook in every game in AFL history. The extra point he made in the game served as the exclamation mark on a riveting professional career. December 5, 1971 was Gino Cappelletti day at Schaefer Stadium, and the fans celebrated his incalculable contributions to the club. Today, Cappelletti is the color commentator for all Patriots games on WBCN Radio in Boston. His voice unmistakable and his analysis invaluable, Cappelletti continues to contribute to the team and city he loves.

Gino Cappelletti

Jim Cheyunski
#50, Linebacker

Jim Cheyunski, who was also known as "Chey," was born in Bridgewater, Massachusetts, and graduated from West Bridgewater High School. From Syracuse University, he was the No. 305 pick in the 1968 College Football Draft.

He was discovered by Rommie Loudd while working at his father's gas station. He took over the middle linebacker duties from Nick Bouniconti, who was traded to the Miami Dolphins. Cheyunski had 16 tackles in the 31–17 loss to the Kansas City Chiefs on 11-17-68; 17 tackles in the 33–14 win over the Cincinnati Bengals on 12-01-68; 20 tackles in the 13–10 loss to the San Diego Chargers on 10-19-69; and 20 tackles in the 34–7 loss to the Detroit Lions on 09-26-71.

Cheyunski was the AFL Defensive Player of the Week and was awarded the game ball as he recovered a fumble and returned a Greg Cook pass 37 yards in the 25–14 win over the Cincinnati Bengals on 11-16-69. Cheyunski returned an interception of a Dan Pastorini pass 24 yards to help set up the Patriots' final touchdown in the 28–20 win over the Houston Oilers on 11-07-71.

Cheyunski was recognized as the NFL Defensive Player of the Week as he played the entire game with a

Jim Cheyunski

cast on his broken thumb and made 18 tackles in the 21–20 win over the Atlanta Falcons at Schaefer Stadium on 09-24-72. Cheyunski returned a John Stofa pass 21 yards in the 33–14 win over the Cincinnati Bengals at Fenway Park on 12-01-68. He returned a Greg Cook pass 37 yards in the 25–14 win over the Bengals at Riverfront Stadium on 11-16-69. Cheyunski returned a Dan Pastorini pass 24 yards in the 24–20 win over the Oilers at Schaefer Stadium on 11-07-71.

Cheyunski sacked Bob Griese twice, Steve Tensi once, and shared in a sack of James Harris and Al Woodall. He recovered a fumble by Jess Phillips on the Bengals' second play in the 25–14 win over Cincy on 11-16-69. He returned a fumble by Ron Sayers three yards in the 28–18 loss to San Diego on 12-07-69. Cheyunski picked up a fumble by Bob Davis and lateraled it to John Bramlett, who took it 17 yards in the 27–23 loss to the Houston Oilers on 12-14-69. Cheyunski recovered a fumble by Larry Brown in the 24–23 win over the Redskins on 10-01-72.

Cheyunski recovered an onside kick in the 41–10 loss to the Oakland Raiders on 10-06-68. Cheyunski was traded to the Buffalo Bills and ended his career playing for the Baltimore Colts.

Raymond Clayborn
#26, Right Side Cornerback

From the University of Texas, Clayborn was chosen with the No. 16 pick by the New England Patriots in the 1977 College Football Draft. (This draft pick was acquired by the Patriots in exchange for trading Jim Plunkett to the 49ers.) Clayborn had a variety of nicknames including "Claybo," "Bones," and "Mr. Reliable."

Clayborn holds the team record (three) for returning kickoffs for touchdowns in a regular season. He took a kickoff 100 yards for a touchdown in the 30–27 loss to the Jets on 10-02-77. He returned a kickoff 93 yards for a touchdown in the 24–14 loss to the Bills on 11-06-77, and he took a kickoff 101 yards for a touchdown in the 30–24 loss to the Baltimore Colts on 12-18-77. Clayborn had the longest kickoff return in the NFL in 1977.

Raymond Clayborn is the only Patriots player to return a kickoff for a touchdown and record a safety in the same season. He forced punter Mike Michel out of the end zone for a safety in the 17–5 loss to Miami on 11-13-77. He had two huge plays as he sacked Steve Bartkowski and returned a kickoff 78 yards at the end of the game to preserve the 16–10 win over the Atlanta Falcons at Fulton County Stadium on 12-04-77.

Clayborn had tremendous agility and athletic ability and is tied with Ty Law for the team record for the most career interceptions. Twenty-one of his 36 career regular season interceptions were at the opponent's home stadium. Among the quarterbacks who he has intercepted in a regular season game for the Patriots are Ken Stabler, Dan Fouts, Tommy Kramer, Bert Jones, John Elway, Dan Marino, Jim Kelly, and Joe Montana. He has also intercepted passes thrown by Pat Ryan, Richard Todd, Bill Troup, Joe Ferguson, Don Strock, David Woodley, Steve DeBerg, David Hum, Danny White, Gary Danielson, Ken O'Brien, Matt Kofler, Bubby Brister, Rusty Hilger, Todd Rutledge, and Chris Miller.

Some of his interceptions saved the game for the Patriots. He picked off a pass by Jim Zorn late in the fourth quarter to seal the 37–31 victory over Seattle at the Kingdome on 09-21-80. His most memorable pass interception was his 85-yard return of a Paul McDonald pass on the last play of the 17–16 win over the Cleveland Browns at Cleveland on 10-07-84. Clayborn caught a pass by Chris Chandler with 23 seconds left to preserve the 21–17 win over the Indianapolis Colts at Sullivan Stadium on 10-02-88. Clayborn returned a pass by Vince Ferragamo 27 yards for a touchdown in the 14–3 win over Buffalo on 10-13-85.

Clayborn, who was overly abrasive in his younger days, became disturbed

Left to right: Phil Dokes and Raymond Clayborn

because he could not get to his locker as reporters talked to No. 29 Harold Jackson after his three-touchdown-reception performance in the 56–3 rout of the New York Jets on 09-09-79. Will McDonough knocked Clayborn into the laundry basket after being jabbed repeatedly, once inadvertently in the eye, by Mr. Clayborn. Clayborn later admitted to McDonough that he was a wrong and they became friends.

Clayborn was at the right place at the right time when he returned a blocked field goal 71 yards for a touchdown in the 21–7 win over the Oilers on 10-18-87.

He recovered fumbles by Wilbert Montgomery, Brian Sipe, Louie Giammona, Tony Nathan, Calvin Thomas, Pete Metzelaars, Boomer Esiason, and George Wonsley.

Raymond Clayborn is the only Patriot player to return an interception for a touchdown, a kickoff for a touchdown, and a blocked field goal for a touchdown. He was recognized as an AFC All-Pro cornerback in 1983, 1985, and 1986 and played in 191 regular season games and seven playoff games for the Patriots. Clayborn finished his career with the Cleveland Browns.

Ben "Winter" Coates
#87, Tight End

Ben Coates was chosen from Livingstone College with the No. 124 pick in the 1991 College Football Draft. This pick was acquired from a trade with the Los Angeles Raiders.

Coates is the most prolific tight end in team history and was a favorite target of Drew Bledsoe. Bledsoe connected with him on 45 of Coates' 50 career regular season touchdown receptions. Among the three touchdown passes from Hugh Millen was his game-tying 2-yard touchdown reception with seven seconds left to force overtime in the 23–17 overtime win vs. the Indianapolis Colts on 12-08-91. Coates' only touchdown reception thrown by Scott Zolak was a 2-yard touchdown catch in the Patriots' 37–34 overtime win vs. the

Indianapolis Colts at the Hoosier Dome on 11-15-92. Coates' only touchdown reception from Scott Secules was a 2-yard game-winning touchdown reception to defeat the Phoenix Cardinals 23–21 at Sun Devil Stadium on 10-10-93.

Big Ben was a player that could make the clutch reception in heavy traffic. Coates grabbed an 8-yard touchdown pass from Drew Bledsoe to defeat the Cincinnati Bengals 7–2 at Foxboro Stadium on 12-12-93. He hauled in a 13 yard touchdown pass from Drew Bledsoe, with under two minutes to go, in the 23–22 comeback win over the New York Giants at Giants Stadium on 12-21-96.

Coates was extremely valuable when recovering an opponent's onside kick. He recovered an onside kick by Chris Gardocki in the 20–17 win over the Indianapolis Colts on 11-30-97. He returned an onside kick by Mike Holis 20 yards to seal the 26–20 win over the Jacksonville Jaguars on 12-07-97. Coates recovered an onside kick by Brad Daluiso in the 16–14 win over the New York Giants on 09-26-99.

Coates is the only Patriots tight end with more than 1,000 yards receiving in a regular season as he accumulated 1,174 yards in the 1994 season. Coates had the most receptions by a tight end in the NFL in 1994. He led the Patriots with the most yards receiving in a season five times.

Coates is the only Patriots tight end with three touchdown receptions on a fourth-down play. He holds the team record with 13 receptions on fourth down. He had a career high three touchdown receptions in the 35–25 win over the Buffalo Bills at Rich Stadium on 11-26-95. Coates is the only Patriots tight end with two game-winning touchdown receptions.

Coates had three rushing attempts during his career, and his most memorable run was for a two-yard gain in the 6–0 loss to the Indianapolis Colts in wind-chill

Ben Coates

weather of six degrees below zero at Foxboro Stadium on 12-06-92. Coates had one reception for a two-point conversion in the 46–38 win over the Baltimore Ravens on 10-06-96.

During his regular season career with the New England Patriots, Coates had 5,471 yards receiving, 50 touchdowns, and was an AFC All-Pro tight end from 1994–98. He played in 142 regular season games and seven playoff games. Coates finished his career with the Baltimore Ravens and was a member of the 2000 Baltimore Ravens championship team.

Sam "Bam" Cunningham
#39, Running Back

Sam Cunningham was chosen from USC with the No. 11 pick in the 1973 College Draft. Cunningham was the MVP of the 1973 Rose Bowl and was inducted into the Rose Bowl Hall of Fame for his performance.

Cunningham led the Patriots in net yards from scrimmage during the 1975–78 seasons and was the team's leading rusher in 1973 and during the 1975–79 seasons. Cunningham holds the team record of 5,453 career yards rushing. He was an AFC Pro Bowl running back in 1978.

Cunningham is the only Patriots player who has caught a touchdown pass and ran for a touchdown on the first offensive play of a regular season game. Cunningham caught a 34-yard touchdown pass on the Patriots' first play in the 30–14 loss to the Dolphins on 10-28-73. He ran 75 yards for a touchdown on the first play of the game and had two other touchdown runs in the 30–28 loss to the Buffalo Bills on 10-20-74. Cunningham was the first Patriots running back with three rushing touchdowns in a regular season game. Cunningham ran for the game-winning touchdown in the 10–3 victory over the Cincinnati Bengals on 10-15-73. Cunningham scored 18 points with two rushing touchdowns and a touchdown reception in the 45–31 loss to the Buffalo Bills on 11-23-75.

Cunningham was the Patriots' top rusher in the record-setting season when they established the NFL team rushing record of 3,165 yards in a season. Cunningham had 768 yards rushing, Horace Ivory had 693, Andy Johnson had 675, and Steve Grogan had 539 yards rushing in 1978. The Patriots are the first NFL team to have four players with more than 500 yards rushing in a season. No other NFL team has rushed for more than 3,165 yards in a regular season.

Cunningham had his career high of 31 carries in the 31–0 shutout of the Seattle Seahawks on 10-09-77. Cunningham rushed for more than 100 yards in a game nine times and had a career-best 141 yards rushing in the 24–20 win over the San Diego Chargers on 10-16-77.

Sam "Bam" Cunningham dove for a 1-yard touchdown in the 14–10 win over the Miami Dolphins on

Sam Cunningham

12-11-77, in the Patriots' coldest regular season home game (14 degrees) without the wind chill factor. The Patriots' coldest regular season home game, with a wind chill factor of -25 degrees, was on 12-11-88. On that date they beat the Tampa Bay Buccaneers 10–7 in overtime at Sullivan Stadium.

Cunningham had 5,453 yards rushing with 43 touchdowns and 1,905 yards receiving with six touchdowns. He played in 107 regular season games and in two playoff games for the New England Patriots. His brother is former NFL Pro-Bowl quarterback Randall Cunningham.

Bob Dee "Bubba"
#89, Defensive End

Hardy? Durable? Resistant? These are just a few of the adjectives that properly describe the career of defensive end Bob Dee. "Bubba" never missed a game during his playing career. He played in 112 consecutive games and built his reputation as a tried and true ironman.

It should come as no surprise that Bob Dee had the perfect blend of athleticism and vigor to play every single week. After all, his mother was a former Olympian, and he himself was a marine.

"Bubba" is a Massachusetts local. He attended Braintree High School in Braintree, Massachusetts.

Left to right: Tom Addison (53), Bob Dee (89), and Larry Eisenhauer (72)

The Best of Bob Dee: The Highlights

- Had 33 sacks.
- Sacked Cotton Davidson five times.
- Had two sacks of Cotton Davidson in the game that the Patriots defense recorded 10 sacks on 09-22-63.
- Had two-and-a-half sacks of John McCormick in the 24–10 win over Denver on 09-18-66.
- Strip-sacked Jacky Lee in the 45–3 rout of the Houston Oilers on 11-01-63.
- Sacked Frank Tripucka, Al Dorow, Hunter Enis, Jacky Lee, MC Reynolds, Randy Duncan, Cotton Davidson, George Blanda, Jack Kemp, Johnny Green, John Hadl, Tobin Rote, Len Dawson, Eddie Wilson, Dick Wood, Joe Namath, Tom Flores, Rick Norton, and Bob Griese.
- Had 13 fumble recoveries: recovered a fumble by Al Carmichael, Art Baker, Wayne Crow, Jacky Lee, Paul Lowe, Bill Tobin, Wray Carlton, and Max Chobian.
- Recovered a lateral from Lee Grosscup in the 43–14 rout of the New York Titans at the Polo Grounds on 10-06-62.
- Recovered his strip sack of Cotton Davidson in the 28–21 win over the Dallas Texans on 11-03-61.
- Returned a fumble by Warren Rabb 30 yards in the Patriots' 52–21 rout of the Bills on 10-22-61.
- Returned a fumble by Len Dawson four yards in the Patriots' 27–27 tie with the Kansas City Chiefs on 11-20-66.
- Returned a pass by Babe Parilli 14 yards in the 27–14 loss to the Oakland Raiders on 10-16-60.
- Recovered an onside kick by George Blair in the 33–28 win over San Diego on 09-20-64.
- Lateraled a kickoff to Dick Christy, who took it 19 yards, in the Patriots' 38–14 loss to Buffalo on 12-04-60.
- Lateraled a kickoff to Jim Crawford, who took it 18 yards, in the Patriots' 21–10 win over Buffalo on 11-23-62.
- Blocked a 37-yard field-goal attempt by Gene Mingo in the 41–16 rout of the Broncos on 09-21-62.
- Blocked a punt by Jim Fraser in the 39–10 rout of the Denver Broncos on 10-04-64.
- Awarded the game ball for his outstanding play in the 34–17 win over Houston on 11-29-64.
- Had two interceptions in the 26–8 American Football League Eastern Divisional Playoff Game victory over Buffalo on 12-28-63.
- Inducted into the Patriots Hall of Fame on 08-18-93.

From there, he went on to play his college football at Holy Cross College where he was an elite three-sport letterman.

Before joining the Boston Patriots, Dee spent two years as a Washington Redskin. However, Dee is a true New England Patriots original. He was one of the initial players signed by the Boston Patriots in the American Football League in 1960. One of Dee's many claims to fame in the AFL occurred during an exhibition game on July 30, 1960. He scored the first touchdown in league history after pouncing on a fumble in the end zone.

His significance to the AFL was appreciated when he became the first player in history to have his jersey (No. 89) retired by the league on October 13, 1968, during a pregame ceremony affectionately called "Dee Day." Quite an honor.

Bob Dee was a perennial All-Star and was named to the American Football League East Team for his efforts during the 1961, 1963, 1964, and 1965 seasons. He was a co-captain of the 1964 team.

"Bubba" is a member of the All-1960s New England Patriots team. Deservedly, he had the ideal finale to an extraordinary career when, on August 8, 1993, he was inducted to the New England Patriots Hall of Fame.

Larry Eisenhauer "The Wild Man"
#72, Defensive End

When Larry Eisenhauer hit you, you knew it. In fact, the 18 quarterbacks Eisenhauer knocked out of games knew it all too well. No player in New England Patriots history had the desire to absolutely thrash an opposing quarterback more than Larry Eisenhauer. As a sixth-round draft pick out of Boston College, he led an impressive array of linemen from Boston College that went on to play for the Patriots.

Blasting past intense and bordering on insane, nobody brought raw emotion to the game like Eisenhauer. His teammates used to say that nobody got as hyped up for a game and judging by his pregame rituals, they were right. "The Wild Man" would smash his head into lockers, walls, and goal posts to fire himself up before kickoff. He once even sprinted onto a snow-covered Municpal Stadium field in Kansas City wearing nothing but his helmet and an athletic supporter. The incident added even more credibility to his moniker.

Although his personality dominated much of the enthrallment with Eisenhauer, it is important to remember how terrific a player he was. Larry was an All-Star defensive end in the American Football League from 1962–64 and again in 1966. He had a wonderful chemistry with his cohorts on the defensive line, and he had the chance to play with the same basic four-man front throughout his Patriots career. It was a defensive unit comprised of Houston Antwine, Jim Lee Hunt, Bob Dee, and, of course, Eisenhauer himself. Collectively, they would wear down offensive lines, interrupt blocking schemes, and pillage their way to the quarterback. Eisenhauer in particular had a penchant for pulverizing the quarterback.

"The Wild Man" compiled 45.5 sacks during his great career, including Len Dawson, George Blanda, Joe Namath, Bob Griese, Frank Tripucka, Harold Stephens, Johnny Green, Butch Songin, Tom Flores, Mickey Slaughter, Dick Wood, Jacky Lee, Tobin Tore, Jack Kemp, Don Trull, John Hadl, Cotton Davidson, Max Chobian, Steve Tensi, Daryle Lamonica, and Pete Beathard.

Eisenhauer never used the most technique as a defensive lineman, but that's not to say he wasn't a skilled player. He relied on unabridged adrenaline and intensity to wildly bash through blockers. The style worked so well in college that it earned him a spot in the Boston College Varsity Club Hall of Fame. It was the same style that brought him endless success in the NFL.

There have been many intense Patriots but none like No. 72. There have been many crazy Patriots—but none like Eisenhauer. There have even been a few wild Patriots, but there is only one "Wild Man." Just ask Pablo the Clown who, after breaking through the Patriots' defense on a live broadcast of Rex Trailer's *Boom Town* TV show, was promptly tackled by Eisenhauer. Truly wild.

The Best of Larry Eisenhauer: The Highlights

- Named the AFL Lineman of the Week for his dominating performance in the Patriots' 23–0 shut out of the Buffalo Bills on 09-24-67. It was the first time that the Buffalo Bills had ever been shut out.
- Picked off a pass that was thrown by Jack Kemp in the Patriots' 17–7 victory over the Buffalo Bills at Fenway Park on 12-01-63.
- Blocked a 35-yard field-goal attempt by Herb Travenio in the Patriots' 22–6 win over San Diego on 10-31-65.
- Had the most sacks by a Patriots player in regular season games played at Boston College Alumni Stadium.

Doug Flutie
#2, Quarterback and Drop Kick Specialist

Doug Flutie was the MVP of the 1982 Tangerine Bowl and the 1983 Liberty Bowl. Flutie was inducted into the Cotton Bowl Hall of Fame for his performance in the 1985 Cotton Bowl. Flutie finished third in the Heisman Trophy voting in 1983 and won the Heisman Trophy in 1984. He also won the Maxwell Award and the Walter Camp Award in 1984. He is a Member of the Boston College Varsity Club Hall of Fame and was inducted in the College Football Hall of Fame in 2006.

Doug Flutie

Flutie played for the New Jersey Generals of the USFL and with the British Columbia Lions, Calgary Stampeders, and Toronto Argonauts of the Canadian Football League. Flutie also played with the Chicago Bears, Buffalo Bills, and San Diego Chargers in the NFL. Flutie was initially acquired by the New England Patriots in a trade with the Chicago Bears on 10-13-87. He signed his last professional football contract with the New England Patriots on April 29, 2005.

Flutie was recognized as the AFC Offensive Player of the Week as he threw a touchdown pass and ran 13 yards on a naked bootleg for the game-winning touchdown with 23 seconds to go to defeat the Indianapolis Colts, 21-17, at Sullivan Stadium on 10-02-88. In his first start as the Patriots' quarterback, he led the team to a 27–21 win over the Cincinnati Bengals on 10-16-88. Flutie tossed an 80-yard touchdown pass to Irving Fryar, on the first play of the game, in the 30–7 rout of the Chicago Bears at Sullivan Stadium on 10-30-88.

On his 26th birthday, Flutie completed a 12-yard touchdown pass to Irving Fryar in the Patriots' 23–20 loss to the Buffalo Bills on 10-23-88. Flutie played against Tom Brady in the Patriots' 29–26 overtime win vs. the San Diego Chargers at Foxboro Stadium on 10-14-01. Flutie was the AFC Special Team Player of the Week as he drop-kicked an extra point in the 28–26 loss to the Miami Dolphins on 01-01-06. It was the first successful drop kick in the NFL since 1941.

Doug Flutie had 1,871 yards passing with 11 touchdowns, 308 yards rushing with one touchdown, and drop-kicked an extra point in his 22 games for the New England Patriots.

Russ Francis "The Kahuna"
#81, Tight End

Few players in New England Patriots history have produced as many stories as Russ Francis. "The Kahuna" would occasionally surf the waves of the Atlantic Ocean the day before a game for what he liked to call "hydrotherapy." Hey, whatever it was, it worked. He had 207 receptions, 3,157 receiving yards, and 28 touchdowns in 92 regular season games with the Patriots. The three-time All-Pro tight end was a force to be reckoned with on the field. He was an amazing athlete and a highly skilled football player who loved the game.

Francis was the 16th pick in the 1975 College Football Draft out of the University of Oregon and had two stints in Foxboro. During his first, he made the All-

NFL team from 1976–78 and again in 1980. He once again donned the Patriots' uniform from 1987–88.

His Hawaiian upbringing is an interesting tale. His father was a professional wrestler, and the former World Wrestling Entertainment Champion Andre the Giant used to be his babysitter. Therefore, it was probably destiny that led to "The Kahuna" squaring off against his former babysitter in the professional wrestler/professional football player "Battle Royal" at WrestleMania II in Chicago in 1986.

Russ was as entertaining as he was talented. He once landed the WBZ Radio helicopter on the 5-yard line of Schaefer Stadium before a practice. During the morning rush hours, the WBZ Radio helicopter would fly around the metropolitan Boston area and provide traffic reports to its many listeners. One morning Russ was a passenger in the WBZ 'copter, and he had to get to practice in Foxboro. As they were flying into the Foxboro area, Russ asked if he could land the helicopter. Just as he was about to land in the parking lot he noticed a layer of snow on the field. He decided to buzz the field and blow the snow away from the grass field

below rather than land in the parking lot. As he hovered and moved down the field the coaching staff and others became very alarmed and ran onto the field. Russ calmly landed the copter on the 50-yard line, proud that he had successfully removed the layer of snow and arrived early for practice as well. As he got out of the 'copter, Chuck Fairbanks and Billy Sullivan started screaming at him. Russ initially thought that his

The Best of Russ Francis: The Highlights

- Upon his retirement, Russ would fly tourists around the Hawaiian mountains and various islands. As the Pro Bowl is played in Hawaii, Pro Bowl linebacker Phil Villapiano and his wife were invited by Russ to tour a private tour of this majestic area. Certainly die-hard Patriot fans remember the mauling that Phil gave Russ in the Patriots' 24–21 playoff game loss to the Raiders in 1976. Russ was unable to raise his hands because of Phil, and no call was made on a key pass play late in that game. Russ informed Phil and his wife that no ill will was left over from that game and that they would truly enjoy this plane trip. As Russ was turning sideways going through the mountain ranges he was able to loosen Phil's seatbelt and open the door, causing Phil to brace himself against the inside frame of the small aircraft. Revenge was sweet.
- Caught a 38-yard touchdown pass on fourth-and-2 from Steve Grogan in the Patriots' 30–27 win over the Pittsburgh Steelers at Three Rivers Stadium on 09-26-76. Russ had six receptions for his career-best 139 yards receiving in this game.
- Had the longest reception of his career with the Patriots with his 53-yard reception in the Patriots' 21–14 win over the Raiders in the Sunday night regular season game played at the Oakland Coliseum on 09-24-78.
- Fell on a fumble by James McAllister with 32 seconds left in the Patriots' 16–6 win over St. Louis on 09-10-78.
- Hauled in a 23-yard pass from Harold Jackson on a wide receiver reverse option pass play, in the Patriots' 34–21 win over the New York Jets on 11-02-80.
- Caught a 12-yard pass form Harold Jackson, on a reverse wide receiver option play, in the Patriots' 16–13 overtime loss to the Dolphins in a *Monday Night Football* game played on 12-08-80.
- Dove for a 38-yard touchdown pass from Matt Cavanaugh just before Howard Cosell announced that John Lennon had been shot on 12-08-80.
- Hauled in two touchdown passes even though he had his bell rung by Don Calhoun's knee in the Patriots' 27–14 loss to the Packers in the first *Monday Night Football* game played at Lambeau Field on 10-01-79.
- He caught a 28-yard pass to help set up the game-tying field goal with no time left in the Patriots' 30–27 overtime loss to the Cleveland Browns in a regular season *Monday Night Football* game on 09-26-77.
- Grabbed eight passes for 101 yards in the Patriots' 31–14 AFC playoff game loss to the Houston Oilers on 12-31-78.
- Had his only pass attempt intercepted by Skip "Dr. Death" Thomas in the Patriots' 24–21 AFC Playoff Game loss to the Raiders on 12-18-76.
- He was traded to the San Francisco 49ers for a draft pick that the Patriots used to select Andre Tippett.
- Russ won a Super Bowl with the 1984 San Francisco 49ers Team.
- Wore No. 49 in the game played on 12-28-87.
- Caught a 26-yard touchdown pass in the playoff game on 12-18-76.
- Caught a 24-yard touchdown pass in the playoff game on 12-31-78.
- Had eight receptions for 101 yards in the Patriots' 31–14 AFC Divisional Playoff Game loss to the Houston Oilers at Schaefer Stadium on 12-31-78.

career with the Patriots was over. Since he was a first-round draft pick and a valued member of the team, he was sternly told never to pull that kind of stunt again. Needless to say he is the first, and he will be the last, NFL player ever to pull that stunt on a football field.

His flare for the dramatic translated into big moments for the Patriots. In the fourth quarter of a September 23, 1979, game against the San Diego Chargers, he caught a game-winning 5-yard touchdown pass from Steve Grogan to give New England the victory at Schaeffer Stadium.

Howard Cosell called Russ Francis an "All World Tight End," and was subsequently criticized for it throughout his career. The criticism became so prevalent that Francis even called Cosell and asked him to stop using the phrase. Cosell replied, "Get tough or get out."

Francis got tough.

"The Kahuna's" legacy is forever in tact in the state of Hawaii where he was inducted into the Hawaii Sports Hall of Fame. Russ Francis won't be forgotten anytime soon.

Russ Francis

Irving Fryar
#80, Wide Receiver/Return Specialist

Irving Fryar was chosen from the University of Nebraska with the first overall pick by the New England Patriots in the 1984 College Football Draft. Fryar had a stellar career for the Huskers and was inducted in the Orange Bowl Hall of Honor for his performance in the 1983 Orange Bowl.

Fryar was a multi talented performer who was used not only as a receiver but as a return-man on special teams. Twice during the 1985 season, he had at least one rushing attempt, one reception, one punt return, and one kickoff return in the same game. On 09-08-85, in the 26–20 opening game victory over the Green Bay Packers, he had a 13-yard run, a 25-yard reception, a 24-yard kickoff return, and three punt returns. On 10-27-85, in the 32–14 win over the Tampa Bay Buccaneers, he had a 2-yard run, two pass receptions, two punt returns, and a kickoff return.

Fryar was recognized as a Pro Bowl Special Team return specialist in 1985. He returned a punt by John Kidd 85 yards for a touchdown, for the longest punt return in the NFL in 1985, in the 17–14 win over the Buffalo Bills at Rich Stadium on 09-22-85. On 11-10-85, in the 34–15 rout of the Colts, not only did he catch a 5-yard touchdown pass from Steve Grogan, but he also returned a punt by Rohn Stark 77 yards for a touchdown. Irving led the NFL with 14.1 yards per punt

Irving Fryar

return during the 1985 season. On 11-02-86, in the 25–17 win over the Atlanta Falcons, Fryar returned a punt 59 yards for a touchdown. Only Irving Fryar and Troy Brown have returned three regular season punts for touchdowns.

Fryar showcased his talent by running a reverse for an 8-yard touchdown and catching the game-winning 13-yard touchdown pass from Steve Grogan in the 20–13 win over the Seattle Seahawks at the Kingdome on 11-17-85. On his 24th birthday, on the last play of the 27–20 loss to the Broncos, he caught a 10-yard touchdown pass from Tony Eason. On 12-07-86, in the 41–7 loss to the Bengals, Fryar led the Patriots with 34 yards rushing.

His most memorable touchdown reception was on the last play of the two-point win over the Los Angeles Rams on 11-16-86. Fryar held onto a 25-yard Hail Mary touchdown pass from Tony Eason, which was tipped by Stanley Morgan, to defeat the Los Angeles Rams 30–28 at Anaheim Stadium.

He was named the AFC Offensive Player of the Week as he had six receptions for 134 yards and hauled in a 50-yard touchdown pass from Hugh Millen, with about 30 seconds left in the half, in the 16–13 win over the Buffalo Bills on 11-24-91. Fryar had his best day as a Patriots receiver with eight catches for 165 yards and two touchdowns in the 30–21 loss to the New York Jets on 10-04-92.

Fryar scored the first touchdown in the Super Bowl for the New England Patriots. He caught an 8-yard touchdown pass on fourth-and-goal from Steve Grogan in Super Bowl XX.

While playing for the Patriots, Fryar had 363 receptions for 5,726 yards with 38 touchdowns, 35 carries for 188 yards with one touchdown, 26 kickoff returns for 495 yards, and 206 punt returns for 2,055 yards and three touchdowns. He participated in 129 regular season games and four playoff games for the New England Patriots and won the Ed Block Courage Award in 1992. He also played for the Miami Dolphins, Philadelphia Eagles, and finished his NFL career with the Washington Redskins.

Larry Garron
#46 and #40, Running Back/Return Specialist

Larry Garron came to the Patriots as a free agent from Western Illinois University. Garron was not used much in the 1960 season but led the team with 5.6 yards per carry during the 1961 season. He sprinted 85 yards for a touchdown, which is the Patriots longest run from scrimmage, and averaged 11.6 yards per carry in the 52–21 rout of the Buffalo Bills on 10-13-61. From that point on Garron was a fixture in the Boston Patriots backfield. In 1962, he led the team with 5.9 yards per carry and caught three touchdown passes as well.

He was a versatile football player as he led the team in kickoff return and yards returned for three consecutive seasons. Garron had back-to-back seasons that he returned at least one kickoff for a touchdown. Garron would go on to return 89 kickoffs for 2,229 yards, averaging 25.8 yards per kickoff return during his 9 year career with Patriots. He is the only Patriot player to receive a kickoff and lateral it to a teammate, hand a kickoff return to a teammate on a reverse return, and receive a lateral on a kickoff return from a teammate. Garron is the first player to return a kickoff for a touchdown. He took it 89 yards for a touchdown in the 31–31 tie with the Houston Oilers at BU Field on 10-13-61.

During the 1961 AFL season he was used as a defensive back for three games and even played as a defensive back in an AFL All-Star Game. Garron caught a 12-yard touchdown pass from Babe Parilli in the 1964

Larry Garron

AFL All-Star Game. He was an AFL All-Star running back in 1961, 1963, 1964, and 1967.

Garron was an excellent receiver and the Patriots utilized his speed and athletic ability by completing 185 passes for 2,502 yards and 26 touchdowns. Garron has the most receptions, yards, and touchdowns by a running back in team history. Garron caught the first fake field pass for a touchdown in the Patriots' 37–30 loss to the New York Titans in 1961. He caught four passes for 120 yards in the 26–8 AFL Eastern Divisional Playoff Game win over the Buffalo Bills on 12-28-63.

Garron played with Ron Burton, "Cowboy" Jim Crawford, and Jim Nance. In 1966, Jim Nance and Larry Garron combined to rush 400 times for 1,777 yards and 15 touchdowns. The Patriots just missed the playoffs that year and could have been the first AFL team in the Super Bowl had they not lost to the New York Jets in the last game of the season. (In November of 1966 the Patriots tied the Kansas City Chiefs 27–27 at Memorial Stadium, and Kansas City went on to lose to the Green Bay Packers in Super Bowl I.)

Garron caught a 27-yard fake field goal touchdown pass from Gino Cappelletti in the 37–30 loss to the NY Titans at the Polo Grounds on 10-01-61. Larry hauled in a 76-yard touchdown pass for the first points scored in the 45–3 rout of the Houston Oilers at Fenway Park on 11-01-63. He caught two touchdown passes and ran for another in the 43–43 tie with the Oakland Raiders at Fenway Park on 10-16-64. He caught two touchdown passes and ran for another in the 35–17 win over the San Diego Chargers at Fenway Park on 10-23-66.

Larry Garron ran for 2,981 yards, had 2,502 yards receiving, had 2,299 kickoff return yards, returned a punt, completed a pass, recovered 11 fumbles, was used as a defensive back, scored 42 touchdowns, and played in 99 regular season games and in two playoff games (scoring two touchdowns) for the Boston Patriots during the 1960–68 seasons.

Bob Gladieux "Harpo"
#24, Running Back/Special Teams Player

The charismatic "Harpo" was adored by the fans, and not just because of his unmistakable curly hair. He was a hard-working, gritty player with an attitude that Boston fans loved. Gladieux loved the game of football and played with an unrelenting passion. Whether he made the big tackle, jumped on the loose ball, or simply pumped up his teammates, his presence was always felt on the field.

Bob Gladieux was the 188th overall pick by the Patriots in the eighth round of the 1969 College Football Draft. He went on to become the special teams captain for the Boston Patriots during his rookie season. He performed on special teams for four years and busted his butt day in and day out. He wasn't necessarily the most skilled player on the field, but he was never outworked or outhustled. His hard work added versatility to his game, and he was used as a backup running back during the 1971 and 1972 seasons.

In addition to his special teams success as a Patriot, Gladieux is nothing short of a Notre Dame legend. He was an offensive juggernaut for the Fighting Irish as both a rusher and a receiver. He became one of the most prolific scorers in school history.

The practiced Gladieux played for the Winnipeg Blue Bombers in the Canadian Football League in addition to the New York Stars and Charlotte Hornets of the World Football League.

The personality, character, and effort Bob Gladieux displayed will not soon be forgotten. In fact, here's a story about "Harpo" that everyone should know:

Bob Gladieux

At the conclusion of training camp in 1970, Bob Gladieux was cut from the Boston Patriots just two days before the first regular season game.

Extremely disappointed that he did not make the final cut, Gladieux made the rounds and hit just about every bar in the south end of Boston during the next few nights. Since the coach told him to stick around, as anything could happen, Gladieux and some of his friends went to the first game of the year as spectators. According to many sources, Gladieux was seen smoking and drinking with his friends while tailgating from his AMC Gremlin.

Certainly, he never imagined that there was even a slight chance that he would be playing football that day. However, it just so happened that two Patriots players, Larry Carwell and John Charles, were not willing to sign contracts before the game and were promptly removed from the roster. The Patriots desperately needed to fill the roster spots so they called John "Outlaw" at home, and he agreed to fill one spot. The team knew that Bob

Gladieux was available as well but did not know how to reach him. Hilariously, the team proceeded to announce over the intercom, "Bob Gladieux please report to the trainer's room."

Although he was in no condition to play professional football, Gladieux suited up and was on the field for the first play of the game—the kickoff. Typical Gladieux, he was fired up. When Jake Scott ran away from his wedge of blockers on the kickoff, he ran right into brick-wall Bob Gladieux. Over the intercom the fans heard, "Tackle made by No. 24 Bob Gladieux." His friend, who was in line buying the first round of beers, drank the beers himself and enjoyed the game.

The Best of Bob Gladieux: The Highlights

- Gladieux was the player who scored the touchdown for Notre Dame in the famous 10–10 tie with Michigan State in 1966.
- Gladieux's name was mentioned in the bar scene of the football movie *Rudy*, but Gladieux became more famous for the tackle that he made on Jake Scott on the opening kickoff in the Patriots opening game of the 1970 regular season.
- He played on special teams in his first year with the Patriots in 1969 and had four kickoff returns and made three fair catches of punts.
- Gladieux also tackled Jack Scott on a punt return in the third quarter of the 27–14 win over the Dolphins at Harvard Stadium on 09-20-70.
- He played in 43 games for the Boston/New England Patriots during the 1969–72 seasons.
- Gladieux is the only left-handed running back to complete a pass in a regular season game for the Patriots.
- Gladieux completed a 48-yard halfback option pass to Hubie Bryant in the 28–20 win over the Houston Oilers at Schaefer Stadium on 11-07-71.
- Recovered a fumble by Hubert Ginn in the Patriots' 34–13 win over Miami on 12-05-71.
- Recovered a fumble by Rickie Harris in the Patriots' 24–23 win over Washington on 10-01-72.
- Played with the NY Stars/Charlotte Stars/Charlotte Hornets of the World Football League.
- Played with the Winnipeg Blue Bombers of the Canadian Football League.

Art Graham
#84, Flanker/Wide Receiver

Art Graham III was born in Somerville, Massachusetts, and was a star at Matignon High School. He was drafted from Boston College by the Boston Patriots with the first round pick in the 1963 College Football Draft. He is a member of the Boston College Varsity Club Hall of Fame.

Graham was a tremendous compliment to AFL All-Star receivers Gino Cappelletti and Jim Colclough. During his rookie season, he averaged 26.1 yards per reception. On 10-05-63, he caught six passes for 156

yards and two touchdowns in the 31–24 loss to the New York Titans at the Polo Grounds.

In 1964, when the Patriots won 10 games, he was the team's second leading receiver. He caught 45 passes for 720 yards and six touchdowns. Graham had a career-best 167 yards receiving in the thrilling 25–24 comeback victory over the Houston Oilers at Fenway Park on 11-06-64. He scored on an 80-yard touchdown pass from Babe Parilli in the 34–17 win over the Houston Oilers on 11-29-64.

He was also a valuable performer on special teams as he made a game-saving tackle on a long punt return by Hoot Gibson in the 17–14 victory over the Oakland Raiders on 09-13-64 and a game-saving tackle on a long punt return by Lance Allworth in the 33–28 win over the San Diego Chargers at Balboa Stadium on 09-20-64.

Graham held the team record for the most receptions in a regular season Patriots game for 33 years. Graham had 11 receptions for 134 yards and two touchdowns in the 27–27 tie with the Kansas City Chiefs on 11-20-66. On 11-27-66, he had one of his most memorable receptions. After losing his shoe during the play, he was still able to score on his 22-yard touchdown reception in the 20–14 win over the Miami Dolphins at the Orange Bowl. (It would take the Patriots 20 years before they won another regular season game at the Orange Bowl)

Graham caught 16 touchdown passes from Babe Parilli, three touchdown passes from Tom Yewcic, and one touchdown pass from Tom Sherman. Art Graham III had 199 receptions for 3,107 yards and 20 touchdowns in 75 regular season games during the 1963–68 regular seasons. His father, Skinny Graham, was an outfielder in 21 games for the Boston Red Sox during the 1934–35 seasons.

Art Graham

Steve Grogan
#14, Quarterback

How is this for juxtaposition? A quarterback, yes a quarterback, is the toughest player in New England Patriots history. Not only that, but one of the hardest tacklers as well. He is Steve Grogan, and in addition to being as tough as nails, he holds nearly every franchise passing record.

Grogan was one of the most entertaining, exciting players to ever play in New England. He was a special athlete who was one of the first quarterbacks mobile enough to be considered a dangerous, multifaceted threat. He became the only Patriots quarterback to rush for 100 yards in a game when he had 103 yards on seven carries during a 41-7 rout of the Jets on October 18, 1976. Then, on December 12 of the same year, Grogan ran for his 12th rushing touchdown of the year. The mark still stands today as the most rushing touchdowns ever scored in a single season by a Patriots quarterback. These are two of the most distinct records that he set.

Grogan threw his first touchdown pass in the National Football League to Russ Francis for 42 yards on October 5, 1975. Despite the accomplishment occurring in the midst of a 36-7 loss at the hands of the New York Jets, it signaled the beginning of something special in Foxboro.

Steve Grogan

Over the course of his magnificent career Grogan was able to play against every existing team in the National Football League. And, in 1987, he played every offensive down during the regular season for the Patriots—truly an amazing feat and a prime example of the dedication and commitment he possessed.

The resilient quarterback won the Ed Block Courage Award in 1984. He finished his stellar career in New England with 26,886 passing yards and 182 touch-downs in 149 regular season games. He added 2,176 rushing yards and 35 rushing touchdowns.

Grogan's legacy of hard work, hard hits, and his never-say-die attitude lives on in the state of Kansas where he has a football stadium named in his honor in Ottawa. He is also a member of the Kansas Sports Hall of Fame. Steve Grogan was inducted into the New England Patriots Hall of Fame during halftime on September 10, 1995.

The Best of Steve Grogan: The Highlights

- Advanced a fumble by Don Calhoun six yards for a touchdown in the Patriots' 41–7 rout of the Jets on 10-18-76.
- Ran for an 11-yard touchdown and a 10-yard touchdown and threw two touchdown passes, allowing the Patriots to qualify for the playoffs, in the 27–6 rout of the Saints on 12-05-76.
- Ran for the game-winning four-yard touchdown to defeat the Chargers 28–23 at Schaefer Stadium on 10-01-78.
- Ran for a touchdown and led the team to the best record in the AFC in the Patriots' 26–24 win over the Bills on 12-10-78.
- Tossed five touchdown passes in the Patriots' 56–3 rout of the Jets on 09-09-79.
- Threw two touchdown passes and caught a 16-yard swing pass from Andy Johnson in the Patriots' 29–28 loss to the Baltimore Colts on 09-06-81.
- Ran 24 yards on a naked reverse play for a touchdown in the Patriots' 38–10 rout of the Houston Oilers on 10-18-81.
- Tossed four touchdown passes and ran for another in the Patriots' 42–20 rout of the New York Jets on 12-13-87.
- Completed 13 consecutive passes and was 20–26 in the second half of the Patriots' 23–20 overtime win vs. the Indianapolis Colts at the Hoosier Dome on 10-29-89.
- Tossed an eight-yard touchdown pass to Irving Fryar on fourth down in Super Bowl XX.
- Ran for at least one touchdown in three consecutive regular season games twice during the 1976 season.
- Built a special neck bar brace in his house that he would hang from in order to stretch out his neck.

Ray "Sugar Bear" Hamilton
#71, Defensive Lineman

Ray Hamilton was chosen from the University of Oklahoma by the New England Patriots with the No. 342 pick in the 1973 College Football Draft.

Hamilton was the starting left defensive end for all 14 games during his rookie season of 1973. In 1974, he was moved inside and played left tackle and nose tackle. He would remain the starting nose tackle for the Patriots through the 1980 season. Ray Hamilton started in 110 consecutive games. "Sugar Bear" was the first Patriots player to sack the quarterback to preserve the win when he sacked Bert Jones with 29 seconds left in the 21–14 win over the Baltimore Colts on 11-14-76.

He had at least two sacks in a regular season game 10 times. On 11-28-76, Hamilton recorded three sacks of Steve Ramsey in the 38–14 rout of the Denver Broncos. He sacked David Woodley three times in the 34–0 shutout of the Miami Dolphins on 10-12-80. His favorite quarterback target was Bob Griese, whom he sacked five times during his career.

On 10-16-77, he had one of his most memorable sacks. He strip-sacked Bill Munson and Tony McGee returned the fumble eight yards that helped set up a touchdown reception by Don Hasselbeck in the 24–20 win over the San Diego Chargers.

Hamilton recovered 14 fumbles, including fumbles by Bobby Douglass, John Hadl, Jim Hart, Ken Stabler, Roland Hooks, Steve Myer, Haskel Stanback, Jim Otis, Joe Ferguson, and Brian Sipe. He returned a fumble by Jim Hart 23 yards for a touchdown in the 24–17 loss to the St. Louis Cardinals on 11-02-75.

Hamilton used his power and great reach to block two field-goal attempts. He blocked a 44-yard field-goal attempt by Jim Bakken in the 24–17 loss to the Cardinals on 11-02-75. On 11-27-77, Hamilton blocked a 19-yard field-goal attempt by Ove Johansson in the 14–6 victory over the Philadelphia Eagles.

Ray Hamilton recorded 54 sacks in 132 regular season games during the 1973–81 seasons. He played in two playoff games and is remembered for hitting Ken Stabler and for being called for roughing the passer by Ben Dreith in the 24–21 playoff game loss to the Oakland Raiders on 12-18-76. Ray Hamilton has continued to work in the NFL as a defensive coach. He was an assistant defensive line coach for the New England Patriots during the 1985–89 seasons and was the defensive line coach for the Patriots during the 1997–99 seasons.

Ray Hamilton

John "Hog" Hannah
#73, Offensive Left Guard

The legendary coach Bear Bryant said that John Hannah was the best offensive lineman that he had ever coached, period. Talk about a solid recommendation. At 6'2" and 265 pounds, John Hannah was a monster of a man and a monster force for the New England Patriots during his 13-year career. During those incredible 13 years, he made the Pro Bowl 10 consecutive times from 1976–85. He was the picture of consistency for the Patriots.

By the time the burly blocker was taken by New England out of Alabama with the fourth pick in the 1973 College Football Draft, he had established himself as one of the best college football players in the country. He was a two-time All-American and was No. 11 in Heisman Trophy voting in 1972. That same year he won the Knute Rockne Award, and in 1999, Hannah was inducted into the College Football Hall of Fame. He is a member of the Alabama Sports Hall of Fame and the Cotton Bowl Hall of Fame as well.

John Hannah's pro career is defined by his unmatched blocking capabilities. Regardless of the play, the scheme, or the objective, Hannah was a brick wall that served and protected his offensive counterparts. In

John Hannah

1978, Hannah was the starting left guard on a historic offensive line that included Leon Gray, Bill Lenkaitis, Sam Adams, and Shelby Jordan. This group is significant for two reasons. They were a phenomenal collection of gifted and accomplished lineman that started every game together during the regular season. And, more memorably, they blocked for the Patriots backfield that set the NFL record for 3,165 rushing yards in a regular season. The Hannah-led group was so good at impeding oncoming rushes and creating canyon-sized holes that it seemed like any Joe Nobody from the street could cut through them. However, that wasn't the case as the Patriots were equipped with a phenomenal backfield that rushed for a staggering 4.7 yards per attempt and found pay dirt 30 times during the '78 campaign. Furthermore, seven players averaged more than four yards per carry, and five players surpassed 390 yards during the year. It was a truly magnificent season of achievement for Hannah, who was named the NFL Offensive Lineman of the Year for the first of four straight years by the Player's Association.

John Hannah announced his retirement from the sport he so thoroughly dominated on June 30, 1986. He was inducted into the Professional Football Hall of Fame on July 27, 1991, after one of the greatest careers in football history. His body of work is without equal. The Patriots retired Hannah's No. 73 jersey during the

The Best of John Hannah: The Highlights

- Recovered an onside kick by John Leypoldt in the Patriots' 37–13 loss to the Buffalo Bills on 12-09-73.
- Recovered a fumbled snap in the end zone for a touchdown in the Patriots' 34–27 loss to the Dolphins on 12-15-74.
- Recovered a fumbled punt return by Chris Farasopoulos in the Patriots' 33–13 loss to the Jets on 11-11-73.
- Recovered three fumbles by Stanley Morgan, and fumbles by Sam Cunningham, Vagas Ferguson, Tom Owen, Steve Grogan, and Tony Collins.
- Played against his brother, Charley, in the Patriots' 35–20 loss to the Los Angeles Raiders on 09-29-85.

halftime ceremony of the game against the Jets on September 30, 1990. It was an appropriate sendoff to a blocker extraordinaire and one of the greatest Patriots of all time.

Mike Haynes

Few players in New England Patriots history have made the immediate impact that Mike Haynes made. The multitalented Haynes of Arizona State University was the fifth overall selection in the 1976 College Football Draft where he was a three-time All-WAC star and the Defensive Most Valuable Player of the 1973 Fiesta Bowl. The Patriots chose Haynes in hopes of adding speed and quickness to the roster and bolstering the defense with a shutdown corner.

During his rookie campaign, Haynes used his lightning-like speed to intercept eight passes. On November 21, 1976, Haynes introduced himself to the legendary Joe Namath in the form of two interceptions. His picks helped neutralize the Jets offense, and the Pats won the game, 38–24. More than a great cornerback, he became the first player in franchise history to return a punt for a touchdown—then he did it again. As his rookie year unfolded, it became apparent that the Patriots had found a new punt return specialist, as well.

His rookie year was a success, and Haynes only got better and more dangerous during his career. He developed into one of the greatest cornerbacks in NFL history with a distinct ability to stay one step ahead of the wide receiver. He was also very sure-handed and recovered fumbles by Franco Harris, Gary Marangi,

Mike Haynes

Sidney Thornton, Larry Csonka, Don Hardeman, Curtis Brown, and Reggie McKenzie in his tenure with New England.

Mike was a perennial Pro Bowl selection as a Patriot, making the AFC team from 1976–80 and again in 1982. At the end of his career in New England, the double threat had 28 interceptions for 388 yards and a touchdown in 90 regular season games to go along with 111 punt returns for 1,159 yards and two touchdowns as a punt return specialist. Mike would go on to play for the Oakland Raiders during the 1980s and enjoyed continued success with the Silver and Black including a Super Bowl victory in 1983.

Mike Haynes was inducted into the Patriots Hall of Fame in 1994, and the team honored him on October 27, 1997, during halftime of the *Monday Night Football* game against the Green Bay Packers. The ultimate recognition of Mike Haynes' amazing career came on July 26, 1997, when he was named to the Professional Football Hall of Fame.

The Best of Mike Haynes: The Highlights

- Returned a Mark Bateman punt 89 yards for a touchdown and had a team record 156 punt return yards in the Patriots' 20–10 win over Buffalo on 11-07-76. (O.J. Simpson and Mel Lunsford were ejected for fighting in this game. His 89-yard punt return is the longest punt return by a Patriots player in a regular season game.)
- Intercepted Matt Robinson twice in the Patriots' 19–17 win over the Jets at Shea Stadium on 11-19-78.
- Returned a pass by Bill Troup 31 yards for a touchdown in the Patriots' 35–14 rout of the Baltimore Colts at Memorial Stadium on 11-26-78.
- Took a Bill Troup pass 31 yards for a touchdown on the third offensive play of the game in the Patriots' 35–14 rout of the Baltimore Colts on 11-26-78.
- Returned a pass by wide receiver Henry Marshall three yards in the Patriots' 33–17 win over the Chiefs on 10-04-81.
- Played against his brother Reggie for the first time in the NFL during the Patriots 16–14 loss to the Washington Redskins at Schaefer Stadium on 09-01-78.
- Took a lateral from John Zamberlin, who had recovered a blocked field-goal attempt, and took it 65 yards for a touchdown in the Patriots' 21–11 win over the New York Jets at Shea Stadium on 10-05-80.

"Mini" Mack Herron
#42, Running Back/Return Specialist

Mack Herron, who was a star player in his senior year at Kansas State, was drafted by the Atlanta Falcons but played three years in the Canadian Football League for the Winnipeg Blue Bombers. Mack was the runner up for the CFL MVP in 1972 and once returned a kickoff 120 yards for a touchdown for Winnipeg. He was given the nickname of "Scoe" because he scored so many touchdowns.

After the 1972 CFL season, his former college coach, Dick Steinberg, who was a scout for the Patriots at the time, discovered that Herron had been waived by the Blue Bombers. Dick notified the Patriots of Herron's availability and enlightened them about his past accomplishments. The Patriots signed Mack Herron, and he quickly became a fan favorite because of his diverse abilities and underdog persona.

At 5'5" and 170 pounds, tiny Mack Herron would hide behind his blockers and make his move when the timing was right. Mack soon became "Mini" Mack.

Many fans can remember the visual image of Mini Mack running behind huge offensive lineman such as John Hannah and Leon Gray on a sweep. He was a crowd favorite.

In 1973, he led the NFL in kickoff return yards and was the first Patriots player to have more than 1,000 kickoff return yards in a season. Mini Mack led the team in punt return yards, as well. He was just as versatile from the backfield, and he had 200 yards rushing and 265 yards receiving during the 1973 regular season. Herron returned a kickoff 92 yards for a touchdown in the Patriots 30–14 win over the San Diego Chargers at Schaefer Stadium on 12-02-73.

In 1974, Herron had one of the best seasons that any running back and return specialist ever produced. He broke the NFL record set by Gale Sayers with 2,444 combined return yards and yards from scrimmage. Mack had 474 yards receiving and led the team with 824 yards rushing, 517 punt return yards, and 629 kickoff return yards. He set the team record with 12 touchdowns scored in a season.

He caught a 12-yard touchdown pass and ran for a 4-yard touchdown in the 28–20 victory over the New York Giants at the Yale Bowl on 09-22-74. Herron had his career-best 199 yards rushing and a career longest run of 53 yards in the 27–10 loss to the Cincinnati Bengals on 10-12-75.

Mini Mack Herron still holds many records for the Patriots. He holds the team record for the longest punt return by a Patriots running back (66 yards). He averaged 14.8 yards per punt return during the regular season. He is the last person to lead the team in punt return yards and yards rushing in the same season. He is the only Patriots player to hold a career average of 12 yards per punt return. Herron still holds the Patriots record for the most kickoff return yards in a season with 1,092.

He played in 10 games for the Patriots in 1975 and finished his professional football career with the Atlanta Falcons. Mack had 353 rushing attempts, 61 receptions, 74 punt returns, and 71 kickoff returns for the New England Patriots in 35 regular season games.

Left to right: Mack Herron and head coach Chuck Fairbanks

Jim Lee Hunt "Earthquake"
#79, Defensive Tackle

Jim Lee Hunt became the "Earthquake" on November 18, 1960, at Boston University Field. After he recovered a Cotton Davidson fumble, the Patriots defensive tackle returned the ball 11 yards, with several members of the Dallas Texans offense giving chase and frantically trying to encumber the 6'1", 255-pounder.

"Earthquake" was considered one of the best pass rushers at his position in the American Football League. The popular star was known for his versatility on the defensive line with the ability to play each position. Hunt's speed and velocity was uncommon for a defensive tackle during his era and it separated him from his counterparts. His attitude and flexibility would make him an ideal Bill Belichick–style player today.

Jim Lee Hunt was a four-time All-Star in the American Football League, making the team in 1961, 1966, 1967, and 1969. In fact, he was one of the constants in the AFL. Hunt is one of a mere 20 players who played in each and every season of the league during its existence.

One of the enduring moments of Jim Lee Hunt's career occurred during "The Game" on December 4, 1964, at Fenway Park. Facing the Buffalo Bills in front of the largest crowd to ever watch the Pats at Fenway Park, Hunt had three sacks and played a critical defensive role in the 14–3 Patriots victory.

Left to right: Jim Lee Hunt and Gino Cappelletti

Jim Lee Hunt's contributions to the New England Patriots are vast and respected. In addition to his No. 79 jersey being retired by the team, he was inducted into the franchise Hall of Fame on August 18, 1993. His legacy lives on in the form of the Jim Lee Hunt Trophy, which is awarded to the most outstanding defensive lineman.

The Best of Jim Lee Hunt: The Highlights

- Sacked Jack Kemp five times
- Recorded 34.5 sacks in 146 regular season games.
- Recorded the most sacks by a Patriots player in regular season games played at Fenway Park.
- Recovered fumbles by Al Dorow, Tom Flores, Mickey Slaughter, Ode Burrell, Daryle Lamonica, Steve Tensi, Bobby Burnett, Bob Cappadona, Marlin Briscoe, Robert Holmes, and Larry Csonka.
- Returned a fumble forced by his hit of Darrell Lester five yards for a touchdown in the 17–10 loss to the Denver Broncos on 11-06-66.
- Awarded the game ball in the 27–21 win over the Houston Oilers at Fenway Park on 11-13-66.
- Returned a fumble by Don Trull 51 yards in the 45–17 loss to the Houston Oilers at the Astrodome on 12-15-68.
- Returned a kickoff eight yards in the 24–10 loss to the Houston Oilers on 11-25-60.
- Outran Billy Cannon and Charlie Tolar on his 78-yard interception return for a touchdown in the 45–3 rout of the Houston Oilers at Fenway Park on 11-01-63.
- Recovered an onside kick by Gino Cappelletti in the Patriots' 26–10 win vs. the New York Jets at Boston College Alumni Stadium on 09-27-64.
- Lateraled a kickoff to J.D. Garrett, who took it 24 yards in the Patriots' 43–43 tie with the Oakland Raiders on 10-16-64.
- Awarded the game ball for his play in the Patriots' 27–21 win over the Houston Oilers at Fenway Park on 11-13-66.
- Sacked Jack Kemp for a safety in the 44–16 loss to the Buffalo Bills at Fenway Park on 12-09-67.

Jesse "Craig" James
#32, Running Back

James was chosen from SMU with the No. 187 pick by the New England Patriots in the 1983 College Football Draft. James was part of the "Pony Express" as he played in the same SMU backfield as Eric Dickerson.

James played two years for the Washington Federals in the USFL before joining the New England Patriots.

James led the Patriots in yards rushing for three consecutive seasons and had 1,227 yards rushing during the 1985 season. James has the longest touchdown reception by a Patriots running back in a regular season game. He scored on a 90-yard touchdown pass from Tony Eason in the 20–7 loss to the Chicago Bears on 09-15-85.

He averaged 4.9 yards per carry in 1984 and 4.7 yards per carry in 1985. James was recognized as an AFC Pro Bowl running back in 1985. James is the only Patriots running back with more halfback option touchdown passes than touchdown receptions. James was the first Patriots running back to toss a touchdown pass on a fourth-down play, and all three of his halfback option touchdown passes were thrown to Tony Collins.

The Patriots won every regular season game when Craig James ran for a touchdown. He played in 52 regular season games and in five playoff games for the Patriots. James currently works as a television sports commentator.

Ty Law
#24, Cornerback

Although the term "shutdown corner" is thrown around a lot, what else can you call Ty Law? During his time with the New England Patriots he defined the term. His hybrid mix of remarkable athleticism with savvy football intelligence made him a nightmare for any opposing quarterback. He was hard to read and not one to be shaken off easily. During the course of his Patriots career, he evolved from promising first-round draft pick to one of the franchise's all-time best players. No. 24 played a vital role in the Patriots' run of three Super Bowl wins in four years. Few fans will ever forget his 47-yard touchdown return of a Kurt Warner interception during the team's first Super Bowl victory ever against the Rams.

Law was drafted out of the University of Michigan 23rd in the 1995 College Football Draft. He brought power, speed, skill, and prowess to the backfield, and he was always psyched for the biggest games and toughest challenges. Law had some of his best moments in games where he was matched up against greats like Marvin Harrison. For instance, who could forget his show-stopping performance during the 2003 AFC Championship Game when he smothered Harrison and rendered the star wide receiver ineffective? In addition to his ability to eat up a wide out, he also had a knack for confusing the quarterback. Law has mystified, bewildered, and perplexed the best in the game, including Peyton Manning. During the very same AFC Championship Game, he intercepted Manning three times during the 24–14 victory at a snowy Gillette Stadium.

Maybe Ty Law just likes to pick on Indianapolis. Several of his peak performances have occurred against the Colts. During his sophomore campaign in 1996, he recorded a career-high 12 tackles against Indy.

While Law continued to make a name for himself during his initial years in the league, it wasn't until 1998 that he finally became an NFL household commodity. He appeared in his first Pro Bowl in 1998, the same year he led the NFL with nine interceptions. This was the first time a Patriots player had ever led the league in interceptions. Three Super Bowls rings and countless records and accolades later, Law firmly established the "Rule of Law" in New England.

For nine years, he patrolled the secondary in Foxboro to a level that is surpassed by none and rivaled by few. He recorded a personal-best 77 tackles in three different seasons as a Patriot; 1997, 2001, and 2003. He shares the franchise record for most interceptions, 36, alongside the outstanding Raymond Clayborne. However, he doesn't share many other franchise records, he owns them unto himself. He has more interceptions returned for a touchdown than any player in franchise history with six.

Ty Law

Ty Law left New England after Super Bowl XXXVIII and has since played for the New York Jets and Kansas City Chiefs. Despite his continued success, his NFL legacy will forever be his nine spectacular years in New England. He has set the bar incredibly high for future defensive backs that have the honor of donning a Patriots jersey.

The Best of Ty Law: The Highlights

- Peyton Manning is not the only quarterback who has become a victim of Ty Law. The list of quarterbacks Law has intercepted reads like a Hall of Fame and Pro Bowl ballot: Jim Kelly, Jim Everert, Boomer Esiason, Glenn Foley, Troy Aikman, Rick Mirer, Bobby Herbert, Alex Van Pelt, Steve McNair, Danny Wuerffel, Dan Marino, Chris Chandler, Kordell Stewart, Steve Young, Damon Huard, Dave Brown, Jay Fielder, Chris Weinke, Trent Green, Brian Griese, Drew Bledsoe, Kelly Holcomb, Quincy Carter, Chad Pennington, and Matt Hasselback have all fought the Law, and the Law won.
- Took a Glenn Foley pass 38 yards for a touchdown in the Patriots' 34–10 win over the Jets on 12-08-96.
- Took a Peyton Manning pass 59 yards for a touchdown in the Patriots' 29–6 rout of the Colts on 09-13-98.
- Took a Damon Huard pass 24 yards for a touchdown in the Patriots' 31–30 loss to the Dolphins on 10-17-99.

- Took a Peyton Manning pass 23 yards for a touchdown in the Patriots' 44–13 rout of the Colts on 09-30-01.
- Took a Chris Weinke pass 46 yards for a touchdown in the Patriots' 38–6 rout of the Panthers on 01-06-02.
- Took a Steve McNair pass 65 yards for a touchdown in the Patriots' 38–30 win over the Tennessee Titans on 10-05-03.
- Had 10 solo tackles in the 27–9 win over the Colts at the RCA Dome on 10-20-96.
- Sacked Jim Harbaugh, Kordell Stewart, and Rob Johnson and shared in sacks of Brad Johnson and Damon Huard.
- Recovered a fumble by Richard Anderson on the Patriots 1-yard line with 15 seconds left in the half in a 27–24 overtime win vs. the Jets on 09-14-97.
- Recovered fumbles by Jerry Rice, Marcus Pollard, and Rod Smith.
- Took a Randall Cunningham pass 67 yards for a touchdown in the 1999 AFC-NFC Pro Bowl and was named the Co-MVP of the game.
- Took a Brad Johnson pass 46 yards for a touchdown in the AFC-NFC Pro Bowl on 02-02-03.
- Returned a pass by Kurt Warner 47 yards for a touchdown in the Patriots first Super Bowl victory.
- Member of the 2001, 2003, and 2004 championship teams.

Joe Kapp
#11, Quarterback

Joe Kapp finished fifth in the voting for the 1958 Heisman Trophy. He played for the British Columbia Lions and the Calgary Stampeders in the Canadian Football League and was inducted into the Canadian Football Hall of Fame in 1984. Kapp was also inducted into the College Football Hall of Fame in 2004. Kapp is the only athlete to play in a NCAA Basketball game, Rose Bowl, Grey Cup Championship Game, and Super Bowl.

Kapp was signed as a free agent after leading the Minnesota Vikings to the Super Bowl. Kapp wore No. 11 and played in 11 games for the Boston Patriots during the 1970 season.

Kapp was a fierce competitor who would get the ball to the receiver any way he could. Many of his passes were not tight spiral passes but were more like fluttering air balls up for grabs, and may the best man come down with it. He only played one year for the Boston Patriots and then retired. Due to a contract dispute with the NFL, the Patriots were able to acquire linebacker Steve King, who played in 124 regular season games and in two playoff games for the Patriots.

As the general manger of the British Columbia Lions, he signed Doug Flutie to his first contract with the Canadian Football League. After football, he had a

Left to right: Gino Cappelletti and Joe Kapp

career in Hollywood. Kapp has appeared in the following sports movies, *The World's Greatest Athlete, 2 Minute Warning, Semi-Tough,* and *The Longest Yard.*

He was the head coach of the University of California team that beat Stanford in John Elway's last collegiate game with the lateral kickoff return through the band on the last play of the game.

Curtis Martin

Curtis Martin was a third-round pick (there were 73 players selected before him) in the 1995 College Football Draft, and he came to the New England Patriots like a locomotive, ready to steamroll over anything in his path. Martin had skill, speed, and strength for days, and stopping him was an unenviable task for any defense in the NFL. Even though Martin was only a Patriot for three seasons, he made sure nobody would forget his name.

Curtis Martin wasted no time cozying up to the Foxboro faithful. In his first career regular season game, his 1-yard touchdown run with 19 seconds left in regulation defeated the Cleveland Browns. His 102 rushing yards on the day marked the first time a Patriots rookie had gone for 100 yards in his first NFL game. Martin's first season in a Patriots jersey was a resounding success, and his impact was deservedly recognized. He was named the NFL Offensive Player of the Year after rushing for a more than 1,400 yards and 14 touchdowns. His sizzling rookie season earned him an all-expense paid trip to Hawaii to compete in the Pro Bowl.

During the 1996 season, he duplicated the success from his rookie season and broke Patriots records along the way. Martin had a rushing touchdown in seven consecutive games during the year, an achievement unmatched in New England. Martin was already considered one of the best running backs in the NFL, and his potency in the backfield made the Drew Bledsoe–led offense that much more dangerous. Bledsoe was able to find his targets with comfort and ease knowing he had a new unyielding force lined up behind him. Martin rushed for 1,152 yards during his sophomore year which, along with Terry Glenn's 1,132 receiving yards, made for a historic combination in Foxboro. It was the first time in franchise history that New England had a 1,000-yard rusher and a 1,000-yard receiver the same season. The dynamic duo opened up

Left to right: Curtis Martin and head coach Pete Carroll

the offensive attack and gave defensive coordinators migraines all the way to Super Bowl XXXI.

Martin's regular season success continued into the postseason. In the Patriots' AFC Divisional Playoff Game on January 5, 1997, Martin broke free of his pursuers and exploded for a 78-yard touchdown sprint. It was one of his three rushing touchdowns of the game and catapulted the Pats to a 28–3 drubbing of the Pittsburgh Steelers.

After the 1997 season, Martin made his way down I-95 to the Meadowlands where he played for the New York Jets until his retirement following the 2006 season. Despite his short stint in Foxboro, Martin remains one of the greatest athletes to ever be handed the ball. Curtis Martin was one of the best running backs of his era and is a candidate for the Professional Football Hall of Fame.

The Best of Curtis Martin: The Highlights

- AFC Offensive Player of the Week as he ran 35 times for 166 yards and two touchdowns in the Patriots' 20–7 win over the New York Jets on 11-05-95.
- AFC Offensive Player of the Week as he had 199 yards rushing and one touchdown in the Patriots' 27–24 overtime win vs. the Jets on 09-14-97.
- AFC Offensive Player of the Week as he had 31 carries for 148 yards and two touchdowns in the Patriots' 31–28 win over the New York Jets in Foxboro on 12-10-95.
- Caught a pass for a two-point conversion in the Patriots' 35–25 win over the Buffalo Bills, as the Patriots scored 22 points in the fourth quarter, in this game played at Rich Stadium on 11-26-95.

- Was the second Patriots player to score 20 points in a regular season game as he caught two touchdown passes, ran for a touchdown, and caught a pass for a two-point conversion in the Patriots' 31–0 shutout of the Arizona Cardinals on 09-15-96.
- AFC Offensive Player of the Week as he had 148 yards rushing and two touchdowns in the Patriots' 31–28 win over the New York Jets on 12-10-96.
- Set the team record with 36 rushing attempts in a game during the Patriots' 27–14 win over Buffalo on 10-23-95.
- Caught a 17-yard touchdown pass from Jim Harbaugh in the 1996 AFC-NFC Pro Bowl Game.

Willie McGinest
#55, Defensive End/Linebacker

Everything about Willie McGinest's game commands respect. Known for his unrelenting intensity, McGinest was an ideal linebacker, model teammate, and perfect representative for an organization. And, for more than a decade, the New England Patriots were fortunate enough to call him their own. McGinest's amazing power and deceptive speed made him a force to be reckoned with for every offensive coordinator. He was at the core of New England's historic defensive teams of the 21st century.

As the No. 4 pick out of Southern Cal in the 1994 College Football Draft, McGinest immediately drew cheers and turned heads at Foxboro Stadium. His brilliant ability to rush the passer, disrupt offensive schemes, and tackle with a brutality that was commonly reserved for a mortal enemy, were all key factors in McGinest's game.

McGinest enjoyed a breakout year of sorts in 1996. In October of that year, he was named the AFC Defensive Player of the Month. The accolade was certainly warranted after he recorded four sacks and returned an interception for a touchdown during the four-week stretch. Moreover, he was voted to his first of two Pro Bowls in 1996. A decade later, McGinest's knack for the sack had not changed. In the Patriots' 28–3 victory over the Jacksonville Jaguars in the 2006 AFC wild card playoff contest, McGinest set a NFL record with 4.5 sacks during the game. His 4.5 sacks gave him 16 in his postseason career and surpassed Bruce Smith for the all-time lead.

One of the greatest moments in Willie's career came on November 30, 2003, in Indianapolis against the Colts. In one of the best games of the NFL season, the Patriots and Colts had slugged it out to a 38–34 score. With the clock running down and the Colts in desperate need of a touchdown to win, they had four tries from the goal line to beat the Pats. After three failed attempts, Willie McGinest put the clamp on the Colts' comeback hopes when he stopped Edgerrin

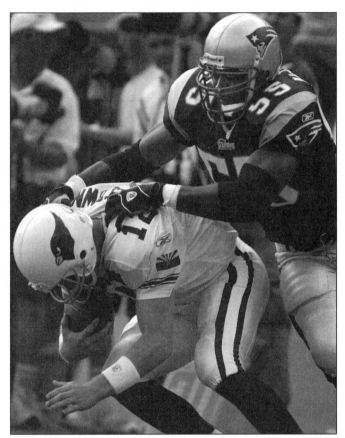

Willie McGinest

James at the goal line to preserve the victory. The usually raucous RCA Dome had never been quieter. Ironically, McGinest had left the game prior to the goal-line stand with a leg injury—an injury that couldn't have come at a better time, as the Colts' drive was looking nearly unstoppable. Wink wink.

Though McGinest's efforts against Indy in 2003 were his most memorable against this opponent, it was not the only time he had come up big against the Colts. The following September at Gillette Stadium he sacked Peyton Manning on third down, which forced a long field-goal attempt by Mike Vanderjagt. The Colts' kicker promptly missed the kick, ensuring the Patriots' 27–24 victory.

Willie McGinest left the New England Patriots after the 2006 season and joined the Cleveland Browns where he reunited with his former defensive coordinator Romeo Crennel. His 78 total sacks as a Patriot are third in franchise history.

Willie McGinest was a stalwart force for the Patriots during his tenure in New England. He was an integral aspect of the Patriots' three Super Bowl championship teams, and few have ever played the outside linebacker position at the level of McGinest.

The Best of Wilie McGinest: The Highlights

- AFC Defensive Player of the Week as he returned a pass 46 yards for a touchdown in the Patriots' 28–25 win over the Buffalo Bills on 10-27-96.
- AFC Defensive Player of the Week as he had two sacks and recovered a fumble for a touchdown in the Patriots' 30–28 win over the Jets on 09-12-99.
- Strip-sacked Jim Kelly, and Chris Slade returned the fumble 27 yards for a touchdown in the Patriots' 35–25 win over the Buffalo Bills at Rich Stadium on 11-26-95. (The Patriots scored 22 points in the fourth quarter of this game.)
- Returned a Jim Kelly pass 46 yards for a touchdown in the Patriots' 28–25 win over Buffalo at Foxboro on 10-27-96.
- Took a Joey Harrington pass two yards in the Patriots' 20–12 win over the Lions on Thanksgiving Day in 2002.
- Intercepted a Matt Hasselbeck pass that was tipped by Richard Seymour 27 yards in the Patriots' 30–20 win over the Seattle Seahawks on 10-17-04.
- Sacked Don Majkowski late in the game to preserve the Patriots' 12–10 win over the Colts at the RCA Dome in the Sunday night game played on 11-27-94.
- Recovered a fumble by Rudi Johnson on the Patriots 12-yard line to stop the Bengals first drive, keeping alive the record of the Patriots scoring first in 18 consecutive regular season games, in the 35–28 win over the Cincinnati Bengals on 12-12-04.
- Led the way for Randall Gay as he returned a fumble by William Green 41 yards for a touchdown in the Patriots' 42–15 rout of the Cleveland Browns on 12-05-04.

Stanley "The Steamer" Morgan
#86, Wide Receiver

Stanley Morgan is the most prolific wide receiver in New England Patriots history. "The Steamer" has left his sure-handed grasp on nearly every franchise receiving record. His 534 receptions, 10,352 yards, and 19.4 yards per catch are all franchise records.

Morgan was a magnificent athlete whose raw natural talent inspired the Foxboro faithful. It is important to remember how scintillating his speed was for his era in the NFL. He dazzled defenses with his blazing speed and fancy footwork, making him an impossible defensive assignment. With his cat-like quickness, it was only right that he became the quickest receiver to reach 10,000 yards in NFL history. He

accomplished this feat on September 17, 1989, against the Miami Dolphins.

As the 25th pick in the 1977 College Football Draft, Morgan's impact out of the University of Tennessee was gargantuan. In his 180 regular season games as a New England Patriot he caught 67 touchdown passes. Moreover, he added three touchdown scores during his seven postseason games for the team. He had several spectacular seasons with the New England Patriots, including 1986, which is considered his best year. During the '86 season Morgan was the definition of consistency—he had nine games with at least 100 receiving yards, which led the NFL. He led the Patriots through the AFC playoffs and straight to Super Bowl XX against the Chicago Bears.

He had incredible games throughout his career, and he picked Buffalo as his victim many times. These games included his seven-catch, 141-yard performance against the Bills on January 2, 1983, his 133-kickoff return yards enabling the Patriots to defeat Buffalo on November 20, 1977, and his 158-yard, two-touchdown performance in the midst of a 26–6 victory over the division rivals on November 4, 1979.

Morgan was named to the Pro Bowl four times in 1979, 1980, 1986, and 1987. Additionally, he held the single-season Patriots record for touchdown receptions until 2007. Randy Moss broke Morgan's previous mark of 12 set during the 1979 season.

"The Steamer" finished his career in 1990 as an Indianapolis Colt. Morgan was named to the New England Patriots Hall of Fame on August 27, 2007. Today, he resides in Memphis, Tennessee, and has been inducted into the Tennessee Sports Hall of Fame.

Stanley Morgan

The Best of Stanley Morgan: The Highlights

- Caught a nine-yard touchdown pass from Brain Sipe in the 1981 AFC-NFC Pro Bowl.
- Caught five passes for 158 yards and two touchdowns, including one for a 63-yard touchdown, in the Patriots' 26–6 win vs. Buffalo on 11-04-79.
- Caught five passes for 182 yards and one touchdown in the 30–27 overtime loss to the Miami Dolphins on 11-08-81.
- Caught three touchdown passes in the Patriots' 38–31 loss to the Seattle Seahawks at Sullivan Stadium on 09-21-86.
- Caught a 12-yard touchdown pass in the final 29 seconds to force overtime in the Patriots' 27–21 overtime loss to the Pittsburgh Steelers at Three Rivers Stadium on 09-27-81.
- Caught a 66-yard touchdown pass from Andy Johnson on a fake reverse halfback option pass in the 33–17 win over the Kansas City Chiefs at Schaefer Stadium on 10-04-81.
- Caught a 62-yard touchdown pass from Steve Grogan on the Patriots' third play of the first possession in the 29–21 win over the Houston Oilers at Schaefer Stadium on 11-28-82.
- Caught a 19-yard touchdown pass and a 45-yard flea flicker pass for a touchdown in the Patriots' 22–17 AFC Divisional Playoff Game loss to the Broncos on 01-04-87.
- Set and tied the Patriots record by having at least one touchdown reception in four consecutive regular season games during the 1980 and the 1986 seasons.
- Hauled in a 75-yard touchdown pass and had 170 yards receiving in the Patriots' 35–14 rout of the Baltimore Colts at Memorial Stadium on 11-26-78.
- Advanced a fumble by Don Calhoun three yards in the Patriots' 37–31 win over Seattle on 09-21-80.
- Advanced a fumble by Tony Collins 20 yards in the Patriots' 30–0 loss to Cleveland on 11-20-83.

Randy Moss
#81, Wide Receiver

In many ways, the arrival of Randy Moss in New England directly contradicted the type of player the Patriots usually acquire. In an organization where success is defined by the accomplishments of the team more than the accolades of the individual, the trade for Moss was met with skepticism. The murmurs and questions of whether Moss could behave himself couldn't be ignored. They said he would break up team chemistry. They said he left his skills in Minnesota. However, the one thing skeptics forgot about is the one fact that always holds true in sports—winning solves everything. After a heartbreaking loss at the hands of the Colts in the 2007 AFC Championship Game, a glaring weakness reared its head. Tom Brady, in all his greatness, had a serious lack of weapons. As rival Peyton Manning continued to tear apart defenses with Marvin Harrison and Reggie Wayne, it was clear that the Patriots needed more firepower to reach the Super Bowl again. So, Bill Belichick and Scott Pioli went out and got the cannon.

That would be Randy Moss.

Tall, fast, with hands like Spider-Man, Randy Moss is a freak of nature. His speed, agility, and superb route-running ability make him the prototypical wide receiver. The ultimate game changer, Moss commands respect from opposing defenses. When the Patriots acquired Moss for a fourth-round draft pick prior to the 2007 season, it was a relatively low-risk move. Already one of the elite receivers in the NFL, Moss was coming off a tumultuous two-year stint in Oakland. Despite the setback in his career, he came to Foxboro with a new attitude and it didn't take long for No. 81 to make a statement. His impact on the team was both monumental and immediate. He recorded more than 100 yards in each of his first four weeks of the 2007 season, adding to his total of 59 100-yard receiving games in his career. Moss caught 23 touchdowns in 2007, surpassing the seemingly unsurpassable single-season record of 22 set by Jerry Rice.

A superior athlete, Moss's most famous trait is to make spectacular one-handed catches. Sometimes it seems that all a quarterback has to do is throw the ball in his general vicinity, and he'll come down with the pigskin. The former West Virginia state track champ is as aggressive as he is flashy and frequently wrestles balls away from cornerbacks. Opposing defenses became so preoccupied with Moss that teammates like Wes Welker, Jabar Gaffney, and Benjamin Watson became even more dangerous weapons for Tom Brady. Brady and Moss—New England's version of the Dynamic Duo—

Randy Moss

couldn't be stopped in 2007, and this killer combo led to one of the greatest single-season offensive performances by any NFL team.

The Randy Moss express didn't lose any steam in 2008. When Tom Brady went down in Week 1 due to injury, Moss' presence provided rookie quarterback Matt Cassel with the confidence he needed to step up and make the big play. Before long, Moss was again the most important player on the field, drawing double teams and leaving the second half of New England's one-two receiving punch, Wes Welker, to make plays. Moss' incredible back-to-back years in New England have added to his legacy, and his maturity and growth as a player, teammate, and person have erased clouds of negativity that surrounded his career. Randy Moss is one of the best wide receivers to ever play the game.

When you are watching Randy Moss, you are watching history. He started his record-breaking career early by catching 17 touchdown passes as a rookie straight out of Marshall. The four-time All-Pro has set countless NFL records throughout his storied career, including the single season touchdown record and is the only NFL player to rack up 1,200 receiving yards in each of his first six seasons.

Jim Nance
#35, Running Back

Jim Nance was the 1965 NCAA heavy weight wrestling champion. Nance was chosen from Syracuse University in the 19th round of the 1965 College Football Draft by the Boston Patriots. Jim ran for 5,323 yards and 45 touchdowns during the 1965–71 seasons for the Boston/New England Patriots.

Nance was the Patriots' leading rusher during the 1965–70 seasons and led the team in net yards from scrimmage in 1966, 1967, and 1970. He holds the Patriots record for having the most games (17) with at least 100 yards rushing. He averaged a team-record 104 yards rushing per game during the 1966 regular season. Nance was the first AFL player to have back-to-back seasons with at least 1,000 yards rushing. He led both leagues with 1,458 yards rushing in 1966 and 1,216 yards rushing in 1967.

Jim Nance was given the nickname "Odd Job" (after the James Bond character) in the locker room after the Patriots defeated the Denver Broncos 24–10 at Bears Stadium on 09-18-66. Nance had a career-high 208 yards rushing and ran for two touchdowns in the 21–21 win over the Oakland Raiders at Fenway Park on 10-30-66.

Nance had his career-long run of 65 yards for a touchdown and made the cover of *Sports Illustrated* as the Patriots defeated the Buffalo Bills 14–3 in "The Game" at Fenway Park on 12-04-66. Nance was recognized as the AFL Offensive Player of the Week as he ran 34 times for 185 yards rushing and one touchdown in the 23–0 shutout of the Buffalo Bills on 09-24-67.

Nance was named the AFL MVP and Player of the Year in 1966 and was an AFL All-Star running back in

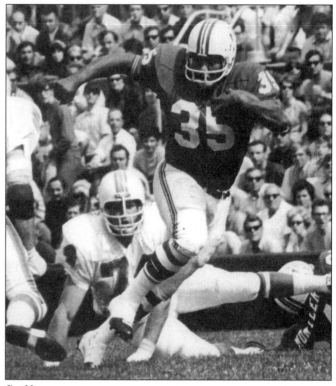

Jim Nance

1966 and 1967. Nance played with the New York Jets in 1973 and with the Houston Texans/Shreveport Steamers of the World Football League in 1974. He was inducted into the Pennsylvania Sports Hall of Fame.

Steve Nelson "Nellie"

Steve Nelson's career should be used as a blueprint for all current and future linebackers in the NFL. Nellie was a Pro Bowl linebacker in the AFC in 1980, 1984, and 1985. He had an eagerness for action and a fervor for competition that were contagious. Nelson made big, crushing hits and was a fearless leader of the defense. He led the Patriots defense in tackles in eight of his 14 seasons, and he was a driving force behind the remarkable 1986 Patriots season that resulted in a Super Bowl XX birth.

Nellie was a proud Patriot from 1974–87. In that time he was a master at reading the quarterback and had several memorable picks during his tenure. The pick most entrenched in the minds of longtime fans came on

September 23, 1979, against the San Diego Chargers. Nelson intercepted Dan Fouts on the 2-yard line and returned the ball to the 20. The interception secured a 27–21 Patriots victory. On September 25, 1983, Nelson intercepted a Cliff Stoudt pass. After returning the pick six yards, he lateraled the ball to teammate Clayton Weishuhn, who proceeded to sprint 27 yards to the end zone. The Patriots defeated the Pittsburgh Steelers on this day at three Rivers Stadium, 28–23.

Nellie was as tough a player as has come down the pike, and it was rare that he'd be kept out of action. If Nelson missed a game, you could almost feel his disappointment and angst. Before the Patriots' November 10, 1985, game against the Colts, using the code name

"Sluggo," Steve sent a telegram to his teammates in the locker room that red, "Rip the faces off." His energy was infectious and New England decimated the opponents 34–15 at Sullivan Stadium. His personality and attitude made him a hometown favorite. When New York Jets field goal kicker Pay Leahy shanked a potential game-winning field goal on November 19, 1978, Nellie made sure to give him a little tap on his helmet, letting him know (as if he didn't already) that he had blown the game.

Nelson not only made his mark in the minds of New England fans, but he left his imprint on the record books as well. Nelson broke the Patriots' fumble recovery record when he snatched up three against the Philadelphia Eagles on October 8, 1978. He made history again when he recorded a personal-best 22 tackles against the Jets on September 19, 1982.

Nelson played the final game of his career on December 28, 1987, against the Miami Dolphins. Nelson went out a winner in the 24–10 victory. Nelson's No. 57 jersey was retired on July 11, 1988, by New England, and the organization inducted Nelson into the franchise Hall of Fame on August 18, 1993. Few are any more deserving to be there than Steve Nelson.

Steve Nelson "Sluggo"

The Best of Steve Nelson: The Highlights

- Both of his interceptions in 1975 were returned four yards in away games that the Patriots lost.
- In 1976, he also had two interceptions. He lost two yards returning a pass by Bob Griese and he took a Gary Marangi pass that was tipped by Steve Zabel 34 yards in home victories against the Dolphins and Bills.
- Had five interceptions and had back-to-back games with an interception twice during the 1978 season. Nelson took a Joe Theisman pass 26 yards in the Patriots' 16–14 loss to the Redskins at Schaefer on 09-03-78.
- Took a Jim Hart pass 37 yards in the Patriots' 16–6 win over the St. Louis Cardinals at Busch Stadium on 09-10-78.
- Returned a Don Strock pass that was tipped by Mike Hawkins three yards in the Patriots' 34–0 shutout of the Dolphins at Schaefer on 10-12-80.
- Rumbled 33 yards with an interception of Vince Ferragamo in the Patriots' 17–14 loss to the Los Angeles Rams at Schaefer on 11-16-80.
- In the Patriots' 47–21 rout of the Baltimore Colts in 1980, he intercepted Bert Jones for the second time in his career.
- Had two interceptions of Jack Trudeau in the 30–21 win over the Colts at the Hoosier Dome in 1986.
- Blocked a 49-yard field-goal attempt by Pat Leahy that was returned for a touchdown in the Patriots' 21–11 win over the New York Jets at Shea Stadium on 10-05-80.
- Returned a Jack Trudeau pass to the 1-yard line to spark the team in the Patriots' 30–21 win vs. the Colts on 11-09-86.
- Had 15 tackles and sacked Craig Morton in the Patriots' 45–10 loss to Denver at Mile High Stadium on 11-11-79. Actual footage of this game was used in filming the movie *Everybody's All American*. During filming, former Patriots All-Pro safety, Tim Fox, who was used an extra, broke the collarbone of lead actor Dennis Quaid in a live-action scene, and the movie was delayed six weeks.

- Sacked Joe Ferguson, Bert Jones, Greg Landry, Brian Sipe, Matt Robinson, Craig Morton, Dave Krieg, Paul McDonald, Matt Kofler, Art Schlitcher, Marc Wilson, Vince Ferragamo, and Jim Kelly.
- Sacked Ron Jaworski twice in the Patriots' 14–6 win over the Eagles on 11-27-77.
- Sacked Bert Jones twice in the Patriots' 30–24 loss to the Baltimore Colts on 12-18-77.
- Forced a fumble by Larry Csonka on the Patriots 11-yard line in the 28–13 win over Miami on 10-21-79.
- Recovered fumbles by Brian Sipe, Terry Bradshaw, Rocky Bleier, Gary Marangi, Benny Malone, Joe Washington, Wilbert Montgomery, Ron Jaworski, Bernie Kosar, Keith Krepfle, Ulysses Norris, Robin Earl, Jim Zorn, Dan Marino, and George Rodgers.
- Fell on a bad pitch from Jim Kelly to Ronnie Harmon in the Patriots' 13–7 win over Buffalo on 12-20-87.

Vito "Babe" Parilli
#15, Quarterback

Babe Parilli is one of the unforgettable personalities in New England Patriots history. Parilli became a star in the 1960s and was a perennial league leader during his stint with the franchise. He and Gino Cappelletti made for an entertaining pair and were a dangerous combination for opposing teams.

Babe Parilli was a star quarterback at the University of Kentucky where he played under the impeccable

Babe Parilli

tutelage of legendary head coach Paul "Bear" Bryant. He was named the 1951 Sugar Bowl Most Valuable Player and one year later was named the Most Outstanding Back in the 1952 Cotton Bowl. He finished a reputable third in Heisman Trophy voting for his efforts in the 1951 season.

Babe Parilli played with the Ottawa Roughriders of the Canadian Football League before being acquired by the Boston Patriots as part of a five-player trade in 1961. From 1961 to 1966 Parilli wowed Patriots fans. The 1964 season was surely his best as he amassed a then-record 3,645 yards and 31 touchdowns.

Steadfast, committed, and sure-handed, Babe's remarkable talent as a placeholder rivaled his outstanding ability as a quarterback. His placeholder/place-kicker combination of Parilli and his favorite target Gino Cappelletti became known as "Grand Opera."

In 1969, Parilli secured the Super Bowl ring that had evaded him throughout his career when he joined the rival New York Jets. His championship ring came as a reserve since the starting quarterback was none other than Joe Namath.

On July 7, 1962, Parilli was inducted into the College Football Hall of Fame. More than a decade later, the New England Patriots honored him with an induction into the franchise Hall of Fame on August 8, 1993.

Babe Parilli's indisputable passion for the sport of football continued long after his playing days had ended. After retirement, Parilli became a head coach for the New York Stars and the Chicago Winds of the now-defunct World Football League. Following his stint in the WFL, he became a head coach for several franchises in the Arena Football League.

Always exciting, always colorful, few will forget Babe Parilli.

The Best of Babe Parilli: Highlights

- Finished fourth in the voting for the Heisman Trophy in 1950 and third in the voting for the 1951 Heisman Trophy.
- Was awarded the game ball as he ran for a 2-yard touchdown and led the Patriots to a 17–7 victory over the Buffalo Bills at Fenway Park on 12-01-63.
- Recovered a fumble by Dainard Paulson, who had just intercepted his pass, in the Patriots' 30–20 loss to the New York Jets at Fenway Park on 11-14-65.
- Was the AFL Offensive Player of the Week as he threw three touchdown passes in the 35–17 win over the San Diego Chargers at Fenway Park on 10-23-66.
- Was the AFL Offensive Player of the Week as he was 16–20 and threw five touchdown passes in the 41–10 rout of the Miami Dolphins at Boston College Alumni Stadium on 10-15-67.
- Ran 32 yards for a touchdown in the 34–21 win over the Houston Oilers at Harvard Stadium on 09-16-62.
- Was a co-captain of the East team in the 1964 AFL All-Star Game.
- Threw two touchdown passes and was named the Offensive Player of the Game in the 1967 AFL All-Star Game.
- Tossed two touchdown passes in the 24–14 loss to the Buffalo Bills in a game that was delayed due to blizzard conditions at Fenway Park on 12-20-64.
- Was the AFL All-Star quarterback in 1963, 1964, and 1966.
- Member of the 1969 New York Jets championship team.

Jim Plunkett
#16, Quarterback

Jim Plunkett won the Heisman Trophy, the Maxwell Award, and the Walter Camp Award as a quarterback for the Stanford Cardinals in 1970. He was also the UPI, *Sporting News*, and *Sport* magazine College Player of the Year. He was the MVP of the 1970 Hula Bowl and the MVP of the 1971 Rose Bowl. Plunkett was chosen by the New England Patriots with the No. 1 overall pick in the 1971 College Football Draft.

During his first NFL training camp, he was asked to stand up and sing his school song from Stanford. Plunkett stood up, said he didn't know the words, and then sat down. Unfortunately for Plunkett, one of the Patriot ball boys, Mike Cataldo, asked if he knew the words to "Jingle Bells." Needless to say Plunkett was up again singing "Jingle Bells."

Plunkett was the first NFL rookie quarterback to play in every offensive play during the entire regular season. Plunkett was recognized as the AFC Rookie of the Year in 1971. In his first NFL regular season game he tossed two touchdown passes and led the Patriots to a 20–6 victory over the Oakland Raiders at Schaefer Stadium.

Plunkett tossed two touchdown passes in the first NFL regular season game where two former Heisman Trophy–winning quarterbacks faced each other as the Patriots lost to Roger Staubach and the Dallas Cowboys 44–21 at Texas Stadium on 10-24-71.

Jim Plunkett

Plunkett completed four touchdown passes in the 38–33 win over the Buffalo Bills at Schaefer Stadium on 11-14-71.

The Patriot fans sang "Happy 24th Birthday" to Plunkett, and he responded by throwing two touchdown passes in the 34–13 win over the Dolphins at Schaefer Stadium on 12-05-71. He led the team to an improbable 21–17 win over the Baltimore Colts at Memorial Stadium on the last game of his rookie year. Plunkett tossed an 88-yard touchdown pass to his former college teammate Randy Vataha in this game as well.

Plunkett was the NFL Offensive Player of the Week twice in his career with the Patriots. Jim tossed two touchdown passes, including one for 88 yards to Randy Vataha, in the fourth quarter of the 21–17 win over the former world champion Baltimore Colts at Memorial Stadium on 12-19-71. Plunkett was the NFL Offensive Player of the Week as he threw two touchdown passes and ran for another in the 33–24 win over the Green Bay Packers at Schaefer Stadium on 11-18-73. (The Patriots scored the final 24 points in this game.)

On 09-15-74, he led the Patriots in the 34–24 defeat of the reigning Super Bowl–champion Miami Dolphins at Schaefer Stadium as he threw a touchdown pass and ran five yards on a fake option play for a touchdown on 09-15-74.

Jim Plunkett was inducted into the Rose Bowl Hall of Fame for his performance in the 1971 Rose Bowl and was inducted into the College Football Hall of Fame, along with former Patriot Player Ron Burton, on 12-04-90. Plunkett had a cameo appearance in the movie *Airport 1975*.

He was traded to the San Francisco 49ers for draft picks that led the Patriots to acquiring Pete Brock, Tim Fox, Tom Owen, Raymond Clayborn, and Horace Ivory. Jim played on the 1980 Oakland Raiders championship team and was the Super Bowl MVP for the 1983 Los Angeles Raiders. Jim Plunkett and Doug Williams are the only Super Bowl MVP quarterbacks who never made it to a Pro Bowl.

Marty Schottenheimer
#54, Linebacker

Marty Schottenheimer played for four seasons with the Buffalo Bills before joining the Boston Patriots in 1969. Schottenheimer, who wore uniform No. 54, was a linebacker for the Boston Patriots in 23 games during the 1969–70 seasons. He had a Patriots career-high 20 tackles in the 23–14 loss to the New York Jets at Boston College Alumni Stadium on 10-05-69. He intercepted a pass by his former teammate Jack Kemp in the Patriots' 23–16 loss to the Buffalo Bills at Rich Stadium on 10-11-69.

Schottenheimer played on special teams and almost had three kickoff returns during his time with the Patriots. He returned a kickoff 13 yards in the 17–16 loss to Miami at Boston College Alumni Stadium on 11-09-69. He returned a kickoff 8 yards in the 27–3 loss to the Colts at Memorial Stadium on 10-25-70. He caught the kickoff but then pitched it back to Odell Lawson, who ran for 17 yards, in the 16–0 loss to the NY Giants on 10-18-70.

Schottenheimer was the starting middle linebacker for the Boston Patriots in the last three games of the 1970 NFL season. On 12-20-70, in the Patriots 45–7 loss to the Cincinnati Bengals, he played in his last professional football game and recorded eight tackles.

Schottenheimer was a linebacker coach for the Portland Storm of the World Football League and the New York Giants and Detroit Lions of the National Football League. He was a defensive coordinator for the New York Giants and the Cleveland Browns. He was the head football coach for the Cleveland Browns, Kansas City Chiefs, Washington Redskins, and San Diego Chargers.

Marty Schottenheimer

Richard Seymour "Big Sey"
#93, Defensive Lineman

Richard Seymour was too big to play Pop Warner football as a child, but his 6'6" 310-pound frame has already made him one of the all-time great defensive linemen in NFL history, and in just a few short years. Bill Belichick once referred to "Big Sey" as his "best player." Quite the compliment from the normally restrained head coach.

The lovable Richard Seymour has a charming personality that has made him a favorite in Foxboro. However, despite his appealing disposition, he is as big and bad as anybody in the National Football League. A true giant amongst men, Seymour is so good that it's scary. His importance to the current Patriots dynasty cannot be overstated. He deserves as much credit as Tom Brady, Bill Belichick, and anyone else for the remarkable run of success the Patriots are currently enjoying.

Since he was selected sixth by the Patriots in the 2001 College Football Draft, Seymour has been an omnipresent force on the defensive side of the ball. His ability to utilize his strength, speed, and agility is second to none and nothing short of incredible. He can rush the pass, stop the run, block field goals, and is one of the few players in the NFL whose mere presence completely changes the game. Quite frankly, there's nothing that the big man can't do.

He has blocked five field goals in five years and amassed 29.5 sacks during his already illustrious career. Furthermore, his 68-yard fumble return for a touchdown on October 3, 2004, was his first career touchdown and the first in team history. The feat came against none other than old friend Drew Bledsoe and the Buffalo Bills.

Big Sey is a regular in Honolulu, Hawaii, as the all-world lineman was selected to the Pro Bowl every year

Richard Seymour

from 2002–06. His five consecutive Pro Bowl appearances had not been done by a Patriots player since Andre Tippett accomplished the feat in the 1980s. Not bad for the former Georgia Bulldog.

Richard Seymour is a simply amazing player who, when it's all said and done, could be one of the best players in the history of the NFL. With each passing week, his accomplishments become more abundant, his accolades continue to pile up, and his legend grows. The tale of Seymour's career may just be getting started.

The Best of Richard Seymour: The Highlights

- Blocked a 43-yard field-goal attempt on 11-25-01.
- Blocked a 49-yard field-goal attempt on 11-17-02.
- Blocked a 43-yard field-goal attempt, shared in a sack of Dante Culpepper, and recovered a fumble in the Patriots' 24–17 win over the Vikings on 11-24-02.
- Blocked a potential game-winning field goal in the 19–13 overtime win vs. the Dolphins on 10-19-03. He won AFC Special Team Player of the Week honors that week.
- Blocked a 45-yard field-goal attempt by Robbie Gould in the 17–13 win over the Bears on 11-26-06.
- Blocked a 31-yard field-goal attempt in the playoff game on 01-10-04.
- Member of the 2001, 2003, and 2004 championship teams.

John Smith
#1, Kicker

John Smith was born in Southampton, England, and was traveling in America as a soccer instructor in 1973. During his visit he was asked to try to kick a football. He was a left-footed kicker and earned a free agent tryout with the Patriots. During the Patriots' 1973 training camp he was traded to the Pittsburgh Steelers. Smith was subsequently waived by the Steelers but signed on with the New England Colonials in the Atlantic Coast League. In April 1974, he signed a free agent contract with the New England Patriots. In August 1974, he ran onto the field to attempt to kick a field goal during an exhibition game against the Washington Redskins without his helmet. His famous quote was, "I forgot my bloody bonnet."

Smith lost three yards attempting to run with the ball in the 24–16 victory over the 49ers at Schaefer Stadium on 10-26-75. John was the only regular NFL kicker to successfully kick every extra point in the 1975 season. He led the NFL in scoring in 1979 and was recognized as an AFC Pro Bowl kicker in 1980.

Smith was the first Patriots kicker to kick an extra point with less than 30 seconds to go to tie the game and force overtime. Smith is the only Patriots player to kick the only field goal in a game that the Patriots won, 3–0.

John Smith

Smith kicked a field goal on the last play of the half four times in his career. He kicked a career-high four field goals in the 33–19 win over the San Diego Chargers on 11-09-75. Smith set the team record by kicking eight extra points in the 56–3 rout of the New York Jets on 09-09-79.

Smith kicked 128 field goals and 308 extra points in 116 regular season games for the New England Patriots. He kicked two field goals and six extra points in three playoff games for the Patriots during the 1974–83 seasons.

Edward "Butch" Songin
#11, Quarterback

Edward Songin was born in Walpole, Massachusetts, and was a tremendous hockey player and baseball All-Star. He was a two-time All American hockey player for Boston College and was a member of the 1948–49 championship team. Songin is a member of the Boston College Varsity Club Hall of Fame.

Songin was a veteran of World War II as he took part in the Normandy invasion in World War II. "Butch" was 36 years old when he played in his first regular season game for the Boston Patriots.

Butch Songin completed the first pass for the Boston Patriots in a regular season game. On 09-09-60, after a 52-yard interception return by Chuck Shonta put the ball on the Broncos 10-yard line, Songin tossed a 10-yard touchdown pass to Jim Colclough for the Patriots' first TD. His longest completion was a 78-yard pass to Billy Wells in the 35–0 shutout of the Los Angeles Chargers on 10-08-60. Butch threw three touchdown passes to former

Butch Songin

Boston College players in the 38–21 win over the New York Titans on 11-11-60.

His presence as the team's quarterback stabilized a group of young and inexperienced men in the Patriots inaugural season in 1960. Chances are that the Patriots team would have failed miserably had Songin not been at the helm for that first year of the AFL. Songin had played football for Boston College and led the

Hamilton Tiger Cats to the Grey Cup championship in his rookie year.

Butch ran for two touchdowns and tossed 36 touchdown passes in 28 games for the Boston Patriots during the 1960–61 seasons. He finished his professional football career with the New York Titans in 1962. His cousin, Tom Songin, played professional hockey for the Boston Bruins

Lennie St. Jean
#60, Defensive End/Offensive Guard

Lennie St. Jean was a ninth-round draft pick of the Boston Patriots in 1964. He played defensive end at Northern Michigan. During the off-season he worked as a lumberjack.

St. Jean was so severely dehydrated after an August 1965 preseason game at Rice University in Houston, Texas, that his body locked up on him so much that they had to carry him on the plane and cover his body with ice in the aisles on the way home. St. Jean was in just about every play during the severe heat, and water was not readily available on the sidelines—Gatorade had not been invented.

St. Jean, who was known as the "Boston Strong Boy," played on both sides of the line of scrimmage. He was used as a defensive end, a linebacker, a tackle, and as an offensive guard. He was the Patriots' starting offensive right guard for 112 games during the 1966–73 seasons. He played in 140 consecutive games. St. Jean was an AFL All-Star offensive guard in 1966 and was the team's Unsung Hero of the Year in 1966 and 1970.

As a defensive end, he recorded 5.5 sacks, and every sack he had was at the opponent's home field. He sacked Mickey Slaughter and Jacky Lee in the 39–10 rout of the Broncos on 10-04-64 and recorded a sack of Don Trull in the 34–17 win over the Houston Oilers on 11-19-64. The only game that he sacked the same quarterback twice (Dick Wood) was in the 30–21 loss to the Raiders on

Lennie St. Jean

10-24-65. He shared in a sack of Joe Namath in the 27–23 win over the New York Jets at Shea Stadium on 11-28-65.

St. Jean was awarded the game ball "for knocking many men down" in the 26–7 loss to the Houston Oilers on 11-26-67. St. Jean played in 140 regular season games during the 1964–73 seasons for the Boston/New England Patriots.

Darryl Stingley
#84, Wide Receiver

Darryl Stingley is an unforgettable part of New England Patriots history. Though his playing career was cut short, his impact on the organization is everlasting. Stingley was chosen out of Purdue with the 19th pick in the College Football Draft. He quickly started burning up the field in Foxboro and became the first Patriots receiver ever to have consecutive games with 100 (or

more) receiving yards. He played the game with style and grace and was a true pleasure for fans to watch. He was known for his unmatched athleticism and his awe-inspiring catches.

During his rookie season, Stingley immediately got fans talking. On November 4, 1973, against the Philadelphia Eagles, Stingley made two equally spectacular touchdown receptions. His leaping, one-handed 16-yard reception of a Jim Plunkett pass is one of the most replayed catches in NFL history.

Another memorable game for Darryl Stingley took place on September 18, 1977, his 26th birthday. Stingley caught a 21-yard touchdown pass and had a 34-yard touchdown run on the day. In fact, Stingley is the only Patriots receiver ever to have two rushing touchdowns. His scores during this game helped lead the Pats to a 21–17 victory over the Kansas City Chiefs at Schaefer Stadium.

Despite his celebrated playing days, Darryl Stingley's career is mired in tragedy. During a preseason game against the Oakland Raiders on August 12, 1978, the great wide receiver was paralyzed after his neck was broken due to an absolutely wicked hit by Jack Tatum. Adding to the misfortune of the situation, Stingley did not have to play in the game because he was not yet under contract for the upcoming season. The fact that Stingley did partake, however, should remind everyone of his character and commitment to the team. Stingley was forever bothered by the fact that Jack Tatum never truly apologized for the incident. Instead, Tatum used the incident as a promotional tool for his autobiography.

One of the most emotionally spellbinding moments in the history of the National Football League came on September 3, 1979. Prior to New England's season-opening game on *Monday Night Football* against the Pittsburgh Steelers, Darryl Stingley was honored by the fans. He received a compassionate ovation that lasted 10 minutes but felt like an eternity.

Stingley continued to be a presence on the team after his retirement. He was an inspirational force on

Darryl Stingley

the sidelines and demonstrated his support for his teammates any chance he got. On October 14, 1979, he was presented with the game ball after the Patriots defeated the Chicago Bears 27–7 at Soldier Field.

Stingley was an inspirational person who cared for the well being of others. Despite his paralysis, he continued to find ways to fuel his passion for sports. He used his tragic situation in many positive ways. For instance, he was instrumental in having wheelchair participants included in the Boston Marathon.

Darryl Stingley passed away on April 5, 2007.

The Best of Darryl Stingley: The Highlights

- Made a leaping one-handed reception of a 16-yard touchdown pass from Jim Plunkett in the Patriots' 24–23 loss to the Philadelphia Eagles on 11-04-73.
- Took a punt by Jeff West on his 3-yard line and on a reverse return handed it to Andy Johnson for a net gain of eight yards in the Patriots' 24–17 loss to the St. Louis Cardinals on 11-02-75.
- Caught two touchdown passes from Jim Plunkett in the Patriots' 34–31 loss to the Dallas Cowboys on 11-16-75.
- Ran 21 yards on a reverse that helped set up a touchdown, ran 27 yards on another reverse to help set up another touchdown, and caught a 21-yard touchdown pass and a 15-yard touchdown pass in the Patriots' 48–17 rout of the Oakland Raiders on 10-03-76.
- Ran for a 34-yard touchdown and caught a 21-yard touchdown pass on his 26th birthday in the Patriots' 21–17 victory over the Kansas City Chiefs at Schaefer Stadium on 09-18-77.
- Recovered an onside kick by Rolf Bernirscke in the Patriots' 24-20 win over San Diego on 10-16-77.
- Had a career-high eight receptions for 121 yards in the Patriots' 24–13 win over the Jets at Schaefer Stadium on 10-30-77.
- Holds the team record for the longest run from scrimmage by a Patriots wide receiver in a regular season game.
- Was the first Patriots receiver drafted in the first round to lead the team in yards receiving in a season.

Mosi Tatupu

#30, Running Back/Special Teams Player

"Mosi Tatupu, Mosi Tatupu." His name transitioned into pop culture when the Island Chief in *The Simpson's* "Treehouse of Horror III" episode used it to mean that the blue-haired woman will make a good sacrifice. If his name wasn't being spoken on the popular sitcom, it was being chanted at the old Foxboro Stadium by "Mosi's Mooses." The popular Mosi Tatupu fan section of the stadium was loud and proud and made sure its presence was felt. He earned the appreciation and admiration of Patriots fans with the heart, passion, and pride he played with on the field.

Perhaps no NFL player is as directly associated with the state of Hawaii as Mosi Tatupu. His name became synonymous with the state after he set the Hawaii high school rushing record. Moreover, the Mosi Tatupu Award given to the collegiate Special Teams Player of the Year, is given out at the Hula Bowl. Tatupu was a star at every level, and in 1978 he began an unforgettable 14-year NFL career. The Patriots chose Tatupu out of Southern California with the 215th pick in the 1978 College Football Draft. He was a hard-working, dedicated fullback and special teams giant for New England.

As a back, a special part of Tatupu's game was his fourth-down potency. The star running back was the go-to-guy when the Pats needed to extend a drive. Tatupu ran for a first down on a fourth-down play on nine occasions during his career. Tatupu's career as a running back can be defined by the 1983 season. His extraordinary 5.5 yards per carry led the National Football League. During the same season he set two personal bests: on November 13, 1983, he rumbled for 55 yards against the Miami Dolphins, the longest run of his career. Three weeks later, Tatupu ran for a career-high 128 yards in the Patriots' victory over the Saints during a snowstorm in Foxboro.

In 1986, Tatupu was an essential part of the Patriots' surge to Super Bowl XX. In the AFC Championship Game against Miami, Tatupu forced a fumble that led to a Pats score and scored the final

Mosi Tatupu

touchdown of the game himself to help snap the Pats 18-game losing streak in the Orange Bowl and secure the spot in the Super Bowl. Furthermore, he was named to the Pro Bowl on special teams, and he was recognized as the Special Teams Player of the Year.

Mosi Tatupu was a talented, unique, versatile running back for the New England Patriots. At the time of his retirement, Mosi Tatupu's 199 games played were the most in NFL history for a running back. The accomplishment shows the reliability, durability, and consistency of Mosi Tatupu. After 13 years in New England, Tatupu played five games with the Los Angeles Rams to conclude his career. Today, Tatupu's son, Lofa, who also attended USC, is a middle linebacker for the Seattle Seahawks and carries on the family tradition.

The Best of Mosi Tatupu: The Highlights

- Recovered an onside kick by Patriots kicker Mike Hubach in the Patriots' 38–34 loss to the Oilers at the Houston Astrodome in a *Monday Night Football* game played on 11-10-80.
- Forced a fumble by Nesby Glasgow on his kickoff return that Rick Sanford returned 22 yards for a touchdown in the Patriots' 47–21 rout of the Colts on 11-23-80.
- Ran four yards for a touchdown on fourth-and-1 in the fourth quarter of the Patriots' 38–27 win over the Saints on 12-21-80.

- Ran two yards for a touchdown on fourth-and-1 in the Patriots' 28–24 loss to the New York Jets on 10-11-81.
- Had his longest reception as a Patriots player (41 yards from Matt Cavanaugh) in the Patriots' 33–17 win over the Kansas City Chiefs at Schaefer Stadium on 10-04-81.
- Had a 26-yard run and finished with 81 yards rushing in the Patriots' 3–0 shutout of the Dolphins during the famous snowstorm at Schaefer Stadium on 12-12-82.
- Fumbled at the end of his 13-yard run into the end zone and Cedric Jones recovered for a Patriots touchdown in the Patriots' 27–17 loss to the Eagles on 12-09-84.
- Was awarded one of the game balls in the Patriots' 16–10 win over the Indianapolis Colts on 12-16-84.
- Recovered an onside kick by Al Del Greco in the Patriots' 26–20 win over the Green Bay Packers at Sullivan Stadium on 09-08-85.
- Had four special team tackles, forced a fumble, and had two receptions and seven carries in the Patriots' 34–0 shutout of the Steelers on 10-19-86.
- Returned a blocked punt 17 yards for a touchdown in the Patriots' 21–20 win over the Saints at the Superdome on 11-30-86.
- Tossed a 15-yard halfback option touchdown pass on fourth down to Tony Collins in the Patriots' 26–23 win over the Oakland Raiders on 11-01-87.
- Caught a career-high eight receptions in the Patriots' 28–24 loss to the Saints on 11-12-89.
- Ran for two touchdowns in the Patriots' biggest comeback victory as they scored the final 38 points in the 38–23 win over the Seattle Seahawks on 09-16-84.
- Scored all three touchdowns—on runs of four, five, and seven yards—in the Patriots' 21–7 win over the Los Angeles Rams on 12-11-83.
- Is the only Patriots player who has touched the ball in all four of the flea-flicker passes that resulted in touchdowns.
- Forced a fumble by Sam Seale on his kickoff return that Jim Bowman recovered in the end zone for the game-winning points scored in the Patriots' 27–20 AFC Divisional Playoff Game victory over the Los Angeles Raiders on 01-05-86.

Andre Tippett
#56, Linebacker

Andre Tippett is one of the greatest linebackers in NFL history. His accomplishments are so vast and his accolades are so abundant, it would be laborious to list them all.

But we'll try.

Andre Tippett was the total package. He was strong, fast, smart, and played with vigor. He pursued quarterbacks like a predator stalks its prey. When the time was right, Tippett made sure his attack was swift, accurate, and always high impact. Tippett was at the core of several of the best Patriots defensive teams of the 1980s. He was voted to the AFC Pro Bowl team five consecutive years from 1984–88, which tied the mark set by John Hannah. He was named the AFC Defensive Player of the Year in 1985. He recorded 778 tackles, 100 sacks, 17 forced fumbles, 18 recovered fumbles, one interception, and a blocked field goal in his impeccable Patriots career. His 100 sacks are a franchise record. Of those

100, he sacked 41 different quarterbacks from the 1983 to 1993 seasons, including Ken O'Brien and Jim Kelly 8.5 times each—Dan Krieg was a victim six times.

Before he introduced his speed and strength to the NFL's top quarterbacks, Tippett was a standout linebacker at the University of Iowa. He was chosen No. 41 in the 1982 College Football Draft by the Patriots and enjoyed a meteoric rise to the top. In 1984, Tippett broke a Patriots franchise record with 18.5 sacks in the regular season. His 18.5 sacks in 1984 combined with his 16.5 sacks in 1985 are the most sacks in a two-year stretch by anyone in NFL history.

The NFL Player's Association honored Tippett with the Linebacker of the Year award from 1985 through 1987, and he was named to the All-NFL First Team in 1985 and 1987.

In total, Tippett played in 151 regular season games and six playoff games during his 11-year career in New

John Elway (on the ground) and Andre Tippett

The Best of Andre Tippett: The Highlights

- Had 30.5 sacks in regular season games played at Sullivan Stadium during the 1983–88 seasons
- Had 28 tackles and recovered a fumble by Theotis Brown during the 1982 season.
- Had 86 tackles, 8.5 sacks, two forced fumbles, and recovered a fumble by Eric Dickerson in 1983.
- Stopped Richard Todd three times on first-and-goal at the 7-yard line in the Patriots' 23–13 win over the Jets at Sullivan Stadium on 09-19-83.
- Had 118 tackles, 18.5 sacks, and two forced fumbles in 1984.
- Sacked Pat Ryan late in the game to preserve the Patriots' 28–21 win over the New York Jets at Shea Stadium on 09-30-84.
- Sacked Joe Ferguson, Dave Krieg, Pat Ryan, Paul McDonald, John Elway, Matt Kofler, Art Schlichter, Danny White, Neil Lomax, and Joe Pisarcik during the 1984 season.
- AFC Defensive Player of the Week on 09-29-85.
- AFC Defensive Player of the Week on 10-18-87.
- Returned a fumble by Roger Vick 29 yards for a touchdown on 09-21-87.
- Returned a poor snap to Ray Guy 25 yards for a touchdown in the Patriots' 35–20 loss to the Raiders on 09-29-85.
- Had 63 tackles, 9.5 sacks, two forced fumbles, and recovered a fumble by Bubby Brister in 1986.
- Advanced a lateral from Johnny Rembert 32 yards and had 3.5 sacks in the Patriots' 23–3 win over Buffalo on 10-26-86.

England. In addition to being named to the Patriots All-Century team in 2000, he was inducted into the Patriots Hall of Fame on November 15, 1999. Tippett's amazing consistency earned him a spot on the NFL 1980s All-Decade team. He is one of the best to ever don a Patriots' jersey. Andre Tippett retired on May 12, 1994, after a career worthy of the highest distinction and praise.

Randy "The Rabbit" Vataha
#18, Wide Receiver

Randy Vataha once played a dwarf at Disneyland in California. Most New England Patriots fans would agree that he made a better wide receiver than a Disneyland character.

Vataha was drafted by the Los Angeles Rams in the 17th round of the 1971 College Football Draft but was signed as a free agent by the New England Patriots prior to the start of his rookie season. The transaction enabled Randy to reunite with quarterback Jim Plunkett who was Vataha's teammate in college. Jim Plunkett and Randy Vataha were excited about the prospect of rekindling the

connection they established while at Stanford University. "The Rabbit" once caught a 97-yard touchdown pass from his former roommate. Randy Vataha played six memorable seasons with the Patriots and was named to the AFC All-Rookie Team in 1971.

"The Rabbit" had many memorable moments in a New England Patriots jersey, several of which came against the Baltimore Colts. On December 19, 1971, he caught an 88-yard touchdown pass, his second of the day, that defeated the Baltimore Colts at Memorial Stadium. He would victimize the Colts again two years later after advancing a Mack Herron fumble 46 yards for a touchdown to give New England a 24–16 win on October 7, 1973. The following year, his 23-yard reverse set up a 33-yard field goal with 14 seconds left in the first half that contributed to the Patriots' 27–27 victory, again over Baltimore, on November 24, 1974, at Memorial Stadium.

He recorded seven receptions for 129 yards and two touchdowns the day after his 23rd birthday on December 5, 1971. His enormous afternoon led the Patriots to a 34–13 victory over the Miami Dolphins at Schaefer Stadium.

Randy Vataha was an exciting part of the Patriots teams during the 1970s and was always a major threat on the offensive end. "The Rabbit" retired as a Green Bay Packer in 1977.

Since his departure from football, Vataha has turned to business. In fact, his business resume is almost as impressive as his football career. He was one of the founders of the United States Football League in 1983, and his sports representation firm has presided over the careers of several notable stars, including Boston's own Larry Bird.

Randy "The Rabbit" Vataha

Adam Vinatieri
#4, Kicker

The images of Adam Vinatieri's heroics are forever immortalized on newspaper front pages, T-shirts, and New England Patriots highlight videos. His exciting career has provided countless classic moments, and the Patriots' quest for greatness rested on the strength of his kicking foot on so many occasions.

His game-winning kicks in Super Bowl XXXVI and Super Bowl XXXVIII gave New England the first two world championships in franchise history. However, the greatest kick of Vinatieri's career came in the famous "Snow Bowl" during the 2001–02 playoffs. With the Patriots trailing by three points, Vinatieri made the most difficult field goal in NFL history from 46 yards out in the midst of a blizzard to send the game into overtime. In the extra frame, Vinatieri connected with a game-winning field goal that sent his team to the AFC Championship Game.

Adam Vinatieri began his professional football career as a member of the Amsterdam Admirals of NFL Europe. From there, the New England Patriots signed No. 4 in 1996 and his remarkable NFL career was off and running. He played 10 seasons in New England

and earned Pro Bowl recognition in 2002 and 2004—not bad for an undrafted free agent.

Vinatieri's best season as a Patriot may have been his 2004 campaign. He was, simply put, a scoring machine (and a Fantasy Football player's dream). He was the NFL's scoring leader during the 2004 season as he accumulated 141 points.

Vinatieri has 20 game-winning field goals with less than 1:00 remaining on the game clock. He has truly earned the nicknames "Mr. Clutch" and "Mr. Automatic." He is considered one of, if not *the* greatest field goal kicker in the history of the NFL. He has four championship rings, including three with the New England Patriots and one as a member of the 2006 Indianapolis Colts.

The argument can be made that Adam Vinatieri is the single most important factor in the Patriots' historical run to three Super Bowls in four years.

Despite playing a position that rarely earns Hall of Fame honors, many analysts have predicted his inevitable induction. This is a true ode to his legacy.

The Best of Adam Vinatieri: The Highlights

- Kicked five field goals, including the game winner, and was named the AFC Special Team Player of the Week in the 28–25 overtime win vs. the Jaguars on 09-22-96.
- Caught Herschel Walker from behind on his long kickoff return in the Patriots 12–6 loss to the Dallas Cowboys at Texas Stadium on 12-15-96.
- Was named the AFC Special Team Player of the Week as he kicked four field goals, including one from 50 yards, and made a tackle in the 33–6 rout of the Bills on 10-12-97.
- Booted a 52-yard field goal that hit the camera on the goal post and bounced back on the field in the 29–6 victory over the Indianapolis Colts in Foxboro on the Sunday night game played on 09-13-98.

Adam Vinatieri, Ken Walter holding

- Kicked the game-winning 27-yard field goal on the last play of the 30–27 win over the New Orleans Saints at the Superdome on 10-04-98.
- Was the AFC Special Team Player of the Week as he kicked four field goals, two extra points, and made two special team tackles in the 26–23 Monday night win over Miami in Foxboro on 11-23-98.
- Ran for a two-point conversion, even though the Buffalo Bills had left the field, in the 25–21 win over the Buffalo Bills on 11-29-98. The Bills were protesting a call that was made by a game official and did not send a team on the field before the play.
- Was named the AFC Special Team Player of the month as he kicked two game-winning field goals and scored 35 points in the three victories in September 1999.
- Kicked a 44-yard field goal and five extra points in the 2005 Pro Bowl Game.
- Kicked the game-winning 23-yard field goal with seven seconds left to beat the Jets 30–28 on 09-12-99.
- Kicked a 22-yard field goal with three seconds left to defeat the Bengals 16–13 at Foxboro on 11-19-00.
- Kicked an overtime game-winning 44-yard field goal to defeat the San Diego Chargers 29–26 on 10-14-01.
- Was the AFC Special Team Player of the Week as he kicked four field goals, including the game winner, in the Patriots' 12–9 overtime win vs. the Buffalo Bills on 12-16-01.
- Kicked a 37-yard field goal with five seconds left in the half and the overtime game-winning 35-yard field goal to defeat the Kansas City Chiefs 41–38 at Gillette Stadium on 09-22-02.
- Was the AFC Special Team Player of the Week as he kicked four field goals—one on the last play of the first half and another to defeat the Miami Dolphins, 27–24, in overtime at Gillette on 12-29-02.
- Was named the AFC Special Team Player of the Week as he kicked four field goals, four extra points and threw a 4-yard touchdown pass to Troy Brown in the 40–22 win over the St. Louis Rams on 11-07-04.
- Was the AFC Special Team Player of the Month as he kicked 14 field goals and threw a touchdown pass in the Patriots' four regular season victories during the month of November 2004.
- Kicked a 48-yard field goal, a 35-yard field goal, and a 43-yard field goal and was named the AFC Special Team Player of the Week in the 23–20 win over the Steelers at Heinz Field on 09-25-05.
- Kicked a 29-yard field goal with 17 seconds left to defeat the Atlanta Falcons 31–28 at the Georgia Dome on 10-09-05.
- Kicked a 46-yard field goal for the game-winning points scored in the 17–14 AFC Divisional Playoff Game win over the Tennessee Titans at Gillette Stadium on 01-10-04.
- Tied the NFL record by kicking five field goals in a playoff game during the 24–14 win over the Colts in the 2003 AFC Championship Game at Gillette Stadium on 01-18-04.
- Member of the 2001, 2003, and 2004 Patriots championship teams.
- Member of the 2006 Indianapolis Colts championship team.

Wes Welker
#83, Wide Receiver

Once viewed by GMs and scouts as a role player, a complimentary piece, or just a return specialist, Wes Welker has emerged as a top-tier wide receiver in the NFL. With his quick feet, speed in the open field, and awe-inspiring maneuvers, the Oklahoma City–boy routinely shakes defenders out of their cleats. Before Welker began setting Patriots franchise records, he was carving out a piece of history at the expense of his current team. As a Dolphin during his rookie season in 2004,

the undrafted return specialist became just the second NFL player to field both a kick and a punt, record a tackle, and kick an extra point and a field goal all in the same game. Later that season he torched the Pats' special teams for a 71-yard touchdown return. For Patriots fans everywhere, Welker's arrival in Foxboro was a collective sigh of relief.

Standing just 5'9", the speedy receiver out of Texas Tech was an integral part of the Patriot's one-two receiving punch in 2007 and 2008. With superstar partner-in-crime Randy Moss commanding so much attention from opposing defenses, Welker has helped open up the Pats offensive attack. He gave Tom Brady an exciting new weapon during the history-making 2007 season. Sure-handed with unparalleled on-field awareness, Welker broke the franchise record for single-season receptions with 112 on the year–a record previously held by Troy Brown. Wes caught 13 balls in a Week 7 game against the Philadelphia Eagles and had 11 receptions in Week 17 against the New York Giants. His 1,175 yards and eight touchdown receptions are also career bests. At Super Bowl XLII, Welker recorded eleven receptions, tying Patriots' Super Bowl XVIII MVP Deion Branch's mark.

When Tom Brady went down in Week 1 of the 2008 season, the universal opinion was that a Matt Cassel–led offense wouldn't produce big numbers. As Cassel took the reigns, Welker's productivity made the quarterback transition as seamless as possible. Welker had six receptions each week for the first 11 games of the season. Arguably the MVP of the offense, he was instrumental in the Patriots success and became the first player in franchise history to record back-to-back 100-reception seasons. Welker was selected as a Pro Bowl reserve, though his accomplishments in '07 and '08 are vastly underrated.

Welker has endeared himself to fans through his fierce play, determination, and everyman work ethic. He's also linked to another fan favorite in New England—Mosi Tatupu. Welker won the 2003 Mosi Tatupu award—the accolade given to the country's best

Wes Welker

special teams player—during his final year at Tech. There are plenty of adjectives used to describe Patriots wide receiver Wes Welker—quick, fast, speedy, and dangerous are all words that come to mind. However, after breaking franchise records and earning a trip to Honolulu, there's a new word to describe him: star.

## 3

All the Team's Men

Here is the alphabetical listing of every player who has participated in at least one regular season or playoff game for the Patriots. Of these 962 players, 43 have played in only one regular season game and 57 have played in exactly two regular season games for the Patriots. Only one player, Smiley Creswell, has participated in two playoff games even though he never played in a regular season game for the Patriots. Ron Burton is the only player to play in the playoff games for that same season. He missed the entire 1963 regular season due to injury.

Many players earned nicknames that stuck with them throughout their Patriots career. Some of these more memorable nicknames include, Babe, Bam, Big Dog, Big House, Big Play, Big T, Blue, Butch, Choo-Choo, Chilly, Comrade, Cowboy, Deep Threat, Dirty, Duke, Earthquake, Harpo, Hawg, King, Mini, My Man, Pinhead, Rambo, Reno, Rocky, Scooter, Sluggo, Spanky, Sugar Bear, Thumper, Thunderfoot, Whimpy, Wildman and three players had the nickname of Hollywood. Certainly you remember The All World Tight End, The Boston Strongboy, The Hitman, The Human Missile, The Italian Stallion, The Jewel, The Pound Puppy, The Rabbit, The Snow Angel, Our Snow Plow, The Steamer, The Undertaker, The Whopper and two players who were known as The Blade. Some nicknames were more formal, such as Mr. Automatic, Mr. Clutch, Mr. Irrelevant, Mr. Reliability, and Mr. Versatility, to name a few.

Each player's uniform number, position, and years played are identified in this chapter. Every player who has touched the ball in some capacity during a game will have his appropriate positive statistics listed such as the number of pass completions, rushing attempts, receptions, returns, and fumble recoveries, along with the total amount of yards and and touchdowns scored. If he was able to advance or return the football then it will so proclaim the longest length of this return and the specific date the yardage occurred. The date of each game is listed for each particular player who has blocked a field goal, punt, extra point, or recorded a safety.

Although many of these men also played for other teams, this section is only about the statistics that they accumulated when they were with the Patriots. In the early years of the AFL, the teams would only suit up 33 players, so many of them had to play multiple positions during the game. Each player's dominant offensive, defensive, or special team position is identified, but if he had an obscure return or briefly played another position that position is in parenthesis.

Each of the 28 AFL All-Star players and 46 AFC Pro Bowl players has been identified by the year he was recognized. The Offensive, Defensive, and Special Team Players of the Week are listed. MVPs and Players of the Year such as Tom Brady, Gino Cappelletti, Jim Nance, and Andre Tippett are highlighted.

We have acknowledged the members of each championship team. If he was drafted and played for the Patriots, it will show the specific pick that he was chosen in that year's draft. Only two of these players did not play college football in North America, kickers John Smith and Mike "Superfoot" Walker. For every other player you will find the name of his dominant college football team.

Also identified are the names of the players who have been inducted into the Patriots Hall of Fame, the College Football Hall of Fame, and the Pro Football Hall of Fame.

KEY
WR: Wide Receiver
RB: Running Back
KR: Kick Returner
LB: Linebacker
PR: Punt Returner
TE: Tight End
DB: Defensive Back
DT: Defensive Tackle
E: End

Abdullah, Rabih, (#27)
Running Back, 2004
13 carries for 13 yards and one touchdown
Ran for a one-yard touchdown on 10-10-04
Longest run was five yards on 12-26-04
Caught a nine-yard pass on 10-17-04
Nine regular season games
Three playoff games
Member of the 2004 championship team
Lehigh Mountain Hawk

Abrams, Bobby (#50)
Linebacker, 1995
Nine games
Michigan Wolverine

Acks, Ron (#51)
Linebacker, 1972–73
Returned an interception 11 yards on 09-16-73
Only sack was made on 10-07-73
Recovered five fumbles
28 games
Illinois Fighting Illini

Adams, Bob (#80)
Tight End/Tackle, 1973–74
31 receptions for 441 yards
Longest reception was 30 yards on 12-09-73
Two carries for seven yards
Longest run was four yards on 12-16-73
25 games
Pacific Tiger

Adams, George (#33)
RB (KR), 1990–91
30 carries for 114 yards
Longest run was 13 yards on 12-30-90
16 receptions for 146 yards and one touchdown
Caught a four-yard touchdown pass on 10-18-90
Longest reception was 28 yards on 11-18-90
Returned a kickoff seven yards on 11-25-90
18 games
Kentucky Wildcat

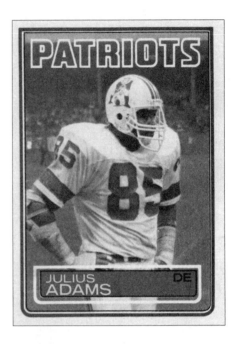

Adams, Julius (#85) and (#69)
"Ju-Ju" and "The Jewel"
Defensive End (LB/DT), 1971–87
80.5 sacks
NFL Defensive Player of the Week on 12-05-71
Blocked an extra-point attempt on 11-03-74
Blocked a 37-yard field-goal attempt on 10-02-77
Blocked a 45-yard field-goal attempt on 12-12-82
Blocked a 42-yard field-goal attempt on 12-16-84
Recovered seven fumbles
Returned a fumble 12 yards on 12-08-85
Wore uniform #69 for two games in 1987
AFC Pro Bowl defensive end in 1980
206 regular season games
Five playoff games
#27 pick in the 1971 College Draft
Texas Southern Tiger

Adams, Sam (#61) "Pimpin"
Guard/Tackle (TE), 1972–80
Recovered four fumbles
Occasionally used as a tight end
119 regular season games
Two playoff games
Pairie View A&M Panther

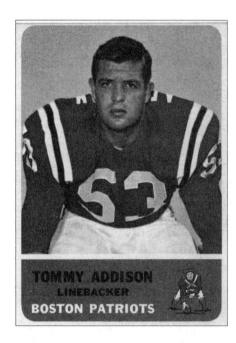

Addison, Tom (#53) "Big T" and "Plugger"
Linebacker, 1960–67
15 sacks
16 interceptions for 103 yards and one touchdown
Returned a pass 10 yards for a touchdown on 10-06-62
Longest return was 17 yards on 09-14-63
Blocked an extra-point attempt on 10-23-60
Recovered four regular season fumbles
AFL All-Star LB in 1960, 1961, 1962, 1963, and 1964
106 regular season games
Two playoff games
South Carolina Gamecock

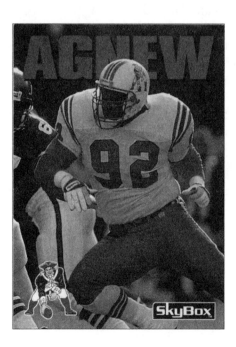

Agnew, Ray (#92)
Defensive Lineman, 1990–94
Eight sacks
Recovered two fumbles
66 regular season games
Only playoff game appearance was on 01-01-95
#10 pick in the 1990 College Draft
North Carolina State Wolfpack

Aiken, Sam (#88)
Wide Receiver, 2008
Eight receptions for 101 yards
Longest reception was 43 yards on 11-13-08
14 games
North Carolina Tarheel

Akbar, Hakin (#29)
Defensive Back, 2001
Six games
#163 pick in the 2001 College Draft
Washington Husky

Akins, Chris (#34)
Safety, 2003
12 regular season games
Three playoff games
Member of the 2003 championship team
Arkansas Pine Bluff Golden Lion

Alexander, Eric (#49) and (#52)
Linebacker/Special Team, 2004–08
31 regular season games
Six playoff games
Member of the 2004 championship team
LSU Fighting Tiger

Alexander, Rogers (#91)
Linebacker (KR), 1987
Returned a kickoff four yards on 10-04-87
Three games
Penn State Nittany Lion

Allard, Don (#12)
Quarterback, 1962
Four games
Boston College Eagle

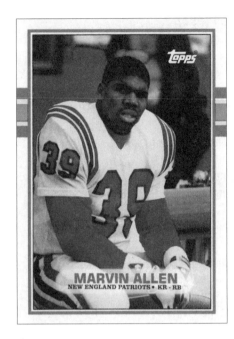

MARVIN ALLEN
NEW ENGLAND PATRIOTS • KR - RB

Allen, Marvin (#39) "Chunky"
RB/KR, 1988–91
94 carries for 378 yards and two touchdowns
Longest run was 29 yards on 12-02-90
Seven receptions for 57 yards
Longest reception was 19 yards on 12-23-90
43 kickoff returns for 844 yards
Longest kickoff return was 34 yards on 12-09-90
Recovered seven fumbles
37 games
#294 pick in the 1988 College Draft
Tulane Green Wave

Allen, Terry (#22)
Running Back, 1999
254 carries for 896 yards and eight touchdowns
Longest run was 39 yards on 10-24-99
14 receptions for 125 yards and one touchdown
Caught an eight-yard touchdown pass on 09-19-99
Longest reception was 38 yards on 10-31-99
Recovered a fumble on 12-19-99
16 games
Clemson Tiger

Andersen, Jason (#67)
Center, 1999–2000
17 games
#211 pick in the 1998 College Draft
BYU Cougar

Anderson, Bobby (#33)
Running Back, 1975
Only rushing attempt was for one yard on 11-02-75
Five games
Colorado Buffalo

Anderson, Darren (#25)
Defensive Back, 1992
Only game played was on 09-27-92
#93 pick in the 1992 College Draft
Toledo Rocket

Anderson, Ralph (#49) "Sticks"
Defensive Back, 1973
Two interceptions for three yards
Only return was for three yards on 11-04-73
Recovered a fumble on 11-25-73
Blocked an extra-point attempt on 12-16-73
13 games
West Texas A&M University Buffalo

Andrews, Willie (#23)
DB/KR, 2006–07
4 kickoff returns for 149 yards and one touchdown
Longest return was a 77-yard touchdown on 10-20-07
30 regular season games
Six playoff games
#229 pick in the 2006 College Draft
Baylor Bear

Andruzzi, Joe (#63) "Italian Stallion"
Offensive Guard, 2000–04
Recovered three fumbles
Advanced a fumble 12 yards on 09-24-00
Caught a pass for no gain on 11-30-03
72 regular season games
Nine playoff games
Member of the 2001, 2003, and 2004 championship
    teams
Ed Block Courage Award in 2002
Southern Connecticut State Owl

Antrum, Glenn (#10)
Wide Receiver, 1989
Only game played was on 11-19-89
UCONN Husky

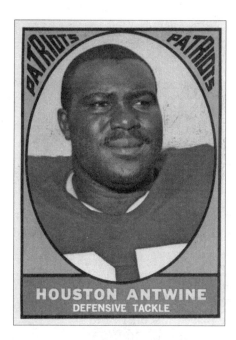

Antwine, Houston (#65) "Twine"
Defensive Tackle (G), 1961–71
39 sacks
Returned an interception two yards on 12-12-65
Recovered four fumbles
Initially played as an offensive guard
AFL Defensive Player of the Week on 09-08-68
AFL All-Star DT in 1963, 1964, 1965, 1966, 1967, and
     1968
142 regular season games
Two playoff games
Southern Illinois Saluki

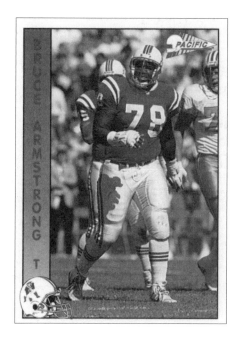

Armstrong, Bruce (#78) "Army"
Offensive Tackle, 1987–2000
Recovered nine fumbles
Advanced a fumble four yards on 10-18-90
AFC Pro Bowl in 1990, 1991, 1994, 1995, 1996, and
     1997
212 regular season games
Seven playoff games
#23 pick in the 1987 College Draft
Ed Block Courage Award in 1993
His uniform #78 was retired by the Patriots
Inducted into the Patriots Hall of Fame on 09-30-01
Louisville Cardinal

Arthur, Mike (#65)
Center, 1993–94
Recovered two fumbles
25 regular season games
Only playoff game appearance was on 01-01-95
Texas A&M Aggie

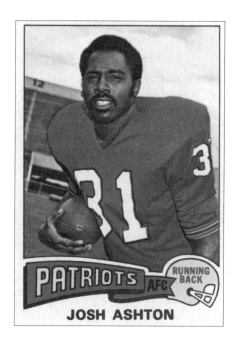

Ashton, Josh (#31)
RB/KR, 1972–74
247 carries for 950 yards and three touchdowns
Longest run was 35 yards on 12-03-72
33 receptions for 320 yards and one touchdown
Caught a 24-yard touchdown pass on 10-01-72
Longest reception was 51 yards on 09-16-73
15 kickoff returns for 309 yards
Longest kickoff return was 31 yards on 11-06-72
Recovered two fumbles
38 games
#209 pick in the 1971 College Draft
Tulsa Golden Hurricane

Ashworth, Tom (#68)
Tackle (FB/TE), 2002–05
Recovered a fumble on 11-07-05
Caught a one-yard touchdown pass on 12-17-05
37 regular season games
Five playoff games
Member of the 2003 and 2004 championship teams
Colorado Buffalo

Atchason, Jack (#85)
Offensive End, 1960
Two receptions for 22 yards
Longest reception ws 14 yards on 09-23-60
Only game played was on 09-23-60
Western Illinois Leatherneck

Atessis, Bill (#73)
Defensive Lineman, 1971
Five games
Texas Longhorn

Atkinson, Ricky (#22)
Defensive Back, 1987
Only game played was on 10-18-87
Southern Connecticut State Owl

Avezzano, Joe (#50)
Center, 1966
Three games
Sixth-round draft pick in 1966
Florida State Seminole

Ayi, Kole (#99)
Linebacker, 2001
Only game played was on 11-18-01
Member of the 2001 championship team
UMASS Minuteman

Baab, Mike (#68)
Center, 1988–89
Recovered a fumble on 11-05-89
31 games
Texas Longhorn

Bahr, Matt (#3)
Kicker (Punter), 1993–95
55 field goals
Longest field goal was 55 yards on 11-12-95
73 extra points
Only punt was for 29 yards on 10-23-95
AFC Special Team Player of the Week on 11-12-95

35 regular season games
Only playoff game appearance was on 01-01-95
Penn State Nittany Lion

Bailey, Bill (#37) "Teddy"
Running Back, 1969
Two games
Cincinnati Bearcat

Bain, Bill (#62)
Offensive Tackle, 1986
Three regular season games
Only playoff game appearance was on 01-04-87
USC Trojan

Baker, Mel (#83)
Special Team, 1975
Only game played was on 10-19-75
Recovered a fumble on 10-19-75
Texas Southern Tiger

Baker, Rashad (#32)
Defensive Back, 2006–07
13 regular season games
Only playoff game appearance was on 01-21-07
Tennessee Volunteer

Baldinger, Rich (#74)
Guard/Tackle, 1993
15 games
Wake Forest Demon Deacon

Ballou, Mike (#51) "Cat"
Linebacker, 1970
14 games
#56 pick in the 1970 College Draft
UCLA Bruin

Banks, Willie (#78)
Guard/Special Team, 1973
Blocked a punt by Julian Fagan on 10-14-73
13 games
Alcorn State Brave

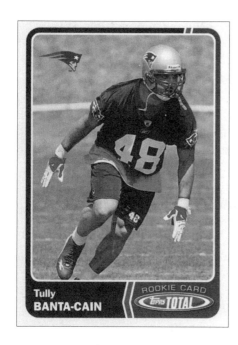

Banta-Cain, Tully (#48) and (#95)
LB/Special Team, 2003–06
8.5 sacks
Returned a pass four yards on 11-14-04
Recovered a fumble on 12-26-04
Returned four kickoffs for 60 yards
Longest kickoff return was 21 yards on 11-22-05
54 regular season games
10 playoff games
Member of the 2003 and 2004 championship teams
#239 pick in the 2002 College Draft
California Golden Bear

Barnard, Brooks (#8)
Punter, 2003
10 punts for 365 yards
Longest punt was 49 yards on 12-07-03
Only game played was on 12-07-03
Member of the 2003 championship team
Maryland Terrapin

Barnes, Bruce (#3)
Punter, 1973–74
100 punts for 3,738 yards
Longest punt was 53 yards on 10-21-73
23 games
#290 pick in the 1973 College Draft
UCLA Bruin

Barnes, Pete (#59)
Linebacker, 1976–77
12 sacks
Returned a pass interception 13 yards on 10-02-77
Recovered two fumbles
Returned a fumble 11 yards on 09-18-77
25 regular season games
Only playoff game appearance was on 12-18-76
Southern University Jaguar

Barnes, Rodrigo (#55)
Linebacker, 1974–75
Recovered a fumble on 11-24-74
Six games
Rice Owl

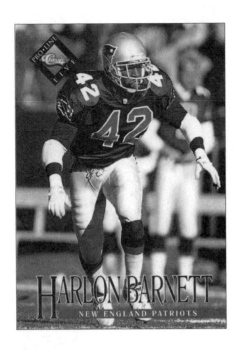

Barnett, Harlon (#42)
Defensive Back, 1993–94
4 interceptions for 91 yards
Longest return was 40 yards on 10-24-93
Returned two fumbles for seven yards
Longest fumble return was five yards on 11-27-94
30 regular season games
Only playoff game appearance was on 01-01-95
Michigan State Spartan

Barnett, Troy (#98) "Laptop"
Defensive End, 1994–96
Three sacks
Recovered a fumble on 11-12-95
Blocked a 38-yard field-goal attempt on 12-24-94
Blocked a 54-yard field-goal attempt on 09-10-95
Blocked an extra-point attempt on 11-26-95
31 regular season games
Only playoff game appearance was on 01-01-95
North Carolina Tar Heel

Bartrum, Mike (#86)
Tight End/Long Snapper, 1996–99
Two receptions for two yards and two touchdowns
Caught a one-yard touchdown pass on 10-06-96
Caught a one-yard touchdown pass on 01-02-00
57 regular season games
Five playoff games
Marshall Thundering Herd

Baty, Greg (#48) and (#85)
Tight End, 1986–87
52 receptions for 469 yards and four touchdowns
Longest reception was 22 yards on 11-30-86
21 regular season games
Only playoff game appearance was on 01-04-87
#220 pick in the 1986 College Draft
Stanford Cardinal

Baumann, Charlie (#8)
Kicker, 1991–92
18 field goals
Longest field goal was 46 yards on 11-24-91
31 extra points
Recovered a fumble on 12-27-92
23 games
West Virginia Mountaineer

Bavaro, David (#52)
Linebacker, 1993–94
Recovered two fumbles
21 regular season games
Only playoff game appearance was on 01-01-95
Syracuse Orangeman

Baxter, Fred (#49) and (#84)
Tight End, 2002–03
13 regular season games
Member of the 2003 championship team
Auburn Tiger

Beach, Walter (#26) and (#41)
RB/KR/PR/DB, 1960–61
Six carries for a net loss of four yards
Longest run was three yards on 10-28-60
Nine receptions for 132 yards and one touchdown
Longest reception was a 59-yard touchdown on
    10-28-60
Nine kickoff returns for 184 yards
Longest kickoff return was 33 yards on 10-08-60
Only punt return was for 21 yards on 09-23-60
Returned an interception 37 yards on 09-09-61
Recovered a fumble on 10-01-61
18 games
Central Michigan Chippewa

Beaudoin, Doug (#27)
DB/KR/PR, 1976–79
4 interceptions for 55 yards
Longest return was 30 yards on 11-25-79
Only sack was made on 12-31-78
10 kickoff returns for 207 yards
Longest kickoff return was 44 yards on 11-14-76
Three punt returns for 18 yards
Longest punt return was 11 yards on 11-07-76
Advanced a blocked punt eight yards for a first down
    on 10-23-77
45 regular season games
Only playoff game appearance was on 12-31-78
#243 pick in the 1976 College Draft
Minnesota Golden Gopher

TOM BEER • TE

Beer, Tom (#82) "Tarzan"
TE (KR), 1970–72
25 receptions for 381 yards and three touchdowns
Longest reception was a 31-yard touchdown on
    10-24-71
Two kickoff returns for 19 yards
Longest kickoff return was 15 yards on 10-29-72
Returned a fumbled punt return five yards on 11-14-71
42 games
Houston Cougar

Beisel, Monty (#52)
Linebacker, 2005
Only sack was made on 10-09-05
15 regular season games
Two playoff games
Kansas State Wildcat

Bell, Bill (#8)
Kicker, 1973
Four extra points
Only field goal was 36 yards on 09-30-73
Three games
Kansas Jayhawk

Bellino, Joe (#27)
RB/WR/KR/PR, 1965–67
30 carries for 64 yards
Longest run was 10 yards on 10-08-65 and on 09-09-67
11 receptions for 151 yards and one touchdown
Longest reception was a 25-yard touchdown on 10-08-66
43 kickoff returns for 905 yards
Longest return was 43 yards on 10-08-66 and on
    12-18-66
19 punt returns for 148 yards
Longest punt return was 18 yards on 10-22-67
Recovered a fumble on 11-12-67
35 games
19th round draft pick in 1961
Inducted into College Football Hall of Fame on
    12-06-77
Navy Midshipman

Bennett, Phil (#52)
Linebacker, 1960
Two games
Miami Hurricane

Benson, Thomas (#53)
Linebacker, 1988
12 games
Oklahoma Sooner

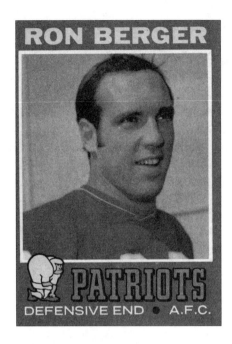

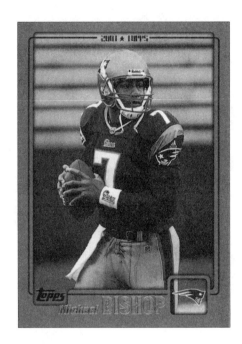

Berger, Ron (#88) "The Whopper"
Defensive End (KR), 1969–72
15.5 sacks
Recovered three fumbles
Returned a kickoff 20 yards on 10-19-69
NFL Defensive Player of the Week on 09-20-70
41 games
Wayne State Tartar

Beverly, Randy (#27)
Defensive Back, 1970–71
Two interceptions for 19 yards
Only return was for 19 yards on 10-31-71
Recovered two fumbles
21 games
Colorado State Ram

Bianchini, Frank (#30)
Running Back, 1987
Only game played was on 10-04-87
Hofstra Flying Dutchman

Billips, Terry (#23)
Defensive Back, 1999
Two games
North Carolina Tar Heel

Biscaha, Joe (#34)
Offensive End, 1960
Two games
Richmond Spider

Bishop, Michael (#7)
Quarterback, 2000
Three completions for 80 yards and one touchdown
Longest pass was a 44-yard touchdown on 10-08-00
Seven carries for a net loss of one yard
Longest run was two yards on 09-11-00
Eight games
#227 pick in the 1999 College Draft
Kansas State Wildcat

Bishop, Richard (#64)
NT/DE, 1976–81
30.5 sacks
Recovered seven fumbles
Recorded a safety on 10-22-78

Blocked a 40-yard field-goal attempt on 09-25-81
85 regular season games
Two playoff games
Louisville Cardinal

Bjornson, Eric (#86)
Tight End, 2000
20 receptions for 152 yards and two touchdowns
Longest reception was 19 yards on 09-11-00
Recovered a Colts onside kick on 10-08-00
Recovered a fumble on 10-22-00
Eight games
Washington Husky

Black, Mel (#94) and (#51)
Linebacker, 1986–87
Six games
Eastern Illinois Panther

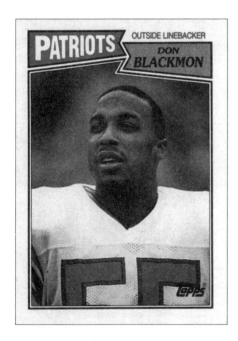

Blackmon, Don (#55) "Gator"
Linebacker, 1981–86
30.5 sacks
Five interceptions for 63 yards
Longest return was 39 yards on 12-11-83
Recorded a safety on 09-08-85
Recorded a safety on 10-27-85
Blocked an extra-point attempt on 09-08-85
Blocked a 53-yard field-goal attempt on 11-02-86
Recovered six fumbles
Returned a fumble 47 yards on 11-28-82
89 regular season games
Six playoff games
#102 pick in the 1981 College Draft
Tulsa Golden Hurricane

Blahak, Joe, (#21)
Defensive Back, 1976
Two regular season games
Only playoff game appearance was on 12-18-76
Nebraska Cornhusker

Blanchard, Dick (#49)
Linebacker, 1972
Returned an interception 20 yards on 12-10-72
14 games
Tulsa Golden Hurricane

Blanks, Sid (#22)
RB/PR/KR, 1969–70
20 carries for 74 yards
Longest run was 12 yards on 11-02-69 and 10-04-70
Seven receptions for 65 yards
Longest reception was 18 yards on 12-20-70
14 punt returns for 93 yards
Longest punt return was 22 yards on 09-20-70
13 kickoff returns for 283 yards
Longest kickoff return was 29 yards on 12-13-70
Recovered a fumble on 11-02-69
28 games
Texas A&I Javelina

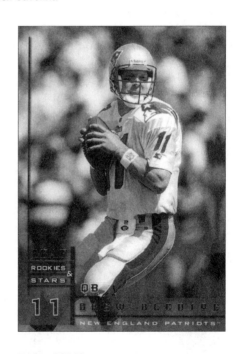

Bledsoe, Drew (#11)
Quarterback, 1993–2001
2,544 completions for 29,657 yards and 166
    touchdowns
Longest completion was an 86-yard touchdown on
    12-06-98
Completed six two-point conversion passes
270 carries for 553 yards and two touchdowns

Longest run was 25 yards on 12-26-99
AFC Offensive Player of the Week on 10-02-94
AFC Offensive Player of the Week on 11-13-94
AFC Offensive Player of the Week on 10-06-96
AFC Offensive Player of the Week on 11-23-98
AFC Offensive Player of the Week on 09-19-99
AFC Offensive Player of the Week on 10-01-00
NFL Player of the Week on 12-01-96
NFL Player of the Week on 11-23-98
NFL Player of the Week on 11-29-98
AFC Pro Bowl quarterback in 1994, 1996, and 1997
Caught a deflected pass on 12-16-95
Recovered 25 fumbles
124 regular season games
Seven playoff games
Member of the 2001 championship team
First overall pick in the 1993 College Draft
Ed Block Courage Award in 1999
Washington State Cougar

Bleier, Bob (#10)
Quarterback, 1987
14 completions for 181 yards and one touchdown
Tossed a six-yard touchdown pass on 10-04-87
Longest completion was 35 yards on 10-04-87
Five carries for a net loss of five yards and one
    touchdown
Longest run was a one-yard touchdown on 10-11-87
Recovered two fumbles
Three games
Richmond Spider

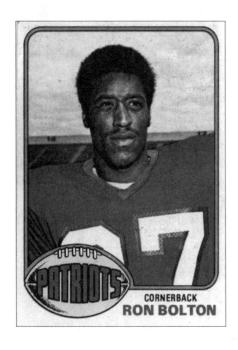

CORNERBACK
RON BOLTON

Bolton, Ron (#27) "Gamebreaker"
Defensive Back, 1972–75
18 interceptions for 116 yards
Longest return was 56 yards on 11-04-73
Blocked a 32-yard field-goal attempt on 09-24-72
Only sack was made on 11-25-73
Recovered a fumble on 10-14-73
55 games
#124 pick in the 1972 College Draft
Norfolk State Spartan

Boudreaux, Jim (#78) and (#64)
OT/DE, 1966–68
Recovered a fumble on 09-09-67
12 games
Second round draft pick in 1966
Louisiana Tech Bulldog

Bowman, Jim (#28)
DB/Special Team, 1985–89
Three interceptions for three yards
Longest return was three yards on 11-22-87
Only sack was made on 11-29-87
Recovered a Saints onside kick on 11-30-86
Recovered three regular season fumbles
Returned a fumble two yards on 11-22-87
73 regular season games
Five playoff games
#52 pick in the 1985 College Draft
Central Michigan Chippewa

Boyd, Greg (#29)
Safety, 1973
Two games
Arizona Wildcat

Boyd, Greg (#65) "Too Strong"
Defensive End, 1977–78
Two sacks
23 games
#170 pick in the 1976 College Draft
San Diego State Aztec

Bradshaw, Morris (#88)
Wide Receiver, 1982
Six receptions for 111 yards and one touchdown
Longest reception was 48 yards on 12-19-82
Only touchdown reception was an 11-yard touchdown
    on 01-02-83
Recovered a fumble on 12-19-82
Eight games
Ohio State Buckeye

Brady, Kyle (#88)

Tight End, 2007

Nine receptions for 70 yards and two touchdowns

Longest reception was 20 yards on 09-23-07

14 regular season games

Three playoff games

Penn State Nittany Lion

Brady, Tom (#12)

Quarterback, 2000–08

2,301 completions for 26,446 yards and 197 touchdowns

Longest completion was a 91-yard touchdown on 10-21-01

Completed four two-point conversion passes

276 carries for 533 yards and five touchdowns

Longest run was for 22 yards on 10-01-06

Caught a 23-yard pass on 12-22-01

Recovered 14 regular season fumbles

AFC Offensive Player of the Week on 10-14-01

AFC Offensive Player of the Week on 11-25-01

AFC Offensive Player of the Week on 09-09-02

AFC Offensive Player of the Week on 11-03-02

AFC Offensive Player of the Week on 11-03-03

AFC Offensive Player of the Week on 12-27-03

AFC Offensive Player of the Week on 10-09-05

AFC Offensive Player of the Week on 09-23-07

AFC Offensive Player of the Week on 10-14-07

AFC Offensive Player of the Week on 10-21-07

AFC Offensive Player of the Week on 12-09-07

AFC Pro Bowl quarterback in 2001, 2004, 2005, and 2007

NFL MVP in 2007

113 regular season games

17 playoff games

Member of the 2001, 2003, and 2004 championship teams

Super Bowl XXXVI MVP

Super Bowl XXXVIII MVP

#199 pick in the 2000 College Draft

Michigan Wolverine

Bramlett, John (#57) "Bull"

Linebacker, 1969–70

Two sacks

Two interceptions for 42 yards

Longest return was 26 yards on 12-07-69

Blocked an extra point on 11-30-69

24 games

Memphis Tiger

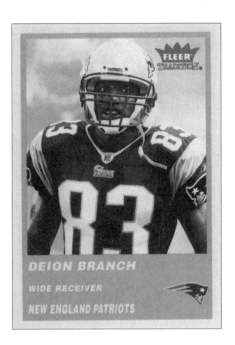

Branch, Deion (#83)

WR/KR/PR, 2002–2005

213 receptions for 2,744 yards and 14 touchdowns

Longest reception was a 66-yard touchdown on 11-03-03

Three carries for 11 yards

Longest run was 11 yards on 09-28-03

36 kickoff returns for 863 yards

Longest kickoff return was 63 yards on 11-28-02

Seven punt returns for 84 yards

Longest punt return was 40 yards on 10-27-02

Recovered two fumbles

53 regular season games

Eight playoff games

Member of the 2003 and 2004 championship teams

Super Bowl XXXIX MVP

#65 pick in the 2002 College Draft

Louisville Cardinal

Brigance, Orenthal (#59) "O.J."

Linebacker, 2002

Only game played was on 09-15-02

Rice Owl

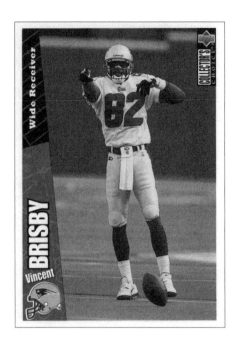

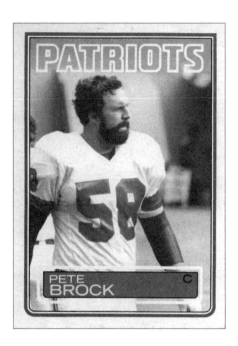

Brisby, Vincent (#82) "Briz"
Wide Receiver, 1993–99
217 receptions for 3,142 yards and 14 touchdowns
Longest reception was 72 yards on 10-01-95
Recovered a fumble on 11-21-93
83 regular season games
Six playoff games
#58 pick in the 1993 College Draft
Northeast Louisiana Indian

Briscoe, Marlin (#88)
Wide Receiver, 1976
10 receptions for 136 yards and one touchdown
Longest reception was 21 yards on 09-12-76
Only touchdown reception was 16 yards on 10-03-76
14 regular season games
Only playoff game appearance was on 12-18-76
Nebraska Cornhusker

Britt, Wesley (#65)
Offensive Tackle, 2006–08
16 regular season games
Alabama Crimson Tide

Brock, Pete (#58) "Deep Threat"
Center/G/T (TE), 1976–87
Caught a six-yard touchdown pass on 11-21-76
Recovered five regular season fumbles
154 regular season games
Eight playoff games
#12 pick in the 1976 College Draft
Ed Block Courage Award in 1985
Colorado Buffalo

Brown, Barry (#63) and (#83) and (#86)
Linebacker/Tight End, 1969–70
21 receptions for 214 yards
Longest reception was 22 yards on 11-01-70
21 games
Florida Gator

Brown, Bill (#54)
Linebacker, 1960
Returned an interception eight yards on 09-17-60
Only sack was made on 11-04-60
14 games
Syracuse Orangeman

Brown, Chad (#98)
Linebacker, 2005 and 2007
17 regular season games
Two playoff games
Colorado Buffalo

Brown, Corwin (#30) "Cornflakes"
Defensive Back, 1991–1996
Recovered three fumbles
Returned a fumble 42 yards for a touchdown on
    12-01-96
Recovered a Ravens onside kick on 10-06-96
61 regular season games
Four playoff games
#110 pick in the 1993 College Draft
Michigan Wolverine

Brown, Monty (#93)
Linebacker, 1996
11 games
Ferris State Bulldog

Brown, Preston (#81)
WR/PR/KR, 1980 and 1982
Four receptions for 114 yards and one touchdown
Longest reception was 41 yards on 12-05-82
Only touchdown reception was 38 yards on 11-21-82
10 punt returns for 42 yards
Longest punt return was 14 yards on 09-07-80
Nine kickoff returns for 156 yards
Longest kickoff return was 26 yards on 09-29-80
14 regular season games
Only playoff game appearance was on 01-08-83
#160 pick in the 1980 College Draft
Vanderbilt Commodore

Brown, Roger (#47)
Defensive Back, 1992
Recovered a fumble on 11-08-92
16 games
Virginia Tech Hokie

Brown, Sidney (#21)
Cornerback, 1978
16 regular season games
Only playoff game appearance was on 12-31-78
#82 pick in the 1977 College Draft
Oklahoma Sooner

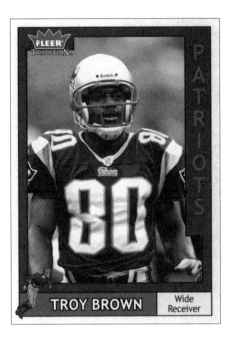

TROY BROWN — Wide Receiver

Brown, Troy (#80), (#86), and (#80) "Mr. Patriot"
WR/KR/PR/DB, 1993–2007
557 receptions for 6,366 yards and 31 touchdowns
Longest reception was an 82-yard touchdown on
    10-19-03
87 kickoff returns for 1,862 yards
Longest kickoff return was 54 yards on 01-02-00
252 punt returns for 2,625 yards and three
    touchdowns
Longest punt return was an 85-yard touchdown on
    12-09-01
Returned a punt for a 66-yard touchdown on 09-03-00
Returned a punt for a 68-yard touchdown on 01-06-02
29 carries for 178 yards
Longest run was 35 yards on 09-03-00
Caught a two-point conversion pass on 11-10-02
Caught a two-point conversion pass on 12-03-06
Recovered a Jaguars onside kick on 12-07-97
Recovered 11 regular season fumbles
Advanced a fumble 75 yards for a touchdown on
    12-10-95
Three interceptions for 22 yards
Longest interception return was 17 yards on 11-14-04
AFC Pro Bowl wide receiver in 2001
192 regular season games
20 playoff games
Member of the 2001, 2003, and 2004 championship
    teams
#198 pick in the 1993 College Draft
Ed Block Courage Award in 1998
Marshall Thundering Herd

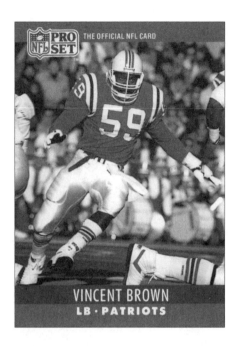

Brown, Vincent (#59) "The Undertaker"
Linebacker, 1988–95
16.5 sacks
10 interceptions for 95 yards and one touchdown
Longest return was a 49-yard touchdown on 11-08-92
Recovered six fumbles
Returned a fumble 25 yards for a touchdown on
    11-01-92
Returned a fumble five yards on 10-16-94
123 regular season games
Only playoff game appearance was on 01-01-95
#43 pick in the 1988 College Draft
Ed Block Courage Award in 1995
Mississippi Valley State Delta Devil

Brown, Wilbert (#60)
Offensive Lineman, 2003
Only regular season game was on 09-21-03
Two playoff games
Houston Cougar

Browning, Dave (#74)
Defensive End, 1983
Two sacks
12 games
Washington Husky

Bruney, Fred (#33) "Fearless"
DB/PR/KR, 1960–62
8 interceptions for 125 yards and one touchdown
Longest return was a 33-yard touchdown on 09-21-62
30 punt returns for 148 yards
Longest punt return was 19 yards on 09-17-60
Two kickoff returns for 39 yards
Longest kickoff return was 20 yards on 09-17-60
Attempted an onside kick on 09-17-60
Recovered three fumbles
Only sack was made on 09-21-62
Holder on extra-point and field-goal attempts
AFL All-Star defensive back in 1961 and 1962
40 games
Ohio State Buckeye

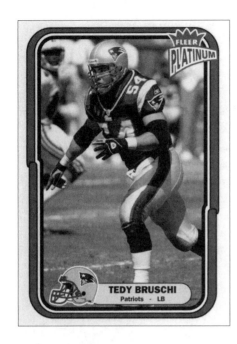

Bruschi, Tedy (#54) "Bru"
Linebacker (KR), 1996–2007
30.5 sacks
12 interceptions for 187 yards and four touchdowns
Returned four consecutive interceptions for a
    touchdown (NFL record)
Longest return was a 48-yard touchdown on 11-17-02
Returned a blocked punt four yards for a touchdown
    on 10-06-96
Recovered six regular season fumbles
Returned a fumble 13 yards on 12-27-03
AFC Defensive Player of the Week on 09-14-03
AFC Defensive Player of the Week on 12-07-03
AFC Defensive Player of the Week on 10-03-04
AFC Defensive Player of the Week on 01-02-05
AFC Defensive Player of the Week on 10-30-05
Six regular season kickoff returns for 47 yards
Longest kickoff return was 11 yards on 11-17-02
AFC Pro Bowl linebacker in 2004
189 regular season games
2 playoff games
Member of the 2001, 2003, and 2004 championship
    teams
#86 pick in the 1996 College Draft
Ed Block Courage Award in 2000 and 2005
Arizona Wildcat

Bryant, Hubie (#45) and (#84)
WR/PR/KR, 1971
14 receptions for 212 yards and one touchdown
Caught a 10-yard touchdown pass on 10-31-71
Longest reception was 48 yards on 11-07-71
Four carries for one yard
Longest run was one yard on 11-28-71 and on 12-12-71
10 punt returns for 24 yards
Longest punt return was 16 yards on 10-03-71
10 kickoff returns for 252 yards
Longest kickoff return was 45 yards on 10-03-71
Recovered a fumble on 10-17-71
13 games
Minnesota Golden Gopher

Buben, Mark (#63)
Defensive Lineman, 1979–81
Returned an interception 49 yards on 10-04-81
Recovered two fumbles
Returned a fumble 31 yards on 09-06-81
32 games
Tufts Jumbo

Buckley, Terrell (#27) and (#22) "T-Buck"
Defensive Back (WR), 2001–02
Seven interceptions for 126 yards and one touchdown
Longest return was a 52-yard touchdown on 11-18-01
Only sack was made on 11-11-01
Was used as a wide receiver occasionally
31 regular season games
Three playoff games
Florida State Seminole

Bugenhagen, Gary (#67)
Offensive Lineman, 1970
10 games
Syracuse Orangeman

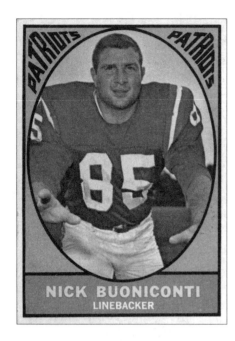

NICK BUONICONTI
LINEBACKER

Buoniconti, Nick (#85) "Skip"
Linebacker (PR), 1962–68
18 sacks
24 interceptions for 223 yards
Longest return was 41 yards on 10-23-66
Recovered six fumbles
Returned a fumble seven yards for a touchdown on 12-08-63
Blocked a 36-yard field-goal attempt on 09-19-65
blocked a 27-yard field goak attempt on 12-12-65
Blocked a 40-yard field-goal attempt on 10-13-68
Blocked an extra-point attempt on 09-25-66
Recorded a safety on 11-05-67
Only punt return was eight yards on 10-06-62
AFL Defensive Player of the Week on 11-05-67
AFL Defensive Player of the Week on 10-20-68
AFL All-Star linebacker in 1963, 1964, 1965, 1966, and 1967
91 regular season games
Two playoff games
13th round draft pick in 1962
Inducted into the Patriots Hall of Fame in 1992
Inducted into the Pro Football Hall of Fame in 2001
Notre Dame Fighting Irish

Burke, John (#85)
Tight End (KR), 1994–96
25 receptions for 241 yards
Longest reception was 21 yards on 10-23-95
Four kickoff returns for 18 yards
Longest kickoff return was seven yards on 12-16-95
Recovered a fumble on 09-10-95

43 regular season games
Four playoff games
#121 pick in the 1994 College Draft
Virginia Tech Hokie

Burks, Steve (#82)
WR/KR, 1975–77
13 receptions for 264 yards
Longest reception was 76 yards on 11-16-75
Only run was two yards on 12-12-76
Four kickoff returns for 65 yards
Longest kickoff return was 25 yards on 11-16-75
34 regular season games
Only playoff game appearance was on 12-18-76
#91 pick in the 1975 College Draft
Arkansas State Indian

RON BURTON
HALFBACK
BOSTON PATRIOTS

Burton, Ron (#22)
HB/KR/PR, 1960–65
429 carries for 1,536 yards and nine touchdowns
Longest run was 77 yards on 10-23-60
111 receptions for 1,205 yards and eight touchdowns
Longest reception was a 73-yard touchdown on 10-17-65
46 kickoff returns for 1,119 yards and one touchdown
Longest return was a 91-yard touchdown on 11-03-61
56 punt returns for 389 yards
Longest punt return was 62 yards on 11-12-61
Returned a missed field goal 91 yards for a touchdown on 11-11-62
Recovered 10 fumbles
69 regular season games

Two playoff games
First overall draft pick of the Boston Patriots
Inducted into College Football Hall of Fame on 12-04-90
Northwestern Wildcat

Butts, Marion (#44)
Running Back, 1994
243 carries for 703 yards and eight touchdowns
Longest run was 26 yards on 12-04-94
Nine receptions for 54 yards
Longest reception was 15 yards on 09-11-94
Recovered a fumble on 10-30-94
16 games
Florida State Seminole

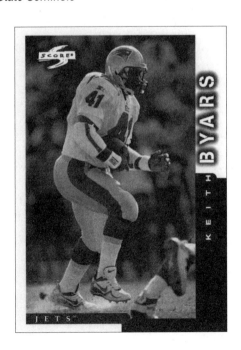

Byars, Keith (#41)
Fullback (TE), 1996–97
13 carries for 26 yards
Longest run was five yards on 09-14-97
47 receptions for 438 yards and five touchdowns
Longest reception was 51 yards on 11-23-97
Caught two-point conversion on 11-17-96
Recovered a Buffalo Bills onside kick on 10-27-96
25 regular season games
Five playoff games
Ohio State Buckeye

Byrd, Dennis (#78)
DE/DT, 1968
3.5 sacks
14 games
Sixth pick in the 1968 College Draft
North Carolina State Wolfpack

Cade, Eddie (#41)
Safety, 1995
10 games
Arizona State Sun Devil

Cagle, Johnny (#62) "Bull"
DT/LB (G), 1969
Played on both sides of the line of scrimmage
Six games
#344 pick in the 1969 College Draft
Clemson Tiger

Caldwell, Reche (#87)
Wide Receiver, 2006
61 receptions for 760 yards and four touchdowns
Longest reception was a 62-yard touchdown on
    12-31-06
Only carry was for five yards on 10-22-06
Recovered a fumble on 11-26-06
16 regular season games
Three playoff games
Florida Gator

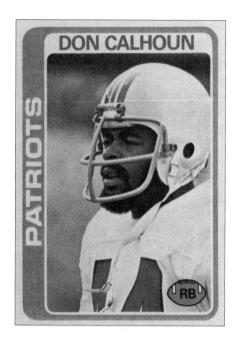

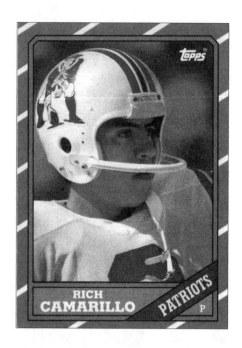

Calhoun, Don (#44) "Houn"
RB (KR), 1975–81
820 carries for 3,391 yards and 23 touchdowns
Longest run was 74 yards on 09-10-78
82 receptions for 614 yards and two touchdowns
Longest reception was a 62-yard touchdown on
    12-14-75
12 kickoff returns for 238 yards
Longest kickoff return was 33 yards on 11-07-76
Recovered a fumble on 12-16-79
93 regular season games
Only playoff game appearance was on 12-18-76
Kansas State Wildcat

Calloway, Chris (#82)
Wide Receiver, 2000
5 receptions for 95 yards
Longest reception was 28 yards on 10-08-00
Seven games
Michigan Wolverine

Camarillo, Rich (#3)
Punter, 1981–87
468 punts for 19,992 yards
Longest punt was 76 yards on 09-19-82
Recovered two fumbles
AFC Pro Bowl punter in 1983
85 regular season games
Six playoff games
Washington Husky

Canale, Justin (#63)
Guard (Kicker), 1965–68
Kicked an extra point on 11-05-67
Attempted an onside kick on 11-19-67
Kicked off in 54 games
Caught a deflected pass on 11-10-68
Recovered a SD Chargers onside kick on 10-31-65
56 games
Sixth round draft pick in 1965
Mississippi State Bulldog

Canale, John (#67) "Whit"
Defensive Lineman, 1968
Recovered a fumble on 12-15-68
13 games
Tennessee Volunteer

Canty, Chris (#26) "The Dancing Bear"
CB/PR/KR, 1997–98

Four sacks
Returned an interception 12 yards on 09-13-98
16 punt returns for 170 yards
Longest punt return was 36 yards on 10-25-98
15 kickoff returns for 313 yards
Longest kickoff return was 63 yards on 09-14-97
Recovered two fumbles
Returned a fumble nine yards on 12-22-97
32 regular season games
Three playoff games
#29 pick in the 1997 College Draft
Kansas State Wildcat

Cappadona, Bob (#33) "Cappy"
RB/KR, 1966–67

50 carries for 188 yards and one touchdown
Longest run was 13 yards on 10-23-66
Ran for a 1-yard touchdown on 12-11-66
Six receptions for 104 yards and one touchdown
Longest reception was 42 yards on 12-09-67
Had a 19-yard touchdown reception on 12-17-67
Caught a two-point conversion pass on 12-17-66
Six kickoff returns for 72 yards
Longest kickoff return was 15 yards on 09-09-67
27 games
Third-round draft pick in 1965
Northeastern University Husky

Cappelletti, Gino (#20) "Duke"
(PR/CB/KR) WR/K (RB), 1960–70

Only punt return was three yards on 09-09-60
Four interceptions for 61 yards during the 1960 season
Longest return was 37 yards on 10-16-60
Four kickoff returns for 100 yards in the 1960 season
Longest kickoff return was 37 yards on 12-18-60
Completed a two-point conversion pass on 10-08-60
292 receptions for 4,589 yards and 42 touchdowns
Longest reception was a 63-yard touchdown on
    11-13-66
Four carries for two yards (ran for a two-yard gain as a
    RB on 10-06-68)
Longest run was four yards on 11-20-64
Ran for three two-point conversions
Threw a fake field goal 27-yard touchdown pass on
    10-01-61
Caught a pass for a two-point conversion on 11-15-64
Recovered two fumbles
Advanced a fumble four yards on 11-20-64
176 field goals
Longest field goal was 53 yards on 11-28-65
346 extra points
AFL All-Star wide receiver in 1961, 1963, 1964, 1966,
    and 1968
AFL All-Star kicker in 1964, 1966, and 1968
AFL MVP and the Player of the Year in 1964
152 consecutive regular season games
Two playoff games
His uniform #20 was retired by the Patriots
Inducted into the Patriots Hall of Fame in 1992
Minnesota Golden Gopher

Carey, Brian (#81)
Wide Receiver, 1987
Two games
AIC Yellow Jacket

Carlson, Jeff (#17)
Quarterback, 1992
18 completions for 232 yards and one touchdown
Tossed a 6-yard touchdown pass on 12-13-92
Longest completion was 40 yards on 12-13-92
11 carries for 32 yards
Longest run was seven yards on 12-20-92
Recovered a fumble on 12-20-92
Three games
Weber State Wildcat

Carpenter, Rob (#81)
Wide Receiver, 1991
Three receptions for 45 yards
Longest reception was 23 yards on 12-08-91
Nine games
Syracuse Orangeman

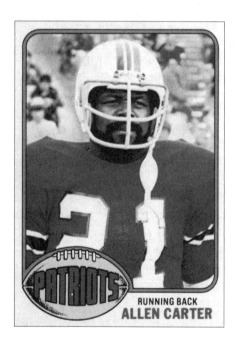

RUNNING BACK
ALLEN CARTER

Carter, Allen (#21)
RB/KR, 1975–76
22 carries for 95 yards
Longest run was 19 yards on 12-21-75
Two receptions for 39 yards
Longest reception was 26 yards on 10-05-75
33 kickoff returns for 898 yards and one touchdown
Longest return was a 99-yard touchdown on 12-21-75
Recovered a fumble on 12-21-75

15 games
#86 pick in the 1975 College Draft
USC Trojan

Carter, Chris (#42)
Safety, 1997–99
Three interceptions for 13 yards
Longest return was eight yards on 09-19-99
Two sacks
Recovered two fumbles
47 regular season games
Three playoff games
#89 pick in the 1997 College Draft
Texas Longhorn

Carter, Kent (#51)
Linebacker, 1974
Two games
USC Trojan

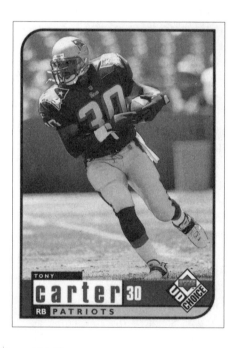

TONY
carter 30
RB PATRIOTS

Carter, Tony (#30)
Running Back (KR), 1998–2000
45 carries for 119 yards
Longest run was nine yards on 09-26-99 and on
    12-17-00
47 receptions for 347 yards
Longest reception was 49 yards on 11-23-98
Returned a kickoff return 16 yards on 12-04-00
Recovered a fumble on 10-31-99
43 regular season games
Only playoff game appearance was on 01-03-99
Minnesota Golden Gopher

Carthen, Jason (#99)
Linebacker, 1993–94
Six games
Ohio University Bobcat

Carwell, Larry (#41)
DB/PR/KR, 1969–72
10 interceptions for 186 yards and one touchdown
Longest return was a 53-yard touchdown on 12-05-71
13 punt returns for 93 yards
Longest punt return was 45 yards on 11-22-70
Two kickoff returns for 58 yards
Longest kickoff return was 30 yards on 11-08-70
Recovered two fumbles
Blocked a 51-yard field-goal attempt on 09-17-72
Returned a blocked FG 45 yards for a touchdown on
    09-17-72
51 games
Iowa State Cyclone

Cash, Rick (#63) "Thumper"
Defensive Tackle, 1972–73
Four sacks
Recovered three fumbles
Blocked a 48-yard field-goal attempt on 11-12-72
28 games
NE Missouri Bulldog

Cassel, Matt (#16)
Quarterback (P), 2005–08
349 completions for 3,946 yards and 23 touchdowns
Longest completion was 76 yards on 12-21-08
85 carries for 298 yards and three touchdowns

Longest run was 19 yards on 11-13-08
Recovered three fumbles
Punted once for 57 yards on 12-28-08
AFC Offensive Player of the Week on 10-20-08
AFC Offensive Player of the Week on 11-23-08
30 regular season games
Four playoff games
#230 pick in the 2005 College Draft
USC Trojan

Catanho, Alcides (#54)
Linebacker, 1995
Recovered a fumble on 11-05-95
12 games
Rutgers Scarlet Knight

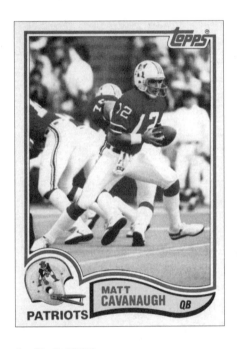

Cavanaugh, Matt (#12)
Quarterback, 1979–82
206 completions for 3,018 yards and 19 touchdowns
Longest completion was a 75-yard touchdown on
    12-26-82
39 carries for 190 yards and three touchdowns
Longest run was 22 yards on 12-14-80
Caught an eight-yard flea-flicker pass on 09-27-81
Recovered a fumble on 11-23-80
52 regular season games
Only playoff game appearance was on 01-08-83
#50 pick in the 1978 College Draft
Pittsburgh Panther

Centers, Larry (#31)
Fullback, 2003
21 carries for 82 yards
Longest run was 13 yards on 09-07-03
19 receptions for 106 yards and one touchdown
Longest reception was 14 yards on 09-28-03
Caught a seven-yard touchdown pass on 09-28-03
Recovered a fumble on 09-21-03
Nine regular season games
Three playoff games
Member of the 2003 championship team
Stephen F. Austin State Lumberjack

Chandler, Al (#87) and (#82)
Tight End, 1976–79
13 receptions for 119 yards and three touchdowns
Longest reception was 29 yards on 09-12-76
Recovered two fumbles
39 regular season games
Only playoff game appearance was on 12-18-76
Oklahoma Sooner

EDGAR CHANDLER   MIDDLE LINEBACKER
PATRIOTS

Chandler, Edgar (#50)
Linebacker, 1973
Recovered two fumbles
Returned a fumble 14 yards on 11-04-73
Recorded a sack on 12-09-73
12 games
Georgia Bulldog

Chapple, Dave (#10)
Punter, 1974
26 punts for 967 yards
Longest punt was 57 yards on 12-15-74
Five games
California Gaucho

Charles, John (#25) "J.C."
Defensive Back, 1967–69
6 interceptions for 110 yards and two touchdowns
Longest return was a 35-yard touchdown on 10-29-67
Blocked an extra-point attempt on 09-03-67
Blocked a 47-yard field-goal attempt on 09-08-68
Blocked a 25-yard field-goal attempt on 10-13-68
Recovered a fumble on 10-19-69
39 games
#21 pick in the 1967 College Draft
Purdue Boilermaker

Chatham, Matt (#58)
Linebacker, 2000–05
2.5 sacks
Recovered two fumbles
Returned a fumble 30 yards for a touchdown on
    10-12-03
66 regular season games
10 playoff games
Member of the 2001, 2003, and 2004 championship
    teams
South Dakota Coyote

Cherry, Je'Rod (#30)
Defensive Back, 2001–2004
Recorded a sack on 09-07-03
Recovered a blocked field goal on 10-21-01
55 regular season games
Six playoff games
Member of the 2001, 2003, and 2004 championship
    teams
California Golden Bear

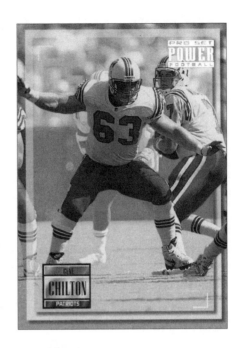

Cheyunski, Jim (#50) "Chey"
Linebacker, 1968–72
Five sacks
Three interceptions for 82 yards
Longest return was 37 yards on 11-16-69
Recovered four fumbles
Returned a fumble three yards on 12-07-69
Recovered a Raiders onside kick on 10-06-68
AFL Defensive Player of the Week on 11-16-69
NFL Defensive Player of the Week on 09-24-72
66 games
#305 pick in the 1968 College Draft
Syracuse Orangeman

Childress, Brandon (#13) "Bam"
WR/DB, 2005–06
Caught five passes for 39 yards
Longest reception was 21 yards on 01-01-06
Three games
Ohio State Buckeye

Childress, Freddie (#61) "The Big Chill"
Guard/Tackle (LS), 1991
Recovered a fumble for a touchdown on 10-20-91
15 games
Arkansas Razorback

Chilton, Gene (#63)
Center/Tackle, 1990–92
Recovered two fumbles
36 games
Texas Longhorn

Christy, Dick (#23)
HB/KR/PR, 1960
78 carries for 363 yards and four touchdowns
Longest run was 48 yards on 09-23-60
26 receptions for 268 yards and two touchdowns
Longest reception was 53 yards on 11-04-60
24 kickoff returns for 617 yards
Longest kickoff return was 52 yards on 11-11-60
Eight punt returns for 73 yards
Longest punt return was 29 yards on 10-16-60
Six completions for 94 yards and two touchdowns
Longest completion was 39 yards on 09-23-60
13 games
North Carolina State Wolfpack

Chung, Eugene (#69)
Offensive Lineman, 1992–94
34 games
#13 pick in the 1992 College Draft
Virginia Tech Hokie

Cindrich, Ralph (#55)
Linebacker, 1972
12 games
Pittsburgh Panther

Clark, Allan (#35) "Kamikazee Kid" and "Smiley"
RB/KR, 1979–80
28 carries for 140 yards and three touchdowns
Longest run was 19 yards on 11-18-79
Two receptions for 35 yards
Longest reception was 20 yards on 11-18-79
40 kickoff returns for 837 yards
Longest kickoff return was 38 yards on 10-14-79
Recovered three fumbles
Returned a fumble 15 yards for a touchdown on
    11-23-80
27 games
#271 pick in the 1979 College Draft
Northern Arizona Lumberjack

Clark, Gail (#54)
Linebacker, 1974
Eight games
Michigan State Spartan

Clark, Phil (#22) "PC"
Defensive Back, 1971
Two games
Northwestern Wildcat

Clark, Rico (#39)
Defensive Back, 1999
Only game played was on 01-02-00
Louisville Cardinal

Clark, Steve (#65)
Defensive End, 1981
Seven games
#130 pick in the 1981 College Draft
Kansas State Wildcat

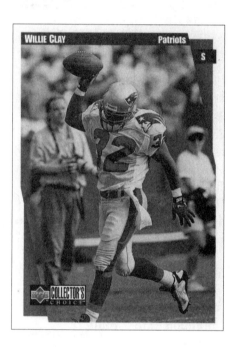

Clay, Willie (#32) "Big Play"
Free Safety, 1996–98
13 interceptions for 178 yards and one touchdown
Longest return was a 53-yard touchdown on 08-31-97
Recovered four fumbles
Returned a fumble 17 yards on 10-20-96
AFC Defensive Player of the Week on 12-20-98
48 regular season games
Six playoff games
Georgia Tech Yellow Jacket

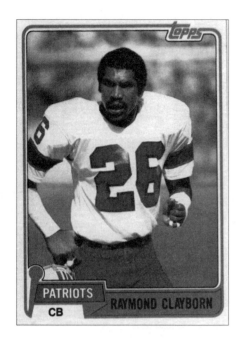

Clayborn, Raymond (#26) "Claybo" and "Bones"
CB/KR, 1977–88
36 interceptions for 555 yards and one touchdown
Longest return was 85 yards on 10-07-84
Returned an interception 27 yards for a touchdown
    on 10-13-85
Recorded a safety on 11-13-77
Recorded a sack on 12-04-77
Recovered nine regular season fumbles
Returned a blocked FG 71 yards for a touchdown on
    10-18-87
57 kickoff returns for 1,538 yards and three
    touchdowns
Longest kickoff return was a 101-yard touchdown on
    12-18-77
Returned a kickoff 100 yards for a touchdown on
    10-02-77
Returned a kickoff 93 yards for a touchdown on
    11-06-77
AFC Pro Bowl cornerback in 1983, 1985 and 1986
191 regular season games
Seven playoff games
#16 pick in the 1977 College Draft
Texas Longhorn

Clayton, Stan (#76)
Guard/Tackle, 1990
11 games
Penn State Nittany Lion

Cleeland, Cam (#85)
Tight End, 2002
16 receptions for 112 yards and one touchdown
Longest reception was 22 yards on 11-17-02
Caught a one-yard touchdown pass on 09-15-02
12 games
Washington Husky

Cloud, Mike (#21)
RB/KR, 2003 and 2005
50 carries for 177 yards and five touchdowns
Longest run was 42 yards on 10-05-03
Only reception was eight yards on 11-23-03
Three kickoff returns for 53 yards
Longest kickoff return was 19 yards on 11-23-03
11 games
Member of the 2003 championship team
Boston College Eagle

Cloutier, Dave (#28)
DB/PR/KR, 1964
20 punt returns for 136 yards
Longest punt return was 40 yards on 10-31-64
Only kickoff return was 46 yards on 10-09-64
12 games
Maine Black Bear

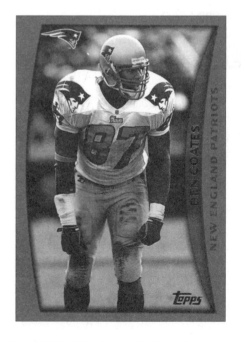

Coates, Ben (#87) "Big" and "Winter"
Tight End (KR), 1991–99
490 receptions for 5,471 yards and 50 touchdowns
Longest reception was an 84-yard touchdown on
    11-03-96
Caught a two-point conversion pass on 10-06-96

Three carries for a net loss of four yards
Longest run was two yards on 12-06-92
Two kickoff returns for 26 yards
Longest kickoff return was 20 yards on 12-07-97
Recovered a Colts onside kick on 11-30-97
Recovered a Giants onside kick on 09-26-99
Recovered two fumbles
AFC Pro Bowl TE in 1994, 1995, 1996, 1997, and 1998
142 regular season games
Seven playoff games
#124 pick in the 1991 College Draft
Livingstone College Fighting Blue Bear

Cobbs, Cedric (#34)
Running Back, 2004
22 carries for 50 yards
Longest run was 13 yards on 01-02-05
Four games
Member of the 2004 championship team
#128 pick in the 2004 College Draft
Arkansas Razorback

Cobbs, Robert (#43) "Duffy"
Defensive Back, 1987
Three games
Penn State Nittany Lion

Coffey, Wayne (#83)
Wide Receiver, 1987
Three receptions for 66 yards
Longest reception was 35 yards on 10-04-87
Three games
Southwest Texas State Bobcat

Cohen, Abe (#62)
Guard/Special Team, 1960
Blocked a Broncos punt on 10-23-60
14 games
Tenn-Chattanooga Moccasin

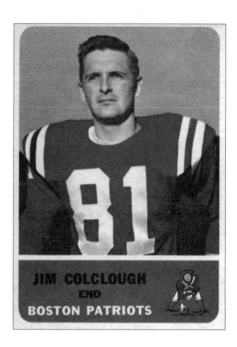

JIM COLCLOUGH
END
BOSTON PATRIOTS

Colclough, Jim (#81) "Coleslaw"
Wide Receiver (KR), 1960–68
283 receptions for 5,001 yards and 39 touchdowns
Longest reception was a 78-yard touchdown on
    11-30-62
Caught a two-point pass on 10-16-64 and on 12-20-64
Four carries for 51 yards
Longest run was 16 yards on 10-29-61 and on 12-09-61
Recovered a fumble on 09-23-61
Returned a kickoff two yards on 11-13-66
AFL All-Star wide receiver in 1962
126 regular season games
Two playoff games
Boston College Eagle

Coleman, Dennis (#53)
Linebacker, 1971
Nine games
Mississippi Rebel

Coleman, Eric (#22)
Defensive Back, 1989–90
Returned an interception one yard on 10-08-89
15 games
#43 pick in the 1989 College Draft
Wyoming Cowboy

Coleman, Fred (#84)
Wide Receiver/Special Team, 2001–02
Two receptions for 50 yards
Longest reception was 46 yards on 12-02-01
Recovered a Patriots onside kick on 12-22-01
Recovered a Dolphins onside kick on 12-22-01
Recovered a fumble on 12-22-01
Nine regular season games
Three playoff games
Member of the 2001 championship team
Washington Husky

Coleman, Pat (#47)
Kickoff Returnman, 1990
Two kickoff returns for 18 yards
Longest kickoff return was 12 yards on 11-25-90
Only game played was on 11-25-90
Mississippi Rebel

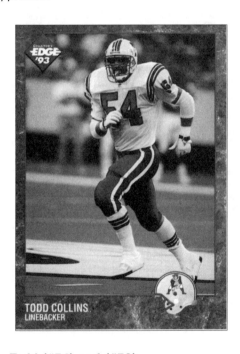

Collins, Todd (#54) and (#59)
Linebacker, 1992–94 and 1996–98
2.5 sacks
Two regular season interceptions for 15 yards
Longest return was eight yards on 09-19-93
Recovered two fumbles
Returned a fumble two yards on 12-19-93
76 regular season games
Five playoff games
#64 pick in the 1994 College Draft
Carson-Newman Eagle

Collins, Tony (#33) "The Blade" and "TC"
RB/KR/PR, 1981–87
1,191 carries for 4,647 yards and 32 touchdowns
Longest run was 54 yards on 09-12-82
261 receptions for 2,356 yards and 12 touchdowns
Longest reception was 49 yards on 10-27-85 and
    11-02-86
65 kickoff returns for 1,335 yards
Longest kickoff return was 46 yards on 11-04-84
Three punt returns for 15 yards
Longest punt return was 15 yards on 12-13-81
Recovered 11 fumbles
AFC Pro Bowl running back in 1983
102 regular season games
Six playoff games
#47 pick in the 1981 College Draft
East Carolina Pirate

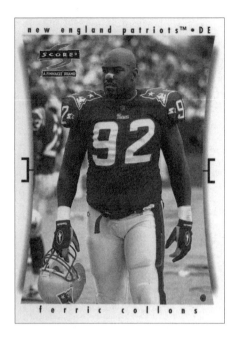

Collons, Ferric (#92)
Defensive End, 1995–99
7.5 sacks
Blocked a 47-yard field-goal attempt on 11-08-98
Returned a fumble five yards on 09-21-97
64 regular season games
Four playoff games
California Golden Bear

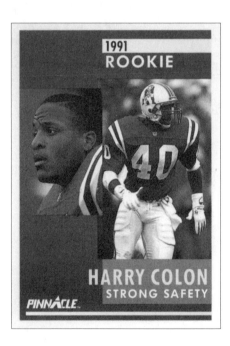

Colon, Harry (#40)
Defensive Back, 1991
Recovered two fumbles
16 games
#196 pick in the 1991 College Draft

Missouri Tiger

Colton, George (#63)
Offensive Guard, 1987
Recovered a fumble on 10-04-87
Three games
#248 pick in the 1986 College Draft
Maryland Terrapin

Colvin, Rosevelt (#59) and (#95) "Rosey"
Linebacker, 2003–08
26.5 sacks
Returned an interception four yards on 09-16-07
Five fumble recoveries
Returned a strip sack 11 yards for a touchdown on
    10-28-07
65 regular season games
Eight playoff games
Member of the 2003 and 2004 championship teams
Ed Block Courage Award in 2004
Purdue Boilermaker

Compton, Mike (#77) "The Thumb"
Offensive Lineman, 2001–03
34 regular season games
Three playoff games
Member of the 2001 and 2003 championship teams
West Virginia Mountaineer

Condon, Tom (#63)
Offensive Guard, 1985
Only game played was on 09-15-85
Boston College Eagle

Conn, Dick (#22)
DB/KR/PR, 1975–79
Returned an interception 24 yards on 09-24-78
Three kickoff returns for 55 yards
Longest return was 26 yards on 12-12-76 and on
    12-18-78
Only punt return was two yards on 10-22-78
46 regular season games
Two playoff games
Georgia Bulldog

MARV COOK

Cook, Marv (#46) and (#85)
TE/LS (KR), 1989–93
210 receptions for 1,843 yards and 11 touchdowns
Longest reception was 49 yards on 09-22-91
Returned a kickoff eight yards on 01-02-94
Recovered three fumbles
AFC Pro Bowl tight end in 1991 and 1992
80 games
#63 pick in the 1989 College Draft
Iowa Hawkeye

Cooks, Terrence (#58)
Linebacker, 1989
Three games
Nicholls State Colonel

Corbett, Steve (#62)
Offensive Guard, 1975
14 games
#30 pick in the 1974 College Draft
Boston College Eagle

Corcoran, Jim (#15) "King"
Quarterback, 1968
Three completions for 33 yards
Longest completion was 14 yards on 11-24-68
Two games
Maryland Terrapin

Corsetti, Rico (#93)
Special Team Player, 1987
Two games
Bates Bobcat

Costict, Ray (#55) "Little Backer"
Linebacker, 1977–79
Two sacks
Returned an interception 22 yards on 09-09-79
Recovered four fumbles
Returned a fumble 16 yards on 10-28-79
46 regular season games
Only playoff game appearance was on 12-31-78
#313 pick in the 1977 College Draft
Mississippi State Bulldog

Cottrell, Dana (#45)
Special Team/Linebacker, 1998
Two regular season games
Only playoff game appearance was on 01-03-99
Syracuse Orangeman

Cowan, Larry (#44)
RB/Special Team, 1982
Six regular season games
Only playoff game appearance was on 01-08-83
Jackson State Tiger

Cox, Bryan (#51)
Linebacker (RB), 2001
Returned a fumble nine yards on 10-14-01
Caught a seven-yard pass, as a RB, on 10-14-01
11 regular season games
Three playoff games
Member of the 2001 championship team
Western Illinois Leatherneck

Crabtree, Eric (#10) "Tree"
Wide Receiver, 1971
Nine receptions for 120 yards and one touchdown
Longest reception was a 31-yard touchdown on
    11-14-71
Two carries for 11 yards
Longest run was 18 yards on 11-14-71
Six games
Pittsburgh Panther

Crawford, Elbert (#65)
Center/Guard, 1990–91
30 games
Arkansas Razorback

Crawford, Jim (#30) "Cowboy"
RB (KR), 1960–64
302 carries for 1,078 yards and five touchdowns
Longest run was a 39-yard touchdown on 11-18-60

52 receptions for 501 yards and two touchdowns
Longest reception was 44 yards on 09-21-62
Caught two two-point conversions
Two kickoff returns for 24 yards
Longest kickoff return was 18 yards on 11-23-62
Both of his pass attempts were completed
Two completions for 27 yards
Longest completion was 15 yards on 09-14-63
Recovered a fumble on 11-23-62
54 games
Wyoming Cowboy

Crawford, Vernon (#99)
LB/Special Team, 1997–99
Recovered a fumble on 12-07-97
41 regular season games
Only playoff game appearance was on 01-03-99
#159 pick in the 1997 College Draft
Florida State Seminole

Creswell, Smiley (#92)
Defensive End, 1985 playoffs
Two playoff games
#118 pick in the 1983 College Draft
Michigan State Spartan

Crittenden, Ray (#81)
WR/KR/PR, 1993–94
44 receptions for 672 yards and four touchdowns
Longest reception was 44 yards on 09-26-93
47 kickoff returns for 938 yards
Longest kickoff return was 44 yards on 09-26-93
21 punt returns for 192 yards
Longest punt return was 30 yards on 09-05-93

Ran for a three-yard loss on 09-26-93
Recovered a fumble on 09-11-94
32 regular season games
Only playoff game appearance was on 01-01-95
Virginia Tech Hokie

Croom, Corey (#26)
RB/KR, 1993–95
73 carries for 252 yards and one touchdown
Ran for a five-yard touchdown on 12-26-93
Longest run was 22 yards on 12-26-93
Nine receptions for 100 yards
Longest reception was 21 yards on 12-05-93
10 kickoff returns for 172 yards
Longest kickoff return was 24 yards on 09-11-94
43 regular season games
Only playoff game appearance was on 01-01-95
Ball State Cardinal

Cross, Bobby (#77)
Offensive Tackle, 1960
Four games
Kilgore Jr. College Ranger

Crouthamel, Jake (#34)
RB/KR, 1960
Four carries for 16 yards
Longest run was six yards on 10-23-60
Two kickoff returns for 27 yards
Longest kickoff return was 15 yards on 10-23-60
Two games
Dartmouth Big Green

Crow, Al (#72)
Defensive Tackle, 1960
Three games
William and Mary Tribe

Crump, George (#91)
Defensive End, 1982
Recorded a safety on 11-28-82
Only sack was made on 11-28-82
Nine regular season games
Only playoff game appearance was on 01-08-83
#85 pick in the 1982 College Draft
East Carolina Pirate

Crump, Harry (#31) "Crunch"
FB/KR (LB), 1963
49 carries for 120 yards and five touchdowns
Longest run was 21 yards on 10-26-63
Six receptions for 46 yards
Longest reception was 12 yards on 11-10-63

Three kickoff returns for 33 yards
Longest kickoff return was 14 yards on 10-05-63
Was occasionally used as a linebacker
14 regular season games
Two playoff games
Boston College Eagle

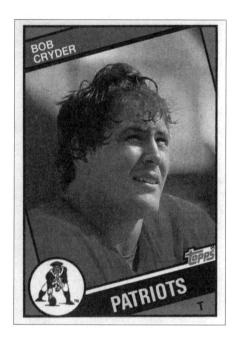

Cryder, Bob (#75)
Offensive Lineman, 1978–83
Recovered three fumbles
75 regular season games
Only playoff game appearance was on 01-08-83
#18 pick in the 1978 College Draft
Alabama Crimson Tide

Cudzik, Walt (#56) and (#54) "Mike"
Center/LS/LB (K), 1960–63
Caught a deflected pass for an 11-yard gain on
    10-28-60
Attempted a 48-yard field goal on 12-11-60
Recovered a Buffalo Bills onside kick on 09-23-61
56 regular season games
Two playoff games
Purdue Boilermaker

Cullors, Derrick (#29) "Flying"
RB/KR, 1997–98
40 carries for 149 yards
Longest run was 24 yards on 11-16-97
16 receptions for 154 yards and one touchdown
Caught a nine-yard touchdown pass on 11-29-98
Longest reception was 43 yards on 10-04-98
60 kickoff returns for 1,471 yards and one touchdown
Longest return was an 86-yard touchdown on 11-09-97
31 regular season games
Three playoff games
Murray State Racer

Cunningham, Jay (#21) "The Dart"
DB/KR/PR, 1965–67
Three interceptions for 70 yards and one touchdown
Longest return was a 54-yard touchdown on 10-15-67
64 kickoff returns 1,372 yards
Longest kickoff return was 45 yards on 11-14-65
22 punt returns for 140 yards
Longest punt return was 44 yards on 10-22-67
Recorded a safety on 10-31-65
Recovered three fumbles
Returned a fumble 12 yards on 09-19-65
40 games
14th round draft pick in 1964
Bowling Green State Falcon

Cunningham, Sam (#39) "Bam"
Running Back, 1973–79 and 1981–82
1,385 carries for 5,453 yards and 43 touchdowns
Longest run was a 75-yard touchdown on 10-20-74
210 receptions for 1,905 yards and six touchdowns
Longest reception was 41 yards on 10-03-76
Recovered eight fumbles
AFC Pro Bowl running back in 1978
107 regular season games
Two playoff games
#11 pick in the 1973 College Draft
USC Trojan

Currier, Bill (#28)
DB-KR, 1980
Six kickoff returns for 98 yards
Longest kickoff return was 26 yards on 10-26-80
16 games
South Carolina Gamecock

Cusick, Pete (#76)
Nose Tackle, 1975
Recorded a sack on 12-07-75
Blocked two field-goal attempts on 12-07-75
13 games
#66 pick in the 1975 College Draft
Ohio State Buckeye

Dalton, Antico (#93)
Special Team/Linebacker, 2000
Recovered a fumble on 12-17-00
Three games
Hampton Pirate

Damkroger, Maury (#51)
Linebacker, 1974–75
13 games
#178 pick in the 1974 College Draft
Nebraska Cornhusker

Danenhauer, Bill (#77)
Defensive End, 1960
Three games
Emporia State Hornet

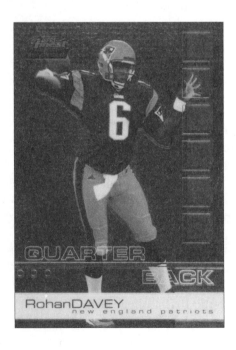

Davey, Rohan (#6)
Quarterback, 2002–2004
Eight completions for 88 yards
Longest completion was 20 yards on 12-05-04
Six carries for a net loss of five yards
Longest run was three yards on 01-02-05
Seven regular season games
Member of the 2003 and 2004 championship teams
#117 pick in the 2002 College Draft
LSU Tiger

Davis, Andre' (#18)
WR/KR, 2005
Nine receptions for 190 yards and one touchdown
Longest reception was a 60-yard touchdown on
    11-20-05
Three kickoff returns for 108 yards
Longest kickoff return was 65 yards on 01-01-06
Nine regular season games
Two playoff games
Virginia Tech Hokie

Davis, Don (#51) "Double D"
LB/DB/Special Team, 2003–06
59 regular season games
Eight playoff games
Member of the 2003 and 2004 championship teams
Kansas Jayhawk

Davis, Elgin (#40)
RB/KR, 1987–88
Nine carries for 43 yards
Longest run was 27 yards on 10-18-87
11 kickoff returns for 240 yards
Longest kickoff return was 43 yards on 11-29-87
Nine games
#330 pick in the 1987 College Draft
Central Florida Golden Knight

Davis, Greg (#5)
Kicker, 1989
16 field goals
Longest field goal was 52 yards on 10-15-89
13 extra points
Nine games
Citadel Bulldog

Davis, Jack (#65)
Offensive Guard, 1960
Returned a blocked punt five yards on 10-23-60
14 games
Maryland Terrapin

Davis, Shockmain (#84)
WR/KR, 2000
Two receptions for 12 yards
Longest reception was nine yards on 11-23-00
Two kickoff returns for 45 yards
Longest kickoff return was 32 yards on 09-17-00
12 games
Angelo State Ram

Dawson, Bill (#83) "Red"
DE/OE/LB, 1965
Played on both sides of the line of scrimmage
Nine games
19th round draft pick in 1964
Florida State Seminole

Dawson, Lin (#87) "The Reverend"
Tight End, 1981–90
117 receptions for 1,233 yards and eight touchdowns
Longest reception was 42 yards on 12-20-81
Recovered two fumbles
105 regular season games
Five playoff games
#212 pick in the 1981 College Draft
Ed Block Courage Award in 1987
North Carolina State Wolfpack

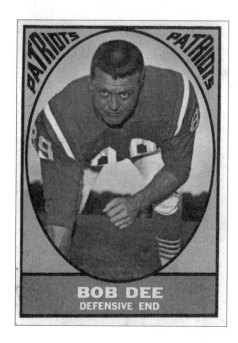

BOB DEE
DEFENSIVE END

Dee, Bob (#89) "Bubba"
Defensive End (LB), 1960–67
33 sacks
13 fumble recoveries
Returned a fumble 30 yards on 10-22-61
Returned a fumble four yards on 11-20-66

Recovered a Chargers onside kick on 09-20-64
Returned an interception 14 yards on 10-16-60
Blocked a 37-yard field-goal attempt on 09-21-62
Blocked a Denver Broncos punt on 10-04-64
AFL All-Star DE in 1961, 1963, 1964, and 1965
112 consecutive regular season games
Two playoff games
His uniform #89 was retired on "Dee Day" on 10-13-68
Inducted into the Patriots Hall of Fame on 08-18-93
Holy Cross Crusader

Dellenbach, Jeff (#66)
Center, 1995–96
17 games
Wisconsin Badger

DeLucca, Jerry (#74)
Tackle (KR), 1960–61 and 1963–64
Returned a kickoff eight yards on 10-28-60
31 games
Middle Tennessee State Blue Raider

Denson, Damon (#61)
Guard (DL), 1997–99
Was a defensive lineman on special teams
14 regular season games
Only playoff game was on 01-03-99
#97 pick in 1997 Draft
Michigan Wolverine

DeOssie, Steve (#50) and (#99)
LB/LS (KR), 1994–95
Returned a kickoff 14 yards on 11-13-94
32 regular season games
Only playoff game appearance was on 01-01-95
Boston College Eagle

DeRiggi, Fred (#71)
Nose Tackle, 1990
Two games
Syracuse Orangeman

DeVree, Tyson (#85)
Tight End, 2008
Two games
Colorado Buffalo

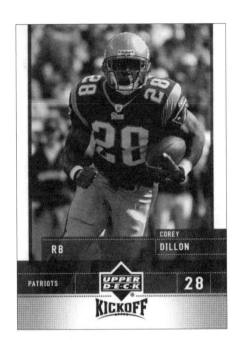

Dillon, Corey (#28) "Clock Killin"
Running Back, 2004–06
753 carries for 3,180 yards and 37 touchdowns
Longest run was 50 yards on 11-12-06
52 receptions for 431 yards and two touchdowns
Longest reception was 52 yards on 12-31-06
Ran for a two-point conversion on 11-28-04
Recovered a fumble on 09-09-04
AFC Pro Bowl running back in 2004
43 regular season games
Eight playoff games
Member of the 2004 championship team
Washington Husky

Dimitroff, Tom (#15)
Quarterback, 1960
Three games
Miami Redskin

Discenzo, Tony (#76)
Tackle (Kicker), 1960
Booted the first AFL preseason kickoff on 07-30-60
Five games
Michigan State Spartan

Doig, Steve (#59)
Linebacker, 1986–87
Recovered a fumble on 12-22-86
Six regular season games
Only playoff game appearance was on 01-04-87
New Hampshire Wildcat

Dombroski, Paul (#47)
DB/KR, 1981–84
Returned an interception 23 yards on 09-16-84
Recovered a fumble on 12-05-82
Three kickoff returns for 66 yards
Longest kickoff return was 24 yards on 12-20-81
36 regular season games
Only playoff game appearance was on 01-08-83
Linfield Wildcat

Donnalley, Kevin (#23)
Defensive Back, 1981
Only game was played on 10-25-81
North Dakota State Bison

Dorsey, Nate (#66)
Defensive End, 1973
Two games
Mississippi Valley State Delta Devil

Douglas, David (#67)
Offensive Lineman, 1989–90
16 games
Tennessee Volunteer

Dowling, Brian (#14) "BD"
Quarterback, 1972–73
29 completions for 383 yards and two touchdowns
Longest completion was 42 yards on 10-22-72
Seven carries for 35 yards and three touchdowns
Longest run was 11 yards on 12-17-72
Recovered a fumble on 09-17-72
25 games
Yale Bulldog

Dressler, Doug (#44)
Running Back, 1975
Three carries for eight yards
Longest run was six yards on 10-05-75
Only reception was a loss of one yard on 10-05-75
Five games
California State Wildcat

Dukes, Mike (#54)
Linebacker (KR), 1964–65
Four sacks
Two interceptions for 16 yards
Longest return was 10 yards on 10-31-65
Recovered five fumbles
Five kickoff returns for 78 yards
Longest kickoff return was 20 yards on 10-17-65
25 games
Clemson Tiger

DuLac, Bill (#68)
Offensive Guard, 1974–75
Recovered two fumbles
26 games
Eastern Michigan Huron

Dumler, Doug (#58)
Center, 1973–75
42 games
#108 pick in the 1973 College Draft
Nebraska Cornhusker

Dupard, Reggie (#21)
RB/KR, 1986–89
186 carries for 571 yards and six touchdowns
Longest run was 49 yards on 12-06-87
43 receptions for 303 yards
Longest reception was 45 yards on 09-17-89
Seven kickoff returns for 111 yards
Longest return was 21 yards on 11-30-86 and 11-15-87
Recovered two fumbles
37 regular season games
Only playoff game appearance was on 01-04-87
#26 pick in the 1986 College Draft
SMU Mustang

Durko, Sandy (#22)
DB/PR, 1973–74
Three interceptions for 26 yards
Longest return was 16 yards on 12-02-73
Four punt returns for 22 yards
Longest punt return was 15 yards on 11-04-73

Co-returned a blocked punt eight yards on 10-14-73
25 games
USC Trojan

Dwight, Tim (#86)
WR/PR/KR, 2005
19 receptions for 332 yards and three touchdowns
Longest reception was 59 yards on 11-13-05
Four carries for 11 yards
Longest run was 12 yards on 11-27-05
32 punt returns for 273 yards
Longest punt return was 29 yards on 11-07-75
10 kickoff returns for 250 yards
Longest kickoff return was 38 yards on 01-01-06
Recovered a fumble on 09-25-05
16 regular season games
Two playoff games
Iowa Hawkeye

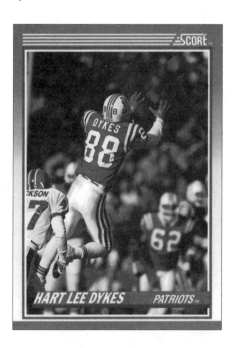

Dykes, Hart Lee (#88) "Bye Bye"
Wide Receiver, 1989–90
83 receptions for 1,344 yards and seven touchdowns
Longest reception was 42 yards on 12-03-89
Recovered a Patriots onside kick on 11-12-89
Recovered a fumble on 11-19-89
26 games
#16 pick in the 1989 College Draft
Oklahoma State Cowboy

Eason, Charles (#11) "Tony"
Quarterback, 1983–89
876 completions for 10,732 yards and 60 touchdowns
Longest completion was a 90-yard touchdown on
      09-15-85
126 carries for 474 yards and six touchdowns
Longest run was 26 yards on 11-16-86
AFC Offensive Player of the Week on 09-16-84
Recovered seven fumbles
72 regular season games
Five playoff games
#15 pick in the 1983 College Draft
Illinois Fighting Illini

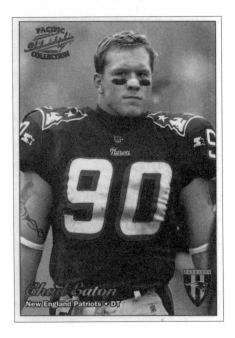

Eaton, Chad (#90)
Defensive Lineman, 1996–2000
14 sacks
Blocked a 38-yard field-goal attempt on 10-19-98
Blocked two field-goal attempts on 12-17-00
Recovered five fumbles
Returned a fumble 30 yards on 12-26-99
Returned a fumble 23 yards for a touchdown on
      01-02-00
AFC Defensive Player of the Week on 12-06-98
65 regular season games
Six playoff games
Washington State Cougar

Eckel, Kyle (#38)
Running Back, 2007
33 carries for 90 yards and two touchdowns
Longest run was 14 yards on 11-18-07
Only reception was for six yards on 11-18-07
12 games
Three playoff games
Navy Midshipman

Edmunds, Randy (#51)
Linebacker, 1971
Recovered a fumble on 12-05-71
14 games
Georgia Tech Yellow Jacket

Edwards, Marc (#44)
FB (KR), 2001–02
82 carries for 237 yards and one touchdown
Ran for a four-yard touchdown on 12-02-01
Longest run was 17 yards on 11-28-02
48 receptions for 362 yards and two touchdowns
Longest reception was 27 yards on 11-24-02
Three kickoff returns for 27 yards
Longest return was 15 yards on 09-29-02
Recovered a fumble on 10-14-01
32 regular season games
Three playoff games
Member of the 2001 championship team
Notre Dame Fighting Irish

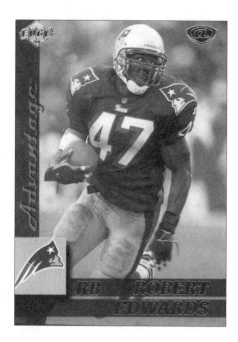

Edwards, Robert (#47)
Running Back, 1998
291 carries for 1,115 yards and nine touchdowns
Longest run was 53 yards on 09-20-98 and on 12-13-98
35 receptions for 331 yards and three touchdowns
Longest reception was 46 yards on 11-23-98
Recovered two fumbles
16 regular season games
Only playoff game appearance was on 01-03-99
#18 pick in the 1998 College Draft
Georgia Bulldog

Edwards, Tim (#98)
Defensive Tackle, 1992
Only sack was made on 11-01-92
14 games
#307 pick in the 1991 College Draft
Delta State Statesman

Egu, Patrick (#33)
RB/KR, 1989
Three carries for 20 yards and one touchdown
Longest run was a 15-yard touchdown on 11-19-89
Two kickoff returns for 26 yards
Longest return was 22 yards on 12-17-89
Recovered a fumble on 12-17-89
Seven games
Nevada Reno Wolf Pack

Eisenhauer, Larry (#72) "Wild Man"
Defensive End, 1961–69
45.5 sacks
Only interception was not returned on 12-01-63
Blocked a nine-yard field-goal attempt on 10-16-64
Blocked a 35-yard field-goal attempt on 10-31-65
Recovered 12 fumbles
Returned a fumble nine yards on 12-09-62
Returned a fumble seven yards on 10-11-63
Returned a fumble three yards on 10-15-67
AFL Defensive Player of the Week on 09-24-67
AFL All-Star DE in 1962, 1963, 1964, and 1966
115 regular season games
Two playoff games
Sixth round draft pick in 1961
Boston College Eagle

Eitzmann, Chris (#46)
Tight End, 2000
Five games
Harvard Crimson

Ellard, Henry (#18)
Wide Receiver, 1998
Five receptions for 86 yards
Longest reception was 19 yards on 11-01-98
Five games
Fresno State Bulldog

Ellis, Edward (#66)
Offensive Tackle, 1997–99
Nine games
#125 pick in 1997 College Draft
Buffalo Bull

Ellison, Jerry (#35)
RB (KR), 1999
Two carries for 10 yards
Longest run was eight yards on 10-31-99
Four receptions for 50 yards
Longest reception was 23 yards on 12-19-99
Only kickoff return was 13 yards on 12-19-99
12 games
Tennessee Chattanooga Moccasin

Emanuel, Bert (#87)
Wide Receiver, 2001
Four receptions for 25 yards
Longest reception was 16 yards on 09-09-01
Two games
Rice Owl

Evans, Heath (#44)
Fullback (KR), 2005–08
123 carries for 453 yards and three touchdowns
Longest run was 35 yards on 10-30-06
24 receptions for 224 yards and one touchdown
Longest reception was 29 yards on 10-21-07
Returned a kickoff 13 yards on 12-03-07
Recovered a fumble on 12-03-06
54 regular season games
Seven playoff games
Auburn Tiger

Fairchild, Paul (#66) "Fingers"
Guard/Center, 1984–90
84 regular season games
Five playoff games
#124 pick in the 1984 College Draft
Kansas Jayhawk

Falcon, Theodore (#68) "Terry"
Offensive Guard, 1978–79
18 regular season games
Only playoff game appearance was on 12-31-78
#198 pick in the 1978 College Draft
Montana Grizzly

Farmer, Lonnie (#55)
Linebacker, 1964–66
Three sacks
Returned an interception 16 yards on 09-11-65
Recovered a fumble on 12-04-66
31 games
20th round draft pick in 1964
Tenn-Chattanooga Moccasin

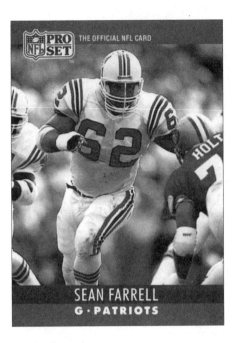

Farrell, Sean (#62)
Offensive Guard, 1987–89
Only reception was four yards on 12-04-88
43 games
Penn State Nittany Lion

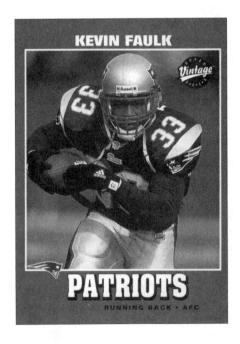

Faulk, Kevin (#33)
RB/KR/PR, 1999–2008
777 carries for 3,170 yards and 14 touchdowns
Longest run was a 45-yard touchdown on 11-03-02
Ran for a two-point conversion on 11-12-00
381 receptions for 3,304 yards and 14 touchdowns
Longest reception was a 52-yard touchdown on
    12-24-00

175 kickoff returns for 3,954 yards and two
  touchdowns
Longest kickoff return was 95 yards on 11-15-99
Returned a kickoff 86 yards for a touchdown on
  11-17-02
Returned a kickoff 87 yards for a touchdown on
  12-22-02
94 punt returns for 901 yards
Longest punt return was 43 yards on 10-01-06
Two completions for 21 yards
Longest completion was 23 yards on 12-22-01
Recovered five fumbles
137 regular season games
17 playoff games
Member of the 2001, 2003, and 2004 championship
  teams
#46 pick in the 1999 College Draft
LSU Tiger

Fauria, Christian (#88)
Tight End (KR), 2002–05
79 receptions for 790 yards and 13 touchdowns
Longest reception was 33 yards on 12-08-02
Caught a two-point conversion pass on 12-29-02
Recovered a Titans onside kick on 10-05-03
Recovered a fumble on 12-26-04
64 regular season games
Eight playoff games
Member of the 2003 and 2004 championship teams
Colorado Buffalo

Feacher, Ricky (#83)
WR/KR, 1976
Two receptions for 38 yards
Longest reception was 21 yards on 09-12-76
10 kickoff returns for 240 yards
Longest kickoff return was 46 yards on 09-26-76
Three games
#270 pick in the 1976 College Draft
Mississippi Valley State Delta Devil

Feagles, Jeff (#6)
Punter, 1988–89
154 punts for 5,874 yards
Longest punt was 74 yards on 10-02-88
Recovered two fumbles
32 games
Miami Hurricane

Feggins, Howard (#27)
Defensive Back, 1989
Returned an interception four yards on 12-02-89
11 games
North Carolina Tar Heel

Feldhausen, Paul (#66)
Offensive Tackle, 1968
Two games
#278 pick in the 1968 College Draft
Northland Community Pioneer

Felt, Dick (#24)
Defensive Back, 1962–66
12 interceptions for 199 yards
Longest return was 35 yards on 09-08-63
Blocked an extra-point attempt on 09-25-66
Recovered two fumbles
Returned a fumble 50 yards on 09-21-62
AFL All-Star defensive back in 1962
52 regular season games
Two playoff games
BYU Cougar

Ferguson, Vasquero (#43) "Vegas"
Running Back, 1980–82
290 carries for 1,163 yards and five touchdowns
Longest run was 44 yards on 10-12-80
26 receptions for 212 yards
Longest reception was 20 yards on 12-13-81
Recovered a fumble on 11-29-81
31 games
#25 pick in the 1980 College Draft
Notre Dame Fighting Irish

Fletcher, Derrick (#64)
Offensive Guard, 2000
Two games
#154 pick in the 1999 College Draft
Baylor University

Flick, Tom (#10)
Quarterback, 1982
Only game played as a QB was on 12-26-82
Three games
Washington Husky

Floyd, Chris (#37)
Fullback, 1998–2000
14 carries for 33 yards
Longest run was 10 yards on 12-20-98
Four receptions for 43 yards
Longest reception was 21 yards on 09-11-00
40 regular season games
Only playoff game appearance was on 01-03-99
#81 pick in the 1998 College Draft
Michigan Wolverine

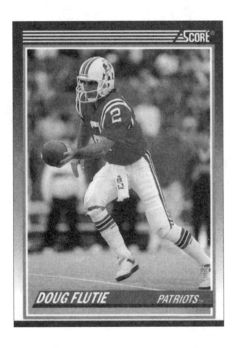

Flutie, Doug (#2)
Quarterback (K), 1987–89 and 2005
148 completions for 1,871 yards and 11 touchdowns
Longest completion was an 80-yard touchdown on
    10-30-88
65 carries for 308 yards and one touchdown
Only touchdown run was a 13-yard touchdown on
    10-02-88
Longest run was 22 yards on 10-01-89
AFC Offensive Player of the Week on 10-02-88

Recovered a fumble on 10-18-87
Drop kicked an extra point on 01-01-06
AFC Special Team Player of the Week on 01-01-06
22 regular season games
Inducted into the College Football Hall of Fame in
    2007
Boston College Eagle

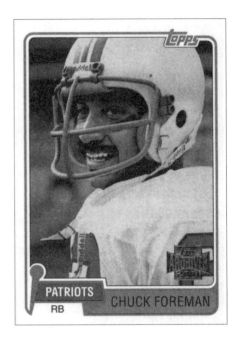

Foreman, Walter (#22) "Chuck"
Running Back, 1980
23 carries for 63 yards and one touchdown
Ran for a 1-yard touchdown on 10-19-80
Longest run was seven yards on 09-14-80
14 receptions for 99 yards
Longest reception was 18 yards on 11-10-80
Recovered a fumble on 11-02-80
16 games
Miami Hurricane

Forte, Donald (#38) "Ike"
RB (PR), 1976–77
87 carries for 257 yards and three touchdowns
Longest run was 26 yards on 11-28-76
11 receptions for 97 yards and one touchdown
Caught a six-yard touchdown pass on 12-05-76
Longest reception was 22 yards on 11-06-77
Two punt returns for nine yards
Longest punt return was six yards on 11-20-77
Recovered a fumble on 12-04-77
23 games
#35 pick in the 1976 College Draft
Arkansas Razorback

Foster, Will (#55)
Linebacker, 1973–74
Recovered a blocked punt for a touchdown on
    10-14-73
Recovered two fumbles
21 games
Eastern Michigan Huron

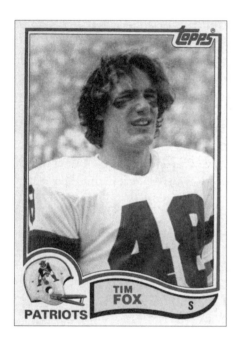

Fox, Tim (#48) "Foxie"
Safety, 1976–81
17 interceptions for 215 yards
Longest return was 29 yards on 11-07-76
Recorded a safety on 12-10-78
Blocked an extra point on 10-01-79
Four sacks
Recovered seven fumbles
Returned a fumble five yards on 11-07-76
Returned a missed field-goal attempt seven yards on
    09-29-80
AFC Pro Bowl safety in 1980
91 regular season games
Two playoff games
#21 pick in the 1976 College Draft
Ohio State Buckeye

Frain, Todd (#44)
Tight End, 1987
Two receptions for 22 yards
Longest was 11 yards on 10-04-87 and on 10-11-87
Three games
Nebraska Cornhusker

Francis, Russ (#81) "All World Tight End"
Tight End, 1975–80 and 1987–88
207 receptions for 3,157 yards and 28 touchdowns
Longest reception was 53 yards on 09-24-78
Two carries for 12 yards
Longest run was eight yards on 10-18-76
Recovered three fumbles
Wore #49 in the game played on 12-28-87
AFC Pro Bowl tight end in 1976, 1977, and 1978
92 regular season games
Two playoff games
#16 pick in the 1975 College Draft
Oregon Duck

Franklin, Arnold (#87)
Tight End, 1987
Three games
North Carolina Tar Heel

Franklin, Tony (#1)
Kicker, 1984–87
93 field goals
Kicked a 50-yard FG on 10-27-85 and on 12-08-85
163 extra points
AFC Pro Bowl kicker in 1986
62 regular season games
Five playoff games
Texas A&M Aggie

Fraser, Jim (#51)
P/LB, 1966
55 punts for 2,044 yards
Longest punt was 68 yards on 09-18-66
1.5 sacks
Returned an interception three yards on 12-04-66
14 games
Wisconsin Badger

Frazier, Charley (#81) "Razor"
Wide Receiver, 1969–70
28 receptions for 392 yards and seven touchdowns
Longest reception was a 50-yard touchdown on
    11-30-69
23 games
Texas Southern Tiger

Freeman, Arturo (#25)
Safety, 2005
Two games
South Carolina Gamecock

Friesz, John (#17)
Quarterback, 1999–2000
11 completions for 66 yards
Longest completion was 17 yards on 11-05-00
Two games
Idaho Vandal

Frisch, David (#88)
Tight End (KR), 1995
Returned a kickoff eight yards on 11-19-95
Two games
Colorado State Ram

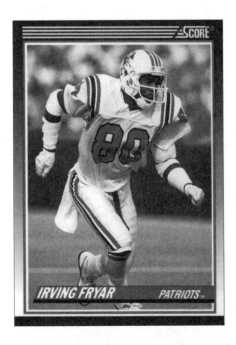

Fryar, Irving (#80) "the Flyer"
WR/KR/PR, 1984–92
363 receptions for 5,726 yards and 38 touchdowns
Longest reception was an 80-yard touchdown on
    10-30-88
35 carries for 188 yards and one touchdown
Ran for an 8-yard touchdown on 11-17-85
Longest run was 31 yards on 10-05-86
26 kickoff returns for 495 yards
Longest kickoff return was 47 yards on 12-24-89
206 punt returns for 2,055 yards and three
    touchdowns
Longest punt return was an 85-yard touchdown on
    09-22-85
Recovered five regular season fumbles
Advanced a lateral eight yards on 10-04-92
AFC Offensive Player of the Week on 11-24-91
AFC Pro Bowl return specialist in 1985
129 regular season games
Four playoff games
First overall pick in the 1984 College Draft
Ed Block Courage Award in 1992
Nebraska Cornhusker

Fullington, Darrell (#29)
Defensive Back, 1991
Five games
Miami Hurricane

Funchess, Tom (#73) "Moose"
Tackle/Guard, 1968–1970
39 games
#32 pick in the 1968 College Draft
Jackson State Tiger

Fussell, Tom (#83)
Defensive End, 1967
12 games
#206 pick in the 1967 College Draft
LSU Fighting Tiger

Gadbois, Dennis (#82) and (#48)
Wide Receiver, 1987–88
Three receptions for 51 yards
Longest reception was 20 yards on 10-18-87
Five games
Boston University Terrier

Gabriel, Doug (#85)
Wide Receiver, 2006
25 receptions for 344 yards and three touchdowns
Longest reception was 45 yards on 10-30-06
12 games
Central Florida Golden Knight

Gaffney, Jabar (#10)
Wide Receiver, 2006–08
85 receptions for 1,059 yards and eight touchdowns
Longest reception was a 56-yard touchdown on
      12-09-07
43 regular season games
Six playoff games
Florida Gator

Gaiter, Tony (#17)
Wide Receiver, 1997
Only game played was on 11-30-97
Miami Hurricane

Gallaher, Allen (#64)
Offensive Tackle, 1974
14 games
#82 pick in the 1973 College Draft
USC Trojan

Gamble, RC (#13)
HB/KR, 1968–69
94 carries for 346 yards and one touchdown
Longest run was a 40-yard touchdown on 09-08-68
18 receptions for 129 yards and one touchdown
Caught a one-yard touchdown pass on 11-17-68
Longest reception was 20 yards on 09-14-69
Two kickoff returns for 23 yards
Longest kickoff return was 23 yards on 11-09-69
Recovered two fumbles
27 games
#88 pick in the 1968 College Draft
South Carolina State Bulldog

Gambol, Chris (#74)
Guard/Tackle, 1990
16 games
Iowa Hawkeye

Gannon, Chris (#91)
DE/TE/LS, 1990–93
Only sack was made on 12-30-90
Recovered a fumble on 11-03-91
Played on both sides of the line of scrimmage

30 games
#73 pick in the 1989 College Draft
Southwest Louisiana Ragin' Cajun

Garcia, Alfonso (#7) "Teddy"
Kicker, 1988
Six field goals
Longest field goal was 50 yards on 9-11-88
11 extra points
16 games
#100 pick in the 1988 College Draft
Northeast Louisiana Indian

Gardin, Ron (#37)
KR/PR, 1971
14 kickoff returns for 321 yards
Longest kickoff return was 34 yards on 11-07-71
Four punt returns for 14 yards
Longest return was five yards on 10-10-71 and 10-31-71
Eight games
Arizona Wildcat

Garrett, Carl (#30) "The Road Runner"
RB/PR/KR, 1969–72
537 carries for 2,235 yards and 15 touchdowns
Longest run was an 80-yard touchdown on 11-09-69
107 receptions for 1,158 yards and three touchdowns
Longest reception was an 80-yard touchdown on
      11-14-71
92 kickoff returns for 2,251 yards
Longest kickoff return was 63 yards on 11-23-69
43 punt returns for 487 yards

Longest punt return was 62 yards on 09-27-70
Recovered eight fumbles
AFL All-Star running back in 1969
AFL Rookie of the Year in 1969
51 games
#58 pick in the 1969 College Draft
New Mexico Highlands Cowboy

Garrett, J.D. (#32) "Red River"
RB/KR/PR, 1964–67
116 carries for 434 yards and three touchdowns
Longest run was 58 yards on 10-04-64
17 receptions for 169 yards and two touchdowns
Longest reception was 57 yards on 10-04-64
48 kickoff returns for 1,054 yards
Longest kickoff return was 42 yards on 09-20-64
Three punt returns for 47 yards
Longest punt return was 28 yards on 10-04-64
Recovered blocked punt for a touchdown on 12-17-67
Recovered three fumbles
50 games
Eighth round draft pick in 1964
Grambling State Tiger

Garron, Larry (#46) and (#40)
RB/KR (DB/PR), 1960–68
759 carries for 2,981 yards and 14 touchdowns
Longest run was a team record 85-yard touchdown on 10-22-61
185 receptions for 2,502 yards and 26 touchdowns
Longest reception was a 76-yard touchdown on 11-01-63
89 kickoff returns for 2,299 yards and two touchdowns

Longest kickoff return was a 95-yard touchdown on 11-03-62
Returned a kickoff 89 yards for a touchdown on 10-13-61
Played in three games as a defensive back in 1961
Recovered 11 fumbles
Returned a fumble two yards on 12-08-63
Only pass completion was 39 yards on 10-26-62
Only punt return was 23 yards on 12-14-63
AFL All-Star running back in 1961, 1963, 1964, and 1967
99 regular season games
Two playoff games
Western Illinois Leatherneck

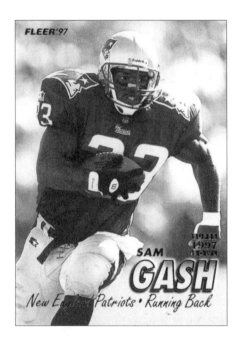

Gash, Sam (#33)
Fullback, 1992–1997
105 carries for 291 yards and two touchdowns
Longest run was 14 yards on 09-05-93
104 receptions for 826 yards and six touchdowns
Longest reception was 30 yards on 09-03-95
Caught a two-point conversion pass on 10-06-96
Recovered two fumbles
88 regular season games
Three playoff games
#205 pick in the 1992 College Draft
Ed Block Courage Award in 1996
Penn State Nittany Lion

Gay, Randall (#21) "Blue"
Cornerback, 2004–07
Five interceptions for 75 yards
Longest return was 31 yards on 10-21-07
Recovered three fumbles
Returned a fumble 41 yards for a touchdown on
      12-05-04
Returned a fumble 15 yards for a touchdown on
      10-07-07
39 regular season games
Six playoff games
Member of the 2004 championship team
LSU Tiger

Geddes, Bob (#59)
Linebacker, 1973–75
Only sack was made on 09-22-74
Two interceptions for 32 yards and one touchdown
Longest return was a 29-yard touchdown on 10-13-74
24 games
UCLA Bruin

George, Tony (#41)
Safety, 1999–2000
Recovered a fumble on 12-17-00
31 games
#91 pick in the 1999 College Draft
Florida Gator

Germany, Willie (#29)
Safety, 1976
10 games
Only playoff game appearance was on 12-18-76
Morgan State Bear

Gibson, Ernest (#43)
DB (PR), 1984–88
Four interceptions for 21 yards
Longest return was 17 yards on 12-28-87
Only punt return was three yards on 09-30-84
Recovered a fumble on 11-11-84
67 regular season games
Five playoff games
#151 pick in the 1984 College Draft
Furman Paladin

Gillen, John (#54)
Linebacker, 1983
Eight games
Illinois Fighting Illini

Gipson, Paul (#46)
Running Back, 1973
Five carries for a net loss of one yard
Longest run was four yards on 09-23-73
Returned a fumble 20 yards on 10-07-73
Five games
Houston Cougar

Gisler, Mike (#67)
Center (KR), 1993–97
Three kickoff returns for 28 yards
Longest kickoff return was 11 yards on 12-03-95
73 regular season games
Three playoff games
Houston Cougar

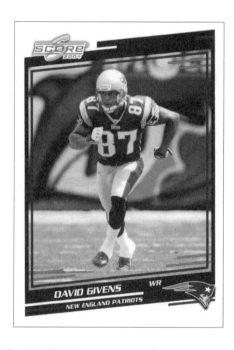

Givens, David (#87)
Wide Receiver, 2002–05
158 receptions for 2,214 yards and 12 touchdowns
Longest reception was 57 yards on 11-16-03
Two kickoff returns for 31 yards
Longest kickoff return was 20 yards on 10-19-03
53 regular season games
Eight playoff games
Member of the 2003 and 2004 championship teams
#253 pick in the 2002 College Draft
Notre Dame Fighting Irish

Gladieux, Bob (#24) "Harpo"
RB/KR/PR, 1969–72
65 carries for 239 yards
Longest run was 31 yards on 11-14-71
25 receptions for 252 yards
Longest reception was 31 yards on 10-01-72
10 kickoff returns for 146 yards
Longest kickoff return was 20 yards on 10-05-69
Only completion was 48 yards on 11-07-71
Six punt returns for minus-6 yards
Recovered two fumbles
43 games
#188 pick in the 1969 College Draft
Notre Dame Fighting Irish

Glenn, Terry (#88)
Wide Receiver, 1996–2001
329 receptions for 4,669 yards and 22 touchdowns
Longest reception was an 86-yard touchdown on
    12-06-98
11 carries for 80 yards
Longest run was 35 yards on 12-04-00
Recovered a fumble on 10-10-99
AFC Offensive Player of the Week on 10-03-99
AFC Pro Bowl wide receiver in 1999
68 regular season games
Five playoff games
Member of the 2001 championship team
Seventh pick in the 1996 College Draft
Ohio State Buckeye

Glenn, Vencie (#25)
Defensive Back, 1986
Four games
#54 pick in the 1986 College Draft
Indiana State Sycamore

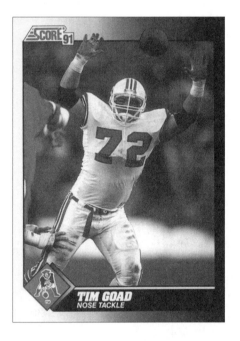

Goad, Tim (#72)
NT/LS (DT and DE), 1988–94
11.5 sacks
Returned four fumbles for 27 yards
Returned a fumble 19 yards for a touchdown on
    12-13-92
109 games
#87 pick in the 1988 College Draft
Ed Block Courage Award in 1994
North Carolina Tar Heel

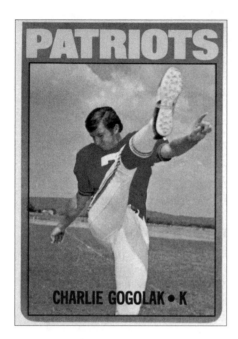

Gogolak, Charlie (#7)
Kicker, 1970–72
20 field goals
Longest field goal was 51 yards on 10-17-71
42 extra points
26 games
Princeton Tiger

Golden, Tim (#59)
Linebacker (KR), 1982–84
Recovered three fumbles
Returned a kickoff 10 yards on 10-02-83
40 regular season games
Only playoff game appearance was on 01-08-83
Florida Gator

Golic, Bob (#51)
DL/LB, 1979–81
Recovered a fumble on 12-20-81
33 games
#52 pick in the 1979 College Draft
Notre Dame Fighting Irish

Gonzalez, Noe (#38)
Running Back, 1974
Two games
Southwest Texas State Bobcat

Gordon, Tim (#41)
Defensive Back, 1991–92
Recovered two fumbles
21 games
Tulsa Golden Hurricane

Gorin, Brandon (#76)
Offensive Tackle, 2003–05
32 regular season games
Seven playoff games
Member of the 2003 and 2004 championship teams
Purdue Boilermaker

Gostkowski, Stephen (#3) "The Kicker"
Kicker, 2006–08
77 field goals
Longest field goal was 52 yards on 11-26-06
157 extra points
AFC Pro Bowl kicker in 2008
48 regular season games
Six playoff games
#118 pick in the 2006 College Draft
Memphis Tiger

Graff, Neil (#15)
Quarterback, 1974–75
19 completions for 241 yards and two touchdowns
Longest completion was a 31-yard touchdown on
    09-28-75
Two carries for two yards
Longest run was for two yards on 09-21-75
Recovered a fumble on 09-28-75
25 games
Wisconsin Badger

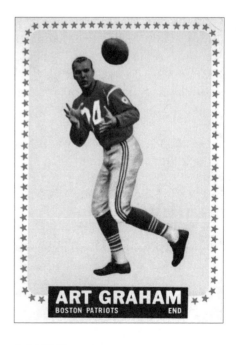

Graham, Art (#84)
WR (PR/KR), 1963–68
199 receptions for 3,107 yards and 20 touchdowns
Longest reception was an 80-yard touchdown on
    11-29-64

Two regular season punt returns for 11 yards
Longest punt return was six yards in 11-03-68
Only kickoff return was nine yards on 12-08-68
Ran for a five-yard loss on 11-05-67
75 regular season games
Two playoff games
First round draft pick in 1963
Boston College Eagle

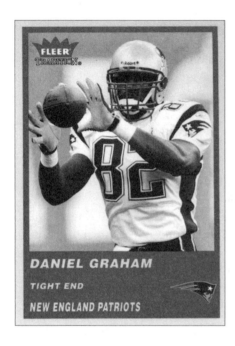

DANIEL GRAHAM

TIGHT END

NEW ENGLAND PATRIOTS

Graham, Daniel (#82)
Tight End, 2002–06
120 receptions for 1,393 yards and 17 touchdowns
Longest reception was 48 yards on 11-22-04
Recovered a fumble on 12-08-02
AFC Offensive Player of the Week on 10-26-03
63 regular season games
11 playoff games
Member of the 2003 and 2004 championship teams
#21 pick in the 2001 College Draft
Colorado Buffalo

Graham, Hason (#81)
Wide Receiver, 1995–96
15 receptions for 220 yards and two touchdowns
Longest reception was a 37-yard touchdown on
    12-10-95
19 games
Georgia Bulldog

Graham, Milt (#70) "Uncle Miltie"
OT/DT, 1961–63
Played on both sides of the line of scrimmage
Recovered a fumble on 10-05-63

28 regular season games
Two playoff games
Colgate Red Raider

Grant, Rupert Jr. (#34)
RB (KR), 1995
Only reception was four yards on 10-08-95
Only kickoff return was seven yards on 10-01-95
Recovered a fumble on 12-23-95
Seven games
Howard Bison

Graves, White (#44) "Whitey"
DB (PR), 1965–67
Three interceptions (no return yards on any
    interception)
Only punt return was five yards on 11-06-06
Recovered two fumbles
40 games
17th round draft pick in 1964
LSU Fighting Tiger

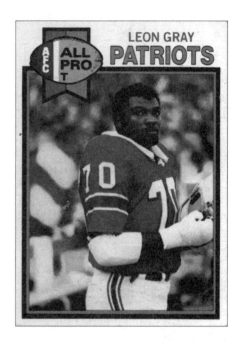

LEON GRAY

PATRIOTS

Gray, Leon (#70) "Big Dog"
Offensive Tackle, 1973–78
Recovered four regular season fumbles
Advanced a fumble four yards on 12-07-75
AFC Pro Bowl tackle in 1976 and 1978
78 regular season games
Two playoff games
Jackson State Tiger

Green, David (#38)
Running Back, 1995
Two games
Boston College Eagle

Green, Jarvis (#97)
DE-NT (KR), 2002–08
27 sacks
Recovered six fumbles
Fell on a fumble for a touchdown on 11-28-04
Returned a kickoff 10 yards on 10-06-02
AFC Defensive Player of the Week on 10-01-06
108 regular season games
14 playoff games
Member of the 2003 and 2004 championship teams
#126 pick in the 2002 College Draft
LSU Tiger

Green, Jerry (#45)
Offensive End, 1960
3 receptions for 52 yards
Longest reception was 31 yards on 09-17-60
Two games
Georgia Tech Yellow Jacket

Green, Victor (#27)
Safety, 2002
Recovered three fumbles
One interception for 90 yards and one touchdown
Returned a pass 90 yards for a touchdown on 09-15-02
16 games
Akron Zip

Greene, Tom (#14)
QB/P/RB (KR), 1960
27 completions for 251 yards and one touchdown
Longest completion was 31 yards on 09-17-60
Threw a 15-yard touchdown pass on 09-17-60
Seven carries for 44 yards
Longest run was 21 yards on 09-23-60
61 punts for 2,253 yards
Longest punt was 66 yards on 10-16-60
Three receptions for 43 yards
Longest reception was 31 yards on 09-17-60
Only kickoff return was three yards on 10-28-60
10 games
Holy Cross Crusader

Green-Ellis, BenJarvus (#42) "The Law Firm of"
Running Back, 2008
74 carries for 275 yards and five touchdowns
Longest run was 15 yards on 10-20-08

Three receptions for 37 yards
Longest reception was 20 yards on 11-30-08
Nine games
Mississippi Rebel

Grier, Marrio (#35)
Running Back, 1996–97
60 carries for 180 yards and two touchdowns
Longest run was 26 yards on 11-24-96
Only reception was eight yards on 12-21-96
Recovered a fumble on 10-20-96
32 regular season games
Five playoff games
#195 pick in the 1996 College Draft
Tennessee-Chattanooga Moccasin

Griffith, Rich (#88)
Tight End, 1993
Three games
#138 pick in the 1993 College Draft
Arizona Wildcat

Grimes, Reggie (#97)
Defensive Tackle, 2000
Eight games
Alabama Crimson Tide

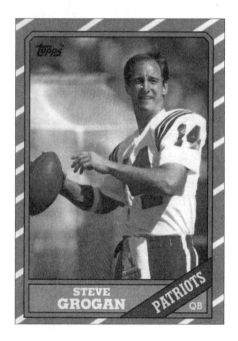

Grogan, Steve (#14) "Grogs" and "Grog"
Quarterback, 1975–90
1,879 completions for 26,886 yards and 182
    touchdowns
Longest pass was a 76-yard touchdown on 11-08-81 and
    09-25-83

445 carries for 2,176 yards and 35 touchdowns
Longest run was a 41-yard touchdown on 10-18-76
Three receptions for 17 yards
Longest reception was 16 yards on 09-06-81
Recovered 35 fumbles
Advanced a fumble six yards for a touchdown on
    10-18-76
149 regular season games
Four playoff games
#116 pick in the 1975 College Draft
Ed Block Courage Award in 1984
Inducted into the Patriots Hall of Fame in 1995
Kansas State Wildcat

Gutierrez, Matt (#7)
Quarterback, 2007
Only completion was 15 yards on 10-21-07
Five carries for minus-13 yards
Four regular season games
Idaho State Bengal

Guyton, Gary (#59)
Linebacker, 2008
Recovered two fumbles
14 games
Georgia Tech Bulldog

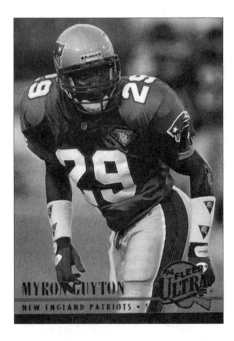

Guyton, Myron (#29)
Safety, 1994–95
Five interceptions for 86 yards
Longest return was 45 yards on 11-12-95
Returned four fumbles for 31 yards

Longest fumble return was 26 yards on 12-18-94
Recovered a Bengals onside kick on 09-18-94
30 regular season games
Only playoff game appearance was on 01-01-95
Eastern Kentucky Colonel

Guzik, John (#97)
Defensive Lineman, 1987
Three games
Ohio University Bobcat

Hagen, Halvor (#62)
Guard/DE (KR), 1971–72
Played on both sides of the line of scrimmage
Only sack was made on 11-12-72
Only kickoff return was seven yards on 10-31-71
26 games
Weber State Wildcat

Haggerty, Mike (#75)
Tackle-DE, 1971
Played on both sides of the line of scrimmage
14 games
Miami Hurricane

Haley, Darryl (#68)
Offensive Tackle, 1982–86
57 regular season games
Only playoff game appearance was on 01-04-87
#55 pick in the 1982 College Draft
Utah Ute

Hall, Ron (#23) "Haystacks"
Defensive Back, 1961–67
29 interceptions for 476 yards and one touchdown
Returned a pass 47 yards for a touchdown on 09-21-62
Longest return was 87 yards on 09-18-66
3.5 sacks
Blocked a 28-yard field-goal attempt on 11-21-65
Recovered three fumbles
AFL All-Star defensive back in 1963
88 regular season games
Two playoff games
Missouri Valley Viking

Hamilton, Bobby (#91)
Defensive End, 2000–03
10.5 sacks
Recovered two fumbles
Intercepted a pass on 11-28-02
Recovered a squibbed kickoff on 12-10-00

64 regular season games
Six playoff games
Member of the 2001 and 2003 championship teams
Southern Mississippi Golden Eagle

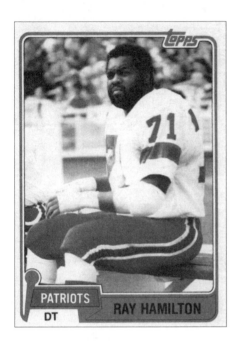

Hamilton, Ray (#71) "Sugar Bear"
NT/DE, 1973–81
54 sacks
Recovered 14 fumbles
Returned a fumble 23 yards for a touchdown on
    11-02-75
Blocked a 44-yard field-goal attempt on 11-02-75
Blocked a 19-yard field-goal attempt on 11-27-77
Recovered a squibbed kickoff on 11-22-81
132 regular season games
Two playoff games
#342 pick in the 1973 College Draft
Oklahoma Sooner

Hammond, Kim (#15)
Quarterback, 1969
Two completions for 31 yards
Longest completion was 18 yards on 12-07-69
Ran for a two-point conversion on 12-07-69
Three games
Florida State Seminole

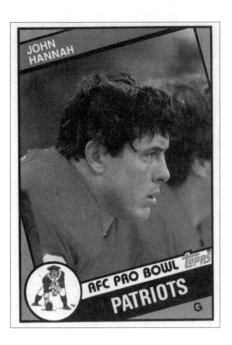

Hannah, John (#73) "Hawg"
Offensive Guard, 1973–85
Recovered 10 fumbles
Recovered an onside kickoff on 12-09-73
Recovered a fumble for a touchdown on 12-15-74
AFC Pro Bowl guard in 1976 and 1978–85
183 regular season games
Seven playoff games
#4 pick in the 1973 College Draft
Inducted into the Pro Football Hall of Fame on
    07-27-91
Inducted into the College Football Hall of Fame on
    12-07-99
His uniform # 73 was retired by the Patriots
Inducted into the Patriots Hall of Fame in 1991
Alabama Crimson Tide

Hanneman, Craig (#74)
Defensive Lineman, 1974–75
4.5 sacks
Recovered a fumble on 12-08-74
20 games
Oregon State Beaver

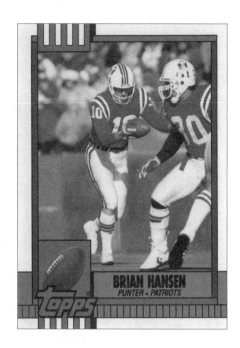

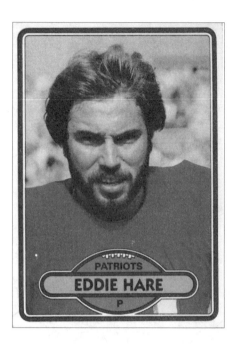

Hansen, Brian (#10)
Punter, 1990
90 punts for 3,752 yards
Longest punt was 69 yards on 09-30-90
Recovered a fumble on 11-04-90
16 games
Sioux Falls Cougar

Hansen, Bruce (#24) and (#35)
FB (KR), 1987
16 carries for 44 yards
Longest run was seven yards on 10-11-87
Only reception was 22 yards on 10-18-87
Only kickoff return was 14 yards on 10-18-87
Recovered a fumble on 10-11-87
Six games
BYU Cougar

Hanson, Chris (#6)
Punter, 2007–08
93 punts for 3,964 yards
Longest punt was 70 yards on 09-07-08
AFC Special Team Player of the Week on 12-28-08
32 regular season games
Three playoff games
Marshall Thundering Herd

Hare, Eddie (#8)
Punter, 1979
83 punts for 3,038 yards
Longest punt was 58 yards on 09-03-79
Only pass completion was four yards on 10-21-79
Recovered two fumbles
16 games
#106 pick in the 1979 College Draft
Tulsa Golden Hurricane

Harlow, Pat (#77)
Offensive Tackle, 1991–95
74 regular season games
Only playoff game appearance was on 01-01-95

#11 pick in the 1991 College Draft
USC Trojan

Harris, Antwan (#23)
Defensive Back, 2000–03
Returned an interception 11 yards on 10-08-00
Recovered a fumble on 11-19-00
Only sack was made on 12-24-00
52 regular season games
Three playoff games
Member of the 2001 and 2003 championship teams
187th pick in the 2000 College Draft
Virginia Cavalier

Harris, Marshall (#78)
Defensive Lineman, 1983
Only sack was recorded on 09-25-83
Six games
Texas Christian Horned Frog

Harris, Raymont (#28)
Running Back, 2000
Three carries for 14 yards
Longest run was seven yards on 12-10-00
Two receptions for one yard
Longest reception was two yards on 12-10-00
Only game played was on 12-10-00
Ohio State Buckeye

RICKIE HARRIS

SAFETY
PATRIOTS

Harris, Rickie (#25)
DB/PR, 1971–72
Three interceptions for 45 yards
Longest return was 32 yards on 10-15-72

Two sacks
Nine punt returns for 24 yards
Longest punt return was nine yards on 12-19-71
Recovered five fumbles
28 games
Arizona Wildcat

Harris, Ronnie (#84)
WR/PR/KR, 1993–94
Only reception was 11 yards on 10-16-94
26 punt returns for 227 yards
Longest punt return was 21 yards on 12-19-93
Six kickoff return for 90 yards
Longest kickoff return was 19 yards on 12-19-93
Recovered a fumble on 12-26-93
Six games
Oregon Duck

Harrison, Rodney (#37) "The Hitman"
Safety, 2003–08
Eight interceptions for 16 yards
Longest interception return was 12 yards on 11-22-04
Nine sacks
Returned a fumble 16 yards on 10-19-03
AFC Defensive Player of the Week on 09-19-04
63 regular season games
Nine playoff games
Member of the 2003 and 2004 championship teams
Western Illinois Leatherneck

Hartley, Ken (#7)
Punter, 1981
Nine punts for 266 yards
Longest punt was 41 yards on 10-11-81
Two games
Catawba Indian

Harvey, Richard (#58)
Linebacker, 1990–91
17 games
Tulane Green Wave

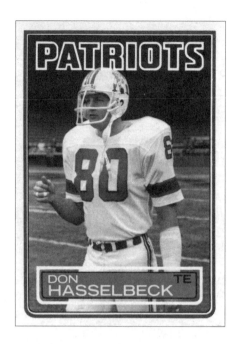

Hasselbeck, Don (#80) "Hass"
Tight End (KR), 1977–83
99 receptions for 1,444 yards and 15 touchdowns
Longest reception was 51 yards on 10-11-81
Only kickoff return was seven yards on 09-21-81
86 regular season games
Two playoff games
#52 pick in the 1977 College Draft
Colorado Buffalo

Hauck, Tim (#40)
Defensive Back, 1990
10 games
Montana Grizzly

Hauser, Art (#67)
G/T (DL), 1960
Played on both sides of the line of scrimmage
Shared in a QB sack on 11-18-60
Eight games
Xavier Musketeer

Hawkins, Artrell (#25)
Defensive Back, 2005–06
Recorded a sack on 12-17-05
Only interception (no return) was on 11-12-06
Recovered a fumble on 11-05-06
19 regular season games
Five playoff games
Cincinnati Bearcat

Hawkins, Mike (#59) "Hawk"
Linebacker, 1978–81
12 sacks
Recovered an onside free kick on 10-22-78
Five interceptions for 56 yards and one touchdown
Longest return was a 35-yard touchdown on 10-21-79
Recovered two fumbles
59 regular season games
Only playoff game appearance was on 12-31-78
#188 pick in the 1978 College Draft
Texas A&I Javelina

Hawkins, Steve (#80)
Wide Receiver, 1994
Two receptions for 22 yards
Longest reception was 14 yards on 11-06-94
Seven games
#166 pick in the 1994 College Draft
Western Michigan Bronco

Hawthorne, Greg (#27)
WR/RB/TE/KR, 1984–86
34 receptions for 361 yards and one touchdown
Longest reception was a 28-yard touchdown on
    11-03-85
Ran for a five-yard gain on 12-22-86
Four kickoff returns for 40 yards
Longest kickoff return was 14 yards on 11-22-84
Recovered a fumble on 12-22-86
43 regular season games
Five playoff games
Baylor Bear

Hayes, Chris (#29)
Safety, 2002
Four games
Washington State Cougar

Hayes, Donald (#81)
Wide Receiver, 2002
12 receptions for 133 yards and two touchdowns
Longest reception was a 40-yard touchdown on
    09-09-02
12 games
Wisconsin Badger

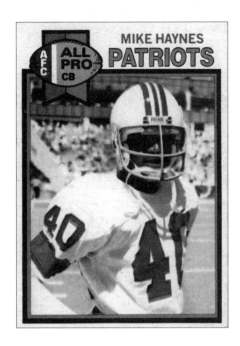

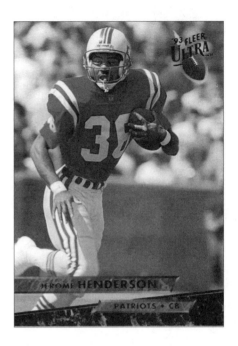

Haynes, Mike (#40)
CB/PR, 1976–82
28 interceptions for 388 yards and one touchdown
Longest return was 50 yards on 10-29-78
Returned a pass 31 yards for a touchdown on 11-26-78
111 punt returns for 1,159 yards and two touchdowns
Returned a punt 89 yards for a touchdown on 11-07-76
Returned a punt 62 yards for a touchdown on 11-28-76
Recovered 10 fumbles
Returned a lateral 65 yards for a touchdown on
    10-05-80
AFC Pro Bowl CB in 1976–80 and 1982
AFC Rookie of the Year in 1976
90 regular season games
Three playoff games
Fifth pick in the 1976 College Draft
Inducted into the Pro Football Hall of Fame on
    07-26-97
His uniform #40 was retired by the Patriots
Inducted into the Patriots Hall of Fame in 1994
Inducted into the College Football Hall of Fame in
    2001
Arizona State Sun Devil

Henderson, Jerome (#36) and (#26)
DB/PR, 1991–93 and 1996
Seven interceptions for 52 yards
Longest return was 34 yards on 10-18-92
27 punt returns for 201 yards
Longest punt return was 39 yards on 10-06-91
Recovered a fumble on 12-15-91
40 games
Three playoff games
#41 pick in the 1991 College Draft
Clemson Tiger

Hendley, David (#28)
Defensive Back, 1987
Two games
Southern Connecticut State Fighting Owl

Henke, Karl (#80)
Defensive Tackle, 1969
Only sack was made on 09-14-69
10 games
Tulsa Golden Hurricane

Hennessey, Tom (#30)
DB/PR, 1965–66
Eight interceptions for 113 yards
Longest return was 34 yards on 10-23-66
12 punt returns for 60 yards
Longest punt return was 11 yards on 10-30-66
28 games
Holy Cross Crusader

Henson, Luther (#70)
Nose Tackle, 1982–1984
Three sacks
21 regular season games
Only playoff game appearance was on 01-08-83
Ohio State Buckeye

Herline, Alan (#6)
Punter, 1987
25 punts for 861 yards
Longest punt was 50 yards on 10-11-87
Three games
Vanderbilt Commodore

Herock, Ken (#36)
LB/TE, 1969
Six games
West Virginia Mountaineer

Hill, Marquise (#91)
Defensive End, 2004–06
13 regular season games
Only playoff game appearance was on 01-14-06
Member of the 2004 championship team
#63 pick in the 2004 College Draft
LSU Fighting Tiger

Hinton, Eddie (#82)
WR-KR, 1974
2 receptions for 36 yards
Longest reception was 20 yards on 12-15-74
Only carry was for one yard on 11-17-74
3 kickoff returns for 83 yards
Longest kickoff return was 53 yards on 11-03-74
Recovered a fumble on 11-10-74
Nine games
Oklahoma Sooner

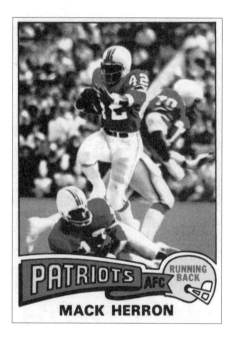

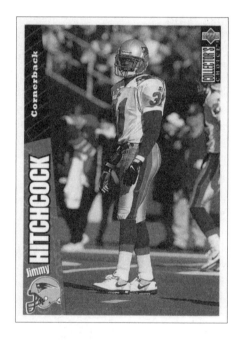

Herron, Mack (#42) "Mini"
RB/KR/PR, 1973–75
353 carries for 1,298 yards and nine touchdowns
Longest run was 53 yards on 10-12-75
61 receptions for 789 yards and six touchdowns
Longest reception was 48 yards on 12-08-74
74 punt returns for 888 yards
Longest punt return was 66 yards on 10-06-74
71 kickoff returns for 1,796 yards and one touchdown
Longest kickoff return was a 92-yard touchdown on
    12-02-73
Recovered eight fumbles
Longest fumble return was six yards on 12-16-73
35 games
Kansas State Wildcat

Hitchcock, Jimmy (#31) and (#37)
Cornerback, 1995–97 and 2002
Four interceptions for 118 yards and one touchdown
Longest return was a 100-yard touchdown on
    11-23-97
37 games
#88 pick in the 1995 College Draft
North Carolina Tar Heel

Hobbs, Ellis (#27) "Mr. 108"
CB/KR, 2005–08
2.5 sacks
Nine interceptions for 87 yards
Longest interception return was 70 yards on 10-30-06
Recovered five fumbles

Returned a fumble 35 yards for a touchdown on
    11-18-07
105 kickoff returns for 2,913 yards and three
    touchdowns
Longest kickoff return was NFL record 108-yard
    touchdown on 09-09-07
AFC Special Team Player of the Week on 09-09-07
AFC Special Team Player of the Week on 12-14-08
63 regular season games
Eight playoff games
#84 pick in the 2005 College Draft
Iowa State Cyclone

Hobby, Marion (#60)
Defensive End, 1990–92
Five sacks
42 games
Tennessee Volunteer

Hochstein, Russ (#71)
Guard/Center (FB/TE), 2002–08
Occasionally used as a FB and a TE
Recovered a fumble on 11-12-06
91 regular season games
14 playoff games
Member of the 2003 and 2004 championship teams
Nebraska Cornhusker

Hodge, Milford (#97)
DE/NT (KR), 1986–89
Three sacks
Recovered a fumble on 09-04-88
Two kickoff returns for 19 yards
Longest kickoff return was 11 yards on 12-24-89
49 regular season games
Only playoff game appearance was on 01-04-87
#224 pick in the 1985 College Draft
Washington State Cougar

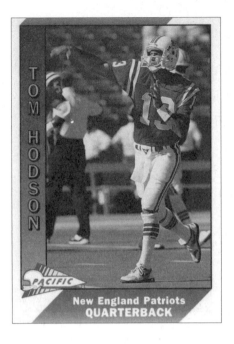

Hodson, Tommy (#13)
Quarterback, 1990–92
171 completions for 1,809 yards and seven
    touchdowns
Longest completion was 56 yards on 12-15-90
21 carries for 90 yards
Longest run was 23 yards on 12-23-90
Caught a deflected pass on 10-18-92
Recovered a fumble on 11-01-92
32 games
#59 pick in the 1990 College Draft
LSU Fighting Tiger

Hoey, George (#23)
DB/KR, 1972–73
Returned an interception 25 yards on 11-26-72
Nine kickoff returns for 210 yards
Longest kickoff return was 30 yards on 10-22-72
25 games
Michigan Wolverine

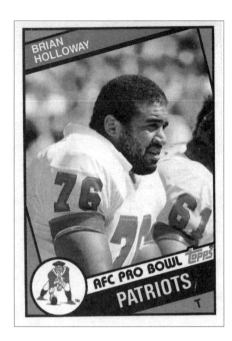

Holloway, Brian (#76)
Offensive Tackle, 1981–86
Recovered four fumbles
Caught a five-yard pass on 10-05-86
AFC Pro Bowl tackle in 1983, 1984, and 1985
88 regular season games
Six playoff games
#19 pick in the 1981 College Draft
Stanford Cardinal

Holmberg, Rob (#50) and (#47)
Linebacker, 2000–01
18 games
Member of the 2001 championship team
Penn State Nittany Lion

Holmes, Darryl (#41)
Defensive Back, 1987–89
Returned an interception four yards on 10-18-87
Recovered two fumbles
44 games
Fort Valley State Wildcat

Holmes, Ernie (#63)
Defensive Lineman, 1978
Recovered a fumble on 12-18-78
Three regular season games
Only playoff game appearance was on 12-31-78
Texas Southern Tiger

Holsey, Bernard (#60)
Defensive Lineman, 2002
Only sack was made on 09-15-02
Eight games
Duke Blue Devil

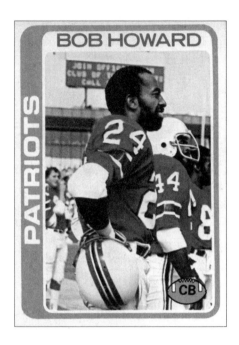

Howard, Bob (#24)
Defensive Back, 1975–1977
10 interceptions for 90 yards and one touchdown
Longest return was a 44-yard touchdown on 11-09-75
Recovered a fumble on 09-21-75
41 regular season games
Only playoff game appearance was on 12-18-76
San Diego State Aztec

Howard, David (#99)
Linebacker, 1991–92
Two sacks
Returned an interception one yard on 10-18-92
Recovered a fumble on 12-13-92
32 games
Long Beach State 49er

Huard, Damon (#19)
Quarterback, 2001–03
Only run was a four-yard QB sneak for a 1st down on
    11-10-02
Four games
Member of the 2001 and 2003 championship teams
Washington Husky

Huarte, John (#7)
Quarterback, 1966–67
Eight completions for 88 yards
Longest completion was 17 yards on 12-11-66
Nine carries for 45 yards
Longest run was 13 yards on 11-27-66
18 games
Notre Dame Fighting Irish

Hubach, Mike (#6)
Punter (K), 1980–81
82 punts for 3,118 yards
Longest punt was 69 yards on 10-12-80
Attempted an onside kick on 11-10-80
Recovered a fumble on 12-14-80
21 games
#293 pick in the 1980 College Draft
Kansas Jayhawk

Hudson, Bill (#61)
DT, 1963
Four games
Clemson Tiger

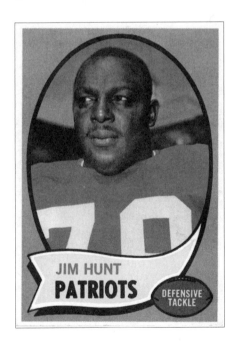

Hunt, Jim Lee (#79) "Earthquake"
DT/DE and (KR), 1960–71
34.5 sacks
Returned an interception 78 yards for a touchdown
    on 11-01-63
Recovered 16 fumbles
Returned a fumble 11 yards on 11-18-60
Returned a fumble five yards for a touchdown on
    11-06-66

Returned a fumble 51 yards on 12-15-68
Recorded a safety on 12-09-67
Only kickoff return was eight yards on 11-25-60
Recovered a Patriots onside kick on 09-27-64
AFL All-Star DT in 1961, 1966, 1967, and 1969
146 regular season games
Two playoff games
His uniform #79 was retired by the Patriots
Inducted into the Patriots Hall of Fame on 08-18-93
Prairie View A&M Panther

Hunt, Kevin (#62)
Offensive Tackle, 1973
Only game played was on 11-11-73
Doanne Tiger

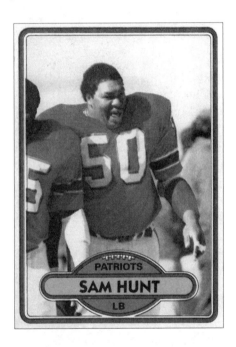

Hunt, Sam (#50) "Big Backer"
Linebacker (KR), 1974–79
Five sacks
Seven interceptions for 189 yards and one touchdown
Longest return was a 68-yard touchdown on 12-12-76
Only kickoff return was 21 yards on 11-17-74
Returned six fumbles for 13 yards
Longest fumble return was seven yards on 12-14-75
84 regular season games
Two playoff games
#374 pick in the 1974 College Draft
Stephen F. Austin State Lumberjack

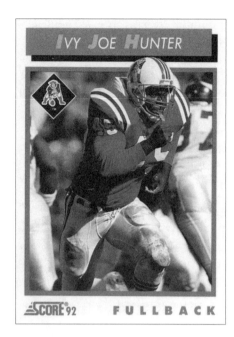

Hunter, Ivy Joe (#45)
Running Back, 1991
18 carries for 53 yards
Longest run was nine yards on 10-06-91
11 receptions for 97 yards
Longest reception was 25 yards on 11-10-91
Recovered two fumbles
13 games
Kentucky Wildcat

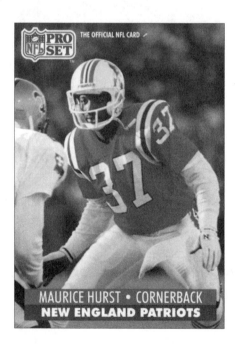

Hurst, Maurice (#37)
Defensive Back (PR), 1989–95
27 interceptions for 263 yards and one touchdown
Longest return was 36 yards on 09-30-90

Returned interception 16 yards for a touchdown on
      11-19-89
Three sacks
Blocked a Pittsburgh Steelers punt on 12-09-90
Only punt return was six yards on 11-12-89
105 regular season games
Only playoff game appearance was on 01-01-95
#96 pick in the 1989 College Draft
Southern Jaguar

Hutson, Brian (#36)
Defensive Back, 1990
Two games
Mississippi State Bulldog

Hyland, Bob (#60)
Center, 1977
Three games
Boston College Eagle

Ilg, Ray (#45)
Linebacker (KR), 1967–68
Two sacks
Returned kickoff 10 yards on 11-19-67
28 games
#336 pick in the 1967 College Draft
Colgate Red Raider

Imhof, Martin (#64) "Tree"
Defensive Lineman, 1975
Recovered a fumble on 12-07-75
Five games
San Diego State Aztec

Ingram, Brian (#51)
Linebacker, 1982–86
39 regular season games
Five playoff games
#111 pick in the 1982 College Draft
Tennessee Volunteer

Irwin, Heath (#63)
Guard/Center, 1996–99
44 regular season games
Three playoff games
#101 pick in the 1996 College Draft
Colorado Buffalo

Isaia, Sale (#72)
Offensive Guard, 2000
Recovered a fumble on 12-10-00
16 games
UCLA Bruin

Israel, Steve (#21)
Cornerback, 1997–99
Four interceptions for 13 yards
Longest return was 12 yards on 12-13-98
Four sacks
Recovered three fumbles
29 regular season games
Three playoff games
Pittsburgh Panther

PATRIOTS
HORACE IVORY
RB

Ivory, Horace (#23)
RB/KR, 1977–81
329 carries for 1,336 yards and 14 touchdowns
Longest run was 52 yards on 11-18-79
49 receptions for 433 yards and two touchdowns
Longest reception was 24 yards on 11-11-79
45 kickoff returns for 1,191 yards and one touchdown
Returned a kickoff 98 yards for a touchdown on 10-19-80
Recovered three fumbles
46 regular season games
Only playoff game appearance was on 12-31-78
#44 pick in the 1977 College Draft
Oklahoma Sooner

Iwuoma, Chidi (#29)
Special Team, 2006
Three games
California Golden Bear

Izzo, Larry (#53) "h to the izzo"
Special Team/LB, 2001–08
Recovered a fumble on 11-18-01

Recovered an onside kick on 12-14-03
Intercepted a pass on 12-27-03
AFC Special Team Player of the Week on 09-22-02
AFC Pro Bowl special team in 2002 and 2004
127 regular season games
17 playoff games
Member of the 2001, 2003, and 2004 championship teams
Rice Owl

Jackson, Chad (#17)
WR/PR (KR), 2006–07
13 receptions for 152 yards and three touchdowns
Longest reception was a 35-yard touchdown on 10-22-06
Four carries for 22 yards
Longest run was 14 yards on 10-22-06
Five punt returns for 83 yards
Longest punt return was 39 yards on 12-31-06
Six kickoff returns for 107 yards
Longest kickoff return was 39 yards on 12-09-07
14 regular season games
Three playoff games
#36 pick in the 2006 College Draft
Florida Gator

Jackson, Curtis (#82)
WR/KR, 2000–01
Seven receptions for 60 yards
Longest reception was 13 yards on 12-10-00
15 kickoff returns for 353 yards
Longest kickoff return was 47 yards on 12-04-00
Seven games
Member of the 2001 championship team
Texas Longhorn

Jackson, Eddie (#29)
DB/Special Team, 2007
Three regular season games
Arkansas Razorback

Jackson, Harold (#29) "Two-Nine" and "Hollywood"
Wide Receiver, 1978–81
156 receptions for 3,162 yards and 18 touchdowns
Longest reception was 59 yards on 09-16-79
11 carries for 42 yards
Longest run was 16 yards on 09-29-80
Two completions for 35 yards
Longest completion was 23 yards on 11-02-80
64 regular season games
Only playoff game appearance was on 12-31-78
Jackson State Tiger

Jackson, Honor (#29)
Defensive Back, 1972–73
Five interceptions for 133 yards
Longest return was 55 yards on 12-10-72
Recovered a fumble on 11-19-72
17 games
Pacific Tiger

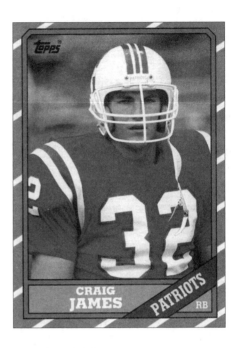

James, Jesse (#32) "Craig"
Running Back, 1984–88
585 carries for 2,469 yards and 11 touchdowns
Longest run was 73 yards on 12-02-84
81 receptions for 819 yards and two touchdowns
Longest reception was a 90-yard touchdown on
    09-15-85
Three completions for 26 yards and three touchdowns
Longest completion was an 11-yard touchdown on
    10-27-85
Recovered four offensive fumbles and one defensive
    fumble
AFC Pro Bowl running back in 1985
52 regular season games
Five playoff games
#187 pick in the 1983 College Draft
SMU Mustang

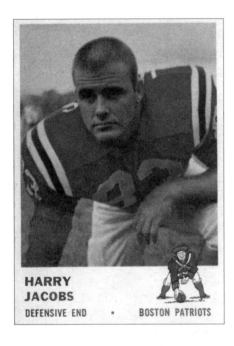

HARRY JACOBS
DEFENSIVE END   •   BOSTON PATRIOTS

Jacobs, Harry (#83) "Baby Face Assassin"
LB/DE, 1960–62
5.5 sacks
Four interceptions for 26 yards
Longest return was 14 yards on 12-18-60
Recovered a fumble on 09-23-61
Blocked a 35-yard field-goal attempt on 10-28-60
Recovered a Broncos onside kick on 11-11-62
37 games
Bradley Brave

Jacobs, Ray (#87)
Defensive Tackle, 1969
Recovered three fumbles
Eight games
Howard Payne Yellow Jacket

Jagielski, Harry (#73) "Moose"
DT/OT, 1960–61
Played on both sides of the line of scrimmage
19 games
Indiana Fighting Hoosier

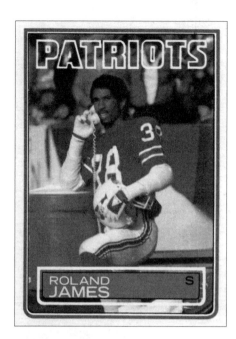

James, Roland (#38)
DB/PR, 1980–90
29 interceptions for 383 yards
Longest return was 46 yards on 10-23-83
Five sacks
42 punt returns for 400 yards and one touchdown
Longest punt return was a 75-yard touchdown on
    11-02-80
Recorded a safety on 11-18-84
Recovered 10 regular season fumbles
145 regular season games
Five playoff games
#14 pick in the 1980 College Draft
Tennessee Volunteer

Janik, Tom (#21) "The Blade"
Punter-DB, 1969–71
243 punts for 9,516 yards
Longest punt was 58 yards on 10-24-71
Returned an interception eight yards on 11-16-69
Recovered two fumbles
42 games
Texas A&I Javelina

Jarostchuk, Ilia (#50)
Linebacker, 1990
12 games
New Hampshire Wildcat

Jarvis, Ray (#87)
Wide Receiver, 1979
Two receptions for 30 yards and one touchdown
Caught a 15-yard touchdown pass on 10-21-79
His other 15 yard reception was on 10-01-79
Seven games
Norfolk State Spartan

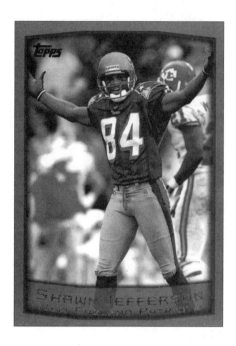

Jefferson, Shawn (#84)
Wide Receiver, 1996–99
178 receptions for 3,081 yards and 14 touchdowns
Longest reception was 76 yards on 11-02-97
Two carries for 21 yards
Longest run was 15 yards on 12-20-98
Recovered two fumbles
63 regular season games
Six playoff games
Central Florida Golden Knight

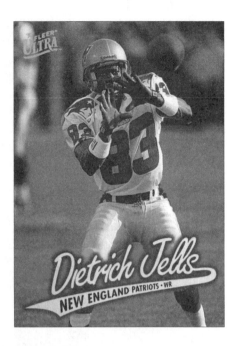

Jells, Deitrich (#18) and (#83)
Wide Receiver, 1996–97
Two receptions for 14 yards
Longest reception was nine yards on 11-16-97
18 games
Pittsburgh Panther

Jenkins, Ed (#30)
Running Back, 1974
Recovered a fumble on 12-15-74
Three games
Holy Cross Crusader

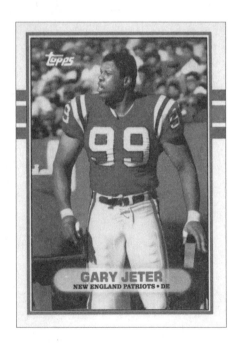

Jeter, Gary (#99)
Defensive Lineman, 1989
Seven sacks
14 games
USC Trojan

Johnson, Andy (#32) "AJ"
RB/WR/KR/PR, 1974–76 and 1978–81
491 carries for 2,017 yards and 13 touchdowns
Longest run was a 69-yard touchdown on 12-12-76
161 receptions for 1,807 yards and nine touchdowns
Longest reception was 53 yards on 12-12-76
Seven completions for 194 yards and four touchdowns
Longest completion was 66 yards on 10-04-81
28 kickoff returns for 544 yards
Longest kickoff return was 41 yards on 11-17-74
Six punt returns for 60 yards
Longest punt return was 15 yards on 12-07-75
Recovered a Bengals onside kick on 09-16-79
Recovered three fumbles
94 regular season games
Three playoff games
#113 pick in the 1974 College Draft
Georgia Bulldog

Johnson, Bethel (#81)
WR/KR (PR), 2003–05
30 receptions for 450 yards and four touchdowns
Longest reception was 48 yards on 10-17-04
Three carries for a net loss of four yards
Longest run was for 11 yards on 01-02-05
102 kickoff returns for 2,557 yards and two
    touchdowns

Returned a kickoff 92 yards for a touchdown on
  11-30-03
Returned a kickoff 93 yards for a touchdown on
  12-05-04
Six punt returns for 21 yards
Longest punt return was 11 yards on 10-30-05
AFC Special Team Player of Week on 11-30-03
Recovered three fumbles
39 regular season games
Six playoff games
Member of the 2003 and 2004 championship teams
#45 pick in the 2003 College Draft
Texas A&M Aggie

Johnson, Billy (#47) "BJ"
DB/KR/PR, 1966–68
Two interceptions for 33 yards
Longest return was 19 yards on 11-17-68
25 kickoff returns for 496 yards
Longest kickoff return was 36 yards on 10-20-68
Recovered a Patriots onside kick on 11-19-67
23 punt returns for 195 yards
Longest punt return was 52 yards on 11-05-67
Recovered four fumbles
Returned a fumble three yards on 10-30-66
Recovered a Broncos onside kick on 11-06-66
32 games
Nebraska Cornhusker

Johnson, Charles (#81)
Wide Receiver, 2001
14 receptions for 111 yards and one touchdown
Longest reception was a 24-yard touchdown on
  11-25-01
14 regular season games
Three playoff games
Member of the 2001 championship team
Colorado Buffalo

Johnson, Damian (#68)
Offensive Guard, 1990
16 games
Kansas State Wildcat

Johnson, Daryl (#23) "TT"
DB/KR/PR, 1968–70
Five interceptions for 85 yards
Longest return was 42 yards on 11-20-70
Recorded a safety on 11-16-69
Only sack was made on 09-20-70
Three kickoff returns for 63 yards
Longest kickoff return was 26 yards on 09-29-68

Three punt returns for 11 yards
Longest punt return was six yards on 11-01-70
Recovered two fumbles
Returned a fumble 32 yards for a touchdown on
  11-02-69
42 games
#197 pick in the 1968 College Draft
Morgan State Bear

Johnson, Ellis (#38)
RB/E/KR/DB, 1965–66
19 carries for 29 yards
Longest run was nine yards on 10-08-65
Four receptions for 29 yards
Longest reception was 23 yards on 09-11-65
Three kickoff returns for 31 yards
Longest kickoff return was 16 yards on 10-03-65
Recovered two fumbles
28 games
Fourth round draft pick in 1965
Southeast Louisiana Lion

Johnson, Garrett (#60) "Mini E"
Nose Tackle, 2000
Recovered a fumble on 12-17-00
Eight games
Illinois Fighting Illini

Johnson, Joe (#24)
Tight End, 1960–61
20 receptions for 268 yards and four touchdowns
Longest reception was a 52-yard touchdown on
  11-25-60
13 games
Boston College Eagle

Johnson, Lee (#10)
Punter, 1999–2001
203 punts for 8,578 yards
Longest punt was 76 yards on 09-09-01
Only completion was for 18 yards on 10-08-00
Only run was for 13 yards on 11-28-99
37 games
Member of the 2001 championship team
BYU Cougar

Johnson, Mario (#98)
Nose Tackle, 1993
Six games
Missouri Tiger

Johnson, Olrick (#51)
Linebacker, 2000
12 games
Florida A&M Rattler

Johnson, Preston (#48)
Running Back, 1968
Two carries for six yards
Longest run was six yards on 11-17-68
Three games
Florida A&M Rattler

Johnson, Steve (#85)
Tight End/Special Team, 1988
Only reception was five yards on 09-25-88
14 games
#154 pick in the 1988 College Draft
Virginia Tech Hokie

Johnson, Ted (#52) "The Pound Puppy"
Linebacker, 1995–2004
11.5 sacks
Only interception was on 12-01-96
AFC Defensive Player of the Week on 01-02-00
Recovered seven fumbles
125 regular season games
14 playoff games appearances
Member of the 2001, 2003, and 2004 championship
    teams
#57 pick in the 1995 College Draft
Ed Block Courage Award in 2001
Colorado Buffalo

Jones, Aaron (#97)
Defensive Lineman, 1993–95
8.5 sacks
Returned three fumbles for 28 yards
Longest fumble return was 21 yards on 11-27-94
37 regular season games
Only playoff game appearance was on 01-01-95
Eastern Kentucky Colonel

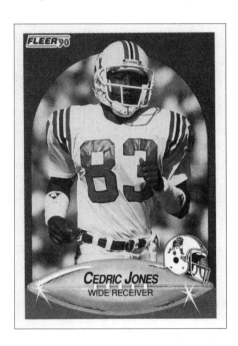

Jones, Cedric (#83)
WR/KR, 1982–90
191 receptions for 2,703 yards and 16 touchdowns
Longest reception was a 65-yard touchdown on
    11-05-89
14 kickoff returns for 207 yards
Longest kickoff return was 23 yards on 09-04-83
Recovered four fumbles
Fell on a fumble in the end zone for a touchdown on
    12-09-84
Returned a fumble 15 yards for a touchdown on
    12-16-85
Two carries for a net loss of four yards
Longest run was three yards on 11-26-89
Recovered a New York Jets onside kick on 11-13-88
120 regular season games
Six playoff games
#56 pick in the 1982 College Draft
Duke Blue Devil

Jones, Ezell (#74) "Easy"
OT/DL, 1969–70
Played on both sides of the line of scrimmage
Recorded a safety on 11-30-69

Blocked a Dolphins punt on 11-30-69
Recovered two fumbles
18 games
Minnesota Golden Gopher

Jones, Kenyatta (#74) "Bear"
Offensive Tackle, 2001–02
18 games
Member of the 2001 championship team
#96 pick in the 2001 College Draft
South Florida Bull

Jones, Mike (#96)
Defensive Lineman, 1994–97
15.5 sacks
Blocked a 29-yard field-goal attempt on 09-14-97
Recovered three fumbles
Returned a fumble 31 yards on 09-15-96
61 regular season games
Six playoff games
North Carolina State Wolfpack

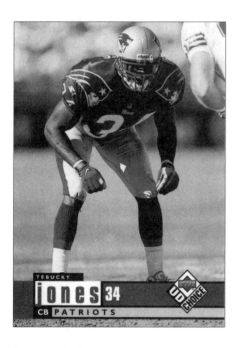

Jones, Tebucky (#34)
DB/KR, 1998–02
Four interceptions for 16 yards
Longest return was 20 yards on 10-08-00
Five kickoff returns for 113 yards
Longest kickoff return was 28 yards on 11-15-99
Blocked a 25-yard field-goal attempt on 10-21-01
Recovered three fumbles for 24 yards and one
     touchdown
Took his strip sack 24 yards for a touchdown on
     09-15-02

1.5 sacks
72 regular season games
Four playoff games
Member of the 2001 championship team
#22 pick in the 1998 College Draft
Syracuse Orangeman

Jones, Todd (#63)
Offensive Tackle, 1993
Four games
Henderson State Reddy

Jordan, LaMont (#32)
Running Back, 2008
80 carries for 363 yards and four touchdowns
Longest run was a 49-yard touchdown on 12-14-08
Recovered his own fumble on 12-07-08
Maryland Terrapin

Jordan, Shelby (#63) and (#74) "the Giant"
Offensive Tackle, 1975 and 1977–82
Recovered three fumbles
Advanced a fumble 12 yards on 11-16-75
95 regular season games
Two playoff games
Washington University Bear

Jordan, Tim (#93)
Linebacker, 1987–89
Three sacks
Returned an interception 31 yards on 10-16-88
Recovered three fumbles
30 games
#107 pick in the 1987 College Draft
Wisconsin Badger

Kaczur, Nick (#77)
Offensive Tackle, 2005–08
54 regular season games
Seven playoff games
#100 Pick in the 2005 College Draft
Toledo Rocket

Kadziel, Ron (#52)
Linebacker, 1972
Recovered a fumble on 12-03-72
14 games
Stanford Cardinal

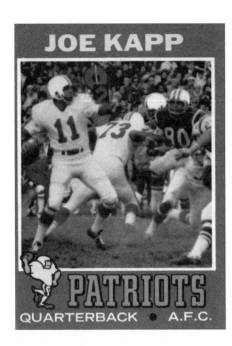

Kapp, Joe (#11) "Injun"
Quarterback, 1970
98 completions for 1,104 yards and three touchdowns
Longest completion was 48 yards on 10-25-70
20 carries for 71 yards
Longest run was 14 yards on 10-18-70
11 games
Inducted into Canadian Football Hall of Fame on
    03-16-84
Inducted into College Football Hall of Fame in 2004
California Golden Bear

Kasper, Kevin, (#10)
KR/WR, 2004
Returned three kickoffs for 61 yards
Longest return was 21 yards on 10-10-04 and on
    12-26-04
Eight games
Member of the 2004 championship team
Iowa Hawkeye

Katzenmoyer, Andy (#59)
Linebacker, 1999–2000
3.5 sacks
Returned a pass 57 yards for a touchdown on 10-17-99
24 games
#28 pick in the 1999 College Draft
Ohio State Buckeye

Kecman, Dan (#45)
Linebacker, 1970
Only game played was on 09-27-70
Maryland Terrapin

Keeton, Durwood (#29)
Defensive Back, 1975
Recovered a fumble on 09-28-75
12 games
Oklahoma Sooner

Kelley, Ethan (#99)
Defensive Tackle, 2004
Only game played was on 01-02-05
Member of the 2004 championship team
#243 pick in the 2003 College Draft
Baylor Bear

Kelly, Ben (#31)
DB/KR, 2001–02
Seven kickoff returns for 123 yards
Longest return was 28 yards on 11-25-01
Recovered his own fumble on 11-25-01
Nine games
Member of the 2001 championship team
Colorado Buffalo

Kerrigan, Mike (#19)
Quarterback, 1983–84
Seven completions for 85 yards
Longest completion was 19 yards on 12-18-83
Only run was for 14 yards on 12-18-83
Two games
Northwestern Wildcat

Key, David (#26)
Defensive Back, 1991
Recovered a fumble on 12-15-91
Three games
#140 pick in the 1991 College Draft
Michigan Wolverine

Khayat, Ed (#73)
Defensive Lineman, 1966
14 games
Tulane Green Wave

Kight, Kelvin (#19)
WR/Special Team, 2006
Caught a nine-yard pass on 12-24-06
Ran for an eight-yard gain on 12-31-06
Four games
Florida Gator

Kimber, Bill (#86)
Offensive End, 1961
Four games
Florida State Seminole

Kinchen, Brian (#46)
Long Snapper, 2003
Two regular season games
Three playoff games
Member of the 2003 championship team
LSU Tiger

Kiner, Steve (#57)
Linebacker, 1971 and 1973
7.5 sacks
Four interceptions for 25 yards
Longest return was 14 yards on 11-07-71
Returned two fumbles for 13 yards
Returned a fumble two yards on 10-10-71
Returned a fumble 11 yards on 09-23-73
NFL Defensive Player of the Week on 11-07-71
Blocked a 39-yard field-goal attempt on 09-23-73
Recorded a safety on 11-25-73
28 games
Inducted into the College Football Hall of Fame on
    12-07-99
Tennessee Volunteer

King, Claude (#41)
RB/KR, 1962
21 carries for 144 yards and one touchdown
Longest run was a 71-yard touchdown on 09-21-62
Five receptions for 42 yards
Longest reception was 33 yards on 09-21-62
Nine kickoff returns for 177 yards
Longest kickoff return was 28 yards on 10-26-62
14 games
Houston Cougar

King, Steve (#52) "Reno"
Linebacker, 1973–81
Eight sacks
Returned an interception nine yards on 10-13-74
124 regular season games
Two playoff games
Tulsa Golden Hurricane

Klecko, Dan (#90)
DT (RB and KR), 2003–05
Two sacks
Returned a fumble four yards on 11-30-03
Two carries for five yards
Longest run was five yards on 10-12-03

Three receptions for 18 yards
Longest reception was 11 yards on 10-17-04
Two kickoff returns for 20 yards
Each return was 10 yards on 10-05-03 and on 12-20-03
Made a fair catch of a short kickoff on 10-10-04
Blocked a 48-yard field-goal attempt on 09-28-03
29 regular season games
Only playoff game appearance was on 01-10-04
Member of the 2003 and 2004 championship teams
#117 pick in the 2003 College Draft
Temple Owl

Klein, Dick (#62)
OT/DT, 1961–62
5.5 sacks
Blocked a Buffalo Bills punt on 10-22-61
Blocked an Oakland Raiders punt on 12-09-61
Recovered a fumble on 12-16-62
Played on both sides on the line of scrimmage
24 games
Iowa Hawkeye

Klemm, Adrian (#70)
Tackle/Guard (TE), 2000 and 2002–04
Occasionally used as a blocking tight end
26 games
Member of the 2003 and 2004 championship teams
#46 pick in the 2000 College Draft
Hawaii Rainbow

Knief, Gayle (#84)
Wide Receiver, 1970
Three receptions for 39 yards and one touchdown
Longest reception was a 22-yard touchdown on
    12-06-70
Three games
Morningside Chief

Koontz, Ed (#54)
Linebacker, 1968
Six games
#440 pick in the 1968 College Draft
Catawba Indian

Kopp, Jeff (#91)
Linebacker, 1999
Six games
USC Trojan

Koppen, Dan (#67)
Center, 2003–08
Recovered five fumbles
AFC Pro Bowl center in 2007

88 regular season games
12 playoff games
Member of the 2003 and 2004 championship teams
#164 pick in the 2003 College Draft
Boston College Eagle

Krakau, Merv (#53)
Linebacker, 1978
Only game played was on 12-10-78
Iowa State Cyclone

Kratch, Bob (#61)
Guard, 1994–96
40 regular season games
Four playoff games
Iowa Hawkeye

Kuberski, Bob (#93)
Defensive Tackle, 1999
Five games
Navy Midshipman

Kuehn, Art (#78)
Center, 1983
Two games
UCLA Bruin

Kurpeikis, Justin (#47)
Special Team, 2004
Five games
Member of the 2004 championship team
Penn State Nittany Lion

Ladd, Anthony (#18)
Special Team, 1998
Four games
Cincinnati Bearcat

Lambert, Dion (#28)
Defensive Back, 1992–93
Only sack was made on 11-22-92
Recovered a fumble on 11-22-92
Only interception was not returned on 12-19-93
30 games
#90 pick in the 1992 College Draft
UCLA Bruin

Lane, Max (#68) "Big Country"
Guard/Tackle and TE, 1994–2000
Recovered five fumbles
Advanced a fumble 30 yards on 10-15-95
Occasionally used as a blocking tight end

100 regular season games
Seven playoff games
#168 pick in the 1994 College Draft
Navy Midshipman

Langham, Antonio (#38)
Defensive Back, 2000
Returned an interception 24 yards on 09-11-00
15 games
Alabama Crimson Tide

Larson, Bill (#34)
Special Team, 1960
Only game played was on 09-09-60
Illinois Wesleyan Titan

Lassiter, Isaac (#87) "Ike"
Defensive End, 1970–71
Seven sacks
Recovered a fumble on 10-04-70
19 games
St. Augustine's Mighty Falcon

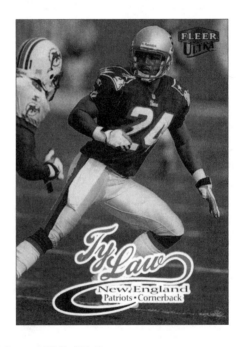

Law, Tajuan (#24) "Ty"
Cornerback, 1995–2004
36 interceptions for 583 yards and six touchdowns
Longest return was a 65-yard touchdown on 10-05-03
Four sacks
Recovered four fumbles
Returned a fumble 17 yards on 12-20-98
AFC Pro Bowl cornerback in 1998 and 2001
Co-MVP in 1998 Pro Bowl
141 regular season games

12 playoff games
Member of the 2001, 2003, and 2004 championship
    teams
#23 pick in the 1995 College Draft
Michigan Wolverine

Lawson, Jamie (#29)
Special Team, 1990
Only game played was on 12-30-90
Nicholls State Colonel

Lawson, Odell (#32)
RB/KR, 1970–71
64 carries for 107 yards
Longest run was 15 yards on 10-04-70
11 receptions for 113 yards
Longest reception was 19 yards on 11-29-70
27 kickoff returns for 593 yards
Longest kickoff return was 52 yards on 11-15-70
Recovered a fumble on 10-04-70
16 games
#160 pick in the 1970 College Draft
Langston Lion

LeBlanc, Michael (#40) and (#27)
RB/KR, 1987
49 carries for 170 yards and one touchdown
Only touchdown run was for three yards on
    10-18-87
Longest run was 42 yards on 10-11-87
Two receptions for three yards
Longest reception was three yards on 10-18-87
Two kickoff returns for 31 yards
Longest kickoff return was 24 yards on 10-04-87
Four games
Stephen F. Austin State Lumberjack

Lee, Bob (#60)
Guard, 1960
Eight games
Missouri Tiger

Lee, John (#66)
Defensive Tackle, 1981
Three sacks
Four games
Nebraska Cornhusker

Lee, Keith (#22)
DB/KR, 1981–84
Only interception was not returned on 10-18-81
10 kickoff returns for 117 yards

Longest kickoff return was 19 yards on 10-16-83
Recovered two regular season fumbles
54 regular season games
Only playoff game appearance was on 01-08-83
Colorado State Ram

Lee, Kevin (#86)
WR/KR, 1995
Eight receptions for 107 yards
Longest reception was 33 yards on 10-08-95
Only run was four yards on 10-23-95
Only kickoff return was 14 yards on 10-23-95
Seven games
#35 pick in the 1994 College Draft
Alabama Crimson Tide

Legette, Burnie (#35)
Special Team, 1993–94
10 games
Michigan Wolverine

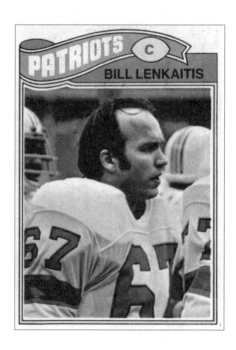

Lenkaitis, Bill (#67) "Missing Link"
Center/Guard, 1971–81
Recovered three fumbles
151 regular season games
Two playoff games
Penn State Nittany Lion

Leo, Bobby (#24)
WR/PR/KR, 1967–68
Only reception was a 25-yard touchdown on 12-09-67
Ran for a seven-yard gain on 12-09-67
Seven punt returns for 66 yards

Longest punt return was 43 yards on 12-09-67
11 kickoff returns for 232 yards
Longest kickoff return was 31 yards on 12-17-67
Recovered three fumbles
Three games
#180 pick in the 1967 College Draft
Harvard Crimson

Leo, Charlie (#63)
Guard, 1960–62
Recovered two fumbles
34 games
AFL All-Star guard in 1960 and 1961
Indiana Fighting Hoosier

LeVoir, Mark (#64)
Tackle, 2008
Recovered a fumble on 10-12-08
15 games
Notre Dame Fighting Irish

Lewis, Bill (#75)
Center, 1993
Seven games
Nebraska Cornhusker

Lewis, Vernon (#43)
Defensive Back, 1993–96
1.5 sacks
Recovered a fumble on 10-29-95
44 regular season games
Only playoff game appearance was on 01-01-95
Pittsburgh Panther

Light, Matt (#72)
Offensive Tackle, 2001–08
Recovered two fumbles
AFC Pro Bowl tackle in 2007
113 regular season games
15 playoff games
Member of the 2001, 2003, and 2004 championship
    teams
#48 pick in the 2001 College Draft
Purdue Boilermaker

Lindquist, Paul (#67)
Defensive Tackle, 1961
Recovered a fumble on 09-16-61
Two games
New Hampshire Wildcat

Linne, Larry (#80)
WR/PR, 1987
11 receptions for 158 yards and two touchdowns
Longest reception was 30 yards on 10-18-87
Five punt returns for 22 yards
Longest punt return was 16 yards on 10-04-87
Recovered a fumble on 10-18-87
Three games
Texas El Paso Miner

Lippett, Ronnie (#42) "Lip"
Defensive Back, 1983–88 and 1990–91
24 interceptions for 420 yards and two touchdowns
Longest return was 73 yards on 09-09-90
Recovered nine fumbles
Blocked an extra-point attempt on 09-18-83

AFC Defensive Player of the Week on 10-05-86
Only sack was made on 10-25-87
Recovered a Colts onside kick on 09-16-90
122 regular season games
Four playoff games
#214 pick in the 1983 College Draft
Ed Block Courage Award in 1990
Miami Hurricane

Livingston, Walt (#24)
RB (KR), 1960
10 carries for 16 yards and one touchdown
Ran for a two-yard touchdown on 09-17-60
Longest run was five yards on 09-09-60
Only reception was for no gain on 09-17-60
Only kickoff return was three yards on 09-09-60
Three games
Heidelberg College Student Prince

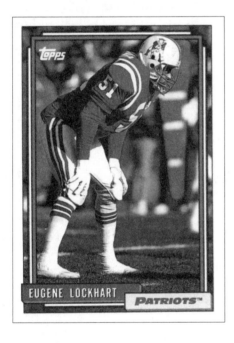

Lockhart, Eugene (#51)
Linebacker, 1991–92
Recovered a fumble on 10-18-92
32 games
Houston Cougar

Lockwood, Scott (#40)
RB/KR, 1992–93
35 carries for 162 yards
Longest run of 23 yards on 12-27-92
11 kickoff returns for 233 yards
Longest kickoff return was 36 yards on 12-13-92
Recovered a fumble on 12-13-92
Six games

#204 pick in the 1992 College Draft
USC Trojan

Lofton, Oscar (#86)
Tight End, 1960
19 receptions for 360 yards and four touchdowns
Longest reception was a 39-yard touchdown on
    12-18-60
14 games
Southeast Louisiana Lion

Lofton, Steve (#38)
Cornerback, 1997–98
10 games
Texas A&M Aggie

Long, Charley (#76) "Choo-choo"
T/OL/DL/TE (KR), 1961–69
Shared in a QB sack on 11-28-65
Recovered two fumbles
Returned a fumble two yards on 10-12-62
Occasionally used as a tight end
Played on both sides of the line of scrimmage
Six kickoff returns for 44 yards
Longest return was 11 yards on 10-01-61 and on 11-03-68
AFL All-Star tackle in 1962 and 1963
124 regular season games
Two playoff games
Eighth round draft pick in 1961
Tenn-Chattanooga Moccasin

Long, Mike (#87)
Offensive End, 1960
Two receptions for 10 yards
Had a five-yard reception on 09-09-60 and 09-17-60
Two games
Brandeis Judge

Lott, Billy (#32)
RB (PR), 1961–63
143 carries for 573 yards and seven touchdowns
Longest run was 38 yards on 10-07-61
36 receptions for 395 yards and seven touchdowns
Longest reception was a 55-yard touchdown on
     09-22-63
Only punt return was eight yards on 10-01-61
35 regular season games
Two playoff games
Mississippi Rebel

Loudd, Rommie (#60) and (#46)
Linebacker/TE (KR), 1961–62
Eight sacks
Returned an interception 12 yards on 12-09-61
Returned four fumbles for 10 yards
Returned a fumble seven yards on 12-17-61
Advanced a fumble three yards on 12-26-62
Was used as a tight end and LB on 12-16-62
Returned a kickoff 15 yards on 10-26-62
27 games
UCLA Bruin

Loukas, Angelo (#66)
Guard, 1970
Two games
Northwestern Wildcat

Lowe, Omare (#23)
Defensive Back, 2004
Three games
Member of the 2004 championship team
Washington Husky

Lowery, Nick (#7)
Kicker, 1978
Seven extra points
Two games
Dartmouth Big Green

Lowry, Orlando (#91)
Linebacker, 1989
Two games
Ohio State Buckeye

Lucas, Ray (#15)
Special Team, 1996
Two regular season games
Two playoff games
Rutgers Scarlet Knight

Lunsford, Mel (#72) "Jaws"
Defensive Lineman, 1973–80
20.5 sacks
Blocked a 39-yard field-goal attempt on 09-26-77
Recovered four regular season fumbles
92 regular season games
Two playoff games
Central State Maurader

Lyle, Rick (#96)
Defensive Lineman, 2002–03
21 games
Member of the 2003 championship team
Missouri Tiger

Maitland, Jack (#40)
RB/KR, 1971–72
26 carries for 58 yards and one touchdown
Ran for a 2-yard touchdown on 11-07-71
Longest run was six yards on 11-28-71 and on 11-26-72
Five receptions for 39 yards
Longest reception was nine yards on 11-13-72
Five kickoff returns for 68 yards
Longest kickoff return was 21 yards on 12-05-71
Recovered four fumbles
Advanced a fourth-down fumble three yards on
     12-12-71
27 games
Williams Ephman

Mallard, Wesley (#96)
Special Team, 2005
Three games
Oregon Duck

Mallory, Irvin (#43)
DB (KR), 1971
Returned a kickoff 19 yards on 09-26-71
Two games
Virginia Union Panther

Mangiero, Dino (#96)
Nose Tackle, 1987
Recorded a sack on 10-11-87
Two games
Rutgers Scarlet Knight

Mangum, John (#74) "Jumbo"
DT (KR), 1966–67
Recovered a fumble on 10-15-67
Returned a kickoff eight yards on 12-04-66

28 games
Fifth round draft pick in 1966
Southern Mississippi Golden Eagle

Mankins, Logan (#70)
Offensive Guard, 2005–08
Recovered a fumble on 11-27-05
Caught a pass for a nine-yard loss on 10-01-07
AFC Pro Bowl offensive guard in 2007
64 regular season games
Eight playoff games
#32 pick in the 2005 College Draft
Fresno State Bulldog

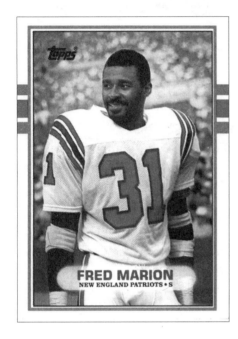

FRED MARION
NEW ENGLAND PATRIOTS • S

Marion, Fred (#31)
Safety (PR), 1982–91
29 interceptions for 457 yards and one touchdown
Longest return was 83 yards on 11-17-85
Returned a pass 37 yards for a touchdown on 10-19-86
Only sack was made on 09-30-84
Two punt returns for 12 yards
Longest punt return was 12 yards on 10-19-86
Recovered 13 regular season fumbles
Returned a fumble nine yards on 11-10-85
AFC Defensive Player of the Week on 11-10-85
AFC Defensive Player of the Week on 10-16-88
AFC Pro Bowl safety in 1985
144 regular season games
Six playoff games
#112 pick in the 1982 College Draft
Ed Block Courage Award in 1991
Miami Hurricane

Maroney, Laurence (#39) "Kool-Aid"
RB/KR, 2006–08
388 carries for 1,673 yards and 12 touchdowns
Longest run was a 59-yard touchdown on 12-23-07
Ran for a two-point conversion on 12-29-07
26 receptions for 310 yards and one touchdown
Caught a 19-yard touchdown pass on 11-19-06
Longest reception was for 43 yards on 12-03-07
28 kickoff returns for 783 yards
Longest kickoff return was 77 yards on 10-30-06
AFC Special Team Player of the Week on 10-30-06
30 regular season games
Six playoff games
#21 pick in the 2006 College Draft
Minnesota Golden Gopher

Marsh, Aaron (#29)
WR/KR, 1968–69
27 receptions for 439 yards and four touchdowns
Longest reception was a 70-yard touchdown on
    09-22-68
Four carries for eight yards
Longest run was 11 yards on 11-03-68
10 kickoff returns for 210 yards
Longest kickoff return was 41 yards on 11-23-69
Recovered a fumble on 09-29-68
28 games
#60 pick in the 1968 College Draft
Eastern Kentucky Colonel

Marshall, Al (#88)
Wide Receiver, 1974
Only reception was a 17-yard touchdown on 12-01-74
Four games
Boise State Bronco

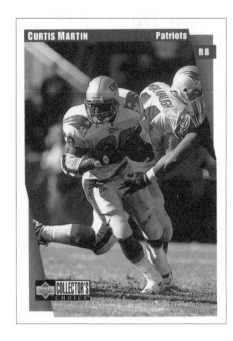

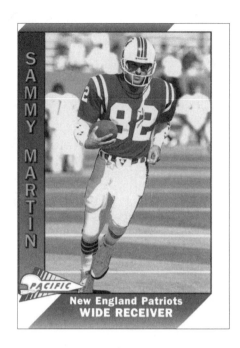

Martin, Curtis (#28) "My Favorite"
Running Back, 1995–97
958 carries for 3,799 yards and 32 touchdowns
Longest regular season run was a 70-yard touchdown
    on 09-21-97
117 receptions for 890 yards and five touchdowns
Longest reception was 41 yards on 11-03-96
Caught a pass for a two-point conversion on 11-26-95
Caught a pass for a two-point conversion on 09-15-96
Recovered four fumbles
AFC Offensive Player of the Week on 11-05-95
AFC Offensive Player of the Week on 12-10-95
AFC Pro Bowl running back in 1995 and 1996
NFL Offensive Rookie of the Year in 1995
45 regular season games
Three playoff games
#74 pick in the 1995 College Draft
Pittsburgh Panther

Martin, Don (#38)
Defensive Back, 1973
Returned a fumble 35 yards on 11-25-73
14 games
Yale Bulldog

Martin, Sammy (#82)
WR/KR/PR, 1988–91
21 receptions for 345 yards and one touchdown
Longest reception was 37 yards on 11-05-89
Caught a 19-yard touchdown pass on 10-28-90
Two carries for 20 yards
Longest run was 13 yards on 11-12-89
88 kickoff returns for 2,012 yards and one touchdown
Returned kickoff 95 yards for a touchdown on
    11-27-88
20 punt returns for 165 yards
Longest punt return was 28 yards on 10-08-89
40 games
#97 pick in the 1988 College Draft
LSU Fighting Tiger

Martin, Steve (#90)
Defensive Tackle, 2002
14 games
Missouri Tiger

Mason, Dave (#28)
Defensive Back, 1973
Recovered a fumble on 12-16-73
Eight games
Nebraska Cornhusker

Mass, Wayne (#75)
Offensive Tackle, 1972
Six games
Clemson Tiger

Massey, Jim (#47)
Defensive Back, 1974–75
Recovered a fumble on 12-21-75
15 games
Linfield Wildcat

Matich, Trevor (#64)
Center/Guard, 1985–88
26 regular season games
Only playoff game appearance was on 01-04-87
#28 pick in the 1985 College Draft
BYU Cougar

Matthews, Bill (#53)
Linebacker (KR), 1978–81
Returned an interception five yards on 10-26-80
Recovered a fumble on 10-25-81
Only kickoff return was five yards on 12-13-81
48 games
#129 pick in the 1978 College Draft
South Dakota State Jack Rabbit

Matthews, Henry (#35)
Kickoff Returnman, 1972
Three kickoff returns for 74 yards
Longest kickoff return was 29 yards on 12-03-72
Three games
Michigan State Spartan

May, Art (#71) "Pop"
Defensive End, 1971
3.5 sacks
11 games
Tuskegee Golden Tiger

Mayer, Shawn (#39)
Safety/Special Team, 2003–04
12 regular season games
Three playoff games
Member of the 2003 and 2004 championship teams
Penn State Nittany Lion

Mayo, Jerod (#51)
Linebacker, 2008
Recovered a fumble on 10-20-08
Defensive Rookie of the Year
16 games
#10 pick in the 2008 College Draft
Tennessee Volunteer

Mays, Corey (#46)
LB/Special Team, 2006–07
Nine regular season games
Three playoff games
Notre Dame Fighting Irish

McAllister, James (#37)
RB/KR, 1978
19 carries for 77 yards and two touchdowns
Longest run was 16 yards on 10-29-78
Only reception was 12 yards on 12-18-78
10 kickoff returns for 186 yards
Longest kickoff return was 32 yards on 10-29-78
16 regular season games
Only playoff game appearance was on 12-31-78
UCLA Bruin

McCabe, Jerry (#52)
Linebacker, 1987
Only sack was made on 10-18-87
Three games
Holy Cross Crusader

McCall, Bob (#24)
RB (KR), 1973
10 carries for 15 yards
Longest run was 14 yards on 11-18-73
Three receptions for 18 yards
Longest reception was 14 yards on 11-11-73
Two kickoff returns for 17 yards
Longest kickoff return was 17 yards on 12-09-73
Recovered two fumbles
Eight games
Arizona Wildcat

McCarthy, Shawn (#11)
Punter, 1991–92
169 punts for 6,877 yards
Longest punt was team record 93 yards on 11-03-91
Completed an 11-yard pass on 11-24-91
Recovered a fumble on 11-01-92
29 games
Purdue Boilermaker

McComb, Don (#85)
Defensive End, 1960
Only game played was on 09-09-60
Villanova Wildcat

McCrary, Fred (#44)
Running Back, 2003
Three carries for three yards
Longest run was four yards on 10-19-03
Two receptions for 12 yards
Longest reception was 12 yards on 11-03-03
Six games
Member of the 2003 championship team
Mississippi State Bulldog

McCray, Prentice (#34) "Pinhead"
Cornerback, 1974–80
15 interceptions for 352 yards and two touchdowns
Longest return was a 63-yard touchdown on 11-21-76
Returned another pass 55 yards for a touchdown on
    11-21-76
Only sack was made on 09-16-79
Recovered six fumbles
Returned a fumble two yards on 10-06-74
81 regular season games
Only playoff game appearance was on 12-18-76
Arizona State Sun Devil

McCurry, Dave (#40)
Defensive Back, 1974
Two games
Iowa State Cyclone

McDermott, Sean (#49)
Long Snapper, 2003
Only game played was on 12-14-03
Member of the 2003 championship team
Kansas Jayhawk

McDougald, Doug (#70)
Defensive End, 1980
Only sack was made on 12-14-80
Eight games
#124 pick in the 1980 College Draft
Virginia Tech Hokie

McGee, George (#75)
Offensive Tackle, 1960
14 games
Southern Jaguar

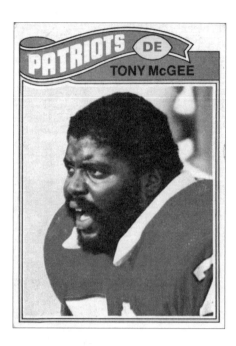

McGee, Tony (#78) "Mac the Sack"
Defensive End, 1974–81
72.5 sacks
Recovered three fumbles
Returned a fumble eight yards on 10-16-77
119 regular season games
Two playoff games
Bishop Cardinal

McGinest, Willie (#55) "Big Mac"
DE/LB, 1994–05
78 sacks
Four interceptions for 90 yards and two touchdowns

Longest interception was a 46-yard touchdown on
    10-27-96
Returned a pass 15 yards for a touchdown on 12-20-03
AFC Defensive Player of the Week on 10-27-96
AFC Defensive Player of the Week on 09-12-99
AFC Defensive Player of the Week on 12-20-03
Recovered 15 fumbles and scored two touchdowns
Recovered a fumble for a touchdown on 12-01-96
Recovered a fumble for a touchdown on 09-12-99
AFC Pro Bowl defensive end in 1996
AFC Pro Bowl linebacker in 2003
171 regular season games
18 playoff games
Member of the 2001, 2003, and 2004 championship
    teams
#4 pick in the 1994 College Draft
USC Trojan

McGovern, Rob (#58)
Linebacker, 1992
Four games
Holy Cross Crusader

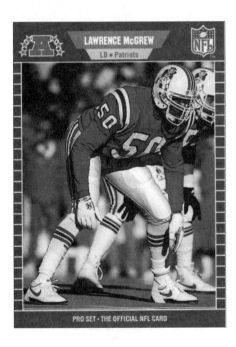

LAWRENCE McGREW
LB • Patriots

PRO SET • THE OFFICIAL NFL CARD

McGrew, Larry (#50)
Linebacker, 1980–89
16.5 sacks
Six interceptions for 49 yards
Longest return was 27 yards on 10-05-86
Blocked a Steelers punt on 10-19-86
Recovered five regular season fumbles
122 regular season games

Six playoff games
#45 pick in the 1980 College Draft
USC Trojan

McGruder, Mike (#27) "Scooter"
Cornerback, 1996–97
1.5 sacks
17 regular season games
Three playoff games
Kent State Golden Flash

McHale, Joe (#55)
Linebacker, 1987
Three games
Delaware Fightin' Blue Hen

McKay, Bob (#66) "Booger"
Guard/Tackle (KR), 1976–78
Two kickoff returns for 39 yards
Longest kickoff return was 23 yards on 09-12-76
Recovered a fumble on 12-11-77
39 regular season games
Only playoff game appearance was on 12-18-76
Texas Longhorn

McKinnon, Don (#51)
Linebacker, 1963–64
17 regular season games
Two playoff games
10th round draft pick in 1963
Dartmouth Big Green

McMahon, Art (#28) "Irish Art"
Defensive Back, 1968–1972
Three interceptions for 99 yards
Longest return was 72 yards on 10-11-70
Recovered two fumbles
43 games
#385 pick in the 1968 College Draft
North Carolina State Wolfpack

McMichael, Steve (#66)
Defensive Tackle, 1980
Six games
#73 pick in the 1980 College Draft
Texas Longhorn

GREG McMURTRY

McMurtry, Greg (#86)
Wide Receiver, 1990–1993
120 receptions for 1,519 yards and four touchdowns
Longest reception was a 65-yard touchdown on
    11-15-92
Two carries for three yards
Longest run was two yards on 12-27-92
Recovered a fumble on 10-17-93
58 games
#80 pick in the 1990 College Draft
Michigan Wolverine

McNeil, Emanuel (#92)
Nose Tackle, 1989
Only game played was on 12-24-89
#267 pick in the 1989 College Draft
Tennessee Martin Skyhawk

McQuay, Leon (#31)
RB/KR, 1975
33 carries for 47 yards
Longest run was nine yards on 09-21-75
Four receptions for 27 yards
Longest reception was 16 yards on 12-01-75
15 kickoff returns for 252 yards
Longest kickoff return was 34 yards on 09-21-75
Recovered a fumble on 10-26-75
13 games
Tampa Spartan

McSwain, Anthony (#32) "Chuck"
RB/KR, 1987
Nine carries for 23 yards
Longest run was nine yards on 10-04-87
Two kickoff returns for 32 yards
Longest kickoff return was 24 yards on 10-04-87
Recovered a fumble on 10-04-87
Three games
Clemson Tiger

McSwain, Rod (#23)
Defensive Back, 1984–90
Six interceptions for 89 yards
Longest return was 42 yards on 11-27-88
Two sacks
Blocked a Los Angeles Rams punt on 11-16-86
Returned the blocked punt 31 yards for a touchdown
    on 11-16-86
Recovered three fumbles
90 regular season games
Five playoff games
Clemson Tiger

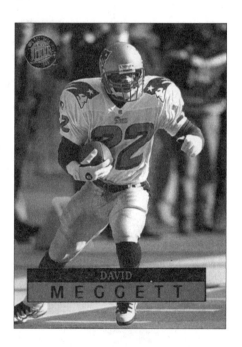

DAVID MEGGETT

Meggett, Dave (#22) "Little Big Man"
RB/PR/KR, 1995–97
120 carries for 432 yards and four touchdowns
Longest run was 25 yards on 10-15-95
104 receptions for 829 yards and one touchdown
Longest reception was a 49-yard touchdown on
    12-13-97
142 punt returns for 1,438 yards and one touchdown
Longest punt return was a 60-yard touchdown on
    12-21-96

105 kickoff returns for 2,561 yards
Longest kickoff return was 61 yards on 11-02-97
Only completion was a 35-yard touchdown pass on
    11-23-97
Ran for a two-point conversion on 09-03-95
Caught a pass for a two-point conversion on 12-16-95
Recovered five regular season fumbles
AFC Pro Bowl return specialist in 1996
48 regular season games
Five playoff games
Ed Block Courage Award in 1997
Towson State Tiger

Megna, Marc (#99)
Special Team, 2000
Four games
Richmond Spider

Meixler, Ed (#52)
Linebacker, 1965
Four games
18th round draft pick in 1965
Boston University Terrier

Melander, Jon (#64)
Guard/Tackle, 1991
11 games
#113 pick in the 1990 College Draft
Minnesota Golden Gopher

Meriweather, Brandon (#31)
DB, 2007–08
Two sacks
Four interceptions for 25 yards
Longest return was 19 yards on 11-23-08
32 regular season games
Three playoff games
#24 pick in the 2007 College Draft
Miami Hurricane

Mickens, Ray (#38)
Defensive Back, 2006
Four regular season games
Three playoff games
Texas A&M Aggie

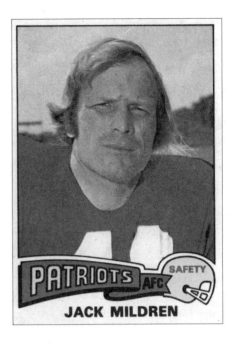

JACK MILDREN

Mildren, Jack (#45)
Defensive Back, 1974
Three interceptions for 51 yards
Longest return was 41 yards on 11-24-74
Recovered two fumbles
Returned a fumble five yards on 11-03-74
14 games
Oklahoma Sooner

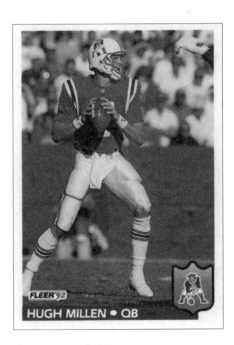

HUGH MILLEN • QB

Millen, Hugh (#7) "Thrillin"
Quarterback, 1991–92
370 completions for 4,276 yards and 17 touchdowns
Longest completion was a 60-yard touchdown on
    12-22-91
48 carries for 200 yards and one touchdown

Ran for a two-yard touchdown on 11-24-91
Longest run was 26 yards on 09-13-92 and 10-04-92
Recovered four fumbles
20 games
Washington Husky

Miller, Alan (#32)
Running Back, 1960
101 carries for 416 yards and one touchdown
Ran for a one-yard touchdown on 10-08-60
Longest run was 33 yards on 10-23-60
29 receptions for 284 yards and two touchdowns
Longest reception was a 48-yard touchdown on
    10-23-60
14 games
Boston College Eagle

Miller, Danny (#6)
Kicker, 1982
Two field goals
Longest field goal was 25 yards on 11-28-82
Four extra points
Two games
Miami Hurricane

Miller, Josh (#8)
Punter, 2004–06
175 punts for 7,629 yards
Longest punt was 69 yards on 12-12-04
42 regular season games
Five playoff games
Member of the 2004 championship team
Arizona Wildcat

Milloy, Lawyer (#36)
Safety, 1996–02
19 interceptions for 123 yards and one touchdown
Longest return was a 30-yard touchdown on 09-20-98
Seven sacks
Recovered seven fumbles
AFC Defensive Player of the Week on 11-01-98
AFC Defensive Player of the Week on 11-19-00
AFC Pro Bowl safety in 1998, 1999, 2001, and 2002
112 regular season games
Nine playoff games
Member of the 2001 championship team
#36 pick in the 1996 College Draft
Washington Husky

Mirich, Rex (#76)
Defensive Lineman, 1970
Seven games
Arizona State Sun Devil

Mitchell, Brandon (#98)
Defensive End, 1997–2001
Six sacks
Blocked a 46-yard field-goal attempt on 10-21-01
Recovered a fumble on 09-19-99
62 regular season games
Five playoff games
Member of the 2001 championship team
#59 pick in the 1997 College Draft
Texas A&M Aggie

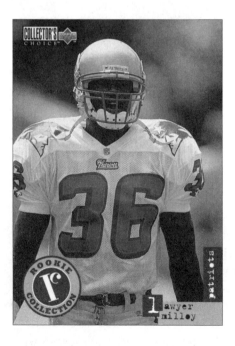

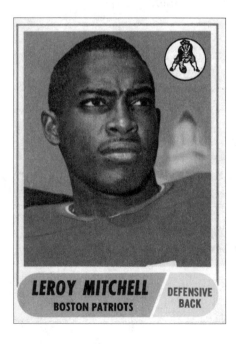

Mitchell, Leroy (#41)
DB, 1967–68
10 interceptions for 50 yards

Longest return was 20 yards on 10-27-68
Recovered two fumbles
AFL All-Star defensive back in 1968
28 games
#283 pick in the 1967 College Draft
Texas Southern Tiger

Mitchell, Mel III (#24)
Special Team/DB, 2007
10 regular season games
Two playoff games
Western Kentucky Hilltopper

Montler, Mike (#64)
Tackle/Guard, 1969–72
Recovered two fumbles
53 games
#32 pick in the 1969 College Draft
Colorado Buffalo

Moore, Art (#75)
NT/DT, 1973–77
Eight sacks
Blocked a 43-yard field-goal attempt on 11-25-73
Blocked a 47-yard field-goal attempt on 12-02-73
Blocked a 41-yard field-goal attempt on 09-29-74
Recovered a fumble on 09-30-73
Co-returned a blocked punt eight yards on 10-14-73
29 games
Tulsa Golden Hurricane

Moore, Brandon (#70)
Tackle, 1993–95
26 games
Duke Blue Devil

Moore, Greg (#54)
Linebacker, 1987
Recovered a fumble on 10-11-87
Three games
Tenn-Chattanooga Moccasin

Moore, LeRoy (#61)
Defensive End, 1961–62
Recovered a deflected punt for a touchdown on
    11-17-61
Recovered two fumbles
19 games
Fort Valley State Wildcat

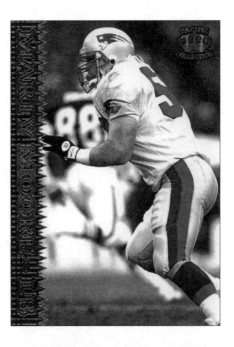

Moore, Marty (#58) and (#90) "Mr. Irrelevant"
Linebacker, 1994–99 and 2001
Two interceptions for seven yards
Longest return was seven yards on 10-12-97
Recovered a fumble on 12-13-98
96 regular season games
Seven playoff games
Member of the 2001 championship team
#222 pick in the 1994 College Draft
Kentucky Wildcat

Moore, Rashad (#95) "Booger"
Defensive Lineman, 2007
Only regular season game was on 12-23-07
Two playoff games
Tennessee Volunteer

Moore, Steve (#67) "Big House"
Tackle (FB), 1983–87
Was a blocking back on 11-03-85 and on 11-10-85
52 regular season games
Four playoff games
#80 pick in the 1983 College Draft
Tennessee State Tiger

Moore, Will (#83)
Wide Receiver, 1995–96
46 receptions for 539 yards and one touchdown
Longest reception was 33 yards on 09-10-95
Only touchdown reception was for six yards on
    10-15-95
16 games
Texas Southern Tiger

Moreland, Earthwind (#29)
Cornerback, 2004
Recovered a fumble on 01-02-05
Nine games
Member of the 2004 championship team
Georgia Southern Eagle

Morey, Sean (#85) "Zsa-Zsa"
Special Team, 1999
Two games
#241 pick in the 1999 College Draft
Brown Bear

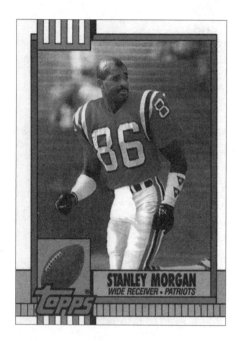

Morgan, Stanley (#86) "The Steamer"
WR/PR/KR, 1977–89
534 receptions for 10,352 yards and 67 touchdowns
Longest reception was a 76-yard touchdown on
    10-21-84
21 carries for 127 yards
Longest run was 17 yards on 09-09-79
92 punt returns for 960 yards and one touchdown
Returned a punt 80 yards for a touchdown on 11-18-79
Two kickoff returns for 29 yards
Longest kickoff return was 17 yards on 12-10-78
Recovered six fumbles
Advanced a fumble three yards on 09-21-80
Advanced a fumble 20 yards on 11-20-83
AFC Pro Bowl WR in 1979, 1980, 1986, and 1987
180 regular season games
Seven playoff games
#25 pick in the 1977 College Draft
Inducted into the Patriots Hall of Fame in 2007
Tennessee Volunteer

Morris, Aric (#29)
Defensive Back, 2003
Returned an interception 33 yards on 09-14-03
Four games
Member of the 2003 championship team
Michigan State Spartan

Morris, Jamie (#24)
RB/KR, 1990
Two carries for four yards
Longest run was three yards on 11-25-90
11 kickoff returns for 202 yards
Longest kickoff return was 22 yards on 12-09-90
Five games
Michigan Wolverine

Morris, Jon (#56)
Center/LS, 1964–74
Recovered three fumbles
AFL All-Star Center from 1964–69
AFC Pro Bowl Center in 1970
130 games
Fourth round draft pick in 1964
Holy Cross Crusader

Morris, Mike (#64)
Offensive Lineman, 1989
11 games
NE Missouri Bulldog

Morris, Sammy (#34)
Running Back, 2007–08
241 carries for 1,111 yards and 10 touchdowns
Longest run was 49 yards on 10-01-07

23 receptions for 196 yards
Longest reception was 42 yards on 12-21-08
Two kickoff returns for 37 yards
Longest return was 24 yards on 12-14-08
Recovered a fumble on 11-23-08
19 regular season games
Ed Block Courage Award in 2008
Texas Tech Red Raider

Morriss, Guy (#75)
Center/Guard, 1984–87
53 regular season games
Five playoff games
Texas Christian Horned Frog

Mosier, John (#88)
Tight End, 1973
Two games
Kansas Jay Hawk

Moss, Randy (#81)
Wide Receiver (DB), 2007–08
167 receptions for 2,501 yards and 34 touchdowns
Longest reception was a 76-yard touchdown on
      12-21-08
Two carries for zero net yards
Longest run was for two yards on 10-05-08
Played in three games as a safety valve defensive back
Recovered three fumbles
AFC Offensive Player of the Week on 11-04-07
AFC Offensive Player of the Week on 11-18-07
AFC Pro Bowl wide receiver in 2007
32 regular season games
Three playoff games
Marshall Thundering Herd

Moss, Roland (#86)
Tight End, 1971
Nine receptions for 124 yards and one touchdown
Longest reception was a 20-yard touchdown on
      09-19-71
Blocked a Buffalo Bills punt on 11-14-71
Returned the blocked punt 10 yards for a touchdown
      on 11-14-71
14 games
Toledo Rocket

Moss, Zefross (#77)
Offensive Tackle, 1997–99
42 regular season games
Three playoff games
Alabama State Hornet

Mowatt, Ezekiel (#81) "Zeke"
Tight End, 1990
Six receptions for 67 yards
Longest reception was 16 yards on 12-09-90
10 games
Florida State Seminole

Mruczkowski, Gene (#64)
Guard/Center, 2004–06
18 regular season games
Four playoff games
Member of the 2004 championship team
Purdue Boilermaker

Murphy, Bill (#31)
Wide Receiver, 1968
18 receptions for 268 yards
Longest reception was 26 yards on 11-17-68
Six games
Cornell Big Red

Myers, Leonard (#25)
Defensive Back, 2001–02
Returned a blocked FG 35 yards on 10-21-01
15 games
Member of the 2001 championship team
#200 pick in the 2001 College Draft
Miami Hurricane

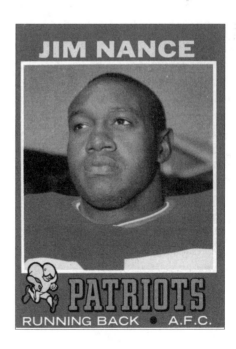

Nance, Jim (#35) "Big Bo"
FB (KR, PR), 1965–71
1,323 carries for 5,323 yards and 45 touchdowns
Longest run was a 65-yard touchdown on 12-04-66
129 receptions for 844 yards and one touchdown

Longest reception was 45 yards on 09-10-66
Only touchdown reception was for 10 yards on 09-03-67
Three kickoff returns for 40 yards
Longest kickoff return was 19 yards on 09-19-65
Only punt return was 16 yards on 10-31-65
Recovered four fumbles
AFL All-Star fullback in 1966 and 1967
AFL Player of the Year in 1966
AFL Offensive Player of the Week on 09-24-67
AFL Comeback Player of Year in 1969
94 games
19th round draft pick in 1965
Inducted into the Patriots Hall of Fame in 2009
Syracuse Orangeman

Naposki, Eric (#49) and (#91)
Linebacker, 1988–89
Four games
UCONN Husky

Neal, Stephen (#61) "Real Deal"
Offensive Guard (KR), 2002, 2004–08
Returned a kickoff 27 yards on 11-30-08
66 regular season games
11 playoff games
Member of the 2004 championship team
Ed Block Courage Award in 2007
California State-Bakersfield Roadrunner

Neighbors, Billy (#73) "Spanky"
Offensive Guard, 1962–65
Recovered two fumbles
AFL All-Star guard in 1963
56 regular season games
Two playoff games
Sixth round draft pick in 1962
Alabama Crimson Tide

Nelson, Edmund (#65)
DE/NT, 1988
12 games
Auburn Tiger

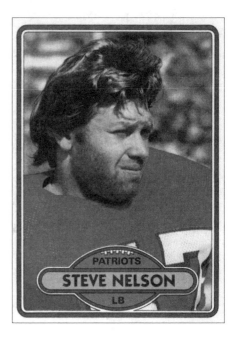

Nelson, Steve (#57) "Nellie"
Linebacker, 1974–87
17 interceptions for 226 yards
Longest return was 37 yards on 09-10-78
19.5 sacks
Recovered 16 fumbles
Blocked a 49-yard field-goal attempt on 10-05-80
Blocked an extra-point attempt on 10-21-84
Blocked an extra-point attempt on 12-02-84
AFC Pro Bowl linebacker in 1980, 1984, and 1985
174 regular season games
Seven playoff games
#34 pick in the 1974 College Draft
Ed Block Courage Award in 1986
His uniform #57 was retired by the Patriots
Inducted into the Patriots Hall of Fame on 08-18-93
North Dakota State Bison

Neumann, Tom (#36)
Running Back, 1963
44 carries for 148 yards
Longest run was 17 yards on 11-01-63
10 receptions for 48 yards and one touchdown
Longest reception was 16 yards on 11-17-63
Only touchdown reception was for 15 yards on
    10-11-63
10 regular season games
Two playoff games
17th round draft pick in 1963
Northern Michigan Wildcat

Neville, Tom (#77)
Offensive Tackle (DT), 1965–77
Defensive tackle for two games in 1965
Recovered five fumbles
Lost eight yards on a rushing attempt on 10-03-71
AFL All-Star tackle in 1966 and 1968
160 regular season games
Only playoff game appearance was on 12-18-76
Seventh round draft pick in 1965
Mississippi State Bulldog

Nichols, Bobby (#87)
Tight End, 1967–68
Only reception was 19 yards on 10-22-67
Blocked a Miami Dolphins punt on 12-17-67
15 games
#440 pick in the 1967 College Draft
Boston University Terrier

Nugent, David (#92)
Defensive End, 2000–01
15 games
Member of the 2001 championship team
Purdue Boilermaker

Oakes, Don (#71) "Tree"
Offensive Tackle, 1963–68
Recovered a squibbed kickoff on 11-20-64
AFL All-Star tackle in 1967
83 regular season games
Two playoff games
Virgina Tech Hokie

O'Callaghan, Ryan (#68)
Offensive Lineman, 2006–07
Recovered a fumble on 10-22-06
25 games
Three playoff games
#136 pick in the 2006 College Draft
California Golden Bear

O'Connell, Kevin (#5)
Quarterback, 2008
Four completions for 23 yards
Longest pass was 12 yards on 09-21-08
Three kneel downs for minus-6 yards
Two games
#94 pick in the 2008 College Draft
San Diego State Aztec

O'Hanley, Ross (#25) "Rocky"
Defensive Back, 1960–65
15 interceptions for 288 yards and one touchdown
Returned pass 47 yards for a touchdown on 11-29-64
Longest return was 61 yards on 10-01-63
Recovered six fumbles
Returned a fumble 10 yards on 09-16-61
AFL All-Star defensive back in 1960
77 regular season games
Two playoff games
Boston College Eagle

O'Neal, Deltha (#21)
Defensive Back (PR), 2008
Three interceptions for 49 yards
Longest interception return was 49 yards on 10-26-08

Two punt returns for two yards
Longest punt return was two yards on 09-07-08
16 games
California Golden Bear

O'Neill, Pat (#5) "Thunderfoot"
Punter (K), 1994–95
110 punts for 4,355 yards
Longest punt was 67 yards on 12-18-94
Kicked off in 24 games
AFC Special Teams Player of the Week on 12-18-94
24 regular season games
Only playoff game appearance was on 01-01-95
#135 pick in the 1994 College Draft
Syracuse Orangeman

Osley, Willie (#37)
DB/Special Team, 1974
Blocked a punt on 10-20-74
Seven games
Illinois Fighting Illini

Outlaw, John (#44)
Defensive Back, 1969–72
Three interceptions for 89 yards and one touchdown
Longest return was a 60-yard touchdown on 12-19-71
Recovered a fumble on 12-12-71
33 games
#249 pick in the 1968 College Draft
Jackson State Tiger

Overton, Don (#29)
RB/KR, 1990
Five carries for eight yards
Longest run was six yards on 10-07-90
Two receptions for 19 yards
Longest reception was 15 yards on 09-23-90
10 kickoff returns for 188 yards
Longest kickoff return was 23 yards on 10-07-90
Seven games
Fairmont State Falcon

Owen, Tom (#17) "T.O."
Quarterback, 1976–81
58 completions for 655 yards and three touchdowns
Longest completion was 32 yards on 10-07-79
Two carries for a net loss of one yard
12 regular season games
Only playoff game appearance was on 12-31-78
Wichita State Shocker

Owens, Dennis (#98)
Nose Tackle, 1982–86
11 regular season sacks
Recovered three fumbles
71 regular season games
Five playoff games
North Carolina State Wolfpack

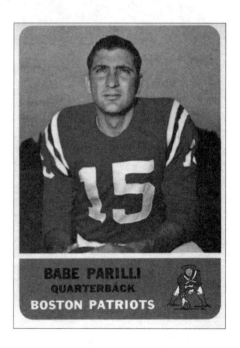

BABE PARILLI
QUARTERBACK
BOSTON PATRIOTS

Parilli, Vito (#15) "Babe"
Quarterback (P), 1961–67
1,140 completions for 16,747 yards and 133
    touchdowns
Longest completion was an 80-yard touchdown on
    11-29-64
228 carries for 949 yards and 15 touchdowns
Longest run was a 32-yard touchdown on 09-16-62
Ran for a two-point conversion on 10-29-61
Completed six two-point conversion passes
Punted five times for 180 yards on 12-20-64
Longest punt was 45 yards on 12-20-64
Recovered 18 fumbles
Advanced a fumble one yard for a touchdown on
    11-03-61
AFL All-Star quarterback in 1963, 1964, and 1966
AFL Player of the Week on 10-23-66
AFL Player of the Week on 10-15-67
AFL Comeback Player of the Year in 1966
AFL All-Star Game MVP on 01-21-67
94 regular season games
Two playoff games
Inducted into College Football Hall of Fame 12-07-82
Inducted into Patriots Hall of Fame on 08-18-93
Kentucky Wildcat

Parker, Riddick (#97)
Defensive Tackle, 2001
Recorded a sack on 09-30-01
Recovered a fumble on 01-06-02
13 regular season games
Two playoff games
Member of the 2001 championship team
North Carolina Tar Heel

Pass, Patrick (#35)
RB/KR, 2000–06
128 carries for 526 yards and three touchdowns
Longest run was 31 yards on 11-20-05
66 receptions for 570 yards and one touchdown
Caught a 23-yard touchdown pass on 12-22-01
Longest reception was 39 yards on 10-16-05
36 kickoff returns for 745 yards
Longest kickoff return was 36 yards on 09-28-03
Recovered three fumbles
78 regular season games
10 playoff games
Member of the 2001, 2003, and 2004 championship
   teams
#239 pick in the 2000 College Draft
Georgia Bulldog

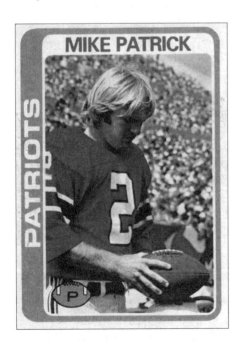

Patrick, Mike (#2)
Punter, 1975–78
222 punts for 8,481 yards
Longest punt was 64 yards on 12-18-77
43 regular season games
Only playoff game appearance was on 12-18-76
Mississippi State Bulldog

Patten, David (#86) "Chief"
WR (KR), 2001–04
165 receptions for 2,513 yards and 16 touchdowns
Longest reception was a 91-yard touchdown on
   10-21-01
Nine carries for 82 yards and one touchdown
Longest run was a 29-yard touchdown on 10-21-01
Three kickoff returns for 60 yards
Longest kickoff return was 24 yards on 11-25-01
Only completion was a 60-yard touchdown pass on
   10-21-01
AFC Offensive Player of the Week on 10-21-01
54 regular season games
Six playoff games
Member of the 2001, 2003, and 2004 championship
   teams
Western Carolina Catamount

Patton, Jerry (#72)
Defensive Tackle, 1975
Blocked an extra-point attempt on 12-14-75
Three games
Nebraska Cornhusker

Paulk, Jeff (#46)
Fullback, 2000
Only game played was on 12-24-00
Arizona State Sun Devil

Paxton, Lonie (#66) "Snow Angel"
Long Snapper, 2000–08
Recovered a fumble on 11-07-04

141 regular season games
14 playoff games
Member of the 2001, 2003, and 2004 championship
    teams
Sacramento State Hornet

Pennywell, Carlos (#88) "Chilly"
Wide Receiver, 1978–81
12 receptions for 143 yards and three touchdowns
Longest reception was 28 yards on 09-18-78
Only carry was three yards on 09-13-81
38 games
#77 pick in the 1977 College Draft
Grambling State Tiger

Peoples, George (#35)
Running Back, 1983
Recovered a fumble on 10-09-83
16 games
Auburn Tiger

Perkins, Willis
Guard, 1961
Only game played was on 09-23-61
Texas Southern Tiger

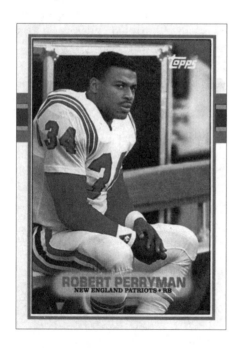

Perryman, Robert (#34)
RB/KR, 1987–90
369 carries for 1,294 yards and nine touchdowns
Longest run was 48 yards on 11-22-87
64 receptions for 430 yards
Longest reception was 18 yards on 11-13-88
Three kickoff returns for 43 yards

Longest kickoff return was 18 yards on 09-21-87
Recovered three fumbles
49 games
#79 pick in the 1987 College Draft
Michigan Wolverine

Peterson, Joe (#45)
Defensive Back, 1987
Only interception was not returned on 10-11-87
Recovered a fumble on 10-18-87
Three games
Nevado Reno Wolf Pack

Phifer, Roman (#95) "Phife"
Linebacker, 2001–04
Four sacks
Two interceptions for 40 yards
Longest return was 26 yards on 11-07-04
Recovered four fumbles
58 regular season games
Nine playoff games
Member of the 2001, 2003, and 2004 championship
    teams
UCLA Bruin

Phillips, Jess (#35) "Banacek"
RB/KR, 1976–77
29 carries for 191 yards and two touchdowns
Longest run was 46 yards on 10-18-76
Only reception was 18 yards on 10-03-76
20 kickoff returns for 490 yards
Longest kickoff return was 71 yards on 10-24-76
Recovered a fumble on 09-26-77
27 regular season games
Only playoff game appearance was on 12-18-76
Michigan State Spartan

Philpott, Ed (#52) "Big Red"
Linebacker, 1967–71
Nine interceptions for 91 yards
Longest return was 23 yards on 10-01-70
Seven sacks
Blocked an extra-point attempt on 11-19-67
Recovered 11 fumbles
Returned a fumble 10 yards for a touchdown on
    09-22-68
68 games
#101 pick in the 1967 College Draft
Miami Redskin

Pickering, Clay (#48)
Wide Receiver, 1987
Only reception was 10 yards on 10-18-87
Only game played was on 10-18-87
Maine Black Bear

Pitts, Mike (#93)
Defensive Lineman, 1993–94
Five sacks
Recovered two regular season fumbles
32 regular season games
Only playoff game appearance was on 01-01-95
Alabama Crimson Tide

Pleasant, Anthony (#98) "A.P."
Defensive End, 2001–03
10 sacks
Two interceptions for no return yards
Returned a fumble six yards on 09-14-03
37 regular season games
Three playoff games
Member of the 2001 and 2003 championship teams
Tennessee State Tiger

Plunkett, Art (#70)
Offensive Tackle, 1985–87
22 regular season games
Four playoff games
Nevada Las Vegas Runnin' Rebel

Plunkett, Jim (#16) "Plunk"
Quarterback, 1971–75
729 completions for 9,932 yards and 62 touchdowns
Longest completion was an 88-yard touchdown on 12-19-71
159 carries for 817 yards and nine touchdowns
Longest run was 37 yards on 12-01-74
Recovered four fumbles
NFL Offensive Player of the Week on 12-19-71
NFL Offensive Player of the Week on 11-18-73
AFC Rookie of the Year in 1971
61 games
First overall pick in the 1971 College Draft
Inducted into the College Football Hall of Fame on 12-04-90
Stanford Cardinal

Pool, David (#27)
Defensive Back, 1991–92
Two interceptions for 54 yards and one touchdown
Longest return was a 41-yard touchdown on 11-15-92
Recovered a fumble on 10-20-91
31 games
Carson-Newman Eagle

Poole, Tyrone (#38)
CB/PR, 2003–05
Seven interceptions for 102 yards
Longest return was 44 yards on 12-14-03
13 punt returns for 81 yards
Longest punt return was 18 yards on 11-23-03
22 regular season games
Three playoff games

Member of the 2003 and 2004 championship teams
Fort Valley State Wildcat

Pope, Ken (#41)
Defensive Back, 1974
Four games
Oklahoma Sooner

Porell, Tom (#65)
Nose Tackle, 1987
Only game played was on 10-04-87
Boston College Eagle

Porter, Willie (#27) "Bubba"
DB/KR/PR, 1968
36 kickoff returns for 812 yards
Longest kickoff return was 61 yards on 11-24-68
22 punt returns for 135 yards
Longest punt return was 24 yards 11-24-68
Recovered six fumbles
Returned a fumble two yards on 11-17-68
13 games
Texas Southern Tiger

Posey, David (#9)
Kicker, 1978
11 field goals
Longest field goal was 47 yards on 11-19-78
29 extra points
11 regular season games
Only playoff game appearance was on 12-31-78
Florida Gator

Poteat, Hank (#31) and (#32)
DB, 2004–06
Recorded a sack on 12-26-05
12 regular season games
Five playoff games
Member of the 2004 championship team
Pittsburgh Panther

President, Andre (#88)
Tight End, 1995
Only game played was on 09-03-95
Angelo State Ram

Prestridge, Luke (#17)
Punter, 1984
44 punts for 1,884 yards
Longest punt was 89 yards on 10-21-84
Nine games
Baylor Bear

Price, Kenny (#54)
Linebacker, 1971
Only game played was on 12-19-71
Iowa Hawkeye

Profit, Eugene (#22)
DB/Special Team, 1986–88
Blocked a New Orleans Saints punt on 11-30-86
Blocked a Philadelphia Eagles punt on 11-29-87
12 regular season games
Only playoff game appearance was on 01-04-87
Yale Bulldog

Pruett, Perry (#39)
Defensive Back, 1971
11 games
North Texas Mean Green Eagle

Puetz, Gary (#77)
Offensive Lineman, 1979–81
36 games
Valparaiso Crusader

Purnell, Lovett (#48) and (#85)
Tight End, 1994–98
17 receptions for 149 yards and five touchdowns
Longest reception was 22 yards on 09-14-98
Recovered a fumble on 11-09-97
34 regular season games
Three playoff games
#216 pick in the 1996 College Draft
West Virginia Mountaineer

Purvis, Vic (#31)
WR/DB/KR, 1966–67
Eight kickoff returns for 185 yards
Longest kickoff return was 34 yards on 09-25-66
Five punt returns for 43 yards
Longest punt return was 18 yards on 09-25-66
Recovered a fumble on 11-20-66
16 games
Southern Mississippi Golden Eagle

Pyne, George (#75)
Defensive Tackle, 1965
Two sacks
Blocked a 30-yard field-goal attempt on 09-11-65
Recovered a squibbed kickoff on 10-03-65
14 games
16th round draft pick in 1965
Olivet Comet

Rademacher, Bill (#33) "RAD"
Wide Receiver, 1969–70
21 receptions for 268 yards and three touchdowns
Longest reception was 16 yards on 11-15-70
Recovered a fumble on 10-18-70
27 games
Northern Michigan Wildcat

Rakoczy, Gregg (#71)
Guard (KR), 1991–92
Only kickoff return was nine yards on 10-20-91
21 games
Miami Hurricane

Ramsey, Derrick (#88)
Tight End, 1983–85
118 receptions for 1,412 yards and 14 touchdowns
Longest reception was 39 yards on 10-09-83
46 games
Four playoff games
Kentucky Wildcat

Ramsey, Tom (#12)
Quarterback, 1986–88
84 completions for 1,005 yards and six touchdowns
Longest completion was 40 yards on 11-29-87
17 carries for 77 yards and one touchdown
Ran for a one-yard touchdown on 11-29-87
Longest run was 19 yards on 12-06-87
Recovered a fumble on 12-06-87
21 games
#267 pick in the 1983 College Draft
UCLA Bruin

Ratkowski, Ray (#23)
Kickoff Returnman, 1961
Only kickoff return was 17 yards on 09-09-61
Only game played was on 09-09-61
17th round draft pick in 1961
Notre Dame Fighting Irish

Ray, Eddie (#36) "Moose"
RB/TE, 1970
Five carries for 13 yards
Longest run was four yards on 10-11-70
Five games
#83 pick in the 1970 College Draft
LSU Tiger

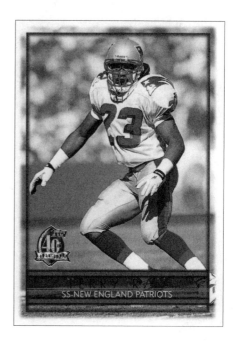

Ray, Terry (#23)
Safety, 1993–96
Four interceptions for 64 yards
Longest return was 21 yards on 10-01-95
Recorded a sack on 10-06-96
Recovered two fumbles
63 regular season games
Four playoff games
Oklahoma Sooner

Redd, Vince (#49)
LB/Special Teams, 2008
Five games
Liberty Flame

Redding, Reggie (#70)
Guard/Tackle, 1992
Recovered a fumble on 11-29-92
14 games
California State Titan

Redmond, Joseph (#21) "J.R."
RB/KR, 2000–02
164 carries for 527 yards and one touchdown
Ran for a one-yard touchdown on 11-05-00
Longest run was 20 yards on 11-12-00
35 receptions for 263 yards and two touchdowns
Longest reception was 20 yards on 10-08-00
Four kickoff returns for 94 yards
Longest kickoff return was 30 yards on 09-09-01
33 regular season games
Three playoff games
Member of the 2001 championship team

#76 pick in the 1999 College Draft
Arizona State Sun Devil

Reed, Benton (#71)
Defensive End, 1987
Three games
Mississippi Rebel

Rehberg, Scott (#60)
Tackle, 1997–98
Eight games
#230 pick in the 1997 College Draft
Central Michigan Chippewa

Rehder, Tom (#76)
Tackle (KR), 1988–89
Only kickoff return was 14 yards on 12-03-89
32 games
#69 pick in the 1988 College Draft
Notre Dame Fighting Irish

Reid, Dexter (#42)
Safety/Special Team, 2004
13 regular season games
Three playoff games
Member of the 2004 championship team
#113 pick in the 2004 College Draft
North Carolina Tar Heel

Reilly, Kevin (#55)
Linebacker, 1975
Returned an interception 54 yards on 12-14-75
Four games
Villanova Wildcat

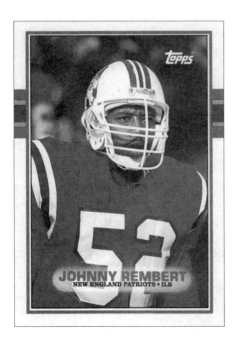

Rembert, Johnny (#52) "Rambo"
Linebacker (KR), 1983–92
Seven interceptions for 70 yards
Longest return was 37 yards on 10-26-86
16 sacks
Recovered 11 regular season fumbles
Recovered a fumble for a touchdown on 10-06-85
Recovered a fumble for a touchdown on 09-07-86
Returned a fumble nine yards on 11-10-85
Returned a fumble 27 yards on 11-19-89
AFC Defensive Player of the Week on 11-06-88
Three kickoff returns for 27 yards
Longest kickoff return was 14 yards on 09-28-86
AFC Pro Bowl linebacker in 1988 and 1989
126 regular season games
Five playoff games
#101 pick in the 1983 College Draft
Clemson Tiger

Reynolds, Bob (#74)
Offensive Tackle, 1972–73
Recovered a fumble on 10-07-73
20 games
Bowling Green State Falcon

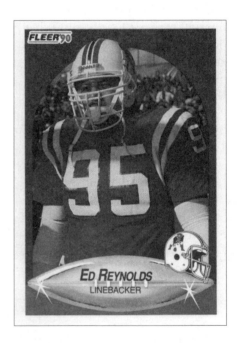

Reynolds, Ed (#95) "Dirty" and "Captain"
Linebacker, 1983–91
Four sacks
Recovered four fumbles
119 regular season games
Five playoff games
Virginia Cavalier

Reynolds, Ricky (#21)
Defensive Back, 1994–96
Six interceptions for 22 yards and one touchdown
Longest return was an 11-yard touchdown on 12-04-94
4.5 sacks
Recovered four fumbles
Returned a fumble 25 yards for a touchdown on
    12-18-94
Advanced a lateral two yards on 11-19-95
42 regular season games
Only playoff game appearance was on 01-01-95
Washington State Cougar

Reynolds, Tom (#21)
Wide Receiver, 1972
Eight receptions for 152 yards and two touchdowns
Longest reception was a 36-yard touchdown on
    12-03-72
12 games
#49 pick in the 1972 College Draft
San Diego State Aztec

Rheams, Leonta (#75)
Defensive Tackle, 1998
Six games
#115 pick in the 1998 College Draft
Houston Cougar

Rice, Rodney (#43)
DB/KR, 1989
Recovered a fumble on 10-01-89
11 kickoff returns for 242 yards
Longest kickoff return was 46 yards on 09-10-89
10 games
#210 pick in the 1989 College Draft
BYU Cougar

Richards, David (#62)
Offensive Lineman, 1996
Five games
UCLA Bruin

Richardson, Al (#79)
Defensive End, 1960
Three games
Grambling State Tiger

Richardson, Jesse (#75) "Big Jess"
Defensive Tackle, 1962–64
6.5 sacks
42 regular season games
Two playoff games
Alabama Crimson Tide

Richardson, Mike (#35)
Defensive Back, 2008
10 games
Notre Dame Fighting Irish

Richardson, Tom (#49) "The Glove"
Wide Receiver, 1969–70
Only reception was five yards on 09-21-69
Recovered a fumble on 11-02-69
15 games
Jackson State Tiger

Rivers, Marcellus (#82)
Tight End, 2007
Three regular season games
Oklahoma State Cowboy

Robbins, Randy (#48)
Defensive Back, 1992
Two interceptions for 27 yards
Longest return was 20 yards on 11-01-92
Recovered a fumble on 09-27-92
15 games
Arizona Wildcat

Roberts, Tim (#94)
Defensive Tackle, 1995
Only sack was made on 12-23-95
13 games
Southern Mississippi Golden Eagle

Roberts, William (#76)
Guard, 1995–96
32 regular season games
Three playoff games
Ohio State Buckeye

Robinson, Bo (#41)
RB/TE/KR, 1984
Four receptions for 32 yards and one touchdown
Caught a four-yard touchdown pass on 09-30-84
Longest reception was 17 yards on 10-21-84
Three kickoff returns for 38 yards
Longest kickoff return was 14 yards on 10-21-84
Recovered a fumble on 10-14-84
16 games
West Texas State Buffalo

Robinson-Randall, Greg (#77) and (#64)
Offensive Tackle, 2000–02
Recovered a fumble on 11-25-01
35 regular season games
Three playoff games

Member of the 2001 championship team
Michigan State Spartan

Robinson, Greg (#61) "Truck"
Offensive Tackle, 1987
Recovered a fumble on 10-04-87
Three games
#137 pick in the 1987 College Draft
Sacramento State Hornet

Robinson, David (#27) "Junior"
DB/KR, 1990
11 kickoff returns for 211 yards
Longest kickoff return was 27 yards on 11-18-90
16 games
#110 pick in the 1990 College Draft
East Carolina Pirate

Robinson, Noble (#7) "Rex"
Kicker, 1982
Five extra points
Only field goal was from 24 yards on 09-12-82
Three games
Georgia Bulldog

Robotti, Frank (#51)
Linebacker, 1961
Two interceptions for 18 yards
Longest return was 11 yards on 11-03-61
Recorded a QB sack on 11-17-61
12 games
Boston College Eagle

Rogers, Doug (#65) "Buck"
Defensive End, 1983–84
2.5 sacks
22 games
Stanford Cardinal

Romaniszyn, Jim (#53)
Linebacker, 1976
Recovered a fumble on 10-18-76
11 games
Edinboro Fighting Scot

Romeo, Tony (#86)
Tight End (KR), 1962–67
110 receptions for 1,724 yards and 10 touchdowns
Longest reception was 62 yards on 09-21-62
Caught a pass for a two-point conversion on 09-18-66
Only kickoff return was five yards on 09-20-64
75 regular season games
Two playoff games
Florida State Seminole

Romine, Al (#46)
Defensive Back, 1961
Only game played was on 09-09-61
North Alabama Lion

Rowe, Dave (#76)
Defensive Tackle, 1971–73
Six sacks
Recovered a fumble on 11-12-72
42 games
Penn State Nittany Lion

Rucci, Todd (#71)
Guard, 1993–2000
85 regular season games
Seven playoff games
#51 pick in the 1993 College Draft
Penn State Nittany Lion

Rucker, Reggie (#33)
WR/KR, 1971–74
126 receptions for 1,884 yards and 10 touchdowns
Longest reception was a 69-yard touchdown on
    10-06-74
15 kickoff returns for 375 yards
Longest kickoff return was 43 yards on 09-30-73
Five carries for four yards
Longest run was five yards on 11-12-72
Recovered three fumbles
Advanced a fumble five yards on 10-14-73
43 games
Boston University Terrier

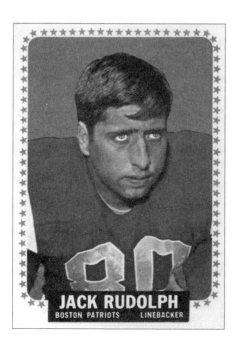

Rudolph, Jack (#80)
Linebacker (KR), 1960–65
Two interceptions for 13 yards
Longest return was 13 yards on 12-11-60
16 sacks
Recorded a safety on 12-08-63
Recorded a safety on 11-20-64
Returned a kickoff four yards on 09-24-65
Recovered 10 fumbles
Returned a fumble two yards on 09-19-65
64 regular season games
Two playoff games
Second round draft pick in 1960
Georgia Tech Yellow Jacket

Ruegamer, Christopher (#67) "Grey"
Center, 2000–02
33 regular season games
Three playoff games
Member of the 2001 championship team
Arizona State Sun Devil

Russ, Bernard (#51)
Linebacker, 1997–99
Nine games
West Virginia Mountaineer

Russell, Leonard (#32)
Running Back, 1991–93
689 carries for 2,437 yards and 13 touchdowns
Longest run was 24 yards on 09-08-91
55 receptions for 350 yards
Longest reception was 38 yards on 09-12-93

Ran 69 yards with a lateral on 10-10-93
Recovered two fumbles
Advanced a fumble 22 yards on 01-02-94
NFL Offensive Rookie of the Year in 1991
43 games
#14 pick in the 1991 College Draft
Arizona State Sun Devil

Ruth, Mike (#65)
Nose Tackle, 1986–87
Recorded a sack on 09-11-86
Recovered a fumble on 10-12-86
Eight regular season games
Only playoff game appearance was on 01-04-87
#42 pick in the 1986 College Draft
Boston College Eagle

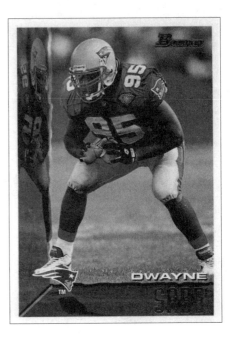

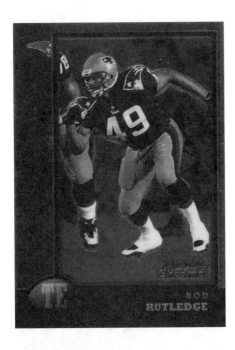

Rutledge, Rod (#83)
Tight End, 1998–2001
Wore No. 49 in the 1998 exhibition season
27 receptions for 204 yards
Longest reception was 16 yards on 10-22-00
Recovered a fumble on 12-17-00
63 regular season games
Four playoff games
Member of the 2001 championship team
#54 pick in the 1998 College Draft
Alabama Crimson Tide

Sabb, Dwayne (#95)
Linebacker, 1992–96
6.5 sacks
Three interceptions for six yards
Longest return was five yards on 09-04-94
74 regular season games
Four playoff games
#116 pick in the 1992 College Draft
New Hampshire Wildcat

Sacco, Frank (#95)
Linebacker, 1987
Two games
Fordham Ram

Sagapolutele, Pio (#75)
Defensive Lineman, 1996
Three sacks
15 games
San Diego State Aztec

Sam, Philip (#14) "P.K."
Wide Receiver, 2004
Three games
Member of the 2004 championship team
#164 pick in the 2004 College Draft
Florida State Seminole

Samuel, Asante (#22)
Cornerback, 2003–2007
22 interceptions for 313 yards and three touchdowns
Longest return was a 55-yard touchdown on 09-21-03
AFC Defensive Player of the Week on 11-26-06

AFC Defensive Player of the Week on 11-25-07
AFC Pro Bowl cornerback in 2007
75 regular season games
14 playoff games
Member of the 2003 and 2004 championship teams
#120 pick in the 2003 College Draft
Central Florida Golden Knight

Sanders, James (#36)
Safety, 2005–08
Five interceptions for 112 yards and one touchdown
Longest return was for 42 yards on 12-03-07
Returned a pass 39 yards for a touchdown on 12-11-05
Recovered two fumbles
Recorded a sack on 12-31-06
55 regular season games
Eight playoff games
#113 pick in the 2005 College Draft
Fresno State Bulldog

Sanders, John (#25) "Colonel"
Defensive Back, 1974–76
Six interceptions for 75 yards and one touchdown
Longest return was a 23-yard touchdown on 12-15-74
Recovered five fumbles
Only fumble return was for three yards on 12-14-75
Blocked a San Francisco 49ers punt on 10-26-75
Blocked an extra-point attempt on 09-28-75
Blocked an extra-point attempt on 10-05-75
30 games
South Dakota Coyote

Sanders, Lewis (#29)
Defensive Back, 2008
10 games
Maryland Terrapin

Sandham, Todd (#72)
Guard, 1987
Two games
Northeastern Husky

Sanford, Rick (#25) "Bat"
DB/KR (PR), 1979–84
16 interceptions for 198 yards and one touchdown
Longest return was a 99-yard touchdown on 12-05-82
Only sack was made on 11-23-80
14 kickoff returns for 261 yards
Longest kickoff return was 27 yards on 11-15-81
Two punt returns for one yard
Longest punt return was one yard on 09-09-79
Blocked a Baltimore Colts punt on 11-18-79

Returned a blocked punt eight yards for a touchdown
    on 11-18-79
Recovered 10 regular season fumbles
Returned a fumble 22 yards for a touchdown on
    11-23-80
Advanced a lateral 27 yards on 11-04-79
89 regular season games
Only playoff game appearance was on 01-08-83
#25 pick in the 1979 College Draft
South Carolina Gamecock

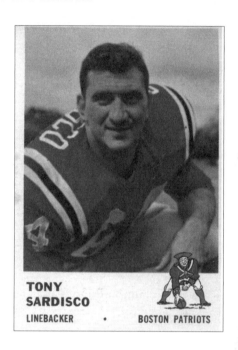

TONY SARDISCO
LINEBACKER   •   BOSTON PATRIOTS

Sardisco, Tony (#64)
LB/DE/Guard, 1960–62
2.5 sacks
Recovered three fumbles
Played on both sides of the line of scrimmage
40 games
Tulane Green Wave

Satcher, Doug (#58) "Scratch"
Linebacker, 1966–68
Only sack was made on 09-03-67
Returned an interception one yard on 11-10-68
Recovered four fumbles
Longest fumble return was for two yards on 09-17-67
Recorded a safety on 12-01-68
42 games
Ninth round draft pick in 1966
Southern Mississippi Golden Eagle

Sauerbrun, Todd (#18)
Punter, 2006
10 punts for 408 yards
Longest punt was 58 yards on 12-31-06
Two regular season games
Three playoff games
West Virginia Mountaineer

Sawyer, Jon (#31)
Defensive Back, 1987
Two games
Cincinnati Bearcat

Saxon, Mike (#7)
Punter, 1993
73 punts for 3,096 yards
Longest punt was 59 yards on 11-21-93
AFC Special Team Player of the Week on 10-10-93
Only run was two yards on 12-26-93
Recovered a fumble on 12-12-93
16 games
San Diego State Aztec

Sayler, Jace (#94)
Defensive End, 2001
Two games
Member of the 2001 championship team
Michigan State Spartan

Scarpitto, Bob (#46)
Punter/WR, 1968
34 punts for 1,382 yards
Longest punt was 87 yards on 09-29-68
Two receptions for 49 yards and one touchdown
Longest reception was a 33-yard touchdown on
    10-27-68
14 games
Notre Dame Fighting Irish

Schaum, Greg (#76)
Defensive End, 1978
14 regular season games
Only playoff game appearance was on 12-31-78
Michigan State Spartan

Schmidt, Bob (#74)
Offensive Lineman, 1964
14 games
Minnesota Golden Gopher

Scholtz, Bruce (#51)
Linebacker, 1989
Eight games
Texas Longhorn

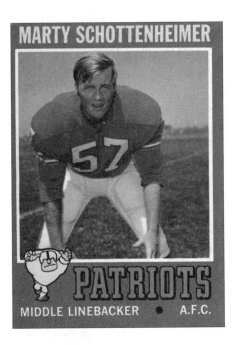

MARTY SCHOTTENHEIMER
57
PATRIOTS
MIDDLE LINEBACKER ● A.F.C.

Schottenheimer, Marty (#54)
Linebacker (KR), 1969–70
Returned an interception three yards on 10-11-69
Two kickoff returns for 21 yards
Longest return was 13 yards on 11-09-69
23 games
Pittsburgh Panther

Schubert, Eric (#1)
Kicker, 1987
Kicked an extra point on 10-04-87
Only field goal was 23 yards on 10-04-87
Only game played was on 10-04-87
Pittsburgh Panther

Schubert, Steve (#87)
WR/KR/PR, 1974
Only reception was a 21-yard touchdown on 10-27-74
Five kickoff returns for 112 yards
Longest kickoff return was 32 yards on 09-22-74
Three punt returns for 15 yards
Longest punt return was 11 yards on 10-20-74
Returned a fumble 13 yards on 09-15-74
Eight games
University of Massachusetts Minuteman

Schwedes, Gerhardt (#31) and (#44)
Running Back, 1960–61
10 carries for 14 yards
Longest run was five yards on 12-17-61
Only reception was 21 yards on 11-12-61
Recovered a Broncos onside kick on 12-03-61
Recovered a fumble on 12-09-61
Seven games
First round territorial draft pick in 1960
Wore No. 16 at Syracuse
Syracuse Orangeman

Scott, Chad (#30)
Cornerback, 2005–06
Two interceptions for 32 yards
Longest return was 32 yards on 11-05-06
17 regular season games
Three playoff games
Maryland Terrapin

Scott, Clarence (#26) "Scotty"
DB/KR, 1969–72
Returned an interception 18 yards on 11-22-70
Six kickoff returns for 43 yards
Longest kickoff return was 14 yards on 11-02-69
Recovered six fumbles
Returned a fumble five yards on 12-13-70
43 games
Morgan State Bear

Scott, Guss (#29)
Safety, 2005–06
Six games
#95 pick in the 2004 College Draft
Florida Gator

Scott, Walter (#94)
Defensive End, 1996
Only game played was on 10-20-96
East Carolina Pirate

Scott, Willie (#88)
Tight End, 1986–88
14 receptions for 84 yards and four touchdowns
Longest reception was 15 yards on 10-18-87
Blocked an Indianapolis Colts punt on 11-22-87
Returned the blocked punt three yards for a
    touchdown on 11-22-87
26 regular season games
Only playoff game appearance was on 01-04-87
South Carolina Gamecock

Sealby, Randy (#59) and (#53)
Linebacker, 1987
Recovered a fumble on 10-04-87
Three games
Missouri Tiger

Seau, Tiaina (#55) "Junior"
Linebacker, 2006–08
4.5 sacks
Three interceptions for 28 yards
Longest return was for 23 yards on 10-07-07
31 regular season games
Three playoff games
USC Trojan

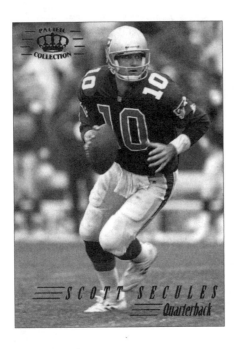

Secules, Scott (#10)
Quarterback, 1993
75 completions for 918 yards and two touchdowns
Longest completion was 82 yards on 10-10-93
Eight carries for 33 yards
Longest run was 13 yards on 11-07-93
Recovered two fumbles
12 games
Virginia Cavalier

Sellers, Ron (#34)
Wide Receiver, 1969–71
79 receptions for 1,477 yards and 13 touchdowns
Longest reception was 77 yards on 12-14-69
AFL Offensive Player of the Week on 11-02-69
AFL All-Star wide receiver in 1969
35 games

Sixth pick in the 1969 College Draft
Inducted in College Football Hall of Fame on 12-06-88
Florida State Seminole

Serwanga, Kato (#31)
Defensive Back, 1999–2000
Three interceptions for two yards
Longest return was two yards on 10-31-99
Three sacks
Recovered three fumbles
31 games
California Golden Bear

Seymour, Richard (#93) "The Quiet Man"
NT/DT/DE, 2001–08
39 sacks
Two interceptions for six yards
Returned an interception six yards on 12-08-02
Blocked a 43-yard field-goal attempt on 11-25-01
Blocked a 49-yard field-goal attempt on 11-17-02
Blocked a 43-yard field-goal attempt on 11-24-02
Blocked a 35-yard field-goal attempt on 10-19-03
Blocked a 45-yard field-goal attempt on 11-26-06
Recovered six fumbles
Returned a fumble 68 yards for a touchdown on 10-03-04
AFC Pro Bowl in 2002, 2003, 2004, 2005, and 2006
111 regular season games
15 playoff games
Member of the 2001, 2003, and 2004 championship teams
Sixth pick in the 2001 College Draft
Georgia Bulldog

Shaw, Harold (#44)
Running Back, 1998–2000
18 carries for 35 yards
Longest run was 12 yards on 01-02-00
Four receptions for 42 yards
Longest reception was 29 yards on 12-26-99
35 games
Only playoff game appearance was on 01-03-99
#176 pick in the 1998 College Draft
Southern Mississippi Golden Eagle

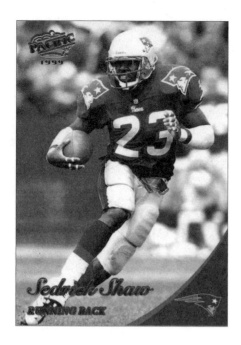

Shaw, Sedrick (#23)
Running Back (KR), 1997–98
48 carries for 236 yards
Longest run was 71 yards on 12-27-98
Six receptions for 30 yards
Longest reception was 11 yards on 11-08-98
Only kickoff return was 16 yards on 09-20-98
Recovered a fumble on 12-27-98
14 regular season games
Three playoff games
#61 pick in the 1997 College Draft
Iowa Hawkeye

Shaw, Terrance (#22)
Defensive Back, 2001
13 regular season games
Three playoff games
Member of the 2001 championship team
Stephen F. Austin State Lumberjack

Shegog, Ron (#42)
Defensive Back, 1987
Returned an interception seven yards on 10-18-87
Three games
Austin Peay State Governor

Sherman, Tom (#14)
Quarterback, 1968–69
90 completions for 1,199 yards and 12 touchdowns
Longest completion was an 87-yard touchdown on
   10-27-68
25 carries for 80 yards
Longest run was 17 yards on 11-24-68

Recovered three fumbles
18 games
Penn State Nittany Lion

Shiner, Dick (#11)
Quarterback, 1973–74
Five completions for 68 yards
Longest completion was 23 yards on 11-25-73
Four games
Maryland Terrapin

Shoate, Rod (#56) "Wolfgang"
Linebacker, 1975–81
Five interceptions for 50 yards and one touchdown
Longest return was a 42-yard touchdown on 11-23-80
22.5 sacks
Recovered seven fumbles
Returned a fumble seven yards on 11-01-81
79 regular season games
Only playoff game appearance was on 12-31-78
#41 pick in the 1975 College Draft
Oklahoma Sooner

Shonta, Chuck (#40) and (#34) "Tonto" and "Kemo"
Defensive Back, 1960–67
15 interceptions for 261 yards
Longest return was 52 yards on 09-09-60
Two sacks
Recovered six fumbles
Returned a fumble 52 yards for a touchdown on
   09-17-60
Caught a nine-yard pass on 12-17-61
AFL All-Star defensive back in 1966

105 regular season games
Two playoff games
Eastern Michigan Huron

Shorts, Peter (#90)
Defensive Tackle, 1989
Only game played was on 12-24-89
Illinois State Redbird

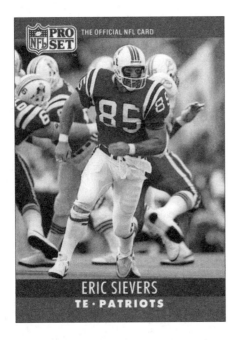

Sievers, Eric (#85)
Tight End, 1989–90
62 receptions for 692 yards
Longest reception was 46 yards on 10-29-89
24 games
Maryland Terrapin

Simerson, John (#75) "Pineapple"
Offensive Tackle, 1961
10 games
Purdue Boilermaker

Simmons, Tony (#81)
WR/KR, 1998–2000
56 receptions for 981 yards and six touchdowns
Longest reception was a 63-yard touchdown on
    11-01-98
10 kickoff returns for 214 yards
Longest kickoff return was 39 yards on 10-08-00
38 regular season games
Only playoff game appearance was on 01-03-99
#52 pick in the 1998 College Draft
Wisconsin Badger

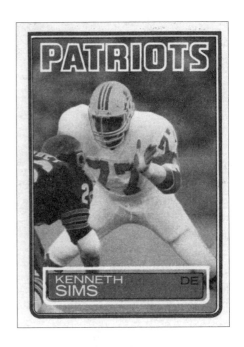

Sims, Kenneth (#77) "Game Day"
Defensive End, 1982–89
17 sacks

Blocked a 40-yard field-goal attempt on 09-08-85
Blocked a 45-yard field-goal attempt on 10-22-89
Recovered five fumbles
74 regular season games
Only playoff game appearance was on 01-08-83
First overall pick in the 1982 College Draft
Ed Block Courage Award in 1989
Texas Longhorn

Singer, Karl (#68)
Tackle (KR), 1966–68
Recovered two fumbles
Three kickoff returns for 56 yards
Longest return was 27 yards on 09-25-66
39 games
First round draft pick in 1966
Purdue Boilermaker

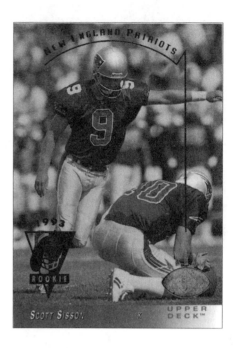

Sisson, Scott (#9)
Kicker, 1993
14 field goals
Longest field goal was 40 yards on 10-31-93 and on
    11-21-93
15 extra points
13 games
#113 pick in the 1993 College Draft
Georgia Tech Yellow Jacket

Skene, Doug (#74)
Guard, 1994
Six games
Michigan Wolverine

Singleton, Chris (#55)
Linebacker, 1990–93
Four sacks
Returned a pass 82 yards for a touchdown on 11-15-92
Returned a fumble 21 yards on 09-29-91
41 games
Eighth pick in the 1990 College Draft
Arizona Wildcat

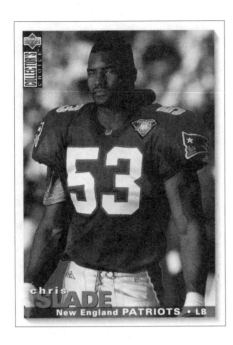

Slade, Chris (#53)
Linebacker, 1993–2000
51 sacks
Three interceptions for three yards and one touchdown
Returned an interception one yard for a touchdown on 11-09-97
Longest return was two yards on 09-08-96
Recovered three regular season fumbles
Returned a fumble 27 yards for a touchdown on 11-26-95
AFC Defensive Player of the Week on 09-03-95
AFC Defensive Player of the Week on 12-28-97
AFC Pro Bowl linebacker in 1997
127 regular season games
Seven playoff games
#31 pick in the 1993 College Draft
Virginia Cavalier

Slater, Matthew (#18)
WR/KR, 2008
11 kickoff returns for 155 yards
Longest return was 31 yards on 10-12-08
14 games
#153 pick in the 2008 College Draft
UCLA Bruin

Small, Torrance (#84)
Wide Receiver, 2001
Four receptions for 29 yards
Longest reception was 11 yards·on 09-30-01
Three games
Member of the 2001 championship team
Alcorn State Brave

Smerlas, Fred (#76)
Nose Tackle, 1991–92
32 games
Boston College Eagle

Smith, Antowain (#32)
Running Back, 2001–03
721 carries for 2,781 yards and 21 touchdowns
Longest run was 44 yards on 12-22-01
Ran for a two-point conversion on 09-22-02
64 receptions for 527 yards and three touchdowns
Longest reception was a 41-yard touchdown on 11-25-01
Recovered four fumbles
45 regular season games
Six playoff games
Member of the 2001 and 2003 championship teams
Houston Cougar

Smith, Donnell (#65)
Defensive End, 1973–74
Four sacks
Blocked an extra point on 12-08-74
Recovered a squibbed kickoff on 12-01-74
Recovered a fumble on 12-15-74
21 games
Southern Jaguar

Smith, Hal (#70)
DT (KR), 1960
Recovered three fumbles
Returned a kickoff 13 yards on 11-11-60
10 games
UCLA Bruin

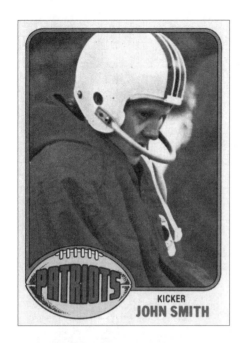

KICKER
JOHN SMITH

Smith, John (#1) "Smitty"
Kicker, 1974–83
128 field goals
Longest field goal was 50 yards on 10-04-81
308 extra points
AFC Pro Bowl kicker in 1980
116 regular season games
Three playoff games
Southampton, England

Smith, Jonathan (#81)
WR/Special Team, 2006
Two games
Georgia Tech Yellow Jacket

Smith, Le Kevin (#65) and (#90)
Defensive Lineman, 2006–08
Recovered a fumble on 10-20-08
31 regular season games
Two playoff games
#206 pick in the 2006 College Draft
Nebraska Cornhusker

Smith, Otis (#45) "My Man"
Defensive Back, 1996 and 2000–02
10 interceptions for 278 yards and two touchdowns
Returned a pass 78 yards for a touchdown on 09-30-01
Returned a pass 76 yards for a touchdown on 01-06-02
Three sacks
Recovered four regular season fumbles
Returned a regular season fumble 12 yards on
    11-19-00
56 regular season games

Six playoff games
Member of the 2001 championship team
Missouri Tiger

Smith, Ricky (#27)
DB/KR/PR, 1982–84
67 kickoff returns for 1,505 yards and one touchdown
Longest return was a 98-yard touchdown on 09-18-82
54 punt returns for 537 yards
Longest punt return was 55 yards on 09-04-83
Recovered eight fumbles
26 regular season games
Only playoff game appearance was on 01-08-83
#141 pick in the 1982 College Draft
Alabama State Hornet

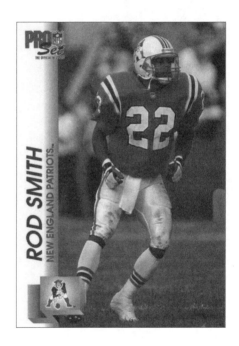

Smith, Rod (#22)
Defensive Back, 1992–94
Three interceptions for 10 yards
Longest return was 10 yards on 10-02-94
Recorded a sack on 09-04-94
48 regular season games
Only playoff game appearance was on 01-01-95
#35 pick in the 1992 College Draft
Notre Dame Fighting Irish

Smith, Sean (#97)
Defensive Tackle, 1990–91
1.5 sacks
17 games
#280 pick in the 1990 College Draft
Georgia Tech Yellow Jacket

Snyder, Al (#38) "Spike"
Wide Receiver, 1964
Only reception was 12 yards on 10-31-64
Two games
23rd round draft pick in 1963
Holy Cross Crusader

Soltis, Bob (#42) and (#46)
Defensive Back, 1960–61
Two interceptions for 33 yards
Longest return was 33 yards on 10-16-60
17 games
Minnesota Golden Gopher

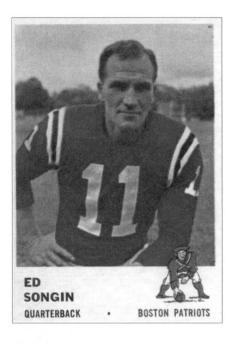

ED
SONGIN
QUARTERBACK • BOSTON PATRIOTS

Songin, Ed (#11) "Butch"
Quarterback, 1960–61
285 completions for 3,905 yards and 36 touchdowns
Longest completion was 78 yards on 10-08-60
19 carries for 79 yards and two touchdowns
Longest run was 20 yards on 12-18-60
Recovered three fumbles
28 games
Boston College Eagle

Spach, Stephen (#82)
Tight End, 2007–08
Five games
Only playoff game appearance was on 01-20-08
Fresno State Bulldog

Spann, Antwain (#31) and (#28)
Defensive Back, 2006–08
19 games
Louisiana-Lafayette Ragin' Cajun

Spears, Ron (#78)
Defensive End, 1982–83
Eight regular season games
Only playoff game appearance was on 01-08-83
San Diego State Aztec

Spires, Greg (#94)
Defensive End, 1998–2000
9.5 sacks
Recovered a fumble on 09-17-00
45 regular season games
Only playoff game appearance was on 01-03-99
#83 pick in the 1998 College Draft
Florida State Seminole

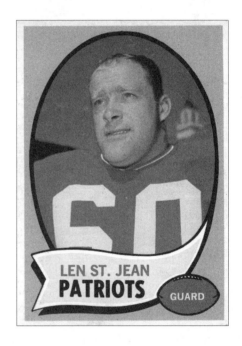

LEN ST. JEAN
PATRIOTS   GUARD

St. Jean, Lennie (#60) "Boston Strongboy"
DE/Guard (LB and T), 1964–73
Recorded 5.5 sacks as a defensive end
Recovered four fumbles
Played on both sides of the line of scrimmage
140 consecutive games
AFL All-Star guard in 1966
Ninth round draft pick in 1964
Northern Michigan Wildcat

Stallworth, Donte' (#18)
Wide Receiver, 2007
46 receptions for 697 yards and three
    touchdowns
Longest reception was a 69-yard touchdown on
    10-14-07
Ran for a 12-yard gain on 10-07-07
16 regular season games

Three playoff games
Tennessee Volunteer

Stanley, Sylvester (#63) "Buster"
Nose Tackle, 1994
Seven games
Michigan Wolverine

Stanley, Walter (#81)
WR/KR/PR, 1992
Three receptions for 63 yards
Longest reception of 36 yards on 10-25-92
29 kickoff returns for 529 yards
Longest return was 40 yards on 10-18-92
28 punt returns for 227 yards
Longest punt return was 50 yards on 10-25-92
Recovered two fumbles
13 games
Colorado Buffalo

Starks, Duane (#23)
Cornerback, 2005
Seven games
Miami Hurricane

Starring, Stephen (#81)
WR/KR/PR (QB), 1983–87
112 receptions for 1,865 yards and 11 touchdowns
Longest reception was a 76-yard touchdown on
    09-25-83
107 kickoff returns for 2,259 yards
Longest kickoff return was 53 yards on 09-22-85
19 punt returns for 108 yards
Longest punt return was 17 yards on 10-25-87
5 carries for a net loss of three yards
Longest run was 10 yards on 12-28-87
Recovered six fumbles
Advanced a fumble eight yards on 09-16-84
Tossed a quarterback run/option pitch on 12-01-85
72 regular season games
Five playoff games
#74 pick in the 1983 College Draft
McNeese State Cowboy

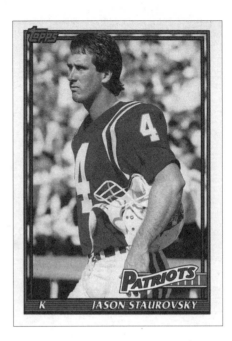

Staurovsky, Jason (#4)
Kicker, 1988–91
50 field goals
Longest field goal was 53 yards on 10-07-90
57 extra points
40 games
Tulsa Golden Hurricane

Steinfort, Fred (#5) "Suitcase"
Kicker, 1983
Six field goals
Longest field goal was 35 yards on 10-16-83
16 extra points
Nine games
Boston College Eagle

Stenger, Brian (#59)
Linebacker, 1973
Recovered two fumbles
10 games
Notre Dame Fighting Irish

Stephens, Calvin (#68)
Guard, 1992
13 games
#56 pick in the 1991 College Draft
South Carolina Gamecock

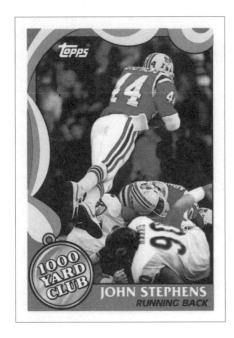

Stephens, John (#44)

Running Back, 1988–92

891 carries for 3,249 yards and 17 touchdowns
Longest run was 52 yards on 12-17-88
100 receptions for 781 yards and one touchdown
Caught an 18-yard touchdown pass on 11-25-90
Longest reception was 43 yards on 12-15-90
Recovered nine fumbles
Recovered a fumble for a touchdown on 10-16-88
AFC Pro Bowl running back in 1988
NFL Offensive Rookie of the Year in 1988
76 games
#17 pick in the 1988 College Draft
Northwestern Louisiana State Demon

Stephens, Tom (#45)

TE/DB/PR/KR, 1960–64

41 receptions for 506 yards and five touchdowns
Longest reception was 53 yards on 12-04-60
19 punt returns for 151 yards
Longest punt return was 26 yards on 11-01-63
Five kickoff returns for 57 yards
Longest kickoff return was 31 yards on 12-16-62
Returned an interception 22 yards on 09-08-63
Recovered three fumbles
Returned a fumble 10 yards for a touchdown on
    10-07-61
Recovered a Chargers onside kick on 09-20-64
49 games
Syracuse Orangeman

Stevens, Matt (#26)

Defensive Back, 2000–01

Returned an interception nine yards on 10-28-01
Recovered a fumble on 10-28-01
15 regular season games
Three playoff games
Member of the 2001 championship team
Appalachian State Mountaineer

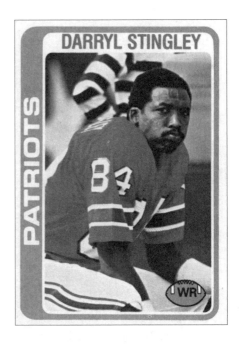

Stingley, Darryl (#84) "The Stinger"

WR/KR/PR, 1973–77

110 receptions for 1,883 yards and 14 touchdowns
Longest reception was 68 yards on 10-23-77
28 carries for 244 yards and two touchdowns
Ran 23 yards for a touchdown on 10-06-74
Longest run was a 34-yard touchdown on 09-18-77
19 punt returns for 136 yards
Longest punt return was 29 yards on 11-16-75
8 kickoff returns for 187 yards
Longest kickoff return was 29 yards on 11-18-73
Returned a fumble 14 yards on 09-28-75
60 regular season games
Only playoff game appearance was on 12-18-76
#19 pick in the 1973 College Draft
Purdue Boilermaker

Stokes, Eric (#78)

Offensive Guard, 1987

Only game played was on 10-04-87
Northeastern University Husky

Stokes, Jerel (#85) "J.J."
Wide Receiver, 2003
Two receptions for 38 yards
Longest reception was 31 yards on 11-23-03
Two games
Member of the 2003 championship team
UCLA Bruin

Stone, Michael (#24)
Safety/Special Team, 2005
13 regular season games
Two playoff games
Memphis Tiger

Striegel, Bill (#72)
Offensive Lineman, 1960
Five games
Pacific Tiger

Stuckey, Shawn (#93)
Linebacker, 1998
Recovered a fumble on 11-15-98
Six regular season games
Only playoff game appearance was on 01-03-99
Troy State Trojan

Studstill, Pat (#2)
Punter, 1972
75 punts for 2,859 yards
Longest punt was 57 yards on 09-24-72
Only run was 11 yards on 11-19-72
14 games
Houston Cougar

Sturt, Fred (#63) "Fred Dog"
Guard, 1976–78
29 regular season games
Only playoff game appearance was on 12-18-76
Bowling Green State Falcon

Suci, Bob (#21)
DB/PR/KR, 1963
Seven interceptions for 277 yards and two touchdowns
Longest return was a 98-yard touchdown on 11-01-63
Returned a pass 52 yards for a touchdown on 12-08-63
25 punt returns for 233 yards
Longest punt return was 22 yards on 10-18-63
17 kickoff returns for 360 yards
Longest kickoff return was 35 yards on 09-08-63
Recovered two fumbles
14 regular season games
Two playoff games
Michigan State Spartan

Sullivan, Chris (#74) "Sully"
Defensive Lineman (KR), 1996–99
Three sacks
Three kickoff returns for 15 yards
Longest kickoff return was nine yards on 11-29-98
Recovered a fumble on 10-26-96
63 regular season games
Six playoff games
#119 pick in the 1996 College Draft
Boston College Eagle

Swanson, Terry (#36)
Punter, 1967–68
127 punts for 5,081 yards
Longest punt was 62 yards on 09-24-67
Recovered three fumbles
24 games
UMASS Minuteman

Sweet, Joe (#81)
Wide Receiver, 1974
Four games
Tennessee State Tiger

Sykes, Alfred (#13) "The Wisp"
Wide Receiver, 1971
Only reception was 15 yards on 10-24-71
Recovered a fumble on 10-10-71
Four games
#339 pick in the 1971 College Draft
Florida A&M Rattler

Taliaferro, Myron (#17) "Mike"
Quarterback, 1968–71
305 completions for 3,920 yards and 27 touchdowns
Longest completion was a 70-yard touchdown on 09-22-68
23 carries for 46 yards
Longest run was 21 yards on 10-20-68
AFL All-Star quarterback in 1969
32 games
Illinois Fighting Illini

Tanner, John (#53) "Craze"
LB/TE/DE, 1973–74
Recorded a sack on 10-07-73
Two receptions for 23 yards and one touchdown
Longest reception was 21 yards on 11-03-74
Caught a 2-yard touchdown pass on 11-24-74
Two kickoff returns for 17 yards
Longest kickoff return was 17 yards on 12-15-74

Played on both sides of the line of scrimmage
26 games
Tennessee Tech Golden Eagle

Tardits, Richard (#53)
Linebacker, 1990–92
Recovered a fumble on 10-20-91
27 games
Georgia Bulldog

Tarver, John (#36)
RB (KR), 1972–74
155 carries for 554 yards and seven touchdowns
Longest run was 28 yards on 10-14-73
29 receptions for 200 yards and one touchdown
Longest reception was 22 yards on 11-26-72
Caught an eight-yard touchdown pass on 12-03-72
Only kickoff return was 17 yards on 09-16-73
Recovered three fumbles
31 games
#186 pick in the 1972 College Draft
Colorado Buffalo

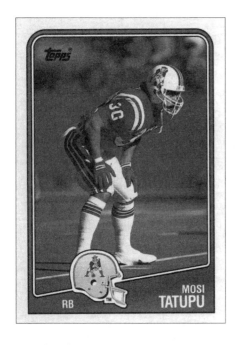

Tatupu, Mosi (#30) "Boo"
RB/Special Team, 1978–90
612 carries for 2,415 yards and 18 touchdowns
Longest run was 55 yards on 11-13-83
96 receptions for 843 yards and two touchdowns
Longest reception was 41 yards on 10-04-81
Two completions for 30 yards and one touchdown
Threw a 15-yard touchdown pass to Tony Collins on
    11-01-87

Completed a 15-yard pass on 11-01-87 and 11-26-89
Seven kickoff returns for 56 yards
Longest kickoff return was 17 yards on 12-18-78
Recovered eight fumbles
Returned a blocked punt 17 yards for touchdown on
    11-30-86
Recovered a Patriots onside kick on 11-10-80
Recovered a Packers onside kick on 09-08-85
AFC Pro Bowl Special Team player in 1986
194 regular season games
Seven playoff games
#215 pick in the 1978 College Draft
USC Trojan

Taylor, Gene (#82)
Wide Receiver, 1991
Only game played was on 11-17-91
#163 pick in the 1987 College Draft
Fresno State Bulldog

Taylor, Greg (#45)
Kickoff Returnman, 1982
Two kickoff returns for 46 yards
Longest kickoff return was 27 yards on 09-12-82
Only game played was on 09-12-82
#308 pick in the 1982 College Draft
Virginia Cavalier

Taylor, Kitrick (#49)
Kickoff Returnman, 1989
Three kickoff returns for 52 yards
Longest kickoff return was 22 yards on 11-19-89
Four games
Washington State Cougar

Testaverde, Vinny (#14)
Quarterback, 2006
Two completions for 29 yards and one touchdown
Longest completion was 23 yards on 12-31-06
Tossed a 6-yard touchdown pass on 12-31-06
Two games
Miami Hurricane

Thomas, Adalius (#96)
Linebacker , 2007–08
11.5 sacks
Returned an interception 65 yards for a touchdown
    on 09-16-07
25 regular season games
Three playoff games
Southern Mississippi Golden Eagle

Thomas, Ben (#99)
Defensive Lineman, 1985–86
Only regular season sack was on 09-28-86
19 regular season games
Four playoff games
#56 pick in the 1985 College Draft
Auburn Tiger

Thomas, Blair (#32)
Running Back (KR), 1994
19 carries for 67 yards and one touchdown
Ran for a 4-yard touchdown on 10-16-94
Longest run was 13 yards on 10-16-94
Two receptions for 15 yards
Longest reception was nine yards on 10-16-94
Three kickoff returns for 40 yards
Longest kickoff return was 16 yards on 10-16-94
Four games
Penn State Nittany Lion

Thomas, David (#86)
Tight End, 2006–08
21 receptions for 261 yards and one touchdown
Caught a 22-yard touchdown pass on 12-24-06
Longest reception was 36 yards on 12-24-06
32 regular season games
Three playoff games
#86 pick in the 2006 College Draft
Texas Longhorn

Thomas, Donnie (#51)
Linebacker, 1976
Three regular season games
Only playoff game was on 12-18-76
#298 pick in the 1976 College Draft
Indiana Fighting Hoosier

Thomas, Gene (#22)
RB (KR), 1968
88 carries for 215 yards and two touchdowns
Longest run was 25 yards on 10-20-68
10 receptions for 85 yards
Longest reception was 32 yards on 09-29-68
Only kickoff return was 22 yards on 09-22-68
Nine games
Florida A&M Rattler

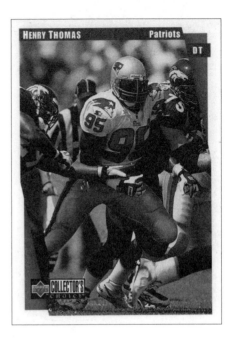

Thomas, Henry (#95)
DT (TE/FB), 1997–2000
20.5 sacks
Two interceptions for 40 yards and one touchdown
Longest return was a 24-yard touchdown on 10-04-98
Recovered three fumbles
Played as a tight end and fullback on 12-17-00
64 regular season games
Three playoff games
LSU Fighting Tiger

Thomas, Santonio (#92)
Defensive Lineman, 2007
Four games
Miami Hurricane

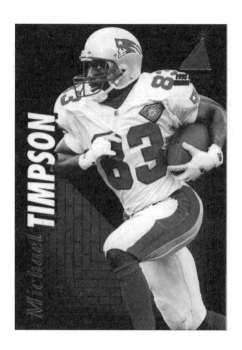

Thompson, Leroy (#36)
RB/KR, 1994

102 carries for 312 yards and two touchdowns

Longest run was 13 yards on 10-02-94, 11-13-94, and 12-04-94

65 receptions for 465 yards and five touchdowns

Longest reception was a 27-yard touchdown on 11-20-94

18 kickoff returns for 376 yards

Longest kickoff return was 30 yards on 12-04-94

Recovered a fumble on 09-04-94

16 regular season games

Only playoff game appearance was on 01-01-95

Penn State Nittany Lion

Thompson, Renya (#21)
Defensive Back, 1993

Returned an interception four yards on 09-05-93

15 games

Baylor Bear

Timpson, Michael (#45) and (#83)
WR/KR/PR, 1989–94

172 receptions for 2,472 yards and eight touchdowns

Longest reception was a 60-yard touchdown on 12-22-91

Three carries for 10 yards

Longest run was 10 yards on 12-24-94

10 kickoff returns for 168 yards

Longest return was 28 yards on 12-20-92 and 09-11-94

Eight punt returns for 47 yards

Longest punt return was 14 yards on 09-13-92

70 regular season games

Only playoff game appearance was on 01-01-95

#100 pick in the 1989 College Draft

Penn State Nitany Lion

ANDRE TIPPETT • LINEBACKER
NEW ENGLAND PATRIOTS

Tippett, Andre (#56) "Tip"
Linebacker (DE), 1982–93
100 sacks
Only interception was returned 10 yards on 09-01-91
Returned a lateral 32 yards on 10-26-86
AFC Defensive Player of the Week on 10-20-85
AFC Defensive Player of the Week on 10-18-87
Blocked a 48-yard field-goal attempt on 10-18-87
Recovered 18 fumbles
Returned a fumble 25 yards for a touchdown on
     09-29-85
Returned a fumble 29 yards for a touchdown on
     09-21-87
AFC Pro Bowl LB in 1984, 1985, 1986, 1987, and 1988
AFC Defensive Player of the Year in 1985
151 regular season games
Six playoff games
#41 pick in the 1982 College Draft
Inducted in the Patriots Hall of Fame on 11-15-99
Inducted in the Pro Football Hall of Fame on 08-02-08
Iowa Hawkeye

Tipton, Dave (#60)
Nose Tackle, 1975–76
Two sacks
Returned a fumble five yards on 11-07-76
12 regular season games
Only playoff game appearance was on 12-18-76
Western Illinois Leatherneck

Toler, Ken (#82)
WR/KR, 1981–82
Seven receptions for 133 yards and two touchdowns
Longest reception was a 33-yard touchdown on
     01-02-83
Only run was four yards on 11-21-82
Nine kickoff returns for 148 yards
Longest kickoff return was 32 yards on 11-08-81
Recovered a fumble on 12-13-81
25 regular season games
Only playoff game appearance was on 01-08-83
#185 pick in the 1981 College Draft
Mississippi Rebel

Toner, Ed (#75)
DT/LB, 1967–69
Recorded a sack on 12-01-68
26 games
Third round draft pick in 1966
University of Massachusetts Minuteman

Towns, Bobby (#34)
Defensive Back, 1961
Two games
Georgia Bulldog

Traylor, Keith (#98)
NT/DT, 2004
16 regular season games
Three playoff games
Member of the 2004 championship team
Central State Maurader

Trull, Don (#10)
Quarterback, 1967
27 completions for 442 yards and one touchdown
Tossed a 40-yard touchdown pass on 11-19-67
Longest completion was 52 yards on 12-17-67
19 carries for 35 yards and three touchdowns
Longest run was 10 yards on 11-19-67
Seven games
Baylor Bear

Tucker, Erroll (#21)
DB/KR/PR, 1989
Two fumble recoveries
13 kickoff returns for 270 yards
Longest kickoff return was 37 yards on 11-26-89
13 punt returns for 102 yards
Longest punt return was 25 yards on 11-19-89
Five games
Utah Ute

Tucker, Ross (#69)
Offensive Lineman, 2005
Only regular season game was on 01-01-06
Only playoff game was on 01-14-06
Princeton Tiger

Tuitele, Maugaula (#96) and (#47) and (#59)
LB/Special Team, 2000–02
Five games
Member of the 2001 championship team
Colorado State Ram

Tupa, Tom (#19)
Punter (QB), 1996–98
215 punts for 9,602 yards
Longest punt was 73 yards on 10-06-97
Took the last two snaps as the quarterback on 10-11-98
45 regular season games
Six playoff games
Ohio State Buckeye

Turner, Robert (#40) "Bake"
Wide Receiver, 1970
28 receptions for 428 yards and two touchdowns
Longest reception was 43 yards on 11-29-70
14 games
Texas Tech Red Raider

Turner, Bill (#74)
Guard, 1987
Two games
Boston College Eagle

Turner, Kevin (#34)
RB (KR), 1992–94
96 carries for 382 yards and one touchdown
Ran for a one-yard touchdown on 09-04-94
Longest run was 49 yards on 12-19-93
98 receptions for 856 yards and six touchdowns
Longest reception was 32 yards on 09-25-94
Only kickoff return was 11 yards on 10-04-92
Recovered six fumbles
Advanced a fumble six yards on 10-17-93
Tossed a lateral to Leonard Russell for an 82 yard play
    on 10-10-93
48 regular season games
Only playoff game appearance was on 01-01-95
#71 pick in the 1992 College Draft
Alabama Crimson Tide

Turner, Thomas (#99) "T.J."
Linebacker, 2001
Two games
Member of the 2001 championship team
#239 pick in the 2001 College Draft
Michigan State Spartan

Twombly, Darren (#64)
Center, 1987
Only game played was on 10-04-87
Boston College Eagle

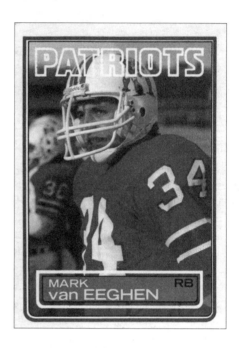

van Eeghen, Mark (#34)
Running Back, 1982–83
177 carries for 744 yards and two touchdowns
Longest run was 17 yards on 12-12-82
12 receptions for 116 yards and one touchdown
Longest reception was 23 yards on 11-06-83
Only touchdown reception was five yards on 12-19-82
Recovered a fumble on 12-04-83
24 regular season games
Only playoff game appearance was on 01-08-83
Colgate Red Raider

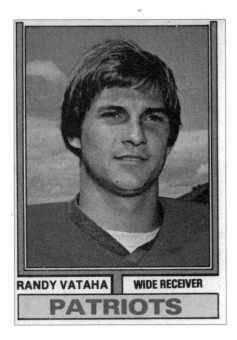

RANDY VATAHA   WIDE RECEIVER
PATRIOTS

Vataha, Randy (#18) "The Rabbit"
WR (DB), 1971–76
178 receptions for 3,055 yards and 23 touchdowns
Longest reception was an 88-yard touchdown on
    12-19-71
Six carries for 10 yards
Longest run was 24 yards on 11-24-74
Recovered two fumbles
Advanced a fumble 46 yards for a touchdown on
    10-07-73
Was a defensive back in the final series on 09-26-76
82 regular season games
Only playoff game appearance was on 12-18-76
Stanford Cardinal

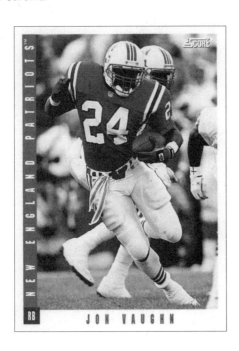

Vaughn, Jon (#24)
RB/KR, 1991–92
144 carries for 597 yards and three touchdowns
Longest run was 36 yards on 10-25-92
22 receptions for 173 yards
Longest reception was 32 yards on 09-08-91
54 kickoff returns for 1,281 yards and two touchdowns
Returned a kickoff 99 yards for a touchdown on
    09-29-91
Returned a kickoff 100 yards for a touchdown on
    12-20-92
Only completion was a 13-yard touchdown pass on
    09-22-91
Recovered two fumbles
32 games
#112 pick in the 1991 College Draft
Michigan Wolverine

Ventrone, Raymond (#41) "The Human Missle"
Special Team, 2007–08
17 regular season games
Two playoff games
Villanova Wildcat

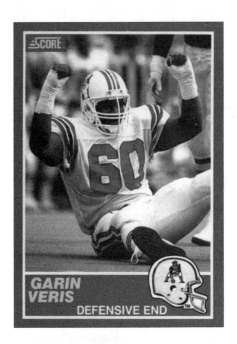

GARIN VERIS   DEFENSIVE END

Veris, Garin (#60) and (#90)
Defensive Lineman, 1985–91
39.5 sacks
Recovered seven regular season fumbles
Blocked an extra-point attempt on 11-03-91
78 regular season games
Five playoff games
#48 pick in the 1985 College Draft
Ed Block Courage Award in 1988
Stanford Cardinal

Viaene, David (#70)
Offensive Tackle, 1989–90
20 games
Minnesota Golden Gopher

Villa, Danny (#73) and (#75)
Tackle/Center/LS, 1987–91 and 1997
Recovered three fumbles
75 regular season games
Two playoff games
#113 pick in the 1987 College Draft
Arizona State Sun Devil

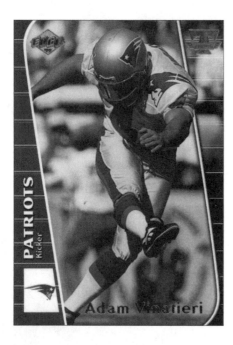

Vinatieri, Adam (#4) "Automatic"
Kicker (P), 1996–2005
263 field goals
Longest field goal was 57 yards on 11-10-02
367 extra points
Two punts for 60 yards
Longest punt was 33 yards on 12-09-01
Ran for a two point conversion on 11-29-98
Tossed a 4-yard touchdown pass on 11-07-04
AFC Special Team Player of the Week on 12-16-01
AFC Special Team Player of the Week on 01-09-02
AFC Special Team Player of the Week on 12-29-02
AFC Special Team Player of the Week on 11-07-04
AFC Special Team Player of the Week on 09-25-05
AFC Pro Bowl kicker in 2002 and 2004
160 regular season games
Kicked the game-winning 23-yard field goal in
    overtime playoff game

Kicked game-winning 48-yard field goal in Super Bowl
    XXXVI
Kicked game-winning 41-yard field goal in Super Bowl
    XXXVIII
17 playoff games
Member of the 2001, 2003, and 2004 championship
    teams
South Dakota State Jack Rabbit

Virkus, Scott (#70)
Defensive End, 1984
Five games
Purdue Boilermaker

Vrabel, Mike (#50) "Vrabes"
LB/DE (TE and KR), 2001–08
48 sacks
11 interceptions for 73 yards and one touchdown
Longest return was a 24-yard touchdown on 09-18-05
Recovered five fumbles
Recovered Buffalo Bills onside kick on 11-11-01
Eight receptions for 11 yards and eight touchdowns
Longest reception was a two-yard touchdown on 11-07-
    04 and 12-26-05
Three kickoff returns for 25 yards
Longest kickoff return was 14 yards on 11-16-03
AFC Defensive Player of the Week on 10-28-07
125 regular season games
17 playoff games
AFC Pro Bowl linebacker in 2007
Member of the 2001, 2003, and 2004 championship
    teams
Ed Block Courage Award in 2003
Ohio State Buckeye

Wagner, Bryan (#8) and (#9)
Punter (K), 1991 and 1995
51 punts for 2,105 yards
Longest punt was 57 yards on 12-23-95
Kicked off in eight games in 1995
11 games
Cal State Northridge Matador

Walker, Bruce (#91)
Nose Tackle, 1995
11 games
UCLA Bruin

Walter, Ken (#13)
Punter, 2001–03 and 2006
211 punts for 8,143 yards
Longest punt was 58 yards on 11-11-01
AFC Special Team Player of Week on 12-22-01
46 regular season games
Recovered a fumble on 09-14-03
Six playoff games
Member of the 2001 and 2003 championship teams
Kent State Golden Flash

Walker, Mike (#12) "Superfoot"
Kicker, 1972
Two field goals
Kicked a 36 yard FG on 11-19-72 and on 12-10-72
15 extra points
Eight games

Ward, David (#94)
Linebacker, 1989
16 games
Southern Arkansas Mulerider

Ward, Dedric (#17)
Wide Receiver, 2003
Seven receptions for 106 yards and one touchdown
Longest reception was a 31-yard touchdown on
    11-30-03
Four games
Member of the 2003 championship team
Northern Iowa Panther

Warren, Lamont (#27)
RB (KR), 1999
35 carries for 120 yards
Longest run was 18 yards on 10-17-99
29 receptions for 262 yards and one touchdown
Longest reception was 21 yards on 10-17-99
Only touchdown reception was a three-yard
    touchdown on 10-31-99
Two kickoff returns for 25 yards
Longest kickoff return was 16 yards on 10-10-99
16 games
Colorado Buffalo

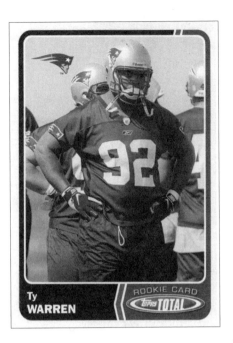

Ty
WARREN
ROOKIE CARD
Topps TOTAL

Warren, Ty (#94) "Boss Hog"
DE/NT, 2003–08
19.5 sacks
Recovered six fumbles
Recorded a safety on 09-10-06
92 regular season games
14 playoff games
Member of the 2003 and 2004 championship teams
#13 pick in the 2003 College Draft
Texas A&M Aggie

Washington, Clyde (#31)
DB/Punter (RB), 1960–61
Seven interceptions for 58 yards
Longest return was 33 yards on 12-17-61
17 punts for 539 yards
Longest punt was 48 yards on 11-25-60
Two carries for six yards
Ran for three yards as a punter on 11-11-60
Ran for three yards as a running back on 09-23-61
Returned a blocked field goal seven yards on 10-28-60
Recovered four fumbles
Advanced a lateral one yard on 10-28-60
27 games
Purdue Boilermaker

Washington, John (#76)
Defensive End, 1993
16 games
Oklahoma State Cowboy

Washington, Kelley (#15)
WR/Special Team, 2007–08
Caught a three-yard pass on 09-07-08
Blocked a New York Jets punt on 12-16-07
24 regular season games
Three playoff games
Tennessee Volunteer

Washington, Mark (#46)
DB (KR), 1979
Only kickoff return was 18 yards on 12-09-79
12 games
Morgan State Bear

Washington, Mickey (#21)
Defensive Back, 1990–91
Two interceptions
No return on either interception
25 games
Texas A&M Aggie

Washington, Ted (#92)
Nose Tackle, 2003
Two sacks
10 regular season games
Three playoff games
Member of the 2003 championship team
Louisville Cardinal

Watson, Benjamin (#84)
Tight End, 2004–08
138 receptions for 1,698 yards and 15 touchdowns
Longest regular season catch was for 40 yards on
    10-30-06
Ran for an 11-yard gain on 10-07-07
Recovered two fumbles
55 regular season games
Eight playoff games
Member of the 2004 championship team
#32 pick in the 2004 College Draft
Georgia Bulldog

Watson, Dave (#67)
Guard (KR), 1963–64
Recovered two fumbles
Recovered a Raiders onside kick on 09-13-64
Only kickoff return was for nine yards on 09-29-63
28 regular season games
Two playoff games
11th round draft pick in 1963
Georgia Tech Yellow Jacket

Weathers, Clarence (#82)
WR/KR/PR, 1983–84
27 receptions for 494 yards and five touchdowns
Longest reception was a 58-yard touchdown on
    11-06-83
Only run was for 28 yards on 10-09-83
Three kickoff returns for 58 yards
Longest kickoff return was 33 yards on 09-04-83
Five punt returns for eight yards
Longest punt return was seven yards on 11-04-84
Recovered a fumble on 11-20-83
25 games
Delaware State Hornet

Weathers, Robert (#24)
RB/KR, 1982–86
159 carries for 733 yards and four touchdowns
Longest run was for 77 yards on 09-04-83
29 receptions for 268 yards
Longest reception was 22 yards on 09-19-82
Four kickoff returns for 86 yards
Longest kickoff return was 29 yards on 10-02-83
44 regular season games
Four playoff games
#40 pick in the 1982 College Draft
Arizona State Sun Devil

Weaver, Jed (#85) "The Dream"
Tight End, 2004
Eight receptions for 93 yards
Longest reception was 25 yards on 01-02-05
Eight games
Member of the 2004 championship team
Oregon Duck

Webb, Don (#42) "Webbie" and "Spider"
DB (KR/HB), 1961–71
21 interceptions for 366 yards and two touchdowns
Longest return was 59 yards on 12-09-61

Returned a pass 27 yards for a touchdown on 10-22-61
Returned a pass 31 yards for a touchdown on 12-17-61
Blocked a San Diego Chargers punt on 12-17-61
Returned the blocked punt 20 yards for a touchdown
    on 12-17-61
Recovered 11 fumbles
Returned a fumble 49 yards for a touchdown on
    10-29-61
Only kickoff return was 15 yards on 10-01-61
Caught an 11-yard pass on 10-06-62
AFL All-Star defensive back in 1969
134 games
24th round draft pick in 1961
Iowa State Cyclone

Webster, George (#90) "Mickey"
Linebacker, 1974–76
Five sacks
Only interception was on 09-28-75
Recovered two fumbles
37 regular season games
Only playoff game appearance was on 12-18-76
Inducted into College Football Hall of Fame 12-08-87
Michigan State Spartan

Webster, Jason (#23)
Defensive Back, 2008
Three games
Texas A&M Aggie

Weisacosky, Ed (#66)
Linebacker, 1971–72
Three sacks
Returned fumble three yards on 10-29-72
28 games
Miami Hurricane

Weishuhn, Clayton (#53) "Happy Warrior of the NFL"
Linebacker, 1982–86
Three sacks
Advanced a lateral 27 yards for a touchdown on
    09-25-83
Recovered four fumbles
30 regular season games
Only playoff game appearance was on 01-08-83
#60 pick in the 1982 College Draft
Angelo State Ram

Welch, Claxton (#43)
Running Back, 1973
Only carry was a loss of two yards on 11-11-73
Six receptions for 22 yards
Longest reception was eight yards on 11-11-73
Recovered a fumble on 11-11-73
Recovered a Patriots onside kick on 11-11-73
Two games
Oregon Duck

Welker, Wes (#83) "The Natural"
WR/KR/PR, 2007–08
223 receptions for 2,340 yards and 11 touchdowns
Longest reception was 64 yards on 11-23-08
Seven carries for 60 yards

Longest run was 27 yards on on 10-01-07
49 punt returns for 486 yards
Longest punt return was 44 yards on 10-20-08
Eight kickoff returns for 202 yards
Longest kickoff return was 33 yards on 10-07-07
Recovered two fumbles
AFC Pro Bowl wide receiver in 2008
32 regular season games
Three playoff games
Texas Tech Red Raider

Wells, Billy (#41)
RB/PR/KR, 1960
14 carries for 59 yards
Longest run was 13 yards on 11-11-60
19 receptions for 206 yards and one touchdown
Longest reception was 78 yards on 10-08-60
Only touchdown reception was for six yards on
     10-23-60
12 punt returns for 66 yards
Longest punt return was 19 yards on 12-18-60
11 kickoff returns for 275 yards
Longest kickoff return was 33 yards on 11-11-60
12 games
Michigan State Spartan

West, Mel (#24) "The Mole"
HB/KR, 1961
26 carries for 90 yards
Longest run was 31 yards on 09-23-61
Five receptions for 42 yards
Longest reception was 18 yards on 09-16-61
Seven kickoff returns for 191 yards
Longest kickoff return was 37 yards on 10-01-61
Four games
11th round draft pick in 1961
Missouri Tiger

Westbrook, Don (#83)
WR/KR/PR, 1977–81
23 receptions for 393 yards and three touchdowns
Longest reception was 38 yards on 11-04-79
Three carries for six yards
Longest run was four yards on 10-28-79 and 11-18-79
19 kickoff returns for 290 yards
Longest kickoff return was 33 yards on 12-03-78
Two punt returns for five yards
Longest punt return was five yards on 09-09-79
Blocked a New York Jets punt on 09-09-79
Two completions for 52 yards
Longest completion was 28 yards on 10-07-79

Recovered three regular season fumbles
71 regular season games
Only playoff game appearance was on 12-31-78
Nebraska Cornhusker

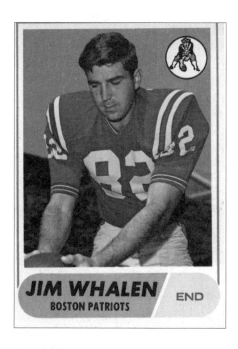

Whalen, Jim (#82)
Tight End/LS, 1965–69
153 receptions for 2,487 yards and 17 touchdowns
Longest reception was an 87-yard touchdown on
     10-27-68
Recovered a fumble on 10-17-65
70 games
Third round draft pick in 1965
Boston College Eagle

Wheatley, Terrence (#22)
Defensive Back, 2008
Six games
#62 pick in the 2008 College Draft
Colorado Buffalo

Wheeler, Dwight (#62) "Whimpy"
Tackle/LS/Center, 1978–83
Recovered a squibbed kickoff on 09-03-78
72 regular season games
Only playoff game appearance was on 01-08-83
#102 pick in the 1978 College Draft
Tennessee State Tiger

Wheeler, Mark (#97)
Defensive Tackle, 1996–98
Five sacks
Recovered a fumble on 11-03-96
40 regular season games
Six playoff games
Texas A&M Aggie

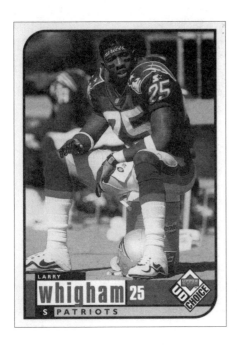

Whigham, Larry (#25) "Hollywood"
DB (Special Team), 1994–2000
Four interceptions for 81 yards and one touchdown
Longest return was a 60-yard touchdown on 11-23-97
Five sacks
Recovered three fumbles
Blocked a Baltimore Ravens punt on 10-04-96
Blocked a Philadelphia Eagles punt on 12-19-99
AFC Defensive Player of the Week on 11-23-97
AFC Pro Bowl Special Team player in 1997
106 regular season games
AFC Special Team Player of the Week on 01-12-97
Seven playoff games
NE Louisiana Indian

White, Adrian (#38)
Defensive Back, 1993
Five games
Florida Gator

White, David (#51)
Linebacker, 1993
Six games
Nebraska Cornhusker

White, Harvey (#10)
QB/RB/TE, 1960
Three completions for 44 yards
Longest completion of 23 yards on 10-28-60
Five carries for seven yards
Longest run was five yards on 10-08-60
Two receptions for 24 yards
Longest reception was 13 yards on 10-23-60
Wore No. 19 at Clemson
Nine games
First round draft pick in 1960
Clemson Tiger

White, Jeff (#2)
Kicker/Punter, 1973
14 field goals
Longest field goal was 48 yards on 11-25-73
21 extra points
Six punts for 163 yards on 10-28-73
Longest punt was 51 yards on 10-28-73
Recovered a fumble on 10-28-73
11 games
Texas El Paso Miner

White, Jim (#87)
Defensive End, 1972
Only sack was made on 11-19-72
13 games
#73 pick in the 1972 College Draft
Colorado State Ram

White, Reggie (#90) "The Other"
Defensive Tackle, 1995
1.5 sacks
16 games
North Carolina A&T Aggie

Whitten, Todd (#15)
Quarterback, 1987
Only game played was on 10-18-87
Stephen F. Austin State Lumberjack

Whittingham, Fred (#53)
Linebacker (KR), 1970
Returned a kickoff 14 yards on 11-15-70
13 games
California Polytechnic Mustang

Wichard, Murray (#90)
Defensive Lineman, 1987
Shared in two quarterback sacks
Recovered two fumbles
Three games
Frostburg State Bobcat

Wiggins, Jermaine (#49) and (#85) "our Snowplow"
Tight End, 2000–01
30 receptions for 336 yards and five touchdowns
Longest reception was 59 yards on 12-24-00
20 regular season games
Three playoff games
Member of the 2001 championship team
Georgia Bulldog

Wilburn, Steve (#99)
Defensive End, 1987
Only sack was made on 10-18-87
Three games
Illinois State Redbird

Wilfork, Vince (#75) "Fat Boy"
Nose Tackle, 2004–08
7.5 sacks
Recovered five fumbles
Blocked an extra-point attempt on 12-14-08
AFC Pro Bowl nose tackle in 2007
77 regular season games
11 playoff games
Member of the 2004 championship team
#21 pick in the 2004 College Draft
Miami Golden Hurricane

Wilhite, Jonathan (#24)
Defensive Back, 2008
Returned an interception 16 yards on 12-14-08
16 games
#129 pick in the 2008 College Draft
Auburn Tiger

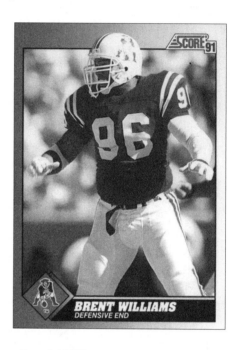

Williams, Brent (#96)
DE (NT), 1986–93
43.5 sacks
Recovered 11 fumbles
Returned a fumble 26 yards on 09-07-86
Returned a fumble seven yards on 11-30-86
Returned a fumble 21 yards for a touchdown on 11-30-86
Returned a fumble 45 yards for a touchdown on 10-07-90
Blocked a 48-yard field-goal attempt on 09-01-91
121 regular season games
Only playoff game appearance was on 01-04-87
#193 pick in the 1986 College Draft
Toledo Rocket

Williams, Brian (#49)
Tight End, 1982
Only game played was on 11-21-82
Southern Jaguar

Williams, Brooks (#80)
Tight End, 1983
13 games
North Carolina Tar Heel

Williams, Derwin (#82)
Wide Receiver, 1985–87
14 receptions for 228 yards
Longest reception was 30 yards on 09-08-85
Recovered a fumble on 11-15-87
42 regular season games
Two playoff games
#192 pick in the 1984 College Draft
New Mexico Lobo

Williams, Ed (#54)
Linebacker, 1984–87 and 1990
Two sacks
Recovered four fumbles
Returned an interception 51 yards on 11-15-87
62 regular season games
Four playoff games
#43 pick in the 1984 College Draft
Texas Longhorn

Williams, Grant (#76)
Offensive Tackle, 2000–01
29 regular season games
Three playoff games
Member of the 2001 championship team
Louisiana Tech Bulldog

Williams, Jon (#44)
KR/Special Team, 1984
23 kickoff returns for 461 yards
Longest return was 29 yards on 09-02-84 and 10-14-84
Nine games
#70 pick in the 1984 College Draft
Penn State Nittany Lion

Williams, Larry (#75)
Guard, 1992
13 games
Recovered a fumble on 12-20-92
Notre Dame Fighting Irish

Williams, Lester (#72)
Nose Tackle, 1982–85
Five sacks
Blocked a 52-yard field-goal attempt on 12-19-82
Recovered two regular season fumbles
40 regular season games
Five playoff games
#27 pick in the 1982 College Draft
Miami Hurricane

Williams, Perry (#38)
Defensive Back, 1987
Only interception was not returned on 10-11-87
Three games
Clemson Tiger

Williams, Toby (#90)
Nose Tackle, 1983–88
15.5 sacks
Recovered a fumble on 10-14-84
80 regular season games
Only playoff game appearance was on 01-04-87
#265 pick in the 1983 College Draft
Nebraska Cornhusker

Williamson, John (#55) "J.R."
Linebacker/Center, 1968–71
Returned an interception two yards on 09-20-70
Recovered two fumbles
39 games
Louisiana Tech Bulldog

Wilson, Darrell (#47)
Defensive Back, 1981
Only game was played on 11-08-81
UCONN Husky

Wilson, Darryal (#48)
Wide Receiver, 1983
Nine games
#47 pick in the 1983 College Draft
Tennessee Volunteer

Wilson, David (#26)
Defensive Back, 1992
Only game was played on 10-25-92
California Golden Bear

Wilson, Eddie (#12)
Quarterback (Punter), 1965
20 completions for 257 yards and one touchdown
Only touchdown pass was for eight yards on
    11-28-65
Longest completion was 30 yards on 10-24-65
Eight carries for four yards
Longest run was 17 yards on 10-24-65
Six punts for 194 yards on 10-17-65
Longest punt was 49 yards on 10-17-65
14 games
Arizona Wildcat

Wilson, Eugene (26) "Geno"
Defensive Back, 2003–07
10 interceptions for 74 yards and one touchdown
Longest return was 24 yards on 12-26-04
Returned a pass five yards for a touchdown on
    12-16-07
Recovered four fumbles
Returned a fumble four yards on 12-16-07
62 regular season games
10 playoff games
Member of the 2003 and 2004 championship teams
#36 pick in the 2003 College Draft
Illinois Fighting Illini

Wilson, Jerrel (#4)
Punter, 1978
54 punts for 1,921 yards
Longest punt was 57 yards on 12-03-78
Recovered a fumble on 11-05-78
14 regular season games
Only playoff game appearance was on 12-31-78
Southern Mississippi Golden Eagle

Wilson, Joe (#23)
RB/KR, 1974
15 carries for 57 yards
Longest run was 12 yards on 12-15-74
Three receptions for 38 yards
Longest reception was 23 yards on 12-15-74
Two kickoff returns for 33 yards
Longest kickoff return was 18 yards on 11-03-74
Recovered a fumble on 12-15-74
12 games
Holy Cross Crusader

Wilson, Marc (#15)
Quarterback, 1989–90
214 completions for 2,631 yards and nine touchdowns
Longest completion was a 65-yard touchdown on
    11-05-89
12 carries for 49 yards
Recovered four fumbles
Longest run was 11 yards on 12-17-89
30 games
Inducted into College Football Hall of Fame in 1996
BYU Cougar

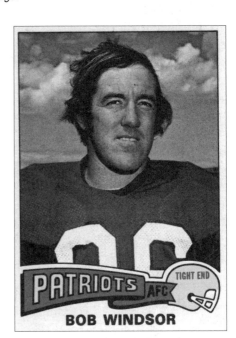

BOB WINDSOR

Windsor, Bob (#86) "Schooner"
Tight End, 1972–75
74 receptions for 915 yards and six touchdowns
Longest reception was 36 yards on 10-21-73
Two carries for a net loss of 10 yards
Longest run was for a four-yard loss on 10-01-72
Recovered a Colts onside kick on 10-07-73
Recovered a fumble on 11-09-75
48 games
Kentucky Wildcat

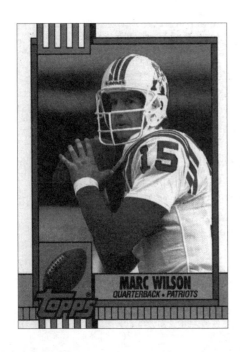

MARC WILSON
QUARTERBACK • PATRIOTS

DENNIS
WIRGOWSKI

DEFENSIVE TACKLE
PATRIOTS

Wirgowski, Dennis (#85) and (#70)
Defensive End (K), 1970–72
Five sacks
Recovered two fumbles
Kicked off on 09-27-70 and 10-04-70
37 games
#212 pick in the 1970 College Draft
Purdue Boilermaker

Witt, Mel (#70) and (#71) "Marvelous Mel"
DE/DT, 1967–70
Returned an interception four yards for a touchdown
    on 09-22-68
35 games
#128 pick in the 1967 College Draft
Arlington State Maverick

Wohlabaugh, Dave (#64)
Center, 1995–98
Recovered three fumbles
57 regular season games
Six playoff games
#112 pick in the 1995 College Draft
Syracuse Orangeman

Wonsley, George (#35)
RB/KR, 1989
Two carries for a net loss of two yards
Longest run was for no gain on 12-17-89
Three kickoff returns for 69 yards
Longest kickoff return was 40 yards on 12-24-89
Five games
Mississippi State Bulldog

Woods, Carl (#34)
Running Back, 1987
Four carries for 20 yards and one touchdown
Longest run was 13 yards on 10-11-87
Only touchdown run was for four yards on 10-11-87
Two games
Vanderbilt Commodore

Woods, Pierre (#58)
LB/Special Team, 2006–08
Recorded a sack on 11-13-08
36 regular season games
Six playoff games
Michigan Wolverine

Woody, Damien (#65)
Center/Guard, 1999–03
Recovered three fumbles
AFC Pro Bowl center in 2002
78 regular season games
Three playoff games
Member of the 2001 and 2003 championship teams
#17 pick in the 1999 College Draft
Boston College Eagle

Wooten, Ron (#61) "Rootin-Tootin"
Guard, 1982–88
Recovered a fumble on 11-23-86
98 regular season games
Six playoff games
#157 pick in the 1981 College Draft
North Carolina Tar Heel

Wren, Darryl (#27)
Defensive Back, 1993–94
Three interception returns for a net loss of seven
    yards
Longest return was two yards on 09-12-93
Recovered a Patriots onside kick on 10-17-93
20 games
Pittsburg State Gorilla

Wright, Elmo (#17)
Wide Receiver, 1975
Four receptions for 46 yards
Longest reception was 20 yards on 11-23-75
Four games
Houston Cougar

Wright, Mike (#99)
Defensive Lineman, 2005–08
Four sacks
Two fumble recoveries
Blocked a 40-yard field goal on 10-08-06
53 regular season games
Three playoff games
Cincinnati Bearcat

Wyman, Devin (#72)
Defensive Tackle, 1996–97
Recorded a sack on 09-22-96
15 games
#206 pick in the 1996 College Draft
Kentucky State Thorobred

Yancy, Carlos (#40)
Cornerback, 1995
Four games
#234 pick in the 1995 College Draft
Georgia Bulldog

Yates, Billy (#74)
Offensive Lineman, 2005–08
22 games
Texas A&M Aggie

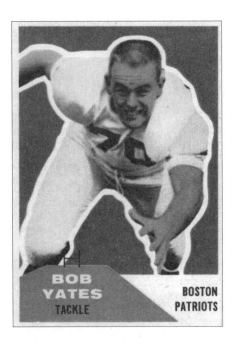

Yates, Bob (#61) and (#50)
Offensive Lineman (K), 1960–65
Recovered a fumble on 10-09-64
Recovered a Raiders onside kick on 10-16-64
Kicked off in 55 games over the 1961–65 seasons

68 regular season games
Two playoff games
Syracuse Orangeman

Yewcic, Tom (#14) "Comrade"
QB/Punter (RB), 1961–66
87 completions for 1,374 yards and 12 touchdowns
Longest completion was a 78-yard touchdown on
   11-30-62
72 carries for 424 yards and four touchdowns
Longest run was 46 yards on 09-29-63
Seven receptions for 69 yards
Longest reception was 46 yards on 09-16-61
377 punts for 14,553 yards
Longest punt was 70 yards on 11-28-65
Recovered three fumbles
77 regular season games
Two playoff games
Michigan State Spartan

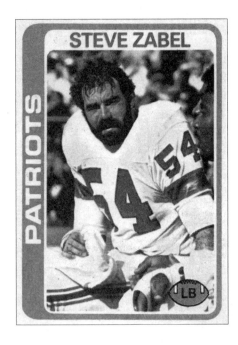

Zabel, Steve (#54) "Zabe"
Linebacker (K), 1975–78
10 sacks
Kicked an extra point on 12-12-76
Only interception was not returned on 10-15-78
Recovered eight fumbles
Returned a fumble eight yards on 09-18-77
Recovered a Buffalo Bills onside kick on 11-05-78
49 regular season games
Two playoff games
Oklahoma Sooner

Zackery, Tony (#25)
Defensive Back, 1990–91
18 games
#223 pick in the 1989 College Draft
Washington Husky

Zamberlin, John (#54) "Zam"
Linebacker, 1979–82
3.5 sacks
Returned an interception 11 yards on 10-18-81
Recovered two fumbles
56 regular season games
Only playoff game appearance was on 01-08-83
#135 pick in the 1979 College Draft
Pacific Lutheran Lute

Zendejas, Joaquin (#5)
Kicker, 1983
Three extra points kicked
Two games
Laverne Tiger

Zereoue, Amos, (#31)
Running Back, 2005
Seven carries for 14 yards
Longest run was 12 yards on 10-16-05
Caught a five-yard pass on 10-16-05
Three regular season games
West Virginia Mountaineer

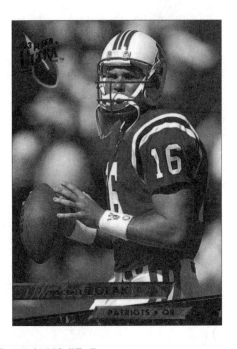

Zolak, Scott (#16) "Zo"
Quarterback, 1992–98
124 completions for 1,314 yards and eight touchdowns
Longest completion was 72 yards on 10-01-95
36 carries for 85 yards
Longest run was 19 yards on 12-06-92
AFC Offensive Player of the Week on 11-15-92
Recovered four fumbles
54 regular season games
Two playoff games
#84 pick in the 1991 College Draft
Maryland Terrapin

The Ball Parks

The Patriots' home games have mostly been played throughout the greater Boston area. The Boston Patriots, however, had to play two home games in other states during the 1967 and 1968 seasons because of scheduling conflicts with its landlord, the Boston Red Sox. Due to the 1967 Baseball World Series, the Patriots had to play a regular season home game in San Diego, California. The team could not get a local field and played a regular season home game against the New York Jets at Legion Field in Birmingham, Alabama on 09-22-68.

The Boston Patriots played 20 regular season games at Boston University Field during the 1960–62 AFL seasons. The Patriots averaged 17,600 fans per game at BU Field. In their only sellout, on 11-3-61, the Boston Patriots defeated the Dallas Texans, 28–21, thanks to Ron Burton, who scored the final touchdown in the Friday game. The Memorable Fan Moment at BU Field happened when a fan on the field interfered with a potential game-tying touchdown pass on the same game's last play.

Boston University Field was built in 1915. It was the home of the National League Boston Braves before the team relocated to Milwaukee after the 1952 baseball season. In September 1963, it was renamed William E. Nickerson Field in honor of a prior member of the BU Board of Trustees who had donated the first field for the school in 1928. (William Nickerson was the principal inventor of the machinery used to manufacture the first Gillette safety razor.) William E. Nickerson Field is located on Harry Agganis Way in Boston, Massachusetts.

Because it was not drawing huge crowds at Boston University Field, the team decided to play elsewhere after the 1962 season. The Patriots became tenants of the Boston Red Sox, and played most of the team's regular season home games during the 1963–68 seasons at Fenway Park in Brookline/Boston, Massachusetts.

There were three times that the Boston Patriots were forced to play regular season games at Boston College Alumni Stadium, which was built in 1957. It is located in Chestnut Hill, Massachusetts.

The Boston Patriots played 10 regular season games there during the 1963–69 seasons. The Boston Patriots played the team's opening home game of the 1963 AFL season at Boston College Alumni Stadium. The Patriots defeated the New York Jets, 38–14, in front of 24,120 fans. It was the first regular season game for the New York Jets as the team changed its name from the New York Titans after the 1962 season. In 1964, the Patriots also opened the regular season at Boston College Alumni Stadium and once again defeated the New York Jets.

Because the Red Sox were in the 1967 World Series, the Patriots had to play another game at Boston College Alumni Stadium. The team continued its home-field dominance crushing the Miami Dolphins, 41–10, on 10-15-67. The Memorable Fan Moment at Boston College Alumni Stadium was a fire in the bleachers that happened just before the Patriots exhibition game against the Washington Redskins on 08-16-70.

The Patriots reached an agreement with Boston College before the 1969 AFL season, and were able to play seven home games at Boston College Alumni Stadium. The Patriots averaged more than 21,300 fans per game during the 1969 season and sold out twice. On 10-05-69, the team lost to the New York Jets, 23–14, and on 11-23-69, the Buffalo Bills were defeated, 35–21, in front of a sold-out capacity crowd of 25,584.

From 1963–68, excluding the three games that were played at Boston College Alumni Stadium, the Boston Patriots played at Fenway Park. Fenway Park opened the day after the Titantic sank on 04-20-1912, and is located at 4 Yawkey Way in Boston, Massachusetts.

In front of its only sellout crowd at Fenway Park (39,350 attended) the team defeated the Buffalo Bills, 14–3 on 12-04-66. The Boston Patriots played 37 regular season games at Fenway Park, and averaged just over 24,200 fans per game. The Memorable Fan Moment at Fenway Park was when the start of a regular season game against the Buffalo Bills on 12-20-64 was delayed for one hour due to a blizzard.

The Boston Patriots played eight regular season games at Harvard Stadium during the 1962 and 1970 AFL seasons. Harvard Stadium, a horseshoe-shaped football stadium built in 1903, is located at 95 North Harvard Street in Allston, Massachusetts. The Boston Patriots defeated the Houston Oilers, 34–21, at Harvard Stadium in front of 32,276 fans on 09-16-62. The Patriots played seven home games at Harvard Stadium during the regular season and averaged just over 35,000 fans per game during the 1970 AFL season. The largest home crowd (39,091) of the season saw the Patriots lose to the New York Giants, 16–0, at Harvard Stadium on 10-18-70. The Memorable Fan Moment at Harvard Stadium was when spectator Bob Galdieux was asked, over the loudspeaker, to report to the Patriots locker room and participate in the game on 09-20-70.

During the spring of 1970, the Patriots received numerous offers to relocate the team. Offers from Tampa and Seattle were discussed, but team owner and Boston native Billy Sullivan wanted to keep the team in the Boston area. The town of Haverhill and the Rockingham Racetrack in New Hampshire were also interested in building a stadium for the team. When local sports reporter Ron Hobson heard about the offer from the Rockingham Racetrack, he suggested that the team move to the vicinity of the Bay State Raceway in Foxboro, Massachusetts.

Elias M. Loew, owner of the Bay State Raceway, offered the land and some money to help build a new stadium in Foxboro. In April 1970, Foxboro,

Luxury Box at Gillette Stadium

Loyal fans

Massachusetts, was selected as the new home of the Patriots. The team changed its name and became the New England Patriots on 03-33-71. F. & M. Schaefer Brewing Company ("The one beer to have when you're having more than one") bought the naming rights for the new stadium. Gino Cappelletti kicked a 36-yard field goal for the first points scored at Schaefer Stadium in an exhibition game in front of 60,423 fans on 08-15-71.

Because of substantial plumbing problems during the first exhibition game, a specialized team was hired to fix the stadium's water control problems. With the local board of health threatening to shut down the stadium before the regular season opening home game, an event known as "The Big Flush" was organized. Various members of the media, stadium workers, and numerous front-office personnel were scattered throughout the restrooms of the stadium. Upon hearing the horn of the public address system, each team flushed the toilets to prove that the updated plumbing system worked properly.

When the original naming rights of the stadium expired, the name was changed to Sullivan Stadium. Victor K. Kiam II ("I liked the [Remington Shaver] product so much I bought the company"), on 10-28-88, agreed to purchase the Patriots from William H. "Billy" Sullivan Jr. Victor K. Kiam II became the majority stockholder, but William H. "Billy" Sullivan Jr. maintained the title of team president. K-Korp, which was co-owned by Robert Kraft, purchased Sullivan Stadium on 11-23-88.

The name of the stadium was changed to Foxboro Stadium on 06-01-90. The Patriots signed a 15-year agreement with the Gillette Company thereby changing the name to Gillette Stadium on 08-05-02. James B. Orthwein bought the controlling interest in the Patriots from Victor Kiam on 05-11-92. Robert Kraft signed an agreement to become the fourth owner of the Patriots on 01-21-94. The sale of the team from James Orthwein to Robert Kraft became official on 02-25-94.

The New England Patriots averaged just over 58,700 fans per game during the 1971 regular season at Schaefer Stadium. The Patriots destroyed the Miami Dolphins, 34–13, in front of the season's largest home crowd (61,457) on 12-05-71. After the 1972 season, the seating capacity of Schaefer Stadium was reduced to 60,999. Although the Patriots went 3–11 in 1972, they sold out every home game. During the offseason, improvements were made to the stadium and the seating capacity increased to 61,279.

The Patriots had two sellout crowds during the 1973 season. They lost to the Miami Dolphins on 10-28-73, but were victorious on Jim Plunkett's birthday (the crowd sang "Happy Birthday" to him) as they defeated

the Green Bay Packers, 33–24. Plunkett was named the NFL Offensive Player of the Week. The Patriots sold out five times in 1974, twice in 1975, three times in 1976, four times in 1977, five times in 1978, and six times in 1979. The team destroyed the Baltimore Colts, 47–21, in front of 60,994 fans on 11-23-80.

The Patriots played in 85 regular season games and averaged more than 57,100 fans per game at Schaefer Stadium. In front of a home capacity crowd of 61,297 fans, the team lost its only home playoff game on 12-13-78.

There were many Memorable Fans Moments at Schaefer Stadium, but two that stand the test of time are the first *Monday Night Football* halftime show and the "Snow Plow" game. "Jumping" Joe Gerlach landed with a cannon-boom thud on an air mattress on the 50-yard line after jumping out of a suspended hot air balloon during the halftime show of the Patriots' 24–17 loss to the Baltimore Colts on 11-06-72. Convict Mark Henderson, who was on work-release parole, drove a snow plow and cleared an area of the field where John Smith was attempting to kick a field goal for the Patriots in the team's 3–0 shutout of the Miami Dolphins on 12-12-82. Dolphins head coach Don Shula is still mad about it, while John Smith remains convinced that the snow plow moved the ice over his plant foot area and made his kick more difficult.

For the 1983–89 seasons, the Patriots' home games were played at Sullivan Stadium. Excluding the two home games in 1987 conducted with replacement players during the NFL players strike, the Patriots averaged more than 52,700 fans per game in 54 regular season games. In front of the largest crowd at Sullivan

Stadium of 60,840 fans, the team defeated the Miami Dolphins, 21–10, on 11-06-88. The Patriots only won twice in front of the four sellout crowds at Sullivan Stadium. The team defeated the Dolphins in 1983, lost to the Dolphins in 1984, lost to the 49ers in 1986, and defeated the Dolphins in 1988.

The Memorable Fan Moment at Sullivan Stadium occurred after the Patriots had defeated the Cincinatti Bengals and were playoff bound. The fans stormed the field, tore down the goal post, and carried it out of the stadium and down Route 1.

From 1990 through the team's first championship season in 2001, the Patriots played at Foxboro Stadium. There, the Patriots played 96 regular season games and four playoff games, averaged more than 52,800 fans per game during 12 regular seasons, and averaged 60,178 fans in the four home playoff game victories. A capacity crowd of 60,292 fans filled Foxboro for every regular season game in the 2000 and 2001 seasons. Every seat was filled for the home playoff game victory over the Oakland Raiders on 01-19-02. The most Memorable Fan Moment of Foxboro Stadium was the overturned fumble call based on the "Tuck Rule" in the overtime AFC Divisional Playoff Game victory over the Oakland Raiders in the last game ever played at Foxboro Stadium.

The current stadium was to be called CMGI Field, but when CMGI ran out of money, Gillette took over the naming rights to the stadium. The initial seating capacity of Gillette Stadium was 68,436, and after the 2003 season it was increased to 68,756. The Patriots have sold out every regular season and playoff game at Gillette Stadium.

Gillette Stadium

Every regular season game played by the Boston Patriots at Boston University (Old Braves) Field

1960 regular season

Lost to the Denver Broncos 13–10 at BU Field on 09-09-60 (Gino Cappelletti scored the first points in the AFL with a 35-yard field goal)

Lost to the Buffalo Bills 13–0 at BU Field on 09-23-60 (Ron Burton was the first Patriots player to run for a first down on a fourth down)

Lost to the Los Angeles Chargers 45–16 at BU Field on 10-28-60 (OL Walt Cudzik ran 11 yards with a deflected pass reception)

Defeated the Oakland Raiders 34–28 at BU Field on 11-04-60 (Dick Christy had 124 yards receiving and one receiving TD, and ran for a TD)

Beat the New York Titans 38–21 at BU Field on 11-11-60 (Former Boston College QB Butch Songin threw three TD passes to former BC receivers)

Destroyed the Dallas Texans 42–14 at BU Field on 11-18-60 (Gino Cappelletti ran for two points and kicked four extra points)

Lost to the Houston Oilers 24–10 at BU Field on 11-25-60 (This is the only sold-out game played in the AFL in 1960)

1961 regular season

Lost to the New York Titans 21–20 at BU Field on 09-09-61 (Gino Cappelletti caught a TD pass, and kicked two field goals and two extra points)

Destroyed the Denver Broncos 45–17 at BU Field on 09-16-61 (World War II veteran Butch Songin tossed four TDs)

Lost to the San Diego Chargers 38–27 at BU Field on 10-07-61 (Tom Stephens returned a fumble 10 yards for a TD)

Tied the Houston Oilers 31–31 at BU Field on 10-13-61 (Larry Garron had the first kickoff return for a TD, 89 yards, by a Patriot)

Destroyed the Buffalo Bills 52–21 at BU Field on 10-22-61 (Larry Garron had the longest run by a Patriots RB of 85 yards for a TD)

Defeated the Dallas Texans 28–21 at BU Field on 11-03-61 (A fan was in the end zone on the last, potentially game-tying pass play)

Beat the Oakland Raiders 20–17 at BU Field on 11-17-61 (LeRoy Moore fell on a punt that hit the crossbar for the last points scored)

1962 regular season
Destroyed the Denver Broncos 41–16 at BU Field on 09-21-62 (Gino Cappelletti caught a TD pass, and kicked two field goals and five PATs)

Lost to the Dallas Texans 27–7 at BU Field on 10-12-62 (Larry Garron caught a pass for a 47-yard TD)

Beat the San Diego Chargers 24–20 at BU Field on 10-19-62 (Jim Crawford caught a two-point pass and ran for the game-winning TD)

Defeated the Oakland Raiders 26–16 at BU Field on 10-26-62 (Gino Cappelletti caught a TD pass, and kicked four field goals and two PATs)

Beat the Buffalo Bills 21–10 at BU Field on 11-23-62 (Punter/QB Tom Yewcic threw three TD passes)

Defeated the New York Titans 24–17 at BU Field on 11-30-62 (Tom Yewcic ran for two TDs and tossed a 78-yard TD pass to win the game)

The Top Five most memorable moments from games played at BU Field
A fan ran onto the field and tried to prevent a last-second, game-tying TD pass in the 28–21 win over Dallas on 11-03-61

Larry Garron dashed 85 yards for a TD for the team's longest run from scrimmage in the 52–21 rout of Buffalo on 10-22-61

Tom Yewcic tossed a 78-yard TD pass to Jim Colclough in the fourth quarter to help defeat the New York Titans 24–17 on 11-30-62

Jim Crawford ran for the game-winning TD in the 24–20 victory over the San Diego Chargers on 10-19-62 LeRoy Moore fell on a punt that deflected off the crossbar for the last points scored in the 20–17 win over Oakland on 11-17-61

The scoring summary of the 52–21 rout of the Buffalo Bills in the game that was rescheduled to October 22, 1961 (The game was to be played on Friday night, but due to a potential hurricane the game was moved to Sunday.)

	Q1	Q2	Q3	Q4	Total
Buffalo	0	0	0	21	21
Boston	17	21	7	7	52

Billy Lott caught a 14-yard TD pass from Babe Parilli. Gino Cappelletti kicked the extra point.

Gino Cappelletti kicked a 12-yard field goal.

Jim Colclough hauled in a 58-yard TD pass from Babe Parilli. Gino Cappelletti kicked the extra point.

Billy Lott scored on a 43-yard pass reception from Babe Parilli. Gino Cappelletti kicked the extra point.

Don Webb returned an interception 26 yards for a TD. Gino Cappelletti kicked the extra point.

Gino Cappelletti caught a 5-yard TD pass from Butch Songin. Gino Cappelletti kicked the extra point.

Billy Lott caught a 25-yard TD pass from Babe Parilli. Gino Cappelletti kicked the extra point.

Perry Richards caught a 4-yard TD pass from Warren Rabb. Billy Atkins kicked the extra point.

Tom Rychlec caught a 9-yard TD pass from Warren Rabb. Billy Atkins kicked the extra point.

Larry Garron sprinted 85 yards for a TD. Gino Cappelletti kicked the extra point.

Tom Rychlec hauled in a 21-yard TD pass from Warren Rabb. Billy Atkins kicked the extra point.

The total points scored by Boston Patriots players in games played at Boston University Field from 1960–62
125 points were scored by kicker Gino Cappelletti

84 points were scored by wide receiver Jim Colclough

48 points were scored by wide receiver Gino Cappelletti

30 points were scored by tight end Tom Stephens and by running back Billy Lott

24 points were scored by running backs Ron Burton, Dick Christy, and Larry Garron

20 points were scored by running back Jim Crawford

18 points were scored by tight end Joe Johnson and by quarterbacks Babe Parilli and Tom Yewcic

6 points by: tight end Oscar Lofton; running backs Walter Beach, Claude King, and Alan Miller; and by defensive backs Fred Bruney, Ron Hall, and Don Webb

6 points were scored by defensive end LeRoy Moore, and two points were scored by the Boston Patriots defensive team

Every regular season game played by the Boston Patriots at Boston College Alumni Stadium

1963 regular season
Defeated the New York Jets 38–14 on 09-08-63 (Babe Parilli ran for a TD and tossed a TD pass)

1964 regular season
Defeated the New York Jets 26–10 on 09-27-64 (Houston Antwine was awarded the game ball)

1967 regular season
Destroyed Miami 41–10 at BC on 10-15-67 (Babe Parilli was the AFL Offensive Player of the Week) (The Game of the Year)

1969 regular season
Lost to the Kansas City Chiefs 31–0 on 09-21-69 (Tom Richardson played against his brother Gloster)

Lost to the Oakland Raiders 38–23 on 09-28-69 (Mike Taliaferro tossed three TDs)

Lost to the New York Jets 23–14 on 10-05-69 (LB Marty Schottenheimer had 20 tackles)

Lost to the San Diego Chargers 13–10 on 10-19-69 (MLB Jim Cheyunski had 20 tackles)

Left to right: Houston Antwine and Jim Lee Hunt

Shutout the Houston Oilers 24–0 on 11-02-69 (Ron Sellers was the AFL Offensive Player of the Week)

Lost to the Miami Dolphins 17–16 on 11-09-69 (Carl Garrett ran for an 80-yard TD)

Defeated Buffalo 35–21 on 11-23-69 (Charley Frazier caught a 34-yard TD pass on the very first play) (The Game of the Year)

The Top Five most memorable moments from games played at Boston College Alumni Stadium

Babe Parilli completed 10 consecutive passes and threw five TD passes in the 41–10 rout of Miami on 10-15-67

Daryl Johnson returned a fumble by Hoyle Granger 32 yards for a TD in the 24–0 shutout of Houston on 11-02-69

Dick Felt intercepted Dick Wood twice in the 38–14 victory over the New York Jets on 09-08-63

Ron Hall intercepted Dick Wood twice in the 26–10 victory over the New York Jets on 09-27-64

A fire broke out in the stands before an exhibition game with the Washington Redskins on 08-16-70

The scoring summary of every regular season game victory by the Patriots at Boston College Alumni Stadium

The Boston Patriots defeated the New York Jets at Boston College Alumni Stadium on 09-08-63

	Q1	Q2	Q3	Q4	Total
NY Jets	7	7	0	0	14
Patriots	7	7	3	21	38

Larry Grantham returned a blocked punt 20 yards for a TD. Dick Guesman kicked the extra point.

Jim Crawford scored on a four-yard TD run. Gino Cappelletti kicked the extra point.

Billy Lott scored on a four-yard TD run. Gino Cappelletti kicked the extra point.

Bake Turner caught a four-yard TD pass from Dick Wood. Dick Guesman kicked the extra point.

Gino Cappelletti kicked a 31-yard field goal.

Babe Parilli ran for a 10-yard TD. Gino Cappelletti kicked the extra point.

Art Graham caught a 33-yard TD pass from Babe Parilli. Gino Cappelletti kicked the extra point.

Billy Lott ran for another four-yard TD. Gino Cappelletti kicked the extra point.

———

The Boston Patriots defeated the New York Jets 26–10 at Boston College Alumni Stadium on 09-27-64

	Q1	Q2	Q3	Q4	Total
NY Jets	3	7	0	0	10
Patriots	0	13	10	3	26

Jim Turner kicked a 40-yard field goal.

Ron Burton caught a 59-yard TD pass from Babe Parilli. Gino Cappelletti kicked the extra point.

Gino Cappelletti kicked a 47-yard field goal.

Bill Mathis ran for a one-yard TD. Jim Turner kicked the extra point.

Gino Cappelletti kicked a 26-yard field goal.

Gino Cappelletti kicked a 41-yard field goal.

Jim Colclough hauled in a 59-yard TD pass from Babe Parilli. Gino Cappelletti kicked the extra point.

———

The Boston Patriots defeated the Miami Dolphins 41–10 at Boston College Alumni Stadium on 10-15-67

	Q1	Q2	Q3	Q4	Total
Dolphins	3	0	7	0	10
Patriots	7	20	7	7	41

Gene Mingo kicked a 34-yard field goal.

Larry Garron caught a 17-yard TD pass from Babe Parilli. Gino Cappelletti kicked the extra point.

Larry Garron hauled in a 41-yard TD pass from Babe Parilli. The extra-point attempt was no good.

Jim Whalen caught a nine-yard TD pass from Babe Parilli. Gino Cappelletti kicked the extra point.

Jim Whalen caught another nine-yard TD pass from Babe Parilli. Gino Cappelletti kicked the extra point.

Jim Whalen hauled in a 41-yard TD pass from Babe Parilli. Gino Cappelletti kicked the extra point.

Joe Auer caught a 29-yard TD pass from Rick Norton. Gene Mingo kicked the extra point.

Jay Cunningham returned an interception 52 yards for a TD. Gino Cappelletti kicked the extra point.

———

The Boston Patriots defeated the Houston Oilers 24–0 at Boston College Alumni Stadium on 11-02-69

	Q1	Q2	Q3	Q4	Total
Houston	0	0	0	0	0
Boston	0	17	7	0	24

Gino Cappelletti kicked a 30-yard field goal.

Ron Sellers caught a 25-yard TD pass from Mike Taliaferro. Gino Cappelletti kicked the extra point.

Daryl Johnson returned a fumble by Hoyle Grainger 32 yards for a TD. Gino Cappelletti kicked the extra point.

Ron Sellers caught a 43-yard TD pass from Mike Taliaferro. Gino Cappelletti kicked the extra point.

———

The Boston Patriots defeated the Buffalo Bills 35–21 at Boston College Alumni Stadium on 11-23-69

	Q1	Q2	Q3	Q4	Total
Buffalo	7	7	7	0	21
Boston	14	7	0	14	35

Charley Frazier caught a 34-yard TD pass from Mike Taliaferro. Gino Cappelletti kicked the extra point.

Wayne Patrick ran for a one-yard TD. Bruce Alford kicked the extra point.

Charley Frazier caught a 24-yard TD pass from Mike Taliaferro. Gino Cappelletti kicked the extra point.

Ron Sellers caught a 35-yard TD pass from Mike Taliaferro. Gino Cappelletti kicked the extra point.

Haven Moses hauled in a 48-yard TD pass from Jack Kemp. Bruce Alford kicked the extra point.

Haven Moses grabbed a two-yard TD pass from Jack Kemp. Bruce Alford kicked the extra point.

Jim Nance scored on a two-yard run. Gino Cappelletti kicked the extra point.

Carl Garrett dashed 44 yards for a TD. Gino Cappelletti kicked the extra point.

The total points scored by Boston Patriots players in regular season games played at Boston College Alumni Stadium

53 points were scored by kicker Gino Cappelletti

24 points were scored by running back Carl Garrett

24 points were scored by wide receiver Ron Sellers

24 points were scored by tight end Jim Whalen

18 points were scored by wide receiver Charley Frazier

12 points were scored by running backs Larry Garron, Billy Lott, and Jim Nance

6 points were scored by running backs Ron Burton and Jim Crawford

6 points were scored by wide receivers Jim Colclough, Art Graham, and Bill Rademacher

6 points were scored by defensive backs Jay Cunningham and Daryl Johnson

6 points were scored by quarterback Babe Parilli

Every regular season game played by the Boston Patriots at Fenway Park

1963 regular season

Beat the Oakland Raiders 20–14 at Fenway Park on 10-11-63 (Tom Neumann caught a 15-yard TD for the last points scored)

Defeated the Broncos 40–21 at Fenway Park on 10-18-63 (Gino Cappelletti caught a TD pass, and kicked four field goals and four PATs)

Destroyed the Houston Oilers 45–3 at Fenway Park on 11-01-63 (DT Jim Lee Hunt returned a pass 78 yards for a TD)

Lost to the San Diego Chargers 7–6 at Fenway Park on 11-10-63 (Gino Cappelletti became the first Patriots player to score every point)

Tied the Kansas City Chiefs 24–24 at Fenway Park on 11-17-63 (The Patriots defense tackled Eddie Wilson for a safety)

Beat the Buffalo Bills 17–7 at Fenway Park on 12-01-63 (Larry Eisenhauer recorded his only interception against Jack Kemp)

1964 regular season

Lost to the San Diego Chargers 26–17 at Fenway Park on 10-09-64 (Larry Garron ran for a TD and caught a TD pass)

Tied the Oakland Raiders 43–43 at Fenway Park on 10-16-64 (Babe Parilli threw for 400 yards, four TDs, and tossed a two-point pass)

Beat the Kansas City Chiefs 24–7 at Fenway Park on 10-23-64 (Jim Colclough caught two TD passes and won the game ball)

Defeated the Houston Oilers 25–24 at Fenway Park on 11-06-64 (Gino kicked a 41-yard field goal on the last play) (The Game of the Year)

Beat the Denver Broncos 12–7 at Fenway Park on 11-20-64 (Gino Cappelletti caught a TD pass and kicked a 52-yard field goal)

Lost to the Buffalo Bills 24–14 at Fenway Park on 12-20-64 (The game was delayed due to a blizzard)

1965 regular season

Lost to the Denver Broncos 27–10 at Fenway Park on 09-24-65 (Joe Bellino led the team in yards rushing)

Lost to the Oakland Raiders 24–10 at Fenway Park on 10-08-65 (Mike Dukes had seven tackles and a 16-yard kickoff return)

Tied the San Diego Chargers 13–13 at Fenway Park on 10-17-65 (Gino Cappelletti kicked a field goal to tie the game)

Lost to the Buffalo Bills 23–7 at Fenway Park on 11-07-65 (Jim Colclough had 114 yards receiving)

Lost to the New York Jets 30–20 at Fenway Park on 11-14-65 (Babe Parilli recovered a fumble by Dainard Paulson on his interception return)

Tied the Kansas City Chiefs 10–10 at Fenway Park on 11-21-65 (Ron Hall blocked a 28-yard field-goal attempt with 26 seconds left)

Destroyed the Houston Oilers 42–14 at Fenway Park on 12-18-65 (Gino Cappelletti set the AFL record by scoring 28 points)

1966 regular season

Lost to the Kansas City Chiefs 43–24 at Fenway Park on 09-25-66 (in overtime Karl Singer returned a kickoff 27 yards)

Tied the New York Jets 24–24 at Fenway Park on 10-02-66 (Tom Hennessey intercepted Joe Namath twice)

Defeated the San Diego Chargers 35–17 at Fenway Park on 10-23-66 (Babe Parilli was the AFL Offensive Player of the Week)

Beat the Oakland Raiders 24–21 at Fenway Park on 10-30-66 (MLB Nick Buoniconti had 10 unassisted tackles)

Lost to the Denver Broncos 17–10 at Fenway Park on 11-06-66 (DT Jim Lee Hunt returned a fumble five yards for a TD)

Defeated the Houston Oilers 27–21 at Fenway Park on 11-13-66 (Gino Cappelletti had TD receptions of 63 yards and 31 yards and scored 21 pts)

Beat the Buffalo Bills 14–3 at Fenway Park on 12-04-66 (Jim Nance rumbled 65 yards for a TD) (The Game of the Year)

1967 regular season

Lost to the Oakland Raiders 48–14 at Fenway Park on 10-22-67 (South Boston native Bobby Nichols had his only reception)

Defeated the Houston Oilers 18–7 at Fenway Park on 11-05-67 (Nick Buoniconti was the AFL Defensive Player of the Week)

Lost to the Chiefs 33–10 at Fenway Park on 11-12-67 (Gino Cappelletti kicked a field goal, caught a TD pass, and booted the PAT)

Lost to the New York Jets 29–24 at Fenway Park on 11-19-67 (Don Trull ran for two TDs and threw a TD pass to Jim Whalen)

Lost to the Buffalo Bills at Fenway Park on 12-09-67 (Bobby Leo had a 44-yard punt return and a 25-yard TD reception)

1968 regular season

Lost to the Houston Oilers 16–0 at Fenway Park on 10-13-68 (The Patriots retired Bob Dee's No. 89 in a pregame ceremony)

Defeated the Buffalo Bills 23–6 at Fenway Park on 10-20-68 (Nick Buoniconti was the AFL Defensive Player of the Week)

Lost to the Denver Broncos 35–14 at Fenway Park on 11-03-68 (Art Graham caught a TD pass and returned two punts)

Lost to the San Diego Chargers 27–17 at Fenway Park on 11-10-68 (Gino Cappelletti was the first AFL player to score 1,000 points)

Lost to the Miami Dolphins 34–10 at Fenway Park on 11-24-68 (Aaron Marsh caught a 60-yard TD pass from Tom Sherman)

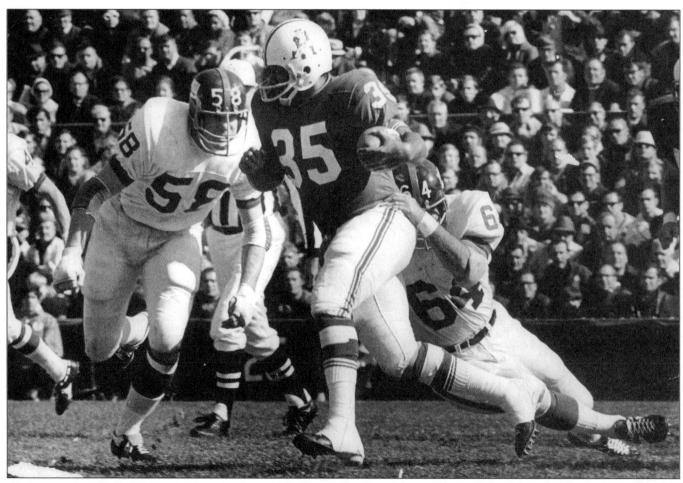

Jim Nance

Defeated the Bengals 33–14 at Fenway Park on 12-01-68 (Tom Sherman threw two TD passes to Jim Whalen and one TD to Gino Cappelletti)

The Top 10 most memorable moments from games played at Fenway Park

Gino Cappelletti set the AFL and team record by scoring 28 points in the 42–14 rout of the Houston Oilers on 12-18-65

Gino Cappelletti kicked a field goal to end the first half and a game-winning 41-yard field goal on the last play in the 25–24 win on 11-06-64

Jim Nance rumbled 65 yards for a TD in the 14–3 victory over the Bills in "The Game" on 12-04-66

Nick Buoniconti intercepted Dan Darragh three times in the 23–6 victory over the Buffalo Bills on 10-20-68

Babe Parilli ran for 10 yards, leaving only one second left, to help set up Gino Cappelletti's 41-yard field goal, in the one-point win on 11-06-64

Jim Lee "Earthquake" Hunt returned a Jacky Lee pass 78 yards for a TD in the 45–3 rout of Houston on 11-01-63

Jim Colclough, Gino Cappelletti, and Ron Burton combined for a 58-yard double-lateral pass completion on 10-16-64

Ron Hall blocked a 28-yard field-goal attempt by Tommy Brooker, with 26 seconds left, to preserve the 10–10 tie on 11-21-65

Joe Bellino caught a deflected pass on his back in the 14–3 win over Buffalo in front of 39,350 fans on 12-04-66

On 12-20-64, the game against the Buffalo Bills was delayed one hour because of blizzard conditions

The scoring summary of every victory by the Boston Patriots in a regular season game played at Fenway Park

The Boston Patriots defeated the Oakland Raiders 20–14 at Fenway Park on 10-11-63

	Q1	Q2	Q3	Q4	Total
Oakland	7	0	7	0	14
Boston	3	0	10	7	20

Gino Cappelletti kicked a 37-yard field goal.

Jim McMillin returned an interception 47 yards for a TD. Mike Mercer kicked the extra point.

Cotton Davidson ran for an 11-yard TD. Mike Mercer kicked the extra point.

Jim Colclough hauled in a 56-yard TD pass from Babe Parilli. Gino Cappelletti kicked the extra point.

Gino Cappelletti kicked a 32-yard field goal.

Tom Neumann caught a 15-yard TD pass from Babe Parilli. Gino Cappelletti kicked the extra point.

———

The Boston Patriots defeated the Denver Broncos 40–21 at Fenway Park on 10-18-63

	Q1	Q2	Q3	Q4	Total
Denver	7	7	7	0	21
Boston	10	13	3	14	40

Gino Cappelletti kicked a 24-yard field goal.

Bob Gaiters hauled in a 74-yard TD pass from Mickey Slaughter. Gene Mingo kicked the extra point.

Gino Cappelletti caught a 24-yard TD pass from Babe Parilli. Gino Cappelletti kicked the extra point.

Billy Joe dashed 68 yards for a TD. Gene Mingo kicked the extra point.

Harry Crump bulled for a one-yard TD. Gino Cappelletti kicked the extra point.

Gino Cappelletti kicked a 34-yard field goal.

Gino Cappelletti kicked a 42-yard field goal.

Gino Cappelletti kicked a 32-yard field goal.

Bob Scarpitto caught a two-yard TD pass from Don Breaux. Gene Mingo kicked the extra point.

Tony Romeo caught a 31-yard TD pass from Babe Parilli. Gino Cappelletti kicked the extra point.

Harry Crump scored on another one-yard run. Gino Cappelletti kicked the extra point.

———

The Boston Patriots destroyed the Houston Oilers 45–3 at Fenway Park on 11-01-63

	Q1	Q2	Q3	Q4	Total
Houston	0	3	0	0	3
Boston	14	14	7	10	45

Larry Garron hauled in a 76-yard TD pass from Babe Parilli. Gino Cappelletti kicked the extra point.

Harry Crump ran for a one-yard TD. Gino Cappelletti kicked the extra point.

Babe Parilli ran for a two-yard TD. Gino Cappelletti kicked the extra point.

George Blanda kicked a 46-yard field goal.

Bob Suci returned an interception 98 yards for a TD. Gino Cappelletti kicked the extra point.

Babe Parilli ran for a one-yard TD. Gino Cappelletti kicked the extra point.

Gino Cappelletti kicked a 37-yard field goal.

Jim Lee Hunt returned an interception 78 yards for a TD. Gino Cappelletti kicked the extra point.

———

The Boston Patriots defeated the Buffalo Bills 17–7 at Fenway Park on 12-01-63

	Q1	Q2	Q3	Q4	Total
Buffalo	0	7	0	0	7
Boston	0	0	14	3	17

Cookie Gilchrist ran for a one-yard TD. Mack Yoho kicked the extra point.

Larry Garron caught a 44-yard TD pass from Babe Parilli. Gino Cappelletti kicked the extra point.

Babe Parilli ran for a two-yard TD. Gino Cappelletti kicked the extra point.

Gino Cappelletti kicked a 43-yard field goal.

———

The Boston Patriots defeated the Kansas City Chiefs 24–7 at Fenway Park on 10-23-64

	Q1	Q2	Q3	Q4	Total
Chiefs	0	0	0	7	7
Patriots	7	0	10	7	24

Jim Colclough caught a 38-yard TD pass from Babe Parilli. Gino Cappelletti kicked the extra point.

Jim Colclough caught an 11-yard TD pass from Babe Parilli. Gino Cappelletti kicked the extra point.

Gino Cappelletti kicked a 26-yard field goal.

Ron Burton ran for a one-yard TD. Gino Cappelletti kicked the extra point.

Mack Lee Hill caught a two-yard TD pass from Eddie Wilson. Marty Brooker kicked the extra point.

———

The Boston Patriots defeated the Houston Oilers 25–24 at Fenway Park on 11-06-64

	Q1	Q2	Q3	Q4	Total
Houston	7	0	7	10	24
Boston	7	6	3	9	25

Charley Tolar ran for a two-yard TD. George Blanda kicked the extra point.

Babe Parilli ran for a one-yard TD. Gino Cappelletti kicked the extra point.

Gino Cappelletti kicked a 25-yard field goal.

Gino Cappelletti kicked a 33-yard field goal on the last play of the first half.

Willie Frazier caught an 80-yard TD pass from George Blanda. George Blanda kicked the extra point.

Gino Cappelletti kicked a 22-yard field goal.

Charley Frazier caught a 37-yard TD pass from George Blanda.

Babe Parilli ran for a five-yard TD. The two-point pass attempt was incomplete.

George Blanda kicked a 10-yard field goal.

Gino Cappelletti kicked a 42-yard field goal on the game's last play.

———

The Boston Patriots defeated the Denver Broncos 12–7 at Fenway Park on 11-20-64

	Q1	Q2	Q3	Q4	Total
Denver	7	0	0	0	7
Boston	2	7	3	0	12

Patriots LB Jack Rudolph sacked Jacky Lee in the end zone for a safety.

Lionel Taylor caught an 11-yard TD pass from Jacky Lee. Dick Guesman kicked the extra point.

Gino Cappelletti caught a 25-yard TD pass from Babe Parilli. Gino Cappelletti kicked the extra point.

Gino Cappelletti kicked a 51-yard field goal.

The Boston Patriots destroyed the Houston Oilers 42–14 at Fenway Park on 12-18-65

	Q1	Q2	Q3	Q4	Total
Houston	0	0	8	6	14
Boston	10	16	3	13	42

Gino Cappelletti kicked a 20-yard field goal.

Jim Nance bulled for a one-yard TD. Gino Cappelletti kicked the extra point.

Jim Colclough caught a 19-yard TD pass from Babe Parilli. Gino Cappelletti kicked the extra point.

The Houston long snapper hiked the ball out of the end zone for a Patriots safety.

Gino Cappelletti caught a 26-yard TD pass from Babe Parilli. Gino Cappelletti kicked the extra point.

Gino Cappelletti kicked a 10-yard field goal.

Charley Hennigan caught a four-yard TD pass from George Blanda. Ode Burrell caught a two-point pass from George Blanda.

Larry Onesti recovered a blocked punt in the end zone for a TD. The two-point rushing attempt failed.

Gino Cappelletti caught a 57-yard TD pass from Babe Parilli. Gino Cappelletti kicked the extra point.

Gino Cappelletti kicked a 24-yard field goal.

Gino Cappelletti kicked a 31-yard field goal.

The Boston Patriots defeated the San Diego Chargers 35–17 at Fenway Park on 10-23-66

	Q1	Q2	Q3	Q4	Total
San Diego	7	3	7	0	17
Boston	0	14	7	14	35

Lance Alworth caught a 42-yard TD pass from John Hadl. Dick Van Raaphorst kicked the extra point.

Larry Garron hauled in a 53-yard TD pass from Babe Parilli. Gino Cappelletti kicked the extra point.

Gino Cappelletti caught a 14-yard TD pass from Babe Parilli. Gino Cappelletti kicked the extra point.

Dick Van Raaphorst kicked a 43-yard field goal.

Lance Alworth hauled in a 66-yard TD pass from John Hadl. Dick Van Raaphorst kicked the extra point.

Larry Garron ran for a two-yard TD. Gino Cappelletti kicked the extra point.

Larry Garron hauled in another 53-yard TD pass from Babe Parilli. Gino Cappelletti kicked the extra point.

Jim Nance ran for a two-yard TD. Gino Cappelletti kicked the extra point.

The Boston Patriots defeated the Oakland Raiders 24–21 at Fenway Park on 10-30-66

	Q1	Q2	Q3	Q4	Total
Oakland	0	7	0	14	21
Boston	14	3	7	0	24

Jim Nance ran for a two-yard TD. Gino Cappelletti kicked the extra point.

Gino Cappelletti caught a 24-yard from Babe Parilli. Gino Cappelletti kicked the extra point.

Clem Daniels hauled in a 51-yard TD pass from Cotton Davidson. Mike Eischeid kicked the extra point.

Gino Cappelletti kicked a 14-yard field goal.

Jim Nance bulled for a one-yard TD. Gino Cappelletti kicked the extra point.

Clem Daniels ran for a 22-yard TD. Mike Eischeid kicked the extra point.

Clem Daniels ran for a one-yard TD. Mike Eischeid kicked the extra point.

The Boston Patriots defeated the Houston Oilers 27–21 at Fenway Park on 11-13-66

	Q1	Q2	Q3	Q4	Total
Houston	7	7	0	7	21
Boston	7	13	7	0	27

Jim Whalen caught a 42-yard TD pass from Babe Parilli. Gino Cappelletti kicked the extra point.

Larry Elkins caught a nine-yard TD pass from Don Trull. George Blanda kicked the extra point.

Gino Cappelletti kicked a 28-yard field goal.

Charley Frazier caught a 42-yard TD pass from Don Trull. George Blanda kicked the extra point.

Gino Cappelletti hauled in a 63-yard TD pass from Babe Parilli. Gino Cappelletti kicked the extra point.

Gino Cappelletti kicked a 44-yard field goal.

Gino Cappelletti caught a 31-yard TD pass from Babe Parilli. Gino Cappelletti kicked the extra point.

Charley Frazier hauled in a 53-yard TD pass from Don Trull. Gino Cappelletti kicked the extra point.

_____

The Boston Patriots defeated the Buffalo Bills 14–3 in "The Game" at Fenway Park on 12-04-66

	Q1	Q2	Q3	Q4	Total
Buffalo	3	0	0	0	3
Boston	7	0	7	0	14

Booth Lusteg kicked an 11-yard field goal.

Jim Nance dashed 65 yards for a TD. Gino Cappelletti kicked the extra point.

Babe Parilli ran for a three-yard TD. Gino Cappelletti kicked the extra point.

_____

The Boston Patriots defeated the Houston Oilers 18–7 at Fenway Park on 11-05-67

	Q1	Q2	Q3	Q4	Total
Houston	0	0	0	7	7
Boston	3	3	5	7	18

Gino Cappelletti kicked a 40-yard field goal.

Gino Cappelletti kicked a 12-yard field goal.

Gino Cappelletti kicked an 18-yard field goal.

Nick Buoniconti tackled Roy Hopkins in the end zone for a safety.

Woody Campbell caught a nine-yard TD pass from Pete Beathard. John Wittenborn kicked the extra point.

Jim Nance ran for a five-yard TD. Justin Canale kicked the extra point.

_____

The Boston Patriots defeated the Buffalo Bills 23–6 at Fenway Park on 10-20-68

	Q1	Q2	Q3	Q4	Total
Buffalo	3	3	0	0	6
Boston	3	3	17	0	23

Gino Cappelletti kicked a 39-yard field goal.

Bruce Alford kicked a 16-yard field goal.

Gino Cappelletti kicked a 20-yard field goal.

Bruce Alford kicked an 11-yard field goal.

Jim Whalen hauled in a 40-yard TD pass from Mike Taliaferro. Gino Cappelletti kicked the extra point.

Gino Cappelletti kicked a 16-yard field goal.

Jim Whalen caught an 18-yard TD pass from Mike Taliaferro. Gino Cappelletti kicked the extra point.

_____

The Boston Patriots defeated the Cincinnati Bengals 33–14 at Fenway Park on 12-01-68

	Q1	Q2	Q3	Q4	Total
Cincinnati	0	0	7	7	14
Boston	2	24	0	7	33

Patriots linebacker Doug Satcher tackled Bengals running back Paul Robinson in the end zone for a safety.

Gino Cappelletti kicked a 27-yard field goal.

Jim Whalen caught an 11-yard TD pass from Tom Sherman. Gino Cappelletti kicked the extra point.

Gino Cappelletti caught an 18-yard TD pass from Tom Sherman. Gino Cappelletti kicked the extra point.

Jim Nance ran for a five-yard TD. Gino Cappelletti kicked the extra point.

Estes Banks caught a five-yard TD pass from John Stofa. Rod Sherman kicked the extra point.

Jim Whalen caught a 21-yard TD pass from Tom Sherman. Gino Cappelletti kicked the extra point.

Rod Sherman caught a 27-yard TD pass from John Stofa. Rod Sherman kicked the extra point.

The total points scored by Boston Patriots players in regular season games played at Fenway Park

215 points were scored by kicker Gino Cappelletti

90 points were scored by running back Larry Garron

84 points were scored by wide receiver Gino Cappelletti

72 points were scored by running back Jim Nance

44 points were scored by wide receiver Jim Colclough

42 points were scored by quarterback Babe Parilli

36 points were scored by tight end Jim Whalen

30 points were scored by tight end Tony Romeo

18 points were scored by running backs Ron Burton, Harry Crump, and J.D. Garrett

18 points were scored by quarterback Don Trull

14 points were scored by defensive tackle Jim Lee Hunt

12 points were scored by wide receiver Art Graham

6 points were scored by offensive guard Charlie Leo

6 points were scored by wide receiver Aaron Marsh

6 points were scored by running back Tom Neumann

6 points were scored by defensive back Bob Suci

4 points were scored by the Boston Patriots defensive team

2 points were scored by linebackers Nick Buoniconti, Jack Rudolph, and Doug Satcher

1 point was scored by kicker Justin Canale

On 10-08-67, the Boston Patriots played a home game at Jack Murphy Stadium in San Diego, California

The Patriots home game against the Chargers was moved to San Diego because Fenway Park was not available as the tenants of the park, the Boston Red Sox, were playing in the 1967 World Series against the St. Louis Cardinals. The Boston Patriots tied the San Diego Chargers 31–31.

———

The Boston Patriots lost to the New York Jets 47–31 in a home game played at Legion Field in Birmingham, Alabama, on 09-22-68

The Patriots could not get a field in the Boston area, so team owner Billy Sullivan moved the game to Alabama.

Gino Cappelletti kicked a 31-yard field goal.

Aaron Marsh caught a 70-yard TD pass from Mike Taliaferro.

Mel Witt returned an interception of Joe Namath four yards for a TD.

Ed Philpott returned a backward lateral/fumble by New York Jets QB Babe Parilli 10 yards for a TD.

Gene Thomas scored on a one-yard TD run.

Gino Cappelletti kicked four extra points as well.

Every regular season game played by the Boston Patriots at Harvard Stadium

1962 regular season

Beat the Houston Oilers 34–21 at Harvard Stadium on 09-16-62 (Gino Cappelletti kicked a 46-yard field goal to end the first half)

1970 regular season

Beat Miami 27–14 at Harvard Stadium on 09-20-70 (Ron Berger was the AFL Defensive Player of the Week) (The Game of the Year)

Lost to the New York Jets 31–21 at Harvard Stadium on 09-27-70 (DT Houston Antwine had 15 tackles)

Lost to the Baltimore Colts 14–6 at Harvard Stadium on 10-04-70 (Ron Sellers had 108 yards receiving)

Lost to the New York Giants 16–0 at Harvard Stadium on 10-18-70 (Houston Antwine partially deflected a successful field goal by Pete Gogolak)

Lost to the Buffalo Bills 45–10 at Harvard Stadium on 11-01-70 (Charlie Gogolak kicked a field goal and an extra point)

Lost to the San Diego Chargers 16–14 at Harvard Stadium on 11-15-70 (Bake Turner caught a TD pass from Joe Kapp)

Lost to the Vikings 35–14 at Harvard Stadium on 12-13-70 (Patriots QB Joe Kapp ran four yards, on fourth and 1, to keep a TD drive alive)

The Top 5 most memorable moments in games played at Harvard Stadium

Bob Gladieux came out of the stands, put on a uniform, and tackled Jake Scott on the opening kickoff in the win on 09-20-70

Ron "The Whopper" Berger sacked Bob Griese three times in the 27–14 victory over the Miami Dolphins on 09-20-70

QB Babe Parilli ran 32 yards for a TD in the 34–21 victory over the Houston Oilers on 09-16-62

Tom Beer lateraled two kickoff returns to Carl Garrett in the 45–10 loss to the Buffalo Bills on 11-01-70

The Patriots lost to the Dallas Texans 24–10 in the first professional sporting charity event at Harvard Stadium on 08-14-60

Joe Kapp

The scoring summary of every regular season victory by the Boston Patriots in a game played at Harvard Stadium

The Boston Patriots defeated the Houston Oilers 34–21 at Harvard Stadium on 09-16-62

	Q1	Q2	Q3	Q4	Total
Houston	7	14	0	0	21
Boston	7	17	0	10	34

Charley Hennigan hauled in a 78-yard TD pass from George Blanda. George Blanda kicked the extra point.

Larry Garron hauled in a 63-yard TD pass from Babe Parilli. Gino Cappelletti kicked the extra point.

Charley Hennigan caught a 49-yard TD pass from George Blanda. George Blanda kicked the extra point.

Ron Burton dashed 59 yards for a TD. Gino Cappelletti kicked the extra point.

Jim Colclough caught a five-yard TD pass from Babe Parilli. Gino Cappelletti kicked the extra point.

Bob MacLeod caught a 40-yard TD pass from George Blanda. George Blanda kicked the extra point.

Gino Cappelletti kicked a 46-yard field goal and a 20-yard field goal.

Babe Parilli scampered 32 yards for a TD. Gino Cappelletti kicked the extra point.

———

The Boston Patriots defeated the Miami Dolphins 27–14 at Harvard Stadium on 09-20-70

	Q1	Q2	Q3	Q4	Total
Miami	7	7	0	0	14
Boston	3	17	0	7	27

Bob Griese ran for a five-yard TD. Karl Kremser kicked the extra point.

Gino Cappelletti kicked a 41-yard field goal.

Jim Kiick ran for a five-yard TD. Karl Kremser kicked the extra point.

Carl Garrett dashed 10 yards for a TD. Gino Cappelletti kicked the extra point.

Jim Nance scored on a one-yard run. Gino Cappelletti kicked the extra point.

Gino Cappelletti kicked a 22-yard field goal.

Ron Sellers caught a 24-yard TD pass from Mike Taliaferro. Gino Cappelletti kicked the extra point.

The total points scored by Boston Patriots players in regular season games played at Harvard Stadium

30 points were scored by running back Jim Nance

28 points were scored by kicker Gino Cappelletti

18 points were scored by running back Carl Garrett

12 points were scored by wide receiver Ron Sellers

8 points were scored by kicker Charlie Gogolak

6 points were scored by running backs Larry Garron and Ron Burton

6 points were scored by wide receivers Jim Colclough and Bake Turner

6 points were scored by quarterback Babe Parilli

Larry Carwell

Every regular season game played by the New England Patriots at Schaefer Stadium

1971 regular season

Beat the Oakland Raiders 20–6 at Schaefer Stadium on 09-19-71 (Jim Plunkett threw two TD passes in his first NFL game)

Lost to the Detroit Lions 34–7 at Schaefer Stadium on 09-26-71 (TKE alumni Jim Cheyunski had 20 tackles)

Lost to the Baltimore Colts 23–3 at Schaefer Stadium on 10-03-71 (John Outlaw intercepted Earl Morrall to set up the field goal)

Shut out the New York Jets 20–0 at Schaefer Stadium on 10-10-71 (The New England Patriots are the first team to shut out the New York Jets)

Defeated the Houston Oilers 28–20 at Schaefer Stadium on 11-07-71 (Steve Kiner was the NFL Defensive Player of the Week)

Defeated the Bills 38–33 at Schaefer Stadium on 11-14-71 (Even though Jim Plunkett only completed nine passes, four went for TDs)

Defeated Miami 34–13 at Schaefer Stadium on 12-05-71 Julius Adams was AFC Defensive Player of the Week (The Game of the Year)

1972 regular season

Lost to the Bengals 31–7 at Schaefer Stadium on 09-17-72 (Larry Carwell blocked a field-goal attempt and returned in 45 yards for a TD)

Beat Atlanta 21–20 at Schaefer Stadium on 09-24-72 (Jim Cheyunski was AFC Defensive Player of the Week) (The Game of the Year)

Defeated the Washington Redskins 24–23 at Schaefer Stadium on 10-01-72 (RB Josh Ashton had 108 yards rushing and scored two TDs)

Lost to the New York Jets 41–13 at at Schaefer Stadium on 10-15-72 (DE Julius Adams was used as LB in a roving defensive scheme)

Lost to the Baltimore Colts 24–17 at Schaefer Stadium on 11-06-72 ("Jumpin Joe Gerlach" lept from a hot air balloon at halftime)

Lost to the Buffalo Bills 27–24 at Schaefer Stadium on 11-19-72 (Mike "Superfoot" Walker kicked a 36-yard field goal and three extra points)

Lost to the Miami Dolphins 37–21 at Schaefer Stadium on 12-03-72 (MLB Ralph Cindrich had 16 unassisted tackles)

1973 regular season

Lost to the Buffalo Bills 31–13 at Schaefer Stadium on 09-16-73 (Sam "Bam" Cunningham ran for his first NFL TD)

Lost to the Kansas City Chiefs 10–7 at Schaefer Stadium on 09-23-73 (Steve Kiner blocked a 34-yard field-goal attempt by Jan Stenerud)

Beat the Baltimore Colts 24–16 at Schaefer Stadium on 10-07-73 (Randy Vataha advanced a fumble by Mack Herron 46 yards for a TD)

Lost to the New York Jets 9–7 at Schaefer Stadium on 10-14-73 (Will Foster recovered a blocked punt by Willie Banks for a TD)

Lost to the Dolphins 30–14 at Schaefer Stadium on 10-28-73 (Sam Cunningham caught a 34-yard TD pass on the Patriots' first play)

Beat Green Bay 33–24 at Schaefer Stadium on 11-18-73 (Jim Plunkett was NFL Offensive Player of the Week) (The Game of the Year)

Defeated the San Diego Chargers 30–14 at Schaefer Stadium on 12-02-73 ("Mini" Mack Herron returned a kickoff 92 yards for a TD)

1974 regular season

Defeated the Miami Dolphins 34–24 at Schaefer Stadium on 09-15-74 (Jim Plunkett ran five yards on a fake option play for a TD)

Defeated the LA Rams 20–14 at Schaefer Stadium on 09-29-74 (Randy Vataha and Darryl Stingley caught TD passes from Jim Plunkett)

Destroyed the Baltimore Colts 42–3 at Schaefer Stadium on 10-06-74 (Three Patriots QBs completed a pass—Shiner, Graff, and Plunkett)

Lost to the Buffalo Bills 29–28 at Schaefer Stadium on 11-03-74 (Mini Mack Herron had two TD receptions and ran for another)

Lost to Cleveland 21–14 at Schaefer Stadium on 11-10-74 (Mack Herron had 18 carries, four receptions, six punt returns, and three kickoff returns)

Lost to the New York Jets 21–16 at Schaefer Stadium on 11-17-74 (Former college QB Jack Mildren had 13 tackles and an interception)

Lost to the Steelers 21–17 at Schaefer Stadium on 12-08-74 ("Sugarbear" Hamilton had 16 tackles and shared in a sack of Terry Bradshaw)

Randy Vataha

1975 regular season

Lost to the Houston Oilers 7–0 at Schaefer Stadium on 09-21-75 (Sam "Bam" Cunningham led the team in yards rushing and receiving)

Lost to the Dolphins 22–14 at Schaefer Stadium on 09-28-75 (Patriots LB George Webster had his only interception against Bob Griese)

Defeated the Baltimore Colts 21–10 at Schaefer Stadium on 10-19-75 (Andy Johnson had the longest run of his career, charging 66 yards for a TD)

Beat the 49ers 24–16 at Schaefer Stadium on 10-26-75 (Kicker John Smith tried to run after his field goal was blocked) (The Game of the Year)

Lost to the Dallas Cowboys 34–31 at Schaefer Stadium on 11-16-75 (Jim Plunkett ran for a TD and tossed two TD passes)

Lost to the New York Jets 30-28 at Schaefer Stadium on 12-07-75 (Randy Vataha caught two TD passes and had career-best 149-yards receiving)

Lost to the Bills 34–14 at Schaefer Stadium on 12-14-75 (Kevin Reilly, in his only NFL start, returned a Joe Ferguson pass 54 yards)

1976 regular season

Lost to the Baltimore Colts 27–13 at Schaefer Stadium on 09-12-76 (OL Bob McKay returned a squibbed kickoff 23 yards)

Beat the Miami Dolphins 30–14 at Schaefer Stadium on 09-19-76 (Steve Grogan ran for a TD and tossed three TD passes)

Destroyed Oakland 48–17 at Schaefer Stadium on 10-03-76 (Darryl Stingley had two TDs and 48 yards rushing) (The Game of the Year)

Destroyed the New York Jets 41–7 at Schaefer Stadium on 10-18-76 (Steve Grogan is the only Patriots QB to rush for more than 100 yards)

Beat the Bills 20–10 at Schaefer Stadium on 11-07-76 (Mike Haynes is the first Patriots player to return a punt 89 yards for a TD)

Crushed the Denver Broncos 38–14 at Schaefer Stadium on 11-28-76 (Mike Haynes returned another punt 62 yards for a TD)

Beat the Saints 27–6 at Schaefer Stadium on 12-05-76 (Patriots qualified for playoffs as Steve Grogan tossed two TDs and ran for two TDs)

Mike Haynes

1977 regular season

Beat the Chiefs 21–17 at Schaefer Stadium on 09-18-77 (Darryl Stingley scored two TDs on his 26th birthday) (The Game of the Year)

Shut out the Seattle Seahawks 31–0 at Schaefer Stadium on 10-09-77 (Steve Grogan had a 41-yard run and threw three TD passes)

Beat the Baltimore Colts 17–3 at Schaefer Stadium on 10-23-77 (Darryl Stingley had 116 of the team's 214 total yards receiving)

Defeated the New York Jets 24–13 at Schaefer Stadium on 10-30-77 (Darryl Stingley had a career-high eight receptions)

Lost to Buffalo 24–14 at Schaefer Stadium on 11-06-77 (Raymond Clayborn returned a kickoff 93 yards for a TD to end first quarter)

Defeated the Eagles 14–6 at Schaefer Stadium on 11-27-77 (Steve Grogan tossed TD passes to Stanley Morgan and Darryl Stingley)

Defeated the Dolphins 14–10 at Schaefer Stadium on 12-11-77 (In 14-degree weather and 17-mph winds, Sam "Bam" Cunningham dove for a TD)

1978 regular season

Lost to the Redskins 16–14 at Schaefer Stadium on 09-03-78 (Mike Haynes played against his brother Reggie for the first time)

Lost to the Baltimore Colts 34–27 in heavy rain on Monday Night at Schaefer Stadium on 09-18-78

Defeated San Diego 28–23 at Schaefer Stadium on 10-01-78 (Fans voted to keep Pat Patriot and Steve Grogan ran for the game-winning TD)

Defeated the Eagles 24–14 at Schaefer Stadium on 10-08-78 (Steve Nelson set the team record with three defensive fumble recoveries)

Defeated the Miami Dolphins 33–24 at Schaefer Stadium on 10-22-78 (Horace Ivory ran for 113 yards and two TDs)

Destroyed the New York Jets 55–21 at Schaefer Stadium on 10-29-78 (Steve Grogan threw four TD passes and the Patriots had four rushing TDs)

Lost to Houston 26–23 at Schaefer Stadium on 11-12-78 (Rod Shoate had nine tackles, one sack, one pass defended, and a fumble recovery)

Beat the Buffalo Bills 26–24 at Schaefer Stadium on 12-10-78 (The Patriots won the team's first divisional title) (The Game of the Year)

1979 regular season

Lost to the Steelers 16–13 in overtime at Schaefer Stadium on 09-03-79 (Tony "Mac the Sack" McGee sacked Terry Bradshaw twice)

Destroyed the New York Jets 56–3 at Schaefer Stadium on 09-09-79 (Steve Grogan completed just 13 passes but five went for a TD)

Darryl Stingley

Defeated San Diego 27–21 at Schaefer Stadium on 09-23-79 (Steve Nelson's late interception sealed the win) (The Game of the Year)

Beat Detroit 24–17 at Schaefer Stadium on 10-07-79 (Don Calhoun handed off to Don Westbrook who threw a 28-yard pass to Russ Francis)

Defeated the Miami Dolphins 28–13 at Schaefer Stadium on 10-21-79 (Mike Hawkins returned a Don Stock pass 35 yards for a TD)

Blew out the Baltimore Colts 50–21 at Schaefer Stadium on 11-18-79 (Stanley Morgan caught a TD and took a punt 80 yards for a TD)

Lost to the Buffalo Bills 16–13 in overtime at Schaefer on 11-25-79 (Steve Nelson had 17 tackles)

Beat the Vikings 27–23 at Schaefer Stadium on 12-16-79 (Harold Jackson and Stanley Morgan finished the year with more than 1,000 yards)

Steve Nelson (Chargers quarterback Dan Fouts is on the ground)

1980 regular season

Defeated the Browns 34–17 at Schaefer Stadium on 09-07-80 (Andy Johnson and Carlos Pennywell each recovered an onside kick)

Lost to the Atlanta Falcons 37–21 at Schaefer Stadium on 09-14-80 (Mosi Tatupu forced a fumble on the opening kickoff to set up a TD)

Defeated the Broncos 23–14 at Schaefer Stadium on 09-29-80 (Harold Jackson had the longest run by a Patriots WR on Monday Night)

Shutout the Miami Dolphins 34–0 at Schaefer Stadium on 10-12-80 (The Patriots had five sacks and four interceptions)

Defeated the New York Jets 34–21 at Schaefer Stadium on 11-02-80 (Roland James had the year's longest punt return, a 75-yard TD, in the NFL)

Lost to the Los Angeles Rams 17–14 at Schaefer Stadium on 11-16-80 (Steve Nelson's 33-yard interception return set up the team's second TD)

Beat the Baltimore Colts 47–21 at Schaefer Stadium on 11-23-80 (This was the first time that the Patriots had two RBs with 100 yards rushing)

Destroyed Buffalo 24–2 at Schaefer Stadium on 12-14-80 (Matt Cavanaugh threw two TDs and had a career-long 22-yard run)

1981 regular season

Lost to the Baltimore Colts 29–28 at Schaefer Stadium on 09-06-81 (Mark Buben returned a fumble 31 yards to set up a TD)

Lost to the Dallas Cowboys 35–21 at Schaefer Stadium on 09-21-81 (Mosi Tatupu had his career-longest TD run of 38 yards)

Defeated the Chiefs 33–17 at Schaefer Stadium on 10-04-81 (Andy Johnson, on a fake reverse, threw a 66-yard TD to Stanley Morgan)

Defeated Houston 38–10 at Schaefer Stadium on 10-18-81 (Steve Grogan ran a naked reverse for a 24-yard TD) (The Game of the Year)

Lost to the Miami Dolphins 30–27 in overtime at Schaefer Stadium on 11-08-81 (John Smith kicked a 34-yard field goal to force OT)

Lost to the New York Jets 17–6 at Schaefer Stadium on 11-15-81 (John Smith kicked two field goals in strong winds and a heavy rainstorm)

Sam Cunningham (39)

Lost to the St. Louis Cardinals 27–20 at Shaefer Stadium on 11-29-81 (Sam Cunningham passed Jim Nance for most career yards rushing)

Lost to the Buffalo Bills 19–10 at Schaefer Stadium on 12-13-81 (LB Bob Golic had 18 tackles)

1982 regular season
Lost to the New York Jets 31–7 at Schaefer Stadium on 09-19-82 (LB Steve Nelson had a career-high 22 tackles)

Defeated the Houston Oilers 29–21 at Schaefer Stadium on 11-28-82 (George Crump sacked Archie Manning for a safety)

Beat Miami 3–0 at Schaefer Stadium on 12-12-83 (John Smith kicked a 33-yard field goal in the "Snow Plow Game") (The Game of the Year)

Defeated the Buffalo Bills 30–19 at Schaefer Stadium on 01-02-83 (Allowed the Patriots to qualify for the play-offs)

The Top 10 most memorable moments in games played at Schaefer Stadium
John Smith kicked a 33-yard field goal, after Mark Henderson plowed a path for him in the snow, in the 3–0 win against Miami on 12-12-83

Steve Grogan ran for a four-yard game-winning TD, with 31 seconds left, in the 28–23 win against the Chargers on 10-01-78

Steve Nelson returned a Dan Fouts pass 18 yards, from the 2-yard line, with 1:37 left, in the 27–21 win over San Diego on 09-23-79

Mike Haynes stopped Keith Moody's 30-yard kickoff return on the last play of the 26–24 playoff-clinching win on 12-10-78

Fans sang "Happy Birthday" to Jim Plunkett, on his 24th birthday, after he led them to a 34–13 rout of Miami on 12-05-71

Darryl Stingley ran for a TD and caught a TD pass, on his 26th birthday, in the 21–17 victory over the Chiefs on 09-18-77

Andy Johnson tossed a 66-yard HB option TD pass to Stanley Morgan in the 33–17 victory over the Chiefs on 10-04-81

Randy Vataha advanced a fumble by Mini Mack Herron 46 yards for a TD in the eight-point win over Baltimore on 10-07-73

Don Westbrook caught a TD pass and blocked a punt, in the Patriots' greatest margin of victory of 53 points, on 09-09-79

The fans voted to keep the Pat Patriot logo at halftime of the 28–23 win during the San Diego Chargers on 10-01-78

The only regular season game that the Patriots had two TD receptions, two rushing TDs, three field goals, a blocked punt that was returned for a TD, a punt return for a TD and at least one extra point
Stanley Morgan caught a 25-yard TD pass from Steve Grogan

Don Calhoun scored on a one-yard TD run

Harold Jackson caught a five-yard TD pass from Steve Grogan

Rick Sanford blocked a punt by Bucky Dilt and returned it eight yards for a TD

John Smith kicked a 24-yard field goal and a 29-yard field goal

Stanley Morgan returned a punt by Bucky Dilt 80 yards for a TD

John Smith kicked a 42-yard field goal

Rick Sanford

Allan Clark ran for a 15-yard TD and John Smith kicked five extra points in the 50–21 rout of the Baltimore Colts at Schaefer Stadium on 11-18-79

The total points scored by New England Patriots players in regular season games played at Schaefer Stadium

323 points were scored by kicker John Smith

138 points were scored by running back Sam Cunningham

120 points were scored by wide receiver Stanley Morgan

114 points were scored by quarterback Steve Grogan

96 points were scored by running backs Don Calhoun and Andy Johnson

84 points were scored by wide receiver Randy Vataha

78 points were scored by wide receiver Harold Jackson and tight end Russ Francis

66 points were scored by wide receiver Darryl Stingley

60 points were scored by running back Mack Herron

54 points were scored by kicker Charlie Gogolak and running back Horace Ivory

48 points were scored by tight end Don Hasselbeck

37 points were scored by kicker David Posey

36 points were scored by running back Tony Collins and quarterback Jim Plunkett

30 points were scored by running backs Vagas Ferguson, Carl Garrett, and John Tarver

30 points were scored by wide receiver Reggie Rucker and kicker Jeff White

18 points were scored by running backs Josh Ashton, Allan Clark, Ike Forte, and Jim Nance

13 points were scored by kicker Mike Walker

12 points were scored by defensive backs Larry Carwell, Mike Haynes, and Rick Sanford

12 points were scored by running backs James McAlister, Jess Phillips, and Mosi Tatupu

12 points were scored by tight ends Al Chandler, Roland Moss, and Bob Windsor

12 points were scored by wide receivers Carlos Pennywell and Ron Sellers

9 points were scored by kicker Dan Miller

6 points were scored by defensive backs Raymond Clayborn and Ricky Smith

6 points were scored by linebackers Will Foster, Mike Hawkins, and Rod Shoate

6 points were scored by quarterback Brian Dowling

6 points were scored by running backs Allan Clark, Craig James, and Jack Maitland

6 points were scored by wide receivers Morris Bradshaw, Marlin Briscoe, Hubie Bryant, and Eric Crabtree

6 points were scored by wide receivers Ray Jarvis, Tom Reynolds, Ken Toler, and Don Westbrook

4 points were scored by kicker Nick Lowery

2 points were scored by kicker Bill Bell

2 points were scored by nose tackle Richard Bishop

2 points were scored by defensive end George Crump

2 points were scored by safety Tim Fox

1 point was scored by kicker Rex Robinson

The scoring summary of the Top 10 most exciting regular season victories by the Patriots at Schaefer Stadium

The New England Patriots defeated the Oakland Raiders 20–6 in the first game played at Schaefer Stadium on 09-19-71

	Q1	Q2	Q3	Q4	Total
Oakland	0	6	0	0	6
New England	0	0	14	6	20

Pete Banaszak ran for a four-yard TD. The extra-point attempt was no good.

Ron Sellers caught a 33-yard TD pass from Jim Plunkett. Charlie Gogolak kicked the extra point.

Roland Moss caught a 20-yard TD pass from Jim Plunkett. Charlie Gogolak kicked the extra point.

Charlie Gogolak kicked a 46-yard field goal.

Charlie Gogolak kicked a 22-yard field goal.

This was Jim Plunkett's first regular season NFL game.

Russ Francis

The New England Patriots defeated the Buffalo Bills 38–33 at Schaefer Stadium on 11-14-71

	Q1	Q2	Q3	Q4	Total
Buffalo	7	13	10	3	33
New England	7	21	7	3	38

Ike Hill returned a punt 68 yards for a TD. John Leypoldt kicked the extra point.

Randy Vataha caught a 16-yard TD pass from Jim Plunkett on the last play of the first quarter. Charlie Gogolak kicked the PAT.

Tom Beer caught a 10-yard TD pass from Jim Plunkett. Charlie Gogolak kicked the extra point.

Marlin Briscoe caught a 15-yard TD pass from James Harris. John Leypoldt kicked the extra point.

John Leypoldt kicked a 17-yard field goal.

Carl Garrett caught an 80-yard TD pass from Jim Plunkett. Charlie Gogolak kicked the extra point.

Roland Moss returned a blocked punt 10 yards for a TD. Charlie Gogolak kicked the extra point.

John Leypoldt kicked a 48-yard field goal with five seconds left in the first half.

Eric Crabtree caught a 31-yard TD pass from Jim Plunkett. Charlie Gogolak kicked the extra point.

John Leypoldt kicked another 17-yard field goal.

Robert James returned a fumble by Carl Garrett two yards for a TD. John Leypoldt kicked the extra point.

John Leypoldt kicked a 12-yard field goal.

Charlie Gogolak kicked a 38-yard field goal.

The New England Patriots defeated the Atlanta Falcons 21–20 at Schaefer Stadium on 09-24-72

	Q1	Q2	Q3	Q4	Total
Atlanta	3	3	14	0	20
New England	0	7	0	14	21

Bill Bell kicked a 38-yard field goal.

Bill Bell kicked a 21-yard field goal.

Josh Ashton ran for a four-yard TD. Mike Walker kicked the extra point.

Ron Bolton blocked a 32-yard field-goal attempt by Bill Bell.

Art Malone ran for a one-yard TD. Bill Bell kicked the extra point.

Dave Hampton ran for a one-yard TD. Bill Bell kicked the extra point.

Randy Vataha caught a 37-yard TD pass from Jim Plunkett. Mike Walker kicked the extra point.

Carl Garrett ran for a 12-yard TD. Mike Walker kicked the extra point.

Bill Bell missed on a 10-yard field-goal attempt with 31 seconds left in the game.

———

The New England Patriots defeated the Washington Redskins 24–23 at Schaefer Stadium on 10-01-72

	Q1	Q2	Q3	Q4	Total
Redskins	0	14	0	9	23
Patriots	0	7	10	7	24

Charley Taylor caught a 30-yard TD pass from Billy Kilmer. Curt Knight kicked the extra point.

Charley Taylor caught a four-yard TD pass from Billy Kilmer. Curt Knight kicked the extra point.

Josh Ashton ran for a two-yard TD. Charlie Gogolak kicked the extra point.

Reggie Rucker caught an 11-yard TD pass from Jim Plunkett. Charlie Gogolak kicked the extra point.

Charlie Gogolak kicked a 42-yard field goal.

Jerry Smith caught a nine-yard TD pass from Billy Kilmer. Curt Knight kicked the extra point.

Josh Ashton caught a 24-yard TD pass from Jim Plunkett. Charlie Gogolak kicked the extra point.

Bill Malinchak blocked a punt by Pat Studstill that went out of the end zone for a safety.

Curt Knight missed on a 50-yard field-goal attempt with 12 seconds left in the game.

David Posey kicks the winning field goal

Tim Fox (48) forces Rusty Jackson (4) out of the end zone for a safety

The New England Patriots defeated the Baltimore Colts 24–16 at Schaefer Stadium on 10-07-73

	Q1	Q2	Q3	Q4	Total
Baltimore	3	0	3	10	16
New England	3	7	7	7	24

Jeff White kicked a 40-yard field goal.

George Hunt kicked a 38-yard field goal.

John Tarver ran for a one-yard TD. Jeff White kicked the extra point.

George Hunt kicked a 27-yard field goal.

John Tarver ran for a three-yard TD. Jeff White kicked the extra point.

George Hunt kicked a 38-yard field goal.

Randy Vataha advanced a fumble by Mini Mack Herron 46 yards for a TD. Jeff White kicked the extra point.

Cotton Speyrer caught a 22-yard TD pass from Bert Jones. George Hunt kicked the extra point.

The New England Patriots defeated the Philadelphia Eagles 14–6 at Schaefer Stadium on 11-27-77

	Q1	Q2	Q3	Q4	Total
Eagles	0	0	0	6	6
Patriots	7	7	0	0	14

Stanley Morgan hauled in a 64-yard TD pass from Steve Grogan. John Smith kicked the extra point.

Ray "Sugar Bear" Hamilton blocked a 19-yard field-goal attempt by Ove Johannson.

Darryl Stingley caught a 16-yard TD pass from Steve Grogan. John Smith kicked the extra point.

Charlie Smith caught a 12-yard TD pass from Ron Jaworski. The extra-point attempt was no good.

Tim Fox recovered an onside kick by Ove Johannson with 52 seconds left in the game.

———

The New England Patriots defeated the San Diego Chargers 28–23 at Schaefer Stadium on 10-01-78

	Q1	Q2	Q3	Q4	Total
San Diego	0	13	7	3	23
New England	7	0	7	14	28

Harold Jackson caught a 30-yard TD pass from Steve Grogan. Nick Lowery kicked the extra point.

Pat Curran caught a three-yard TD pass from Dan Fouts. The extra-point attempt was no good.

John Jefferson caught a 21-yard TD pass from Dan Fouts. Rolf Benirschke kicked the extra point.

John Jefferson caught a 40-yard TD pass from Dan Fouts. Rolf Benirschke kicked the extra point.

Harold Jackson caught a 14-yard TD pass from Steve Grogan. Nick Lowery kicked the extra point.

Russ Francis caught a six-yard TD pass from Steve Grogan. Nick Lowery kicked the extra point.

Rolf Benirschke kicked a 41-yard field goal.

Steve Grogan ran for a four-yard TD with 36 seconds left in the game. Nick Lowery kicked the extra point.

———

The New England Patriots defeated the Buffalo Bills 26–24 at Schaefer Stadium on 12-10-78

	Q1	Q2	Q3	Q4	Total
Buffalo	0	10	7	7	24
New England	0	7	7	12	26

Roland Hooks ran for a 28-yard TD. Tom Dempsey kicked the extra point.

Sam Cunningham ran for a four-yard TD. David Posey kicked the extra point.

Tom Dempsey kicked a 26-yard field goal.

Terry Miller ran for a 32-yard TD. Tom Dempsey kicked the extra point.

Steve Grogan ran for a four-yard TD. David Posey kicked the extra point.

Horace Ivory dashed 20 yards for a TD. David Posey kicked the extra point.

Frank Lewis caught a 21-yard TD pass from Joe Ferguson. Tom Dempsey kicked the extra point.

Tim Fox forced Bills punter Rusty Jackson out of the end zone for a safety.

David Posey kicked a 21-yard field goal.

———

The New England Patriots defeated the Baltimore Colts 47–21 at Schaefer Stadium on 11-23-80

	Q1	Q2	Q3	Q4	Total
Baltimore	0	0	7	14	21
New England	7	3	10	27	47

Don Calhoun ran for a one-yard TD. John Smith kicked the extra point.

John Smith kicked a 22-yard field goal.

Rod Shoate returned an interception 42 yards for a TD. John Smith kicked the extra point.

Joe Washington caught a 23-yard TD pass from Greg Landry. Steve Mike-Mayer kicked the extra point.

John Smith kicked a 35-yard field goal.

Rick Sanford returned a fumble 22 yards for a TD. John Smith kicked the extra point.

Curtis Dickey ran for a 28-yard TD. Steve Mike-Mayer kicked the extra point.

Carlos Pennywell caught a nine-yard TD pass from Matt Cavanaugh. The extra-point attempt was no good.

Curtis Dickey ran for a one-yard TD. Steve Mike-Mayer kicked the extra point.

Don Calhoun ran for a three-yard TD. John Smith kicked the extra point.

Allan Clark returned a fumble 15 yards for a TD. John Smith kicked the extra point.

———

The New England Patriots defeated the Buffalo Bills 30–19 in the last game played at Schaefer Stadium on 01-02-83

	Q1	Q2	Q3	Q4	Total
Buffalo	0	13	3	3	19
New England	3	7	6	14	30

John Smith kicked a 42-yard field goal.

Joe Cribbs ran for a 14-yard TD. Effren Herrera kicked the extra point.

Jerry Butler caught a 22-yard TD pass from Joe Ferguson. The extra-point attempt was no good.

Morris Bradshaw caught an 11-yard TD pass from Steve Grogan. John Smith kicked the extra point.

Ken Toler caught a 33-yard TD pass from Steve Grogan. The extra-point attempt was no good.

Effren Herrera kicked a 46-yard field goal.

Tony Collins ran for a one-yard TD. John Smith kicked the extra point.

Effren Herrera kicked a 25-yard field goal.

Don Hasselbeck caught a two-yard TD pass from Steve Grogan. John Smith kicked the extra point.

This win propelled the Patriots and eliminated the Buffalo Bills from the playoffs.

Every regular season game played by the New England Patriots at Sullivan Stadium

1983 regular season
Lost to the Colts 29–23 in overtime at Sullivan Stadium on 09-04-83 (Robert Weathers had 100 yards rushing and Clarence Weathers had 17 yards receiving)

Defeated the New York Jets 23–13 at Sullivan Stadium on 09-18-83 (Andre Tippett stopped Richard Todd three times inside the 10-yard line)

Lost to the San Francisco 49ers 33–13 at Sullivan Stadium on 10-02-83 (Clayton Weishuhn had 20 tackles)

Defeated the San Diego Chargers 37–21 at Sullivan Stadium on 10-16-83 (The Patriots scored 24 points in the fourth quarter)

Defeated the Buffalo Bills 21–7 at Sullivan Stadium on 11-06-83 (Ronnie Lippett deflected five passes and made six tackles)

Defeated Miami 17–6 at Sullivan Stadium on 11-13-83 (Center Pete Brock tears knee up on first play, plays full game and is given game ball)

Lost to the Cleveland Browns 30–0 at Sullivan Stadium on 11-20-83 (DE Julius Adams plays in his 160th game)

Shutout the Saints 7–0 in a rain/snowstorm at Sullivan Stadium on 12-04-83 (Stanley Morgan had the only receptions for the Patriots)

1984 regular season
Defeated Seattle 38–23 at Sullivan Stadium on 09-16-84 (Tony Eason was AFC Offensive Player of the Week) (The Game of the Year)

Lost to the Washington Redskins at Sullivan Stadium on 09-23-84 (Steve Nelson and Rick Sanford each had 11 tackles)

Defeated the Cincinnati Bengals 20–14 at Sullivan Stadium on 10-14-84 (Tony Eason had a 13-yard TD run and a 25-yard TD run)

Lost to the Miami Dolphins 44–24 at Sullivan Stadium on 10-21-84 (Luke Prestridge boomed a career long 89-yard punt)

Defeated the New York Jets 30–20 at Sullivan Stadium on 10-28-84 (The Patriots scored the last 27 points and Luke Prestridge had an 82-yard punt)

Defeated the Buffalo Bills 38–10 at Sullivan Stadium on 11-11-84 (Ronnie Lippett had his first two NFL interceptions)

Lost to the St. Louis Cardinals 33–10 at Sullivan Stadium on 12-02-84 (Steve Nelson blocked a PAT by Neil O'Donoghue)

Defeated the Indianapolis Colts 16–10 at Sullivan Stadium on 12-16-84 (Ronnie Lippett intercepted Art Schlitcher with 38 ticks left)

Steve Nelson

1985 regular season

Defeated the Packers 26–20 at Sullivan Stadium on 09-08-85 (This is the only game that the Patriots blocked a field goal and a PAT)

Lost to the Los Angeles Raiders 35–20 at Sullivan Stadium on 09-29-85 (John Hannah played against his brother Charley for the first time)

Defeated the Bills 14–3 at Sullivan Stadium on 10-13-85 (Raymond Clayborn returned a Vince Ferragamo pass 27 yards for a TD)

Beat the Jets 20–13 at Sullivan Stadium on 10-20-85 (Andre Tippett was AFC Defensive Player of the Week) (The Game of the Year)

Defeated the Miami Dolphins 17–13 at Sullivan Stadium on 11-03-85 (Steve Grogan ran for the game-winning TD)

Defeated the Indianapolis Colts 34–15 at Sullivan Stadium on 11-10-85 (Fred Marion was the AFC Defensive Player of the Week)

Defeated the Lions 23–6 at Sullivan Stadium on 12-08-85 (Toby Williams played against his brother Jimmy for the first time in the NFL)

Defeated the Bengals 34–23 at Sullivan Stadium on 12-22-85 (Robert Weathers ran for a 42-yard TD on fourth down with two minutes left)

1986 regular season

Destroyed the Indianapolis Colts 33–3 at Sullivan Stadium on 09-07-86 (LB Johnny Rembert recovered a fumble for a TD)

Lost to the Seattle Seahawks 38–31 at Sullivan Stadium on 09-21-86 (Stanley Morgan had three TD receptions)

Destroyed the Dolphins 34–7 at Sullivan Stadium on 10-05-86 (Ronnie Lippett was the AFC Defensive Player of the Week)

Lost to the New York Jets 31–24 at Sullivan Stadium on 10-12-86 (Steve Grogan threw for a career high 401 yards)

Defeated the Atlanta Falcons 25–17 at Sullivan Stadium on 11-02-86 (Irving Fryar returned a punt 59 yards for a TD)

Defeated the Bills 22–19 at Sullivan Stadium on 11-23-86 (Tony Franklin set a team record by kicking a field goal in 17 consecutive games)

Lost to the Bengals 31–7 at Sullivan Stadium on 12-07-86 (Irving Fryar is the first Patriots WR to lead the team in yards rushing)

Lost to the 49ers 29–24 at Sullivan Stadium on 12-14-86 (Stanley Morgan caught a 15-yard TD on fourth-and-4 for the team's final TD)

1987 regular season

Defeated the Dolphins 28–21 at Sullivan Stadium on 09-13-87 (Ronnie Lippett took a Marino pass 20 yards for the game-winning TD)

Lost to the Cleveland Browns 20–10 at Sullivan Stadium on 10-04-87 (Bob Bleier tossed a six-yard TD pass to Larry Linne)

Defeated the Buffalo Bills 14–7 at Sullivan Stadium on 10-11-87 (Bob Bleier ran one yard for the game-winning TD)

Defeated the Los Angeles Raiders 26–23 at Sullivan Stadium on 11-01-87 (Tony Franklin kicked a 29-yard field goal with one second left)

Lost to the Cowboys 23–17 in overtime at Sullivan Stadium on 11-15-87 (Stanley Morgan caught a five-yard TD on fourth down to force overtime)

Shutout Indianapolis 24–0 at Sullivan Stadium on 11-22-87 (Jim Bowman had two interceptions, a fumble recovery, and eight tackles) (The Game of the Year)

Lost to the Eagles 34–31 in overtime at Sullivan Stadium on 11-29-87 (Tom Ramsey threw three TDs and ran for a TD to force overtime)

Routed the New York Jets 42–20 at Sullivan Stadium on 12-13-87 (Steve Grogan threw four TDs and ran for another in the first half)

1988 regular season

Destroyed the New York Jets 28–3 at Sullivan Stadium on 09-04-88 (Irving Fryar caught two TD passes from Steve Grogan)

Lost to the Buffalo Bills 16–14 at Sullivan Stadium on 09-18-88 (Fred Marion intercepted Jim Kelly twice and had 11 tackles)

Defeated the Indianapolis Colts 21–17 at Sullivan Stadium on 10-02-88 (Doug Flutie was the AFC Offensive Player of the Week)

Defeated the Cincinnati Bengals 27–21 at Sullivan Stadium on 10-16-88 (Fred Marion was the AFC Defensive Player of the Week)

Defeated Chicago 30–7 at Sullivan Stadium on 10-30-88 (Irving Fryar caught an 80-yard TD on the very first play) (The Game of the Year)

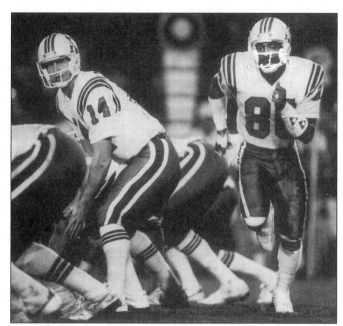

Steve Grogan (14) and Irving Fryar (80)

Defeated the Miami Dolphins 21–10 at Sullivan Stadium on 11-06-88 (Johnny Rembert was the AFC Defensive Player of the Week)

Defeated Seattle 13–7 at Sullivan Stadium on 12-04-88 (Kicker Teddy Garcia made a game-saving tackle on a 43-yard kickoff return)

Defeated Tampa Bay 10–7 in overtime at Sullivan Stadium in minus-25 degree wind chill weather on 12-11-88 (The Patriots first overtime victory)

1989 regular season

Lost to the Dolphins 24–10 at Sullivan Stadium on 09-17-89 (Hart Lee Dykes caught a 10-yard TD pass on the game's last play)

Lost to the Seattle Seahawks 24–3 at Sullivan Stadium on 09-24-89 (Jim Bowman led the team with 10 tackles)

Defeated the Houston Oilers 23–13 at Sullivan Stadium on 10-08-89 (Doug Flutie had a 22-yard run to set up a field goal)

Lost to the New York Jets 27–26 at Sullivan Stadium on 11-05-89 (Marc Wilson tossed an 11-yard TD to Hart Lee Dykes with one minute left)

Lost to the Saints 28–24 at Sullivan Stadium on 11-12-89 (Hart Lee Dykes caught a fourth-down TD and recovered a Patriots onside kick)

Defeated the Bills 33–24 at Sullivan Stadium on 11-19-89 (Maurice Hurst took a Jim Kelly pass 16 yards for a TD late in the fourth quarter)

Defeated the Indianapolis Colts 22–16 at Sullivan Stadium on 12-03-89 (John Stephens ran for a 10-yard TD with 25 seconds left)

Lost to the LA Rams 24–20 at Sullivan on 12-24-89 (Irving Fryar had a 47-yard kickoff return and a 47-yard TD reception)

The Top 10 most memorable moments in games played at Sullivan Stadium

Robert Weathers ran for a 42-yard TD, on fourth down, to propel the Patriots into the playoffs in the 11-point win on 12-22-85

Doug Flutie caused the fans to go "icky balooky" as he ran for the game-winning TD in the four-point win on 10-02-88

Andre Tippett stopped Richard Todd and the Jets three times within the Patriots 10-yard line late in the 23–13 win on 09-18-83

Mike Haynes became the first Patriots player to return a punt for a TD in the team's 10-point win over Buffalo on 11-07-76

Irving Fryar caught an 80-yard TD pass from Doug Flutie on the game's first play in the team's 23-point win on 10-30-88

Steve Grogan ran a three-yard bootleg left for a TD for the game-winning TD in the 20–13 win against the Jets on 10-20-85

John Stephens ran for a 10-yard TD, with 25 seconds left, to defeat the Indianapolis Colts 22–16 on 12-03-89

Jason Staurovsky kicked an overtime game-winning field goal to beat Tampa 10–7, in minus-25 degree wind chill weather, on 12-11-88

Ronnie Lippett returned a Dan Marino pass 20 yards for a TD for the last points scored in the 28–21 win on 09-13-87

The total points scored by New England Patriots players in regular season games played at Sullivan Stadium

230 points were scored by kicker Tony Franklin

132 points were scored by running back Tony Collins

108 points were scored by wide receiver Irving Fryar

102 points were scored by wide receiver Stanley Morgan

65 points were scored by kicker Jason Staurovsky

48 points were scored by wide receiver Cedric Jones

42 points were scored by running back Craig James

36 points were scored by quarterback Steve Grogan

36 points were scored by running backs Robert Perryman and John Stephens

30 points were scored by tight end Derrick Ramsey

26 points were scored by kicker Greg Davis

24 points were scored by tight end Lin Dawson

24 points were scored by wide receivers Hart Lee Dykes and Stephen Starring

24 points were scored by quarterback Tony Eason

22 points were scored by kicker Fred Steinfort

18 points were scored by running backs Reggie Dupard and Mosi Tatupu

18 points were scored by kicker Teddy Garcia

18 points were scored by tight end Willie Scott

18 points were scored by wide receiver Clarence Weathers

12 points were scored by tight end Greg Baty

12 points were scored by defensive back Ronnie Lippett

12 points were scored by running back Robert Weathers

11 points were scored by kicker John Smith

6 points were scored by running backs Marvin Allen, Patrick Egu, Mark van Eeghen, and Carl Woods

6 points were scored by quarterbacks Bob Bleier, Doug Flutie, and Tom Ramsey

6 points were scored by defensive backs Raymond Clayborn and Maurice Hurst

6 points were scored by wide receivers Greg Hawthorne and Larry Linne

6 points were scored by linebackers Johnny Rembert and Andre Tippett

4 points were scored by kicker Eric Schubert

2 points were scored by linebacker Don Blackmon

2 points were scored by the New England Patriots defensive team

The scoring summary of the Top 10 most exciting victories by the Patriots in a regular season game at Sullivan Stadium

The New England Patriots defeated the New York Jets 23–13 at Sullivan Stadium on 09-18-83

	Q1	Q2	Q3	Q4	Total
New York	0	13	0	0	13
New England	13	3	7	0	23

Tony Collins dashed 39 yards for a TD. John Smith kicked the extra point.

Tony Collins ran for a seven-yard TD. The extra-point attempt was no good.

Dwayne Crutchfield ran for a one-yard TD. Pat Leahy kicked the extra point.

John Smith kicked a 43-yard field goal.

Wesley Walker caught a 13-yard TD pass from Richard Todd. Ronnie Lippett blocked the extra point.

Tony Collins ran for a 23-yard TD. John Smith kicked the extra point.

Andre Tippett stymied Richard Todd on three consecutive plays inside the 8-yard line early in the fourth quarter.

———

The New England Patriots defeated the Cincinnati Bengals 20–14 at Sullivan Stadium on 10-14-84

	Q1	Q2	Q3	Q4	Total
Cincinnati	7	7	0	0	14
New England	3	0	7	10	20

Tony Franklin kicked a 20-yard field goal.

M.L. Harris caught a 34-yard TD pass from Boomer Esiason. Jim Breech kicked the extra point.

Cris Collinsworth caught a seven-yard TD pass from Boomer Esiason. Jim Breech kicked the extra point.

Tony Eason ran for a 13-yard TD. Tony Franklin kicked the extra point.

Tony Eason dashed 25 yards down the sideline for a TD. Tony Franklin kicked the extra point.

Tony Franklin kicked a 27-yard field goal with just under two minutes to go in the game.

The New England Patriots defeated the New York Jets 30–20 at Sullivan Stadium on 10-28-84

	Q1	Q2	Q3	Q4	Total
New York	10	10	0	0	20
New England	0	6	10	14	30

Raymond Berry's first game as the head coach of the Patriots

Pat Leahy kicked a 46-yard field goal.

Rocky Klever caught a six-yard TD pass from Ken O'Brien on the last play of the first quarter. Pat Leahy kicked the extra point.

Tony Franklin kicked a 20-yard field goal.

Pat Leahy kicked an 18-yard field goal.

Marion Barber ran for a two-yard TD. Pat Leahy kicked the extra point.

Tony Franklin kicked a 27-yard field goal on the last play of the first half.

Tony Franklin kicked a 47-yard field goal.

Craig James ran for a 25-yard TD. Tony Franklin kicked the extra point.

Stephen Starring caught a five-yard TD pass from Tony Eason. Tony Franklin kicked the extra point.

Tony Collins ran for a four-yard TD. Tony Franklin kicked the extra point.

Steve Nelson intercepted a pass by Pat Ryan with two minutes left in the game.

Roland James intercepted a pass by Pat Ryan with 36 seconds left in the game.

The New England Patriots defeated the Green Bay Packers 26–20 at Sullivan Stadium on 09-08-85

	Q1	Q2	Q3	Q4	Total
Green Bay	0	6	0	14	20
New England	7	12	0	7	26

Tony Collins ran for an 11-yard TD. Tony Franklin kicked the extra point.

Kenneth Sims blocked a 40-yard field-goal attempt by Al DelGreco.

Tony Franklin kicked a 34-yard field goal.

Don Blackmon sacked Lynn Dickey in the end zone for a safety.

Gerry Ellis ran for a one-yard TD. Don Blackmon blocked the extra-point attempt.

Cedric Jones caught a three-yard TD pass from Tony Eason with eight seconds left in the half. Tony Franklin kicked the extra point.

Craig James sprinted 65 yards on a "Toss 38 Play" for a TD. Tony Franklin kicked the extra point.

Paul Coffman caught an eight-yard TD pass from Lynn Dickey. Al DelGreco kicked the extra point.

Jessie Clark ran for a 23-yard TD. Al DelGreco kicked the extra point.

Mosi Tatupu recovered the onside kick attempt with 34 seconds left in the game.

This is the only time that the Patriots blocked an extra point and a field-goal attempt in the same game.

The New England Patriots defeated the Cincinnati Bengals 34–23 at Sullivan Stadium on 12-22-85

	Q1	Q2	Q3	Q4	Total
Cincinnati	3	3	7	10	23
New England	10	10	0	14	34

Tony Franklin kicked a 25-yard field goal.

Jim Breech kicked a 42-yard field goal.

Stanley Morgan hauled in a 50-yard TD pass from Tony Eason. Tony Franklin kicked the extra point.

Jim Breech kicked a 22-yard field goal.

Tony Collins ran for a nine-yard TD. Tony Franklin kicked the extra point.

Tony Collins kicked a 30-yard field goal.

Eddie Brown caught a 33-yard TD pass from Boomer Esiason. Jim Breech kicked the extra point.

Jim Breech kicked a 30-yard field goal.

Craig James ran for an 11-yard TD. Tony Franklin kicked the extra point.

Cris Collinsworth caught an eight-yard TD pass from Boomer Esiason. Jim Breech kicked the extra point.

Robert Weathers dashed 42 yards on fourth down with two minutes left for a TD. Tony Franklin kicked the extra point.

———

The New England Patriots defeated the Buffalo Bills 22–19 at Sullivan Stadium on 11-23-86

	Q1	Q2	Q3	Q4	Total
Buffalo	0	3	3	13	19
New England	9	6	0	7	22

Larry McGrew strip-sacked Jim Kelly on the second play of the game and the ball went out of the end zone for a safety.

Craig James ran for a four-yard TD. Tony Franklin kicked the extra point.

Bills lineman Fred Smerlas was penalized for unnecessary roughness on the extra-point attempt.

Tony Franklin kicked a 37-yard field goal.

Tony Franklin kicked a 47-yard field goal.

Scott Norwood kicked a 48-yard field goal with eight seconds left in the first half.

Scott Norwood kicked a 34-yard field goal.

Scott Norwood kicked a 33-yard field goal.

Scott Norwood kicked a 28-yard field goal.

Robb Riddick caught a 31-yard TD pass from Jim Kelly. Scott Norwood kicked the extra point.

Greg Baty caught a 13-yard TD pass from Tony Eason with 1:46 left. Tony Franklin kicked the extra point.

Ronnie Lippett intercepted Jim Kelly with 1:10 left in the game.

Jim Bowman and Mosi Tatupu tackled Ron Pitts after his 18-yard punt return on the last play of the game.

———

The New England Patriots defeated the Los Angeles Raiders 26–23 at Sullivan Stadium on 11-01-87

	Q1	Q2	Q3	Q4	Total
Los Angeles	3	3	0	17	23
New England	3	7	6	10	26

Chris Bahr kicked a 31-yard field goal.

Tony Franklin kicked a 50-yard field goal.

Tony Collins caught a 15-yard HB option TD pass from Mosi Tatupu. Tony Franklin kicked the extra point.

Chris Bahr kicked another 31-yard field goal.

Tony Franklin kicked a 27-yard field goal.

Tony Franklin kicked a 25-yard field goal.

Irving Fryar caught a 25-yard TD pass from Steve Grogan. Tony Franklin kicked the extra point.

Todd Christensen caught an eight-yard TD pass from Rusty Hilger. Chris Bahr kicked the extra point.

Marcus Allen ran for a two-yard TD. Chris Bahr kicked the extra point.

Chris Bahr kicked a 39-yard field goal.

Tony Franklin missed a 34-yard field-goal attempt with nine seconds left, but the Raiders were offside.

Tony Franklin kicked the game-winning 29-yard field goal with five seconds left in the game.

Mosi Tatupu

The New England Patriots defeated the Indianapolis Colts 21–17 at Sullivan Stadium on 10-02-88

	Q1	Q2	Q3	Q4	Total
Indianapolis	0	7	0	10	17
New England	0	7	0	14	21

Robert Perryman dove for a one-yard TD. Teddy Garcia kicked the extra point.

Eric Dickerson ran for a one-yard TD. Dean Biasucci kicked the extra point.

Stanley Morgan caught a 26-yard TD pass from Doug Flutie. Teddy Garcia kicked the extra point.

Dean Biasucci kicked a 20-yard field goal.

Bill Brooks caught a 48-yard TD pass from Chris Chandler. Dean Biasucci kicked the extra point.

Doug Flutie ran a 13-yard bootleg left for the game-winning TD with 29 seconds left. Teddy Garcia kicked the extra point.

Raymond Clayborn intercepted Chris Chandler with 23 seconds left to seal the victory.

The New England Patriots defeated the Cincinnati Bengals 27–21 at Sullivan Stadium on 10-16-88

	Q1	Q2	Q3	Q4	Total
Cincinnati	0	0	14	7	21
New England	7	7	6	7	27

John Stephens recovered a fumble by Robert Perryman in the end zone for a TD. Teddy Garcia kicked the extra point.

Mosi Tatupu ran for a three-yard TD with 23 seconds left in the first half. Teddy Garcia kicked the extra point.

Reggie Dupard ran for a three-yard TD. The extra-point attempt was no good.

Ickey Woods ran for a one-yard TD. Jim Breech kicked the extra point.

Eddie Brown caught a 26-yard TD pass from Boomer Esiason. Jim Breech kicked the extra point.

Reggie Dupard ran for a 10-yard TD. Teddy Garcia kicked the extra point.

Eddie Brown caught a 16-yard TD pass from Boomer Esiason. Jim Breech kicked the extra point.

Jim Bowman intercepted Boomer Esiason on the Patriots' 5-yard line on the last play of the game.

The New England Patriots defeated the Indianapolis Colts 22–16 at Sullivan Stadium on 12-03-89

	Q1	Q2	Q3	Q4	Total
Indianapolis	0	3	7	6	16
New England	6	0	3	13	22

Jason Staurovsky kicked a 44-yard field goal.

Jason Staurovsky kicked a 37-yard field goal.

Dean Biasucci kicked an 18-yard field goal with three seconds left in the first half.

Jason Staurovsky kicked a 24-yard field goal.

Albert Bentley caught a nine-yard TD pass from Jack Trudeau. Dean Biasucci kicked the extra point.

Jason Staurovsky kicked a 50-yard field goal.

Jason Staurovsky kicked a 23-yard field goal.

Eric Dickerson caught an eight-yard TD pass from Jack Trudeau. The extra-point attempt was no good.

John Stephen ran 10 yards for the game-winning TD with 25 seconds left. Jason Staurovsky kicked the extra point.

Every regular season game played by the New England Patriots at Foxboro Stadium
1990 regular season

Lost to the Dolphins 27–24 at Foxboro Stadium on 09-09-90 (Ronnie Lippett had a 73-yard interception return to set up a TD and returned a fumble)

Lost to the New York Jets 37–13 at Foxboro Stadium on 09-30-90 (John Hannah's No. 73 was retired during halftime ceremony)

Lost to the Seattle Seahawks 33–20 at Foxboro Stadium on 10-07-90 (Brent Williams returned a fumble 45 yards for a TD)

Lost to the Buffalo Bills 27–10 at Foxboro Stadium on 10-28-90 (RB Robert Perryman led the team in receptions)

Lost to the Indianapolis Colts 13–10 at Foxboro Stadium on 11-11-90 (Tim Goad had 10 tackles)

John Hannah

Lost to the Chiefs 37–7 at Foxboro Stadium on 12-02-90 (Marvin Allen had three carries, one reception, five kickoff returns, and a recovered fumble)

Lost to the Redskins 25–10 at Foxboro Stadium on 12-15-90 (LS Chris Gannon had 0 yards rushing as his long snap went out of the end zone)

Lost to the New York Giants 13–10 at Foxboro Stadium on 12-30-90 (Irving Fryar caught a 40-yard TD from Tommy Hodson)

1991 regular season
Lost to the Cleveland Browns 20–0 at Foxboro Stadium on 09-08-91 (Leonard Russell had his longest run as a Patriots RB)

Defeated the Houston Oilers 24–20 at Foxboro Stadium on 09-22-91 (Marv Cook was the AFC Offensive Player of the Week)

Lost to the Miami Dolphins 20–10 at Foxboro Stadium on 10-06-91 (Jerome Henderson's 39-yard punt return set up the team's only TD)

Beat the Vikings 26–23 in overtime on Jason Staurovsky's 42-yard field goal on the last play of overtime at Foxboro Stadium on 10-20-91 (The Game of the Year)

Lost to the Denver Broncos 9–6 at Foxboro Stadium on 10-27-91 (NT Fred Smerlas shared in a tackle of Robert Perryman)

Lost to the Jets 28–21 at Foxboro Stadium on 11-17-91 (Former Patriots center Trevor Matich caught the game-winning TD for the Jets)

Defeated the Buffalo Bills 16–13 at Foxboro Stadium on 11-24-91 (Irving Fryar was the AFC Offensive Player of the Week)

Defeated Indianapolis 23–17 in overtime at Foxboro Stadium on 12-08-91 (Michael Timpson caught the game-winning TD in overtime from Hugh Millen)

1992 regular season
Lost to the Seattle Seahawks 10–6 at Foxboro Stadium on 09-20-92 (Irving Fryar caught a 36-yard TD from Hugh Millen)

Lost to the Buffalo Bills 41–7 at Foxboro Stadium on 09-27-92 (Hugh Millen completed 14 consecutive passes)

Lost to the San Francisco 49ers 24–12 at Foxboro Stadium on 10-11-92 (Kevin Turner tackled punter Klaus Wilmsmeyer)

Lost to the Cleveland Browns 19–17 at Foxboro Stadium on 10-25-92 (Walter Stanley caught a 36-yard pass as time expired)

Lost to the New Orleans Saints 31–14 at Foxboro Stadium on 11-08-92 (Vincent "Undertaker" Brown returned a pass 49 yards for a TD)

Defeated the New York Jets 24–3 at Foxboro Stadium on 11-22-92 (Jon Vaughn had a career-best 110 yards rushing)

Lost to Indianapolis 6–0 at Foxboro Stadium (in minus-6 degree wind chill) on 12-06-92 (Scott Zolak had his career's longest run of 19 yards)

Lost to the Dolphins 16–13 in overtime at Foxboro Stadium on 12-27-92 (Shawn McCarthy had team-best 103 punts in a year)

1993 regular season
Lost to Detroit 19–16 in overtime at Foxboro Stadium on 09-12-93 (Vincent Brisby had a two-yard TD reception with 12 ticks left to force overtime)

Lost to the Seattle Seahawks 17–14 at Foxboro Stadium on 09-19-93 (Sam Gash ran four yards for his last TD as a Patriots RB)

Lost to the Houston Oilers 28–14 at Foxboro Stadium on 10-17-93 (Darryl Wren recovered a Patriots' onside kick by Scott Sisson)

Lost to the Buffalo Bills 13–10 in overtime at Foxboro Stadium on 11-07-93

Lost to the New York Jets 6–0 in a heavy rainstorm at Foxboro on 11-28-93 (Leonard Russell had career-best 147 yards rushing)

Defeated the Cincinnati Bengals 7–2 at Foxboro Stadium on 12-12-93 (Terry Ray intercepted David Klinger to end the game)

Shutout the Indianapolis Colts 38–0 at Foxboro Stadium on 12-26-93 (Corey Croom scored his only NFL TD on a five-yard run)

Beat Miami 33–27 in overtime at Foxboro Stadium on 01-02-94 (Michael Timpson caught overtime game-winning TD) (The Game of the Year)

1994 regular season
Lost to the Buffalo Bills 38–35 at Foxboro Stadium on 09-11-94 (Marion Butts had TD runs of 19 yards and six yards)

Defeated the Green Bay Packers 17–16 at Foxboro Stadium on 10-02-94 (Drew Bledsoe was the AFC Offensive Player of the Week)

Lost to the Los Angeles Raiders 21–17 at Foxboro Stadium on 10-09-94 (Ben Coates had nine receptions for 123 yards)

Lost to the Dolphins 23–3 at Foxboro Stadium on 10-30-94 (Harlon Barnett's interception set up a 48-yard field goal by Matt Bahr)

Beat Minnesota 26–20 in overtime at Foxboro Stadium on 11-13-94 (Drew Bledsoe was AFC Offensive Player of Week) (The Game of the Year)

Defeated the San Diego Chargers 23–17 at Foxboro Stadium on 11-20-94 (Marion Butts scored on a one-yard TD against his former team)

Beat the New York Jets 24–13 at Foxboro Stadium on 12-04-94 (Pat O'Neill's pooched punt was downed by Todd Rucci on the 1-yard line)

Defeated the Indianapolis Colts 24–13 at Foxboro Stadium on 12-11-94 (Leroy Thompson had a TD reception and a TD run)

1995 regular season
Defeated the Cleveland Browns 17–14 at Foxboro Stadium on 09-03-95 (Curtis Martin scored TD with 19 ticks left to win it)

Lost to the Miami Dolphins 20–3 at Foxboro Stadium on 09-10-95 (Steve Grogan was inducted into Patriots Hall of Fame at halftime)

Lost to the Denver Broncos 37–3 at Foxboro Stadium on 10-08-95 (Matt Bahr kicked a 51-yard field goal)

Defeated the Buffalo Bills 27–14 at Foxboro Stadium on 10-23-95 (Curtis Martin set team record with 36 rushing attempts)

Lost to the Carolina Panthers 20–17 in overtime at Foxboro Stadium on 10-29-95 (Curtis Martin scored on a two-yard TD to force overtime)

Lost to the Indianapolis Colts 24–10 at Foxboro Stadium on 11-19-95 (Ben Coates caught an 11-yard pass on fourth down to set up TD)

Lost to the New Orleans Saints 31–17 at Foxboro Stadium on 12-03-95 (Scott Zolak ran eight yards for a first down on a fake field goal)

Defeated the New York Jets 31–28 at Foxboro Stadium on 12-10-95 (Curtis Martin was the AFC Offensive Player of the Week)

1996 regular season
Shutout the Arizona Cardinals 31–0 at Foxboro Stadium on 09-15-96 (Curtis Martin scored 20 points)

Defeated the Jaguars 28–25 in overtime at Foxboro Stadium on 09-22-96 (Adam Vinatieri was the AFC Special Team Player of the Week)

Lost to the Washington Redskins 27–22 at Foxboro Stadium on 10-13-96 (Curtis Martin had 164 of the team's 177 total yards rushing)

Defeated the Buffalo Bills 28–25 at Foxboro Stadium on 10-27-96 (Willie McGinest was the AFC Defensive Player of the Week)

Defeated Miami 42–23 at Foxboro Stadium on 11-03-96 (Curtis Martin had three TDs and Ben Coates had TD receptions of 23 and 84 yards)

Lost to the Denver Broncos 34–8 at Foxboro Stadium on 11-17-96 (Lawyer Milloy's first NFL interception against John Elway)

Defeated the Indianapolis Colts 27–13 at Foxboro Stadium on 11-24-96 (Curtis Martin scored a TD in 7th consecutive game)

Defeated the New York Jets 34–10 at Foxboro Stadium on 12-08-96 (Terry Glenn set the NFL record with 75 rookie receptions)

Lawyer Milloy

1997 regular season

Destroyed San Diego 41–7 at Foxboro Stadium on 08-31-97 (The only year that the Patriots won the home opening game in August)

Defeated the New York Jets 27–24 in overtime at Foxboro Stadium on 09-14-97 (Curtis Martin was the AFC Offensive Player of the Week)

Troy Brown

Beat the Chicago Bears 31–3 at Foxboro Stadium on 09-21-97 (Drew Bledsoe threw two TD passes and Scott Zolak tossed a TD pass)

Destroyed the Bills 33–6 at Foxboro Stadium on 10-12-97 (Adam Vinatieri was the AFC Special Team Player of the Week)

Lost to the Green Bay Packers 28–10 at Foxboro Stadium on 10-27-97 (Pro Football Hall of Fame player Mike Haynes was honored)

Defeated the Miami Dolphins 27–24 at Foxboro Stadium on 11-23-97 (Dave Meggett threw a HB option TD pass to Troy Brown)

Defeated the Indianapolis Colts 20–17 at Foxboro Stadium on 11-30-97 (Troy Brown caught an 18-yard game-winning TD pass)

Lost to the Pittsburgh Steelers 24–21 in overtime at Foxboro Stadium on 12-13-97 (Dave Meggett caught a 49-yard TD pass)

1998 regular season

Defeated the Indianapolis Colts 29–6 at Foxboro Stadium on 09-13-98 (Adam Vinatieri's 52-yard field goal hit the camera and bounced back)

Beat the Tennessee Oilers 27–16 at Foxboro Stadium on 09-20-98 (Lawyer Milloy returned a Steve McNair pass 30 yards for a TD)

Destroyed the Kansas City Chiefs 40–10 at Foxboro Stadium on 10-11-98 (Robert Edwards ran for a TD and caught a TD pass)

Lost to the New York Jets 24–14 at Foxboro Stadium on 10-19-98 (Robert Edwards was the first NFL player to score a TD in his first six games)

Lost to the Atlanta Falcons 41–10 at Foxboro Stadium on 11-08-98 (Ferric Collons blocked a 47-yard field-goal attempt by Morton Andersen)

Defeated the Miami Dolphins 26–23 at Foxboro Stadium on 11-23-98 (Drew Bledsoe was the NFL Player of the Week)

Beat the Bills 25–21 at Foxboro Stadium on 11-29-98 (Drew Bledsoe was the NFL Player of the Week again) (The Game of the Year)

Defeated the 49ers 24–21 at Foxboro Stadium on 12-20-98 (Willie Clay was the AFC Defensive Player of the Week)

1999 regular season

Beat the Colts 31–28 at Foxboro Stadium on 09-19-99 (Adam Vinatieri kicked the game-winning 26-yard field goal) (The Game of the Year)

Defeated the New York Giants 16–14 at Foxboro Stadium on 09-26-99 (Ben Coates recovered an onside kick to preserve the win)

Lost to the Miami Dolphins 31–30 at Foxboro Stadium on 10-17-99 (Drew Bledsoe set team record for career passing attempts)

Defeated the Denver Broncos 24–23 at Foxboro Stadium on 10-24-99 (Terry Allen ran for two TDs including game winner)

Lost to the Jets 24–14 at Foxboro Stadium on 11-15-99 (Kevin Faulk set the team record of longest non-scoring kickoff return, 95 yards)

Defeated the Dallas Cowboys 13–6 at Foxboro Stadium on 12-05-99 (Beat Dallas for the first time as Terry Allen had fourth quarter TD run)

Lost to the Buffalo Bills 13–10 in overtime at Foxboro Stadium on 12-26-99 (Drew Bledsoe had career's longest run of 25 yards)

Defeated the Baltimore Ravens 20–3 at Foxboro Stadium on 01-02-00 (Chad Eaton returned a fumble 23 yards for a TD)

Drew Bledsoe

2000 regular season

Lost to Tampa Bay 21–16 at Foxboro Stadium on 09-03-00 (Troy Brown took a punt 66 yards for a TD and led team in rushing yards)

Lost to the Minnesota Vikings 21–13 at Foxboro Stadium on 09-17-00 (Kato Serwanga played against his brother Wasswa)

Beat the Colts 24–16 at Foxboro Stadium on 10-08-00 (Tony Simmons caught a 44-yard TD from Michael Bishop to end the first half)

Lost to the New York Jets 34–17 at Foxboro Stadium on 10-15-00 (Drew Bledsoe ran 13 yards for his first NFL TD)

Lost to the Buffalo Bills 16–13 in overtime at Foxboro Stadium on 11-05-00 (J.R. Redmond's only rushing TD for the Patriots)

Beat the Bengals 16–13 at Foxboro Stadium on 11-19-00 (Adam Vinatieri kicked a 22-yard field goal, with three seconds left, to win the game)

Defeated the Kansas City Chiefs 30–24 at Foxboro Stadium on 12-04-00 (Adam Vinatieri kicked a 53-yard field goal to end the first half)

Lost to the Miami Dolphins 27–24 at Foxboro Stadium on 12-24-00 (Terry Glenn caught a 16-yard TD pass to end the first half)

2001 Championship Season

Lost to the New York Jets 10–3 at Foxboro Stadium on 9-23-01 (Drew Bledsoe was severely injured after being hit by LB Mo Lewis)

Destroyed the Indianapolis Colts 44–13 at Foxboro Stadium on 09-30-01 (Tom Brady's first NFL start)

Beat San Diego 29–26 in overtime at Foxboro Stadium on 10-14-01 (Jermaine Wiggins caught a three-yard TD to force overtime) (The Game of the Year)

Defeated the Bills 21–11 at Foxboro Stadium on 11-11-01 (Antowain Smith had a 42-yard TD run against his former team)

Lost to the St. Louis Rams 24–17 at Foxboro Stadium on 11-18-01 (Terrell Buckley returned a Kurt Warner pass 52 yards for a TD)

Destroyed the New Orleans Saints 34–17 at Foxboro Stadium on 11-25-01 (Tom Brady was the NFL Player of the Week)

Defeated the Cleveland Browns 27–16 at Foxboro Stadium on 12-09-01 (Troy Brown returned a punt 85 yards for a TD)

Defeated the Dolphins 20–13 at Foxboro Stadium on 12-22-01 (Ken Walter was the AFC Special Team Player of the Week)

The Top 10 most memorable moments in games played at Foxboro Stadium

Tom Brady's incomplete pass, that was initially ruled as a fumble, in the team's 16–13 overtime playoff game win on 01-19-02

Adam Vinatieri's 45-yard field goal to tie the game in the snow in the team's 16–13 overtime playoff game win on 01-19-02

Drew Bledsoe threw a 25-yard TD with a broken finger to Shawn Jefferson with 29 ticks left in the three-point win on 11-23-98

Drew Bledsoe tossed a one-yard TD pass to Ben Coates, with no time left, in the 25–21 win over Buffalo on 11-29-98

Willie McGinest returned a pass by Jim Kelly 46 yards for a TD, with 41 ticks left, in the three-point win over Buffalo on 10-27-96

Curtis Martin dashed 78 yards for a TD (his career-longest run) in the 28–3 playoff game rout of the Steelers on 01-05-97

Otis Smith returned a fumble by James Stewart 47 yards for a TD in the 20–6 playoff game win against the Jaguars on 01-12-97

Jimmy Hitchcock returned a Dan Marino pass 100 yards for a TD in the three-point win against the Dolphins on 11-23-97

Troy Brown advanced a fumbled kickoff return by Dave Meggett 75 yards for a TD in the three-point win over the Jets on 12-10-95

Tom Brady caught a 23-yard swing pass from Kevin Faulk in the 20–13 victory over the Miami Dolphins on 12-22-01

The total points scored by New England Patriots players in regular season games played at Foxboro Stadium

383 points were scored by kicker Adam Vinatieri

182 points were scored by running back Curtis Martin

162 points were scored by tight end Ben Coates

109 points were scored by kicker Matt Bahr

62 points were scored by kicker Jason Staurovsky

60 points were scored by wide receiver Troy Brown

60 points were scored by running back Antowain Smith

54 points were scored by wide receiver Terry Glenn

48 points were scored by running backs Robert Edwards and Kevin Faulk

42 points were scored by wide receiver Vincent Brisby

42 points were scored by running back Leonard Russell

39 points were scored by kicker Charlie Baumann

36 points were scored by running backs Sam Gash, Leroy Thompson, John Stephens, and Terry Allen

30 points were scored by wide receiver Irving Fryar

24 points were scored by running backs Marion Butts and Kevin Turner

24 points were scored by tight end Marv Cook

24 points were scored by wide receivers Shawn Jefferson and Michael Timpson

24 points were scored by defensive back Ty Law

20 points were scored by running back Keith Byars

19 points were scored by kicker Scott Sisson

18 points were scored by tight end Lovett Purnell

18 points were scored by running back Jon Vaughn

14 points were scored by running back Dave Meggett

12 points were scored by defensive back Otis Smith

12 points were scored by running back Tony Carter

12 points were scored by wide receivers Greg McMurtry and Tony Simmons

12 points were scored by tight end Jermaine Wiggins

6 points were scored by defensive backs Terrell Buckley, Willie Clay, Jimmy Hitchcock, and Lawyer Milloy

6 points were scored by defensive backs Ricky Reynolds and Larry Whigham

6 points were scored by linebackers Vincent Brown, Todd Collins, Andy Katzenmoyer, and Willie McGinest

6 points were scored by running backs Marvin Allen, Derrick Cullors, Corey Croom, and Marc Edwards

6 points were scored by running backs Marrio Grier, Patrick Pass, and Robert Perryman

6 points were scored by wide receivers Ray Crittenden, Hart Lee Dykes, Hason Graham, and Charles Johnson

Shawn Jefferson

6 points were scored by wide receivers Sammy Martin and David Patten

6 points were scored by tight ends Mike Bartrum and Eric Bjornson

6 points were scored by quarterbacks Drew Bledsoe and Hugh Millen

6 points were scored by offensive guard Freddie Childress

6 points were scored by nose tackle Chad Eaton

6 points were scored by defensive end Brent Williams

2 points were scored by the New England Patriots defensive team

The scoring summary of the Top 10 most exciting regular season victories by the Patriots at Foxboro Stadium

The New England Patriots defeated the Buffalo Bills 16–13 at Foxboro Stadium on 11-24-91

	Q1	Q2	Q3	Q4	Total
Buffalo	3	7	3	0	13
New England	0	9	0	7	16

Scott Norwood kicked a 23-yard field goal.

Thurman Thomas caught a 10-yard TD pass from Jim Kelly. Scott Norwood kicked the extra point.

Charlie Baumann kicked a 46-yard field goal.

Irving Fryar caught a 50-yard TD pass from Hugh Millen with 33 seconds left in the half. The extra-point attempt was blocked.

Scott Norwood kicked a 29-yard field goal.

Hugh Millen ran for a two-yard TD early in the fourth quarter. Charlie Baumann kicked the extra point.

———

The New England Patriots defeated the Green Bay Packers 17–16 at Foxboro Stadium on 10-02-94

	Q1	Q2	Q3	Q4	Total
Green Bay	3	7	0	6	16
New England	0	0	7	10	17

Chris Jacke kicked a 27-yard field goal.

Sterling Sharpe caught an 11-yard TD pass from Brett Favre. Chris Jacke kicked the extra point.

Vincent Brisby caught a 10-yard TD pass from Drew Bledsoe. Matt Bahr kicked the extra point.

Vincent Brisby caught a 37-yard TD pass from Drew Bledsoe. Matt Bahr kicked the extra point.

Reggie Cobb ran for a one-yard TD with 1:14 left in the game. The extra-point attempt was no good.

The ensuing kickoff by Chris Jacke went out-of-bounds

Matt Bahr kicked the game-winning 33-yard field goal with seven seconds left.

Sam Gash tackled the Packers kickoff returnman Corey Harris on the game's last play.

———

The New England Patriots defeated the New York Jets 31–28 at Foxboro Stadium on 12-10-95

	Q1	Q2	Q3	Q4	Total
New York	0	7	7	14	28
New England	0	7	7	17	31

Ryan Yarborough caught a 31-yard TD pass from Boomer Esiason. Nick Lowery kicked the extra point.

Hason Graham caught a 37-yard TD pass from Drew Bledsoe. Matt Bahr kicked the extra point.

Johnny Mitchell caught a three-yard TD pass from Boomer Esiason. Nick Lowery kicked the extra point.

Curtis Martin ran nine yards for a TD. Matt Bahr kicked the extra point.

Matt Bahr kicked a 31-yard field goal.

Adrian Murrell caught three-yard TD pass from Boomer Esiason. Nick Lowery kicked the extra point.

Troy Brown advanced a fumbled kickoff return by Dave Meggett 75 yards for a TD. Matt Bahr kicked the extra point.

Curtis Martin ran for a one-yard TD. Matt Bahr kicked the extra point.

Ryan Yarborough caught a three-yard TD pass from Boomer Esiason with eight seconds left. Nick Lowery kicked the extra point.

———

The New England Patriots defeated the Buffalo Bills 28–25 at Foxboro Stadium on 10-27-96

	Q1	Q2	Q3	Q4	Total
Buffalo	0	0	10	15	25
New England	7	6	2	13	28

Curtis Martin caught a four-yard TD pass from Drew Bledsoe. Adam Vinatieri kicked the extra point.

Adam Vinatieri kicked a 40-yard field goal.

Adam Vinatieri kicked a 32-yard field goal on the last play of the first half.

Steve Christie kicked a 33-yard field goal.

Darick Holmes caught a six-yard TD pass from Jim Kelly. Steve Christie kicked the extra point.

Mike Jones forced Jim Kelly to intentionally ground the ball in the end zone for a safety.

Thurman Thomas ran for a one-yard TD. Darick Holmes ran for a two-point conversion.

Curtis Martin ran for a 10-yard TD. The extra-point attempt was no good.

Willie McGinest returned an interception 46 yards for a TD with 51 seconds left. Adam Vinatieri kicked the extra point.

Andre Reed hauled in a 48-yard TD pass from Jim Kelly with 33 seconds left. Steve Christie kicked the extra point.

Keith Byars recovered the onside kick by Steve Christie.

———

The New England Patriots defeated the Miami Dolphins 27–24 at Foxboro Stadium on 11-23-97

	Q1	Q2	Q3	Q4	Total
Miami	0	3	7	14	24
New England	3	21	3	0	27

Adam Vinatieri kicked a 36-yard field goal.

Olindo Mare kicked a 26-yard field goal.

Troy Brown caught a 35-yard HB option TD pass from Dave Meggett. Adam Vinatieri kicked the extra point.

Larry Whigham returned an interception 60 yards for a TD. Adam Vinatieri kicked the extra point.

Jimmy Hitchcock returned an interception 100 yards for a TD with 11 seconds left in the first half. Adam Vinatieri kicked the PAT.

Adam Vinatieri kicked a 27-yard field goal.

Karim Abdul Jabbar ran for a one-yard TD. Olindo Mare kicked the extra point.

Karim Abdul Jabbar ran for another one-yard TD. Olindo Mare kicked the extra point.

Larry Whigham

Karim Abdul Jabbar scored his third TD on a one-yard run with 10 seconds left. Olindo Mare kicked the extra point.

———

The New England Patriots defeated the Miami Dolphins 26–23 at Foxboro Stadium on 11-23-98

	Q1	Q2	Q3	Q4	Total
Miami	7	7	3	6	23
New England	7	3	6	10	26

Oronde Gadsden caught a 35-yard TD pass from Dan Marino. Olindo Mare kicked the extra point.

Ben Coates caught an eight-yard TD pass from Drew Bledsoe. Adam Vinatieri kicked the extra point.

Oronde Gadsden caught an 11-yard TD pass from Dan Marino. Olindo Mare kicked the extra point.

Adam Vinatieri kicked a 25-yard field goal.

Adam Vinatieri kicked a 44-yard field goal.

Olindo Mare kicked a 21-yard field goal.

Adam Vinatieri kicked a 45-yard field goal.

Adam Vinatieri kicked a 24-yard field goal.

Karim Abdul Jabbar ran for a four-yard TD. The two-point pass attempt was incomplete.

Shawn Jefferson caught a 12-yard pass, on fourth-and-7, with 43 seconds left, to set up the final touchdown.

Shawn Jefferson caught a 25-yard TD pass from Drew Bledsoe with 29 seconds left. Vinatieri kicked the extra point.

———

The New England Patriots defeated the San Francisco 49ers 24–21 at Foxboro Stadium on 12-20-98

	Q1	Q2	Q3	Q4	Total
San Francisco	0	21	0	0	21
New England	7	7	0	10	24

Robert Edwards caught a 19-yard TD pass from Scott Zolak. Adam Vinatieri kicked the extra point.

Jerry Rice hauled in a 75-yard TD pass from Steve Young. Wade Richey kicked the extra point.

Shawn Jefferson hauled in a 61-yard TD pass from Scott Zolak. Adam Vinatieri kicked the extra point.

Drew Bledsoe

Terrell Owens caught a seven-yard TD pass from Steve Young. Wade Richey kicked the extra point.

Irv Smith caught a 25-yard TD pass from Ty Detmer on a fumbled field-goal attempt on the last play of the half. Wade Richey hit the PAT.

Robert Edwards ran for a five-yard TD. Adam Vinatieri kicked the extra point.

"Big Play" Willie Clay intercepted Steve Young to set up the final field goal.

Adam Vinatieri kicked a game-winning 35-yard field goal with three seconds left in the game.

———

The New England Patriots defeated the Denver Broncos 24–23 at Foxboro Stadium on 10-24-99

	Q1	Q2	Q3	Q4	Total
Denver	0	10	3	10	23
New England	10	7	7	0	24

Kevin Faulk ran for a 15-yard TD. Adam Vinatieri kicked the extra point.

Adam Vinatieri kicked a 28-yard field goal.

Jason Elam kicked a 40-yard field goal.

Rod Smith caught a 28-yard TD pass from Brian Griese. Jason Elam kicked the extra point.

Terry Allen ran for a one-yard TD. Adam Vinatieri kicked the extra point.

Jason Elam kicked a 28-yard field goal.

Terry Allen ran for a another one-yard TD. Adam Vinatieri kicked the extra point.

Brian Griese ran for a seven-yard TD. Jason Elam kicked the extra point.

Jason Elam kicked a 30-yard field goal.

―――――

The New England Patriots defeated the Kansas City Chiefs 30–24 at Foxboro Stadium on 12-04-00

	Q1	Q2	Q3	Q4	Total
Kansas City	3	7	0	14	24
New England	10	10	7	3	30

Adam Vinatieri kicked a 48-yard field goal.

Todd Peterson kicked a 42-yard field goal.

Kevin Faulk ran for a one-yard TD. Adam Vinatieri kicked the extra point.

Derrick Alexander hauled in an 81-yard TD pass from Elvis Grbac. Todd Peterson kicked the extra point.

Troy Brown caught a 17-yard TD pass from Drew Bledsoe. Adam Vinatieri kicked the extra point.

Adam Vinatieri kicked a 53-yard field goal on the last play of the first half.

Jermaine Wiggins caught a one-yard TD pass from Drew Bledsoe. Adam Vinatieri kicked the extra point.

Tony Gonzalez caught a four-yard TD pass from Drew Bledsoe. Adam Vinatieri kicked the extra point.

Adam Vinatieri kicked a 27-yard field goal.

Kevin Lockett caught a 19-yard TD pass from Elvis Grbac. Todd Peterson kicked the extra point.

Tebucky Jones tackled Tony Gonzalez on the Patriots 7-yard line on the game's last play.

―――――

The New England Patriots defeated the Indianapolis Colts 44–13 at Foxboro Stadium on 09-30-01

	Q1	Q2	Q3	Q4	Total
Indianapolis	0	0	7	6	13
New England	7	13	3	21	44

Antowain Smith ran for a four-yard TD. Adam Vinatieri kicked the extra point.

Adam Vinatieri kicked a 47-yard field goal.

Otis Smith returned an interception 78 yards for a TD. Adam Vinatieri kicked the extra point.

Adam Vinatieri kicked a 48-yard field goal on the last play of the first half.

Adam Vinatieri kicked a 35-yard field goal.

Peyton Manning ran for a 10-yard TD. Mike Vanderjagt kicked the extra point.

Kevin Faulk ran for an eight-yard TD. Adam Vinatieri kicked the extra point.

Ty Law returned an interception 23 yards for a TD. Adam Vinatieri kicked the extra point.

Marcus Pollard caught a 17-yard TD pass from Peyton Manning. The two-point pass attempt was incomplete.

Antowain Smith ran for a two-yard TD. Adam Vinatieri kicked the extra point.

Every regular season game played by the New England Patriots at Gillette Stadium

2002 regular season

Defeated the Steelers 30–14 at Gillette Stadium on 09-09-02 (Tom Brady was AFC Offensive Player of Week) (The Game of the Year)

Defeated the Chiefs 41–38 in overtime at Gillette Stadium on 09-22-02 (Larry Izzo was the AFC Special Team Player of the Week)

Lost to the Packers 28–10 at Gillette Stadium on 10-13-02 (Antowain Smith caught a 14-yard pass on the game's last play)

Lost to the Denver Broncos 24–16 at Gillette Stadium on 10-27-02 (Deion Branch's 40-yard punt return set up the team's final TD)

Defeated the Vikings 24–17 at Gillette Stadium on 11-24-02 (Richard Seymour blocked a field goal, shared in a sack, and recovered a fumble)

Defeated the Buffalo Bills 27–17 at Gillette Stadium on 12-08-02 (Richard Seymour sacked and intercepted Drew Bledsoe)

Richard Seymour

Lost to the New York Jets 30–17 at Gillette Stadium on 12-22-02 (Kevin Faulk returned a kickoff 87 yards for a TD)

Defeated the Dolphins 27–24 in overtime at Gillette Stadium on 12-29-02 (Adam Vinatieri was the AFC Special Team Player of the Week)

2003 Championship Season

Beat the Jets 23–16 at Gillette Stadium on 09-21-03 (Asante Samuel returned a Vinny Testaverde pass 55 yards for a TD in the fourth quarter)

Defeated the Tennessee Titans 38–30 at Gillette Stadium on 10-05-03 (Ty Law returned a Steve McNair pass 65 yards for a TD)

Defeated the New York Giants 17–6 at Gillette Stadium on 10-12-03 (Matt Chatham took a Tiki Barber fumble 38 yards for a TD)

Defeated the Cleveland Browns 9–3 at Gillette Stadium on 10-26-03 (Daniel Graham was the AFC Offensive Player of the Week)

Shut out the Dallas Cowboys 12–0 at Gillette Stadium on 11-16-03 (Mike Vrabel had the only kickoff return for the Patriots)

Shut out the Miami Dolphins 12–0 at Gillette Stadium on 12-07-03 (Tedy Bruschi was the AFC Defensive Player of the Week)

Defeated the Jacksonville Jaguars 27–13 at Gillette Stadium on 12-14-03 (Larry Izzo recovered an onside kick by Seth Marler)

Shut out the Buffalo Bills 31–0 at Gillette Stadium on 12-27-03 (Tom Brady was the AFC Offensive Player of the Week)

2004 Championship Season

Beat the Colts 27–24 at Gillette Stadium on 09-09-04 (Willie McGinest sacked Peyton Manning forcing a long field-goal attempt that was missed)

Defeated the Miami Dolphins 24–10 at Gillette Stadium on 10-10-04 (Rahib Addulah ran for a one-yard TD)

Defeated Seattle 30–20 at Gillette Stadium on 10-17-04 (Bethel Johnson had a leaping 48-yard reception to set up the team's final TD)

Defeated the New York Jets 13–7 at Gillette Stadium on 10-24-04 (The Patriots set the NFL record with the team's 21st consecutive win)

Beat the Bills 29–6 at Gillette Stadium on 11-14-04 (The Red Sox shared the championship trophy with the home crowd)

Destroyed the Baltimore Ravens 24–3 at Gillette Stadium on 11-28-04 (Jarvis Green recovered a Kyle Boller fumble for a TD)

Beat the Bengals 35–28 at Gillette Stadium on 12-12-04 (Willie McGinest recovered a fumble allowing the team to score first for the 18th time)

Defeated the 49ers 21–7 at Gillette Stadium on 01-02-05 (Corey Dillon set the team record with 1,635 yards rushing)

2005 regular season

Defeated the Oakland Raiders 30–20 at Gillette Stadium on 09-08-05 (Corey Dillon ran for a TD in the third quarter and the fourth quarter)

Lost to the San Diego Chargers 41–17 at Gillette Stadium on 10-02-05 (The Patriots 21 home-game winning streak ended)

Defeated the Buffalo Bills 21–16 at Gillette Stadium on 10-30-05 (Tedy Bruschi was the AFC Defensive Player of the Week)

Lost to the Indianapolis Colts 40–21 at Gillette Stadium on 11-07-05 (Six Patriots players had at least three receptions)

Defeated the Saints 24–17 at Gillette Stadium on 11-20-05 (Eugene Wilson intercepted Aaron Brooks to end the game)

Defeated the New York Jets 16–3 at Gillette Stadium on 12-04-05 (Tom Brady ran for a three-yard gain, on fourth-and-1, on the last play)

Shut out the Tampa Bay Buccaneers 28–0 at Gillette Stadium on 12-17-05 (OL/TE Tom Ashworth caught a one-yard TD pass)

Lost to the Miami Dolphins 28–26 at Gillette Stadium on 01-01-06 (Doug Flutie drop-kicked an extra point)

2006 regular season

Beat the Bills 19–17 at Gillette Stadium on 09-10-06 (Ty Warren sacked J.P. Losman for a safety and the last points scored)

Lost to the Denver Broncos 17–7 at Gillette Stadium on 09-24-06 (Doug Gabriel caught an eight-yard TD pass from Tom Brady)

Defeated the Miami Dolphins 20–10 at Gillette Stadium on 10-08-06 (Heath Evans caught a one-yard TD pass in the fourth quarter)

Lost to the Indianapolis Colts 27–20 at Gillette Stadium on 11-05-06 (Junior Seau had a sack and led the team in tackles)

Lost to the New York Jets 17–14 at Gillette Stadium on 11-12-06 (Reche Caldwell had a 15-yard TD reception and a two-point conversion reception)

Beat the Bears 17–13 at Gillette Stadium on 11-26-06 (Asante Samuel was AFC Defensive Player of the Week) (The Game of the Year)

Defeated the Detroit Lions 28–21 at Gillette Stadium on 12-03-06 (Mike Vrabel had two interceptions and recovered a fumble)

Beat the Houston Texans 40–7 at Gillette Stadium on 12-17-06 (Ellis Hobbs was first Patriots DB with a kickoff return TD and pass interception)

2007 Undefeated Regular Season

Defeated the San Diego Chargers 38–14 at Gillette Stadium on 09-16-07 (Adalius Thomas returned an interception 65 yards for a TD)

Defeated the Buffalo Bills 38–7 at Gillette Stadium on 09-23-07 (Tom Brady was the AFC Offensive Player of the Week)

Defeated the Cleveland Browns 34–17 at Gillette Stadium on 10-07-07 (Junior Seau intercepted Derek Anderson twice)

Destroyed the Washington Redskins 52–7 at Gillette Stadium on 10-28-07 (Mike Vrabel had three strip-sacks and a TD reception)

Defeated the Philadelphia Eagles 31–28 at Gillette Stadium on 11-25-07 (Laurence Maroney ran for the game-winning TD)

Beat the Steelers 34–13 at Gillette Stadium on 12-09-07 (Tom Brady and Randy Moss combined on a 56-yard TD pass to Jabar Gaffney)

Defeated the New York Jets 20–10 at Gillette Stadium on 12-16-07 (Patriots tied the NFL season record with 21 players scoring a TD)

Defeated the Dolphins 28–7 at Gillette Stadium on 12-23-07 (This was the first time that the Patriots won every divisional game)

2008 regular season

Beat the Kansas City Chiefs 17–10 at Gillette Stadium on 09-07-08 (Tom Brady suffered a knee injury and was replaced by Matt Cassel)

Lost to the Miami Dolphins 38–13 at Gillette Stadium on 09-21-08 (Ellis Hobbs set the team record with 237 kickoff return yards)

Destroyed the Denver Broncos 41–7 at Gillette Stadium on 10-20-08 (Sammy Morris had 138 yards rushing and one TD)

Beat the St. Louis Rams 23–16 at Gillette Stadium on 10-26-08 (Kevin Faulk caught a game-winning 15-yard TD pass from Matt Cassel)

Defeated the Buffalo Bills 20–10 at Gillette Stadium on 11-09-08 (Ben Jarvus Green-Ellis had 105 yards rushing and one TD)

Lost to the New York Jets 34–31 in overtime at Gillette Stadium on 11-13-08 (Randy Moss caught a 16-yard TD with one tick left to force overtime)

Lost to the Pittsburgh Steelers 33–10 at Gillette Stadium on 11-30-08 (Lineman Stephen Neal had a 27-yard kickoff return)

Destroyed the Arizona Cardinals 47–7 at Gillette Stadium on 12-21-08 (Junior Seau and Jerod Mayo led the team with seven tackles)

The Top 10 most memorable moments in games played at Gillette Stadium

Unveiling the World Championship banners on the opening day games played in 2002, 2004, and 2005

Tedy Bruschi returning from a stroke and being the AFC Defensive Player of the Week in the team's five-point win on 10-30-05

Tom Brady set the NFL Playoff Game Record by completing 92.9% of his passes in the Patriots' 11-point victory on 01-12-08

Ty Law's three interceptions of Peyton Manning in the team's 10-point win during the Colts in the AFC Championship Game on 01-18-04

Willie McGinest's NFL record 4.5 sacks in the Patriots' 25-point Wild Card playoff game rout of the Jaguars on 01-07-06

Tedy Bruschi falling to his knees after his interception return for a TD in the 12–0 shutout of Miami in the snow on 12-07-03

Mike Vrabel had three strip-sacks and a TD reception in the 45-point blowout of the Redskins on 10-28-07

Willie McGinest's sack of Peyton Manning forcing a long field-goal attempt that was missed in the three-point win on 09-09-04

Doug Flutie became the first player since 1941 to successfully drop-kick a football in an NFL regular season game on 01-01-06

The Red Sox shared the 2004 World Championship trophy with the fans at halftime of the team's 23-point victory on 11-14-04

The Longest

The Patriots player with the longest run from scrimmage in a regular season game at Gillette Stadium
2007 undefeated regular season
Laurence Maroney dashed 59 yards for a TD in the 28–7 victory over the Miami Dolphins on 12-23-07

The Patriots player with the longest reception in a regular season game at Gillette Stadium
2007 undefeated regular season
Randy Moss caught a 76-yard TD pass in the team's 47–7 rout of the Arizona Cardinals on 12-21-08

Wes Welker

The Patriots player with the longest completion in a regular season game at Gillette Stadium
2007 undefeated regular season
Matt Cassel tossed a 76-yard TD pass to Randy Moss in the 47–7 rout of the Arizona Cardinals on 12-21-08

The Patriots player with the longest kickoff return in a regular season game at Gillette Stadium
2002 regular season
Kevin Faulk returned a kickoff 87 yards for a TD in the 30–17 loss to the New York Jets on 12-22-02

The Patriots player with the longest punt return in a regular season game at Gillette Stadium
2008 regular season
Wes Welker returned a punt 44 yards in the 41–7 rout of the Denver Broncos on 10-20-08

The Patriots player with the longest punt in a regular season game at Gillette Stadium
2004 championship season
Josh Miller punted the football 69 yards in the 35–28 victory over the Cincinnati Bengals on 12-12-04

The Patriots Defensive Back with the longest interception return in a regular season game at Gillette Stadium
2003 championship season
Ty Law returned a pass by Steve McNair 65 yards for a TD in the 38–30 win against the Tennessee Titans on 10-05-03

The Patriots Linebacker with the longest interception return in a regular season game at Gillette Stadium
2007 undefeated regular season
Adalius Thomas returned a pass by Philip Rivers 65 yards for a TD in the 38–14 rout of the San Diego Chargers on 09-16-07

The Patriots Kicker with the longest field goal in a regular season game at Gillette Stadium
2006 regular season
Stephen Gostkowski kicked a 52-yard field goal, with six seconds left in the half, in the 17–13 win over the Chicago Bears on 11-26-06

The Most

The Patriots player with the most yards rushing in a regular season game at Gillette Stadium
2007 undefeated regular season
Laurence Maroney had 156 yards rushing in the 28–7 rout of the Miami Dolphins on 12-23-07

The Patriots Quarterback with the most yards passing in a regular season game at Gillette Stadium
2002 regular season
Tom Brady threw for 410 yards in the 41–38 overtime win against the Kansas City Chiefs on 09-22-02

The Patriots player with the most yards receiving in a regular season game at Gillette Stadium
2002 regular season
Troy Brown had 176 yards receiving in the 41–38 overtime win against the Kansas City Chiefs on 09-22-02

Two-Point Conversions

Every Patriots player who has run for a two-point conversion in a regular season game at Gillette Stadium
2002 regular season
Antowain Smith ran for a two-point conversion in the 41–38 overtime win against the Kansas City Chiefs on 09-22-02

2004 championship season
Corey Dillon ran for a two-point conversion in the 24–3 rout of the Baltimore Ravens on 11-28-04

Safeties

The only time that the Patriots completed a pass for a two-point conversion in a regular season game at Gillette Stadium
Matt Cassel tossed a two-point pass to Jabar Gaffney in the 34–31 overtime loss to the New York Jets on 11-13-08

Every Patriots Defensive Lineman who has recorded a safety in a regular season game at Gillette Stadium
2003 championship season
Jarvis Green tackled Jay Fiedler in the end zone for a safety in the 12–0 shutout of the Miami Dolphins on 12-07-03

2006 regular season

Ty Warren sacked JP Losman for a safety, for the game-winning score, in the 19–17 win against the Buffalo Bills on 09-10-06

Scoring Feats

The only Patriots player who has kicked the overtime game-winning field goal in a regular season game at Gillette Stadium

2002 regular season

Adam Vinatieri kicked a 35-yard field goal to defeat the Kansas City Chiefs 41–38 at Gillette Stadium on 09-22-02

Adam Vinatieri kicked a 35-yard field goal to defeat the Miami Dolphins 27–24 at Gillette Stadium on 12-29-02

The only Patriots player to score on three rushing TDs in a regular season game at Gillette Stadium

Corey Dillon had TD runs of six yards, two yards, and four yards in the 28–21 victory over the Detroit Lions on 12-03-06

Every Patriots player who has returned a kickoff for a TD in a regular season game at Gillette Stadium

2002 regular season

Kevin Faulk returned a kickoff 87 yards for a TD in the 30–17 loss to the New York Jets on 12-22-02

2006 regular season

Ellis Hobbs returned a kickoff 93 yards for a TD in the 40–7 rout of the Houston Texans on 12-17-06

Every Patriots player who has returned a fumble for a TD in a regular season game at Gillette Stadium

2007 undefeated regular season

Randall Gay returned a fumble 15 yards for a TD in the 34–17 win over the Cleveland Browns on 10-07-07

Rosevelt Colvin took a strip-sacked fumble 11 yards for a TD in the 52–7 rout of the Washington Redskins on 10-28-07

Every Patriots Defensive Back who has returned an interception for a TD in a regular season game at Gillette Stadium

2003 championship season

Ty Law returned a pass 65 yards for a TD in the 38–30 win against the Tennessee Titans on 10-05-03

Asante Samuel returned a pass 55 yards for a TD in the 23–16 win against the New York Jets on 09-21-03

2004 championship season

Asante Samuel returned a pass 34 yards for a TD in the 35–28 victory over the Cincinnati Bengals on 12-12-04

2007 undefeated regular season

Asante Samuel returned a pass 40 yards for a TD in the 31–28 victory over the Philadelphia Eagles on 11-25-07

Eugene Wilson returned a pass five yards for a TD in the 20–10 victory over the New York Jets on 12-16-07

Every Patriots Linebacker who has returned an interception for a TD in a regular season game at Gillette Stadium

2003 championship season

Tedy Bruschi returned a pass five yards for a TD in the 12–0 shutout of the Miami Dolphins on 12-07-03

2007 undefeated regular season

Adalius Thomas returned a pass 65 yards for a TD in the 38–14 rout of the San Diego Chargers on 09-16-07

Every Patriots player who has blocked a field-goal attempt in a regular season game at Gillette Stadium

2002 regular season

Richard Seymour blocked a 43-yard field-goal attempt by Gary Anderson in the 24–17 win against the Minnesota Vikings on 11-24-02

2006 regular season

Mike Wright blocked a 40-yard field-goal attempt by Olindo Mare in the 20–10 win against the Miami Dolphins on 10-08-06

Richard Seymour blocked a 45-yard field-goal attempt by Robbie Gould in the 17–13 win against the Chicago Bears on 11-26-06

The total points scored by New England Patriots players in regular season games played at Gillette Stadium

233 points were scored by kicker Adam Vinatieri

196 points have been scored by kicker Stephen Gostkowski

110 points were scored by running back Corey Dillon

78 points have been scored by wide receiver Randy Moss

56 points were scored by wide receiver Troy Brown

48 points were scored by wide receiver Deion Branch

48 points have been scored by running back Kevin Faulk

44 points were scored by running back Antowain Smith and tight end Christian Fauria

44 points were scored by wide receiver Jabar Gaffney

42 points were scored by wide receiver David Patten

42 points have been scored by tight end Benjamin Watson

36 points were scored by tight end Donald Graham

30 points were scored by running back Sammy Morris

24 points have been scored by wide receiver Wes Welker and by wide receiver David Givens

24 points were scored by running back Laurence Maroney

18 points have been scored by quarterback Tom Brady

18 points were scored by running back Mike Cloud, wide reciever Tim Dwight, and defensive back Asante Samuel

18 points were scored by tight end Mike Vrabel

18 points were scored by running back Ben Jarvus Green-Ellis

12 points were scored by running back Heath Evans

12 points were scored by wide receiver Donald Hayes

12 points were scored by running back Lamont Jordan

12 points were scored by quarterback Matt Cassel

8 points were scored by defensive lineman Jarvis Green

8 points were scored by wide receiver Reche Caldwell

6 points were scored by running back Rabih Abdullah

6 points were scored by wide receivers Bethel Johnson, André Davis, Doug Gabriel, and Donte Stallworth

6 points were scored by defensive backs Randall Gay, Ty Law, and Eugene Wilson

6 points were scored by kick returner Ellis Hobbs

6 points were scored by linebackers Tedy Bruschi, Matt Chatham, Rosevelt Colvin, and Adalius Thomas

6 points were scored by tight end Tom Ashworth

2 points were scored by defensive lineman Ty Warren

1 extra point was drop-kicked by quarterback Doug Flutie

The scoring summaries of the Top 10 most exciting regular season victories by the Patriots at Gillette Stadium

The New England Patriots defeated the Pittsburgh Steelers 30–14 at Gillette Stadium on 09-09-02

	Q1	Q2	Q3	Q4	Total
Pittsburgh	7	0	0	7	14
New England	7	3	17	3	30

Christian Fauria caught a four-yard TD pass from Tom Brady. Adam Vinatieri kicked the extra point.

Hines Ward caught a 13-yard TD pass from Kordell Stewart. Todd Peterson kicked the extra point.

Adam Vinatieri kicked a 45-yard field goal.

Donald Hayes caught a 40-yard TD pass from Tom Brady. Adam Vinatieri kicked the extra point.

Deion Branch caught a 22-yard TD pass from Tom Brady. Adam Vinatieri kicked the extra point.

Adam Vinatieri kicked a 28-yard field goal.

Adam Vinatieri kicked a 27-yard field goal.

Kordell Stewart scored on a 1-yard run on the last play of the game. Todd Peterson kicked the extra point.

Corey Dillon

The New England Patriots defeated the Miami Dolphins 27–24 in overtime at Gillette Stadium on 12-29-02

	Q1	Q2	Q3	Q4	OT	Total
Miami	7	14	0	3	0	24
New England	0	10	3	11	3	27

Ricky Williams ran for an eight-yard TD. Olindo Mare kicked the extra point.

Ricky Williams ran for a 14-yard TD. Olindo Mare kicked the extra point.

Antowain Smith ran for an 11-yard TD. Adam Vinatieri kicked the extra point.

James McKnight caught a 32-yard TD pass from Jay Fiedler. Olindo Mare kicked the extra point.

Adam Vinatieri kicked a 41-yard field goal.

Adam Vinatieri kicked a 36-yard field goal.

Olindo Mare kicked a 28-yard field goal.

Troy Brown caught a three-yard TD pass from Tom Brady. Christian Fauria caught a two-point pass from Tom Brady.

Adam Vinatieri kicked a 43-yard field goal with 1:09 left in the fourth quarter.

Adam Vinatieri kicked a 35-yard field goal to win the game in overtime.

———

The New England Patriots defeated the Tennessee Titans 38–30 at Gillette Stadium on 10-05-03

	Q1	Q2	Q3	Q4	Total
Tennessee	6	7	3	14	30
New England	7	0	14	17	38

Craig Hentrich kicked a 48-yard field goal.

Gary Anderson kicked a 43-yard field goal.

Troy Brown caught a 58-yard TD pass from Tom Brady. Adam Vinatieri kicked the extra point.

Steve McNair ran for a one-yard TD. Gary Anderson kicked the extra point.

Antowain Smith ran for a one-yard TD. Adam Vinatieri kicked the extra point.

Gary Anderson kicked a 33-yard field goal.

Mike Cloud scored on a one-yard run. Adam Vinatieri kicked the extra point.

Gary Anderson kicked a 37-yard field goal.

Adam Vinatieri kicked a 48-yard field goal.

Steve McNair ran for another one-yard TD. Gary Anderson kicked the extra point.

Mike Cloud dashed 15 yards for a TD. Adam Vinatieri kicked the extra point.

With 1:49 left, Ty Law returned a Steve McNair pass 65 yards for a TD. Adam Vinatieri kicked the extra point.

Gary Anderson kicked a 41-yard field goal.

———

The New England Patriots shut out the Miami Dolphins 12–0 at Gillette Stadium on 12-07-03

	Q1	Q2	Q3	Q4	Total
Miami	0	0	0	0	0
New England	3	0	0	9	12

Adam Vinatieri kicked a 29-yard field goal.

Tedy Bruschi returned a Jay Fiedler pass five yards for a TD. Adam Vinatieri kicked the extra point.

Jarvis Green sacked Jay Fiedler for a safety.

———

The New England Patriots defeated the Indianapolis Colts 27–24 at Gillette Stadium on 09-09-04

	Q1	Q2	Q3	Q4	Total
Indianapolis	0	17	0	7	24
New England	3	10	14	0	27

Adam Vinatieri kicked a 32-yard field goal.

Mike Vanderjagt kicked a 32-yard field goal.

Dominic Rhodes ran for a three-yard TD. Mike Vanderjagt kicked the extra point.

Deion Branch caught a 16-yard TD pass from Tom Brady. Adam Vinatieri kicked the extra point.

Marvin Harrison caught a three-yard TD pass from Peyton Manning. Mike Vanderjagt kicked the extra point.

Adam Vinatieri kicked a 43-yard field goal on the last play of the first half.

David Patten caught a 25-yard TD pass from Tom Brady.

Adam Vinatieri kicked the extra point.

Daniel Graham caught an eight-yard TD pass from Tom Brady. Adam Vinatieri kicked the extra point.

Brandon Stokley caught a seven-yard TD pass from Peyton Manning. Mike Vanderjagt kicked the extra point.

Willie McGinest sacked Peyton Manning for a 12-yard loss with 49 seconds left in the game.

Mike Vanderjagt was wide right on his 48-yard field-goal attempt with 24 seconds left in the game.

———

The New England Patriots defeated the New Orleans Saints 24–17 at Gillette Stadium on 11-20-05

	Q1	Q2	Q3	Q4	Total
New Orleans	0	7	0	10	17
New England	7	7	7	3	24

Deion Branch caught a two-yard TD pass from Tom Brady. Adam Vinatieri kicked the extra point.

Mike Vrabel caught a one-yard TD pass from Tom Brady. Adam Vinatieri kicked the extra point.

Donte Stallworth caught a seven-yard TD pass from Aaron Brooks. John Carney kicked the extra point.

André Davis hauled in a 60-yard TD pass from Tom Brady. Adam Vinatieri kicked the extra point.

Adam Vinatieri kicked a 37-yard field goal.

Donte Stallworth caught a 12-yard TD pass from Aaron Brooks. John Carney kicked the extra point.

John Carney kicked a 46-yard field goal.

Eugene Wilson intercepted a pass by Aaron Brooks in the end zone on the game's last play.

———

The New England Patriots defeated the Buffalo Bills 19–17 at Gillette Stadium on 09-10-06

	Q1	Q2	Q3	Q4	Total
Buffalo	10	7	0	0	17
New England	7	0	7	5	19

London Fletcher-Baker took a strip-sack fumble five yards for a TD on the first play of the game. Ryan Lindell hit the PAT.

Troy Brown caught a nine-yard TD pass from Tom Brady. Stephen Gostkowski kicked the extra point.

Ryan Lindell kicked a 53-yard field goal.

Anthony Thomas dashed 18 yards for a TD. Ryan Lindell kicked the extra point.

Kevin Faulk caught a 17-yard TD pass from Tom Brady. Stephen Gostkowski kicked the extra point.

Stephen Gostkowski kicked a 32-yard field goal.

Ty Warren sacked J.P. Losman for a safety.

———

The New England Patriots defeated the Chicago Bears 17–13 at Gillette Stadium on 11-26-06

	Q1	Q2	Q3	Q4	Total
Chicago	0	3	0	10	13
New England	0	10	0	7	17

Laurence Maroney scored on a one-yard run. Stephen Gostkowski kicked the extra point. Richard Seymour blocked a 45-yard field-goal attempt by Robbie Gould.

Robbie Gould kicked a 46-yard field goal.

Stephen Gostkowski kicked a 52-yard field goal with six seconds left in the first half.

Cedric Benson ran for a two-yard TD. Robbie Gould kicked the extra point.

Benjamin Watson caught a two-yard TD pass from Tom Brady. Stephen Gostkowski kicked the extra point.

Robbie Gould kicked a 32-yard field goal.

Asante Samuel intercepted his third pass of the game, with 1:52 left, to seal the victory.

———

The New England Patriots destroyed the San Diego Chargers 38–14 at Gillette Stadium on 09-16-07

	Q1	Q2	Q3	Q4	Total
San Diego	0	0	7	7	14
New England	14	10	7	7	38

Benjamin Watson caught a seven-yard TD pass from Tom Brady. Stephen Gostkowski kicked the extra point.

Randy Moss caught a 23-yard TD pass from Tom Brady. Stephen Gostkowski kicked the extra point.

Stephen Gostkowski kicked a 24-yard field goal.

Adalius Thomas returned a Philip Rivers pass 65 yards for a TD. Stephen Gostkowski kicked the extra point.

Lorenzo Neal ran for a one-yard TD. Nate Kaeding kicked the extra point.

Randy Moss caught a 24-yard TD pass from Tom Brady. Stephen Gostkowski kicked the extra point.

Antonio Gates caught a 12-yard TD pass from Philip Rivers. Nate Kaeding kicked the extra point.

Sammy Morris ran for a three-yard TD. Stephen Gostkowski kicked the extra point.

———

The New England Patriots defeated the Philadelphia Eagles 31–28 at Gillette Stadium on 11-25-07

	Q1	Q2	Q3	Q4	Total
Philadelphia	7	14	7	0	28
New England	14	10	0	7	31

Asante Samuel returned a pass by A.J. Feeley 40 yards for a TD. Stephen Gostkowski kicked the extra point.

Brian Westbrook ran for a one-yard TD. David Akers kicked the extra point.

Heath Evans scored on a one-yard run. Stephen Gostkowski kicked the extra point.

Greg Lewis caught a 28-yard TD pass from A.J. Feeley. David Akers kicked the extra point.

Stephen Gostkowski kicked a 23-yard field goal.

Greg Lewis caught an 18-yard TD pass from A.J. Feeley. David Akers kicked the extra point.

Jabar Gaffney caught a 19-yard TD pass from Tom Brady. Stephen Gostkowski kicked the extra point.

Reggie Brown caught an eight-yard TD pass from A.J. Feeley. David Akers kicked the extra point.

Laurence Maroney ran for a four-yard TD. Stephen Gostkowski kicked the extra point.

James Sanders intercepted a pass by A.J. Feeley with 18 seconds left to seal the victory.

Prime Time Games

## 5

The Patriots have played a regular season game on *Monday Night Football* 37 times. Of these, only 15 were played in front of the home crowd, and the Patriots were victorious in only seven. The team went 2–4 in games played at Schaefer Stadium and did not play a regular season game on *Monday Night Football* at Sullivan Stadium. In fact, there was a 14-year gap between games played in front of their home crowd in Foxborough, Massachusetts.

One of the most unusual halftime entertainment shows happened in the Patriots' first appearance on *Monday Night Football.* "Jumpin" Joe Gerlach, former Hungarian Olympic high diver and stuntman, lept out of a hot air balloon that was suspended above midfield onto an air matrress at halftime during the game against the Baltimore Colts at Schaefer Stadium on 11-06-72.

The most unforgettable moment in a *Monday Night Football* game was when Howard Cosell announced to the world that John Lennon had been shot in front of his New York apartment during the Patriots game against the Miami Dolphins in 1980. Patriots tight end Russ Francis hauled in a 38-yard TD pass from Matt Cavanaugh prior to this devasting announcement. The Patriots lost the game 16–13 in overtime at the Orange Bowl on 12-08-80.

The most inspiring moment in a *Monday Night Football* game was the appearance of wheelchair-bound former Patriots wide receiver Darryl Stingley. The home crowd gave him a seven-minute standing ovation during the Patriots' 16–13 overtime loss to the Pittsburgh Steelers at Schaefer Stadium on 09-03-79.

The most memorable victory on *Monday Night Football* was against the Denver Broncos at Invesco Field on 11-03-03

Clinton Portis scored the first TD with a 15-yard run. Deion Branch hauled in a 66-yard TD pass from Tom Brady to tie the score. Jason Elam kicked a 43-yard field goal, and Adam Vinatieri matched him with a 40-yard field goal of his own. Danny Kanell tossed a 1-yard pass to Mike Anderson with 24 seconds left in the first half. Bethel Johnson took the ensuing kickoff 63 yards, and with one second left in the half, Vinatieri kicked a 46-yard field goal.

Tom Brady tossed a six-yard TD pass to Daniel Graham, and with Adam Viantieri's extra point the Patriots had the lead for the first time in the game. Deltha O'Neal returned a punt 57 yards for a TD, and with Micah Knorr's extra point the Broncos were up by four points. (Jason Elam was hurt during the game.) Adam Vinatieri kicked a 28-yard field goal to cut the Denver lead to only one point.

With just under three minutes to go, Patriots long snapper Lonie Paxton snapped the ball over the head of punter Ken Walter. The intentional high snap went out of the end zone for a safety. Although the Broncos scored two points on the play and were going to get the ball back as well, the Patriots coaching staff had full faith that their defense would stop the Broncos' attack. Their faith was rewarded. With 30 seconds left in the game, Tom Brady tossed an 18-yard TD pass to David Givens for the game-winning score. The final score was Patriots 30 Broncos 26. Tom Brady was the AFC Offensive Player of the Week.

The only Patriots player to be the *NFL Player of the Week* for his performance in a game played on Monday Night

Drew Bledsoe threw for 423 yards and two TDs in the 26–23 win over the Miami Dolphins at Foxboro on 11-23-98

Every Patriots player who was the AFC Offensive Player of the Week in a regular season game played on Monday Night

2002 regular season

Tom Brady threw three TD passes in the 30–14 victory over the Pittsburgh Steelers at Gillette Stadium on 09-09-02

2003 championship season

Tom Brady tossed a TD pass with 30 seconds left to defeat the Denver Broncos 30–26 at Invesco Field on 11-03-03

2008 regular season

Matt Cassel threw three TD passes in the 41–7 rout of the Denver Broncos at Gillette Stadium on 10-20-08

The only Patriots player to be the *AFC Special Team Player of the Week* in a game played on Monday Night

Adam Vinatieri kicked four field goals and made two tackles in the 26–23 win over the Miami Dolphins at Foxboro on 11-23-98

Bruce Armstrong (78) and Drew Bledsoe (11)

Every regular season game played by the Patriots on Monday Night

1972 regular season

Lost to the Baltimore Colts 24–17 at Schaefer Stadium on 11-06-72 ("Jumpin" Joe Gerlach performed at halftime)

1975 regular season

Lost to the Miami Dolphins 20–7 at the Orange Bowl on 12-01-75 (Steve Grogan ran for a TD)

1976 regular season

Destroyed the New York Jets 41–7 at Schaefer Stadium on 10-18-76 (The only game the Patriots had five TDs on the ground)

1977 regular season

Lost to the Cleveland Browns 30–27 in overtime at Cleveland Stadium on 09-26-77 (John Smith's 28-yard field goal forced overtime)

1978 regular season

Lost to the Colts 34–27 at Schaefer on 09-18-78 (The Colts' Joe Washington threw and caught a TD and returned a kickoff for a TD)

Lost to the Dolphins 23–3 at the Orange Bowl on 12-18-78 (Patriots set NFL record with 3,165 yards rushing in the year)

1979 regular season

Lost to the Pittsburgh Steelers 16–13 in overtime at Schaefer Stadium on 09-03-79 (Darryl Stingley received seven-minute ovation)

Lost to the Green Bay Packers 27–14 at Lambeau Field on 10-01-79 (Russ Francis had two TD receptions)

1980 regular season

Beat the Broncos 23–14 at Schaefer Stadium on 09-29-80 (WRs Stanley Morgan and Harold Jackson had positive yards rushing)

Lost to the Houston Oilers 38–34 at the Astrodome on 11-10-80 (Steve Grogan was 21-of-28 for 308 yards and three TDs in second half)

Lost to Miami 16–13 in overtime at the Orange Bowl on 12-08-80 (Russ Francis snared a TD pass away from two defenders)

1981 regular season

Lost to the Dallas Cowboys 35–21 at Schaefer Stadium on 09-21-81 (Cowboys RB Tony Dorsett ran for a 75-yard TD)

1985 regular season

Lost to the Dolphins 30–27 at the Orange Bowl on 12-16-85 (Cedric Jones took a fumbled kickoff return 15 yards for a TD)

1986 regular season

Beat Miami 34–27 at the Orange Bowl on 12-22-86 (Stanley Morgan caught a game-winning TD pass) (The Game of the Year)

1987 regular season

Lost to the New York Jets 43–24 at the Meadowlands on 09-21-87 (Andre Tippett returned a fumble 29 yards for a TD)

Beat the Miami Dolphins 24–10 at Joe Robbie Stadium on 12-28-87 (Steve Nelson's last regular season game)

Steve Nelson

1995 regular season
Beat the Buffalo Bills 27–14 at Foxboro Stadium on 10-23-95 (Matt Bahr kicked two field goals and three extra points and pooched a punt)

1997 regular season
Lost to the Denver Broncos 34–13 at Mile High Stadium on 10-06-97 (Keith Byars had a 44-yard TD reception)

Lost to the Green Bay Packers 28–10 at Foxboro Stadium on 10-27-97 (Terry Glenn had 163 yards receiving)

Beat the Miami Dolphins 14–12 at Pro Player Stadium on 12-22-97 (Lawyer Milloy's fourth-down interception sealed the victory)

1998 regular season
Lost to the Denver Broncos 27–21 at Mile High Stadium on 09-07-98 (Tom Tupa made a tackle after a blocked field-goal attempt)

Lost to the Jets 24–14 at Foxboro on 10-19-98 (Robert Edwards had a career-high 104 yards rushing in consecutive games)

Beat Miami 26–23 at Foxboro on 11-23-98 (Drew Bledsoe threw a game-winning TD with a broken finger) (The Game of the Year)

1999 regular season
Lost to the New York Jets 24–17 at Foxboro on 11-15-99 (Former Patriots WR Ray Lucas threw two TD passes for the New York Jets)

2000 regular season
Lost to the New York Jets 20–19 at the Meadowlands on 09-11-00 (Eric Bjornson caught a 6-yard TD pass)

Beat the Kansas City Chiefs 30–24 at Foxboro Stadium on 12-04-00 (NT Henry Thomas was used in the offensive backfield)

2002 regular season
Beat the Steelers 30–14 at Gillette Stadium on 09-09-02 (Roman Phifer had 12 tackles and a fumble recovery) (The Game of the Year)

Lost to Tennessee 24–7 at the Coliseum on 12-16-02 (Tom Brady ran 10 yards for a TD)

2003 championship season
Beat the Denver Broncos 30–26 at Invesco Field on 11-03-03 (Tom Brady was the AFC Offensive Player of the Week)

2004 championship season
Beat the Chiefs 27–19 at Arrowhead Stadium on 11-22-04 (Rodney Harrison returned a pass 12 yards from the end zone with 54 seconds left in the half)

Lost to the Miami Dolphins 29–28 at Pro Player Stadium on 12-20-04 (Wes Welker had 226 return yards for the Dolphins)

2005 regular season
Lost to Indianapolis 40–21 at Gillette Stadium on 11-07-05 (Tom Brady threw TD passes to D. Branch, D. Givens, and T. Brown)

Beat the New York Jets 31–21 at the Meadowlands on 12-26-05 (LB/TE Mike Vrabel caught two TD passes)

2006 regular season
Destroyed the Vikings 31–7 at the Metrodome on 10-30-06 (Ben Watson caught a nine-yard TD with 24 seconds left in the first half)

2007 undefeated regular season
Blew out the Bengals 34–13 at Paul Brown Stadium on 10-01-07 (For third time in four games, the Patriots only punted once)

Beat the Ravens 27–24 at M&T Bank Stadium on 12-03-07 (Tom Brady had a 12-yard run on fourth-and-6 to set up the final TD)

2008 regular season
Destroyed the Broncos 41–7 at Gillette Stadium on 10-20-08 (Matt Cassel threw three TDs and completed 75% of his passes)

The 10 most memorable moments from games played by the Patriots on Monday Night
The Patriots displayed their 2001 World Championship banner before beating the Steelers by 16 points on 09-09-01

Drew Bledsoe threw a 25-yard TD pass with a broken index finger with 29 seconds left in the three-point win on 11-23-98

Stanley Morgan caught a 30-yard game-winning TD pass with 44 seconds left in the seven-point win over Miami on 12-22-86

Russ Francis caught a TD pass just before Howard Cosell announced that John Lennon had been shot on 12-08-80

Tom Brady threw an 18-yard TD pass to David Givens with 30 seconds left in the four-point win over Denver on 11-03-03

Long snapper Lonie Paxton snapped the ball out of the end zone for a safety in the 30–26 win over Denver on 11-03-03

Jabar Gaffney caught an eight-yard TD pass with 44 seconds left in the three-point win over the Ravens on 12-03-07

Steve Grogan had a 41-yard TD run and 103 yards rushing along with advancing a fumble for a TD in the 41–7 win on 10-18-76

Larry Whigham forced Lamar Thomas to fumble which forced three laterals on the last play of the two-point win on 12-22-97

Former Patriot receiver Darryl Stingley received a seven-minute standing ovation at Schaefer Stadium on 09-03-79

The scoring summary of every Patriots victory in a regular season game played on Monday Night

The New England Patriots defeated the New York Jets 41–7 at Schaefer Stadium on 10-18-76

	Q1	Q2	Q3	Q4	Total
Jets	0	0	7	0	7
Patriots	7	13	21	0	41

Andy Johnson ran for a six-yard TD. John Smith kicked the extra point.

Steve Grogan advanced a fumble by Don Calhoun six yards for a TD. John Smith kicked the extra point.

Andy Johnson caught a 10-yard TD pass from Steve Grogan. The extra-point attempt was blocked.

Steve Grogan dashed 41 yards for a TD. John Smith kicked the extra point.

Clark Gaines caught a 12-yard TD pass from Joe Namath. Pat Leahy kicked the extra point.

Sam Cunningham ran for a 14-yard TD. John Smith kicked the extra point.

Don Calhoun ran for an 11-yard TD. John Smith kicked the extra point.

_____

The New England Patriots defeated the Denver Broncos 23–14 at Schaefer Stadium on 09-29-80

	Q1	Q2	Q3	Q4	Total
Broncos	7	0	7	0	14
Patriots	3	7	7	6	23

Haven Moses caught a 17-yard TD pass from Matt Robinson. Fred Steinfort kicked the extra point.

John Smith kicked a 26-yard field goal.

Vegas Ferguson ran for a two-yard TD. John Smith kicked the extra point.

Otis Armstrong ran for an eight-yard TD. Fred Steinfort kicked the extra point.

Stanley Morgan hauled in a 45-yard TD pass from Steve Grogan. John Smith kicked the extra point.

John Smith kicked a 19-yard field goal and a 36-yard field goal.

_____

The New England Patriots defeated the Miami Dolphins 34–27 at the Orange Bowl on 12-22-86

	Q1	Q2	Q3	Q4	Total
Patriots	7	6	7	14	34
Dolphins	0	10	17	0	27

Stanley Morgan caught a 22-yard TD pass from Tony Eason. Tony Franklin kicked the extra point.

Tony Franklin kicked a 47-yard field goal.

Fuad Reveiz kicked a 42-yard field goal.

Tony Franklin kicked a 44-yard field goal.

Bruce Hardy caught a one-yard TD pass from Dan Marino. Fuad Reveiz kicked the extra point.

Fuad Reveiz kicked a 21-yard field goal.

Mark Clayton caught a 32-yard TD pass from Dan Marino. Fuad Reveiz kicked the extra point.

Steve Grogan ran for a seven-yard TD. Tony Franklin kicked the extra point.

Mark Clayton caught a 19-yard TD pass from Dan Marino. Fuad Reveiz kicked the extra point.

Tony Collins caught a 12-yard TD pass from Steve Grogan. Tony Franklin kicked the extra point.

Stanley Morgan hauled in a 30-yard TD pass from Steve Grogan. Tony Franklin kicked the extra point.

_____

The New England Patriots defeated the Miami Dolphins 24–10 at Joe Robbie Stadium on 12-28-87

	Q1	Q2	Q3	Q4	Total
Patriots	14	10	0	0	24
Dolphins	3	0	0	7	10

Irving Fryar caught a three-yard TD pass from Steve Grogan. Tony Franklin kicked the extra point.

Fuad Reveiz kicked a 47-yard field goal.

Stephen Starring caught a 34-yard TD pass from Steve Grogan. Tony Franklin kicked the extra point.

Tony Collins ran for a five-yard TD. Tony Franklin kicked the extra point.

Tony Franklin kicked a 31-yard field goal.

James Pruitt caught a nine-yard TD pass from Dan Marino. Fuad Reveiz kicked the extra point.

_____

The New England Patriots defeated the Buffalo Bills 27–14 at Foxboro Stadium on 10-23-95

	Q1	Q2	Q3	Q4	Total
Buffalo	6	8	0	0	14
New England	7	14	3	3	27

Curtis Martin dashed 20 yards for a TD. Matt Bahr kicked the extra point.

Steve Christie kicked a 23-yard field goal.

Steve Christie kicked another 23-yard field goal.

Vincent Brisby caught a five-yard TD pass from Drew Bledsoe. Matt Bahr kicked the extra point.

Dave Meggett ran for a three-yard TD. Matt Bahr kicked the extra point.

Bill Brooks hauled in a 45-yard TD pass from Jim Kelly. Carwell Gardner caught a two-point pass from Jim Kelly.

Matt Bahr kicked a 39-yard field goal and a 24-yard field goal.

_____

The New England Patriots defeated the Miami Dolphins 14–12 at Pro Player Stadium on 12-22-97

	Q1	Q2	Q3	Q4	Total
Patriots	0	0	7	7	14
Dolphins	3	3	0	6	12

Olindo Mare kicked a 50-yard field goal.

Olindo Mare kicked a 41-yard field goal.

Marrio Grier ran for a two-yard TD. Adam Vinatieri kicked the extra point.

Dave Meggett ran for a five-yard TD. Adam Vinatieri kicked the extra point.

Lamar Thomas caught an eight-yard TD pass from Dan Marino. The two point pass attempt was incomplete.

_____

The New England Patriots defeated the Miami Dolphins 26–23 at Foxboro Stadium on 11-23-98

	Q1	Q2	Q3	Q4	Total
Dolphins	7	7	3	6	23
Patriots	7	3	6	10	26

Oronde Gadsden caught a 35-yard TD pass from Dan Marino. Olindo Mare kicked the extra point.

Ben Coates caught an eight-yard TD pass from Drew Bledsoe. Adam Vinatieri kicked the extra point.

Oronde Gadsden caught an 11-yard TD pass from Dan Marino. Olindo Mare kicked the extra point.

Adam Vinatieri kicked a 25-yard field goal.

Adam Vinatieri kicked a 44-yard field goal.

Olindo Mare kicked a 21-yard field goal.

Adam Vinatieri kicked a 45-yard field goal.

Adam Vinatieri kicked a 24-yard field goal.

Karim Abdul-Jabbar ran for 4-yard TD. The two-point pass attempt was incomplete.

Shawn Jefferson grabbed a 25-yard TD pass from Drew Bledsoe. Adam Vinatieri kicked the extra point.

The New England Patriots defeated the Kansas City Chiefs 30–24 at Foxboro Stadium on 12-04-00

	Q1	Q2	Q3	Q4	Total
Chiefs	3	7	0	14	24
Patriots	10	10	7	3	30

Adam Vinatieri kicked a 48-yard field goal.

Todd Peterson kicked a 42-yard field goal.

Kevin Faulk ran for a one-yard TD. Adam Vinatieri kicked the extra point.

Derrick Alexander hauled in an 81-yard TD pass from Elvis Grbac. Todd Peterson kicked the extra point.

Troy Brown caught a 17-yard TD pass from Drew Bledsoe. Adam Vinatieri kicked the extra point.

Adam Vinatieri kicked a 53-yard field goal on the last play of the first half.

Jermaine Wiggins caught a one-yard TD pass from Drew Bledsoe. Adam Vinatieri kicked the extra point.

Tony Gonzalez caught a four-yard TD pass from Elvis Grbac. Todd Peterson kicked the extra point.

Adam Vinatieri kicked a 27-yard field goal.

Kevin Lockett caught a 19-yard TD pass from Elvis Grbac. Todd Peterson kicked the extra point.

———

The New England Patriots defeated the Pittsburgh Steelers 30–14 at Gillette Stadium on 09-09-02

	Q1	Q2	Q3	Q4	Total
Pittsburgh	7	0	0	7	14
New England	7	3	17	3	30

Christian Fauria caught a four-yard TD pass from Tom Brady. Adam Vinatieri kicked the extra point.

Hines Ward caught a 13-yard TD pass from Kordell Stewart. Todd Peterson kicked the extra point.

Adam Vinatieri kicked a 45-yard field goal.

Donald Hayes hauled in a 40-yard TD pass from Tom Brady. Adam Vinatieri kicked the extra point.

Deion Branch caught a 22-yard TD pass from Tom Brady. Adam Vinatieri kicked the extra point.

Adam Vinatieri kicked a 28-yard field goal.

Adam Vinatieri kicked a 27-yard field goal.

Kordell Stewart ran a QB sneak for a one-yard TD on the last play of the game. Todd Peterson kicked the extra point.

———

The New England Patriots defeated the Denver Broncos 30–26 at Invesco Field on 11-03-03

	Q1	Q2	Q3	Q4	Total
Patriots	7	6	7	10	30
Broncos	7	10	7	2	26

Clinton Portis ran for a 15-yard TD. Jason Elam kicked the extra point.

Deion Branch hauled in a 66-yard TD pass from Tom Brady. Adam Vinatieri kicked the extra point.

Jason Elam kicked a 43-yard field goal.

Adam Vinatieri kicked a 40-yard field goal.

Mike Anderson caught a one-yard TD pass from Danny Kanell. Micah Knorr kicked the extra point.

Adam Vinatieri kicked a 46-yard field goal.

Daniel Graham caught a six-yard TD pass from Tom Brady. Adam Vinatieri kicked the extra point.

Deltha O'Neal returned a fumble 57 yards for a TD. Micah Knorr kicked the extra point.

Adam Vinatieri kicked a 28-yard field goal.

Long snapper Lonie Paxton snapped the ball out of the end zone for a two point safety.

David Givens caught an 18-yard TD pass from Tom Brady with 30 seconds left. Adam Vinatieri kicked the extra point.

———

The New England Patriots defeated the Kansas City Chiefs 27–19 at Arrowhead Stadium on 11-22-04

	Q1	Q2	Q3	Q4	Total
Patriots	7	10	7	3	27
Chiefs	10	0	3	6	19

Corey Dillon ran for a five-yard TD. Adam Vinatieri kicked the extra point.

Lawrence Tynes kicked a 44-yard field goal.

Eddie Kennison hauled in a 65-yard TD pass from Trent Green. Lawrence Tynes kicked the extra point.

Corey Dillon bulled for a one-yard TD. Adam Vinatieri kicked the extra point.

Adam Vinatieri kicked a 37-yard field goal.

Lawrence Tynes kicked a 24-yard field goal.

Deion Branch caught a 26-yard TD pass from Tom Brady. Adam Vinatieri kicked the extra point.

Eddie Kennison caught a 26-yard TD pass from Trent Green. The two-point conversion attempt was incomplete.

Adam Vinatieri kicked a 28-yard field goal.

———

The New England Patriots defeated the New York Jets 31–21 at the Meadowlands on 12-26-05

	Q1	Q2	Q3	Q4	Total
Patriots	7	14	7	3	31
Jets	7	0	0	14	21

Tight end eligible (LB) Mike Vrabel caught a 1-yard TD pass from Tom Brady. Adam Vinatieri kicked the extra point.

Jets cornerback Ty Law returned an interception 74 yards for a TD. Mike Nugent kicked the extra point.

Mike Vrabel caught a two-yard TD pass from Tom Brady. Adam Vinatieri kicked the extra point.

Corey Dillon ran for a one-yard TD. Adam Viantieri kicked the extra point.

Corey Dillon ran for another one-yard TD. Adam Vinatieri kicked the extra point.

Laveranues Coles caught an 11-yard TD pass from Brooks Bollinger. Mike Nugent kicked the extra point.

Adam Vinatieri kicked a 26-yard field goal.

Laveranues Coles caught a 27-yard TD pass from Vinny Testaverde. Mike Nugent kicked the extra point.

———

The New England Patriots defeated the Minnesota Vikings 31–7 at the Metrodome on 10-30-06

	Q1	Q2	Q3	Q4	Total
Patriots	7	10	14	0	31
Vikings	0	0	7	0	7

Reche Caldwell caught a six-yard TD pass from Tom Brady. Stephen Gostkowski kicked the extra point.

Stephen Gostkowski kicked a 23-yard field goal.

Benjamin Watson caught a nine-yard TD pass from Tom Brady. Stephen Gostkowski kicked the extra point.

Mewelde Moore returned a punt 71 yards for a TD. Ryan Longwell kicked the extra point.

Troy Brown caught a seven-yard TD pass from Tom Brady. Stephen Gostkowski kicked the extra point.

Chad Jackson caught a 10-yard TD pass from Tom Brady. Stephen Gostkowski kicked the extra point.

———

The New England Patriots defeated the Cincinnati Bengals 34–13 at Paul Brown Stadium on 10-01-07

	Q1	Q2	Q3	Q4	Total
Patriots	10	7	7	10	34
Bengals	0	7	3	3	13

Stephen Gostkowski kicked a 31-yard field goal.

Tight end eligible (LB) Mike Vrabel caught a one-yard TD pass from Tom Brady. Stephen Gostkowski kicked the exta point.

T.J. Houshmandzadeh caught a one-yard TD pass from Carson Palmer. Shayne Graham kicked the extra point.

Randy Moss caught a seven-yard TD pass from Tom Brady. Stephen Gostkowski kicked the extra point.

Sammy Morris ran for a seven-yard TD. Stephen Gostkowski kicked the extra point.

Shayne Graham kicked a 40-yard field goal.

Stephen Gostkowski kicked a 36-yard field goal.

Shayne Graham kicked a 48-yard field goal.

Randy Moss caught a 14-yard TD pass from Tom Brady. Stephen Gostkowski kicked the extra point.

———

The New England Patriots defeated the Baltimore Ravens 27–24 at M&T Bank Stadium on 12-03-07

	Q1	Q2	Q3	Q4	Total
Patriots	3	7	7	10	27
Ravens	7	3	7	7	24

Stephen Gostkowski kicked a 21-yard field goal.

Derrick Mason caught a four-yard TD pass from Kyle Boller. Matt Stover kicked the extra point.

Matt Stover kicked a 29-yard field goal.

Heath Evans bulled for a one-yard TD. Stephen Gostkowski kicked the extra point.

Willis McGahee dashed for a 17-yard TD. Matt Stover kicked the extra point.

Randy Moss caught a three-yard TD pass from Tom Brady. Stephen Gostkowski kicked the extra point.

Daniel Wilcox caught a one-yard TD pass from Kyle Boller. Matt Stover kicked the extra point.

Stephen Gostkowski kicked a 38-yard field goal.

(The Patriots had third-and-10, fourth-and-1, fourth-and-6, and fourth-and-5 on their last drive with less than two minutes to go in the game.)

Jabar Gaffney caught an eight-yard TD pass from Tom Brady with 44 seconds left. Stephen Gostkowski kicked the extra point.

———

The New England Patriots destroyed the Denver Broncos 41–7 at Gillette Stadium on 10-20-08

	Q1	Q2	Q3	Q4	Total
Broncos	0	0	0	7	7
Patriots	6	14	14	7	41

Stephen Gostkowski kicked a 31-yard field goal.

Stephen Gostkowski kicked a 40-yard field goal.

Sammy Morris ran for a four-yard TD. Stephen Gostkowski kicked the extra point.

Randy Moss caught a 13-yard TD pass from Matt Cassel. Stephen Gostkowski kicked the extra point.

Randy Moss caught a 27-yard TD pass from Matt Cassel. Stephen Gostkowski kicked the extra point.

Wes Welker grabbed a six-yard TD pass from Matt Cassel. Stephen Gostkowski kicked the extra point.

Daniel Graham caught a 10-yard TD pass from Jay Cutler. Matt Prater kicked the extra point.

Ben Jarvus Green-Ellis scored on a one-yard TD run. Stephen Gostkowski kicked the extra point.

Fumble Advancement for a TD
The only Patriots player who has advanced a teammate's fumble for a TD in a game played on Monday Night
Steve Grogan advanced a fumble by Don Calhoun six yards for a TD in the 41–7 rout of the Jets at Schaefer on 10-18-76

Every Patriots player who has scored the game-winning TD
Every Patriots player who has caught a TD pass with less than one minute left in a game played on Monday Night
Stanley Morgan caught a 30-yard TD pass with 44 seconds left to defeat the Dolphins 34–27 at the Orange Bowl on 12-22-86

Shawn Jefferson caught a 25-yard TD pass with 29 seconds left to defeat the Dolphins 26–23 at Foxboro Stadium on 11-23-98

David Givens caught an 18-yard TD pass with 30 seconds left to defeat the Broncos 30–26 at Invesco Field on 11-03-03

Jabar Gaffney caught an eight-yard TD pass with 44 seconds left to defeat the Ravens 27–24 at M&T Bank Stadium on 12-03-07

Blocked Field-Goal Attempts
Every Patriots player who has blocked a field-goal attempt in a regular season game played on Monday Night
Mel Lunsford blocked a 39-yard field-goal attempt by Don Cockroft in the 30–27 overtime loss to the Browns at Cleveland on 09-26-77

Chad Eaton blocked a 38-yard field-goal attempt by John Hall in the 24–14 loss to the New York Jets at Foxboro Stadium on 10-19-98

Last second field goals
Every Patriots kicker who has hit a field goal with one second left in the first half of a game played on Monday Night
John Smith hit a 32-yard field goal with one tick left in the half in the 16–13 overtime loss to Pittsburgh at Schaefer Stadium on 09-03-79

Adam Vinatieri hit a 53-yard field goal with one tick left in the half in the 30–24 win over the Chiefs at Foxboro on 12-04-00

The Longest

The Patriots player with the longest run from scrimmage in a regular season game played on Monday Night
Jess Phillips rumbled for a 46-yard gain in the 41–7 rout of the New York Jets at Schaefer Stadium on 10-18-76

The Patriots player with the longest reception in a regular season game played on Monday Night

Deion Branch caught a 66-yard TD pass in the 30–26 comeback win over Denver at Invesco Field on 11-03-03

The Patriots player with the longest completion in a regular season game played on Monday Night

Tom Brady tossed a 66-yard TD pass in the 30–26 win over the Broncos at Invesco Field on 11-03-03

The Patriots player with the longest interception return in a regular season game played on Monday Night

Ellis Hobbs returned a pass by Brooks Bollinger 70 yards in the 31–7 rout of the Vikings at the Metrodome on 10-30-06

The Patriots player with the longest punt return in a regular season game played on Monday Night

Mike Haynes returned a punt 46 yards in the 30–27 overtime loss to the Browns at Cleveland on 09-26-77

The Patriots player with the longest kickoff return in a regular season game played on Monday Night

Kevin Faulk returned a kickoff 95 yards in the 24–17 loss to the New York Jets at Foxboro Stadium on 11-15-99

The Patriots player with the longest field goal in a regular season game played on Monday Night

Adam Vinatieri hit a 53-yard field goal, on the last play of the half, in the 30–24 win over the Chiefs at Foxboro on 12-04-00

The Patriots player with the longest punt in a regular season game played on Monday Night

Tom Tupa booted it 73 yards in the 34–13 loss to the Denver Broncos at Mile High Stadium on 10-06-97

The Patriots Special Team player with the longest fumble return in a regular season game played on Monday Night

Cedric Jones took a fumbled kickoff return 15 yards for a TD in the 30–27 loss to Miami at the Orange Bowl on 12-16-85

The Patriots Defensive player with the longest fumble return in a regular season game played on Monday Night

Andre Tippett returned a fumble 29 yards for a TD in the 43–24 loss to the New York Jets at the Meadowlands on 09-21-87

The Most

The Patriots Quarterback with the most yards passing in a regular season game played on Monday Night

Drew Bledsoe threw for 423 yards in the 26–23 win over the Miami Dolphins at Foxboro Stadium on 11-23-98

The Patriots Receiver with the most yards receiving in a regular season game played on Monday Night

Terry Glenn had 163 yards receiving in the 28–10 loss to the Green Bay Packers at Foxboro Stadium on 10-27-97

The Patriots player with the most yards rushing in a regular season game played on Monday Night

Sammy Morris ran for 138 yards in the 41–7 rout of the Denver Broncos at Gillette Stadium on 10-20-08

The Patriots Quarterback with the most yards rushing in a regular season game played on Monday Night

Steve Grogan ran for 103 yards in the 41–7 rout of the New York Jets at Schaefer Stadium on 10-18-76

The Patriots Receiver with the most yards rushing in a regular season game played on Monday Night

Terry Glenn had 37 yards rushing in the 30–24 win over the Kansas City Chiefs at Arrowhead Stadium on 12-04-00

The Patriots players with the most special team return yards in a regular season game played on Monday Night

1998 regular season

Derrick Cullors had 170 kickoff return yards in the 27–21 loss to the Denver Broncos at Mile High Stadium on 09-07-98

1999 regular season

Kevin Faulk had 170 kickoff return yards in the 24–17 loss to the New York Jets at Foxboro Stadium on 11-15-99

The progression of the most points scored by a Patriots player in a regular season game played on Monday Night

Three points were scored by Charlie Gogolak in the 24–17 loss to the Baltimore Colts at Schaefer Stadium on 11-06-72

6 points were scored by Jim Plunkett in the 24–17 loss to the Baltimore Colts at Schaefer Stadium on 11-06-72

6 points were scored by Carl Garrett in the 24–17 loss to the Baltimore Colts at Schaefer Stadium on 11-06-72

6 points were scored by Steve Grogan in the 20–7 loss to the Miami Dolphins at the Orange Bowl on 12-01-75

6 points were scored by Andy Johnson in the 41–7 rout of the New York Jets at Schaefer Stadium on 10-18-76

6 points were scored by Steve Grogan in the 41–7 rout of the New York Jets at Schaefer Stadium on 10-18-76

12 points were scored by Andy Johnson in the 41–7 rout of the New York Jets at Schaefer Stadium on 10-18-76

12 points were scored by Steve Grogan in the 41–7 rout of the New York Jets at Schaefer Stadium on 10-18-76

12 points were scored by Russ Francis in the 27–14 loss to the Green Bay Packers at Lambeau Field on 10-01-79

12 points were scored by Russ Francis in the 38–34 loss to the Houston Oilers at the Astrodome on 11-10-80

12 points were scored by Stanley Morgan in the 34–27 win over the Miami Dolphins at the Orange Bowl on 12-22-86

13 points were scored by Adam Vinatieri in the 20–19 loss to the New York Jets at the Meadowlands on 09-11-00

Every regular season game played by the Patriots on Thanksgiving Day
1984 regular season
Lost to Dallas 20–17 at Texas Stadium on 11-22-84 (Tony Eason had a one-yard QB sneak for a TD with two minutes left)

2000 regular season
Lost to the Detroit Lions 34–9 at the Pontiac Silverdome on 11-23-00 (Adam Vinatieri kicked three field goals)

2002 regular season
Beat the Detroit Lions 20–12 at Ford Field on 11-28-02 (Tedy Bruschi returned a Joey Harrington pass 27 yards for a TD)

The Longest

The Patriots player with the longest run from scrimmage in a regular season game played on Thanksgiving Day
Craig James dashed for a 43-yard gain in the 20–17 loss to the Dallas Cowboys at Texas Stadium on 11-22-84

The Patriots player with the longest reception in a regular season game played on Thanksgiving Day
Derrick Ramsey caught a 27-yard pass in the 20–17 loss to the Dallas Cowboys at Texas Stadium on 11-22-84

The Patriots player with the longest completion in a regular season game played on Thanksgiving Day
Tony Eason threw a 27-yard pass to Derrick Ramsey in the 20–17 loss to the Cowboys at Texas Stadium on 11-22-84

The Patriots Defensive Back with the longest interception return in a regular season game played on Thanksgiving Day
Raymond Clayborn returned a Danny White pass 17 yards in the 20–17 loss to the Cowboys at Texas Stadium on 11-22-84

The Patriots Linebacker with the longest interception return in a regular season game played on Thanksgiving Day
Tedy Bruschi returned a Joey Harrington pass 27 yards for a TD in the 20–12 win over the Lions at Ford Field on 11-28-02

The Patriots player with the longest punt return in a regular season game played on Thanksgiving Day
Irving Fryar returned a punt 14 yards in the 20–17 loss to the Dallas Cowboys at Texas Stadium on 11-22-84

The Patriots player with the longest kickoff return in a regular season game played on Thanksgiving Day
Deion Branch returned a kickoff 63 yards in the 20–12 victory over the Detroit Lions at Ford Field on 11-28-02

The Patriots Kicker with the longest field goal in a regular season game played on Thanksgiving Day
Adam Vinatieri kicked a 47-yard field goal in the 34–9 loss to the Detroit Lions at the Silverdome on 11-23-00

The Patriots player with the longest punt in a regular season game played on Thanksgiving Day

Lee Johnson booted it 62 yards in the 34–9 loss to the Detroit Lions at the Pontiac Silverdome on 11-23-00

The Most

The Patriots player with the most yards rushing in a regular season game played on Thanksgiving Day

Craig James had 112 yards rushing in the 20–17 loss to the Dallas Cowboys at Texas Stadium on 11-22-84

The Patriots player with the most yards passing in a regular season game played on Thanksgiving Day

Tom Brady had 210 yards passing in the 20–12 victory over the Detroit Lions at Ford Field on 11-28-02

The Patriots player with the most yards receiving in a regular season game played on Thanksgiving Day

Troy Brown had 111 yards receiving in the 20–12 victory over the Detroit Lions at Ford Field on 11-28-02

The Patriots player with the most special team return yards in a regular season game played on Thanksgiving Day

Deion Branch had 141 special team return yards in the 20–12 victory over the Detroit Lions at Ford Field on 11-28-02

The progression of the *most points scored* by a Patriots player in a regular season game played on Thanksgiving Day

3 points were scored by Tony Franklin in the 20–17 loss to the Dallas Cowboys at Texas Stadium on 11-22-84

6 points were scored by Derrick Ramsey in the 20–17 loss to the Dallas Cowboys at Texas Stadium on 11-22-84

6 points were scored by Tony Eason in the 20-17 loss to the Dallas Cowboys at Texas Stadium on 11-22-84

9 points were scored by Adam Vinatieri in the 34-9 loss to the Detroit Lions at the Pontiac Silverdome on 11-23-00

Every regular season game played by the New England Patriots on Thursday Night

1979 regular season
Lost to the Miami Dolphins 39–24 at the Orange Bowl on 11-29-79 (Carlos Pennywell caught a 13-yard TD pass on the last play)

1986 regular season
Defeated the New York Jets 20–6 at Shea Stadium on 09-11-86 (Craig James tossed HB Option TD pass to Tony Collins)

1990 regular season
Lost to the Dolphins 17–10 at Joe Robbie Stadium on 10-18-90 (Marvin Allen caught a four-yard TD pass on fourth down)

2004 championship season
Defeated the Indianapolis Colts 27–24 at Gillette Stadium on 09-09-04 (Deion B., David P. and Daniel G. caught TD passes)

2005 regular season
Defeated the Oakland Raiders 30–20 at Gillette Stadium on 09-08-05 (The Patriots had a PAT blocked and a punt blocked)

2008 regular season
Lost to the Jets 34–31 in overtime at Gillette Stadium on 11-13-08 (Randy Moss caught a 16-yard TD to end the fourth quarter and force overtime)

The scoring summary of every Patriots victory in a regular season game played on Thursday Night

The New England Patriots defeated the New York Jets 20–6 at Shea Stadium on 09-11-86

	Q1	Q2	Q3	Q4	Total
NE Patriots	7	0	10	3	20
New York Jets	0	6	0	0	6

Tony Collins caught a six-yard TD pass from Tony Eason. Tony Franklin kicked the extra point.

Pat Leahy kicked a 33-yard field goal.

Pat Leahy kicked a 47-yard field goal.

Tony Collins caught a 10-yard HB option TD pass from Craig James. Tony Franklin kicked the extra point.

Tony Franklin kicked a 45-yard field goal.

Tony Franklin kicked a 42-yard field goal.

The New England Patriots defeated the Indianapolis Colts 27–24 at Gillette Stadium on 09-09-04

	Q1	Q2	Q3	Q4	Total
Colts	0	17	0	7	24
Patriots	3	10	14	0	27

Dominic Rhodes ran for a three-yard TD. Mike Vanderjagt kicked the extra point.

Deion Branch caught a 16-yard TD pass from Tom Brady. Adam Vinatieri kicked the extra point.

Marvin Harrison caught a three-yard TD pass from Peyton Manning. Mike Vanderjagt kicked the extra point.

Adam Vinatieri kicked a 43-yard field goal on the last play of the first half.

David Patten caught a 25-yard TD pass from Tom Brady. Adam Vinatieri kicked the extra point.

Daniel Graham grabbed an eight-yard TD pass from Tom Brady. Adam Vinatieri kicked the extra point.

Brandon Stockley caught a seven-yard TD pass from Peyton Manning. Mike Vanderjagt kicked the extra point.

———

The New England Patriots defeated the Oakland Raiders 30–20 at Gillette Stadium on 09-08-05

	Q1	Q2	Q3	Q4	Total
Raiders	7	7	0	6	20
Patriots	10	7	6	7	30

Courtney Anderson caught a two-yard TD pass from Kerry Collins. Sebastian Janikowski kicked the extra point.

Adam Vinatieri kicked a 26-yard field goal.

Deion Branch caught an 18-yard TD pass from Tom Brady. Adam Vinatieri kicked the extra point.

Randy Moss corralled a 73-yard TD pass from Kerry Collins. Sebastian Janikowski kicked the extra point.

Tim Dwight caught a five-yard TD pass from Tom Brady. Adam Vinatieri kicked the extra point.

Corey Dillon ran for an eight-yard TD. Adam Vinatieri kicked the extra point.

Corey Dillon ran for a five-yard TD. Adam Vinatieri kicked the extra point.

Courtney Anderson caught a five-yard TD pass from Kerry Collins. The two-point conversion pass failed.

The Longest

The Patriots player with the longest run from scrimmage in a regular season game played on Thursday Night
Corey Dillon bolted for a 38-yard gain in the 27–24 victory over the Indianapolis Colts at Gillette on 09-09-04

The Patriots player with the longest reception in a regular season game played on Thursday Night
Sam Aiken caught a 43-yard pass from Matt Cassel in the 34–31 overtime loss to the Jets at Gillette Stadium on 11-13-08

The Patriots Quarterback with the longest completion in a regular season game played on Thursday Night
Steve Grogan threw a 38-yard TD to Stanley Morgan in the 39–24 loss to Miami at the Orange Bowl on 11-29-79

The Patriots Defensive Back with the longest interception return in a regular season game played on Thursday Night
Prentice McCray had a 22-yard interception return in the 39–24 loss to the Dolphins at the Orange Bowl on 11-29-79

The Patriots Linebacker with the longest interception return in a regular season game played on Thursday Night
Tedy Bruschi returned a Peyton Manning pass five yards in the 27–24 win over the Colts at Gillette Stadium on 09-09-04

The Patriots player with the longest punt return in a regular season game played on Thursday Night
Tim Dwight had a 27-yard punt return in the 30–20 victory over the Oakland Raiders at Gillette Stadium on 09-11-86

The Patriots player with the longest kickoff return in a regular season game played on Thursday Night
Ellis Hobbs had a 37-yard kickoff return in the 30–20 victory over the Oakland Raiders at Gillette Stadium on 09-08-05

The Patriots Kicker with the longest field goal in a regular season game played on Thursday Night

Tony Franklin kicked a 45-yard field goal in the 20–6 victory over the New York Jets at Shea Stadium on 09-11-86

The Patriots player with the longest punt in a regular season game played on Thursday Night

Rich Camarillo punted the football 56 yards in the 20–6 win over the New York Jets at the Meadowlands on 09-11-86

The Most

The Patriots player with the most yards rushing in a regular season game played on Thursday Night

Corey Dillon had 86 yards rushing in the 27–24 victory over the Indianapolis Colts at Gillette Stadium on 09-09-04

The Patriots Quarterback with the most yards passing in a regular season game played on Thursday Night

Matt Cassel threw for 400 yards in the 34–31 overtime loss to the New York Jets at Gillette Stadium on 11-13-08

The Patriots Receiver with the most yards receiving in a regular season game played on Thursday Night

Stanley Morgan had 124 yards receiving in the 39–24 loss to the Miami Dolphins at the Orange Bowl on 11-29-79

The Patriots player with the most special team return yards in a regular season game played on Thursday Night

Ellis Hobbs had 135 kickoff return yards in the 34–31 overtime loss to the New York Jets at Gillette Stadium on 11-13-08

The progression of the most points scored by a Patriots player in a regular season game played on Thursday Night

6 points were scored by Harold Jackson in the 39–24 loss to the Miami Dolphins at the Orange Bowl on 11-29-79

6 points were scored by Stanley Morgan in the 39–24 loss to the Miami Dolphins at the Orange Bowl on 11-29-79

6 points were scored by Carlos Pennywell in the 39–24 loss to the Miami Dolphins at the Orange Bowl on 11-29-79

6 points were scored by John Smith in the 39–24 loss to the Miami Dolphins at the Orange Bowl on 11-29-79

12 points were scored by Tony Collins in the 20–6 victory over the New York Jets at Shea Stadium on 09-11-86

12 points were scored by Corey Dillon in the 30–20 win over the Oakland Raiders at Gillette Stadium on 09-08-05

The most memorable Thursday Night Game was a 27–24 win over the Indianapolis Colts at Gillette on 09-09-04

The Patriots won the toss and elected to receive the opening kickoff. Bethel Johnson was pushed out of bounds after his 32-yard kickoff return. Tom Brady's first pass was completed to David Givens for 19 yards. On the Patriots' second offensive play, Deion Branch grabbed a 14-yard pass from Tom Brady. On third-and-8, Benjamin Watson hauled in a 14-yard pass—good for another first down. Their drive stalled on the Colts' 15-yard line, and Adam Vinatieri kicked a 32-yard field goal.

Peyton Manning marched his team down the field with the help of a 42-yard pass completion to Reggie Wayne, inside the 10-yard line of the Patriots. The Patriots defense bent but it did not break. LB Tedy Bruschi intercepted a Peyton Manning pass on the Patriots' 1-yard line and he returned it to the 6-yard line. The Colts were denied.

On the fourth play of the second quarter, however, Mike Vanderjagt kicked a 32-yard field goal to tie the game. After the Patriots were forced to punt, the Colts marched down the field again. This time Dominic Rhodes finished the drive with a three-yard run for a TD. Mike Vanderjagt kicked the extra point.

About five minutes later, the Patriots tied the score. Corey Dillon dashed for a 38-yard gain to get them onto the Colts side of the field. Bethel Johnson caught a 5-yard pass on third-and-2 and David Patten had a 20-yard reception. Tom Brady connected with Deion Branch for a 16-yard TD, and Adam Vinatieri kicked the extra point to tie the game at 10–10.

Dallas Clark hauled in a 64-yard pass from Peyton Manning and just like that the Colts were in the red zone of the Patriots. On third-and-5, Peyton Manning hit Marvin Harrison for an eight-yard gain to keep the drive alive. With 45 seconds left in the half, Manning fired a three-yard TD pass to Marvin Harrison. Mike Vangerderjagt kicked the extra point.

Bethel Johnson had a nice 34-yard kickoff return to give the Patriots' offense the ball on its own 41-yard line. On third-and-2, Tom Brady tossed a 5-yard pass to Daniel Graham and the Patriots were in Colts territory. Daniel Graham caught a 21-yard pass and took it to the Colts 25-yard line. On the last play of the first half, Adam Vinatieri kicked a 43-yard field goal.

On the first Patriots drive of the second half, David Patten finished a seven-play drive with a 25-yard TD reception. Adam Vinatieri kicked the extra point.

Peyton Maning took his team to the Patriots' 22-yard line before the Patriots defense forced another turnover. Ty Warren forced Edgerrin James to fumble, and Eugene Wilson recovered the loose ball for the Patriots.

Just seven plays later, the Patriots were in the end zone again. David Patten had receptions of 12 and 29 yards on this drive. David Givens hauled in a 25-yard pass and took the ball to the Colts' 15-yard line. On second-and-3 from the 8-yard line, Tom Brady tossed an eight-yard pass to Daniel Graham for the TD. Adam Vinatieri kicked the extra point.

Persistent Peyton Manning methodically took his team on an 11-play drive that ended with a seven-yard TD reception by Brandon Stokley. Mike Vanderjagt kicked the extra point. The Colts were only down by three points with more than 11 minutes to go in the game.

Neither team would score again. Eugene Wilson forced Edgerrin James to fumble on the Patriots' 1-yard line and Vince Wilfork recovered the loose ball for the Patriots. With 1:43 left in the game, the Colts had the ball back, and Peyton Mannning connected with Brandon Stokley for a 45-yard gain. With 49 seconds left in the game, on third-and-8 from the Patriots' 17-yard line Willie McGinest sacked Peyton Manning for a loss of 12 yards. Mike Vanderjagt's 48-yard field-goal attempt was no good, wide right. (Mike Vanderjagt had kicked 42 consecutive field goals before this miss.) Tom Brady knelt for the final play in the 27–24 victory over the Colts.

Every regular season game played by the Boston Patriots on Friday Night
1960 regular season
Lost to the Denver Broncos 13–10 at BU Field on 09-09-60 (Jim Colclough caught a 10-yard TD pass from Butch Songin)

Lost to the Buffalo Bills 13–0 at BU Field on 09-23-60 (The Patriots defense blocked an extra-point attempt by Billy Atkins)

Lost to the Los Angeles Chargers 45–16 at BU Field on 10-28-60 (Walter Beach caugh a 59-yard TD pass for his only AFL TD)

Defeated the Oakland Raiders 34–28 at BU Field on 11-04-60 (Butch Songin threw three TD passes)

Beat the New York Titans 38–21 at BU Field on 11-11-60 (Dick Christy had a 46-yard TD run and threw a HB Option TD pass)

Destroyed the Dallas Texans 42–14 at BU Field on 11-18-60 (Dick Christy tossed a HB option TD pass and ran for a six-yard TD)

Lost to the Houston Oilers 24–10 at BU Field on 11-25-60 (Joe Johnson caught a 51-yard TD and had 123 yards receiving)

1961 regular season
Tied the Houston Oilers 31–31 at BU Field on 10-13-61 (Gino Cappelletti caught a 43-yard TD from Butch Songin in the fourth quarter)

Beat the Dallas Texans 28–21 at BU Field on 11-03-61 (Ron Burton returned a kickoff 91 yards for the game-winning score)

Beat the Oakland Raiders 20–17 at BU Field on 11-17-61 (Tom Addison intercepted Tom Flores to help set up a FG)

1962 regular season
Destroyed the Denver Broncos 41–16 at BU Field on 09-21-62 (Fred Bruney and Ron Hall returned an interception for a TD)

Lost to the Dallas Texans 27–7 at BU Field on 10-12-62 (Larry Garron caught a 47-yard TD pass from Babe Parilli)

Beat the San Diego Chargers 24–20 at BU Field on 10-19-62 (Jim Crawford caught a two-point pass and ran for the game-winning TD)

Defeated the Oakland Raiders 26–16 at BU Field on 10-26-62 (Larry Garron had a career-best 140 yards rushing)

Beat the Buffalo Bills 21–10 at BU Field on 11-23-62 (Ron Burton caught a 69-yard TD pass from Tom Yewcic)

Defeated the NY Titans 24–17 at BU Field on 11-30-62 (Tom Yewcic tossed a game-winning 78-yard TD to Jim Colclough)

1963 regular season
Beat the Raiders 20–14 at Fenway Park on 10-11-63 (Tom Neumann caught a 15-yard TD in the fourth quarter) (The Game of the Year)

Defeated the Denver Broncos 40–21 at Fenway Park on 10-18-63 (Harry "Crunch" Crumb ran for two TDs)

Destroyed the Houston Oilers 45–3 at Fenway Park on 11-01-63 (Larry Garron had a 76-yard TD reception)

1964 regular season
Lost to the San Diego Chargers 26–17 at Fenway Park on 10-09-64 (Larry Garron ran for a TD and had a TD reception)

Tied the Oakland Raiders 43–43 at Fenway Park on 10-16-64 (Larry Garron ran for a TD and had two TD receptions)

Beat the Kansas City Chiefs 24–7 at Fenway Park on 10-23-64 (The Chiefs scored their TD with just three seconds left)

Defeated the Houston Oilers 25–24 at Fenway Park on 11-06-64 (Babe Parilli ran for 98 yards and two TDs (The Game of the Year)

Beat the Denver Broncos 12–7 at Fenway Park on 11-20-64 (Jack Rudolph tackled Jacky Lee in the end zone for a safety)

1965 regular season
Lost to the Denver Broncos 27–10 at Fenway Park on 09-24-65 (Tony Romeo caught a four-yard TD pass from Babe Parilli)

Lost to the Oakland Raiders 24–10 at Fenway Park on 10-08-65 (Defensive Tackle Tom Neville had seven tackles)

The only regular season game that the Patriots scored with two TD receptions, an offensive fumble return for a TD, a kickoff return for a TD, and at least one extra point

Jim Colclough caught a 14-yard TD pass from Butch Songin. Gino Cappelletti caught a seven-yard TD pass from Babe Parilli. Babe Parilli advanced a fumble by Larry Garron one yard for a TD. Ron Burton returned a kickoff 91 yards for the game-winning points, and Gino Cappelletti kicked four extra points in the 28–21 victory over the Dallas Texans at BU Field on 11-03-61.

The 10 most memorable moments in games played by the Patriots on Friday Night

A fan ran onto the field and tried to prevent a game-tying TD reception on the last play in the Patriots' seven-point win on 11-03-61

Gino Cappelletti kicked a 42-yard field goal on the last play of the game in the one-point win over Houston on 11-06-64

Babe Parilli ran out of bounds after a 10-yard jaunt, leaving just one second left for Gino Cappelletti to kick a game-winning field goal on 11-06-64

Gino Cappelletti scored 20 of the Patriots' 26 points in the 10-point win over the Oakland Raiders on 10-26-62

Ron Burton returned a kickoff for the final points scored in the 28–21 win over the Texans on 11-03-61

Larry Garron had two TD receptions and ran for another TD in the 43–43 tie with the Raiders on 10-16-64

Jim Lee Hunt returned a pass by Jacky Lee 78 yards for a TD in the 42-point victory over Houston on 11-01-63

Tom Yewcic had 231 yards passing, three TDs, and punted five times for 191 yards in the 21–10 win over Buffalo on 11-23-62

Tom Yewcic ran for a fourth-quarter TD and then tossed a game-winning 78-yard TD in the 24–17 win over the Titans on 11-30-62

LeRoy Moore fell on a punt that deflected off the goal post for a TD and the final points scored on 11-17-61

The scoring summary of every Patriots victory in a regular season game that was played on Friday Night

The Boston Patriots defeated the Oakland Raiders 34–28 at BU Field on 11-04-60

	Q1	Q2	Q3	Q4	Total
Oakland	0	7	7	14	28
Boston	14	6	7	7	34

Tom Stephens caught a 19-yard TD pass from Butch Songin. Gino Cappelletti kicked the extra point.

Dick Christy caught a 28-yard TD pass from Butch Songin. Gino Cappelletti kicked the extra point.

Tony Teresa bulled for a one-yard TD. Larry Barnes kicked the extra point.

Gino Cappelletti kicked a 27-yard field goal.

Gino Cappelletti kicked another 27-yard field goal.

Tom Flores ran for an eight-yard TD. Larry Barnes kicked the extra point.

Dick Christy ran for a one-yard TD. Gino Cappelletti kicked the extra point.

Jim Colclough caught a 38-yard TD pass from Butch Songin. Gino Cappelletti kicked the extra point.

Tony Teresa ran for a three-yard TD. Larry Barnes kicked the extra point.

Tony Teresa dashed 20 yards for a TD. Larry Barnes kicked the extra point.

The Boston Patriots defeated the New York Titans 38–21 at BU Field on 11-11-60

	Q1	Q2	Q3	Q4	Total
NY Titans	0	14	7	0	21
Boston Patriots	7	10	7	14	38

Alan Miller caught a 48-yard TD pass from Butch Songin. Gino Cappelletti kicked the extra point.

Joe Pagliei ran for a one-yard TD. Bill Shockley kicked the extra point.

Gino Cappelletti kicked a 30-yard field goal.

Jim Colclough caught a 31-yard TD pass from Butch Songin. Gino Cappelletti kicked the extra point.

Dewey Bohling ran for a 6-yard TD. Bill Shockley kicked the extra point.

Jim Colclough caught a 9-yard TD pass from Butch Songin. Gino Cappelletti kicked the extra point.

Don Maynard caught a 32-yard TD pass from Al Dorow. Bill Shockley kicked the extra point.

Dick Christy dashed 46 yards for a TD. Gino Cappelletti kicked the extra point.

Tom Stephens caught a 10-yard HB option TD pass from Dick Christy. Gino Cappelletti kicked the extra point.

The Boston Patriots destroyed the Dallas Texans 42–14 at BU Field on 11-18-60

	Q1	Q2	Q3	Q4	Total
Dallas	0	7	0	7	14
Boston	13	7	22	0	42

Tom Stephens caught a 10-yard HB option TD pass from Dick Christy. Gino Cappelletti kicked the extra point.

Dick Christy ran for a 6-yard TD. Gino Cappelletti was stopped on his rushing attempt for the two-point conversion.

Jim Colclough caught a 9-yard TD pass from Butch Songin. Gino Cappelletti kicked the extra point.

Hunter Enis ran a QB sneak for a 1-yard TD. Jack Spikes kicked the extra point.

Joe Johnson caught a 6-yard TD pass from Butch Songin. Gino Cappelletti kicked the extra point.

Joe Johnson caught an 18-yard TD pass from Butch Songin. Gino Cappelletti kicked the extra point.

Jim Crawford rumbled for a 39-yard TD. Gino Cappelletti kicked the extra point.

Jack Spikes ran for a 2-yard TD. Jack Spikes kicked the extra point.

The Boston Patriots defeated the Dallas Texans 28–21 at BU Field on 11-03-61

	Q1	Q2	Q3	Q4	Total
Dallas	7	7	7	0	21
Boston	14	0	14	0	28

Jim Colclough caught a 14-yard TD pass from Butch Songin. Gino Cappelletti kicked the extra point.

Gino Cappelletti caught a 7-yard TD pass from Babe Parilli. Gino Cappelletti kicked the extra point.

Abner Hayes ran for a 3-yard TD. Ben Agajanian kicked the extra point.

Babe Parilli advanced a fumble by Larry Garron one yard for a TD. Gino Cappelletti kicked the extra point.

Bo Dickinson hauled in a 48-yard TD pass from Cotton Davidson. Ben Agajanian kicked the extra point.

Ron Burton returned the ensuing kickoff 91 yards for a TD. Gino Cappelletti kicked the extra point.

———

The Boston Patriots defeated the Oakland Raiders 20–17 at BU Field on 11-17-61

	Q1	Q2	Q3	Q4	Total
Oakland	0	14	3	0	17
Boston	7	6	0	7	20

Ron Burton ran for a 6-yard TD. Gino Cappelletti kicked the extra point.

Charlie Hardy caught a 31-yard TD pass from Tom Flores. George Fleming kicked the extra point.

Gino Cappelletti kicked a 29-yard field goal.

Doug Asad caught a 5-yard TD pass from Tom Flores. George Fleming kicked the extra point.

George Fleming kicked a 16-yard field goal.

LeRoy Moore fell on a punt that hit the goal post and landed in the end zone for a TD. Gino Cappelletti kicked the extra point.

———

The Boston Patriots defeated the Denver Broncos 41–16 at BU Field on 09-21-62

	Q1	Q2	Q3	Q4	Total
Denver	0	3	0	13	16
Boston	3	14	10	14	41

Gino Cappelletti kicked a 28-yard field goal.

Gene Mingo kicked an 18-yard field goal.

Jim Crawford caught a 13-yard TD pass from Babe Parilli. Gino Cappelletti kicked the extra point.

Gino Cappelletti kicked a 33-yard field goal.

Fred Bruney returned an interception 33 yards for a TD. Gino Cappelletti kicked the extra point.

Jerry Tarr caught a 31-yard TD pass from Frank Tripucka. Gene Mingo kicked the extra point.

Ron Hall returned an interception 47 yards for a TD. Gino Cappelletti kicked the extra point.

Jerry Tarr hauled in a 97-yard TD pass from Dennis Shaw. Dennis Shaw was stopped on his run for a two-point conversion.

Claude King galloped 71 yards for a TD. Gino Cappelletti kicked the extra point.

———

The Boston Patriots defeated the San Diego Chargers 24–20 at BU Field on 10-19-62

	Q1	Q2	Q3	Q4	Total
San Diego	10	10	0	0	20
Boston	3	0	14	7	24

Gino Cappelletti kicked a 13-yard field goal.

Dave Kocourek caught a 36-yard TD pass from Dick Wood. George Blair kicked the extra point.

George Blair kicked a 43-yard field goal.

Bobby Jackson ran for a 2-yard TD. George Blair kicked the extra point.

George Blair kicked a 27-yard field goal.

Jim Colclough caught a 9-yard TD pass from Babe Parilli. The extra-point attempt was no good.

Jim Colclough caught a 25-yard TD pass from Babe Parilli. Jim Crawford caught a two-point pass from Babe Parilli.

Jim Crawford ran for a 1-yard TD. Gino Cappelletti kicked the extra point.

———

The Boston Patriots defeated the Oakland Raiders 26–16 at BU Field on 10-26-62

	Q1	Q2	Q3	Q4	Total
Oakland	7	6	0	3	16
Boston	3	3	10	10	26

Gino Cappelletti kicked a 25-yard field goal.

Dobie Craig caught a 34-yard TD pass from Cotton Davidson. Cotton Davidson kicked the extra point.

Gino Cappelletti kicked a 17-yard field goal.

Bo Roberson sprinted for a 63-yard TD. The extra-point attempt was no good.

Gino Cappelletti caught a 13-yard TD pass from Babe Parilli. Gino Cappelletti kicked the extra point.

Gino Cappelletti kicked a 31-yard field goal.

Cotton Davidson kicked a 19-yard field goal.

Larry Garron dashed 41 yards for a TD. Gino Cappelletti kicked the extra point.

Gino Cappelletti kicked an 11-yard field goal.

———

The Boston Patriots defeated the Buffalo Bills 21–10 at BU Field on 11-23-62

	Q1	Q2	Q3	Q4	Total
Buffalo	7	0	3	0	10
Boston	0	14	0	7	21

Jack Kemp ran for a six-yard TD. Cookie Gilchrist kicked the extra point.

Jim Colclough caught a 31-yard TD pass from Tom Yewcic. Gino Cappelletti kicked the extra point.

Ron Burton hauled in a 69-yard TD pass from Tom Yewcic. Gino Cappelletti kicked the extra point.

Mack Yoho kicked a 36-yard field goal.

Gino Cappelletti caught a 19-yard TD pass from Tom Yewcic. Gino Cappelletti kicked the extra point.

———

The Boston Patriots defeated the New York Titans 24–17 at BU Field on 11-30-62

	Q1	Q2	Q3	Q4	Total
NY Titans	7	3	7	0	17
Boston Patriots	0	3	7	14	24

Don Maynard caught a two-yard TD pass from Johnny Green. Bill Shockley kicked the extra point.

Gino Cappelletti kicked a 32-yard field goal.

Bill Shockley kicked a 37-yard field goal.

Tom Yewcic ran for a 27-yard TD. Gino Cappelletti kicked the extra point.

Larry Grantham recovered a fumble in the end zone for a TD. Bill Shockley kicked the extra point.

Tom Yewcic ran for a four-yard TD. Gino Cappelletti kicked the extra point.

Jim Colclough hauled in a 78-yard TD pass from Tom Yewcic. Gino Cappelletti kicked the extra point.

———

The Boston Patriots defeated the Oakland Raiders 20–14 at Fenway Park on 10-11-63

	Q1	Q2	Q3	Q4	Total
Oakland	7	0	7	0	14
Boston	3	0	10	7	20

Gino Cappelletti kicked a 37-yard field goal.

Jim McMillin returned an interception 47 yards for a TD. Mike Mercer kicked the extra point.

Cotton Davidson ran for an 11-yard TD. Mike Mercer kicked the extra point.

Jim Colclough hauled in a 56-yard TD pass from Babe Parilli. Gino Cappelletti kicked the extra point.

Gino Cappelletti kicked a 32-yard field goal.

Tom Neumann caught a 15-yard TD pass from Babe Parilli. Gino Cappelletti kicked the extra point.

———

The Boston Patriots defeated the Denver Broncos 40–21 at Fenway Park on 10-18-63

	Q1	Q2	Q3	Q4	Total
Denver	7	7	7	0	21
Boston	10	13	3	14	40

Gino Cappelletti kicked a 24-yard field goal.

Bob Gaiters hauled in a 74-yard TD pass from Mickey Slaughter. Gene Mingo kicked the extra point.

Gino Cappelletti caught a 24-yard TD pass from Babe Parilli. Gino Cappelletti kicked the extra point.

Billy Joe dashed 68 yards for a TD. Gene Mingo kicked the extra point.

Harry Crump bulled for a one-yard TD. Gino Cappelletti kicked the extra point.

Gino Cappelletti kicked a 34-yard field goal.

Gino Cappelletti kicked a 42-yard field goal.

Gino Cappelletti kicked a 32-yard field goal.

Bob Scarpitto caught a two-yard TD pass from Don Breaux. Gene Mingo kicked the extra point.

Tony Romeo caught a 31-yard TD pass from Babe Parilli. Gino Cappelletti kicked the extra point.

Harry Crump scored on another one-yard run. Gino Cappelletti kicked the extra point.

———

The Boston Patriots destroyed the Houston Oilers 45–3 at Fenway Park on 11-01-63

	Q1	Q2	Q3	Q4	Total
Houston	0	3	0	0	3
Boston	14	14	7	10	45

Larry Garron hauled in a 76-yard TD pass from Babe Parilli. Gino Cappelletti kicked the extra point.

Harry Crump ran for a one-yard TD. Gino Cappelletti kicked the extra point.

Babe Parilli ran for a two-yard TD. Gino Cappelletti kicked the extra point.

George Blanda kicked a 46-yard field goal.

Bob Suci returned an interception 98 yards for an interception. Gino Cappelletti kicked the extra point.

Babe Parilli ran for a one-yard TD. Gino Cappelletti kicked the extra point.

Gino Cappelletti kicked a 37-yard field goal.

Jim Lee Hunt returned an interception 78 yards for a TD. Gino Cappelletti kicked the extra point.

———

The Boston Patriots defeated the Kansas City Chiefs 24–7 at Fenway Park on 10-23-64

	Q1	Q2	Q3	Q4	Total
Chiefs	0	0	0	7	7
Patriots	7	0	10	7	24

Jim Colclough caught a 38-yard TD pass from Babe Parilli. Gino Cappelletti kicked the extra point.

Jim Colclough caught an 11-yard TD pass from Babe Parilli. Gino Cappelletti kicked the extra point.

Gino Cappelletti kicked a 26-yard field goal.

Ron Burton ran for a one-yard TD. Gino Cappelletti kicked the extra point.

Mack Lee Hill caught a two-yard TD pass from Eddie Wilson. Marty Brooker kicked the extra point.

———

The Boston Patriots defeated the Houston Oilers 25–24 at Fenway Park on 11-06-64

	Q1	Q2	Q3	Q4	Total
Houston	7	0	7	10	24
Boston	7	6	3	9	25

Charley Tolar ran for a two-yard TD. George Blanda kicked the extra point.

Babe Parilli ran for a one-yard TD. Gino Cappelletti kicked the extra point.

Gino Cappelletti kicked a 25-yard field goal.

Gino Cappelletti kicked a 33-yard field goal on the last play of the first half.

Willie Frazier caught an 80-yard TD pass from George Blanda. George Blanda kicked the extra point.

Gino Cappelletti kicked a 22-yard field goal.

Charley Frazier caught a 37-yard TD pass from George Blanda.

Babe Parilli ran for a five-yard TD. The two-point pass attempt was incomplete.

George Blanda kicked a 10-yard field goal.

Gino Cappelletti kicked a 42-yard field goal on the last play of the game.

———

The Boston Patriots defeated the Denver Broncos 12–7 at Fenway Park on 11-20-64

	Q1	Q2	Q3	Q4	Total
Denver	7	0	0	0	7
Boston	2	7	3	0	12

LB Jack Rudolph sacked Jacky Lee in the end zone for a safety.

Lionel Taylor caught an 11-yard TD pass from Jacky Lee. Dick Guesman kicked the extra point.

Gino Cappelletti caught a 25-yard TD pass from Babe Parilli. Gino Cappelletti kicked the extra point.

Gino Cappelletti kicked a 51-yard field goal.

The scoring details of the Boston Patriots 43–43 tie with the Oakland Raiders at Fenway Park on 10-16-64

Mike Mercer kicked a 42-yard field goal for the only points scored in the first quarter. Ron Burton ran for a two-yard TD on the first play of the second quarter and Gino Cappelletti kicked the extra point. Cotton Davidson tossed a 26-yard swing pass to Clem Daniels for a TD and Mike Mercer kicked the PAT.

Larry Garron lost two yards on a fourth-and-1 running play, and the Raiders took over on downs at midfield. Cotton Davidson connected on a 50-yard TD pass to Bo Roberson on the next play. Mike Mercer kicked the extra point.

Patriots Defensive Tackle Jim Lee Hunt caught the ensuing kickoff and lateraled it to J.D. Garrett who took it 24 yards to the 42-yard line. Two plays later, Babe Parilli lofted a 36-yard TD pass to Jim Colclough. Gino Cappelletti kicked the extra point. Cotton Davidson completed a 39-yard TD pass to Art Powell, and Mike Mercer kicked the PAT.

In the third quarter, Billy Cannon dashed for a 34-yard TD and Mike Mercer kicked a 37-yard field goal for the Raiders. Babe Parilli tossed a 10-yard TD pass to Larry Garron, and with Gino Cappelletti's extra point, the Patriots were only down by 13 points heading into the fourth quarter. Larry Garron bulled for a one-yard TD for the first points scored in the fourth quarter. Gino Cappelletti kicked another extra point.

Jack Rudolph recovered a fumble by Clem Daniels, and three plays later the Patriots were in the end zone. Babe Parilli fired an eight-yard TD pass to Art Graham. Gino Cappelletti kicked his fifth extra point to put the Patriots up by one point 35–34.

Bo Roberson had a 54-yard reception to help set up the next score for the Raiders. Cotton Davidson tossed his fourth TD pass, this one from nine yards out to Art Powell, but his two-point pass attempt went incomplete. The Raiders led 40–35.

Archie Matsos returned an interception of Babe Parilli 22 yards to the Patriots' 16-yard line. The Raiders had a great chance to put the game out of reach. The Patriots defense stood their ground and collectively blocked a nine-yard field-goal attempt by Mike Mercer. Don Webb recovered the loose ball on the 11-yard line, and the Patriots took it to the house in three plays.

Jim Colclough caught a 37-yard pass and then lateraled it to Gino Cappelletti, who took it another 14 yards, before he lateraled it to Ron Burton, who took it another seven yards, for a 58-yard play. Cappelletti caught a 20-yard pass and Larry Garron scored for the third time in the game with an 11-yard reception from Babe Parilli. Jim Colclough caught a pass for a two-point conversion from Babe Parilli. Mike Mercer kicked a 38-yard field goal for the final points scored in the 43–43 tie.

The only Patriots Defensive Lineman who has intercepted a pass in a regular season game played on Friday Night

Jim Lee Hunt took a Jacky Lee pass 78 yards for a TD in the 45–3 rout of the Houston Oilers at Fenway Park on 11-01-63

The only Patriots player who has recovered a fumble in the end zone in a regular season game played on Friday Night

LeRoy Moore recovered a blocked punt in the end zone for a TD in the 20–17 win over the Oakland Raiders on 11-17-61

The Longest

The Patriots player with the longest run from scrimmage in a regular season game played on Friday Night

Claude King galloped 71 yards for a TD in the 41–16 rout of the Denver Broncos at BU Field on 09-21-62

The Patriots Quarterback with the longest completion in a regular season game played on Friday Night

Tom Yewcic threw a 78-yard TD to Jim Colclough in the 24–17 win over the New York Titans at BU Field on 11-30-62

The Patriots player with the longest interception return in a regular season game played on Friday Night

Bob Suci returned a George Blanda pass 98 yards for a TD in the 45–3 rout of the Houston Oilers at Fenway Park on 11-01-63

The Patriots player with the longest punt return in a regular season game played on Friday Night

Tom Stephens returned a punt 26 yards in the 45–3 rout of the Houston Oilers at Fenway Park on 11-01-63

The Patriots player with the longest kickoff return in a regular season game played on Friday Night

Ron Burton returned it 91 yards for a TD in the 28–21 victory over the Dallas Texans at BU Field on 11-03-61

The Patriots Kicker with the longest field goal in a regular season game played on Friday Night

Gino Cappelletti nailed a 51-yard field goal in the 12–7 win over the Denver Broncos at Fenway Park on 11-20-64

The Patriots player with the longest punt in a regular season game played on Friday Night

Tom Greene punted the football 66 yards in the 45–16 loss to the Los Angeles Chargers at BU Field on 10-28-60

The Most

The Patriots player with the most yards rushing in a regular season game played on Friday Night

Larry Garron had 140 yards rushing in the 26–16 victory over the Oakland Raiders at BU Field on 10-26-62

The Patriots Receiver with the most yards receiving in a regular season game played on Friday Night

Art Graham had 167 yards receiving in the 25–24 victory over the Houston Oilers at Fenway Park on 11-06-64

The Patriots Quarterback with the most yards passing in a regular season game played on Friday Night

Babe Parilli threw for 422 yards in the 43–43 tie with the Oakland Raiders at Fenway Park on 10-16-64

The Patriots player with the most special team return yards in a regular season game played on Friday Night

Ron Burton had 148 kickoff return yards in the 28–21 victory over the Dallas Texans at BU Field on 11-03-61

The progression of the most points scored by a Patriots player in a regular season game played on Friday Night

3 points were scored by Gino Cappelletti in the 13–10 loss to the Denver Broncos at BU Field on 09-09-60

6 points were scored by Jim Colclough in the 13–10 loss to the Denver Broncos at BU Field on 09-09-60

6 points were scored by Walter Beach in the 45–16 loss to the Los Angeles Chargers at BU Field on 10-28-60

6 points were scored by Oscar Lofton in the 45–16 loss to the Los Angeles Chargers at BU Field on 10-28-60

6 points were scored by Tom Stephens in the 34–28 victory over the Oakland Raiders at BU Field on 11-04-60

6 points were scored by Dick Christy in the 34–28 victory over the Oakland Raiders at BU Field on 11-04-60

8 points were scored by Gino Cappelletti in the 34–28 victory over the Oakland Raiders at BU Field on 11-04-60

12 points were scored by Dick Christy in the 34–28 victory over the Oakland Raiders at BU Field on 11-04-60

12 points were scored by Jim Colclough in the 38–21 victory over the New York Titans at BU Field on 11-11-60

12 points were scored by Joe Johnson in the 42–14 rout of the Dallas Texans at BU Field on 11-18-60

13 points were scored by Gino Cappelletti in the 31–31 tie with the Houston Oilers at BU Field on 10-13-61

17 points were scored by Gino Cappelletti in the 41–16 rout of the Denver Broncos at BU Field on 09-21-62

20 points were scored by Gino Cappelletti in the 26–16 victory over the Oakland Raiders at BU Field on 10-26-62

22 points were scored by Gino Cappelletti in the 40–21 rout of the Denver Broncos at Fenway Park on 10-18-63

Every regular season game played by the Patriots on Saturday Afternoon

1961 regular season
Beat the Oakland Raiders 35–21 at Candlestick Park on 12-09-61 (Billy Lott ran for two TDs and caught a TD pass)

1963 regular season
Lost to the Kansas City Chiefs 35–3 at Municipal Stadium in 11-degree weather on 12-14-63 (The Patriots scored first)

1965 regular season
Destroyed the Houston Oilers 42–14 at Fenway Park on 12-18-65 (Gino Cappelletti set an AFL record by scoring 28 points)

1966 regular season
Lost to the New York Jets 38–28 at Shea Stadium on 12-17-66 (Jim Nance finished 1966 with AFL- and NFL-best 1,458 yards rushing)

1967 regular season
Lost to the Bills 44–16 at Fenway Park on 12-09-67 (Bills LB Marty Schottenheimer intercepted two passes and took one for a TD)

1990 regular season
Lost to the Washington Redskins 25–10 at Foxboro Stadium on 12-15-90 (John Stephens had his career longest reception)

1994 regular season
Beat the Chicago Bears 13–3 at Soldier Field on 12-24-94 (Drew Bledsoe set an NFL record with 691 passing attempts for the year)

1996 regular season
Beat the Giants 23–22 at Giants Stadium on 12-21-96 (Troy Brown caught a third-down pass on his back) (The Game of the Year)

1997 regular season
Lost to the Pittsburgh Steelers 24–21 in overtime at Foxboro Stadium on 12-13-97 (Tedy Bruschi had two special team tackles)

2001 championship season
Defeated the Dolphins 20–13 at Foxboro Stadium on 12-22-01 (Fred Coleman recovered an onside kick by Olindo Mare)

2003 championship season
Shut out the Buffalo Bills 31–0 at Gillette Stadium on 12-27-03 (Larry Izzo preuserved the shutout with his late interception)

2005 regular season
Shut out the Tampa Bay Buccaneers 28–0 at Gillette Stadium on 12-17-05 (David Givens had 137 yards receiving and one TD)

The 10 most memorable moments in games played by the Patriots on Saturday Afternoon

Gino Cappelletti set the AFL and team record by scoring 28 points in the 28-point win over Houston on 12-18-65

On third-and-13, Troy Brown caught a 13-yard pass on his back during the game-winning drive in the one-point win on 12-21-96

Ben Coates caught a 13-yard TD pass from Drew Bledsoe with 1:23 left to beat the Giants 23–22 on 12-21-96

Dave Meggett returned a punt 60 yards for a TD against his former team in the 23–22 win over the Giants on 12-21-96

Tom Brady caught a 23-yard swing pass from Kevin Faulk in the seven-point victory over the Dolphins on 12-22-01

Larry Izzo intercepted a pass in the end zone for a touchback to preserve the 31–0 shutout of the Bills on 12-27-03

Tight end eligible Tom Ashworth caught a one-yard TD pass from Tom Brady in the 28-0 shutout of Tampa on 12-17-05

Richard Seymour was used in the backfield as a blocking fullback on Antowain Smith's two-yard TD run on 12-22-01

Jim Nance set AFL season record of 1,458 yards rushing when he ran for 78 yards in the last game of the 1966 AFL season

Drew Bledsoe set NFL season record for the most pass attempts and threw it downfield on the last play of the win on 12-24-94

The scoring summary of every Patriots victory in a regular season game played on Saturday Afternoon

The Boston Patriots defeated the Oakland Raiders 35–21 at Candlestick Park on 12-09-61

	Q1	Q2	Q3	Q4	Total
Patriots	7	14	7	7	35
Raiders	7	0	7	7	21

Jim Colclough caught a five-yard TD pass from Babe Parilli. Gino Cappelletti kicked the extra point.

Bob Coolbaugh caught a 36-yard TD pass from Tom Flores. George Fleming kicked the extra point.

Billy Lott ran for a one-yard TD. Gino Cappelletti kicked the extra point.

Billy Lott caught an 18-yard TD pass from Babe Parilli. Gino Cappelletti kicked the extra point.

Jerry Burch hauled in a 54-yard TD pass from Tom Flores. George Fleming kicked the extra point.

Billy Lott ran for a three-yard TD. Gino Cappelletti kicked the extra point.

Riley Morris returned an interception 35 yards for a TD. George Fleming kicked the extra point.

Larry Garron caught an eight-yard TD pass from Babe Parilli. Gino Cappelletti kicked the extra point.

_____

The Boston Patriots destroyed the Houston Oilers 42–14 at Fenway Park on 12-18-65

	Q1	Q2	Q3	Q4	Total
Houston	0	0	8	6	14
Boston	10	16	3	13	42

Gino Cappelletti kicked a 20-yard field goal.

Jim Nance ran for a one-yard TD. Gino Cappelletti kicked the extra point.

Jim Colclough caught a 19-yard TD pass from Babe Parilli. Gino Cappelletti kicked the extra point.

Houston's long snapping center Wayne Frazier snapped the ball out of the end zone for a two-point safety.

Gino Cappelletti caught a 26-yard TD pass from Babe Parilli. Gino Cappelletti kicked the extra point.

Gino Cappelletti kicked a 10-yard field goal.

Charley Hennigan caught a four-yard TD pass from George Blanda. Ode Burrell caught a two-point pass from George Blanda.

Larry Onesti recovered a blocked punt in the end zone for a TD. The attempt for a two-point conversion failed.

Gino Cappelletti hauled in a 57-yard TD pass from Babe Parilli. Gino Cappelletti kicked the extra point.

Gino Cappelletti kicked a 24-yard field goal.

Gino Cappelletti kicked a 31-yard field goal.

_____

The New England Patriots defeated the Chicago Bears 13–3 at Soldier Field on 12-24-94

	Q1	Q2	Q3	Q4	Total
Patriots	3	3	0	7	13
Bears	3	0	0	0	3

Kevin Butler kicked a 44-yard field goal.

Matt Bahr kicked a 29-yard field goal.

Matt Bahr kicked a 22-yard field goal.

Leroy Thompson caught a three-yard TD pass from Drew Bledsoe. Matt Bahr kicked the extra point.

_____

The New England Patriots defeated the New York Giants 23–22 at Giants Stadium on 12-21-96

	Q1	Q2	Q3	Q4	Total
Patriots	0	0	3	20	23
Giants	2	20	0	0	22

Drew Bledsoe was penalized for intentional grounding in the end zone resulting a two-point safety for the Giants.

Charles Way ran for a one-yard TD. Brad Deluiso kicked the extra point.

Brad Deluiso kicked a 30-yard field goal.

Brad Deluiso kicked a 27-yard field goal.

Jason Sehorn returned an interception 23 yards for a TD. Brad Deluiso kicked the extra point.

Adam Vinatieri kicked a 40-yard field goal.

Terry Glenn caught a 26-yard TD pass from Drew Bledsoe. Adam Vinatieri kicked the extra point.

Dave Meggett returned a punt 60 yards against his former team for a TD. Adam Vinatieri kicked the extra point.

Ben Coates caught a 13-yard TD pass from Drew Bledsoe. Adam Vinatieri kicked the extra point.

_____

The New England Patriots defeated the Miami Dolphins 20–13 at Foxboro Stadium on 12-22-01

	Q1	Q2	Q3	Q4	Total
Dolphins	0	3	0	10	13
Patriots	0	20	0	0	20

Antowain Smith ran for a two-yard TD. Adam Vinatieri kicked the extra point.

Patrick Pass caught a 23-yard TD pass from Tom Brady. Adam Vinatieri kicked the extra point.

Adam Vinatieri kicked a 32-yard field goal.

Adam Vinatieri kicked a 23-yard field goal.

Olindo Mare kicked a 36-yard field goal.

Jeff Ogden caught a 10-yard TD pass from Jay Fiedler. Olindo Mare kicked the extra point.

Highlights from the 20–13 win over the Dolphins that put the Patriots in first place in the AFC Eastern Division on 12-22-01

Neither team scored in the first quarter, but the Patriots scored all of their points in the second quarter of this game. Antowain Smith scored a TD on a two-yard run, and Patrick Pass caught a 23-yard TD pass from Tom Brady less than four minutes later. Adam Vinatieri kicked an extra point after each TD. Vinatieri kicked a 32-yard field goal and a 23-yard field goal in the second quarter. With three seconds left in the first half, Olindo Mare kicked a 36-yard field goal for the Dolphins.

Neither team scored in the third quarter. Olindo Mare kicked a 36-yard field goal early in the fourth quarter. Jeff Ogden caught a 10-yard TD pass from Jay Fiedler, and Olindo Mare kicked the extra point for the Dolphins' final points.

The Patriots had 44 rushing attempts for 196 yards. Antowain Smith had his best day as a running back for the Patriots with 26 carries for 156 yards, and averaged six yards per carry. Tom Brady caught a 23-yard pass from Kevin Faulk.

———

The New England Patriots shut out the Buffalo Bills 31–0 at Gillette Stadium on 12-27-03

	Q1	Q2	Q3	Q4	Total
Buffalo	0	0	0	0	0
New England	14	14	0	3	31

Daniel Graham caught a one-yard TD pass from Tom Brady. Adam Vinatieri kicked the extra point.

Bethel Johnson caught a nine-yard TD pass from Tom Brady. Adam Vinatieri kicked the extra point.

Troy Brown caught a 19-yard TD pass from Tom Brady. Adam Vinatieri kicked the extra point.

David Givens caught a 10-yard TD pass from Tom Brady. Adam Vinatieri kicked the extra point.

Adam Vinatieri kicked a 24-yard field goal.

———

The New England Patriots shut out the Tampa Bay Buccaneers 28–0 at Gillette Stadium on 12-17-05

	Q1	Q2	Q3	Q4	Total
Tampa Bay	0	0	0	0	0
New England	7	14	0	7	28

Tight End eligible Tom Ashworth caught a 1-yard TD pass from Tom Brady. Adam Vinatieri kicked the extra point.

Corey Dillon ran for a three-yard TD. Adam Vinatieri kicked the extra point.

David Givens caught a 16-yard TD pass from Tom Brady. Adam Vinatieri kicked the extra point.

Corey Dillon ran for a two-yard TD. Adam Vinatieri kicked the extra point.

Every Patriots player who was the AFC Special Team Player of the Week in a regular season Saturday Afternoon Game

1996 regular season
Dave Meggett returned a fourth-quarter punt 60 yards for a TD in the 23–22 win over the New York Giants at Giants Stadium on 12-21-96

2001 championship season
Ken Walter averaged over 42 yards per punt and had two within the 20-yard line in the 20–13 win over Miami at Foxboro Stadium on 12-22-01

The Longest

The Patriots player with the longest run from scrimmage in a regular season game played on Saturday Afternoon

Antowain Smith rumbled for a 44-yard gain in the 20–13 victory over the Miami Dolphins at Foxboro on 12-22-01

The Patriots player with the longest reception in a regular season game played on Saturday Afternoon

Jim Colclough caught a 47-yard pass in the 35–21 victory over the Oakland Raiders at Candlestick Park on 12-09-61

The Patriots player with the longest completion in a regular season game played on Saturday Afternoon

Babe Parilli tossed a 47-yard pass to Jim Colclough in the 35–21 win over the Raiders at Candlestick Park on 12-09-61

The Patriots DB with the longest interception return in a regular season game played on Saturday Afternoon

Chuck Shonta returned a pass by Tom Flores 18 yards in the 44–16 loss to the Buffalo Bills at Fenway Park on 12-09-67

The Patriots Linebacker with the longest interception return in a regular season game played on Saturday Afternoon

Mike Vrabel returned a Drew Bledsoe pass 14 yards in the 31–0 shutout of the Buffalo Bills at Gillette Stadium on 12-27-03

The Patriots player with the longest fumble return in a regular season game played on Saturday Afternoon

Willie McGinest returned a fumble by Chris Simms 19 yards in the 28–0 shutout of Tampa Bay at Gillette Stadium on 12-17-05

The Patriots player with the longest punt return in a regular season game played on Saturday Afternoon

Dave Meggett took a punt 60 yards for a TD in the fourth quarter of the 23–22 win over the New York Giants at Giants Stadium on 12-21-96

The Patriots player with the longest kickoff return in a regular season game played on Saturday Afternoon

Dave Meggett had a 45-yard kickoff return in the 24–21 overtime loss to the Pittsburgh Steelers at Foxboro on 12-13-97

The Patriots player with the longest field goal in a regular season game played on Saturday Afternoon

Gino Cappelletti kicked a 31-yard field goal in the 42–14 rout of the Houston Oilers at Fenway Park on 12-18-65

The Patriots player with the longest punt in a regular season game played on Saturday Afternoon

Tom Yewcic had two 50-yard punts in the 35–3 loss to the Kansas City Chiefs at Municipal Stadium on 12-14-63

The Most

The Patriots player with the most yards rushing in a regular season game played on Saturday Afternoon

Antowain Smith had 156 yards rushing in the 20–13 win over the Miami Dolphins at Foxboro Stadium on 12-22-01

The Patriots Quarterback with the most yards passing in a regular season game played on Saturday Afternoon

Babe Parilli had 379 yards passing in the 38–28 loss to the New York Jets at Shea Stadium on 12-17-66

The Patriots Receiver with the most yards receiving in a regular season game played on Saturday Afternoon

Gino Cappelletti had 111 yards receiving in the 38–28 loss to the New York Jets at Shea Stadium on 12-17-66

The Patriots player with the most special team return yards in a regular season game played on Saturday Afternoon

Bobby Leo had 160 special team return yards in the 44–16 loss to the Buffalo Bills at Fenway Park on 12-09-67

The progression of the most points scored by a Patriots player in a regular season game played on Saturday Afternoon

6 points were scored by Jim Colclough in the 35–21 victory over the Oakland Raiders at Candlestick Park on 12-09-61

18 points were scored by Billy Lott in the 35–21 victory over the Oakland Raiders at Candlestick Park on 12-09-61

28 points were scored by Gino Cappelletti in the 42–14 rout of the Houston Oilers at Fenway Park on 12-18-65

The only Patriots Defensive Player to record a safey in a regular season game played on Saturday Afternoon

Jim Lee Hunt sacked Jack Kemp for a safety in the 44–16 loss to the Buffalo Bills at Fenway Park on 12-09-67

Every regular season game played by the Patriots on Saturday Night

1960 regular season

Beat the New York Titans 28–24 at the Polo Grounds on 09-17-60 (Chuck Shonta took a fumble 54 yards for a TD on the last play)

Shut out the Los Angeles Chargers 35–0 at the LA Coliseum on 10-08-60 (Gino Cappelletti kicked off seven times) (The Game of the Year)

1961 regular season

Lost to the New York Titans 21–20 at BU Field on 09-09-61 (Gino Cappelletti caught a TD pass, kicked two field goals and two PATs)

Destroyed the Denver Broncos 45–17 at BU Field on 09-16-61 (Tom Yewcic tossed an 18-yard halfback option TD pass)

Beat the Buffalo Bills 23–21 at War Memorial Stadium on 09-23-61 (Walt Cudzik recovered an onside kick to seal the win)

Lost to the San Diego Chargers 38–27 at BU Field on 10-07-61 (Don Webb attempted an onside kick for the Patriots)

1962 regular season

Lost to the Dallas Texans 42–28 at the Cotton Bowl on 09-08-62 (LB Rommie Loudd and DB Don Webb played on offense)

Destroyed the New York Titans 43–14 at the Polo Grounds on 10-06-62 (Gino Cappelletti scored 19 points)

Tied Buffalo 28–28 at War Memorial on 11-03-62 (Larry Garron had a 95-yard TD kickoff return and TD catch to tie the game in fourth quarter)

1963 regular season

Lost to the San Diego Chargers 17–13 at Balboa Stadium on 09-14-63 (The first pro football game played at night in San Diego)

Lost to the New York Jets 31–24 at the Polo Grounds on 10-05-63 (Tom Yewcic tossed three TDs and had a career-best 311 yards passing)

Lost to the Buffalo Bills 28–21 at War Memorial Stadium on 10-26-63 (Art Graham had a 77-yard TD reception)

1964 regular season

Lost to the New York Jets 35–14 at Shea Stadium on 10-31-64 (Gino Cappelletti had a career-best 147 yards receiving)

1965 regular season

Lost to the Buffalo Bills 24–7 at War Memorial Stadium on 09-11-65 (George Pyne blocked a field-goal attempt by Pete Gogolak)

1966 regular season

Lost to the San Diego Chargers 24–0 at Balboa Stadium on 09-10-66 (Jim Nance had a career-long 45-yard pass reception)

Defeated the Buffalo Bills 20–10 at War Memorial Stadium on 10-08-66 (Joe Bellino caught a 25-yard TD for his only AFL TD)

1967 regular season

Lost to the San Diego Chargers 28–14 at Jack Murphy Stadium on 09-09-67 (Jim Whalen and Art Graham had TD receptions)

1969 regular season

Lost to Buffalo 23–16 at War Memorial Stadium on 10-11-69 (Marty Schottenheimer had his only interception as a Patriot LB)

1995 regular season

Lost to the Pittsburgh Steelers 41–27 at Three Rivers Stadium on 12-16-95 (Drew Bledsoe threw three TDs and a two-point pass)

Lost to the Indianapolis Colts 10–7 at the RCA Dome on 12-23-95 (Hason Graham caught a 31-yard TD from Drew Bledsoe)

2003 championship season

Beat the New York Jets 21–16 at the Meadowlands on 12-20-03 (Tedy Bruschi intercepted Chad Pennington on the Jets' second play)

2007 undefeated regular season
Beat the New York Giants 38–35 at Giants Stadium on 12-20-07 (Tom Brady threw his NFL-record 50th TD pass in the season)

The 10 most memorable moments in games played by the Patriots on Saturday Night

Tom Brady threw a 65-yard TD pass to Randy Moss setting numerous NFL records in the three-point win on 12-20-07

Randy Moss hauled in a 65-yard TD pass from Tom Brady setting numerous NFL records in the three-point win on 12-20-07

Chuck Shonta returned a poor exchange to the punter 52 yards for a TD on the last play of the four-point win on 09-17-60

Gino Cappelletti scored 19 points in the 29-point victory over the New York Titans on 10-06-62

Larry Garron took a kickoff 95 yards for a TD and caught a TD pass for the final points scored in the tie with Buffalo on 11-03-62

Heisman Trophy–winner Joe Bellino caught a 25-yard TD pass from Babe Parilli in the 10-point win on 10-08-66

Tedy Bruschi intercepted Chad Pennington on the Jets' second play from scrimmage to help set up a TD pass on the Patriots' first play on 12-20-03

David Givens caught a 35-yard TD pass from Tom Brady on the Patriots' first play in the 21–16 win over the Jets on 12-20-03

Willie McGinest returned a pass by Chad Pennington 15 yards for a TD in the five-point win over the Jets on 12-20-03

Mike Vrabel recovered an onside kick with 1:04 left to preserve the undefeated regular season on 12-20-07

The scoring summary of every Patriots victory in a regular season game that was played on Saturday Night

The Boston Patriots defeated the New York Titans 28–24 at the Polo Grounds on 09-17-60

	Q1	Q2	Q3	Q4	Total
Boston Patriots	7	0	7	14	28
NY Titans	3	14	7	0	24

Walt Livingston ran for a one-yard TD. Gino Cappelletti kicked the extra point.

Bill Shockley kicked a 23-yard field goal.

Dewey Bohling caught an eight-yard TD pass from Al Dorow. Bill Shockley kicked the extra point.

Ted Wegert caught a 16-yard TD pass from Al Dorow. Bill Shockley kicked the extra point.

Thurlow Cooper hauled in a 38-yard TD pass from Al Dorow. Bill Shockley kicked the extra point.

Oscar Lofton caught a 15-yard TD pass from Tom Greene. Gino Cappelletti kicked the extra point.

Jim Colclough caught a six-yard TD pass from Babe Parilli. Gino Cappelletti kicked the extra point.

Chuck Shonta returned a misplayed snap to the punter, on the last play of the game, 52 yards for a TD. Gino Cappelletti hit the PAT.

————

The Boston Patriots shut out the Los Angeles Chargers 35–0 at the Los Angeles Memorial Coliseum on 10-08-60

	Q1	Q2	Q3	Q4	Total
Boston Patriots	18	7	10	0	35
LA Chargers	0	0	0	0	0

Gino Cappelletti kicked a 23-yard field goal.

Ron Burton ran for a four-yard TD. Jim Crawford caught a two point pass from Gino Cappelletti.

Jim Colclough caught a 19-yard TD pass from Butch Songin. Gino Cappelletti kicked the extra point.

Jim Crawford ran for a one-yard TD. Gino Cappelletti kicked the extra point.

Alan Miller ran for a one-yard TD. Gino Cappelletti kicked the extra point.

Gino Cappelletti kicked a field goal.

Highlights from the Boston Patriots first regular season victory

Tony Discenzo kicked off for the Patriots and Gino Cappelletti made the tackle of kickoff returnman Leon Burton. The Titans went three-and-out and Rick Sapienza punted it to the Patriots. Tom Greene completed a 31-yard pass to RB Jerry Green but the drive stalled and Tom Greene punted it back to the Titans.

Patriots LB Jack Rudolph recovered a fumble pitch out by Al Dorow and the Patriots had the ball on the Titans' 17-yard line. Jim "Cowboy" Crawford ran for 15 yards taking it to the 2-yard line. On second-and-goal,

Walt Livingston scored on a one-yard run. Gino Cappelletti kicked the extra point.

Roger Donnahoo recovered a fumble by Walt Livingston, and the Titans were in prime position to score. Bill Shockley put the Titans on the scoreboard with a 23-yard field goal.

Roger Donnahoo returned a pass by Tommy Greeen 30 yards yards on the last play of the first quarter. This turnover led to the Titans' first TD of the game. Titans QB Al Dorow tossed an eight-yard pass to Dewey Bohling for a TD. Bill Shockley kicked the extra point.

On the Titans' next possession, they scored again. Art Powell had a 36-yard reception and the Patriots were called for a 30-yard pass-interference penalty. Al Dorow tossed a 16-yard pass to Ted Wegert for a TD. Bill Shockley kicked the extra point.

Patriots LB Bill Brown intercepted a pass by Al Dorow but the Patriots couldn't punch it in for a TD. On fourth-and-1 from the 5-yard line, Patriots RB Alan Miller was stuffed by Titans LB Bill Mathis for no gain. The Titans responded by taking it 95 yards for a TD. Ted Wegert had a 32-yard reception. The Patriots had a 45-yard pass interference penalty. Al Dorow put it in the end zone with his two-yard pass to Thurlow Cooper for a TD. Bill Shockley kicked the extra point.

Boston came back with a 10-play scoring drive of their own. Tom Greene finished off the impressive drive with an 18-yard TD pass to tight end Oscar Lofton. Gino Cappelletti kicked the extra point.

The Patriots defense held and forced the Titans to punt. Rick Sapienza had his best punt of the day of 42 yards late in the fourth quarter. The Patriots took over on their own 20-yard line. With just under two minutes left in the game, the Patriots were faced with fourth-and-goal from the 6-yard line. Patriots QB Butch Songin simply tossed a 6-yard TD pass to Jim Colclough. The Patriots tried for a two-point conversion. Holder Fred Bruney tossed a two-point pass to Alan Miller but it was nullified by a penalty. Gino Cappelletti kicked the extra point.

Tony Discenzo's onside kick was recovered by Titans tight end Thurlow Cooper. The Titans tried to run out the clock, but officials stopped the clock twice, much to the dismay of Titans head coach Sammy Baugh. On fourth-and-4 with 30 seconds left in the game and the Patriots out of timeouts, Rick Sapienza came on to punt. This was the last play of the game. The snap hit Rick in the hands, but he dropped it and then kicked it. The ball squirted away, and Tony Sardisco and Gino Cappelletti kicked the ball forward. Patriots defensive back Chuck Shonta picked up the

ball near the 25-yard line and took it in for the game-winning TD. The Patriots defeated the New York Titans 28–24 at the Polo Grounds on the last play of the game for their first victory.

———

The Boston Patriots defeated the Buffalo Bills 23–21 at War Memorial Stadium on 09-23-61

	Q1	Q2	Q3	Q4	Total
Boston	3	3	14	3	23
Buffalo	7	0	7	7	21

Gino Cappelletti kicked a 36-yard field goal.

Wray Carlton ran for a one-yard TD. Billy Atkins kicked the extra point.

Gino Cappelletti kicked a 35-yard field goal.

Larry Garron scampered 67 yards for a TD. Gino Cappelletti kicked the extra point.

Tom Stephens caught a one-yard TD pass from Butch Songin.

M.C. Reynolds ran for a one-yard TD. Billy Atkins kicked the extra point.

Gino Cappelletti kicked a 46-yard field goal.

Albert Dubenion caught a 10-yard TD pass from M.C. Reynolds. Billy Atkins kicked the extra point.

———

The Boston Patriots destroyed the New York Titans 43–14 at the Polo Grounds on 10-06-62

	Q1	Q2	Q3	Q4	Total
Boston Patriots	3	21	13	6	43
NY Titans	0	7	7	0	14

Gino Cappelletti kicked a 28-yard field goal.

Jim Colclough hauled in a 63-yard TD pass from Babe Parilli. Gino Cappelletti kicked the extra point.

Ron Burton caught a 13-yard TD pass from Babe Parilli. Gino Cappelletti kicked the extra point.

Gino Cappelletti caught a 36-yard TD pass from Babe Parilli. Gino Cappelletti kicked the extra point.

Art Powell hauled in a 73-yard TD pass from Lee Grosscup. Bill Shockley kicked the extra point.

Don Maynard corralled an 86-yard TD pass from Lee Grosscup. Bill Shockley kicked the extra point.

Gino Cappelletti kicked a 12-yard field goal.

Tom Addison returned an interception 12 yards for a TD. Gino Cappelletti kicked the extra point.

Gino Cappelletti kicked a 38-yard field goal.

Jim Crawford ran for a three-yard TD. The extra-point attempt missed.

———

The Boston Patriots defeated the Buffalo Bills 20–10 at War Memorial Stadium on 10-08-66

	Q1	Q2	Q3	Q4	Total
Boston	10	3	7	0	20
Buffalo	0	0	3	7	10

Gino Cappelletti kicked a 10-yard field goal.

Jim Nance rumbled for a 19-yard TD. Gino Cappelletti kicked the extra point.

Gino Cappelletti kicked a 31-yard field goal.

Booth Lusteg kicked a 37-yard field goal.

Joe Bellino caught a 25-yard TD pass from Babe Parilli. Gino Cappelletti kicked the extra point.

Wray Carlton ran for a one-yard TD. Booth Lusteg kicked the extra point.

———

The Boston Patriots defeated the New York Jets 21–16 at the Meadowlands on 12-20-03

	Q1	Q2	Q3	Q4	Total
New England	7	7	7	0	21
New York	7	3	0	6	16

David Givens caught a 35-yard TD pass from Tom Brady on the first offensive play. Adam Vinatieri kicked the extra point.

Chad Pennington ran a QB sneak for a one-yard TD. Doug Brien kicked the extra point.

Willie McGinest returned an interception 15 yards for a TD. Adam Vinatieri kicked the extra point.

Doug Brien kicked a 29-yard field goal.

David Givens caught a five-yard TD pass from Tom Brady. Adam Vinatieri kicked the extra point.

Chad Pennington ran for a 10-yard TD. The two-point conversion pass attempt was incomplete.

———

The New England Patriots defeated the New York Giants 38–35 at Giants Stadium on 12-29-07

	Q1	Q2	Q3	Q4	Total
New England	3	13	7	15	38
New York	7	14	7	7	35

Brandon Jacobs caught a seven-yard TD pass from Eli Manning. Lawrence Tynes kicked the extra point.

Stephen Gostkowski kicked a 37-yard field goal.

Randy Moss caught a four-yard TD pass from Tom Brady. Stephen Gostkowski kicked the extra point.

Domenik Hixon returned the ensuing kickoff 74 yards for a TD. Lawrence Tynes kicked the extra point.

Stephen Gostkowski kicked a 45-yard field goal.

Stephen Gostkowski kicked a 37-yard field goal.

Kevin Boss caught a three-yard TD pass from Eli Manning with 18 seconds left in the half. Lawrence Tynes kicked the PAT.

Plaxico Burress caught a 19-yard TD pass from Eli Manning. Lawrence Tynes kicked the extra point.

Laurence Maroney ran for a six-yard TD. Stephen Gostkowski kicked the extra point.

Randy Moss hauled in a 65-yard TD pass from Tom Brady. (Setting two NFL records). Laurence Maroney ran for two points.

Laurence Maroney ran for a five-yard TD. Stephen Gostkowski kicked the extra point.

Plaxico Burress caught a three-yard TD pass from Eli Manning. Lawrence Tynes kicked the extra point. (Mike Vrabel recovered the ensuing onside kick with 1:04 left in the game.)

The only Boston Patriots player who has blocked a field-goal attempt in a game played on Saturday Night

George Pyne blocked a 30-yard field goal by Pete Gogolak in the 24–7 loss to Buffalo at War Memorial Stadium on 09-11-65

The only Patriots player who has returned a fumble for a TD in a regular season game played on Saturday Night

Tom Stephens returned a Paul Lowe fumble 10 yards for a TD in the 38–27 loss to the Chargers at BU Field on 10-07-61

The only Patriots player to be the AFC Defensive Player of the Week for his performance in a Saturday Night Game

Willie McGinest returned an interception 15 yards for a TD in the 21–16 win over the Jets at the Meadowlands on 12-20-03

The only Patriots player to be the AFC Offensive Player of the Week for his performance in a Saturday Night Game

Tom Brady was 32–42 for 356 yards and two TDs as the team overcame a 12-point deficit in the 38–35 win over the Giants on 12-29-07

The Longest

The Patriots player with the longest run from scrimmage in a regular season game played on Saturday Night

Larry Garron dashed 67 yards for a TD in the 23–21 win over the Buffalo Bills at War Memorial Stadium on 09-23-61

The Patriots player with the longest reception in a regular season game played on Saturday Night

Billy Wells snared a 78-yard TD pass from Butch Songin in the 35–0 win over the Los Angeles Chargers at the Los Angeles Coliseum on 10-08-60

The Patriots Quarterback with the longest completion in a regular season game played on Saturday Night

Butch Songin threw a 78-yard TD to Billy Wells in the 35–0 shutout of the Los Angeles Chargers at the Los Angeles Coliseum on 10-08-60

The Patriots Defensive Back with the longest interception return in a regular season game played on Saturday Night

Ron Hall returned a Jack Kemp pass 29 yards in the 24–7 loss to the Buffalo Bills at War Memorial Stadium on 09-11-65

The Patriots Linebacker with the longest interception return in a regular season game played on Saturday Night

Tom Addison returned a Tobin Rote pass 17 yards in the 17–13 loss to the Chargers at Balboa Stadium on 09-14-63

The Patriots player who has the longest fumble advancement of a teammate's fumble in a game played on Saturday Night

Jim Colclough advanced a fumble by Billy Lott 10 yards on the 23–21 win over Buffalo at War Memorial Stadium on 09-23-61

The Patriots player with the longest fumble return in a regular season game played on Saturday Night

Chuck Shonta returned a fumbled snap by the punter 52 yards for a TD on the last play in the 28–24 win over the New York Titans on 09-17-60

The Patriots player with the longest punt return in a regular season game played on Saturday Night

Dave Cloutier returned a punt 40 yards in the 35–14 loss to the New York Jets at Shea Stadium on 10-31-64

The Patriots player with the longest kickoff return in a regular season game played on Saturday Night

Larry Garron returned a kickoff 95 yards for a TD in the 28–28 tie with Buffalo at War Memorial Stadium on 11-03-62

The Patriots player with the longest punt in a regular season game played on Saturday Night

Tom Yewcic booted it 65 yards in the 17–13 loss to the San Diego Chargers at Balboa Stadium on 09-14-63

The Patriots Kicker with the longest field goal in a regular season game played on Saturday Night

Gino Cappelletti booted a 46-yard field goal in the 23–21 win over the Buffalo Bills at War Memorial Stadium on 09-23-61

The Most

The Patriots player with the most yards rushing in a regular season game played on Saturday Night

Jim Crawford had 95 yards rushing in the 35–0 shutout of the Los Angeles Chargers at the Los Angeles Coliseum on 10-08-60

The Patriots Receiver with the most yards receiving in a regular season game played on Saturday Night

Gino Cappelletti had 147 yards receiving in the 35–14 loss to the New York Jets at Shea Stadium on 10-31-64

The Patriots Quarterback with the most yards passing in a regular season game played on Saturday Night

Babe Parilli threw for 379 yards in the 38–28 loss to the New York Jets at Shea Stadium on 12-17-66

The Patriots player with the most special team return yards in a regular season game played on Saturday Night

Carl Garrett had 174 special team return yards in the 23–16 loss to the Bills at War Memorial Stadium on 10-11-69

The progression of the most points scored by a Patriots player in a regular season game played on Saturday Night

6 points were scored by Walt Livingston in the 28–24 win over the New York Titans at the Polo Grounds on 09-17-60

6 points were scored by Oscar Lofton in the 28–24 victory over the New York Titans at the Polo Grounds on 09-17-60

6 points were scored by Jim Colclough in the 28–24 victory over the New York Titans at the Polo Grounds on 09-17-60

6 points were scored by Chuck Shonta on the last play of the 28–24 win over the New York Titans at the Polo Grounds on 09-17-60

6 points were scored by Ron Burton in the 35–0 shutout of the Los Angeles Chargers at the LA Coliseum on 10-08-60

6 points were scored by Jim Colclough in the 35–0 shutout of the Los Angeles Chargers at the LA Coliseum on 10-08-60

6 points were scored by Jim Crawford in the 35–0 shutout of the Los Angeles Chargers at the LA Coliseum on 10-08-60

6 points were scored by Alan Miller in the 35–0 shutout of the Los Angeles Chargers at the LA Coliseum on 10-08-60

9 points were scored by Gino Cappelletti in the 35–0 shutout of the Los Angeles Chargers at the LA Coliseum on 10-08-60

12 points were scored by Gino Cappelletti in the 21–20 loss to the New York Titans at BU Field on 09-09-61

15 points were scored by Gino Cappelletti in the 45–17 rout of the Denver Broncos at BU Field on 09-16-61

19 points were scored by Gino Cappelletti in the 43–14 romp over the New York Titans at the Polo Grounds on 10-06-62

Every regular season game played by the Patriots on Sunday Afternoon

1960 regular season

Lost to the Oakland Raiders 27–14 at Kezar Stadium on 10-16-60 (Gino Cappelletti was second AFL player with three interceptions in a game)

Lost to the Denver Broncos 31–24 at Bears Stadium on 10-23-60 (Ron Burton had 127 yards rushing)

Lost to the Buffalo Bills 38–14 at War Memorial Stadium on 12-04-60 (Butch Songin threw a TD pass and ran for another)

Lost to the Dallas Texans 34–0 at the Cotton Bowl on 12-11-60 (Walt Cudzik's 41-yard field-goal attempt was short)

Lost to the Houston Oilers 37–21 at Jeppesen Stadium on 12-18-60 (Gino Cappelletti scored his third two-point conversion in 1960)

1961 regular season

Lost to the New Tork Titans 37–30 at the Polo Grounds on 10-01-61 (Gino Cappelletti threw a 27-yard TD pass on a fake field goal)

Destroyed the Buffalo Bills 52–21 at BU Field on 10-22-61 (The game was rescheduled due to a hurricane that never arrived)

Beat the Dallas Texans 18–17 at the Cotton Bowl on 10-29-61 (Gino Cappelletti kicked a game-winning 24-yard field goal) (The Game of the Year)

Lost to the Oilers 27–15 at Jeppesen Stadium on 11-12-61 (Butch Songin threw a TD pass and Babe Parilli ran for a TD)

Beat the Denver Broncos 28–24 at Bears Stadium on 12-03-61 (Ger Schwedes recovered an onside kick to secure the victory)

Shut out the San Diego Chargers 41–0 at Balboa Stadium on 12-17-61 (Don Webb returned a pass and a blocked punt for a TD)

1962 regular season
Defeated the Houston Oilers 34–21 at Harvard Stadium on 09-16-62 (Babe Parilli ran for a 32-yard TD) (The Game of the Year)

Beat Denver 33–29 at Bears Stadium on 11-11-62 (Ron Burton returned a missed field goal 91 yards for the game-winning TD)

Lost to the Houston Oilers 21–17 at Jeppesen Stadium on 11-18-62 (Ron Burton caught a 69-yard TD pass from Tom Yewcic)

Defeated the San Diego Chargers 20–14 at Balboa Stadium on 12-09-62 (Jim Crawford and Jim Colclough caught TD passes)

Lost to the Oakland Raiders 20–0 at Frank Youell Field on 12-16-62 (Tom Addison intercepted a pass on the 1-yard line)

1963 regular season
Defeated the New York Jets 38–14 at Boston College Alumni Stadium on 09-08-63 (Billy Lott had two four-yard TD runs)

Defeated the Oakland Raiders 20–14 at Frank Youell Field on 09-22-63 (The Patriots recorded 10 sacks in this game)

Lost to the Denver Broncos 14–10 at Bears Stadium on 09-29-63 (Gino Cappelletti scored every point for the Patriots)

Lost to the Chargers 7–6 at Fenway Park on 11-10-63 (Chargers WR Lance Alworth had 217 yards receiving and a TD)

Tied the Kansas City Chiefs 24–24 at Fenway Park on 11-17-63 (Tony Romeo had a career-high 149 yards receiving)

Beat the Buffalo Bills 17–7 at Fenway Park on 12-01-63 (Babe Parilli, who had a TD pass and a TD run, was given the game ball)

Beat the Oilers 46–28 at Jeppesen Stadium on 12-08-63 (Bob Suci returned a pass 52 yards for a TD after hearing audible "purple")

1964 regular season
Beat Oakland 17–14 at Frank Youell Field on 09-13-64 (Art Graham made a game-saving tackle on Hoot Gibson's punt return)

Beat the San Diego Chargers 33–28 at Balboa Stadium on 09-20-64 (Art Graham had game-saving tackle of Lance Alworth in the fourth quarter)

Defeated the New York Jets 26–10 at Boston College Alumni Stadium on 09-27-64 (Babe Parilli threw two 59-yard TD passes)

Destroyed the Denver Broncos 39–10 at Bears Stadium on 10-04-64 (Gino Cappelletti kicked six field goals)

Defeated the Buffalo Bills 36–28 at War Memorial Stadium on 11-15-64 (Gino Cappelletti scored 24 points)

Defeated the Houston Oilers 34–17 at Jeppesen Stadium on 11-29-64 (Art Graham caught an 80-yard TD pass)

Defeated the Kansas City Chiefs 31–24 at Municipal Stadium on 12-06-64 (Don Webb's late interception sealed the victory)

Lost to the Bills 24–14 at Fenway Park on 12-20-64 (Gino Cappelletti scored 155 points in the season and was league MVP)

1965 regular season
Lost to the Houston Oilers 31–10 at Rice Stadium on 09-19-65 (Nick Buoniconti blocked a 36-yard field-goal attempt by George Blanda)

Lost to the Kansas City Chiefs 27–17 at Municipal Stadium on 10-03-65 (Jim Nance ran for two TDs)

Tied the San Diego Chargers 13–13 at Fenway Park on 10-17-65 (Ron Burton had a 73-yard TD reception)

Lost to the Oakland Raiders 30–21 at Frank Youell Field on 10-24-65 (Ron Burton had a TD reception and ran for a TD)

Defeated the San Diego Chargers 22–6 at Balboa Stadium on 10-31-65 (Gino Cappelletti scored 20 points)

Lost to the Buffalo Bills 23–7 at Fenway Park on 11-07-65 (J.D. Garrett ran for a one-yard TD)

Lost to the New York Jets 30–20 at Fenway Park on 11-14-65 (Gino Cappelletti caught a TD pass and kicked two field goals and two PATs)

Tied the Kansas City Chiefs 10–10 at Fenway Park on 11-21-65 (J.D. Garrett caught a 10-yard TD pass in the fourth quarter)

Beat the Jets 27–23 at Shea Stadium on 11-28-65 (Tony Romeo caught a game-winning fourth-down TD pass) (The Game of the Year)

Defeated the Denver Broncos 28–20 at Bears Stadium on 12-12-65 (Houston Antwine had his only career interception)

1966 regular season

Beat the Broncos 24–10 at Bears Stadium on 09-18-66 (Jim Nance was given the nickname of "Odd Job" after this game)

Lost to the Kansas City Chiefs 43–24 at Fenway Park on 09-25-66 (Jim Nance ran for two TDs)

Tied the New York Jets 24–24 at Fenway Park on 10-02-66 (Larry Garron and Gino Cappelletti each scored 12 points)

Defeated the San Diego Chargers 35–17 at Fenway Park on 10-23-66 (Larry Garron had two 53-yard TD receptions and ran for another)

Defeated the Oakland Raiders 24–21 at Fenway Park on 10-30-66 (Jim Nance and Gino Cappelletti each scored 12 points)

Lost to the Denver Broncos 17–10 at Fenway Park on 11-06-66 (White Graves blocked a punt and each team lost five fumbles)

Defeated the Houston Oilers 27–21 at Fenway Park on 11-13-66 (Gino Cappelletti scored 21 points)

Tied the Kansas City Chiefs 27–27 at Municipal Stadium on 11-20-66 (Gino Cappelletti kicked game-tying field goal with 24 seconds left)

Defeated the Dolphins 20–14 at the Orange Bowl on 11-27-66 (Art Graham caught a TD pass while wearing only one shoe)

Beat Buffalo 14–3 at Fenway Park on 12-04-66 (The largest football crowd at Fenway Park) (The Game of the Year)

Destroyed the Houston Oilers 38–14 at Rice Stadium on 12-11-66 (Two Heisman Trophy winners connected on a 15-yard pass)

1967 regular season

Lost to Denver 26–21 at Bears Stadium on 09-03-67 (Art Graham's 79-yard TD reception was the longest in the AFL in 1967)

Lost to the Oakland Raiders 35–7 at the Oakland Coliseum on 09-17-67 (Maurice Hurst was born and Art Graham had a TD)

Shut out Buffalo 23–0 at War Memorial Stadium on 09-24-67 (Larry Eisenhauer and Jim Nance are AFL Players of the Week)

Tied the San Diego Chargers 31–31 at Jack Murphy Stadium on 10-08-67 (Game was played in San Diego because of 1967 World Series)

Destroyed the Dolphins 41–10 at Boston College Alumni Stadium on 10-15-67 (Babe Parilli threw five TDs) (The Game of the Year)

Lost to the Oakland Raiders 48–14 at Fenway Park on 10-22-67 (Jim Nance and Gino Cappelletti scored a TD)

Lost to the New York Jets 30–23 at Shea Stadium on 10-29-67 (The biggest crowd, 62,784, attended to watch the Boston Patriots)

Beat the Houston Oilers 18–7 at Fenway Park on 11-05-67 (Billy Johnson was the first Patriots special team player to get game ball)

Lost to the Kansas City Chiefs 33–10 at Fenway Park on 11-12-67 (Curt Gowdy and Paul Christman called the game for NBC)

Lost to the New York Jets 29–24 at Fenway Park on 11-19-67 (The Patriots scored 21 points in the fourth quarter on Cape Cod Day)

Lost to the Houston Oilers 27–6 at Rice Stadium on 11-26-67 (Jim Nance is first AFL RB with 1,000+ yards rushing in consecutive seasons)

Lost to the Miami Dolphins 41–32 at the Orange Bowl on 12-17-67 (Bob Cappadona caught a 19-yard TD pass for his only TD)

1968 regular season

Beat Buffalo 16–7 at War Memorial Stadium on 09-08-68 (Houston Antwine was AFL Defensive Player of the Week)

Lost to the New York Jets 47–31 at Legion Field on 09-22-68 (This home game was played in Birmingham, Alabama)

Beat Denver 20–17 at Bears Stadium on 09-29-68 (Gino Cappelletti kicked a tough-angled field goal to win game) (The Game of the Year)

Lost to the Oakland Raiders 41–10 at the Oakland Coliseum on 10-06-68 (Gene Thomas ran for a TD)

Lost to the Houston Oilers 16–0 at Fenway Park on 10-13-68 (Nick Buoniconti and John Charles each blocked a field-goal attempt)

Defeated the Buffalo Bills 23–6 at Fenway Park on 10-20-68 (MLB Nick Buoniconti had three interceptions)

Lost to the New York Jets 48–14 at Shea Stadium on 10-27-68 (Jim Whalen caught an 87-yard TD pass from Tom Sherman)

Lost to the Denver Broncos 35–14 at Fenway Park on 11-03-68 (Leroy Mitchell intercepted Steve Tensi and Marlin Briscoe)

Lost to San Diego 27–17 at Fenway Park on 11-10-68 (Doug Satcher and Billy Johnson had an interception and a fumble recovery)

Lost to the Kansas City Chiefs 31–17 at Municipal Stadium on 11-17-68 (R.C. Gamble and Aaron Marsh have TD receptions)

Lost to the Miami Dolphins 34–10 at Fenway Park on 11-24-68 (Aaron Marsh caught a 60-yard TD pass from Tom Sherman)

Defeated the Cincinnati Bengals 33–14 at Fenway Park on 12-01-68 (Tom Sherman threw three TD passes)

Lost to the Miami Dolphins 38–7 at the Orange Bowl on 12-08-68 (Jim Nance rumbled for a 30-yard TD)

Lost to the Houston Oilers 45–17 at the Astrodome on 12-15-68 (Jim Whalen led AFL tight ends with 47 receptions in 1968)

1969 regular season
Lost to the Denver Broncos 35–7 at Mile High Stadium on 09-14-69 (Carl Garrett ran for the only TD)

Lost to Kansas City 31–0 at BC Stadium on 09-21-69 (The Patriots had six first downs; two rushing, two passing, and two by penalty)

Lost to the Raiders 38–23 at BC Stadium on 09-28-69 (Larry Carwell had a 28-yard kickoff return and a 28-yard interception return)

Lost to the New York Jets 23–14 at Boston College Alumni Stadium on 10-05-69 (Bob Gladieux had a career-high three kickoff returns)

Lost to the San Diego Chargers 13–10 at Boston College Alumni Stadium on 10-19-69 (DE Ron Berger had a 20-yard kickoff return)

Lost to the New York Jets 23–17 at Shea Stadium on 10-26-69 (John Charles returned a Joe Namath pass for a TD)

Shut out the Houston Oilers 24–0 at Boston College Alumni Stadium on 11-02-69 (Daryl Johnson returned a fumble by Hoyle Granger 32 yards for a TD)

Lost to the Dolphins 17–16 at Boston College Alumni Stadium on 11-09-69 (Both completions were to Bill Rademacher)

Beat the Bengals 25–14 at Nippert Stadium on 11-16-69 (Jim Cheyunski was the AFL Defensive Player of the Week)

Beat the Bills 35–21 at Boston College Alumni Stadium on 11-23-69 (Mike Taliaferro threw three TDs) (The Game of the Year)

Defeated the Miami Dolphins 38–23 at Tampa Stadium on 11-30-69 (Ezell Jones tackled Mercury Morris for a safety)

Lost to the San Diego Chargers 28–18 at Jack Murphy Stadium on 12-07-69 (QB Kim Hammond ran a bootleg play for two points)

Lost to the Houston Oilers 27–23 at the Houston Astrodome on 12-14-69 (Ron Sellers had a career-best 158 yards receiving)

1970 regular season
Beat Miami 27–14 at Harvard Stadium on 09-20-70 (The game ball was given to Billy Sullivan) (The Game of the Year)

Lost to the New York Jets 31–21 at Harvard Stadium on 09-27-70 (Ron Sellers caught a 40-yard TD pass from Mike Taliaferro)

Lost to the Baltimore Colts 14–6 at Harvard Stadium on 10-04-70 (The Colts went on to win Super Bowl IV)

Lost to the Kansas City Chiefs 23–10 at Municipal Stadium on 10-11-70 (Art McMahon had a 72-yard interception return)

Lost to the New York Giants 16–0 at Harvard Stadium on 10-18-70 (Joe Kapp led the Patriots with 41 yards rushing)

Lost to the Baltimore Colts 27–3 at Memorial Stadium on 10-25-70 (Charlie Gogolak kicked a 15-yard field goal)

Lost to the Buffalo Bills 45–10 at Harvard Stadium on 11-01-70 (Tom Beer lateraled a kickoff to Carl Garrett twice)

Lost to the St. Louis Cardinals 31–0 at Busch Memorial Stadium on 11-08-70 (Clarence Scott had his only interception)

Lost to the San Diego Chargers 16–14 at Harvard Stadium on 11-15-70 (Odell Lawson had a career-long 52-yard kickoff return)

Lost to the New York Jets 17–3 at Shea Stadium on 11-22-70 (Marty Schottenheimer made the tackle on the opening kickoff)

Beat Buffalo 14–10 at War Memorial Stadium on 11-29-70 (H. Antwine's fumble recovery and J. Bramlett's interception set up TDs)

Lost to the Miami Dolphins 37–20 at the Orange Bowl on 12-06-70 (Gayle Knief had his only TD reception)

Lost to the Minnesota Vikings 35–14 at Harvard Stadium on 12-13-70 (Daryl Johnson led the team with 10 tackles)

Lost to the Cincinnati Bengals 45–7 at Riverfront Stadium on 12-20-70 (Ron Sellers caught a 12-yard TD pass from Joe Kapp)

1971 regular season
Beat the Oakland Raiders 20–6 at Schaefer Stadium on 09-19-71 (Ron Sellers and Roland Moss had TD receptions)

Lost to the Detroit Lions 34–7 at Schaefer Stadium on 09-26-71 (Randy Vatha caught a 61-yard TD pass from Jim Plunkett)

Lost to the Baltimore Colts 23–3 at Schaefer Stadium on 10-03-71 (Steve Kiner had 15 tackles)

Shutout the New York Jets 20–0 in heavy rain at Schaefer Stadium on 10-10-71 (Randy Vataha and Ron Sellers had TD receptions)

Lost to the Miami Dolphins 41–3 at the Orange Bowl on 10-17-71 (Charlie Gogolak kicked a 51-yard field goal)

Lost to the Cowboys 44–21 at Texas Stadium on 10-24-71 (The first NFL game that Heisman Trophy QBs played each other)

Lost to the San Francisco 49ers 27–10 at Candlestick Park on 10-31-71 (OG Halvor Hagen had a seven-yard kickoff return)

Beat the Houston Oilers 28–20 at Schaefer Stadium on 11-07-71 (Bob Gladiuex threw a left-handed 48-yard HB option pass)

Defeated the Buffalo Bills 38–33 at Schaefer Stadium on 11-14-71 (Roland Moss blocked a punt and took it 10 yards for a TD)

Lost to the Cleveland Browns 27–7 at Municipal Stadium on 11-21-71 (Tom Beer caught a TD pass from Jim Plunkett)

Lost to the Buffalo Bills 27–20 at War Memorial Stadium on 11-28-71 (Carl Garrett had a career-high 127 yards rushing)

Beat the Dolphins 34–13 at Schaefer Stadium on 12-05-71 (Fans sang "Happy Birthday" to Jim Plunkett) (The Game of the Year)

Lost to the New York Jets 13–6 at Shea Stadium on 12-12-71 (John Outlaw stopped a Jets drive with an end zone fumble recovery)

Beat the Baltimore Colts 21–17 at Memorial Stadium on 12-19-71 (Jim Plunkett was the NFL Offensive Player of the Week)

1972 regular season
Lost to the Bengals 31–7 at Schaefer Stadium on 09-17-72 (Mike "Superfoot" Walker's opening kickoff goes out of the end zone)

Beat the Atlanta Falcons 21–20 at Schaefer Stadium on 09-24-72 (Carl Garrett ran for the game-winning TD) (The Game of the Year)

Defeated the Washington Redskins 24–23 at Schaefer Stadium on 10-01-72 (The Patriots second consecutive one-point win)

Lost to the Buffalo Bills 38–14 at War Memorial Stadium on 10-08-72 (The Patriots scored first and last in this game)

Lost to the New York Jets 41–13 at Schaefer Stadium on 10-15-72 (Carl Garrett dashed 41 yards for a TD)

Lost to the Pittsburgh Steelers 33–3 at Three Rivers Stadium on 10-22-72 (Brian Dowling had his longest pass completion)

Lost to the New York Jets 34–10 at Shea Stadium on 10-29-72 (Brian Dowling scored a TD with 20 seconds left)

Lost to the Miami Dolphins 52–0 at the Orange Bowl on 11-12-72 (Rick "Thumper" Cash blocked a field-goal attempt)

Lost to the Bills 27–24 at Schaefer Stadium on 11-19-72 (Punter Pat Studstill ran 11 yards for a first down to set up a TD)

Lost to the Baltimore Colts 31–0 at Memorial Stadium on 11-26-72 (George Hoey halted Marty Domres no interception streak)

Lost to the Miami Dolphins 37–21 at Schaefer Stadium on 12-03-72 (John Tarver had his only NFL TD reception)

Beat the New Orleans Saints 17–10 at the Superdome on 12-10-72 (Reggie Rucker caught two TDs within 60 seconds)

Lost to Denver 45–21 at Mile High Stadium on 12-17-72 (Tom Reynolds caught a 28-yard TD pass from Brian Dowling)

1973 regular season
Lost to the Bills 31–13 at Schaefer Stadium on 09-16-73 (Ron Bolton deflected an OJ Simpson pass that was completed)

Lost to the Kansas City Chiefs 10–7 at Schaefer Stadium on 09-23-73 (Sam "Bam" Cunningham dove for a TD with 1:02 left)

Lost to the Miami Dolphins 44–23 at the Orange Bowl on 09-30-73 (John Tarver ran for two TDs)

Defeated the Baltimore Colts 24–16 at Schaefer Stadium on 10-07-73 (Mack Herron's 54-yard punt return set up a TD)

Lost to the New York Jets 9–7 at Schaefer Stadium on 10-14-73 (Rick "Thumper" Cash had 16 tackles and a sack)

Defeated the Chicago Bears 13–10 at Soldier Field on 10-21-73 (Jim Plunkett's TD run was the game-winning score in fourth quarter)

Lost to the Miami Dolphins 30–14 at Schaefer Stadium on 10-28-73 (Sam Cunningham had a TD reception and a TD run)

Lost to Philly 24–23 at Veterans Stadium on 11-04-73 (Darryl Stingley had a one-handed TD catch and a leaping TD reception)

Lost to the New York Jets 33–13 at Shea Stadium on 11-11-73 (Bob Windsor caught two TD passes from Jim Plunkett)

Defeated the Packers 33–24 at Schaefer Stadium on 11-18-73 (The Patriots scored the final 24 points) (The Game of the Year)

Shut out the Houston Oilers 32–0 at the Astrodome on 11-25-73 (Steve Kiner sacked Dan Pastorini for a safety)

Defeated the San Diego Chargers 30–14 at Schaefer Stadium on 12-02-73 (Jim Plunkett ran for two TDs and threw a TD pass)

Lost to the Buffalo Bills 37–13 at Rich Stadium on 12-09-73 (Jim Plunkett ran for a 5-yard TD)

Lost to the Baltimore Colts 18–13 at Memorial Stadium on 12-16-73 (Randy Vataha and Mack Herron had TD receptions)

1974 regular season
Defeated the Miami Dolphins 34–24 at Schaefer Stadium on 09-15-74 (The Dolphins won the 1973 Super Bowl)

Defeated the New York Giants 28–20 at the Yale Bowl on 09-22-74 (Mack Herron had a TD reception and a TD run)

Defeated the Los Angeles Rams 20–14 at Schaefer Stadium on 09-29-74 (Art May blocked a 41-yard field-goal attempt by David Ray)

Destroyed the Baltimore Colts 42–3 at Schaefer Stadium on 10-06-74 (Reggie Rucker had two TD receptions)

Shut out the New York Jets 24–0 at Shea Stadium on 10-13-74 (Steve King intercepted Joe Namath for his only career interception)

Lost to Buffalo 30–28 at Rich Stadium on 10-20-74 (Sam Cunningham had three TDs and ran 75 yards for a TD on the first play)

Beat Minnesota 17–14 at Metropolitan Stadium on 10-27-74 (Bob Windsor scored the game-winning TD) (The Game of the Year)

Lost to the Buffalo Bills 29–28 at Schaefer Stadium on 11-03-74 (Mel Lunsford blocked an extra point)

Lost to the Cleveland Browns 21–14 at Schaefer Stadium on 11-10-74 (Sam Cunningham scored on successive drives)

Lost to the New York Jets 21–16 at Schaefer Stadium on 11-17-74 (LB Sam Hunt returned a kickoff 21 yards)

Defeated the Baltimore Colts 27–17 at Memorial Stadium on 11-24-74 (LB/TE John Tanner caught a two-yard TD pass)

Lost to the Oakland Raiders 41–26 at the Oakland Coliseum on 12-01-74 (Jim Plunkett had his longest run of 37 yards)

Mack Herron

Lost to the Pittsburgh Steelers 21–17 at Schaefer Stadium on 12-08-74 (Mack Herron had a TD reception and ran for a TD)

Lost to the Dolphins 34–27 at the Orange Bowl on 12-15-74 (Mack Herron set NFL record with 2,444 all-purpose yards)

1975 regular season
Lost to the Houston Oilers 7–0 at Schaefer Stadium on 09-21-75 (Seven Patriots players had at least one rushing attempt)

Lost to Miami 22–14 at Schaefer Stadium on 09-28-75 (Neil Graff threw a TD passs to Randy Vataha and Russ Francis)

Lost to the New York Jets 36–7 at Shea Stadium on 10-05-75 (Steve Grogan's first TD pass was a 42-yard TD to Russ Francis)

Lost to the Cincinnati Bengals 27–10 at Riverfront Stadium on 10-12-75 (Mack Herron had a career-best 119 yards rushing)

Defeated the Baltimore Colts 21–10 at Schaefer Stadium on 10-19-75 ("Nellie" had 16 tackles, a sack, and a pass deflection)

Beat the 49ers 24–16 at Schaefer Stadium on 10-26-75 (AJ had consecutive games with 100+ yards rushing) (The Game of the Year)

Lost to the St. Louis Cardinals 24–17 at Busch Stadium on 11-02-75 ("Sugarbear" Hamilton scored a TD and blocked a field goal)

Beat the San Diego Chargers 33–19 at Jack Murphy Stadium on 11-09-75 (Bob Howard returned a Dan Fouts pass for a TD)

Lost to the Dallas Cowboys 34–31 at Schaefer Stadium on 11-16-75 (Steve Burks had his longest reception of 76 yards)

Lost to the Buffalo Bills 45–31 at Rich Stadium on 11-23-75 (Sam Cunningham ran for two scores and caught a TD pass)

Lost to the New York Jets 30–28 at Schaefer Stadium on 12-07-75 (Pete Cusick blocked two field-goal attempts by Pat Leahy)

Lost to the Bills 34–14 at Schaefer Stadium on 12-14-75 (Don Calhoun had a 62-yard TD reception and 100 yards receiving)

Lost to the Baltimore Colts 34–21 at Memorial Stadium on 12-21-75 (Allen Carter took the opening kickoff 99 yards for a TD)

1976 regular season
Lost to the Baltimore Colts 27–13 at Schaefer Stadium on 09-12-76 (Julius Adams sacked Bert Jones for a loss of 24 yards)

Beat the Miami Dolphins 30–14 at Schaefer Stadium on 09-19-76 (Andy Johnson had two TD receptions)

Beat the Pittsburgh Steelers 30–27 at Three Rivers Stadium on 09-26-76 (Russ Francis caught a 38-yard TD pass on fourth-and-2)

Destroyed the Oakland Raiders 48–17 at Schaefer Stadium on 10-03-76 (Oakland won the Super Bowl) (The Game of the Year)

Lost to the Lions 30–10 at Pontiac Stadium on 10-10-76 (Darryl Stingley and Russ Francis made a tackle on interception returns)

Don Calhoun (44) and John Hannah (73)

Beat the Buffalo Bills 26–22 at Rich Stadium on 10-24-76 (Steve Grogan ran a 10-yard bootleg play for the game-winning TD)

Lost to the Miami Dolphins 10–3 at the Orange Bowl on 10-31-76 (John Smith kicked a field goal with three seconds left in the half)

Beat the Buffalo Bills 20–10 at Schaefer Stadium on 11-07-76 (Mel Lunsford and OJ Simpson were ejected for fighting)

Defeated the Baltimore Colts 21–14 at Memorial Stadium on 11-14-76 (Steve Grogan ran for two TDs and threw a TD pass)

Beat the New York Jets 38–24 at Shea Stadium on 11-21-76 (Prentice McCray returned two Joe Namath passes for TDs)

Crushed the Denver Broncos 38–14 at Schaefer Stadium on 11-28-76 (Patriots set team record with 332 yards rushing)

Beat the New Orleans Saints 27–6 at Schaefer Stadium on 12-05-76 (John Smith hit the upright on a 30-yard extra-point attempt)

Beat the Tampa Bay Buccaneers 31–14 at Tampa Stadium on 12-12-76 (Steve Grogan set NFL record with 12 rushing TDs)

1977 regular season
Beat the Chiefs 21–17 at Schaefer Stadium on 09-18-77 (Darryl Stingley ran for a TD and caught a TD) (The Game of the Year)

Lost to the New York Jets 30–27 at Shea Stadium on 10-02-77 (Raymond Clayborn returned a kickoff 100 yards for a TD)

Shut out the Seattle Seahawks 31–0 at Schaefer Stadium on 10-09-77 (Russ Francis recovered a fumble on the Patriots first play)

Defeated the San Diego Chargers 24–20 at Jack Murphy Stadium on 10-16-77 (Sam Cunningham had a career-best 141 yards rushing)

Beat the Baltimore Colts 17–3 at Schaefer Stadium on 10-23-77 (Doug Beaudoin advanced a blocked punt eight yards for a first down)

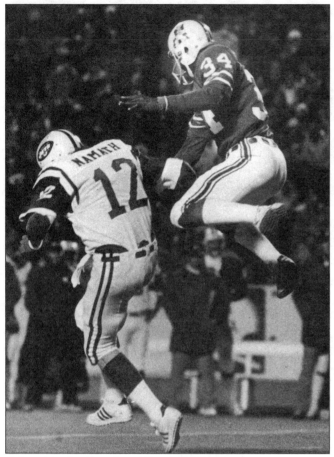

Left to right: Joe Namath and Prentice McCray

Defeated the New York Jets 24–13 at Schaefer Stadium on 10-30-77 (Darryl Stingley had a career-best eight receptions)

Lost to the Buffalo Bills 24–14 at Schaefer Stadium on 11-06-77 (Tim Fox and Steve King had 14 tackles)

Lost to Miami 17–5 at the Orange Bowl on 11-13-77 (Raymond Clayborn forced Miami's punter out of the end zone for a safety)

Defeated the Buffalo Bills 20–7 at Rich Stadium on 11-20-77 (Sam Cunningham ran for two TDs)

Beat the Eagles 14–6 at Schaefer Stadium on 11-27-77 (Roman Gabriel tackled Sam Hunt on his six-yard return of a blocked field-goal attempt)

Beat the Atlanta Falcons 16–10 at Fulton County Stadium on 12-04-77 (Ray Clayborn's 78-yard kickoff return sealed the win)

Defeated the Miami Dolphins 14–10 at Schaefer Stadium on 12-11-77 (Steve Grogan had seven carries and six completions)

Lost to the Baltimore Colts 30–24 at Memorial Stadium on 12-18-77 (Steve Grogan called all 922 offensive plays in the year)

1978 regular season

Lost to the Washington Redskins 16–14 at Schaefer Stadium on 09-03-78 (Harold Jackson caught a 45-yard TD pass)

Defeated the St. Louis Cardinals 16–6 at Busch Stadium on 09-10-78 (Don Calhoun had a 74-yard run from scrimmage)

Beat the San Diego Chargers 28–23 at Schaefer Stadium on 10-01-78 (Steve Grogan threw three TDs and ran for the game-wininng TD)

Defeated the Philadelphia Eagles 24–14 at Schaefer Stadium on 10-08-78 (Stanley Morgan caught a 58-yard TD pass)

Beat the Cincinnati Bengals 10–3 at Riverfront Stadium on 10-15-78 (Sam "Bam" Cunningham ran for the game-winning TD)

Defeated the Miami Dolphins 33–24 at Schaefer Stadium on 10-22-78 (Richard Bishop sacked Bob Griese for a safety)

Darryl Stingley

Beat the New York Jets 55–21 at Schaefer Stadium on 10-29-78 (The second consecutive game that the Patriots had four rushing TDs)

Beat the Buffalo Bills 14–10 at Rich Stadium on 11-05-78 (Horace Ivory scored two TDs and had a career-best 128 yards rushing)

Lost to the Houston Oilers 26–23 at Schaefer Stadium on 11-12-78 (The Patriots led 23–0 and missed two field goals)

Beat the New York Jets 19–17 at Shea Stadium on 11-19-78 (Steve Nelson tapped Pat Leahy on the helmet after he missed a field goal)

Defeated the Baltimore Colts 35–14 at Memorial Stadium on 11-26-78 (Mike Haynes returned an interception for a TD)

Lost to the Dallas Cowboys 17–10 at Texas Stadium on 12-03-78 (Sam Cunningham bolted 52 yards for a TD)

Beat the Bills 26–24 at Schaefer Stadium on 12-10-78 (David Posey kicked a game-winning field goal) (The Game of the Year)

1979 regular season
Destroyed the New York Jets 56–3 at Schaefer Stadium on 09-09-79 (Mike Hawkins had four sacks) (The Game of the Year)

Defeated the Cincinnati Bengals 20–14 at Riverfront Stadium on 09-16-79 (Andy Johnson recovered an onside kick)

Beat San Diego 27–21 at Schaefer Stadium on 09-23-79 (Shelby Jordan made a game-saving tackle on an interception return)

Defeated the Detroit Lions 24–17 at Schaefer Stadium on 10-07-79 (Don Calhoun caught a TD pass in the fourth quarter)

Defeated the Chicago Bears 27–7 at Soldier Field on 10-14-79 (Pete Brock was a LT, LS, TE, and Wing Back on the same drive)

Defeated the Miami Dolphins 28–13 at Schaefer Stadium on 10-21-79 (Ray Jarvis caught a 15-yard TD pass from Steve Grogan)

Lost to the Baltimore Colts 31–26 at Memorial Stadium on 10-28-79 (Steve Grogan threw two TDs and ran for another)

Defeated the Buffalo Bills 26–6 at Rich Stadium on 11-04-79 (Stanley Morgan had 69-yard and 34-yard TD receptions)

Lost to Denver 45–10 at Mile High Stadium on 11-11-79 (Game footage was used in the movie *Everybody's All American*)

Destroyed the Baltimore Colts 50–21 at Schaefer Stadium on 11-18-79 (Rick Sanford blocked a punt and took it eight yards for a TD)

Lost to Buffalo 16–13 in overtime at Schaefer Stadium on 11-25-79 (Bills LB Jim Haslett's second interception help set up their final field goal)

Lost to the New York Jets 27–26 at Shea Stadium on 12-09-79 (Stanley Morgan had 48-yard and 39-yard TD receptions)

Defeated the Vikings 27–23 at Schaefer Stadium on 12-16-79 (Don Westbrook made a tackle for a loss on a fake punt play)

1980 regular season
Defeated the Cleveland Browns 34–17 at Schaefer Stadium on 09-07-80 (Stanley Morgan had a 67-yard TD reception)

Lost to the Atlanta Falcons 37–21 at Schaefer Stadium on 09-14-80 (Don Hasselbeck and Don Calhoun each scored a TD)

Defeated the Seattle Seahawks 37–31 at the Kingdome on 09-21-80 (Ray Clayborn's interception sealed the win) (The Game of the Year)

Defeated the New York Jets 21–11 at Shea Stadium on 10-05-80 (Harold Jackson caught a TD pass from Matt Cavanaugh)

Shut out the Miami Dolphins 34–0 at Schaefer Stadium on 10-12-80 (Steve Grogan and Matt Cavanaugh threw a TD pass)

Defeated the Baltimore Colts 37–21 at Memorial Stadium on 10-19-80 (Chuck Foreman lept on fourth down for a one-yard TD)

Lost to the Buffalo Bills 31–13 at Rich Stadium on 10-26-80 (Tim Fox had an interception on the last play of the first half)

Defeated the New York Jets 34–21 at Schaefer Stadium on 11-02-80 (On a WR reverse, Harold Jackson threw a 23-yard pass)

Lost to the LA Rams 17–14 at Schaefer Stadium on 11-16-80 (Steve Grogan made TD-saving tackle on an 80-yard interception return)

Defeated the Baltimore Colts 47–21 at Schaefer Stadium on 11-23-80 (Rick Sanford took a fumbled kickoff return for a TD)

Lost to the San Francisco 49ers 21–17 at Candlestick Park on 11-30-80 (Mosi Tatupu ran for two TDs)

Beat the Bills 24–2 at Schaefer (with wind chill minus-10 degrees) on 12-14-80 (Mike Haynes recovered a fumble by OL Reggie McKenzie)

Defeated the New Orleans Saints 38–27 at the Louisiana Superdome on 12-21-80 (Pete Brock played against his brother Stan)

1981 regular season
Lost to the Colts 29–28 at Schaefer on 09-06-81 (RB Andy Johnson completed a pass to "Grogs" and Mosi Tatupu)

Lost to the Eagles 13–3 at Veterans Stadium on 09-13-81 (The only game John Smith and Tony Franklin played against each other)

Lost to Pittsburgh 27–21 in overtime at Three Rivers Stadium on 09-27-81 (Matt Cavanaugh ran eight yards on fourth down to set up game-tying TD)

Beat the Chiefs 33–17 at Schaefer Stadium on 10-04-81 (Mark Buben had a 49-yard interception return of a ball that popped up in the air)

Lost to the New York Jets 28–24 at Shea Stadium on 10-11-81 (TE Don Hasselbeck had his career-longest reception)

Beat the Houston Oilers 38–10 at Schaefer Stadium on 10-18-81 (Steve Grogan ran a 24-yard naked reverse for a TD) (The Game of the Year)

Lost to the Redskins 24–22 at RFK Stadium on 10-25-81 (Mosi Tatupu recovered a fumble on the opening kickoff)

Lost to the Raiders 27–17 at the Oakland Coliseum on 11-01-81 (Rich Camarillo booted the longest punt in the NFL in 1981)

Lost to Miami 30–27 in overtime at Schaefer Stadium on 11-08-81 (Stanley Morgan caught a 76-yard TD pass on the Patriots' fifth play)

Lost to the Jets 17–6 at Schaefer Stadium on 11-15-81 (The Jets sacked Steve Grogan three times and Matt Cavanaugh five times)

Lost to the Buffalo Bills 20–17 at Rich Stadium on 11-22-81 (Don Hasselbeck caught a five-yard TD pass with two minutes left)

Lost to the St. Louis Cardinals 27–20 at Schaefer Stadium on 11-29-81 (Matt Cavanaugh threw a 41-yard flea flicker pass to S. Morgan)

Lost to the Miami Dolphins 24–14 at the Orange Bowl on 12-06-81 (Matt Cavanaugh threw a TD pass and ran for another)

Lost to the Buffalo Bills 19–10 at Schaefer Stadium on 12-13-81 (Vagas Ferguson ran 19 yards for a TD)

Lost to Baltimore 23–21 at Memorial Stadium on 12-20-81 (Don Westbrook caught TDs from Tom Owen and Matt Cavanaugh)

1982 regular season
Defeated the Baltimore Colts 24–13 at Memorial Stadium on 09-12-82 (Rex Robinson kicked his only field goal in the NFL)

Lost to the New York Jets 31–7 at Schaefer Stadium on 09-19-82 (Ricky Smith returned a kickoff 98 yards for a TD)

Lost to the Cleveland Browns 10–7 at Municipal Stadium on 11-21-82 (Mark van Eeghen became 19th player with 6,000+ yards)

Defeated the Houston Oilers 29–21 at Schaefer Stadium on 11-28-82 (Don Blackmon returned an Earl Campbell fumble 47 yards)

Mosi Tatupu (30)

Lost to the Chicago Bears 26–13 at Soldier Field on 12-05-82 (Rick Sanford returned a Jim McMahon pass 99 yards for a TD)

Shut out the Miami Dolphins 3–0 at Schaefer Stadium on 12-12-82 (Mark van Eeghen had 100 yards rushing)

Shut out the Seattle Seahawks 16–0 at the Kingdome on 12-19-82 (Lester Williams blocked a field goal to preserve shutout)

Lost to the Pittsburgh Steelers 37–14 at Three Rivers Stadium on 12-26-82 (QB Tom Flick played in three series to start second half)

Beat Buffalo 30–19 at Schaefer Stadium on 01-02-83 (Stanley Morgan had 141 yards receiving) (The Game of the Year)

1983 regular season
Lost to the Baltimore Colts 29–23 in overtime at Sullivan Stadium on 09-04-83 (Stephen Starring had a 73-yard TD reception)

Lost to Miami 34–24 at the Orange Bowl on 09-11-83 (Ronnie Lippett had eight tackles, deflected a pass, and recovered a fumble)

Defeated the New York Jets 23–13 at Sullivan Stadium on 09-18-83 (Tony Collins set a team record with 212 yards rushing)

Beat the Steelers 28–23 at Three Rivers Stadium on 09-25-83 (Clayton Weishuhn took a lateral 27 yards for a TD) (The Game of the Year)

Lost to the 49ers 33–13 at Sullivan Stadium on 10-02-83 (Former Patriot TE Russ Francis caught an 8-yard TD pass from Joe Montana)

Lost to the Baltimore Colts 12–7 at Memorial Stadium on 10-09-83 (Cedric Jones caught a TD pass from Steve Grogan)

Defeated the San Diego Chargers 37–21 at Sullivan Stadium on 10-16-83 (The Patriots had four rushing TDs)

Shut out the Buffalo Bills 31–0 at Rich Stadium on 10-23-83 (Roland James intercepted Joe Ferguson three times in third quarter)

Lost to the Falcons 24–13 at Fulton County Stadium on 10-30-83 (Mosi Tatupu recovered a Patriots onside kick to no avail)

Defeated the Buffalo Bills 21–7 at Sullivan Stadium on 11-06-83 (Clarence Weathers had a 40-yard TD and a 58-yard TD reception)

Defeated the Dolphins 17–6 at Sullivan Stadium on 11-13-83 (Ken "Game Day" Sims stopped Woody Bennett on fourth-and-goal)

Lost to the Browns 30–0 at Sullivan Stadium on 11-20-83 (Stanley Morgan advanced a Tony Collins fumble 20 yards)

Lost to the New York Jets 26–3 at Shea Stadium on 11-27-83 (Fred "Suitcase" Steinfort kicked a 33-yard field goal)

Shut out the New Orleans Saints 7–0 at Sullivan Stadium on 12-04-83 (Mosi Tatupu had a career-best 128 yards rushing)

Defeated the Los Angeles Rams 21–7 at Anaheim Stadium on 12-11-83 (Andre Tippett stole the ball from Eric Dickerson)

Lost to the Seattle Seahawks 24–6 at the Kingdome on 12-18-83 (Derrick Ramsey caught a 33-yard TD pass from Tony Eason)

1984 regular season
Beat the Buffalo Bills 21–17 at Rich Stadium on 09-02-84 (Stephen Starring caught a 65-yard TD pass from Steve Grogan)

Lost to the Miami Dolphins 28–7 at the Orange Bowl on 09-09-84 (Lin Dawson caught a 9-yard TD pass from Steve Grogan)

Beat the Seahawks 38–23 at Sullivan Stadium on 09-16-84 (The Patriots scored the final 38 points) (The Game of the Year)

Lost to the Redskins 26–10 at Sullivan Stadium on 09-23-84 (Stephen Starring caught a TD pass from Tony Eason)

Defeated the New York Jets 28–21 at Shea Stadium on 09-30-84 (Tony Eason completed a pass to 10 Patriots players)

Beat the Browns 17–16 at Cleveland Stadium on 10-07-84 (Ray Clayborn had an 85-yard interception return on the last play)

Defeated the Cincinnati Bengals 20–14 at Sullivan Stadium on 10-14-84 (Tony Franklin and Tony Eason scored all of the points)

Lost to the Dolphins 44–24 at Sullivan Stadium on 10-21-84 (Stanley Morgan caught a 76-yard TD pass from Tony Eason)

Defeated the Miami Dolphins 30–20 at Sullivan Stadium on 10-28-84 (Patriots celebrated their 25th aniversary at halftime)

Lost to the Denver Broncos 26–19 at Mile High Stadium on 11-04-84 (Tony Franklin kicked four field goals and an extra point)

Defeated the Buffalo Bills 38–10 at Sullivan Stadium on 11-11-84 (Andre Tippett recorded his only fourth-down sack)

Destroyed the Indianapolis Colts 50–17 at the Hoosier Dome on 11-18-84 (Derrick Ramsey had three TD receptions)

Lost to the St. Louis Cardinals 33–10 at Sullivan Stadium on 12-02-84 (Craig James had his career-longest run of 73 yards)

Lost to the Eagles 27–17 at Veterans Stadium on 12-09-84 (Cedric Jones returned a fumbled kickoff return for a TD)

Beat the Indianapolis Colts 16–10 at Sullivan Stadium on 12-16-84 (Ed Williams recovered a fumbled punt return to set up a TD)

1985 regular season
Beat the Green Bay Packers 26–20 at Sullivan Stadium on 09-08-85 (Craig James scored a 65-yard TD on "Toss 38" in the fourth quarter)

Lost to the Chicago Bears 20–7 at Soldier Field on 09-15-85 (Craig James caught a 90-yard TD pass from Tony Eason)

Defeated the Buffalo Bills 17–14 at Rich Stadium on 09-22-85 (Irving Fryar had an NFL season-best 85-yard punt return for TD in 1985)

Lost to the Los Angeles Raiders 35–20 at Sullivan Stadium on 09-29-85 (Andre Tippett took a high snap 25 yards for a TD)

Lost to the Cleveland Browns 24–20 at Cleveland Stadium on 10-06-85 (Johnny Rembert recovered a fumble for a TD)

Beat Buffalo 14–3 at Sullivan Stadium on 10-13-85 (Steve Grogan threw a 56-yard pass to Irving Fryar to end the first half)

Beat the New York Jets 20–13 at Sullivan Stadium on 10-20-85 (Steve Grogan scored the game-winning TD) (The Game of the Year)

Defeated the Tampa Bay Buccaneers 32–14 at Tampa Stadium on 10-27-85 (Tony Collins had 109 yards receiving and one TD)

Defeated the Miami Dolphins 17–13 at Sulllivan Stadium on 11-03-85 (Steve "Big House" Moore was used in the backfield)

Defeated the Indianapolis Colts 34–15 at Sullivan Stadium on 11-10-85 (Irving Fryar had a TD reception and a punt return TD)

Defeated the Seattle Seahawks 20–13 at the Kingdome on 11-17-85 (Irving Fryar had game-winning TD reception in fourth quarter)

Lost to the Jets 16–13 in overtime at Shea Stadium on 11-24-85 (Tony Franklin kicked a field goal with 16 seconds left to force overtime)

Defeated the Indianapolis Colts 38–31 at the Hoosier Dome on 12-01-85 (QB Stephen Starring pitched it to Tony Collins)

Defeated the Detroit Lions 23–6 at Sullivan Stadium on 12-08-85 (Tony Eason ran for a TD and threw a TD pass)

Defeated the Cincinnati Bengals 34–23 at Sullivan Stadium on 12-22-85 (Craig James had a career-best 142 yards rushing)

Johnny Rembert (52) and Brian Ingram (51)

1986 regular season

Beat the Indianapolis Colts 33–3 at Sullivan Stadium on 09-07-86 (Brent Williams took a fumble 26 yards to set up a TD)

Lost to the Seahawks 38–31 at Sullivan on 09-21-86 (S. Morgan, I. Fryar, and C. Jones had 345 combined yards receiving)

Lost to the Denver Broncos 27–20 at Mile High Stadium on 09-28-86 (Irving Fryar caught a TD pass on the last play)

Destroyed the Dolphins 34–7 at Sullivan Stadium on 10-05-86 (Tony Eason threw two TDs and Steve Grogan threw a TD pass)

Lost to the New York Jets 31–24 at Sullivan Stadium on 10-12-86 (Stanley Morgan and Irving Fryar had 288 combined yards receiving)

Shutout the Pittsburgh Steelers 34–0 at Three Rivers Stadium on 10-19-86 (Larry McGrew blocked a punt)

Defeated the Buffalo Bills 23–3 at Rich Stadium on 10-26-86 (Andre Tippett had 3-1/2 sacks and advanced a lateral 32 yards)

Defeated the Atlanta Falcons 25–17 at Sullivan Stadium on 11-02-86 (Don Blackmon blocked a field-goal attempt)

Defeated the Indianapolis Colts 30–21 at the Hoosier Dome on 11-09-86 (Steve Nelson returned a pass to the 1-yard line)

Beat the Los Angeles Rams 30–28 at Anaheim Stadium on 11-16-86 (Irving Fryar caught a tipped "Hail Mary" TD pass on the last play)

Beat the Buffalo Bills 22–19 at Sullivan Stadium on 11-23-86 (Greg Baty caught a game-winning TD pass from Tony Eason)

Defeated the Saints 21–20 at the Superdome on 11-30-86 (Brent Williams returned a fumble for the game-winning TD)

Lost to the Bengals 31–7 at Sullivan Stadium on 12-07-86 (Irving Fryar had a 54-yard punt return, 34 yards rushing, and 68 yards receiving)

Lost to the 49ers 29–24 at Sullivan Stadium on 12-14-86 (Greg Baty caught an eight-yard TD pass on the Patriots third play)

Left to right: Tony Eason (11), head coach Raymond Berry, and Steve Grogan (14)

1987 regular season

Beat the Dolphins 28–21 at Sullivan Stadium on 09-13-87 (Steve Grogan's key block allowed Tony Collins to run for a TD)

Lost to the Browns 20–10 at Sullivan Stadium on 10-04-87 (34,780 tickets were returned and 10,501 were not used due to players' strike)

Defeated the Buffalo Bills 14–7 at Sullivan Stadium on 10-11-87 (Dino Mangiero sacked Willie Totten on the last play)

Defeated the Houston Oilers 21–7 at the Houston Astrodome on 10-18-87 (Ray Clayborn returned a blocked field goal for a TD)

Lost to the Indianapolis Colts 30–16 at the Hoosier Dome on 10-25-87 (The first game played after players' strike was settled)

Defeated the LA Raiders 26–23 at Sullivan Stadium on 11-01-87 (Mosi Tatupu threw a fourth-down TD pass to Tony Collins)

Lost to the Dallas Cowboys 23–17 in overtime at Sullivan Stadium on 11-15-87 (Andre Tippett sacked Danny White three times)

Shut out the Indianapolis Colts 24–0 at Sullivan Stadium on 11-22-87 (Andre Tippett had three sacks) (The Game of the Year)

Lost to the Philadelphia Eagles 34–31 in overtime at Sullivan Stadium on 11-29-87 (RB Tony Collins had 11 receptions)

Lost to the Denver Broncos 31–20 at Mile High Stadium on 12-06-87 (Reggie Dupard had his longest run of 49 yards)

Routed the New York Jets 42–20 at Sullivan Stadium on 12-13-87 (Cedric Jones had two TD receptions and recovered an onside kick)

Defeated the Buffalo Bills 13–7 at Rich Stadium on 12-20-87 (Reggie Dupard dashed 36 yards for a TD)

1988 regular season
Destroyed the New York Jets 28–3 at Sullivan Stadium on 09-04-88 (Irving Fryar caught two TD passes from Steve Grogan)

Lost to the Minnesota Vikings 36–6 at the Metrodome on 09-11-88 (Eight Patriots players combined to rush for only 102 yards)

Lost to the Bills 16–14 at Sullivan Stadium on 09-18-88 (Steve Grogan threw two TDs within a four-minute span in the second quarter)

Lost to the Houston Oilers 31–6 at the Houston Astrodome on 09-25-88 (Steve Grogan ran for a TD)

Beat the Indianapolis Colts 21–17 at Sullivan Stadium on 10-02-88 (Doug Flutie ran for the game-winning TD)

Lost to the Green Bay Packers at Milwaukee County Stadium on 10-09-88 (Reggie Dupard had a career-high seven receptions)

Beat the Cincinnati Bengals 27–21 at Sullivan Stadium on 10-16-88 (Robert Perryman almost scored a TD on his birthday)

Lost to the Buffalo Bills 23–20 at Rich Stadium on 10-23-88 (Doug Flutie completed a TD pass on his birthday)

Defeated the Chicago Bears 30–7 at Sullivan Stadium on 10-30-88 (Doug Flutie tossed four TDs) (The Game of the Year)

Beat Miami 21–10 at Sullivan Stadium on 11-06-88 (John Stephens had his third consecutive game with 100+ yards rushing)

Defeated the New York Jets 14–13 at Shea Stadium on 11-13-88 (Cedric Jones recovered an onside kick to secure the victory)

Lost to the Colts 24–21 at the Hoosier Dome on 11-27-88 (Sammy Martin took the opening kickoff 95 yards for a TD)

Stanley Morgan (86) and Irving Fryar (80)

Defeated the Seattle Seahawks 13–7 at Sullivan Stadium on 12-04-88 (Robert Perryman ran for a TD)

Beat Tampa 10–7 in overtime at Sullivan Stadium on 12-11-88 (Stanley Morgan advanced a lateral seven yards to end regulation)

1989 regular season
Defeated the New York Jets 27–24 at Shea Stadium on 09-10-89 (Reggie Dupard ran for a TD with less than two minutes to go)

Lost to the Miami Dolphins 24–10 at Sullivan Stadium on 09-17-89 (Stanley Morgan exceeded 10,000 career yards receiving)

Lost to the Seattle Seahawks 24–3 at Sullivan Stadium on 09-24-89 (Marv Cook had two receptions and made two tackles)

Lost to Buffalo 31–10 at Rich Stadium on 10-01-89 (Doug Flutie ran 12 yards on fourth-and-1 and then lateraled to Reggie Dupard)

Defeated the Houston Oilers 23–13 at Sullivan Stadium on 10-08-89 (Marvin Allen recovered a fumble return to set up his TD run)

Lost to the Atlanta Falcons 16–15 at Fulton County Stadium on 10-15-89 (Greg Davis kicked a career-long 52-yard field goal)

Lost to the 49ers 37–20 at Stanford Stadium on 10-22-89 (The game was moved beause of an earthquake)

Beat the Colts 23–20 in overtime at the Hoosier Dome on 10-29-89 ("Grogs" had 13 consecutive completions) (The Game of the Year)

Lost to the New York Jets 27–26 at Sullivan Stadium on 11-05-89 (Marc Wilson had 12 completions and Steve Grogan had 13)

Lost to the New Orleans Saints 28–24 at Sullivan Stadium on 11-12-89 (Mosi Tatupu had a career-high eight receptions)

Defeated the Buffalo Bills 33–24 at Sullivan Stadium on 11-19-89 (Patrick Egu ran for a 15-yard TD on his first NFL carry)

Lost to the Los Angeles Raiders 24–21 at the Los Angeles Memorial Coliseum on 11-26-89 (Steve Grogan threw three TDs)

Beat the Indianapolis Colts 22–16 at Sullivan Stadium on 12-03-89 (John Stephens had 124 yards rushing and the game-winning TD)

Lost to the Pittsburgh Steelers 28–10 at Three Rivers Stadium on 12-17-89 (Hart Lee Dykes had a career-high 130 yards receiving)

Lost to the Los Angeles Rams 24–20 at Sullivan Stadium on 12-24-89 (Steve Grogan's eight-yard completion on fourth-and-5 set up their final TD)

1990 regular season
Lost to the Dolphins 27–24 at Foxboro Stadium on 09-09-90 (Jason Staurovsky missed a 57-yard field goal with 27 seconds left)

Beat the Indianapolis Colts 16–14 at the Hoosier Dome on 09-16-90 (Rod Rust was given the game ball) (The Game of the Year)

Lost to the Cincinnati Bengals 41–7 at Riverfront Stadium on 09-23-90 (Marv Cook caught a seven-yard TD pass from Marc Wilson)

Lost to the New York Jets 37–13 at Foxboro Stadium on 09-30-90 (Robert Perryman ran for a TD)

Lost to the Seattle Seahawks 33–20 at Foxboro Stadium on 10-07-90 (Jason Staurovsky kicked a career-long 53-yard field goal)

Lost to the Buffalo Bills 27–10 at Foxboro Stadium on 10-28-90 (Sammy Martin had his only TD reception)

Lost to the Philadelphia Eagles 48–20 at Veterans Stadium on 11-04-90 (Irving Fryar and Marv Cook had TD receptions)

Lost to the Indianapolis Colts 13–10 at Foxboro on 11-11-90 (Marvin Allen led both teams with 71 yards rushing and one TD)

Lost to the Buffalo Bills 14–0 at Rich Stadium on 11-18-90 (The Patriots had first-and-goal from the 1-yard line and didn't score)

Lost to the Phoenix Cardinals 34–14 at Sun Devil Stadium on 11-25-90 (Tommy Hodson threw two TD passes)

Lost to the Chiefs 37–7 at Foxboro Stadium on 12-02-90 (Chiefs QB Steve DeBerg threw an 86-yard TD pass on the first play)

Lost to the Steelers 24–3 at Three Rivers Stadium on 12-09-90 (Maurice Hurst blocked a punt with only 10 men on the field)

Lost to the New York Jets 42–7 at the Meadowlands on 12-23-90 (Irving Fryar caught a TD pass from Marc Wilson)

Lost to the New York Giants 13–10 at Foxboro on 12-30-90 (Both Jason Staurovsky and Matt Bahr missed a field-goal attempt)

1991 regular season
Defeated the Indianapolis Colts 16–7 at the Hoosier Dome on 09-01-91 (Brent Williams blocked a field-goal attempt by Dean Biasucci)

Lost to the Cleveland Browns 20–0 at Foxboro Stadium on 09-08-91 (Ronnie Lippett recovered a fumble by Irving Fryar)

Lost to the Pittsburgh Steelers 20–6 at Three Rivers Stadium on 09-15-91 (Jason Staurovsky kicked two field goals)

Defeated the Houston Oilers 24–20 at Foxboro Stadium on 09-22-91 (Greg McMurtry caught a 34-yard TD with six seconds left)

Lost to the Phoenix Cardinals 24–10 at Sun Devil Stadium on 09-29-91 (Jon Vaughn returned a kickoff 99 yards for a TD)

Lost to the Miami Dolphins 20–10 at Foxboro Stadium on 10-06-91 (Hugh Millen was sacked on the last play of the game)

Beat the Minnesota Vikings 26–23 in overtime at Foxboro Stadium on 10-20-91 (Freddie Childress fell on a fumble for a TD)

Lost to Denver 9–6 at Foxboro Stadium on 10-27-91 (Scored just two field goals even though they had first-and-goal from the 5- and 8-yard lines)

Lost to the Buffalo Bills 22–17 at Rich Stadium on 11-03-91 (Shawn McCarthy set team record with a 93-yard punt)

Lost to the New York Jets 28–21 at Foxboro Stadium on 11-17-91 (Hugh Millen had a career-high 372 yards passing)

Defeated the Buffalo Bills 16–13 at Foxboro Stadium on 11-24-91 (Hugh Millen ran for the game-winning TD)

Lost to the Denver Broncos 20–3 at Mile High Stadium on 12-01-91 (Charlie Baumann kicked a 23-yard field goal)

Beat the Indianapolis Colts 23–17 in overtime at Foxboro on 12-08-91 (Ben Coates caught a game-tying TD) (The Game of the Year)

Defeated the New York Jets 6–3 at the Meadowlands on 12-15-91 (Leonard Russell had 112 yards rushing)

Lost to the Bengals 29–7 at Riverfront Stadium on 12-22-91 (Michael Timpson had a career-high 150 yards receiving)

1992 regular season

Lost to the Los Angeles Rams 14–0 at Anaheim Stadium on 09-13-92 (QB Hugh Millen had a career-long 26-yard run)

Lost to the Seattle Seahawks 10–6 at Foxboro Stadium on 09-20-92 (Irving Fryar caught a 36-yard TD pass from Hugh Millen)

Lost to the Buffalo Bills 41–7 at Foxboro Stadium on 09-27-92 (Hugh Millen was 13–13 in the first half)

Lost to the 49ers 24–12 at Foxboro Stadium on 10-11-92 (Kevin Turner and Sam Gash recovered a fumbled punt return)

Lost to the Cleveland Browns 19–17 at Foxboro Stadium on 10-25-92 (Walter Stanley's 50-yard punt return set up the field goal)

Lost to the Bills 16–7 at Rich Stadium on 11-01-92 (Vincent Brown returned a Thurman Thomas fumble 25 yards for a TD)

Scott Zolak

Lost to the New Orleans Saints 31–14 at Foxboro Stadium on 11-08-92 (Tim Goad tipped a pass that was returned for a TD)

Beat the Colts 37–34 in overtime at the Hoosier Dome on 11-15-92 (Scott Zolak was AFC Offensive Player of Week) (The Game of the Year)

Defeated the New York Jets 24–3 at Foxboro Stadium on 11-22-92 (Jon Vaughn had a career-high 110 yards rushing)

Lost to the Atlanta Falcons 34–0 at the Georgia Dome on 11-29-92 (Vincent "Undertaker" Brown had 12 tackles)

Lost to the Indianapolis Colts 6–0 at Foxboro Stadium on 12-06-92 (Hugh Millen and Scott Zolak were sacked eight times)

Lost to the Kansas City Chiefs 27–20 at Arrowhead Stadium on 12-13-92 (Tim Goad took a fumble for a TD on the first play)

Lost to the Bengals 20–10 at Riverfront Stadium on 12-20-92 (Jon Vaughn had NFL's longest kickoff return in 1992)

Lost to Miami 16–13 in overtime at Foxboro Stadium on 12-27-92 (Scott Lockwood had 123 yards rushing and 89 kickoff return yards)

1993 regular season

Lost to the Buffalo Bills 38–14 at Rich Stadium on 09-05-93 (Ben Coates caught a 54-yard TD pass on fourth down)

Lost to the Lions 19–16 in overtime at Foxboro Stadium on 09-12-93 (Vincent Brisby caught a TD with 12 seconds left to force overtime)

Lost to Seattle 17–14 at Foxboro Stadium on 09-19-93 (Scott Sisson's 54-yard field-goal attempt hit the cross bar with 30 seconds left)

Beat the Phoenix Cardinals 23–21 at Sun Devil Stadium on 10-10-93 (Mike Saxon was AFC Special Team Player of Week)

Lost to the Houston Oilers 28–14 at Foxboro Stadium on 10-17-93 (Scott Secules had 280 yards passing and one TD)

Lost to the Seattle Seahawks 10–9 at the Kingdome on 10-24-93 (Seattle QB Rick Mirer tossed a TD with 25 seconds left)

Lost to the Indianapolis Colts 9–6 at the Hoosier Dome on 10-31-93 (Scott Sisson kicked a field goal to end the first half)

Lost to the Bills 13–10 in overtime at Foxboro on 11-07-93 (Scott Secules had 16 yards rushing and Drew Bledsoe had 14)

Lost to the Miami Dolphins 17–13 at Joe Robbie Stadium on 11-21-93 (Ray Crittenden had a 40-yard TD reception)

Lost to the New York Jets 6–0 at Foxboro (heavy rain and gusty winds) on 11-28-93 (Leonard Russell had career high 147 yards rushing)

Lost to the Pittsburgh Steelers 17–14 at Three Rivers Stadium on 12-05-93 (Ronnie Harris set team record with 10 punt returns)

Beat the Bengals 7–2 at Foxboro Stadium on 12-12-93 (Ben Coates caught an eight-yard TD with 25 seconds left in the first half)

Defeated the Cleveland Browns 20–17 at Cleveland Stadium on 12-19-93 (Leonard Russell ran for a TD with two minutes left)

Shutout the Colts 38–0 at Foxboro Stadium (wind chill was minus-21 degrees) on 12-26-93 (Corey Croom scored the last TD on fourth down)

Beat Miami 33–27 in overtime at Foxboro on 01-02-94 (Drew Bledsoe threw a TD on second drive of overtime) (The Game of the Year)

1994 regular season

Lost to the Miami Dolphins 39–35 at Joe Robbie Stadium on 09-04-94 (Ben Coates had a career-high 161 yards receiving)

Lost to Buffalo 38–35 at Foxboro Stadium on 09-11-94 (On a fourth-down play that was the game's last, Drew Bledsoe ran for first down)

Beat the Bengals 31–28 at Riverfront Stadium on 09-18-94 (Bledsoe had 365 yards passing, Coates and Timpson each had 100+ yards receiving)

Defeated the Detroit Lions 23–17 at Pontiac Stadium on 09-25-94 (Myron Guyton's late interception sealed the win)

Defeated the Green Bay Packers 17–16 at Foxboro Stadium on 10-02-94 (Matt Bahr kicked a field goal with four seconds left)

Lost to the LA Raiders 21–17 at Foxboro Stadium on 10-09-94 (Kevin Turner and Leroy Thompson had TD receptions)

Lost to the New York Jets 24–17 at the Meadowlands on 10-16-94 (Blair Thomas scored his only TD for the Patriots)

Lost to the Miami Dolphins 23–3 at Foxboro Stadium on 10-30-94 (Harlon Barnett intercepted Dan Marino twice)

Lost to the Cleveland Browns 13–6 at Cleveland Stadium on 11-06-94 (Matt Bahr kicked two field goals)

Defeated the Vikings 26–20 in overtime at Foxboro Stadium on 11-13-94 (Bledsoe threw 70 passes) (The Game of the Year)

Defeated the San Diego Chargers 23–17 at Foxboro Stadium on 11-20-94 (Chris Slade had 3.5 sacks)

Beat the New York Jets 24–13 at Foxboro on 12-04-94 (Jets WR Art Monk tied the NFL record of at least one reception in 177 straight games)

Defeated the Indianapolis Colts 24–13 at Foxboro Stadium on 12-11-94 (Troy Barnett partially deflected the Colts' first punt)

Defeated the Buffalo Bills 41–17 at Rich Stadium on 12-18-94 (Pat O'Neill was AFC Special Team Player of the Week)

1995 regular season
Defeated the Cleveland Browns 17–14 at Foxboro Stadium on 09-03-95 (Curtis Martin scored a TD with 19 seconds left)

Lost to the Miami Dolphins 20–3 at Foxboro Stadium on 09-10-95 (Troy Barnett blocked a field-goal attempt)

Lost to the San Francisco 49ers 28–3 at 3Com Park on 09-17-95 (Matt Bahr kicked a 43-yard field goal)

Lost to Atlanta 30–17 at Georgia Dome on 10-01-95 (Dave Meggett had 215 yards rushing, receiving, returning punts and kickoffs)

Lost to the Kansas City Chiefs 31–26 at Arrowhead Stadium on 10-15-95 (Max Lane advanced an airborne fumble 30 yards)

Lost to the Carolina Panthers 20–17 in overtime at Foxboro Stadium on 10-29-95 (DE Tim Roberts led the Patriots with 12 tackles)

Defeated the New York Jets 20–7 at the Meadowlands on 11-05-95 (Curtis Martin was AFC Offensive Player of the Week)

Defeated the Dolphins 34–17 at Joe Robbie Stadium on 11-12-95 (Matt Bahr was AFC Special Team Player of the Week)

Lost to the Indianapolis Colts 24–10 at Foxboro on 11-19-95 (Vincent Brown and Ted "Pound Puppy" Johnson had 13 tackles)

Beat the Bills 35–25 at Rich Stadium on 11-26-95 (Chris Slade took a fumble 27 yards for a TD) (The Game of the Year)

Lost to the Saints 31–17 at Foxboro Stadium on 12-03-95 (Scott Zolak ran eight yards for a first down on a fake field goal)

Beat the Jets 31–28 at Foxboro on 12-10-95 (Troy Brown advanced Dave Meggett's fumbled return 75 yards for a TD)

1996 regular season
Lost to the Miami Dolphins 24–10 at Pro Player Park on 09-01-96 (Ben Coates caught a 29-yard TD pass on fourth down)

Lost to the Bills 17–10 at Rich Stadium on 09-08-96 (Adam Vinatieri hit the right upright and missed on a field-goal attempt)

Shut out the Arizona Cardinals 31–0 at Foxboro Stadium on 09-15-96 (Adam Vinatieri hit the upright and missed on a PAT)

Beat the Jacksonville Jaguars 28–25 in overtime at Foxboro Stadium on 09-22-96 (Adam Vinatieri kicked a 40-yard field goal in overtime)

Defeated the Baltimore Ravens 46–38 at Memorial Stadium on 10-06-96 (Drew Bledsoe threw four TDs and two two-point conversion passes)

Lost to the Washington Redskins 27–22 at Foxboro Stadium on 10-13-96 (Adam Vinatieri hit the upright on a missed field-goal attempt)

Defeated the Indianapolis Colts 27–9 at the RCA Dome on 10-20-96 (Ty Law recorded 10 solo tackles)

Defeated the Miami Dolphins 42–23 at Foxboro Stadium on 11-03-96 (Curtis Martin had three TDs and Ben Coates had two TDs)

Beat the New York Jets 31–27 at the Meadowlands on 11-10-96 (Keith Byars caught a game-winning TD pass from Drew Bledsoe)

Lost to the Denver Broncos 34–8 at Foxboro Stadium on 11-17-96 (Keith Byars caught a pass for a two-point conversion)

Defeated the Indianapolis Colts 27–13 at Foxboro Stadium on 11-24-96 (seven Patriots players had at least a 12-yard reception)

Routed the Jets 34–10 at Foxboro Stadium on 12-08-96 (Adam Vinatieri pooched a punt to the Jets 3-yard line on the first drive)

Lost to the Dallas Cowboys 12–6 at Texas Stadium on 12-15-96 (Adam Vinatieri caught Herschel Walker from behind)

1997 regular season
Destroyed the Chargers 41–7 at Foxboro Stadium on 08-31-97 (Drew Bledsoe threw for 271 yards and four TDs in the first half)

Crushed the Colts 31–6 at the RCA Dome on 09-07-97 (Drew Bledsoe was the first NFL QB with four TD passes in the first and second games of the season)

Destroyed the Chicago Bears 31–3 at Foxboro Stadium on 09-21-97 (Marty Moore intercepted Rick Mirer to end the game)

Destroyed the Buffalo Bills 33–6 at Foxboro Stadium on 10-12-97 (Adam Vinatieri kicked four field goals and made a tackle)

Lost to the New York Jets 24–19 at the Meadowlands on 10-19-97 (Defense forced Neil O'Donnell to ground ball for a safety)

Lost to the Vikings 23–18 at the Metrodome on 11-02-97 (Adam Vinatieri set the team record with his 24th consecutive field goal)

Beat Buffalo 31–10 at Rich Stadium on 11-09-97 (first time offense, defense, and special team scored a TD) (The Game of the Year)

Lost to the Tampa Bay Buccaneers 27–7 at Houlihan Stadium on 11-16-97 (Lovett Purnell caught a TD pass from Scott Zolak)

Beat Miami 27–24 at Foxboro Stadium on 11-23-97 (Larry Whigham and Jimmy Hitchcock returned a Dan Marino pass for a TD)

Defeated the Indianapolis Colts 20–17 at Foxboro Stadium on 11-30-97 (Adam Vinatieri kicked a 48-yard field goal to end the first half)

Defeated the Jacksonville Jaguars 26–20 at Alltel Stadium on 12-07-97 (Troy Brown and Ben Coates recovered onside kicks)

1998 regular season
Defeated the Tennessee Oilers 27–16 at Foxboro Stadium on 09-20-98 (Chad Eaton had a 13-yard kickoff return)

Beat the New Orleans Saints 30–27 at the Superdome on 10-04-98 (Tom Tupa made game-saving tackle on a long punt return)

Destroyed the Kansas City Chiefs 40–10 at Foxboro Stadium on 10-11-98 (Robert Edwards and Ben Coates scored two TDs)

Lost to the Dolphins 12–9 in overtime at Pro Player Stadium on 10-25-98 (Adam Vinatieri kicked three field goals and made a tackle)

Defeated the Colts 21–16 at the RCA Dome on 11-01-98 (Lawyer Milloy was the AFC Defensive Player of the Week)

Lost to the Atlanta Falcons 41–10 at Foxboro Stadium on 11-08-98 (Atlanta went on to play in the Super Bowl)

Lost to Buffalo 13–10 at Ralph Wilson Stadium on 11-15-98 (Tony Simmons scored a TD after his previous TD was called back)

Larry Whigham

Beat Buffalo 25–21 at Foxboro Stadium on 11-29-98 (Adam Vinatieri ran for two points after Bills defense left the field) (The Game of the Year)

Defeated the Pittsburgh Steelers 23–9 at Three Rivers Stadium on 12-06-98 (Chad Eaton was AFC Defensive Player of the Week)

Lost to the St. Louis Rams 32–18 at the Trans World Dome on 12-13-98 (Robert Edwards had career-high 196 yards rushing)

Beat the 49ers 24–21 at Foxboro on 12-20-98 (Scott Zolak's team was victorious over Steve Young, Jerry Rice, and Ty Detmer)

Lost to the New York Jets 31–10 at the Meadowlands on 12-27-98 (Tony Simmons caught a 44-yard TD pass from Scott Zolak)

1999 regular season
Beat the Jets 30–28 at the Meadowlands on 09-12-99 (Adam Vinatieri kicked a 23-yard field goal with seven ticks left) (The Game of the Year)

Defeated the Colts 31–28 at Foxboro Stadium on 09-19-99 (Drew Bledsoe threw four TDs and the Patriots scored the final 24 points)

Beat the New York Giants 16–14 at Foxboro Stadium on 09-26-99 (Terry Glenn had a key reception on every Patriots scoring drive)

Defeated the Cleveland Browns 19–7 at Cleveland Browns Stadium on 10-03-99 (Terry Glenn had 214 yards receiving)

Lost to the Chiefs 16–14 at Arrowhead Stadium on 10-10-99 (Adam Vinatieri hit the upright on his 32-yard field-goal attempt with nine seconds left)

Lost to the Dolphins 31–30 at Foxboro Stadium on 10-17-99 (Andy Katzenmoyer returned a pass for a TD and had two sacks)

Defeated Denver 24–23 at Foxboro Stadium on 10-24-99 (Kevin Faulk had a 15-yard TD run and 210 special team return yards)

Beat the Arizona Cardinals 27–3 at Sun Devil Stadium on 10-31-99 (Shawn Jefferson had a 64-yard and a 35-yard TD reception)

Lost to the Miami Dolphins 27–17 at Pro Player Stadium on 11-21-99 (Shawn Jefferson had a 68-yard TD reception)

Lost to the Buffalo Bills 17–7 at Ralph Wilson Stadium on 11-28-99 (Punter Lee Johnson ran for 13 yards on fourth-and-3)

Lost to the Indianapolis Colts 20–15 at the RCA Dome on 12-12-99 (Punter Lee Johnson attempted an onside kick)

Lost to the Philadelphia Eagles 24–9 at Veterans Stadium on 12-19-99 (Larry Whigham blocked a punt by Sean Landeta)

Lost to Buffalo 13–10 in overtime at Foxboro on 12-26-99 (Patriots RB Terry Allen had a career-high 126 yards rushing)

Beat the Ravens 20–3 at Foxboro on 01-02-00 (Mike Bartrum caught a TD pass and was the long snapper on special teams)

2000 regular season

Lost to the Buccaneers 21–16 at Foxboro Stadium on 09-03-00 (Troy Brown led team in yards rushing, receiving, and returning)

Lost to the Vikings 21–13 at Foxboro on 09-17-00 (Kevin Faulk had the longest run, reception, and return for the Patriots)

Lost to the Miami Dolphins 10–3 at Pro Player Stadium on 09-24-00 (Joe Andruzzi advanced a fumble two yards)

Defeated Denver 28–19 at Mile High on 10-01-00 (Drew Bledsoe was AFC Offensive Player of the Week) (The Game of the Year)

Beat the Indianapolis Colts 24–16 at Foxboro Stadium on 10-08-00 (Punter Lee Johnson threw an 18-yard pass to Eric Bjornson)

Lost to the New York Jets 34–17 at Foxboro Stadium on 10-15-00 (Curtis Martin ran for three TDs for the Jets)

Lost to the Indianapolis Colts 30–23 at the RCA Dome on 10-22-00 (J.R. Redmond scored his only TD as a RB for the Patriots)

Lost to Buffalo 16–13 in overtime at Foxboro on 11-05-00 (Drew Bledsoe, John Friesz, and Michael Bishop attempted a pass)

Lost to the Cleveland Browns 19–11 at Cleveland Browns Stadium on 11-12-00 (Rod Rutledge caught a TD pass)

Beat the Bengals 16–13 at Foxboro on 11-19-00 (Terry Glenn had 129 yards receiving and Troy Brown had 110 yards receiving)

Lost to the Bears 24–17 at Soldier Field on 12-10-00 (Former Bear Raymont Harris played in his only game for the Patriots)

Beat Buffalo 13–10 in overtime at Ralph Wilson Stadium on 12-17-00 (Chad Eaton was the AFC Special Team Player of the Week)

Lost to the Miami Dolphins 27–24 at Foxboro Stadium on 12-24-00 (Tedy Bruschi had nine tackles and a six-yard kickoff return)

2001 championship season

Lost to the Bengals 23–17 at Paul Brown Stadium on 09-09-01 (Troy Brown and Jermaine Wiggins had TD receptions)

Lost to the New York Jets 10–3 at Foxboro Stadium on 9-23-01 (Tom Brady replaced a severely injured Drew Bledsoe)

Destroyed the Indianapolis Colts 44–13 at Foxboro on 09-30-01 (Otis Smith and Ty Law returned an interception for a TD)

Lost to the Dolphins 30–10 at Pro Player Stadium on 10-07-01 (Mike Vrabel intercepted Jay Fiedler on Miami's first play)

Beat San Diego 29–26 in overtime at Foxboro on 10-14-01 (Jermaine Wiggins scored a TD with 36 seconds left) (The Game of the Year)

Destroyed the Indianapolis Colts 38–17 at the RCA Dome on 10-21-01 (David Patten was the NFL Player of the Week)

Lost to the Denver Broncos 31–20 at Invesco Field on 10-28-01 (Seven Patriots players had at least one rushing attempt)

Beat the Atlanta Falcons 24–10 at the Georgia Dome on 11-04-01 (Kevin Faulk, Marc Edwards, and Troy Brown scored a TD)

Defeated the Buffalo Bills 21–11 at Foxboro Stadium on 11-11-01 (Tom Brady's pass to Terrell Buckley was intercepted)

Destroyed the New Orleans Saints 34–17 at Foxboro Stadium on 11-25-01 (Antowain Smith caught a 41-yard TD pass)

Defeated the New York Jets 17–16 at the Meadowlands on 12-02-01 (Fred Coleman's 46-yard reception helped set up Patriots first TD)

Troy Brown

Beat the Browns 27–16 at Foxboro on 12-09-01 (Terrell Buckley, Anthony Pleasant, and Tebucky Jones had interceptions)

Beat Buffalo 12–9 in overtime at Ralph Wilson Stadium on 12-16-01 (Adam Vinatieri was AFC Special Team Player of the Week)

Pasted the Carolina Panthers 38–6 at Ericsson Stadium on 01-06-02 (Ty Law and Otis Smith returned an interception for a TD)

2002 regular season

Destroyed the New York Jets 44–7 at the Meadowlands on 09-15-02 (Tebucky Jones had a strip-sack and returned it for a TD)

Defeated the Kansas City Chiefs 41–38 in overtime at Gillette Stadium on 09-22-02 (Antowain Smith ran for a TD and for two points)

Lost to the San Diego Chargers 21–14 at Qualcomm Stadium on 09-29-02 (Christian Fauria and Mike Vrabel had TD receptions)

Lost to the Miami Dolphins 26–13 at Pro Player Stadium on 10-06-02 (David Patten had two TD receptions)

Lost to the Green Bay Packers 28–10 at Gillette Stadium on 10-13-02 (The Patriots scored first and last in this game)

Lost to the Denver Broncos 24–16 at Gillette Stadium on 10-27-02 (Deion Branch had a career long 40-yard punt return)

Blasted Buffalo 38–7 at Ralph Wilson Stadium on 11-03-02 (Tom Brady was the AFC Offensive Player of the Week)

Defeated the Chicago Bears 33–30 at Memorial Stadium on 11-10-02 (David Patten caught a TD pass with 21 seconds left)

Defeated the Vikings 24–17 at Gillette Stadium on 11-24-02 (Richard Seymour blocked a FGA for the second consecutive game)

Defeated the Buffalo Bills 27–17 at Gillette Stadium on 12-08-02 (Tom Brady threw two TDs within 21 seconds of each other)

Beat Miami 27–24 in overtime at Gillette Stadium on 12-29-02 (Kevin Faulk had 232 yards rushing, receiving, and returning kicks and punts)

2003 championship season

Lost to Buffalo 31–0 at Ralph Wilson Stadium on 09-07-03 (The son of former Patriot OL Sam Adams scored a TD for the Bills)

Destroyed the Eagles 31–10 at Lincoln Financial Field on 09-14-03 (Tedy Bruschi was AFC Defensive Player of the Week)

Defeated the New York Jets 23–16 at Gillette Stadium on 09-21-03 (Asante Samuel returned a pass 55 yards for a TD in the fourth quarter)

Lost to the Washington Redskins 20–17 at FedEx Field on 09-28-03 (David Givens and Larry Centers had TD receptions)

Beat the Tennessee Titans 38–30 at Gillette on 10-05-03 (Ty Law had his career-longest pass return of 65 yards for a TD)

Defeated the New York Giants 17–6 at Gillette Stadium on 10-12-03 (Tyrone Poole intercepted a pass on the first play of the game)

Beat Miami 19–13 in overtime at Pro Player Stadium on 10-19-03 (Troy Brown caught an 82-yard game-winning TD pass in overtime)

Defeated the Cleveland Browns 9–3 at Gillette Stadium on 10-26-03 (Daniel Graham had seven receptions for 110 yards)

Beat the Houston Texans 23–20 in overtime at Reliant Stadium on 11-23-03 (Daniel Graham caught a fourth-down TD to force overtime)

Beat the Colts 38–34 at the RCA Dome on 11-30-03 (Bethel Johnson was AFC Special Team Player of the Week) (The Game of the Year)

Shut out the Miami Dolphins 12–0 at Gillette Stadium on 12-07-03 (Jarvis Green and Mike Vrabel sacked Jay Fiedler for a safety)

Defeated the Jacksonville Jaguars 27–13 at Gillette Stadium on 12-14-03 (Tyrone Poole intercepted Byron Leftwich twice)

2004 championship season

Beat the Arizona Cardinals 23–12 at Sun Devil Stadium on 09-19-04 (Rodney Harrison was AFC Defensive Player of the Week)

Defeated the Bills 31–17 at Ralph Wilson Stadium on 10-03-04 (Tedy Bruschi was AFC Defensive Player of the Week)

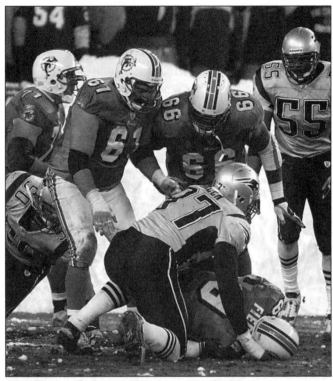

Jarvis Green and Mike Vrabel sacked Jay Fiedler for a safety

Defeated the Miami Dolphins 24–10 at Gillette Stadium on 10-10-04 (Patriots set NFL record with 19th consecutive victory)

Defeated the Seahawks 30–20 at Gillette Stadium on 10-17-04 (Ty Law tied Ray Clayborn with his 36th career interception)

Beat the New York Jets 13–7 at Gillette Stadium on 10-24-04 (Patriots set NFL record with 18th consecutive regular season victory)

Lost to the Pittsburgh Steelers 34–20 at Heinz Field on 10-31-04 (The Patriots had six carries for just five total yards)

Defeated the St. Louis Rams 40–23 at the Edward Jones Dome on 11-07-04 (Adam Vinatieri threw a TD pass to Troy Brown)

Beat the Bills 29–6 at Gillette Stadium on 11-14-04 (Troy Brown is first Patriots player with a reception and interception in the same game)

Destroyed the Baltimore Ravens 24–3 at Gillette Stadium on 11-28-04 (The Ravens kicked a field goal to end the first half)

Destroyed Cleveland 42–15 at Browns Stadium on 12-05-04 (Bethel Johnson took the first kickoff for a TD) (The Game of the Year)

Defeated the Cincinnati Bengals 35–28 at Gillette Stadium on 12-12-04 (The Patriots scored two TDs within 12 seconds)

Beat the Jets 23–7 at the Meadowlands on 12-26-04 (Set NFL record by scoring first in 20th consecutive regular season game)

Defeated the San Francisco 49ers 21–7 at Gillette Stadium on 01-02-05 (Patrick Pass led the team with five receptions)

2005 regular season
Lost to the Carolina Panthers 27–17 at Bank of America Stadium on 09-18-05 (Mike Vrabel returned a pass 24 yards for a TD)

Beat the Steelers 23–20 at Heinz Field on 09-25-05 (Adam Vinatieri was AFC Special Team Player of Week) (The Game of the Year)

Lost to the San Diego Chargers 41–17 at Gillette Stadium on 10-02-05 (This loss ended their 21 home game winning streak)

Defeated the Atlanta Falcons 31–28 at the Georgia Dome on 10-09-05 (Tom Brady was AFC Offensive Player of the Week)

Lost to the Denver Broncos 28–20 at Invesco Field on 10-16-05 (Patrick Pass led the team in yards rushing and receiving)

Defeated the Miami Dolphins 23–16 at Dolphin Stadium on 11-13-05 (Heath Evans ran for a two-point conversion)

Defeated the New Orleans Saints 24–17 at Gillette Stadium on 11-20-05 (LB/TE Mike Varbel caught a one-yard TD pass)

Lost to the Chiefs 26–16 at Arrowhead on 11-27-05 (Tim Dwight had 17 yards rushing, 76 receiving, and 147 returning)

Beat the New York Jets 16–3 at Gillette Stadium on 12-04-05 (Adam Vinatieri passed Gino Cappelletti for career points scored)

Destroyed the Buffalo Bills 35–7 at Ralph Wilson Stadium on 12-11-05 (James Sanders returned a tipped pass for a TD)

Lost to Miami 28–26 at Gillette on 01-01-06 (Doug Flutie joined Steve Zabel as nonkickers who have booted an extra point)

Left to right: Asante Samuel, Rodney Harrison, Mike Vrabel

2006 regular season

Beat Buffalo 19–17 at Gillette on 09-10-06 (Corey Dillon ran six yards on fourth down to allow the Patriots to run out the clock)

Defeated the New York Jets 24–17 at the Meadowlands on 09-17-06 (Tedy Bruschi intercepted a tipped pass with 15 seconds left)

Beat the Cincinanti Bengals 38–13 at Paul Brown Stadium on 10-01-06 (Jarvis Green was AFC Defensive Player of the Week)

Beat Miami 20–10 at Gillette Stadium on 10-08-06 (Ben Watson's fourth-down reception allowed the Patriots to run out the clock)

Blasted the Bills 28–6 at Ralph Wilson Stadium on 10-22-06 (Laurence Maroney was AFC Special Team Player of the Week)

Lost to the New York Jets 17–14 at Gillette Stadium on 11-12-06 (Russ Hochstein fell on a fumble by Tom Brady on the last play)

Shut out the Green Bay Packers 35–0 at Lambeau Field on 11-19-06 (Tom Brady threw four TD passes)

Defeated the Chicago Bears 17–13 at Gillette Stadium on 11-26-06 (Richard Seymour blocked a field goal) (The Game of the Year)

Defeated the Detroit Lions 28–21 at Gillette Stadium on 12-03-06 (Corey Dillon ran for just 25 yards but had and three TDs)

Lost to Miami 21–0 at Dolphin Stadium on 12-10-06 (Tom Brady's illegal forward pass for a TD was voided due to penalty)

Defeated the Houston Texans 40–7 at Gillette Stadium on 12-17-06 (Samuel, Sanders, Hobbs, and Seymour had interceptions)

Beat the Jaguars 24–21 at Alltel Stadium on 12-24-06 (Rodney Harrison's recovery of Jarvis Green's strip-sack sealed the win)

Defeated the Tennessee Titans 40–23 at LP Field on 12-31-06 (Vinny Testaverde tossed a TD pass to Troy Brown)

2007 undefeated regular season

Defeated the New York Jets 38–14 at the Meadowlands on 09-09-07 (Ellis Hobbs set NFL record with 108-yard kickoff return)

Beat Buffalo 38–7 at Gillette on 09-23-07 (Brady threw for 331 yards, Maroney ran for 103 yards, and Moss had 115 yards receiving)

Beat the Cleveland Browns 34–17 at Gillette Stadium on 10-07-07 (Randall Gay forced and returned a fumble 15 yards for a TD)

Defeated the Dallas Cowboys 48–27 at Texas Stadium on 10-14-07 (Tom Brady was AFC Offensive Player of the Week)

Defeated the Miami Dolphins 49–28 at Dolphin Stadium on 10-21-07 (Tom Brady was the AFC Offensive Player of the Week)

Routed the Redskins 52–7 at Gillette Stadium on 10-28-07 (Tom Brady has led his team to victories over every NFL team)

Beat the Indianapolis Colts 24–20 at the RCA Dome on 11-04-07 (Randy Moss was the AFC Offensive Player of the Week)

Defeated the Pittsburgh Steelers 34–13 at Gillette Stadium on 12-09-07 (Jabar Gaffney hauled in a 56-yard flea-flicker TD pass)

Defeated the New York Jets 20–10 at Gillette Stadium on 12-16-07 (Kelley Washington blocked a punt by Chris Hanson)

Beat the Dolphins 28–7 at Gillette Stadium on 12-23-07 (Jabar Gaffney caught a 48-yard TD pass that should have been intercepted)

2008 regular season

Defeated the Kansas City Chiefs 17–10 at Gillette on 09-07-08 (Matt Cassel replaced Tom Brady who was injured)

Defeated the New York Jets 19–10 at the Meadowlands on 09-14-08 (Adalius Thomas spun Brett Favre for a 20-yard loss)

Lost to the Miami Dolphins 38–13 at Gillette Stadium on 09-21-08 (Ronnie Brown ran for four TDs and tossed a TD pass for Miami)

Defeated the 49ers 30–21 at Monster Park on 10-05-08 (Randy Moss hauled in a 66-yard TD pass from Matt Cassel)

Defeated the St. Louis Rams 23–16 at Gillette on 10-26-08 (Kevin Faulk caught a 15-yard TD pass for the final points scored)

Defeated the Buffalo Bills 20–10 at Gillette Stadium on 11-09-08 (Matt Cassel ran up the middle for a 13-yard TD on their first drive)

Defeated the Dolphins 48–28 at Dolphin Stadium on 11-23-08 (Matt Cassel was the AFC Offensive Player of the Week)

Lost to the Pittsburgh Steelers 33–10 at Gillette Stadium on 11-30-08 (Mike Vrabel's interception set up the only Patriots TD)

Routed the Oakland Raiders 49–26 at McAfee Coliseum on 12-14-08 (The Patriots averaged 7.1 yards rushing (39-for-277)

Crushed the Cardinals 47–7 at Gillette on 12-21-07 (Randy Moss dashed 76 yards on a screen pass for a TD to start the third quarter)

Beat the Bills 13–0 at Ralph Wilson Stadium on 12-28-08 (Chris Hanson was the AFC Special Team Player of the Week)

The 10 most memorable moments in regular season games played by the Patriots on Sunday Afternoon

Bob Gladieux came out of the stands, made two special team tackles, and tossed his pregame meal in the 13-point win over the Miami Dolphins on 09-20-70

Drew Bledsoe led his team to consecutive wins with a broken finger and was the NFL Player of the Week each time in November 1998

Tom Brady had a perfect QB rating of 158.3—going 21-of-25 for 354 yards and six TDs in the 21-point win on 10-21-07

David Patten ran for a TD, threw a TD pass, and caught two TD passes (one for 91 yards) in the 21-point win on 10-21-01

Troy Brown was the first Patriots player with a reception and an interception in the same game in the 23-point win on 11-14-04

Irving Fryar caught a 25-yard TD pass that was tipped by Stanley Morgan on the last play of the two-point win on 11-16-86

Jim Plunkett tossed an 88-yard TD to Randy Vataha much to the dismay of GM Upton Bell in the four-point win on 12-19-71

Steve Nelson tapped Pat Leahy on his helmet after his potentially game-winning field goal missed in the two-point win on 11-19-78

Andre Tippett stole the ball from future Pro Football Hall of Fame running back Eric Dickerson in the 14-point win on 12-11-83

Art Graham caught a 22-yard TD pass while wearing only one shoe in the six-point win over the Dolphins on 11-27-66

Every Patriots player who was the NFL Player of the Week for his performance in a game played on Sunday Afternoon

1998 regular season
With a broken finger, Drew Bledsoe threw a TD pass to Ben Coates to defeat the Buffalo Bills 25–21 at Foxboro on 11-29-98

2001 champixonship season
Tom Brady threw for 364 yards and two TDs in the 29–26 overtime win vs the San Diego Chargers at Foxboro on 10-14-01

David Patten ran for a TD, threw a TD pass, and caught two TD passes in the 38–17 rout of the Colts at RCA Dome on 10-21-01

Tom Brady threw four TD passes in the 34–17 victory over the New Orleans Saints at Foxboro Stadium on 11-25-01

The only Patriots to be the NFL Offensive Player of the Week for his performance in a Sunday Afternoon game

1971 regular season
Jim Plunkett threw two TD passes in the 21–17 win over the Baltimore Colts at Memorial Stadium on 12-19-71

1973 regular season
Jim Plunkett threw for 348 yards and two TDs in the 33–24 win over the Green Bay Packers at Schaefer Stadium on 11-18-73

The only Patriots player to be the NFL Defensive Player of the Week for his performance in a Sunday Afternoon game

1971 regular season
Steve Kiner led the defense and had a key interception in the 28–20 win over the Houston Oilers at Schaefer Stadium on 11-07-71

Holder Babe Parilli and kicker Gino Cappelletti

Boston Patriots who were the AFL Offensive Player of the Week for their performance in a Sunday Afternoon game

1966 regular season
Babe Parilli threw three TD passes in the 35–17 win over the San Diego Chargers at Fenway Park on 10-23-66

1967 regular season
Jim Nance ran 34 times for 185 yards and one TD in the 23–0 shutout of the Buffalo Bills at War Memorial Stadium on 09-24-67

Babe Parilli threw five TD passes in the 41–10 rout of the Miami Dolphins at BC Alumni Stadium on 10-15-67

1969 regular season
Ron Sellers caught two TD passes in the 24–0 shutout of the Houston Oilers at BC Alumni Stadium on 11-02-69

Every Patriots player who was the AFC Offensive Player of the Week for his perfomance in a Sunday Afternoon game

1984 regular season
Tony Eason ran for a TD and threw two TD passes in the 38–23 comeback win over Seattle at Sullivan Stadium on 09-16-84

1986 regular season
Tony Eason tossed a 25-yard TD pass on the last play to defeat the Los Angeles Rams 30–28 at Anaheim Stadium on 11-16-86

1988 regular season
Doug Flutie ran for a TD with 13 seconds left to defeat the Indianapolis Colts 21–17 at Sullivan Stadium on 10-02-88

1991 regular season
Marv Cook caught 10 passes for 99 yards and one TD in the 24–20 win over the Houston Oilers at Foxboro on 09-22-91

1992 regular season
Scott Zolak threw for 261 yards and two TDs in the 37–34 overtime win vs the Colts at the Hoosier Dome on 11-15-92

1994 regular season
Drew Bledsoe led the team to a game-winning field goal in the 17–16 win over the Green Bay Packers at Foxboro on 10-02-94

Drew Bledsoe was 45-for-70 for 426 yards and led the team to a 26–20 overtime win vs the Vikings at Foxboro on 11-13-94

1995 regular season
Curtis Martin had 35 carries for 166 yards and two TDs in the 20–7 win over the New York Jets at the Meadowlands on 11-05-95

Curtis Martin had 31 carries for 148 yards and two TDs in the 31–28 win over the New York Jets at Foxboro on 12-10-95

1996 regular season
Drew Bledsoe threw for 310 yards and four TDs in the 46–38 win over the Baltimore Ravens at Memorial Stadium on 10-06-96

1999 regular season

Terry Glenn had 13 receptions for 214 yards and one TD in the 19–7 win over the Cleveland Browns at Cleveland on 10-03-99

2000 regular season

Drew Bledsoe threw four TD passes in the 28–19 victory over the Denver Broncos at Mile High Stadium on 10-01-00

2002 regular season

Tom Brady threw three TD passes in the 38–7 rout of the Buffalo Bills at Ralph Wilson Stadium on 11-03-02

2003 championship season

Daniel Graham had seven receptions, five for a first down, in the 9–3 win over the Cleveland Browns at Gillette Stadium on 10-26-03

Tom Brady threw four TD passes in the first half of the 31–0 shutout of the Buffalo Bills at Gillette Stadium on 12-27-03

2005 regular season

Tom Brady threw for 350 yards and three TDs in the 31–28 win over the Atlanta Falcons at the Georgia Dome on 10-09-05

2007 undefeated regular season

Tom Brady was 23-for-29 for 311 yards and four TDs in the 38–7 rout of the Buffalo Bills at Gillette Stadium on 09-23-07

Tom Brady threw for 388 yards and five TDs in the 48–27 win over the Dallas Cowboys at Texas Stadium on 10-14-07

Tom Brady was 21-25 for 354 yards and six TDs in the 49–28 win over the Miami Dolphins at Dolphin Stadium on 10-21-07

Randy Moss caught nine passes for 145 yards and one TD in the 24–20 win over the Colts at the RCA Dome on 11-04-07

Tom Brady threw for 399 yards and four TDs in the 34–13 win over the Pittsburgh Steelers at Gillette Stadium on 12-09-07

Boston Patriots who were the AFL Defensive Player of the Week for their perfomance in a Sunday Afternoon Game

1967 regular season

Larry Eisenhauer led the defense as the Patriots became the first AFL team to shutout the Bills in the 23–0 victory on 09-24-67

Nick Buoniconti recorded a safety and led the defense in the 18–7 victory over Houston at Fenway Park on 11-05-67

1968 regular season

Houston Antwine had three sacks in the 16–7 victory over the Buffalo Bills at War Memorial Stadium on 09-08-68

Nick Buoniconti forced a fumble and intercepted three passes in the 23–6 win over the Buffalo Bills at Fenway Park on 10-20-68

1969 regular season

Jim Cheyunski had 14 tackles in the 25–14 victory over the Cincinnati Bengals at Riverfront Stadium on 11-16-69

Every Patriots player who was the AFC Defensive Player of the Week for his performance in a Sunday Afternoon Game

1970 regular season

Ron Berger led the Patriots defense in the 27–14 win over the Miami Dolphins at Harvard Stadium on 09-20-70

1971 regular season

Julius Adams led the Patriots defense in the 34–13 win over the Super Bowl–bound Dolphins at Schaefer Stadium on 12-05-71

1972 regular season

Jim Cheyunski had 18 tackles in the 21–20 victory over the Atlanta Falcons at Schaefer Stadium on 09-24-72

1985 regular season

Andre Tippett was dominant as he had three sacks in the 20–13 victory over the New York Jets at Sullivan Stadium on 10-20-85

Fred Marion forced and recovered a fumble and returned an interception 36 yards in the 34–15 rout of the Colts on 11-10-85

1986 regular season

Ronnie Lippett had two key interceptions in the 34–7 rout of the Miami Dolphins at Sullivan Stadium on 10-05-86

1987 regular season

Andre Tippett had 14 tackles, three sacks, and blocked a field goal in the 21–7 win over Houston at the Astrodome on 10-18-87

1988 regular season

Fred Marion recovered a fumble, deflected a pass, and had an interception in the 27–21 win over the Bengals on 10-16-88

Johnny Rembert had 16 tackles in the 27–10 victory over the Miami Dolphins at Sullivan Stadium on 11-06-88

1995 regular season

Chris Slade had 11 tackles and one sack in the 17–14 win over the Cleveland Browns at Foxboro Stadium on 09-03-95

1997 regular season

Larry Whigham returned an interception 60 yards for a TD in the 27–24 win over the Dolphins at Foxboro on 11-23-97

1998 regular season

Lawyer Milloy had 10 tackles and two interceptions in the 21–16 win over the Indianapolis Colts at Foxboro Stadium on 11-01-98

Chad Eaton had three sacks in the 23–9 victory over the Pittsburgh Steelers at Three Rivers Stadium on 12-06-98

Willie Clay intercepted a pass to set up the game-winning field goal in the 24–21 win over the 49ers at Foxboro on 12-20-98

1999 regular season

Willie McGinest recovered a fumble for a TD and had two sacks in the 30–28 win over the Jets at the Meadowlands on 09-12-99

Ted Johnson had two sacks and forced a fumble that was recovered for a TD in the 20–3 rout of the Baltimore Ravens on 01-02-00

2000 regular season

Lawyer Milloy had 14 tackles and an interception in the 16–13 win over the Cincinnati Bengals at Foxboro on 11-19-00

2003 championship season

Tedy Bruschi returned an interception 18 yards for a TD in the 31–10 rout of the Philadelphia Eagles on 09-14-03

Tedy Bruschi returned an interception five yards for a TD in the snow during the 12–0 win over Miami at Gillette on 12-07-03

2004 championship season

Rodney Harrison had two sacks and forced a fumble in the 23–12 win over the Arizona Cardinals at Sun Devil Stadium on 09-19-04

Tedy Bruschi had two sacks and forced a fumble that was returned for a TD in the 31–17 win over the Buffalo Bills on 10-03-04

Tedy Bruschi had 15 tackles in the 21–7 victory over the San Francisco 49ers at Gillette Stadium on 01-02-05

2005 regular season

Tedy Bruschi had 10 tackles in his first game back after his stroke in the 21–16 win over Buffalo at Gillette Stadium on 10-30-05

2006 regular season

Jarvis Green had three sacks, forced a fumble and recovered a fumble in the 38–13 win over the Cincinnati Bengals on 10-01-06

Asante Samuel had three interceptions in the 17–13 victory over the Chicago Bears at Gillette Stadium on 11-26-06

2007 undefeated regular season

Mike Vrabel had three strip-sacks and 15 tackles in the 52–7 rout of the Washington Redskins at Gillette Stadium on 10-28-07

Every Patriots player who was the AFC Special Team Player of the Week for his performance in a Sunday Afternoon Game

1993 regular season

Mike Saxon had three punts inside the 20-yard line in the 23–21 win over the Phoenix Cardinals at Sun Devil Stadium on 10-10-93

1994 regular season

Pat O'Neill had a 67-yard punt in the 41–17 rout of the Buffalo Bills at Rich Stadium on 12-18-94

1995 regular season

Matt Bahr kicked a 55-yard field goal in the 34–17 win over the Miami Dolphins at Joe Robbie Stadium on 11-12-95

1997 regular season

Adam Vinatieri kicked four field goals, including one from 52 yards, in the 33–6 rout of the Buffalo Bills at Foxboro on 12-12-97

1998 regular season

Adam Vinatieri kicked a game-winning field goal to defeat the New Orleans Saints 30–27 at the Superdome on 10-04-98

2000 regular season

Chad Eaton blocked two field-goal attempts in the 13–10 overtime win vs the Bills at Ralph Wilson Stadium on 12-17-00

2001 championship season

Adam Vinatieri scored every point in the 12–9 overtime win vs the Buffalo Bills at Ralph Wilson Stadium on 12-16-01

2002 regular season

Larry Izzo had six special team tackles in the 41–38 overtime win vs the Kansas City Chiefs at Gillette Stadium on 09-22-02

Adam Vinatieri kicked the game-winning field goal to defeat the Miami Dolphins 27–24 at Gillette Stadium on 12-29-02

2003 championship season

Richard Seymour blocked a potential game-winning field goal in the 19–13 overtime win vs the Miami Dolphins on 10-19-03

Bethel Johnson had a 92-yard kickoff return for a TD and a 67-yard kickoff return in the 38–34 win over the Colts on 11-30-03

2004 championship season

Adam Vinatieri kicked four field goals and tossed a 4-yard TD pass in the 40–22 victory over the St. Louis Rams on 11-07-04

2005 regular season

Adam Vinatieri kicked a game-winning 43-yard field goal to defeat the Pittsburgh Steelers 23–20 at Heinz Field on 09-25-05

Doug Flutie drop-kicked an extra point in the 28–26 loss to the Miami Dolphins at Gillette Stadium on 01-01-06

2006 regular season

Laurence Maroney had a 74-yard kickoff return in the 28–6 victory over Buffalo at Ralph Wilson Stadium on 10-22-06

2007 undefeated regular season

Ellis Hobbs set the NFL record with a 108-yard kickoff return in the 38–14 win over the Jets at Giants Stadium on 09-09-07

2008 regular season

Chris Hanson punted well in extremely windy weather in the 13–0 shutout of Buffalo at Ralph Wilson Stadium on 12-28-08

The Longest

The Patriots player with the longest run from scrimmage in a regular season game played on Sunday Afternoon

Larry Garron sprinted 85 yards for a TD in the 52–21 rout of the Buffalo Bills at BU Field on 10-22-61

The Patriots player with the longest reception in a regular season game played on Sunday Afternoon

David Patten caught a 91-yard TD pass in the 38–17 rout of the Indianapolis Colts at the RCA Dome on 10-21-01

The Patriots player with the longest completion in a regular season game played on Sunday Afternoon

Tom Brady tossed a 91-yard TD pass to David Patten in the 38–17 rout of the Indianapolis Colts at the RCA Dome on 10-21-01

The Patriots Defensive Back with the longest interception return in a regular season game played on Sunday Afternoon

Jimmy Hitchcock took a Dan Marino pass 100 yards for a TD in the 27–24 win over Miami at Foxboro on 11-23-97

The Patriots Linebacker with the longest interception return in a regular season game played on Sunday Afternoon

Chris Singleton took a Jeff George pass 82 yards for a TD in the 37–34 overtime win vs the Colts at the Hoosier Dome on 11-15-92

The Patriots player with the longest kickoff return in a regular season game played on Sunday Afternoon

Ellis Hobbs returned a kickoff 108 yards for a TD in the 38–14 rout of the New York Jets at the Meadowlands on 09-09-07 (NFL Record)

Jimmy Hitchcock

The Patriots player with the longest punt return in a regular season game played on Sunday Afternoon

Mike Haynes returned a punt 89 yards for a TD in the 20–10 win over the Buffalo Bills at Schaefer Stadium on 11-07-76

The Patriots player with the longest advancement of his own fumble in a regular season game on Sunday Afternoon

Jon Vaughn returned his own fumbled kickoff return 100 yards for a TD in the 20–10 loss to the Bengals on 12-20-92

The Patriots player with the longest advancement of a teammate's fumbled kickoff return in a Sunday Afternoon game

Troy Brown took Dave Meggett's fumble 75 yards for a TD in the 31–28 win over the Jets at Foxboro Stadium on 12-10-95

The Patriots player with the longest advancement of a teammate's fumbled rushing attempt on Sunday Afternoon

Randy Vataha advanced Mack Herron's fumble 46 yards for a TD in the 24–16 win over Baltimore at Schaefer Stadium on 10-07-73

The Patriots player with the longest return of a blocked punt in a regular season game played on Sunday Afternoon

Rod McSwain took a blocked punt 31 yards for a TD in the 30–28 win over the Los Angeles Rams at Anaheim Stadium on 11-16-86

The Patriots player with the longest return of a blocked field-goal attempt in a Sunday Afternoon game

Raymond Clayborn took a blocked field goal 71 yards for a TD in the 21–7 win over Houston at the Astrodome on 10-18-87

The Patriots player with the longest field goal in a regular season game played on Sunday Afternoon

Adam Vinatieri kicked a 57-yard field goal in the 33–30 win over the Chicago Bears at Memorial Stadium on 11-10-02

The Patriots player with the longest punt in a regular season game played on Sunday Afternoon

Shawn McCarthy boomed a punt 93 yards in the 22–17 loss to the Buffalo Bills at Rich Stadium on 11-03-91

The Most

The Patriots player with the most yards rushing in a regular season game played on Sunday Afternoon

Tony Collins had 212 yards rushing in the 23–13 victory over the New York Jets at Sullivan Stadium on 09-18-83

The Patriots player with the most yards passing in a regular season game played on Sunday Afternoon

Drew Bledsoe had 426 yards passing in the 26–20 overtime win vs the Vikings at Foxboro Stadium on 11-13-94

The Patriots player with the most yards receiving in a regular season game played on Sunday Afternoon

Terry Glenn had 214 yards receiving in the 19–7 win over the Browns at Cleveland Browns Stadium on 10-03-99

The Patriots player with the most special team return yards in a regular season game played on Sunday Afternoon

Ellis Hobbs had 237 special team return yards in the 38–13 loss to the Miami Dolphins at Gillette Stadium on 09-21-08

The progression of the most points scored by a Patriots player in a regular season game played on Sunday Afternoon

6 points were scored by Dick Christy in the 27–14 loss to the Oakland Raiders at Kezar Stadium on 10-16-60

6 points were scored by Jim Colclough in the 31–24 loss to the Denver Broncos at Bears Stadium on 10-23-60

6 points were scored by Gino Cappelletti in the 31–24 loss to the Denver Broncos at Bears Stadium on 10-23-60

12 points were scored by Oscar Lofton in the 37–21 loss to the Houston Oilers at Jeppesen Stadium on 12-18-60

18 points were scored by Gino Cappelletti in the 37–30 loss to the New York Titans at the Polo Grounds on 10-01-61

18 points were scored by Billy Lott in the 52–21 rout of the Buffalo Bills at BU Field on 10-22-61

21 points were scored by Gino Cappelletti in the 33–28 win over the San Diego Chargers at Balboa Stadium on 09-20-64

21 points were scored by Gino Cappelletti in the 39–10 rout of the Denver Broncos at Bears Stadium on 10-04-64

24 points were scored by Gino Cappelletti in the 36–28 victory over the Buffalo Bills at War Memorial Stadium on 11-15-64

Every regular season game played by the New England Patriots on Sunday Night

1978 regular season
Beat the Raiders 21–14 at the Oakland Coliseum on 09-24-78 (Sam Cunningham scored on a one-yard TD with 16 seconds left)

1987 regular season
Lost to the New York Giants 17–10 at Giants Stadium on 11-08-87 (Steve Grogan has played against every NFL team)

1988 regular season
Beat Miami 6–3 at Joe Robbie Stadium on 11-20-88 (The first NFL regular season game with no turnovers by either team)

1989 regular season
Lost to the Miami Dolphins 31–10 at Joe Robbie Stadium on 12-10-89 (Eric Sievers had a career-best 117 yards receiving)

1991 regular season
Lost to the Miami Dolphins 30–20 at Joe Robbie Stadium on 11-10-91 (The Patriots used four different long snappers)

1992 regular season
Lost to the New York Jets 30–21 at the Meadowlands on 10-04-92 ("Thrillin" Hugh Millen tossed three TD passes)

Lost to the Miami Dolphins 38–17 at Joe Robbie Stadium on 10-18-92 (Game was rescheduled due to Hurricane Andrew)

1993 regular season
Lost to the New York Jets 45–7 at the Meadowlands on 09-26-93 (Ray Crittenden had career longest pass reception)

1994 regular season
Beat the Indianapolis Colts 12–10 at the RCA Dome on 11-27-94 (Willie McGinest sacked Don Majkowski to seal the win)

1995 regular season
Lost to the Denver Broncos 37–3 at Foxboro Stadium on 10-08-95 (Matt Bahr kicked a 51-yard field goal)

1996 regular season
Beat Buffalo 28–25 at Foxboro on 10-27-96 (Willie McGinest returned a pass 46 yards for a TD) (The Game of the Year)

Destroyed the San Diego Chargers 45–7 at Jack Murphy Stadium on 12-01-96 (Drew Bledsoe was NFL Player of the Week)

1997 regular season

Beat the New York Jets 27–24 in overtime at Foxboro on 09-14-97 (Mike Jones blocked a 29-yard field-goal attempt attempt to force overtime)

1998 regular season

Beat the Indianapolis Colts 29–6 at Foxboro Stadium on 09-13-98 (Ty Law returned a Peyton Manning pass 59 yards for a TD)

1999 regular season

Defeated the New York Giants 16–14 at Foxboro Stadium on 09-26-99 (Terry Glenn's 45-yard reception set up the Patriots' only TD)

Beat the Dallas Cowboys 13–6 at Foxboro Stadium on 12-05-99 (Terry Allen ran for a TD in the fourth quarter)

2001 championship season

Lost to the St. Louis Rams 24–17 at Foxboro on 11-18-01 (David Patten caught a TD in this loss and in the Super Bowl win)

2002 regular season

Lost to the Oakland Raiders 27–20 at the Network Assoc. Coliseum on 11-17-02 (Tedy Bruschi took a pass 48 yards for a TD)

Lost to the New York Jets 30–17 at Gillette Stadium on 12-22-02 (Kevin Faulk had 271 total yards rushing, receiving, and returning)

2003 championship season

Shutout the Cowboys 12–0 at Gillette Stadium on 11-16-03 (Ty Law returned a pass 45 yards on the last play of the game)

2004 championship season

Beat the Buffalo Bills 29–6 at Gillette Stadium on 11-14-04 (Adam Vinatieri kicked five field goals and two extra points)

2005 regular season

Defeated the Buffalo Bills 21–16 at Gillette Stadium on 10-30-05 (Tedy Bruschi returned to the lineup after his stroke)

2006 regular season

Lost to the Denver Broncos 17–7 at Gillette Stadium on 09-24-06 (David Thomas started at tight end)

Lost to the Indianapolis Colts 27–20 at Gillette Stadium on 11-05-06 (Corey Dillon ran for two TDs)

2007 undefeated regular season

Routed the Chargers 38–14 at Gillette Stadium on 09-16-07 (Randy Moss had two TD receptions for the first of three consecutive games)

Blasted Buffalo 56–10 at Ralph Wilson Stadium on 11-18-07 (Randy Moss was the AFC Offensive Player of the Week)

Beat the Philadelphia Eagles 31–28 at Gillette Stadium on 11-25-07 (James Sanders sealed the win with his late interception)

2008 regular season

Lost to the San Diego Chargers 30–10 at Qualcomm Stadium on 10-12-08 (Wes Welker caught nine of the 22 pass completions)

Lost to the Indianapolis Colts 18–15 at Lucas Oil Stadium on 11-02-08 (Chris Hanson's only punt was for 64 yards)

Beat the Seattle Seahawks 24–21 at Qwest Field on 12-07-08 (Brandon Meriweather's strip-sack sealed the win)

The 10 most memorable moments in regular season games played by the Patriots on Sunday Night

Tedy Bruschi returned to the lineup after his recovery from a stroke and was named the AFC Defensive Player of the Week in the five-point win on 10-30-05

Randy Moss had four TD receptions in the first half of the 46-point win over the Buffalo Bills on 11-18-07

Drew Bledsoe threw a TD pass to Terry Glenn, Keith Byars, Sam Gash, and Shawn Jefferson in the 38-point win on 12-01-96

Sam "Bam" Cunningham dove for a 1-yard TD with 16 seconds left in the seven-point win over Oakland on 09-24-78

Curtis Martin had 42 of his 199 yards rushing in the overtime period to help set up the game-winning field goal on 09-14-97

Willie McGinest returned a pass by Jim Kelly 46 yards for a TD with 41 seconds left in the three-point win on 10-27-96

Tom Brady completed a pass to nine different receivers in the first half of their 23-point win over the Bills on 11-14-04

Willie McGinest strip-sacked Don "The Magic Man" Majkowski late in the game to seal the two-point win on 11-27-94

James Sanders intercepted A.J. Feeley with 11 seconds left to seal the three-point win over the Eagles on 11-25-07

Mike Vrabel had the only kickoff return for the Patriots in the 12–0 shutout of the Dallas Cowboys on 11-16-03

The only Patriot to be the NFL Player of the Week for his perfomance in a regular season Sunday Night Game

Drew Bledsoe threw four TD passes in the 45–7 rout of the San Diego Chargers at Jack Murphy Stadium on 12-01-96

Every Patriot who was the AFC Offensive Player of the Week for his work in a regular season Sunday Night Game

1997 regular season

Curtis Martin had 40 carries for 199 yards and one TD in the 27–24 overtime win vs the New York Jets at Foxboro on 09-14-97

2007 regular season

Randy Moss had 10 receptions for 128 yards and four TDs in the 56–10 rout of the Bills at Ralph Wilson Stadium on 11-18-07

The only Patriot to be the AFC Special Team Player of the Week for his work in a regular season Sunday Night Game

Tom Tupa averaged 50 yards per punt in the 28–25 victory over the Buffalo Bills at Foxboro Stadium on 10-27-96

The Longest

The Patriots player with the longest run from scrimmage in a regular season game played on Sunday Night

Sedrick Shaw dashed for a 51-yard gain in the 29–6 win over the Indianapolis Colts at Foxboro Stadium on 09-13-98

The Patriots player with the longest reception in a regular season game played on Sunday Night

Russ Francis had a 53-yard pass reception in the 21–14 win over Oakland at the Oakland Coliseum on 09-24-78

The Patriots Quarterback with the longest completion in a regular season game played on Sunday Night

Steve Grogan tossed a 53-yard pass to Russ Francis in the 21–14 win over the Raiders at the Oakland Coliseum on 09-24-78

The Patriots Defensive Back with the longest interception return in a regular season game played on Sunday Night

Ty Law took a Peyton Manning pass 59 yards for a TD in the 29–6 win over the Indianapolis Colts at Foxboro on 09-13-98

The Patriots Linebacker with the longest interception return in a regular season game played on Sunday Night

Tedy Bruschi returned a Rich Gannon pass 48 yards for a TD in the 27–20 loss to the Oakland Raiders at the Coliseum on 11-17-02

The Patriots player with the longest punt return in a regular season game played on Sunday Night

Troy Brown returned a punt 38 yards in the 29–6 rout of the Indianapolis Colts at Foxboro on 09-13-98

The Patriots player with the longest kickoff return in a regular season game played on Sunday Night

Chris Canty returned a kickoff 63 yards in the 27–24 overtime win vs the New York Jets at Foxboro on 09-14-97

The Patriots Kicker with the longest field goal in a regular season game played on Sunday Night

Adam Vinatieri hit a 52-yard field goal on the last play of the half in the 29–6 win over the Colts at Foxboro on 09-13-98

The Patriots player with the longest punt in a regular season game played on Sunday Night

Lee Johnson booted it 58 yards in the 16–14 victory over the New York Giants at Foxboro Stadium on 09-26-99

The Most

The Patriots player with the most yards rushing in a regular season game played on Sunday Night

Curtis Martin had 199 yards rushing in the 27–24 overtime win vs the New York Jets at Foxboro Stadium on 09-14-97

The Patriots QB with the most yards passing in a regular season game played on Sunday Night

Drew Bledsoe threw for 373 yards in the 28–25 victory over the Buffalo Bills at Foxboro Stadium on 10-27-96

The Patriots Receiver with the most yards receiving in a regular season game played on Sunday Night

Irving Fryar had 165 yards receiving in the 30–21 loss to the New York Jets at the Meadowlands on 10-04-92

The Patriots player with the most special team return yards in a regular season game played on Sunday Night

Kevin Faulk had 220 kickoff return yards in the 30–17 loss to the New York Jets at Gillette Stadium on 12-22-02

The progression of the most points scored by a Patriots player in a regular season game played on Sunday Night

6 points were scored by Russ Francis in the 21–14 victory over the Oakland Raiders at the Oakland Coliseum on 09-24-78

6 points were scored by Horace Ivory in the 21–14 victory over the Oakland Raiders at the Oakland Coliseum on 09-24-78

6 points were scored by Sam Cunningham in the 21–14 win over the Oakland Raiders at the Oakland Coliseum on 09-24-78

6 points were scored by Greg Baty in the 17–10 loss to the New York Giants at Giants Stadium on 11-08-87

6 points were scored by Jason Staurovsky in the 6–3 win over the Miami Dolphins at Joe Robbie Stadium on 11-20-88

6 points were scored by John Stephens in the 31–10 loss to the Miami Dolphins at Joe Robbie Stadium on 12-10-89

6 points were scored by George Adams in the 17–10 loss to the Miami Dolphins at Joe Robbie Stadium on 10-18-90

6 points were scored by Charlie Baumann in the 30–20 loss to the Miami Dolphins at Joe Robbie Stadium on 11-10-91

6 points were scored by Irving Fryar in the 30–20 loss to the Miami Dolphins at Joe Robbie Stadium on 11-10-91

8 points were scored by Charlie Baumann in the 30–20 loss to the Miami Dolphins at Joe Robbie Stadium on 11-10-91

12 points were scored by Matt Bahr in the 12–10 victory over the Indianapolis Colts at the RCA Dome on 11-27-94

12 points were scored by Curtis Martin in the 28–25 victory over the Buffalo Bills at Foxboro Stadium on 10-27-96

12 points were scored by Corey Dillon in the 21–16 victory over the Buffalo Bills at Gillette Stadium on 10-30-05

12 points were scored by Randy Moss in the 38–14 victory over the San Diego Chargers at Gillette Stadium on 09-16-07

24 points were scored by Randy Moss in the 56–10 rout of the Buffalo Bills at Ralph Wilson Stadium on 11-18-07

Every Patriots player who has blocked a field-goal attempt in a regular season game played on Sunday Night

1997 regular season

Mike Jones blocked a 29-yard field-goal attempt by John Hall with 16 seconds left in the 27–24 overtime win vs the New York Jets on 09-14-97

2002 regular season

Richard Seymour blocked a 49-yard field-goal attempt by Sebastian Janikowski in the 27–20 loss to the Raiders on 11-17-02

Every Patriots Defensive Back who has returned a pass for a TD in a regular season game played on Sunday Night

1998 regular season

Ty Law took a Peyton Manning pass 59 yards for a TD in the 29–6 win over the Indianapolis Colts at Foxboro on 09-13-98

2001 championship season

Terrell Buckley took a Kurt Warner pass 52 yards for a TD in the 24–17 loss to the St. Louis Rams at Foxboro on 11-18-01

The only Patriots Linebacker who has returned a pass for a TD in a regular season game played on Sunday Night

Tedy Bruschi took a Rich Gannon pass 48 yards for a TD in the 27–20 loss to Oakland at Network Assoc. Coliseum on 11-17-02

Every Playoff Game that was played by the Patriots on Saturday Afternoon
1963 AFL Divisional Playoff Game
Beat the Buffalo Bills 26–8 at War Memorial Stadium on 12-28-63 (Ron Burton played after missing the regular season with disc surgery)

1976 AFC Divisional Playoff Game
Lost to the Oakland Raiders 24–21 at the Oakland Coliseum on 12-18-76 (Julius Adams sacked Ken Stabler three times)

1982 AFC first round Playoff Game
Lost to the Dolphins 28–13 at the Orange Bowl on 01-08-83 (Only tight ends have more than one reception for the Patriots)

1985 AFC Wild Card Playoff Game
Defeated the New York Jets 26–14 at the Meadowlands on 12-28-85 (Garin Veris had three sacks, an interception, and a fumble recovery)

1997 AFC Divisional Playoff Game
Lost to the Pittsburgh Steelers 7–6 at Three Rivers Stadium on 01-03-98 (Robert Edwards ran for the only TD)

The scoring summary of every Patriots victory in a playoff game that was played on Saturday Afternoon
The Boston Patriots defeated the Buffalo Bills 26–8 at War Memorial Stadium on 12-28-63

	Q1	Q2	Q3	Q4	Total
Boston	10	6	0	10	26
Buffalo	0	0	8	0	8

Gino Cappelletti kicked a 28-yard field goal.

Larry Garron hauled in a 59-yard TD pass from Babe Parilli. Gino Cappelletti kicked the extra point.

Gino Cappelletti kicked a 12-yard field goal.

Gino Cappelletti kicked a 33-yard field goal.

Elbert Dubenion hauled in a 93-yard TD pass from Daryle Lamonica. John Tracey caught a two-point pass from Daryle Lamonica.

Larry Garron caught a 17-yard TD pass from Babe Parilli. Gino Cappelletti kicked the extra point.

Gino Cappelletti kicked a 36-yard field goal.

_____

The New England Patriots defeated the New York Jets 26–14 at the Meadowlands on 12-28-85

	Q1	Q2	Q3	Q4	Total
New England	3	10	10	3	26
New York	0	7	7	0	14

Tony Franklin kicked a 33-yard field goal.

Johnny Hector caught an 11-yard TD pass from Ken O'Brien. Pat Leahy kicked the extra point.

Tony Franklin kicked a 41-yard field goal.

Stanley Morgan caught a 36-yard TD pass from Tony Eason. Tony Franklin kicked the extra point.

Tony Franklin kicked a 20-yard field goal.

Johnny Rembert returned a fumble by Johnny Hector 15 yards for a TD. Tony Franklin kicked the extra point.

Mickey Shuler caught a 12-yard TD pass from Pat Ryan. Pat Leahy kicked the extra point.

Tony Franklin kicked a 26-yard field goal.

Every Playoff Game that was played by the New England Patriots on Saturday Night
2001 AFC Divisional Playoff Game
Beat the Oakland Raiders 16–13 in overtime at Foxboro Stadium on 01-19-02 (David Patten's fourth-down reception set up final field goal)

2003 AFC Divisional Playoff Game
Beat the Tennessee Titans 17–14 at Gillette Stadium (minus-11 degree wind chill) on 01-10-04 (Adam Vinatieri kicked a 46-yard field goal)

2005 AFC Wild Card Playoff Game
Defeated the Jacksonville Jaguars 28–3 at Gillette Stadium on 01-07-06 (Willie McGinest set NFL Record with 4.5 sacks)

2005 AFC Divisional Playoff Game
Lost to the Denver Broncos 27–13 at Invesco Field on 01-14-06 (Deion Branch had eight receptions for 153 yards)

2007 AFC Divisional Playoff Game
Beat the Jacksonville Jaguars 31–20 at Gillette on 01-12-08 (Tom Brady was 26-for-28 for an NFL record 92.8 completion percentage)

The scoring summary of every Patriots victory in a playoff game that was played on Saturday Night.

The New England Patriots defeated the Oakland Raiders 16–13 in overtime at Foxboro Stadium on 01-19-02

	Q1	Q2	Q3	Q4	OT	Total
Oakland	0	7	6	0	0	13
New England	0	0	3	10	3	16

James Jett caught a 13-yard TD pass from Rich Gannon. Sebastian Janikowski kicked the extra point.

Adam Vinatieri kicked a 23-yard field goal.

Sebastian Janikowski kicked a 38-yard field goal.

Sebastian Janikowski kicked a 45-yard field goal.

Tom Brady ran up the middle for a six-yard TD. Adam Vinatieri kicked the extra point.

Adam Vinatieri kicked a 45-yard field goal.

Adam Vinatieri kicked a 23-yard field goal.

———

The New England Patriots defeated the Tennessee Titans 17–14 at Gillette Stadium on 01-10-04

	Q1	Q2	Q3	Q4	Total
Tennessee	7	0	7	0	14
New England	7	7	0	3	17

Bethel Johnson hauled in a 41-yard TD pass from Tom Brady. Adam Vinatieri kicked the extra point.

Chris Brown ran for a five-yard TD. Gary Anderson kicked the extra point.

Antowain Smith ran for a one-yard TD. Adam Vinatieri kicked the extra point.

Derrick Mason caught an 11-yard TD pass from Steve McNair. Gary Anderson kicked the extra point.

Adam Vinatieri kicked a 46-yard field goal.

———

The New England Patriots defeated the Jacksonville Jaguars 28–3 at Gillette Stadium on 01-07-06

	Q1	Q2	Q3	Q4	Total
Jacksonville	0	3	0	0	3
New England	0	7	14	7	28

Troy Brown caught an 11-yard TD pass from Tom Brady. Adam Vinatieri kicked the extra point.

Josh Scobee kicked a 36-yard field goal.

David Givens caught a three-yard TD pass from Tom Brady. Adam Vinatieri kicked the extra point.

Benjamin Watson hauled in a 63-yard TD pass from Tom Brady. Adam Vinatieri kicked the extra point.

Asante Samuel returned an interception 73 yards for a TD. Adam Vinatieri kicked the extra point.

———

The New England Patriots defeated the Jacksonville Jaguars 31–20 at Gillette Stadium on 01-12-08

	Q1	Q2	Q3	Q4	Total
Jacksonville	7	7	3	3	20
New England	7	7	14	3	31

Matt Jones caught an eight-yard TD pass from David Garrard. Josh Scobee kicked the extra point.

Benjamin Watson caught a three-yard TD pass from Tom Brady. Stephen Gostkowski kicked the extra point.

Laurence Maroney scored on a one-yard run. Stephen Gostkowski kicked the extra point.

Ernest Wilford caught a six-yard TD pass from David Garrard. Josh Scobee kicked the extra point.

Wes Welker caught a six-yard TD pass from Tom Brady after a fake snap to Kevin Faulk. Stephen Gostkowski kicked the PAT.

Josh Scobee kicked a 39-yard field goal.

Benjamin Watson caught a nine-yard TD pass from Tom Brady. Stephen Gostkowski kicked the extra point.

Josh Scobee kicked a 25-yard field goal.

Stephen Gostkowski kicked a 35-yard field goal.

Tom Brady completed 16 consecutive passes.

Every playoff game that was played by the Patriots on Sunday Afternoon

1963 AFL Championship Game

Lost to the San Diego Chargers 51–10 at Balboa Stadium on 01-05-64 (Larry Garron ran for their only TD)

1978 AFC Divisional Playoff Game

Lost to the Houston Oilers 31–14 at Schaefer Stadium on 12-31-78 (Russ Francis had 101 yards receiving and one TD)

1985 AFC Divisional Playoff Game

Beat the Los Angeles Raiders 27–20 at the Los Angeles Coliseum on 01-05-86 (Jim Bowman recovered a fumble in the end zone)

1985 AFC Championship Game

Defeated the Dolphins 31–14 at the Orange Bowl on 01-12-86 (Patriots ended their 18-game losing streak at the Orange Bowl)

1986 AFC Divisional Playoff Game

Lost to the Denver Broncos 22–17 at Mile High Stadium on 01-04-87 (Stanley Morgan caught a 45-yard flea-flicker TD pass)

1994 AFC Wild Card Playoff Game

Lost to the Browns 20–13 at Cleveland Stadium on 01-01-95 (Corwin Brown recovered a Patriots onside kick and caught a pass)

1996 AFC Divisional Playoff Game

Defeated the Pittsburgh Steelers 28–3 at Foxboro Stadium on 01-05-97 (Curtis Martin ran for three TDs including one from 78 yards)

1996 AFC Championship Game

Defeated the Jacksonville Jaguars 20–6 at Foxboro Stadium on 01-12-97 (Otis Smith returned a fumble 47 yards for a TD)

1997 AFC Wild Card Playoff Game

Defeated the Miami Dolphins 17–3 at Foxboro Stadium on 12-28-97 (Chris Slade was the AFC Defensive Player of the Week)

1998 AFC Wild Card Playoff Game

Lost to the Jacksonville Jaguars 25–10 at Alltel Stadium on 01-03-99 (Robert Edwards ran for the only TD)

2001 AFC Championship Game

Defeated the Pittsburgh Steelers 24–17 at Heinz Field on 01-27-02 (Antwan Harris took a blocked FGA and lateral for a TD)

2003 AFC Championship Game

Defeated the Indianapolis Colts 24–14 at Gillette Stadium on 01-18-04 (Ty Law intercepted Peyton Manning three times)

Left to right: Tebucky Jones, Antwan Harris, Ty Law

2004 AFC Divisional Playoff Game
Defeated the Indianapolis Colts 20–3 at Gillette Stadium on 01-16-05 (Tedy Bruschi was NFL Defensive Player of the Week)

2006 AFC Wild Card Playoff Game
Routed the New York Jets 37–16 at Gillette Stadium on 01-07-07 (Daniel Graham caught a TD pass with 11 seconds left in the half)

2006 AFC Divisional Playoff Game
Beat the San Diego Chargers 24–21 at Qualcomm Stadium on 01-14-07 (Stephen Gostkowski kicked a 31-yard field goal to win game)

2007 AFC Championship Game
Beat the San Diego Chargers 21–12 at Gillette Stadium on 01-20-08 (Heath Evans had more yards rushing than LaDanian Tomlinson)

The 10 most memorable moments in playoff games played by the Patriots on Sunday Afternoon

Antwan Harris took a lateral from Troy Brown for a TD, after Brandon Mitchell's blocked field goal, in the seven-point win on 01-27-02

Troy Brown forced Marlon McCree to fumble on his fourth quarter interception return in the three-point win over San Diego on 01-14-07

Troy Brown returned a punt by Josh Miller 55 yards for a TD in the seven-point win over Pittsburgh on 01-27-02

Ty Law intercepted Peyton Manning three times in the 10-point victory over the Indianapolis Colts on 01-18-04

Curtis Martin ran for three TDs, including one for 78 yards, in the 25-point victory over the Steelers on 01-05-97

Tedy Bruschi stole the ball from Dominic Rhodes after stopping him for a loss in the 17-point win over the Colts on 01-16-05

Chris Slade intercepted, sacked, and recovered a fumble by Dan Marino in the 14-point win on 12-28-97

Otis Smith returned a James Stewart fumble that was forced by Chris Slade 47 yards for a TD in the 14-point win on 01-12-97

Tom Brady threw a 49-yard pass on third-and-10 to Reche Caldwell during the game-winning drive in the three-point win on 01-14-07

Jim Bowman fell on a fumble by Sam Seale that was forced by Mosi Tatupu for the last points scored in the win on 01-05-86

Chris Slade

The only Patriots player who was named the NFL Defensive Player of the Week in a playoff game

Tedy Bruschi had eight tackles, forced a fumble, and recovered two fumbles in the 20–3 rout of the Colts on 01-16-05

The only Patriots player who was named the AFC Defensive Player of the Week in a playoff game

Chris Slade returned a Dan Marino pass 22 yards, had a sack, and recovered a fumble by Dan Marino in the 17–3 win on 12-28-97

Every Playoff Game that was played by the New England Patriots on Sunday Night (5:00 PM or later)

Super Bowl XX
Lost to the Bears 46–10 at the Louisiana Superdome on 01-26-86 (Tony Franklin kicked a 36-yard field goal just 1:14 into the game)

Super Bowl XXXVI
Lost to the Green Bay Packers 35–21 at the Superdome on 01-26-97 (Keith Byars, Curtis Martin, and Ben Coates scored a TD)

Super Bowl XXXVI
Beat the St. Louis Rams 20–17 at the Lousiana Superdome on 02-03-02 (Adam Vinatieri kicked a 48-yard field goal to win the game)

Super Bowl XXXVIII
Beat the Carolina Panthers 32–29 at Reliant Stadium on 02-01-04 (Adam Vinatieri kicked a 41-yard field goal with four seconds left)

2004 AFC Championship Game
Defeated the Pittsburgh Steelers 41–27 at Heinz Field on 01-23-05 (Deion Branch had a 60-yard reception and a 23-yard TD run)

Super Bowl XXXIX
Defeated the Philadelphia Eagles 24–21 at Alltel Stadium on 02-06-05 (Deion Branch had 133 yards receiving and was the MVP)

Adam Vinatieri

Deion Branch, Super Bowl XXXIX MVP

2006 AFC Championship Game
Lost to the Indianapolis Colts 38–34 at the RCA Dome on 01-21-07 (Logan Makins recovered a fumble for a TD)

Every Patriots player who was named the AFC Special Team Player of the Week in a playoff game
Larry Whigham tackled the Jaguars Punter on the 4-yard line in the 20–6 victory over Jacksonville on 01-12-97

Troy Brown returned a punt for a TD and lateraled a blocked field-goal attempt that resulted in a TD in the 24–17 win on 01-27-01

Every Patriots player who was named the MVP of a Super Bowl
Tom Brady led the Patriots to their first Super Bowl victory on 02-03-02

Tom Brady set a Super Bowl record with 32 completions in the Patriots' second Super Bowl victory on 02-01-04

Deion Branch had 11 receptions for 133 yards in the Patriots' third Super Bowl victory on 02-06-05

The scoring summary of every Patriots victory in a playoff game that was played on Sunday Night

The New England Patriots defeated the St. Louis Rams 20–17 at the Superdome on 02-03-02

	Q1	Q2	Q3	Q4	Total
St. Louis	3	0	0	14	17
New England	0	14	3	3	20

Jeff Wilkins kicked a 50-yard field goal.

Ty Law returned an interception 47 yards for a TD. Adam Vinatieri kicked the extra point.

David Patten caught an eight-yard TD pass from Tom Brady. Adam Vinatieri kicked the extra point.

Adam Vinatieri kicked a 37-yard field goal.

Kurt Warner ran for a two-yard TD. Jeff Wilkins kicked the extra point.

Ricky Proehl caught a 26-yard TD pass from Kurt Warner. Jeff Wilkins kicked the extra point.

Adam Vinatieri kicked a 48-yard field goal on the last play of the game.

———

The New England Patriots defeated the Carolina Panthers 32–29 at Reliant Stadium on 02-01-04

	Q1	Q2	Q3	Q4	Total
Carolina	0	10	0	19	29
New England	0	14	0	18	32

Deion Branch caught a five-yard TD pass from Tom Brady. Adam Vinatieri kicked the extra point.

Steve Smith caught a 39-yard TD pass from Jake Delhomme. John Kasay kicked the extra point.

David Givens cuaght a five-yard TD pass from Tom Brady. Adam Vinatieri kicked the extra point.

John Kasay kicked a 50-yard field goal on the last play of the first half.

Antowain Smith ran for a 2-yard TD. Adam Vinatieri kicked the extra point.

DeShaun Foster ran for a 33-yard TD. Jake Delhomme's two-point pass attempt was incomplete.

Muhsin Muhammad hauled in an 85-yard TD pass from Jake Delhomme. The two-point conversion pass attempt was incomplete.

Mike Vrabel caught a one-yard TD pass from Tom Brady. Kevin Faulk ran for a two-point conversion.

Ricky Proehl caught a 12-yard TD pass from Jake Delhomme. John Kasay kicked the extra point.

Adam Vinatieri kicked a 41-yard field goal.

———

The New England Patriots defeated the Pittsburgh Steelers 41–27 at Heinz Field on 01-23-05

	Q1	Q2	Q3	Q4	Total
New England	10	14	7	10	41
Pittsburgh	3	0	14	10	27

Adam Vinatieri kicked a 48-yard field goal.

Deion Branch caught a 60-yard TD pass from Tom Brady. Adam Vinatieri kicked the extra point.

Jeff Reed kicked a 43-yard field goal.

David Givens caught a nine-yard TD pass from Tom Brady. Adam Vinatieri kicked the extra point.

Rodney Harrison returned an interception 87 yards for a TD. Adam Vinatieri kicked the extra point.

Jerome Bettis ran for a five-yard TD. Jeff Reed kicked the extra point.

Corey Dillon dashed 25 yards for a TD. Adam Vinatieri kicked the extra point.

Hines Ward caught a 30-yard TD pass from Ben Roethlisberger. Jeff Reed kicked the extra point.

Jeff Reed kicked a 20-yard field goal.

Adam Vinatieri kicked a 31-yard field goal.

Wide receiver Deion Branch scampered 23 yards for a TD. Adam Vinatieri kicked the extra point.

Plaxico Burress caught a seven-yard TD pass from Ben Roethlisberger. Jeff Reed kicked the extra point.

———

The New England Patriots defeated the Philadelphia Eagles 24–21 at Alltel Stadium on 02-06-05

	Q1	Q2	Q3	Q4	Total
New England	0	7	7	10	24
Philadelphia	0	7	7	7	21

L.J. Smith caught a six-yard TD pass from Donovan McNabb. David Akers kicked the extra point.

David Givens caught a four-yard TD pass from Tom Brady. Adam Vinatieri kicked the extra point.

Mike Vrabel caught a two-yard TD pass from Tom Brady. Adam Vinatieri kicked the extra point.

Brian Westbrook caught a 10-yard TD pass from Donovan McNabb. David Akers kicked the extra point.

Corey Dillon ran for a two-yard TD. Adam Vinatieri kicked the extra point.

Adam Vinatieri kicked a 22-yard field goal.

Greg Lewis caught a 30-yard TD pass from Donovan McNabb. David Akers kicked the extra point.

Rodney Harrison returned a pass by Donovan McNabb six yards, with 17 seconds left, to seal the victory.

Every regular season game that was played by the Boston Patriots that ended in a tie

The Boston Patriots tied the Houston Oilers 31–31 at BU Field on 10-13-61

	Q1	Q2	Q3	Q4	Total
Houston	0	14	7	10	31
Boston	7	3	14	7	31

Babe Parilli scored on a one-yard QB sneak. Gino Cappelletti kicked the extra point.

Bill Groman caught a 44-yard TD pass from Jacky Lee. George Blanda kicked the extra point.

Charley Hennigan hauled in a 48-yard TD pass from Jacky Lee. George Blanda kicked the extra point.

Gino Cappelletti kicked a 17-yard field goal.

Larry Garron returned a kickoff 89 yards for a TD. Gino Cappelletti kicked the extra point.

Charley Tolar ran for a two-yard TD. George Blanda kicked the extra point.

Ron Burton scored on a one-yard run. Gino Cappelletti kicked the extra point.

Billy Cannon ran for a two-yard TD. George Blanda kicked the extra point.

Gino Cappelletti caught a three-yard TD pass from Butch Songin. Gino Cappelletti kicked the extra point.

George Blanda kicked a 25-yard field goal with five seconds left in the game.

The Boston Patriots tied the Buffalo Bills 28–28 at War Memorial Stadium on 11-03-62

	Q1	Q2	Q3	Q4	Total
Boston	14	7	7	0	28
Buffalo	14	0	7	7	28

Cookie Gilchrist ran for a two-yard TD. Cookie Gilchrist kicked the extra point.

Larry Garron returned a kickoff 95 yards for a TD. Gino Cappelletti kicked the extra point.

Ron Burton caught a 29-yard TD pass from Babe Parilli. Gino Cappelletti kicked the extra point.

Elbert Dubenion returned a kickoff 93 yards for a TD. Cookie Gilchrist kicked the extra point.

LeRoy Moore returned an interception three yards for a TD. Cookie Gilchrist kicked the extra point.

Cookie Gilchrist ran for a seven-yard TD. Cookie Gilchrist kicked the extra point.

Gino Cappelletti caught a six-yard TD pass from Babe Parilli. Gino Cappelletti kicked the extra point.

Larry Garron hauled in a 23-yard TD pass from Babe Parilli. Gino Cappelletti kicked the extra point.

Cookie Gilchrist missed on a 46-yard field-goal attempt on the last play of the game.

The Boston Patriots tied the Kansas City Chiefs 24–24 at Fenway Park on 11-17-63

	Q1	Q2	Q3	Q4	Total
Kansas City	7	3	7	7	24
Boston	0	15	2	7	24

Frank Jackson caught an 11-yard TD pass from Edie Wilson. Jack Spikes kicked the extra point.

Gino Cappelletti kicked a 32-yard field goal.

Tony Romeo caught an eight-yard TD pass from Babe Parilli. The extra-point attempt was no good.

Jack Spikes kicked a 27-yard field goal.

Babe Parilli ran a QB sneak for a one-yard TD. The two-point conversion attempt failed.

Eddie Wilson was tackled in the end zone by the Patriots defense for a safety.

Larry Garron dashed 47 yards for a TD. Gino Cappelletti kicked the extra point.

Curtis McClinton caught a 28-yard TD pass from Eddie Wilson. Jack Spikes kicked the extra point.

———

The Boston Patriots tied the Oakland Raiders 43–43 at Fenway Park on 10-16-64

	Q1	Q2	Q3	Q4	Total
Oakland	3	21	10	9	43
Boston	0	14	7	22	43

Mike Mercer kicked a 42-yard field goal.

Ron Burton ran for a two-yard TD. Gino Cappelletti kicked the extra point.

Clem Daniels caught a 26-yard TD pass from Cotton Davidson. Mike Mercer kicked the extra point.

Bo Roberson hauled in a 50-yard TD pass from Cotton Davidson. Mike Mercer kicked the extra point.

Jim Colclough caught a 36-yard TD pass from Babe Parilli. Gino Cappelletti kicked the extra point.

Art Powell hauled in a 39-yard TD pass from Cotton Davidson. Mike Mercer kicked the extra point.

Billy Cannon dashed 34 yards for a TD. Mike Mercer kicked the extra point.

Mike Mercer kicked a 37-yard field goal.

Larry Garron caught a 10-yard TD pass from Babe Parilli. Gino Cappelletti kicked the extra point.

Larry Garron scored on a one-yard run. Gino Cappelletti kicked the extra point.

Art Graham caught an eight-yard TD pass from Babe Parilli. Gino Cappelletti kicked the extra point.

Art Powell grabbed a nine-yard TD pass from Cotton Davidson, The two-point conversion attempt failed.

Larry Garron caught an 11-yard TD pass from Babe Parilli. Parilli tossed a two-point pass to Jim Colclough.

Mike Mercer kicked a 38-yard field goal.

Bob Yates recovered the onside kick attempt by Mike Mercer with five seconds left in the game.

———

The Boston Patriots tied the San Diego Chargers 13–13 at Fenway Park on 10-17-65

	Q1	Q2	Q3	Q4	Total
San Diego	3	10	0	0	13
Boston	0	7	3	3	13

Herb Travenio kicked a 40-yard field goal.

Ron Burton hauled in a 73-yard TD pass from Babe Parilli. Gino Cappelletti kicked the extra point.

Lance Alworth hauled in an 85-yard TD pass from John Hadl. Herb Travenio kicked the extra point.

Herb Travenio kicked a 10-yard field goal.

Gino Cappelletti kicked a 21-yard field goal.

Gino Cappelletti kicked a 22-yard field goal.

———

The Boston Patriots tied the Kansas City Chiefs 10–10 at Fenway Park on 11-21-65

	Q1	Q2	Q3	Q4	Total
Kansas City	0	7	0	3	10
Boston	0	3	0	7	10

Gino Cappelletti kicked a 17-yard field goal.

Chris Burford caught an eight-yard TD pass from Len Dawson. Tommy Brooker kicked the extra point.

Tommy Brooker kicked a 32-yard field goal.

J.D. Garrett caught a 10-yard TD pass from Babe Parilli. Gino Cappelletti kicked the extra point.

Ron Hall blocked a 28-yard field-goal attempt by Tommy Brooker with 26 seconds left to preserve the tie.

———

The Boston Patriots tied the New York Jets 24–24 at Fenway Park on 10-02-66

	Q1	Q2	Q3	Q4	Total
New York	0	7	0	17	24
Boston	7	3	14	0	24

Larry Garron ran for a six-yard TD. Gino Cappelletti kicked the extra point.

Matt Snell rumbled for a five-yard TD. Jim Turner kicked the extra point.

Gino Cappelletti kicked a 17-yard field goal.

Gino Cappelletti caught a 19-yard TD pass from Babe Parilli. Gino Cappelletti kicked the extra point.

Larry Garron scored on a two-yard run. Gino Cappelletti kicked the extra point.

Matt Snell caught a 10-yard TD pass from Joe Namath. Jim Turner kicked the extra point.

Pete Lammons caught a 12-yard TD pass from Joe Namath. Jim Turner kicked the extra point.

Jim Turner kicked a 17-yard field goal with 32 seconds left in the game.

———

The Boston Patriots tied the Kansas City Chiefs 27–27 at Municipal Stadium on 11-20-66

	Q1	Q2	Q3	Q4	Total
Boston	0	17	7	3	27
Kansas City	10	0	17	0	27

Mike Mercer kicked a 23-yard field goal.

Frank Pitts returned a blocked punt for a TD. Mike Mercer kicked the extra point.

Art Graham caught a 21-yard TD pass from Babe Parilli. Gino Cappelletti kicked the extra point.

Art Graham hauled in a 38-yard TD pass from Babe Parilli. Gino Cappelletti kicked the extra point.

Gino Cappelletti kicked a 31-yard field goal.

Mike Mercer kicked a 40-yard field goal.

Otis Taylor caught a 21-yard TD pass from Len Dawson. Mike Mercer kicked the extra point.

Jim Whalen caught a 13-yard TD pass from Babe Parilli. Gino Cappelletti kicked the extra point.

Otis Taylor hauled in a 26-yard TD pass from Len Dawson. Mike Mercer kicked the extra point.

Gino Cappelletti kicked a 19-yard field goal with 24 seconds left in the game.

———

The Boston Patriots tied the San Diego Chargers 31–31 at Jack Murphy Stadium on 10-08-67

	Q1	Q2	Q3	Q4	Total
Boston	7	14	10	0	31
San Diego	7	10	0	14	31

Brad Hubbert caught a 20-yard TD pass from John Hadl. Dick Van Raaphorst kicked the extra point.

Larry Garron hauled in a 64-yard TD pass from Babe Parilli. Gino Cappelletti kicked the extra point.

John Hadl ran a QB sneak for a one-yard TD. Dick Van Raaphorst kicked the extra point.

Jim Nance dove for a one-yard TD. Gino Cappelletti kicked the extra point.

Dick Van Raaphorst kicked a 32-yard field goal.

Jim Nance rumbled for a 18-yard TD. Gino Cappelletti kicked the extra point.

Art Graham caught an eight-yard TD pass from Babe Parilli. Gino Cappelletti kicked the extra point.

Gino Cappelletti kicked a 41-yard field goal.

Willie Frazier caught a four-yard TD pass from John Hadl. Dick Van Raaphorst kicked the extra point.

Lance Alworth hauled in a 24-yard TD pass from John Hadl. Dick Van Raaphorst kicked the extra point.

Every regular season overtime game that was played by the New England Patriots

1977 regular season

Lost to the Browns 30–27 in overtime on Monday Night at Cleveland Stadium 09-26-77 (John Smith's late field goal forced overtime)

1979 regular season

Lost to the Steelers 16–13 in overtime on Monday Night at Schaefer Stadium on 09-03-79 (Matt Bahr kicked the final field goal)

Lost to the Buffalo Bills 16–13 in overtime at Schaefer Stadium on 11-25-79 (John Smith tackled Mike Collier in the fourth quarter)

1980 regular season

Lost to Miami 16–13 in overtime on Monday Night at the Orange Bowl on 12-08-80 (John Smith's last-second 35-yard field-goal attempt was blocked)

1981 regular season

Lost to Pittsburgh 27–21 in overtime at Three Rivers Stadium on 09-27-81 (Andy Johnson threw a 9-yard pass to QB Matt Cavanaugh)

Lost to the Miami Dolphins 30–27 in overtime at Schaefer Stadium on 11-08-81 (John Smith's late field goal forced overtime)

1983 regular season

Lost to the Colts 29–23 in overtime at Sullivan Stadium on 09-04-83 (Steve Grogan threw a 73-yard TD and a 50-yard TD in the second quarter)

1985 regular season

Lost to the New York Jets 16–13 in overtime at the Meadowlands on 11-24-85 (Tony Franklin's late field goal forced overtime)

1987 regular season

Lost to the Dallas Cowboys 23–17 in overtime at Sullivan Stadium on 11-15-87 (Herschel Walker dashed 60 yards for the final TD)

Lost to the Philadelphia Eagles 34–31 in overtime at Sullivan Stadium on 11-29-87 (Tom Ramsey threw for 402 yards and three TDs)

1988 regular season

Beat the Tampa Bay Buccaneers 10–7 in overtime (18 degrees) at Sullivan Stadium on 12-11-88 (Jason Staurovsky kicked the field goal)

1989 regular season

Beat the Colts 23–20 in overtime at the Hoosier Dome on 10-29-89 (Greg Davis kicked a 51-yard field goal) (The Game of the Year)

1991 regular season

Defeated the Minnesota Vikings 26–23 in overtime at Foxboro Stadium on 10-20-91 (Jason Staurovsky kicked the final FG)

Beat the Colts 23–17 in overtime at Foxboro on 12-08-91 (Hugh Millen threw a game-tying and game-winning TD (The Game of the Year)

1992 regular season

Beat the Colts 37–34 in overtime at the Hoosier Dome on 11-15-92 (Charlie Baumann kicked the field goal) (The Game of the Year)

Lost to Miami 16–13 in overtime at Foxboro Stadium on 12-27-92 (Charlie Baumann recovered a fumbled kickoff return)

1993 regular season

Lost to Detroit 19–16 in overtime at Foxboro on 09-12-93 (Willie Clay took Troy Brown's opening kickoff return fumble for a TD)

Lost to Buffalo 13–10 in overtime at Foxboro on 11-07-93 (Scott Secules had 16 yards rushing and Drew Bledsoe had 14 yards rushing)

Beat Miami 33–27 in overtime at Foxboro Stadium on 01-02-94 (Michael Timpson scored the final TD) (The Game of the Year)

1994 regular season

Beat the Vikings 26–20 in overtime at Foxboro Stadium on 11-13-94 (Kevin Turner scored the final TD) (The Game of the Year)

1995 regular season

Lost to the Carolina Panthers 20–17 in overtime at Foxboro Stadium on 10-29-95 (Curtis Martin had two fourth-quarter TDs)

1996 regular season

Defeated the Jacksonvillle Jaguars 28–25 in overtime at Foxboro Stadium on 09-22-96 (Adam Vinatieri kicked the final field goal)

1997 regular season

Defeated the New York Jets 27–24 in overtime at Foxboro Stadium on 09-14-97 (Mike Jones blocked a field-goal attempt with 16 seconds left)

Lost to the Steelers 24–21 in overtime at Foxboro Stadium on 12-13-97 ("Swede" Hanson and "Spam" Seymour won free tickets)

Kevin Turner (34) scored the winning TD on 11-13-94

1998 regular season
Lost to the Miami Dolphins 12–9 in overtime at Pro Player Stadium on 10-25-98 (Shawn Jefferson had 116 yards receiving)

1999 regular season
Lost to Buffalo 13–10 in overtime at Foxboro on 12-26-99 (Terry Allen had more yards rushing than Drew Bledsoe had passing)

2000 regular season
Lost to the Bills 16–13 in overtime at Foxboro on 11-05-00 (Willie McGinest recovered a fumble to help set up late first-half field goal)

Beat Buffalo 13–10 in overtime (wind chill of 6 degrees) at Ralph Wilson Stadium on 12-17-00 (Adam Vinatieri kicked the final field goal)

2001 championship season
Beat the Chargers 29–26 in overtime at Foxboro Stadium on 10-14-01 (Adam Vinatieri kicked the final FG) (The Game of the Year)

Beat the Buffalo Bills 12–9 in overtime at Ralph Wilson Stadium on 12-16-01 (Adam Vinatieri kicked the final field goal)

2002 regular season
Defeated the Kansas City Chiefs 41–38 in overtime at Gillette Stadium on 09-22-02 (Adam Vinatieri kicked the final field goal)

Defeated the Miami Dolphins 27–24 in overtime at Foxboro Stadium on 12-29-02 (Adam Vinatieri kicked the final field goal)

2003 championship season
Defeated Miami 19–13 in overtime at Pro Player Stadium on 10-19-03 (Troy Brown caught an 82-yard TD pass to win the game)

Defeated the Houston Texans 23–20 in overtime at Reliant Stadium on 11-23-03 (Adam Vinatieri kicked the final field goal)

2008 regular season
Lost to the New York Jets 34–31 in overtime at Gillette Stadium on 11-13-08 (Randy Moss caught a TD pass to end regulation)

Every Patriots player who has kicked a PAT to tie the game and force the overtime period
1981 regular season
John Smith kicked a PAT with 29 seconds left to tie the game in the 27–21 overtime loss to the Steelers on 09-27-81

1987 regular season
Tony Franklin kicked a PAT with 65 seconds left to tie the game in the 34–31 overtime loss to the Eagles on 11-29-87

1988 regular season
Jason Staurovsky kicked a PAT to tie the game in the 10–7 overtime win vs the Tampa Bay Buccaneers on 12-11-88

1991 regular season
Charlie Baumann kicked a PAT with seven seconds left to tie the game in the 23–17 overtime win vs the Colts on 12-08-91

1993 regular season
Scott Sisson kicked a PAT with 12 seconds left to tie the game in the 19–16 overtime loss to the Lions on 09-12-93

1995 regular season
Matt Bahr kicked a PAT with 52 seconds left to tie the game in the 20–17 overtime loss to the Panthers on 10-29-95

2000 regular season
Adam Vinatieri kicked a PAT in the fourth quarter to tie the game in the 13–10 overtime win vs the Buffalo Bills on 12-17-00

Every Patriots player who has kicked the overtime game-winning field goal in a regular season game
1988 regular season
Jason Staurovsky kicked a 27-yard field goal to defeat the Tampa Bay Buccaneeers 10–7 at Sullivan Stadium on 12-11-88

1989 regular season
Greg Davis kicked a 51-yard field goal to defeat the Indianapolis Colts 23–20 at the Hoosier Dome on 10-29-89

1991 regular season
Jason Staurovsky kicked a 42-yard field goal to defeat the Minnesota Vikings 26–23 at Foxboro Stadium on 10-20-91

1992 regular season
Charlie Baumann kicked an 18-yard field goal to defeat the Indianapolis Colts 37–34 at the Hoosier Dome on 11-15-92

1996 regular season
Adam Vinatieri kicked a 40-yard field goal to defeat the Jacksonville Jaguars 28–25 at Foxboro Stadium on 09-22-96

1997 regular season
Adam Vinatieri kicked a 34-yard field goal to defeat the New York Jets 27–24 at Foxboro Stadium on 09-14-97

2000 regular season
Adam Vinatieri kicked a 22-yard field goal to defeat the Cincinnati Bengals 16–13 at Foxboro Stadium on 11-19-00

Adam Vinatieri kicked a 24-yard field goal to defeat the Buffalo Bills 13–10 at Ralph Wilson Stadium on 12-17-00

2001 championship season
Adam Vinatieri kicked a 44-yard field goal to defeat the San Diego Chargers 29–26 at Foxboro Stadium on 10-14-01

Adam Vinatieri kicked a 23-yard field goal to defeat the Buffalo Bills 12–9 at Ralph Wilson Stadium on 12-16-01

2002 regular season
Adam Vinatieri kicked a 35-yard field goal to defeat the Kansas City Chiefs 41–38 at Gillette Stadium on 09-22-02

Adam Vinatieri kicked a 35-yard field goal to defeat the Miami Dolphins 27–24 at Gillette Stadium on 12-29-02

2003 championship season
Adam Vinatieri kicked a 28-yard field goal to defeat the Houston Texans 23–20 at Reliant Stadium on 11-23-03

2005 regular season
Adam Vinatieri kicked a 43-yard field goal with one second left to defeat the Steelers 23–20 at Heinz Field on 09-25-05

Adam Vinatieri kicked a 29-yard field goal with 17 seconds left to defeat the Falcons 31–28 at the Georgia Dome on 10-09-05

Every Patriots player who has blocked a field-goal attempt in a victorious regular season overtime game

Mike Jones blocked a 29-yard field-goal attempt by John Hall with 16 seconds left in the 27–24 overtime win vs the Jets on 09-14-97

Chad Eaton blocked a 23-yard field-goal attempt and then a 30-yard field-goal attempt in overtime of the 13–10 win vs the Bills on 12-17-00

Richard Seymour blocked a 35-yard field-goal attempt by Olinda Mare with 1:52 left in the 19–13 overtime win vs Miami on 10-19-03

Every Patriots player who has caught a TD pass to win a regular season overtime game

1991 regular season
Michael Timpson hauled in a 45-yard TD pass from Hugh Millen to defeat the Colts 23–17 in overtime on 12-08-91

1993 regular season
Michael Timpson hauled in a 36-yard TD pass from Drew Bledsoe to defeat the Dolphins 33–27 in overtime on 01-02-94

1994 regular season
Kevin Turner grabbed a 14-yard TD pass from Drew Bledsoe to defeat the Vikings 26–20 in overtime on 11-13-94

2003 championship season
Troy Brown caught an 82-yard TD pass from Tom Brady to defeat the Dolphins 19–13 in overtime on 10-19-03

The Longest

The Patriots player with the longest run from scrimmage in a regular season overtime game

Robert Weathers galloped for a 77-yard gain in the 29–23 overtime loss to the Baltimore Colts on 09-04-83

The Patriots player with the longest reception in a regular season overtime game

Troy Brown hauled in an 82-yard TD pass from Tom Brady to defeat the Miami Dolphins 19–13 in overtime on 10-19-03

The Patriots player with the longest kickoff return in a regular season overtime game

Chris Canty had a 63-yard kickoff return in the 27–24 overtime win vs the New York Jets on 09-14-97

The Patriots player with the longest punt return in a regular season overtime game

Ricky Smith returned a punt 55 yards in the 29–23 overtime loss to the Baltimore Colts on 09-04-83

The Patriots player with the longest interception return in a regular season overtime game

Chris Singleton took a Jeff George pass 82 yards for a TD in the 37–34 overtime win vs the Colts on 11-15-92

The Patriots player with the longest punt in a regular season overtime game

Jeff Feagles had a 66-yard punt in the 10–7 overtime win vs the Tampa Bay Buccaneers on 12-11-88

The Patriots player with the longest field goal in a regular season overtime game

Greg Davis kicked a 51-yard field goal to defeat the Indianapolis Colts 23–20 in overtime on 10-29-89

The Most

The Patriots player with the most yards rushing in a regular season overtime game

Curtis Martin had 40 carries for 199 yards and one TD in the 27–24 overtime win vs the New York Jets on 09-14-97

The Patriots player with the most yards receiving in a regular season overtime game

Stanley Morgan had 182 yards receiving in the 30–27 overtime loss to the Miami Dolphins on 11-08-81

The Patriots Quarterback with the most yards passing in a regular season overtime game

Drew Bledsoe threw for 426 yards in the 26–20 overtime win vs the Minnesota Vikings on 11-13-94

The Patriots player with the most special team return yards in a regular season overtime game

Deion Branch had 201 kickoff return yards in the 41–38 overtime win vs the Kansas City Chiefs on 09-22-02

## 6

Postseason Stories

As fans witnessed during the 2007–08 season, it is awfully tough to win a Super Bowl in the National Football League. Even if you are the perfect team with the greatest offense of all time, the best quarterback in the sport, and a defensive genius for a head coach, there are no sure things in this league. For the Patriots to have won three titles in four years during the salary-cap era is nothing short of astonishing. In a time where parity is the buzz word in NFL circles, the Patriots have destroyed the very notion. Even in postseason defeat, New England is still the preeminent team in the National Football League because of its ability to go deep into the postseason year after year. The difficulty of capturing Super Bowl glory has been somewhat taken for granted over the years in New England. Winning has become expected, and anything less than a Super Bowl victory is considered a disappointment. What's even more amazing is that prior to their upset of the St. Louis Rams in 2002, the Patriots had a fate similar to the pre-2004 Boston Red Sox. They were a team that couldn't win the biggest games, that didn't come through in the greatest moments, and that blew the most important opportunities.

Boy did that change.

The postseason lineage of the New England Patriots is established as among the best in professional sports. There have been so many games, so many moments, and enough memories to last the lifetime of a New England sports fan (Or, until the next season). This chapter focuses on the most memorable playoff games in Patriots history. Though the spotlight is on the victories, such as their Super Bowl wins and the playoff runs leading up to them, we have included a loss. The earliest game profiled is the 1976 Divisional Playoff Game against the Oakland Raiders. It was a game mired in controversy and plagued with missed opportunities. It had a lasting effect on how the Patriots were defined in the postseason, thus it must be included.

As we know, the Patriots have more than enough postseason positives to keep even the most demanding fan satisfied. The heroes of these games live on in this chapter: the Tom Bradys, the Adam Vinatieris, the Tedy Bruschis and more. The goal is to allow you to remember the way you felt when you saw your favorite Patriots players in a state of childlike glee, making snow angels after defeating the Oakland Raiders in the "Snow Bowl." The intention is to make you as proud as you were when the Patriots fended off the multifaceted threat of Donavan McNabb and Terrell Owens, thus establishing the team's dynasty with a third championship ring. The idea is to get you to forget the pain and agony of 1976 and recount the euphoria you felt when the Patriots went on to "Squish the Fish" in the 1985 AFC Championship Game.

This is the stuff that legends are made of; the games that define a franchise. These games and these performances can never be diminished and never be dismissed. As Junior Seau once said, these moments are a part of "ever."

—Ben Cafardo

December 18, 1976

New England Patriots vs. Oakland Raiders
1976 American Football Conference Divisional Playoff
Oakland Coliseum, Oakland, California

Scoring Summary:

AFC: Oakland Raiders 24, New England Patriots 21

	Q1	Q2	Q3	Q4	Total
Patriots	7	0	14	0	21
Raiders	3	7	0	14	24

NE—Johnson one-yard run (Smith kick), NE 7–0
OAK—Mann 40-yard field goal, NE 7–3
OAK—Biletnikoff 31-yard pass from Stabler (Mann kick), OAK 10–7
NE—Francis 26-yard pass from Grogan (Smith kick), NE 14–10
NE—Phillips three-yard run (Smith kick), NE 21–10
OAK—Van Eeghen one-yard run (Mann kick), NE 21–17
OAK—Stabler one-yard run (Mann kick), OAK 24–21

Not every Patriots postseason has ended with confetti, the acceptance of the Lombardi trophy, and parades through downtown Boston. Prior to the "dynasty era," the Patriots playoff history wasn't quite as joyous.

This was never more evident than during the 1976 Divisional Playoff Game against the Oakland Raiders. Let's just say that any true, longtime Patriots fan will remember the name Ben Dreith for a long, long time.

When head coach Chuck Fairbanks led the 1976 New England Patriots into the Oakland Coliseum, expectations were high. This was the greatest Patriots team assembled to date, featuring a who's who of Patriots legends. The roster included legends such as Darryl Stingley, Randy Vataha, Steve Grogan, Sam Cunningham, Russ Francis, Leon Gray, John Hannah, Mike Haynes, Julius Adams, Steve Nelson, Tim Fox, and Ray Hamilton.

These stars led New England to an impressive 11–3 regular season record. The team finished the season tied with the Baltimore Colts atop the AFC East.

On the other side of the field were John Madden's Oakland Raiders, who boasted quite a roster of who's who talent as well. The roster included Cliff Branch,

Bobby Hamilton makes snow angels

Fred Biletnikoff, Ken Stabler, Mark Van Eeghen, Dave Casper, Art Shell, Gene Upshaw, Ted Hendricks, George Atkinson, Jack Tatum, and Phil Villapiano.

Oakland had amassed a jaw-dropping 13–1 regular season record, including an undefeated mark at home. However, the one notable blemish on its record was a 48–17 clubbing at Schaefer Stadium courtesy of the Patriots.

It was time for the battle to commence, and New England struck first on its second drive of the game. Russ Francis caught a 10-yard pass on a big third-and-4 play, and he followed it with a 40-yard reception on third-and-7. The completion brought the Patriots deep into Raiders territory. Steve Grogan's 24-yard pass to Darryl Stingley took the ball to the 1-yard line, and the 85-yard drive culminated with a 1-yard Andy Johnson touchdown run.

The silver and black marched down the field in the next series, but Ray Hamilton knocked down a third-down pass that forced the Raiders to settle for a 40-yard field goal by Errol Mann.

After fumbles by Patriots running back Sam Cunningham and Raiders running back Clarence Davis, the Patriots went on a long drive into Oakland territory. Things were looking good until a curious tight end-around option pass by Russ Francis was intercepted by Skip "Dr. Death" Thomas. With just over two minutes left in the half, the Raiders made the Patriots pay for the ill-advised call. Kenny Stabler found Fred Biletnikoff in the end zone for a 31-yard touchdown.

Oakland had jumped back into the game, and the Patriots found themselves trailing, 10–7, at halftime.

In the third quarter, the Patriots gave fans something to feel good about. The team scored twice: first on a 26-yard touchdown pass from Steve Grogan to tight end Russ Francis, and again on a 3-yard touchdown run by fullback Jess Phillips.

New England's offense came to life to firmly put the Red and White ahead, 21–10. The tide had seemingly turned. However, like all things, nothing was guaranteed.

Oakland scored a touchdown in the fourth quarter to cut the deficit to 21–17. With 6:24 left in the game, the Patriots took possession of the ball on the Raiders' 48-yard line. After a 10-yard run by tough guy Steve Grogan, Sam Cunningham's rushing attempt fell just inches short of the first down. After an offside call made it third-and-5, Grogan hit Russ Francis in the chest, *literally*. The Big Kahuna was unable to grasp the ball because he was the victim of a bear hug from Raider linebacker Phil Villapiano that would make Andre the Giant proud. Since no official seemed to notice, John Smith came on to try a 50-yard field goal, but the kick was low. Frustration was mounting.

The Raiders took over on downs with 4:12 left in the game facing a four-point deficit. On third-and-7, Stabler hit his targets; Branch for eight yards and Casper for 21 yards. After the Patriots put Stabler in reverse with an eight-yard sack, victory was in sight.

What happened next was a play that lives in infamy among longtime Patriots supporters across the country. The Oakland Raiders faced a third-and-18 with 57 seconds remaining when Kenny Stabler dropped back for a pass. The pass went incomplete and Patriots nation rejoiced in unison—they had forced fourth-and-long late in the game, and the lead would remain intact.

But there was a problem.

Referee Ben Dreith called Ray "Sugar Bear" Hamilton for roughing the passer, despite Hamilton making no contact with Stabler. Nevertheless, the call stood and proceeded to change the fortunes of the 1976 Patriots.

It was first down Raiders on the Patriots' 13-yard line. On third-and-1 from the 4-yard line, Pete Banaszak ran one yard for the first down and Mel Lunsford was called for unsportsmanlike conduct. Finally, with 14 seconds remaining, Ken Stabler rolled over to the left side for a one-yard game-winning touchdown. Patriots fans were in disbelief.

The silver and black surged past New England, 24–21, after an implausible come-from-behind, controversy-riddled sequence of events.

The phantom roughing the passer call has been played, replayed, and played again, and the reaction was, and still is unanimous—referee Ben Dreith got it wrong, really wrong. However, this game was not simply about Dreith. The Patriots had opportunities to win, but fell short.

The Patriots victory over Oakland in the 2002 Divisional playoff was particularly sweet for Patriots fans who vividly remember the disappointment suffered in 1976.

Whenever two of the NFL's original eight get together, fireworks go off, controversy ensues, and memories are made. However, the memory of the phantom pass interference call on Ray Hamilton left Patriots fans with a bitter taste in their mouths. It is one they would all like to forget.

January 12, 1986
New England Patriots vs. Miami Dolphins
1986 American Football Championship Conference Championship
Orange Bowl, Miami, FL

Scoring Summary:
AFC: New England Patriots 31, Miami Dolphins 14

	Q1	Q2	Q3	Q4	Total
Patriots	3	14	7	7	31
Dolphins	0	7	0	7	14

NE—Franklin 23-yard field goal, NE 3–0
MIA—Johnson 11-yard pass from Marino (Reveiz kick), MIA 3–7
NE—Collins four-yard pass from Eason (Franklin kick), NE 10–7
NE—Ramsey one-yard pass from Eason (Franklin kick), NE 17–7
NE—Weathers two-yard pass from Eason (Franklin kick), NE 24–7
MIA—Nathan 10-yard pass from Marino (Reveiz kick), MIA 24–14
NE—Tatupu one-yard run (Franklin kick), NE 31–14

About 15 years before the Cinderella season of the 2001–02 Patriots took place, there was another Cinderella Patriots team that roamed the field in Foxboro. The 1985–86 Patriots went 11–5 during the regular season, and had captured the imagination of fans throughout the region. Despite the team's success, the Patriots were treated as an afterthought in the Super Bowl picture (sound familiar?) as the NFL nation was looking toward a Miami/Chicago showdown.

The 1986 American Football Conference Championship game held special significance for the New England Patriots organization. A victory over the Miami Dolphins would enable New England to reach the Super Bowl for the first time in its storied history. It was a goal that Patriots fans wanted to see come to fruition since the infamous roughing the passer call in the playoffs a decade earlier.

The Patriots, led by head coach Raymond Berry, were confident in the team's chances. New England had already pulled off two upsets on the road against the Jets and Raiders, respectively.

Still, reaching Super Bowl XX was a different story. The Patriots had not won a game in the Orange Bowl since 1966—18 years and were not projected to snap that streak this year.

In spite of this, the Patriots were ready, and defense was the name of the game. New England's success against Miami was based on converting turnovers into points and controlling the clock with a stellar ground game. The Patriots turned four fumble recoveries into 24 points and outrushed the Dolphins 255 to 68.

On the Dolphins first offensive play of the game Tony Nathan was hit by Steve Nelson and Garin Veris returned the loose ball to the Dolphins 20-yard line. Field goal kicker Tony Franklin converted the turnover into three points.

After Dan Marino led an 80-yard scoring drive that ended with an 11-yard touchdown pass, Patriots quarterback Tony Eason had an answer.

Eason took charge of his offense and led his own 66-yard scoring drive, culminating in a four-yard pass to Tony Collins.

The Dolphins second turnover also directly led to a New England score. Dan Marino fumbled the snap and Lester Williams recovered it on the Dolphins 36-yard line. Six plays later, Tony Eason tossed a one-yard touchdown pass to Derrick Ramsey.

The Patriots were up, 17–7, at the break and the fantasy scenario of a Miami/Chicago Super Bowl match up was starting to look like a pipedream.

In the second half, it was more of the same. The Patriots defensemen were like vultures swarming to the ball, creating plays, and making the Dolphins pay for every mistake.

So when Lorenzo Hampton fumbled the opening kickoff of the half, it wasn't entirely a surprise. Nor was it a surprise when Tony Eason converted the mistake into points. Eason found running back Robert Weathers for a two-yard touchdown and the Patriots were firmly in control.

Though Robert Weathers contributed for six, it was Patriots running back Craig James who rushed for 105 yards, broadening the Patriots offensive attack.

After Miami cut the lead to 10 points, Mosi Tatupu, another Patriots player who made an impact, ended Miami's comeback hopes with a one-yard touchdown run.

New England had pulled off three-straight playoff road wins to become champions of the American Football Conference.

Though the Cinderella season of the Patriots would eventually come to an end at the hands of the mighty Chicago Bears, few fans will forget New England's march through the AFC postseason en route to Super Bowl XX.

January 12, 1997

New England Patriots vs. Jacksonville Jaguars
1997 American Football Conference Championship Game
Foxboro Stadium, Foxboro, MA

Scoring Summary:

New England Patriots 20, Jacksonville Jaguars 6

	Q1	Q2	Q3	Q4	Total
Jaguars	0	3	3	0	6
Patriots	7	6	0	7	20

NE—Martin one-yard run (Vinatieri kick), NE 7–0
JAC—Hollis 32-yard field goal, NE 7–3
NE—Vinatieri 29-yard field goal, NE 10–3
NE—Vinatieri 20-yard field goal, NE 13–3
JAC—Hollis 28-yard field goal, NE 13–6
NE—Smith 47-yard fumble return (Vinatieri kick), NE 20–6

The 1996–1997 New England Patriots roster was comprised of many of the team's historically best players at early stages in their careers. Many of whom would became stalwarts of the Patriots championship teams in the coming years. Even Bill Belichick roamed the sideline as the team's defensive coordinator, an often-overlooked occurrence today.

It was the first time the New England Patriots had reached the American Football Conference championship game in 11 years. With Drew Bledsoe leading a new era of Patriots, fans were thirsty for the club's first Super Bowl berth of the decade.

The Patriots entered the 1997 AFC Championship Game against the Jaguars with a defense as hot as the game-time temperature was cold (zero degrees with the windchill chill factor). The Patriots postseason run had not only been defined by the cannon that was Drew Bledsoe's arm, but by the team's defensive intensity and aptitude.

Not to be shortchanged, the Jaguars were also hot, boasting an offense led by strong-armed quarterback Mark Brunell and a solid running game led by Natrone Means.

Larry Whigham was the AFC Special Team Player of the Week as he tackled Bryan Barker for a 16-yard loss on the Jaguars first punt of the game during the team's opening drive. The Patriots now had possession at the 4-yard line.

Two plays later, New England lit up the scoreboard when superstar running back Curtis Martin ran in a touchdown from the 1-yard line. Scoring would be hard to come by in this contest, so hard in fact, that this would prove to be the contest's lone offensive touchdown.

The two clubs added field goals though the middle of the game, including an Adam Vinatieri field goal from 20 yards out on the last play of the first half. However, neither team was able to mount any significant offensive drives.

New England's defense was superb, harassing Mark Brunell and suffocating Natrone Means. Chris Hudson fumbled after being hit by Marty "Mr. Irrelevant" Moore on a 6-yard punt return and Mike Bartrum recovered the loose ball. Four plays later Vinatieri kicked a 29-yard field goal.

Jacksonville never reached the end zone as the Patriots defense held Brunell to a mere 190 passing yards and picked off two of his passes. One of these, by safety Willie Clay, came in the end zone with 3:43 left in regulation.

Despite the Patriots' defensive success, the game was still close. With the score New England 13, Jacksonville 6, the Jaguars had another chance to tie the game. With 2:36 left in regulation, Patriots linebacker Chris Slade rattled the ball loose from the hands of Jaguars halfback James Stewart, and cornerback Otis Smith scooped it up.

Smith proceeded to run the pigskin back 47 yards for the touchdown, thus putting the game out of reach for the Jaguars. Tedy Bruschi added an interception that he returned to the 12-yard line to put the exclamation point on the victory.

The Patriots were champions of the American Football Conference for 1996.

Despite the impressive victory, this game is mostly remembered for the power outage at Foxboro Stadium that occurred minutes before halftime. The lights went out in the stadium, and then the Patriots turned the lights out on Jacksonville's Super Bowl dreams.

Did You Know?

If "death comes in threes," then the parity in Dave Meggett's stat line: three carries, three receptions, three punt returns, and three kickoff returns was a sign of the beginning of the end for Jacksonville's season.

January 19, 2002
New England Patriots vs. Oakland Raiders "Snow Bowl"
2002 American Football Conference Divisional Playoff
Foxboro Stadium, Foxboro, MA

Scoring Summary:
New England Patriots 16, Oakland Raiders 13 (OT)

	Q1	Q2	Q3	Q4	OT	Total
Raiders	0	7	6	0	0	13
Patriots	0	0	3	10	3	16

OAK—Jett 13-yard pass from Gannon (Janikowski kick), OAK 7–0

NE—Vinatieri 23-yard field goal, OAK 7–3

OAK—Janikowski 38-yard field goal, OAK 10–3

OAK—Janikowski 45-yard field goal, OAK 13–3

NE—Brady six-yard run (Vinatieri kick), OAK 13–10

NE—Vinatieri 45-yard field goal, tie 13–13

NE—Vinatieri 23-yard field goal, NE 16–13

The New England Patriots team has defined itself in countless ways throughout its storied history. From the Super Bowl wins to the countless come-from-behind victories to the one-game-at-a-time mantra, Patriots fans have no shortage of stories and no shortage of memories to fondly look back upon. This franchise continues to feed the fans' desire for more.

Perhaps no story, no memory, and no game have become as much a part of Patriots mystique than the famous "Snow Bowl."

The snow was there, the fans were there, the Raiders were cold, and the tuck rule. Oh, right, the tuck rule. That was there, too.

Patriots fans had seen the season begin with a devastating injury to franchise quarterback Drew Bledsoe. But by January 19, the Patriots had gone 11–5, with one improbable victory after another, giving the team home-field advantage in what would be the final game ever played in old Foxboro Stadium.

As to be expected, the game didn't feature much scoring early on. Neither team was able to conjure up a scoring drive in the first quarter. Tom Brady's offense was unable to establish consistency.

Unsung Hero:
David Patten hauled in eight receptions for 104 yards on the day including a critical reception on fourth-and-4 to set up Vinatieri's game-tying field goal with 32 seconds left.

It was not until the end of the second quarter when points, not the ones wanted by Patriots fans, were finally put up on the scoreboard. Raiders quarterback Rich Gannon hit James Jett for a 13-yard touchdown; the first of the game. Jett's touchdown gave Oakland a 7–0 half-time advantage.

While the first half of the game saw New England feeling out the Raiders and the conditions, the second half was all about the Patriots and Tom Brady breaking out.

After the Raiders made it a 13–3 game with two field goals, Brady put the Patriots right back into it. After hitting a wide array of receivers. Brady ran it in from the 6-yard line and emphatically slammed the ball down in the end zone in a moment of emotional triumph. It was the first rushing touchdown of his career. More late-game dramatics would follow.

As the game headed toward its unforgettable end, Charles Woodson seemingly had strip-sacked Tom Brady with a blow to the helmet, assuring the victory for Oakland.

However, the play was overturned when the referees determined that Brady was tucking the ball in, not throwing it forward as previously thought. The play was deemed an incomplete pass, and the Patriots' drive and season, continued much to the chagrin of the Raiders players, fans, and organization. (Remember Ben Dreith or Phil Villapiano bear hugging Russ Francis on a crucial third-down pass late in the game?)

On the next play from scrimmage Brady hit David Patten for 13 yards to get to the Raiders 29-yard line.

Then, the time had arrived. Who could forget the moment? With no timeouts, the clock ticking down, and 32 seconds left in the game Adam Vinatieri hit the most difficult and most dramatic field goal in modern postseason history. Vinatieri had sent the game into overtime and Foxboro fans into a frenzy.

In overtime, Tom Brady was magic. He orchestrated a 14-play drive for 64 yards. On fourth-and-4, with the weight of the world on his shoulders, Brady completed a six-yard pass to David Patten; his eighth catch of the game.

This time, Vinatieri's job was a bit easier, as he connected from 23 yards out, and that was it. The New England Patriots had overcome adversity once again, and in the most dramatic of fashions.

Maybe it was irony; maybe the salty past between these two clubs had come full circle. After all, it was 25 years earlier that the Patriots had seen the team's playoff chances go down the drain against this very same franchise in a game mired by controversy.

In the most improbable of ways, amidst the most undesirable conditions, the Patriots' Cinderella march to the Lombardi Trophy lived on, not just for the moment, but forever, in New England Patriots folklore.

January 27, 2002
New England Patriots vs. Pittsburgh Steelers
Heinz Field, Pittsburgh, PA

Scoring Summary:
New England Patriots 24, Pittsburgh Steelers 17

	Q1	Q2	Q3	Q4	Total
Patriots	7	7	7	3	24
Steelers	0	3	14	0	17

NE—Brown 55-yard punt return (Vinatieri kick), NE 7–0
PIT—Brown 30-yard field goal, NE 7–3
NE—Patten 11-yard pass from Bledsoe (Vinatieri kick), NE 14–3
NE—Harris 45-yard lateral from Brown (Vinatieri kick), NE 21–3
PIT—Bettis one-yard run (Brown kick), NE 21–10
PIT—Zereouqe 11-yard run (Brown kick), NE 21–17
NE—Vinatieri 44-yard field goal, NE 24–17

Fresh off one of the most dramatic games in National Football League history, the New England Patriots traveled to Heinz Field for a battle with the AFC's top-ranked team: the Pittsburgh Steelers. Would there be an emotional letdown? Were the Patriots drained from a week earlier? Hardly. There was no shortage of dramatics in Pittsburgh.

In what had been a miraculous season for the Red and Blue, the unexpected twists and turns kept coming week after week. Who would have thought prior to the start of the AFC Championship Game that No. 11 would make a guest cameo for the ages?

In front of 64,450 strong in Pittsburgh, most of whom were looking for "one for the thumb," the New England offense, defense, and special teams were prominently showcased.

In the first quarter, the Patriots defense established itself early, stuffing "The Bus" Jerome Bettis, and sacking the elusive Kordell Stewart. In fact, the Steelers were only able to gain 17 yards rushing from its running backs.

Although New England was hard-pressed to get any offense going early, the Patriots special teams made the first statement of the game.

Troy Brown, who led all receivers with eight receptions and 121 yards, returned a Pittsburgh punt from his own 45-yard line for the touchdown. It was a 7–0 Patriots advantage.

In the second quarter, Patriots fans were forced to hold their collective breaths as Tom Brady went down with an injury. During a 28-yard pass completion to Troy Brown, Lee Flowers effectively took Brady out of the game by taking out his legs.

Tom Brady's replacement? Probably the most famous backup quarterback in the NFL at this point, Drew Bledsoe. The Brady/Bledsoe controversy was a passionate discussion topic that flooded local and national newspaper columns, talk-radio banter, and television interviews throughout the season. Those loyal to Bledsoe felt he should have been given a chance to resume his job as starter, while those in favor of Brady pointed to the team's success with the sixth-rounder from Michigan at the helm.

All the same, Bledsoe entered the game and instantly made an impact. With no signs of rust, Bledsoe conducted a brilliant two-minute drill that saw him utilize David Patten three times, including an 11-yard touchdown. Bledsoe was back, the Patriots were winning, and NFL fans across the country were in disbelief.

In the second half the defense and special teams figured prominently. Tedy Bruschi recovered a botched snap by Kordell Stewart, and on the next drive, Brandon Mitchell blocked a field goal try by the Steelers. Troy Brown was in the right place at the right time, as always, and picked up the loose ball. After a graceful lateral to Antwan Harris, Harris took the ball all the way in for the score and gave New England an 18-point lead, silencing the usually fiery Steelers' faithful.

Despite the lead, Pittsburgh made a game of it. Its offense got back on track with two solid drives, including one that started at New England's 32-yard line. Two touchdowns later, the seemingly safe lead had dissipated to four points.

Again, New England called on its defense and special teams to pick up the slack and give the team a boost. Adam Vinatieri muscled a field goal through the uprights, giving his team a 24–17 lead. Interceptions by Tebucky Jones and Lawyer Milloy followed, which helped to finalize what was a stellar all-around effort.

New England continued to find new ways of beating its opponents, and each week someone new stepped up and got in on the act.

The incredible season lived on, and the Patriots were AFC Champions! The team was one step closer to completing its impossible journey to Super Bowl glory.

February 3, 2002
New England Patriots vs. St. Louis Rams
Super Bowl XXXVI
Louisiana Superdome, New Orleans, LA

Scoring Summary:
New England Patriots 20, St. Louis Rams 17

	Q1	Q2	Q3	Q4	Total
Rams	3	0	0	14	17
Patriots	0	14	3	3	20

STL—Jeff Wilkins 50-yard field goal, STL 3–0

NE—Ty Law 47-yard interception return (Adam Vinatieri kick), NE 7–3

NE—David Patten eight-yard pass from Tom Brady (Adam Vinatieri kick), NE 14–3

NE—Adam Vinatieri 37-yard field goal, NE 17–3

STL—Kurt Warner two-yard run (Jeff Wilkins kick), NE 17–10

STL—Ricky Proehl 26-yard pass from Kurt Warner (Jeff Wilkins kick), tie 17–17

NE—Adam Vinatieri 48-yard field goal, NE 20–17

MVP: Tom Brady

The spread was Rams by 14. The talk around the water-bubblers in every office coast-to-coast was that the Patriots shouldn't even bother showing up. The Patriots were lucky, not good; Tom Brady could "manage" but not lead the offense; and because of these "facts of life" Super Bowl XXXVI would be the setting when the clock struck midnight on the Cinderella season of the New England Patriots.

A lot of people were wrong.

Even the most loyal Patriots supporters had to feel skeptical of the team's chances of upstaging the much-ballyhooed St. Louis Rams. After all, the Rams were "The Greatest Show on Turf" and the Patriots should be awestruck.

Wrong again.

From the onset of the contest, the team mantra that the New England Patriots had embraced all year long was on display. Scrapping the traditional individual player introductions, this Patriots team insisted on being introduced as a unit. The team was a singular,

solitary collection of like-minded players led by a no-nonsense coach that took it one game at a time, one step at a time.

The Rams struck first with a field goal in the first quarter by Jeff Wilkins, but the Patriots' "bend but don't break," big-play defense came alive. Mike Vrabel disrupted a Kurt Warner pass that Ty Law picked and took 45 yards to the house. From there, Antwan Harris knocked a Ricky Proehl reception loose, and Terrell Buckley recovered the fumble. Tom Brady managed to drive the Patriots into the red zone, spreading the ball to Troy Brown and Jermaine Wiggins before finding David Patten in the end zone for the eight-yard touchdown pass. The perennial underdogs took the fight to

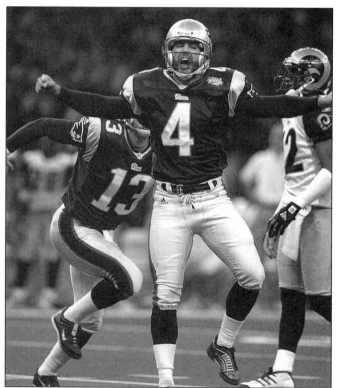

Adam Vinatieri

the Rams in the first half and compiled a 14–3 lead at the break.

In the third quarter, the Patriots defense continued to keep Kurt Warner and the Rams in check. After Adam Vinatieri added a 37-yard field goal, the Rams offense finally came to life and made its run.

There was a moment of temporary bliss for Patriots fans when it appeared that Tebucky Jones had recovered a fumble and ran it back 97 yards for the score. However, no such luck as the play was called back and the Rams offense kept pressing forward. Kurt Warner ran in for a one-yard touchdown to pull the Rams within seven.

The Greatest Show on Turf was beginning to live up to its moniker, and Patriots fans held their collective breath.

With the game now tied at 17, it was time for Tom Brady to cement his postseason legend. With no time-outs remaining, the Patriots offensive leader was cool under pressure, and steadily moved the Patriots to the St. Louis 31-yard line, setting up one of the greatest moments in Boston sports history.

Adam Vinatieri was called upon to play the role of hero, as he had against the Oakland Raiders two games earlier. As time ticked off the Superdome game clock, Vinatieri's 48-yard field goal attempt soared through the uprights and into NFL lore where it will remain forever.

The New England Patriots were the champions of the National Football League for the first time in the team's storied history. The great players, the close calls, the triumphs, and the tragedies that defined Patriots franchise history had all led to this moment.

Little did the world know, this was not simply a Cinderella story fully realized, it was the birth of the next great NFL dynasty.

January 10, 2004
New England Patriots vs. Tennessee Titans
2004 American Football Conference Divisional Playoff
Gillette Stadium, Foxboro, MA

Scoring Summary:
New England Patriots 17, Tennessee Titans 14

	Q1	Q2	Q3	Q4	Total
Titans	7	0	7	0	14
Patriots	7	7	0	3	17

NE—Johnson 41-yard pass from Brady (Vinatieri kick), NE 7–0
TEN—Brown five-yard run (Anderson kick), tie 7–7
NE—Smith one-yard run (Vinatieri kick), NE 14–7
TEN—Mason 11-yard pass from McNair (Anderson kick), tie 14–14
NE—Vinatieri 46-yard field goal, NE 17–14

After a disappointing 2002 campaign that saw New England miss the playoffs entirely, the Patriots were back and ready to strike in 2003. By the time the AFC Divisional Playoffs came around, New England looked better than ever. The team's defense was more disciplined, its special teams more timely, and its quarterback was arguably the game's best.

The Tennessee Titans were a gritty, hard-nosed bunch that brought a brand of smash-mouth football to the arctic field at Gillette Stadium. The temperature at kickoff was a frigid four degrees, with windchills reaching minus-10 degrees.

To no one's surprise, the temperature never killed the spirits of the Foxboro faithful who came *en masse* and bared the icy conditions to cheer on the Patriots.

As is usually the case, the Patriots started strong. Forcing Tennessee to a three-and-out, Brady hit speedy wide receiver Bethel Johnson for a 41-yard score.

Tennessee tied the game on a five-yard run by Chris Brown, but the Patriots defense continued to play hard against league co-MVP Steve McNair.

Tom Brady went back to work on the following drive, spreading the ball around in true Brady fashion. Not one of New England's 10 receivers who caught balls from Brady on the evening had more than four catches individually. It took a much needed team effort to keep Tennessee's defense off guard.

On the defensive side, Rodney Harrison, perhaps the Patriots' most important preseason pickup, picked off Air McNair on the Titans' next possession.

After the Harrison interception, Brady took his boys on an 11-yard drive for a touchdown. On third-and-10 from New England's own 40-yard line, Tom Brady threw a three-yard pass to wide receiver Bethel Johnson, who was bottled up on his side of the field. Ever the speedster, Johnson reversed his direction. With the help of a killer block by his fearless quarterback; he utilized his elusiveness to go for a 14-yard gain. Eight plays later, Antowain Smith ran over the left guard for a one-yard touchdown.

New England took a 14–7 lead into the half, but not before defensive end Richard Seymour blocked a Tennessee field goal attempt with just over a minute remaining on the clock. The Patriots had the momentum as the team made its way to the locker room.

In the second half, Tennessee put together its best drive of the game, a 70-yard sequence capped off by an 11-yard touchdown pass from McNair to the talented Derrick Mason.

Conversely, most of the second half was a defensive struggle as Tennessee had difficulty mustering up more offense against the NFL's top-ranked defense.

Unfortunately for the fans at Gillette, the Patriots offense didn't fair much better.

With the game in a 14–14 deadlock late in the fourth quarter, the Patriots caught a break. With 6:49 left on the game clock, Troy Brown returned a 32-yard punt by Craig Hentrich nine yards, and the Patriots had the ball on the Titans' 40. On fourth-and-3 from the Titans' 33-yard line, the Patriots had a critical decision to make. Bill Belichick elected to go for it, and his decision paid dividends. Tom Brady completed a four-yard pass to the ever-reliable Troy Brown for the first down.

The play set up a 46-yard field goal try for, you guessed it, Mr. Clutch.

In the midst of the coldest game in Patriots history, with the season on the line, and the frozen fingers of more than 68,000 fans clasped together in a fit of half anxiety, half excitement—would Vinatieri be able to deliver yet again?

Yes.

The field goal gave the Patriots a 17–14 lead that the defense would hold onto. On fourth-and-12, with 1:45 left in the game, the Titans took one more shot downfield. Steve McNair threw it up and hit Drew Bennett in the hands. It would have been a difficult catch, and alas it went incomplete. The Patriots regained possession and ran out the clock despite one last effort by the Titans offense.

The win gave New England its ninth win of the season at The Razor. It was also the first of two-straight playoff contests in which New England defeated a co-MVP.

New England had met its first postseason challenge.

January 18, 2004
New England Patriots vs. Indianapolis Colts
2004 American Football Conference Championship
Gillette Stadium, Foxboro, MA

Scoring Summary:
New England Patriots 24, Indianapolis Colts 14

	Q1	Q2	Q3	Q4	Total
Colts	0	0	7	7	14
Patriots	7	8	6	3	24

NE—Givens seven-yard pass from Brady (Vinatieri kick), NE 7–0
NE—Vinatieri 31-yard field goal, NE 10–0
NE—Vinatieri 25-yard field goal, NE 13–0
NE—Smith kicked ball out of end zone resulting in a safety, NE 15–0
IND—James two-yard run (Vanderjagt kick), NE 15–7
NE—Vinatieri 27-yard field goal, NE 18–7
NE—Vinatieri 21-yard field goal, NE 21–7
IND—Pollard seven-yard pass from Manning (Vanderjagt kick), NE 21–14
NE—Vinatieri 34-yard field goal, NE 24–14

The rivalry between the New England Patriots and the Indianapolis Colts is among the best in sports and features the game's two best quarterbacks in the primes of their respective careers, each trying to outgun the other and lead their team to victory. No matter the outcome, it has been great football and great theatre.

By the time the 2004 divisional playoffs had begun, Peyton Manning had developed a reputation for being unable to "win the big one." Not only had he not reached a Super Bowl, he had not won a chess match against coach Bill Belichick.

Though the game was played in Foxboro, most national media experts were calling for a Colts victory, citing the amazing Colts offense as the juggernaut that simply could not be stopped.

As for the Patriots, the team found itself back in the playoffs after missing out entirely the year prior. Coming off a hard-fought victory over an excellent Tennessee Titans team, the Patriots had a renewed sense of resolve. With the end goal in sight, the Patriots continued to march back to the Super Bowl.

A major factor in the game was New England's home field advantage, which brought snowy conditions that have become predictable at Patriots playoff home games. New England thrives in games with poor weather conditions, and the snow that fell that day in Foxboro worked in the Patriots' favor.

Though the attention was largely on Peyton Manning, it was Tom Brady who struck first. The

Rodney Harrison (37) and Marvin Harrison (88)

Patriot's superstar quarterback drove the Patriots into the red zone, and on first-and-goal hit David Givens to throw a crooked number on the scoreboard.

For a moment, it appeared that the Patriots and Colts would be entangled in a battle of back and forth, as Manning moved his offense the length of the field. However, Rodney Harrison stepped in front of a pass headed for the end zone, stopping the Colts dead. Manning faired no better on his second possession, as the first time he dropped back to throw, Ty Law picked him off.

The Patriots offense continued to move and continued to rack up points, including six on the leg of Mr. Automatic, Adam Vinatieri.

Even the New England special teams got into the act securing a rare safety on a bungled long snap by Justin Snow. The Patriots had recorded the team's first safety in postseason history, and it was 15–0.

Meanwhile, the Patriots defense continued to perplex the league's Co-MVP. Ty Law covered Marvin Harrison flawlessly, and intercepted Manning three times, in the first, third, and fourth quarters.

In addition to Law's brilliance, defensive end Jarvis Green introduced himself to Manning, sacking the starting quarterback three times. He was a thorn in Manning's side all afternoon.

Nevertheless, Manning wasn't an MVP for nothing, and he threw a touchdown pass to his tight end Pollard to make it a seven-point game in the fourth quarter. However, every time it seemed the Colts were about to get back into the game, the Patriots made a big play on defense.

In the wintry conditions, the New England ground game played a vital role in keeping Manning off the field. Antowain Smith racked up 100 yards rushing and exhausted Indy's defense.

Brady was his efficient self, leading his team into field goal range consistently throughout the game. Even though Adam Vinatieri wasn't called on for any late-game dramatics, he did earn his paycheck on this day. Vinatieri made five field goals and gave New England a 10-point lead late in the game, putting victory out of reach for the Colts.

Tom Brady had outplayed both Steve McNair and Peyton Manning (the league's co-MVPs) in consecutive weeks to stake his claim as the game's best quarterback.

The final score was 24–14 Patriots—on to Super Bowl XXXVII!

February 1, 2004

New England Patriots vs. Carolina Panthers
Super Bowl XXXVIII
Reliant Stadium, Houston, TX

Scoring Summary:

New England Patriots 32, Carolina Panthers 29

	Q1	Q2	Q3	Q4	Total
Panthers	0	10	0	19	29
Patriots	0	14	0	18	32

NE—Deion Branch five-yard pass from Tom Brady (Adam Vinatieri kick), NE 7–0

CAR—Steve Smith 39-yard pass from Jake Delhomme (John Kasay kick), tie 7–7

NE—David Givens five-yard pass from Tom Brady (Adam Vinatieri kick), NE 14–7

CAR—John Kasay 50-yard field goal, NE 14–10

NE—Antowain Smith two-yard run (Adam Vinatieri kick), NE 21–10

CAR—DeShaun Foster 33-yard run (two-point conversion: pass failed), NE 21–16

CAR—Muhsin Muhammad 85-yard pass from Jake Delhomme (two-point conversion: pass failed), CAR 22–21

NE—Mike Vrabel one-yard pass from Tom Brady (two-point conversion: Kevin Faulk run), NE 29–22

CAR—Ricky Proehl 12-yard pass from Jake Delhomme (John Kasay kick), tie 29–29

NE—Adam Vinatieri 41-yard field goal, NE 32–29

MVP: Tom Brady

For the second time since the turn-of-the-century, the New England Patriots represented the American Football Conference in the Super Bowl. After overcoming the AFC's best during the 2004 postseason, the Patriots were primed and ready to test the team's talents against the best of the NFC: the Carolina Panthers. Packing Houston's Reliant Stadium were 71,525 rabid fans ready to witness the instant classic.

In Super Bowl XXXVI against the Rams, the Patriots were the underdogs, the Cinderella team that should have just been happy to be there in the presence of the revered "Greatest Show on Turf." Fast forward two years later, and it was the Carolina Panthers who were the underdog, unafraid of Tom Brady, undaunted by the vaunted Patriots defense. The Panthers embraced the team concept and rallied around head coach John Fox. Is any of this sounding familiar? Comparisons to the Patriots of two years prior were abundant, and the pregame analysis pointed to two similar, equally matched teams, each with the ability to beat any opponent on any given Sunday.

This game could be summed up as a tale of two halves, the first half was largely slow and conservative, but as halftime approached, the game got a high-octane injection that led to a second half for the ages.

Whether it was smothering defense, offensive ineptitude, or a little of both that led to a scoreless first quarter, both teams appeared to be playing out of character. Understandably, neither team had much of a history playing against each other, and the good old "feeling out" process was well underway.

Uncharacteristically, Adam Vinatieri was unable to connect on two field goal tries. He was wide right on his 31-yard field goal attempt on the Patriots' first drive of the game, and he had his 36-yard field goal attempt blocked on the Patriots' first drive of the second quarter. It could have been the Panthers, or it could have been the stadium. All of Vinatieri's missed indoor field goals until this point had come in Houston.

As the second quarter winded down, the game started to heat up. Tom Brady marched the Patriots downfield and found familiar target Deion Branch in the end zone for the first score of the game with only three minutes remaining until halftime. Remarkably, after being stopped all game by the New England defense, Jake Delhomme led the Panthers on a 95-yard all-out blast in less than two minutes, culminating in a 39-yard touchdown pass to the ultra-talented wideout Steve Smith with 1:14 left.

Then, just like lightning, Brady hit Branch for 52, Givens for nine, and Givens again with a five-yard touchdown pass with 23 seconds remaining in the half. The pace had quickened.

The short kickoff by Vinatieri backfired, and after a 21-yard dash by Stephen Davis, John Kasay kicked a 50-yard field goal on the last play of the first half.

The Panthers got three back as the first-half clock ticked away and 24 points were on the board in just three minutes. If these final moments were any indication of the second half, fans were about to witness a classic that they wouldn't soon forget.

The Patriots came out for the second half guns a blazing, and nobody was safe; not even a local streaker, who was laid out by big Matt Chatam much to the crowd's delight.

The Patriots dominated time of possession during the third quarter behind Tom Brady's mastery and Antowain Smith's contributions to the ground attack.

With 14:49 remaining in the game, Smith reached the end zone on a two-yard run and gave the Patriots a 21–10 advantage.

The Panthers, however, were not to be deterred, and Jake Delhomme led a masterful no-huddle attack on the Patriots defense resulting in a touchdown. Reggie Howard gave the Panthers a boost on third-and-9 from the Panthers' 9-yard line when he intercepted a Tom Brady pass two yards deep in the end zone and brought it back to the 10-yard line.

One 85-yard bomb to Muhsin Muhammed later, and Carolina was on top. The Patriots were only down by one, fortunately, due to two botched two-point conversion attempts by Carolina.

With less than seven minutes remaining, the Patriots relied on the team's star. Tom Brady led his potent offense and found one of his favorite red zone targets, Mike Vrabel, who had come into the game as the third tight end. Vrabel's touchdown reception was followed by a successful two-point conversion by Kevin Faulk who took the snap directly and ran it in. In this game of one-upmanship it was once again advantage Patriots.

The advantage, however, was short-lived as Jake Delhomme led the Panthers offense down field within a blink of an eye, feasting on a secondary that lost Rodney Harrison (broken arm) and Eugene Wilson (leg). A 12-yard touchdown pass to Ricky Proehl tied the game at 29 with 1:08 left.

It seemed like whichever team had the ball last would win the game, and the Panthers handed the Patriots a gift—a penalty on the ensuing kickoff gave New England possession at its 40-yard line.

Tom Brady then added to his postseason legacy. On the game's final drive, he completed four consecutive passes for a total of 47 yards including a 17-yard pass on third-and-3 to Deion Branch.

That left :09 seconds on the clock.

Enter Mr. Clutch.

The 41-yard field goal was good.

Was there ever a doubt? Matt Chatham made the tackle of Rod "He Hate Me" Smart on the ensuing kickoff, and the game was over.

Scoring came in sprints, and the game became an instant classic. The Patriots had tasted Super Bowl glory for the second time in three years, and it tasted just as sweet the second time around.

January 16, 2005
New England Patriots vs. Indianapolis Colts
2005 American Football Conference Divisional Playoff
Gillette Stadium, Foxboro, MA

Scoring Summary:
New England Patriots 20, Indianapolis Colts 3

	Q1	Q2	Q3	Q4	Total
Colts	0	3	0	0	3
Patriots	0	6	7	7	20

NE—Vinatieri 24-yard field goal, NE 3–0
NE—Vinatieri 31-yard field goal, NE 6–0
IND—Vanderjagt 23-yard field goal, NE 6–3
NE—Givens five-yard pass from Brady (Vinatieri kick), NE 13–3
NE—Brady one-yard run (Vinatieri kick), NE 20–3

The energy at Gillette Stadium was unforgettable as 68,756 of the Patriots' faithful passed through the turnstiles in Foxboro to bear witness to the first game of New England's Super Bowl title defense. After charting an amazing 14–2 regular season mark, New England had its eyes on the prize. First up was a familiar foe, Peyton Manning and the Indianapolis Colts.

The Colts had burned through the NFL during their 2004–05 campaign, and lit up every scoreboard they came across. Manning had broken the legendary Dan Marino's single season touchdown record with an amazing 49 touchdown strikes. The experts believed this was finally the year Manning and the Colts would overcome their demons and outmaneuver a Bill Belichick–led Patriots defense.

The Patriots defense was more focused than perhaps at any moment in its dynasty era. Even with an injury-riddled secondary, the Patriots' front seven were able to disrupt Manning's rhythm throughout the game, thus taking away his ability to attack down field. On the offensive end, the Patriots utilized the ground game, namely Corey Dillon, to the maximum. Dillon racked up 144 yards rushing, as he systematically wore down the Colts defense throughout the game.

Adam Vinatieri added the first points of the contest on a 24-yard field goal with 10:40 remaining in the second quarter. A stellar defensive series followed including a Mike Vrabel strip-sack of Manning, which was recovered by Indianapolis. Dillon marched the Patriots into field goal range and Mr. Automatic drilled a 34-yard kick through the uprights giving New England a 6–0 lead.

With the Colts driving, Big-Play Bruschi recovered his forced fumble by Dominic Rhodes. The Patriots did not take advantage of this turnover, however.

On the last play of the half, Mike Vanderjagt kicked a 23-yard field goal to make it 6–3. However, the Patriots marched into the locker room with a hard-fought 6–3 lead, much to the delight of the Foxboro onlookers as the snow began to fall.

The second half was all about hard-nosed grind-it-out football, a style of play that few teams do better than the Patriots. The hometown team dominated time of possession, and Brady found David Givens in the end zone for a five-yard touchdown score. Tom Brady snuck up the middle for a one-yard touchdown ending a 14-play, 94-yard drive that took 7:24 off the clock. The Patriots defense smothered Manning the entire second half. When Tedy Bruschi recovered a Reggie Wayne

---

Patriots' Keys to Victory:

Key Statistic: Tedy Bruschi's two fumble recoveries, and he was only player to return a kickoff for the Patriots.

---

fumble later in the fourth quarter, it was time to celebrate in the snow.

In true Patriots fashion, Harrison provided the exclamation, the insult to injury, and picked off Manning with 12 seconds left in the game. Even at home, the defensive ascendancy over the Colts' high-powered attack was an outstanding achievement. Furthermore, Corey Dillon's relentless rushing performance ensured the Patriots had the ball for an astounding 37 minutes and 43 seconds. The great Colts offense had been repelled for a second straight postseason. The Colts had averaged 32.6 points per game in the regular season and torched the Broncos for 49 in the Wild Card game, but were held to only 3.

January 23, 2005
New England Patriots vs. Pittsburgh Steelers
2005 American Football Conference Championship
Heinz Field, Pittsburgh, PA

Scoring Summary:

New England Patriots 41, Pittsburgh Steelers 27

	Q1	Q2	Q3	Q4	Total
Patriots	10	14	7	10	41
Steelers	3	0	14	10	27

NE—Vinatieri 48-yard field goal, NE 3–0

NE—Branch 60-yard pass from Brady (Vinatieri kick), NE 10–0

PIT—Reed 43-yard field goal, NE 10–3

NE—Givens nine-yard pass from Brady (Vinatieri kick), NE 17–3

NE—Harrison 87-yard interception return (Vinatieri kick), NE 24–3

PIT—Bettis five-yard run (Reed kick), NE 24–10

NE—Dillon 25-yard run (Vinatieri kick), NE 31–10

PIT—Ward 30-yard pass from Roethlisberger (Reed kick), NE 31–17

PIT—Reed 20-yard field goal, NE 31–20

NE—Vinatieri 31-yard field goal, NE 34–20

NE—Branch 23-yard run (Vinatieri kick), NE 41–20

PIT—Burress seven-yard pass from Roethlisberger (Reed kick), NE 41–27

By the time the Patriots entered the arctic Heinz Field in Pittsburgh for the AFC Championship Game showdown with the Steelers, it had become difficult to call the team underdogs. The dominance displayed by the Patriots during the 2005 AFC playoffs was nothing short of astounding. One week after stopping the

unstoppable Peyton Manning in the Divisional matchup, the Patriots launched an offensive assault against a defense that the experts said couldn't be assaulted.

On the third play of the game, Eugene Wilson asserted Patriots dominance with a nice interception of a tipped ball thrown by Big Ben Roethlisberger.

After a tough 48-yard field goal into the wind by Adam Vinatieri, Mike Vrabel recovered a Jerome Bettis fumble on fourth-and-1 that was forced by Rosevelt Colvin and returned it to the Patriots' 40-yard line.

On the very next play, the brilliant Brady hit Deion Branch with a 60-yard touchdown bomb, and the normally boisterous Heinz Field crowd was silenced.

After a 27-yard punt by Josh Miller, the Steelers had possession on the Patriots' 48-yard line. Just five plays later, Jeff Reed kicked a 43-yard field goal to put Pittsburgh on the board.

With 10 minutes left in the second quarter, Tom Brady took his team to pay dirt once again. His completion of 45 yards to his new favorite target, Deion Branch, put the ball on the Steelers' 14-yard line. Two plays later he tossed a five-yard touchdown strike to David Givens. At 11 degrees, it was the coldest home game in Pittsburgh Steelers history, but the Patriots were simply on fire.

The defense kept the Steelers offense guessing in the first half. Even though Big Ben had practiced throughout the week how to look off the strong safety on a particular pass play, he threw a ball right into the hands of arguably the league's strongest safety, Rodney Harrison, who took it 87 yards for the touchdown. The good guys rolled into halftime with a shocking 24–3 lead.

It was a blitzkrieg in Blitzburgh, and the only challenge was to keep the pressure on and the intensity up during the second half.

On the Steelers first drive of the third quarter, Big Ben hit Antwaan Randle El for a 34-yard gain, and Jerome Bettis punched it in for a five-yard touchdown. Nobody said the Steelers would roll over and die.

However, the Patriots kept the pressure on. Throughout the season Corey Dillon had provided the Patriots with an element the team had never had during its mighty run—a true force in the backfield. Dillon made his presence felt in the third quarter with a 25-yard dash for a touchdown and sent the score to 31–10.

Despite New England's all-around intensity, Pittsburgh fought to stay in the game. On a crucial fourth-and-5, Big Ben tossed a 30-yard touchdown pass to Hines Ward to make the score 31–17. Then, on the fourth play of the fourth quarter, Jeff Reed kicked a 20-yard field goal to make the score 31–20. Not to be outdone, the Patriots answered with a 31-yard field goal by Adam Vinatieri.

As usual, Tom Brady was a wizard, finding every open receiver and spreading the ball around as he does best.

The defense continued to confuse Roethlisberger, and Eugene Wilson recorded his second interception of the contest. After Deion Branch scored on a 23-yard end around play, the final seconds mercifully ticked off the clock. Branch became the first Patriots receiver to record both a rushing and receiving touchdown in the same playoff game.

It had become customary for New England to beat the teams it wasn't supposed to beat, overcome the challenges it wasn't supposed to overcome, and find cracks in the armor of its adversaries when they were supposed to fall.

No one could have predicted the sheer dominance the Patriots displayed to upend the talented Steelers. However, the Patriots were more aggressive on all sides of the ball, and were once again headed to the Super Bowl to pursue their destiny.

February 6, 2005
New England Patriots vs. Philadelphia Eagles
Super Bowl XXXIX
ALLTEL Stadium, Jacksonville, FL

Scoring summary:

New England Patriots 24, Philadelphia Eagles 21

	Q1	Q2	Q3	Q4	Total
Patriots	0	7	7	10	24
Eagles	0	7	7	7	21

PHI—L.J. Smith six-yard touchdown pass from Donovan McNabb (David Akers kick), PHI 7–0

NE—David Givens four-yard pass from Tom Brady (Adam Vinatieri kick), tie 7–7

NE—Mike Vrabel two-yard pass from Tom Brady (Adam Vinatieri kick), NE 14–7

PHI—Brian Westbrook 10-yard pass from Donovan McNabb (David Akers kick), tie 14–14

NE—Corey Dillon two-yard run (Adam Vinatieri kick), NE 21–14

NE—Adam Vinatieri 22-yard field goal, NE 24–14

PHI—Greg Lewis 30-yard pass from Donovan McNabb (David Akers kick), NE 24–21

MVP: Deion Branch

Freddie Mitchell should have known better. You don't tug on Superman's cape, you don't spit into the wind, and you certainly don't disrespect the New England Patriots. If New England needed any extra motivation prior to its Super Bowl battle with the Philadelphia Eagles, it got it from Mitchell. Some say when the extraneous Eagles receiver called out Patriots pit bull Rodney Harrison and the New England secondary; he signed his team's season over as well.

And it certainly didn't hurt that Bill Belichick read to his team the exact route of the victory parade through the streets of Philadelphia prior to the game.

After amassing a 14–2 regular season record and steamrolling through familiar adversaries in the AFC playoffs, New England was a seven-point favorite against the brash boys from Philadelphia. With victories now expected, and the word "dynasty" on every New England fan's mind, the Patriots quickly went to work.

On defense, the Patriots had mastered the 3-4 during the regular season, but played a flexible 4-3 defensive alignment in Super Bowl XXXIX in an effort to keep the versatile Donavan McNabb contained. In the first quarter, things went according to plan.

On the Eagles' first drive of the game Tedy Bruschi sacked Donovan McNabb for a 10-yard loss on third down and the Eagles were forced to punt. On the Eagles' third drive of the game, Rodney Harrison intercepted a pass that was intended for Brian Westbrook on the Patriots' 4-yard line.

With 52 seconds left in the scoreless first quarter, Randall Gay forced L.J. Smith to fumble after his eight-yard reception, and Eugene Wilson recovered it for the Patriots.

With no score heading into the second quarter, Philadelphia finally shook the Patriots stingy defense and struck first on a six-yard touchdown pass from McNabb to tight end L.J. Smith. With 1:10 left in the half, Brady evened things up with a four-yard touchdown pass to David Givens, who celebrated his score by flapping his wings, much to the dismay of the Eagles, but to the delight of Patriots fans.

Tom Brady came out firing at the start of the third quarter, driving New England 69 yards. Deion Branch was here, there, and everywhere for the Patriots, recording four of his Super Bowl record-tying 11 receptions on the drive. Then, a familiar site for Patriots fans, as Tom Brady tossed a two-yard touchdown pass to linebacker/third tight end Mike Vrabel, who also showed the Eagles his wings after putting the Patriots up, 14–7.

Following a Brian Westbrook 10-yard touchdown reception, the game was knotted back up at 14. Patriots running back Kevin Faulk's 12-yard run and 14-yard reception on a screen from Brady set up a two-yard touchdown score by Corey Dillon.

For the third time in as many Super Bowls, an Adam Vinatieri field goal was the deciding factor in the outcome. Though this time less dramatic, Vinatieri's three points with 8:40 remaining in the fourth quarter put the Patriots ahead, 24–14.

Following the 22-yard field goal by Mr. Automatic, the Eagles were stopped when Tedy Bruschi intercepted a pass that was intended for L.J. Smith.

The Eagles, refusing to vanish, went on an impressive 11 play, 79-yard drive for the game's final score that took 3:52 off the clock. With 1:48 left, Donovan McNabb connected on a 30-yard touchdown pass to Gregory Lewis.

The multitalented Philadelphia quarterback led a late-game Eagle comeback, but the steadfast Patriots never seemed to lose any footing. In what was perhaps a piece of poetic justice, with 17 seconds left in the game McNabb's final pass from his own 5-yard line was intercepted by Rodney Harrison—his second pick of the game doubled Freddie Mitchell's reception total for the game.

For the third time in four years, the Patriots became football royalty and the toast of the town.

Deion Branch was named the Most Valuable Player of Super Bowl XXXIX after a Jerry Rice–like performance. Branch finished with 133 receiving yards. His 11 catches, combined with his 10 receptions in Super Bowl XXXVIII, gave him the record for most receptions in consecutive Super Bowls.

The win boosted Tom Brady's undefeated postseason record to 9–0, and gave Bill Belichick 10 playoff victories, one more than famed Packers head coach Vince Lombardi.

The dynasty became official, and with Tom Brady at the helm, Patriots fans could rest assured that the good times would keep on rollin'.

January 7, 2006
New England Patriots vs. Jacksonville Jaguars
2006 American Football Conference Wild Card Game
Gillette Stadium, Foxboro, MA

Scoring Summary:

New England Patriots 28, Jacksonville Jaguars 3

	Q1	Q2	Q3	Q4	Total
Jaguars	0	3	0	0	3
Patriots	0	7	14	7	28

NE—Brown 11-yard pass from Brady (Vinatieri kick), NE 7–0

JAX—Scobee 36-yard field goal, NE 7–3

NE—Givens 3-yard pass from Brady (Vinatieri kick), NE 14–3

NE—Watson 63-yard pass from Brady (Vinatieri kick), NE 21–3

NE—Samuel 73-yard interception return (Vinatieri kick), NE 28–3

The New England Patriots had experienced it all throughout the dynasty era when it came to postseason play. There were Super Bowls, Snow Bowls, AFC Championship Games, you name it. However, at the onset of the 2005–06 postseason campaign, the team found itself in an unfamiliar situation—a Wild Card game. For the first time in the team's dynasty era, it did not earn a first round bye during the regular season.

Jacksonville rolled into a cold Gillette Stadium looking for the glory that comes with knocking off a back-to-back Super Bowl champion. Needless to say, that didn't happen. As a matter of fact, it didn't even come close to happening.

This game can be summed up by two words: absolute domination. Supremacy in every facet of the game is what the Patriots showcased against Jacksonville. Save for a field goal in the second quarter, Jacksonville was unable to put together scoring drives, as New England's defense outplayed, outhit, and out-maneuvered the Jaguars.

Willie McGinest was the defensive star on this day with a record-breaking defensive performance. McGinest's four-and-a-half sacks are the most in NFL postseason history. His game total pushed his career postseason tally to 16, and he passed the legendary Bruce Smith for first on the all-time list. It was an incredible accomplishment for the fierce and relentless competitor who is all guts on the field.

Though New England's offense didn't immediately overwhelm, it bided its time and played the game of field position. Adam Vinatieri pooched a punt from the 46-yard line, which was downed at Jacksonville's own 4-yard line. After forcing a three-and-out the Patriots had desirable field position, and after a pair of Corey Dillon runs, Tom Brady found Troy Brown in the end zone for seven.

In the second half, it was all Patriots. On the team's first offensive drive, Tom Brady marched his Brady

Did You Know?

The Patriots defense was so dominant that it didn't allow a Jacksonville first down until there was 9:40 remaining in the second quarter.

Bunch 82 yards over 11 efficient plays, hooking up with David Givens for his second touchdown pass of the game.

After another Jacksonville punt, which had become customary, Brady continued to attack the Jacksonville defense in the third quarter. Benjamin Watson broke free of defenders for a huge 63-yard touchdown, and blew the game wide open.

In the fourth quarter, the Patriots dished out more punishment. Byron Leftwich attempted to get something resembling a scoring drive going, but it was to no avail. Asante Samuel intercepted a Leftwich pass and took it back 73 yards to pay dirt. The rout was on. The Patriots defense played hard the entire game and kept the 28–3 margin intact. The Jaguars went home conquered, and the fans rejoiced in Foxboro.

The victory was the 10th straight in the postseason for head coach Bill Belichick, as he surpassed the legendary Vince Lombardi's streak.

January 7, 2007
New England Patriots vs. New York Jets
2007 American Football Conference Wild Card Game
Gillette Stadium, Foxboro, MA

Scoring Summary:

New England Patriots, 37 New York Jets 16

	Q1	Q2	Q3	Q4	Total
Jets	3	7	3	3	16
Patriots	7	10	6	14	37

NE—Corey Dillon 11-yard run (Gostkowski kick), NE 7–0

NYJ—Mike Nugent 28-yard field goal, NE 7–3

NYJ—Jerricho Cotchery 77-yard pass from Chad Pennington (Nugent kick), NYJ 10–7

NE—Stephen Gostkowski 20-yard field goal, tie 10–10

NE—Daniel Graham one-yard pass from Tom Brady (Gostkowski kick), NE 17–10

NYJ—Mike Nugent 21-yard field goal, NE 17–13

NE—Stephen Gostkowski 40-yard field goal, NE 20–13

NE—Stephen Gostkowski 28-yard field goal, NE 23–13

NYJ—Mike Nugent 37-yard field goal, NE 23–16

NE—Kevin Faulk 7-yard pass from Tom Brady (Gostkowski kick), NE 30–16

NE—Asante Samuel 36-yard interception return (Gostkowski kick), NE 37–16

The Foxboro faithful were primed and ready for the 2007 NFL playoffs to kickoff, and what better way to start the festivities than with a game against the team's ultimate division rival, the New York Jets?

There is no team in Patriots' history that the team has played more times than the New York Jets. Just how many times have the Patriots played the Jets? The total is 91 times, the same as the Buffalo Bills in the regular season, and the playoffs before this game. These two teams know each other very well, especially with the advent of former Patriots defensive coordinator Eric Mangini at the helm of the Jets team.

Like New England had done so many times in the past, the game started on the right foot. After winning the coin toss, Tom Brady took the reigns of his offense and immediately went into the no-huddle.

Jabar Gaffney was his receiver of choice early, and he hit Gaffney for three passes on the drive before handing off to Corey Dillon who bounced into the end zone uncontested.

After a field goal made the game 7–3, the Jets temporarily stunned the Foxboro fans when Chad Pennington hit Jerricho Cotchery for a 77-yard touchdown sprint that put New York ahead. The play was particularly alarming as the New England defense, rarely, if ever, gave up the big play.

However, any jubilation felt by the Jets would be short-lived and unequivocally reversed.

New England knotted the game up on a Stephen Gostkowski field goal, but it was not taking over the game as was largely expected.

Finally, as halftime approached, Tom Brady spread the ball out to wide receivers Jabar Gaffney, Reche Caldwell, and Benjamin Watson to drive the Patriots downfield. Then, with 14 seconds remaining on third-and-goal from the 1-yard line, Brady found tight end Daniel Graham in the back of the end zone for the score.

In half two, the waiting game continued. Although New York was a solid club, it clearly did not have the talent or ability to defeat New England at Gillette Stadium. Nonetheless, the Patriots were unable to establish authority over the proceedings. The teams traded a pair of field goals with Stephen Gostkowski kicking a 28-yard field goal with seven seconds left in the third quarter.

Although the offense couldn't pull away early, the defense was its typically stellar self. A 31-yard return by Vince Wilfork on a backward pass that was deflected by Rosevelt Colvin put the ball on the Jets 15-yard line. This play gave New England prime real estate that set up its only third-quarter score.

Though the Patriots had not blown the game open, their offensive balance kept the Jets defense on its toes throughout the game. New England's ground attack amassed 158 rushing yards between Lawrence Maroney,

> ## Drive of the Game:
> Tom Brady orchestrated an efficient 63-yard drive in the fourth quarter that put New England in front, 30–16, and put the game out of reach for the Jets. Troy Brown's reception on third-and-8 assured the drive's success. Jabar Gaffney was also targeted on the drive. Gaffney charted 104 receiving yards in the game. This was the first of two consecutive playoff games that Gaffney broke the 100-yard barrier.

Corey Dillon, and Kevin Faulk. It helped to keep the Jets defense off guard, and enabled Tom Brady to put together another solid playoff effort: 212 yards and two touchdowns for No. 12.

It wasn't until the fourth quarter that New England separated itself from the pesky Jets. In need of a solid touchdown drive, Tom Brady led his offense on a 63-yard drive that included a key third-and-8 completion to "Mr. Third Down" Troy Brown, and climaxed with a seven-yard touchdown flip to Kevin Faulk.

This is just what the crowd had been looking for, but New England wasn't done scoring.

All that was missing was the exclamation point: Asante Samuel. Samuel picked off a Pennington pass and took it 36 yards to pay dirt. With the interception return for a touchdown, Samuel became the only player in Patriots history to return two interceptions for a touchdown in the postseason.

The final score was 37–16, though the game was much closer than indicated. It was a hard-fought victory for the Patriots. That was that. Another playoff game, another playoff win, and New England was off and running in the 2007 postseason.

January 14, 2007
New England Patriots vs. San Diego Chargers
2007 American Football Conference Divisional Playoff
Qualcomm Stadium, San Diego, CA

Scoring Summary:
New England Patriots 24, San Diego Chargers 21

	Q1	Q2	Q3	Q4	Total
Patriots	3	7	3	11	24
Chargers	0	14	0	7	21

NE—Stephen Gostkowski 50-yard field goal, NE 3–0

SD—LaDainian Tomlinson two-yard run (Kaeding kick), SD 7–3

SD—Michael Turner six-yard run (Kaeding kick), SD 14–3

NE—Jabar Gaffney six-yard pass from Tom Brady (Gostkowski kick), SD 14–10

NE—Stephen Gostkowski 34-yard field goal, SD 14–13

SD—LaDainian Tomlinson three-yard run (Kaeding kick), SD 21–13

NE—Reche Caldwell four-yard pass from Tom Brady (Kevin Faulk two-point conversion run), tie 21–21

NE—Stephen Gostkowski 31-yard field goal, NE 24–21

When the New England Patriots entered Qualcomm Stadium to play the top-seeded San Diego Chargers, the team was in a familiar position: underdog. Once again the Patriots looked overmatched, and once again the experts were predicting the team's demise.

And how could they not? The Chargers were the "it" team of the 2006 season. The Chargers were undefeated at home, LaDainian Tomlinson was the league's Most Valuable Player, and the Charger defense was a cocky, menacing bunch led by all-world linebacker Shawn "Lights Out" Merriman.

However, as Patriots fans knew, the team had built a legacy by stopping the "it" team dead in its tracks, chopping most valuable players down to size, and finding weaknesses in the most unbreakable of defenses.

On this afternoon, it was the Patriots defense that played a vital role in the game's outcome. The Chargers started with excellent field position throughout the game, making the Patriots defensive unit work extra hard to keep San Diego's dangerous offense at bay.

Linebacker Tully Banta-Cain recovered a crucial fumble that was forced by Mike Vrabel late in the first quarter. The timely play set up a Stephen Gostkowski field goal from 50 yards out to put the Patriots on the scoreboard first.

The Chargers answered in the second frame as young quarterback Philip Rivers led his unit into the Patriots red zone before handing off to Tomlinson. LaDainain knew what to do, and found pay dirt giving the Bolts a 7–3 advantage with 7:19 remaining in the half.

San Diego quickly added another score on a six-yard touchdown scamper after intercepting a Brady pass and then stuffing New England's offense three-and-out.

To say Brady was being put to the test was an understatement. The running game was basically nonexistent averaging a dismal 2.4 yards-per-carry.

Nevertheless, more often than not, Brady will find a way. As the end of the second quarter drew near, he relied on Jabar Gaffney to get the Patriots back in the game. The Brady-Gaffney connection was clicking on all cylinders, with four of the team's ten receptions on the day, including a six-yard touchdown catch to put the Patriots right back into contention. New England had driven 72 yards in less than two minutes.

The two defenses continued to make big plays in the third quarter. Tom Brady threw an unBrady-like second interception, but his defense bailed him out on the Chargers ensuing drive. On the other side of the field, it was Rosevelt Colvin with a beautiful over-the-shoulder pick of a Rivers pass, stopping what appeared to be a promising Chargers drive.

Stephen Gostkowski put three more points on the board and the Patriots had a one-point game heading into the final frame.

Play of the Game:
The Play of the Game was the Reche Caldwell fumble recovery that immediately followed a Morton McCree interception of Tom Brady. Troy Brown made a great hit jarring the ball from McCree's hands giving the ball and a fresh set of downs right back to Brady. It was the break that New England had been looking for after a frustrating offensive day where the team couldn't establish any rhythm.

In the first three quarters, neither team was able to break out, but at the start of the fourth it was San Diego who finally hit its stride.

With just over eight-and-a-half minutes remaining in the game, San Diego quickly drove down to the New England 2-yard line. From there, a handoff to Tomlinson resulted in another six, and the home team was up, 21–13.

With the hearts of Patriots fans firmly planted in their stomachs, New England had to make its move. On the next drive, the Patriots reminded the sports world that they were not to be counted out of a game.

With the prospect of a game-tying drive looking grim, New England was forced to go for it on a fourth-and-5 from the Chargers' 41-yard line. What happened next was the kind of magic moment that Patriots fans had come to expect.

Marlon McCree intercepted Brady's pass and began his return when Johnny-on-the-spot Troy Brown made a solid hit on the ball carrier. Reche Caldwell recovered the loose ball and the ever-attentive New England offense was back in business. San Diego had committed the fatal flaw of giving Tom Brady another chance to win—and that he did.

Brady found Reche Caldwell in the end zone on a beautifully crafted play-action pass. A direct snap to Kevin Faulk followed as Faulk took it to the house for the two-point conversion and it was all tied up in San Diego.

After a five-yard run and two incomplete passes, the Patriots got the ball back with 3:30 left with a chance to win. A huge 49-yard pass play to Caldwell set up a 31-yard game-winning field goal by Stephen Gostkowski, and New England had done it again.

With 1:05 left the Chargers had a chance, but their 54-yard field goal attempt with eight seconds left was short. Another giant slain by the never-say-die New England Patriots and the "lights" were turned out on Shawn Merriman and the Chargers season.

## 7

Offensive Stats

Rushing

Rushing the ball requires a team effort and starts with the offensive line. The New England Patriots have had some tremendous offensive lineman. Many experts acknowledge that Pro Football Hall of Famer and New England Patriots offensive guard John Hannah was the best offensive lineman ever. John Hannah was an AFC Pro Bowl offensive lineman nine times in his career. Two Patriots offensive lineman have been recognized six times as either an AFL All-Star or an AFC Pro Bowl player: center Jon Morris and tackle Bruce Armstrong.

The Boston Patriots had four guards, two tackles, and one center who were recognized as AFL All-Stars. They were offensive guards Charlie Leo, Charlie Long, Billy Neighbors, and Lennie St. Jean; offensive tackles Tom Neville and Don Oakes; and center Jon Morris. The New England Patriots have had two guards, four tackles, and three centers recognized as AFC Pro Bowl offensive lineman. They were offensive guards John Hannah and Logan Mankins; offensive tackles Leon Gray, Brian Holloway, Bruce Armstrong, and Matt Light; and centers Jon Morris, Damien Woody, and Dan Koppen.

In 1960, the Patriots had 13 different players attempt a rushing play from the line of scrimmage, and averaged 4.2 yards per carry as a team. Alan Miller, Dick Christy, Ron Burton, and Jim Crawford all ran for more than 200 yards that season. In 1961, only Billy Lott, Larry Garron, and Ron Burton ran for more than 200 yards. In 1962, Tom Yewcic became the first Patriots player to play both as a quarterback and a running back and rush for more than 200 yards. The Patriots had four players (Larry Garron,

Tom Yewcic, Babe Parilli, and Claude King) average more than 5.8 yards per carry in the 1962 regular season.

In 1963, Larry Garron became the first Patriots player with at least 750 yards rushing in a season. During the 1964 and 1965 regular seasons, the Patriots became more of a passing team than a rushing team. In 1966 and 1967, Jim Nance ran for 1,458 yards and 1,216 yards respectively. Did you know that Nance was the only AFL rusher to lead the league in yards rushing in consecutive years? Jim Nance also led the Patriots in yards rushing during the 1968–70 regular seasons. Carl Garrett was the first running back to lead the New England Patriots in yards rushing with 784 yards in 1971. Quarterback Jim Plunkett averaged 4.7 yards per carry in 1971, 6.4 yards per carry in 1972, 4.8 yards per carry in 1973, 5.4 yards per carry in 1974, and rushed for 817 yards during the 1971–75 regular seasons.

Sam "Bam" Cunningham led the Patriots in rushing yards in 1973, 1975, 1976, 1977, 1978, and 1979. He finished his career with 62 more carries than Jim Nance and had 130 more yards rushing than Nance. Cunningham holds the team record with 1,385 carries for 5,453 yards. "Mini" Mack Herron, who set an NFL record with 2,444 all-purpose yards (rushing, receiving, and returning), also led the Patriots with 824 yards rushing during the 1974 regular season.

The Patriots set and still own the NFL record for the most yards rushing in a regular season with 3,165 yards rushing during the 1978 regular season. Seven Patriots players averaged more than four yards per carry, and four Patriots players had more than 500 yards rushing that season. Running backs Horace Ivory, Andy Johnson, Steve Grogan, Don Calhoun,

James McAllister, and wide receivers Stanley Morgan and Harold Jackson averaged more than four yards per carry during the 1978 regular season. Sam Cunningham led the team with 768 yards rushing, Horace Ivory had 693, Andy Johnson had 675, and Steve Grogan had 539 yards rushing during that season. The stability achieved by having the tremendous offensive line of Leon Gray, John Hannah, Bill Lenkaitis, Sam Adams, and Shelby Jordan start every game of that season contributed to the success of the running game.

Although the dynamic duo of Vegas Ferguson and Don Calhoun combined for 1,605 yards and 11 TDs in 1980, the Patriots just missed making the playoffs. Tony Collins led the team in yards rushing in 1982, 1983, and 1987. Craig James led the team in yards rushing in 1984, 1985, and 1986, as the Patriots made it to the Super Bowl once and the playoffs twice during that three-year span. John Stephens, who was the NFL Offensive Rookie of the Year in 1988, led the team in yards rushing during the 1988–90 regular seasons. Leonard Russell, who was the NFL Offensive Rookie of the Year in 1991, led the team in yards rushing in 1991 and 1993. Jon Vaughn, who led the led team in kickoff return yards, led the team in yards rushing during the 1992 regular season. With Marion Butts leading the team with 703 yards rushing in 1994, the Patriots made the playoffs for the first time in eight seasons.

Tom Brady

Third-round draft pick Curtis Martin had 1,487 yards rushing and 14 rushing TDs during his rookie season in 1995. Martin was the first Patriots running back to have three consecutive regular seasons with at least 1,000 yards rushing. First-round draft pick Robert Edwards led the Patriots with 1,115 yards rushing during the 1998 regular season, and he was the first NFL running back to score a rushing TD in his first six NFL regular season games.

Kevin Faulk led the Patriots in yards rushing during the 2000 regular season, and Antowain Smith led the team during the 2001–03 regular seasons including the two Super Bowl championship seasons. Corey Dillon set the Patriots record with 1,635 yards rushing, and led the team to another Super Bowl championship following the 2004 regular season. Corey Dillon led the Patriots in yards rushing in 2005 and 2006. Laurence Maroney had the most yards rushing for the Patriots in the undefeated regular season in 2007. Sammy Morris led the team with 727 yards rushing in 2008. Kevin Faulk led the NFL with the best rushing average as he gained 6.1 yards per rushing attempt in 2008.

The 10 greatest Patriots rushing plays

Tom Brady ran for a six-yard TD in the fourth quarter of the 16–13 overtime playoff game win on 01-19-02

Kevin Faulk ran for a two-point conversion in the 32–29 Super Bowl win on 02-01-04

Robert Weathers ran for a 42-yard TD on fourth down (that propelled the Patriots into the playoffs) in the 34–23 win on 12-22-85

Jim Nance bolted 65 yards for a TD in the 14–3 victory in "The Game" on 12-04-66

Darryl Stingley dashed 34 yards for a TD in the 21–17 win on 09-18-77 (his 26th birthday)

Steve Grogan ran left on a bootleg for a three-yard TD in the fourth quarter for the final points scored in the 20–13 win on 10-30-85

Doug Flutie ran left on a naked bootleg for a 13-yard TD with 23 seconds left in the 21–17 victory on 10-02-88

Larry Garron set the Team Record with his 85-yard TD run in the 52–21 blowout victory on 10-22-61

Curtis Martin galloped 78 yards for a TD in the 28–3 playoff game win on 01-05-97

Craig James scampered 65 yards for a TD in the fourth quarter of the 26–20 victory on 09-08-85

The yearly list of players who have led the Patriots in yards rushing, rushing TDs, and have had the longest run of the year

	Most yards rushing	Most rushing TDs	The longest run
1960	Alan Miller	Dick Christy	Ron Burton
1961	Billy Lott	Billy Lott and Babe Parilli	Larry Garron
1962	Ron Burton	*5 Patriots players had two TDs	Claude King
1963	Larry Garron	Harry Crump and Babe Parilli	Larry Garron
1964	Larry Garron	Ron Burton	JD Garrett
1965	Jim Nance	Jim Nance	Larry Garron
1966	Jim Nance	Jim Nance	Jim Nance
1967	Jim Nance	Jim Nance	Jim Nance
1968	Jim Nance	Jim Nance	RC Gamble
1969	Jim Nance	Jim Nance	Carl Garrett
1970	Jim Nance	Jim Nance	Carl Garrett
1971	Carl Garrett	Jim Nance	Jim Nance
1972	Josh Ashton	Carl Garrett	Carl Garrett
1973	Sam Cunningham	Jim Plunkett	Josh Ashton
1974	Mack Herron	Sam Cunningham	Sam Cunningham
1975	Sam Cunningham	Sam Cunningham	Andy Johnson
1976	Sam Cunningham	Steve Grogan	Andy Johnson
1977	Sam Cunningham	Sam Cunningham and Don Calhoun	Steve Grogan
1978	Sam Cunningham	Horace Ivory	Don Calhoun
1979	Sam Cunningham	Sam Cunningham and Don Calhoun	Horace Ivory
1980	Vagas Ferguson	Don Calhoun	Vagas Ferguson
1981	Tony Collins	Tony Collins	Mosi Tatupu
1982	Tony Collins	**3 Patriots players had one TD	Tony Collins
1983	Tony Collins	Tony Collins	Robert Weathers
1984	Craig James	Tony Collins and Tony Eason	Craig James
1985	Craig James	Craig James	Craig James
1986	Craig James	Craig James	Irving Fryar
1987	Tony Collins	Tony Collins and Reggie Dupard	Reggie Dupard
1988	John Stephens	Robert Perryman	John Stephens
1989	John Stephens	John Stephens	John Stephens
1990	John Stephens	John Stephens	Marvin Allen
1991	Leonard Russell	Leonard Russell	Leonard Russell
1992	Jon Vaughn	Leonard Russell and John Stephens	Jon Vaughn
1993	Leonard Russell	Leonard Russell	Kevin Turner
1994	Marion Butts	Marion Butts	Marion Butts
1995	Curtis Martin	Curtis Martin	Curtis Martin
1996	Curtis Martin	Curtis Martin	Curtis Martin
1997	Curtis Martin	Curtis Martin	Curtis Martin
1998	Robert Edwards	Robert Edwards	Sedrick Shaw
1999	Terry Allen	Terry Allen	Kevin Faulk
2000	Kevin Faulk	Kevin Faulk	Troy Brown and Terry Glenn
2001	Antowain Smith	Antowain Smith	Antowain Smith
2002	Antowain Smith	Antowain Smith	Kevin Faulk
2003	Antowain Smith	Mike Cloud	Mike Cloud
2004	Corey Dillon	Corey Dillon	Corey Dillon
2005	Corey Dillon	Corey Dillon	Patrick Pass
2006	Corey Dillon	Corey Dillon	Corey Dillon
2007	Laurence Maroney	Laurence Maroney	Laurence Maroney
2008	Sammy Morris	Sammy Morris	Lamont Jordan

*Run Burton, Jim Crawford, Larry Garron, Tom Yewcic, and Babe Parilli each ran for two TDs in 1962
**Tony Collins, Robert Weathers, and Steve Grogan each ran for one TD in the strike-shortened 1982 season

Mike Cloud

The progression of the most yards rushing by a Patriots Running Back in a regular season game

29 yards rushing by Jim Crawford in the 13–10 loss to the Denver Broncos at BU Field on 09-09-60

44 yards rushing by Alan Miller in the 28–24 victory over the New York Titans at the Polo Grounds on 09-17-60

93 yards rushing by Dick Christy in the 13–0 loss to the Buffalo Bills at BU Field on 09-23-60

93 yards rushing by Jim Crawford in the 35–0 shutout of the Los Angeles Chargers at the Los Angeles Coliseum on 10-08-60

94 yards rushing by Alan Miller in the 27–14 loss to the Oakland Raiders at Kezar Stadium on 10-16-60

127 yards rushing by Ron Burton in the 31–24 loss to the Denver Broncos at Bears Stadium on 10-23-60

140 yards rushing by Larry Garron in the 26–16 victory over the Oakland Raiders at BU Field on 10-26-62

208 yards rushing by Jim Nance in the 24–21 victory over the Oakland Raiders at Fenway Park on 10-30-66

212 yards rushing by Tony Collins in the 23-13 victory over the New York Jets at Sullivan Stadium on 09-18-83

The progression of the most yards rushing by a Patriots Quarterback in a regular season game

2 yards rushing by Butch Songin in the 13–10 loss to the Denver Broncos at BU Field on 09-09-60

33 yards rushing by Tom Greene in the 13–0 loss to the Buffalo Bills at BU Field on 09-23-60

46 yards rushing by Babe Parilli in the 35–21 victory over the Oakland Raiders at Candlestick Park on 12-09-61

90 yards rushing by Tom Yewcic in the 24–17 victory over the New York Titans at BU Field on 11-30-62

96 yards rushing by Babe Parilli in the 25–24 victory over the Houston Oilers at Fenway Park on 11-06-64

103 yards rushing by Steve Grogan in the 41–7 rout of the New York Jets at Schaefer Stadium on 10-18-76

The progression of the most yards rushing by a Patriots Wide Receiver in a regular season game

10 yards rushing by Jim Colclough in the 23–21 win over the Buffalo Bills at War Memorial Stadium on 09-23-61

16 yards rushing by Jim Colclough in the 18–17 victory over the Dallas Texans at the Cotton Bowl on 10-29-61

16 yards rushing by Jim Colclough in the 35–21 victory over the Oakland Raiders at Candlestick Park on 12-09-61

18 yards rushing by Eric Crabtree in the 38–33 victory over the Buffalo Bills at Schaefer Stadium on 11-14-71

18 yards rushing by Darryl Stingley in the 33–24 victory over the Green Bay Packers at Schaefer Stadium on 11-18-73

19 yards rushing by Darryl Stingley in the 32–0 shutout of the Houston Oilers at the Astrodome on 11-25-73

20 yards rushing by Darryl Stingley in the 28–20 victory over the New York Giants at Giants Stadium on 09-22-74

22 yards rushing by Darryl Stingley in the 42–3 rout of the Baltimore Colts at Schaefer Stadium on 10-06-74

48 yards rushing by Darryl Stingley in the 48–17 rout of the Oakland Raiders at Schaefer Stadium on 10-03-76

The progression of the most yards rushing by a Patriots Tight End in a regular season game

3 yards rushing by Bob Adams in the 30–14 victory over the San Diego Chargers at Schaefer Stadium on 12-02-73

4 yards rushing by Bob Adams in the 18–13 loss to the Baltimore Colts at Memorial Stadium on 12-16-73

4 yards rushing by Russ Francis in the 27–13 loss to the Baltimore Colts at Schaefer Stadium on 09-12-76

8 yards rushing by Russ Francis in the 41–7 rout of the New York Jets at Schaefer Stadium on 10-18-76

11 yards rushing by Benjamin Watson in the 34–17 win over the Cleveland Browns at Gillette Stadium on 10-07-07

The progression of the most yards rushing by a Patriots Running Back in a regular season

416 yards rushing by Alan Miller in 1960

461 yards rushing by Billy Lott in 1961

548 yards rushing by Ron Burton in 1962

750 yards rushing by Larry Garron in 1963

1,458 yards rushing by Jim Nance in 1966

1,487 yards rushing by Curtis Martin in 1995

1,635 yards rushing by Corey Dillon in 2004

The progression of the most yards rushing by a Patriots Quarterback in a regular season

44 yards rushing by Tom Greene in 1960

183 yards rushing by Babe Parilli in 1961

200 yards rushing by Babe Parilli in 1965

210 yards rushing by Jim Plunkett in 1971

230 yards rushing by Jim Plunkett in 1972

397 yards rushing by Steve Grogan in 1976

539 yards rushing by Steve Grogan in 1978

The progression of the most yards rushing by a Patriots Wide Receiver in a regular season

37 yards rushing by Jim Colclough in 1961

64 yards rushing by Darryl Stingley in 1973

80 yards rushing by Irving Fryar in 1986

91 yards rushing by Troy Brown in 2001

Every Patriots Wide Receiver who has led the team in yards rushing in a regular season game

1986 regular season
Irving Fryar led the team with 34 yards rushing in the 41–7 loss to the Bengals at Sullivan Stadium on 12-07-86

2000 regular season
Troy Brown led the team with 33 yards rushing in the 21–16 loss to the Buccaneers at Foxboro Stadium on 09-03-00

Every Patriots Quarterback who has led the team in yards rushing in a regular season game

1961 regular season
Babe Parilli led the team with 29 yards rushing in the 27–15 loss to the Oilers at Jeppesen Stadium on 11-12-61

1962 regular season
Tom Yewcic led the team with 35 yards rushing in the 21–17 loss to the Oilers at Jeppesen Stadium on 11-18-62

1963 regular season
Tom Yewcic led the team with 64 yards rushing in the 14–10 loss to the Broncos at Bears Stadium on 09-29-63

1964 regular season
Babe Parilli led the team with 96 yards rushing in the 25–24 win over the Oilers at Fenway Park on 11-06-64

1967 regular season
Don Trull led the team with 38 yards rushing in the 29–24 loss to the New York Jets at Fenway Park on 11-19-67

1970 regular season
Joe Kapp led the team with 41 yards rushing in the 16–0 loss to the New York Giants at Harvard Stadium on 10-18-70

1971 regular season
Jim Plunkett led the team with 14 yards rushing in the 41–3 loss to the Miami Dolphins at the Orange Bowl on 10-17-71

Jim Plunkett led the team with 52 yards rushing in the 13–6 loss to the New York Jets at Shea Stadium on 12-12-71

1976 regular season
Steve Grogan led the team with 103 yards rushing in the 41–7 rout of the New York Jets at Schaefer Stadium on 10-18-76

1978 regular season
Steve Grogan led the team with 65 yards rushing in the 21–14 win over the Raiders at the Oakland Coliseum on 09-24-78

Steve Grogan led the team with 48 yards rushing in the 10–7 win over the Bengals at Riverfront Stadium on 10-15-78

1986 regular season

Tony Eason led the team with 55 yards rushing in the 23–3 win over the Buffalo Bills at Rich Stadium on 10-26-86

Tony Eason led the team with 35 yards rushing in the 30–21 win over the Colts at the Hoosier Dome on 11-09-86

1992 regular season

Hugh Millen led the team with 37 yards rushing in the 30–21 loss to the New York Jets at the Meadowlands on 10-04-92

Every Patriots Running Back who has rushed for at least 100 yards in at least five consecutive regular season games

1966 regular season

Jim Nance ran for 104 yards in the 27–21 victory over the Houston Oilers at Fenway Park on 11-13-66

Jim Nance ran for 107 yards in the 27–27 tie with the Kansas City Chiefs at Municipal Stadium on 11-20-66

Jim Nance ran for 133 yards in the 20–14 victory over the Miami Dolphins at the Orange Bowl on 11-27-66

Curtis Martin

Jim Nance ran for 109 yards in the 14–3 victory over the Buffalo Bills at Fenway Park on 12-04-66

Jim Nance ran for 146 yards in the 38–14 rout of the Houston Oilers at Rice Stadium on 12-11-66

1995 regular season

Curtis Martin ran for 148 yards in the 35–25 victory over the Buffalo Bills at Rich Stadium on 11-26-95

Curtis Martin ran for 112 yards in the 31–17 loss to the New Orleans Saints at Foxboro Stadium on 12-03-95

Curtis Martin ran for 148 yards in the 31–28 victory over the New York Jets at Foxboro Stadium on 12-10-95

Curtis Martin ran for 120 yards in the 41–27 loss to the Pittsburgh Steelers at Three Rivers Stadium on 12-16-95

Curtis Martin ran for 103 yards in the 10–7 loss to the Indianapolis Colts at the RCA Dome on 12-23-95

The progression of the most career yards rushing by a Patriots Running Back

416 career yards rushing by Alan Miller in the 1960 season

1,536 career yards rushing by Ron Burton during the 1960–65 seasons

2,981 career yards rushing by Larry Garron during the 1960–68 seasons

5,323 career yards rushing by Jim Nance during the 1965–71 seasons

5,453 career yards rushing by Sam Cunningham during the 1973–79 and 1981–82 seasons

The progression of the most career yards rushing by a Patriots Quarterback

44 career yards rushing by Tom Greene in the 1960 season

949 career yards rushing by Babe Parilli during the 1961–67 seasons

2,176 career yards rushing by Steve Grogan during the 1975–90 seasons

The progression of the most career yards rushing by a Patriots Receiver

51 career rushing yards by Jim Colclough during the 1961–62 seasons

244 career rushing yards by Darryl Stingley during the 1973–77 seasons

The progression of the most yards rushing by the Patriots team in a regular season

1,512 total yards rushing by the Boston Patriots in 1960

1,675 total yards rushing by the Boston Patriots in 1961

1,970 total yards rushing by the Boston Patriots in 1962

2,134 total yards rushing by the New England Patriots in 1974

2,948 total yards rushing by the New England Patriots in 1976 (14 game regular season)

3,165 total yards rushing by the New England Patriots in 1978 (16 game regular season) NFL record

The 10 greatest offensive lineman of the Patriots

John Hannah—acknowledged as the most intense and greatest offensive lineman ever

Bruce Armstrong—started in a team-record 212 games, 44 as right tackle and 168 as left tackle

Jon Morris—an AFL All-Star center for six consecutive seasons and the Patriots' first AFC Pro Bowl Player (in 1970)

Leon Gray—played alongside John Hannah for six years and was a two-time AFC Pro Bowl offensive tackle

Bruce Armstrong

(Tie) Sam Adams, Bill Lenkaitis, and Shelby Jordan—they made up the rest of the Patriots' starting offensive line in 1978

Matt Light—has three championship rings and helped the Patriots achieve numerous offensive rushing and scoring records

Logan Mankins—made the Pro Bowl in 2007 and is the only Patriots offensive lineman to score a TD in a playoff game

Tom Neville—played in two games as a DT in 1965, took a handoff from Jim Plunkett in 1971, and was a two-time AFL All-Star

Pete Brock—earned the nickname "Mr. Versatility" when he played every position on the offensive line during the same drive

Len St. Jean—played LB and DE, earned 5.5 sacks in the process, and was an AFL All-Star offensive guard in 1966

The progression of the best average yards rushing per game by a Patriots Running Back in a season

30 yards rushing per game by Alan Miller, who had 416 yards rushing in 1960

33 yards rushing per game by Billy Lott, who had 461 yards rushing in 1961

39 yards rushing per game by Ron Burton, who had 548 yards rushing in 1962

54 yards rushing per game by Larry Garron, who had 750 yards rushing in 1963

104 yards rushing per game by Jim Nance, who had 1,458 yards rushing in 1966

John Hannah

The progression of the best average yards rushing per game by a Patriots Quarterback in a season

3 yards rushing per game by Tom Greene, who had 44 yards rushing in 1960

13 yards rushing per game by Babe Parilli, who had 183 yards rushing in 1961

15 yards rushing per game by Tom Yewcic, who had 215 yards rushing in 1962

16 yards rushing per game by Jim Plunkett, who had 230 yards rushing in 1972

28 yards rushing per game by Steve Grogan, who had 397 yards rushing in 1976

33 yards rushing per game by Steve Grogan, who had 539 yards rushing in 1978

The progression of the career average yards rushing per game by a Patriots Running Back

29.7 career average yards rushing per game by Alan Miller in 1960

30.1 career average yards rushing per game by Larry Garron over the 1960–1968 seasons

56.6 career average yards rushing per game by Jim Nance over the 1965–1971 seasons

84.4 career average yards rushing per game by Curtis Martin over the 1995–1997 seasons

Every Patriots player who has run for at least 100 yards and averaged more than 10 yards per carry in a game

Larry Garron averaged 11.6 yards per carry in the 55–21 rout of the Buffalo Bills at BU Field on 10-22-61

Larry Garron averaged 10.8 yards per carry in the 26–16 win over the Oakland Raiders at BU Field on 10-26-62

J.D. Garrett averaged 10.1 yards per carry in the 39–10 rout of the Denver Broncos at Bears Stadium on 10-04-64

Sam Cunningham averaged 11.4 yards per carry in the 30–28 loss to the Buffalo Bills at Rich Stadium on 10-20-74

Steve Grogan averaged 14.7 yards per carry in the 41–7 rout of the New York Jets at Schaefer Stadium on 10-18-76

Robert Weathers averaged 16.7 yards per carry in the 29–23 overtime loss to the Baltimore Colts at Sullivan Stadium on 09-04-83

Laurence Maroney averaged 11.1 yards per carry in the 28–7 rout of the Miami Dolphins at Gillette Stadium on 12-23-07

The progression of the most rushing attempts by a Patriots player in a regular season game

8 carries by Jim Crawford in the 13–10 loss to the Denver Broncos at BU Field on 09-09-60

9 carries by Alan Miller in the 28–24 victory over the New York Titans at the Polo Grounds on 09-17-60

9 carries by Dick Christy in the 13–0 loss to the Buffalo Bills at BU Field on 09-23-60

19 carries by Jim Crawford in the 35–0 shutout of the Los Angeles Chargers at Los Angeles Coliseum on 10-08-60

24 carries by Jim Nance in the 24–10 victory over the Denver Broncos at Bears Stadium on 09-18-66

25 carries by Jim Nance in the 35–17 victory over the San Diego Chargers at Fenway Park on 10-23-66

38 carries by Jim Nance in the 24–21 victory over the Oakland Raiders at Fenway Park on 10-30-66

40 carries by Curtis Martin in the 27–24 overtime win vs the New York Jets at Foxboro Stadium on 09-14-97

The progression of the most rushing attempts by a Patriots Quarterback in a regular season game

2 carries by Tom Greene in the 28–24 victory over the New York Titans at the Polo Grounds on 09-17-60

3 carries by Tom Greene in the 13–0 loss to the Buffalo Bills at BU Field on 09-23-60

3 carries by Babe Parilli in the 21–20 loss to the New York Titans at BU Field on 09-09-61

3 carries by Tom Yewcic in the 45–17 rout of the Denver Broncos at BU Field on 09-16-61

4 carries by Babe Parilli in the 18–17 victory over the Dallas Texans at the Cotton Bowl on 10-29-61

6 carries by Babe Parilli in the 27–15 loss to the Houston Oilers at Jeppesen Stadium on 11-12-61

9 carries by Tom Yewcic in the 24–17 victory over the New York Titans at BU Field on 11-30-62

9 carries by Tom Yewcic in the 20-14 victory over the San Diego Chargers at Balboa Stadium on 12-09-62

The progression of the most rushing attempts by a Patriots Wide Receiver in a regular season game

2 carries by Darryl Stingley in the 48–17 rout of the Oakland Raiders at Schaefer Stadium on 10-03-76

2 carries by Irving Fryar in the 17–14 victory over the Buffalo Bills at Rich Stadium on 09-22-85

2 carries by Irving Fryar in the 31–7 loss to the Cincinnati Bengals at Sullivan Stadium on 12-07-86

3 carries by Irving Fryar in the 42–20 victory over the New York Jets at Sullivan Stadium on 12-13-87

3 carries by Irving Fryar in the 36–6 loss to the Minnesota Vikings at the Metrodome on 09-11-88

The progression of the most rushing attempts by a Patriots player in a regular season

101 carries by Alan Miller in 1960

139 carries by Jim Crawford in 1962

179 carries by Larry Garron in 1963

183 carries by Larry Garron in 1964

299 carries by Jim Nance in 1966

300 carries by Leonard Russell in 1993

368 carries by Curtis Martin in 1995

The progression of the most rushing attempts by a Patriots Quarterback in a regular season

11 carries by Butch Songin in 1960

38 carries by Babe Parilli in 1961

50 carries by Babe Parilli in 1965

60 carries by Steve Grogan in 1976

61 carries by Steve Grogan in 1977

81 carries by Steve Grogan in 1978

The progression of the most rushing attempts by a Patriots Wide Receiver in a regular season

3 carries by Jim Colclough in 1961

3 carries by Reggie Rucker in 1972

6 carries by Darryl Stingley in 1973

6 carries by Darryl Stingley in 1975

8 carries by Darryl Stingley in 1976

9 carries by Irving Fryar in 1987

11 carries by Troy Brown in 2001

The progression of the most rushing attempts by a Patriots Tight End in a regular season

1 carry by Bob Windsor in 1972

2 carries by Bob Adams in 1973

2 carries by Russ Francis in 1976

The progression of the most rushing attempts by a Patriots Kicker in a regular season

4 two-point conversion attempts (three were successful) by Gino Cappelletti in 1960

Two-point conversions

The only Patriots player who has run for a two-point conversion while the opposing team was on the sideline

Adam Vinatieri ran for a two-point conversion in the 25–21 victory over the Buffalo Bills at Foxboro Stadium on 11-29-98 (The Bills defense had left the field)

Every Patriots Quarterback who has run for a two-point conversion in a regular season game

1961 regular season

Babe Parilli ran for a two-point conversion in the 18–17 victory over the Dallas Texans at the Cotton Bowl on 10-29-61

1969 regular season

Kim Hammond ran for a two-point conversion in the 28–18 loss to the Chargers at Jack Murphy Stadium on 12-07-69

Every Patriots Running Back who has run for a two-point conversion in a regular season game

1995 regular season

Dave Meggett ran for a two-point conversion in the 17–14 victory over the Cleveland Browns at Foxboro Stadium on 09-03-95

2000 regular season

Kevin Faulk ran for a two-point conversion in the 19–11 loss to the Cleveland Browns at Browns Stadium on 11-12-00

2002 regular season

Antowain Smith ran for a two-point conversion in the 41–38 overtime win vs the Kansas City Chiefs at Gillette Stadium on 09-22-02

2004 championship season
Corey Dillon ran for a two-point conversion in the 24–3 rout of the Baltimore Ravens at Gillette Stadium on 11-28-04

2007 undefeated regular season
Laurence Maroney ran for a two-point conversion in the 38–35 win over the New York Giants at Giants Stadium on 12-29-07

Every Patriots Wide Receiver who has run for a TD in a regular season game

1974 regular season
Darryl Stingley sprinted 23 yards for a TD in the 42–3 rout of the Baltimore Colts at Schaefer Stadium on 10-06-74

1977 regular season
Darryl Stingley galloped 34 yards for a TD in the 21–17 win over the Kansas City Chiefs at Schaefer Stadium on 09-18-77 (it was his 26th birthday)

1985 regular season
Irving Fryar dashed eight yards for a TD in the 20–13 win over the Seattle Seahawks at the Kingdome on 11-17-85

2001 championship season
David Patten dashed 29 yards for a TD on the Patriots' first play in the 38–17 rout of the Colts at the RCA Dome on 10-21-01

Every Patriots Quarterback who has run for two TDs in a regular season game

1962 regular season
Tom Yewcic had TD runs of 27 yards and four yards in the 24–17 win over the New York Titans at BU Field on 11-30-62

1963 regular season
Babe Parilli had TD runs of two yards and one yard in the 45–3 rout of the Houston Oilers at Fenway Park on 11-01-63

1964 regular season
Babe Parilli had TD runs of one yard and five yards in the 25–24 win over the Houston Oilers at Fenway Park on 11-06-64

1967 regular season
Don Trull had TD runs of one yard and two yards in the 29–24 loss to the New York Jets at Fenway Park on 11-19-67

1973 regular season
Jim Plunkett had TD runs of one yard and three yards in the 30–14 win over the San Diego Chargers at Schaefer Stadium on 12-02-73

1976 regular season
Steve Grogan had TD runs of two yards and 10 yards in the 48–17 rout of the Oakland Raiders at Schaefer Stadium on 10-03-76

Steve Grogan had TD runs of two yards and three yards in the 21–14 win over the Baltimore Colts at Memorial Stadium on 11-14-76

Steve Grogan ran for a 11-yard TD and a 10-yard TD in the 27–6 victory over the Saints at Schaefer Stadium on 12-05-76

1984 regular season
Tony Eason had TD runs of 13 yards and 25 yards in the 20–14 win over the Cincinnati Bengals at Sullivan Stadium on 10-14-84

2007 regular season
Tom Brady had TD runs of three yards and two yards in the 52–7 rout of the Washington Redskins at Gillette Stadium on 10-28-07

Every Patriots player who has run for three TDs in a regular season game

1974 regular season
Sam Cunningham ran for three TDs in the 30–28 loss to the Buffalo Bills at Rich Stadium on 10-20-74

1983 regular season
Tony Collins ran for three TDs in the 23–13 victory over the New York Jets at Sullivan Stadium on 09-18-83

Mosi Tatupu rumbled for three TDs in the 21–7 victory over the Los Angeles Rams at the Los Angeles Coliseum on 12-11-83

1996 regular season
Curtis Martin ran for three TDs in the 42–23 victory over the Miami Dolphins at Foxboro Stadium on 11-03-96

The progression of the most rushing TDs by a Patriots Running Back in a regular season

4 rushing TDs by Dick Christy in 1960

5 rushing TDs by Billy Lott in 1961

5 rushing TDs by Harry Crump in 1963

5 rushing TDs by Jim Nance in 1965

Robert Edwards

11 rushing TDs by Jim Nance in 1966

11 rushing TDs by Horace Ivory in 1978

14 rushing TDs by Curtis Martin in 1995

14 rushing TDs by Curtis Martin in 1996

The progression of the most rushing TDs by a Patriots Quarterback in a regular season

2 rushing TDs by Butch Songin in 1960

5 rushing TDs by Babe Parilli in 1961

5 rushing TDs by Babe Parilli in 1963

5 rushing TDs by Jim Plunkett in 1973

12 rushing TDs by Steve Grogan in 1976 (NFL record for QBs)

The progression of the most career regular season rushing TDs by a Patriots Running Back

4 career rushing TDs by Dick Christy in the 1960 season

8 career rushing TDs by Billy Lott during the 1961–63 seasons

9 career rushing TDs by Ron Burton during the 1960–65 seasons

15 career rushing TDs by Babe Parilli during the 1961–67 seasons

45 career rushing TDs by Jim Nance during the 1965–71 seasons

The progression of the most career regular season rushing TD by a Patriots Quarterback

2 career rushing TDs by Butch Songin in the 1960 season

15 career rushing TDs by Babe Parilli during the 1961–67 seasons

35 career rushing TD by Steve Grogan during the 1975–90 seasons

The only Patriots Receiver who has rushed for two TDs during his career with the Patriots

Darryl Stingley ran for a TD during the 1974 regular season and ran for a TD during the 1977 regular season

The progression of the longest run by a Patriots player in a regular season game

5-yard run by Jim Crawford in the 13–10 loss to the Denver Broncos at BU Field on 09-09-60

15-yard run by Jim Crawford in the 13–10 loss to the Denver Broncos at BU Field on 09-09-60

15-yard run by Alan Miller in the 28–24 victory over the New York Titans at the Polo Grounds on 09-17-60

48-yard run by Dick Christy in the 13–0 loss to the Buffalo Bills at BU Field on 09-23-60

77-yard run by Ron Burton in the 31–24 loss to the Denver Broncos at Bears Stadium on 10-23-60

85-yard run for a TD by Larry Garron in the 52–21 rout of the Buffalo Bills at BU Field on 10-22-61

The progression of the longest run by a Patriots Quarterback in a regular season game

2-yard run by Butch Songin in the 13–10 loss to the Denver Broncos at BU Field on 09-09-60

21-yard run by Tom Greene in the 13–0 loss to the Buffalo Bills at BU Field on 09-23-60

24-yard run by Babe Parilli in the 35–21 victory over the Oakland Raiders at Candlestick Park on 12-09-61

32-yard run for a TD by Babe Parilli in the 34–21 victory over the Houston Oilers at BU Field on 09-16-62

46-yard run by Tom Yewcic in the 14–10 loss to the Denver Broncos at Bears Stadium on 09-29-63

The progression of the longest run by a Patriots Wide Receiver in a regular season game

10-yard run by Jim Colclough in the 23–21 victory over the Buffalo Bills at War Memorial Stadium on 09-23-61

16-yard run by Jim Colclough in the 18–17 victory over the Dallas Texans at the Cotton Bowl on 10-29-61

18-yard run by Eric Crabtree in the 38–33 victory over the Buffalo Bills at Schaefer Stadium on 11-14-71

18-yard run by Darryl Stingley in the 33–24 victory over the Green Bay Packers at Schaefer Stadium on 11-18-73

19-yard run by Darryl Stingley in the 32–0 shutout of the Houston Oilers at the Houston Astrodome on 11-25-73

23-yard run for a TD by Darryl Stingley in the 42–3 romp over the Baltimore Colts at Schaefer Stadium on 10-06-74

27-yard run by Darryl Stingley in the 48–17 rout of the Oakland Raiders at Schaefer Stadium on 10-03-76

34-yard run for a TD by Darryl Stingley in the 21–17 victory over the Kansas City Chiefs at Schaefer Stadium on 09-18-77

35-yard run by Troy Brown in the 21–16 loss to the Tampa Bay Buccaneers at Foxboro Stadium on 09-03-00

35-yard run by Terry Glenn in the 30–24 victory over the Kansas City Chiefs at Foxboro Stadium on 12-04-00

The progression of the longest run by a Patriots Tight End in a regular season game

3-yard run by Bob Adams in the 30–14 victory over the San Diego Chargers at Schaefer Stadium on 12-02-73

4-yard run by Bob Adams in the 18–13 loss to the Baltimore Colts at Memorial Stadium on 12-16-73

4-yard run by Russ Francis in the 27–13 loss to the Baltimore Colts at Schaefer Stadium on 09-12-76

8-yard run by Russ Francis in the 41–7 rout of the New York Jets at Schaefer Stadium on 10-18-76

11-yard run by Benjamin Watson in the 34–17 victory over the Cleveland Browns at Gillette Stadium on 10-07-07

The longest run by a Patriots Punter in a regular season game

Tom Yewcic ran for a 20-yard gain on fourth-and-4 in the 26–16 victory over the Oakland Raiders at BU Field on 10-26-62

Did you know that?

Jim Plunkett, who was in the process of being sacked, handed the ball to offensive tackle Tom Neville, who was subsequently tackled for an eight-yard loss, in the 23–3 loss to the Baltimore Colts at Schaefer Stadium on 10-03-71

The career-longest run by every Patriots Kicker in a regular season game

1960 regular season

Gino Cappelletti ran for a two-point conversion in the 27–14 loss to the Oakland Raiders at Kezar Stadium 10-16-60

Gino Cappelletti ran for a two-point conversion in the 42–14 rout of the Dallas Texans at BU Field on 11-18-60

Gino Cappelletti ran for a two-point conversion in the 37–21 loss to the Houston Oilers at Jeppesen Stadium on 12-18-60

1975 regular season

John Smith lost three yards attempting to run with the ball in the 24–16 win over the San Francisco 49ers at Schaefer Stadium on 10-26-75

1985 regular season

Tony Franklin lost five yards attempting to run with the ball in the 20–13 win over the Seahawks at the Kingdome on 11-17-85

1998 regular season

Adam Vinatieri ran for a two-point conversion in the 25–21 victory over the Buffalo Bills at Foxboro Stadium on 11-29-98

The only Patriots Quarterback who has run for a first down on a fake punt play in a regular season game

Damon Huard, on a fake punt, ran four yards on fourth-and-1 in the 33–30 win over the Bears at Memorial Stadium on 11-10-02

The only Patriots Field Goal Holder who has run for a first down on a fake field-goal attempt in a regular season game

Scott Zolak ran for eight yards on fourth-and-2 in the 31–17 loss to the New Orleans Saints at Foxboro Stadium on 12-03-95

Every Patriots Kicker who has attempted to run with a lateral after a poor field goal snap in a regular season game

1960 regular season

Gino Cappelletti lost six yards after receiving a lateral from Ross O'Hanley in the 27–14 loss to Oakland on 10-16-60

1985 regular season

Tony Franklin lost five yards after receiving a lateral from Tony Eason in the 20–13 victory over Seattle on 11-17-85

The only Patriots player who has advanced a lateral on a fourth down play in a regular season game

1989 regular season

Reggie Dupard advanced a lateral from Doug Flutie seven yards on fourth-and-1 in the 31–10 loss to Buffalo on 10-01-89

Fourth Down Runs for a TD

Every Patriots Running Back who has run for a TD on a fourth-down play in a regular season game

1961 regular season

Ron Burton ran for a one-yard TD on fourth-and-goal in the 31–31 tie with the Houston Oilers at BU Field 10-13-61

1964 regular season

J.D. Garrett dashed 42 yards for a TD on fourth-and-1 in the 39–10 rout of the Denver Broncos at Bears Stadium on 10-04-64

1965 regular season

Ron Burton ran for a one-yard TD on fourth-and-goal in the 30–21 loss to the Raiders at Frank Youell Field on 10-24-65

1969 regular season

Carl Garrett ran for a one-yard TD on fourth-and-goal in the 23–16 loss to the Buffalo Bills at War Memorial Stadium on 10-11-69

1971 regular season

Jim Nance dove for a one-yard TD on fourth-and-goal in the 27–20 loss to the Buffalo Bills at War Memorial Stadium on 11-28-71

1974 regular season

Mack Herron ran two yards for a TD on fourth-and-goal in the 29–28 loss to the Buffalo Bills at Schaefer Stadium on 11-03-74

1975 regular season

Andy Johnson dashed 20 yards for a TD on fourth-and-1 in the 34–14 loss to the Buffalo Bills at Schaefer Stadium on 12-14-75

1977 regular season

Ike Forte ran one yard for a TD on fourth-and-goal in the 14–10 win over the Miami Dolphins at Schaefer Stadium on 12-11-77

1979 regular season

Horace Ivory ran for a one-yard TD on fourth-and-goal in the 28–13 win over the Miami Dolphins at Schaefer Stadium on 10-21-79

Don Calhoun scored on a one-yard TD on fourth-and-goal in the 50–21 rout of the Baltimore Colts at Schaefer Stadium on 11-18-79

1980 regular season

Chuck Foreman dove for a one-yard TD on fourth-and-goal in the 37–21 win over the Baltimore Colts at Memorial Stadium on 10-19-80

Mosi Tatupu ran four yards for a TD on fourth-and-1 in the 38–27 victory over the Saints at the Superdome on 12-21-80

1981 regular season

Mosi Tatupu ran for a two-yard TD on fourth-and-1 in the 28–24 loss to the New York Jets at Shea Stadium on 10-11-81

Sam Cunningham dove for a one-yard TD on fourth-and-goal in the 27–17 loss to the Raiders at the Coliseum on 11-01-81

1985 regular season

Robert Weathers bolted 42 yards for a TD on fourth-and-1 in the 34–23 victory over the Bengals at Sullivan Stadium on 12-22-85

1988 regular season

Robert Perryman scored on a one-yard TD on fourth-and-goal in the 24–21 loss to the Colts at the Hoosier Dome on 11-27-88

1991 regular season

Jon Vaughn dashed three yards for a TD on fourth-and-1 in the 28–21 loss to the New York Jets at Foxboro Stadium on 11-17-91

1993 regular season

Leonard Russell ran for a one-yard TD on fourth-and-goal in the 28–14 loss to the Houston Oilers at Foxboro Stadium on 10-17-93

Leonard Russell ran three yards for a TD on fourth-and-1 in the 38–0 shutout of the Indianapolis Colts at Foxboro Stadium on 12-26-93

1994 regular season

Marion Butts dove for a one-yard TD on fourth-and-goal in the 28–13 win over the Indianapolis Colts at Foxboro Stadium on 12-11-94

1995 regular season

Curtis Martin bulled two yards for a TD on fourth-and-1 in the 20–7 win over the New York Jets at the Meadowlands on 11-05-95

Curtis Martin ran for a three-yard TD on fourth-and-1 in the 34–17 win over the Miami Dolphins at Joe Robbie Stadium on 11-12-95

1998 regular season

Robert Edwards dove for a one-yard TD on fourth-and-goal in the 24–14 loss to the New York Jets at Foxboro Stadium on 10-19-98

2000 regular season

J.R. Redmond dove for a one-yard TD on fourth-and-goal in the 16–13 overtime loss to the Buffalo Bills at Foxboro Stadium on 11-05-00

Kevin Faulk ran for a one-yard TD on fourth-and-goal in the 30–24 win over the Kansas City Chiefs at Foxboro Stadium on 12-04-00

2007 undefeated regular season

Sammy Morris ran for a three-yard TD on fourth-and 1 in the 38–14 rout of the San Diego Chargers at Gillette Stadium on 09-16-07

Sammy Morris ran for a seven-yard TD on fourth-and-1 in the 34–13 win over the Bengals at Paul Brown Stadium on 10-01-07

Kyle Eckel ran for a one-yard TD on fourth-and-goal with 19 seconds left in the 48–27 win over Dallas at Texas Stadium on 10-14-07

2008 regular season

Kevin Faulk took a direct snap for a two-yard TD on fourth-and-1 in the 30–21 win over the 49ers at Candlestick Park on 10-05-08

Ben Jarvus Green-Ellis ran for a one-yard TD on fourth-and-1 with 40 seconds left in the 48–28 rout of Miami at Dolphin Stadium on 11-23-08

Sammy Morris scored a one-yard TD on fourth-and-goal with 2:44 left in the 24–21 win over Seattle at Qwest Field on 12-07-08

Every Patriots Quarterback who has run for a TD on a fourth-down play in a regular season game

1972 regular season

Brian Dowling ran for a one-yard TD on fourth-and-goal in the 38–14 loss to the Buffalo Bills at War Memorial Stadium on 10-08-72

Jim Plunkett swept right for a two-yard TD on fourth-and-goal in the 24–17 loss to the Baltimore Colts at Schaefer Stadium on 11-06-72

1981 regular season

Matt Cavanaugh dashed eight yards for a TD on fourth-and-1 in the 33–17 win over the Kansas City Chiefs at Schaefer Stadium on 10-04-81

2000 regular season

Drew Bledsoe dove for a one-yard TD on fourth-and-goal in the 30–23 loss to the Colts at the RCA Dome on 10-22-00

Long runs for a TD in the fourth quarter

Every Patriots RB who has run for at least 50 yards for a TD in the fourth quarter of a regular season game

1961 regular season

Larry Garron ran 85 yards for a TD in the fourth quarter of the 52–21 rout of the Buffalo Bills at BU Field on 10-22-61

1962 regular season

Claude King dashed 71 yards for a TD in the fourth quarter of the 41–16 rout of the Denver Broncos at BU Field on 09-21-62

1969 regular season

Carl Garrett ran 80 yards for a TD in the fourth quarter of the 17–16 loss to the Dolphins at BC Alumni Stadium on 11-09-69

1971 regular season

Jim Nance rumbled 50 yards for a TD in the fourth quarter of the 20–0 shutout of the New York Jets at Schaefer Stadium on 10-10-71

1975 regular season

Andy Johnson dashed 66 yards for a TD in the fourth quarter of the 24–16 win over the 49ers at Schaefer Stadium on 10-19-75

1985 regular season

Craig James ran 65 yards for a TD in the fourth quarter of the 26–20 win over the Green Bay Packers at Sullivan Stadium on 09-08-85

Game-Winning Runs for a TD

Every Patriots Quarterback who has run for the game-winning TD in a regular season game

1973 regular season

Jim Plunkett ran for a game-winning five-yard TD with 1:56 left to defeat the Chicago Bears 13–10 at Soldier Field on 10-21-73

1976 regular season

Steve Grogan ran for a three-yard TD for the final points scored in the 21–14 win over Baltimore at Memorial Stadium on 11-14-76

1978 regular season

Steve Grogan ran for a four-yard TD with 31 seconds left to defeat the San Diego Chargers 28–23 at Schaefer Stadium on 10-01-78

1985 regular season

Steve Grogan ran for a three-yard TD with 3:23 left to defeat the New York Jets 20–13 at Sullivan Stadium on 10-20-85

Steve Grogan ran over the right side for a one-yard TD with 3:03 left to defeat the Dolphins 17–13 at Sullivan Stadium on 11-03-85

1988 regular season

Doug Flutie ran a naked bootleg for a 13-yard TD with 23 seconds left to defeat the Colts 21–17 at Sullivan Stadium on 10-02-88

1991 regular season

Hugh Millen ran for a two-yard TD with under two minutes left to defeat the Buffalo Bills 16–13 at Foxboro Stadium on 11-24-91

Every Patriots Running Back who has run for the game-winning TD in a regular season game

1962 regular season

Jim Crawford ran for a one-yard TD for the final points scored in the 24–20 win over San Diego at BU Field on 10-19-62

1972 regular season

Carl Garrett ran for a 12-yard TD with 7:09 left to defeat the Atlanta Falcons 21–20 at Schaefer Stadium on 09-24-72

1978 regular season

Sam Cunningham dove for a one-yard TD with 16 seconds left to defeat the Raiders 21–14 at Oakland Coliseum on 09-24-78

Sam Cunningham ran three yards for a TD with 6:56 left to defeat the Bengals 10–3 at Riverfront Stadium on 10-15-78

1983 regular season

Tony Collins ran three yards for the only TD in the 7–0 shutout of the New Orleans Saints at Sullivan Stadium on 12-04-83

1984 regular season

Tony Collins ran for a two-yard TD on the second play of the fourth quarter to defeat the Browns 17–16 at Cleveland Municipal Stadium on 10-07-84

1989 regular season

Reggie Dupard scored on a four-yard TD run with 1:55 left to defeat the Jets 27–24 at the Meadowlands on 09-10-89

John Stephens ran for a 10-yard TD with 25 seconds left to defeat the Indianapolis Colts 22–16 at Sullivan Stadium on 12-03-89

1993 regular season

Leonard Russell ran for a four-yard TD with 2:02 left to defeat the Cleveland Browns 20–17 at Cleveland Stadium on 12-19-93

1995 regular season

Curtis Martin ran for a one-yard TD with 19 seconds left to beat the Cleveland Browns 17–14 at Foxboro Stadium on 09-03-95

2008 regular season

Sammy Morris scored on a one-yard run with 2:44 left to defeat the Seattle Seahawks 24–21 at Qwest Field on 12-07-08

Every regular season game that the Patriots had a 100-yard rusher, a 100-yard receiver, and a 300-yard passer

1975 regular season

Sam Cunningham ran for 100 yards, Russ Francis had 125 yards receiving, and Steve Grogan threw for 365 yards in the New England Patriots' 45–31 loss to the Buffalo Bills at Rich Stadium on 11-23-75

1981 regular season

Tony Collins ran for 103 yards, Don Hasselbeck had 112 yards receiving, and Steve Grogan threw for 306 yards in the New England Patriots' 24–22 loss to the Washington Redskins at RFK Stadium on 10-25-81

1984 regular season

Craig James ran for 120 yards, Stanley Morgan had 122 yards receiving, and Tony Eason threw for 313 yards in the New England Patriots' 26–19 loss to the Denver Broncos at Mile High Stadium on 11-04-84

1995 regular season

Curtis Martin ran for 102 yards, Ben Coates had 106 yards receiving, and Drew Bledsoe threw for 302 yards in the New England Patriots' 17–14 victory over the Cleveland Browns at Foxboro Stadium on 09-03-95

1997 regular season

Curtis Martin ran for 104 yards, Shawn Jefferson had 108 yards receiving, and Drew Bledsoe threw for 313 yards in the New England Patriots' 23–18 loss to the Minnesota Vikings at the Metrodome on 11-02-97

2007 undefeated regular season

Laurence Maroney ran for 103 yards, Randy Moss had 115 yards receiving, and Tom Brady threw for 311 yards in the New England Patriots' 38–7 rout of the Buffalo Bills at Gillette Stadium on 09-23-07

The 10 Greatest Patriots Running Backs

Curtis Martin—averaged a career team-best 84 yards rushing per regular season game

Jim Nance—holds the team record of five regular season games with a run of at least 50 yards

Corey Dillon—scored a rushing TD 37 times in just 43 regular season games played for the Patriots

Sam Cunningham—the longest run from scrimmage by a Patriots player on the first play of the game

Tony Collins—the only Patriots RB to run for over 200 yards and have three rushing TDs in the same game

Kevin Faulk—the only Patriots RB with more than 3,000 career yards rushing and 3,000 career yards receiving

Larry Garron—the only Patriots RB to lead the league in average yards per carry in consecutive seasons

Craig James—ran for at least one TD as the Patriots won every regular season game (11–11)

John Stephens—was the NFL Rookie of the Year and was an AFC Pro Bowl running back in 1988

Carl Garrett—the only Patriots RB to lead the AFL and the NFL with the best yards per carry in a specific season (1969)

The 10 greatest running Quarterbacks of the Patriots

Steve Grogan—set the NFL record with 12 TDs in a season and set team record with four game-winning TDs by a QB

Babe Parilli—tied for the team lead with the most rushing TDs for three consecutive seasons

Doug Flutie

Jim Plunkett—mostly ran for his life but did average 6.4 yards per carry in 1972 and led the team with five TDs in 1973

Doug Flutie—averaged 7.2 yards per carry in 1987 and ran for a game-winning TD on 10-02-88

Tom Brady—ran for the Patriots' only TD in the 16–13 overtime playoff game win on 01-19-02

Tony Eason—the only Patriots QB to have two TD runs of at least 25 yards in a regular season

Hugh Millen—ran for a game-winning TD on 11-24-91 and had two 26-yard runs in the 1992 season

Tom Yewcic—the longest run by a Patriots QB in a regular season game

Matt Cassel—the only NFL QB to throw for more than 400 yards and run for more than 60 yards in a game

Drew Bledsoe—ran for a nine-yard gain but was hit by Mo Lewis and suffered a severe injury on 09-23-01

The Patriots player with the best offensive performance in regular season games played against the:

Arizona Cardinals (The Patriots have won all three games against the Arizona Cardinals since 1996)

Passing: Drew Bledsoe threw for 276 yards and four TDs in the 31–0 shutout of the Arizona Cardinals on 09-15-96

Rushing: Corey Dillon ran for 158 yards in the 23–12 victory over the Arizona Cardinals on 09-19-04

Receiving: David Givens had 120 yards receiving in the 23–12 win over the Arizona Cardinals on 09-19-04

Atlanta Falcons (The Patriots have only won four of the 10 games against the Atlanta Falcons during the 1972–2008 seasons)

Passing: Tom Brady threw for 350 yards and three TDs in the 31–28 win over Atlanta on 10-09-05

Rushing: Antowain Smith ran for 117 yards in the 24–10 win over the Atlanta Falcons on 11-04-01

Receiving: Vincent Brisby had 161 yards receiving in the 30–17 loss to the Atlanta Falcons on 10-01-95

Baltimore Colts (The Patriots' record was 12–15 vs the Baltimore Colts during the 1970–83 seasons)

Passing: Steve Grogan threw for 317 yards and two TDs in the 31–26 loss to the Baltimore Colts on 10-28-79

Rushing: Don Calhoun ran for 141 yards in the 21–14 victory over the Baltimore Colts on 11-14-76

Receiving: Stanley Morgan had 170 yards receiving and one TD in the 35–14 rout of the Baltimore Colts on 11-26-78

Baltimore Ravens (The Patriots have won all four of their games against the Baltimore Ravens since 1996)

Passing: Drew Bledsoe threw for 310 yards and four TDs in the 46–38 victory over the Ravens on 10-06-96

Rushing: Corey Dillon had 123 yards rushing and one TD in the 24–3 rout of the Baltimore Ravens on 11-28-04

Receiving: Terry Glenn and Shawn Jefferson had 88 yards receiving in the 46–38 win over the Ravens on 10-06-96

Buffalo Bills (The Patriots' regular season record is 56–40–1 vs the Buffalo Bills during the 1960–2008 seasons)

Passing: Drew Bledsoe threw for 380 yards and three TDs in the 38–35 loss to the Buffalo Bills on 09-11-94

Rushing: Jim Nance ran for 185 yards and one TD in the 23–0 shutout of the Buffalo Bills on 09-24-67

Receiving: Stanley Morgan had 158 yards receiving and two TDs in the 26–6 rout of the Bills on 11-04-79

Carolina Panthers (The Patriots have lost two of the three regular season games played against the Carolina Panthers since 1995)

Passing: Tom Brady threw for 270 yards and one TD in the 27–17 loss to the Carolina Panthers on 09-18-05

Rushing: Curtis Martin ran for 85 yards and two TDs in the 20–17 overtime loss to the Panthers on 10-29-95

Receiving: Troy Brown had 87 yards receiving in the 27–17 loss to the Carolina Panthers on 09-18-05

Chicago Bears (The Patriots regular season record vs the Chicago Bears is 7–3 during the 1973–2008 seasons)

Passing: Tom Brady threw for 328 yards and three TDs in the 33–30 victory over the Chicago Bears on 11-10-02

Rushing: John Stephens ran for 124 yards in the 30–7 rout of the Chicago Bears on 10-30-88

Receiving: Stanley Morgan had 130 yards receiving in the 26–13 loss to the Chicago Bears on 12-05-82

Cincinnati Bengals (The Patriots' record vs the Cincinnati Bengals is 13–8 during the 1968–2008 seasons)

Passing: Drew Bledsoe threw for 365 yards and one TD in the 31–28 victory over the Cincinnati Bengals on 09-18-94

Rushing: Craig James ran for 142 yards and one TD in the playoff-clinching 34–23 win over the Bengals on 12-22-85

Receiving: Michael Timpson had 150 yards receiving and one TD in the 29–7 loss to the Cincinnati Bengals on 12-22-91

Cleveland Browns (The Patriots' regular season record vs the Cleveland Browns is 9–11 during the 1971–2008 seasons)

Passing: Drew Bledsoe threw for 393 yards and one TD in the 19–7 victory over Cleveland on 10-03-99

Rushing: Corey Dillon ran for 100 yards in the 42–15 rout of the Cleveland Browns on 12-05-04

Receiving: Terry Glenn had 214 yards receiving in the 19–7 win over the Cleveland Browns on 10-03-99

Dallas Cowboys (The Patriots have only won three of the 10 regular season games played against the Dallas Cowboys since 1971)

Passing: Tom Brady threw for 388 yards and five TDs in the 48–27 rout of the Dallas Cowboys on 10-14-07

Rushing: Craig James ran for 112 yards in the 20–17 loss to the Dallas Cowboys on 11-22-84

Receiving: Donte Stallworth had 136 yards receiving and one TD in the 48–27 rout of the Cowboys on 10-14-07

Dallas Texans (The Boston Patriots won three of the six games played against the Dallas Texans during the 1960–62 seasons)

Passing: Babe Parilli threw for 253 yards and one TD in the 27–7 loss to the Dallas Texans on 10-12-62

Rushing: Ron Burton ran for 63 yards in the 18–17 victory over the Dallas Texans on 10-29-61

Receiving: Tony Romeo had 84 yards receiving and one TD in the 42–28 loss to Dallas on 09-08-62, and Jim Colclough had 84 yards receiving in the 27–7 loss to the Dallas Texans on 10-12-62

Denver Broncos (The Patriots' regular season record vs the Denver Broncos is 16–24 through the 2008 season)

Passing: Tom Brady threw for 350 yards and three TDs in the 30–26 comeback win over the Broncos on 11-03-03

Rushing: Don Calhoun ran for 177 yards in the 38–14 rout of the Denver Broncos on 11-28-76

Receiving: Jim Colclough had 123 yards receiving in victories over the Broncos on 09-16-61 and 11-11-62

Detroit Lions (The Patriots record vs the Detroit Lions is 5–4 over the 1971–2008 regular seasons)

Passing: Tom Brady had 305 yards passing in the 28–21 victory over the Detroit Lions on 12-03-06

Rushing: Craig James ran for 115 yards in the 23–6 victory over the Detroit Lions on 12-08-85

Receiving: Reche Caldwell had 112 yards receiving in the 28–21 win over the Detroit Lions on 11-28-02

Green Bay Packers (The Patriots regular season record vs the Green Bay Packers is 4–4 since the 1973 season)

Passing: Jim Plunkett threw for 348 yards and two TDs in the 33–24 win over the Green Bay Packers on 11-18-73

Rushing: Craig James ran for 99 yards and one TD in the 26–20 victory over the Green Bay Packers on 09-08-85

Receiving: Terry Glenn had 163 yards receiving in the 28–10 loss to the Green Bay Packers on 10-27-97

Houston Oilers (The Patriots' regular season record was 16–15–1 vs the Houston Oilers during the 1960–93 seasons)

Passing: Steve Grogan threw for 374 yards and three TDs in the 38–34 loss to the Houston Oilers on 11-10-80

Rushing: Tony Collins ran for 161 yards in the 29–21 victory over the Houston Oilers on 11-28-82

Receiving: Art Graham had 167 yards receiving in the dramatic last second 25–24 win over Houston on 11-06-64

Houston Texans (The Patriots have won both games against the Houston Texans since 2003)

Passing: Tom Brady threw for 368 yards and two TDs in the 23–20 comeback win in overtime vs the Texans on 11-23-03

Rushing: Kevin Faulk ran for 80 yards in the 23–20 overtime win vs the Houston Texans on 11-23-03

Receiving: Kevin Faulk had 108 yards receiving in the 23–20 overtime win vs the Houston Texans on 11-23-03

Indianapolis Colts (The Patriots' regular season record vs the Indianapolis Colts is 30–11 since 1994)

Passing: Drew Bledsoe threw for 379 yards and one TD in the 20–15 loss to the Indianapolis Colts on 12-12-99

Rushing: Curtis Martin ran for 141 yards and one TD in the 27–13 win over the Indianapolis Colts on 11-24-96

Receiving: Terry Glenn had 148 yards receiving in the 20–15 loss to the Indianapolis Colts on 12-12-99

Jacksonville Jaguars (The Patriots have won all four of their regular season games against the Jaguars since 1996)

Passing: Drew Bledsoe threw for 255 yards and one TD in the 28–25 overtime win over the Jaguars on 09-22-96

Rushing; Curtis Martin ran for 95 yards and one TD in the 28–25 overtime win vs the Jacksonville Jaguars on 09-22-96

Receiving: Terry Glenn had 89 yards receiving in the 28–25 overtime win vs the Jacksonville Jaguars on 09-22-96

Kansas City Chiefs (The Patriots record is 8–13–3 vs the Kansas City Chiefs during the 1963–2008 seasons)

Passing: Tom Brady threw for 410 yards and four TDs in the 41–38 overtime win vs the Kansas City Chiefs on 09-22-02

Rushing: Jim Nance had 107 yards in the 27–27 tie with the Kansas City Chiefs on 11-20-66

Receiving: Troy Brown had 176 yards receiving and one TD in the 41–38 overtime win vs the Chiefs on 09-22-02

Los Angeles Chargers (The Boston Patriots record was 1–1 vs the Los Angeles Chargers during the 1960 AFL Season)

Passing: Butch Songin threw for 182 yards and one TD in the 35–0 shuout of the Los Angeles Chargers on 10-08-60

Rushing: Jim Crawford ran for 93 yards and one TD in the 35–0 victory over the Los Angeles Chargers on 10-08-60

Receiving: Billy Wells had 89 yards receiving in the 35–0 shutout of the Los Angeles Chargers on 10-08-60

Los Angeles Raiders (The Patriots' record was 1–3 vs the Los Angeles Raiders was during the 1982–94 seasons)

Passing: Drew Bledsoe threw for 321 yards and two TDs in the 21–17 loss to the Los Angeles Raiders on 10-09-94

Rushing: Tony Collins ran for 75 yards in the 26–23 comeback win over the Los Angeles Raiders on 11-01-87

Receiving: Stanley Morgan had 146 yards receiving in the last-second 26–23 win over the Los Angeles Raiders on 11-01-87

Los Angeles Rams (The Patriots' record was 3–3 vs the Los Angeles Rams during the 1974–94 seasons)

Passing: Tony Eason threw for 375 yards and two TDs in the 30–28 comeback win over the Rams on 11-16-86

Rushing: Mosi Tatupu ran for 73 yards and three TDs in the 21–7 victory over the Los Angeles Rams on 12-11-83

Receiving: Stanley Morgan had 118 yards receiving in the 30–28 last-second victory over the Los Angeles Rams on 11-16-86

Miami Dolphins (The Patriots' regular season record vs the Miami Dolphins is 36–48 over the 1966–2008 seasons)

Passing: Drew Bledsoe threw for 423 yards and two TDs in the 26–23 win over the Miami Dolphins on 11-23-98

Rushing: Jim Nance ran for 164 yards and two TDs in the 41–32 loss to the Miami Dolphins on 12-17-67

Receiving: Stanley Morgan had 182 yards receiving and one TD in the 30–27 overtime loss to the Dolphins on 11-08-81

Minnesota Vikings (The Patriots' regular season record vs the Minnesota Vikings is 6–4 during the 1970–2008 seasons)

Passing: Drew Bledsoe threw for 426 yards and three TDs in the 26–23 overtime win vs the Vikings on 11-13-94

Rushing: Sam Cunningham ran for 129 yards in the dramatic last-second 17–14 victory over the Vikings on 10-27-74

Receiving: Irving Fryar had 161 yards receiving in the 26–23 overtime win vs the Minnesota Vikings on 10-20-91

New Orleans Saints (The Patriots' record vs the New Orleans Saints is 8–3 during the 1972–2008 seasons)

Passing: Drew Bledsoe threw for 317 yards and one TD in the 30–27 win over the New Orleans Saints on 10-04-98

Rushing: Mosi Tatupu had 128 yards rushing in the 7–0 shutout of the New Orleans Saints on 12-04-83

Receiving: Hart Lee Dykes had 105 yards receiving and one TD on 11-12-89, and Terry Glenn had 105 yards on 10-04-98

New York Giants (The Patriots' regular season record vs the New York Giants is 5–3 during the 1970–2008 seasons)

Passing: Drew Bledsoe threw for 301 yards and two TDs in the 23–22 comeback win over the Giants on 12-21-96

Rushing: Kevin Faulk had 87 yards rushing in the 17–6 victory over the New York Giants on 10-12-03

Receiving: Terry Glenn had 124 yards receiving and one TD in the dramatic 23–22 win over the Giants on 12-21-96

New York Jets (The Patriots' regular season record vs the New York Jets is 43–47 during the 1963–2008 seasons)

Passing: Steve Grogan threw for 401 yards and three TDs in the 31–24 loss to the New York Jets on 10-12-86

Rushing: Tony Collins ran for 212 yards and three TDs in the 23–13 victory over the New York Jets on 09-18-83

Receiving: Irving Fryar had 165 yards receiving and two TDs in the 30–21 loss to the New York Jets on 10-04-92

New York Titans (The Boston Patriots' record vs the New York Titans was 4–2 during the 1960–1962 AFL seasons)

Passing: Babe Parilli threw for 234 yards and three TDs in the 43–14 rout of the New York Titans on 10-06-62

Rushing: Dick Christy ran for 105 yards in the 38–21 win over the New York Titans on 11-11-60

Receiving: Jim Colclough had 142 yards receiving and one TD in the 43–14 win over the Titans on 10-06-62

Oakland Raiders (The Patriots' regular season record vs the Oakland Raiders is 13–11–1 during the 1960–82 and 1995–2008 seasons)

Passing: Babe Parilli threw for 400 yards and four TDs in the 43–43 tie with the Oakland Raiders on 10-16-64

Rushing: Jim Nance ran for 208 yards and two TDs in the 24–21 victory over the Oakland Raiders on 10-30-66

Receiving: Russ Francis had 126 yards receiving and one TD in the 21–14 win over the Oakland Raiders on 09-24-78

Philadelphia Eagles (The Patriots' regular season record vs the Philadelphia Eagles is 4–6 over the 1973–2008 seasons)

Passing: Tom Ramsey threw for 402 yards and three TDs in the 34–31 overtime loss to the Eagles on 11-19-87

Rushing: Craig James had 92 yards rushing in the 27–17 loss to the Philadelphia Eagles on 12-04-84

Receiving: Irving Fryar had 115 yards receiving and one TD in the 48–20 loss to the Philadelphia Eagles on 11-04-90

Phoenix Cardinals (The Patriots' record was 1–2 vs the Phoenix Cardinals over the 1988–94 seasons)

Passing: Scott Secules threw for 214 yards and one TD in the 23–21 win over the Phoenix Cardinals on 10-10-93

Rushing: Leonard Russell ran for 116 yards in the 23–21 victory over the Phoenix Cardinals on 10-10-93

Receiving: Leonard Russell had 82 yards receiving in the 23–21 win over the Phoenix Cardinals on 10-10-93

Pittsburgh Steelers (The Patriots' regular season record vs the Pittsburgh Steelers is 7–13 during the 1972–2008 seasons)

Passing: Drew Bledsoe threw for 336 yards and three TDs in the 41–27 loss to the Pittsburgh Steelers on 12-16-95

Rushing: Curtis Martin ran for 120 yards in the 41–27 loss to the Pittsburgh Steelers on 12-16-95

Receiving: Terry Glenn had 193 yards receiving and one TD in the 23–9 win over the Pittsburgh Steelers on 12-06-98

Sam Cunningham

San Diego Chargers (The Patriots' regular season record vs the San Diego Chargers is 18–13–2 during the 1961–2008 seasons)

Passing: Tom Brady threw for 364 yards and two TDs in the 29–26 overtime win vs the San Diego Chargers on 10-14-01

Rushing: Sam Cunningham ran for 141 yards in the 24–20 win over the San Diego Chargers on 10-16-77

Receiving: Deion Branch had 128 yards receiving in the 21–14 loss to the San Diego Chargers on 09-29-02

San Francisco 49ers (The Patriots record vs the San Francisco 49ers is 4–7 during the 1971–2008 seasons)

Passing: Steve Grogan threw for 274 yards in the 21–17 loss to the San Francisco 49ers on 11-30-80

Rushing: Corey Dillon ran for 116 yards and one TD in the 21–7 victory over the San Francisco 49ers on 01-02-05

Receiving: Stanley Morgan had 142 yards receiving in the 21–17 loss to the San Francisco 49ers on 11-30-80

Seattle Seahawks (The Patriots' record vs the Seattle Seahawks is 8–7 during the 1977–2008 regular seasons)

Passing: Tony Eason threw for 414 yards and three TDs in the 38–31 loss to the Seattle Seahawks on 09-21-86

Rushing: John Stephens ran for 121 yards in the 13–7 victory over the Seattle Seahawks on 12-04-88

Receiving: Stanley Morgan had 161 yards receiving and three TDs in the 38–31 loss to the Seattle Seahawks on 09-21-86

St. Louis Cardinals (The Patriots' record vs the St. Louis Cardinals was 1–4 during the 1970–84 seasons)

Passing: Matt Cavanaugh threw for 245 yards in the 27–20 loss to the St. Louis Cardinals on 11-29-81

Rushing: Don Calhoun ran for 143 yards in the 16–6 victory over the St. Louis Cardinals on 09-10-78

Receiving: Stanley Morgan had 94 yards receiving in the 27–20 loss to the St. Louis Cardinals on 11-29-81

St. Louis Rams (The Patriots' regular season record vs the St. Louis Rams is 1–2 over the 1998–2008 seasons)

Passing: Tom Brady threw for 234 yards in the 40–22 victory over the St. Louis Rams on 11-07-04

Rushing: Robert Edwards ran for 196 yards in the 32–18 loss to the St. Louis Rams on 12-13-98

Receiving: David Givens had 100 yards receiving in the 40–22 victory over the St. Louis Rams on 11-07-04

Tampa Bay Buccaneers (The Patriots' record vs the Tampa Bay Buccaneers is 4–2 over the 1976–2008 regular seasons)

Passing: Tom Brady had 258 yards passing and three TDs in the 28–0 shutout of the Tampa Bay Buccaneers on 12-17-05

Rushing: Andy Johnson ran for 127 yards and two TDs in the 31–14 win over the Tampa Bay Buccaneers on 12-12-76

Receiving: David Givens had 137 yards receiving and one TD in the 28–0 shutout of the Buccaneers on 12-17-05

Tennessee Oilers (The Patriots won their only regular season game played against the Tennessee Oilers)

Passing: Drew Bledsoe threw for 250 yards and one TD in the 27–16 victory over the Tennessee Oilers on 09-20-98

Rushing: Robert Edwards ran for 92 yards and one TD in the 27–16 win over the Tennessee Oilers on 09-20-98

Receiving: Terry Glenn had 102 yards receiving and one TD in the 27–16 victory over the Tennessee Oilers on 09-20-98

Tennessee Titans (The Patriots have won two of the three regular season games played against the Tennessee Titans since 2002)

Passing: Tom Brady threw for 225 yards and one TD in the 40–23 win over the Tennessee Titans on 12-31-06

Rushing: Antowain Smith ran for 80 yards and one TD in the 38–30 victory over the Tennessee Titans on 10-05-03

Receiving: Reche Caldwell had 134 yards receiving and one TD in the 40–23 win over the Tennessee Titans on 12-31-06

Washington Redskins (The Patriots' record vs the Washington Redskins is 2–6 during the 1972–2008 regular seasons)

Passing: Tom Brady threw for 306 yards and three TDs in the 52–7 rout of the Washington Redskins on 10-28-07

Rushing: Curtis Martin ran for 164 yards and two TDs in the 27–22 loss to the Washington Redskins on 10-13-96

Receiving: Harold Jackson had 124 yards receiving and one TD in the 16–14 loss to the Redskins on 09-03-78

The Playoffs

The progression of the most yards rushing by a Patriots Running Back in a playoff game

44 yards rushing by Larry Garron in the 26–8 victory over the Buffalo Bills at War Memorial Stadium on 12-28-63

68 yards rushing by Sam Cunningham in the 24–21 loss to the Oakland Raiders at Oakland Coliseum on 12-18-76

104 yards rushing by Craig James in the 27–20 win over the Los Angeles Raiders at the Los Angeles Coliseum on 01-05-86

105 yards rushing by Craig James in the 31–14 victory over the Miami Dolphins at the Orange Bowl on 01-12-86

166 yards rushing by Curtis Martin in the 28–3 rout of the Pittsburgh Steelers at Foxboro Stadium on 01-05-97

The progression of the most yards rushing by a Patriots Quarterback in a playoff game

14 yards rushing by Tom Yewcic in the 51–10 loss to the San Diego Chargers at Balboa Stadium on 01-05-64

35 yards rushing by Steve Grogan in the 24–21 loss to the Oakland Raiders at the Oakland Coliseum on 12-18-76

The progression of the most yards rushing by a Patriots Wide Receiver in a playoff game

-2 yards rushing by Stanley Morgan in the 28–13 loss to the Miami Dolphins at the Orange Bowl on 01-08-83

3 yards rushing by Irving Fryar in the 27–20 victory over the Los Angeles Raiders at the Los Angeles Coliseum on 01-05-86

22 yards rushing by David Patten in the 20–17 victory over the St. Louis Rams at the Superdome on 02-03-02

37 yards rushing by Deion Branch in the 41–27 victory over the Pittsburgh Steelers at Heinz Field on 01-23-05

Every Patriots Running Back who has run for at least 100 yards in a playoff game

1985 AFC Divisional playoff game
Craig James ran for 104 yards in the 27–20 victory over the Los Angeles Raiders at the Los Angeles Coliseum on 01-05-86

1985 AFC Championship Game
Craig James ran for 105 yards in the 31–14 victory over the Miami Dolphins at the Orange Bowl on 01-12-86

1996 AFC Divisional playoff game
Curtis Martin ran for 166 yards in the 28–3 rout of the Pittsburgh Steelers at Foxboro Stadium on 01-05-97

2003 AFC Championship Game
Antowain Smith ran for 100 yards in the 24–14 victory over the Indianapolis Colts at Gillette Stadium on 01-18-04

2004 Divisional playoff game
Corey Dillon ran for 144 yards in the 20–3 rout of the Indianapolis Colts at Gillette Stadium on 01-16-05

2007 Divisional playoff game

Laurence Maroney ran for 122 yards in the 31–20 win over the Jacksonville Jaguars at Gillette Stadium on 01-12-08

The only Patriots Running Back who has run for at least 100 yards in consecutive playoff games

1985 Playoffs

Craig James ran for 104 yards in the 27–20 victory over the Los Angeles Raiders at the Los Angeles Coliseum on 01-05-86

Craig James ran for 105 yards in the 31–14 victory over the Miami Dolphins at the Orange Bowl on 01-12-86

The progression of the most career yards rushing by a Patriots player in the playoffs

59 career yards rushing by Larry Garron in two playoff games

110 career yards rushing by Sam Cunningham in two playoff games

290 career yards rushing by Craig James in five playoff games

456 career yards rushing by Antowain Smith in six playoff games

508 career rushing yards by Corey Dillon in eight playoff games

Antowain Smith

The progression of the most rushing attempts by a Patriots player in a playoff game

19 carries by Larry Garron in the 26–8 victory over the Buffalo Bills at War Memorial Stadium on 12-28-63

20 carries by Sam Cunningham in the 24–21 loss to the Oakland Raiders at the Oakland Coliseum on 12-18-76

23 carries by Craig James in the 26–14 victory over the New York Jets at the Meadowlands Stadium on 12-28-85

23 carries by Craig James in the 27–20 victory over the Los Angeles Raiders at Los Angeles Coliseum on 01-05-86

26 carries by Antowain Smith in the 32–29 victory over the Carolina Panthers at Reliant Stadium on 02-01-04

The progression of the most rushing attempts by a Patriots Quarterback in a playoff game

1 carry by Babe Parilli in the 26–8 victory over the Buffalo Bills at War Memorial Stadium on 12-28-63

1 carry by Babe Parilli in the 51–10 loss to the San Diego Chargers at Balboa Stadium on 01-05-64

1 carry by Tom Yewcic in the 51–10 loss to the San Diego Chargers at Balboa Stadium on 01-05-64

7 carries by Steve Grogan in the 24–21 loss to the Oakland Raiders at the Oakland Coliseum on 12-18-76

The progression of the most rushing attempts by a Patriots Wide Receiver in a playoff game

1 carry by Stanley Morgan in the 28–13 loss to the Miami Dolphins at the Orange Bowl on 01-08-83

1 carry by Irving Fryar in the 27–20 victory over the Los Angeles Raiders at the Oakland Coliseum on 01-05-86

1 carry by Irving Fryar in the 22–17 loss to the Denver Broncos at Mile High Stadium on 01-04-87

1 carry by Troy Brown in the 16–13 overtime win vs the Oakland Raiders at Foxboro Stadium on 01-19-02

1 carry by David Patten in the 20–17 victory over the St. Louis Rams at the Louisiana Superdome on 02-03-02

1 carry by Bethel Johnson in the 24–14 victory over the Indianapolis Colts at Gillette Stadium on 01-18-04

1 carry by Troy Brown in the 32–29 victory over the Carolina Panthers at Reliant Stadium on 02-01-04

1 carry by Deion Branch in the 20–3 rout of the Indianapolis Colts at Gillette Stadium on 01-16-05

2 carries by Deion Branch in the 41–27 victory over the Pittsburgh Steelers at Heinz Field on 01-23-05

The progression of the most career rushing attempts by a Patriots player in the playoffs

22 career rushing attempts by Larry Garron in two playoff games

30 career rushing attempts by Sam Cunningham in two playoff games

82 career rushing attempts by Craig James in five playoff games

117 career rushing attempts by Antowain Smith in six playoff games

120 career rushing attempts by Corey Dillon in eight playoff games

The most consecutive rushing attempts without a fumble by a Patriots Running Back in a playoff game

19 carries without a fumble by Larry Garron in the 26–8 rout of the Buffalo Bills at War Memorial Stadium on 12-28-63

23 carries without a fumble by Craig James in the 27–20 win over the Los Angeles Raiders at the Los Angeles Coliseum on 01-05-86

26 carries without a fumble by Antowain Smith in the 32–29 win over the Panthers at Reliant Stadium on 02-01-04

The progression of the most consecutive carries without a fumble by a Patriots player in the playoffs

22 consecutive rushing attempts in the playoffs without a fumble by Larry Garron

56 consecutive rushing attempts in the playoffs without a fumble by Craig James

Corey Dillon

117 consecutive rushing attempts in the playoffs without a fumble by Antowain Smith

The progression of the longest run by a Patriots player in a playoff game

15-yard run by Ron Burton in the 26–8 victory over the Buffalo Bills at War Memorial Stadium on 12-28-63

16-yard run by Tom Neumann in the 26–8 victory over the Buffalo Bills at War Memorial Stadium on 12-28-63

22-yard run by Sam Cunningham in the 24–21 loss to the Oakland Raiders at the Oakland Coliseum on 12-18-76

22-yard run by Mosi Tatupu in the 27–20 win over the Los Angeles Raiders at the Los Angeles Coliseum on 01-05-86

45-yard run by Robert Weathers in the 31–14 victory over the Miami Dolphins at the Orange Bowl on 01-12-86

78-yard dash for a TD by Curtis Martin in the 28–3 rout of the Pittsburgh Steelers at Foxboro Stadium on 01-05-97

The progression of the longest run by a Patriots Quarterback in a playoff game

14-yard run by Tom Yewcic in the 51–10 loss to the San Diego Chargers at Balboa Stadium on 01-05-64

16-yard run by Steve Grogan in the 31–14 loss to the Houston Oilers at Schaefer Stadium on 12-31-78

The progression of the longest run by a Patriots Wide Receiver in a playoff game

-2-yard run by Stanley Morgan in the 28–13 loss to the Miami Dolphins at the Orange Bowl on 01-08-83

3-yard run by Irving Fryar in the 27–20 victory over the Los Angeles Raiders at the Los Angeles Coliseum on 01-05-86

22-yard run by David Patten in the 20–17 victory over the St. Louis Rams at the Louisiana Superdome on 02-03-02

23-yard run for a TD by Deion Branch in the 41–27 win over the Pittsburgh Steelers at Heinz Field on 01-23-05

The only Patriots Running Back who has run for a two-point conversion in a playoff game
Super Bowl XXXVIII
Kevin Faulk ran for a two-point conversion in the 32–29 win over the Carolina Panthers at Reliant Stadium on 02-01-04

2006 AFC Divisional playoff game

Kevin Faulk ran for a two-point conversion in the 24–21 win over the Chargers at Qualcomm Stadium on 01-14-07

The only Patriots Quarterback who has run for a TD in a playoff game

2001 AFC Divisional playoff game

Tom Brady ran for a six-yard TD in the fourth quarter of the 16–13 overtime win vs the Oakland Raiders at Foxboro Stadium on 01-19-02

2004 AFC Divisional playoff game

Tom Brady scored on a one-yard run in the fourth quarter of the 20–3 rout of the Indianapolis Colts at Gillette Stadium on 01-16-05

The only Patriots Wide Receiver who has run for a TD in a playoff game

2004 AFC Championship Game

Deion Branch dashed for a 23-yard TD in the fourth quarter of the 41–27 win over the Pittsburgh Steelers at Heniz Field on 01-23-05

The only Patriots player who has run for three TDs in a playoff game

1996 AFC Divisional playoff game

Curtis Martin rumbled for three TDs in the 28–3 rout of the Pittsburgh Steelers at Foxboro Stadium on 01-05-97

The progression of the most career rushing TDs by a Patriots player in the playoffs

1 career rushing TD by Larry Garron in two playoff games

1 career rushing TD by Andy Johnson in two playoff games

1 career rushing TD by Jess Phillips in one playoff game

1 career rushing TD by Craig James in five playoff games

1 career rushing TD by Mosi Tatupu in seven playoff games

5 career rushing TDs by Curtis Martin in three playoff games

Passing

Forty-two Patriots quarterbacks have thrown for 155,980 yards during the last 49 regular seasons. Twelve running backs, three punters, three receivers and two kickers have completed a pass for the Patriots during this time span as well. Tom Yewcic is the only Patriots quarterback who has thrown an halfback option pass. Although Yewcic was primarily the team's punter, he was so versatile that he played in five games as a quarterback, five games as a running back, and was a flanker in one game for the Boston Patriots during the 1961 season.

The Boston Patriots had five different players attempt a pass during the 1960 season. Butch Songin was the Patriots starting quarterback as he attempted 84 percent of the passes and tossed 22 of the 25 TD passes during the 14-game season. When Babe Parilli arrived in 1961, Songin and Parilli alternated at quarterback. Songin quarterbacked on one play, and Parilli brought the next play from the bench to the huddle. Their passing statistics in 1961 were very similar. Songin was 98-of-212 for 1,429 yards and 14 TDs, and Parilli was 104-of-198 for 1,314 yards and 13 TDs. They both led the league with the fewest interceptions with nine during this season.

From 1962–67, Babe Parilli was the starting quarterback for the Boston Patriots. Babe led the Patriots to their first championship playoff game in 1963, and he led the AFL with 3,465 yards passing and 31 TDs during the 1964 season. Parilli was an AFL All-Star quarterback in 1963, 1964, and 1966, and was the AFL Comeback Player of the Year in 1966. Babe Parilli then went on to be the backup quarterback to Joe Namath of the New York Jets during the 1968–69 seasons.

From 1968–70, the Patriots had five different quarterbacks complete a pass during the regular season. Tom Sherman and Mike Taliaferro shared the quarterback position during the 1968 season. In 1969, Mike Taliaferro was named to the AFL All-Star team. Mike Taliaferro and Joe Kapp shared the quarterbacking duties for the Boston Patriots during the 1970 season.

With the first overall draft pick in 1971, the New England Patriots selected Heisman Trophy winner Jim Plunkett. He was the first NFL quarterback to play in every offensive play in his rookie season and he was the AFC Rookie of the Year in 1971. He passed for 9,932 yards and 62 TDs during the 1971–75 seasons.

Steve Grogan was the Patriots quarterback in 1976—perhaps the third-best team the Patriots have ever assembled. Grogan led the Patriots to an 11–3 regular season record. This team lost to the Oakland Raiders 24–21 in the 1976 AFC Divisional playoff game at the Oakland Coliseum. Earlier that year, the Patriots destroyed Oakland 48–17 at Schaefer Stadium.

From 1976 to 1990, Steve Grogan completed 1,879 passes for 26,886 yards and 182 TDs. During those 15 seasons other Patriots players who attempted a pass in a regular season game include Tom Owen, Andy Johnson, Marlin Briscoe, Don Westbrook, Matt Cavanaugh, Eddie Hare, Harold Jackson, Tony Collins, Tom Flick, Tony Eason, Mike Kerrigan, Craig James, Tom Ramsey, Bob Bleier, Doug Flutie, Cedric Jones, Mosi Tatupu, Marc Wilson, Jeff Feagles, Tommy Hodson, and John Stephens.

The New England Patriots made the playoffs in 1985 after Steve Grogan led them on a six-game winning streak. Tony Eason, who replaced Steve Grogan after he was injured in the game against the New York Jets on 11-24-85, led the Patriots to three straight playoff game victories. Unfortunately, the Patriots met the dominant Chicago Bears in the Super Bowl that year.

The Patriots quarterbacks who led the team in passing yards during the 1986–91 seasons were Tony Eason, Steve Grogan, Doug Flutie, Steve Grogan, Marc Wilson, and Hugh Millen, respectively. In 1992, the Patriots had four quarterbacks throw a TD pass, Hugh Millen, Scott Zolak, Tommy Hodson, and Jeff Carlson.

Babe Parilli

With the first overall draft pick in 1993, the New England Patriots selected quarterback Drew Bledsoe. He led the NFL with 400 completions for 4,555 yards in the 1994 season. Bledsoe was an AFC Pro Bowl quarterback in 1994, 1996, and 1997, and led the Patriots to seven playoff games and one Super Bowl.

Tom Brady was chosen with the 199th pick by the New England Patriots in the 2000 College Draft. Brady has never lost an overtime game, and he holds the NFL record for the most overtime wins without a loss(7). Brady set the Patriots records for the best completion percentage in a single regular season game and during the regular season. He did not throw an interception in his first 162 passing attempts, and he did not throw an interception in 241 home game passing attempts during the 2003 regular season. Tom Brady was an AFC Pro Bowl quarterback in 2001, 2004, 2005, and 2007, and has led the Patriots to three Super Bowl championships. Matt Cassel led the Patriots with 3,693 yards passing in 2008.

The 10 Greatest Patriots Quarterbacks

Tom Brady—led his team to three Super Bowl World Championships and was the NFL MVP in 2007

Drew Bledsoe—the only Patriots player to be named the NFL Player of the Week for consecutive games

Babe Parilli—the only Patriots quarterback to complete a TD pass of at least 63 yards in six consecutive seasons

Tony Eason—led the Patriots to their biggest comeback victory when they were down 23–0 to Seattle on 09-16-84

Steve Grogan—holds the team record of the most yards per passing attempt in a regular season

Jim Plunkett— trading him to the 49ers brought Pete Brock, Tim Fox, Raymond Clayborn, and Horace Ivory to the Patriots

Butch Songin—holds the team record for the most games started as the Patriots quarterback after the age of 36

Matt Cassel—the only Patriots quarterback to throw for at least 400 yards in consecutive regular season games

Hugh Millen—the only Patriots quarterback to complete 100% of at least 10 passing attempts in the first half of a game

Doug Flutie—threw an 80-yard TD pass on the first play of a game and ran for a game-winning 13-yard TD in 1988

The yearly list of the Patriots player with the most yards passing, most TD passes, and longest pass completion in the year

	Most yards passing	Most TD passes	Longest pass completion
1960	Butch Songin	Butch Songin	Butch Songin
1961	Butch Songin	Butch Songin and Babe Parilli	Butch Songin
1962	Babe Parilli	Babe Parilli	Tom Yewcic
1963	Babe Parilli	Babe Parilli	Babe Parilli
1964	Babe Parilli	Babe Parilli	Babe Parilli
1965	Babe Parilli	Babe Parilli	Babe Parilli
1966	Babe Parilli	Babe Parilli	Babe Parilli
1967	Babe Parilli	Babe Parilli	Babe Parilli
1968	Tom Sherman	Tom Sherman	Tom Sherman
1969	Mike Taliaferro	Mike Taliaferro	Mike Taliaferro
1970	Joe Kapp	Mike Taliaferro	Joe Kapp
1971	Jim Plunkett	Jim Plunkett	Jim Plunkett
1972	Jim Plunkett	Jim Plunkett	Jim Plunkett
1973	Jim Plunkett	Jim Plunkett	Jim Plunkett
1974	Jim Plunkett	Jim Plunkett	Jim Plunkett
1975	Steve Grogan	Steve Grogan	Jim Plunkett
1976	Steve Grogan	Steve Grogan	Steve Grogan
1977	Steve Grogan	Steve Grogan	Steve Grogan
1978	Steve Grogan	Steve Grogan	Steve Grogan
1979	Steve Grogan	Steve Grogan	Steve Grogan
1980	Steve Grogan	Steve Grogan	Steve Grogan
1981	Steve Grogan	Steve Grogan	Steve Grogan
1982	Steve Grogan	Steve Grogan	Matt Cavanaugh
1983	Steve Grogan	Steve Grogan	Steve Grogan
1984	Tony Eason	Tony Eason	Tony Eason
1985	Tony Eason	Tony Eason	Tony Eason
1986	Tony Eason	Tony Eason	Steve Grogan
1987	Steve Grogan	Steve Grogan	Tony Eason
1988	Doug Flutie	Doug Flutie	Doug Flutie
1989	Steve Grogan	Steve Grogan	Marc Wilson
1990	Marc Wilson	Marc Wilson	Tommy Hodson
1991	Hugh Millen	Hugh Millen	Hugh Millen
1992	Hugh Millen	Hugh Millen	Scott Zolak
1993	Drew Bledsoe	Drew Bledsoe	Scott Secules
1994	Drew Bledsoe	Drew Bledsoe	Drew Bledsoe
1995	Drew Bledsoe	Drew Bledsoe	Scott Zolak
1996	Drew Bledsoe	Drew Bledsoe	Drew Bledsoe
1997	Drew Bledsoe	Drew Bledsoe	Drew Bledsoe
1998	Drew Bledsoe	Drew Bledsoe	Drew Bledsoe
1999	Drew Bledsoe	Drew Bledsoe	Drew Bledsoe
2000	Drew Bledsoe	Drew Bledsoe	Drew Bledsoe
2001	Tom Brady	Tom Brady	Tom Brady
2002	Tom Brady	Tom Brady	Tom Brady
2003	Tom Brady	Tom Brady	Tom Brady
2004	Tom Brady	Tom Brady	Tom Brady
2005	Tom Brady	Tom Brady	Tom Brady
2006	Tom Brady	Tom Brady	Tom Brady
2007	Tom Brady	Tom Brady	Tom Brady
2008	Matt Cassel	Matt Cassel	Matt Cassel

The progresssion of the most yards passing by a Patriots Quarterback in a regular season game

145 yards passing by Butch Songin in the 13–10 loss to the Denver Broncos at BU Field on 09-09-60

182 yards passing by Butch Songin in the 35–0 shutout of the Los Angeles Chargers at the Los Angeles Coliseum on 09-23-60

223 yards passing by Butch Songin in the 31–24 loss to the Denver Broncos at Bears Stadium on 10-23-60

327 yards passing by Butch Songin in the 37–21 loss to the Houston Oilers at Jeppesen Stadium on 12-18-60

400 yards passing by Babe Parilli in the 43–43 tie with the Oakland Raiders at Fenway Park on 10-16-64

426 yards passing by Drew Bledsoe in the 26–20 overtime win vs the Minnesota Vikings at Foxboro Stadium on 11-13-94

The fewest yards passing by a Patriots Quarterback in a victorious regular season game

1982 regular season

Steve Grogan had just 13 yards passing in the 3–0 victory over the Miami Dolphins at Schaefer Stadium on 12-12-82

Every Patriots Quarterback who has thrown for at least 300 yards in a game only once during his career with the Patriots

1960 regular season

Butch Songin threw for 327 yards in the 37–21 loss to the Houston Oilers at Jeppesen Stadium on 12-18-60

1963 regular season

Tom Yewcic threw for 304 yards in the 31–24 loss to the New York Jets at the Polo Grounds on 10-05-63

1973 regular season

Jim Plunkett threw for 348 yards in the 33–24 victory over the Green Bay Packers at Schaefer Stadium on 11-18-73

1981 regular season

Matt Cavanaugh threw for 325 yards in the 27–21 overtime loss to the Pittsburgh Steelers at Three Rivers Stadium on 09-27-81

1987 regular season

Tom Ramsey threw for 414 yards in the 34–31 overtime loss to the Philadelphia Eagles at Veterans Stadium on 11-29-87

The progression of the most career regular season games that a Patriots Quarterback had at least 300 yards passing

1 game with at least 300 yards passing by Tom Yewcic, who had 304 yards passing in the 31–24 loss to the Jets on 10-05-63

5 games with at least 300 yards passing by Babe Parilli during his career with the Boston Patriots

11 games with at least 300 yards passing by Steve Grogan during his career with the New England Patriots

26 games with at least 300 yards passing by Drew Bledsoe during his career with the New England Patriots

The progression of the most consecutive regular season games that a Patriots Quarterback had at least 300 yards passing

1 game by Tom Yewcic, who had 304 yards passing in the 31–24 loss to the New York Jets on 10-05-63

1 game by Babe Parilli, who had 331 yards passing in the 40–21 victory over the Denver Broncos on 10-18-63

1 game by Babe Parilli, who had 354 yards passing in the 24–24 tie with the Kansas City Chiefs on 11-17-63

1 game by Babe Parilli, who had 400 yards passing in the 43–43 tie with the Oakland Raiders on 10-16-64

1 game by Babe Parilli, who had 333 yards passing in the 34–17 victory over the Houston Oilers on 11-29-64

1 game by Babe Parilli, who had 379 yards passing in the 38–28 loss to the New York Jets on 12-17-66

1 game by Jim Plunkett, who had 348 yards passing in the 33–24 victory over the Green Bay Packers on 11-18-73

1 game by Steve Grogan, who had 365 yards passing in the 45–31 loss to the Buffalo Bills on 11-23-75

1 game by Steve Grogan, who had 315 yards passing in the 56–3 rout of the New York Jets on 09-09-79

2 consecutive games where Steve Grogan had at least 300 yards passing during the 1979 regular season

3 consecutive games where Drew Bledsoe had at least 300 yards passing during the 1994 regular seasons

3 consecutive games where Tom Brady had at least 300 yards passing during the 2007 regular season

The most consecutive regular season games that a Patriots Quarterback had at least 400 yards passing

2 consecutive games where Matt Cassel had at least 400 yards passing in the 2008 season (on 11-13-08 and 11-23-08)

Every Patriots Quarterback who has thrown for more than 400 yards in a victorious regular season regulation game

1996 regular season

Drew Bledsoe threw for 419 yards in the 42–23 victory over the Miami Dolphins at Foxboro Stadium on 11-03-96

1998 regular season

Drew Bledsoe threw for 423 yards in the 26–23 victory over the Miami Dolphins at Foxboro Stadium on 11-23-98

2008 regular season

Matt Cassel threw for 415 yards in the 48–28 rout of the Miami Dolphins at Dolphin Stadium on 11-23-08

Every Patriots Quarterback who has thrown for more than 400 yards in a victorious overtime game

1994 regular season

Drew Bledsoe threw for 426 yards in the 26–20 overtime win vs the Minnesota Vikings at Foxboro Stadium on 11-13-94

2002 regular season

Tom Brady threw for 410 yards in the 41–38 overtime win vs the Kansas City Chiefs at Gillette Stadium on 09-22-02

The Boston Patriots Quarterback who led the AFL with the most yards passing during a specific season

3,465 yards passing by Babe Parilli during the 1964 season

The New England Patriots Quarterbacks who have led the NFL with the most yards passing during the season

1994 regular season

4,555 yards passing by Drew Bledsoe in 1994

2005 regular season

4,110 yards passing by Tom Brady in 2005

2007 undefeated regular season

4,806 yards passing by Tom Brady in 2007

Tom Brady

The progression of the most yards passing by a Patriots Quarterback in a regular season

2,476 yards passing by Butch Songin in 1960 (14 games)

3,465 yards passing by Babe Parilli in 1964 (14 games)

4,555 yards passing by Drew Bledsoe in 1994 (16 games)

4,806 yards passing by Tom Brady in 2007 (16 games)

The progression of the most career regular season yards passing by a Patriots Quarterback

3,905 career yards passing by Butch Songin during the 1960–61 seasons

16,747 career yards passing by Babe Parilli during the 1961–67 seasons

26,886 career yards passing by Steve Grogan during the 1975–90 seasons

29,657 career yards passing by Drew Bledsoe during the 1993–2001 seasons

The progression of the most consecutive passing attempts without an interception in the regular season by a Patriots Quarterback

13 attempts by Butch Songin on 09-09-60

33 attempts by Tom Greene from 09-17-60 to 09-23-60

40 attempts by Butch Songin from 09-23-60 to 10-16-60

105 attempts by Butch Songin from 11-04-60 to 11-18-60

128 attempts by Butch Songin from 12-08-60 to 10-07-61

141 attempts by Tony Eason from 12-18-83 to 10-14-84

178 attempts by Tony Eason from 12-22-85 to 10-26-86

179 attempts by Drew Bledsoe from 10-23-95 to 11-26-95

*Tom Brady did not throw an interception until his 163rd passing attempt for the best start in NFL History

**Tom Brady did not throw an interception in a home game during the 2003 regular season (241 attempts)

The progession of the most passing attempts by a Patriots Quarterback in a regular season game

24 attempts by Butch Songin in the 13–10 loss to the Denver Broncos at BU Field on 09-09-60

30 attempts by Butch Songin in the 28–24 victory over the New York Titans at the Polo Grounds on 09-17-60

35 attempts by Butch Songin in the 42–14 rout of the Dallas Texans at BU Field on 11-18-60

43 attempts by Butch Songin in the 24–10 loss to the Houston Oilers at BU Field on 11-25-60

50 attempts by Babe Parilli in the 30–20 loss to the New York Jets at Fenway Park on 11-14-65

52 attempts by Tony Eason in the 30–28 victory over the Los Angeles Rams at Anaheim Stadium on 11-16-86

53 attempts by Tom Ramsey in the 34–31 overtime loss to the Philadelphia Eagles at Sullivan Stadium on 11-29-87

59 attempts by Steve Grogan in the 28–24 loss to the New Orleans Saints at Sullivan Stadium on 11-12-89

70 attempts by Drew Bledsoe in the 26–20 overtime win vs the Minnesota Vikings at Foxboro Stadium on 11-13-94 (Drew Bledsoe did not throw an interception in the 26–20 overtime win vs the Minnesota Vikings on 11-13-94)

The progression of the most consecutive pass completions (10 or more) by a Patriots Quarterback in a regular season game

10 consecutive completions by Babe Parilli in the 41–10 rout of Miami at Boston College Alumni Stadium on 10-15-67

13 consecutive completions by Steve Grogan in the 23–20 overtime win vs the Colts at the Hooiser Dome on 10-29-89

13 consecutive completions by Hugh Millen in the 41–7 loss to the Buffalo Bills at Foxboro Stadium on 09-27-92

The progression of the most pass completions by a Patriots Quarterback in a regular season game

12 completions by Butch Songin in the 13–10 loss to the Denver Broncos at BU Field on 09-09-60

15 completions by Butch Songin in the 28–24 victory over the New York Titans at the Polo Grounds on 09-17-60

25 completions by Butch Songin in the 42–14 rout of the Dallas Texans at BU Field on 11-18-60

25 completions by Babe Parilli in the 24–24 tie with the Kansas City Chiefs at Fenway Park on 11-17-63

25 completions by Babe Parilli in the 43–43 tie with the Oakland Raiders at Fenway Park on 10-16-64

25 completions by Steve Grogan in the 45–31 loss to the Buffalo Bills at Rich Stadium on 11-23-75

25 completions by Steve Grogan in the 38–34 loss to the Houston Oilers at the Houston Astrodome on 11-10-80

28 completions by Tony Eason in the 28–21 victory over the New York Jets at the Meadowlands on 09-30-84

29 completions by Tony Eason in the 50–17 rout of the Indianapolis Colts at the Hoosier Dome on 11-18-84

36 completions by Tony Eason in the 30–28 victory over the Los Angeles Rams at Anaheim Stadium on 11-16-86

45 completions by Drew Bledsoe in the 26–20 overtime win vs the Minnesota Vikings at Foxboro Stadium on 11-13-94

The progression of the most passing attempts by a Patriots Quarterback in a regular season

392 passing attempts by Butch Songin in 1960

473 passing attempts by Babe Parilli in 1964

691 passing attempts by Drew Bledsoe in 1994

The NFL Quarterback with the most passing attempts during a specific regular season

1994 regular season

691 passing attempts by New England Patriots QB Drew Bledsoe in 1994

1995 regular season

636 passing attempts by New England Patriots QB Drew Bledsoe in 1995

1996 regular season

623 passing attempts by New England Patriots QB Drew Bledsoe in 1996

The progression of the best average passing attempts per game by a Patriots Quarterback in a regular season

28 attempts per game by Butch Songin, who had 392 attempts in 14 games during the 1960 season

34 attempts per game by Babe Parilli, who had 473 attempts in 14 games during the 1964 season

43 attempts per game by Drew Bledsoe, who had 691 attempts in 16 games during the 1994 season

The most passing attempts by a Patriots Running Back in a regular season

11 passing attempts by Dick Christy in 1960

The progression of the most pass completions by a Patriots Running Back in a regular season

6 pass completions by Dick Christy in 1960

7 pass completions by Andy Johnson in 1981

The most passing attempts by a Patriots Wide Receiver in a regular season

2 passing attempts by Don Westbrook in 1979

The progression of the most pass completions by a Patriots Wide Receiver in a regular season

2 pass completions by Don Westbrook in 1979

2 pass completions by Harold Jackson in 1980

The progession of the most pass completions by a Patriots Quarterback in a regular season

187 pass completions by Butch Songin in 1960

228 pass completions by Babe Parilli in 1964

259 pass completions by Tony Eason in 1984

276 pass completions by Tony Eason in 1986

400 pass completions by Drew Bledsoe in 1994

The NFL Quarterback with the most pass completions in a specific regular season

400 pass completions by Drew Bledsoe in 1994

373 pass completions by Drew Bledsoe in 1996

The progression of the best average yards per pass attempt by a Patriots Quarterback in a season (100 or more attempts)

6.32 yards per attempt by Butch Songin in 1960

6.74 yards per attempt by Butch Songin in 1961

7.86 yards per attempt by Babe Parilli in 1962

8.09 yards per attempt by Steve Grogan in 1980

8.43 yards per attempt by Matt Cavanaugh in 1980

8.61 yards per attempt by Steve Grogan in 1981

9.57 yards per attempt by Steve Grogan in 1986

The progression of the highest Quarterback Rating in a regular season (10 or more attempts)

70.9 QB Rating by Butch Songin in 1960

73.0 QB Rating by Butch Songin in 1961

76.5 QB Rating by Babe Parilli in 1961

91.8 QB Rating by Babe Parilli in 1962

95.9 QB Rating by Matt Cavanaugh in 1980

113.8 QB Rating by Steve Grogan in 1986

117.2 QB Rating by Tom Brady in 2007

The NFL Quarterback with the most yards passing per pass attempt during a specific season

8.09 yards per attempt by Steve Grogan in 1980

8.61 yards per attempt by Steve Grogan in 1981

The progression of the best average of completions per game by a Patriots Quarterback in a season

13 completions per game by Butch Songin in 1960

16 completions per game by Babe Parilli in 1964

17 completions per game by Tony Eason in 1986

25 completions per game by Drew Bledsoe in 1994

The progression of the longest pass completion by a Patriots Quarterback in a regular season game

1-yard pass by Butch Songin to Jim Colclough in the 13–10 loss to the Denver Broncos at BU Field on 09-09-60

6-yard pass by Butch Songin to Jim Colclough in the 13–10 loss to the Denver Broncos at BU Field on 09-09-60

13-yard pass by Butch Songin to Oscar Lofton in the 13–10 loss to the Denver Broncos at BU Field on 09-09-60

17-yard pass by Butch Songin to Oscar Lofton in the 13–10 loss to the Denver Broncos at BU Field on 09-09-60

19-yard pass by Butch Songin to Jim Colclough in the 13–10 loss to the Denver Broncos at BU Field on 09-09-60

40-yard pass by Butch Songin to Jim Crawford in the 13–10 loss to the Denver Broncos at BU Field on 09-09-60

78-yard pass by Butch Songin to Billy Wells in the 35–0 shutout of the Los Angeles Chargers at the Los Angeles Coliseum on 10-08-60

78-yard TD pass by Tom Yewcic to Jim Colclough in the 24–17 win over the New York Titans at BU Field on 11-30-62

80-yard TD pass by Babe Parilli to Art Graham in the 34–17 win over the Oilers at Jeppesen Stadium on 11-29-64

87-yard TD pass by Tom Sherman to Jim Whalen in the 48–14 loss to the New York Jets at Shea Stadium on 10-27-68

90-yard TD pass by Tony Eason to Craig James in the 30–7 loss to the Chicago Bears at Sullivan Stadium on 09-15-85

91-yard TD pass by Tom Brady to David Patten in the 38–17 rout of the Colts at the RCA Dome on 10-21-01

The progression of the longest pass completion by a Patriots Running Back in a regular season game

39-yard halfback option pass by Dick Christy to Walter Beach in the 13–10 loss to Buffalo at BU Field on 09-23-60

39-yard halfback option pass by Larry Garron to Ron Burton in the 26–16 win over Oakland at BU Field on 10-26-62

48-yard halfback option pass by Bob Gladieux to Hubie Bryant in the 28–20 win over Houston at Schaefer Stadium on 11-07-71

66-yard halfback option TD pass by Andy Johnson to Stanley Morgan in the 33–17 win over the Chiefs at Schaefer Stadium on 10-04-81

The progression of the longest pass completion by a Patriots Wide Receiver in a regular season game

28-yard pass by Don Westbrook to Russ Francis in the 24–17 victory over the Detroit Lions at Schaefer Stadium on 10-07-79

60-yard TD pass by David Patten to Troy Brown in the 38–17 rout of the Indianapolis Colts at the RCA Dome on 10-21-01

The longest pass completion by a Patriots Kicker in a regular season game

27-yard TD pass from Gino Cappelletti to Larry Garron in the 37–30 loss to the New York Titans at the Polo Grounds on 10-01-61

Every Patriots player who has completed a pass for a two-point conversion in a regular season game

1960 regular season
Gino Cappelletti to Jim Crawford in the 35–0 shutout of the Los Angeles Chargers at the Los Angeles Coliseum on 10-08-60

1962 regular season
Babe Parilli to Jim Crawford in the 24–20 win over the San Diego Chargers at BU Field on 10-19-62

1964 regular season
Babe Parilli to Jim Colclough in the 43–43 tie with the Oakland Raiders at Fenway Park on 10-16-64

Babe Parilli to Gino Cappelletti in the 36–28 victory over the Buffalo Bills at War Memorial Stadium on 11-15-64

Babe Parilli to Jim Colclough in the 24–14 loss to the Buffalo Bills at Fenway Park on 12-20-64

1966 regular season
Babe Parilli to Tony Romeo in the 24–10 victory over the Denver Broncos at Bears Stadium on 09-18-66

Babe Parilli to Bob Cappadona in the 38–28 loss to the New York Jets at Shea Stadium on 12-17-66

1995 regular season
Drew Bledsoe to Curtis Martin in the 35–25 victory over the Buffalo Bills at Rich Stadium on 11-26-95

Drew Bledsoe to Dave Meggett in the 41–27 loss to the Pittsburgh Steelers at Three Rivers Stadium on 12-16-95

1996 regular season
Drew Bledsoe to Curtis Martin in the 31–0 shutout of the Arizona Cardinals at Foxboro Stadium on 09-15-96

Drew Bledsoe to Sam Gash in the 46–38 victory over the Baltimore Ravens at Memorial Stadium on 10-06-96

Drew Bledsoe to Ben Coates in the 46–38 victory over the Baltimore Ravens at Memorial Stadium on 10-06-96

Drew Bledsoe to Keith Byars in the 34–8 loss to the Denver Broncos at Foxboro Stadium on 11-17-96

2002 regular season
Tom Brady to Troy Brown in the 33–30 victory over the Chicago Bears at Memorial Stadium on 11-10-02

Tom Brady to Christian Fauria in the 27–24 overtime win vs the Miami Dolphins at Gillette Stadium on 12-29-02

2008 regular season
Matt Cassel to Jabar Gaffney in the 34–31 overtime loss to the New York Jets at Gillette Stadium on 11-13-08

Matt Cassel to Wes Welker for the final points scored in the 24–21 win over Seattle at Qwest Field on 12-07-08

The combination of Patriots players who have completed a flea-flicker TD pass in a regular season game

1984 regular season
Tony Eason to Mosi Tatupu back to Eason to Stephen Starring for a 42-yard TD in the 17–16 win vs Cleveland on 10-07-84

1985 regular season
Steve Grogan to Mosi Tatupu back to Grogan to Greg Hawthorne for a 28-yard TD in the 17–13 win over Miami on 11-03-85

1989 regular season
Steve Grogan to Mosi Tatupu back to Grogan to Stanley Morgan for a 55-yard TD in the 37–20 loss to the 49ers on 10-22-89

The only time that the Patriots completed a double lateral TD pass in a regular season game

Tom Brady lateraled to Randy Moss, who then lateraled it back to Brady, who threw a 56-yard TD pass to Jabar Gaffney in the 34–13 win over the Pittsburgh Steelers on 12-09-07

The only pass completion by a left-handed Patriots Running Back in a regular season game

Bob Gladieux threw a 48-yard pass to Hubie Bryant in the 28–20 victory over the Oilers at Schaefer Stadium on 11-07-71

Every pass completion by a left-handed Patriots Wide Receiver in a regular season game

1979 regular season
Don Westbrook completed a 28-yard pass to Russ Francis in the 24–17 victory over the Lions at Schaefer Stadium on 10-07-79

Don Westbrook threw a 24-yard pass to Don Hasselbeck in the 27–23 win over the Vikings at Schaefer Stadium on 12-16-79

Every Patriots Wide Receiver who has completed a pass in a regular season game

1979 regular season
Don Westbrook tossed a 28-yard pass to Russ Francis in the 24–17 win over the Detroit Lions at Schaefer Stadium on 10-07-79

Don Westbrook threw a 24-yard pass to Don Hasselbeck in the 27–23 win over the Vikings at Schaefer Stadium on 12-16-79

1980 regular season
Harold Jackson completed a 23-yard pass to Russ Francis in the 34–21 win over the New York Jets at Schaefer Stadium on 11-03-80

Harold Jackson threw a 12-yard pass to Russ Francis in the 16–13 overtime loss to Miami at the Orange Bowl on 12-08-80

2001 championship season
David Patten tossed a 60-yard TD pass to Troy Brown in the 38–17 win over the Colts at the RCA Dome on 10-21-01

The only Patriots Quarterback to complete a pass to a Patriots Linebacker/Running Back in a regular season game

Tom Brady threw a seven-yard pass to Bryan Cox in the 29–26 overtime win vs the San Diego Chargers at Foxboro Stadium on 10-14-01

Every Patriots Quarterback who has completed a TD pass to a Patriots Linebacker/TE in a regular season game

1974 regular season
Jim Plunkett lofted a two-yard TD to John Tanner in the 29–28 loss to the Buffalo Bills at Schaefer Stadium on 11-03-74

2002 regular season
Tom Brady threw a one-yard TD to Mike Vrabel in the 21–14 loss to San Diego at Qualcomm Stadium on 09-29-02

2004 championship season
Tom Brady lofted a two-yard TD to Mike Vrabel in the 40–22 win vs the Rams at the Edward Jones Dome on 11-07-04

Tom Brady tossed a one-yard TD to Mike Vrabel in the 21–7 win over the San Francisco 49ers at Gillette Stadium on 01-20-05

2005 regular season
Tom Brady fired a one-yard TD to Mike Vrabel in the 24–17 win over the New Orleans Saints at Gillette Stadium on 11-20-05

Tom Brady tossed a one-yard TD and a two-yard TD to Mike Vrabel in the 31–21 win over the New York Jets at the Meadowlands on 12-26-05

2007 undefeated regular season
Tom Brady tossed a one-yard TD to Mike Vrabel in the 34–13 win over the Bengals at Paul Brown Stadium on 10-01-07

Tom Brady fired a two-yard TD to Mike Vrabel in the 52–7 rout of the Washington Redskins at Gillette Stadium on 10-28-07

Every Patriots Quarterback who has completed a TD pass to a Patriots Offensive Lineman/TE in a regular season game
1976 regular season
Steve Grogan tossed a six-yard TD pass to Pete Brock in the 38–24 win over the New York Jets at Shea Stadium on 11-21-76

2005 regular season
Tom Brady tossed a one-yard TD pass to Tom Ashworth in the 28–0 shutout of the Tampa Bay Buccaneers at Gillette Stadium on 12-17-05

The only Patriots Punter who has completed a pass for a first down in a regular season game
Lee Johnson hit Eric Bjornson for 18 yards on fourth-and-2 in the 24–16 victory over the Colts at Foxboro Stadium on 10-08-00

Adam Vinatieri to Troy Brown for a touchdown

Every Patriots Kicker who has completed a pass in a regular season game
1961 regular season
Gino Cappelletti tossed a 27-yard TD to Larry Garron in the 37–30 loss to the New York Titans at the Polo Grounds on 10-01-61

2004 championship season
Adam Vinatieri tossed a four-yard TD to Troy Brown in the 40–22 win over the Rams at the Edward Jones Dome 11-07-04

Every Patriots Quarterback who has completed a pass to himself in a regular season game
1983 regular season
Steve Grogan caught his deflected pass for an eight-yard loss on the first play of the 21–7 win vs Buffalo at Sullivan Stadium on 11-06-83

1992 regular season
Tom Hodson caught his deflected pass for a six-yard loss in the 30–17 loss to Miami at Joe Robbie Stadium on 10-18-92

1995 regular season

Drew Bledsoe caught his deflected pass for a nine-yard loss in the 41–27 loss to Pittsburgh at Three Rivers Stadium on 12-16-95

The only Patriots player to attempt every pass for the Patriots during a regular season

Steve Grogan was the only Patriots player to attempt to throw a pass during the 1977 season

Every regular season that only one Patriots player completed at least one pass

1977 regular season

Steve Grogan was the only Patriots player to complete a pass during the 1977 season

1999 regular season

Drew Bledsoe completed 305 passes, and Troy Brown's only passing attempt was unsuccessful in the 1999 season

The Boston Patriots Quarterbacks who have led the AFL with the fewest interceptions during the season

1961 regular season

Babe Parilli threw only nine interceptions (in 198 attempts) during the 1961 season

Butch Songin threw only nine interceptions (in 212 attempts) during the 1961 season

1962 regular season

Babe Parilli threw only eight interceptions (in 252 attempts) during the 1962 season

The NFL Quarterback with the most passing attempts in a game without an interception

Drew Bledsoe threw 70 passes in the 26–20 overtime win vs the Minnesota Vikings at Foxboro Stadium on 11-13-94

The NFL Quarterback who was not intercepted in a home game during an entire regular season

Tom Brady attempted 241 passes without throwing an interception in the eight home games during the 2003 season

The only Boston Patriots Quarterback who was named the AFL Offensive Player of the Week

1966 regular season

Babe Parilli threw three TD passes in the 35–17 win over the San Diego Chargers at Fenway Park on 10-23-66

1967 regular season

Babe Parilli threw five TDs in the 41–10 rout of the Miami Dolphins at Boston College Alumni Stadium on 10-15-67

Every Patriots Quarterback who was named the AFC Offensive Player of the Week

1984 regular season

Tony Eason threw two TDs and ran for a TD in the 38–23 comeback win over the Seahawks at Sullivan Stadium on 09-16-84

1988 regular season

Doug Flutie threw a TD pass and ran for the game-winning TD to defeat the Colts 21–17 at Sullivan Stadium on 10-02-88

1992 regular season

Scott Zolak threw for 261 yards and two TDs in the 37–34 overtime win vs the Colts at the Hoosier Dome on 11-15-92

1994 regular season

Drew Bledsoe threw for 334 yards and two TDs in the 17–16 win vs the Green Bay Packers at Foxboro Stadium on 10-02-94

Drew Bledsoe threw for 426 yards and three TDs in the 26–20 overtime win vs the Vikings at Foxboro Stadium on 11-13-94

1996 regular season

Drew Bledsoe was 25-of-39 for 310 yards and four TDs in the 46–38 win over the Baltimore Ravens at Memorial Stadium on 10-06-96

1998 regular season

Drew Bledsoe threw for 423 yards and two TDs in the 26–23 victory over the Miami Dolphins at Foxboro Stadium on 11-23-98

1999 regular season

Drew Bledsoe threw for 299 yards and four TDs in the 31–28 comeback win over the Indianapolis Colts at Foxboro Stadium on 09-19-99

2000 regular season

Drew Bledsoe threw for 271 yards and four TDs in the 28–19 win over the Denver Broncos at Mile High Stadium on 10-01-00

2001 championship season
Tom Brady completed 33 passes for 364 yards and two TDs in the 29–26 overtime win vs San Diego at Foxboro Stadium on 10-14-01

Tom Brady threw four TD passes in the 34–17 victory over the New Orleans Saints at Foxboro Stadium on 11-25-01

2002 regular season
Tom Brady threw for 294 yards and three TDs in the 30–14 win over the Pittsburgh Steelers at Gillette Stadium on 09-09-02

Tom Brady was 22-of-26 for 265 yards and three TDs in the 38–7 rout of Buffalo at Ralph Wilson Stadium on 11-03-02

2003 championship season
Tom Brady threw for 350 yards and three TDs in the 30–26 comeback win over the Broncos at Invesco Field on 11-03-03

Tom Brady threw four TD passes in the 31–0 shutout of the Buffalo Bills at Gillette Stadium on 12-27-03

2005 regular season
Tom Brady threw for 350 yards and three TDs in the 31–28 win over the Atlanta Falcons at the Georgia Dome on 10-09-05

2007 undefeated regular season
Tom Brady was 23-of-29 for 311 yards and four TDs in the 38–7 rout of the Buffalo Bills at Gillette Stadium on 09-23-07

Tom Brady threw for 388 yards and five TDs in the 48–27 win over the Dallas Cowboys at Texas Stadium on 10-14-07

Tom Brady was 21-of-25 for 354 yards and six TDs in the 49–28 rout of the Dolphins at Dolphin Stadium on 10-21-07

2008 regular season
Matt Cassel threw three TD passes in the 41–7 rout of the Denver Broncos at Gillette Stadium on 10-20-08

Matt Cassel threw for 415 yards and three TDs in the 48–28 rout of the Miami Dolphins at Dolphin Stadium on 11-23-08

The only Patriots player who was named the AFC Offensive Player of the Month
2007 undefeated regular season
Tom Brady was the AFC Offensive Player of the Month in September 2007

Ben Coates

Tom Brady was the AFC Offensive Player of the Month in October 2007

Every New England Patriots Quarterback who was named the NFL Offensive Player of the Week
1971 regular season
Jim Plunkett was 10-of-17 for 170 yards and two TDs in the 21–17 win over the Baltimore Colts at Memorial Stadium on 12-19-71

1973 regular season
Jim Plunkett threw for 348 yards and two TDs and ran for a TD in the 33–24 win over the Packers at Schaefer Stadium on 11-18-73

1996 regular season
Drew Bledsoe was 19-of-29 for 232 yards and four TDs in the 45–7 rout of the Chargers at Jack Murphy Stadium on 12-01-96

1998 regular season
Drew Bledsoe threw a TD pass with a broken finger and 29 seconds left to defeat the Miami Dolphins 26–23 on 11-23-98

Drew Bledsoe fired a one-yard TD pass to Ben Coates with no time left in the 25–21 win over Buffalo at Foxboro Stadium on 11-29-98 (Bledsoe became the first NFL player to win the award in consecutive weeks and his jersey was sent to the Hall of Fame)

2001 championship season

Tom Brady threw four TD passes in the 34–17 victory over the New Orleans Saints at Foxboro Stadium on 11-25-01

2007 undefeated regular season

Tom Brady threw five TDs passes in the 48–27 victory over the Dallas Cowboys at Texas Stadium on 10-14-07

Tom Brady tossed six TDs and had a perfect QB rating of 158.3 in the 49–28 win over the Miami Dolphins at Miami on 10-21-07

The progression of the highest pass completion percentage by a Patriots Quarterback with more than 20 attempts in a game

50% of Butch Songin's passes were completed (12-of-24) in the 13–10 loss to the Broncos at BU Field on 09-09-60

71% of Butch Songin's passes were completed (25-of-35) in the 42–14 rout of the Texans at BU Field on 11-18-60

80% of Babe Parilli's passes were completed (16-of-20) in the 41–10 rout of Miami at BC Stadium on 10-15-67

80% of Tom Brady's passes were completed (16-of-20) in the 38–17 victory over the Colts at the RCA Dome on 10-21-01

84.6% of Tom Brady's passes were completed (22-of-26) in the 38–7 rout of the Bills at Buffalo on 11-03-02

Jim Plunkett

The only Patriots Quarterback who has completed at least 84% of his passes in a regular season game (at least 10 attempts)

2002 regular season

84.6% by Tom Brady, who was 22-of-26 in the 38–7 rout of the Buffalo Bills at Ralph Wilson Stadium on 11-03-02

2007 undefeated regular season

84% by Tom Brady, who was 21-of-25 in the 49–28 rout of the Miami Dolphins at Dolphin Stadium on 10-21-07

The only Patriots Quarterback who completed 100% of his passes in the first half of a regular season game (at least 10 attempts)

100% by Hugh Millen, who was 13-of-13 in the 41–7 loss to the Buffalo Bills at Foxboro Stadium on 09-27-92

Every Patriots Quarterback who has completed at least 90% of his passes in the second half of a regular season game (at least 10 attempts)

1982 regular season

92% by Steve Grogan, who was 12-of-13 in the 30–19 victory over the Buffalo Bills at Schaefer Stadium on 01-02-83

1985 regular season

91% by Tony Eason, who was 10-of-11 in the 38–31 win over the Indianapolis Colts at the Hoosier Dome on 12-01-85

2002 regular season

92% by Tom Brady, who was 12-of-13 in the 38–7 rout of the Buffalo Bills at Ralph Wilson Stadium on 11-03-02

The most attempts, completions, and yards passing by a Patriots Quarterback in the second half of a regular season game

Drew Bledsoe was 37-of-53 for 354 yards in the second half of the 26–20 overtime win vs Minnesota at Foxboro Stadium on 11-13-94

The only Patriots Quarterback who completed 100% of his passes in the overtime period of a regular season game (at least five attempts)

100% by Drew Bledsoe, who was 6-of-6 in the 26–20 overtime win vs the Minnesota Vikings at Foxboro Stadium on 11-13-94

Every Patriots player who has completed a fourth-down pass for a TD in a regular season game

1960 regular season
Butch Songin tossed a six-yard TD to Jim Colclough on fourth-and-goal in the 28–24 win vs the Titans at New York on 09-17-60

1961 regular season
Butch Songin tossed a one-yard TD to Tom Stephens on fourth-and-goal in the 23–21 win over the Bills at Buffalo on 09-23-61

Gino Cappelletti to Larry Garron for a 27-yard TD on fourth-and-13 in the 37–30 loss to the Titans at New York on 10-01-61

1964 regular season
Babe Parilli tossed a 15-yard TD to Tony Romeo on fourth-and-11 in the 24–14 loss to Buffalo at Fenway Park on 12-20-64

1965 regular season
Babe Parilli tossed a two-yard TD to Tony Romeo on fourth-and-goal in the 27–23 win vs the New York Jets at Shea Stadium on 11-28-65

1976 regular season
Steve Grogan to Russ Francis for a 38-yard TD on fourth-and-2 in the 30–27 win over the Steelers at Three Rivers Stadium on 09-26-76

1983 regular season
Steve Grogan to Stanley Morgan for a 32-yard TD on fourth-and-2 in the 33–13 loss to the 49ers at Sullivan Stadium on 10-02-83

1984 regular season
Tony Eason tossed a five-yard TD to Derrick Ramsey on fourth-and-5 in the 44–24 loss to Miami at Sullivan Stadium on 10-21-84

1985 regular season
Steve Grogan to Greg Hawthorne for a 28-yard TD on fourth-and-1 in the 17–13 win over Miami at Sullivan Stadium on 11-03-85

1986 regular season
Craig James tossed a 10-yard TD to Tony Collins on fourth-and-1 in the 20–6 win over the Jets at Shea Stadium on 09-11-86

Tony Eason tossed a 15-yard TD to Stanley Morgan on fourth-and-4 in the 29–24 loss to the 49ers at Sullivan Stadium on 12-14-86

1987 regular season
Mosi Tatupu tossed a 15-yard TD to Tony Collins on fourth-and-1 in the 26–23 win vs the Raiders at Sullivan Stadium on 11-01-87

Tom Ramsey to Stanley Morgan for a five-yard TD on fourth-and-goal in the 23–17 overtime loss to Dallas at Sullivan Stadium on 11-15-87

1988 regular season
Doug Flutie tossed a four-yard TD pass to Lin Dawson on fourth-and-1 in the 30–7 rout of the Bears at Sullivan Stadium on 10-30-88

1989 regular season
Steve Grogan to Hart Lee Dykes for a 13-yard TD on fourth-and-4 in the 28–24 loss to the Saints at Sullivan Stadium on 11-12-89

1990 regular season
Marc Wilson tossed a four-yard TD to George Adams on fourth-and-goal, in the 17–10 loss to Miami at Miami on 10-18-90

1992 regular season
Hugh Millen tossed a five-yard TD to Marv Cook on fourth-and-2 in the 30–21 loss to the Jets at the Meadowlands on 10-04-92

1993 regular season
Drew Bledsoe to Ben Coates for a 54-yard TD on fourth-and-1 in the 38–14 loss to the Bills at Rich Stadium on 09-05-93

Drew Bledsoe to Kevin Turner for a six-yard TD on fourth-and-1 in the 20–17 win vs the Browns at Cleveland Municipal Stadium on 12-19-93

1994 regular season
Drew Bledsoe to Ray Crittenden for a three-yard TD on fourth-and-goal in the 24–17 loss to the New York Jets at the Meadowlands on 10-16-94

1996 regular season

Drew Bledsoe tossed a 29-yard TD to Ben Coates on fourth-and-1 in the 24–10 loss to Miami at Pro Player Stadium on 09-01-96

Drew Bledsoe to Ben Coates for a 13-yard TD on fourth-and-7 in the 23–22 win vs the Giants at the Meadowlands on 12-21-96

2000 regular season

Drew Bledsoe to Jermaine Wiggins for a one-yard TD on fourth-and-l in the 30–24 win over Kansas City at Foxboro Stadium on 12-04-00

Drew Bledsoe to Troy Brown for a seven-yard TD on fourth-and-goal in the 24–17 loss to Chicago at Soldier Field on 12-10-00

2003 championship season

Tom Brady to Daniel Graham for a one-yard TD on fourth-and-1 to force overtime in the 23–20 overtime win at Houston on 11-23-03

2004 championship season

Adam Vinatieri to Troy Brown for a four-yard TD on fourth-and-goal in the 40–22 win vs the Rams at St. Louis on 11-07-04

2006 regular season

Tom Brady tossed a two-yard TD to Daniel Graham on fourth-and-1 in the 35–0 shutout of Green Bay at Lambeau Field on 11-19-06

2007 undefeated regular season

Tom Brady tossed a three-yard TD to Ben Watson on fourth-and-1 in the 56–10 rout of the Bills at Ralph Wilson Stadium on 11-18-07

The progression of the longest TD pass by a Patriots Quarterback in a regular season game

10-yard TD pass from Butch Songin to Jim Colclough in the 13–10 loss to the Denver Broncos at BU Field on 09-09-60

15-yard TD pass from Tom Greene to Oscar Lofton in the 28–24 win over the New York Titans at the Polo Grounds on 09-17-60

19-yard TD pass from Butch Songin to Jim Colclough in 35–0 shutout of the Los Angeles Chargers at the Los Angeles Coliseum on 10-08-60

47-yard TD pass from Butch Songin to Alan Miller in the 31–24 loss to Denver Broncos at Bears Stadium on 10-23-60

59-yard TD pass from Butch Songin to Walter Beach in the 45–16 loss to the Los Angeles Chargers at BU Field on 10-28-60

63-yard TD pass from Babe Parilli to Larry Garron in the 34–21 victory over the Oilers at Harvard Stadium on 09-16-62

63-yard TD pass from Babe Parilli to Jim Colclough in the 43–14 rout of the New York Titans at the Polo Grounds on 10-06-62

Randy Vataha

67-yard TD pass from Babe Parilli to Jim Colclough in the 33–29 win over the Broncos at Bears Stadium on 11-11-62

78-yard TD pass from Tom Yewcic to Jim Colclough in the 24–17 victory over the New York Titans at BU Field on 11-30-62

80-yard TD pass from Babe Parilli to Art Graham in the 34–17 win over the Oilers at Jeppesen Stadium on 11-29-64

87-yard TD pass from Tom Sherman to Jim Whalen in the 48–14 loss to the New York Jets at Shea Stadium on 10-27-68

88-yard TD pass from Jim Plunkett to Randy Vataha in the 21–17 upset win over the Colts at Memorial Stadium on 12-19-71

90-yard TD pass from Tony Eason to Craig James in the 30–7 loss to the Chicago Bears at Soldier Field on 09-15-85

91-yard TD pass from Tom Brady to David Patten in the 38–17 rout of the Colts at the RCA Dome on 10-21-01

Every Quarterback who has completed only one TD pass for the Patriots
1960 regular season
Tom Greene threw a 15-yard TD to Oscar Lofton in the 28–24 win over the New York Titans at the Polo Grounds on 10-16-60

1965 regular season
Eddie Wilson threw an eight-yard TD to Jim Colclough in the 27–23 victory over the New York Jets at Shea Stadium on 11-28-65

1967 regular season
Don Trull threw a 40-yard TD to Jim Whalen in the 29–24 loss to the New York Jets at Fenway Park on 11-19-67

1987 regular season
Bob Bleier threw a six-yard TD to Larry Linne in the 20–10 loss to the Cleveland Browns at Sullivan Stadium on 10-04-87

1992 regular season
Jeff Carlson threw a six-yard TD pass to Kevin Turner in the 27–20 loss to the Kansas City Chiefs at Arrowhead Stadium on 12-13-92

2006 regular season
Vinny Testaverde tossed a six-yard TD pass to Troy Brown in the 40–23 win over the Tennessee Titans at LP Field on 12-31-06

The progression of the most TD passes by a Patriots Running Back in a regular season
2 halfback option TD passes were thrown by Dick Christy in 1960

4 halfback option TD passes were thrown by Andy Johnson in 1981

The only Patriots Quarterback who has thrown a TD pass of at least 80 yards on the first play of a regular season game
Doug Flutie tossed an 80-yard TD pass to Irving Fryar on the first play in the 30–7 win over the Chicago Bears on 10-30-88

Every Patriots Quarterback who has thrown a TD pass on the last play of a regulation game
1979 regular season
Steve Grogan tossed a 13-yard TD to Carlos Pennywell in the 39–24 loss to Miami at the Orange Bowl on 11-29-79

1986 regular season
Tony Eason tossed a 10-yard TD to Irving Fryar in the 27–20 loss to the Broncos at Mile High Stadium on 09-28-86

Tony Eason tossed a 25-yard "Hail Mary" TD to Irving Fryar to beat the Los Angeles Rams 30–28 at Anaheim Stadium on 11-16-86

1998 regular season
Drew Bledsoe tossed a one-yard TD to Ben Coates to defeat the Buffalo Bills 25–21 at Foxboro Stadium on 11-29-98

Every Patriots Quarterback who has thrown a game-winning TD pass in the fourth quarter of a regular season game
1962 regular season
Tom Yewcic threw a 78-yard TD to Jim Colclough in the 24–17 win over the New York Titans at BU Field on 11-30-62

1963 regular season
Babe Parilli threw a 15-yard TD to Tom Neumann in the 20–14 win over the Oakland Raiders at Fenway Park on 10-11-63

1965 regular season
Babe Parilli lofted a two-yard TD to Tony Romeo with 54 seconds left to defeat the New York Jets 27–23 at Shea Stadium on 11-28-65

1972 regular season
Jim Plunkett threw a 24-yard TD to Josh Ashton with 4:12 left to defeat the Redskins 24–23 at Schaefer Stadium on 10-01-72

1974 regular season
Jim Plunkett tossed a 10-yard TD to Bob Windsor with three seconds left to defeat the Vikings 17–14 at Metropolitan Stadium on 10-27-74

1977 regular season
Steve Grogan fired a 33-yard TD to Stanley Morgan with 4:40 left to defeat Atlatnta 16–10 at Fulton County Stadium on 12-04-77

1980 regular season
Steve Grogan threw a 16-yard TD to Don Hasselbeck with 2:52 left to beat the Seahawks 37–31 at the Kingdome on 09-21-80

1983 regular season
Steve Grogan tossed a 76-yard TD to Stephen Starring with 3:59 left to beat Pittsburgh 28–23 at Three Rivers Stadium on 09-25-83

1985 regular season
Steve Grogan tossed a 13-yard TD to Irving Fryar with 2:39 left to defeat the Seahawks 20–13 at the Kingdome on 11-17-85

1986 regular season
Tony Eason threw a 25-yard TD to Irving Fryar on the last play to defeat the Los Angeles Rams 30–28 at Anaheim Stadium on 11-16-86

Tony Eason threw a 13-yard TD pass to Greg Baty with 1:40 left to beat the Bills 22–19 at Sullivan Stadium on 11-23-86

Steve Grogan threw a 30-yard TD to Stanley Morgan with 44 seconds left to defeat Miami 34–27 at Miami Stadium on 12-22-86

1991 regular season
Hugh Millen tossed a 34-yard TD to Greg McMurtry with six seconds left to defeat Houston 24–20 at Foxboro Stadium on 09-22-91

1993 regular season
Scott Secules lofted a two-yard TD to Ben Coates with 3:56 left to beat the Phoenix Cardinals 23–21 at Sun Devil Stadium on 10-10-93

1996 regular season
Drew Bledsoe threw a two-yard TD to Keith Byars with 4:06 left to defeat the New York Jets 31–27 at the Meadowlands on 11-10-96

Drew Bledsoe threw a 13-yard TD to Ben Coates with 1:23 left to defeat the New York Giants 23–22 at Giants Stadium on 12-21-96

1998 regular season
Drew Bledsoe rifled a 25-yard TD pass to Shawn Jefferson with 29 seconds left to beat Miami 26–23 at Foxboro Stadium on 11-23-98

Drew Bledsoe fired a one-yard TD pass to Ben Coates with no time left in the 25–21 win over Buffalo at Foxboro Stadium on 11-29-98

2002 regular season
Tom Brady tossed a 20-yard TD to David Patten with 21 seconds left to beat Chicago 33–30 at Memorial Stadium on 11-10-02

2003 championship season
Tom Brady threw an 18-yard TD pass to David Givens with 30 seconds left to beat Denver 30–26 at Invesco Field on 11-03-03

David Givens

Every Patriots Quarterback who has thrown a TD pass with less than 30 seconds left to force the overtime period

1981 regular season

Matt Cavanaugh threw a 12-yard TD to Stanley Morgan with 24 seconds left to force overtime in the 27–21 overtime loss on 09-27-81

1991 regular season

Hugh Millen tossed a two-yard TD to Ben Coates with seven seconds left to force overtime in the 23–17 overtime loss on 12-08-91

1993 regular season

Drew Bledsoe tossed a two-yard TD to Vincent Brisby with 12 seconds left to force overtime in the 19–16 overtime loss on 09-12-93

2008 regular season

Matt Cassel fired a 16-yard TD pass to Randy Moss with one second left to force overtime in the 34–31 overtime loss on 11-13-08

Every Patriots Quarterback who has thrown a regular season overtime game-winning TD pass

1991 regular season

Hugh Millen threw a 45-yard TD to Michael Timpson to defeat the Indianapolis Colts 23–17 at Foxboro Stadium on 12-08-91

1993 regular season

Drew Bledsoe threw a 36-yard TD to Michael Timpson to defeat the Miami Dolphins 33–27 at Foxboro Stadium on 01-02-94

1994 regular season

Drew Bledsoe tossed a 14-yard TD to Kevin Turner to defeat the Minnesota Vikings 26–20 at Foxboro Stadium on 11-13-94

2003 championship season

Tom Brady threw an 82-yard TD to Troy Brown to defeat the Miami Dolphins 19–13 at Pro Player Stadium on 10-19-03

The progression of the most consecutive games that a Patriots Quarterback has thrown at least one TD pass

2 consecutive games where Butch Songin threw a TD pass (from 09-09-60 to 09-17-60)

7 consecutive games where Butch Songin threw a TD pass (from 10-23-60 to 12-04-60)

14 consecutive games where Babe Parilli threw a TD pass (from 12-03-61 to 09-08-63)

16 consecutive games where Tom Brady threw a TD pass (from 12-17-06 to 12-09-07)

The number of consecutive regular season games that every Patriots Quarterback has thrown a TD pass

2 consecutive games where Tommy Hodson threw a TD pass (on 11-25-90 and 12-02-90)

2 consecutive games where Scott Secules threw a TD pass (on 10-10-93 and 10-17-93)

2 consecutive games where Scott Zolak threw a TD pass (on 12-20-98 and 12-27-98)

3 consecutive games where Matt Cavanaugh threw a TD pass (from 12-08-80 to 12-21-80)

4 consecutive games where Tom Yewcic threw a TD pass (from 11-18-62 to 12-09-62)

4 consecutive games where Tom Ramsey threw a TD pass (from 11-15-87 to 12-06-87)

4 consecutive games where Doug Flutie threw a TD pass (from 10-23-88 to 11-13-88)

4 consecutive games where Hugh Millen threw a TD pass (from 09-20-92 to 10-11-92)

6 consecutive games where Tom Sherman threw a TD pass (from 10-27-68 to 12-01-68)

7 consecutive games where Butch Songin threw a TD pass (from 10-23-60 to 12-04-60)

7 consecutive games where Jim Plunkett threw a TD pass (from 10-24-71 to 12-05-71)

8 consecutive games where Steve Grogan threw a TD pass (from 12-18-76 to 10-30-77)

10 consecutive games where Mike Taliaferro threw a TD pass (from 09-28-69 to 11-30-69)

11 consecutive games where Tony Eason threw a TD pass (from 10-21-84 to 09-15-85)

11 consecutive games where Tom Brady threw a TD pass (from 12-16-01 to 11-10-02)

12 consecutive games where Drew Bledsoe threw a TD pass (from 12-05-93 to 10-16-94)

14 consecutive games where Babe Parilli threw a TD pass (from 12-03-61 to 09-08-63)

16 consecutive games where Tom Brady threw a TD pass (from 12-17-06 to 12-09-07)

The most consecutive regular season games that a Patriots Quarterback threw at least two TD passes in a game

2 consecutive games by Matt Cavanaugh (on 12-14-80 and 12-21-80)

2 consecutive games by Matt Cassel (on 11-13-08 and 11-23-08 and 12-14-08 and 12-21-08)

3 consecutive games by Mike Taliaferro (from 11-16-69 to 11-30-69)

3 consecutive games by Tony Eason (from 09-21-86 to 10-05-86)

4 consecutive games by Babe Parilli (from 12-11-66 to 09-09-67)

4 consecutive games by Jim Plunkett (from 11-04-73 to 11-25-73)

4 consecutive games by Drew Bledsoe (from 08-31-97 to 09-21-97)

5 consecutive games by Butch Songin (from 10-23-60 to 11-18-60)

6 consecutive games by Steve Grogan (from 11-29-79 to 09-21-80)

10 consecutive games by Tom Brady (from 09-09-07 to 11-18-07)

The most consecutive regular season games that a Patriots Quarterback threw at least three TD passes in a game

2 consecutive games by Mike Taliaferro (on 11-23-69 and 11-30-69)

2 consecutive games by Tony Eason (on 11-11-84 and 11-18-84)

2 consecutive games by Steve Grogan (on 10-12-86 and 10-19-86)

2 consecutive games by Matt Cassel (on 11-13-08 and 11-23-08 and 12-14-08 and 12-21-08)

3 consecutive games by Butch Songin (from 11-04-60 to 11-18-60)

3 consecutive games by Babe Parilli (from 12-11-66 to 09-03-67)

3 consecutive games by Drew Bledsoe (from 01-02-94 to 09-11-94)

10 consecutive games by Tom Brady (from 09-09-07 to 11-18-07)

The most consecutive games that a Patriots Quarterback threw at least four TD passes in a regular season game

2 consecutive games that Tom Brady threw at least five TD passes (on 10-14-07 and 10-21-07)

The most consecutive games that a Patriots Quarterback threw at least five TD passes in a regular seaosn game

2 consecutive games by Tom Brady in victories over the Cowboys and the Dolphins in October 2007

The progression of the most times that a Patriots Quarterback had consecutive regular season games with at least three TDs passes

5 times that Babe Parilli threw at least three TD passes in back-to-back regular season games

9 times that Tom Brady threw at least three TD passes in back-to-back regular season games

The most consecutive TD passes thrown by a Patriots Quarterback to the same receiver

4 consecutive during the 1960 season
Butch Songin tossed four consecutive TD passes to Jim Colclough (from 09-09-60 to 10-23-60)

5 consecutive during the 1971–72 seasons
Jim Plunkett completed five consecutive TD passes to Randy Vataha over three games (on 12-05-71, 12-19-71, and 09-24-72)

Every Patriots Quarterback who has thrown four TD passes in the first half of a regular season game

1967 regular season
Babe Parilli threw four TDs in the first half of the 41–10 rout of the Miami Dolphins at Fenway Park on 10-15-67

1978 regular season
Steve Grogan threw four TDs in the first half of the 55–21 rout of the New York Jets at Schaefer Stadium on 10-29-78

1979 regular season
Steve Grogan threw four TDs in the first half of the 56–3 rout of the New York Jets at Schaefer Stadium on 09-09-79

1987 regular season
Steve Grogan threw four TDs in the first half of their 42–20 win over the New York Jets at Sullivan Stadium on 12-13-87

1997 regular season
Drew Bledsoe threw four TDs in the first half of the 41–7 rout of the San Diego Chargers at Foxboro Stadium on 08-31-97

2003 championship season
Tom Brady threw four TDs in the first half of the 31–0 shutout of the Buffalo Bills at Gillette Stadium on 12-27-03

2007 undefeated regular season
Tom Brady threw four TDs in the first half of the 56–10 rout of the Bills at Ralph Wilson Stadium on 11-18-07

The only Patriots Quarterback who has thrown five TD passes in the first half of a regular season game

Tom Brady threw five TDs in the first half of the 49–28 rout of the Miami Dolphins at Dolphin Stadium on 10-21-07

Every Patriots Quarterback who has thrown at least five TD passes in a regular season game

1964 regular season
Babe Parilli completed five TDs in the 36–28 win over the Buffalo Bills at War Memorial Stadium on 11-15-64

1967 regular season
Babe Parilli tossed five TDs in the 41–10 rout of the Miami Dolphins at Boston College Alumni Stadium on 10-15-67

1979 regular season
Steve Grogan completed five TD passes in the 56–3 blowout of the New York Jets at Schaefer Stadium on 09-09-79

2007 undefeated regular season
Tom Brady completed five TDs in the 48–27 win over the Dallas Cowboys at Texas Stadium on 10-14-07

Tom Brady completed six TDs in the 49–28 rout of the Miami Dolphins at Dolphin Stadium on 10-21-07

The only Patriots Quarterback to throw four TD passes in a regular season overtime game

Tom Brady threw four TD passes in the 41–38 overtime win vs the Kansas City Chiefs at Gillette Stadium on 09-22-02

The progression of the most TD passes by a Patriots Quarterback in a regular season

22 TD passes were thrown by Ed "Butch" Songin in the 1960 season

31 TD passes were thrown by Vito "Babe" Parilli in the 1964 season

50 TD passes were thrown Tom Brady in the 2007 season

The AFL Quarterback with the most TD passes during a specific regular season

1964 regular season
31 TD passes were thrown by Boston Patriots QB Babe Parilli during the 1964 season

The NFL Quarterback with the most TD passes during a specifc regular season

1979 regular season
28 TD passes were thrown by New England Patriots QB Steve Grogan during the 1979 season (tied with Brian Sipe)

2002 regular season
28 TD passes were thrown by New England Patriots QB Tom Brady during the 2002 season

2007 undefeated regular season
50 TD passes were thrown by New England Patriots QB Tom Brady during the 2007 season

The NFL Quarterback with the most TD passes to a different receiver in a specific regular season

2002 regular season
Tom Brady tied the NFL record by completing at least one TD pass to 11 different receivers in the 2002 season

The progression of the most career regular season TD passes thrown by a Patriots Quarterback

36th TD pass thrown by Butch Songin was to Billy Lott in the 28–24 win over Denver on 12-03-61

37th TD pass thrown by Babe Parilli was to Gino Cappelletti in the 40–21 win over Denver on 10-18-63

132nd TD pass thrown by Babe Parilli was to Bob Cappadona in the 41–32 loss to Miami on 12-17-67

133rd TD pass thrown by Steve Grogan was to Derrick Ramsey in the 24–13 loss to the Falcons on 10-30-83

182nd TD pass thrown by Steve Grogan was to Sammy Martin in the 27–10 loss to the Bills on 10-28-90

183rd TD pass thrown by Tom Brady was to Randy Moss in the 56–10 rout of the Redskins on 11-18-07

The progression of the best percentage of TD passes per attempt by a Patriots Quarterback in a season

5.6% of Butch Songin's passes resulted in a TD during the 1960 season

6.6% of Butch Songin's passes resulted in a TD during the 1961 season

7.1% of Babe Parilli's passes resulted in a TD during the 1962 season

8.6% of Matt Cavanaugh's passes resulted in a TD during the 1980 season

8.8% of Steve Grogan's passes resulted in a TD during the 1986 season

The NFL Quarterback with the best TD percentage per pass attempt in a specific regular season

1979 regular season

6.6% of Steve Grogan's passes resulted in a TD during the 1979 season with 28 TD passes in 423 passing attempts

The progession of the best average yards per pass completion by a Patriots Quarterback in a regular season

13.2 yards per completion by Butch Songin in 1960

14.6 yards per completion by Butch Songin in 1961

15.3 yards per completion by Babe Parilli in 1963

15.6 yards per completion by Steve Grogan in 1978

16.0 yards per completion by Steve Grogan in 1979

The progression of the highest pass completion percentage by a Patriots Quarterback in a regular season

47.7% completion rate by Butch Songin in 1960

52.5% completion rate by Babe Parilli in 1961

55.3% completion rate by Babe Parilli in 1962

57.2% completion rate by Steve Grogan in 1980

60.1% completion rate by Tony Eason in 1984

61.6% completion rate by Tony Eason in 1986

63.9% completion rate by Tom Brady in 2001

68.9% completion rate by Tom Brady in 2007

The progression of the most yards passing by a Patriots Quarterback in a regular season

2,476 yards passing by Butch Songin in 1960

3,465 yards passing by Babe Parilli in 1964

4,555 yards passing by Drew Bledsoe in 1994

4,806 yards passing by Tom Brady in 2007

The progression of the most yards passing by a Patriots RB in a regular season

94 yards passing by Dick Christy in 1960

194 yards passing by Andy Johnson in 1981

The progression of the most yards passing by a Patriots WR in a regular season

52 yards passing by Don Westbrook in 1979

60 yards passing by David Patten in 2001

The progression of the most yards passing by a Patriots Punter in a regular season

4 yards passing by Eddie Hare in 1979

11 yards passing by Shawn McCarthy in 1991

18 yards passing by Lee Johnson in 2000

The progression of the most yards passing by a Patriots Kicker in a regular season

27 yards passing by kicker Gino Cappelletti in 1961

The progression of the most regular season career yards passing by a Patriots Quarterback

3,905 yards passing by Patriots QB Butch Songin from 09-09-60 to 12-03-61

16,747 yards passing by Patriots QB Babe Parilli from 09-09-61 to 12-17-67

26,886 yards passing by Steve Grogan from 09-21-75 to 11-04-90

29,257 yards passing by Patriots QB Drew Bledsoe from 09-05-93 to 09-23-01

The Patriots regular season record when a Patriots Quarterback tossed at least one TD pass

The New England Patriots have won 71-of-81 regular season games when Tom Brady has tossed at least one TD pass

The New England Patriots were 63–40 for the 103 regular season games that Steve Grogan tossed at least one TD pass

The Patriots were 53–39 for the 92 regular season games when Drew Bledsoe tossed at least one TD pass

The Boston Patriots were 39–24–8 for the 71 regular season games when Babe Parilli tossed at least one TD

The New England Patriots won 21 of the 39 regular season games when Tony Eason completed at least one TD pass

The New England Patriots won 18 of the 35 games when Jim Plunkett tossed a TD pass

The Boston Patriots were 10–8–1 in the 19 games when Butch Songin tossed a TD pass

The New England Patriots won eight of the 11 games when Matt Cassel tossed at least one TD pass

The New England Patriots won seven of the 14 games when Matt Cavanaugh tossed at least one TD pass

The New England Patriots won five of the eight games when Doug Flutie tossed a TD pass

The Boston Patriots won five of the seven regular season games when Tom Yewcic completed a TD pass

The New England Patriots won three of the six regular season games when Scott Zolak completed a TD pass

The Boston Patriots won the only game where Tom Greene tossed at least one TD pass

The New England Patriots won the only game when Vinny Testaverde tossed at least one TD pass

The Patriots regular season record when the Quarterback tossed at least two TD passes

The Patriots have won 55-of-62 games when Tom Brady has thrown at least two TD passes in the game

The Patriots won 35-of-55 games when Steve Grogan tossed at least two TD passes in the game

The Patriots won 31-of-46 games when Drew Bledsoe tossed at least two TDs passes in the game

The Boston Patriots were 24–9–4 when Babe Parilli tossed at least two TD passes in the game

The Patriots won 13-of-21 games when Jim Plunkett tossed at least two TD passes in the game

The Patriots won nine of the 14 games when Tony Eason tossed at least two TD passes in the game

The Boston Patriots won five of the nine games when Butch Songin tossed at least two TD passes in the game

The Boston Patriots won 5-of-6 games when Mike Taliaferro tossed at least two TD passes in the game

The New England Patriots won 4-of-5 games when Matt Cassel tossed at least two TD passes in the game

The Patriots were 3–1 when Matt Cavanaugh completed at least two TD passes in the game

The New England Patriots won both of the games when Scott Zolak tossed at least two TD passes

The Patriots won the only game when Doug Flutie tossed at least two TD passes in the game

The Boston Patriots won 2-of-3 games when Tom Yewcic tossed at least two TD passes in the game

The Patriots won 1-of-4 games when Hugh Millen tossed at least two TD passes in the game

The Patriots won 1-of-4 games when Tom Sherman tossed at least two TD passes in the game

The New England Patriots lost both of the games when Marc Wilson tossed at least two TD passes in the game

The Patriots lost the only game when Neil Graff tossed two TD passes in the game

The Patriots lost the only game when Tom Ramsey tossed at least two TD passes in the game

The Patriots regular season record when the Quarterback tossed at least three TD passes

The New England Patriots won 21-of-23 games when Tom Brady tossed at least three TD passes in the game

The New England Patriots won 16-of-19 games when Steve Grogan tossed at least three TD passes in the game

The New England Patriots won 15-of-19 games when Drew Bledsoe tossed at least three TD passes in the game

The Boston Patriots were 13–2–3 in the 18 games when Babe Parilli tossed at least three TD passes

The New England Patriots won 4-of-6 games when Tony Eason tossed at least three TD passes in the game

The Boston Patriots won 4-of-6 games when Butch Songin tossed at least three TD passes in the game

The New England Patriots won 4-of-5 games when Matt Cassel tossed at least three TD passes in the game

The New England Patriots won 3-of-4 games when Jim Plunkett tossed at least three TD passes in the game

The Boston Patriots won 2-of-3 games when Mike Taliaferro tossed at least three TD passes in the game

The Boston Patriots won 1-of-2 games when Tom Yewcic tossed at least three TD passes in the game

The Boston Patriots defeated the Bengals 33–14 in the only game when Tom Sherman tossed at least three TD passes

The New England Patriots defeated the New Orleans Saints 38–27 in the only game when Matt Cavanaugh threw three TDs

The Patriots destroyed the Chicago Bears 30–7 in the only game when Doug Flutie tossed at least three TD passes

The New England Patriots lost the only game when Tom Ramsey tossed at least three TD passes in the game

The New England Patriots lost the only game when Hugh Millen tossed at least three TD passes in the game

The Patriots regular season record when the Quarterback tossed at least four TD passes

The New England Patriots won 8-of-9 games when Drew Bledsoe tossed at least four TD passes in a game

The New England Patriots have won all eight games when Tom Brady has tossed at least four TD passes in the game

The New England Patriots won all three of the games when Steve Grogan tossed at least four TD passes in the game

The Boston Patriots won two and tied one of the three games when Babe Parilli tossed at least four TD passes in the game

The Boston Patriots destroyed the Denver Broncos 45–17 in the only game when Butch Songin tossed four TD passes

The New England Patriots beat the Buffalo Bills 38–33 in the only game when Jim Plunkett threw four TD passes

The New England Patriots crushed the Indianapolis Colts 50–17 in the only game when Tony Eason threw four TDs

The New England Patriots routed the Chicago Bears 30–7 in the only game when Doug Flutie tossed four TD passes

The New England Patriots routed the Oakland Raiders 49–26 in the only game when Matt Cassel tossed four TD passes

The number of TD passes and the receivers who have caught a TD pass by every Patriots Quarterback who has thrown at least two TDs

Drew Bledsoe
Drew Bledsoe completed 56 regular season TD passes (11 yard average) to a Patriots Tight End
Bledsoe threw 45 TD passes to Ben Coates; three TD passes to Lovett Purnell; two TD passes to Mike Bartrum, Eric Bjornson, and Jermaine Wiggins; and one TD pass to Marv Cook and Rod Rutledge

Drew Bledsoe completed 33 regular season TD passes (13 yard average) to a Patriots Running Back
Bledsoe threw five TD passes to Keith Byars, Sam Gash, Curtis Martin, and Leroy Thompson, three TD passes to Kevin Turner, two TD passes to Kevin Faulk, J.R. Redmond, and Robert Edwards, and one TD pass to Terry Allen, Derrick Cullors, Dave Meggett, and Lamont Warren

Drew Bledsoe completed 77 TD passes (23 yard average) to a Patriots Wide Receiver
Bledsoe completed 21 TD passes to Terry Glenn, 14 TD passes to Vincent Brisby, 13 TD passes to Shawn Jefferson, 12 TD passes to Troy Brown, five TD passes to

Dave Meggett

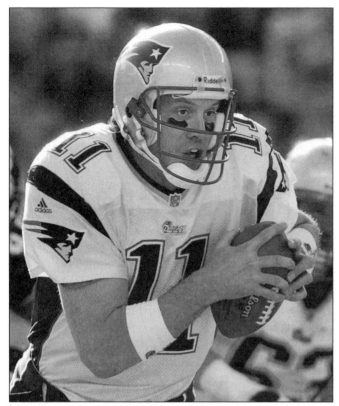

Drew Bledsoe

Michael Timpson, four TD passes to Ray Crittenden and Tony Simmons, two TD passes to Hason Graham, and one TD pass to Greg McMurtry and Will Moore

Tom Brady
Tom Brady has thrown 58 regular season TD passes (9 yard average) to a Patriots Tight End
Brady has thrown 16 TD passes to Daniel Graham, 14 TDs to Christian Fauria, 12 TDs to Benjamin Watson, eight regular season TD passes to Mike Vrabel, three TDs to Jermaine Wiggins, two TDs to Kyle Brady, and one regular season TD pass to Tom Ashworth, Cam Cleeland, and David Thomas

Tom Brady has thrown 20 regular season TD passes (17 yard average) to a Patriots Running Back
Brady has thrown nine TD passes to Kevin Faulk, three TD passes to Antowain Smith, two TD passes to Marc Edwards and Corey Dillon, and one TD pass to Larry Centers, Heath Evans, Laurence Maroney, and Patrick Pass

Tom Brady has thrown 119 regular season TD passes (22 yard average) to a Patriots Wide Receiver
Brady threw 23 TD passes to Randy Moss, 16 TD passes to David Patten, 15 TD passes to Troy Brown, 14 TDs to Deion Branch, 12 TDs to David Givens, eight TDs to

Wes Welker, five TDs to Jabar Gaffney, four TDs to Reche Caldwell and Bethel Johnson, three TDs to Doug Gabriel, Chad Jackson, and Donte Stallworth, two TDs to Donald Hayes and Tim Dwight, and one TD pass to Andre' Davis, Jabar Gaffney, Terry Glenn, Charles Johnson, and Dedric Ward

Matt Cassel
Matt Cassel has thrown 17 regular season TD passes (21 yard average) to a Patriots Wide Receiver
Cassel threw 11 TD passes to Randy Moss, three TDs to Wes Welker, two TD passes to Jabar Gaffney, and one TD pass to Tim Dwight

Matt Cassel has thrown three regular season TD passes (12 yard average) to a Patriots RB (Kevin Faulk)

Matt Cassel has thrown three regular season TD passes (7 yard average) to a Patriots Tight End (Benjamin Watson)

Matt Cavanaugh
Matt Cavanaugh completed eight TD passes (17 yard average) to a Patriots Tight End
Cavanaugh threw four TD passes to Russ Francis, three TDs to Don Hasselbeck, and one TD pass to Lin Dawson

Matt Cassel

Matt Cavanaugh completed five TD passes (8 yard average) to a Patriots Running Back

Cavanaugh threw four TD passes to Andy Johnson and one TD pass to Tony Collins

Matt Cavanaugh completed six TD passes (38 yard average) to a Patriots Wide Receiver

Cavanaugh threw a TD pass to Harold Jackson, Carlos Pennywell, Don Westbrook, Ken Toler, Preston Brown, and Stanley Morgan

Brian Dowling

Brian Dowling tossed an eight-yard TD pass to a Patriots RB (John Tarver)

Brian Dowling completed a 28-yard TD pass to a Patriots WR (Bob Reynolds)

Tony Eason

Tony Eason completed 16 regular season TD passes (9 yard average) to a Patriots Tight End

Eason threw eight TD passes to Derrick Ramsey, three TD passes to Greg Baty and Lin Dawson, and two TD passes to Willie Scott

Tony Eason completed four TD passes (32 yard average) to a Patriots Running Back

Eason tossed two TD passes to Tony Collins and one TD pass to Craig James and Bo Robinson

Tony Eason completed 40 regular season TD passes (23 yard average) to a Patriots Wide Receiver

Eason threw 18 regular season TD passes to Stanley Morgan, 10 TD passes to Irving Fryar, five TD passes to Stephen Starring, four TD passes to Cedric Jones, two TD passes to Clarence Weathers, and one TD pass to Hart Lee Dykes

Doug Flutie

Doug Flutie completed two TD passes (8 yard average) to a Patriots Tight End

Flutie threw two TD passes to Lin Dawson

Doug Flutie completed nine TD passes (25 yard average) to a Patriots Wide Receiver

Flutie threw three TD passes to Stanley Morgan and Irving Fryar, two TDs to Cedric Jones, and one TD pass to Larry Linne

Neil Graff

Neil Graff threw a five-yard TD pass to TE Russ Francis and a 31-yard TD pass to WR Randy Vataha

Tom Greene

Tom Greene tossed a 15-yard TD pass to TE Oscar Lofton

Steve Grogan

Steve Grogan completed 50 regular season TD passes (14 yard average) to a Patriots Tight End

Grogan threw 22 TD passes to Russ Francis, 12 TD passes to Don Hasselbeck, six TD passes to Derrick Ramsey, three TD passes to Al Chandler, two TD passes to Lin Dawson, and one TD pass to Pete Brock, Greg Baty, Marv Cook, Greg Hawthorne, and Willie Scott

Steve Grogan completed 19 regular season TD passes (14 yard average) to a Patriots Running Back

Grogan threw six TD passes to Andy Johnson, three TDs to Tony Collins and Sam Cunningham, two TDs to Horace Ivory, and one TD pass to Don Calhoun, Ike Forte, Mark van Eeghen, Mosi Tatupu, and Craig James

Steve Grogan completed 113 regular season TD passes (31 yard average) to a Patriots Wide Receiver

Grogan threw 39 TD passes to Stanley Morgan, 17 TD passes to Harold Jackson, 14 TD passes to Irving Fryar, nine TDs to Darryl Stingley, eight TDs to Cedric Jones, six TD passes to Stephen Starring and Randy Vataha, four TDs to Hart Lee Dykes, three to Clarence Weathers, two TD passes to Carlos Pennywell, and one TD pass to Marlin Briscoe, Ray Jarvis, Ken Toler, Morris Bradshaw, and Sammy Martin

Steve Grogan

Tommy Hodson

Tommy Hodson completed three TD passes (16 yard average) to a Patriots Tight End (Marv Cook)

Tommy Hodson completed an 18-yard TD pass to a Patriots Running Back (John Stephens)

Tommy Hodson completed three TD passes (36 yard average) to a Patriots Wide Receiver
Hodson threw two TD passes to Irving Fryar and one TD pass to Michael Timpson

Joe Kapp

Joe Kapp completed three TD passes (13 yard average) to a Patriots Wide Receiver
Joe Kapp completed two TD passes to Wide Receiver Bake Turner and one TD pass to Ron Sellers

Hugh Millen

Hugh Millen completed six TD passes (8 yard average) to a Patriots Tight End
Millen threw three TD passes to New England Patriots Tight Ends Marv Cook and Ben Coates

Hugh Millen completed a 19-yard TD pass to Patriots Running Back Kevin Turner

Hugh Millen completed nine TD passes (40 yard average) to a Patriots Wide Receiver
Millen threw six TD passes to Irving Fryar and two TD passes to Greg McMurtry and Michael Timpson

Joe Kapp

Tom Owen

The average length of a Tom Owen TD pass was 15 yards
Owen completed a two regular season TD passes to Wide Receiver Don Westbrook and one TD pass to RB Don Calhoun

Babe Parilli

Babe Parilli completed 18 TD passes (18 yard average) to a Patriots Tight End
Parilli threw 10 TD passes to Tony Romeo and eight TD passes to Jim Whalen

Babe Parilli completed 43 regular season TD passes (29 yard average) to a Patriots Running Back
Parilli threw 25 TD passes to Larry Garron, six TD passes to Ron Burton, five TD passes to Billy Lott, two TD passes to JD Garrett, and one TD pass to Jim Crawford, Tom Neumann, Joe Bellino, Jim Nance, and Bob Cappadona

Babe Parilli completed 69 TD passes (27 yard average) to a Patriots Wide Receiver
Parilli threw 34 TD passes to Gino Cappelletti, 18 TD passes to Jim Colclough, 16 TD passes to Art Graham, and one TD pass to Bobby Leo

Jim Plunkett

Jim Plunkett completed 11 TD passes (17 yard average) to a Patriots Tight End
Plunkett threw six TD passes to Bob Windsor, three TD passes to Tom Beer, and one TD pass to Russ Francis and John Tanner

Jim Plunkett completed 11 TD passes (24 yard average) to a Running Back
Plunkett threw six TD passes to Mack Herron, three TD passes to Sam Cunningham, and one TD pass to Carl Garrett and Josh Ashton

Jim Plunkett completed 40 TD passes (26 yard average) to a Patriots Wide Receiver
Plunkett threw 16 TD passes to Randy Vataha, 10 TD passes to Reggie Rucker, five TD passes to Darryl Stingley, three TD passes to Ron Sellers, and one TD pass to Eric Crabtree, Steve Schubert, Hubie Bryant, Tom Reynolds, Al Marshall, and Roland Moss

Tom Ramsey

Tom Ramsey tossed a three-yard TD pass to Patriots TE Willie Scott

Tom Ramsey completed two TD passes (14 yard average) to Patriots RB Tony Collins

Jim Plunkett

Butch Songin

Butch Songin completed 10 TD passes (20 yard average) to a Patriots Tight End
Songin threw four TD passes to Joe Johnson and three TD passes to Oscar Lofton and Tom Stephens

Butch Songin completed eight TD passes (29 yard average) to a Patriots Running Back
Songin threw two TD passes to Alan Miller, Dick Christy, and Billy Lott, and one TD pass to Billy Wells and Walter Beach

Butch Songin completed 18 TD passes (21 yard average) to a Patriots Wide Receiver
Songin threw 14 TD passes to Jim Colclough and four TD passes to Gino Cappelletti

Mike Taliaferro

Mike Taliaferro threw four TD passes (19 yard average) to Patriots TE Jim Whalen

Mike Taliaferro tossed two TD passes (4 yard average) to Patriots RB Carl Garrett

Mike Taliaferro completed 21 TD passes (28 yard average) to a Patriots Wide Receiver
Taliaferro threw nine TD passes to Ron Sellers, seven to Charley Frazier, three to Bill Rademacher, and one to Aaron Marsh and Gayle Knief

Tom Ramsey completed three TD passes (9 yard average) to a Patriots Wide Receiver
Ramsey completed two TD passes to Stanley Morgan and one TD pass to Irving Fryar

Scott Secules

Scott Secules fired a game-winning two-yard TD pass to TE Ben Coates in the 23–21 win over the Cardinals on 10-10-93

Scott Secules tossed a seven-yard TD pass to RB Kevin Turner in the 28–14 loss to the Houston Oilers on 10-17-93

Tom Sherman

Tom Sherman completed four TD passes (37 yard average) to a Patriots TE Jim Whalen

Tom Sherman threw a five-yard TD pass to Boston Patriots RB R.C. Gamble

Tom Sherman completed seven TD passes (21 yard average) to a Patriots Wide Receiver
Sherman threw three TD passes to Aaron Marsh, two TD passes to Gino Cappelletti, and one TD pass to Bob Scarpitto and Art Graham

Marc Wilson

Marc Wilson completed two TD passes (10 yard average) to Patriots TE Marv Cook

Marc Wilson completed a four-yard TD pass to Patriots RB George Adams

Marc Wilson completed six TD passes (31 yard average) to a Patriots Wide Receiver
Marc tossed two TD passes to Hart Lee Dykes, Irving Fryar, and Cedric Jones

Tom Yewcic

Tom Yewcic completed three TD passes (60 yard average) to a Patriots Running Back
Yewcic tossed two TD passes to Ron Burton and one TD pass to Jim Crawford

Scott Zolak

Tom Yewcic completed nine TD passes (33 yard average) to a Patriots Wide Receiver
Yewcic tossed five TD passes to Jim Colclough, three TD passes to Art Graham, and one TD pass to Gino Cappelletti

Scott Zolak
Scott Zolak completed three TD passes (9 yard average) to a Patriots Tight End
Zolak tossed two TD passes to Lovett Purnell and one TD pass to Ben Coates

Scott Zolak completed two TD passes (10 yard average) to a Patriots Running Back
Zolak threw a TD pass to Sam Gash and Robert Edwards

Scott Zolak completed three TD passes (53 yard average) to a Patriots Wide Receiver
Zolak threw a TD pass to Greg McMurtry, Shawn Jefferson, and Tony Simmons

The Playoffs

The progression of the most yards passing by a Patriots Quarterback in a playoff game
300 yards passing by Babe Parilli in the 26–8 victory over the Buffalo Bills at War Memorial Stadium on 12-28-63

312 yards passing by Tom Brady in the 16–13 overtime win vs the Oakland Raiders at Foxboro Stadium on 01-19-02

354 yards passing by Tom Brady in the 32–29 victory over the Carolina Panthers at Reliant Stadium on 02-01-04

The Patriots Quarterback with the most yards passing in an overtime playoff game
2001 AFC Divisional playoff game
Tom Brady threw for 312 yards in the 16–13 overtime win vs the Oakland Raiders at Foxboro Stadium on 01-19-02

The progression of the most career yards passing by a Patriots Quarterback in the playoffs
489 career yards passing by Babe Parilli in two playoff games

571 career yards passing by Steve Grogan in four playoff games

1,335 career yards passing by Drew Bledsoe in seven playoff games

3,954 career yards passing by Tom Brady in 17 playoff games

The progression of the most pass attempts by a Patriots Quarterback in a playoff game
35 attempts by Babe Parilli in the 26–8 victory over the Buffalo Bills at War Memorial Stadium on 12-28-63

50 attempts by Drew Bledsoe in the 20–13 loss to the Cleveland Browns at Cleveland Stadium on 01-01-95

52 attempts by Tom Brady in the 16–13 overtime win vs the Oakland Raiders at Foxboro Stadium on 01-19-02

The progression of the most pass attempts without an interception by a Patriots Quarterback in a playoff game
2 pass attempts without an interception by Babe Parilli in the 26–8 victory over the Buffalo Bills on 12-28-63

32 pass attempts without an interception by Babe Parilli in the 26–8 victory over the Buffalo Bills on 12-28-63

32 pass attempts without an interception by Drew Bledsoe in the 17–3 win over Miami on 12-28-97

44 pass attempts without an interception by Tom Brady in the 16–13 overtime win vs the Raiders on 01-19-02

The progression of the most career passing attempts by a Patriots Quarterback in the playoffs
64 career passing attempts by Babe Parilli in two playoff games

95 career passing attempts by Steve Grogan in four playoff games

252 career passing attempts by Drew Bledsoe in seven playoff games

595 career passing attempts by Tom Brady in 17 playoff games

The progression of the most pass completions by a Patriots Quarterback in a playoff game

14 completions by Babe Parilli in the 26–8 victory over the Buffalo Bills at War Memorial Stadium on 12-28-63

14 completions by Babe Parilli in the 51–10 loss to the San Diego Chargers at Balboa Stadium on 01-05-64

16 completions by Steve Grogan in the 28–13 loss to the Miami Dolphins at the Orange Bowl on 01-08-83

17 completions by Steve Grogan in the 46–10 loss to the Chicago Bears at the Louisiana Superdome on 01-26-86

21 completions by Drew Bledsoe in the 20–13 loss to the Cleveland Browns at Cleveland Stadium on 01-01-95

25 completions by Drew Bledsoe in the 35–21 loss to the Green Bay Packers at the Louisiana Superdome on 01-26-97

32 completions by Tom Brady in the 16–13 overtime win vs the Oakland Raiders at Foxboro Stadium on 01-19-02

32 completions by Tom Brady in the 32–29 victory over the Carolina Panthers at Reliant Stadium on 02-01-04

Every Patriots Running Back who completed his only pass attempt in a playoff game

1978 AFC Divisional playoff game
Andy Johnson threw a 24-yard TD to Harold Jackson in the 31–14 loss to the Oilers at Schaefer Stadium on 12-31-78

1985 AFC Divisional playoff game
Craig James tossed an eight-yard pass to Tony Collins in the 27–20 win over the Los Angeles Raiders at the Los Angeles Coliseum on 01-05-86

The only pass completion by a Patriots Punter in a playoff game

Pat O'Neill tossed a 21-yard pass to Corwin Brown in the 20–13 loss to the Browns at Cleveland Municipal Stadium on 01-01-95

The most consecutive completions by a Patriots Quarterback in a playoff game

16 consecutive passes were completed (12-of-12 in the first half) by Tom Brady in the 31–20 win over the Jaguars on 01-12-08

The most attempts, completions, and yards passing by a Patriots Quarterback in the second half of a playoff game

2001 AFC Divisional playoff game
Tom Brady was 26-of-39 for 238 yards in the second half of the 16–13 overtime win vs the Raiders at Foxboro Stadium on 01-19-02

The progression of the most career pass completions by a Patriots Quarterback in the playoffs

28 career pass completions by Babe Parilli in two playoff games

48 career pass completions by Steve Grogan in four playoff games

129 career pass completions by Drew Bledsoe in seven playoff games

372 career pass completions by Tom Brady in 17 playoff games

The progression of the highest pass completion percentage by a Patriots Quarterback in a playoff game

40% of Babe Parilli's passes were completed (14-of-35) in the 26–8 victory over the Buffalo Bills on 12-28-63

49% of Babe Parilli's passes were completed (14-of-29) in the 51–10 loss to the San Diego Chargers on 01-05-64

52% of Steve Grogan's passes were completed (12-of-23) in the 24–21 loss to the Oakland Raiders on 12-18-76

54.5% of Tom Owen's passes were completed (12-of-22) in the 31–14 loss to the Houston Oilers on 12-31-78

75% of Tony Eason's passes were completed (12-of-16) in the 26–14 victory over the New York Jets on 12-28-85

83% of Tony Eason's passes were completed (10-of-12) in the 31–14 victory over the Dolphins on 01-12-86

92.9% of Tom Brady's passes were completed (26-of-28) for an NFL record in the 31–20 win over the Jaguars on 01-12-08

The progression of the best pass career completion percentage by a Patriots Quarterback in the playoffs

43.7% of Babe Parilli's career playoff passes were completed in two playoff games for the Boston Patriots

54.5% of Tom Owen's career playoff passes were completed in the 31–14 loss to the Houston Oilers on 12-31-78

58.3% of Tony Eason's career playoff passes were completed in five playoff games

62.5% of Tom Brady's career playoff passes were completed in 17 playoff games

The progression of the longest pass completion by a Patriots Quarterback in a playoff game

9-yard pass by Babe Parilli to Ron Burton in the 26–8 victory over the Bills at War Memorial Stadium on 12-28-63

9-yard pass by Babe Parilli to Jim Colclough in the 26–8 win over the Bills at War Memorial Stadium on 12-28-63

22-yard pass by Babe Parilli to Gino Cappelletti in the 26–8 victory over the Bills at War Memorial Stadium on 12-28-63

59-yard TD pass by Babe Parilli to Larry Garron in the 26–8 win over Buffalo at War Memorial Stadium on 12-28-63

60-yard TD pass by Tom Brady to Deion Branch in the 41–27 win over the Steelers at Heinz Field on 01-23-05

63-yard TD pass by Tom Brady to Benjamin Watson in the 28–3 rout of the Jaguars at Gillette Stadium on 01-07-06

73-yard pass by Tom Brady to Deion Branch in the 27–13 loss to the Broncos at Invesco Field on 01-14-06

The only pass completion by a Patriots Running Back in a playoff game
1978 AFC Divisional playoff game
24-yard TD pass by Andy Johnson to Harold Jackson in the 31–14 loss to Houston at Schaefer Stadium on 12-31-78

The only flea-flicker TD Pass by the Patriots in a playoff game
1986 AFC Divisional playoff game
Tony Eason to Mosi Tatupu to Tony Eason to Stanley Morgan for a 45-yard TD in the 22–17 loss to the Broncos

Every Patriots player who has thrown a fourth-down TD pass in a playoff game
1985 AFC Championship Game
Tony Eason tossed a two-yard TD to Robert Weathers on fourth-and-1 in the 31–14 win over the Dolphins on 01-12-86

Stanley Morgan

Super Bowl XX
Steve Grogan tossed an eight-yard TD to Irving Fryar on fourth-and-goal in the 46–10 loss to the Bears on 01-26-86

The only Patriots Punter to complete a fourth-down pass for a first down in a playoff game
1994 AFC Wild Card playoff game
Pat O'Neill threw a 21-yard pass to Corwin Brown on fourth-and-10 in the 20–13 loss to the Browns on 01-01-95

The only Patriots QB to complete a TD pass to a Patriots Linebacker/Tight End in a playoff game
Super Bowl XXXVIII
Tom Brady threw a one-yard TD to Mike Vrabel in the 32–29 win over the Carolina Panthers at Reliant Stadium on 02-01-04

Super Bowl XXXIX
Tom Brady tossed a two-yard TD to Mike Vrabel in the 24–21 victory over the Eagles at Alltel Stadium on 02-06-05

The progression of the most TD passes by a Patriots Quarterback in a playoff game
2 TD passes by Babe Parilli in the 26–8 victory over the Buffalo Bills at War Memorial Stadium on 12-28-63

3 TD passes by Tony Eason in the 31–14 victory over the Miami Dolphins at the Orange Bowl on 01-12-86

3 TD passes by Tom Brady in the 32–29 victory over the Carolina Panthers at Reliant Stadium on 02-01-04

3 TD passes by Tom Brady in the 28–3 rout of the Jacksonville Jaguars at Gillette Stadium on 01-07-06

3 TD passes by Tom Brady in the 31–20 victory over the Jacksonville Jaguars at Gillette Stadium on 01-12-08

The progression of the most career TD passes by a Patriots Quarterback in the playoffs

2 career TD passes were thrown by Babe Parilli in two playoff games for the Boston Patriots

3 career TD passes were thrown by Steve Grogan in four playoff games for the New England Patriots

7 career TD passes were thrown by Tony Eason in five playoff games for the New England Patriots

26 career TD passes have been thrown by Tom Brady in 17 playoff games

Receiving

At least one pass has been caught by 94 wide receivers, 84 running backs, 44 tight ends, eight offensive linemen, and five quarterbacks for the Patriots during the regular season. Among these players 12 wide receivers, 12 running backs, four tight ends, and four quarterbacks only had one reception in the regular season during their career with the Patriots. Since 1960, 61 wide receivers, 49 running backs, and 32 tight ends have caught at least one TD pass during the regular season for the Patriots.

Gino Cappelletti was recognized as the first AFL All-Star receiver for the Patriots and he finished second to George Blanda for the league MVP in 1961. Jim Colclough was recognized as an AFL Star receiver in 1962. Both Cappelletti and Colclough finished with more than 5,000 yards receiving during their careers. Randy Vataha had some success catching balls thrown by Jim Plunkett and Steve Grogan in the early- and mid-1970s. Stanley Morgan, who reached the milestone of 10,000 career yards receiving quicker than any other NFL receiver at that time, was the team's most prolific receiver for many years through the late 1970s and 1980s. Irivng Fryar had the first TD reception by a Patriots player in a Super Bowl when he caught an eight-yard TD pass from Steve Grogan on a fourth-down play in Super Bowl XX. Terry Glenn, Troy Brown, David Givens, and Deion Branch have also led the team in yards receiving in a regular season.

Tight ends have played an important role in the receiving department, and the Patriots have had many stellar performers from this position. Oscar Lofton, Tony Romeo, and Jim Whalen had success as tight ends for the Boston Patriots. Bob Windsor had one of the most dramatic receptions by a New England Patriots tight end as he was injured scoring the game-winning

TD on the last play of the 17–14 win over the Minnesota Vikings in 1974. Other memorable tight ends include Russ Francis, Don Hasselbeck, Derrick Ramsey, Lin Dawson, Eric Sievers, Marv Cook, Ben Coates, Christian Fauria, Daniel Graham, and Benjamin Watson.

Some of the Patriots running backs who have excelled in receiving the forward pass include Billy Lott, who had six TD receptions in 1961, and Larry Garron, who had seven TD receptions in 1964. Mini-Mack Herron had five TD receptions in 1974, and Andy Johnson had six TD receptions in 1976. Tony Collins had five TD receptions in 1986, and Leroy Thompson had five TD receptions during the 1994 regular season.

Jim Colclough led the team in yards receiving in 1960, 1962, and 1963 and Gino Cappelletti led the team in yards receiving in 1961, 1964, 1965, and 1966. Ron Sellers, who was an AFL All-Star wide receiver in 1969, led the Boston Patriots with 705 yards receiving in 1969 and 550 yards receiving in 1970. Randy Vataha led the Patriots with 872 yards in 1971, 561 yards in 1974, and 720 yards receiving in 1975. Reggie Rucker led the team with 681 yards in 1972 and 743 yards receiving during the 1973 regular season. Darryl Stingley was the first player who was drafted in the first round by the Patriots to lead the team in receiving yards as he led the team with 370 yards receiving in 1976 and 657 yards receiving in 1977. Stanley Morgan led the team in 1978, 1980, 1981, 1982, 1983, 1985, 1986, 1987, and 1988. Harold Jackson led the team with 1,013 yards receiving in 1984, and Hart Lee Dykes led the team with 795 yards receiving in 1989. Irving Fryar led the team in yards receiving in 1990, 1991, and 1992 and Vincent Brisby led the team with 974 yards receiving in 1995. Terry Glenn led the team in yards receiving in 1996, 1998, 1999, and 2000, and Troy Brown led the team in

Troy Brown

this category in the 2001 championship season and their 2002 regular season. Deion Branch was the team leader during the 2003 championship season and David Givens led the team in yards receiving during the 2004 championship season. Deion Branch led the team again in 2005. Reche Caldwell led the Patriots with 760 yards receiving in 2006. Randy Moss set the team record with 1,493 yards receiving in the 2007 regular season. Wes Welker was the first Patriots receiver to have consecutive seasons with at least 1,000 yards receiving, and he led the team with 1,165 yards in 2008.

Jim Whalen, Derrick Ramsey, and Ben Coates are the three tight ends who have led the Patriots in yards receiving during a regular season. Jim Whalen had 651 yards receiving in 1967 and 718 yards receiving in 1968. Derrick Ramsey had 794 yards receiving in 1984, and Ben Coates had 659 yards receiving in 1993 and 1,174 yards receiving in 1994.

Harold Jackson and Stanley Morgan were the first Patriots teammates to each have more than 1,000 yards receiving in the same season. Ben Coates is the only Patriots tight end with more than 1,000 yards receiving in a season. The eight Patriots receivers who had more than 1,000 yards receiving in a regular season are Harold Jackson, Stanley Morgan, Irving Fryar, Ben Coates, Terry Glenn, Troy Brown, Randy Moss, and Wes Welker. Stanley Morgan had three regular seasons with more than 1,000 yards receiving. Terry Glenn is the only other Patriots receiver to have two regular seasons with more than 1,000 yards receiving.

The 10 Greatest Receivers of the Patriots

Stanley Morgan—at the time, was the NFL receiver who reached 10,000 career yards receiving in the shortest amount of time

Randy Moss—set the NFL record with 23 regular season TD receptions in a regular season

Ben Coates—holds the team record of having a reception in 63 consecutive regular season games

Wes Welker—set the NFL record of having at least six receptions in the first 11 games of a regular season

Gino Cappelletti—the only player to win the AFL MVP (1964) and finish second for the AFL MVP (1961)

Deion Branch—had at least 115 yards receiving in four playoff games and was the MVP of Super Bowl XXXIX

Troy Brown—set the team record with 16 receptions in a regular season game

Harold Jackson—the only starting Patriots receiver to average more than 20 yards per reception for his career

Terry Glenn—set the team record with 214 yards receiving in a regular season game

Irving Fryar—the only player with a TD reception on the Patriots first play of a game and on the last play of a game

The yearly list of the Patriots player with the most yards receiving, TD receptions, and the longest reception in the year

	Most yards receiving	Most TD receptions	Longest reception in the year
1960	Jim Colclough	Jim Colclough	Billy Wells
1961	Gino Cappelletti	Jim Colclough	Jim Colclough
1962	Jim Colclough	Jim Colclough	Jim Colclough
1963	Jim Colclough	Art Graham	Art Graham
1964	Gino Cappelletti	Gino Cappelletti and Art Graham	Art Graham
1965	Gino Cappelletti	Gino Cappelletti	Ron Burton
1966	Gino Cappelletti	Gino Cappelletti	Gino Cappelletti
1967	Jim Whalen	Larry Garron and Jim Whalen	Art Graham
1968	Jim Whalen	Jim Whalen	Jim Whalen
1969	Ron Sellers	Charley Frazier	Ron Sellers
1970	Ron Sellers	Ron Sellers	Ron Sellers
1971	Randy Vataha	Randy Vataha	Randy Vataha
1972	Reggie Rucker	Reggie Rucker	Reggie Rucker
1973	Reggie Rucker	Bob Windsor	Reggie Rucker
1974	Randy Vataha	Mack Herron	Reggie Rucker
1975	Randy Vataha	Randy Vataha	Steve Burks
1976	Darryl Stingley	Darryl Stingley and Andy Johnson	Darryl Stingley
1977	Darryl Stingley	Darryl Stingley	Darryl Stingley
1978	Stanley Morgan	Harold Jackson	Stanley Morgan
1979	Harold Jackson	Stanley Morgan	Stanley Morgan
1980	Stanley Morgan	Russ Francis	Stanley Morgan
1981	Stanley Morgan	Stanley Morgan and Don Hasselbeck	Stanley Morgan
1982	Stanley Morgan	Stanley Morgan	Stanley Morgan
1983	Stanley Morgan	Derrick Ramsey	Stephen Starring
1984	Derrick Ramsey	Derrick Ramsey	Stanley Morgan
1985	Stanley Morgan	Irving Fryar	Craig James
1986	Stanley Morgan	Stanley Morgan	Irving Fryar
1987	Stanley Morgan	Irving Fryar	Stanley Morgan
1988	Stanley Morgan	Irving Fryar	Irving Fryar
1989	Hart Lee Dykes	Cedric Jones	Cedric Jones
1990	Irving Fryar	Marv Cook	Irving Fryar
1991	Irving Fryar	Marv Cook and Irving Fryar	Michael Timpson
1992	Irving Fryar	Irving Fryar	Greg McMurtry
1993	Ben Coates	Ben Coates	Leonard Russell (after lateral)
1994	Ben Coates	Ben Coates	Ben Coates
1995	Vincent Brisby	Ben Coates	Vincent Brisby
1996	Terry Glenn	Ben Coates	Ben Coates
1997	Shawn Jefferson	Ben Coates	Shawn Jefferson
1998	Terry Glenn	Ben Coates	Terry Glenn
1999	Terry Glenn	Shawn Jefferson	Shawn Jefferson
2000	Terry Glenn	Terry Glenn	Jermaine Wiggins
2001	Troy Brown	Troy Brown	David Patten
2002	Troy Brown	Christian Fauria	Deion Branch
2003	Deion Branch	David Givens	Troy Brown
2004	David Givens	Daniel Graham and David Patten	David Givens
2005	Deion Branch	Deion Branch	Troy Brown
2006	Reche Caldwell	Troy Brown and Reche Caldwell	Reche Caldwell
2007	Randy Moss	Randy Moss	Donte Stallworth
2008	Wes Welker	Randy Moss	Randy Moss

The progression of the most yards receiving by a Patriots player in a regular season game

42 yards receiving by Jim Colclough in the 13–10 loss to the Denver Broncos at BU Field on 09-09-60

65 yards receiving by Oscar Lofton in the 28–24 victory over the New York Titans at the Polo Grounds on 09-17-60

89 yards receiving by Billy Wells in the 35–0 shutout of Los Angeles Chargers at the Los Angeles Coliseum on 10-08-60

124 yards receiving by Dick Christy in the 34–28 victory over the Oakland Raiders at BU Field on 11-04-60

131 yards receiving by Gino Cappelletti in the 31–31 tie with the Houston Oilers at BU Field on 10-13-61

142 yards receiving by Jim Colclough in the 43–14 rout of the New York Titans at the Polo Grounds on 10-06-62

149 yards receiving by Tony Romeo in the 24–24 tie with the Kansas City Chiefs at Fenway Park on 11-17-63

167 yards receiving by Art Graham in the 25–24 victory over the Houston Oilers at Fenway Park on 11-06-64

Art Graham

170 yards receiving by Stanley Morgan in the 35–14 win over the Baltimore Colts at Memorial Stadium on 11-26-78

182 yards receiving by Stanley Morgan in the 30–27 overtime loss to the Miami Dolphins at Schaefer Stadium on 11-08-81

193 yards receiving by Terry Glenn in the 23–9 victory over the Pittsburgh Steelers at Three Rivers Stadium on 12-06-98

214 yards receiving by Terry Glenn in the 19–7 victory over the Cleveland Browns at Cleveland Stadium on 10-03-99

The progression of the most yards receiving by a Patriots Wide Receiver in a regular season game

42 yards receiving by Jim Colclough in the 13–10 loss to the Denver Broncos at BU Field on 09-09-60

84 yards receiving by Jim Colclough in the 31–24 loss to the Denver Broncos at Bears Stadium on 10-23-60

85 yards receiving by Jim Colclough in the 38–21 victory over the New York Titans at BU Field on 11-11-60

85 yards receiving by Jim Colclough in the 42–14 rout of the Dallas Texans at BU Field on 11-18-60

123 yards receiving by Jim Colclough in the 45–17 rout of the Denver Broncos at BU Field on 09-16-61

131 yards receiving by Gino Cappelletti in the 31–31 tie with the Houston Oilers at BU Field on 10-13-61

142 yards receiving by Jim Colclough in the 43–14 rout of the New York Titans at the Polo Grounds on 10-06-62

147 yards receiving by Gino Cappelletti in the 35–14 loss to the New York Jets at Shea Stadium on 10-31-64

167 yards receiving by Art Graham in the 25–24 victory over the Houston Oilers at Fenway Park on 11-06-64

170 yards receiving by Stanley Morgan in the 35–14 victory over the Baltimore Colts at Memorial Stadium on 11-26-78

182 yards receiving by Stanley Morgan in the 30–27 overtime loss to the Miami Dolphins at Schaefer Stadium on 11-08-81

193 yards receiving by Terry Glenn in the 23–9 victory over the Pittsburgh Steelers at Three Rivers Stadium on 12-06-98

214 yards receiving by Terry Glenn in the 19–7 victory over the Cleveland Browns at Cleveland Stadium on 10-03-99

The progression of the most yards receiving by a Patriots Running Back in a regular season game

40 yards receiving by Jim Crawford in the 13–10 loss to the Denver Broncos at BU Field on 09-09-60

50 yards receiving by Walter Beach in the 13–0 loss to the Buffalo Bills at BU Field on 09-23-60

89 yards receiving by Billy Wells in the 35–0 shutout of the Los Angeles Chargers at the Los Angeles Coliseum on 10-08-60

124 yards receiving by Dick Christy in the 34–28 victory over the Oakland Raiders at BU Field on 11-04-60

The progression of the most yards receiving by a Patriots Tight End in a regular season game

40 yards receiving by Oscar Lofton in the 13–10 loss to the Denver Broncos at BU Field on 09-09-60

65 yards receiving by Oscar Lofton in the 28–24 victory over the New York Titans at the Polo Grounds on 09-17-60

123 yards receiving by Joe Johnson in the 24–10 loss to the Houston Oilers at BU Field on 11-25-60

149 yards receiving by Tony Romeo in the 24–24 tie with the Kansas City Chiefs at Fenway Park on 11-17-63

161 yards receiving by Ben Coates in the 39–35 loss to the Miami Dolphins at Joe Robbie Stadium on 09-04-94

The progression of the most games in a season that a Patriots Tight End had at least one game with 100 yards receiving

1 game by Joe Johnson, who had 123 yards receiving in the 24–10 loss to the Houston Oilers at BU Field on 11-25-60

1 game by Tony Romeo, who had 121 yards receiving in the 41–16 rout of the Denver Broncos at BU Field on 09-21-62

1 game by Tony Romeo, who had 149 yards receiving in the 24–24 tie with the Chiefs at Fenway Park on 11-17-63

1 game by Jim Whalen, who had 109 yards receiving in the 30–21 loss to the Raiders at Frank Youell Field on 10-24-65

2 games that Jim Whalen had at least 100 yards receiving during the 1967 regular season

3 games that Don Hasselbeck had at least 100 yards receiving during the 1981 regular season

5 games that Ben Coates had at least 100 yards receiving during the 1994 regular season

The progression of the most games in a season that a Patriots RB had at least one game with at least 100 yards receiving

1 game by Dick Christy, who had 124 yards receiving in the 34–28 win over the Oakland Raiders at BU Field on 11-04-60

1 game by Billy Lott, who had 108 yards receiving in the 52–21 rout of the Buffalo Bills at BU Field on 10-22-61

2 games by Larry Garron, who had 106 yards receiving and 113 yards receiving in the wins over the Chargers and the Oilers in 1966

The progression of the most games in a season that a Patriots WR had at least one game with at least 100 yards receiving

1 game by Jim Colclough, who had 123 yards receiving in the 45–17 rout of the Denver Broncos at BU Field on 09-16-61

1 game by Gino Cappelletti, who had 131 yards receiving in the 31–31 tie with the Houston Oilers at BU Field on 10-13-61

2 games by Jim Colclough, who had 142 yards receiving and 127 yards receiving in the two victories over the New York Titans in 1962

2 games that Jim Colclough had at least 100 yards receiving during the 1963 regular season

2 games that Gino Cappelletti had at least 100 yards receiving during the 1964 regular season

2 games that Gino Cappelletti had at least 100 yards receiving during the 1966 regular season

4 games that Ron Sellers had at least 100 yards receiving during the 1969 regular season

5 games that Stanley Morgan had at least 100 yards receiving during the 1979 regular season

8 games that Stanley Morgan had at least 100 yards receiving during the 1986 regular season

9 games that Randy Moss had at least 100 yards receiving during the 2007 regular season

The progression of the most seasons that a Patriots Receiver had at least one game with at least 100 yards receiving

5 regular seasons that Jim Colclough had at least one game with at least 100 yards receiving (from 1961–65)

10 regular seasons that Stanley Morgan had at least one game with at least 100 yards receiving (from 1978–87)

Every time that two Patriots Wide Receivers had at least 100 yards receiving in the same regular season game

1979 regular season
Harold Jackson had 121 yards and Stanley Morgan had 102 yards in the 56–3 rout of the New York Jets at Schaefer Stadium on 09-09-79

Stanley Morgan had 124 yards and Harold Jackson had 105 yards in the 39–24 loss to Miami at the Orange Bowl on 11-29-79

1986 regular season
Stanley Morgan had 116 yards and Stephen Starring had 102 yards in the 33–3 rout of the Colts at Sullivan Stadium on 09-07-86

Stanley Morgan had 161 yards and Irving Fryar had 110 yards in the 38–31 loss to the Seattle Seahawks at Sullivan Stadium on 09-21-86

Stanley Morgan had 162 yards and Irving Fryar had 126 yards in the 31–24 loss to the New York Jets at Sullivan Stadium on 10-12-86

1987 regular season
Stanley Morgan had 146 yards and Irving Fryar had 107 yards in the 26–23 win over the Los Angeles Raiders at Sullivan Stadium on 11-01-87

2000 regular season
Terry Glenn had 129 yards and Troy Brown had 110 yards in the 16–13 win over the Bengals at Foxboro Stadium on 11-19-00

2001 championship season
Troy Brown had 117 yards and Terry Glenn had 110 yards in the 29–26 overtime win vs the Chargers at Foxboro Stadium on 10-14-01

Troy Brown had 120 yards and David Patten had 117 yards in the 38–17 rout of the Colts at the RCA Dome on 10-21-01

2002 regular season
Troy Brown had 176 yards and David Patten had 108 yards in the 41–38 overtime win vs the Chiefs at Gillette Stadium on 09-22-02

2007 undefeated regular season
Donte Stallworth had 136 yards and Wes Welker had 124 yards in the 48–27 rout of Dallas at Texas Stadium on 10-14-07

Wes Welker had 138 yards and Randy Moss had 122 yards in the 49–28 win over the Dolphins at Miami on 10-21-07

Randy Moss had 135 yards and Jabar Gaffney had 122 yards in the 34–13 rout of the Steelers at Gillette Stadium on 12-09-07

Wes Welker had 122 yards and Randy Moss had 100 yards in the 38–35 win over the Giants at Giants Stadium on 12-29-07

2008 regular season
Randy Moss had 125 yards and Wes Welker had 120 yards in the 48–28 rout of Miami at Dolphin Stadium on 11-23-08

Every Patriots Running Back who had at least 100 yards receiving in a regular season game

1960 regular season
Dick Christy had 124 yards receiving in the 34–28 victory over the Oakland Raiders at BU Field on 11-04-60

1961 regular season
Billy Lott had 108 yards receiving in the 52–21 rout of the Buffalo Bills at BU Field on 10-22-61

1966 regular season
Larry Garron had 106 yards receiving in the 35–17 victory over the San Diego Chargers at Fenway Park on 10-23-66

Larry Garron had 113 yards receiving in the 38–14 victory over the Houston Oilers at Rice Stadium on 12-11-66

1975 regular season
Don Calhoun had 100 yards receiving in the 34–14 loss to the Buffalo Bills at Schaefer Stadium on 12-14-75

Andy Johnson had 103 yards receiving in the 34–21 loss to the Baltimore Colts at Memorial Stadium on 12-21-75

1985 regular season
Tony Collins had 109 yards receiving in the 32–14 win over the Tampa Bay Buccaneers at Tampa Stadium on 10-27-85

Kevin Faulk

1987 regular season
Tony Collins had 100 yards receiving in the 34–31 overtime loss to the Philadelphia Eagles at Sullivan Stadium on 11-29-87

2002 regular season
Kevin Faulk had 109 yards receiving in the 33–30 victory over the Chicago Bears at Memorial Stadium on 11-10-02

Ben Coates (87)

2003 championship season
Kevin Faulk had 108 yards receiving in the 23–20 overtime win vs the Houston Texans at Reliant Stadium on 11-23-03

The only Patriots Tight End who had at least 100 yards receiving in three consecutive games
1994 regular season
Ben Coates had 161 yards receiving in the 39–35 loss to the Miami Dolphins at Joe Robbie Stadium on 09-04-94

Ben Coates had 124 yards receiving in the 38–35 loss to the Buffalo Bills at Foxboro Stadium on 09-11-94

Ben Coates had 108 yards receiving in the 31–28 win over the Cincinnati Bengals at Riverfront Stadium on 09-18-94

Every time that a Patriots TE and a Patriots WR had at least 100 yards receiving in the same regular season game
1963 regular season
Tony Romeo had 149 yards and Jim Colclough had 137 yards in the 24–24 tie with the Chiefs at Fenway Park on 11-17-63

1967 regular season
Jim Whalen had 122 yards and Jim Colclough had 112 yards in the 41–32 loss to Miami at the Orange Bowl on 12-17-67

1994 regular season
Ben Coates had 124 yards and Michael Timpson had 101 yards in the 38–35 loss to Buffalo at Foxboro Stadium on 09-11-94

Ben Coates had 108 yards and Michael Timpson had 125 yards in the 31–28 win over Cincinnati at Riverfront Stadium on 09-18-94

1996 regular season
Ben Coates had 135 yards and Terry Glenn had 112 yards in the 42–23 win over Miami at Foxboro Stadium on 11-03-96

2005 regular season
Daniel Graham had 119 yards and Deion Branch had 107 yards in the 31–28 win over Atlanta at the Georgia Dome on 10-09-05

The only Patriots Receiver who had at least 100 yards receiving in four consecutive regular season games

2007 regular season

Randy Moss had 183 yards, 105 yards, 115 yards, and 102 yards receiving in the first four games of the 2007 regular season

The progression of the most yards receiving by a Patriots player in a regular season

666 yards receiving by Jim Colclough in 1960

768 yards receiving by Gino Cappelletti in 1961

868 yards receiving by Jim Colclough in 1962

872 yards receiving by Randy Vataha in 1971

1,013 yards receiving by Harold Jackson in 1979

1,029 yards receiving by Stanley Morgan in 1981

1,491 yards receiving by Stanley Morgan in 1986

1,493 yards receiving by Randy Moss in 2007

The progression of the most yards receiving by a Patriots Running Back in a regular season

284 yards receiving by Alan Miller in 1960

341 yards receiving by Larry Garron in 1961

461 yards receiving by Ron Burton in 1962

507 yards receiving by Larry Garron in 1967

549 yards receiving by Tony Collins in 1985

684 yards receiving by Tony Collins in 1986

The progression of the most yards receiving by a Patriots Tight End in a regular season

360 yards receiving by Oscar Lofton in 1960

608 yards receiving by Tony Romeo in 1962

651 yards receiving by Jim Whalen in 1967

718 yards receiving by Jim Whalen in 1968

808 yards receiving by Don Hasselbeck in 1981

808 yards receiving by Marv Cook in 1991

1,174 yards receiving by Ben Coates in 1994

The progression of the most career yards receiving by a Patriots Wide Receiver

5,001 yards receiving by Jim Colclough over the 1960–68 regular seasons

10,352 yards receiving by Stanley Morgan over the 1977–89 regular seasons

The progression of the most career yards receiving by a Patriots Running Back

2,502 career yards receiving by Larry Garron over the 1960–68 regular seasons

3,304 career yards receiving by Kevin Faulk

The progression of the most career yards receiving by a Patriots Tight End

360 career yards receiving by Oscar Lofton during the 1960 regular season

506 career yards receiving by Tom Stephens over the 1960–64 regular seasons

1,724 carer yards receiving by Tony Romeo over the 1962–67 regular seasons

2,487 career yards receiving by Jim Whalen over the 1965–69 regular seasons

3,157 career yards receiving by Russ Francis over the 1975–80 and 1987–88 regular seasons

5,471 career yards receiving by Ben Coates over the 1991–99 regular seasons

The progression of the most receptions by a Patriots player in a regular season game

4 receptions by Jim Colclough in the 13–10 loss to the Denver Broncos at BU Field on 09-09-60

5 receptions by Ron Burton in the 31–24 loss to the Denver Broncos at Bears Stadium on 10-23-60

9 receptions by Jim Colclough in the 42–14 rout of the Dallas Texans at BU Field on 11-18-60

10 receptions by Tony Romeo in the 24–24 tie with the Kansas City Chiefs at Fenway Park on 11-17-63

11 receptions by Art Graham in the 27–27 tie with the Kansas City Chiefs at Municipal Stadium on 11-20-66

12 receptions by Ben Coates in the 12–10 victory over the Indianapolis Colts at the RCA Dome on 11-27-94

13 receptions by Terry Glenn in the 19–7 victory over the Cleveland Browns at Cleveland Stadium on 10-03-99

16 receptions by Troy Brown in the 41–38 overtime win vs the Kansas City Chiefs at Gillette Stadium on 09-22-02

The progression of the most receptions by a Patriots Wide Receiver in a regular season game

4 receptions by Jim Colclough in the 13–10 loss to the Denver Broncos at BU Field on 09-09-60

6 receptions by Jim Colclough in the 38–21 victory over the New York Titans at BU Field on 11-11-60

9 receptions by Jim Colclough in the 42–14 rout of the Dallas Texans at BU Field on 11-18-60

11 receptions by Art Graham in the 27–27 tie with the Kansas City Chiefs at Municipal Stadium on 11-20-66

13 receptions by Terry Glenn in the 19–7 victory over the Cleveland Browns at Cleveland Stadium on 10-03-99

16 receptions by Troy Brown in the 41–38 overtime win vs the Kansas City Chiefs at Gillette Stadium on 09-22-02

The Receiver who caught the most passes in a regular season game during the 2002 NFL Season

Troy Brown caught 16 passes in the 41–38 overtime victory vs the Kansas City Chiefs at Gillette Stadium on 09-22-02

The progression of the most receptions by a Patriots Running Back in a regular season game

3 receptions by Alan Miller in the 13–10 loss to the Denver Broncos at BU Field on 09-09-60

5 receptions by Ron Burton in the 31–24 loss to the Denver Broncos at Bears Stadium on 10-23-60

6 receptions by Walter Beach in the 45–16 loss to the Los Angeles Chargers at BU Field on 10-28-60

8 receptions by Mack Herron in the 18–13 loss to the Baltimore Colts at Memorial Stadium on 12-16-73

10 receptions by Tony Collins in the 30–28 victory over the Los Angeles Rams at Anaheim Stadium on 11-16-86

11 receptions by Tony Collins in the 34–31 Overtime loss to the Philadelphia Eagles at Sullivan Stadium on 11-29-87

11 receptions by Leroy Thompson in the 26–20 Overtime win vs the Minnesota Vikings at Foxboro Stadium on 11-13-94

11 receptions by Kevin Faulk in the 21–16 loss to the Tampa Bay Buccaneers at Foxboro Stadium on 09-03-00

The progression of the most receptions by a Patriots Tight End in a regular season game

2 receptions by Oscar Lofton in the 13–10 loss to the Denver Broncos at BU Field on 09-09-60

4 receptions by Oscar Lofton in the 28–24 victory over the New York Titans at the Polo Grounds on 09-17-60

5 receptions by Joe Johnson in the 24–10 loss to the Houston Oilers at BU Field on 11-25-60

6 receptions by Tom Stephens in the 35–21 victory over the Oakland Raiders at Candlestick Park on 12-09-61

6 receptions by Tony Romeo in the 38–14 victory over the New York Jets at Boston College Alumni Stadium on 09-08-63

10 receptions by Tony Romeo in the 24–24 tie with the Kansas City Chiefs at Fenway Park on 11-17-63

10 receptions by Marv Cook in the 24–20 victory over the Houston Oilers at Foxboro Stadium on 09-22-91

10 receptions by Ben Coates in the 26–20 overtime win vs the Minnesota Vikings at Foxboro Stadium on 11-13-94

12 receptions by Ben Coates in the 12–10 victory over the Indianapolis Colts at the RCA Dome on 11-27-94

The progression of the most consecutive regular season games with a pass reception by a Patriots Player

42 consecutive games that Jim Colclough caught at least one pass from 09-09-60 to 12-16-62

63 consecutive games that Ben Coates caught at least one pass from 12-27-92 to 12-15-96

The progression of the most consecutive regular season games that a Patriots Receiver had at least five receptions

2 consecutive games that Gino Cappelletti had at least five receptions (from 10-07-61 to 10-31-61)

2 consecutive games that Jim Colclough had at least five receptions (from 11-03-61 to 11-17-61)

2 consecutive games that Art Graham had at least five receptions (from 10-09-64 to 10-16-64)

3 consecutive games that Gino Cappelletti had at least five receptions (from 11-15-64 to 11-29-64)

3 consecutive games that Gino Cappelletti had at least five receptions (from 10-02-66 to 10-23-66)

3 consecutive games that Jim Whalen had at least five receptions (from 11-17-68 to 12-01-68)

4 consecutive games that Reggie Rucker had at least five receptions (from 11-04-73 to 11-25-73)

4 consecutive games that Stanley Morgan had at least five receptions (from 12-07-86 to 09-13-87)

5 consecutive games that Marv Cook had at least five receptions (from 09-22-91 to 10-13-91)

5 consecutive games that Terry Glenn had at least five receptions (from 09-08-96 to 10-27-96) and (11-24-96 to 12-21-96)

5 consecutive games that Terry Glenn had at least five receptions (from 09-12-99 to 10-10-99)

5 consecutive games that Troy Brown had at least five receptions (from 10-07-01 to 11-04-01)

10 consecutive games that Troy Brown had at least five receptions (from 11-18-01 to 09-22-02)

13 consecutive regular season games that Wes Welker had at least five receptions (from 12-23-07 to 11-30-08)

NFL record set in the 2008 regular season
Wes Welker set an NFL Record with at least six receptions in each of the first 11 regular season games

The progression of the most regular season receptions by a Patriots Player
49 receptions by Jim Colclough in 1960

49 receptions by Gino Cappelletti in 1964

51 receptions by Art Graham in 1966

51 receptions by Randy Vataha in 1971

53 receptions by Reggie Rucker in 1973

58 receptions by Stanley Morgan in 1983

84 receptions by Stanley Morgan in 1986

96 receptions by Ben Coates in 1994

101 receptions by Troy Brown in 2001

112 receptions by Wes Welker in 2007 (Tied for NFL lead)

The progression of the most regular season receptions by a Patriots Wide Receiver
49 receptions by Jim Colclough in 1960

49 receptions by Gino Cappelletti in 1964

51 receptions by Art Graham in 1966

51 receptions by Randy Vataha in 1971

53 receptions by Reggie Rucker in 1973

58 receptions by Stanley Morgan in 1983

Did you know that?
Darryl Stingley was the inspiration for Russ Francis attempting to catch the ball with one hand over the middle of the field.

Some of Russ Francis' most memorable receptions were made with one hand and Francis credits his roommate, Darryl Stingley, for providing the attitude and the fortitude that gave Francis the courage to make those dangerous receptions in the open field.

84 receptions by Stanley Morgan in 1986

90 receptions by Terry Glenn in 1996

101 receptions by Troy Brown in 2001

112 receptions by Wes Welker in 2007 (Tied for NFL lead)

The progression of the most regular season receptions by a Patriots Running Back
29 receptions by Alan Miller in 1960

32 receptions by Billy Lott in 1961

40 receptions by Ron Burton in 1962

40 receptions by Larry Garron in 1964

Darryl Stingley

Russ Francis

42 receptions by Sam Cunningham in 1977

52 receptions by Tony Collins in 1985

77 receptions by Tony Collins in 1986

The progession of the most receptions by a Patriots Tight End in a regular season

19 receptions by Oscar Lofton in 1960

34 receptions by Tony Romeo in 1962

39 receptions by Jim Whalen in 1967

47 receptions by Jim Whalen in 1968

66 receptions by Derrick Ramsey in 1984

82 receptions by Marv Cook in 1991

96 receptions by Ben Coates in 1994

The Tight End with the most receptions in the NFL in 1991

New England Patriots tight end Marv Cook led the NFL with 82 receptions in 1991

The Tight End with the most receptions in the NFL in a regular season

New England Patriots tight end Ben Coates set the NFL record with 96 receptions by a tight end in the 1994 regular season

Every Patriots player who had more than 100 yards receiving and averaged more than 50 yards per reception in a game

Larry Garron averaged 53 yards per reception in the 35–17 victory over the San Deigo Chargers at Fenway Park on 10-23-66

Jim Whalen averaged 56.5 yards per reception in the 48–14 loss to the New York Jets at Shea Stadium on 10-27-68

Ron Sellers averaged 52.7 yards per reception in the 27–23 loss to the Houston Oilers at the Astrodome on 12-14-69

Stanley Morgan averaged 54 yards per reception in the 37–31 win over Seattle at the Kingdome on 09-21-80

Stephen Starring averaged 54 yards per reception in the 28–23 win over the Steelers at Three Rivers Stadium on 09-25-83

The progression of the most yards per reception by a Patriots player in a season (10 or more receptions)

18.9 yards per reception by Oscar Lofton in 1960

26.1 yards per reception by Art Graham in 1963

26.1 yards per reception by Ron Sellers in 1969

The progression of the most yards per reception by a Patriots Wide Receiver in a season (10 or more receptions)

13.6 yards per reception by Jim Colclough in 1960

18.0 yards per reception by Jim Colclough in 1961

21.7 yards per reception by Jim Colclough in 1962

26.1 yards per reception by Art Graham in 1963

26.1 yards per reception by Ron Sellers in 1969

The Patriots Receiver who led the AFL with the most yards per reception in a specific season

Jim Colclough led the AFL with 21.7 yards per reception during the 1962 AFL season

The only Patriots Receiver who has led the NFL with the most yards per reception in a specific season

1979 regular season

Stanley Morgan led the NFL with 22.8 yards per reception during the 1979 regular season

1980 regular season

Stanley Morgan led the NFL with 22.0 yards per reception during the 1980 regular season

1981 regular season

Stanley Morgan led the NFL with 23.4 yards per reception during the 1981 regular season

The progression of the most yards per reception by a Patriots Running Back in a season (5 or more receptions)

14.7 yards per reception by Walter Beach in 1960

14.7 yards per reception by Billy Wells in 1960

14.8 yards per reception by Larry Garron in 1965

14.8 yards per reception by Joe Bellino in 1965

16.9 yards per reception by Larry Garron in 1967

17.3 yards per reception by Bob Cappadona in 1967

18.4 yards per reception by Andy Johnson in 1974

22.2 yards per reception by Don Calhoun in 1975

The most yards per reception by a Patriots Tight End in a regular season (5 or more receptions)

18.9 yards per reception by Oscar Lofton in 1960

The progression of the career-best average yards per reception by a Patriots WR

17.7 yards per reception by Jim Colclough over the 1960–68 seasons

20.3 yards per reception by Harold Jackson over the 1978–81 seasons

The career best average yards per reception by a Patriots RB

14.67 yards per reception by Walter Beach in 1960

14.71 yards per reception by Billy Wells in 1960

The career-best average yards per reception by a Patriots Tight End

18.9 yards per reception by Oscar Lofton in 1960

The progression of the most career regular season receptions by a Patriots Wide Receiver

283 career receptions by Jim Colclough over the 1960–68 regular seasons

292 career receptions by Gino Cappelletti over the 1960–70 regular seasons

534 career receptions by Stanley Morgan over the 1977–89 regular season

The progression of the most career regular season receptions by a Patriots Running Back

185 career receptions by Larry Garron over the 1960–68 regular seasons

210 career receptions by Sam Cunningham over the 1973–79 and 1981–82 regular seasons

261 career receptions by Tony Collins over the 1981–87 regular seasons

381 career receptions by Kevin Faulk over the 1999–2008 regular seasons

The progression of the most career regular season receptions by a Patriots Tight End

41 career receptions by Tom Stephens over the 1960–64 regular seasons

110 career receptions by Tony Romeo over the 1962–67 regular seasons

153 career receptions by Jim Whalen over the 1965–69 regular seasons

207 career receptions by Russ Francis over the 1975–80 and 1987–88 regular seasons

490 career receptions by Ben Coates over the 1991–99 regular seasons

The progression of the longest reception by a Patriots player in a regular season game

1 yard reception by Jim Colclough in the 13–10 loss to the Denver Broncos at BU Field on 09-09-60

6 yard reception by Jim Colclough in the 13–10 loss to the Denver Broncos at BU Field on 09-09-60

13 yard reception by Oscar Lofton in the 13–10 loss to the Denver Broncos at BU Field on 09-09-60

17 yard reception by Oscar Lofton in the 13–10 loss to the Denver Broncos at BU Field on 09-09-60

19 yard reception by Jim Colclough in the 13–10 loss to the Denver Broncos at BU Field on 09-09-60

40 yard reception by Jim Crawford in the 13–10 loss to the Denver Broncos at BU Field on 09-09-60

78 yard reception by Billy Wells in the 35–0 shutout of the Los Angeles Chargers at the Los Angeles Coliseum on 10-08-60

78-yard TD reception by Jim Colclough in the 24–17 victory over the New York Titans at BU Field on 11-30-62

80-yard TD reception by Art Graham in the 37–17 victory over the Houston Oilers at Jeppesen Stadium on 11-29-64

87-yard TD reception by Jim Whalen in the 48–14 loss to the New York Jets at Shea Stadium on 10-27-68

88-yard TD reception by Randy Vataha in the 21–17 victory over the Baltimore Colts at Memorial Stadium on 12-19-71

90-yard TD reception by Craig James in the 20–7 loss to the Chicago Bears at Soldier Field on 09-15-85

91-yard TD reception by David Patten in the 38–17 victory over the Indianapolis Colts at the RCA Dome on 10-21-01

The progression of the longest reception by a Patriots Wide Receiver in a regular season game

1 yard reception by Jim Colclough in the 13–10 loss to the Denver Broncos at BU Field on 09-09-60

6 yard reception by Jim Colclough in the 13–10 loss to the Denver Broncos at BU Field on 09-09-60

19 yard reception by Jim Colclough in the 13–10 loss to the Denver Broncos at BU Field on 09-09-60

31 yard reception by Jerry Green in the 28–24 victory over the New York Titans at the Polo Grounds on 09-17-60

61 yard reception by Jim Colclough in the 31–24 loss to the Denver Broncos at Bears Stadium on 10-23-60

78-yard TD reception by Jim Colclough in the 24–17 victory over the New York Titans at BU Field on 11-30-62

80-yard TD reception by Art Graham in the 34–17 victory over the Houston Oilers at Jeppesen Stadium on 11-29-64

88-yard TD reception by Randy Vataha in the 21–17 victory over the Baltimore Colts at Memorial Stadium on 12-19-71

91-yard TD reception by David Patten in the 38–17 rout of the Indianapolis Colts at the RCA Dome on 10-21-01

David Patten

The Wide Receiver with the longest reception in the AFL in 1967

Art Graham hauled in a 79-yard TD pass in the 26–21 loss to the Denver Broncos on 09-03-67

The Wide Receiver with the longest reception in the NFL in 2001

David Patten hauled in a 91-yard TD pass in the 38–17 rout of the Indianapolis Colts on 10-21-01

The progression of the longest reception by a Patriots Running Back in a regular season game

40-yard reception by Jim Crawford in the 13–10 loss to the Denver Broncos at BU Field on 09-09-60

78-yard reception by Billy Wells in the 35–0 shutout of the Los Angeles Chargers at the Los Angeles Coliseum on 10-08-60

80-yard TD reception by Carl Garrett in the 38–33 victory over the Buffalo Bills at Schaefer Stadium on 11-14-71

90-yard TD reception by Craig James in the 20–7 loss to the Chicago Bears at Soldier Field on 09-15-85

Carl Garrett

The progression of the longest reception by a Patriots Tight End in a regular season game

13-yard reception by Oscar Lofton in the 13–10 loss to the Denver Broncos at BU Field on 09-09-60

17-yard reception by Oscar Lofton in the 13–10 loss to the Denver Broncos at BU Field on 09-09-60

23-yard reception by Oscar Lofton in the 13–10 loss to the Denver Broncos at BU Field on 09-09-60

24-yard reception by Tom Stephens in the 45–16 loss to the Los Angeles Chargers at BU Field on 10-28-60

52-yard TD reception by Joe Johnson in the 24–10 loss to the Houston Oilers at BU Field on 11-25-60

53-yard reception by Tom Stephens in the 38–14 loss to the Buffalo Bills at War Memorial Stadium on 12-04-60

62-yard reception by Tony Romeo in the 41–16 rout of the Denver Broncos at BU Field on 09-21-62

67-yard reception by Jim Whalen in the 30–21 loss to the Oakland Raiders at Frank Youell Field on 10-24-65

87-yard TD reception by Jim Whalen in the 48–14 loss to the New York Jets at Shea Stadium on 10-27-68

The progression of the longest reception by a Patriots Quarterback in a regular season game

16-yard reception by Steve Grogan in the 29–28 loss to the Baltimore Colts at Schaefer Stadium on 09-06-81

23-yard reception by Tom Brady in the 20–13 victory over the Miami Dolphins at Foxboro Stadium on 12-22-01

The longest reception by a Patriots Lineman, who had reported as a Tight End, in a regular season game

6-yard TD reception by Pete Brock in the 38–24 victory over the New York Jets at Shea Stadium on 11-21-76

(Upon delivering the play from the sideline Brock told Steve Grogan that it was "200 to me" rather than "200 Tight End Delay")

The longest reception by a Patriots Offensive Lineman who caught a deflected pass in a regular season game

11 yard reception by Walt Cudzik in the 45–16 loss to the Los Angeles Chargers at BU Field on 10-28-60

The only Patriots Defensive Lineman, who was lined up as a RB, with a pass reception in a regular season game

2004 championship season

Dan Klecko caught an 11-yard pass, on a third-down play, in the 30–20 win over Seattle at Gillette Stadium on 10-17-04

Dan Klecko caught an eight-yard pass, on the first play from scrimmage, in the 13–7 win vs the Jets at Gillette Stadium on 10-24-04

Dan Klecko lost one yard on another reception in the 13–7 victory over the New York Jets at Gillette Stadium on 10-24-04

Every Patriots Offensive Lineman who has caught a deflected pass in a regular season game

1960 regular season

Walt Cudzik caught a deflected pass for an 11 yard gain in the 45–16 loss to the Los Angeles Chargers at BU Field on 10-28-60

1968 regular season

Justin Canale caught a deflected pass for no gain in the 27–17 loss to the San Diego Chargers at Fenway Park on 11-10-68

1986 regular season

Brian Holloway caught a deflected pass for a five yard gain in the 34–7 rout of the Dolphins at Sullivan Stadium on 10-05-86

1988 regular season

Sean Farrell caught a deflected pass for a four yard gain in the 13–7 win over the Seattle Seahawks at Sullivan Stadium on 12-04-88

2003 championship season

Joe Andruzzi caught a deflected pass for no gain in the 38–34 win over the Indianapolis Colts at the RCA Dome on 11-30-03

Every Patriots Offensive Lineman, who was lined up as a Tight End, with a pass reception in a regular season game

1976 regular season

Pete Brock caught a six-yard TD pass in the 38–24 victory over the New York Jets at Shea Stadium on 11-21-76

2005 regular season

Tom Ashworth caught a one-yard TD pass in the 28–0 shutout of the Tampa Bay Buccaneers at Gillette Stadium on 12-17-05

Every reception by a Patriots Defensive Back, who had reported as a Receiver, in a regular season game

1961 regular season

Chuck Shonta caught a nine-yard pass in the 41–0 shutout of the San Diego Chargers at Balboa Stadium on 12-17-61

1962 regular season

Don Webb caught an 11-yard pass in the 43–14 rout of the New York Titans at the Polo Grounds on 10-06-62

The only Patriots Linebacker, who was lined up as a Running Back, with a reception in a regular season game

Bryan Cox caught a seven-yard pass in the 29–26 Overtime win vs the San Diego Chargers at Foxboro Stadium on 10-14-01

Every Patriots LB/TE who had at least one reception in a regular season

1974 regular season

John Tanner had two receptions, one for a TD, in 1974

2002 regular season

Mike Vrabel caught a one-yard TD pass on 09-29-02

2004 championship season

Mike Vrabel had three receptions, two for a TD, in 2004

2005 regular season

Mike Vrabel had four receptions, three for a TD, in 2005

2007 undefeated regular season

Mike Vrabel had two TD receptions in 2007

The progression of the longest reception and lateral after the reception by the Patriots in a regular season game

1960 regular season

5 yards; as Jim Colclough caught a pass on the line of scrimmage and lateraled to Dick Christy, who ran five yards on 11-18-60

1964 regular season

58 yards; as Jim Colclough caught a 37-yard pass then he lateraled it to Gino Cappelletti, who ran for 14 additional yards before lateraling it to Ron Burton, who ran for seven more yards, in the game played on 10-16-64

1993 regular season

82 yards; as Kevin Turner caught a 13-yard pass and then lateraled it to Leonard Russell who ran an additional 69 yards on 10-19-93

Notable Patriots players who have received a lateral from another receiver after his initial pass reception

1960 regular season

Dick Christy ran five yards with a lateral from Jim Colclough in the 42–14 rout of the Dallas Texans on 11-18-60

1964 regular season

Gino Cappelletti ran 14 yards with a lateral from Jim Colclough in the 43–43 tie with the Oakland Raiders on 10-16-64

Ron Burton then ran seven yards with the lateral from Gino Cappelletti in the 43–43 tie with the Oakland Raiders on 10-16-64

1988 regular season

Craig James ran 20 yards with a lateral from Willie Scott, on the last play, in the 16–14 loss to Bufffalo on 09-18-88

Stanley Morgan ran seven yards with a lateral from Cedric Jones, to end the fourth Quarter, in the 10–7 overtime win vs Tampa on 12-11-88

1993 regular season

Kevin Turner caught a 13-yard pass and lateraled to Leonard Russell for an 82-yard play in the 23–21 win vs Phoenix on 10-10-93

The only Patriots player who has caught a TD pass on a double lateral pass play in a regular season game

Jabar Gaffney caught a 56-yard TD pass from Tom Brady who just had lateraled to Randy Moss in the 34–13 win on 12-09-07

The progression of the longest reception by a Patriots Player on a fourth down play in a regular season game

6-yard TD reception by Jim Colclough in the 28–24 victory over the New York Titans at the Polo Grounds on 09-17-60

22 yard reception by Jim Colclough in the 45–16 loss to the Los Angeles Chargers at BU Field on 10-28-60

27-yard TD reception by Larry Garron in the 37–30 loss to the New York Titans at the Polo Grounds on 10-01-61

40 yard reception by Bill Rademacher in the 17–16 loss to Miami Dolphins at Boston College Alumni Stadium on 11-09-69

54-yard TD reception by Ben Coates in the 38–14 loss to the Buffalo Bills at Rich Stadium on 09-05-93

The progression of the longest reception by a Patriots Wide Receiver on a fourth down play in a regular season game

6-yard TD reception by Jim Colclough, on fourth-and-goal, in the 28–24 win over the New York Titans at the Polo Grounds on 09-17-60

22 yard reception by Jim Colclough, on fourth-and-16, in the 45–16 loss to the Los Angeles Chargers at BU Field on 10-28-60

40 yard reception by Bill Rademacher, on fourth-and-15, in the 17–16 loss to the Dolphins at BC Alumni Stadium on 11-09-69

The progression of the longest reception by a Patriots Running Back on a fourth-down play in a regular season game

27-yard TD reception by Larry Garron, on fourth-and-13, in the 37–30 loss to the New York Titans at the Polo Grounds on 10-01-61

28 yard reception by Kevin Faulk, on fourth-and-3, in the 44–13 rout of the Indianapolis Colts at Foxboro Stadium on 09-30-01

The progression of the longest reception by a Patriots Tight End on a fourth down play in a regular season game

1-yard TD reception by Tom Stephens, on fourth-and-goal, in the 23–21 win over the Bills at War Memorial Stadium on 09-23-61

15-yard TD reception by Tony Romeo, on fourth-and-11, in the 24–14 loss to the Buffalo Bills at Fenway Park on 12-20-64

28-yard TD reception by Bob Windsor, on fourth-and-2, in the 33–24 win over the Packers at Schaefer Stadium on 11-18-73

38-yard TD reception by Russ Francis, on fourth-and-2, in the 30–27 win over the Steelers at Three Rivers Stadium on 09-26-76

54-yard TD reception by Ben Coates, on fourth-and-1, in the 38–14 loss to the Buffalo Bills at Rich Stadium on 09-05-93

The only Patriots player with a TD reception on a fourth-down flea-flicker play in a regular season game

Greg Hawthorne caught a 28-yard TD pass, on fourth-and-1, in the 17–13 win over the Miami Dolphins at Sullivan Stadium on 11-03-85

The only Patriots player with a TD reception on a fourth-down Halfback Option Pass in a regular season game

1986 regular season
Tony Collins caught a 10-yard TD pass, on fourth-and-1, in the 20–6 victory over the New York Jets at the Meadowlands on 09-11-86

1987 regular season
Tony Collins caught a 15-yard TD pass, on fourth-and-1, in the 26–23 victory over the Los Angeles Raiders at Sullivan Stadium on 11-01-87

The only Patriots Running Back who has caught a TD pass on a fake field-goal attempt in a regular season game

Larry Garron caught a 27-yard TD pass, on fourth-and-13, in the 37-30 loss to the New York Titans at the Polo Grounds on 10-01-61

The only Patriots Wide Receiver who has caught a fake field goal TD pass in a regular season game

Troy Brown snared a four-yard TD, on fourth-and-goal, in the 40–22 win over the St. Louis Rams at the Edward Jones Dome on 11-07-04

The only Patriots player who had a game-winning TD reception on a fourth down play in a regular season game

Tony Romeo caught a two-yard TD pass from Babe Parilli, on fourth-and-goal, in the 27–23 win over the New York Jets at Shea Stadium on 11-28-65

Every Patriots Wide Receiver who had a fourth down TD reception in a regular season game

1960 regular season
Jim Colclough scored on a six-yard TD pass, on fourth-and-goal, in the 28–24 win over the New York Titans at the Polo Grounds on 09-17-60

1983 regular season
Stanley Morgan caught a 32-yard TD pass, on fourth-and-2, in the 33–13 loss to the San Francisco 49ers at Sullivan Stadium on 10-02-83

1986 regular season
Stanley Morgan scored on a 15-yard TD, on fourth-and-4, in the 29–24 loss to the San Francisco 49ers at Sullivan Stadium on 12-14-86

1987 regular season
Stanley Morgan caught a five-yard TD pass, on fourth-and-goal, in the 23–17 overtime loss to the Dallas Cowboys at Sullivan Stadium on 11-15-87

1989 regular season
Hart Lee Dykes scored on a 13-yard TD pass, on fourth-and-4, in the 28–24 loss to the New Orleans Saints at Sullivan Stadium on 11-12-89

1994 regular season
Ray Crittenden scored on a three-yard TD pass, on fourth-and-goal, in the 24–17 loss to the New York Jets at the Meadowlands on 10-16-94

2000 regular season
Troy Brown caught a seven-yard TD pass, on fourth-and-goal, in the 24–17 loss to the Chicago Bears at Soldier Field on 12-10-00

2004 championship season
Troy Brown caught a four-yard TD, on fourth-and-goal, in the 40–22 win over the St. Louis Rams at the Edward Jones Dome on 11-07-04

2008 regular season
Jabar Gaffney caught a five-yard TD pass, on fourth-and-3, in the 38–13 loss to the San Diego Chargers at Gillette Stadium on 09-21-08

Randy Moss caught a 16-yard TD, on fourth-and-1, with eight seconds left, in the 34–31 overtime loss to the Jets at Gillette Stadium on 11-13-08

Every Patriots Running Back who had a fourth-down TD reception in a regular season game

1961 regular season
Larry Garron grabbed a 27-yard TD pass, on fourth-and-13, in the 37–30 loss to the New York Titans at the Polo Grounds on 10-01-61

1986 regular season
Tony Collins caught a 10-yard TD pass, on fourth-and-1, in the 20–6 win over the New York Jets at the Meadowlands on 09-11-86

1987 regular season
Tony Collins snared a 15-yard TD pass, on fourth-and-1, in the 26–23 win over the Los Angeles Raiders at Sullivan Stadium on 11-01-87

1990 regular season
George Adams cradled a four-yard TD pass, on fourth-and-goal, in the 17–10 loss to the Dolphins at Joe Robbie Stadium on 10-18-90

1993 regular season
Kevin Turner caught a six-yard TD pass, on fourth-and-1, in the 20–17 win over the Browns at Cleveland Stadium on 12-19-93

Every Patriots Tight End who had a fourth-down TD reception in a regular season game

1961 regular season
Tom Stephens caught a one-yard TD pass, on fourth-and-goal, in the 23–21 win over the Buffalo Bills at War Memorial Stadium on 09-23-61

1964 regular season
Tony Romeo grabbed a 15-yard TD pass, on fourth-and-11, in the 24–14 loss to the Buffalo Bills at Fenway Park on 12-20-64

1965 regular season
Tony Romeo caught a two-yard TD pass, on fourth-and-goal, in the 27–23 win over the New York Jets at Shea Stadium on 11-28-65

1973 regular season
Bob Windsor caught a 28-yard TD pass, on fourth-and-2, in the 33–24 win over the Packers at Schaefer Stadium on 11-18-73

1976 regular season
Russ Francis hauled in a 38-yard TD pass, on fourth-and-2, in the 30–27 win over the Pittsburgh Steelers at Three Rivers Stadium on 09-26-76

1984 regular season
Derrick Ramsey snared a five-yard TD pass, on fourth-and-goal, in the 44–24 loss to the Miami Dolphins at Sullivan Stadium on 10-21-84

1985 regular season
Greg Hawthorne caught a 28-yard flea-flicker TD pass, on fourth-and-1, in the 17–13 win over Miami at Sullivan Stadium on 11-03-85

1988 regular season
Lin Dawson caught a four-yard TD pass, on fourth-and-1, in the 30–7 win over the Chicago Bears at Sullivan Stadium on 10-30-88

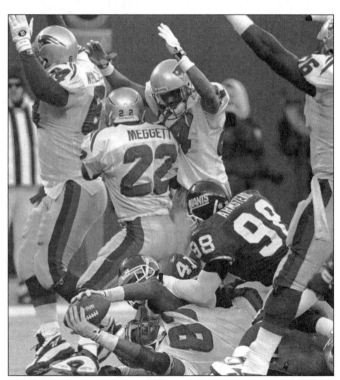

Ben Coates scores a touchdown

1992 regular season

Marv Cook grabbed a five-yard TD pass on fourth-and-2 in the 30–21 loss to the New York Jets at the Meadowlands on 10-04-92

1993 regular season

Ben Coates hauled in a 54-yard TD pass on fourth-and-1 in the 38–14 loss to the Buffalo Bills at Rich Stadium on 09-05-93

1996 regular season

Ben Coates caught a 29-yard TD pass on fourth-and-1 in the 24–10 loss to the Miami Dolphins at Pro Player Park on 09-01-96

Ben Coates caught a 13-yard TD pass on fourth-and-7 in the 23–22 win over the New York Giants at Giants Stadium on 12-21-96

2000 regular season

Jermaine Wiggins cradled a one-yard TD on fourth-and-goal in the 30–24 win over the Kansas City Chiefs at Foxboro Stadium on 12-04-00

2003 championship season

Daniel Graham caught a one-yard TD on fourth-and-1 in the 23–20 overtime win vs the Houston Texans at Reliant Stadium on 11-23-03

2007 undefeated regular season

Benjamin Watson caught a three-yard TD on fourth-and-1 in the 56–10 rout of the Bills at Ralph Wilson Stadium on 11-18-07

The 10 most memorable pass receptions by a Patriots Player

Troy Brown made a contorted 13 yard reception on third-and-13 to set up the game-winning TD, in the one-point win on 12-21-96

Stanley Morgan caught a 30-yard TD with 44 seconds left to end the 17-year regular season losing streak at Miami on 12-22-86

Randy Moss made an amazing one-handed 50-yard TD reception at Miami in the 2007 undefeated regular season

Ben Coates muscled his way to the end zone on his 13-yard game-winning TD reception in the one-point win on 12-21-96

Irving Fryar

Russ Francis caught a 38-yard TD pass on fourth-and-2 in the three-point win over the two time defending Super Bowl champs on 09-26-76

Bob Windsor injured his knee on his 10 yard game-winning TD reception, with three seconds left, in the three-point win on 10-27-74

David Patten caught a six-yard pass on fourth down from his knees to set up a field goal in the overtime playoff game win on 01-19-02

Irving Fryar caught a game-winning TD, that was tipped by Stanley Morgan, on the last play in the two-point win on 11-16-86

Mike Vrabel caught a two-yard TD pass that he tipped to himself in the Patriots third Super Bowl Victory, on 02-06-05

David Patten caught a pass, was knocked unconscious, and fumbled off himself out of bounds, in the 12–9 overtime win on 12-16-01

Two-point conversions

Every Patriots Running Back who has caught a pass for a two-point conversion in a regular season game

1960 regular season
Jim Crawford caught a two-point pass from Gino Cappelletti in the 35–0 shutout of the Chargers at the Los Angeles Coliseum on 10-08-60

1961 regular season
Jim Crawford cradled a two-point pass from Babe Parilli in the 18–17 win over the Texans at the Cotton Bowl on 10-29-61

1966 regular season
Bob Cappadona caught a two-point pass from Babe Parilli in the 38–28 loss to the New York Jets at Shea Stadium on 12-17-66

1995 regular season
Curtis Martin grabbed a two-point pass from Drew Bledsoe in the 35–25 win over the Bills at Rich Stadium on 11-26-95

Dave Meggett cradled a two-point pass from Drew Bledsoe in the 41–27 loss to the Steelers at Three Rivers Stadium on 12-16-95

Curtis Martin

1996 regular season
Curtis Martin caught a two-point pass from Drew Bledsoe in the 31–0 shutout of the Cardinals at Foxboro Stadium on 09-15-96

Sam Gash caught a two-point pass from Drew Bledsoe in the 46–38 win over the Ravens at Memorial Stadium on 10-06-96

Keith Byars caught a two-point pass from Drew Bledsoe in the 34–8 loss to the Broncos at Foxboro Stadium on 11-17-96

Every Patriots Wide Receiver who has caught a pass for a two-point conversion

1964 regular season
Jim Colclough caught a two-point pass from Babe Parilli in 43–43 tie with the Raiders at Fenway Park on 10-16-64

Gino Cappelletti caught a two-point pass from Babe Parilli the 36–28 win over the Bills at War Memorial Stadium on 11-15-64

Jim Colclough caught a two-point pass from Babe Parilli in the 24–14 loss to the Buffalo Bills at Fenway Park on 12-20-64

2002 regular season
Troy Brown caught a two point pass from Tom Brady in the 33–30 win over the Chicago Bears at Memorial Stadium on 11-10-02

2008 regular season
Jabar Gaffney caught a two-point pass from Matt Cassel in the 34–31 overtime loss to the New York Jets at Gillette Stadium on 11-13-08

Wes Welker caught a two-point pass from Matt Cassel for the last points scored in the 24–21 win vs Seattle at Qwest Field on 12-07-08

Every Patriots Tight End who has caught a pass for a two-point conversion

1966 regular season
Tony Romeo caught a two point pass from Babe Parilli in the 24–10 win over the Broncos at Bears Stadium on 09-18-66

1996 regular season
Ben Coates caught two point pass from Drew Bledsoe in the 46–38 win over the Baltimore Ravens at Memorial Stadium on 10-06-96

2002 regular season
Christian Fauria caught a two-point pass from Tom Brady in the 27–24 overtime win vs the Miami Dolphins at Gillette Stadium on 12-29-02

Every Patriots Quarterback who has caught a pass in a regular season game

1981 regular season
Steve Grogan caught a 16-yard pass from Andy Johnson in the 29–28 loss to the Baltimore Colts at Schaefer Stadium on 09-06-81

Matt Cavanaugh caught an eight-yard pass from Andy Johnson in the 27–21 loss to the Steelers at Three Rivers Stadium on 09-27-81

Steve Grogan caught a nine-yard pass from Andy Johnson in the 27–17 loss to the Oakland Raiders at Oakland on 11-01-81

1983 regular season
Steve Grogan caught a deflected pass for an eight yard loss, on the first play, in the 21–7 win over Buffalo at Sullivan Stadium on 11-06-83

1992 regular season
Tommy Hodson caught a deflected pass for a six yard loss in the 30–17 loss to Miami at Joe Robbie Stadium on 10-18-92

1995 regular season
Drew Bledsoe caught a deflected pass for a nine yard loss in the 41–27 loss to the Steelers at Three Rivers Stadium on 12-16-95

2001 championship season
Tom Brady cradled a 23-yard pass from Kevin Faulk in the 20–13 victory over the Dolphins at Foxboro Stadium on 12-22-01

Every Patriots player who has caught a pass thrown by a Patriots Wide Receiver in a regular season game

1979 regular season
Russ Francis grabbed a 28-yard pass from Don Westbrook in the 24–17 win over the Detroit Lions at Schaefer Stadium on 10-07-79

Don Hasselbeck caught a 24-yard pass from Don Westbrook in the 27–23 win over Minnesota Vikings at Schaefer Stadium on 12-16-79

1980 regular season
Russ Francis caught a 23-yard pass from Harold Jackson in the 34–21 win over the New York Jets at Schaefer Stadium on 11-03-80

Russ Francis cradled a 12-yard pass from Harold Jackson in the 16–13 overtime loss to the Dolphins at Orange Bowl on 12-08-80

2001 championship season
Troy Brown scored on a 60-yard TD pass from David Patten in the 38–17 rout of the Colts at the RCA Dome on 10-21-01

Every Patriots player who has caught a Halfback Option Pass for a TD in a regular season game

1960 regular season
Tom Stephens scored on a 10-yard TD pass from Dick Christy in the 38–21 win over the New York Titans at BU Field on 11-11-60

Tom Stephens grabbed a 10-yard TD pass from Dick Christy in the 42–14 rout of the Dallas Texans at BU Field on 11-18-60

1961 regular season
Jim Colclough cradled an 18-yard TD pass from Tom Yewcic in the 45–17 rout of the Broncos at BU Field on 09-16-61

1981 regular season
Mosi Tatupu caught an eight-yard TD pass from Andy Johnson in the 29–28 loss to the Baltimore Colts at Schaefer Stadium on 09-06-81

Stanley Morgan hauled in a 66-yard TD pass from Andy Johnson in the 33–17 win over the Chiefs at Schaefer Stadium on 10-04-81

Stanley Morgan caught a 28-yard TD pass from Andy Johnson in the 38–10 rout of the Oilers at Schaefer Stadium on 10-18-81

Stanley Morgan scored on a 56-yard TD pass from Andy Johnson in the 20–17 loss to the Bills at Rich Stadium on 11-22-81

1985 regular season
Tony Collins grabbed a five-yard TD pass from Craig James in the 17–14 win over the Buffalo Bills at Rich Stadium on 09-22-85

Tony Collins cradled an 11-yard TD pass from Craig James in the 32–14 win over the Buccaneers at Tampa on 10-27-85

1986 regular season

Tony Collins snared a 10-yard TD pass from Craig James in the 20–6 win over the New York Jets at the Meadowlands on 09-11-86

1987 regular season

Tony Collins scored on a 15-yard TD pass from Mosi Tatupu in the 26–23 win over the Los Angeles Raiders at Sullivan Stadium on 11-01-87

1991 regular season

Marv Cook cradled a 13-yard TD pass from Jon Vaughn in the 24–20 win over the Houston Oilers at Foxboro Stadium on 09-22-91

1997 regular season

Troy Brown snared a 35-yard TD pass from Dave Meggett in the 27–24 win over the Miami Dolphins at Foxboro Stadium on 11-23-97

The only Patriots player who has caught a TD pass even though he was only wearing one shoe at the time

Art Graham caught a 22-yard TD pass, after losing his shoe, in the 20–14 win over Miami at the Orange Bowl on 11-27-66

Every Patriots player who has caught a TD in the fourth Quarter of a game, to tie the game, that ended in a tie

1962 regular season

Larry Garron caught a 23-yard TD pass in the fourth Quarter of the 28–28 tie with the Buffalo Bills at War Memorial Stadium on 11-03-62

1965 regular season

JD Garrett caught a 10-yard TD in the fourth quarter of their 10–10 tie with the Kansas City Chiefs at Fenway Park on 11-21-65

Every Patriots player with a TD reception on the Patriots first play in a regular season game

1969 regular season

Charley Frazier caught a 34-yard TD from Mike Taliaferro, on the Patriots' first play, in the 35–21 win over the Bills on 11-23-69

(Ed Philpott intercepted a pass by Jack Kemp on the Bills first play from scrimmage to set up this TD reception)

1973 regular season

Sam Cunningham caught a 34-yard TD pass from Jim Plunkett, on the Patriots' first play, in the 30–14 loss to Miami on 10-28-73

1988 regular season

Irving Fryar caught an 80-yard TD pass from Doug Flutie, on the first play, in the 30–7 win over the Chicago Bears on 10-30-88

2003 championship season

David Givens caught a 35-yard TD pass from Tom Brady, on the first play, in the 21–16 win over the New York Jets on 12-20-03

The Patriots player with the longest pass reception on the second play in a regular season game

1984 regular season

Stephen Starring caught a 65-yard TD from Steve Grogan, on the second play, in the 21–17 win over the Buffalo Bills on 09-02-84

Every TD reception by a Patriots Wide Receiver that was scored late in the game for the game-winning points

1962 regular season

Jim Colclough hauled in a 78-yard TD pass in the fourth quarter to beat the New York Titans 24–17 at BU Field on 11-30-62

1977 regular season

Stanley Morgan caught a 33-yard TD pass, with 4:40 left, to beat the Atlanta Falcons 16–10 at Fulton County on 12-04-77

1983 regular season

Stephen Starring snared a 76-yard TD pass, with 3:59 left, to beat the Pittsburgh Steelers 28–23 at Three Rivers Stadium on 09-25-83

1985 regular season

Irving Fryar cradled a 13-yard TD pass in the fourth quarter to beat the Seattle Seahawks 20–13 at the Kingdome on 11-17-85

1986 regular season

Irving Fryar caught a 25-yard TD, that was tipped by Stanley Morgan, on the last play to beat the Los Angeles Rams 30–28 at Anaheim Stadium on 11-16-86

Stanley Morgan caught a 30-yard TD pass, with 44 seconds left, to defeat Miami 34–27 at the Orange Bowl on 12-22-86

1991 regular season

Greg McMurtry caught a 34-yard TD, with six seconds left, to beat the Houston Oilers 24–20 at Foxboro Stadium on 09-22-91

1998 regular season

Shawn Jefferson grabbed a 25-yard TD pass, with 29 seconds left, to beat the Miami Dolphins 26–23 at Foxboro Stadium on 11-23-98

Every TD reception by a Patriots Running Back that was scored late in the game for the game-winning points

1972 regular season

Josh Ashton caught a 24-yard TD pass, with 4:12 left, to beat the Washington Redskins 24–23 at Schaefer Stadium on 10-01-72

1996 regular season

Keith Byars caught a two-yard TD pass, with 4:06 left, to beat the New York Jets 31–27 at the Meadowlands on 11-10-96

Every TD reception by a Patriots Tight End that was scored late in the game for the game-winning points

1965 regular season

Tony Romeo cradled a two-yard TD pass, with 54 seconds left, to beat the New York Jets 27–23 at Shea Stadium on 11-28-65

1974 regular season

Bob Windsor injured his knee on a 10-yard TD reception, with three seconds left, to defeat the Vikings 17–14 at Metropolitan Stadium on 10-27-74

1977 regular season

Don Hasselbeck cradled a four-yard TD pass, with 2:52 left, to beat the San Diego Chargers 24–20 at Jack Murphy on 10-16-77

1986 regular season

Greg Baty snared a 13-yard TD pass, with 1:40 left, to beat the Buffalo Bills 22–19 at Sullivan Stadium on 11-23-86

1993 regular season

Ben Coates cradled a two-yard TD pass, with 3:56 left, to beat the Phoenix Cardinals 23–21 at Sun Devil Stadium on 10-10-93

1996 regular season

Ben Coates snared a 13-yard TD pass, with 1:23 left, in the 23–22 win over the New York Giants at Giants Stadium on 12-21-96

1998 regular season

Ben Coates caught a one-yard TD pass, with no time left, in the 25–21 victory over the Buffalo Bills at Foxboro Stadium on 11-19-98

The only Patriots player who has caught two TD passes in a regular season overtime game

Ben Coates caught two TD passes in the 33–27 overtime win vs the Miami Dolphins at Foxboro Stadium on 01-02-94

Every Patriots player who has caught a TD pass on the last play of a regulation game

1979 regular season

Carlos Pennywell snared a 13-yard TD pass on the last play of the 39–24 loss to the Dolphins at the Orange Bowl on 11-29-79

1986 regular season

Irving Fryar caught a 10-yard TD pass, on the last play, in the 27–20 loss to the Denver Broncos at Mile High on 09-28-86

Irving Fryar grabbed a 25-yard TD pass, on the last play, to beat the Los Angeles Rams 30–28 at Anaheim Stadium on 11-16-86

1989 regular season

Hart Lee Dykes snared a 10-yard TD pass on the last play of the 24–10 loss to the Miami Dolphins at Sullivan Stadium on 09-17-89

1998 regular season

Ben Coates cradled a one-yard TD pass, with no time left, to defeat the Buffalo Bills 25–21 at Foxboro Stadium on 11-29-98

The only Patriots player to catch a TD pass on the last play of the game to tie the game and force overtime

Ben Coates cradled a two-yard TD on the last play and the PAT forced overtime in the 23–17 win over the Colts at Foxboro Stadium on 12-08-91

Every Patriots Wide Receiver who has caught a TD pass to win the game in overtime

1991 regular season

Michael Timpson hauled in a 45-yard TD pass to defeat the Indianapolis Colts 23–17 at Foxboro Stadium on 12-08-91

1993 regular season

Michael Timpson caught a 36-yard TD pass to defeat the Miami Dolphins 33–27 at Foxboro Stadium on 01-02-94

2003 regular season

Troy Brown scored with an 82-yard TD reception to defeat the Miami Dolphins 19–13 at Pro Player Stadium on 10-19-03

The only Patriots Running Back with an overtime game-winning TD reception

Kevin Turner snared a 14-yard TD pass to defeat the Minnesota Vikings 26–20 at Foxboro Stadium on 11-13-94

The Wide Receiver who caught the most consecutive passes for a TD in a game played in 1979

Harold Jackson caught three consecutive passes for TDs in the 56–3 rout of the New York Jets at Schaefer Stadium on 09-09-79

The Receiver who caught the most consecutive passes for a TD in a game played in 1984

Derrick Ramsey caught three consecutive passes for a TD in the 50–17 rout of the Colts at the Hoosier Dome on 11-18-84

The progression of the most consecutive regular season games that a Patriots player had a TD reception

2 consecutive games that Jim Colclough caught a TD pass (from 09-09-60 to 09-17-60)

3 consecutive games that Jim Colclough caught a TD pass (from 11-04-60 to 11-18-60)

4 consecutive games that Gino Cappelletti caught a TD pass (from 10-01-61 to 10-22-61)

5 consecutive games that Jim Colclough caught a TD pass (from 11-11-62 to 12-09-62)

5 consecutive games that Michael Timpson caught a TD pass (from 12-26-93 to 09-18-94)

5 consecutive games that Randy Moss caught a TD pass (from 10-14-07 to 11-18-07)

The progression of the most consecutive regular season games that a Patriots player had at least two TD receptions

2 consecutive games that Gino Cappelletti caught at least two TD passes (12-12-65 and 12-18-65)

2 consecutive games that Stanley Morgan caught at least two TD passes (10-28-79 and 11-04-79)

3 consecutive games that Ben Coates caught at least two TD passes (01-02-94; 09-08-94 and 09-11-94)

3 consecutive games that Randy Moss caught at least two TD passes (09-16-07 to 10-01-07)

The progression of the most regular season TD receptions by a Patriots Player

9 TD receptions by Jim Colclough in 1960

10 TD receptions by Jim Colclough in 1962

12 TD receptions by Stanley Morgan in 1979

23 TD receptions by Randy Moss in 2007

The progression of the most regular season TD receptions by a Patriots Running Back

2 TD receptions by Alan Miller in 1960

2 TD receptions by Dick Christy in 1960

6 TD receptions by Billy Lott in 1961

7 TD receptions by Larry Garron in 1964

The progression of the most regular season TD receptions by a Patriots Tight End

4 TD receptions by Oscar Lofton in 1960

5 TD receptions by Jim Whalen in 1967

7 TD receptions by Jim Whalen in 1968

8 TD receptions by Russ Francis in 1980

9 TD receptions by Ben Coates in 1996

The progression of the most career TD receptions by a Patriots Player

38th TD reception by Jim Colclough was for 19 yards in the 42–14 rout of the Houston Oilers at Fenway Park on 12-18-65

39th TD reception by Gino Cappelletti was for 16 yards in the 30–23 loss to the New York Jets at Shea Stadium on 10-29-67

42nd TD reception by Gino Cappelletti was for 18 yards in the 33–14 win over the Bengals at Fenway Park on 12-01-68

43rd TD reception by Stanley Morgan was for 22 yards in the 24–20 loss to the Browns at Cleveland Stadium on 10-06-85

67th TD reception by Stanley Morgan was a 19-yard TD in the 37–20 loss to the San Francisco 49ers at Stanford on 10-22-89

The most career TD receptions by a Patriots Running Back

26 career TD receptions by Larry Garron over the 1961–67 regular seasons

The progression of the most career TD receptions by a Patriots Tight End

4 TD receptions by Oscar Lofton in 1960

4 career TD receptions by Joe Johnson over the 1960–61 regular seasons

10 career TD receptions by Tony Romeo over the 1962–65 regular seasons

17 career TD receptions by Jim Whalen over the 1965–69 regular seasons

28 career TD receptions by Russ Francis over the 1975–80 regular seasons

50 career TD receptions by Ben Coates over the 1991–99 regular seasons

The Wide Receiver with the most TD receptions in the NFL in 1979

Stanley Morgan led the NFL with 12 TD receptions during the 1979 regular season

The Wide Receiver with the most TD receptions in any regular season

Randy Moss set the NFL record with his 23 TD receptions during the 2007 regular season

The Playoffs

The progression of the most receptions by a Patriots player in a playoff game

4 receptions by Gino Cappelletti in the 26–8 victory over the Buffalo Bills at War Memorial Stadium on 12-28-63

4 receptions by Larry Garron in the 26–8 victory over the Buffalo Bills at War Memorial Stadium on 12-28-63

4 receptions by Ron Burton in the 51–10 loss to the San Diego Chargers at Balboa Stadium on 01-05-64

4 receptions by Russ Francis in the 24–21 loss to the Oakland Raiders at the Oakland Coliseum on 12-18-76

8 receptions by Russ Francis in the 31–14 loss to the Houston Oilers at Schaefer Stadium on 12-31-78

9 receptions by Shawn Jefferson in the 7–6 loss to the Pittsburgh Steelers at Three Rivers Stadium on 01-03-98

10 receptions by Jermaine Wiggins in the 16–13 overtime win vs the Oakland Raiders at Foxboro Stadium on 01-19-02

10 receptions by Deion Branch in the 32–29 victory over the Carolina Panthers at Reliant Stadium on 02-01-04

11 receptions by Deion Branch in the 24–21 victory over the Philadelphia Eagles at Alltel Stadium on 02-06-05

11 receptions by Wes Welker in the 17–14 loss to the New York Giants at the University of Phoenix Stadium on 02-03-08

The progression of the most receptions by a Patriots Wide Receiver in a playoff game

4 receptions by Gino Cappelletti in the 26–8 victory over the Buffalo Bills at War Memorial Stadium on 12-28-63

4 receptions by Stanley Morgan in the 26–14 victory over the New York Jets at the Meadowlands Stadium on 12-28-85

7 receptions by Stanley Morgan in the 46–10 loss to the Bears at the Louisiana Superdome on 01-26-86

9 receptions by Shawn Jefferson in the 7–6 loss to the Pittsburgh Steelers at Three Rivers Stadium on 01-03-98

10 receptions by Deion Branch in the 32–29 victory over the Carolina Panthers at Reliant Stadium on 02-01-04

11 receptions by Deion Branch in the 24–21 victory over the Philadelphia Eagles at Alltel Stadium on 02-06-05

11 receptions by Wes Welker in the 17–14 loss to the New York Giants at the University of Phoenix Stadium on 02-03-08

The progression of the most receptions by a Patriots Running Back in a playoff game

4 receptions by Larry Garron in the 26–8 victory over the Buffalo Bills at War Memorial Stadium on 12-28-63

4 receptions by Ron Burton in the 51–10 loss to the San Diego Chargers at Balboa Stadium on 01-05-64

4 receptions by Tony Collins in the 22–17 loss to the Denver Broncos at Mile High Stadium on 01-04-87

4 receptions by Keith Byars in the 28–3 victory over the Pittsburgh Steelers at Foxboro Stadium on 01-05-97

4 receptions by Keith Byars in the 20–6 victory over the Jacksonville Jaguars at Foxboro Stadium on 01-12-97

4 receptions by Keith Byars in the 35–21 loss to the Green Bay Packers at the Louisiana Superdome on 01-26-97

4 receptions by J.R. Redmond in the 16–13 overtime win vs the Oakland Raiders at Foxboro Stadium on 01-19-02

4 receptions by Marc Edwards in the 24–17 victory over the Pittsburgh Steelers at Heinz Field on 01-27-02

5 receptions by Corey Dillon in the 20–3 rout of the Indianapolis Colts at Gillette Stadium on 01-16-05

The progression of the most receptions by a Patriots Tight End in a playoff game

4 receptions by Russ Francis in the 24–21 loss to the Oakland Raiders at the Oakland Coliseum on 12-18-76

8 receptions by Russ Francis in the 31–14 loss to the Houston Oilers at Schaefer Stadium on 12-31-78

10 receptions by Jermaine Wiggins in the 16–13 overtime win vs the Oakland Raiders at Foxboro Stadium on 01-19-02

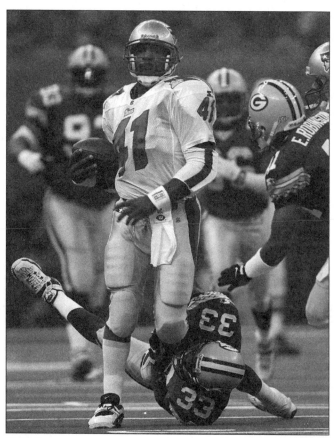

Keith Byars

The progression of the most career receptions by a Patriots player in the Playoffs

7 career playoff receptions by Ron Burton in two playoff games

12 career playoff receptions by Russ Francis in two playoff games

19 career playoff receptions by Stanley Morgan in seven playoff games

21 career playoff receptions by Terry Glenn in five playoff games

22 career playoff receptions by Ben Coates in seven playoff games

58 career playoff receptions by Troy Brown in 20 playoff games

The progression of the most career receptions by a Patriots Wide Receiver in the playoffs

6 career playoff receptions by Gino Cappelletti in two playoff games

19 career playoff receptions by Stanley Morgan in seven playoff games

21 career playoff receptions by Terry Glenn in five playoff games

58 career playoff receptions by Troy Brown in 20 playoff games

The progression of the most career receptions by a Patriots Running Back in the playoffs

7 career playoff receptions by Ron Burton in two playoff games

13 career playoff receptions by Tony Collins in six playoff games

14 career playoff receptions by Keith Byars in five playoff games for the Patriots

45 career playoff receptions by Kevin Faulk in 17 playoff games

The progression of the most career receptions by a Patriots Tight End in the playoffs

12 career playoff receptions by Russ Francis in two playoff games

22 career playoff receptions by Ben Coates in seven playoff games

The progression of the most yards receiving by a Patriots player in a playoff game

120 yards receiving by Larry Garron in the 26–8 victory over the Buffalo Bills at War Memorial Stadium on 12-28-63

121 yards receiving by Troy Brown in the 24–17 victory over the Pittsburgh Steelers at Heinz Field on 01-27-02

143 yards receiving by Deion Branch in the 32–29 win over the Carolina Panthers at Reliant Stadium on 02-01-04

153 yards receiving by Deion Branch in the 27–13 loss to the Denver Broncos at Invesco Field on 01-14-06

The progression of the most yards receiving by a Patriots Wide Receiver in a playoff game

109 yards receiving by Gino Cappelletti in the 26–8 victory over the Buffalo Bills at War Memorial Stadium on 12-28-63

121 yards receiving by Troy Brown in the 24–17 victory over the Pittsburgh Steelers at Heinz Field on 01-27-02

133 yards receiving by Deion Branch in the 24–21 victory over the Philadelphia Eagles at Altell Stadium on 02-06-05

153 yards receiving by Deion Branch in the 27–13 loss to the Denver Broncos at Invesco Field on 01-14-06

The progression of the most yards receiving by a Patriots Tight End in a playoff game

96 yards receiving by Russ Francis in the 24–21 loss to the Oakland Raiders at the Oakland Coliseum on 12-18-76

101 yards receiving by Russ Francis in the 31–14 loss to the Houston Oilers at Schaefer Stadium on 12-31-78

Every Patriots Wide Receiver who had at least 100 yards receiving in a playoff game

1963 AFL Divisional playoff game
Gino Cappelletti had 109 yards receiving in the 26–8 win over the Buffalo Bills at War Memorial Stadium on 12-28-63

1986 AFC Divisional playoff game
Stanley Morgan had 100 yards receiving in the 22–17 loss to the Denver Broncos at Mile High Stadium on 01-04-87

1997 AFC Divisional playoff game
Shawn Jefferson had 104 yards receiving in the 7–6 loss to the Pittsburgh Steelers at Three Rivers Stadium on 01-03-98

2001 AFC Divisional playoff game
David Patten had 107 yards receiving in the 16–13 overtime win vs the Oakland Raiders at Foxboro Stadium on 01-19-02

2001 AFC Championship Game
Troy Brown had 121 yards receiving in the 24–17 victory over the Pittsburgh Steelers at Heinz Field on 01-27-02

Super Bowl XXXVIII
Deion Branch had 143 yards receiving in the 32–29 win over the Carolina Panthers at Reliant Stadium on 02-01-04

2004 AFC Championship Game
Deion Branch had 116 yards receiving in the 41–27 victory over the Pittsburgh Steelers at Heinz Field on 01-23-05

2005 AFC Divisional playoff game
Deion Branch had 153 yards receiving in the 27–13 loss to the Denver Broncos at Invesco Field on 01-14-06

Shawn Jefferson

Super Bowl XXXIX
Deion Branch had 133 yards receiving in the 24–21 win over the Philadelphia Eagles at Alltel Stadium on 02-06-05

2006 AFC Wild Card playoff game
Jabar Gaffney had 104 yards receiving in the 37–16 rout of the New York Jets at Gillette Stadium on 01-07-07

2006 AFC Divisional playoff game
Jabar Gaffney had 103 yards receiving in the 24–21 win over the San Diego Chargers at Qualcomm Stadium on 01-14-07

Super Bowl XLII
Wes Welker had 103 yards receiving in the 17–14 loss to the New York Giants at the University of Phoenix Stadium on 02-03-08

The only Patriots Running Back with at least 100 yards receiving in a playoff game
1963 AFL Eastern Divisional playoff game
Larry Garron had 120 yards receiving in the 26–8 win over the Buffalo Bills at War Memorial Stadium on 12-28-63

The only time that two Patriots players had at least 100 yards receiving in the same playoff game
1963 AFL Divisional playoff game
Larry Garron had 120 yards receiving and Gino Cappelletti had 109 yards receiving in the 26–8 win over Buffalo on 12-28-63

The only time that a Patriots RB and a Patriots WR had at least 100 yards receiving in the same playoff game
1963 AFL Eastern Divisional playoff game
RB Larry Garron had 120 yards and WR Gino Cappelletti had 109 yards in the 26–8 win over the Buffalo Bills on 12-28-63

The progression of the most career yards receiving by a Patriots player in the Playoffs
126 career yards receiving by Larry Garron in two playoff games

181 career yards receiving by Gino Cappelletti in two playoff games

197 career yards receiving by Russ Francis in two playoff games

321 career yards receiving by Stanley Morgan in six playoff games

553 career yards receiving by Troy Brown in 15 playoff games

The progression of the most career yards receiving by a Patriots Wide Receiver in the playoffs
181 career yards receiving by Gino Cappelletti in two playoff games

321 career yards receiving by Stanley Morgan in six playoff games

553 career yards receiving by Troy Brown in 15 playoff games

The progression of the most career yards receiving by a Patriots Running Back in the playoffs
126 career yards receiving by Larry Garron in two playoff games

375 career yards receiving by Kevin Faulk in 17 playoff games

The progression of the most career yards receiving by a Patriots Tight End in the playoffs
197 career yards receiving by Russ Francis in two playoff games

204 career yards receiving by Ben Coates in seven playoff games

The only NFL Receiver to have at least 100 yards receiving and at least eight receptions in consecutive playoff games
2006 AFC Wild Card game and 2006 AFC Divisional playoff game
Jabar Gaffney had eight receptions for 104 yards and 10 receptions for 103 yards in consecutive playoff games in 2007

The progression of the longest reception by a Patriots player in a playoff game
9 yard reception by Ron Burton in the 26–8 victory over the Buffalo Bills at War Memorial Stadium on 12-28-63

9 yard reception by Jim Colclough in the 26–8 victory over the Buffalo Bills at War Memorial Stadium on 12-28-63

22 yard reception by Gino Cappelletti in the 26–8 victory over the Buffalo Bills at War Memorial Stadium on 12-28-63

59-yard TD reception by Larry Garron in the 26–8 victory over the Buffalo Bills at War Memorial Stadium on 12-28-63

60-yard TD reception by Deion Branch in the 41–27 victory over the Pittsburgh Steelers at Heinz Field on 01-23-05

The progression of the longest reception by a Patriots Wide Receiver in a playoff game

9-yard reception by Jim Colclough in the 26–8 victory over the Buffalo Bills at War Memorial Stadium on 12-28-63

22-yard reception by Gino Cappelletti in the 26–8 victory over the Buffalo Bills at War Memorial Stadium on 12-28-63

51-yard reception by Gino Cappelletti in the 26–8 victory over the Buffalo Bills at War Memorial Stadium on 12-28-63

53 yard reception by Terry Glenn in the 28–3 rout of the Pittsburgh Steelers at Foxboro Stadium on 01-05-97

60-yard TD reception by Deion Branch in the 41–27 victory over the Pittsburgh Steelers at Heinz Field on 01-23-05

73 yard reception by DeionBranch in the 27-13 loss to Denver at Invesco Field on 01-14-06

The progression of the longest reception by a Patriots Running Back in a playoff game

9-yard reception by Ron Burton in the 26–8 victory over the Buffalo Bills at War Memorial Stadium on 12-28-63

59-yard TD reception by Larry Garron in the 26–8 victory over the Buffalo Bills at War Memorial Stadium on 12-28-63

The progression of the longest reception by a Patriots Tight End in a playoff game

10-yard reception by Russ Francis in the 24–21 loss to the Oakland Raiders at the Oakland Coliseum on 12-18-76

40-yard reception by Russ Francis in the 24–21 loss to the Oakland Raiders at the Oakland Coliseum on 12-18-76

63-yard TD by Benjamin Watson in the 28–3 rout of Jacksonville on 01-07-06

The only reception by a Patriots Defensive Back, who had reported as a Wide Receiver, in a playoff game
1994 AFC Wild Card playoff game
Corwin Brown caught a 21-yard pass in the 20–13 AFC Wild Card loss to the Browns at Cleveland Stadium on 01-01-95

Every reception by a Patriots Linebacker, who had reported as a Tight End, in a playoff game
Super Bowl XXXVIII
Mike Vrabel caught a one-yard TD in the 32–29 victory over the Carolina Panthers at Reliant Stadium on 02-01-04

Super Bowl XXXIX
Mike Vrabel tipped a pass to himself for a two-yard TD in the 24–21 win over the Eagles at Alltel Stadium on 02-06-05

The progression of the longest reception by a Patriots Player, on a fourth down play, in a playoff game

2-yard TD reception by Robert Weathers, on fourth-and-1, in the 31–14 win over the Dolphins at the Orange Bowl on 01-12-86

8-yard TD reception by Irving Fryar, on fourth-and-goal, in the 46–10 loss to the Bears at the Louisiana Superdome on 01-21-86

21-yard reception by Corwin Brown, on fourth-and-10, in the 20–13 loss to the Browns at Cleveland Stadium on 01-01-95

Every Patriots Wide Receiver who has caught a pass on a fourth down play in a playoff game
Super Bowl XX
Irving Fryar caught an eight-yard TD from Steve Grogan, on fourth-and-goal, in the 46–10 loss to the Bears at Superdome on 01-21-86

1994 AFC Wild Card playoff game
Corwin Brown caught a 21-yard pass from Pat O'Neill, on fourth-and-10, in the 20–13 loss to the Browns at Cleveland on 01-01-95

2001 AFC Divisional playoff game
David Patten caught a six-yard pass on his knees on fourth-and-4 in the 16–13 overtime win vs the Raiders at Foxboro Stadium on 01-19-02

2003 AFC Divisional playoff game
Troy Brown caught a four-yard pass from Tom Brady on fourth-and-3 in the 17–14 win over the Titans at Gillette Stadium on 01-10-04

2003 AFC Championship Game
Troy Brown caught a 16-yard pass from Tom Brady on fourth-and-8 in the 24–14 win over the Colts at Gillette Stadium on 01-18-04

The only Patriots Running Back with a pass reception on a fourth-down play in a playoff game

1986 AFC Championship playoff game

Robert Weathers caught a two-yard TD from Tony Eason on fourth-and-1 in the 31–14 win over Miami at Orange Bowl on 01-12-86

Every Patriots Tight End who has caught a pass on a fourth down play in a playoff game

1996 AFC Championship Game

Ben Coates caught a five-yard pass from Drew Bledsoe on fourth-and-2 in the 20–6 win over the Jaguars at Foxboro Stadium on 01-12-97

2003 AFC Divisional playoff game

Christian Fauria caught a nine-yard pass from Tom Brady on fourth-and-1 in the 17–14 win over the Titans at Gillette Stadium on 01-10-04

The only Patriots Running Back who has caught a TD pass on a fourth-down play in a playoff game

1985 AFC Championship playoff game

Robert Weathers caught a two-yard TD on fourth-and-1 in the 31–14 win over the Dolphins at the Orange Bowl on 01-12-86

Mosi Tatupu

The only Patriots Wide Receiver who has caught a fourth-down TD pass in a playoff game

Super Bowl XX

Irving Fryar snared an eight-yard TD pass on fourth-and-goal in the 46–10 loss to the Chicago Bears at the Superdome on 01-21-86

The only time that the Patriots had a successful flea-flicker pass for a TD in a playoff game

1986 AFC Divisional playoff game

Tony Eason to Mosi Tatupu to Tony Eason to Stanley Morgan for a 45-yard TD in the 22–17 loss to Denver at Mile High Stadium on 01-04-87

The only Patriots player who has caught a Halfback Option pass for a TD in a playoff game

1978 AFC Divisional playoff game

Harold Jackson caught a 24-yard TD from Andy Johnson in the 31–14 loss to the Houston Oilers at Schaefer Stadium on 12-31-78

The Patriots player with the longest pass reception on the first play of a playoff game

1997 AFC Divisional playoff game

Terry Glenn hauled in a 53-yard pass from Drew Bledsoe on the first play of the 28–3 rout of the Steelers on 01-05-97

The progression of the most TD receptions by a Patriots Wide Receiver in a playoff game

1 TD reception by Harold Jackson in the 31–14 loss to the Houston Oilers at Schaefer Stadium on 12-31-78

1 TD reception by Stanley Morgan in the 26–14 victory over the New York Jets at the Meadowlands on 12-28-85

1 TD reception by Irving Fryar in the 46–10 loss to the Chicago Bears at the Louisiana Superdome on 01-26-85

2 TD receptions by Stanley Morgan in the 22–17 loss to the Denver Broncos at Mile High Stadium on 01-04-87

The most TD receptions by a Patriots Running Back in a playoff game

1963 AFL Eastern Divisional playoff game

2 TD receptions by Larry Garron in the 26–8 victory over the Buffalo Bills at War Memorial Stadium on 12-28-63

The progression of the most TD receptions by a Patriots Tight End in a playoff game

1 TD reception by Russ Francis in the 24–21 loss to the Oakland Raiders at the Oakland Coliseum on 12-18-76

1 TD reception by Russ Francis in the 31–14 loss to the Houston Oilers at Schaefer Stadium on 12-31-78

1 TD reception by Don Hasselbeck in the 28–13 loss to the Miami Dolphins at the Orange Bowl on 01-08-83

1 TD reception by Lin Dawson in the 27–20 victory over the Los Angeles Raiders at the Los Angeles Coliseum on 01-05-86

1 TD reception by Derrick Ramsey in the 31–14 victory over the Miami Dolphins at the Orange Bowl on 01-12-86

1 TD reception by Ben Coates in the 35–21 loss to the Green Bay Packers at the Louisiana Superdome on 01-26-97

1 TD reception by Mike Vrabel in the 32–29 victory over the Carolina Panthers at Reliant Stadium on 02-01-04

1 TD reception by Mike Vrabel in the 24–21 victory over the Philadelphia Eagles at Alltel Stadium on 02-06-05

2 TD receptions by Benjamin Watson in the 31–20 win over the Jacksonville Jaguars at Gillette Stadium on 01-12-08

Every Patriots Running Back who has caught a TD pass in a playoff game

1963 AFL Eastern Divisional Playoff Game

Larry Garron had a 59-yard TD and a 17-yard TD reception in the 26–8 win over the Buffalo Bills at War Memorial Stadium on 12-28-63

1985 AFC Championship Game

Tony Collins caught a four-yard TD pass in the 31–14 victory over the Miami Dolphins at the Orange Bowl on 01-12-86

Did you know that?

The New England Patriots have won both of the Super Bowl Games in which Mike Vrabel has caught a TD pass.

The New England Patriots lost both of the playoff games that Russ Francis caught a TD pass.

1994 AFC Wild Card playoff game

Leroy Thompson caught a 13-yard TD pass in the 20-13 loss to the Cleveland Browns at Cleveland Stadium on 01-01-95

1996 AFC Divisional playoff game

Keith Byars hauled in a 34-yard TD pass in the 28–3 rout of the Pittsburgh Steelers at Foxboro Stadium on 01-05-97

Super Bowl XXXI

Keith Byars snared a one-yard TD pass in the 35–21 loss to the Green Bay Packers at the Superdome on 01-26-97

The progression of the most career TD receptions by a Patriots player in the playoffs

2 career TD receptions by Larry Garron in two playoff games

2 career TD receptions by Russ Francis in two playoff games

3 career TD receptions by Stanley Morgan in seven playoff games

7 career TD receptions by David Givens in eight playoff games

Points Scored

## 8

From 1960–69, Gino Cappelletti scored the most points in every season for the Boston Patriots. Jim Nance then led the team with 42 points scored during the 1970 regular season. Charlie Gogolak led the New England Patriots by scoring 64 points during the 1971 season. Carl Garrett was the second running back to lead the team in points scored, as he scored 30 points during the 1972 season. Place-kicker Jeff White led the Patriots with 63 points scored in the 1973 season.

John Smith scored the most points for the New England Patriots in each of the next four regular seasons. Horace Ivory led the 1978 team with 66 points scored. John Smith then scored the most points for the Patriots over the next four regular seasons. In 1983, Tony Collins led the 1983 team with 60 points scored.

Tony Franklin scored the most points for the New England Patriots in each of the next four regular seasons. Robert Perryman led the 1988 team with 36 points scored. Greg Davis led the 1989 team with 61 total points scored. Jason Staurovsky led the team in points scored over the next two regular seasons. Charlie Baumann and Scott Sisson had the most total points scored over the 1992 and 1993 seasons, respectively. Matt Bahr scored the most points for the New England Patriots during the 1994 and 1995 regular seasons. Adam Vinatieri was the leading scorer for the New England Patriots in every regular season from 1996–2005. Stephen Gostkowski led the team in scoring in the 2006 regular season. Randy Moss set the NFL record with 23 touchdown receptions and scored one more point than Stephen Gostkowski in 2007. Stephen Gostkowski was recognized as an All-Pro kicker and he scored the most points by a Patriots player in 2008.

Adam Vinatieri holds the team record of scoring at least 100 points during the regular season for nine consecutive seasons. Gino Cappelletti, however, still holds the team record by scoring 155 points in a regular season, and he did this with a 14-game regular season in 1964. Adam Vinatieri has led the NFL in scoring once, Tony Franklin did it once, John Smith did it twice, and Gino Cappelletti led the AFL and the NFL five times over a six-year period from 1961–66. Adam Vinatieri and Gino Cappelletti are the only Patriots kickers who have tossed a touchdown pass in a regular season game. Gino Cappelletti scored at least 34 percent of the total points scored in a season for the Patriots for eight consecutive years. Tony Franklin scored at least 34 percent of the team's total points scored in a season in 1986, and Adam Vinatieri did this for three consecutive years from 1998–2000.

Gino Cappelletti scored 18 points or more in a game 10 times during his career and scored 20 points or more in a game eight times. Cappelletti averaged 9.5 points per game when the Patriots' record was 47–29–8. Over his 11-year career with the Patriots, Cappelletti averaged 7.5 points per game. Cappelletti holds the AFL record by scoring 28 points in a game and by scoring 1,130 points in his career. Not only was Gino Cappelletti an AFL All-Star receiver, but he also set a record that lasted 34 years by successfully kicking all of his six field-goal attempts in a game. Cappelletti also holds the AFL record by scoring on four two-point conversions.

Mack Herron was the first Patriots player to score 12 or more touchdowns in a season, as he ran for seven touchdowns and had five touchdown receptions in 1974. Steve Grogan set the NFL record by rushing for 12 touchdowns during the 1976 season, and he advanced a fumble six yards for a touchdown during that season as well.

Stanley Morgan was the first wide receiver for the Patriots to score in double digits in a regular season— he had 12 touchdown receptions, and he returned a punt for a touchdown during the 1979 season. Morgan holds the team record with 68 total touchdowns scored, as he had 67 career touchdown receptions and one special teams return for a touchdown.

Irving Fryar was the first Patriots player to score at least 10 total touchdowns by running for a touchdown, scoring on a special teams return, and by receiving one or more touchdown passes. Irving rushed for a touchdown, returned two punts for a touchdown, and caught seven touchdown passes during the 1985 regular season.

Curtis Martin scored 15 touchdowns during the 1995 season and he set the team record by scoring 17 touchdowns during the 1996 season. Curtis Martin and Gino Cappelletti are the only Patriots players who have scored 20 points or more in a regular season game for the Patriots. Curtis set the team record by scoring 18 points in a playoff game for the Patriots.

Robert Edwards set the NFL record by a scoring a touchdown in his first seven NFL games, and he finished his 1998 rookie season with 12 total touchdowns scored. Antowain Smith scored 13 touchdowns for the 2001 World Champion New England Patriots team. Corey Dillon scored 13 touchdowns for the 2004 World Champion New England Patriots team.

Jim Nance holds the team record with 45 career rushing touchdowns. Ben Coates holds the team record for the most career touchdown receptions by a tight end with 50. Larry Garron holds the team record for the most career touchdown receptions by a running back with 25.

Raymond Clayborn holds the team record of three kickoff returns for a touchdown. Irving Fryar and Troy Brown each have had three punt returns for a touchdown during the regular season. Ty Law set the team record by returning six interceptions for a touchdown during the regular season. Tedy Bruschi set an NFL record by returning four consecutive interceptions for a touchdown.

Tom Brady holds the team record by throwing 50 touchdown passes during the 2007 undefeated regular season. Tom Brady holds the team record with 197 regular season career touchdown passes. Adam Vinatieri holds the team record of 1,158 career points scored in the regular season.

The Patriots player with the most points scored, his points-scored total, and how the points were scored in each season

Most Points Scored	Total Points Scored	How Points were Scored
1960 Gino Cappelletti	60 points	8 field goals, 33 extra points, and 3 two-point conversions
1961 Gino Cappelletti	147 points	17 field goals, 48 PATs, and TD receptions
1962 Gino Cappelletti	128 points	20 field goals, 38 PATs, and 5 TD receptions
1963 Gino Cappelletti	113 points	22 field goals, 35 PATs, and 2 TD receptions
1964 Gino Cappelletti	155 points	25 field goals, 37 PATs, 7 TD receptions, and 1 two-point conversion
1965 Gino Cappelletti	132 points	17 field goals, 27 PATs, and 9 TD receptions
1966 Gino Cappelletti	119 points	16 field goals, 35 PATs, and 6 TD receptions
1967 Gino Cappelletti	95 points	16 field goals, 29 PATs, and 3 TD receptions
1968 Gino Cappelletti	83 points	15 field goals, 26 PATs, and 2 TD receptions
1969 Gino Cappelletti	68 points	14 field goals and 26 extra points
1970 Jim Nance	42 points	7 rushing TDs
1971 Charlie Gogolak	64 points	12 field goals and 28 extra points
1972 Carl Garrett	30 points	5 rushing TDs
1973 Jeff White	63 points	14 field goals and 21 extra points
1974 John Smith	90 points	16 field goals and 42 extra points
1975 John Smith	60 points	9 field goals and 33 extra points
1976 John Smith	87 points	15 field goals and 42 extra points
1977 John Smith	78 points	15 field goals and 33 extra points
1978 Horace Ivory	66 points	11 rushing TDs
1979 John Smith	115 points	23 field goals and 46 extra points
1980 John Smith	129 points	26 field goals and 51 extra points
1981 John Smith	82 points	15 field goals and 37 extra points
1982 John Smith	21 points	5 field goals and 6 extra points (strike season of 9 games)
1983 Tony Collins	60 points	10 rushing TDs
1984 Tony Franklin	108 points	22 field goals and 42 extra points
1985 Tony Franklin	112 points	24 field goals and 40 extra points
1986 Tony Franklin	140 points	32 field goals and 44 extra points
1987 Tony Franklin	82 points	15 field goals and 37 PATs (strike season of 15 games)
1988 Robert Perryman	36 points	6 rushing TDs
1989 Greg Davis	61 points	16 field goals and 13 extra points
1990 Jason Staurovsky	67 points	16 field goals and 19 extra points
1991 Jason Staurovsky	49 points	13 field goals and 10 extra points
1992 Charlie Baumann	55 points	11 field goals and 22 extra points
1993 Scott Sisson	57 points	14 field goals and 15 extra points
1994 Matt Bahr	117 points	27 field goals and 36 extra points
1995 Matt Bahr	96 points	23 field goals and 27 extra points
1996 Adam Vinatieri	120 points	27 field goals and 39 extra points
1997 Adam Vinatieri	115 points	25 field goals and 40 extra points
1998 Adam Vinatieri	127 points	31 field goals, 32 extra points, and 1 two-point conversion
1999 Adam Vinatieri	107 points	26 field goals and 29 extra points
2000 Adam Vinatieri	106 points	27 field goals and 25 extra points
2001 Adam Vinatieri	113 points	24 field goals and 41 extra points
2002 Adam Vinatieri	117 points	27 field goals and 36 extra points
2003 Adam Vinatieri	112 points	25 field goals and 37 extra points
2004 Adam Vinatieri	141 points	31 field goals and 48 extra points
2005 Adam Vinatieri	100 points	20 field goals and 40 extra points
2006 Stephen Gostkowski	103 points	20 field goals and 43 extra points
2007 Randy Moss	138 points	NFL record 23 TD receptions
2008 Stephen Gostkowski	148 points	36 field goals and 40 extra points

The progression of the best percentage of the team's total points scored in a season by a Patriots player

21 percent of the team's total points scored during the 1960 season were scored by Gino Cappelletti

35.6 percent of the team's total points scored during the 1961 season were scored by Gino Cappelletti

37 percent of the team's total points scored during the 1962 season were scored by Gino Cappelletti

42.5 percent of the team's total points scored during the 1964 season were scored by Gino Cappelletti

54 percent of the team's total points scored during the 1965 season were scored by Gino Cappelletti

The Top 10 memorable scoring accomplishments by a Patriots player in a game

Adam Vinatieri kicking a 45-yard field goal, in the snow, to tie the game in the 16–13 overtime playoff game win on 01-19-02

Adam Vinatieri kicking a Super Bowl game-winning 48-yard field goal, on the last play, in the three-point win on 02-03-02

Randy Moss catching four TD passes in the first half of the 56–10 rout of the Buffalo Bills on 11-18-07

David Patten running for a TD, catching two TD passes, and throwing a TD pass in the 17-point win on 11-25-01

Gino Cappelletti scoring an AFL-record 28 points in the 42–14 rout of the Houston Oilers on 12-18-65

Steve Grogan throwing four TD passes and running for two TDs in the 22-point victory over the Jets on 12-13-87

Darryl Stingley running for a TD and catching a TD pass on his 26th birthday in the four-point win on 09-18-77

Prentice McCray returning two Joe Namath passes for a TD in the 14-point win on 11-21-76

Ron Burton returning a missed field-goal attempt 91 yards for a TD in the four-point win on 11-11-62

Antwan Harris advancing a lateral from Troy Brown for a TD, after a blocked field-goal attempt, in the seven-point playoff game win on 1-27-02

The only Patriots player who has scored every point in the game by catching a TD pass and kicking a field goal and a PAT

1963 regular season

Gino Cappelletti caught a TD pass, kicked a field goal and an extra point in the 14–10 loss to the Broncos on 09-29-63

1967 regular season

Gino Cappelletti caught a TD pass, kicked a field goal and an extra point in the 33–10 loss to the Kansas City Chiefs on 11-12-67

The only Patriots quarterback to score every point for the Patriots in a regular season game

Steve Grogan ran one yard for a TD in the 31–6 loss to the Houston Oilers at the Houston Astrodome on 09-25-88

The only Patriots wide receiver to score every point for the Patriots in a regular season game

Irving Fryar caught a 36-yard TD pass from Hugh Millen in the 10–6 loss to the Seattle Seahawks on 09-20-92

The only Patriots tight end to score every point for the Patriots in a regular season game

Derrick Ramsey caught a 33-yard TD pass from Tony Eason in the 24–6 loss to the Seattle Seahawks on 12-18-83

Every Patriots player who has scored at least 20 points in a regular season game

1962 regular season

Gino Cappelletti scored 20 points in the 26–16 victory over the Oakland Raiders at Boston University on 10-26-62

1963 regular season

Gino Cappelletti scored 22 points in the 40–21 victory over the Denver Broncos at Fenway Park on 10-18-63

1964 regular season

Gino Cappelletti scored 21 points in the 33–28 victory over the San Diego Chargers at Balboa Stadium on 09-20-64

Gino Cappelletti scored 21 points in the 39–10 rout of the Denver Broncos at Bears Stadium on 10-04-64

Gino Cappelletti scored 24 points in the 36–28 victory over the Buffalo Bills at War Memorial Stadium on 11-15-64

1965 regular season

Gino Cappelletti scored 20 points in the 22–6 victory over the San Diego Chargers at Balboa Stadium on 10-31-65

Gino Cappelletti scored (an AFL record) 28 points in the 42–14 rout of the Houston Oilers at Fenway Park on 12-18-65

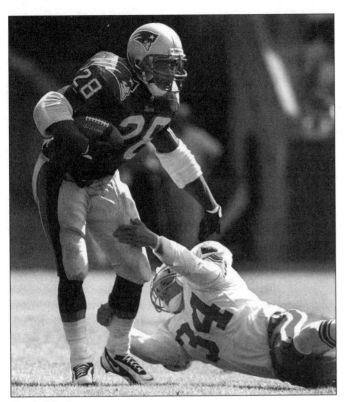

Curtis Martin

1966 regular season
Gino Cappelletti scored 21 points in the 27–21 victory over the Houston Oilers at Fenway Park on 11-13-66

1996 regular season
Curtis Martin scored 20 points in the 31–0 shutout of the Arizona Cardinals at Foxboro Stadium on 09-15-96

2007 undefeated regular season
Randy Moss scored 24 points in the 56–10 rout of the Buffalo Bills at Ralph Wilson Stadium on 11-18-07

The only Patriots player who has scored 28 points in a game (AFL game record)
Gino Cappelletti had two TD receptions, kicked four field goals and four PATs in the 42–14 rout of the Houston Oilers on 12-18-65

The progression of the most points scored by a Patriots player in a regular season game
3 points were scored by Gino Cappelletti in the 13–10 loss to the Denver Broncos at BU Field on 09-09-60

6 points were scored by Jim Colclough in the 13–10 loss to the Denver Broncos at BU Field on 09-09-60

6 points were scored by Walt Livingston in the 28–24 win over the New York Titans at the Polo Grounds on 09-17-60

6 points were scored by Oscar Lofton in the 28–24 win over the New York Titans at the Polo Grounds on 09-17-60

6 points were scored by Jim Colclough in the 28–24 win over the New York Titans at the Polo Grounds on 09-17-60

6 points were scored by Chuck Shonta, on the final play, in the 28–24 win over the New York Titans at the Polo Grounds on 09-17-60

6 points were scored by Ron Burton in the 35–0 shutout of the Los Angeles Chargers at the Los Angeles Coliseum on 10-08-60

6 points were scored by Jim Colclough in the 35–0 shutout of the Los Angeles Chargers at the Los Angeles Coliseum on 10-08-60

6 points were scored by Jim Crawford in the 35–0 shutout of the Los Angeles Chargers at the Los Angeles Coliseum on 10-08-60

6 points were scored by Alan Miller in the 35–0 shutout of the Los Angeles Chargers at the Los Angeles Coliseum on 10-08-60

9 points were scored by Gino Cappelletti in the 35–0 shutout of the Los Angeles Chargers at the Los Angeles Coliseum on 10-08-60

12 points were scored by Dick Christy in the 34–28 victory over the Oakland Raiders at BU Field on 11-04-60

12 points were scored by Jim Colclough in the 38–21 win over the New York Titans at BU Field on 11-11-60

12 points were scored by Joe Johnson in the 42–14 rout of the Dallas Texans at BU Field on 11-18-60

12 points were scored by Oscar Lofton in the 37–21 loss to the Houston Oilers at Jeppesen Stadium on 12-18-60

12 points were scored by Gino Cappelletti in the 21–20 loss to the New York Titans at BU Field on 09-09-61

15 points were scored by Gino Cappelletti in the 45–17 rout of the Denver Broncos at BU Field on 09-16-61

18 points were scored by Gino Cappelletti in the 37–30 loss to the New York Titans at the Polo Grounds on 10-01-61

18 points were scored by Billy Lott in the 52–21 rout of the Buffalo Bills at BU Field on 10-22-61

19 points were scored by Gino Cappelletti in the 43–14 rout of the New York Titans at the Polo Grounds on 10-06-62

20 points were scored by Gino Cappelletti in the 26–16 victory over the Oakland Raiders at BU Field on 10-26-62

22 points were scored by Gino Cappelletti in the 40–21 victory over the Denver Broncos at Fenway Park on 10-18-63

24 points were scored by Gino Cappelletti in the 36–28 win over the Buffalo Bills at War Memorial Stadium on 11-15-64

28 points were scored by Gino Cappelletti in the 42–14 rout of the Houston Oilers at Fenway Park on 12-18-65

The progression of the most points scored by a Patriots running back in a regular season game

6 points were scored by Walt Livingston in the 28–24 victory over the New York Titans at the Polo Grounds on 09-17-60

6 points were scored by Ron Burton in the 35–0 shutout of the Los Angeles Chargers at the Los Angeles Coliseum on 10-08-60

6 points were scored by Jim Crawford in the 35–0 shutout of the Los Angeles Chargers at the Los Angeles Coliseum on 10-08-60

6 points were scored by Alan Miller in the 35–0 shutout of the Los Angeles Chargers at the Los Angeles Coliseum on 10-08-60

6 points were scored by Walter Beach in the 45–16 loss to the Los Angeles Chargers at BU Field on 10-28-60

12 points were scored by Dick Christy in the 34–28 victory over the Oakland Raiders at BU Field on 11-04-60

18 points were scored by Billy Lott in the 52–21 rout of the Buffalo Bills at BU Field on 10-22-61

18 points were scored by Larry Garron in the 35–17 win over the San Diego Chargers at Fenway Park on 10-23-66

18 points were scored by Sam Cunningham in the 30–28 loss to the Buffalo Bills at Rich Stadium on 10-20-74

18 points were scored by Sam Cunningham in the 45–31 loss to the Buffalo Bills at Rich Stadium on 11-23-75

18 points were scored by Tony Collins in the 23–13 victory over the New York Jets at Sullivan Stadium on 09-18-83

18 points were scored by Mosi Tatupu in the 21–7 win over the Los Angeles Rams at Anaheim Stadium on 12-11-83

20 points were scored by Curtis Martin in the 31–0 shutout of the Arizona Cardinals at Foxboro on 09-15-96

The progression of the most points scored by a Patriots wide receiver in a regular season game

6 points were scored by Jim Colclough in the 13–10 loss to the Denver Broncos at BU Field on 09-09-60

12 points were scored by Jim Colclough in the 38–21 victory over the New York Titans at BU Field on 11-11-60

18 points were scored by Gino Cappelletti in the 36–28 win over the Buffalo Bills at War Memorial Stadium on 11-15-64

18 points were scored by Harold Jackson in the 56–3 rout of the New York Jets at Schaefer Stadium on 09-09-79

18 points were scored by Stanley Morgan in the 38–31 loss to the Seattle Seahawks at Sullivan Stadium on 09-21-86

18 points were scored by David Patten in the 38–17 rout of the Indianapolis Colts at the RCA Dome on 10-21-01

24 points were scored by Randy Moss, in the first half, in the 56–10 rout of the Buffalo Bills at Ralph Wilson Stadium on 11-18-07

Every Patriots player who scored an offensive TD and a special teams TD in the same game

Larry Garron caught a TD pass and returned a kickoff for a TD in the 28–28 tie with Buffalo on 11-03-62

Stanley Morgan caught a TD pass and returned a punt for a TD in the 50–21 rout of Baltimore on 11-18-79

Irving Fryar caught a TD pass and returned a punt for a TD in the 34–15 rout of Indianapolis on 11-10-85

David Patten

The only Patriots player who scored a defensive TD and a special teams TD in the same game

Don Webb returned an interception for a TD and returned a blocked punt for a TD in the 41–0 rout of San Diego on 12-17-61

The progression of the most points scored by a Patriots tight end in a regular season game

6 points were scored by Oscar Lofton in the 28–24 victory over the New York Titans at the Polo Grounds on 09-17-60

6 points were scored by Oscar Lofton in the 45–16 loss to the Los Angeles Chargers at BU Field on 10-28-60

6 points were scored by Tom Stephens in the 34–28 victory over the Oakland Raiders at BU Field on 11-04-60

6 points were scored by Tom Stephens in the 38–21 victory over the New York Titans at BU Field on 11-11-60

6 points were scored by Tom Stephens in the 42–14 rout of the Dallas Texans at BU Field on 11-18-60

12 points were scored by Joe Johnson in the 42–14 rout of the Dallas Texans at BU Field on 11-18-60

18 points were scored by Jim Whalen in the 41–10 rout of the Miami Dolphins at Boston College Alumni Stadium on 10-15-67

18 points were scored by Derrick Ramsey in the 50–17 rout of the Indianapolis Colts at the Hoosier Dome on 11-18-84

18 points were scored by Ben Coates in the 35–25 victory over the Buffalo Bills at Rich Stadium on 11-26-95

The progression of the most points scored by a Patriots quarterback in a regular season game

6 points were scored by Butch Songin in the 27–14 loss to the Oakland Raiders at Kezar Stadium on 10-16-60

6 points were scored by Butch Songin in the 38–14 loss to the Buffalo Bills at War Memorial Stadium on 12-04-60

6 points were scored by Babe Parilli in the 21–20 loss to the New York Titans at BU Field on 09-09-61

6 points were scored by Tom Yewcic in the 45–17 rout of the Denver Broncos at BU Field on 09-16-61

6 points were scored by Babe Parilli in the 31–31 tie with the Houston Oilers at BU Field on 10-13-61

6 points were scored by Babe Parilli in the 28–21 victory over the Dallas Texans at BU Field on 11-03-61

6 points were scored by Babe Parilli in the 27–15 loss to the Houston Oilers at Jeppesen Stadium on 11-12-61

6 points were scored by Babe Parilli in the 28–24 victory over the Denver Broncos at Bears Stadium on 12-03-61

6 points were scored by Babe Parilli in the 42–28 loss to the Dallas Texans at the Cotton Bowl on 09-08-62

6 points were scored by Babe Parilli in the 34–21 victory over the Houston Oilers at Harvard Stadium on 09-16-62

12 points were scored by Tom Yewcic in the 24–17 win over the New York Titans at BU Field on 11-30-62

12 points were scored by Babe Parilli in the 45–3 rout of the Houston Oilers at Fenway Park on 11-01-63

12 points were scored by Babe Parilli in the 25–24 victory over the Houston Oilers at Fenway Park on 11-06-64

12 points were scored by Don Trull in the 29–24 loss to the New York Jets at Fenway Park on 11-19-67

12 points were scored by Jim Plunkett in the 30–14 victory over the San Diego Chargers at Schaefer Stadium on 12-02-73

12 points were scored by Steve Grogan in the 48–17 rout of the Oakland Raiders at Schaefer Stadium on 10-03-76

12 points were scored by Steve Grogan in the 21–14 victory over the Baltimore Colts at Memorial Stadium on 11-14-76

12 points were scored by Steve Grogan in the 27–6 rout of the New Orleans Saints at Schaefer Stadium on 12-05-76

12 points were scored by Tony Eason in the 20–14 victory over the Cincinnati Bengals at Sullivan Stadium on 10-14-84

12 points were scored by Tom Brady in the 52–7 rout of the Washington Redskins at Gillette Stadium on 10-28-07

Every Patriots player who has scored with at least one TD run and at least one TD reception in consecutive regular season games

Billy Lott ran for a TD and had a TD reception on 12-03-61, and had two TD runs and one TD reception on 12-09-61

Larry Garron ran for a TD and had a TD reception on 10-09-64, and ran for a TD and had two TD receptions on 10-16-64

Every Patriots player who has run for three TDs in a regular season game

1974 regular season

Sam Cunningham ran for a 75-yard TD, a 12-yard TD, and a one-yard TD in the 30–28 loss to the Buffalo Bills on 10-20-74

1983 regular season

Tony Collins ran for a 39-yard TD, a seven-yard TD, and a 23-yard TD in the 23–13 win over the New York Jets on 09-18-83

Mosi Tatupu ran for a four-yard TD, a five-yard TD, and a seven-yard TD in the 21–7 win over the Los Angeles Rams on 12-11-83

1996 regular season

Curtis Martin ran for a one-yard TD, a one-yard TD, and a two-yard TD in the 42–23 win over the Miami Dolphins on 11-03-96

The only Patriots running back with three TD receptions in a regular season game

Billy Lott caught three TD passes in the 52–21 rout of the Buffalo Bills at BU Field on 10-22-61

Every Patriots player who has run for at least one TD, caught at least one TD pass, and scored at least 18 points in the same game

Billy Lott ran for two TDs and caught a TD pass in the 35–21 win over the Oakland Raiders on 12-09-61

Larry Garron ran for a TD and caught two TD passes in the 43–43 tie with the Oakland Raiders on 10-16-64

Sam Cunningham ran for two TDs and caught a TD pass in the 45–31 loss to the Buffalo Bills on 11-23-75

Curtis Martin ran for a TD and caught two TD passes in the 31–0 shutout of the Arizona Cardinals on 09-15-96

David Patten ran for a TD and caught two TD passes in the 34–17 victory over the Indianapolis Colts on 11-25-01

The progression of the most consecutive regular season games during which a Patriots player scored at least one TD

3 consecutive games that Dick Christy scored at least one TD during the 1960 season

3 consecutive games that Harry Crump scored at least one TD during the 1963 season

3 consecutive games that Larry Garron scored at least one TD during the 1966 season

4 consecutive games that Jim Nance scored at least one TD during the 1966 season

5 consecutive games that Horace Ivory scored at least one TD during the 1978 season

5 consecutive games that Curtis Martin scored at least one TD during the 1995 season

7 consecutive games that Curtis Martin scored at least one TD during the 1996 season

The progression of the most consecutive regular season games during which a Patriots player scored at least two TDs

2 consecutive games that Billy Lott scored at least two TDs during the 1961 season

2 consecutive games that Larry Garron scored at least two TDs during the 1964 season

2 consecutive games that Gino Cappelletti scored at least two TDs during the 1965 season

2 consecutive games that Jim Nance scored at least two TDs during the 1969 season

2 consecutive games that John Tarver scored at least two TDs during the 1973 season

3 consecutive games that Horace Ivory scored at least two TDs during the 1978 season

3 consecutive games that Curtis Martin scored at least two TDs during the 1995 season

4 consecutive games that Curtis Martin scored at least two TDs during the 1996 season

The progression of the most consecutive regular season games during which a Patriots receiver had at least one TD reception

2 consecutive games that Jim Colclough caught at least one TD pass during the 1960 season

3 consecutive games that Jim Colclough caught at least one TD pass during the 1960 season

4 consecutive games that Gino Cappelletti caught at least one TD pass during the 1961 season

5 consecutive games that Jim Colclough caught at least one TD pass during the 1962 season

5 consecutive games that Michael Timpson caught at least one TD pass over the 1993-1994 seasons

5 consecutive games that Randy Moss caught at least one TD pass during the 2007 season

Every Patriots receiver who had at least two TD receptions in consecutive regular season games

Gino Cappelletti had two TD receptions in the consecutive wins over the Broncos and the Oilers in the last two games of 1965

Stanley Morgan had two TD receptions in the 31–26 loss to the Ravens and in the 26–6 win over the Bills in 1979

Ben Coates had two TD receptions in consecutive losses to the Dolphins and the Bills to start the 1994 season

Randy Moss had two TD receptions in three consecutive games during the 2007 undefeated regular season

Wes Welker had two TD receptions in consecutive victories over the Cowboys and the Dolphins in the 2007 regular season

Randy Moss had two TD receptions in the final two games to cap the 2007 undefeated regular season

Every Patriots wide receiver with at least three TD receptions in a regular season game

1964 regular season
Gino Cappelletti caught three TD passes in the 36–28 win over the Buffalo Bills at War Memorial Stadium on 11-15-64

1979 regular season
Harold Jackson caught three TD passes in the 56–3 rout of the New York Jets at Schaefer Stadium on 09-09-79

1986 regular season
Stanley Morgan caught three TD passes in the 31–28 loss to the Seattle Seahawks at Sullivan Stadium on 09-21-86

2007 undefeated regular season
Randy Moss caught four TD passes in the first half in the 56–10 rout of the Buffalo Bills at Ralph Wilson Stadium on 11-18-07

2008 regular season
Randy Moss caught three TD passes in the 48–28 rout of the Miami Dolphins at Dolphin Stadium on 11-23-08

Every Patriots tight end with three TD receptions in a regular season game

1967 regular season
Jim Whalen caught three TD passes in the 41–10 rout of the Miami Dolphins at Fenway Park on 10-15-67

1984 regular season
Derrick Ramsey caught three TD passes in the 50–17 rout of the Indianapolis Colts at the Hoosier Dome on 11-18-84

1995 regular season
Ben Coates caught three TD passes in the 35–25 victory over the Buffalo Bills at Rich Stadium on 11-26-95

The progression of the most points scored by a Patriots kicker in a regular season game

4 points by Gino Cappelletti, who kicked a field goal and a PAT in the 13–10 loss to the Denver Broncos at BU Field on 09-09-60

4 points by Gino Cappelletti, who kicked four PATs in the 28–24 win over the New York Titans at the Polo Grounds on 09-17-60

9 points by Gino Cappelletti, (two field goals and three PATs) in the 35–0 shutout of the San Diego Chargers at the Los Angeles Coliseum on 10-08-60

11 points by Gino Cappelletti, (two field goals and five PATs) in the 34–28 win over the Oakland Raiders at BU Field on 11-04-60

11 points by Gino Cappelletti, (three field goals and two PATs) in the 23–21 win over the Buffalo Bills at War Memorial Stadium on 09-23-61

12 points by Gino Cappelletti, (three field goals and three PATs) in the 37–30 loss to the New York Titans at the Polo Grounds on 10-01-61

13 points by Gino Cappelletti, (three field goals and four PATs) in the 43–14 rout of the New York Titans at the Polo Grounds on 10-06-62

14 points by Gino Cappelletti, (four field goals and two PATs) in the 26–16 win over Oakland Raiders at BU Field on 10-26-62

15 points by Gino Cappelletti, (four field goals and three PATs) in the 33–29 win over the Denver Broncos at Bears Stadium on 11-11-62

16 points by Gino Cappelletti, (four field goals and four PATs) in the 40–21 win over the Denver Broncos at Fenway Park on 10-18-63

21 points by Gino Cappelletti, (six field goals and three PATs) in the 39–10 rout of the Denver Broncos at Bears Stadium on 10-04-64

The progression of the most points scored by a Patriots offensive lineman in a regular season game

6 points by John Hannah on a fumble recovery in the 34–27 loss to the Miami Dolphins at Schaefer Stadium on 12-15-74

6 points by Freddie Childress on a fumble recovery in the 26–23 overtime win vs the Minnesota Vikings at Foxboro on 10-20-91

The progression of the most points scored by a Patriots defensive lineman in a regular season game

6 points by Jim Lee Hunt, who returned an interception 78 yards for a TD in the 45–3 rout of the Houston Oilers on 11-01-63

6 points by Jim Lee Hunt, who returned a fumble five yards for a TD in the 17–10 loss to the Denver Broncos on 11-06-66

6 points by Mel Witt, who returned an interception four yards for a TD in the 47–31 loss to the New York Jets on 09-22-68

6 points by Ray Hamilton, who returned a fumble 23 yards for a TD in the 24–17 loss to the St. Louis Cardinals on 11-02-75

6 points by Brent Williams, who returned a fumble 21 yards for a TD to beat the Seattle Seahawks, 21–20, on 11-30-86

6 points by Brent Williams, who returned a fumble 45 yards for a TD in the 33–20 loss to the Seattle Seahawks on 10-07-90

6 points by Tim Goad, who returned a fumble 19 yards for a TD in the 27–20 loss to the Kansas City Chiefs on 12-13-92

6 points by Willie McGinest, who returned a pass 46 yards for a TD in the 28–25 win over the Buffalo Bills on 10-27-96

6 points by Willie McGinest, who recovered a fumble in the end zone in the 45–7 rout of the San Diego Chargers on 12-01-96

6 points by Henry Thomas, who returned a pass 24 yards for a TD in the 30–27 win over the New Orleans Saints on 10-24-98

6 points by Chad Eaton, who returned a fumble 23 yards for a TD in the 20–3 win over the Baltimore Ravens on 01-02-00

6 points by Richard Seymour, who returned a fumble 68 yards for a TD in the 31–17 win over the Buffalo Bills on 10-03-04

6 points by Jarvis Green, who recovered a fumble in the end zone in the 24–3 rout of the Baltimore Ravens on 11-28-04

The progression of the most points scored by a Patriots linebacker in a regular season game

6 points by Tom Addison, who returned a pass 12 yards for a TD in the 43–14 win over the New York Titans on 10-06-62

6 points by Nick Buoniconti, who returned a fumble seven yards for a TD in the 46–28 win over the Houston Oilers on 12-08-63

6 points by Ed Philpott, who returned a fumble 10 yards for a TD in the 47–31 loss to the New York Jets on 09-22-68

6 points by Bob Geddes, who returned a pass 29 yards for a TD in the 24–0 shutout of the New York Jets on 10-13-74

6 points by Sam Hunt, who returned a pass 68 yards for a TD in the 31–14 win over Tampa Bay Buccaneers on 12-12-76

6 points by Mike Hawkins, who returned a pass 35 yards for a TD in the 28–13 win over the Miami Dolphins on 10-21-79

6 points by Rod Shoate, who returned a pass 42 yards for a TD in the 47–21 rout of the Baltimore Colts on 11-23-80

6 points by Clayton Weishuhn, who returned a lateral 27 yards for a TD in the 28–23 win over the Pittsburgh Steelers on 09-25-83

6 points by Andre Tippett, who returned a fumble 25 yards for a TD in the 35–20 loss to the Los Angeles Raiders on 09-29-85

6 points by Johnny Rembert, who recovered a fumble in the end zone in the 33–3 rout of the Indianapolis Colts on 09-07-86

6 points by Andre Tippett, who returned a fumble 29 yards for a TD in the 43–24 loss to the New York Jets on 09-21-87

6 points by Vincent Brown, who returned a fumble 25 yards for a TD in the 16–7 loss to the Buffalo Bills on 11-01-92

6 points by Vincent Brown, who returned a pass 49 yards for a TD in the 31–14 loss to the New Orleans Saints on 11-08-92

6 points by Chris Singleton, who returned a pass 82 yards for a TD in the 37–34 overtime win vs the Indianapolis Colts on 11–15-92

6 points by Chris Slade, who returned a fumble 27 yards for a TD in the 35–25 win over the Buffalo Bills on 11-26-95

6 points by Tedy Bruschi, who returned a blocked punt four yards for a TD in the 46–38 win over the Baltimore Ravens on 10-06-96

6 points by Chris Slade, who returned a pass one yard for a TD in the 31–10 win over the Buffalo Bills on 11-09-97

6 points by Andy Katzenmoyer, who returned a pass 57 yards for a TD in the 31–30 loss to the Miami Dolphins on 10-17-99

6 points by Tedy Bruschi, who returned a pass 48 yards for a TD in the 27–20 loss to the Oakland Raiders on 11-17-02

6 points by Tedy Bruschi, who returned a pass 27 yards for a TD in the 20–12 win over the Detroit Lions on 11-28-02

6 points by Tedy Bruschi, who returned a pass 18 yards for a TD in the 31–10 rout of the Philadelphia Eagles on 09-14-03

6 points by Tedy Bruschi, who returned a pass 5 yards for a TD in the 12–0 shutout of the Miami Dolphins on 12-07-03

6 points by Willie McGinest, who returned a pass 15 yards for a TD in the 21–16 win over the New York Jets on 12-20-03

6 points by Mike Vrabel, who took a pass 24 yards for a TD in the 27–17 loss to the Carolina Panthers on 09-18-05

6 points by Adalius Thomas, who took a pass 65 yards for a TD in the 38–14 rout of the San Diego Chargers on 09-16-07

6 points by Rosevelt Colvin, who returned a strip-sack 11 yards for a TD in the 52–7 rout of the Washington Redskins on 10-28-07

The progression of the most points scored by a Patriots defensive back in a regular season game

6 points by Chuck Shonta, who returned a fumble 52 yards for a TD to beat the New York Titans 28–24 on 09-17-60

6 points by Tom Stephens, who returned a fumble 10 yards for a TD in the 38–27 loss to the San Diego Chargers on 10-07-61

6 points by Don Webb, who returned a pass 27 yards for a TD in the 52–21 rout of the Buffalo Bills on 10-22-61

6 points by Don Webb, who returned a fumble 49 yards for a TD in the 18–17 win over the Dallas Texans on 10-29-61

6 points by Don Webb, who returned a blocked punt 20 yards for a TD in the 41–0 shutout of the San Diego Chargers on 12-17-61

6 points by Don Webb, who returned a pass 31 yards for a TD in the 41–0 shutout of the San Diego Chargers on 12-17-61

6 points by Fred Bruney, who returned a pass 33 yards for a TD in the 41–16 win over the Denver Broncos on 09-21-62

6 points by Ron Hall, who returned a pass 47 yards for a TD in the 41–16 win over the Denver Broncos on 09-21-62

6 points by Bob Suci, who returned a pass 98 yards for a TD in the 45–3 rout of the Houston Oilers on 11-01-63

6 points by Bob Suci, who returned a pass 52 yards for a TD in the 46–28 win over the Houston Oilers on 12-08-63

6 points by Ross O'Hanley, who returned a pass 47 yards for a TD in the 34–17 win over the Houston Oilers on 11-29-64

6 points by Jay Cunningham, who returned a pass 54 yards for a TD in the 41–10 rout of the Miami Dolphins on 10-15-67

6 points by John Charles, who returned a pass 35 yards for a TD in the 30–23 loss to the New York Jets on 10-29-67

6 points by John Charles, who returned a pass 25 yards for a TD in the 23–17 loss to the New York Jets on 10-26-69

6 points by Daryl Johnson, who returned a fumble 32 yards for a TD in the 24–0 shutout of the Houston Oilers on 11-02-69

6 points by Larry Carwell, who returned a pass 53 yards for a TD in the 34–13 win over the Miami Dolphins on 12-05-71

6 points by John Outlaw, who returned a pass 60 yards for a TD in the 21–17 win over the Baltimore Colts on 12-19-71

6 points by Larry Carwell, who returned a blocked field goal 45 yards for a TD in the 31–7 loss to the Cincinnati Bengals on 09-17-72

6 points by John Sanders, who returned a pass 23 yards for a TD in the 34–27 loss to the Miami Dolphins on 12-15-74

6 points by Bob Howard, who returned a pass 44 yards for a TD in the 33–19 win over the San Diego Chargers on 11-09-75

12 points by Prentice McCray, who returned two passes for a TD in the 38–24 win over the New York Jets on 11-21-76

The only regular season game that the Patriots scored with two TD receptions, an offensive fumble return for a TD, a kickoff return for a TD, and at least one extra point

1961 regular season

Jim Colclough caught a 14-yard TD pass from Butch Songin; Gino Cappelletti caught a seven-yard TD pass from Babe Parilli; Babe Parilli advanced a fumble by Larry Garron one yard for a TD; Ron Burton returned a kickoff 91 yards for the game-winning points; Gino Cappelletti kicked four extra points in the 28–21 victory over the Dallas Texans at BU Field on 11-03-61

The only regular season game that the Patriots had two TD receptions, two rushing TDs, three field goals, a blocked punt that was returned for a TD, a punt return for a TD, and at least one extra point

1979 regular season

Stanley Morgan and Harold Jackson had TD receptions; Don Calhoun and Allan Clark ran for a TD; John Smith kicked three field goals; Rick Sanford blocked a Bucky Dilt punt and returned it eight yards for a TD; Stanley Morgan returned a punt by Bucky Dilt 80 yards for a TD; John Smith kicked five extra points in the 50–21 rout of the Baltimore Colts at Schaefer Stadium on 11-18-79

The only regular season game that the Patriots scored with a kickoff return for a TD, a field goal, a TD reception, an interception return for a TD, a TD run, and at least one extra point

1997 regular season

Derrick Cullors returned a kickoff 86 yards for a TD; Adam Vinatieri kicked a 42-yard field goal; Ben Coates caught a six-yard TD pass from Drew Bledsoe; Chris Slade returned a Todd Collins pass one yard for a TD; Curtis Martin dove one yard for a TD; Adam Vinatieri kicked four extra points in the 31–10 rout of the Buffalo Bills at Rich Stadium on 11-09-97

The only regular season game that the Patriots scored with a field goal, a punt return for a TD, a TD run, a TD reception, two interception returns for a TD, and at least one extra point

2001 championship season

Adam Vinatieri kicked a 19-yard field goal; Ty Law returned a Chris Weinke pass 46 yards for a TD; Troy Brown returned a punt by Todd Sauerbrun 61 yards for a TD; Antowain Smith ran 32 yards for a TD; Jermaine Wiggins caught a five-yard TD pass from Tom Brady; Otis Smith returned a Chris Weinke pass 76 yards for a TD; Adam Vinatieri kicked five extra points in the 38–6 rout of the Carolina Panthers at Ericsson Stadium on 01-06-02

The only game that the Patriots scored a TD with defense and special teams but not with its offense

2002 regular season

Tedy Bruschi returned a Rich Gannon pass 48 yards for a TD; Kevin Faulk returned a kickoff 86 yards for a TD; Adam Vinatieri kicked two field goals and two extra points in the 26–20 loss to the Oakland Raiders at the Network Associates Coliseum on 11-17-02

The only regular season game that the Patriots scored with a kickoff return for a TD, at least one rushing TD, at least one TD reception, a defensive fumble return for a TD, and at least one extra point

2004 championship season

Bethel Johnson returned the opening kickoff 93 yards for a TD; Corey Dillon had two TD runs; Kevin Faulk ran 10 yards for a TD; Randall Gay returned a William Green fumble 41 yards for a TD; David Patten caught a 44-yard TD pass from Tom Brady; Adam Vinatieri kicked six extra points in the 42–15 rout of the Cleveland Browns at Cleveland Browns Stadium on 12-05-04

Every special teams player who has scored a TD in a regular season game for the Patriots

1960 regular season

Chuck Shonta took a bad snap to the punter 52 yards for a TD on the last play to defeat the New York Titans 28–24 on 09-17-60

1961 regular season

Larry Garron returned a kickoff 89 yards for a TD in the 31–31 tie with the Houston Oilers on 10-13-61

Ron Burton returned a kickoff 91 yards for a TD for the final points scored to beat the Dallas Texans 28–21 on 11-03-61

LeRoy Moore recovered a blocked punt in the end zone in the 20–17 win over the Oakland Raiders on 12-17-61

Don Webb returned a blocked punt 20 yards for a TD in the 41–0 shutout of the San Diego Chargers on 12-17-61

1962 regular season

Larry Garron returned a kickoff 95 yards for a TD in the 28–28 tie with the Buffalo Bills on 11-03-62

Ron Burton returned a missed field goal 91 yards for a TD in the 33–29 win over the Denver Broncos on 11-11-62

1967 regular season

J.D. Garrett recovered a blocked punt in the end zone for a TD in the 41–32 loss to the Miami Dolphins on 12-17-67

1971 regular season

Roland Moss returned a blocked punt 10 yards for a TD in the 38–33 victory over the Buffalo Bills on 11-14-71

1972 regular season

Larry Carwell returned a blocked field goal 45 yards for a TD in the 31–7 loss to the Cincinnati Bengals on 09-17-72

1973 regular season

Will Foster recovered a blocked punt in the end zone in the 9–7 loss to the New York Jets on 10-14-73

Mack Herron returned a kickoff 92 yards for a TD in the 30–14 win over the San Diego Chargers on 12-02-73

1975 regular season

Allen Carter took the opening kickoff 99 yards for a TD in the 32–21 loss to the Baltimore Colts on 12-21-75

1976 regular season

Mike Haynes returned a punt 89 yards for a TD in the 20–10 victory over the Buffalo Bills on 11-07-76

Mike Haynes returned a punt 62 yards for a TD in the 38–14 rout of the Denver Broncos on 11-28-76

1977 regular season

Stanley Morgan returned a kickoff 100 yards for a TD in the 30–27 loss to the New York Jets on 10-02-77

Stanley Morgan returned a kickoff 93 yards for a TD in the 24–14 loss to the Buffalo Bills on 11-06-77

Stanley Morgan returned a kickoff 101 yards for a TD in the 30–24 loss to the Baltimore Colts on 12-18-77

1979 regular season

Rick Sanford returned a blocked punt eight yards for a TD in the 50–21 rout of the Baltimore Colts on 11-18-79

Stanley Morgan returned a punt 80 yards for a TD in the 50–21 rout of the Baltimore Colts on 11-18-79

1980 regular season

Mike Haynes returned a blocked field goal 65 yards for a TD in the 21–11 victory over the New York Jets on 10-05-80

Horace Ivory returned a kickoff 98 yards for a TD in the 37–21 win over the Baltimore Colts on 10-19-80

Roland James returned a punt 75 yards for a TD in the 34–21 win over the New York Jets on 11-02-80

Rick Sanford returned a fumbled kickoff return 22 yards for a TD in the 47–21 rout of the Baltimore Colts on 11-23-80

Allan Clark returned a fumbled kickoff return 15 yards for a TD in the 47–21 rout of the Baltimore Colts on 11-23-80

1982 regular season

Ricky Smith returned a kickoff 98 yards for a TD in the 31–7 loss to the New York Jets on 09-18-82

1985 regular season

Irving Fryar returned a punt 85 yards for a TD in the 17–14 victory over the Buffalo Bills on 09-22-85

Irving Fryar returned a punt 77 yards for a TD in the 34–15 rout of the Indianapolis Colts on 11-10-85

1986 regular season

Irving Fryar returned a punt 59 yards for a TD in the 25–17 victory over the Atlanta Falcons on 11-02-86

Rod McSwain returned a blocked punt 31 yards for a TD in the 30–28 win over the Los Angeles Rams on 11-16-86

Mosi Tatupu returned a blocked punt 21 yards for a TD in the 21–20 win over the New Orleans Saints on 11-30-86

1987 regular season
Raymond Clayborn returned a blocked field goal 71 yards for a TD in the 21–7 win over the Houston Oilers on 10-18-87

Willie Scott returned a blocked punt three yards for a TD in the 24–0 shutout of the Indianapolis Colts on 11-22-87

1988 regular season
Sammy Martin took the opening kickoff 95 yards for a TD in the 24–21 loss to the Indianapolis Colts on 11-27-88

1991 regular season
Jon Vaughn returned a kickoff 99 yards for a TD in the 24–10 loss to the Phoenix Cardinals on 09-29-91

1992 regular season
Jon Vaughn took a kickoff 100 yards for a TD in the 20–10 loss to the Cincinnati Bengals on 12-20-92

1995 regular season
Troy Brown advanced a fumble by Dave Meggett 75 yards for a TD in the 31–28 win over the New York Jets on 12-10-95

1996 regular season
Tedy Bruschi returned a blocked punt four yards for a TD in the 46–38 win over the Baltimore Ravens on 10-06-96

Troy Brown

Dave Meggett returned a punt 60 yards for a TD in the 23–22 comeback win over the New York Giants on 12-21-96

1997 regular season
Derrick Cullors returned a kickoff 86 yards for a TD in the 31–10 win over the Buffalo Bills on 11-09-97

2000 regular season
Troy Brown returned a punt 66 yards for a TD in the 21–16 loss to the Tampa Bay Buccaneers on 09-03-00

2001 championship season
Troy Brown returned a punt 85 yards for a TD in the 27–16 win over the Cleveland Browns on 12-09-01

Troy Brown returned a punt 68 yards for a TD in the 38–6 rout of the Carolina Panthers on 01-06-02

2002 regular season
Kevin Faulk returned a kickoff 86 yards for a TD in the 27–20 loss to the Oakland Raiders on 11-17-02

Kevin Faulk returned a kickoff 87 yards for a TD in the 30–17 loss to the New York Jets on 12-22-02

2003 championship season
Bethel Johnson took a kickoff 92 yards for a TD, on the last play of the half, in the 38–34 win over the Indianapolis Colts on 11-30-03

2004 championship season
Bethel Johnson took the opening kickoff 93 yards for a TD in the 42–15 rout of the Cleveland Browns on 12-05-04

2006 regular season
Ellis Hobbs returned a kickoff 93 yards for a TD in the 40–7 rout of the Houston Texans on 12-17-06

2007 undefeated regular season
Ellis Hobbs set the NFL record with a kickoff return of 108 yards for a TD in the 38–14 rout of the New York Jets on 09-09-07

Willie Andrews returned a kickoff 77 yards for a TD in the 49–28 win over the Miami Dolphins on 10-21-07

2008 regular season
Ellis Hobbs returned a kickoff 95 yards for a TD in the 49–26 rout of the Oakland Raiders on 12-14-08

Extra Points

The only kicker who kicked an extra point for the last point scored by the Patriots in a game that ended in a tie

1961 regular season
Gino Cappelletti kicked an extra point in the fourth quarter of the 31–31 tie with the Houston Oilers on 10-13-61

1962 regular season
Gino Cappelletti kicked an extra point in the fourth quarter of the 28–28 tie with the Buffalo Bills on 11-03-62

1963 regular season
Gino Cappelletti kicked an extra point in the fourth quarter of the 24–24 tie with the Kansas City Chiefs on 11-17-63

1964 regular season
Gino Cappelletti kicked an extra point in the fourth quarter of the 43–43 tie with the Oakland Raiders on 10-16-64

1965 regular season
Gino Cappelletti kicked the extra point for the final point scored in the 10–10 tie with the Kansas City Chiefs on 11-21-65

The only Patriots player who has drop-kicked the football for an extra point in a regular season game

Doug Flutie drop-kicked an extra point in the 28–26 loss to the Miami Dolphins at Gillette Stadium on 01-01-06

Every Patriots player who has kicked a PAT to tie the game and force the overtime period

1981 regular season
John Smith kicked a PAT, with 29 seconds left, to tie the game in the 27–21 loss overtime loss to the Pittsburgh Steelers on 09-27-81

1987 regular season
Tony Franklin kicked a PAT, with 65 seconds left, to tie the game in the 34–31 overtime loss to the Philadelphia Eagles on 11-29-87

1988 regular season
Jason Staurovsky kicked a PAT, to tie the game in the 10–7 overtime win vs the Tampa Bay Buccaneers on 12-11-88

1991 regular season
Charlie Baumann kicked a PAT, with seven seconds left, to tie the game in the 23–17 overtime win vs the Indianapolis Colts on 12-08-91

1993 regular season
Scott Sisson kicked a PAT, with 12 seconds left, to tie the game in the 19–16 overtime loss to the Detroit Lions on 09-12-93

1995 regular season
Matt Bahr kicked a PAT, with 52 seconds left, to tie the game in the 20–17 overtime loss to the Carolina Panthers on 10-29-95

2000 regular season
Adam Vinatieri kicked a PAT, in the fourth quarter, to tie the game in the 13–10 overtime win vs the Buffalo Bills on 12-17-00

2008 regular season
Stephen Gostkowski kicked a PAT, with one second left, to tie the game in the 34–31 overtime loss to the New York Jets on 11-13-08

Every Patriots player who kicked the game-winning extra point in a regular season game

1972 regular season
Mike Walker kicked the extra point to defeat the Atlanta Falcons, 21–20, at Schaefer Stadium on 09-24-72

Charlie Gogolak kicked the extra point to defeat the Washington Redskins, 24–23, at Schaefer Stadium on 10-01-72

1984 regular season
Tony Franklin kicked the extra point to defeat the Cleveland Browns, 17–16, at Cleveland Stadium on 10-07-84

1986 regular season
Tony Franklin kicked the extra point to defeat the New Orleans Saints, 21–20, at the Superdome on 11-30-86

1988 regular season
Jason Staurovsky kicked the extra point to defeat the New York Jets, 14–13, at the Meadowlands on 11-13-88

1999 regular season
Adam Vinatieri kicked the extra point to defeat the Denver Broncos, 24–23, at Foxboro Stadium on 10-24-99

The first time that two different Patriots kickers have scored a point in a regular season game

Gino Cappelletti kicked two field goals and Justin Canale kicked an extra point in the 18–7 win over Houston on 11-05-67

Two-Point Conversions

The only Patriots player who has run for a two-point conversion while the opposing team was on the sidelines

Adam Vinatieri ran for a two-point conversion in the 25–21 victory over the Buffalo Bills at Foxboro Stadium on 11-29-98

Every Patriots player who has run for a two-point conversion in a regular season game

1960 regular season

Gino Cappelletti ran for a two-point coversion in the 27–14 loss to the Oakland Raiders at Kezar Stadium on 10-16-60

Gino Cappelletti ran for a two-point conversion in the 42–14 win over the Dallas Texans at BU Field on 11-18-60

Gino Cappelletti ran for a two-point conversion in the 37–21 loss to the Houston Oilers at Jeppesen Stadium on 12-18-60

1961 regular season

Babe Parilli ran for a two-point conversion in the 18–17 victory over the Dallas Texans at the Cotton Bowl on 10-29-61

1969 regular season

Kim Hammond ran for two points in the 28–18 loss to the San Diego Chargers at Jack Murphy Stadium on 12-07-69

1995 regular season

Dave Meggett ran for a two-point conversion in the 17–14 win over the Cleveland Browns at Foxboro on 09-03-95

1998 regular season

Adam Vinatieri ran for a two-point conversion in the 25–21 win over the Buffalo Bills at Foxboro Stadium on 11-29-98

2000 regular season

Kevin Faulk ran for a two-point conversion in the 19–11 loss to the Cleveland Browns at Browns Stadium on 11-12-00

Corey Dillon

2002 regular season

Antowain Smith ran for a two-point conversion in the 41–38 overtime win vs the Kansas City Chiefs at Gillette Stadium on 09-22-02

2004 championship season

Corey Dillon ran for a two-point conversion in the 24–3 rout of the Baltimore Ravens at Gillette Stadium on 11-28-04

2007 undefeated regular season

Laurence Maroney ran for a two-point conversion in the 38–35 win over the New York Giants at Giants Stadium on 12-29-07

The only Patriots player who has thrown for two, two-point conversion passes in the same game

Drew Bledsoe threw a two-point pass to Sam Gash and one to Keith Byars in the 46–38 win over the Ravens on 10-06-96

Drew Bledsoe

Every Patriots player who completed a pass for a two-point conversion

1960 regular season
Gino Cappelletti tossed a two-point pass to Jim Crawford in the 35–0 shutout of the Los Angeles Chargers at Los Angeles on 10-08-60

1962 regular season
Babe Parilli threw a two-point pass to Jim Crawford in the 24–20 win over the San Diego Chargers at BU Field on 10-19-62

1964 regular season
Babe Parilli tossed a two-point pass to Jim Colclough in the 43–43 tie with the Oakland Raiders at Fenway Park on 10-16-64

Babe Parilli threw a two-point pass to Gino Cappelletti in the 36–28 win over the Buffalo Bills at War Memorial Stadium on 11-15-64

Babe Parilli tossed a two-point pass to Jim Colclough in the 24–14 loss to the Buffalo Bills at Fenway Park on 12-20-64

1966 regular season
Babe Parilli lofted a two-point pass to Tony Romeo in the 24–10 win over the Denver Broncos at Bears Stadium on 09-18-66

Babe Parilli threw a two-point pass to Bob Cappadona in the 38–28 loss to the New York Jets at Shea Stadium on 12-17-66

1995 regular season
Drew Bledsoe tossed a two-point pass to Curtis Martin in the 35–25 victory over the Buffalo Bills at Rich Stadium on 11-26-95

Drew Bledsoe fired a two-point pass to Dave Meggett in the 41–27 loss to the Pittsburgh Steelers at Three Rivers Stadium on 12-16-95

1996 regular season
Drew Bledsoe threw a two-point pass to Curtis Martin in the 31–0 shutout of the Arizona Cardinals at Foxboro Stadium on 09-15-96

Drew Bledsoe fired a two-point pass to Ben Coates in the 46–38 win over the Baltimore Ravens at Memorial Stadium on 10-06-96

Drew Bledsoe tossed a two-point pass to Sam Gash in the 46–38 win over the Baltimore Ravens at Memorial Stadium on 10-06-96

Drew Bledsoe threw a two-point pass to Keith Byars in the 34–8 loss to the Denver Broncos at Foxboro Stadium on 11-17-96

2002 regular season
Tom Brady drilled a two-point pass to Troy Brown in the 33–30 win over the Chicago Bears at Memorial Stadium on 11-10-02

Tom Brady tossed a two-point pass to Christian Fauria in the 27–24 overtime win vs the Miami Dolphins at Gillette Stadium on 12-29-02

2006 regular season
Tom Brady tossed a two-point pass to Reche Caldwell in the 17–14 loss to the New York Jets at Gillette Stadium on 11-12-06

Tom Brady fired a two-point pass to Troy Brown in the 28–21 win over the Detroit Lions at Gillette Stadium on 12-03-06

Tom Brady

2008 regular season
Matt Cassel tossed a two-point pass to Jabar Gaffney in the 34–31 overtime loss to the New York Jets at Gillette Stadium on 11-13-08

Matt Cassel tossed a two-point pass to Wes Welker for the final points scored in the 24–21 win over the Seattle Seahawks at Qwest Field on 12-07-08

Every Patriots player who caught a TD pass and a two-point conversion pass in the same game
1964 regular season
Jim Colclough caught a 36-yard TD pass and a two-point conversion in the 43–43 tie with the Raiders on 10-16-64

1996 regular season
Ben Coates caught a one-yard TD pass and a two-point conversion in the 46–38 win over the Ravens on 10-06-96

The only Patriots player who caught two TDs, ran for a TD, and caught a two-point pass in the same game
Curtis Martin caught a 13-yard TD, a 7-yard TD pass, ran one yard for a TD, and caught a two-point conversion on 09-15-96

The only Patriots player who caught three TD passes and a two-point conversion pass in the same game
Gino Cappelletti caught three TD passes and a two-point conversion pass in the 36–28 win over the Bills on 11-15-64

The only Patriots player to kick a field goal and throw a two-point conversion pass in the same game
Gino Cappelletti kicked a 23-yard field goal and a 33-yard field goal and threw a two-point pass to Jim Crawford in the 35–0 shutout on 10-08-60

The only Patriots player to kick a field goal and run for a two-point conversion in the same game
Adam Vinatieri kicked a 44-yard field goal and ran for a two-point conversion in the 25–21 win over Buffalo on 11-29-98

The only Patriots player to lead the league with two-point conversions scored in a season
Gino Cappelletti ran for three two-point conversions during the 1960 AFL season

The only Patriots player to hold the league record for the most career two-point conversions
Gino Cappelletti holds the AFL record with four career two-point conversions

Safeties

The only safety recorded by a Patriots player even though the quarterback was tackled on the 2-yard line
George Crump tackled Archie Manning on 2-yard line for a safety in the 29–21 win over the Houston Oilers at Schaefer Stadium on 11-28-82

Every Patriots defensive end who tackled the quarterback in the end zone for a safety
1967 regular season
Jim Lee Hunt tackled Jack Kemp for a safety in the 44–16 loss to the Buffalo Bills at Fenway Park on 12-09-67

1982 regular season
George Crump tackled Archie Manning for a safety in the 29–21 win over the Houston Oilers at Schaefer Stadium on 11-28-82

2003 championship season

Jarvis Green tackled Jay Fiedler in the end zone for a safety in the 12–0 shutout of the Miami Dolphins at Gillette Stadium on 12-07-03

2006 regular season

Ty Warren sacked J.P. Losman for a safety for the last points scored in the 19–17 win over the Buffalo Bills at Gillette Stadium on 09-10-06

The only Patriots nose tackle who sacked the quarterback in the end zone for a safety

Richard Bishop tackled Bob Griese for a safety in the 33–24 win over the Miami Dolphins at Schaefer Stadium on 10-22-78

Every Patriots linebacker who tackled the quarterback in the end zone for a safety

1963 regular season

Jack Rudolph sacked Jacky Lee for a safety in the 46–28 win over the Houston Oilers at Jeppesen Stadium on 12-08-63

1964 regular season

Jack Rudolph sacked Jacky Lee for a safety in the 12–7 win over the Denver Broncos at Fenway Park on 11-20-64

1973 regular season

Steve Kiner sacked Dan Pastorini for a safety in the 32–0 shutout of the Houston Oilers at the Astrodome on 11-25-73

1985 regular season

Don Blackmon sacked Lynn Dickey for a safety in the 26–20 win over the Green Bay Packers at Sullivan Stadium on 09-08-85

Don Blackmon sacked Steve DeBerg for a safety in the 32–14 win over the Tampa Bay Buccaneers at Tampa on 10-27-85

The only game during which the Patriots defensive team sacked the quarterback and the fumble went out of the end zone for a safety

The defense hit Jim Kelly forcing him to fumble out of the end zone in the 22–19 win over the Buffalo Bills at Sullivan Stadium on 11-23-86

Every game a safety was recorded by the Patriots because of an intentional grounding penalty by a quarterback

1996 regular season

Mike Jones forced Jim Kelly to ground the ball in the 28–25 win over the Buffalo Bills at Foxboro Stadium on 10-27-96

1997 regular season

Henry Thomas forced Neil O'Donnell to ground the ball in the 24–19 loss to the New York Jets at the Meadowlands on 10-19-97

The only time the Patriots defensive team tackled the opposing center, after a fumble, for a safety

The defense tackled center Don Rogers in the end zone in the 45–16 loss to the Los Angeles Chargers at BU Field on 10-28-60

The only time the Patriots defensive team gang-tackled the opposing quarterback for a safety

The defense sacked quarterback Eddie Wilson in the end zone in the 24–24 tie vs the Kansas City Chiefs at Fenway Park on 11-17-63

Every Patriots defensive back who tackled a running back in the end zone for a safety

1965 regular season

Jay Cunningham tackled Les "Speedy" Duncan for a safety in the 22–6 win over the San Diego Chargers at Balboa Stadium on 10-31-65

1969 regular season

Daryl Johnson tackled Jess Phillips for a safety in the 25–14 victory over the Cincinnati Bengals at Nippert Stadium on 11-16-69

1984 regular season

Roland James tackled Frank Middleton for a safety in the 50–17 rout of the Indianapolis Colts at the Hoosier Dome on 11-18-84

Every Patriots linebacker who tackled a running back in the end zone for a safety

1967 regular season

Nick Buoniconti tackled Roy Hopkins for a safety in the 18–7 win over the Houston Oilers at Fenway Park on 11-05-67

1968 regular season

Doug Satcher tackled Paul Robinson for a safety in the 33–14 victory over the Cincinnati Bengals at Fenway Park on 12-01-68

The only Patriots special teams player who has tackled a punt returner in the end zone for a safety

Ezell Jones tackled punt returner Mercury Morris for a safety in the 38–23 win over Miami at Tampa on 11-30-69

Every Patriots defensive back who has forced the punter to run out of the end zone for a safety

1977 regular season

Raymond Clayborn forced Mike Michel out of the end zone in the 17–5 loss to Miami at the Orange Bowl on 11-13-77

1978 regular season

Tim Fox forced Rusty Jackson out of the end zone in the 26–24 win over the Bills at Schaefer Stadium on 12-10-78

The only game during which the Patriots defensive team forced the punter to run out of the end zone for a safety

The defense forced punter Chuck Ramsey out of the end zone in the 27–26 loss to the New York Jets at Shea Stadium on 12-09-79

The only regular season game the opposing center snapped the ball out of the end zone for a safety

Wayne Frazier snapped the ball out of the end zone in the 42–14 rout of the Houston Oilers at Fenway Park on 12-18-65

Safeties and Interceptions

The only Patriots defensive back who has recorded a safety and intercepted a pass in the same game

Daryl Johnson tackled Jess Phillips for a safety and intercepted a Greg Cook pass in the 25–14 win over the Bengals on 11-16-69

The only Patriots linebacker who has recorded a safety and intercepted a pass in the same game

Don Blackmon sacked Steve DeBerg for a safety and returned a Steve DeBerg pass 14 yards in the 32–14 win over the Tampa Bay Buccaneers on 10-27-85

Game-Winning Field Goals

The only Patriots player to kick a field goal for the only points scored in a regular season game

John Smith kicked a 33-yard field goal in the 3–0 "Snow Plow" win over the Miami Dolphins at Schaefer Stadium on 12-12-82

Every Patriots player who kicked a game-winning field goal on the last play of a regular season game

1961 regular season

Gino Cappelletti kicked a 24-yard field goal to defeat the Dallas Texans, 18–17, at the Cotton Bowl on 10-29-61

1964 regular season

Gino Cappelletti kicked a 41-yard field goal to defeat the Houston Oilers, 25–24, at Fenway Park on 11-06-64

1994 regular season

Matt Bahr kicked a 33-yard field goal to defeat the Green Bay Packers, 17–16, at Foxboro Stadium on 10-02-94

1998 regular season

Adam Vinatieri kicked a 27-yard field goal to defeat the New Orleans Saints, 30–27, at the Superdome on 10-04-98

Adam Vinatieri kicked a 35-yard field goal to defeat the San Francisco 49ers, 24–21, at Foxboro Stadium on 12-20-98

Every Patriots player who kicked the overtime game-winning field goal in a regular season game

1988 regular season

Jason Staurovsky kicked a 27-yard field goal to defeat the Tampa Bay Buccaneeers, 10–7, at Sullivan Stadium on 12-11-88

1989 regular season

Greg Davis kicked a 51-yard field goal to defeat the Indianapolis Colts, 23–20, at the Hoosier Dome on 10-29-89

1991 regular season

Jason Staurovsky kicked a 42-yard field goal to defeat the Minnesota Vikings, 26–23, at Foxboro Stadium on 10-20-91

1992 regular season
Charlie Baumann kicked an 18-yard field goal to defeat the Indianapolis Colts, 37–34, at the Hoosier Dome on 11-15-92

1996 regular season
Adam Vinatieri kicked a 40-yard field goal to defeat the Jacksonville Jaguars, 28–25, at Foxboro Stadium on 09-22-96

1997 regular season
Adam Vinatieri kicked a 34-yard field goal to defeat the New York Jets, 27–24, at Foxboro Stadium on 09-14-97

2000 regular season
Adam Vinatieri kicked a 22-yard field goal to defeat the Cincinnati Bengals, 16–13, at Foxboro Stadium on 11-19-00

Adam Vinatieri kicked a 24-yard field goal to defeat the Buffalo Bills, 13–10, at Ralph Wilson Stadium on 12-17-00

2001 championship season
Adam Vinatieri kicked a 44-yard field goal to defeat the San Diego Chargers, 29–26, at Foxboro Stadium on 10-14-01

Adam Vinatieri kicked a 23-yard field goal to defeat the Buffalo Bills, 12–9, at Ralph Wilson Stadium on 12-16-01

2002 regular season
Adam Vinatieri kicked a 35-yard field goal to defeat the Kansas City Chiefs, 41–38, at Gillette Stadium on 09-22-02

Adam Vinatieri kicked a 35-yard field goal to defeat the Miami Dolphins, 27–24, at Gillette Stadium on 12-29-02

2003 championship season
Adam Vinatieri kicked a 28-yard field goal to defeat the Houston Texans, 23–20, at Reliant Stadium on 11-23-03

2005 regular season
Adam Vinatieri kicked a 43-yard field goal, with one second left, to defeat the Steelers, 23–20, at Heinz Field on 09-25-05

Adam Vinatieri kicked a 29-yard field goal, with 17 seconds left, to defeat the Falcons, 31–28, at the Georgia Dome on 10-09-05

TD Runs

Every Patriots wide receiver who has run for a TD in a regular season game

1974 regular season
Darryl Stingley ran 23 yards for a TD in the 42–3 rout of the Baltimore Colts at Schaefer Stadium on 10-06-74

1977 regular season
Darryl Stingley ran 34 yards for a TD in the 21–17 win over the Kansas City Chiefs at Schaefer Stadium on 09-18-77

1985 regular season
Irving Fryar ran eight yards for a TD in the 20–13 win over the Seattle Seahawks at the Kingdome on 11-17-85

Irving Fryar

2001 championship season
David Patten ran 29 yards for a TD in the 38–17 rout of the Indianapolis Colts at the RCA Dome on 10-21-01

Every Patriots quarterback who has run for a TD on a fourth-down play in a regular season game

1972 regular season
Brian Dowling ran for a one-yard TD on fourth-and-goal in the 38–14 loss to the Buffalo Bills on 10-08-72

Jim Plunkett ran for a two-yard TD on fourth-and-goal in the 24–17 loss to the Baltimore Colts on 11-06-72

1981 regular season
Matt Cavanaugh ran eight yards for a TD on fourth-and-1 in the 33–17 victory over the Kansas City Chiefs on 10-04-81

2000 regular season
Drew Bledsoe ran for a one-yard TD on fourth-and-goal in the 30–23 loss to the Indianapolis Colts on 10-22-00

Game-Winning Runs for a TD

Every Patriots quarterback who has run for a game-winning TD in a regular season game

1961 regular season
Babe Parilli ran for a game-winning seven-yard TD to defeat the Denver Broncos, 28–24, at Bears Stadium on 12-03-61

1973 regular season
Jim Plunkett ran for a game-winning five-yard TD to defeat the Chicago Bears, 13–10, at Soldier Field on 10-21-73

1976 regular season
Steve Grogan ran for a game-winning 10-yard TD to defeat the Buffalo Bills, 26–22, at Rich Stadium on 10-24-76

Steve Grogan ran for a three-yard TD to defeat the Baltimore Colts, 21–14, at Memorial Stadium on 11-14-76

1978 regular season
Steve Grogan ran for a four-yard TD to defeat the San Diego Chargers, 28–23, at Schaefer Stadium on 10-01-78

1985 regular season
Steve Grogan ran for a game-winning three-yard TD to defeat the New York Jets, 20–13, at Sullivan Stadium on 10-20-85

Steve Grogan ran for a game-winning one-yard TD to defeat the Miami Dolphins, 17–13, at Sullivan Stadium on 11-03-85

1987 regular season
Bob Bleier ran for a game-winning one-yard TD to defeat the the Buffalo Bills, 14–7, at Sullivan Stadium on 10-11-87

1988 regular season
Doug Flutie ran a naked bootleg 13-yard TD to defeat the Indianapolis Colts, 21–17, at Sullivan Stadium on 10-02-88

1991 regular season
Hugh Millen ran for a game-winning two-yard TD to defeat the Buffalo Bills, 16–13, at Foxboro Stadium on 11-24-91

Every Patriots running back who has run for the game-winning TD in a regular season game

1962 regular season
Jim Crawford ran for a game-winning one-yard TD to defeat the San Diego Chargers, 24–20, at BU Field on 10-19-62

1964 regular season
J.D. Garrett ran for a game-winning one-yard TD to beat the Kansas City Chiefs, 31–24, at Municipal Stadium on 12-06-64

1972 regular season
Carl Garrett ran for a game-winning 12-yard TD to defeat the Atlanta Falcons, 21–20, at Schaefer Stadium on 09-24-72

1977 regular season
Jess Phillips ran for a game-winning 11-yard TD to defeat the Kansas City Chiefs, 21–17, at Schaefer Stadium on 09-18-77

1978 regular season
Sam Cunningham dove one yard for the game-winning TD to defeat the Raiders, 21–14, at the Oakland Coliseum on 09-24-78

Sam Cunningham ran three yards for the game-winning TD to defeat the Bengals, 10–3, at Riverfront Stadium on 10-15-78

Horace Ivory ran for a game-winning five-yard TD to defeat the Buffalo Bills, 14–10, at Rich Stadium on 11-05-78

1983 regular season
Tony Collins ran for a game-winning three-yard TD to defeat the New Orleans Saints, 7–0, at Sullivan Stadium on 12-04-83

1984 regular season
Tony Collins ran for a game-winning two-yard TD to defeat the Cleveland Browns, 17–16, at Cleveland on 10-07-84

1989 regular season
Reggie Dupard ran for a game-winning four-yard TD to defeat the New York Jets, 27–24, at the Meadowlands on 09-10-89

John Stephens ran for a 10-yard TD to defeat the Indianapolis Colts, 22–16, at Sullivan Stadium on 12-03-89

1993 regular season
Leonard Russell ran for a four-yard TD to defeat the Cleveland Browns, 20–17, at Cleveland Stadium on 12-19-93

1995 regular season
Curtis Martin ran for a game-winning one-yard TD to beat the Cleveland Browns, 17–14, at Foxboro Stadium on 09-03-95

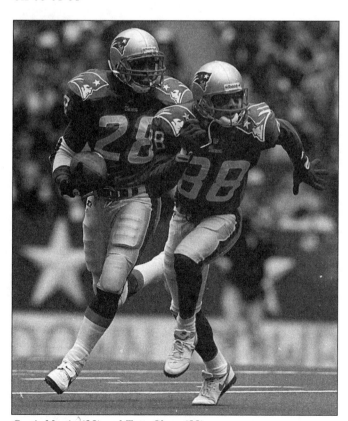
Curtis Martin (28) and Terry Glenn (88)

Curtis Martin ran for a game-winning one-yard TD to defeat the New York Jets, 31–28, at Foxboro Stadium on 12-10-95

1999 regular season
Terry Allen ran for a game-winning three-yard TD to defeat the Dallas Cowboys, 13–6, at Foxboro Stadium on 12-05-99

2008 regular season
Sammy Morris ran for a game-winning one-yard TD to defeat the Seattle Seahawks, 24–21, at Qwest Field on 12-07-08

Game-Winning TD Receptions

Every Patriots wide receiver who has caught a game-winning TD pass in a regulation game

1962 regular season
Jim Colclough caught a 78-yard TD pass to defeat the New York Titans, 24–17, at BU Field on 11-30-62

1977 regular season
Stanley Morgan caught a 33-yard TD pass to defeat the Falcons, 16–10, at Fulton County Stadium on 12-04-77

1983 regular season
Stephen Starring caught a game-winning 76-yard TD to defeat the Steelers, 28–23, at Three Rivers Stadium on 09-25-83

1985 regular season
Irving Fryar caught a game-winning 13-yard TD to defeat the Seattle Seahawks, 20–13, at the Kingdome on 11-17-85

1986 regular season
Irving Fryar caught a 25-yard TD pass on the last play to defeat the Los Angeles Rams, 30–28, at Anaheim Stadium on 11-16-86

Stanley Morgan caught an AFC East title-winning 30-yard TD to beat the Dolphins, 34–27, at the Orange Bowl on 12-22-86

1991 regular season
Greg McMurtry caught a 34-yard TD pass with six seconds left to defeat the Houston Oilers, 24–20, at Foxboro Stadium on 09-22-91

1998 regular season

Shawn Jefferson caught a 25-yard TD pass with 29 seconds left to defeat the Miami Dolphins, 26–23, at Foxboro Stadium on 11-23-98

2002 regular season

David Patten caught a 20-yard TD pass with 21 seconds left to defeat the Bears, 33–30, at Memorial Stadium on 11-10-02

2003 championship season

David Givens caught an 18-yard TD pass with 30 seconds left to defeat the Broncos, 30–26, at Invesco Field on 11-03-03

2007 undefeated regular season

Jabbar Gaffney caught an 8-yard TD pass with 44 seconds left to defeat the Ravens, 27–24, at M&T Bank Stadium on 12-03-07

David Givens

Every Patriots wide receiver who caught a TD pass to win a regular season game in overtime

1991 regular season

Michael Timpson caught a 45-yard TD to defeat the Indianapolis Colts, 23–17, in overtime at Foxboro Stadium on 12-08-91

1993 regular season

Michael Timpson caught a 36-yard TD to defeat the Miami Dolphins, 33–27, in overtime at Foxboro Stadium on 01-02-94

2003 championship season

Troy Brown caught an 82-yard TD to defeat the Miami Dolphins, 19–13, in overtime at Pro Player Stadium on 10-19-03

Every Patriots tight end who caught a game-winning TD reception in a regulation game

1965 regular season

Tony Romeo caught a game-winning two-yard TD to defeat the New York Jets, 27–23, at Shea Stadium on 11-28-65

1974 regular season

Bob Windsor caught a game-winning 10-yard TD to defeat the Minnesota Vikings, 17–14, at Metropolitan Stadium on 10-27-74

1980 regular season

Don Hasselbeck caught a 16-yard TD pass to defeat the Seattle Seahawks, 37–31, at the Kingdome on 09-21-80

1986 regular season

Greg Baty caught a game-winning 13-yard TD to defeat the Buffalo Bills, 22–19, at Sullivan Stadium on 11-23-86

1993 regular season

Ben Coates grabbed a two-yard TD pass to defeat the Phoenix Cardinals, 23–21, at Sun Devil Stadium on 10-10-93

1996 regular season

Ben Coates caught a game-winning 13-yard TD to defeat the New York Giants, 23–22, at Giants Stadium on 12-12-96

Every Patriots running back who caught a game-winning TD reception in a regulation game

1963 regular season

Tom Neumann caught a game-winning 15-yard TD pass to defeat the Oakland Raiders, 20–14, at Fenway Park on 10-11-63

1972 regular season

Josh Ashton caught a game-winning 24-yard TD pass to beat the Washington Redskins, 24–23, at Schaefer Stadium on 10-01-72

1996 regular season

Keith Byars caught a game-winning two-yard TD pass to defeat the New York Jets, 31–27, at the Meadowlands on 11-10-96

The only Patriots running back who has caught a TD pass to win a regular season game in overtime

Kevin Turner caught a 14-yard TD pass to defeat the Minnesota Vikings, 26–20, in overtime at Foxboro Stadium on 11-13-94

Halfback Option Passes for a TD

Every Patriots running back who has thrown a halfback option touchdown pass in a regular season game

1960 regular season

Dick Christy threw a 10-yard TD pass to Tom Stephens in the 38–21 win over the New York Titans at BU Field on 11-11-60

Dick Christy threw a 10-yard TD pass to Tom Stephens in the 42–14 rout of the Dallas Texans at BU Field on 11-18-60

1961 regular season

Tom Yewcic threw an 18-yard TD pass to Jim Colclough in the 45–17 rout of the Denver Broncos at BU Field on 09-16-61

1981 regular season

Andy Johnson threw an eight-yard TD pass to Mosi Tatupu in the 29–28 loss to the Baltimore Colts at Schaefer Stadium on 09-06-81

Andy Johnson threw a 66-yard TD pass to Stanley Morgan in the 33–17 win over the Kansas City Chiefs at Schaefer Stadium on 10-04-81

Andy Johnson threw a 28-yard TD pass to Stanley Morgan in the 38–10 rout of the Houston Oilers at Schaefer Stadium on 10-18-81

Andy Johnson threw a 56-yard TD pass to Stanley Morgan in the 20–17 loss to the Buffalo Bills at Rich Stadium on 11-22-81

1985 regular season

Craig James threw a five-yard TD pass to Tony Collins in the 17–14 victory over the Buffalo Bills at Rich Stadium on 09-22-85

Craig James threw an 11-yard TD pass to Tony Collins in the 32–14 win over the Tampa Bay Buccaneers at Tampa on 10-27-85

1986 regular season

Craig James threw a 10-yard TD pass to Tony Collins in the 20–6 victory over the New York Jets at Shea Stadium on 09-11-86

1987 regular season

Mosi Tatupu threw a 15-yard TD pass to Tony Collins in the 26–23 victory over the Los Angeles Raiders at Sullivan Stadium on 11-01-87

1991 regular season

Jon Vaughn threw a 13-yard TD pass to Marv Cook in the 24–20 win over the Houston Oilers at Foxboro Stadium on 09-22-91

1997 regular season

Dave Meggett threw a 35-yard TD pass to Troy Brown in the 27–24 win over the Miami Dolphins at Foxboro Stadium on 11-23-97

Stanley Morgan

Every Flea Flicker TD Pass in a Regular Season Game

The combination of Patriots players who have completed a flea-flicker TD pass in a regular season game

1984 regular season
Tony Eason to Mosi Tatupu back to Eason to Stephen Starring for a 42-yard TD in the 17–16 win vs Cleveland on 10-07-84

1985 regular season
Steve Grogan to Mosi Tatupu back to Grogan to Greg Hawthorne for a 28-yard TD in the 17–13 win over Miami on 11-03-85

1989 regular season
Steve Grogan to Mosi Tatupu back to Grogan to Stanley Morgan for a 55-yard TD in the 37–20 loss to the 49ers on 10-22-89

2007 undefeated regular season
Tom Brady to Randy Moss back to Brady to Jabar Gaffney for a 56-yard TD in the 34–13 win over Pittsburgh on 12-09-07

Overtime Game-Winning Touchdown Passes

Every Patriots quarterback who has thrown an overtime game-winning TD pass

1991 regular season
Hugh Millen threw a 45-yard TD pass to Michael Timpson to defeat the Colts, 23–17, in overtime at Foxboro Stadium on 12-08-91

1993 regular season
Drew Bledsoe threw a 36-yard TD pass to Michael Timpson to defeat the Dolphins, 33–27, in overtime at Foxboro Stadium on 01-02-94

1994 regular season
Drew Bledsoe threw a 14-yard TD pass to Kevin Turner to defeat the Vikings, 26–20, in overtime at Foxboro Stadium on 11-13-94

2003 championship season
Tom Brady tossed an 82-yard TD pass to Troy Brown to defeat the Dolphins, 19–13, in overtime at Pro Player Stadium on 10-19-03

Touchdown Passes Thrown on the Last Play of a Regulation Game

Every Patriots quarterback who has thrown a TD pass on the last play of a regulation game

1967 regular season
Babe Parilli threw a 25-yard TD to Bobby Leo with five seconds left in the 44–16 loss to the Buffalo Bills at Fenway Park on 12-09-67

1974 regular season
Jim Plunkett threw a 10-yard TD pass to Bob Windsor to defeat the Minnesota Vikings 17–14 at the Met on 10-27-74

1979 regular season
Steve Grogan threw a 13-yard TD pass to Carlos Pennywell in the 39–24 loss to the Miami Dolphins at the Orange Bowl on 11-29-79

1986 regular season
Tony Eason threw a 10-yard TD pass to Irving Fryar in the 27–20 loss to the Denver Broncos at Mile High Stadium on 09-28-86

Left to right: Tony Eason and Steve Grogan

Tony Eason threw a 25-yard Hail Mary pass to Irving Fryar to defeat the Los Angeles Rams 30–28 at Anaheim on 11-16-86

1989 regular season
Tony Eason threw a 10-yard TD pass to Hart Lee Dykes in the 24–10 loss to the Miami Dolphins at Sullivan Stadium on 09-17-89

1991 regular season
Hugh Millen threw a 34-yard TD pass to Greg McMurtry to defeat the Houston Oilers 24–20 at Foxboro Stadium on 09-22-91

Hugh Millen threw a two-yard TD pass to Ben Coates in the 23–17 overtime win vs the Indianapolis Colts at Foxboro Stadium on 12-08-91

1998 regular season
Drew Bledsoe threw a one-yard TD pass to Ben Coates to defeat the Buffalo Bills, 25–21, at Foxboro Stadium on 11-29-98

Players Who Have Thrown a TD Pass and Run for a TD

The only Patriots player to run for a TD, catch a TD pass, and throw a TD pass in the same game
David Patten ran for a 29-yard TD, caught two TD passes, and threw a 60-yard TD pass in the 38–17 win on 10-21-01

Every Patriots quarterback who has thrown a TD pass and run for two TDs in a regular season game
1962 regular season
Tom Yewcic threw a 78-yard TD pass and ran for two TDs in the 24–17 win over the New York Titans on 11-30-62

1963 regular season
Babe Parilli threw a 76-yard TD pass and ran for two TDs in the 45–3 rout of the Houston Oilers on 11-01-63

1973 regular season
Jim Plunkett threw a 14-yard TD pass and ran for two TDs in the 30–14 win over the San Diego Chargers on 12-02-73

1976 regular season
Steve Grogan threw a two-yard TD pass and ran for two TDs in the 21–14 victory over the Baltimore Colts on 11-14-76

The only Patriots quarterback who has thrown two TD passes and run for two TDs in a regular season game
Steve Grogan threw two TD passes and ran for two TDs in the 27–6 win over the New Orleans Saints on 12-05-76

Every Patriots quarterback who has thrown three TD passes and run for two TDs in a regular season game
1976 regular season
Steve Grogan threw three TD passes and ran for two TDs in the 48–17 rout of the Oakland Raiders on 10-03-76

2007 undefeated regular season
Tom Brady threw three TD passes and ran for two TDs in the 52–7 rout of the Washington Redskins on 10-28-07

The only Patriots quarterback who has thrown four TD passes and run for a TD in a regular season game
Steve Grogan threw four TD passes and ran two yards for a TD in the 42–20 win over the New York Jets on 12-13-87

Players Who Have Returned a Punt for a TD

Every Patriots player who returned a punt for a TD in a regular season game
1976 regular season
Mike Haynes returned a punt 89 yards for a TD in the 20–10 win over the Buffalo Bills at Schaefer Stadium on 11-07-76

Mike Haynes returned a punt 62 yards for a TD in the 38–14 rout of the Denver Broncos at Schaefer Stadium on 11-28-76

1979 regular season
Stanley Morgan returned a punt 80 yards for a TD in the 50–21 rout of the Baltimore Colts at Schaefer Stadium on 11-18-79

1980 regular season
Roland James returned a punt 75 yards for a TD in the 34–21 win over the New York Jets at Schaefer Stadium on 11-02-80

1985 regular season
Irving Fryar returned a punt 85 yards for a TD in the 17–14 win over the Buffalo Bills at Rich Stadium on 09-22-85

Irving Fryar returned a punt 77 yards for a TD in the 34–15 win over the Indianapolis Colts at Sullivan Stadium on 11-10-85

1986 regular season
Irving Fryar returned a punt 59 yards for a TD in the 25–17 win over the Atlanta Falcons at Sullivan Stadium on 11-02-86

1996 regular season
Dave Meggett returned a punt 60 yards for a TD in the 23–22 win over the New York Giants at Giants Stadium on 12-21-96

2000 regular season
Troy Brown returned a punt 66 yards for a TD in the 21–16 loss to the Tampa Bay Buccaneers at Foxboro Stadium on 09-03-00

2001 championship season
Troy Brown returned a punt 85 yards for a TD in the 27–16 win over the Cleveland Browns at Foxboro Stadium on 12-09-01

Troy Brown returned a punt 68 yards for a TD in the 38–6 rout of the Carolina Panthers at Ericsson Stadium on 01-06-02

Players Who Have Returned a Blocked Punt Return for a TD

Every Patriots player who has returned a blocked punt for a TD in a regular season game
1961 regular season
Don Webb returned a blocked punt 20 yards for a TD in the 41–0 shutout of the San Diego Chargers on 12-17-61

1971 regular season
Roland Moss returned a blocked punt 10 yards for a TD in the 38–33 win over the Buffalo Bills on 11-14-71

1979 regular season
Rick Sanford returned a blocked punt eight yards for a TD in the 50–21 rout of the Baltimore Colts on 11-18-79

1986 regular season
Rod McSwain returned a blocked punt 31 yards for a TD in the 30–28 win over the Los Angeles Rams on 11-16-86

Mosi Tatupu returned a blocked punt 21 yards for a TD in the 21–20 win over the New Orleans Saints on 11-30-86

1987 regular season
Willie Scott returned a blocked punt three yards for a TD in the 24–0 shutout of the Indianapolis Colts on 11-22-87

1996 regular season
Tedy Bruschi returned a blocked punt four yards for a TD in the 46–38 win over the Baltimore Ravens on 10-06-96

Every Patriots player who has recovered a blocked punt in the end zone for a TD
1961 regular season
LeRoy Moore recovered a blocked punt in the end zone for a TD in the 20–17 win over the Oakland Raiders on 11-17-61

1967 regular season
J.D. Garrett recovered a blocked punt in the end zone for a TD in the 41–32 loss to the Miami Dolphins on 12-17-67

1973 regular season
Will Foster recovered a blocked punt in the end zone for a TD in the 9–7 loss to the New York Jets on 10-14-73

The only Patriots player to recover a punt from the end zone that deflected off the goal post for a TD
LeRoy Moore recovered a deflected punt for a TD in the 20–17 win over the Oakland Raiders at BU Field on 11-17-61

Players Who Have Returned a Kickoff for a TD

Every Patriots player who has returned a kickoff for a TD in a regular season game
1961 regular season
Larry Garron returned a kickoff 89 yards for a TD in the 31–31 tie with the Houston Oilers at BU Field on 10-13-61

Ron Burton returned a kickoff 91 yards for a TD in the 28–21 win over the Dallas Texans at BU Field on 11-03-61

1962 regular season
Larry Garron returned a kickoff 95 yards for a TD in the 28–28 tie with the Buffalo Bills at War Memorial Stadium on 11-03-62

1973 regular season

Mack Herron returned a kickoff 92 yards for a TD in the 30–14 win over the Chargers at Schaefer Stadium on 12-02-73

1975 regular season

Allen Carter took the opening kickoff 99 yards for a TD in the 34–21 loss to the Baltimore Colts at Memorial Stadium on 12-21-75

1977 regular season

Raymond Clayborn returned a kickoff 100 yards for a TD in the 30–27 loss to the New York Jets at Shea Stadium on 10-02-77

Raymond Clayborn returned a kickoff 93 yards for a TD in the 24–14 loss to the Buffalo Bills at Schaefer Stadium on 11-06-77

Raymond Clayborn returned a kickoff 101 yards for a TD in the 30–24 loss to the Baltimore Colts at Memorial Stadium on 12-18-77

1980 regular season

Horace Ivory returned a kickoff 98 yards for a TD in the 37–21 win over the Baltimore Colts at Memorial Stadium on 10-19-80

1982 regular season

Ricky Smith returned a kickoff 98 yards for a TD in the 31–7 loss to the New York Jets at Schaefer Stadium on 09-18-82

1988 regular season

Sammy Martin took the opening kickoff 95 yards for a TD in the 24–21 loss to the Indianapolis Colts at the Hoosier Dome on 11-27-88

1991 regular season

Jon Vaughn returned a kickoff 99 yards for a TD in the 24–10 loss to the Phoenix Cardinals at Sun Devil Stadium on 09-29-91

1992 regular season

Jon Vaughn returned a kickoff 100 yards for a TD in the 20–10 loss to the Cincinnati Bengals at Riverfront Stadium on 12-20-92

1997 regular season

Derrick Cullors returned a kickoff 86 yards for a TD in the 31–10 win over the Buffalo Bills at Rich Stadium on 11-09-97

2002 regular season

Kevin Faulk returned a kickoff 86 yards for a TD in the 27–20 loss to the Oakland Raiders at Network Coliseum on 11-17-02

Kevin Faulk returned a kickoff 87 yards for a TD in the 30–17 loss to the New York Jets at Gillette Stadium on 12-22-02

2003 championship season

Bethel Johnson took it 92 yards for a TD on the last play of the half in the 38–34 win over the Indianapolis Colts on 11-30-03

2004 championship season

Bethel Johnson took the opening kickoff 93 yards for a TD in the 42–15 rout of the Cleveland Browns at Cleveland on 12-05-04

2006 regular season

Ellis Hobbs returned a kickoff 93 yards for a TD in the 40–7 rout of the Houston Texans at Gillette Stadium on 12-17-06

2007 undefeated regular season

Ellis Hobbs took a kickoff 108 yards for a TD in the 38–14 rout of the New York Jets at the Meadowlands on 09-09-07

Willie Andrews returned a kickoff 77 yards for a TD in the 49–28 win over the Miami Dolphins at Dolphin Stadium on 10-21-07

Other Special Team Returns for a TD

The only Patriots player to return a missed field goal for a TD in a regular season game

Ron Burton returned a missed field goal 91 yards for a TD in the 33–29 win over the Denver Broncos at Bears Stadium on 11-11-62

Every Patriots player who has returned a blocked field goal for a TD in a regular season game

1972 regular season

Larry Carwell returned a blocked field goal 45 yards for a TD in the 31–7 loss to the Cincinnati Bengals on 09-17-72

1980 regular season

Mike Haynes returned a lateral, after a blocked field goal, 65 yards for a TD in the 21–11 win over the New York Jets on 10-05-80

1987 regular season

Raymond Clayborn returned a blocked field goal 71 yards for a TD in the 21–7 win over the Houston Oilers on 10-18-87

Players Who Have Returned an Interception for a TD

Every Patriots defensive back who has returned an interception for a TD in a regular season game

1961 regular season

Don Webb returned a pass 27 yards for a TD in the 52–21 rout of the Buffalo Bills at BU Field on 10-22-61

Don Webb returned a pass 31 yards for a TD in the 41–0 shutout of the San Diego Chargers at Balboa Stadium on 12-17-61

1962 regular season

Fred Bruney returned a pass 33 yards for a TD in the 41–16 rout of the Denver Broncos at BU Field on 09-21-62

Ron Hall returned a pass 47 yards for a TD in the 41–16 rout of the Denver Broncos at BU Field on 09-21-62

1963 regular season

Bob Suci returned a pass 98 yards for a TD in the 45–3 rout of the Houston Oilers at Fenway Park on 11-01-63

Bob Suci returned a pass 52 yards for a TD in the 46–28 win over the Houston Oilers at Jeppesen Stadium on 12-08-63

1964 regular season

Ross O'Hanley returned a pass 47 yards for a TD in the 34–17 win over the Houston Oilers at Jeppesen Stadium on 11-29-64

1967 regular season

Jay Cunningham returned a pass 54 yards for a TD in the 41–10 rout of the Miami Dolphins at BC Alumni Stadium on 10-15-67

John Charles returned a pass 35 yards for a TD in the 30–23 loss to the New York Jets at Shea Stadium on 10-29-67

1969 regular season

John Charles returned a pass 25 yards for a TD in the 23–17 loss to the New York Jets at Shea Stadium on 10-26-69

1971 regular season

Larry Carwell returned a pass 53 yards for a TD in the 34–13 win over the Miami Dolphins at Schaefer Stadium on 12-05-71

John Outlaw returned a pass 60 yards for a TD in the 21–17 victory over the Baltimore Colts at Memorial on 12-19-71

1974 regular season

John Sanders returned a pass 23 yards for a TD in the 34–27 loss to the Miami Dolphins at the Orange Bowl on 12-15-74

1975 regular season

Bob Howard returned a pass 44 yards for a TD in the 33–19 win over the San Diego Chargers at Jack Murphy Stadium on 11-09-75

1976 regular season

Prentice McCray returned a pass 63 yards for a TD in the 38–24 win over the New York Jets at Shea Stadium on 11-21-76

Prentice McCray returned a pass 55 yards for a TD in the 38–24 win over the New York Jets at Shea Stadium on 11-21-76

1978 regular season

Mike Haynes returned a pass 31 yards for a TD in the 35–14 win over the Baltimore Colts at Memorial Stadium on 11-26-78

1982 regular season

Rick Sanford returned a pass 99 yards for a TD in the 26–13 loss to the Chicago Bears at Soldier Field on 12-05-82

1985 regular season

Raymond Clayborn returned a pass 27 yards for a TD in the 14–3 win over the Buffalo Bills at Sullivan Stadium on 10-13-85

1986 regular season

Fred Marion returned a pass 37 yards for a TD in the 34–0 shutout of the Pittsburgh Steelers at Three Rivers Stadium on 10-19-86

1987 regular season
Ronnie Lippett returned a pass 20 yards for a TD in the 28–21 win over the Miami Dolphins at Sullivan Stadium on 09-13-87

Ronnie Lippett returned a pass 45 yards for a TD in the 24–0 shutout of the Indianapolis Colts at Sullivan Stadium on 11-22-87

1989 regular season
Maurice Hurst returned a pass 16 yards for a TD in the 33–24 win over the Buffalo Bills at Sullivan Stadium on 11-19-89

1992 regular season
David Pool returned a pass 41 yards for a TD in the 37–34 overtime win vs the Indianpolis Colts at the Hoosier Dome on 11-15-92

1994 regular season
Ricky Reynolds returned a pass 11 yards for a TD in the 24–13 win over the New York Jets at Foxboro Stadium on 12-04-94

1996 regular season
Ty Law returned a pass 38 yards for a TD in the 34–10 win over the New York Jets at Foxboro Stadium on 12-08-96

Jimmy Hitchcock

1997 regular season
Willie Clay returned a pass 53 yards for a TD in the 41–7 rout of the San Diego Chargers at Foxboro Stadium on 08-31-97

Larry Whigham returned a pass 60 yards for a TD in the 27–24 win over the Miami Dolphins at Foxboro Stadium on 11-23-97

Jimmy Hitchcock returned a pass 100 yards for a TD in the 27–24 win over the Miami Dolphins at Foxboro Stadium on 11-23-97

1998 regular season
Ty Law returned a pass 59 yards for a TD in the 29–6 victory over the Indianapolis Colts at Foxboro Stadium on 09-13-98

Lawyer Milloy returned a pass 30 yards for a TD in the 27–16 win over the Tennessee Oilers at Foxboro Stadium on 09-20-98

1999 regular season
Ty Law returned a pass 24 yards for a TD in the 31–30 loss to the Miami Dolphins at Foxboro Stadium on 10-17-99

2001 championship season
Otis Smith returned a pass 78 yards for a TD in the 44–13 rout of the Indianapolis Colts at Foxboro Stadium on 09-30-01

Willie Clay

Ty Law returned a pass 23 yards for a TD in the 44–13 rout of the Indianapolis Colts at Foxboro Stadium on 09-30-01

Terrell Buckley returned a pass 52 yards for a TD in the 24–17 loss to the St. Louis Rams at Foxboro Stadium on 11-18-01

Otis Smith returned a pass 76 yards for a TD in the 38–6 rout of the Carolina Panthers at Ericsson Stadium on 01-06-02

Ty Law returned a pass 46 yards for a TD in the 38–6 rout of the Carolina Panthers at Ericsson Stadium on 01-06-02

2002 regular season
Victor Green returned a pass 90 yards for a TD in the 44–7 rout of the New York Jets at the Meadowlands on 09-15-02

2003 championship season
Ty Law returned a pass 65 yards for a TD in the 38–30 win over the Tennessee Titans at Gillette Stadium on 10-05-03

Asante Samuel returned a pass 55 yards for a TD in the 23–16 win over the New York Jets at Gillette Stadium on 09-21-03

2004 championship season
Asante Samuel returned a pass 34 yards for a TD in the 35–28 victory over the Cincinnati Bengals at Gillette Stadium on 12-12-04

2005 regular season
James Sanders returned a pass 39 yards for a TD in the 35–7 rout of the Buffalo Bills at Ralph Wilson Stadium on 12-11-05

2007 undefeated regular season
Asante Samuel returned a pass 40 yards for a TD in the 31–28 win over the Philadelphia Eagles at Gillette Stadium on 11-25-07

Eugene Wilson returned a pass five yards for a TD in the 20–10 victory over the New York Jets at Gillette Stadium on 12-16-07

Every Patriots linebacker who has returned an interception for a TD in a regular season game
1962 regular season
Tom Addison returned a pass 12 yards for a TD in the 43–14 rout of the New York Titans at the Polo Grounds on 10-06-62

1974 regular season
Bob Geddes returned a pass 29 yards for a TD in the 24–0 shutout of the New York Jets at Shea Stadium on 10-13-74

1976 regular season
Sam Hunt returned a pass 68 yards for a TD in the 31–14 over the Tampa Bay Buccaneers at Tampa Stadium on 12-12-76

1979 regular season
Mike Hawkins returned a pass 35 yards for a TD in the 28–13 win over the Miami Dolphins at Schaefer Stadium on 10-21-79

1980 regular season
Rod Shoate returned a pass 42 yards for a TD in the 47–21 rout of the Baltimore Colts at Schaefer Stadium on 11-23-80

1992 regular season
Vincent Brown returned a pass 49 yards for a TD in the 31–14 loss to the New Orleans Saints at Foxboro Stadium on 11-08-92

Chris Singleton returned a pass 82 yards for a TD in the 37-34 overtime win vs the Indianapolis Colts at the Hoosier Dome on 11-15-92

1997 regular season
Chris Slade returned a pass one yard for a TD in the 31–10 win over the Buffalo Bills at Rich Stadium on 11-09-97

1999 regular season
Andy Katzenmoyer returned a pass 57 yards for a TD in the 31–30 loss to the Miami Dolphins at Foxboro Stadium on 10-17-99

2002 regular season
Tedy Bruschi returned a pass 48 yards for a TD in the 27–20 loss to the Oakland Raiders at the Network Coliseum on 11-17-02

Tedy Bruschi returned a pass 27 yards for a TD in the 20–12 victory over the Detroit Lions at Ford Field on 11-28-02

2003 championship season
Tedy Bruschi returned a pass 18 yards for a TD in the 31–10 rout of the Philadelphia Eagles at Lincoln Financial Field on 09-14-03

Tedy Bruschi returned a pass five yards for a TD in the 12–0 shutout of the Miami Dolphins at Gillette Stadium on 12-07-03

Willie McGinest returned a pass 15 yards for a TD in the 21–16 win over the New York Jets at the Meadowlands on 12-20-03

2005 regular season
Mike Vrabel returned a pass 24 yards for a TD in the 27–17 loss to the Carolina Panthers at Bank of America Stadium on 09-18-05

2007 undefeated regular season
Adalius Thomas returned a pass 65 yards for a TD in the 38–14 rout of the San Diego Chargers at Gillette Stadium on 09-16-07

Every Patriots defensive lineman who returned an interception for a TD in a regular season game

1963 regular season
Jim Lee Hunt returned a pass 78 yards for a TD in the 45–3 rout of the Houston Oilers at Fenway Park on 11-01-63

1968 regular season
Mel Witt returned a pass four yards for a TD in the 47–31 loss to the New York Jets at Legion Field on 09-22-68

1996 regular season
Willie McGinest returned a pass 46 yards for a TD in the 28–25 win over the Buffalo Bills at Foxboro Stadium on 10-27-96

1998 regular season
Henry Thomas returned a pass 24 yards for a TD in the 30–27 win over the New Orleans Saints at the Superdome on 10-24-98

Every Fumble That was Recovered for a TD

Every Patriots player who has recovered a fumble in the end zone for a TD in a regular season game

1961 regular season
LeRoy Moore recovered a fumble in the end zone for a TD in the 20–17 win over the Oakland Raiders on 11-17-61

1967 regular season
J.D. Garrett recovered a fumble in the end zone for a TD in the 41–32 loss to the Miami Dolphins on 12-17-67

1973 regular season
Will Foster recovered a fumble, after a blocked punt, in the end zone for a TD in the 9–7 loss to the New York Jets on 10-14-73

1974 regular season
John Hannah recovered a fumble, after a bad snap, in the end zone for a TD in the 34–27 loss to the Miami Dolphins on 12-15-74

1984 regular season
Cedric Jones recovered a fumble in the end zone for a TD in the 27–17 loss to the Philadelphia Eagles on 12-09-84

1985 regular season
Johnny Rembert recovered a fumble in the end zone for a TD in the 24–20 loss to the Cleveland Browns on 10-06-85

1986 regular season
Johnny Rembert recovered a fumble in the end zone for a TD in the 33–3 rout of the Indianapolis Colts on 09-07-86

1988 regular season
John Stephens recovered a fumble in the end zone for a TD in the 27–21 victory over the Cincinnati Bengals on 10-16-88

1991 regular season
Freddie Childress recovered an end zone fumble for a TD in the 26–23 overtime win vs Minnesota Vikings on 10-20-91

1996 regular season
Willie McGinest recovered a fumble in the end zone for a TD in the 45–7 rout of the San Diego Chargers on 12-01-96

1999 regular season
Willie McGinest recovered a fumble in the end zone for a TD in the 30–28 victory over the New York Jets on 09-12-99

2004 championship season
Jarvis Green recovered a fumble in the end zone for a TD in the 24–3 rout of the Baltimore Ravens on 11-28-04

Every Fumble Returned for a TD

Every Patriots linebacker who returned a fumble for a TD in a regular season game

1963 regular season
Nick Buoniconti returned a Bill Tobin fumble seven yards for a TD in the 46–28 win over the Houston Oilers on 12-08-63

1968 regular season
Ed Philpott returned a Babe Parilli lateral 10 yards for a TD in the 47–31 loss to the New York Jets on 09-22-68

1987 regular season
Andre Tippett returned a Roger Vick fumble 29 yards for a TD in the 43–24 loss to the New York Jets on 09-21-87

1992 regular season
Vincent Brown took a Thurman Thomas fumble 25 yards for a TD in the 16–7 loss to the Buffalo Bills on 11-01-92

1995 regular season
Chris Slade returned a Jim Kelly fumble 27 yards for a TD in the 35–25 victory over the Buffalo Bills on 11-26-95

2007 undefeated regular season
Rosevelt Colvin returned a fumble by Jason Campbell 11 yards for a TD in the 52–7 rout of the Washington Redskins on 10-28-07

Every Patriots defensive back who has returned a fumble for a TD in a regular season game

1961 regular season
Don Webb returned a Johnny Robinson fumble 49 yards for a TD in the 18–17 victory over the Dallas Texans on 10-29-61

1969 regular season
Daryl Johnson returned a Hoyle Granger fumble 32 yards for a TD in the 24–0 shutout of the Houston Oilers on 11-02-69

1994 regular season
Ricky Reynolds returned a Carwell Gardner fumble 25 yards for a TD in the 41–17 victory over the Buffalo Bills on 12-18-94

1996 regular season
Corwin Brown returned a Bryan Still fumble 42 yards for a TD in the 45–7 rout of the San Diego Chargers on 12-01-96

2002 regular season
Tebucky Jones returned a Vinny Testaverde fumble 24 yards for a TD in the 44–7 rout of the New York Jets on 09-15-02

2007 undefeated regular season
Randall Gay returned a Kellen Winslow fumble 15 yards for a TD in the 34–17 win over the Cleveland Browns on 10-07-07

Ellis Hobbs returned a fumble by Dwayne Wright 35 yards for a TD in the 56–10 rout of the Buffalo Bills on 11-18-07

Every Patriots defensive lineman who returned a fumble for a TD in a regular season game

1966 regular season
Jim Lee Hunt returned a Darrell Lester fumble five yards for a TD in the 17–10 loss to the Denver Broncos on 11-06-66

1975 regular season
Ray Hamilton returned a Jim Hart fumble 23 yards for a TD in the 24–17 loss to the St. Louis Cardinals on 11-02-75

1986 regular season
Brent Williams took a Dave Wilson fumble 21 yards for the game-winning TD in the 21–20 win over the New Orleans Saints on 11-30-86

1990 regular season
Brent Williams returned a Dave Krieg fumble 45 yards for a TD in the 33–20 loss to the Seattle Seahawks on 10-07-90

1992 regular season
Tim Goad returned a Christian Okoye fumble 19 yards for a TD in the 27–20 loss to the Kansas City Chiefs on 12-13-92

1999 regular season
Chad Eaton returned a Tony Banks fumble 23 yards for a TD in the 20–3 rout of the Baltimore Ravens on 01-02-00

2004 championship season
Richard Seymour returned a Drew Bledsoe fumble 68 yards for a TD in the 31–17 victory over the Buffalo Bills on 10-03-04

Every Patriots special team player who returned a fumble for a TD in a regular season game

1960 regular season
Chuck Shonta returned a fumble by the punter 52 yards for a TD in the 28–24 win over the New York Titans on 09-17-60

1961 regular season
Tom Stephens returned a fumbled punt return by Paul Lowe 10 yards for a TD in the 38–27 loss to the San Diego Chargers on 10-07-61

Don Webb returned a fumble after a blocked punt 20 yards for a TD in the 41–0 shutout of the San Diego Chargers on 12-17-61

1971 regular season
Roland Moss returned a fumble after a blocked punt 10 yards for a TD in the 38–33 win over the Buffalo Bills on 11-14-71

1972 regular season
Larry Carwell returned a blocked field goal 45 yards for a TD in the 31–7 loss to the Cincinnati Bengals on 09-17-72

1979 regular season
Rick Sanford returned a blocked punt eight yards for a TD in the 50–21 rout of the Baltimore Colts on 11-18-79

1980 regular season
Rick Sanford took a fumbled kickoff return by Nesby Glasgow 22 yards for a TD in the 47–21 rout of the Baltimore Colts on 11-23-80

Allan Clark took a fumbled kickoff return by Kim Anderson 15 yards for a TD in the 47–21 rout of the Baltimore Colts on 11-23-80

1985 regular season
Andre Tippett returned a poor snap to Ray Guy 25 yards for a TD in the 35–20 loss to the Los Angeles Raiders on 09-29-85

Cedric Jones returned a fumbled kickoff return by Joe Carter 15 yards for a TD in the 30–27 loss to Miami Dolphins on 12-16-85

1986 regular season
Rod McSwain returned a fumble after a blocked punt 31 yards for a TD in the 30–28 win over the Los Angeles Rams on 11-16-86

Mosi Tatupu returned a fumble after a blocked punt 21 yards for a TD in the 21–20 win over the New Orleans Saints on 11-30-86

1987 regular season
Raymond Clayborn returned a blocked field goal 71 yards for a TD in the 21–7 win over the Houston Oilers on 10-18-87

Willie Scott returned a fumble after a blocked punt three yards for a TD in the 24–0 shutout of the Indianapolis Colts on 11-22-87

1996 regular season
Tedy Bruschi returned a fumble after a blocked punt four yards for a TD in the 46–38 win over the Baltimore Ravens on 10-06-96

Fumbles Advanced for a TD

Every Patriots player who advanced a fumble for a TD in a regular season game

1961 regular season
Babe Parilli advanced a fumble one yard for a TD in the 28–21 victory over the Dallas Texans on 11-03-61

1973 regular season
Randy Vataha advanced a Mack Herron fumble 46 yards for a TD in the 24–16 win over the Baltimore Colts on 10-07-73

1976 regular season
Steve Grogan advanced a Don Calhoun fumble six yards for a TD in the 41–7 rout of the New York Jets on 10-18-76

1992 regular season
Jon Vaughn advanced his own fumble 100 yards for a TD in the 20–10 loss to the Cincinnati Bengals on 12-20-92

1995 regular season
Troy Brown advanced a fumbled kickoff return by Dave Meggett 75 yards for a TD in the 31–28 win over the New York Jets on 12-10-95

Laterals Advanced for a TD

Every Patriots player who has advanced a lateral for a TD in a regular season game

1980 regular season

Mike Haynes took a lateral 65 yards for a TD in the 21–11 win over the New York Jets on 10-05-80

1983 regular season

Clayton Weishuhn took a lateral 27 yards for a TD in the 28–23 win over the Pittsburgh Steelers on 09-25-83

Points Scored by a Patriots Player on His Birthday

Every Patriots player who has kicked a field goal in a regular season game played on his birthday

1984 regular season

Tony Franklin, on his 28th birthday, kicked a 28-yard and a 40-yard field goal in the 50–17 rout of Indianapolis Colts on 11-18-84

1989 regular season

Greg Davis, on his 34th birthday, kicked a 47-yard field goal, a 48-yard field goal, and the overtime game-winning 51-yard field goal on 10-29-89

Every Patriots Player who kicked an extra point in a regular season game played on his birthday

1984 regular season

Tony Franklin, on his 28th birthday, kicked six extra points in the 50–17 rout of the Indianapolis Colts on 11-18-84

1989 regular season

Greg Davis, on his 34th birthday, kicked two extra points in the 23–20 overtime win vs the Indianapolis Colts on 10-29-89

Every Patriots quarterback who completed a TD pass in a game played on his birthday

1971 regular season

Jim Plunkett, on his 24th birthday, threw two TD passes to Randy Vataha in the 34–13 win over the Miami Dolphins on 12-05-71

1988 regular season

Doug Flutie, on his 26th birthday, threw a 12-yard TD pass to Irving Fryar in the 23–20 loss to Buffalo Bills on 10-23-88

Doug Flutie (head coach Raymond Berry to his right)

The only Patriots running back who has run for a TD and caught a TD pass on his birthday

Andy Johnson, on his 24th birthday, had a four-yard TD run and a 10-yard TD reception in the 41–7 rout of New York Jets on 10-18-76

The only Patriots wide receiver who has run for a TD and caught a TD pass in a game played on his birthday

Darryl Stingley, on his 26th birthday, had a 34-yard TD run and caught a 21-yard TD in the 21–17 win vs the Kansas City Chiefs on 09-18-77

Every Patriots player who caught a TD pass in a regular season game played on his birthday

1976 regular season

Andy Johnson, on his 24th birthday, caught a 10-yard TD pass in the 41–7 rout of the New York Jets on 10-18-76

1977 regular season

Darryl Stingley, on his 26th birthday, caught a 21-yard TD pass in the 21–17 win over the Kansas City Chiefs on 09-18-77

1986 regular season

Irving Fryar, on his 24th birthday, caught a 10-yard TD pass in the 27–20 loss to the Denver Broncos on 09-28-86

The only Patriots player who caught two TD passes in a regular season game played on the day after his birthday

Randy Vataha caught a 26-yard TD pass and a 25-yard TD pass on the day after his 23rd birthday on 12-05-71

The only Patriots player who *almost* scored a TD in a regular season game played on his birthday

Robert Perryman, on his 24th birthday, fumbled into the end zone and John Stephens recovered it for the TD on 10-16-88

The only Patriots player who kicked a field goal in a playoff game on his birthday

1997 AFC wild-card playoff game

Adam Vinatieri kicked a 22-yard field goal on his 25th birthday in the 17–3 win over the Miami Dolphins on 12-28-97

The only Patriots player who kicked a field goal in a playoff game on his birthday

1997 AFC wild-card playoff game

Adam Vinatieri kicked two extra points on his 25th birthday in the 17–3 win over the Miami Dolphins on 12-28-97

The progression of the most points scored by a Patriots player in a regular season

60 points were scored by Gino Cappelletti in 1960

147 points were scored by Gino Cappelletti in 1961

155 points were scored by Gino Cappelletti in 1964

The progression of the most points scored by a Patriots running back in a regular season

36 points were scored by Dick Christy in 1960

66 points were scored by Billy Lott in 1961

66 points were scored by Jim Nance in 1966

72 points were scored by Mack Herron in 1974

92 points were scored by Curtis Martin in 1995

104 points were scored by Curtis Martin in 1996

The progression of the most points scored by a Patriots wide receiver/special team player in a regular season

54 points were scored by Jim Colclough in 1960

54 points were scored by Jim Colclough in 1961

60 points were scored by Jim Colclough in 1962

78 points were scored by Stanley Morgan in 1979

138 points were scored by Randy Moss in 2007

The progression of the most points scored by a Patriots tight end in a regular season

24 points were scored by Oscar Lofton in 1960

24 points were scored by Tony Romeo in 1964

24 points were scored by Jim Whalen in 1966

30 points were scored by Jim Whalen in 1967

42 points were scored by Jim Whalen in 1968

48 points were scored by Russ Francis in 1980

48 points were scored by Ben Coates in 1993

56 points were scored by Ben Coates in 1996

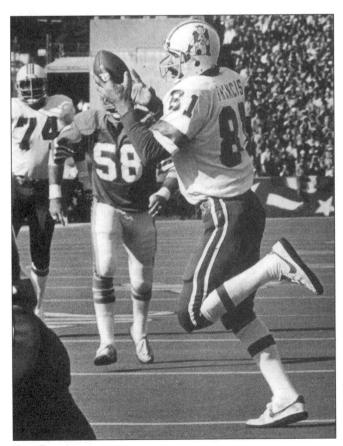

Russ Francis

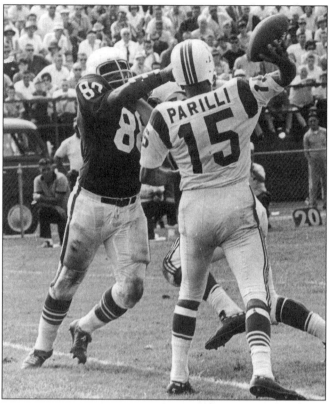

Babe Parilli

The most points scored by a Patriots tight end/special team player in a regular season

18 points were scored by Tom Stephens in 1961

The progression of the most points scored by a Patriots quarterback in a regular season

12 points were scored by Butch Songin in 1960

32 points were scored by Babe Parilli in 1961

78 points were scored by Steve Grogan in 1976

The progression of the most points scored by a Patriots kicker in a regular season

60 points were scored by Gino Cappelletti in 1960

99 points were scored by Gino Cappelletti in 1961

101 points were scored by Gino Cappelletti in 1963

113 points were scored by Gino Cappelletti in 1964

115 points were scored by John Smith in 1979

129 points were scored by John Smith in 1980

140 points were scored by Tony Franklin in 1986

141 points were scored by Adam Vinatieri in 2004

148 points by Stephen Gostkowski in 2008

The progression of the most points scored by a Patriots defensive back/special teams player in a regular season

6 points were scored by Chuck Shonta in 1960

24 points were scored by Don Webb in 1961

The progression of the most points scored by a Patriots linebacker/special teams player in a regular season

6 points were scored by Tom Addison in 1962

6 points were scored by Nick Buoniconti in 1963

6 points were scored by Ed Philpott in 1868

6 points were scored by Will Foster in 1973

6 points were scored by Bob Geddes in 1974

6 points were scored by Sam Hunt in 1976

6 points were scored by Mike Hawkins in 1979

6 points were scored by Rod Shoate in 1980

6 points were scored by Clayton Weishuhn in 1983

6 points were scored by Andre Tippett in 1985

6 points were scored by Johnny Rembert in 1985

6 points were scored by Johnny Rembert in 1986

6 points were scored by Andre Tippett in 1987

12 points were scored by Vincent Brown in 1992

12 points were scored by Tedy Bruschi in 2002

12 points were scored by Tedy Bruschi in 2003

Tedy Bruschi

Mike Vrabel

The progression of the most points scored by a Patriots linebacker/tight end in a regular season

6 points were scored by John Tanner in 1974

12 points were scored by Mike Vrabel in 2004

24 points were scored by Mike Vrabel in 2005

The progression of the most points scored by a Patriots defensive lineman in a regular season

6 points were scored by LeRoy Moore in 1961

6 points were scored by Jim Lee Hunt in 1963

6 points were scored by Jim Lee Hunt in 1966

6 points were scored by Mel Witt in 1968

6 points were scored by Ray Hamilton in 1975

6 points were scored by Brent Williams in 1986

6 points were scored by Brent Williams in 1990

6 points were scored by Tim Goad in 1992

12 points were scored by Willie McGinest in 1996

Every Patriots player who has led the NFL with the most points scored in a specific regular season

Gino Cappelletti led both leagues with 147 points scored during the 1961 season

Gino Cappelletti led both leagues with 113 points scored during the 1963 season

Gino Cappelletti led both leagues with 155 points scored during the 1964 season

Gino Cappelletti tied with Gale Sayers with 132 points scored during the 1965 season

Gino Cappelletti led both leagues with 119 points scored during the 1966 season

John Smith was the NFL scoring leader with 115 points scored during the 1979 season

John Smith was the NFL scoring leader with 129 points scored during the 1980 season

Tony Franklin was the NFL scoring leader with 140 points scored during the 1986 season

Adam Vinatieri was the NFL scoring leader with 141 points scored during the 2004 season

Stephen Gostkowski was the NFL scoring leader with 148 points scored during the 2008 season

The progression of the most career points scored by a Patriots player

1,130 career points were scored by Gino Cappelletti over the 1960–70 seasons

1,158 career points were scored by Adam Vinatieri over the 1996–2005 seasons

The progression of the most career points scored by a Patriots running back/special teams player

36 points were scored by Dick Christy in 1960

252 career points were scored by Larry Garron over the 1960–68 seasons

276 career points were scored by Jim Nance over the 1965–71 seasons

294 career points were scored by Sam Cunningham over the 1973–79 and 1981 seasons

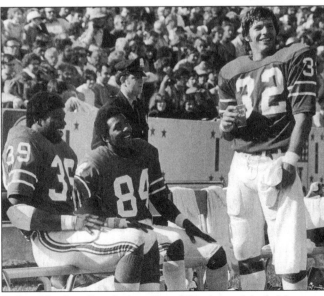

Left to right: Sam Cunningham, Darryl Stingley, and Andy Johnson

The progression of the most career points scored by a Patriots wide receiver/special teams player

238 career points were scored by Jim Colclough over the 1960–67 seasons

408 career points were scored by Stanley Morgan over the 1977–89 seasons

The progression of the most career points scored by a Patriots tight end/special teams player

24 points were scored by Oscar Lofton during the 1960 season

36 points were scored by Tom Stephens over the 1960–61 seasons

62 points were scored by Tony Romeo over the 1962–66 seasons

102 points were scored by Jim Whalen over the 1966–69 seasons

168 points were scored by Russ Francis over the 1975–80 seasons

302 points were scored by Ben Coates over the 1991–99 seasons

The progression of the most career points scored by a Patriots quarterback

12 points were scored by Butch Songin during the 1960 season

92 points were scored Babe Parilli over the 1961–67 seasons

216 points were scored by Steve Grogan over the 1975–88 seasons

The progression of the most career points scored by a Patriots defensive back/special teams player

6 points were scored by Chuck Shonta during the 1960 season

24 points were scored by Don Webb during the 1961 season

30 points were scored by Raymond Clayborn over the 1977–87 seasons

36 points were scored by Ty Law over the 1996–2003 seasons

The progression of the most career points scored by a Patriots linebacker

6 points were scored by Tom Addison during the 1962 season

8 points were scored by Nick Buoniconti over the 1962–67 seasons

12 points were scored by Johnny Rembert over the 1985–86 seasons

12 points were scored by Andre Tippett over the 1985–87 seasons

12 points were scored by Vincent Brown during the 1992 season

30 points were scored by Tedy Bruschi over the 1996–2003 seasons

The most career points scored by a Patriots defensive lineman

14 points were scored by Jim Lee Hunt over the 1963-1966 seasons

The Playoffs

The progression of the most points scored by a Patriots player in a playoff game

3 points were scored by Gino Cappelletti in the 26–8 victory over the Buffalo Bills at War Memorial Stadium on 12-28-63

6 points were scored by Larry Garron in the 26–8 victory over the Buffalo Bills at War Memorial Stadium on 12-28-63

14 points were scored by Gino Cappelletti in the 26–8 victory over the Buffalo Bills at War Memorial Stadium on 12-28-63

14 points were scored by Tony Franklin in the 26–14 win over the New York Jets at the Meadowlands on 12-28-85

18 points were scored by Curtis Martin in the 28–3 rout of the Pittsburgh Steelers at Foxboro Stadium on 01-05-97

The progression of the most points scored by a Patriots wide receiver in a playoff game

6 points were scored by Harold Jackson in the 31–14 loss to the Houston Oilers at Schaefer Stadium on 12-31-78

6 points were scored by Stanley Morgan in the 26–14 victory over the New York Jets at the Meadowlands on 12-28-85

6 points were scored by Irving Fryar in the 46–10 loss to the Bears at the Louisiana Superdome on 01-26-86

12 points were scored by Stanley Morgan in the 22–17 loss to the Denver Broncos at Mile High Stadium on 01-04-87

12 points were scored by Deion Branch in the 41–27 victory over the Pittsburgh Steelers at Heinz Field on 01-23-05

The progression of the most points scored by a Patriots tight end in a playoff game

6 points were scored by Russ Francis in the 24–21 loss to the Oakland Raiders at the Oakland Coliseum on 12-18-76

6 points were scored by Russ Francis in the 31–14 loss to the Houston Oilers at Schaefer Stadium on 12-31-78

6 points were scored by Don Hasselbeck in the 28–13 loss to the Miami Dolphins at the Orange Bowl on 01-08-83

6 points were scored by Lin Dawson in the 27–20 victory over the Los Angeles Raiders at the Los Angeles Coliseum on 01-05-86

6 points were scored by Derrick Ramsey in the 31–14 victory over the Miami Dolphins at the Orange Bowl on 01-12-86

6 points were scored by Ben Coates in the 35–21 loss to the Green Bay Packers at the Superdome on 01-26-97

6 points were scored by Mike Vrabel in the 32–29 victory over the Carolina Panthers at Reliant Stadium on 02-01-04

6 points were scored by Mike Vrabel in the 24–21 victory over the Philadelphia Eagles at Alltel Stadium on 02-06-05

6 points were scored by Benjamin Watson in the 28–3 rout of the Jacksonville Jaguars at Gillette Stadium on 01-07-06

12 points were scored by Benjamin Watson in the 31–20 win over the Jacksonville Jaguars at Gillette Stadium on 01-12-08

The progression of the most points scored by a Patriots running back in a playoff game

12 points were scored by Larry Garron in the 26–8 victory over the Buffalo Bills at War Memorial Stadium on 12-28-63

18 points were scored by Curtis Martin in the 28–3 rout of the Pittsburgh Steelers at Foxboro Stadium on 01-05-97

The only Patriots quarterback who scored a TD in a playoff game

6 points were scored by Tom Brady in the 16–13 overtime victory vs the Oakland Raiders at Foxboro Stadium on 01-19-02

6 points were scored by Tom Brady in the 20–3 rout of the Indianapolis Colts at Gillette Stadium on 01-16-05

The progression of the most points scored by a Patriots kicker in a playoff game

14 points were scored by Gino Cappelletti in the 26–8 win over the Buffalo Bills at War Memorial Stadium on 12-28-63

14 points were scored by Tony Franklin in the 26–8 victory over the Buffalo Bills at War Memorial Stadium on 12-28-63

16 points were scored by Adam Vinatieri in the 24–14 victory over the Indianapolis Colts at Gillette Stadium on 01-18-04

The only points scored by a Patriots offensive lineman in a playoff game

6 points were scored by Logan Mankins in the 38–34 loss to the Indianapolis Colts at the RCA Dome on 01-27-07

The only points scored by a Patriots linebacker in a playoff game

6 points were scored by Todd Collins in the 17–3 victory over the Miami Dolphins at Foxboro Stadium on 12-28-97

The progression of the most points scored by a defensive back in a playoff game

6 points were scored by Otis Smith in the 20–6 victory over the Jacksonville Jaguars at Foxboro Stadium on 01-12-97

6 points were scored by Ty Law in the 20–17 victory over the St. Louis Rams at the Superdome on 02-03-02

6 points were scored by Rodney Harrison in the 41–27 win over the Pittsburgh Steelers at Heinz Field on 01-23-05

6 points were scored by Asante Samuel in the 28–3 rout of the Jacksonville Jaguars at Gillette Stadium on 01-07-06

6 points were scored by Asante Samuel in the 37–16 rout of the New York Jets at Gillette Stadium on 01-07-07

6 points were scored by Asante Samuel in the 38–34 loss to the Indianapolis Colts at the RCA Dome on 01-21-07

Otis Smith (45)

Adam Vinatieri

The progression of the most points scored by a Patriots special teams player (not a kicker) in a playoff game

6 points were scored by Johnny Rembert in the 26–14 victory over the New York Jets at the Meadowlands on 12-28-85

6 points were scored by Jim Bowman in the 27–20 win over the Los Angeles Raiders at the Los Angeles Coliseum on 01-05-86

6 points were scored by Troy Brown in the 24–17 victory over the Pittsburgh Steelers at Heinz Field on 01-27-02

6 points were scored by Antwan Harris in the 24–17 victory over the Pittsburgh Steelers at Heinz Field on 01-27-02

The only Patriots player who has run for a two-point conversion in a playoff game
Super Bowl XXXVIII
Kevin Faulk ran for a two-point conversion in the 32–29 win over the Carolina Panthers at Reliant Stadium on 02-03-04

2006 AFC Divisional playoff game
Kevin Faulk ran for a two-point conversion in the 24–21 win over the San Diego Chargers at Qualcomm Stadium on 01-14-07

The only Patriots player who kicked the game-winning field goal on the last play of a regulation playoff game
Super Bowl XXXVI
Adam Vinatieri kicked a 48-yard field goal to defeat the St. Louis Rams 20–17 at the Superdome on 02-03-02

The only Patriots player who kicked the game-winning field goal on the next-to-last play of a playoff game
Super Bowl XXXVIII
Adam Vinatieri kicked a 41-yard field goal with four seconds left to defeat the Carolina Panthers 32–29 at Reliant Stadium on 02-01-04

The only Patriots player who kicked an overtime game-winning field goal in a playoff game
2001 AFC Divisional playoff game
Adam Vinatieri kicked a 23-yard field goal to defeat the Oakland Raiders 16–13 in overtime at Foxboro Stadium on 01-19-02

The only Patriots quarterback who has run for a TD in a playoff game
2001 AFC Divisional playoff game
Tom Brady ran for a six-yard TD in the 16–13 overtime win vs the Oakland Raiders at Foxboro Stadium on 01-19-02

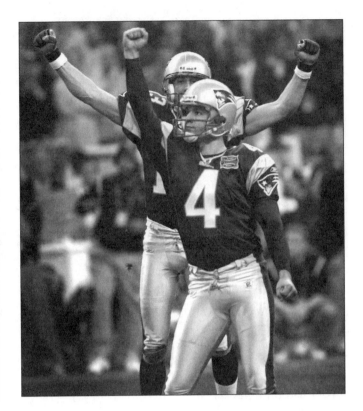

Adam Vinatieri

2004 AFC Divisional playoff game
Tom Brady ran for a one-yard TD in the 20–3 rout of the Indianapolis Colts at Gillette Stadium on 01-16-05

The only Patriots wide receiver who has run for a TD in a playoff game
2004 AFC Championship Game
Deion Branch ran 23 yards for a TD in the 41–27 victory over the Pittsburgh Steelers at Heinz Field on 01-23-05

The only Patriots running back with two TD receptions in a playoff game
1963 AFL Eastern Divisional playoff game
Larry Garron caught a 59-yard TD pass and a 17-yard TD pass in the 26–8 win over the Buffalo Bills on 12-28-63

The only Patriots wide receiver with two TD receptions in a playoff game
1986 AFC Divisional playoff game
Stanley Morgan caught a 19-yard TD pass and a 45-yard TD pass in the 22–17 loss to the Denver Broncos on 01-04-87

The only Patriots tight end with two TD receptions in a playoff game
2007 AFC Divisional playoff game
Benjamin Watson caught a three-yard TD pass and a nine-yard TD pass in the 31–20 win over the Jacksonville Jaguars on 01-12-08

The only Patriots running back who has thrown a halfback option touchdown pass in a playoff game
1978 AFC Divisional playoff game
Andy Johnson threw a 24-yard TD pass to Harold Jackson in the 31–14 loss to the Houston Oilers at Schaefer Stadium on 12-31-78

The only Patriots flea-flicker TD pass in a playoff game
1986 AFC Divisional playoff game at Mile High Stadium on 01-04-87
Tony Eason to Mosi Tatupu to Tony Eason to Stanley Morgan for a 45-yard TD in the 22–17 loss to the Denver Broncos

The only Patriots player to return a punt for a TD in a playoff game
2001 AFC Championship Game
Troy Brown returned a punt 55 yards for a TD in the 24–17 victory over the Pittsburgh Steelers at Heinz Field on 01-27-02

The combination of two Patriots players who returned a blocked field goal for a TD in a playoff game

2001 AFC Championship Game

Troy Brown lateraled to Antwan Harris, who ran 49 yards for a TD in the 24–17 win over the Pittsburgh Steelers on 01-27-02

The only Patriots player who returned a lateral, after a field goal was blocked, for a TD in a playoff game

2001 AFC Championship Game

Antwan Harris returned a lateral after a blocked field goal 49 yards for a TD in the 24–17 win over Pittsburgh on 01-27-02

The combination of Patriots players who have returned a loose ball (blocked FGA) for a TD in a playoff game

2001 AFC Championship Game

Troy Brown advanced the ball 11 yards and lateraled it to Antwan Harris, who ran 49 yards for a TD in the 24–17 win on 01-27-02

Every Patriots player who returned an interception for a TD in a playoff game

1997 AFC wild-card playoff game

Todd Collins returned a Dan Marino pass 40 yards for a TD in the 17–3 win over the Miami Dolphins on 12-28-97

Super Bowl XXXVI

Ty Law returned a Kurt Warner pass 47 yards for a TD in the 20–17 win over the St. Louis Rams on 02-03-02

2004 AFC Championship Game

Rodney Harrison returned a Ben Roethlisberger pass 87 yards for a TD in the 41–27 win over the Pittsburgh Steelers on 01-23-05

2005 AFC wild-card playoff game

Asante Samuel returned a Byron Leftwich pass 73 yards for a TD in the 28–3 rout of the Jacksonville Jaguars on 01-07-06

2006 AFC wild-card playoff game

Asante Samuel returned a Chad Pennington pass 36 yards for a TD in the 37–16 rout of the New York Jets on 01-07-07

2006 AFC Championship Game

Asante Samuel returned a Peyton Manning pass 39 yards for a TD in the 38–34 loss to the Indianapolis Colts on 1-21-07

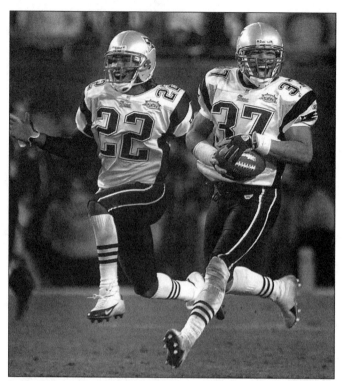

Left to right: Asante Samuel (22) and Rodney Harrison (37)

The only Patriots special teams player who returned a fumble for a TD in a playoff game

1985 AFC wild-card playoff game

Johnny Rembert returned a fumbled kickoff return 15 yards for a TD in the 26–14 win over the New York Jets on 12-28-85

The only Patriots defensive back who returned a fumble for a TD in a playoff game

1996 AFC Championship Game

Otis Smith returned a fumble by a running back 47 yards for a TD in the 20–6 win over the Jacksonville Jaguars on 01-12-97

The progression of the most career points scored by a Patriots player in the playoffs

18 career points scored by Gino Cappelletti in two playoff games

18 career points scored by Larry Garron in two playoff games

18 career points scored by Stanley Morgan in seven playoff games

39 career points scored by Tony Franklin in five playoff games

117 career points scored by Adam Vinatieri in 17 playoff games

Stanley Morgan

The progression of the most career points scored by a Patriots running back in the playoffs

18 points were scored by Larry Garron in two playoff games

30 points were scored by Curtis Martin in three playoff games

The progression of the most career points scored by a Patriots wide receiver in the playoffs

6 points were scored by Harold Jackson on 12-31-78

18 points were scored by Stanley Morgan in seven playoff games

42 points were scored by David Givens in eight playoff games

The progresson of the most career points scored by a Patriots tight end in the playoffs

12 points were scored by Russ Francis in two playoff games

18 points were scored by Benjamin Watson in eight playoff games

The only Patriots quarterback who scored in the playoffs

12 points have been scored by Tom Brady in 17 playoff games

Every Patriots special teams player who scored a TD in the playoffs

6 points were scored by Johnny Rembert on 12-28-85

6 points were scored by Jim Bowman on 01-05-86

6 points were scored by Troy Brown on 01-27-02

6 points were scored by Antwan Harris on 01-27-02

The progression of the most career points scored by a Patriots defensive back in the playoffs

6 points were scored by Otis Smith on 01-12-97

6 points were scored by Ty Law on 02-03-02

6 points were scored by Rodney Harrison on 01-23-05

18 points were scored by Asante Samuel in 14 playoff games

The only Patriots linebacker who scored a TD in the playoffs

6 points were scored by Todd Collins on 12-28-97

The only Patriots linebacker/tight end who scored in the playoffs

12 points were scored by Mike Vrabel in 17 playoff games

The only Patriots offensive lineman who scored in the playoffs

6 points were scored by Logan Mankins on 01-27-07

AFL All-Star Games and NFL Pro Bowl Games

The only Patriots player who kicked an extra point in an AFL All-Star Game

Gino Cappelletti kicked three extra points in the 1964 AFL East/West All-Star Game played on 01-19-64

Gino Cappelletti kicked two extra points in the 1965 AFL East/West All-Star Game played on 01-16-65

Gino Cappelletti kicked three extra points in the 1966 AFL East/West All-Star Game played on 01-15-66

Gino Cappelletti kicked four extra points in the 1967 AFL East/West All-Star Game played on 01-21-67

Every Patriots player who kicked an extra point in an NFL Pro Bowl game

John Smith kicked the extra point in the 12–7 loss to the NFC in the 1981 Pro Bowl game on 02-01-81

Tony Franklin kicked the extra point in the 10–6 win over the NFC in the 1987 Pro Bowl game on 02-01-87

Adam Vinatieri kicked six extra points in the 45–20 win over the NFC in the 2003 Pro Bowl game on 02-02-03

Adam Vinatieri kicked five extra points in the 38–27 win over the NFC in the 2004 Pro Bowl game on 02-13-05

The only Patriots player who kicked a field goal in an AFL All-Star Game

Gino Cappelletti kicked a 35-yard field goal in the AFL East/West All-Star Game on 01-19-64

Gino Cappelletti kicked a 46-yard, 14-yard, and a 32-yard field goal in the AFL East/West All-Star Game on 01-15-66

Every Patriots player who kicked a field goal in a NFL Pro Bowl game

Tony Franklin kicked a 26-yard field goal in the 10–6 victory over the NFC in the NFL Pro Bowl game on 02-01-87

Adam Vinatieri kicked a 20-yard field goal in the 45–20 victory over the NFC in the NFL Pro Bowl game on 02-02-03

Adam Vinatieri kicked a 44-yard field goal in the 38–27 victory over the NFC in the NFL Pro Bowl game on 02-13-05

The only Patriots quarterback to throw two TD passes in an AFL All-Star Game

1964 AFL All-Star Game
Babe Parilli completed two TD passes in the 27–24 loss to the West AFL All-Stars on 01-19-64

1967 AFL All-Star Game
Babe Parilli tossed two TD passes and was named the Offensive MVP of the 1967 AFL All-Star Game on 01-21-67

The only Patriots player who returned an interception for a TD in a NFL Pro Bowl game

Ty Law returned a pass by Randall Cunningham 67 yards for a TD in the 23–10 win over the NFC on 02-07-99

Ty Law returned a pass by Brad Johnson 46 yards for a TD in the 45–20 win over the NFC on 02-02-03

The only Boston Patriots player who scored a TD in an AFL All-Star Game

Gino Cappelletti caught a five-yard TD pass from George Blanda in the 47–27 loss to the West All-Stars on 01-07-62

Gino Cappelletti

Ty Law

The only Boston Patriots running back who scored in an AFL All-Star Game

Larry Garron caught a 12-yard TD pass from Babe Parilli in the 27–24 loss to the West AFL All-Stars on 01-19-64

The only Boston Patriots linebacker who scored in an AFL All-Star Game

Nick Buoniconti returned a fumble 17 yards for a TD in the 38–14 loss to the West AFL All-Stars on 01-16-65

The only Boston Patriots kicker who scored in an AFL All-Star Game

Gino Cappelletti kicked three extra points and a 35-yard field goal in the 27–24 loss to the West All-Stars on 01-19-64

Gino Cappelletti kicked two extra points in the 38–14 loss to the West AFL All-Stars on 01-16-65

Gino Cappelletti kicked a 46-yard field goal, a 14-yard field goal, a 32-yard field goal and three PATs in the 30–19 win over Buffalo on 01-15-66

Gino Cappelletti kicked four extra points in the 30–23 win over the West AFL All-Stars on 01-21-67

The only New England Patriots defensive back who scored a TD in an NFL Pro Bowl game

Ty Law returned a Randall Cunningham pass 67 yards for a TD in the 23–10 win over the NFC on 02-07-99

Ty Law returned a Brad Johnson pass 46 yards for a TD in the 45–20 win over the NFC on 02-02-03

The only Boston Patriots quarterback who has thrown a TD pass in an AFL All-Star Game

Babe Parilli threw a 12-yard TD pass to Larry Garron and a three-yard TD pass to Bill Mathis in the 27–24 loss on 01-19-64

Babe Parilli threw a three-yard TD pass to Wray Carlton and a 17-yard TD pass to Willie Frazier in the 30–23 win on 01-21-67

The only New England Patriots quarterback who has thrown a TD pass in a NFL Pro Bowl game

Drew Bledsoe threw a 14-yard TD pass to Jimmy Smith in the 29–24 win over the NFC on 02-01-98

Special Teams

This chapter is about the many men who have performed on special teams. It contains information regarding those who have kicked and punted, and returned kickoffs and punts for the Patriots. It also lists every Patriots player who has blocked a field goal, a punt, or extra-point attempt.

In the early years of the Boston Patriots, the team only had 33 total players on its roster. That meant just about every player was on special teams. Here are a few examples of some linemen who contributed to the Patriots' kicking game. Offensive lineman Tony Discenzo kicked off in five games during the 1960 season. Offensive lineman Walt Cudzik missed on a 48-yard field-goal attempt on 12-11-60. Offensive lineman Bob Yates kicked off in 55 games during the 1961–65 seasons.

Offensive lineman Justin Canale kicked off in 54 games during the 1965–68 seasons and kicked an extra point on 11-05-67. Defensive lineman Dennis Wirgowski kicked off in two games for the Boston Patriots during the 1970 season. Defensive back Fred Bruney attempted an onside kick in the Boston Patriots first regular season victory on 09-16-60. Linebacker Steve Zabel kicked an extra point for the New England Patriots on 12-12-76.

Some of these players are easily recognized because of their success with the Patriots. The stars of this chapter include Gino Cappelletti, Adam Vinatieri, Tom Yewcic, Ron Burton, Larry Garron, Mini-Mack Herron, Raymond Clayborn, Mike Haynes, Irving Fryar, Dave Meggett, Troy Brown, Ellis Hobbs, and Kevin Faulk.

As you might have noticed, many of these players were successful at various positions on the team. Gino Cappelletti was an AFL All-Star receiver. Adam Vinatieri tossed a touchdown pass and caught Herschel Walker from behind. Tom Yewcic was a punter, quarterback, and a running back. Ron Burton, Larry Garron, Mack Herron, Dave Meggett, and Kevin Faulk were excellent running backs and dynamic return men as well.

Mike Haynes and Raymond Clayborn were AFC All-Pro cornerbacks. Patriots cornerback Ellis Hobbs has the record for the longest kickoff return in NFL history. Receiver Irving Fryar was an AFC return specialist, and AFC All-Pro receiver Troy Brown has more career punt returns than any other player for the Patriots.

Of course, we need to mention that both Mosi Tatupu and Larry Izzo were recognized as Pro Bowl special teams players. Mosi was an AFC special teams Pro Bowl player in 1986, and Larry Izzo was selected to the Pro Bowl in 2002 and 2004. The Hula Bowl recognizes the best college special teams player of the year with the Mosi Tatupu Award and Wesley Walker is the only Patriots player who has won this coveted award.

There are 10 types of special teams. The teams are either trying to kick an extra point, score via a two-point conversion or field goal kick, or are trying prevent the opposing team from scoring one point, two points, or three points. The teams are either trying to return a punt or a kickoff or are trying to prevent the opposing team from advancing up the field via a punt return or a kickoff return. Twice the Patriots have confused an opponent with a fake field-goal attempt and thrown a touchdown pass instead. The team has also had its quarterback pooch a punt, thereby forcing the opposing team to start inside its own 10-yard line.

Certainly the most unique play on special teams was the dropped extra point that was kicked by back-up quarterback Doug Flutie in his last professional football game.

The Top 10 most memorable Patriots Special Teams players whose main duty was to stop the other team from scoring

Richard Seymour—blocked five field goals during the regular season and one field-goal attempt in the playoffs

Johnny Rembert—the only Patriots player to score a TD on a fumbled kickoff return in the regular season and in the playoffs

Mosi Tatupu—the only Patriots player to force a special teams fumble that resulted in a TD in the regular season and in the playoffs

Jim Bowman—recovered a fumbled kickoff return for the final TD in the playoff game win on 01-05-86

Larry Izzo—was voted the Patriots special teams captain for eight consecutive seasons

Larry Whigham—was the AFC Special Teams Player of the Week in the playoff game win on 01-12-97

Chad Eaton—the only Patriots player to block two FGAs in a game and the only Patriots player to block a FGA in overtime

Rick Sanford—the only Patriots player to return a blocked punt for a TD and a fumbled kickoff return for a TD

Art Graham—made two game-saving tackles on long punt returns by Hoot Gibson and Lance Alworth in 1964

Bob Gladieux—made the tackle on the opening kickoff even though he was tailgaiting an hour before the game

Kicking

The first place-kicker for the Boston Patriots was Gino Cappelletti. Cappelletti was a straight-ahead kicker who used a special flat-toed shoe to kick an extra point or a field goal. Cappelletti scored the first points in the AFL, and he scored the most points in the league's history. Cappelletti led the AFL in many kicking categories, including having the best percentage of field goals kicked in 1964, kicking the longest field goal in the league in consecutive years, and being the only AFL kicker to lead the league with the most field goals made three times in the 10-year history of the league. Cappelletti is the only AFL player to be first runner-up as the league's MVP (he finished second to George Blanda in 1961) and also be named the league's MVP (he won the award in 1964). Cappelletti not only led the AFL three times with the most field goals attempted and made, he also tied with Jim Bakken for the most field goals made in the NFL in 1964. Cappelletti was an AFL All-Star kicker in 1961, 1963, 1964, 1966, and 1968. He was one of only two AFL kickers to boot four field goals in a regular season game for three consecutive games. Cappelletti only kicked one field goal in college.

Charlie Gogolak was the first soccer-style kicker to play for the Patriots. He was the place-kicker for the Patriots in four games during the 1970 season and kicked through the mid-point of the 1972 season. Mike

"Super Foot" Walker, who won a contest to become the Patriots kicker, was with the team along with Bill Bell and Jeff White during the 1972–73 seasons. John Smith, who had never played in a football game before joining the Patriots, was the team's kicker from the 1974–77 and through the 1979–83 seasons. John Smith was the first Patriots kicker to be named to the NFL Pro Bowl. Due to an injury to John Smith, Nick Lowery and David Posey kicked for the Patriots during the 1978 season. Other kickers for the Patriots during the 1982–83 seasons included Rex Robinson, Dan Miller, and Fred Steinfort.

Tony Franklin was brought in as a free agent from the Philadelphia Eagles, and he is the only Patriots player to kick with a bare foot. In 1985, Franklin became the first Patriots player to kick two field goals of 50 yards during the season. He was the team's kicker from 1984–87 and was an AFC Pro Bowl kicker in 1986.

In 1988, Teddy Garcia and Jason Staurovsky shared the kicking duties. Greg Davis and Jason Staurovsky shared the kicking duties during the 1989 season. Jason Staurovsky was the only kicker to attempt a field goal for the Patriots during the 1990 season. In 1991, Staurovsky shared the duties with Charlie Baumann. Baumann held this position through the end of the 1992 season, as Scott Sisson was the kicker in 1993.

Matt Bahr replaced Scott Sisson with three games left in the 1993 season. Bahr was named the AFC Special Teams Player of the Week as he became the oldest NFL player to kick a field goal of 55 yards on 11-12-95. Bahr relinquished his role as the Patriots kicker to Adam Vinatieri at the beginning of the 1996 regular season. Vinatieri was the Patriots kicker during the 1996–2005 seasons, including the first three Super Bowl championships. Adam Vinatieri was a two-time Pro Bowl kicker for the Patriots. Steven Gostkowski, who was chosen with the 118th pick in the 2006 College Football Draft, has been the place-kicker since the 2006 season. Stephen Gostkowski was a Pro Bowl kicker for the Patriots in 2008.

Every Patriots Kicker named the AFC Special Teams Player of the Week

The AFC Special Teams Player of the Week on 11-12-95
Matt Bahr kicked a 55-yard field goal to set the team record and help defeat the Miami Dolphins 34–17

The AFC Special Teams Player of the Week on 09-22-96
Adam Vinatieri kicked five field goals including the game-winner to defeat the Jacksonville Jaguars 28–25 in overtime

The AFC Special Teams Player of the Week on 10-12-97
Adam Vinatieri kicked four field goals including one from 52 yards in the 33–6 victory over the Buffalo Bills

The AFC Special Teams Player of the Week on 10-04-98
Adam Vinatieri kicked three field goals including a game-winning 27-yard field goal to beat the Saints 30–27

The AFC Special Teams Player of the Week on 11-23-98
Adam Vinatieri kicked four field goals to help defeat the Miami Dolphins 26–23

The AFC Special Teams Player of the Week on 12-16-01
Adam Vinatieri kicked a 25-yard field goal to tie the game and a 23-yard field goal to beat the Buffalo Bills 12–9 in overtime

The AFC Special Teams Player of the Week on 09-25-05
Adam Vinatieri kicked three field goals including a 43-yard field goal with one second left in the 23–20 win vs Pittsburgh on 09-25-05

Every Patriots Kicker named the AFC Special Teams Player of the Month

AFC Special Teams Player of the Month for October 1998
Adam Vinatieri kicked a game-winning field goal, was 10-of-11 in FGAs, and 9-of-9 on PATs in October 1998

AFC Special Teams Player of the Month for September 1999
Adam Vinatieri kicked two game-winning field goals, was 9-of-10 in FGAs, and 9-of-9 on PATs in September 1999

AFC Special Teams Player of the Month for October 2008
Stephen Gostkowski scored 38 points and kicked three field goals in a game twice in October 2008

The Patriots player who has kicked the most field goals, the longest field goal, and most extra points every year

	Most Field Goals	Longest Field Goal	Most Extra Points
1960	Gino Cappelletti	Gino Cappelletti	Gino Cappelletti
1961	Gino Cappelletti	Gino Cappelletti	Gino Cappelletti
1962	Gino Cappelletti	Gino Cappelletti	Gino Cappelletti
1963	Gino Cappelletti	Gino Cappelletti	Gino Cappelletti
1964	Gino Cappelletti	Gino Cappelletti	Gino Cappelletti
1965	Gino Cappelletti	Gino Cappelletti	Gino Cappelletti
1966	Gino Cappelletti	Gino Cappelletti	Gino Cappelletti
1967	Gino Cappelletti	Gino Cappelletti	Gino Cappelletti
1968	Gino Cappelletti	Gino Cappelletti	Gino Cappelletti
1969	Gino Cappelletti	Gino Cappelletti	Gino Cappelletti
1970	Gino Cappelletti	Gino Cappelletti	Gino Cappelletti
1971	Charlie Gogolak	Charlie Gogolak	Charlie Gogolak
1972	Charlie Gogolak	Charlie Gogolak and Mike Walker	Mike Walker
1973	Jeff White	Jeff White	Jeff White
1974	John Smith	John Smith	John Smith
1975	John Smith	John Smith	John Smith
1976	John Smith	John Smith	John Smith
1977	John Smith	John Smith	John Smith
1978	David Posey	David Posey	David Posey
1979	John Smith	John Smith	John Smith
1980	John Smith	John Smith	John Smith
1981	John Smith	John Smith	John Smith
1982	John Smith	John Smith	John Smith
1983	Fred Steinfort	John Smith	Fred Steinfort
1984	Tony Franklin	Tony Franklin	Tony Franklin
1985	Tony Franklin	Tony Franklin	Tony Franklin
1986	Tony Franklin	Tony Franklin	Tony Franklin
1987	Tony Franklin	Tony Franklin	Tony Franklin
1988	Jason Staurovsky	Teddy Garcia	Jason Staurovsky
1989	Greg Davis	Greg Davis	Jason Staurovsky
1990	Jason Staurovsky	Jason Staurovsky	Jason Staurovsky
1991	Jason Staurovsky	Charlie Baumann	Jason Staurovsky
1992	Charlie Baumann	Charlie Baumann	Charlie Baumann
1993	Scott Sisson	Scott Sisson	Scott Sisson
1994	Matt Bahr	Matt Bahr	Matt Bahr
1995	Matt Bahr	Matt Bahr	Matt Bahr
1996	Adam Vinatieri	Adam Vinatieri	Adam Vinatieri
1997	Adam Vinatieri	Adam Vinatieri	Adam Vinatieri
1998	Adam Vinatieri	Adam Vinatieri	Adam Vinatieri
1999	Adam Vinatieri	Adam Vinatieri	Adam Vinatieri
2000	Adam Vinatieri	Adam Vinatieri	Adam Vinatieri
2001	Adam Vinatieri	Adam Vinatieri	Adam Vinatieri
2002	Adam Vinatieri	Adam Vinatieri	Adam Vinatieri
2003	Adam Vinatieri	Adam Vinatieri	Adam Vinatieri
2004	Adam Vinatieri	Adam Vinatieri	Adam Vinatieri
2005	Adam Vinatieri	Adam Vinatieri	Adam Vinatieri
2006	Stephen Gostkowski	Stephen Gostkowski	Stephen Gostkowski
2007	Stephen Gostkowski	Stephen Gostkowski	Stephen Gostkowski
2008	Stephen Gostkowski	Stephen Gostkowski	Stephen Gostkowski

The progression of the most field goals kicked by a Patriots player in a regular season game

1 field goal was kicked by Gino Cappelletti in the 13–10 loss to the Denver Broncos at BU Field on 09-09-60

2 field goals were kicked by Gino Cappelletti in the 35–0 shutout of the Los Angeles Chargers at the Los Angeles Coliseum on 10-08-60

3 field goals were kicked by Gino Cappelletti in the 23–21 victory over the Buffalo Bills at War Memorial Stadium on 09-23-61

3 field goals were kicked by Gino Cappelletti in the 37–30 loss to the New York Titans at the Polo Grounds on 10-01-61

3 field goals were kicked by Gino Cappelletti in the 43–14 rout of the New York Titans at the Polo Grounds on 10-06-62

4 field goals were kicked by Gino Cappelletti in the 26–16 victory over the Oakland Raiders at BU Field on 10-26-62

4 field goals were kicked by Gino Cappelletti in the 33–29 win over the Denver Broncos at Bears Stadium on 11-11-62

4 field goals were kicked by Gino Cappelletti in the 40–21 rout of the Denver Broncos at Fenway Park on 10-18-63

4 field goals were kicked by Gino Cappelletti in the 33–28 win over San Diego Chargers at Balboa Stadium on 09-20-64

6 field goals were kicked by Gino Cappelletti in the 39–10 rout of the Denver Broncos at Bears Stadium on 10-04-64*

6 field goals kicked in a game is the AFL record for most field goals kicked in a game. Cappelletti held this NFL record of kicking six field goals without missing in a regulation game until 11-18-96.

The progression of the most consecutive regular season field goals by a Patriots Kicker

2nd consecutive field goal by Gino Cappelletti was from 33 yards in the 35–0 shutout of the Los Angeles Chargers on 10-08-60

3rd consecutive field goal by Gino Cappelletti was from 35 yards in the 23–21 win over the Buffalo Bills on 09-23-61

7th consecutive field goal by Gino Cappelletti was from 38 yards in the 43–14 rout of the New York Titans on 10-06-62

9th consecutive field goal by Tony Franklin was from 40 yards in the 26–19 loss to the Denver Broncos on 11-04-84

14th consecutive field goal by Tony Franklin was from 47 yards in the 22–19 win over the Buffalo Bills on 11-23-86

15th consecutive field goal by Adam Vinatieri was from 26 yards in the 34–13 loss to the Denver Broncos on 10-06-97

25th consecutive field goal by Adam Vinatieri was from 42 yards in the 31–10 rout of the Buffalo Bills on 11-09-97

The progression of the most consecutive regular season games that a Patriots player kicked a field goal

2 consecutive games that Gino Cappelletti kicked a field goal (from 11-04-60 to 11-11-60)

4 consecutive games that Gino Cappelletti kicked a field goal (from 10-01-61 to 10-22-61)

7 consecutive games that Gino Cappelletti kicked a field goal (from 09-08-63 to 10-18-63)

11 consecutive games that Gino Cappelletti kicked a field goal (from 11-01-63 to 10-09-64)

12 consecutive games that Tony Franklin kicked a field goal (from 10-07-84 to 09-08-85)

17 consecutive games that Tony Franklin kicked a field goal (from 11-24-85 to 11-23-86)

17 consecutive games that Matt Bahr kicked a field goal (from 12-18-94 to 12-16-95)

The progression of the most successful field goals kicked by a Patriots player in a regular season

8 field goals were kicked by Gino Cappelletti in 1960

17 field goals were kicked by Gino Cappelletti in 1961 (the most in the AFL in 1961)

20 field goals were kicked by Gino Cappelletti in 1962

22 field goals were kicked by Gino Cappelletti in 1963 (the most in the AFL in 1963)

25 field goals were kicked by Gino Cappelletti in 1964 (the most in the AFL in 1964)

26 field goals were kicked by John Smith in 1980

32 field goals were kicked by Tony Franklin in 1986 (the most in the NFL in 1986)

36 field goals were kicked by Stephen Gostkowski in 2008 (the most in the NFL in 2008)

The progression of the most career field goals kicked by a Patriots player

176 field goals were kicked by Gino Cappelletti over the 1960–70 seasons

263 field goals were kicked by Adam Vinatieri over the 1996–2005 seasons

The amount of career regular season field goals by every kicker of the Patriots

263 career regular season field goals by Adam Vinatieri during the 1996–2005 seasons

176 career regular season field goals by Gino Cappelletti during the 1960–70 seasons

128 career regular season field goals by John Smith during the 1974–84 seasons

93 career regular season field goals by Tony Franklin during the 1984–87 seasons

77 career regular season field goals by Stephen Gostkowski during the 2006–08 seasons

55 career regular season field goals by Matt Bahr during the 1993–95 seasons

50 career field goals by Jason Staurovsky during the 1993–95 seasons

20 career field goals by Charlie Gogolak during the 1970–72 seasons

18 career field goals by Charlie Baumann during the 1991–92 seasons

16 field goals were kicked by Greg Davis during the 1989 season

14 field goals were kicked by Jeff White during the 1973 season

14 field goals were kicked by Scott Sisson during the 1993 season

11 field goals were kicked by David Posey during the 1978 season

6 field goals were kicked by Fred Steinfort during the 1983 season

6 field goals were kicked by Teddy Garcia during the 1988 season

2 field goals were kicked Mike Walker during the 1972 season

2 field goals were kicked by Danny Miller during the 1982 season

Bill Bell kicked a 36-yard field goal in the 44–23 loss to the Miami Dolphins at the Orange Bowl on 09-30-73

Rex Robinson kicked a 24-yard field goal in the 24–13 win over the Baltimore Colts at Memorial Stadium on 09-12-82

Eric Schubert kicked a 23-yard field goal in the 20–10 loss to the Cleveland Browns at Sullivan Stadium on 10-04-87

The progression of the longest field goal kicked by a Patriots player in a regular season game

35-yard field goal by Gino Cappelletti in the 13–10 loss to the Denver Broncos at BU Field on 09-09-60

36-yard field goal by Gino Cappelletti in the 23–21 win over the Buffalo Bills at War Memorial Stadium on 09-23-61

46-yard field goal by Gino Cappelletti in the 23–21 win over the Buffalo Bills at War Memorial Stadium on 09-23-61

46-yard field goal by Gino Cappelletti in the 20–14 victory over the Oakland Raiders at Frank Youell Field on 09-22-63

47-yard field goal by Gino Cappelletti in the 20–14 victory over the Oakland Raiders at Frank Youell Field on 09-22-63

48-yard field goal by Gino Cappelletti in the 17–14 win over the Oakland Raiders at Frank Youell Field on 09-13-64

51-yard field goal by Gino Cappelletti in the 12–7 victory over the Denver Broncos at Fenway Park on 11-20-64

53-yard field goal by Gino Cappelletti in the 27–23 victory over the New York Jets at Shea Stadium on 11-28-65

53-yard field goal by Jason Staurovsky in the 33–20 loss to the Seattle Seahawks at Foxboro Stadium on 10-07-90

55-yard field goal by Matt Bahr in the 34–17 victory over the Miami Dolphins at Joe Robbie Stadium on 11-12-95

55-yard field goal by Adam Vinatieri in the 32–18 loss to the St. Louis Rams at the Trans World Dome on 12-13-98

57-yard field goal by Adam Vinatieri in the 33–30 victory over the Chicago Bears at Memorial Stadium on 11-10-02

The career longest field goal by a Patriots Kicker that also happened to be on the last play of the first half of a game

1973 regular season

Bill Bell hit his career longest field goal of 36 yards on the last play of the half in the 44–23 loss to the Miami Dolphins on 09-30-73

1993 regular season

Scott Sisson hit his career longest field goal of 40 yards to end the first half in the 9–6 loss to the Indianapolis Colts on 10-31-93

1995 regular season

Matt Bahr booted a 55-yard field goal on the last play of the half in the 34–17 win over the Miami Dolphins on 11-12-95

The only Patriots Kicker who hit a field goal to end the first half and hit a field goal to win the game on the last play

Gino Cappelletti hit a 33-yard field goal to end the first half and booted a 41-yard field goal to defeat the Houston Oilers, 25–24, on 11-06-64

Every Patriots player who has kicked a game-winning field goal on the last play of a regulation regular season game

1961 regular season

Gino Cappelletti hit a 24-yard field goal on the last play to defeat the Dallas Texans, 18–17, at the Cotton Bowl on 10-29-61

1964 regular season

Gino Cappelletti hit a 41-yard field goal with one second left to defeat the Houston Oilers, 25–24, at Fenway Park on 11-06-64

1994 regular season

Matt Bahr kicked a 33-yard field goal with four seconds left to defeat the Green Bay Packers, 17–16, at Foxboro Stadium on 10-02-94

1998 regular season

Adam Vinatieri kicked a 27-yard field goal with three seconds left to defeat the New Orleans Saints, 30–27, at the Superdome on 10-04-98

Adam Vinatieri kicked a 35-yard field goal with six seconds left to defeat the San Francisco 49ers, 24–21, at Foxboro Stadium on 12-20-98

2005 regular season

Adam Vinatieri kicked a 43-yard field goal with one second left to defeat the Pittsburgh Steelers, 23–20, at Heinz Field on 09-25-05

Other Patriots players who have kicked the game-winning field goal in the fourth quarter of a regular season game

1964 regular season

Gino Cappelletti kicked a 48-yard field goal in the fourth quarter to beat the Los Angeles Raiders, 17–14, at Frank Youell Field on 09-13-64

1968 regular season

Gino Cappelletti kicked a seven yard field goal in the fourth quarter to defeat the Denver Broncos, 20–17, at Bears Stadium on 09-29-68

1978 regular season

David Posey kicked a 24-yard field goal in the fourth quarter to defeat the New York Jets, 19–17, at Shea Stadium on 11-19-78

David Posey kicked a 21-yard field goal in the fourth quarter to defeat the Buffalo Bills, 26–24, at Schaefer Stadium on 12-10-78

1987 regular season

Tony Franklin kicked a 29-yard field goal in the fourth quarter to defeat the Los Angeles Raiders, 26–23, at Sullivan Stadium on 11-01-87

1994 regular season

Matt Bahr kicked a 42-yard field goal in the fourth quarter to beat the Indianapolis Colts, 12–10, at the Hoosier Dome on 11-27-94

1999 regular season

Adam Vinatieri kicked a 23-yard field goal with seven seconds left to defeat the New York Jets, 30–28, at the Meadowlands on 09-12-99

Adam Vinatieri kicked a 26-yard field goal in the fourth quarter to defeat the Indianapolis Colts, 31–28, at Foxboro Stadium on 09-19-99

Adam Vinatieri kicked a 41-yard field goal in the fourth quarter to defeat the New York Giants, 16–14, at Foxboro Stadium on 09-26-99

2001 championship season

Adam Vinatieri kicked a 28-yard field goal in the fourth quarter to defeat the New York Jets, 17–16, at the Meadowlands on 12-02-01

2005 regular season

Adam Vinatieri kicked a 29-yard field goal with 17 seconds left to defeat the Atlanta Falcons, 31–28, at the Georgia Dome on 10-09-05

The only Patriots player who kicked a game-tying field goal in a game that ended in a tie

Gino Cappelletti kicked a 22-yard field goal in the fourth quarter in the 13–13 tie with the San Diego Chargers at Fenway Park on 10-17-65

The only Patriots player who kicked a field goal to take a three-point lead late in a game that ended in a tie

Gino Cappelletti kicked a 19-yard field goal, to take a three-point lead, in the 27–27 tie with the Kansas City Chiefs at Municipal Stadium on 11-20-66

Other kickers who booted a field goal for the game-winning points scored for the Patriots

1982 regular season

John Smith kicked a 33-yard field goal in the 3–0 "Snow Plow" win over the Miami Dolphins at Schaefer Stadium on 12-12-82

1988 regular season

Jason Staurovsky kicked a 34-yard field goal in the 6–3 win over the Miami Dolphins at Joe Robbie Stadium on 11-20-88

1991 regular season

Charlie Baumann kicked a 41-yard field goal in the 6–3 victory over the New York Jets at the Meadowlands on 12-15-91

1994 regular season

Matt Bahr kicked a 42-yard field goal in the 12–10 win over the Indianapolis Colts at the Hoosier Dome on 11-27-94

Every Patriots player who kicked a field goal in the fourth quarter of a regular season game to force overtime

1977 regular season

John Smith hit a 28-yard field goal on last play to tie it up in the 30–27 overtime loss to the Cleveland Browns at Cleveland on 09-26-77

1981 regular season

John Smith kicked a 34-yard field goal with 10 seconds left in the 30–27 overtime loss to the Miami Dolphins at Schaefer Stadium on 11-08-81

1985 regular season

Tony Franklin hit a 28-yard field goal with 16 seconds left in the 16–13 overtime loss to the New York Jets at the Meadowlands on 11-24-85

1992 regular season

Charlie Baumann hit a 44-yard field goal on the last play of the fourth quarter in the 37–34 overtime win over the Indianapolis Colts on 11-15-92

1994 regular season

Matt Bahr hit a 23-yard field goal with 14 seconds left in the 26–20 overtime win over the Minnesota Vikings at Foxboro Stadium on 11-13-94

2000 regular season

Adam Vinatieri hit a 21-yard field goal with 38 seconds left in the 16–13 overtime win over the Cincinnati Bengals at Foxboro Stadium on 11-19-00

2001 championship season

Adam Vinatieri hit a 25-yard field goal with 2:45 left in the 12–9 overtime win over Buffalo at Ralph Wilson Stadium on 12-16-01

The chronological listing of Patriots Kickers who kicked a field goal to win a regular season overtime game

1988 regular season

Jason Staurovsky kicked a 27-yard field goal to defeat the Tampa Bay Buccaneers, 10–7, at Sullivan Stadium on 12-11-88

1989 regular season

Greg Davis boomed a 51-yard field goal to defeat the Indianapolis Colts, 23–20, at the Hoosier Dome on 10-29-89

1991 regular season

Jason Staurovsky kicked a 42-yard field goal, on the last play of overtime, in the 26–23 win over the Minnesota Vikings at Foxboro Stadium on 10-20-91

1992 regular season

Charlie Baumann kicked an 18-yard field goal to defeat the Indianapolis Colts, 37–34, at the Hoosier Dome on 11-15-92

1996 regular season

Adam Vinatieri nailed a 40-yard field goal with 36 seconds left in overtime to defeat the Jacksonville Jaguars, 28–25, at Foxboro Stadium on 09-22-96

1997 regular season

Adam Vinatieri booted a 34-yard field goal to defeat the New York Jets, 27–24, at Foxboro Stadium on 09-14-97

2000 regular season

Adam Vinatieri kicked a 22-yard field goal to defeat the Cincinnati Bengals, 16–13, at Foxboro Stadium on 11-19-00

Adam Vinatieri kicked a 24-yard field goal to defeat the Buffalo Bills, 13–10, at Ralph Wilson Stadium on 12-17-00

2001 championship season

Adam Vinatieri nailed a 44-yard field goal to defeat the San Diego Chargers, 29–26, at Foxboro Stadium on 10-14-01

Adam Vinatieri kicked a 23-yard field goal to defeat the Buffalo Bills, 12–9, at Ralph Wilson Stadium on 12-16-01

2002 regular season

Adam Vinatieri booted a 35-yard field goal to defeat the Kansas City Chiefs, 41–38, at Gillette Stadium on 09-22-02

Adam Vinatieri booted a 35-yard field goal to defeat the Miami Dolphins, 27–24, at Gillette Stadium on 12-29-02

2003 championship season

Adam Vinatieri kicked a 28-yard field goal to defeat the Houston Texans, 23–20, at Reliant Stadium on 11-23-03

Every player who attempted an onside kick even though he was not the regular kicker for the Patriots

1960 regular season

(DB) Fred Bruney attempted an onside kick in the 28–24 win over the New York Titans at the Polo Grounds on 09-17-60

1980 regular season

(Punter) Mike Hubach attempted an onside kick in the 38–34 loss to the Houston Oilers at the Astrodome on 11-10-80

The only Patriots running back who kicked a field goal in a regular season game

Running back Gino Cappelletti ran for two yards and two plays later kicked a 15-yard field goal in the 34–10 loss to Miami on 11-24-68

The Patriots regular season record when their kicker has kicked just one field goal in the game

The Patriots won 30 of 57 regular season games when Adam Vinatieri kicked just one field goal

The Patriots won 19 of 39 regular season games when John Smith kicked just one field goal

The Patriots won 18, lost 31, and tied in five of their 54 regular season games when Gino Cappelletti kicked just one field goal

The Patriots have won 14 of 15 regular season games when Stephen Gostkowski kicked just one field goal

The Patriots won nine of 21 regular season games when Tony Franklin kicked just one field goal

The Patriots won four of six games when David Posey kicked just one field goal

The Patriots won four of 14 regular season games when Matt Bahr kicked just one field goal

The Patriots won three of seven games when Charlie Baumann kicked just one field goal

The Patriots won three of 17 games when Jason Staurovsky kicked just one field goal

The Patriots won two of 10 games when Charlie Gogolak kicked just one field goal

The Patriots won two of three games when Fred Steinfort kicked just one field goal

The Patriots won two of three games when Jeff White kicked just one field goal

The Patriots won once and lost once when Mike Walker kicked just one field goal

The Patriots lost all three of their games when Greg Davis kicked just one field goal

Rex Robinson kicked a 24-yard field goal in the 24–13 victory over the Baltimore Colts on 09-12-82

Bill Bell kicked a 36-yard field goal in the 44–23 loss to the Miami Dolphins on 09-30-73

Eric Schubert kicked a 23-yard field goal in the 20–10 loss to the Cleveland Browns on 10-04-87

Teddy Garcia kicked a 43-yard field goal in the 45–3 loss to the Green Bay Packers on 10-09-88

Scott Sisson kicked a 27-yard field goal in the 13–10 overtime loss to the Buffalo Bills on 11-07-93

The Patriots regular season record when just two field goals were kicked in the game by its kicker

The Patriots won 24 of 33 regular season games when Adam Vinatieri has kicked two field goals

The Patriots won 17, lost seven, and tied in two of its 26 regular season games when Gino Cappelletti kicked two field goals

The Patriots won 16 of 29 regular season games when John Smith kicked two field goals

The Patriots won 13 of 16 regular season games when Stephen Gostkowski kicked two field goals

The Patriots won 10 of 16 regular season games when Tony Franklin kicked two field goals

The Patriots won nine of 12 regular season games when Matt Bahr kicked two field goals

The Patriots won three of nine games when Jason Staurovsky kicked two field goals

The Patriots won two of five games when Charlie Gogolak kicked two field goals

The Patriots won one of four games when Charlie Baumann kicked two field goals

The Patriots won once and lost once when Jeff White kicked two field goals

The Patriots lost both of the games when Greg Davis kicked two field goals

The Patriots lost both of the games when Scott Sisson kicked two field goals

Danny Miller kicked a 23-yard field goal and a 25-yard field goal in the 29–21 victory over the Houston Oilers on 11-28-82

David Posey kicked a 47-yard field goal and a 24-yard field goal in the 19–17 victory over the New York Jets on 11-19-79

Teddy Garcia kicked a 50-yard field goal and a 23-yard field goal in the 36–6 loss to the Minnesota Vikings on 09-11-88

The Patriots regular season record when exactly three field goals were kicked by their kicker in the game

The Patriots won 23 of 30 regular season games when Adam Vinatieri kicked three field goals

The Patriots won nine of 12 regular season games when Gino Cappelletti kicked three field goals

The Patriots won eight of nine regular season games when John Smith kicked three field goals

The Patriots won seven of eight regular season games when Tony Franklin kicked three field goals

The Patriots have won four of six regular season games when Stephen Gostkowski kicked three field goals

The Patriots won all three of regular season games when Matt Bahr kicked three field goals

The Patriots won two of three games when Greg Davis kicked three field goals

The Patriots won both games when Jason Staurovsky kicked three field goals

The Patriots won only one of three games when Scott Sisson kicked three field goals

Jeff White kicked three field goals in the 32–0 shutout of the Houston Oilers on 11-25-73

David Posey kicked three field goals in the 26–23 loss to the Houston Oilers on 11-12-78

Fred Steinfort kicked three field goals in the 37–21 victory over the San Diego Chargers on 10-16-83

Teddy Garcia kicked three field goals in the 28–3 rout of the New York Jets on 09-04-88

Charlie Baumann kicked three field goals in the 37–34 overtime win vs the Indianapolis Colts on 11-15-92

The Patriots regular season record when four field goals were kicked by their kicker in the game

The Patriots won all seven regular season games when Gino Cappelletti kicked four field goals

The Patriots have won eight of 10 games when Adam Vinatieri has kicked four field goals

The Patriots won three of four regular season games when Tony Franklin kicked four field goals

The Patriots have won all three regular season games when Stephen Gostkowski kicked four field goals

The Patriots won both regular season games when Matt Bahr kicked four field goals

Jeff White kicked four field goals in the 33–24 victory over the Green Bay Packers on 11-18-73

John Smith kicked four field goals in the 33–19 victory over the San Diego Chargers on 11-09-75

Jason Staurovsky kicked four field goals in the 33–24 victory over the Buffalo Bills on 11-19-89

The Patriots have won all three regular season games when their kicker has booted five field goals

1989 regular season
Jason Staurovsky kicked five field goals in the 22–16 victory over the Indianapolis Colts on 12-03-89

1996 regular season
Adam Vinatieri kicked five field goals in the 28–25 overtime win over the Jacksonville Jaguars on 09-22-96

2004 championship season
Adam Vinatieri kicked five field goals in the 29–6 rout of the Buffalo Bills on 11-14-04

The only Patriots player who kicked six field goals in a regular season game

Gino Cappelletti kicked six field goals in the 39–10 rout of the Denver Broncos on 10-04-64

The progression of the most consecutive games a Patriots player scored by kicking a PAT or a field goal

2 consecutive games that Gino Cappelletti scored by kicking a PAT or a field goal (09-09-60 to 09-17-60)

7 consecutive games that Gino Cappelletti scored by kicking a PAT or a field goal (10-23-60 to 12-04-60)

28 consecutive games that Gino Cappelletti scored by kicking a PAT or a field goal (12-18-60 to 12-09-62)

31 consecutive games that Gino Cappelletti scored by kicking a PAT or a field goal (09-18-66 to 10-06-68)

45 consecutive games that John Smith scored by kicking an extra point or a field goal (09-28-75 to 09-18-78)

48 consecutive games that John Smith scored by kicking an extra point or a field goal (09-03-79 to 12-20-81)

55 consecutive games that Tony Franklin scored by kicking an extra point or a field goal (09-02-84 to 09-21-87)

110 consecutive games that Adam Vinatieri scored by kicking a PAT or a field goal (11-24-96 to 12-29-02)

The progression of the most points scored by a Patriots Kicker in a regular season game

4 points by Gino Cappelletti (one field goal and one PAT) in the 13–10 loss to the Denver Broncos at BU Field on 09-09-60

4 points by Gino Cappelletti (four extra points) in the 28–24 win over the New York Titans at the Polo Grounds on 09-17-60

9 points by Gino Cappelletti (two field goals and three PATs) in the 35–0 shutout of the Los Angeles Chargers at Los Angeles Coliseum on 10-08-60

11 points by Gino Cappelletti (two field goals and five PATs) in the 34–28 win over the Oakland Raiders at BU Field on 11-04-60

11 points by Gino Cappelletti (three field goals and two PATs) in the 23–21 win over the Buffalo Bills at War Memorial on 09-23-61

12 points by Gino Cappelletti (three field goals and three PATs) in the 37–30 loss to the New York Titans at the Polo Grounds on 10-01-61

13 points by Gino Cappelletti (three field goals and four PATs) in the 43–14 rout of the New York Titans at the Polo Grounds on 10-06-62

14 points by Gino Cappelletti (four field goals and two PATs) in the 26–16 win over the Oakland Raiders at BU Field on 10-26-62

15 points by Gino Cappelletti (four field goals and three PATs) in the 33–29 win over the Denver Broncos at Bears Stadium on 11-11-62

16 points by Gino Cappelletti (four field goals and four PATs) in the 40–21 rout of the Denver Broncos at Fenway Park on 10-18-63

21 points by Gino Cappelletti (six field goals and three PATs) in the 39–10 rout of the Denver Broncos at Bears Stadium on 10-04-64

The progression of the most points scored by a Patriots Kicker in a regular season

60 points were scored by Gino Cappelletti in 1960

99 points were scored by Gino Cappelletti in 1961

101 points were scored by Gino Cappelletti in 1963 (the most in the AFL in 1963)

111 points were scored by Gino Cappelletti in 1964 (the most in the AFL in 1964)

115 points were scored by John Smith in 1979

129 points were scored by John Smith in 1980

140 points were scored by Tony Franklin in 1986 (the most in the NFL in 1986)

141 points were scored by Adam Vinatieri in 2004 (the most in the NFL in 2004)

148 points were scored by Stephen Gostkowski in 2008 (the most in the NFL in 2008)

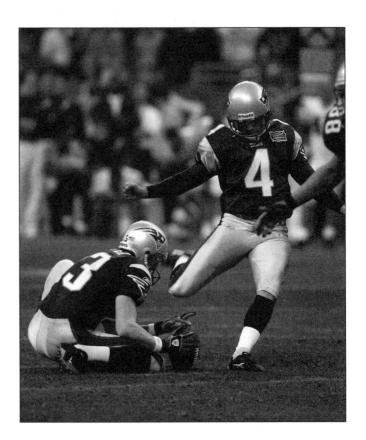

Adam Vinatieri

The Top 10 greatest Patriots field goals

2001 AFC Divisional playoff game
Adam Vinatieri kicked a 45-yard field goal in the snow to tie the game in the 16–13 overtime win over the Oakland Raiders on 01-19-02

Super Bowl XXXVI
Adam Vinatieri kicked a Super Bowl game-winning 48-yard field goal to defeat the St. Louis Rams, 20–17, on 02-03-02

2003 AFC Divisional playoff game
Adam Vinatieri kicked a 46-yard field goal in four degree weather to defeat the Tennessee Titans, 17–14, on 01-10-04

Super Bowl XXXVIII
Adam Vinatieri kicked a 41-yard field goal for the last points scored in the 32–29 Super Bowl win over the Carolina Panthers on 02-01-04

1964 regular season
Gino Cappelletti kicked a 41-yard field goal with one second left to defeat the Houston Oilers, 25–24, on 11-06-64

1988 regular season
Jason Staurovsky kicked a 27-yard field goal in minus-25 windchill weather to defeat the Tampa Bay Buccaneers, 10-7, in overtime on 12-11-88

1982 regular season
John Smith kicked a 33-yard field goal on a field of ice and snow in the 3–0 win over the Miami Dolphins on 12-12-82

1991 regular season
Jason Staurovsky kicked a 42-yard field goal on the last play of overtime to defeat the Minnesota Vikings, 26–23, on 10-20-91

1996 regular season
Adam Vinatieri kicked a 40-yard field goal with 36 seconds left in overtime to defeat the Jacksonville Jaguars, 28–25, on 09-22-96

1968 regular season
Gino Cappelletti kicked a tough-angled, seven-yard field goal to defeat the Denver Broncos, 20–17, on 09-29-68

League Leaders

The AFL leader with the most FGAs in a specific regular seeason

32 FGAs by Gino Cappelletti in 1961

38 FGAs by Gino Cappelletti in 1963

39 FGAs by Gino Cappelletti in 1964

The NFL leader with the most FGAs in a specific regular season

39 FGAs by Gino Cappelletti in 1964

33 FGAs by John Smith in 1979

41 FGAs by Tony Franklin in 1986

The AFL leader with the most field goals made in a specific regular season

17 field goals kicked by Gino Cappelletti in 1961

22 field goals kicked by Gino Cappelletti in 1963

25 field goals kicked by Gino Cappelletti in 1964

The NFL leader with the most field goals made in a specific regular season

25 field goals were kicked by Gino Cappelletti (and by St. Louis Cardinals kicker Jim Bakken) in 1964

32 field goals were kicked by Tony Franklin in 1986

31 field goals were kicked by Adam Vinatieri in 2004

The Patriots Kicker who had the best field-goal percentage by any kicker in the AFL in 1964

Gino Cappelletti led the AFL in field-goal percentage in the 1964 season

The Patriots Kicker who had the best field-goal percent of any kicker who played in every NFL game in 2004

Adam Vinatieri was 31–34 (.939) and had the best field-goal percentage of any NFL kicker who played in every game in 2004

The Playoffs

The progression of the longest field goal kicked by a Patriots player in a playoff game

28-yard field goal by Gino Cappelletti in the 26–8 win over the Buffalo Bills at War Memorial Stadium on 12-28-63

33-yard field goal by Gino Cappelletti in the 26–8 win over the Buffalo Bills at War Memorial Stadium on 12-28-63

36-yard field goal by Gino Cappelletti in the 26–8 win over the Buffalo Bills at War Memorial Stadium on 12-28-63

42-yard field goal by John Smith in the 28–13 loss to the Miami Dolphins at the Orange Bowl on 01-08-83

45-yard field goal by Tony Franklin in the 27–20 win over the Los Angeles Raiders at the Los Angeles Coliseum on 01-05-86

46-yard field goal by Adam Vinatieri in the 7–6 loss to the Pittsburgh Steelers at Three Rivers Stadium on 01-03-98

48-yard field goal by Adam Vinatieri to defeat the St. Louis Rams 20–17 at the Louisiana Superdome on 02-03-02

50-yard field goal by Stephen Gostkowski in the 24–21 win over the San Diego Chargers at Qualcomm on 01-14-07

The alphabetical listing of every Patriots Kicker and his longest field goal for his team in a playoff game

Matt Bahr hit a 33-yard field goal in the 20–13 loss to the Cleveland Browns at Cleveland Stadium on 01-01-95

Gino Cappelletti kicked a 36-yard field goal in the 26–8 win over the Buffalo Bills at War Memorial Stadium on 12-28-63

Tony Franklin kicked a 45-yard field goal in the 27–20 win over the Los Angeles Raiders at Los Angeles Coliseum on 01-05-86

Stephen Gostkowski kicked a 50-yard field goal in the 24–21 win over the San Diego Chargers at Qualcomm on 01-14-07

John Smith kicked a 42-yard field goal in the 28–13 loss to the Miami Dolphins at the Orange Bowl on 01-08-83

Adam Vinatieri kicked a 48-yard field goal to beat the St. Louis Rams, 20–17, at Louisiana Superdome on 02-03-02

Every Patriots Kicker who hit a field goal with less than 30 seconds to go in the first half of a playoff game

1986 AFC Divisional playoff game

Tony Franklin kicked a 38-yard field goal with two seconds left in the first half in the 22–17 loss to Denver on 01-04-87

1994 AFC wild-card playoff game

Matt Bahr kicked a 23-yard field goal with 30 seconds left in the first half in the 20–13 loss to the Browns on 01-01-95

The only Patriots player who kicked a game-winning field goal on the last play of a playoff game

Super Bowl XXXVI

Adam Vinatieri kicked a 48-yard field goal with seven seconds left to beat the Rams, 20–17, at the Superdome on 02-03-02

Super Bowl XXXVIII

Adam Vinatieri kicked a 41-yard field goal with four seconds left to defeat Carolina, 32–29, at Reliant Stadium on 02-01-04

The only Patriots player who kicked a game-tying field goal in the fourth quarter to force overtime in a playoff game

2001 AFC Divisional playoff game

Adam Vinatieri hit a game-tying, 45-yard field goal with 27 seconds left in the 16–13 overtime win over Oakland on 01-19-02

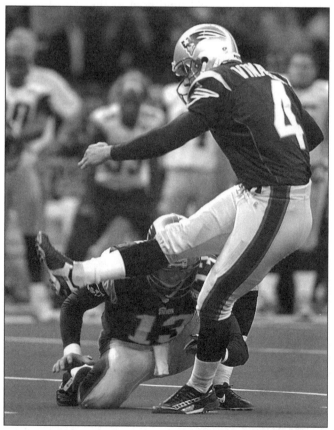

Adam Vinatieri

The only Patriots player who has kicked an overtime game-winning field goal in a playoff game

2001 AFC Divisional playoff game

Adam Vinatieri kicked a 23-yard field goal to defeat the Oakland Raiders, 16–13, in overtime at Foxboro Stadium on 01-19-02

The progression of the most field goals kicked by a Patriots player in a playoff game

4 field goals were kicked by Gino Cappelletti in the 26–8 victory over the Buffalo Bills at War Memorial Stadium on 12-28-63

4 field goals were kicked by Tony Franklin in the 26–14 win over the New York Jets at the Meadowlands on 12-28-85

5 field goals were kicked by Adam Vinatieri in the 24–14 victory over the Indianapolis Colts at Gillette Stadium on 01-18-04

The progression of the most consecutive playoff games in which a Patriots player kicked a field goal

2 consecutive playoff games that Gino Cappelletti kicked a field goal (from 12-28-63 to 01-05-64)

4 consecutive playoff games that Tony Franklin kicked a field goal (from 01-05-86 to 01-04-87)

12 consecutive playoff games that Adam Vinatieri kicked a field goal (from 01-28-97 to 02-06-05)

The progression of the most consecutive field goals by a Patriots Kicker in a playoff game

3rd consecutive field goal by Gino Cappelletti was from 33 yards in the 26–8 win over the Bills on 12-28-63

3rd consecutive field goal by Tony Franklin was from 20 yards in the 26–14 win over the Jets on 12-28-85

4th consecutive field goal by Tony Franklin was from 23 yards in the 31–14 win over Miami on 01-12-86

4th consecutive field goal by Adam Vinatieri was from 27 yards in the 25–10 win over Jacksonville on 01-03-99

8th consecutive field goal by Adam Vinatieri was from 44 yards in the 24–17 win over Pittsburgh on 01-27-02

The progression of the most points scored by a Patriots Kicker in a playoff game

14 points by Gino Cappelletti (4 field goals and two PATs) in the 26–8 win over the Bills at War Memorial Stadium on 12-28-63

14 points by Tony Franklin (4 field goals and two PATs) in the 26–14 win over the Jets at the Meadowlands on 12-28-85

16 points by Adam Vinatieri (5 field goals and one PAT) in the 24–14 win over the Colts at Gillette Stadium on 01-18-04

The Patriots playoff record when they kicked only one field goal in the game

The Patriots have won five of the six playoff games that Adam Vinatieri has kicked only one field goal

The Patriots lost both of the playoff games that Tony Franklin kicked only one field goal

Stephen Gostkowski kicked a 35-yard field goal in the 31–20 win over the Jacksonville Jaguars on 01-12-08

Gino Cappelletti kicked a 15-yard field goal in the AFL Championship Game loss to the San Diego Chargers on 01-05-64

The Patriots playoff record when they kicked exactly two field goals in the game

The Patriots have won four of the six playoff games when Adam Vinatieri has kicked two field goals

The Patriots lost in the only playoff games when its kicker Stephen Gostkowski kicked two field goals

The Patriots lost in the only playoff game when its kicker Tony Franklin booted two field goals

The Patriots lost in the only playoff game when its kicker Matt Bahr kicked two field goals

Every Patriots player who has kicked exactly three field goals in a playoff game

2001 AFC Divisional playoff game
Adam Vinatieri kicked three field goals in the 16–13 overtime win over the Oakland Raiders at Foxboro Stadium on 01-19-02

2006 AFC Wild Card playoff game
Stephen Gostkowski kicked three field goals in the 37–16 rout of the New York Jets at Gillette Stadium on 01-07-07

2006 AFC Divisional playoff game
Stephen Gostkowski kicked three field goals in the 24–21 win over the San Diego Chargers at Qualcomm on 01-14-07

The Patriots have won both playoff games when it kicked four field goals

1963 AFL Eastern Divisional playoff game
Gino Cappelletti kicked four field goals in the 26–8 victory over the Buffalo Bills on 12-28-63

1985 AFC Wild Card playoff game
Tony Franklin kicked four field goals in the 26–14 victory over the New York Jets on 12-28-85

The only Patriots player who has kicked five field goals in a playoff game

2003 AFC Championship playoff game
Adam Vinatieri kicked five field goals in the 24–14 AFC Championship Game win over the Colts on 01-18-04

The only player who has scored every point for the Patriots in a playoff game

1997 AFC Divisional playoff game
Adam Vinatieri kicked a 31-yard field goal and a 46-yard field goal in the 7–6 loss to the Steelers at Three Rivers Stadium on 01-03-98

The only Patriots Kicker who tied for the most field goals kicked in an AFL playoff game

1963 AFL Eastern Divisional playoff game
Gino Cappelletti kicked four field goals in the 26–8 win over the Buffalo Bills at War Memorial Stadium on 12-28-63

Every Patriots Kicker who has tied for the most field goals kicked in a NFL playoff game

1985 AFC Wild Card playoff game
Tony Franklin kicked four field goals in the 26–14 win over the New York Jets at the Meadowlands on 12-28-85

2003 AFC Championship Game
Adam Vinatieri kicked five field goals in the 24–14 victory over the Indianapolis Colts at Gillette Stadium on 01-18-04

Extra Point Section

The progression of the most extra points kicked by a Patriots player in a regular season game

1 extra point was kicked by Gino Cappelletti in the 13–10 loss to the Denver Broncos at BU Field on 09-09-60

4 extra points were kicked by Gino Cappelletti in the 28–24 win over the New York Titans at the Polo Grounds on 09-17-60

5 extra points were kicked by Gino Cappelletti in the 35–0 shutout of the Los Angeles Chargers at the Los Angeles Coliseum on 10-08-60

7 extra points were kicked by Gino Cappelletti in the 52–21 rout of the Buffalo Bills at BU Field on 10-22-61

8 extra points were kicked by John Smith in the 56–3 rout of the New York Jets at Schaefer Stadium on 09-09-79

8 extra points were kicked by Stephen Gostkowski in the 56–10 rout of the Buffalo Bills at Gillette Stadium on 11-18-07

The progression of the most consecutive games in which a Patriots player has kicked an extra point

2 consecutive games in which Gino Cappelletti kicked an extra point from 09-09-60 to 09-17-60

7 consecutive games in which Gino Cappelletti kicked an extra point from 10-23-60 to 12-04-60

10 consecutive games in which Gino Cappelletti kicked an extra point from 12-18-60 to 11-03-61

17 consecutive games in which Gino Cappelletti kicked an extra point from 11-17-61 to 12-09-62

21 consecutive games in which Gino Cappelletti kicked an extra point from 09-18-66 to 10-29-67

34 consecutive games in which John Smith kicked an extra point from 12-31-78 to 09-06-81

54 consecutive games in which Tony Franklin kicked an extra point from 09-02-84 to 09-21-87

The progression of the most extra points kicked by a Patriots player in a regular season

33 extra points were kicked by Gino Cappelletti in 1960

48 extra points were kicked by Gino Cappelletti in 1961

51 extra points were kicked by John Smith in 1980

74 extra points were kicked by Stephen Gostkowski in 2007

Every Patriots player who has kicked an extra point to force an overtime period in a regular season game

1981 regular season
John Smith kicked a PAT to tie the game with 29 seconds left in the 27–21 overtime loss to the Steelers on 09-27-81

1987 regular season
Tony Franklin kicked a PAT to tie the game with 65 seconds left in the 34–31 overtime loss to the Eagles on 11-29-87

1988 regular season
Jason Staurovsky kicked a PAT to tie the game in the third quarter in the 10–7 overtime win over the Buccaneers on 12-11-88

1991 regular season
Charlie Baumann kicked a PAT to tie the game with seven seconds left in the 23–17 overtime win over the Colts on 12-08-91

1993 regular season
Scott Sisson kicked a PAT with 12 seconds left to tie the game in the 19–16 overtime loss to the Lions on 09-12-93

1995 regular season
Matt Bahr kicked a PAT with 52 seconds left to tie the game in the 20–17 overtime loss to the Panthers on 10-29-95

2000 regular season
Adam Vinatieri kicked a PAT to tie the game with five minutes left in the 13–10 overtime win over the Bills on 12-17-00

Every Patriots player who kicked a PAT for the final point scored in regulation in a victorious overtime game

1988 regular season
Jason Staurovsky kicked a PAT in the third quarter to tie the game in the 10–7 overtime win over the Buccaneers on 12-11-88

1991 regular season
Charlie Baumann kicked a PAT with seven seconds left to tie the game in the 23–17 overtime win over the Colts on 12-08-91

2000 regular season
Adam Vinatieri kicked a PAT with five minutes left to tie the game in the 13–10 overtime win over the Bills on 12-17-00

The only Patriots player who has kicked a PAT for the last points scored for the Patriots in a tie game

1961 regular season

Gino Cappelletti kicked a PAT in the fourth quarter in the 31–31 tie with the Oilers at BU Field on 10-13-61

1962 regular season

Gino Cappelletti kicked a PAT in the fourth quarter in the 28–28 tie with the Bills at War Memorial Stadium on 11-03-62

1963 regular season

Gino Cappelletti kicked a PAT in the fourth quarter in the 24–24 tie with the Chiefs at Fenway Park on 11-17-63

1964 regular season

Gino Cappelletti kicked a PAT in the fourth quarter in the 43–43 tie with the Raiders at Fenway Park on 10-16-64

1965 regular season

Gino Cappelletti booted the final point scored in the 10–10 tie with the Chiefs at Fenway Park on 11-21-65

Every Patriots player who has kicked the extra point for the game-winning point scored in the game

1972 regular season

Mike Walker kicked a PAT for the final point in the 21–20 win over the Falcons at Schaefer Stadium on 09-24-72

Charlie Gogolak kicked a PAT in the fourth quarter in the 24–23 win over the Redskins at Schaefer Stadium on 10-01-72

1984 regular season

Tony Franklin kicked a PAT for the final point in the 17–16 win over the Browns at Cleveland on 10-07-84

1986 regular season

Tony Franklin kicked a PAT with 99 seconds left in the 21–20 win over the Saints at the Superdome on 11-30-86

1988 regular season

Jason Staurovsky kicked a PAT in the fourth quarter in the 14–13 win over the New York Jets at the Meadowlands on 11-13-88

1999 regular season

Adam Vinatieri kicked a PAT in the third quarter in the 24–23 win over the Denver Broncos at Foxboro Stadium on 10-24-99

Every Patriots Kicker who had 100 percent accuracy with his extra points kicked in a regular season

Gino Cappelletti kicked 36 consecutive extra points in 1964, 27 extra points in 1965, and 26 extra points in 1968

Charlie Gogolak kicked five extra points in 1970 and nine extra points in 1972

Mike Walker kicked 15 consecutive extra points in 1972

John Smith booted 33 consecutive extra points in 1975, 33 extra points in 1977, and 51 extra points in 1980

Nick Lowery kicked seven extra points in 1978

Dan Miller was 2-of-2 in 1982

Rex Robinson was 5-of-5 in 1982

Tony Franklin kicked 42 consecutive extra points in 1984

Jason Staurovsky kicked 14 consecutive extra points in 1989 and 19 extra points in 1990

Matt Bahr booted 10 consecutive extra points in 1993, 36 PATs in 1994, and 27 consecutive PATs in 1995

Scott Sisson kicked 15 consecutive extra points in 1993

Adam Vinatieri kicked 40 consecutive in 1997, 32 PATs in 1998, 25 PATs in 2000, 36 in 2002, and 48 in 2004

Stephen Gostkowski kicked 74 consecutive extra points in 2007 and 40 PATs in 2008

Every Patriots Kicker who was 100 percent accurate with his only extra-point attempt in the regular season

Justin Canale was 1-1 in the 18–7 victory over the Houston Oilers at Fenway Park on 11-05-67

Steve Zabel was 1-1 in the 31–14 victory over the Tampa Bay Buccaneers at Tampa Stadium on 12-12-76

Doug Flutie drop-kicked an extra point in the 28–26 loss to the Miami Dolphins at Gillette Stadium on 01-01-06

The amount of career regular season extra points by every Patriots Kicker

367 extra points by Adam Vinatieri over the 1996-2005 seasons

346 extra points by Gino Cappelletti over the 1960–70 regular seasons

308 extra points by John Smith over the 1974–83 regular seasons

163 extra points by Tony Franklin over the 1984–87 regular seasons

157 extra points by Stephen Gostkowski over the 2006–08 regular seasons

73 extra points by Matt Bahr over the 1993–95 regular seasons

57 extra points by Jason Staurovsky over the 1988–91 seasons

42 extra points by Charlie Gogolak over the 1970–72 seasons

31 extra points by Charlie Baumann over the 1991–92 seasons

29 extra points by David Posey during the 1978 season

21 extra points by Jeff White during the 1973 season

16 extra points by Fred Steinfort during the 1983 season

15 extra points by Mike "Superfoot" Walker during the 1972 season

15 extra points by Scott Sisson during the 1993 season

13 extra points by Greg Davis during the 1989 season

11 extra points by Teddy Garcia during the 1988 season

7 extra points by Nick Lowery during the 1978 season

5 extra points by Rex Robinson during the 1982 season

4 extra points by Bill Bell during the 1973 season

4 extra points by Danny Miller during the 1982 season

1 PAT by Justin Canale, who kicked an extra point in the 18–7 victory over the Houston Oilers on 11-05-67

1 PAT by Eric Schubert, who kicked an extra point in the 20–10 loss to the Cleveland Browns on 10-04-87

1 PAT by Steve Zabel, who kicked an extra point to end the game in the 31–14 win over the Tampa Bay Buccaneers on 12-12-76

1 PAT by Doug Flutie, who drop-kicked an extra point in the 28–26 loss to the Miami Dolphins on 01-01-06

Every Patriots Kicker who has run for a two-point conversion in a regular season game
1960 regular season
Gino Cappelletti ran for a two-point conversion in the 27–14 loss to the Oakland Raiders at Kezar Stadium on 10-16-60

Gino Cappelletti ran for a two-point conversion in the 42–14 rout of the Dallas Texans at BU Field on 11-18-60

Gino Cappelletti ran for a two-point conversion in the 37–21 loss to the Houston Oilers at Jeppsen Stadium on 12-18-60

1998 regular season
Adam Vinatieri ran for a two-point conversion in the 25–21 win over the Buffalo Bills at Foxboro Stadium on 11-29-98

The progression of the most career regular season points scored by a Patriots Kicker
874 career kicking points were scored by Gino Cappelletti from 09-09-60 to 12-20-70

1,156 career kicking points were scored by Adam Vinatieri during the 1996–2005 regular seasons

The progression of the most consecutive extra points kicked by a Patriots Kicker
109 consecutive extra points, including playoff games, were kicked by Gino Cappelletti from 11-17-63 to 12-17-66

129 consecutive extra points, including playoff games, were kicked by Adam Vinatieri from 10-27-96 to 10-31-99

The Playoffs

The progression of the most extra points kicked by a Patriots player in a playoff game
2 extra points by Gino Cappelletti in the 26–8 win over the Buffalo Bills at War Memorial Stadium on 12-28-63

3 extra points by John Smith in the 24–21 loss to the Oakland Raiders at the Oakland Coliseum on 12-18-76

3 extra points by Tony Franklin in the 27–20 win over the Los Angeles Raiders at the Los Angeles Coliseum on 01-05-86

4 extra points by Tony Franklin in the 31–14 victory over the Miami Dolphins at the Orange Bowl on 01-12-86

4 extra points by Adam Vinatieri in the 28–3 rout of the Pittsburgh Steelers at Foxboro Stadium on 01-05-97

5 extra points by Adam Vinatieri in the 41–27 victory over the Pittsburgh Steelers at Heinz Field on 01-23-05

The progression of the most consecutive extra points kicked by a Patriots player in the playoffs
3 consecutive extra points were kicked by Gino Cappelletti in the playoff games from 12-28-63 to 01-05-64

6 consecutive extra points were kicked by John Smith in the playoff games from 12-18-76 to 01-08-83

12 consecutive extra points were kicked by Tony Franklin in the playoff games from 12-28-85 to 01-04-87

39 consecutive extra points were kicked by Adam Vinatieri in the playoff games from 01-05-97 to 01-14-06

The progression of the most consecutive playoff games in which a Patriots player kicked an extra point

2 consecutive playoff games in which Gino Cappelletti kicked an extra point for the Boston Patriots

3 consecutive playoff games in which John Smith kicked an extra point for the New England Patriots

5 consecutive playoff games in which Tony Franklin kicked an extra point for the New England Patriots

12 consecutive playoff games in which Adam Vinatieri kicked an extra point for the New England Patriots

The progression of the most career extra points kicked by a Patriots player in the playoffs

3 extra points were kicked by Gino Cappelletti in the playoff games on 12-28-63 and 01-05-64

6 extra points were kicked by John Smith in the playoff games from 12-18-76 to 01-08-83

12 extra points were kicked by Tony Franklin in the playoff games from 12-28-85 to 01-04-87

39 extra points were kicked by Adam Vinatieri in the playoff games from 01-05-97 to 01-14-06

The alphabetical listing of every player who has kicked an extra point for the Patriots in the playoffs

Matt Bahr kicked an extra point in the 20–13 AFC playoff game loss to the Cleveland Browns on 01-01-95

Gino Cappelletti kicked three extra points for the Boston Patriots in the playoffs

Tony Franklin kicked 12 extra points for the New England Patriots in the playoffs

Stephen Gostkowski has kicked 18 extra points for the New England Patriots in the playoffs

John Smith kicked six extra points for the New England Patriots in the playoffs

Adam Vinatieri kicked 39 extra points for the New England Patriots in the playoffs

The progression of the most career points scored by a Patriots player in the playoffs

18 points were scored by Gino Cappelletti in the two playoff games on 12-28-63 and 01-05-64

39 points were scored by Tony Franklin in the five playoff games from 12-28-85 to 01-04-87

117 points have been scored by Adam Vinatieri in the 17 playoff games from 01-05-97 to 01-14-06

The amount of playoff games played by every Kicker for the Patriots

17 playoff games by Adam Vinatieri for the New England Patriots

6 playoff games by Stephen Gostkowski for the New England Patriots

5 playoff games by Tony Franklin for the New England Patriots

3 playoff games by John Smith for the New England Patriots

2 playoff games by Gino Cappelletti for the Boston Patriots

1 playoff game by Matt Bahr, as he was the Patriots kicker in the 1994 AFC Wild Card playoff game on 01-01-95

Punting

Since 1960, 39 players have punted the football in a regular season game for the Patriots. There have been six quarterbacks who have punted in a regular season game for the Patriots: Tom Greene, Tom Yewcic, Babe Parilli, Eddie Wilson, Tom Brady, and Matt Cassel. Tom Greene is the only Patriots player who has returned a kickoff, completed a pass, and punted in the same regular season game. Tom Greene ran seven times, completed 27 passes (including one for a touchdown), punted the ball 61 times, and returned a kickoff during the 1960 season. Boston Patriots quarterback Babe Parilli punted the

ball five times in the 24–14 loss to the Buffalo Bills at Fenway Park on 12-20-64.

The Boston Patriots had a player who not only punted but was also used as a quarterback, a running back, and a flanker/receiver. Tom Yewcic threw 12 touchdown passes, ran for four touchdowns, caught seven passes, and punted 377 times over his six-year career with the Patriots. He has the longest run by a Patriots punter as he ran 20 yards for a first down in the 26–16 victory over the Oakland Raiders at BU Field on 10-26-62.

Clyde Washington is the only player who has played on both the offensive and defensive sides of the ball, and has punted for the Patriots in a regular season game. Clyde carried the ball three times, intercepted seven passes, and punted 17 times over the 1960–61 seasons.

There have been three defensive players who have punted in a regular season game for the Patriots: Clyde Washington, Jim Fraser, and Tom Janik. Linebacker Jim Fraser had 1.5 sacks, intercepted a pass, and punted 55 times for the Boston Patriots during the 1966 season. Tom Janik is the only Patriots player who has punted and attempted to return a punt in the same game. Janik had five punts for 178 yards and he returned a punt by Larry Seiple for no gain in the 17–16 loss to the Miami Dolphins at Boston College Alumni Stadium on 11-09-69.

This section will have a listing for the longest punt, the most punts, and other punting statistics of every Patriots player who has punted the football in a game for the Patriots. You will know every game in which there were no punts by a Patriots punter and every game in which there was only one punt by a Patriots punter. This section contains the names of every Patriots player who has punted the football 70 yards or more in a regular season game. If you were interested in finding the progression of the most punts by a Patriots player in the first half of a game, and in the second half of a game this is the place to find that information. We have the names of every Patriots punter who was named the AFC Special Teams Player of the Week.

Tom Greene was the primary punter for the Boston Patriots during the 1960 season. Tom Yewcic was the only punter for the team during the 1961–63 seasons and only missed two games as punter for the team during the 1964–65 seasons. Jim Fraser then led the team with 55 punts during the 1966 season. Terry Swanson had the most punts for the Boston Patriots during the 1967 and 1968 seasons. Tom Janik was the only punter for the Patriots in the 1969–71 seasons. Pat Studstill punted 75 times for the team during the 1972 season. Bruce Barnes had the most punts for the New England Patriots in the 1973 and 1974 seasons. Mike Patrick was the Patriots only punter during the 1975–77 seasons. Former Kansas City Chiefs punter Jerrel Wilson was the Patriots punter during the 1978 season. Eddie Hare was the only punter for the Patriots in 1979, and Mike Hubach was the only punter for the team in 1980.

Rich Camarillo is the arguably best punter ever to play for the Patriots, as he led the team for seven consecutive years. Rich was the only Patriots punter to be named to the Pro Bowl. Rich holds the team record with 468 punts for 19,922 yards and averaged 42.6 yards per punt during the 1981–87 seasons.

Jeff Feagles was the first Patriots player to punt more than 90 times during the season as he had 91 punts during the 1988 season. Jeff was the only punter for the Patriots during the 1989 season as well. Brian Hansen punted 90 times for the Patriots in the 1990 season. Shawn McCarthy had the most punts for the Patriots in 1991, and he set the team record with 103 punts during the 1992 season. Mike Saxon was the only punter for the Patriots in 1993. Fifth-round draft pick Pat O'Neill led the team in punting over the 1994–95 seasons. Former NFL quarterback Tom Tupa led the Patriots in punting over the 1996–98 seasons. Lee Johnson was the punter for the New England Patriots over the 1999–2000 seasons. Ken Walter was the Patriots leading punter over the 2001–03 seasons and he was the punter in the first two World Championship games. Josh Miller was the only punter for the 2004 World Championship New England Patriots team and the 2005 team. Josh Miller, Ken Walter, and Todd Sauerbrun shared the punting duties for the Patriots during the 2006 regular season. Chris Hanson was the only punter for the Patriots during the 2007 undefeated regular season. Chris Hanson led the team in yards punted in 2008.

Every Patriots punter who was named the AFC Special Teams Player of the Week

Mike Saxon had a 50-yard punt and had three inside the 20 in the 23–21 win over the Cardinals at Sun Devil Stadium on 10-10-93

Pat O'Neill had a 67-yard punt and three punts for 143 yards in the 41–17 rout of the Bills at Rich Stadium on 12-18-94

Tom Tupa had a 62-yard punt and four punts for 201 yards in the 28–25 win over the Bills at Foxboro Stadium on 10-27-96

Ken Walter had five punts inside the 20-yard line in the 20–13 win over the Miami Dolphins at Foxboro Stadium on 12-22-01

Chris Hanson punted well in windy conditions in the 13–0 win over the Bills at Ralph Wilson Stadium on 12-28-08

The Patriots player with the most punts, the longest punt, and the best punting average in each season

Year	Most Punts	Longest Punt	Best Punting Average
1960	Tom Greene	Tom Greene	Tom Greene
1961	Tom Yewcic	Tom Yewcic	Tom Yewcic
1962	Tom Yewcic	Tom Yewcic	Tom Yewcic
1963	Tom Yewcic	Tom Yewcic	Tom Yewcic
1964	Tom Yewcic	Tom Yewcic	Tom Yewcic
1965	Jim Fraser	Jim Fraser	Jim Fraser
1966	Terry Swanson	Terry Swanson	Terry Swanson
1967	Terry Swanson	Bob Scarpitto	Bob Scarpitto
1968	Tom Janik	Tom Janik	Tom Janik
1969	Tom Janik	Tom Janik	Tom Janik
1970	Tom Janik	Tom Janik	Tom Janik
1971	Pat Studstill	Pat Studstill	Pat Studstill
1972	Bruce Barnes	Bruce Barnes	Bruce Barnes
1973	Bruce Barnes	Dave Chapple	Dave Chapple
1974	Mike Patrick	Mike Patrick	Mike Patrick
1975	Mike Patrick	Mike Patrick	Mike Patrick
1976	Mike Patrick	Mike Patrick	Mike Patrick
1977	Mike Patrick	Mike Patrick	Mike Patrick
1978	Jerrel Wilson	Jerrel Wilson	Jerrel Wilson
1979	Eddie Hare	Eddie Hare	Eddie Hare
1980	Mike Hubach	Mike Hubach	Mike Hubach
1981	Rich Camarillo	Rich Camarillo	Rich Camarillo
1982	Rich Camarillo	Rich Camarillo	Rich Camarillo
1983	Rich Camarillo	Rich Camarillo	Rich Camarillo
1984	Rich Camarillo	Luke Prestridge	Luke Prestridge
1985	Rich Camarillo	Rich Camarillo	Rich Camarillo
1986	Rich Camarillo	Rich Camarillo	Rich Camarillo
1987	Rich Camarillo	Rich Camarillo	Rich Camarillo
1988	Jeff Feagles	Jeff Feagles	Jeff Feagles
1989	Jeff Feagles	Jeff Feagles	Jeff Feagles
1990	Brian Hansen	Brian Hansen	Brian Hansen
1991	Shawn McCarthy	Shawn McCarthy	Shawn McCarthy
1992	Shawn McCarthy	Shawn McCarthy	Shawn McCarthy
1993	Mike Saxon	Mike Saxon	Mike Saxon
1994	Pat O'Neill	Pat O'Neill	Pat O'Neill
1995	Pat O'Neill	Bryan Wagner	Pat O'Neill and Bryan Wagner
1996	Tom Tupa	Tom Tupa	Tom Tupa
1997	Tom Tupa	Tom Tupa	Tom Tupa
1998	Tom Tupa	Tom Tupa	Tom Tupa
1999	Lee Johnson	Lee Johnson	Lee Johnson
2000	Lee Johnson	Lee Johnson	Lee Johnson
2001	Ken Walter	Lee Johnson	Lee Johnson
2002	Ken Walter	Ken Walter	Ken Walter
2003	Ken Walter	Ken Walter	Ken Walter
2004	Josh Miller	Josh Miller	Josh Miller
2005	Josh Miller	Josh Miller	Josh Miller
2006	Josh Miller	Josh Miller	Josh Miller
2007	Chris Hanson	Chris Hanson	Chris Hanson
2008	Chris Hanson	Chris Hanson	Chris Hanson

The only AFC Pro Bowl Punter for the New England Patriots

Rich Camarillo was an AFC Pro Bowl punter for the New England Patriots in 1983

Every regular season game in which there were no punts by the Patriots Punter

1966 regular season

There were no punts by the Patriots in the 38–14 win over the Houston Oilers at Rice Stadium on 12-11-66

1967 regular season

There were no punts by the Patriots in the 41–32 loss to the Miami Dolphins at the Orange Bowl on 12-17-67

1978 regular season

There were no punts by the Patriots in the 26–23 loss to the Houston Oilers at Schaefer Stadium on 11-12-78

Every Patriots Punter who only had to punt once in a regular season game

1960 regular season

*Clyde Washington punted once for 38 yards in the 42–14 rout of the Dallas Texans at BU Field on 11-18-60

1961 regular season

Tom Yewcic punted once for 49 yards in the 35–21 win over the Oakland Raiders at Candlestick Park on 12-09-61

1962 regular season

Tom Yewcic punted once for 28 yards in the 33–29 victory over the Denver Broncos at Bears Stadium on 11-11-62

1963 regular season

Tom Yewcic punted once for 33 yards in the 31–24 loss to the New York Jets at the Polo Grounds on 10-05-63

1965 regular season

Tom Yewcic punted once for 51 yards in the 42–14 rout of the Houston Oilers at Fenway Park on 12-18-65

1978 regular season

Jerrel Wilson punted once for 31 yards in the 55–21 rout of the New York Jets at Schaefer Stadium on 10-29-78

1980 regular season

Mike Hubach punted once for 37 yards in the 34–17 win over the Cleveland Browns at Schaefer Stadium on 09-07-80

Mike Hubach punted once for 28 yards in the 24–2 rout of the Buffalo Bills at Schaefer Stadium on 12-14-80

1981 regular season

Mike Hubach punted once for 21 yards in the 33–17 win over the Kansas City Chiefs at Schaefer Stadium on 10-04-81

1994 regular season

Pat O'Neill punted once for 50 yards in the 31–28 victory over the Cincinnati Bengals at Riverfront on 09-18-94

1996 regular season

Tom Tupa punted once for 47 yards in the 31–27 victory over the New York Jets at the Meadowlands on 11-10-96

2006 regular season

Josh Miller punted once for 46 yards in the 27–20 loss to the Indianapolis Colts at Gillette Stadium on 11-05-06

2007 undefeated regular season

Chris Hanson punted once for 53 yards in the 38–14 rout of the New York Jets at the Meadowlands on 09-09-07

Chris Hanson punted once for 34 yards in the 38–14 rout of the San Diego Chargers at Gillette Stadium on 09-16-07

Chris Hanson punted once for 38 yards in the 34–13 win over the Cincinnati Bengals at Paul Brown Stadium on 10-01-07

Chris Hanson punted once for 36 yards in the 56–10 rout of the Buffalo Bills at Ralph Wilson Stadium on 11-18-07

2008 regular season

Chris Hanson punted once for 64 yards in the 18–15 loss to the Indianapolis Colts at Lucas Oil Stadium on 11-02-08

*Clyde Washington actually punted twice, but the Texans were penalized for roughing the kicker on 11-18-60

The progression of the longest punt by a Patriots Punter in a regular season game

44-yard punt by Tom Greene in the 13–10 loss to the Denver Broncos at BU Field on 09-09-60

50-yard punt by Tom Greene in the 13–10 loss to the Denver Broncos at BU Field on 09-09-60

66-yard punt by Tom Greene in the 27–14 loss to the Oakland Raiders at Kezar Stadium on 10-16-60

66-yard punt by Tom Greene in the 45–16 loss to the Los Angeles Chargers at BU Field on 10-28-60

70-yard punt by Tom Yewcic in the 27–23 victory over the New York Jets at Shea Stadium on 11-28-65

87-yard punt by Bob Scarpitto in the 20–17 victory over the Denver Broncos at Bears Stadium on 09-29-68

89-yard punt by Luke Prestridge in the 44–24 loss to the Miami Dolphins at Sullivan Stadium on 10-21-84

93-yard punt by Shawn McCarthy in the 22–17 loss to the Buffalo Bills at Rich Stadium on 11-03-91

Every Patriots Quarterback who has punted in a regular season game
1960 regular season

Tom Greene had six punts for 243 yards in the 13–10 loss to the Denver Broncos at BU Field on 09-09-60

Tom Greene punted five times for 190 yards in the 28–24 win over the New York Titans at the Polo Grounds on 09-17-60

Tom Greene had three punts for 124 yards in the 13–0 loss to the Buffalo Bills at BU Field on 09-23-60

Tom Greene punted four times for 171 yards in the 45–16 loss to the Los Angeles Chargers at BU Field on 10-28-60

Tom Greene had nine punts for 293 yards in the 38–14 loss to the Bills at War Memorial Stadium on 12-04-60

Tom Greene punted nine times for 275 yards in the 34–0 loss to the Dallas Texans at the Cotton Bowl on 12-11-60

1964 regular season
Babe Parilli punted five times for 180 yards in the 24–14 loss to the Buffalo Bills at Fenway Park on 12-20-64

1965 regular season
Ed Wilson punted six times for 194 yards in the 13–13 tie with the San Diego Chargers at Fenway Park on 10-17-65

2003 championship season
Tom Brady punted the football 36 yards in the 12–0 shutout of the Dolphins at Gillette Stadium on 12-07-03

2008 regular season
Matt Cassel's 57-yard punt was downed on the 2-yard line in the 13–0 win over Buffalo at Ralph Wilson Stadium on 12-28-08

Every Patriots Place-Kicker who has punted in a regular season game
1973 regular season
Jeff White punted six times in the 30–14 loss to the Miami Dolphins at Schaefer Stadium on 10-28-73

1995 regular season
Matt Bahr punted the football 29 yards in the 27–14 victory over the Buffalo Bills at Foxboro Stadium on 10-23-95

1996 regular season
Adam Vinatieri punted the football 27 yards in the 34–10 rout of the New York Jets at Foxboro Stadium on 12-08-96

2001 championship season
Adam Vinatieri punted the football 33 yards in the 27–16 win over the Cleveland Browns at Foxboro Stadium on 12-09-01

The only Patriots player who has punted, returned a kickoff, and completed a pass in the same game
Tom Greene punted four times, had a three-yard kickoff return, and completed three passes in the 45–16 loss to Los Angeles on 10-28-60

The only Patriots player who has punted the football and attempted to return a punt in the same game
Tom Janik punted five times and returned a punt for no gain in the 17–16 loss to Miami at BC Stadium on 11-09-69

Every Patriots player who has punted the football at least 80 yards in a regular season game
1968 regular season
Bob Scarpitto punted it 87 yards to the 3-yard line in the 20–17 win over Denver Broncos at Bears Stadium on 09-29-68

1984 regular season
Luke Prestridge punted it 89 yards for a touchback in the 44–24 loss to the Miami Dolphins at Sullivan on 10-21-84

Luke Prestridge punted it 82 yards to the 1-yard line in the 30–20 win over the New York Jets at Sullivan on 10-28-84

1991 regular season

Shawn McCarthy punted it 93 yards to the 1-yard line in the 22–17 loss to the Buffalo Bills at Rich Stadium on 11-03-91

The two most recent times that a Patriots Punter helped set up a two-point safety for the Patriots

1996 regular season

Tom Tupa's punt was downed on the 1-yard line, which set up a safety in the 28–25 win over the Bills on 10-27-96 (Mike Jones forced Buffalo's quarterback Jim Kelly to down the ground the ball for the two-point safety at Foxboro Stadium)

2003 championship season

Tom Brady's punt was downed on the 1-yard line, which set up a safety in the 12–0 shutout of Miami on 12-07-03 (Jarvis Green and Mike Vrabel sacked Jay Fiedler on fourth down for a two-point safety at Gillette Stadium)

The progression of the highest average yards per punt by a Patriots Punter in a regular season

36.9 average yards per punt by Tom Greene in 1960

37.6 average yards per punt by Tom Yewcic in 1961

38.5 average yards per punt by Tom Yewcic in 1962

38.7 average yards per punt by Tom Yewcic in 1964

40.7 average yards per punt by Tom Yewcic in 1965

41.5 average yards per punt by Tom Janik in 1969

41.7 average yards per punt by Rich Camarillo in 1981

43.7 average yards per punt by Rich Camarillo in 1982

44.6 average yards per punt by Rich Camarillo in 1983

45.8 average yards per punt by Tom Tupa in 1997

The only New England Patriots Punter/Quarterback to kneel on the last two plays of a game

Tom Tupa knelt on the last two plays of the game in the 40–10 rout of the Kansas City Chiefs at Foxboro Stadium on 10-11-98

Did you know that?

Tom Tupa played quarterback for the Arizona Cardinals and the New York Jets in games against the New England Patriots. In fact, Tupa was sacked by Patriots players Vincent Brown, Steve Israel, and Willie McGinest.

The progression of the most punts by a Patriots Punter in a regular season game

6 punts by Tom Greene in the 13–10 loss to the Denver Broncos at BU Field on 09-09-60

7 punts by Tom Greene in the 28–24 victory over the New York Titans at the Polo Grounds on 09-17-60

9 punts by Tom Greene in the 38–14 loss to the Buffalo Bills at War Memorial Stadium on 12-04-60

10 punts by Tom Greene in the 37–21 loss to the Houston Oilers at Jeppesen Stadium on 12-18-60

11 punts by Jim Fraser in the 24–24 tie with the New York Jets at Fenway Park on 10-02-66

11 punts by Rich Camarillo in the 20–17 loss to the Dallas Cowboys at Texas Stadium on 11-22-84

11 punts by Rich Camarillo in the 20–7 loss to the Chicago Bears at Soldier Field on 09-15-85

11 punts by Shawn McCarthy in the 31–14 loss to the New Orleans Saints at Foxboro Stadium on 11-08-92

The most punts by a Patriots Punter in the first half of a regular season game

7 punts by Tom Greene in the 37–21 loss to the Houston Oilers at Jeppesen Stadium on 12-18-60

7 punts by Tom Yewcic in the 17–7 victory over the Buffalo Bills at Fenway Park on 12-01-63

7 punts by Jim Fraser in the 24–0 loss to the San Diego Chargers at Balboa Stadium on 09-10-66

7 punts by Rich Camarillo in the 20–17 loss to the Dallas Cowboys at Texas Stadium on 11-22-84

The most punts by a Patriots Punter in the second half of a regular season game

7 punts by Mike Patrick in the 21–10 victory over the Baltimore Colts at Schaefer Stadium on 10-19-75

The progression of the most yards punted by a Patriots Punter in a regular season game

243 yards punted by Tom Greene in the 13–10 loss to the Denver Broncos at BU Field on 09-09-60

262 yards punted by Tom Greene in the 28–24 victory over the New York Titans at the Polo Grounds on 09-17-60

293 yards punted by Tom Greene in the 38–14 loss to the Buffalo Bills at War Memorial Stadium on 12-04-60

373 yards punted by Tom Greene in the 37–21 loss to the Houston Oilers at Jeppesen Stadium on 12-18-60

417 yards punted by Tom Yewcic in the 36–28 win over the Buffalo Bills at War Memorial Stadium on 11-15-64

436 yards punted by Bob Scarpitto in the 41–10 loss to the Oakland Raiders at the Oakland Coliseum on 10-06-68

479 yards punted by Rich Camarillo in the 20–17 loss to the Dallas Cowboys at Texas Stadium on 11-22-84

514 yards punted by Rich Camarillo in the 20–7 loss to the Chicago Bears at Soldier Field on 09-15-85

The progression of the most punts and kickoffs by the same Patriots player in a regular season game

9: Jeff White punted six times and kicked off three times in the 30–14 loss to the Dolphins at Schaefer Stadium on 10-28-73

10: Mike Hubach punted six times and kicked off four times in the 37–21 loss to the Falcons at Schaefer Stadium on 09-14-80

11: Mike Hubach punted four times and kicked off seven times in the 37–31 win over Seattle at the Kingdome on 09-21-80

11: Mike Hubach punted six times and kicked off five times in the 21–11 win over the NY Jets at Shea Stadium on 10-05-80

11: Mike Hubach punted four times and kicked off seven times in the 34–0 shutout of Miami at Schaefer Stadium on 10-12-80

13: Mike Hubach punted six times and kicked off seven times in the 34–21 win over the Jets at Schaefer Stadium on 11-02-80

13: Pat O'Neill punted seven times and kicked off six times in the 31–26 loss to the Chiefs at Arrowhead Stadium on 10-15-95

13: Bryan Wagner punted seven times and kicked off six times in the 31–28 win over the Jets at Foxboro Stadium on 12-10-95

The only Patriots player who has sacked a quarterback, intercepted a pass, and punted the football in the same season

Jim Fraser recorded 1.5 sacks, returned a pass three yards, and punted 55 times for the Patriots during the 1966 season

The only Patriots player who has punted the ball and caught a TD pass in the same season

Bob Scarpitto caught two passes for 49 yards and punted 34 times for 1,382 yards during the 1968 season

The progression of the most punts by a Patriots Punter in a regular season

61 punts by Tom Greene in 1960

64 punts by Tom Yewcic in 1961

69 punts by Tom Yewcic in 1962

75 punts by Tom Yewcic in 1963

76 punts by Tom Yewcic in 1965

86 punts by Tom Janik in 1970

87 punts by Tom Janik in 1971

92 punts by Rich Camarillo in 1985

103 punts by Shawn McCarthy in 1992

The progression of the most yards punted by a Patriots Punter in a regular season

2,253 yards punted by Tom Greene in 1960

2,406 yards punted by Tom Yewcic in 1961

2,654 yards punted by Tom Yewcic in 1962

2,880 yards punted by Tom Yewcic in 1963

3,094 yards punted by Tom Yewcic in 1965

3,364 yards punted by Tom Janik in 1970

3,615 yards punted by Rich Camarillo in 1983

3,953 yards punted by Rich Camarillo in 1985

4,212 yards punted by Shawn McCarthy in 1992

Did you know that?

Tom Janik is the only Patriots player who has intercepted a pass, recovered two fumbles, and punted during his career.

Janik intercepted a pass by Greg Cook, recovered two of his own fumbles, and punted 243 times during the 1969–71 seasons.

Did you know that?

Tom Yewcic and Tom Brady are the only Patriots who have punted, thrown a TD pass, caught a pass, and run for a TD.

The amount of career regular season punts by every Patriots player

468 punts by Rich Camarillo during the 1981–87 seasons

377 punts by Tom Yewcic during the 1961–66 seasons

243 punts by Tom Janik during the 1969–71 seasons

222 punts by Mike Patrick during the 1975–78 seasons

215 punts by Tom Tupa during the 1996–98 seasons

211 punts by Ken Walter during the 2001–03 and 2006 seasons

203 punts by Lee Johnson during the 1999–2001 seasons

175 punts by Josh Miller during the 2004–06 seasons

169 punts by Shawn McCarthy during the 1991–92 seasons

154 punts by Jeff Feagles during the 1988–89 seasons

127 punts by Terry Swanson during the 1967–68 seasons

110 punts by Pat O'Neill during the 1994–95 seasons

100 punts by Bruce Barnes during the 1973–74 seasons

93 punts by Chris Hanson during the 2007–08 seasons

90 punts by Brian Hansen in the 1990 season

83 punts by Eddie Hare in the 1979 season

82 punts by Mike Hubach, who had 63 punts in the 1980 season and 19 punts in the 1981 season

75 punts by Pat Studstill in the 1972 season

73 punts by Mike Saxon in the 1993 season

61 punts by Tom Greene in the 1960 season

55 punts by Jim Fraser in the 1966 season

54 punts by Jerrel Wilson in the 1978 season

51 punts by Bryan Wagner, who had 14 punts in the 1991 season and 37 punts in the 1995 season

44 punts by Luke Prestridge in the 1984 season

44 punts by Chris Hanson in the 2007 season

34 punts by Bob Scarpitto in the 1968 season

26 punts by Dave Chapple in five games in the 1974 season

25 punts by Alan Herline in three games in the 1987 season

17 punts by Clyde Washington in the 1960 season

10 punts by Brooks Barnard in the 12–0 shutout of the Miami Dolphins on 12-07-03

10 punts by Todd Sauerbrun in the 2006 season

9 punts by Ken Hartley in two games in the 1981 season

6 punts by Jeff White in the 30–14 loss to the Miami Dolphins on 10-28-73

6 punts by Eddie Wilson in the 13–13 tie with the San Diego Chargers on 10-17-65

5 punts by Babe Parilli in the 24–14 loss to the Buffalo Bills on 12-20-64

2 punts by Adam Vinatieri; one was for 27 yards on 12-08-96 and the other punt went for 33 yards on 12-09-01

1 punt by Matt Bahr for 29 yards in the 27–14 victory over the Buffalo Bills on 10-23-95

1 punt by Tom Brady for 36 yards in the 12–0 shutout of the Miami Dolphins on 12-07-03

1 punt by Matt Cassel for 57 yards in the 13–0 shutout of the Buffalo Bills on 12-28-08

The progression of the most career regular season yards punted by a Patriots player

2,253 career yards punted by Tom Greene in the 1960 season

14,553 career yards punted by Tom Yewcic over the 1961–66 seasons

19,922 career yards punted by Rich Camarillo over the 1981–87 seasons

Patriots Punters Who have Led the League in a Particular Punting Category

The only Patriots Punter to lead the NFL with the best average net yards per punt

Rich Camarillo led the NFL with a 37.1 average net yards per punt in the 1983 season

The only Patriots player to lead the NFL with best average yards per punt

Tom Tupa led the NFL with a 44.5 average yards per punt in the 1998 season

The only Patriots Punter to lead the NFL with the most yards punted during the season

Rich Camarillo led the NFL with 3,953 yards punted during the 1985 season

The only Patriots Punter to lead the NFL with the most punts during the season

Rich Camarillo led the NFL with 92 punts during the 1985 season

Every Patriots Punter who had the longest punt in the NFL during a specific regular season

1981 regular season
Rich Camarillo had the longest punt in the NFL of 75 yards in the 27–17 loss to the Raiders at Oakland on 11-01-81

1983 regular season
Rich Camarillo had the longest punt in the NFL of 70 yards in the 7–0 shutout of the Saints at Sullivan Stadium on 12-04-83

1984 regular season
Luke Prestridge had the longest punt in the NFL of 89 yards in the 44–24 loss to Miami at Sullivan Stadium on 10-21-84

1985 regular season
Rich Camarillo had the longest punt in the NFL of 75 yards in the 20–7 loss to the Bears at Soldier Field on 09-15-85

1988 regular season
Jeff Feagles had the longest punt in the NFL of 74 yards in the 21–17 win over the Colts at Sullivan on 10-02-88

1991 regular season
Shawn McCarthy hit the NFL's longest punt of 93 yards in the 22–17 loss to Buffalo at Rich Stadium on 11-03-91

The first time that a NFL Punter had two punts of more than 80 yards during the regular season

1984 regular season
Luke Prestridge boomed an 89-yard punt in the 44–24 loss to the Miami Dolphins at Sullivan Stadium on 10-21-84

Luke Prestridge booted an 82-yard punt in the 30–20 win over the New York Jets at Sullivan Stadium on 10-28-84

The only Patriots Punter to tie for the league lead with the most punts in a game during the regular season

Rich Camarillo tied for the league lead with 11 punts in the 20–7 loss to the Bears at Soldier Field on 09-15-85

The Top 10 greatest punts by a Patriots Punter

1968 regular season
Bob Scarpitto punted it 87 yards to the 3-yard line in the 20–17 win over the Denver Broncos on 09-22-68

1983 regular season
Rich Camarillo punted it 70 yards to the 8-yard line in the 7–0 shutout of the New Orleans Saints on 12-04-83

1991 regular season
Shawn McCarthy booted it 93 yards to the 1-yard line in the 22–17 loss to the Buffalo Bills on 11-03-91

1984 regular season
Luke Prestridge punted it 82 yards to the 1-yard line in the 30–20 win over the New York Jets on 10-28-84

1996 regular season
Tom Tupa's punt was downed on the 1-yard line that helped set up a safety in the 28–25 win over Buffalo on 10-27-96

2003 championship season
Tom Brady's 36-yard punt to the 1-yard line, helped set up a safety in the 12–0 shutout of Miami on 12-07-03

1994 regular season
Pat O'Neill, on a fake field goal pooch, punted the ball to the 1-yard line in the 24–13 win over the Jets on 12-04-94

1963 AFL Championship Game
Tom Yewcic set the team playoff record with his 68-yard punt in the 51–10 loss to San Diego on 01-05-64

1977 regular season
Mike Patrick's fourth-quarter punt was downed on the 4-yard line in the 21–17 win over the Kansas City Chiefs on 09-18-77

2003 championship season
Ken Walter's fourth-quarter punt was downed on the 1-yard line in the 9–3 win over the Cleveland Browns on 10-26-03

The Playoffs

The progression of the longest punt by a Patriots Punter in a playoff game

20-yard punt by Tom Yewcic in the 26–8 victory over the Buffalo Bills at War Memorial Stadium on 12-28-63

46-yard punt by Tom Yewcic in the 26–8 victory over the Buffalo Bills at War Memorial Stadium on 12-28-63

68-yard punt by Tom Yewcic in the 51–10 loss to the San Diego Chargers at Balboa Stadium on 01-05-64

The career longest punt by every Patriots player in a playoff game

Tom Yewcic punted it 68 yards in the 51–10 loss to the San Diego Chargers at Balboa Stadium on 01-05-64

Mike Patrick had a 51-yard punt in the 24–21 loss to the Oakland Raiders at the Oakland Coliseum on 12-18-76

Jerrel Wilson punted the football 55 yards in the 31–14 loss to the Houston Oilers at Schaefer Stadium on 12-31-78

Rich Camarillo had a 62-yard punt in the 46–10 loss to the Chicago Bears at the Louisiana Superdome on 01-26-86

Pat O'Neill punted the football 51 yards in the 20–13 loss to the Cleveland Browns at Cleveland on 01-01-95

Tom Tupa had a 58-yard punt in the 25–10 loss to the Jacksonville Jaguars at Alltel Stadium on 01-03-99

Ken Walter punted the football 53 yards in the 20–17 win over the St. Louis Rams at the Superdome on 02-03-02

Josh Miller had a 52-yard punt in the 20–3 rout of the Indianapolis Colts at Gillette Stadium on 01-16-05

Todd Sauerbrun punted it 59 yards in the 38–34 loss to the Indianapolis Colts at the RCA Dome on 01-21-07

Chris Hanson had a 49-yard punt in the 17–14 loss to the New York Giants at the University of Phoenix Stadium on 02-03-08

The progression of the most punts in a playoff game by a Patriots Punter

7 punts by Tom Yewcic in the 26–8 victory over the Buffalo Bills at War Memorial Stadium on 12-28-63

7 punts by Tom Yewcic in the 51–10 loss to the San Diego Chargers at Balboa Stadium on 01-05-64

9 punts by Rich Camarillo in the 22–17 loss to the Denver Broncos at Mile High Stadium on 01-04-87

The progression of the most yards punted by a Patriots Punter in a playoff game

226 yards punted by Tom Yewcic in the 26–8 victory over the Buffalo Bills at War Memorial Stadium on 12-28-63

329 yards punted by Tom Yewcic in the 51–10 loss to the San Diego Chargers at Balboa Stadium on 01-05-64

452 yards punted by Rich Camarillo in the 22–17 loss to the Denver Broncos at Mile High Stadium on 01-04-87

The progression of the most career yards punted by a Patriots Punter in the playoffs

523 career yards punted in two playoff games by Tom Yewcic

1,559 career yards punted in six playoff games by Rich Camarillo

1,833 career yards punted in six playoff games by Tom Tupa

Special Teams Returns

In this section you can review the kickoff return statistics of every Patriots running back, wide receiver, tight end, offensive lineman, defensive lineman, linebacker, and defensive back since the 1960 season. You can recall the length, opponent, score, and location of every player's longest kickoff return by each position in both a regular season game and in a playoff game. A total of 79 running backs, 42 wide receivers, 33 defensive backs, 16 linebackers, nine tight ends, 11 defensive linemen, and 11 offensive linemen have returned a kickoff for a the Patriots in a regular season game.

Dick Christy was the first Patriots player to return at least 20 kickoffs in a regular season. Over the next three seasons, Larry Garron led the team in kickoff returns and he averaged more than 24 yards per kickoff return. For the next five years, either J.D. Garrett, Jay Cunningham, Joe Bellino, or Willie Porter led the Patriots in the number of kickoff returns. Carl Garrett led the team in kickoff returns during the 1969 season and over the 1971–72 seasons. Odell Lawson led the Boston Patriots in kickoff returns during the last season in 1970.

Mini-Mack Herron was a crowd favorite and led the New England Patriots with 41 returns in 1973 and 28 kickoff returns in 1974. Allen Carter and Jess Phillips had the most returns during the 1975 and 1976 seasons, respectively. Rookie sensation Raymond Clayborn set numerous team records in 1977 as he averaged 31 yards per kickoff return and returned three kickoffs for a touchdown that year.

The leaders in kickoff returns from 1978–81 were Raymond Clayborn, Allan Clark, Horace Ivory, and Tony Collins. Ricky Smith had 24 kickoff returns in 1982, and 42 kickoff returns in 1983, to lead the team in that department. Once again, Tony Collins led the team in kickoff returns during the 1984 season. Receiver Stephen Starring was the dominant kickoff returnman for the Patriots over the 1985–87 seasons. Sammy Martin led the team for the next three years until Jon Vaughn and Walter Stanley took the honors.

Ray Crittenden led the team in kickoff returns in 1993 and 1994. Dave Meggett was the kickoff return leader for the team for the next three seasons. Derrick "Flying" Cullors had 45 kickoff returns during the 1998 season. Running back Kevin Faulk then led the team over the 1999–2001 seasons before receiver Deion Branch took the job and had the most kickoff returns during the 2002 season. Bethel Johnson led the team in kickoff returns over the 2003–05 regular seasons.

Rookie Laurence Maroney led the team with 28 kickoff returns, averaging 28 yards per return, during the 2006 season. Ellis Hobbs led the team with 35 kickoff returns for 911 yards, and set the NFL record with a 108-yard kickoff return for a touchdown during the 2007 undefeated regular season.

You will know every Patriots player who has recovered or returned an onside kick or a squibbed short kickoff. Did you know that the Patriots have only 11 successful advancements with a lateral during a kickoff return? I could find only two occasions in which the Patriots accomplished a reverse kickoff return.

Running backs Larry Garron, Jon Vaughn, and Kevin Faulk, who have each returned two kickoffs for a touchdown during their careers with the Patriots, are among the best kickoff returnmen for the Patriots. Other Patriots running backs who have returned a kickoff for a touchdown include Ron Burton, Allen Carter, Derrick Cullors, Mack Herron, and Horace Ivory. In fact, Allen Carter was the first Patriots player to return the opening kickoff for a touchdown when he returned a kickoff 99 yards in the 34–21 loss to the Baltimore Colts at Memorial Stadium on 12-21-75.

The four most productive wide receivers who have returned a kickoff are Stephen Starring, Deion Branch, Troy Brown, and Bethel Johnson. They are the only Patriots receivers with at least two kickoff returns of at least 50 yards in a game. In fact, Bethel Johnson is the only Patriots player to return two kickoffs at least 65 yards in the same game. On November 30, 2003, Bethel returned a kickoff 92 yards for a touchdown on the last play of the first half and he returned another kickoff 67 yards to help set up the final touchdown in the 38–34 victory over the Indianapolis Colts at the RCA Dome on 11-30-03.

Arguably, the most productive kickoff returnman in the history is defensive back Raymond Clayborn. Clayborn is the only Patriots player to return three kickoffs for a touchdown and he is the only Patriots player to return four kickoffs of at least 75 yards in the same season. Defensive backs Ricky Smith, Willie Andrews, and Ellis Hobbs (twice) have also returned a kickoff for a touchdown. Ellis Hobbs set the NFL record by returning a kickoff 108 yards for a touchdown in the 38–14 rout of the New York Jets at the Meadowlands on 09-09-07.

Since the first regular season game on September 9, 1960, only three Patriots players have returned the opening kickoff for a touchdown. Only two Patriots defensive backs have recovered an opponent's onside kick attempt and intercepted a pass in the same game. Only two Patriots linebackers have returned at least one kickoff and returned a pass interception for a touchdown during their careers. Ron Burton is the only Patriots player to return a missed field-goal attempt for a touchdown. Jon Vaughn is the only Patriots player to advance his own fumble on a kickoff return for a touchdown. Troy Brown is the only Patriots player to advance a teammate's (Dave Meggett) fumble on a kickoff return for a touchdown.

The Patriots player who had the most kickoffs, most yards, best average return, and longest return for each year

	Most Kickoffs	Most Return Yards	Best Return Average	Longest Kickoff Return
1960	Dick Christy	Dick Christy	Ron Burton	Ron Burton
1961	Larry Garron	Larry Garron	Larry Garron	Ron Burton
1962	Larry Garron	Larry Garron	Larry Garron	Larry Garron
1963	Larry Garron	Larry Garron	Larry Garron	Larry Garron
1964	J.D. Garrett	J.D. Garrett	Dave Cloutier	Dave Cloutier
1965	Jay Cunningham	Jay Cunningham	Larry Garron	Jay Cunningham
1966	Joe Bellino	Joe Bellino	Karl Singer	Joe Bellino
1967	Jay Cunningham	Jay Cunningham	Larry Garron	Jay Cunningham
1968	Willie Porter	Willie Porter	Willie Porter	Willie Porter
1969	Carl Garrett	Carl Garrett	Carl Garrett	Carl Garrett
1970	Odell Lawson	Odell Lawson	Larry Carwell	Odell Lawson
1971	Carl Garrett	Carl Garrett	Hubie Bryant	Hubie Bryant
1972	Carl Garrett	Carl Garrett	Reggie Rucker	Carl Garrett
1973	Mack Herron	Mack Herron	Mack Herron	Mack Herron
1974	Mack Herron	Mack Herron	Eddie Hinton	Mack Herron
1975	Allen Carter	Allen Carter	Mack Herron	Allen Carter
1976	Jess Phillips	Jess Phillips	Jess Phillips	Jess Phillips
1977	Raymond Clayborn	Raymond Clayborn	Raymond Clayborn	Raymond Clayborn
1978	Raymond Clayborn	Raymond Clayborn	Dick Conn	Raymond Clayborn
1979	Allan Clark	Allan Clark	Allan Clark	Allan Clark
1980	Horace Ivory	Horace Ivory	Horace Ivory	Horace Ivory
1981	Tony Collins	Tony Collins	Paul Dombroski	Ken Toler
1982	Ricky Smith	Ricky Smith	Ricky Smith	Ricky Smith
1983	Ricky Smith	Ricky Smith	Robert Weathers	Ricky Smith
1984	Tony Collins	Tony Collins	Ricky Smith	Tony Collins
1985	Stephen Starring	Stephen Starring	Stephen Starring	Stephen Starring
1986	Stephen Starring	Stephen Starring	Stephen Starring	Stephen Starring
1987	Stephen Starring	Stephen Starring	Elgin Davis	Elgin Davis and S. Starring
1988	Sammy Martin	Sammy Martin	Sammy Martin	Sammy Martin
1989	Sammy Martin	Sammy Martin	Irving Fryar	Irving Fryar
1990	Sammy Martin	Sammy Martin	Michael Timpson	Sammy Martin
1991	Jon Vaughn	Jon Vaughn	Sammy Martin	Jon Vaughn
1992	Walter Stanley	Jon Vaughn	Jon Vaughn	Jon Vaughn
1993	Ray Crittenden	Ray Crittenden	Ray Crittenden	Ray Crittenden
1994	Ray Crittenden	Ray Critenden	Michael Timpson	Ray Crittenden
1995	Dave Meggett	Dave Meggett	Dave Meggett	Dave Meggett
1996	Dave Meggett	Dave Meggett	Dave Meggett	Dave Meggett
1997	Dave Meggett	Dave Meggett	Chris Canty	Derrick Cullors
1998	Derrick Cullors	Derrick Cullors	Derrick Cullors	Derrick Cullors
1999	Kevin Faulk	Kevin Faulk	Troy Brown	Kevin Faulk
2000	Kevin Faulk	Kevin Faulk	J.R. Redmond	Curtis Jackson
2001	Kevin Faulk	Kevin Faulk	J.R. Redmond	Kevin Faulk
2002	Deion Branch	Deion Branch	Kevin Faulk	Kevin Faulk
2003	Bethel Johnson	Bethel Johnson	Bethel Johnson	Bethel Johnson
2004	Bethel Johnson	Bethel Johnson	Bethel Johnson	Bethel Johnson
2005	Bethel Johnson	Bethel Johnson	André Davis	André Davis
2006	Laurence Maroney	Laurence Maroney	Ellis Hobbs	Ellis Hobbs
2007	Ellis Hobbs	Ellis Hobbs	Willie Andrews	Ellis Hobbs
2008	Ellis Hobbs	Ellis Hobbs	Ellis Hobbs	Ellis Hobbs

The Most Kickoff Returns

The progression of the most kickoff returns by a Patriots player in a regular season game

1 kickoff return by Larry Garron in the 13–10 loss to the Denver Broncos at BU Field on 09-09-60

1 kickoff return by Walt Livingston in the 13–10 loss to the Denver Broncos at BU Field on 09-09-60

4 kickoff returns by Dick Christy in the 28–24 win over the New York Titans at Polo Grounds on 09-17-60

4 kickoff returns by Walter Beach in the 45–16 loss to the Los Angeles Chargers at BU Field on 10-28-60

4 kickoff returns by Larry Garron in the 31–31 tie with the Houston Oilers at BU Field on 10-13-61

6 kickoff returns by Larry Garron in the 27–7 loss to the Dallas Cowboys at BU Field on 10-12-62

6 kickoff returns by J.D. Garrett in the 43–43 tie with the Oakland Raiders at Fenway Park on 10-16-64

6 kickoff returns by J.D. Garrett in the 35–14 loss to the New York Jets at Shea Stadium on 10-31-64

6 kickoff returns by Jay Cunningham in the 35–7 loss to the Oakland Raiders at the Oakland Coliseum on 09-17-67

6 kickoff returns by Bobby Leo in the 44–16 loss to the Buffalo Bills at Fenway Park on 12-09-67

8 kickoff returns by Willie Porter in the 47–31 loss to the New York Jets at Legion Field on 09-22-68

The progression of the most kickoff return yards by a Patriots player in a regular season game

21 kickoff return yards by Larry Garron in the 13–10 loss to the Denver Broncos at BU Field on 09-09-60

123 kickoff return yards by Dick Christy in the 28–24 win over the New York Titans at the Polo Grounds on 09-17-60

141 kickoff return yards by Larry Garron in the 31–31 tie with the Houston Oilers at BU Field on 10-13-61

148 kickoff return yards by Ron Burton in the 28–21 win over the Dallas Texans at BU Field on 11-03-61

173 kickoff return yards by Larry Garron in the 28–28 tie with the Buffalo Bills at War Memorial on 11-03-62

175 kickoff return yards by Carl Garrett in the 23–16 loss to the Buffalo Bills at Rich Stadium on 10-11-69

206 kickoff return yards by Allen Carter in the 34–21 loss to the Baltimore Colts at Memorial Stadium on 12-21-75

220 kickoff return yards by Kevin Faulk in the 30–17 loss to the New York Jets at Gillette Stadium on 12-22-02

237 kickoff return yards by Ellis Hobbs in the 38–13 loss to the Miami Dolphins at Gillette Stadium on 09-21-08

The progression of the most kickoff return yards by a Patriots player in a regular season

617 kickoff return yards by Dick Christy in 1960

686 kickoff return yards by Larry Garron in 1962

693 kickoff return yards by Larry Garron in 1963

749 kickoff return yards by JD Garrett in 1964

812 kickoff return yards by Willie Porter in 1968

1,092 kickoff return yards by Mack Herron in 1973

1,281 kickoff return yards by Ellis Hobbs in 2008

The progression of the most career kickoff return yards by a Patriots player

617 kickoff return yards by Dick Christy (averaging 25.7 yards/return) during the 1960 season

2,299 kickoff return yards by Larry Garron (averaging 25.8 yards/return) over the 1960–67 seasons

2,561 kickoff return yards by Dave Meggett (averaging 24.4 yards/return) over the 1995–97 seasons

3,918 kickoff return yards by Kevin Faulk (averaging 22.6 yards/return) over the 1999–2007 seasons

The progression of the most kickoff returns by a Patriots player in a regular season

24 kickoff returns by Dick Christy in 1960

28 kickoff returns by Larry Garron in 1963

32 kickoff returns by J.D. Garrett in 1964

36 kickoff returns by Willie Porter in 1968

41 kickoff returns by Mack Herron in 1973

42 kickoff returns by Ricky Smith in 1983

48 kickoff returns by Stephen Starring in 1985

The progression of the most career kickoff returns by a Patriots player

24 career kickoff returns by Dick Christy in the 1960 season

89 career kickoff returns by Larry Garron over the 1960–67 seasons

92 career kickoff returns by Carl Garrett over the 1969–72 seasons

107 career kickoff returns by Stephen Starring over the 1984–87 seasons

173 career kickoff returns by Kevin Faulk over the 1999–2007 seasons

The progression of the best average kickoff return by a Patriots player in a regular season game

21-yard kickoff return by Larry Garron in the 13–10 loss to the Denver Broncos on 09-09-0

30.7 average yards per kickoff return by Dick Christy in the 28–24 win over the New York Titans on 09-17-60

35.2 average yards per kickoff return by Larry Garron in the 31–31 tie with the Houston Oilers on 10-13-61

49.3 average yards per kickoff return by Ron Burton in the 28–21 win over the Dallas Texans on 11-03-61

The progression of the best average kickoff return (more than 10) by a Patriots player in a regular season

28.5 average yards per kickoff return by Billy Wells in 1960

28.6 average yards per kickoff return by Larry Garron in 1962

31.0 average yards per kickoff return by Raymond Clayborn in 1977

The progression of the best career average kickoff return by a Patriots player

25.8 career average yards per kickoff return by Larry Garron over the 1960–68 seasons

27.2 career average yards per kickoff return by Allen Carter over the 1975–76 seasons

28.0 career average yards per kickoff return by Laurence Maroney over the 2006–07 seasons

The progression of the longest kickoff return by a Patriots player in a regular season game

21-yard return by Larry Garron in the 13–10 loss to the Denver Broncos at BU Field on 09-09-60

41-yard return by Dick Christy in the 28–24 win over the New York Titans at the Polo Grounds on 09-17-60

41-yard return by Dick Christy in the 27–14 loss to the Oakland Raiders at Kezar Stadium on 10-16-60

52-yard return by Dick Christy in the 38–21 win over the New York Titans at BU Field on 11-11-60

59-yard return by Ron Burton in the 42–14 rout of the Dallas Texans at BU Field on 11-18-60

89-yard TD return by Larry Garron in the 31–31 tie with the Houston Oilers at BU Field on 10-13-61

91-yard TD return by Ron Burton in the 28–21 victory over the Dallas Texans at BU Field on 11-03-61

95-yard TD return by Larry Garron in the 28–28 tie with the Buffalo Bills at War Memorial Stadium on 11-03-62

100-yard TD return by Raymond Clayborn in the 30–27 loss to the New York Jets at Shea Stadium on 10-02-77

101-yard TD return by Raymond Clayborn in the 30–24 loss to the Baltimore Colts at Memorial Stadium on 12-18-77

108-yard TD return by Ellis Hobbs in the 38–14 rout of the New York Jets at the Meadowlands on 09-09-07

The progression of the longest kickoff return by a Patriots Running Back in a regular season game

21-yard return by Larry Garron in the 13–10 loss to the Denver Broncos at BU Field on 09-09-60

41-yard return by Dick Christy in the 28–24 victory over the New York Titans at the Polo Grounds on 09-17-60

52-yard return by Dick Christy in the 27–14 loss to the Oakland Raiders at Kezar Stadium on 10-16-60

59-yard return by Ron Burton in the 42–14 rout of the Dallas Texans at BU Field on 11-18-60

89-yard return for a TD by Larry Garron in the 31–31 tie with the Houston Oilers at BU Field on 10-13-61

91-yard return for a TD by Ron Burton in the 28–21 victory over the Dallas Texans at BU Field on 11-03-61

95-yard return for a TD by Larry Garron in the 28–28 tie with the Buffalo Bills at War Memorial Stadium on 11-03-62

99-yard return for a TD by Allen Carter in the 34–21 loss to the Baltimore Colts at Memorial Stadium on 12-21-75

100-yard return for a TD by Jon Vaughn in the 20–10 loss to the Cincinnati Bengals at Riverfront Stadium on 12-20-92

The progression of the longest kickoff return by a Patriots Wide Receiver in a regular season game

34-yard return by Vic Purvis in the 43–24 loss to the Kansas City Chiefs at Fenway Park on 09-25-66

41-yard return by Aaron Marsh in the 23–16 victory over the Buffalo Bills at Rich Stadium on 11-23-69

45-yard return by Hubie Bryant in the 23–3 loss to the Baltimore Colts at Schaefer Stadium on 10-03-71

53-yard return by Eddie Hinton in the 29–28 loss to the Buffalo Bills at Schaefer Stadium on 11-03-74

53-yard return by Ricky Smith in the 7–0 shutout of the New Orleans Saints at Sullivan Stadium on 12-04-83

53-yard return by Stephen Starring in the 17–14 victory over the Buffalo Bills at Rich Stadium on 09-22-85

95-yard return for a TD by Sammy Martin in the 24–21 loss to the Colts at the Hoosier Dome on 11-27-88

The progression of the longest kickoff return by a Patriots Tight End in a regular season game

6-yard return by Tom Stephens in the 27–15 loss to the Houston Oilers at Jeppesen Stadium on 11-12-61

15-yard return by Tom Beer in the 34–10 loss to the New York Jets at Shea Stadium on 10-29-72

20-yard return by Ben Coates in the 26–20 win over the Jacksonville Jaguars at Alltel Stadium on 12-07-97

The progression of the longest kickoff return by a Patriots Offensive Lineman in a regular season game

8-yard return by Gerry Delucca in the 45–16 loss to the Los Angeles Chargers at BU Field on 10-28-60

11-yard return by Charlie Long in the 37–30 loss to the New York Titans at the Polo Grounds on 10-01-61

27-yard return by Karl Singer in the 43–24 loss to the Kansas City Chiefs at Fenway Park on 09-25-66

The progression of the longest kickoff return by a Patriots Defensive Back in a regular season game

20-yard return by Fred Bruney in the 28–24 victory over the New York Titans at the Polo Grounds on 09-17-60

33-yard return by Walter Beach in the 35–0 shutout of the Los Angeles Chargers at the Los Angeles Coliseum on 10-08-60

37-yard return by Gino Cappelletti in the 37–21 loss to the Houston Oilers at Jeppesen Stadium on 12-18-60

46-yard return by Dave Cloutier in the 26–17 loss to the San Diego Chargers at Fenway Park on 10-09-64

61-yard return by Willie Porter in the 34–10 loss to the Miami Dolphins at Fenway Park on 11-24-68

100-yard return for a TD by Raymond Clayborn in the 30–27 loss to the New York Jets at Shea Stadium on 10-02-77

101-yard return for a TD by Raymond Clayborn in the 30–24 loss to the Baltimore Colts at Memorial Stadium on 12-18-77

108-yard return for a TD by Ellis Hobbs in the 38–14 rout of the New York Jets at the Meadowlands on 09-09-07

The progression of the longest kickoff return by a Patriots Linebacker in a regular season game

15-yard return by Rommie Loudd in the 26–16 win over the Oakland Raiders at BU Field on 10-26-62

16-yard return by Mike Dukes in the 12–7 victory over the Denver Broncos at Fenway Park on 11-20-64

17-yard return by Mike Dukes in the 24–14 loss to the Buffalo Bills at Fenway Park on 12-20-64

20-yard return by Mike Dukes in the 13–13 tie with the San Diego Chargers at Fenway Park on 10-17-65

21-yard return by Sam Hunt in the 21–16 loss to the New York Jets at Schaefer Stadium on 11-17-74

21-yard return by Tully Banta-Cain in the 27–19 win over the Kansas City Chiefs at Arrowhead Stadium on 11-22-04

The progression of the longest kickoff return by a Patriots defensive lineman in a regular season game

13-yard return by Hal Smith in the 38–21 victory over the New York Titans at BU Field on 11-11-60

14-yard return by Bob Dee in the 24–17 victory over the New York Titans at BU Field on 11-30-62

20-yard return by Ron Berger in the 13–10 loss to the San Diego Chargers at BC Alumni Stadium on 10-19-69

The Patriots player with the longest kickoff return in a regular season overtime game

Chris Canty returned a kickoff 63 yards in the 27–24 overtime win over the New York Jets at Foxboro Stadium on 09-14-97

Kickoffs That Were Returned for a TD

The only Patriots player who has returned a kickoff for a TD in a game that ended in a tie
1961 regular season
Larry Garron returned a kickoff 89 yards for a TD in the 31–31 tie with Houston at BU Field on 10-13-61

1962 regular season
Larry Garron returned a kickoff 95 yards for a TD in the 28–28 tie with Buffalo at War Memorial Stadium on 11-03-62

Every Patriots player who has returned the opening kickoff for a TD in a regular season game
1975 regular season
Allen Carter took the opening kickoff 99 yards for a TD in the 34–21 loss to the Colts at Memorial Stadium on 12-21-75

1988 regular season
Sammy Martin returned it 95 yards for a TD in the 24–21 loss to the Colts at the Hoosier Dome on 11-27-88

2004 championship season
Bethel Johnson took it 93 yards for a TD in the 42–15 rout of the Browns at Cleveland on 12-05-04

Every Patriots Running Back who has returned a kickoff for a TD in a regular season game
1961 regular season
Larry Garron took it 89 yards for a TD in the 31–31 tie with the Oilers at BU Field on 10-13-61

Ron Burton returned it 91 yards for a TD in the 28–21 win over the Texans at BU Field on 11-03-61

1962 regular season
Larry Garron returned it 95 yards for a TD in the 28–28 tie with the Bills at War Memorial Stadium on 11-03-62

1973 regular season
Mack Herron returned it 92 yards for a TD in the 30–14 win over the Chargers at Schaefer Stadium on 12-02-73

1975 regular season
Allen Carter took the opening kickoff 99 yards for a TD in the 34–21 loss to Baltimore at Memorial Stadium on 12-21-75

1980 regular season
Horace Ivory returned a kickoff 98 yards for a TD in the 37–21 win over the Colts at Memorial Stadium on 10-19-80

1991 regular season
Jon Vaughn returned it 99 yards for a TD in the 24–10 loss to the Cardinals at Sun Devil Stadium on 09-29-91

1992 regular season
Jon Vaughn returned a kickoff 100 yards for a TD in the 20–10 loss to the Bengals at Riverfront Stadium on 12-20-92

1997 regular season
Derrick Cullors returned it 86 yards for a TD in the 31–10 win over Buffalo at Rich Stadium on 11-09-97

2002 regular season
Kevin Faulk returned a kickoff 86 yards for a TD in the 27–20 loss to the Raiders at Oakland on 11-17-02

Kevin Faulk returned a kickoff 87 yards for a TD in the 30–17 loss to the Jets at Gillette Stadium on 12-22-02

Every Patriots Wide Receiver who has returned a kickoff for a TD in a regular season game
1988 regular season
Sammy Martin took the opening kickoff 95 yards for a TD in the 24–21 loss to the Colts on 11-27-88

2003 championship season
Bethel Johnson took it 92 yards for a TD on the last play of the first half in the 38–34 win over the Colts on 11-30-03

2004 championship season
Bethel Johnson took the opening kickoff 93 yards for a TD in the 42–15 rout of Cleveland on 12-05-04

Every Patriots Defensive Back who has returned a kickoff for a TD in a regular season game
1977 regular season
Raymond Clayborn returned a kickoff 100 yards for a TD in the 30–27 loss to the Jets at Shea Stadium on 10-02-77

Ray Clayborn took it 93 yards for a TD to end the first quarter in the 24–14 loss to Buffalo at Schaefer Stadium on 11-06-77

Raymond Clayborn returned it 101 yards for a TD in the 30–24 loss to Baltimore at Memorial Stadium on 12-18-77

1982 regular season

Ricky Smith returned a kickoff 98 yards for a TD in the 31–7 loss to the Jets at Schaefer Stadium on 09-19-82

2006 regular season

Ellis Hobbs returned a kickoff 93 yards for a TD in the 40–7 rout of the Texans at Gillette Stadium on 12-17-06

2007 regular season

Ellis Hobbs took a kickoff 108 yards for a TD in the 38–14 rout of the Jets at the Meadowlands on 09-09-07
Willie Andrews took a kickoff 77 yards for a TD in the 49–28 win over Miami at Dolphin Stadium on 10-21-07

2008 regular season

Ellis Hobbs took a kickoff 95 yards for a TD in the 49–26 rout of the Raiders at McAfee Coliseum on 12-14-08

The only Patriots player to advance a teammate's fumble on a kickoff return for a TD

Troy Brown advanced Dave Meggett's fumble 75 yards for a TD in the 31–28 win over the New York Jets on 12-10-96

Recoveries of an Onside Kick

Every Patriots Running Back who has recovered an opponent's onside kick in a regular season game

1961 regular season

Ger Schwedes fell on the onside kick by Gene Mingo on the last play of the 28–24 win over Denver on 12-03-61

1975 regular season

Andy Johnson fell on a Steve Mike-Mayer onside kick with 50 seconds left in the 24–16 win over the 49ers on 10-26-75

1979 regular season

Andy Johnson fell on the onside kick by Chris Bahr with two minutes left in the 20–14 win over Cincinnati on 09-16-79

1980 regular season

Andy Johnson fell on a Don Cockroft onside kick with four minutes left in the 34–17 win over the Browns on 09-07-80

1985 regular season

Mosi Tatupu recovered an onside kick by Al Del Greco with 30 seconds left in the 26–20 win over Green Bay on 09-08-85

Craig James fell on the onside kick by Raul Allegre with two minutes left in the 38–31 win over the Colts on 12-01-85

1996 regular season

Keith Byars fell on the onside kick by Steve Christie with 24 seconds left in the 28–25 win over Buffalo on 10-27-96

Every Patriots Wide Receiver who has recovered an opponent's onside kick in a regular season game

1977 regular season

Darryl Stingley fell on the onside kick by Rolf Bernirscke with 1:45 left in the 24–20 win over the San Diego Chargers on 10-16-77

1980 regular season

Carlos Pennywell fell on a Don Cockroft onside kick with eight minutes left in the 34–17 win over Cleveland on 09-07-80

1988 regular season

Cedric Jones fell on a Pat Leahy onside kick with two minutes left in the 14–13 win over the New York Jets on 11-13-88

1997 regular season

Troy Brown recovered an onside kick by Mike Hollis with 5:50 left in the 26–20 win over the Jaguars on 12-07-97

2001 championship season

Fred Coleman fell on an onside kick by Olindo Mare with 1:28 left in the 20–13 win over Miami on 12-22-01

Every Patriots Tight End who has recovered an opponent's onside kick in a regular season game

1973 regular season

Bob Windsor recovered an onside kick by George Hunt with 2:30 left in the 24–16 win over Baltimore on 10-07-73

1997 regular season

Ben Coates fell on a Chris Gardocki onside kick with 1:08 left in the 20–17 win over the Colts on 11-30-97

Ben Coates took a Mike Hollis onside kick 20 yards with 2:15 left in the 26–20 win over the Jaguars on 12-07-97

1999 regular season

Ben Coates recovered a Brad Daluiso onside kick with 1:14 left in the 16–14 win over the Giants on 09-26-99

2000 regular season

Eric Bjornson recovered a Danny Knight onside kick with 36 seconds left in the 24–16 win over the Colts on 10-08-00

2002 championship season

Christian Fauria fell on a Craig Hentrich onside kick with 36 seconds left in the 38–30 win over the Titans on 10-05-03

2005 regular season

Ben Watson took the Mike Nugent onside kick one yard with 2:10 left in the 31–21 win over the Jets on 12-26-05

The only Patriots Tight End who recovered a short kickoff by the opponent's kicker in a regular season game

1994 regular season

John Burke fell on a short kickoff by Nick Lowery to end the first half in the 24–13 win over the Jets on 12-04-94

Every Patriots Offensive Lineman who has recovered an opponent's onside kick in a regular season game

1961 regular season

Walt Cudzik fell on the Billy Atkins onside kick with one minute left in the 23–21 win over Buffalo on 09-23-61

1964 regular season

Dave Watson recovered a Mike Mercer onside kick in the first quarter of the 17–14 win over Oakland on 09-13-64

Bob Yates fell on the Mike Mercer onside kick with five seconds left in the 43–43 tie with the Raiders on 10-16-64

Every Patriots Defensive Back/Special Teams player who recovered an opponent's onside kick in a regular season game

1964 regular season

Tom Stephens fell on a George Blair onside kick with 2:47 left in the 33–28 win over San Diego on 09-20-64

1966 regular season

Billy Johnson fell on an onside kick by Gary Kroner on the last play in the 17–10 loss to the Broncos on 11-06-66

1971 regular season

Tom Janik recovered an onside kick by John Leypoldt to end the half in the 38–33 win over the Bills on 11-14-71

Don Webb fell on an onside kick by Jim O'Brien with 26 seconds left in the 21–17 win over the Colts on 12-19-71

1974 regular season

Sandy Durko fell on an onside kick by Garo Yepremian with 4:26 left in the 34–24 win over Miami on 09-15-74

1977 regular season

Tim Fox fell on an onside kick by Ove Johansson with 52 seconds left in the 14–6 win over the Eagles on 11-27-77

1986 regular season

Jim Bowman fell on a Morton Andersen's kick with 28 seconds left in the 21–20 win over the Saints on 11-30-86

1990 regular season

Ronnie Lippett fell on an onside kick by Dean Biasucci with 2:16 left in the 16–14 win over the Colts on 09-16-90

1994 regular season

Myron Guyton fell on an onside kick by Doug Pelfrey with 1:13 left in the 31–28 win over Cincinnati on 09-18-94

1996 regular season

Corwin Brown fell on an onside kick by Matt Stover with 1:58 left in the 46–38 win over the Ravens on 10-06-96

Every Patriots Linebacker who has recovered an opponent's onside kick in a regular season game

1962 regular season

Harry Jacobs fell on the onside kick by Jim Fraser to end the 33–29 victory over Denver on 11-11-62

1968 regular season

Jim Cheyunski recovered a George Blanda onside kick in the third quarter of the 41–10 loss to Oakland on 10-06-68

1970 regular season

Barry Brown recovered an onside kick by Grant Guthrie with 1:58 left in the 14–10 win over Buffalo on 11-29-70

1978 regular season

Steve Zabel recovered an onside kick by Tom Dempsey with 1:47 left in the 14–10 win over Buffalo on 11-05-78

Mike Hawkins recovered an onside free kick by George Roberts in the 33–24 win over Miami on 10-22-78

2001 championship season

Mike Vrabel recovered an onside kick by Jake Arians with 2:43 left in the 21–11 win over Buffalo on 11-11-01

2003 championship season

Larry Izzo recovered an onside kick by Seth Marler with 3:22 left in the 27–13 win over the Jaguars on 12-14-03

2005 regular season

Larry Izzo fell on the onside kick by Lawrence Tynes to end the half in the 26–16 loss to the Chiefs on 11-27-05

2007 regular season

Mike Vrabel had a three-yard return of an onside kick by Shaun Suisham in the 52–7 rout of the Redskins on 10-28-07

Mike Vrabel fell on the kick by Lawrence Tynes with 1:04 left in the 38–35 win over the Giants on 12-29-07

Every Patriots defensive lineman who has recovered an opponent's squibbed kickoff

1965 regular season

George Pyne recovered a squibbed kick by Jim Fraser in the 27–17 loss to the Chiefs on 10-03-65

1974 regular season

Donnell Smith recovered a short kick by George Jakowenko in the 41–26 loss to the Raiders on 12-01-74

1981 regular season

Ray Hamilton recovered a squibbed kick by Nick Mike-Mayer in the 20–17 loss to the Bills on 11-22-81

2000 regular season

Bobby Hamilton recovered a squibbed kick by Paul Edinger in the 24–17 loss to the Bears on 12-10-00

The only Patriots player who punted and recovered an onside kick in the same regular season game

Tom Janik punted seven times for 278 yards and recovered an onside kick in the 38–33 win over Buffalo on 11-14-71

The only Patriots players who kicked off and recovered a short kickoff in a regular season game

1964 regular season

Bob Yates kicked off seven times and fell on an onside kick on the last play in the 43–43 tie with Oakland on 10-16-64

1965 regular season

Justin Canale kicked off four times and recovered a squibbed kick in the 13–13 tie with San Diego on 10-17-65

Squibbed Kickoff Recoveries and Returns

Every Patriots Offensive Lineman who has recovered a squibbed kickoff in a regular season game

1964 regular season

Don Oakes recovered a squibbed kick by Dick Guesman in the first quarter of the 12–7 win over Denver on 11-20-64

1965 regular season

Justin Canale fell on a squibbed kick by Herb Travenio to end the half in the 13–13 tie with the San Diego Chargers on 10-17-65

Justin Canale fell on a squibbed kick by Herb Travenio with eight minutes left in the 22–6 win over San Diego on 10-31-65

1973 regular season

John Hannah fell on a squibbed kick by John Leypoldt with 2:27 left in the 37–13 loss to the Bills on 12-09-73

1978 regular season

Dwight Wheeler fell on Mark Moseley's short kick, with 2:40 left, in the 16–14 loss to Washington on 09-03-78

The only Patriots defensive lineman to call for a fair catch on a short kickoff in a regular season game

Dan Klecko caught a 40-yard kickoff by Wes Welker in the 24–10 win over Miami at Gillette Stadium on 10-10-04

The only Patriots Linebacker to call for a fair catch on a short kickoff in a regular season game

Johnny Rembert caught a short kickoff by David Treadwell in the 20–3 loss to the Broncos on 12-01-91

Every Patriots Linebacker who has returned a squibbed kickoff in a regular season game

1974 regular season

John Tanner took a squibbed kick by Garo Yepremian 17 yards in the 34–27 loss to the Dolphins on 12-15-74

1981 regular season

Bill Matthews took a squibbed kick by Nick Mike-Mayer five yards in the 19–10 loss to the Bills on 12-13-81

The only Patriots defensive lineman who has recovered an opponent's onside kick in a regular season game

Bob Dee fell on an onside kick attempt by George Blair to end the half in the 33–28 win over San Diego on 09-20-64

Recoveries of an Onside Kick by the Patriots

Every Patriots player who recovered an onside kick by the Patriots in a regular season game

1964 regular season

Jim Lee Hunt recovered a Gino Cappelletti onside kick in the 26–10 win over the New York Jets at BC Stadium on 09-27-64

1967 regular season

Billy Johnson recovered a Justin Canale onside kick in the 29–24 loss to the New York Jets at Fenway Park on 11-19-67

1969 regular season

Carl Garrett recovered a Gino Cappelletti onside kick in the 38–23 loss to Oakland at BC Stadium on 09-28-69

1970 regular season

Clarence Scott recovered a Charlie Gogolak onside kick in the 35–14 loss to Minnesota at Harvard Stadium on 12-13-70

1972 regular season

Clarence Scott recovered a Charlie Gogolak onside kick in the 24–17 loss to Baltimore at Schaefer Stadium on 11-06-72

1973 Regular Season

Claxton Welch recovered an onside kick by Jeff White in the 33–13 loss to the New York Jets at Shea Stadium on 11-11-73

1978 regular season

Don Westbrook recovered a John Smith onside kick in the 34–27 loss to Baltimore at Schaefer Stadium on 09-18-78

1980 regular season

Mosi Tatupu recovered a Mike Hubach onside kick in the 38–34 loss to the Oilers at the Astrodome on 11-10-80

1989 regular season

Hart Lee Dykes recovered a Jason Staurovsky kick in the 28–24 loss to the Saints at Sullivan Stadium on 11-12-89

1993 regular season

Darryl Wren recovered a Scott Sisson onside kick in the 28–14 loss to the Oilers at Foxboro Stadium on 10-17-93

Lateral Returns on a Kickoff

Every Patriots Offensive Lineman who has lateraled the ball to a teammate on a kickoff return

1961 regular season

John Simerson lateraled it to Larry Garron, who ran 26 yards in the 45–17 rout of the Broncos on 09-16-61

1963 regular season

Bob Yates lateraled it to Bob Suci, who ran 22 yards in the 35–3 loss to the Chiefs on 12-14-63

1973 regular season

Len St. Jean lateraled it to Mack Herron, who ran 30 yards in the 24–23 loss to the Eagles on 11-04-73

Every Patriots player who has handed off the ball to a teammate during a reverse kickoff return

1961 regular season

Larry Garron ran seven yards and gave it to Don Webb, who ran for 15 more in the 37–30 loss to New York on 10-01-61

Larry Garron gave it to Walter Beach, who ran for 20 yards in the 38–27 loss to the Chargers on 10-07-61

Ron Burton gave it to Larry Garron, who ran for 11 yards in the 31–31 tie with the Oilers on 10-13-61

The only Patriots Tight End who has lateraled the ball to a teammate on a kickoff return

1970 regular season

Tom Beer lateraled it to Carl Garrett, who took it 21 yards in the 27–3 loss to the Colts at Memorial Stadium on 10-25-70

Tom Beer lateraled it to Carl Garrett, who took it 27 yards in the 45–10 loss to the Bills at Harvard Stadium on 11-01-70

Tom Beer lateraled it to Carl Garrett, who took it 15 yards in the 45–10 loss to the Bills at Harvard Stadium on 11-01-70

Every Patriots Linebacker who has lateraled the ball to a teammate on a kickoff return

1962 regular season

Rommie Loudd lateraled to Larry Garron, who ran 36 yards in the 26–16 win over the Raiders on 10-26-62

1970 regular season

Marty Schottenheimer lateraled to Odell Lawson, who ran 17 yards in the 16–0 loss to the Giants on 10-18-70

Every Patriots defensive lineman who has lateraled the ball to a teammate during a kickoff return

1960 regular season

Bob Dee lateraled to Dick Christy, who advanced it 19 yards in the 38–14 loss to the Buffalo Bills on 12-04-60

1962 regular season

Bob Dee lateraled to Jim Crawford, who advanced it 18 yards in the 21–10 win over the Buffalo Bills on 11-23-62

1964 regular season

Jim Hunt lateraled to J.D. Garrett, who advanced it 24 yards in the 43–43 tie with the Oakland Raiders on 10-16-64

Missed FGA Returns

The only Patriots player to return a FGA on the last play of the first half in a regular season game

Tim Fox had a seven-yard return of a 73-yard FGA by Fred Steinfort in the 23–14 win over Denver at Schaefer Stadium on 09-29-80

The only Patriots player who has returned a missed FGA for the game-winning TD

Ron Burton took a missed FGA and caught his own fumble during his 91-yard TD return in the 33–29 win on 11-11-62

Offensive Linemen Who Have Returned a Kickoff and Recovered a Fumble in the Same Regular Season Game

The only Patriots offensive lineman who has returned two kickoffs in the same regular season game

Charlie Long had kickoff returns of two yards and 11 yards in the 37–30 loss to the New York Titans on 10-01-61

The only Patriots offensive lineman who has returned a kickoff and recovered a fumble in the same game

Karl Singer took a kickoff nine yards and recovered a fumble in the 33–10 loss to the Kansas City Chiefs on 11-12-67

The only Patriots Defensive Back who has recovered an onside kick and intercepted a pass in the same game

Ronnie Lippett recovered an onside kick and intercepted a pass in the 16–14 win over the Colts on 09-16-90

The only Patriots Linebacker who has returned a kickoff and returned an interception in the same game

Tedy Bruschi returned a kickoff 11 yards and a pass 48 yards for a TD in the 27–20 loss to Oakland on 11-17-02

The only Patriots Defensive Lineman who has returned two kickoffs in the same game

Milford Hodge returned a kickoff eight yards and took a kickoff 11 yards in the 24–20 loss to the Los Angeles Rams on 12-24-89

The only Patriots player to recover and advance his own fumble on a kickoff return for a TD

Jon Vaughn advanced his own fumble 100 yards for a TD in the 20–10 loss to the Bengals on 12-20-92

The only Patriots player to return a kickoff for the game-winning TD in a regular season game

Ron Burton returned it 91 yards for the game-winning TD in the 28–21 win over the Dallas Texans on 11-03-61

The progression of the best average return per kickoff (10 or more kickoffs returned in a season)

28.5 yards per kickoff return by Billy Wells in 1960

28.6 yards per kickoff return by Larry Garron in 1962

31.0 yards per kickoff return by Raymond Clayborn in 1977

Every Patriots Kickoff Returnman who was named the Special Teams Player of the Week in the regular season

2003 championship season

Bethel Johnson had a 92-yard TD return and a 67-yard return to set up a TD in the 38–34 win over the Colts on 11-30-03

2006 regular season
Lawrence Maroney had a 77-yard kickoff return in the 31–7 rout of the Minnesota Vikings on 10-30-03

2007 undefeated regular season
Ellis Hobbs set the NFL record with his 108-yard kickoff return in the 38–14 rout of the New York Jets on 09-09-07

NFL League Leaders

The four Patriots players who have led the NFL with the longest kickoff return in a game during the season

1977 regular season
Raymond Clayborn had the longest kickoff return of 101 yards in the NFL during the 1977 season

1982 regular season
Ricky Smith had the longest kickoff return of 98 yards in the NFL during the 1982 season

1992 regular season
Jon Vaughn had the longest kickoff return of 100 yards in the NFL during the 1992 season

2007 undefeated regular season
Ellis Hobbs had the longest kickoff return in the history of the NFL of 108 yards during the 2007 season

The five Patriots players who have tied for the most in the league by returning one kickoff for a TD in a season

1961 regular season
Larry Garron tied for the most in the AFL by returning a kickoff for a TD in 1961

Ron Burton tied for the most in the AFL by returning a kickoff for a TD in 1961

1962 regular season
Larry Garron tied for the most in the AFL by returning a kickoff for a TD in 1962

1980 regular season
Horace Ivory tied for the most in the NFL by returning a kickoff for a TD in 1980

1982 regular season
Ricky Smith tied for the most in the NFL by returning a kickoff for a TD in 1982

1988 regular season
Sammy Martin tied for the most in the NFL by returning a kickoff for a TD in 1988

The only Patriots player to tie for the most kickoff returns for a TD in the NFL during that season

Kevin Faulk tied for the NFL lead by returning two kickoffs for a TD during the 2002 season

The only Patriots player to lead the AFL with the most kickoff returns in a game during a season

Willie Porter led the AFL with eight kickoff returns in a game (in the 47–31 loss to the New York Jets on 09-22-68)

Every Patriots player who has led the NFL with the most kickoff return yards in a particular season

1973 regular season
Mack Herron led the NFL with 1,092 kickoff return yards in 1973

1980 regular season
Horace Ivory led the NFL with 992 kickoff return yards in 1980

The two Patriots players who have led the NFL with the most kickoff returns in a season

1973 regular season
Mack Herron led the NFL with 41 kickoff returns in 1973

1985 regular season
Stephen Starring led the NFL with 48 kickoff returns in 1985

The only Patriots player to lead the NFL with the most kickoff returns in a specific season

Horace Ivory led the NFL with 36 kickoff returns in 1980

Every Patriots player who has led the NFL with the best kickoff return average in a season

1977 regular season
Raymond Clayborn had the NFL best kickoff return average of 31.0 yards per return in 1977

1980 regular season
Horace Ivory had the NFL best kickoff return average of 27.6 yards per return in 1980

1992 regular season

Jon Vaughn had the NFL best kickoff return average of 28.2 yards per return in 1992

The Playoffs

The progression of the most kickoff returns by a Patriots player in a playoff game

2 kickoff returns by Bob Suci in the 26–8 victory over the Buffalo Bills at War Memorial Stadium on 12-28-63

2 kickoff returns by Harry Crump in the 51–10 loss to the San Diego Chargers at Balboa Stadium on 01-05-64

2 kickoff returns by Larry Garron in the 51–10 loss to the San Diego Chargers at Balboa Stadium on 01-05-64

2 kickoff returns by Ron Burton in the 51–10 loss to the San Diego Chargers at Balboa Stadium on 01-05-64

4 kickoff returns by Jess Phillips in the 24–21 loss to the Raiders at the Oakland Coliseum on 12-18-76

7 kickoff returns by Stephen Starring in the 46–10 loss to the Chicago Bears at the Superdome on 01-26-86 (Stephen Starring set a Super Bowl record with seven kickoff returns)

The progression of the most kickoff return yards by a Patriots player in a playoff game

38 kickoff return yards by Bob Suci in the 26–8 win over the Bills at War Memorial Stadium on 12-28-63

67 kickoff return yards by Jess Phillips in the 24–21 loss to the Raiders at the Oakland Coliseum on 12-18-76

68 kickoff return yards by Raymond Clayborn in the 31–14 loss to the Oilers at Schaefer Stadium on 12-31-78

68 kickoff return yards by James McAlister in the 31–14 loss to the Oilers at Schaefer Stadium on 12-31-78

153 kickoff return yards by Stephen Starring in the 46–10 loss to the Bears at the Superdome on 01-26-86

220 kickoff return yards by Ellis Hobbs in the 38–34 loss to the Colts at the RCA Dome on 01-21-07

The progression of the most career kickoff returns by a Patriots player in the playoffs

3 career kickoff returns by Bob Suci in two playoff games

4 career kickoff returns by Jess Phillips in one playoff game

15 career kickoff returns by Stephen Starring in five playoff games

15 career kickoff returns by Patrick Pass in 10 playoff games

17 career kickoff returns by Ellis Hobbs in eight playoff games

The progression of the most career kickoff return yards by a Patriots player in the playoffs

56 career kickoff return yards by Bob Suci in two playoff games for the Boston Patriots

67 career kickoff return yards by Jess Phillips in the AFC Divisional playoff game on 12-18-76

68 career kickoff return yards by Raymond Clayborn in the AFC Divisional playoff game on 12-31-78

68 career kickoff return yards by Jim McAlister in the AFC Divisional playoff game on 12-31-78

315 career kickoff return yards by Stephen Starring in five playoff games

336 career kickoff return yards by Patrick Pass in 10 playoff games

471 kickoff return yards by Ellis Hobbs in eight playoff games

The progression of the most consecutive playoff games that a Patriots player returned at least one kickoff

2 consecutive playoff games that Bob Suci returned at least one kickoff

5 consecutive playoff games that Stephen Sarring returned at least one kickoff

5 consecutive playoff games that Ellis Hobbs returned at least one kickoff

The Longest Kickoff Returns

The progression of the longest return of the opening kickoff by a Patriots player in a playoff game

15 yards that Jess Phillips took the opening kickoff from Ray Guy in the 24–21 loss to the Raiders on 12-18-76

19 yards that Stephen Starring took the opening kickoff from Pat Leahy in the 26–14 win over the Jets on 12-28-85

24 yards that Stephen Starring took the opening kickoff by Chris Bahr in the 27–20 win over the Raiders on 01-05-86

37 yards that Stephen Starring took the opening kickoff by Faud Reveiz in the 31–14 win over Miami on 01-12-86

The progression of the longest kickoff return by a Patriots player in a playoff game

15-yard return by Bob Suci in the 26–8 win over the Buffalo Bills at War Memorial Stadium on 12-28-63

23-yard return by Bob Suci in the 26–8 win over the Buffalo Bills at War Memorial Stadium on 12-28-63

47-yard return by Raymond Clayborn in the 31–14 loss to the Houston Oilers at Schaefer Stadium on 12-31-78

80-yard return by Ellis Hobbs in the 38–34 loss to the Indianapolis Colts at the RCA Dome on 01-21-07

The progression of the longest kickoff return by a Patriots Running Back in a playoff game

22-yard return by Harry Crump in the 51–10 loss to the San Diego Chargers at Balboa Stadium on 01-05-64

22-yard return by Jess Phillips in the 24–21 loss to the Oakland Raiders at the Oakland Coliseum on 12-18-76

28-yard return by Jim McAlister in the 31–14 loss to the Houston Oilers at Schaefer Stadium on 12-31-78

35-yard return by Patrick Pass in the 24–17 victory over the Pittsburgh Steelers at Heinz Field on 01-27-02

35-yard return by Patrick Pass in the 20–14 victory over the St. Louis Rams at the Superdome on 02-03-02

The progression of the longest kickoff return by a Patriots Wide Receiver in a playoff game

19-yard return by Stephen Starring in the 26–14 win over the New York Jets at the Meadowlands on 12-28-85

25-yard return by Stephen Starring in the 27–20 victory over the Los Angeles Raiders at the Los Angeles Coliseum on 01-05-86

37-yard return by Stephen Starring in the 31–14 win over the Miami Dolphins at the Orange Bowl on 01-12-86

The progression of the longest kickoff return by a Patriots Defensive Back in a playoff game

15-yard return by Bob Suci in the 26–8 victory over the Buffalo Bills at War Memorial Stadium on 12-28-63

23-yard return by Bob Suci in the 26–8 victory over the Buffalo Bills at War Memorial Stadium on 12-28-63

47-yard return by Raymond Clayborn in the 31–14 loss to the Houston Oilers at Schaefer Stadium on 12-31-78

80-yard return by Ellis Hobbs in the 38–34 loss to the Indianapolis Colts at the RCA Dome on 01-21-07

Every Patriots Tight End who has returned a kickoff in a playoff game
1963 AFL Championship Game
Tony Romeo took it nine yards in the 51–10 loss to the San Diego Chargers at Balboa Stadium on 01-05-64

Super Bowl XXIX
Christian Fauria returned a kickoff two yards in the 24–21 win over the Eagles at Alltel Stadium on 02-06-05

The only Patriots Offensive Lineman who has returned a kickoff in a playoff game

Bob Yates returned a kickoff five yards in the 51–10 loss to the San Diego Chargers at Balboa Stadium on 01-05-64

The only Patriots Linebacker who has recovered a squibbed kickoff in a playoff game

George Webster recovered a squibbed kick by Ray Guy in the 24–21 loss to the Raiders at Oakland on 12-18-76

The only Patriots player who has returned a free kick after a Patriots safety in a playoff game

Troy Brown returned a punt by Hunter Smith 16 yards in the 24–14 win over the Colts at Gillette Stadium on 01-18-04

The only Patriots Tight End who has recovered an opponent's onside kick in a playoff game
2003 AFC Championship Game
Christian Fauria recovered a Mike Vanderjagt onside kick in the 24–14 win over the Colts on 01-18-04

2003 AFC Championship Game
Christian Fauria recovered a Jeff Reed onside kick in the 41–27 victory over the Steelers on 01-23-05

Super Bowl XXXIX
Christian Fauria returned a David Akers onside kick two yards in the 24–21 win over the Eagles on 02-06-05

The only Patriots player who has recovered an onside kick by a Patriots Kicker in a playoff game

Corwin Brown recovered an onside kick by teammate Matt Bahr in the 20–13 loss to Cleveland on 01-01-95

Punt Returns

Since the team's first regular season game on September 9, 1960, there have been 1,797 punt returns by the Patriots. In only 11 of these 724 regular season games has a Patriots player returned a punt for a touchdown. In fact, only six Patriots players have accomplished this feat. Mike Haynes was the first Patriots player to return a punt for a touchdown, and he did it twice during the month of November 1976. Stanley Morgan, Roland James, and Dave Meggett have each returned a punt for a touchdown in a regular season game for the New England Patriots. Irving Fryar and Troy Brown share the team record with three regular season punts that have been returned for a touchdown. Finally, you should know that Troy Brown is the only Patriots player to return a punt for a touchdown in a playoff game.

The Patriots have had 36 defensive backs, 25 wide receivers, 20 running backs, and only one linebacker attempt to return a punt. Bob Suci is the only Patriots defensive back to lead the team in punt return yards and interception return yards in the same season. Ron Burton, Carl Garrett, and Mack Herron have led the team with the most punt return yards and the most yards rushing in the same season. Troy Brown is the only Patriots player to lead the team with the most punt return yards and the most net yards from scrimmage in the same year. Nick Buoniconti is the only Patriots linebacker to attempt to return a punt.

From 1960 to 1968, the following players led the Boston Patriots with the most punt returns in a season: Billy Wells; Fred Bruney; Ron Burton; Bob Suci; Dave Cloutier; Ron Burton; Tom Hennessey; Jay Cunningham; and Willie Porter. Carl Garrett was the first Patriots player to lead the team with the most punt returns in consecutive seasons as he led the Patriots in this category from 1969–72. Mini-Mack Herron had the most punt returns during the 1973–74 seasons for the Patriots. Darryl Stingley was the first Patriots wide receiver to lead the team with the most punt returns with 15 returns during the 1975 season.

Mike Haynes led the AFC with 45 punt returns during the 1976 season and was the third player to lead the Patriots in consecutive seasons. Stanley Morgan was the first Patriots wide receiver to return a punt for a touchdown and led the team with the most punt returns during the 1978, 1979, and 1981 seasons. Roland James was the second Patriots defensive back to return a punt for a touchdown, and he led the team

with 33 punt returns during the 1980 season. Ricky Smith led the Patriots with the most punt returns during the 1982 and 1983 seasons.

Irving Fryar was the first Patriots player to lead the team with the most punt returns in a season for five consecutive seasons as he led the team from 1984–88. Fryar was the first Patriots player to return at least one punt for a touchdown in consecutive seasons. Fryar also led the team with 28 punt returns during the 1990 season. Sammy Martin led the Patriots with 19 punt returns during the 1989 season. Jerome Henderson and Walter Stanley led the team during the 1991 and 1992 seasons, respectively.

Troy Brown was the first Patriots player to lead the team with the most returns during eight seasons. Brown led the team with the most punt returns over the 1993–94 seasons and over the 1998–2003 seasons. Brown was the second Patriots player to return at least one punt for a touchdown in consecutive seasons. Dave Meggett led the Patriots over the 1995–97 seasons and Kevin Faulk led the team during the 2004 championship season. Tim Dwight led the team in 2005, Kevin Faulk led the team in 2006, and Wes Welker led the team during the 2007 undefeated regular season.

Boston Patriots defensive back Fred Bruney led the AFL with the most punt returns in 1961. Boston Patriots running back Ron Burton led the AFL with the most punt returns in 1962. Irving Fryar and Troy Brown led the NFL with the most yards per return during the 1985 season and 2001 season, respectively.

The Patriots player with the most punt returns, return yards, best return average, and longest return of each year

	Most Kickoffs	Most Return Yards	Best Return Average	Longest Kickoff Return
1960	Billy Wells	Billy Wells	Walter Beach	Dick Christy
1961	Fred Bruney	Fred Bruney	Ron Burton	Ron Burton
1962	Ron Burton	Ron Burton	Nick Buoniconti	Ron Burton
1963	Bob Suci	Bob Suci	Larry Garron	Tom Stephens
1964	Dave Cloutier	Dave Cloutier	J.D. Garrett	Dave Cloutier
1965	Ron Burton	Ron Burton	J.D. Garrett	J.D. Garrett
1966	two players tied	Vic Purvis	Vic Purvis	Vic Purvis
1967	Jay Cunningham	Joe Bellino	Billy Johnson	Billy Johnson
1968	Willie Porter	Willie Porter	Willie Porter	Willie Porter
1969	Carl Garrett	Carl Garrett	Carl Garrett	Carl Garrett
1970	Carl Garrett	Carl Garrett	Larry Carwell	Carl Garrett
1971	Hubie Bryant	Carl Garrett	Carl Garrett	Carl Garrett
1972	Carl Garrett	Carl Garrett	Carl Garrett	Carl Garrett
1973	Mack Herron	Mack Herron	Mack Herron	Mack Herron
1974	Mack Herron	Mack Herron	Mack Herron	Mack Herron
1975	Darryl Stingley	Darryl Stingley	Andy Johnson	Darryl Stingley
1976	Mike Haynes	Mike Haynes	Mike Haynes	Mike Haynes
1977	Mike Haynes	Stanley Morgan	Stanley Morgan	Stanley Morgan
1978	Stanley Morgan	Stanley Morgan	Mike Haynes	Stanley Morgan
1979	Stanley Morgan	Stanley Morgan	Stanley Morgan	Stanley Morgan
1980	Roland James	Roland James	Roland James	Roland James
1981	Stanley Morgan	Stanley Morgan	Roland James	Stanley Morgan
1982	Ricky Smith	Ricky Smith	Ricky Smith	Ricky Smith
1983	Ricky Smith	Ricky Smith	Ricky Smith	Ricky Smith
1984	Irving Fryar	Irving Fryar	Irving Fryar	Irving Fryar
1985	Irving Fryar	Irving Fryar	Irving Fryar	Irving Fryar
1986	Irving Fryar	Irving Fryar	Fred Marion	Irving Fryar
1987	Irving Fryar	Irving Fryar	Stephen Starring	Irving Fryar
1988	Irving Fryar	Irving Fryar	Irving Fryar	Irving Fryar
1989	Sammy Martin	Sammy Martin	Irving Fryar	Sammy Martin
1990	Irving Fryar	Irving Fryar	Irving Fryar	Irving Fryar
1991	Jerome Henderson	Jerome Henderson	Jerome Henderson	Jerome Henderson
1992	Walter Stanley	Walter Stanley	Walter Stanley	Walter Stanley
1993	Troy Brown	Troy Brown	Ray Crittenden	Ray Crittenden
1994	Troy Brown	Troy Brown	Ronnie Harris	Troy Brown
1995	Dave Meggett	Dave Meggett	Dave Meggett	Dave Meggett
1996	Dave Meggett	Dave Meggett	Dave Meggett	Dave Meggett
1997	Dave Meggett	Dave Meggett	Dave Meggett	Dave Meggett
1998	Troy Brown	Troy Brown	Troy Brown	Troy Brown
1999	Troy Brown	Troy Brown	Troy Brown	Troy Brown
2000	Troy Brown	Troy Brown	Troy Brown	Troy Brown
2001	Troy Brown	Troy Brown	Troy Brown	Troy Brown
2002	Troy Brown	Troy Brown	Deion Branch	Deion Branch
2003	Troy Brown	Troy Brown	Kevin Faulk	Troy Brown
2004	Kevin Faulk	Kevin Faulk	Troy Brown	Troy Brown
2005	Tim Dwight	Tim Dwight	Bethel Johnson	Tim Dwight
2006	Kevin Faulk	Kevin Faulk	Chad Jackson	Kevin Faulk
2007	Wes Welker	Wes Welker	Wes Welker	Wes Welker
2008	Wes Welker	Wes Welker	Kevin Faulk	Wes Welker

*Tom Hennessey and Billy Johnson each had seven punt returns in the 1966 AFL season for the Patriots

The Most Punt Returns

The progression of the most punt returns by a Patriots player in a regular season game

1 punt return by Jim Colclough in the 13–10 loss to the Denver Broncos at BU Field on 09-09-60

1 punt return by Fred Bruney in the 13–10 loss to the Denver Broncos at BU Field on 09-09-60

1 punt return by Gino Cappelletti in the 13–10 loss to the Denver Broncos at BU Field on 09-09-60

2 punt returns by Fred Bruney in the 28–24 victory over the New York Titans at the Polo Grounds on 09-17-60

3 punt returns by Dick Christy in the 13–0 loss to the Buffalo Bills at BU Field on 09-23-60

3 punt returns by Billy Wells in the 34–28 victory over the Oakland Raiders at BU Field on 11-04-60

3 punt returns by Billy Wells in the 37–21 loss to the Houston Oilers at Jeppesen Stadium on 12-18-60

6 punt returns by Fred Bruney in the 23–21 victory over the Buffalo Bills at War Memorial Stadium on 09-23-61

6 punt returns by Ron Burton in the 17–14 victory over the Oakland Raiders at Frank Youell Field on 09-13-64

6 punt returns by Mack Herron in the 21–14 loss to the Cleveland Browns at Schaefer Stadium on 11-10-74

6 punt returns by Roland James in the 17–14 loss to the Los Angeles Rams at Schaefer Stadium on 11-16-80

7 punt returns by Irving Fryar in the 20–17 loss to the Dallas Cowboys at Texas Stadium on 11-22-84

10 punt returns by Ronnie Harris in the 17–14 loss to the Pittsburgh Steelers at Three Rivers Stadium on 12-05-93

The progression of the most punt return yards by a Patriots player in a regular season game

5 punt return yards by Fred Bruney in the 13–10 loss to the Denver Broncos at BU Field on 09-09-60

20 punt return yards by Fred Bruney in the 28–24 win over the New York Titans at the Polo Grounds on 09-17-60

21 punt return yards by Walter Beach in the 13–0 loss to the Buffalo Bills at BU Field on 09-23-60

23 punt return yards by Dick Christy in the 35–0 shutout of the Los Angeles Chargers at the Los Angeles Coliseum on 10-08-60

34 punt return yards by Dick Christy in the 27–14 loss to the Oakland Raiders at Kezar Stadium on 10-16-60

34 punt return yards by Billy Wells in the 37–21 loss to the Houston Oilers at Jeppesen Stadium on 12-18-60

39 punt return yards by Fred Bruney in the 23–21 win over the Buffalo Bills at War Memorial Stadium on 09-23-61

62 punt return yards by Ron Burton in the 27–15 loss to the Houston Oilers at Jeppesen Stadium on 11-12-61

126 punt return yards by Billy Johnson in the 18–7 victory over the Houston Oilers at Fenway Park on 11-05-67

156 punt return yards by Mike Haynes in the 20–10 victory over the Buffalo Bills at Schaefer Stadium on 11-07-76

The progression of the most consecutive years that a Patriots player returned at least one punt in a season

3 consecutive years that Fred Bruney returned at least one punt (from 1960–62)

3 consecutive years that Ron Burton returned at least one punt (from 1960–62)

3 consecutive years that Billy Johnson returned at least one punt (from 1966–68)

4 consecutive years that Carl Garrett returned at least one punt (from 1969–72)

6 consecutive years that Mike Haynes returned at least one punt (from 1976–81)

8 consecutive years that Irving Fryar returned at least one punt (from 1984–91)

The progression of the most punt returns by a Patriots player in a regular season

12 punt returns by Billy Wells in 1960

23 punt returns by Fred Bruney in 1961 (Fred Bruney led the AFL in 1961)

25 punt returns by Bob Suci in 1963

27 punt returns by Mack Herron in 1973

35 punt returns by Mack Herron in 1974

45 punt returns by Mike Haynes in 1976

45 punt returns by Dave Meggett in 1995

52 punt returns by Dave Meggett in 1996

The progression of the most punt return yards by a Patriots player in a regular season

66 punt return yards by Billy Wells in 1960

128 punt return yards by Ron Burton in 1961

233 punt return yards by Bob Suci in 1963

282 punt return yards by Mack Herron in 1973

517 punt return yards by Mack Herron in 1974

608 punt return yards by Mike Haynes in 1976

The progression of the most career punt returns by a Patriots player

56 career punt returns by Ron Burton over the 1960–65 seasons

74 career punt returns by Mack Herron over the 1973–75 seasons

111 career punt returns by Mike Haynes over the 1976–81 seasons

206 career punt returns by Irving Fryar over the 1984–91 seasons

270 career punt returns by Troy Brown over the 1993–2007 seasons

The progression of the most career punt return yards by a Patriots player

389 career punt return yards by Ron Burton over the 1960–65 seasons

487 career punt return yards by Carl Garrett over the 1969–72 seasons

888 career punt return yards by Mack Herron over the 1973–75 seasons

1,159 career punt return yards by Mike Haynes over the 1976–81 seasons

2,055 career punt return yards by Irving Fryar over the 1984–91 seasons

2,625 career punt return yards by Troy Brown over the 1993–2007 seasons

The progression of the best average yards per punt return (more than three returns) in a regular season game

4-yard average per punt return by Dick Christy in the 13–0 loss to the Buffalo Bills on 09-23-60

4.6 average yards per punt return by Billy Wells in the 34–28 win over the Oakland Raiders on 11-04-60

11.3 average yards per punt return by Billy Wells in the 37–21 loss to the Houston Oilers on 12-18-60

25.2 average yards per punt return by Billy Johnson in the 18–7 victory over the Houston Oilers on 11-05-67

26.7 average yards per punt return by Mack Herron in the 24–16 victory over the Baltimore Colts on 10-07-73

39.0 average yards per punt return by Mike Haynes in the 20–10 victory over the Buffalo Bills on 11-07-76

The progression of the best punt return average (more than 10 returns) by a Patriots player in a season

5.6 average yards per punt return by Billy Wells in 1960

5.8 average yards per punt return by Ron Burton in 1962

9.3 average yards per punt return by Bob Suci in 1963

13.3 average yards per punt return by Carl Garrett in 1969

14.8 average yards per punt return by Mack Herron in 1974

The progression of the best career average yards per punt return (more than 10 returns) by a Patriots player

5.6 career average yards per punt return by Billy Wells in 1960

9.3 career average yards per punt return by Bob Suci in 1963

11.3 career average yards per punt return by Carl Garrett over the 1969–72 seasons

12.0 career average yards per punt return by Mack Herron over the 1973–75 seasons

The Longest Punt Returns

The progression of the longest punt return by a Patriots player in a regular season game

No return by Jim Colclough in the 13–10 loss to the Denver Broncos at BU Field on 09-09-60

5-yard punt return by Fred Bruney in the 13–10 loss to the Denver Broncos at BU Field on 09-09-60

19-yard return by Fred Bruney in the 28–24 victory over the New York Titans at the Polo Grounds on 09-17-60

21-yard punt return by Walter Beach in the 13–0 loss to the Buffalo Bills at BU Field on 09-23-60

29-yard punt return by Dick Christy in the 27–14 loss to the Oakland Raiders at Kezar Stadium on 10-16-60

62-yard punt return by Ron Burton in the 27–15 loss to the Houston Oilers at Jeppesen Stadium on 11-12-61

62-yard punt return by Carl Garrett in the 31–21 loss to the New York Jets at Harvard Stadium on 09-27-70

66-yard punt return by Mack Herron in the 42–3 rout of the Baltimore Colts at Schaefer Stadium on 10-06-74

89-yard return for a TD by Mike Haynes in the 20–10 victory over the Buffalo Bills at Schaefer Stadium on 11-07-76

The progression of the longest punt return by a Patriots Running Back in a regular season game

7-yard return by Dick Christy in the 28–24 victory over the New York Titans at the Polo Grounds on 09-17-60

21-yard return by Walter Beach in the 13–0 loss to the Buffalo Bills at BU Field on 09-23-60

29-yard return by Dick Christy in the 27–14 loss to the Oakland Raiders at Kezar Stadium on 10-16-60

62-yard return by Ron Burton in the 27–15 loss to the Houston Oilers at Jeppesen Stadium on 11-12-61

66-yard return by Mack Herron in the 42–3 rout of the Baltimore Colts at Schaefer Stadium on 10-06-74

The progression of the longest punt return by a Patriots Wide Receiver in a regular season game

No return by Jim Colclough in the 13–10 loss to the Denver Broncos at BU Field on 09-09-60

43-yard return by Bobby Leo in the 44–16 loss to the Buffalo Bills at Fenway Park on 12-09-67

53-yard return by Stanley Morgan in the 20–7 victory over the Buffalo Bills at Rich Stadium on 11-20-77

80-yard return for a TD by Stanley Morgan in the 50–21 rout of the Baltimore Colts at Schaefer Stadium on 11-18-79

85-yard return for a TD by Irving Fryar in the 17–14 victory over the Buffalo Bills at Rich Stadium on 09-22-85

85-yard return for a TD by Troy Brown in the 27–16 win over the Cleveland Browns at Foxboro Stadium on 12-09-01

The progression of the longest punt return by a Patriots Defensive Back in a regular season game

5-yard return by Fred Bruney in the 13–10 loss to the Denver Broncos at BU Field on 09-09-60

19-yard return by Fred Bruney in the 28–24 win over the New York Titans at the Polo Grounds on 09-17-60

22-yard return by Bob Suci in the 40–21 victory over the Denver Broncos at Fenway Park on 10-18-63

26-yard return by Tom Stephens in the 45–3 rout of the Houston Oilers at Fenway Park on 11-01-63

40-yard return by Dave Cloutier in the 35–14 loss to the New York Jets at Shea Stadium on 10-31-64

44-yard return by Jay Cunningham in the 48–14 loss to the Oakland Raiders at Fenway Park on 10-22-67

52-yard return by Billy Johnson in the 18–7 victory over the Houston Oilers at Fenway Park on 11-05-67

89-yard return for a TD by Mike Haynes in the 20–10 victory over the Buffalo Bills at Schaefer Stadium on 11-07-76

Every Punt Returned for a TD in the Regular Season

The only Patriots Defensive Back/Returnman who has returned a punt for a TD in a regular season game

Mike Haynes returned a punt 89 yards for a TD in the 20–10 win over the Buffalo Bills at Schaefer Stadium on 11-07-76

Mike Haynes returned a punt 62 yards for a TD in the 38–14 rout of the Denver Broncos at Schaefer Stadium on 11-28-76

Every Patriots Wide Receiver/Returnman who has returned a punt for a TD in a regular season game

1979 regular season

Stanley Morgan returned a punt 80 yards for TD in the 50–21 rout of the Baltimore Colts at Schaefer Stadium on 11-18-79

1980 regular season

Roland James returned a punt 75 yards for a TD in the 34–21 win over the New York Jets at Schaefer Stadium on 11-02-80

1985 regular season

Irving Fryar returned a punt 85 yards for TD in the 17–14 win over the Buffalo Bills at Rich Stadium on 09-22-85

Irving Fryar returned a punt 77 yards for TD in the 34–15 rout of the Indianapolis Colts at Sullivan Stadium on 11-10-85

1986 regular season

Irving Fryar returned a punt 59 yards for a TD in the 25–17 win over the Atlanta Falcons at Sullivan Stadium on 11-02-86

2000 regular season

Troy Brown returned a punt 66 yards for a TD in the 21–16 loss to the Buccaneers at Foxboro Stadium on 09-03-00

2001 championship season

Troy Brown took it 85 yards for a TD in the 27–16 victory over the Browns at Foxboro Stadium on 12-09-01

Troy Brown took it 68 yards for a TD in the 38–6 rout of the Panthers at Ericsson Stadium on 01-06-02

The only Patriots Running Back/Returnman who has returned a punt for a TD in a regular season game

Dave Meggett returned it 60 yards for a TD in the 23–22 win over the New York Giants at Giants Stadium on 12-21-96

The only Patriots player who has returned a punt for a TD for the game-winning points

Irving Fryar took a punt 85 yards for a TD in the 17–14 victory over the Buffalo Bills at Rich Stadium on 09-22-85

The only Patriots Wide Receiver who handed off on a reverse punt return to a Running Back in a game

Darryl Stingley took a Jeff West punt on his 3-yard line and on a reverse return handed off to Andy Johnson

(This reverse return gained eight total yards in the 24–17 loss to the St. Louis Cardinals at Busch Stadium on 11-02-75)

Every Patriots Running Back who has returned only one punt during his career with the team

1961 regular season

Billy Lott returned a punt eight yards in the 37–30 loss to the New York Titans at the Polo Grounds on 10-01-61

1963 regular season

Larry Garron returned a punt 23 yards in the 35–3 loss to the Kansas City Chiefs at Municipal Stadium on 12-14-63

1965 regular season

Jim Nance returned a punt 16 yards in the 22–6 win over the Chargers at Balboa Stadium on 10-31-65

The only Patriots Wide Receiver who attempted to return just one punt during his career with the Patriots

Jim Colclough returned a punt for no yards in the 13–10 loss to the Denver Broncos at BU Field on 09-09-60

The only Patriots Linebacker who returned a punt in a regular season game

Nick Buoniconti returned a punt eight yards in the 43–14 rout of the New York Titans at the Polo Grounds on 10-06-62

Every Patriots Defensive Back who has returned only one punt during his career with the Patriots

1960 regular season

Gino Cappelletti returned a punt three yards in the 13–10 loss to the Denver Broncos at BU Field on 09-09-60

Walter Beach returned a punt 21 yards in the 13–10 loss to the Buffalo Bills at BU Field on 09-23-60

1966 regular season

White Graves returned a punt five yards in the 17–10 loss to the Denver Broncos at Fenway Park on 11-06-66

1978 regular season

Dick Conn returned a punt two yards in the 33–24 victory over the Miami Dolphins at Schaefer Stadium on 10-22-78

1984 regular season

Ernest Gibson returned a punt three yards in the 28–21 victory over the New York Jets at the Meadowlands on 09-30-84

1989 regular season

Maurice Hurst returned a punt six yards in the 28–24 loss to the New Orleans Saints at Sullivan Stadium on 11-12-89

League Leaders

The Patriots players who were the NFL leader for the longest punt return in a specific regular season

1980 regular season

Roland James tied for the longest punt return in the NFL during the 1980 season

1985 regular season

Irving Fryar had the longest punt return in the NFL during the 1985 season

The NFL leader for the most punts returned for a TD during the season

1985 regular season

Irving Fryar tied for the NFL lead with two punt returns for a TD during the 1985 season

2001 championship season

Troy Brown led the NFL by returning two punts for a TD during the 2001 regular season

The NFL leader for the most average yards per punt return during the season

1985 regular season

Irving Fryar led the NFL with 14.1 yards per punt return during the 1985 season

2001 championship season

Troy Brown led the NFL with 14.2 yards per punt return during the 2001 season

The AFL leader with the most punt returns during a specific regular season

1961 regular season

Fred Bruney led the AFL with 23 punt returns during the 1961 season

1962 regular season

Ron Burton led the AFL with 21 punt returns during the 1962 season

The only Patriots player who was NFL leader with the most punt returns in a specific regular season

Irving Fryar led the NFL with 37 punt returns during the 1985 season

The Playoffs

The only Patriots Punt Returnman who was named the AFC Special Teams Player of the Week in a playoff game

Troy Brown took a punt 55 yards for a TD and lateraled a blocked FGA in the 24–17 win over Pittsburgh on 01-27-02

The progression of the most punt returns by a Patriots player in a playoff game

2 punt returns by Art Graham in the 26–8 win over the Buffalo Bills at War Memorial Stadium on 12-28-63

2 punt returns by Stanley Morgan in the 31–14 loss to the Houston Oilers at Schaefer Stadium on 12-31-78

4 punt returns by Irving Fryar in the 26–14 victory over the New York Jets at the Meadowlands on 12-28-85

7 punt returns by Dave Meggett in the 28–3 rout of the Pittsburgh Steelers at Foxboro Stadium on 01-05-97

The progression of the most punt return yards by a Patriots player in a playoff game

34 punt return yards by Art Graham in the 26–8 win over the Buffalo Bills at War Memorial Stadium on 12-28-63

72 punt return yards by Dave Meggett in the 28–3 rout of the Pittsburgh Steelers at Foxboro Stadium on 01-05-97

80 punt return yards by Troy Brown in the 24–17 victory over the Pittsburgh Steelers at Heinz Field on 01-27-02

The progression of the most career punt returns by a Patriots player in the playoffs

2 career punt returns by Art Graham in the 28–6 victory over the Buffalo Bills on 12-28-63

2 career punt returns by Mike Haynes in two playoff games for the New England Patriots

2 career punt returns by Stanley Morgan in the 31–14 loss to the Houston Oilers on 12-31-78

8 career punt returns by Irving Fryar in three playoff games for the New England Patriots

18 career punt returns by Dave Meggett in five playoff games for the New England Patriots

33 career punt returns by Troy Brown in 20 playoff games for the New England Patriots

The progression of the most career punt return yards by a Patriots player in the playoffs

34 career punt return yards by Art Graham in the 28–6 win over the Buffalo Bills on 12-28-63

47 career punt return yards by Irving Fryar in three playoff games for the New England Patriots

165 career punt return yards by Dave Meggett in five playoff games for the New England Patriots

315 career punt return yards by Troy Brown in 20 playoff games for the New England Patriots

The progression of the most consecutive playoff games that a Patriots player returned at least one punt

2 consecutive playoff games that Irving Fryar returned at least one punt

5 consecutive playoff games that Dave Meggett returned at least one punt

10 consecutive playoff games that Troy Brown returned at least one punt

The progression of the longest punt return by a Patriots player in a playoff game

6-yard punt return by Art Graham in the 26–8 victory over the Bills at War Memorial Stadium on 12-28-63

28-yard punt return by Art Graham in the 26–8 victory over the Bills at War Memorial Stadium on 12-28-63

55-yard punt return for a TD by Troy Brown in the 24–17 win over the Steelers at Heinz Field on 01-27-02

The progression of the longest punt return by a Patriots Running Back in a playoff game

8-yard return by Dave Meggett in the 28–3 rout of the Pittsburgh Steelers at Foxboro Stadium on 01-05-97

14-yard return by Dave Meggett in the 28–3 rout of the Pittsburgh Steelers at Foxboro Stadium on 01-05-97

20-yard return by Dave Meggett in the 35–21 loss to the Green Bay Packers at the Superdome on 01-26-97

The progression of the longest punt return by a Patriots Wide Receiver in a playoff game

6-yard return by Art Graham in the 26–8 win over the Buffalo Bills at War Memorial Stadium on 12-28-63

28-yard return by Art Graham in the 26–8 win over the Buffalo Bills at War Memorial Stadium on 12-28-63

55-yard return for a TD by Troy Brown in the 24–17 victory over the Pittsburgh Steelers at Heinz Field on 01-27-02

The progression of the longest punt return by a Patriots Defensive Back in a playoff game

13-yard return by Mike Haynes in the 24–21 loss to the Oakland Raiders at the Oakland Coliseum on 12-18-76

20-yard return by Troy Brown in the 20–3 rout of the Indianapolis Colts at Gillette Stadium on 01-16-05 (Troy Brown, who caught two passes for 13 yards, was used as a defensive back in this 20–3 rout of the Colts)

The only Patriots player who has returned a punt for a TD in a playoff game

Troy Brown returned a punt 55 yards for a TD in the 24–17 win over the Pittsburgh Steelers on 01-27-02

The progression of the highest punt return average by a Patriots player in a playoff game

17.0 yards per return by Art Graham in the 26–8 win over Buffalo at War Memorial Stadium on 12-28-63

26.7 yards per return by Troy Brown in the 24–17 win over the Pittsburgh Steelers at Heinz Field on 01-27-02

The progression of the career highest punt return average (3+ returns) by a Patriots player in the playoffs

5.8 career average yards per punt return by Irving Fryar in five playoff games

9.1 career average yards per punt return by Dave Meggett in five playoff games

9.7 career average yards per punt return by Tim Dwight in two playoff games

Blocked Punts, Blocked Extra Points, and Blocked Field Goals

This section provides the names of every Patriots player who has blocked a punt, an extra point, and/or a field-goal attempt. There have been 56 different Patriots players who have accomplished at least one of these feats. You will also find the name of the opposing team's punter or kicker whose attempt was blocked, and the outcome, score, location, and date of the game.

You will find the name of every defensive lineman, linebacker, and defensive back of the Patriots who has blocked a punt, a field-goal attempt, or an extra-point attempt. Of the 47 field-goal attempts that have been blocked by a Patriots player, seven have been blocked by a defensive back, 33 have been blocked by a defensive lineman, and seven have been blocked by a linebacker. Did you know that Richard Seymour is the only first-round draft pick of the Patriots who has blocked a field-goal attempt in consecutive regular season games?

Every Linebacker/Special Teams player of the Patriots who blocked a punt in a regular season game

1963 regular season

Jack Rudolph blocked a punt by Curley Johnson in the 31–24 loss to the New York Jets at the Polo Grounds on 10-05-63

1986 regular season

Larry McGrew blocked a punt by Harry Newsome in the 34–0 shutout of the Steelers at Three Rivers Stadium on 10-19-86

The only Patriots player to block a punt even though his team had only 10 men on the field at the time

Maurice Hurst blocked a punt by Dan Stryzinski in the 24–3 loss to the Pittsburgh Steelers at Three Rivers Stadium on 12-09-90

Every Tight End/Special Teams player of the Patriots who blocked a punt in a regular season game

1967 regular season

Bobby Nichols blocked a punt by Larry Seiple on the fourth play in the 41–32 loss to Miami at Miami on 12-17-67

1971 regular season

Roland Moss blocked a punt by Spike Jones in the 38–33 win over the Buffalo Bills at Schaefer Stadium on 11-14-71

1987 regular season

Willie Scott blocked a punt by Rohn Stark in the 24–0 shutout of the Indianapolis Colts at Sullivan Stadium on 11-22-87

Every Wide Receiver/Special Teams player of the Patriots who has blocked a punt in a game

1979 regular season

Don Westbrook partially blocked a punt by Chuck Ramsey in the 56–3 rout of the New York Jets at Schaefer Stadium on 09-09-79 (Stanley Morgan made a leaping 37-yard TD reception on the Patriots' next play)

2007 undefeated regular season

Kelley Washington blocked a punt by Ben Graham in the 20–10 victory over the New York Jets at Gillette Stadium on 12-16-07 (Laurence Maroney scored two plays later on a one-yard TD run with 1:08 left in the first half)

The Patriots player who has deflected two punts that were not officially recognized as a blocked punt

1996 regular season

Larry Whigham deflected a 17-yard punt by Jeff Feagles in the 31–0 shutout of the Arizona Cardinals on 09-15-96

1998 regular season

Larry Whigham deflected a 13-yard punt by Mark Royals in the 30–27 win over the New Orleans Saints on 10-04-98

Every Defensive Lineman of the Patriots who has blocked a punt in a regular season game

1960 regular season

Abe Cohen blocked a punt by George Herring in the 31–24 loss to the Broncos at Bears Stadium on 10-23-60

1961 regular season

Dick Klein blocked a punt by Billy Atkins in the 52–21 rout of the Bills at BU Field on 10-22-61

Dick Klein blocked a punt by Jerry Burch in the 20–17 win over the Raiders at Candlestick Park on 12-09-61

1964 regular season

Bob Dee blocked a punt by Jim Fraser in the 39–10 rout of the Broncos at Bears Stadium on 10-04-64

1969 regular season

Ezell Jones blocked a punt by Larry Seiple in the 38–23 win over the Dolphins at Tampa Stadium on 11-30-69

1973 regular season

Willie Banks blocked a punt by Julian Fagan in the 9–7 loss to the Jets at Schaefer Stadium on 10-14-73

Every Defensive Back/special teams player of the Patriots who blocked a punt in a regular season game

1961 regular season

Don Webb blocked a punt by Paul Maguire in the 41–0 shutout of the Chargers at Balboa Stadium on 12-17-61

1966 regular season

White Graves blocked a punt by Bob Scarpitto in the 17–10 loss to the Broncos at Fenway Park on 11-06-66

1975 regular season

John Sanders blocked a punt by Tom Wittum in the 24–16 win over the 49ers at Schaefer Stadium on 10-26-75

1979 regular season

Rick Sanford blocked a punt by Bucky Dilt in the 50–21 rout of the Colts at Schaefer Stadium on 11-18-79

1986 regular season

Rod McSwain blocked a punt by Dale Hatcher in the 30–28 win over the Rams at Anaheim Stadium on 11-16-86

Eugene Profit blocked a punt by Brian Hansen in the 21–20 victory over the Saints at the Superdome on 11-30-86

1987 regular season

Eugene Profit blocked a punt by John Teltschik in the 34–31 overtime loss to the Eagles at Sullivan Stadium on 11-29-87

1990 regular season

Maurice Hurst blocked a punt by Dan Stryzinski in the 24–3 loss to the Steelers at Three Rivers Stadium on 12-09-90

1996 regular season

Larry Whigham blocked a punt by Greg Montgomery in the 46–38 win over the Ravens at Memorial Stadium on 10-06-96

1999 regular season

Larry Whigham blocked a punt by Sean Landeta in the 24–9 loss to the Eagles at Veterans Stadium on 12-19-99

The only Patriots who has returned an interception for a TD and took a blocked punt for a TD in the same game

Don Webb returned a pass 31 yards for a TD and blocked a punt, which he took 20 yards for a TD on 12-17-61

The only Patriots player who has blocked a punt and intercepted a pass in the same game

Don Webb blocked a Paul Maguire punt and intercepted Jack Kemp in the 41–0 shutout of San Diego on 12-17-61

The only Patriots player to recover a punt, that was blocked by the goal post, in the end zone for a TD

LeRoy Moore fell on Wayne Crow's punt in the end zone for a TD in the 20–17 win over Oakland at BU Field on 11-17-61 (The punt was booted from the end zone, hit the goal line goal post crossbar, and deflected back into the end zone)

The combination of Patriots players who have blocked a punt and recovered the ball in the end zone for a TD

1967 regular season

Bobby Nichols blocked a punt that J.D. Garrrett recovered for a TD in the 41–32 loss to the Dolphins on 12-17-67

1973 regular season

Willie Banks blocked a punt that Will Foster recovered for a TD in the 9–7 loss to the Jets on 10-14-73 (Art Moore and Sandy Durko initially recovered the loose ball before they fumbled it into the end zone)

The combination of Patriots players who have blocked and returned the blocked punt for a TD

1986 regular season

Eugene Profit blocked a punt that Mosi Tatupu took 17 yards for a TD in the 21–20 win over the Saints on 11-30-86

1996 regular season

Larry Whigham blocked a punt that Tedy Bruschi took four yards for a TD in the 46–38 win over the Ravens on 10-06-96

The only Patriots player who advanced the loose ball after a Patriots punt was blocked for a first down

Mike Patrick's punt was blocked, but Doug Beaudoin picked up the loose ball and advanced it eight yards for a first down in the Patriots 17–3 victory over the Baltimore Colts at Schaefer Stadium on 10-23-77

The only Patriots player who has blocked an extra-point attempt and intercepted a pass in the same game

John Sanders blocked a Garo Yepremian PAT and returned a Bob Griese pass 18 yards in the 22–14 loss on 09-28-75

Every Patriots player who has blocked a punt, recovered and returned it for a TD

1961 regular season

Don Webb blocked a punt and took it 20 yards for a TD in the 41–0 shutout of the San Diego Chargers on 12-17-61

1971 regular season

Roland Moss blocked a punt and returned it 10 yards for a TD in the 38–33 win over the Buffalo Bills on 11-14-71

1979 regular season

Rick Sanford blocked a punt and returned it eight yards for a TD in the 50–21 rout of the Baltimore Colts on 11-18-79

1986 regular season

Rod McSwain blocked a punt and returned it 31 yards for a TD in the 30–28 win over the LA Rams on 11-16-86

1987 regular season

Willie Scott blocked a punt and took it three yards for a TD in the 24–0 shutout of the Indianapolis Colts on 11-22-87

Every Defensive Lineman of the Patriots who has blocked an extra-point attempt in a regular season game

1974 regular season

Julius Adams blocked a PAT by John Leypoldt in the 29–28 loss to the Buffalo Bills at Schaefer Stadium on 11-03-74

Donnell Smith blocked a PAT by Roy Gerela in the 21–17 loss to the Pittsburgh Steelers at Schaefer Stadium on 12-08-74

1975 regular season

Jerry Patton blocked an extra-point attempt by John Leypoldt in the 34–14 loss to Buffalo at Schaefer Stadium on 12-14-75

1991 regular season

Garin Veris blocked a PAT by Scott Norwood in the 22–17 loss to the Buffalo Bills at Rich Stadium on 11-03-91

1995 regular season

Troy Barnett blocked a PAT by Doug Christie in the 35–25 win over the Bills at Rich Stadium on 11-26-95

Every Linebacker of the Patriots who has blocked an extra-point attempt in a regular season game

1960 regular season

Tom Addison blocked an extra point by Gene Mingo in the 31–24 loss to Denver at Bears Stadium on 10-23-60

1966 regular season

Nick Buoniconti blocked a Fletcher Smith PAT in the 43–24 loss to the Chiefs at Fenway Park on 09-25-66

1967 regular season

Ed Philpott blocked an extra-point attempt by Jim Turner in the 29–24 loss to the Jets at Fenway Park on 11-19-67

1969 regular season

John Bramlett blocked a PAT by Karl Kremser in the 38–23 win over Miami at Tampa Stadium on 11-30-69

1984 regular season

Steve Nelson blocked a PAT by Uwe Von Schamann in the 44–24 loss to the Dolphins at Sullivan on 10-21-84

Steve Nelson blocked a Neil O'Donoghue PAT in the 33–10 loss to the Cardinals at Sullivan Stadium on 12-02-84

1985 regular season

Don Blackmon blocked a PAT by Al DelGreco in the 26–20 win over the Packers at Sullivan Stadium on 09-08-85

Every Defensive Back of the Patriots who has blocked an extra-point attempt in a regular season game

1966 regular season

Dick Felt blocked a PAT by Fletcher Smith in the 43–24 loss to the Chiefs at Fenway Park on 09-25-66

1967 regular season
John Charles blocked an extra point by Gary Kroner in the 26–21 loss to Denver at Bears Stadium on 09-03-67

1973 regular season
Ralph Anderson blocked an extra point by George Hunt in the 18–13 loss to the Colts at Memorial on 12-16-73

1974 regular season
Willie Osley blocked a John Leypoldt PAT in the 30–28 loss to the Bills at Rich Stadium on 10-20-74

1975 regular season
John Sanders blocked a Garo Yepremian PAT in the 22–14 loss to the Dolphins at Schaefer Stadium on 09-28-75

John Sanders blocked an extra-point attempt by Pat Leahy in the 36–7 loss to the Jets at Shea Stadium on 10-05-75

1979 regular season
Tim Fox blocked a PAT by Chester Marcol in the 27–13 loss to the Packers at Lambeau Field on 10-01-79

1983 regular season
Ronnie Lippett blocked an extra-point attempt by Pat Leahy in the 23–13 win over the Jets at Sullivan Stadium on 09-18-83

2002 regular season
Tebucky Jones blocked a PAT by Olindo Mare in the 26–13 loss to Miami at Pro Player Stadium on 10-06-02

The only Patriots Hall of Fame player who has blocked a FGA by another Pro Football Hall of Fame player

Nick Buoniconti blocked a 36-yard FGA by George Blanda in the 31–10 loss to Houston on 09-19-65

The only Patriots player who has blocked a field goal that was returned by a teammate for a TD

Andre Tippett blocked a 48-yard FGA that was returned 71 yards for a TD by Raymond Clayborn on 10-18-87

The combination of Patriots players who have blocked a field goal, recovered, lateraled, and returned it for a TD

Steve Nelson blocked a FGA that John Zamberlin recovered and then lateraled to Mike Haynes. (Haynes took this lateral 65 yards for a TD in the 21–11 victory over the New York Jets on 10-05-80)

The only Patriots player who blocked a FGA in the overtime period

Chad Eaton blocked a 30-yard FGA by Steve Christie in overtime of the 13–10 overtime win over the Bills on 12-17-00

The only Patriots player to block a field goal with less than 30 seconds left in the fourth quarter to force overtime

Mike Jones blocked a 29-yard FGA with 16 seconds left in the 27–24 overtime win over the Jets at Foxboro Stadium on 09-14-97

Every Linebacker of the Patriots who has blocked a FGA in a regular season game

1960 regular season
Harry Jacobs blocked a 35-yard FGA by Ben Agajanian in the 45–16 loss to the Chargers at BU Field on 10-28-60

1965 regular season
Nick Buoniconti blocked a 36-yard FGA by George Blanda in the 31–10 loss to Houston at Rice Stadium on 09-19-65

Nick Buoniconti blocked a 27-yard FGA by Gary Kroner in the 28–20 win over Denver at Bears Stadium on 12-12-65

1968 regular season
Nick Buoniconti blocked a 40-yard FGA by John Wittenborn in the 16–0 loss to Houston at Fenway Park on 10-13-68

1973 regular season
Steve Kiner blocked a 39-yard FGA by Jan Stenerud in the 10–7 loss to the Chiefs at Schaefer Stadium on 09-23-73

1980 regular season
Steve Nelson blocked a 49-yard FGA by Pat Leahy in the 21–11 win over the Jets at Shea Stadium on 10-05-80

1986 regular season
Don Blackmon blocked a 53-yard FGA by Mick Luckhurst in the 25–17 win over Atlanta at Sullivan Stadium on 11-02-86

1987 regular season
Andre Tippett blocked a 48-yard FGA by Tony Zendejas in the 21–7 win vs Houston at the Astrodome on 10-18-87

Every Defensive Back of the Patriots who has blocked a FGA in a regular season game

1965 regular season

Ron Hall blocked a Tommy Brooker 28-yard FGA with 26 seconds left in the 10–10 tie with the Chiefs on 11-21-65

1968 regular season

John Charles blocked a 47-yard FGA by Mike Mercer in the 16–7 win over Buffalo at War Memorial on 09-08-68

John Charles blocked a 25-yard FGA by John Wittenborn in the 16–0 loss to Houston at Fenway Park on 10-13-68

1972 regular season

Larry Carwell blocked a 51-yard FGA by Horst Mulmann in the 31–7 loss to the Bengals at Schaefer Stadium on 09-17-72

Ron Bolton blocked a 32-yard FGA by Bill Bell to end the half in the 21–20 win over Atlanta at Schaefer Stadium on 09-24-72

1989 regular season

Darryl Holmes blocked a 33-yard FGA by Mike Cofer in the 37–20 loss to San Francisco at Stanford Stadium on 10-22-89

2001 championship season

Tebucky Jones blocked a 25-yard FGA by Mike Vanderjagt in the 38–17 rout of the Colts at the Dome on 10-21-01

The only Defensive Lineman of the New England Patriots who has tipped but not blocked a FGA

Richard Seymour tipped a 50-yard FGA by Adam Vinatieri in the 24–20 win over Indianapolis at the RCA Dome on 11-04-07

Every Defensive Lineman of the Patriots who blocked a FGA in a regular season game

1962 regular season

Bob Dee blocked a 37-yard FGA by Gene Mingo in the 41–16 rout of the Broncos at BU Field on 09-21-62

1964 Regular Season

Larry Eisenhauer blocked a nine-yard FGA by Mike Mercer in the 43–43 tie with the Raiders at Fenway Park on 10-16-64

1965 regular season

George Pyne blocked a 30-yard FGA by Pete Gogolak in the 24–7 loss to the Bills at War Memorial Stadium on 09-11-65

Larry Eisenhauer blocked a 35-yard FGA by Herb Travenio in the 22–6 win over the Chargers at Balboa on 10-31-65

1972 regular season

Rick Cash blocked a 48-yard FGA by Garo Yepremian in the 52–0 loss to Miami at the Orange Bowl on 11-12-72

1973 regular season

Art Moore blocked a 43-yard FGA by Skip Butler in the 32–0 shutout of the Oilers at the Astrodome on 11-25-73

Art Moore blocked a 47-yard FGA by Dennis Partee in the 30–14 win over the Chargers at Schaefer Stadium on 12-02-73

1974 regular season

Art Moore blocked a 41-yard FGA by David Ray in the 20–14 victory over the Rams at Schaefer Stadium on 09-29-74

1975 regular season

Ray Hamilton blocked a 44-yard FGA by Jim Bakken in the 24–17 loss to St. Louis at Busch Stadium on 11-02-75

Pete Cusick blocked a 48-yard FGA by Pat Leahy in the 30–28 loss to the Jets at Schaefer Stadium on 12-07-75

Pete Cusick blocked a 46-yard FGA by Pat Leahy in the 30–28 loss to the Jets at Schaefer Stadium on 12-07-75

1977 regular season

Mel Lunsford blocked a 39-yard FGA by Don Cockroft in the 30–27 overtime loss to Cleveland at Cleveland on 09-26-77

Julius Adams blocked a 3-yard FGA by Pat Leahy in the 30–27 loss to the Jets at Shea Stadium on 10-02-77

Ray Hamilton blocked a 19-yard FGA by Ove Johansson in the 14–6 win over the Eagles at Schaefer Stadium on 11-27-77

1981 regular season

Richard Bishop blocked a 40-yard FGA by Mark Moseley to end the half in the 24–22 loss at RFK on 10-25-81

1982 regular season
Julius Adams blocked a 45-yard FGA by Uwe Von Schamann in the 3–0 shutout of Miami at Schaefer Stadium on 12-12-82

Lester Williams blocked a 52-yard FGA by Norm Johnson in the 16–0 win vs Seattle at the Kingdome on 12-19-82

1984 regular season
Julius Adams blocked a 42-yard FGA by Raul Allegre in the 16–10 victory over the Colts at Sullivan Stadium on 12-16-84

1985 regular season
Kenneth Sims blocked a 40-yard FGA by Al DelGreco in the 26–20 win over the Packers at Sullivan Stadium on 09-08-85

1989 regular season
Kenneth Sims blocked a 45-yard FGA by Mike Cofer in the 37–20 loss to the 49ers at Stanford on 10-22-89

1991 regular season
Brent Williams blocked a 48-yard FGA by Dean Biasucci in the 16–7 win over the Colts on 09-01-91

1994 regular season
Troy Barnett blocked a 38-yard FGA by Kevin Butler in the 13–3 win over the Bears at Soldier Field on 12-24-94

1995 regular season
Troy Barnett blocked a 54-yard FGA by Pete Stoyanovich in the 20–3 loss to the Dolphins at Foxboro Stadium on 09-10-95

1997 regular season
Mike Jones blocked a John Hall 29-yard FGA with 16 seconds left in the 27–24 overtime home win vs the Jets on 09-14-97

1998 regular season
Chad Eaton blocked a 38-yard FGA by John Hall in the 24–14 loss to the Jets at Foxboro Stadium on 10-19-98

Ferric Collons blocked a 47-yard FGA by Morton Andersen in the 41–10 loss to Atlanta at Foxboro Stadium on 11-08-98

2000 regular season
Chad Eaton blocked a 23-yard FGA by Steve Christie in the 13–10 overtime win over Buffalo at Ralph Wilson Stadium on 12-17-00

Chad Eaton blocked a 30-yard FGA by Steve Christie in the 13–10 overtime win over Buffalo at Ralph Wilson Stadium on 12-17-00

2001 championship season
Brandon Mitchell blocked a 46-yard FGA by Mike Vanderjagt in the 38–17 rout of Indianapolis at the Hoosier Dome on 10-21-01

Richard Seymour blocked a 43-yard FGA by John Carney in the 34–17 win over the Saints at Foxboro Stadium on 11-25-01

2002 regular season
Richard Seymour blocked a 49-yard FGA by Sebastian Janikowski in the 27–20 road loss to Oakland on 11-17-02

Richard Seymour blocked a 43-yard FGA by Gary Anderson in the 24–17 win over Minnesota at Gillette Stadium on 11-24-02

2003 championship season
Dan Klecko blocked a 48-yard FGA by John Hall in the 20–17 loss to the Redskins at FedEx Field on 09-28-03

Richard Seymour blocked a 35-yard FGA by Olindo Mare late in the 19–13 overtime road win over Miami on 10-19-03

2006 regular season
Mike Wright blocked a 40-yard FGA by Olino Mare in the 20–10 win over the Dolphins at Gillette Stadium on 10-08-06

Richard Seymour blocked a 45-yard FGA by Robbie Gould in the 17–13 win over the Bears at Gillette Stadium on 11-26-06

The only Patriots player to block a FGA with less than 30 seconds left in the game to preserve a tie
Ron Hall blocked a 28-yard FGA with 26 seconds left to preserve the 10–10 tie with the Chiefs at Fenway Park on 11-21-65

The only Patriots player who has blocked a FGA and returned the loose ball for a TD
Larry Carwell blocked a 51-yard FGA by Horst Mulmann and took it 45 yards for a TD at Schaefer Stadium on 09-17-72

The Playoffs

Every Patriots Defensive Lineman who has blocked a FGA in a playoff game

1994 AFC Wild Card playoff game

Troy Barnett blocked a 50-yard FGA by Matt Stover to end the half in the 20–13 loss to Cleveland on 01-01-95

2001 AFC Championship Game

Brandon Mitchell blocked a 34-yard FGA by Kris Brown in the 24–17 win over the Pittsburgh Steelers on 01-27-02

2003 AFC Divisional playoff game

Richard Seymour blocked a 31-yard FGA by Gary Anderson in the 17–14 win over the Tennessee Titans on 01-10-04

The players who have blocked a field goal, recovered, lateraled, and returned it for a TD in a Patriots playoff game

2001 AFC Championship playoff game

Brandon Mitchell blocked a field goal and Troy Brown recovered and returned it 11 yards before he lateraled to Antwan Harris, who took the ball 49 yards for a TD in the 24–17 victory over the Steelers on 01-27-02

Defense

Interceptions

In this chapter you will find the progression of the most interceptions, the longest interception returns, and the most return yards by a Patriots defensive lineman, linebacker, and defensive back. It includes details of every interception that was returned for a touchdown by a Patriots player, the quarterback who was intercepted, the score, outcome, location, and date of the game as well. Two passes that were intercepted by a Patriots defender were thrown by a wide receiver rather than by a quarterback. Coincidentally, both of these receivers (Henry Marshall and Otis Taylor) played for the Kansas City Chiefs.

In total, 96 defensive backs, 56 linebackers, and 11 defensive lineman have intercepted a pass for the Boston/New England Patriots over the course of the 1960–2008 regular seasons. Twenty-two of these defensive backs only recorded one regular season interception. Roland James and Ty Law hold the team record of intercepting at least one pass in 10 consecutive seasons. Twenty-eight Patriots linebackers only had one regular season interception. Patriots linebacker Nick Buoniconti intercepted at least one pass in seven consecutive seasons. Henry Thomas and Anthony Pleasant are the only defensive linemen with multiple career regular season interceptions for the Patriots.

Gino Cappelletti was the first Patriots defensive back to lead the team with the most interceptions in a regular season with four interceptions during the 1960 season. Don Webb and Ross O'Hanley had five interceptions during the 1961 and 1962 seasons, respectively. Bob Suci had eight interceptions for the Boston Patriots in 1963. Ron Hall was the first Patriots defensive back to lead the team for three consecutive regular seasons as he had 11, three, and six interceptions during the 1964–66 seasons. Nick Buoniconti tied Harry Jacobs' record of four interceptions by a Patriots linebacker during the 1967 season. Don Webb also had four interceptions in the 1967 season for the Boston Patriots.

From 1968–72, the following defensive backs where the leading interceptors of the team, Leroy Mitchell, Larry Carwell, Daryl Johnson, Larry Carwell, and Honor Jackson. Ron Bolton and Mike Haynes had three consecutive years leading the team with the most interceptions during the 1973–78 seasons. Raymond Clayborn had back to back years with five interceptions. Rick Sanford and Tim Fox were the first pair of defensive backs to tie for the team lead in 1981. From 1982–86, the following defensive backs led the team with the most interceptions, Mike Haynes, Rick Sanford, Raymond Clayborn, Fred Marion, and Ronnie Lippett. Fred Marion had the most interceptions in 1987 and tied for the most with Raymond Clayborn and Roland James in 1988.

Maurice Hurst was the first defensive back to lead the Patriots with the most interceptions in a season for six consecutive seasons, although he did tie for the team lead with Ronnie Lippett and Fred Marion in 1990 and with Jerome Henderson in 1992. Vincent Brown was the only Patriots linebacker to have more interceptions in a season than any defensive back as he had four during the 1995 season. Willie "Big Play" Clay led the Patriots with four interceptions and six interceptions during the 1996 and 1997 seasons. Ty Law was the NFL leader with nine interceptions during the 1998 regular season. Lawyer Milloy led the team in 1999 and tied for the team lead with Ty Law and Tebucky Jones during the 2000 season.

Otis "My Man" Smith led the team with five interceptions during the team's first championship season in 2001. Ty Law and Terrell Buckley tied for the team lead with four interceptions each during the 2002 regular season. Ty Law and Tyrone Poole tied for the team lead with six interceptions each during their second championship season in 2003. Eugene Wilson was the AFC Defensive Player of the Month in September 2004, and he led the team during its third

championship season in 2004. Ellis Hobbs and Asante Samuel tied for the team lead with three inteceptions during the 2005 regular season. Asante Samuel had 10 interceptions in 2006 and six interceptions in the 2007 undefeated regular season. Brandon Meriweather led the Patriots with four interceptions in 2008.

The six AFL All-Star Defensive Backs of the Boston Patriots who have intercepted a pass in a regular season game

Ross O'Hanley, Fred Bruney, Dick Felt, Ron Hall, Chuck Shonta, and Leroy Mitchell

The four AFL All-Star Defensive Linemen of the Boston Patriots who have intercepted a pass in a regular season game

Houston Antwine, Bob Dee, Larry Eisenhauer, and Jim Lee Hunt

The two AFL All-Star Linebackers of the Boston Patriots who have intercepted a pass in a regular season game

Tom Addison and Nick Buoniconti

The seven AFC Pro Bowl Defensive Backs of the New England Patriots who have intercepted a pass in a regular season game

Raymond Clayborn, Tim Fox, Mike Haynes, Ty Law, Fred Marion, Lawyer Milloy, and Asante Samuel

The two AFC Pro Bowl Defensive Lineman of the New England Patriots who have intercepted a pass in a regular season game

Willie McGinest and Richard Seymour

The six AFC Pro Bowl Linebackers of the New England Patriots who have intercepted a pass in a regular season game

Tedy Bruschi, Willie McGinest, Steve Nelson, Johnny Rembert, Chris Slade, Andre Tippett, and Mike Vrabel

The list of every Patriots player who had the most interceptions, most return yards, and the longest interception return each year

Year	Most Interceptions	Most Int Return Yards	The longest interception return
1960	Gino Cappelletti and Harry Jacobs	Chuck Shonta	Chuck Shonta
1961	Don Webb	Don Webb	Don Webb
1962	Three players had five interceptions	Ron Hall	Ron Hall
1963	Bob Suci	Bob Suci (team record 277)	Bob Suci
1964	Ron Hall (team record of 11)	Ron Hall	Ron Hall
1965	Ron Hall and Nick Buoniconti	Chuck Shonta	Don Webb
1966	Ron Hall and Tom Hennessey	Ron Hall	Ron Hall
1967	Don Webb and Nick Buoniconti	Don Webb	Jay Cunningham
1968	Leroy Mitchell	Leroy Mitchell	John Charles
1969	Three players had four interceptions	Larry Carwell	Larry Carwell
1970	Daryl Johnson	Art McMahon	Art McMahon
1971	Larry Carwell	John Outlaw	John Outlaw
1972	Honor Jackson	Honor Jackson	Honor Jackson
1973	Ron Bolton	Ron Bolton	Ron Bolton
1974	Ron Bolton	Sam Hunt	Jack Mildren
1975	Ron Bolton	Kevin Reilly	Kevin Reilly
1976	Mike Haynes	Prentice McCray	Sam Hunt
1977	Mike Haynes	Prentice McCray	Prentice McCray
1978	Mike Haynes	Mike Haynes	Mike Haynes
1979	Raymond Clayborn	Mike Haynes	Mike Hawkins
1980	Raymond Clayborn	Raymond Clayborn	Rod Shoate
1981	Rick Sanford and Tim Fox	Mark Buben	Mark Buben
1982	Mike Haynes	Rick Sanford	Rick Sanford (99-yard return for a TD)
1983	Rick Sanford	Roland James	Roland James
1984	Ray Clayborn and Ron Lippett	Raymond Clayborn	Raymond Clayborn
1985	Feed Marion	Fred Marion	Fred Marion
1986	Ronnie Lippett	Ronnie Lippett	*Two players combined for the longest
1987	Fred Marion	Ronnie Lippett	Ed Williams
1988	Three players had four interceptions	Raymond Clayborn	Rod McSwain
1989	Maurice Hurst	Roland James	Roland James
1990	Three players had four interceptions	Ronnie Lippett	Ronnie Lippett
1991	Maurice Hurst	Fred Marion	Fred Marion
1992	Jerome Henderson and M. Hurst	Chris Singleton	Chris Singleton
1993	Maurice Hurst	Maurice Hurst	Harlon Barnett
1994	Maurice Hurst	Maurice Hurst	Maurice Hurst and Harlon Barnett
1995	Vincent Brown	Myron Guyton	Myron Guyton
1996	Willie Clay	Willie Clay	Willie McGinest
1997	Willie Clay	Willie Clay	Jimmy Hitchcock (100-yard return for a TD)
1998	Ty Law	Ty Law	Ty Law
1999	Lawyer Milloy	Andy Katzenmoyer	Andy Kaztenmoyer
2000	Three players had two interceptions	Otis Smith	Otis Smith
2001	Otis Smith	Otis Smith	Otis Smith
2002	Terrell Buckley and Ty Law	Victor Green	Victor Green (90-yard return for a TD)
2003	Ty Law and Tyrone Poole	Ty Law	Ty Law
2004	Eugene Wilson	Tedy Bruschi	Tedy Bruschi
2005	Asante Samuel and Ellis Hobbs	James Sanders	James Sanders
2006	Asante Samuel	Asante Samuel	Ellis Hobbs
2007	Asante Samuel	Asante Samuel	Adalius Thomas
2008	Brandon Meriweather	Deltha O'Neal	Deltha O'Neal

* 1962: Ross O'Hanley, Dick Felt, and Tom Addison each had five interceptions; 1969: Larry Carwell, John Charles, and Ed Philpott each had four interceptions; 1988: Raymond Clayborn, Fred Marion, and Roland James each had four interceptions; 1990: Ronnie Lippett, Maurcice Hurst, and Fred Marion each had four interceptions; 2000: Ty Law, Tebucky Jones, and Lawyer Milloy each had two interceptions

* Johnny Rembert returned a pass 37 yards and then lateraled it to Andre Tippett who took it an additional 32 yards in 1986

The progression of the most interceptions in a regular season game

The progression of the most interceptions by a Patriots Defensive Back in a regular season game

1 interception by Chuck Shonta in the 13–10 loss to the Denver Broncos at BU Field on 09-09-60

3 interceptions by Gino Cappelletti in the 27–14 loss to the Oakland Raiders at Kezar Stadium on 10-16-60

3 interceptions by Ross O'Hanley in the 21–17 loss to the Houston Oilers at Jeppesen Stadium on 11-18-62

3 interceptions by Ron Hall in the 33–28 victory over the San Diego Chargers at Balboa Stadium on 09-20-64

3 interceptions by Mike Haynes in the 38–24 victory over the New York Jets at Shea Stadium on 11-21-76

3 interceptions by Roland James in the 31–0 shutout of the Buffalo Bills at Rich Stadium on 10-23-83

3 interceptions by Asante Samuel in the 17–13 victory over the Chicago Bears at Gillette Stadium on 11-26-06

The only Patriots Defensive Back who has intercepted three passes in just one quarter of a game

Roland James intercepted three Joe Ferguson passes in the third quarter of the 31–0 shutout of the Buffalo Bills at Rich Stadium on 10-23-83

Every Patriots Defensive Back who has intercepted two different Quaterbacks in the same regular season game

Don Webb intercepted George Herring and Frank Tripucka in the 28–24 win over the Denver Broncos on 12-03-61

Fred Bruney intercepted Jack Kemp and Hunter Enis in the 41–0 shutout of the San Diego Chargers on 12-17-61

Bob Suci intercepted George Blanda and Jacky Lee in the 45–3 rout of the Houston Oilers on 11-01-63

Bob Suci intercepted Jacky Lee and George Blanda in the 46–28 win over the Houtson Oilers on 12-08-63

Ron Hall intercepted Tobin Rote twice and John Hadl once in the 33–28 win over the San Diego Chargers on 09-20-64

Ronnie Lippett

Dick Felt intercepted Dick Wood and Mike Taliaferro in the 26–10 victory over the New York Jets on 09-27-64

Ross O'Hanley intercepted Jacky Lee and Mickey Slaughter in the 12–7 win over the Denver Broncos on 11-20-64

Leroy Mitchell intercepted Steve Tensi and Marlin Briscoe in the 35–14 loss to the Denver Broncos on 11-03-68

Honor Jackson intercepted Earl Morrall and Jim Del Gaizo in the 37–21 loss to the Miami Dolphins on 12-03-72

Mike Haynes intercepted Joe Namath twice and Richard Todd once in the 38–24 win over the New York Jets on 11-21-76

Raymond Clayborn intercepted Don Strock and David Woodley in the 34–0 shutout of the Miami Dolphins on 10-12-80

Ronnie Lippett intercepted Jim Kelly and Frank Reich in the 23–3 rout of the Buffalo Bills on 10-26-86

Every Patriots Defensive Back who has intercepted a Pro Football Hall of Fame Quarterback twice in the same regular season game

Dick Felt intercepted George Blanda twice in the 34–21 win over the Houston Oilers on 09-16-62

Ross O'Hanley intercepted George Blanda three times in the 21–17 loss to the Houston Oilers on 11-18-62

Tom Hennessey intercepted Joe Namath twice in the 24–24 tie with the New York Jets on 10-02-66

Leroy Mitchell intercepted Joe Namath twice in the 48–14 loss to the New York Jets on 10-27-68

Ron Bolton intercepted Fran Tarkenton twice in the 17–14 victory over the Minnesota Vikings on 10-27-74

Mike Haynes intercepted Joe Namath twice in the 38–24 win over the New York Jets on 11-21-76

Prentice McCray intercepted Joe Namath twice in the 38–24 victory over the New York Jets on 11-21-76

Doug Beaudoin intercepted Bob Griese twice in the 33–24 win over the Miami Dolphins on 10-22-78

Ronnie Lippett intercepted Dan Marino twice in the 34–7 rout of the Miami Dolphins on 10-05-86

Fred Marion intercepted Jim Kelly twice in the 16–14 loss to the Buffalo Bills on 09-18-88

Ronnie Lippett intercepted Dan Marino twice in the 27–24 loss to the Miami Dolphins on 09-09-90

Maurice Hurst intercepted Jim Kelly twice in the 16–13 win over the Buffalo Bills on 11-24-91

Harlon Barnett intercepted Dan Marino twice in the 23–3 loss to the Miami Dolphins on 10-30-94

Willie Clay intercepted John Elway twice in the 34–13 loss to the Denver Broncos on 10-06-97

Larry Whigham intercepted Dan Marino twice in the 27–24 win over the Miami Dolphins on 11-23-97

Every Patriots Defensive Back who has intercepted at least two passes in consecutive regular season games

Ron Hall had three interceptions in the 33–28 win over SD on 09-20-64, and two interceptions in the 26–10 win over the New York Jets on 09-27-64

Leroy Mitchell had two interceptions in the 48–14 loss to the Jets on 10-27-68, and three interceptions in the 35–14 loss to the Denver Broncos on 11-03-68

Mike Haynes had two interceptions in the 21–14 win over the Colts on 11-14-76, and three interceptions in the 38–24 win over the New York Jets on 11-21-76

Every Patriots Defensive Back who has intercepted at least two passes in three games during the regular season

Ron Hall in 1964, Ronnie Lippett in 1986, Asante Samuel in 2006.

The progression of the most career regular season games that a Patriots Defensive Back had at least two interceptions

2 games that Bob Suci had at least two interceptions during the 1963 season

3 games that Dick Felt had at least two interceptions during the 1962–64 seasons

3 games that Ross O'Hanley had at least two interceptions during the 1962–64 seasons

3 games that Ron Hall had at least two interceptions during the 1964 season

3 games that Ron Bolton had at least two interceptions during the 1973–74 seasons

6 games that Mike Haynes had at least two interceptions during the 1976–82 seasons

The only Patriots Linebacker who has intercepted at least two passes in multiple regular season games

4 games that Nick Buoniconti intercepted at least two passes duing the 1963–68 seasons

The progression of the most interceptions by a Patriots Linebacker in a regular season game

1 interception by Bill Brown in the 28–24 victory over the New York Titans at the Polo Grounds on 09-17-60

2 interceptions by Harry Jacobs in the 37–21 loss to the Houston Oilers at Jeppesen Stadium on 12-18-60

2 interceptions by Tom Addison in the 24–20 victory over the San Diego Chargers at BU Field on 10-19-62

2 interceptions by Nick Buoniconti in the 20–14 victory over the Oakland Raiders at Frank Youell Field on 09-22-63

2 interceptions by Nick Buoniconti in the 23–0 shutout of the Buffalo Bills at War Memorial Stadium on 09-24-67

2 interceptions by Nick Buoniconti in the 27–6 loss to the Houston Oilers at Rice Stadium on 11-26-67

Nick Buoniconti

Mike Vrabel

3 interceptions by Nick Buoniconti in the 23–6 victory over the Buffalo Bills at Fenway Park on 10-20-68

Every Patriots Linebacker who has intercepted two different Quarterbacks in a regular season game

1960 regular season
Harry Jacobs intercepted Jacky Lee and George Blanda in the 37–21 loss to the Houston Oilers on 12-18-60

1963 regular season
Nick Buoniconti intercepted Cotton Davidson and Tom Flores in the 20–14 win over the Oakland Raiders on 09-22-63

1979 regular season
Mike Hawkins intercepted Don Strock and Bob Griese in the 28–13 victory over the Miami Dolphins on 10-21-79

Every Patriots Linebacker who has intercepted the same Quarterback twice in a regular season game

1962 regular season
Tom Addison intercepted Dick Wood twice in the 24–20 victory over the San Diego Chargers on 10-19-62

1967 regular season
Nick Buoniconti intercepted Tom Flores twice in the 23–0 shutout of the Buffalo Bills on 09-24-67

Nick Buoniconti intercepted Pete Beathard twice in the 27–6 loss to the Houston Oilers on 11-26-67

1969 regular season
Ed Philpott intercepted Jack Kemp twice in the 35–21 win over the Buffalo Bills on 11-23-69

1986 regular season
Steve Nelson intercepted Jack Trudeau twice in the 30–21 victory over the Indianapolis Colts on 11-09-86

2006 regular season
Mike Vrabel intercepted Jon Kitna twice in the 28–21 win over the Detroit Lions on 12-03-06

2007 undefeated regular season
Junior Seau intercepted Derek Anderson twice in the 34–17 victory over the Cleveland Browns on 10-07-07

The most consecutive regular season games with an interception

The progression of the most consecutive regular season games that by a Patriots Linebacker had an interception

2 consecutive games that Harry Jacobs intercepted a pass (on 12-11-60 and 12-18-60)

2 consecutive games that Jack Rudolph intercepted a pass (on 12-11-60 and 12-18-60)

2 consecutive games that Tom Addison intercepted a pass (on 11-17-61 and 12-03-61)

2 consecutive games that Nick Buoniconti intercepted a pass (on 10-12-62 and 10-19-62)

2 consecutive games that Nick Buoniconti intercepted a pass (on 09-27-64 and 10-04-64)

2 consecutive games that Nick Buoniconti intercepted a pass (on 11-20-66 and 11-27-66)

3 consecutive games that Ed Philpott intercepted a pass (from 09-22-68 to 10-06-68)

The progression of the most consecutive regular season games that a Patriots Defensive Back had an interception

3 consecutive games that Fred Bruney intercepted a pass (from 11-04-60 to 11-18-60)

3 consecutive games that Fred Bruney intercepted a pass (from 09-16-62 to 10-05-62)

3 consecutive games that Don Webb intercepted a pass (from 11-19-64 to 12-20-64)

3 consecutive games that Ron Hall intercepted a pass (from 09-18-66 to 10-02-66)

Mike Haynes

3 consecutive games that Tom Hennessey intercepted a pass (from 11-20-66 to 12-04-66)

3 consecutive games that Leroy Mitchell intercepted a pass (from 10-20-68 to 11-03-68)

3 consecutive games that Honor Jackson intercepted a pass (from 11-26-72 to 12-10-72)

3 consecutive games that Ron Bolton intercepted a pass (from 11-18-73 to 12-02-73)

3 consecutive games that Ron Bolton intercepted a pass (from 09-21-75 to 10-02-75)

4 consecutive regular season games that Mike Haynes intercepted a pass (from 11-07-76 to 11-28-76)

Other Patriots Defensive Backs who have intercepted a pass in three consecutive regular season games

3 consecutive games that Myron Guyton intercepted a pass (from 11-12-95 to 11-26-95)

3 consecutive games that Ty Law intercepted a pass (from 11-26-95 to 12-10-95)

The most interceptions in a regular season

The progression of the most interceptions by a Patriots player in a regular season

4 interceptions by Gino Cappelletti in 1960

4 interceptions by Harry Jacobs in 1960

5 interceptions by Don Webb in 1961

5 interceptions by Ross O'Hanley in 1962

5 interceptions by Dick Felt in 1962

5 interceptions by Tom Addison in 1962

7 interceptions by Bob Suci in 1963

11 interceptions by Ron Hall in 1964

The progression of the most interceptions by a Patriots Linebacker in a regular season

4 interceptions by Harry Jacobs in 1960

4 interceptions by Tom Addison in 1961

5 interceptions by Tom Addison in 1962

5 interceptions by Nick Buoniconti in 1964

5 interceptions by Steve Nelson in 1978

The most career interceptions

The progression of the most career regular season interceptions by a Defensive Back of the Patriots

4 career interceptions by Gino Cappelletti during the 1960 season

7 career interceptions by Clyde Washington during the 1960–61 seasons

8 career interceptions by Fred Bruney during the 1960–62 seasons

15 career interceptions by Ross O'Hanley during the 1960–65 seasons

15 career interceptions by Chuck Shonta during the 1960–67 seasons

29 career interceptions by Ron Hall during the 1961–67 seasons

36 career interceptions by Raymond Clayborn during the 1977–89 seasons

36 career interceptions by Ty Law during the 1995–2004 seasons

The progression of the most career interceptions by a Linebacker of the Patriots

1 interception by Bill Brown in the 28–24 win over the New York Titans on 09-17-60

4 career interceptions by Harry Jacobs during the 1960 season

16 career interceptions by Tom Addison during the 1960–67 seasons

24 career interceptions by Nick Buoniconti during the 1962–68 seasons

The most interception return yards in a game

The progression of the most interception return yards by a Patriots Defensive Back in a regular season game

52 interception return yards by Chuck Shonta in the 13–10 loss to the Denver Broncos at BU Field on 09-09-60

80 interception return yards by Don Webb in the 28–24 victory over the Denver Broncos at Bears Stadium on 12-03-61

118 interception return yards by Prentice McCray in the 38–24 victory over the New York Jets at Shea Stadium on 11-21-76

The progression of the most interception return yards by a Patriots Linebacker in a regular season game

8 interception return yards by Bill Brown in the 28–24 win over the New York Titans at the Polo Grounds on 09-17-60

12 interception return yards by Harry Jacobs in the 35–0 shutout of the Los Angeles Chargers at the LA Coliseum on 10-08-60

13 interception return yards by Jack Rudolph in the 34–0 loss to the Dallas Texans at the Cotton Bowl on 12-11-60

14 interception return yards by Harry Jacobs in the 37–21 loss to the Houston Oilers at Jeppesen Stadium on 12-18-60

16 interception return yards by Tom Addison in the 24–20 win over the San Diego Chargers at BU Field on 10-19-62

26 interception return yards by Nick Buoniconti in the 38–14 rout of the New York Jets at BC Alumni Stadium on 09-08-63

26 interception return yards by Nick Buoniconti in the 25–24 victory over the Houston Oilers at Fenway Park on 11-06-64

26 interception return yards by Nick Buoniconti in the 27–10 loss to the Denver Broncos at Fenway Park on 09-24-65

41 interception return yards by Nick Buoniconti in the 35–17 win over the San Diego Chargers at Fenway Park on 10-23-66

54 interception return yards by Kevin Reilly in the 34–14 loss to the Buffalo Bills at Schaefer Stadium on 12-14-75

68 interception return yards by Sam Hunt in the 31–14 victory over the Tampa Bay Buccaneers at Tampa Stadium on 12-12-76

82 interception return yards by Chris Singleton in the 37–34 overtime win vs the Colts at the Hoosier Dome on 11-15-92

The progression of the most interception return yards by a Patriots Defensive Lineman in a regular season game

14 interception return yards by Bob Dee in the 27–14 loss to the Oakland Raiders at Kezar Stadium on 10-16-60

78 interception return yards by Jim Lee Hunt in the 45–3 rout of the Houston Oilers at Fenway Park on 11-01-63

The most interception return yards in a season

The progression of most interception return yards by a Patriots Defensive Back in a regular season

101 interception return yards by Chuck Shonta in 1960

153 interception return yards by Don Webb in 1961

277 interception return yards by Bob Suci in 1963

The progression of the most interception return yards by a Patriots Linebacker in a regular season

26 interception return yards by Harry Jacobs in 1960

42 interception return yards by Tom Addison in 1962

42 interception return yards by Nick Buoniconti in 1963

75 interception return yards by Nick Buoniconti in 1964

106 interception return yards by Sam Hunt in 1976

The most career interception return yards

The progression of the most career regular season interception return yards by a Defensive Back of the Patriots

261 career interception return yards by Chuck Shonta during the 1960–67 regular seasons

476 career interception return yards by Ron Hall during the 1961–67 regular seasons

555 career interception return yards by Raymond Clayborn during the 1977–89 regular seasons

583 career interception return yards by Ty Law during the 1995–2004 regular seasons

The progression of the most career regular season interception return yards by a Linebacker of the Patriots

26 interception return yards by Harry Jacobs in 1960

103 career interception return yards by Tom Addison during the 1961–65 regular seasons

223 career interception return yards by Nick Buoniconti during the 1962–68 regular seasons

The progession of the longest interception return

The progression of the longest interception return by a Patriots Defensive Back in a regular season game

52-yard return by Chuck Shonta in the 13–10 loss to the Denver Broncos at BU Field on 09-09-60

59-yard return by Don Webb in the 28–24 victory over the Denver Broncos at Bears Stadium on 12-03-61

61-yard return by Ross O'Hanley in the 20–14 victory over the Oakland Raiders at Fenway Park on 10-11-63

62-yard return by Bob Suci in the 40–21 victory over the Denver Broncos at Fenway Park on 10-18-63

98-yard return for a TD by Bob Suci in the 45–3 rout of the Houston Oilers at Fenway Park on 11-01-63

99-yard return for a TD by Rick Sanford in the 26–13 loss to the Chicago Bears at Soldier Field on 12-05-82

100-yard return for a TD by Jimmy Hitchcock in the 27–24 win over the Miami Dolphins at Foxboro Stadium on 11-23-97

The progression of the longest interception return by a Patriots Linebacker in a regular season game

8-yard return by Bill Brown in the 28–24 victory over the New York Titans at the Polo Grounds on 09-17-60

12-yard return by Harry Jacobs in the 35–0 shutout of the Los Angeles Chargers at the Los Angeles Coliseum on 10-08-60

13-yard return by Jack Rudolph in the 34–0 loss to the Dallas Texans at the Cotton Bowl on 12-11-60

14-yard return by Harry Jacobs in the 37–21 loss to the Houston Oilers at Jeppesen Stadium on 12-18-60

16-yard return by Tom Addison in the 24–20 victory over the San Diego Chargers at BU Field on 10-19-62

26-yard return by Nick Buoniconti in the 38–14 win over the New York Jets at Boston College Alumni Stadium on 09-08-63

26-yard return by Nick Buoniconti in the 25–24 victory over the Houston Oilers at Fenway Park on 11-06-64

26-yard return by Nick Buoniconti in the 27–10 loss to the Denver Broncos at Fenway Park on 09-24-65

41-yard return by Nick Buoniconti in the 35–17 victory over the San Diego Chargers at Fenway Park on 10-23-66

54-yard return by Kevin Reilly in the 34–14 loss to the Buffalo Bills at Schaefer Stadium on 12-14-75

68-yard return for a TD by Sam Hunt in the 31–14 victory over the Tampa Bay Buccaneers at Tampa Stadium on 12-12-76

82-yard return for a TD by Chris Singleton in the 37–34 overtime win vs the Indianapolis Colts at the Hoosier Dome on 11-15-92

The progression of the longest interception return by a Patriots Defensive Lineman in a regular season game

14-yard return by Bob Dee in the 27–14 loss to the Oakland Raiders at Kezar Stadium on 10-16-60

78-yard return for a TD by Jim Lee Hunt in the 45–3 rout of the Houston Oilers at Fenway Park on 11-01-63

The progression of the longest interception return by two different players of the Patriots in a regular season game

21 total return yards by Gino Cappelletti and Clyde Washington in the 45–16 loss to the Los Angeles Chargers on 10-28-60

27 total interception return yards by Rod Shoate and Rick Sanford in the 26–6 victory over the Buffalo Bills on 11-04-79

33 total return yards by Steve Nelson and Clayton Weishun in the 28–23 win over the Pittsburgh Steelers on 09-25-83

69 total interception return yards by Johnny Rembert and Andre Tippett in the 23–3 rout of the Buffalo Bills on 10-26-86

The longest interception return in the American Football League during the 1963 season

Bob Suci had a 98-yard interception return for a TD on 11-01-63

The longest interception return in the National Football League during the 1982 Season

Rick Sanford had a 99-yard interception return for a TD on 12-05-82

The longest interception return in the National Football League during the 1997 Season

Jimmy Hitchcock had a 100-yard return for a TD on 11-23-97

Patriot Players who have advanced a lateral after an interception

Every Patriots Defensive Back who has advanced a lateral from another Patriots Defensive Back on his interception return

1960 regular season

Clyde Washington ran one yard with a lateral from Gino Cappelletti in the 45–16 loss to the Los Angeles Chargers on 10-28-60

1995 regular season

Ricky Reynolds ran two yards with a lateral from Myron Guyton in the 24–10 loss to the Indianapolis Colts on 11-19-95

The only Patriots Defensive Back who advanced a lateral from a Patriots Linebacker on his interception return

Rick Sanford ran 27 yards with a lateral from Rod Shoate in the 26–6 victory over the Buffalo Bills on 11-04-79

Every Patriots Linebacker who has advanced a lateral from another Patriots Linebacker on his interception return

1983 regular season

Clayton Weishuhn ran 27 yards for a TD with a lateral from Steve Nelson in the 28–23 win over Pittsburgh on 09-25-83

1986 regular season

Andre Tippett ran 32 yards with a lateral from Johnny Rembert in the 23–3 rout of the Buffalo Bills on 10-26-86

The 10 Greatest Defensive Backs of the Patriots

Mike Haynes—is in the Pro Football Hall of Fame

Ty Law—returned a pass for a TD in the Super Bowl and set the team record with six returns for a TD in the regular season

Rodney Harrison—has the team's longest interception return for a TD in a playoff game

Raymond Clayborn—holds the team record with three game saving interceptions, with less than two minutes to go, in a regular season game

Lawyer Milloy—was recognized as an AFC Pro Bowl safety four times

Asante Samuel—holds the team record with three career interception returns for a TD in the playoffs

Ron Hall—holds the team record with 11 interceptions in a regular season

Fred Marion—the only Patriots defensive back with an interception return and a fumble return in two regular season games

Roland James—holds the team record with three interceptions in just one quarter of a regular season game

Ronnie Lippett—the only Patriots defensive back to return a pass for the last points scored and the game-winning touchdown

The longest interception return by a Patriots player that helped set up the game-winning touchdown pass

Fred Marion returned a Dave Krieg pass 83 yards in the 20–13 win over the Seattle Seahawks at the Kingdome on 11-17-85 (Larry McGrew tipped the pass that Marion returned to Seattle's 15-yard line. Two plays later, Steve Grogan tossed a 13-yard TD pass to Irving Fryar for the game-winning TD with 2:39 left in the game.)

The only Patriots Linebacker whose late interception helped set up the game tying field goal in a game that ended in a tie

Nick Buoniconti intercepted a Len Dawson pass, with 2:57 left, in the 27–27 tie with the Kansas City Chiefs on 11-20-66 (This interception set up Gino Cappelletti's 19-yard field goal for the final points scored in the game)

The only Patriots Defensive Back whose interception helped set up the overtime game-winning field goal

Jerome Henderson returned a Jeff George pass nine yards in the 37–34 overtime win vs the Indianapolis Colts on 11-15-92 (Four plays later Charlie Baumann kicked an 18-yard field goal to win the game in overtime)

The only Patriots Defensive Back whose interception helped set up the overtime game-winning touchdown

Tyrone Poole had no return on his interception of Jay Fiedler in the 19–13 overtime win vs the Miami Dolphins on 10-19-03 (Tom Brady threw an 82-yard game-winning TD pass to Troy Brown on the Patriots' next play)

The only Patriots Defensive Back with an interception on the first play of a regular season game

Tyrone Poole returned a pass by Kerry Collins 13 yards on the first play of the game in the 17–6 win over the New York Giants on 10-12-03

The only Patriots Linebacker with an interception on the second play of a regular season game

Tedy Bruschi took a Chad Pennington pass three yards on the second play of the game in the 21–16 win over the New York Jets on 12-20-03

Game saving interceptions

Every Patriots Linebacker who has intercepted a pass late in a regular season game to seal the victory

1963 regular season
Nick Buoniconti intercepted a Tom Flores pass with less than two minutes left in the 20–14 win over the Oakland Raiders on 09-22-63

1979 regular season
Steve Nelson intercepted a Dan Fouts pass on his 2-yard line in the 27–21 victory over the San Diego Chargers on 09-23-79

1982 regular season
Don Blackmon intercepted a David Woodley pass on his 10-yard line in the 3–0 "Snow Plow" win over the Miami Dolphins on 12-12-82

2006 regular season
Tedy Bruschi intercepted a pass by Chad Pennington with 15 seconds left to preserve the 24–17 win over the New York Jets on 09-17-06

Mike Vrabel returned a Jon Kitna pass one yard with two minutes left to help seal the 28–21 victory over the Detroit Lions on 12-03-06

The only Patriots Linebacker who has intercepted a pass in the end zone with less that 20 seconds left to preserve a shutout

Larry Izzo caught a Travis Brown pass in the end zone with 13 seconds left to preserve the 31–0 shutout of the Buffalo Bills on 12-27-03

Every Patriots Defensive Back who has intercepted a pass late in a regular season game to seal the victory

1964 regular season

Ron Hall intercepted a John Hadl pass with 72 seconds to go in the 33–28 win over the San Diego Chargers on 09-20-64

Ross O'Hanley caught a Mickey Slaughter pass on the last play on the 10-yard line in the 12–7 win over the Denver Broncos on 11-20-64

Don Webb intercepted a pass by Len Dawson with 20 seconds left in the 31–24 win over the Kansas City Chiefs on 12-06-64

1966 regular season

Chuck Shonta intercepted a Cotton Davidson pass with about two minutes left in the 24–21 win over the Oakland Raiders on 10-30-66

Ron Hall intercepted Dick Wood on the last play in the 20–14 victory over the Miami Dolphins on 11-27-66

1972 regular season

Rickie Harris intercepted an Archie Manning pass with 1:28 left in the 17–10 win over the New Orleans Saints on 12-10-72

1973 regular season

Honor Jackson intercepted a pass by Bobby Douglass on the last play in the 13–10 win over the Chicago Bears on 10-21-73

1974 regular season

Prentice McCray returned a John Hadl pass 39 yards with 1:39 left in the 20–14 win over the Los Angeles Rams on 09-29-74

1977 regular season

Tim Fox intercepted a Steve Bartkowski pass with 56 seconds left in the 16–10 win over the Atlanta Falcons on 12-04-77

1978 regular season

Dick Conn intercepted a Ken Stabler pass on the last play in the 21–14 victory over the Oakland Raiders on 09-24-78

Tim Fox intercepted a Ken Anderson pass with 13 seconds left in the 10–3 win over the Cincinnati Bengals on 10-15-78

1980 regular season

Raymond Clayborn intercepted a Jim Zorn pass with two minutes left in the 37–31 win over the Seahawks on 09-21-80

1982 regular season

Roland James intercepted a David Woodley pass on the last play of their 3–0 "Snow Plow" win over Miami on 12-12-82

1984 regular season

Raymond Clayborn returned a Paul McDonald pass 85 yards on the last play in the 17–16 win over the Browns on 10-07-84

Ronnie Lippett intercepted an Art Schlichter pass with 38 seconds left in the 16–10 win over the Colts on 12-16-84

1985 regular season

Roland James intercepted a Dave Krieg pass with 17 seconds left in the 20–13 win over Seattle at the Kingdome on 11-17-85

1986 regular season

Ronnie Lippett intercepted a pass by Jim Kelly with 1:10 left in the 22–19 victory over the Buffalo Bills on 11-23-86

Rod McSwain intercepted a Dan Marino pass with 38 seconds left in the 34–27 win over the Miami Dolphins on 12-22-86

1988 regular season

Raymond Clayborn intercepted a Chris Chandler pass with 23 seconds left in the 21–17 win over the Indianapolis Colts on 10-02-88

Jim Bowman intercepted a Boomer Esiason pass on the last play in the 27–21 win over the Cincinnati Bengals on 10-16-88

1993 regular season

Darryl Wren intercepted a Steve Beuerlein pass with about four minutes left in the 23–21 win over the Cardinals on 10-10-93

Terry Ray intercepted a David Klinger pass on the last play of the 7–2 win over the Cincinnati Bengals on 12-12-93

Maurice Hurst intercepted a Vinny Testaverde pass with about two minutes left in the 20–17 win over the Browns on 12-19-93

1994 regular season
Myron Guyton intercepted a Scott Mitchell pass with 2:10 left in the 23–17 win over the Detroit Lions on 09-25-94

1997 regular season
Lawyer Milloy intercepted a fourth-down pass from Dan Marino with 1:18 left in the 14–12 win over Miami on 12-22-97

1998 regular season
Lawyer Milloy intercepted a Peyton Manning pass with 44 seconds left in the 21–16 win over the Colts on 11-01-98

1999 regular season
Chris Carter intercepted a Peyton Manning pass with 12 seconds left in the 31–28 win over the Colts on 09-19-99

2001 championship season
Terrell Buckley intercepted a Vinny Testaverde pass with 2:07 left in the 17–16 win over the New York Jets on 12-02-01

2003 championship season
Ty Law intercepted a Kelly Holcomb pass with 51 seconds left in the 9–3 victory over the Cleveland Browns on 10-26-03

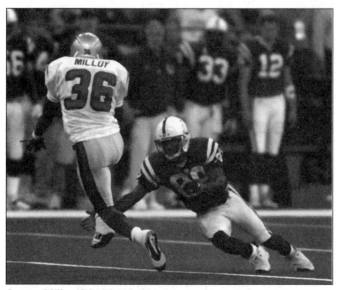

Lawyer Milloy (36), Marvin Harrison on the ground

Eugene Wilson returned a Chad Pennington pass 10 yards with 45 seconds left in the 21–16 win over the New York Jets on 12-20-03

2005 regular season
Eugene Wilson picked off a pass by Aaron Brooks in the end zone on the last play in the 24–17 win over the New Orleans Saints on 11-20-05

2006 regular season
Asante Samuel lost one yard on his interception return of Rex Grossman with 1:52 left in the 17–13 win over the Chicago Bears on 11-26-06

2007 undefeated regular season
James Sanders had a one-yard return on his interception of A.J. Feeley with 11 seconds left in the 31–28 win over the Philadelphia Eagles on 11-25-07

Interceptions that were returned for a touchdown

Every Patriots Defensive Lineman who has returned an interception for a touchdown in a regular season game
1963 regular season
Jim Lee Hunt returned a Jacky Lee pass 78 yards for a TD in the 45–3 rout of the Houston Oilers at Fenway Park on 11-01-63

1968 regular season
Mel Witt returned a Joe Namath pass four yards for a TD in the 47–31 loss to the New York Jets at Legion Field on 09-22-68

1996 regular season
Willie McGinest took a Jim Kelly pass 46 yards for a TD with 41 seconds left in the 28–25 win over the Buffalo Bills at Foxboro Stadium on 10-27-96

1998 regular season
Henry Thomas returned a Danny Wuerffel pass 24 yards for a TD in the 30–27 win over the New Orleans Saints at the Superdome on 10-04-98

The only Patriots Defensive Back who has returned an interception for the game-winning touchdown
Ronnie Lippett took a Dan Marino pass 20 yards for a TD for the last points scored in the 28–21 win over the Miami Dolphins on 09-13-87

Mel Witt

Every Patriots Defensive Back who has returned an interception for a touchdown in a regular season game

1961 regular season

Don Webb returned pass by M.C. Reynolds 27 yards for a TD in the 52–21 rout of the Buffalo Bills at BU Field on 10-22-61

Don Webb returned a Jack Kemp pass 31 yards for a TD in the 41–0 shutout of the Chargers at Balboa Stadium on 12-17-61

1962 regular season

Fred Bruney returned a George Shaw pass 33 yards for a TD in the 41–16 rout of the Denver Broncos at BU Field on 09-21-62

Ron Hall took a George Shaw pass 47 yards for a TD in the 41–16 rout of the Denver Broncos at BU Field on 09-21-62

1963 regular season

Bob Suci returned a George Blanda pass 98 yards for a TD in the 45–3 rout of the Houston Oilers at Fenway Park on 11-01-63

Bob Suci took a Jacky Lee pass 52 yards for a TD in the 46–28 win over the Houston Oilers at Jeppesen Stadium on 12-08-63

1964 regular season

Ross O'Hanley returned a George Blanda pass 47 yards for a TD in the 34–17 win over the Houston Oilers at Jeppesen Stadium on 11-29-64

1967 regular season

Jay Cunningham returned a Rick Norton pass 54 yards for a TD in the 41–10 rout of the Miami Dolphins at BC Alumni Stadium on 10-15-67

John Charles returned a Joe Namath pass 35 yards for a TD in the 30–23 loss to the New York Jets at Shea Stadium on 10-29-67

1969 regular season

John Charles returned a Joe Namath pass 25 yards for a TD in the 23–17 loss to the New York Jets at Shea Stadium on 10-26-69

1971 regular season

Larry Carwell returned a Bob Griese pass 53 yards for a TD in the 34–13 win over the Miami Dolphins at Schaefer Stadium on 12-05-71

John Outlaw took a Johnny Unitas pass 60 yards for TD in the 21–17 win over the Baltimore Colts at Memorial Stadium on 12-19-71

1974 regular season

John Sanders returned an Earl Morrall pass 23 yards for a TD in the 34–27 loss to the Miami Dolphins at the Orange Bowl on 12-15-74

1975 regular season

Bob Howard returned a Dan Fouts pass 44 yards for a TD in the 33–19 win over the San Diego Chargers at Jack Murphy Stadium on 11-09-75

1976 regular season

Prentice McCray returned a Joe Namath pass 63 yards for a TD in the 38–24 win over the New York Jets at Shea Stadium on 11-21-76

Prentice McCray returned a Joe Namath pass 55 yards for a TD in the 38–24 win over the New York Jets at Shea Stadium on 11-21-76

1978 regular season

Mike Haynes took a Bill Troup pass 31 yards for a TD on the third play, in the 35–14 rout of the Baltimore Colts at Memorial Stadium on 11-26-78

1982 regular season
Rick Sanford returned a Jim McMahon pass 99 yards for a TD in the 26–13 loss to the Chicago Bears at Soldier Field on 12-05-82

1985 regular season
Raymond Clayborn returned a Vince Ferragamo pass 27 yards for a TD in the 14–3 win over the Buffalo Bills at Sullivan Stadium on 10-13-85

1986 regular season
Fred Marion returned a Bubby Brister pass 37 yards for a TD in the 34–0 shutout of the Pittsburgh Steelers at Three Rivers Stadium on 10-19-86

1987 regular season
Ronnie Lippett returned a Dan Marino pass 20 yards for a TD in the 28–21 win over the Miami Dolphins at Sullivan Stadium on 09-13-87

Ronnie Lippett took a Gary Hogenboom pass 45 yards for a TD in the 24–0 shutout of the Indianapolis Colts at Sullivan Stadium on 11-22-87

1989 regular season
Maurice Hurst returned a Jim Kelly pass 16 yards for a TD in the 33–24 win over the Buffalo Bills at Sullivan Stadium on 11-19-89

1992 regular season
David Pool returned a Jeff George pass 41 yards for a TD in the 37–34 overtime win vs the Indianapolis Colts at the Hoosier Dome on 11-15-92

1994 regular season
Ricky Reynolds returned a Boomer Esiason pass 11 yards for a TD in the 24–13 win over the New York Jets at Foxboro Stadium on 12-04-94

1996 regular season
Ty Law returned a Glenn Foley pass 38 yards for a TD in the 34–10 rout of the New York Jets at Foxboro Stadium on 12-08-96

1997 regular season
Willie Clay returned a Jim Everett pass 53 yards for a TD in the 41–7 rout of the San Diego Chargers at Foxboro Stadium on 08-31-97

Larry Whigham returned a Dan Marino pass 60 yards for a TD in the 27–24 win over the Miami Dolphins at Foxboro Stadium on 11-23-97

Jimmy Hitchcock took a Dan Marino pass 100 yards for a TD late in the second quarter, in the 27–24 win over the Miami Dolphins at Foxboro Stadium on 11-23-97

1998 regular season
Ty Law returned a Peyton Manning pass 59 yards for a TD in the 29–6 win over the Indianapolis Colts at Foxboro Stadium on 09-13-98

Lawyer Milloy took a Steve McNair pass 30 yards for a TD in the 27–16 win over the Tennessee Oilers at Foxboro Stadium on 09-20-98

1999 regular season
Ty Law returned a Damon Huard pass 24 yards for a TD in the 31–30 loss to the Miami Dolphins at Foxboro Stadium on 10-17-99

2001 championship season
Otis Smith took a Peyton Manning pass 78 yards for a TD in the 44–13 rout of the Indianapolis Colts at Foxboro Stadium on 09-30-01

Ty Law returned a Peyton Manning pass 23 yards for a TD in the 44–13 rout of the Indianapolis Colts at Foxboro Stadium on 09-30-01

Terrell Buckley returned a Kurt Warner pass 52 yards for a TD in the 24–17 loss to the St. Louis Rams at Foxboro Stadium on 11-18-01

Otis Smith took a Chris Weinke pass 76 yards for a TD in the 38–6 rout of the Carolina Panthers at Ericsson Stadium on 01-06-02

Otis Smith

Victor Green

Ty Law returned a Chris Weinke pass 46 yards for a TD in the 38–6 rout of the Carolina Panthers at Ericsson Stadium on 01-06-02

2002 regular season
Victor Green returned a Vinny Testaverde pass 90 yards for a TD in the 44–7 rout of the New York Jets at the Meadowlands on 09-15-02

2003 championship season
Asante Samuel took a Vinny Testaverde pass 55 yards for a TD in the 23–16 win over the New York Jets at Gillette Stadium on 09-21-03

Ty Law took a Donovan McNabb pass 65 yards for TD in the 31–10 rout of the Philadelphia Eagles at Lincoln Financial Field on 10-05-03

2004 championship season
Asante Samuel returned a Carson Palmer pass 34 yards for a TD in the 35–28 victory over the Cincinnati Bengals at Gillette Stadium on 12-12-04

2005 regular season
James Sanders took a J.P. Losman pass 39 yards for a TD in the 35–7 rout of the Buffalo Bills at Ralph Wilson Stadium on 12-11-05

2007 undefeated regular season
Asante Samuel took a A.J. Feeley pass 40 yards for a TD on the third play in the 31–28 win over the Philadelphia Eagles at Gillette Stadium on 11-25-07

Eugene Wilson took a pass by Kellen Clemens five yards for a TD in the 20–10 win over the New York Jets at Gillette Stadium on 12-16-07

Every Patriots Linebacker and Defensive Back who have each returned an interception for a TD in the same game
1992 regular season
Chris Singleton and David Pool each returned an interception for a TD in the 37–34 overtime win over the Indianapolis Colts on 11-15-92

Asante Samuel

Asante Samuel

1999 regular season

Andy Katzenmoyer and Ty Law each returned an interception for a TD in the 31–30 loss to the Miami Dolphins on 10-17-99

Every Patriots Linebacker who has returned an interception for a touchdown in a regular season game

1962 regular season

Tom Addison took a Lee Grosscup pass 12 yards for a TD in the 43–14 rout of the New York Titans at the Polo Grounds on 10-06-62

1974 regular season

Bob Geddes returned an Al Woodall pass 29 yards for a TD in the 24–0 shutout of the New York Jets at Shea Stadium on 10-13-74

1976 regular season

Sam Hunt returned a Steve Spurrier pass 68 yards for a TD in the 31–14 win over the Tampa Bay Buccaneers at Tampa Stadium on 12-12-76

1979 regular season

Mike Hawkins returned a Don Strock pass 35 yards for a TD in the 28–13 win over the Miami Dolphins at Schaefer Stadium on 10-21-79

1980 regular season

Rod Shoate returned a Bert Jones pass 42 yards for a TD in the 47–21 rout of the Baltimore Colts at Schaefer Stadium on 11-23-80

1992 regular season

Vincent Brown took a Bobby Hebert pass 49 yards for a TD in the 31–14 loss to the New Orleans Saints at Foxboro Stadium on 11-08-92

Chris Singleton took a Jeff George pass 82 yards for a TD in the 37–34 overtime win vs the Indianapolis Colts at the Hoosier Dome on 11-15-92

1997 regular season

Chris Slade returned a Todd Collins pass one yard for a TD in the 31–10 rout of the Buffalo Bills at Rich Stadium on 11-09-97

1999 regular season

Andy Katzenmoyer took a Dan Marino pass 57 yards for a TD on the fifth play of the 31–30 loss to the Miami Dolphins at Foxboro Stadium on 10-17-99

2002 regular season

Tedy Bruschi returned a Rich Gannon pass 48 yards for a TD in the 27–20 loss to the Oakland Raiders at Oakland Stadium on 11-17-02

Tedy Bruschi returned a Joey Harrington pass 27 yards for a TD in the 20–12 win over the Detroit Lions at Ford Field on 11-28-02

2003 championship season

Tedy Bruschi took a Donovan McNabb pass 18 yards for a TD in the 31–10 rout of the Philadelphia Eagles at Lincoln Field on 09-14-03

Tedy Bruschi returned a Jay Fiedler pass five yards for a TD in the 12–0 shutout of the Miami Dolphins at Gillette Stadium on 12-07-03

Willie McGinest took a Chad Pennington pass 15 yards for a TD in the 23–16 win over the New York Jets at the Meadowlands on 12-20-03

2005 regular season

Mike Vrabel took a Jake Delhomme pass 24 yards for a TD in the 27–17 loss to the Carolina Panthers at Charlotte Stadium on 09-18-05

2007 undefeated regular season

Adalius Thomas returned a Philip Rivers pass 65 yards for a TD in the 38–14 rout of the San Diego Chargers at Gillette Stadium on 09-16-07

The only Patriots Defensive Lineman who has returned an interception for a TD for the game-winning points

Willie McGinest returned a Jim Kelly pass, 46 yards for a TD, in the 28–25 win over the Buffalo Bills at Foxboro on 10-27-96

The Patriots Regular Season Won-Loss-Tie Record when;

The Patriots had only one interception in a regular season game

The Patriots record is 90–81–4 when a Patriots defensive back had the only interception for his team in the game

The Patriots record is 24–23 when a Patriots linebacker had the only interception for his team in the game

The only Patriots Defensive Lineman to record the only interception for his team in a regular season game

Willie McGinest returned a Jim Kelly pass 46 yards for a TD in the 28–25 win over the Bills at Foxboro on 10-27-96

The Patriots had two interceptions in a regular season game

The Patriots record is 23–29–2 when there was one interception by a Patriots defensive back and one interception by a linebacker

The Patriots record is 68–35 when there were two interceptions by the defensive backfield of the Patriots

The two regular season games that the two interceptions by the Patriots were recorded by a Patriots Linebacker

1963 regular season

Nick Buoniconti intercepted Cotton Davidson and Tom Flores in the 20–14 win over the Oakland Raiders on 09-22-63

1967 regular season

Nick Buoniconti intercepted Pete Beathard *twice* in the 27–6 loss to the Houston Oilers at Rice Stadium on 11-26-67

The two regular season games that the only Patriots interceptions were by two Patriots Linebackers

2003 championship season

Mike Vrabel and Larry Izzo had interceptions in the 31–0 shutout of the Buffalo Bills at Gillette Stadium on 12-27-03

2007 undefeated regular season

Adalius Thomas and Rosevelt Colvin intercepted Philip Rivers in the 38–14 rout of the San Diego Chargers at Gillette Stadium on 09-16-07

The two regular season games that a Patriots Linebacker and a Defensive Lineman had an interception

1965 regular season

Nick Buoniconti and Houston Antwine had interceptions in the 28–20 win over the Denver Broncos at Bears Stadium on 12-12-65

1968 regular season

Ed Philpott and Mel Witt had interceptions in the 47–31 loss to the New York Jets at Legion Field on 09-22-68

Rosevelt Colvin

The games that there was one interception by a Patriots Defensive Back and one by a Patriots Defensive Lineman

1963 regular season

Ron Hall and Larry Eisenhauer intercepted a Jack Kemp pass in the 17–7 win over the Buffalo Bills at Fenway Park on 12-01-63

1998 regular season

Ty Law and Henry Thomas intercepted a Danny Wuerffel pass in the 30–27 win over the New Orleans Saints at the Superdome on 10-04-98

2000 regular season

Ty Law and Henry Thomas intercepted a Jay Fiedler pass in the 10–3 loss to the Miami Dolphins at Pro Player Stadium on 09-24-00

2001 Championship Season

Lawyer Milloy and Anthony Pleasant intercepted an Aaron Brooks pass in the 34–17 win over the New Orleans Saints at Foxboro Stadium on 11-25-01

The Patriots had three interceptions in a regular season game

The Patriots record is 22–7 when there were two interceptions by a defensive back and one interception by a linebacker

The only game that the three Patriots interceptions were recorded by two Patriots Linebackers

Harry Jacobs had two interceptions and Jack Rudolph had the other interception in the 37–21 loss to the Houston Oilers on 12-18-60

Every game that there was one interception by a Patriots Defensive Back and two interceptions by a Patriots Linebacker

1979 regular season

Mike Haynes had an interception and Mike Hawkins had two interceptions in the 28–13 win over the Miami Dolphins at Schaefer Stadium on 10-21-79

2006 regular season

Asante Samuel had an interception and Mike Vrabel had two interceptions in the 28–21 win over the Detroit Lions at Gillette Stadium on 12-03-06

2007 undefeated regular season

Asante Samuel had an interception and Junior Seau had two interceptions in the 34–17 win over the Cleveland Browns at Gillette Stadium on 10-07-07

The only game that there was an interception by two Patriots Linebackers and an interception by a Patriots Defensive Lineman

Tedy Bruschi, Willie McGinest, and Bobby Hamilton had interceptions in the 20–12 win vs the Detroit Lions at Ford Field on 11-28-02

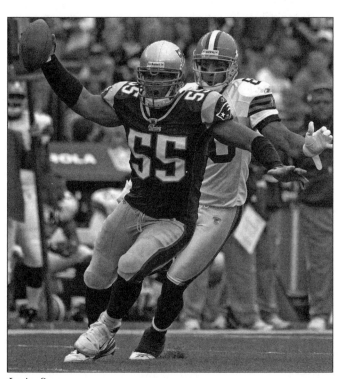

Junior Seau

Every regular season game that there were three total interceptions, each by the same Patriots Defensive Back

1964 regular season

Ron Hall had all three interceptions in the 33–28 victory over the San Diego Chargers at Balboa Stadium on 09-20-64

1983 regular season

Roland James had all three interceptions in the third quarter of the 31–0 shutout of the Buffalo Bills at Rich Stadium on 10-23-83

2006 regular season

Asante Samuel had all three interceptions in the 17–13 victory over the Chicago Bears at Gillette Stadium on 11-26-06

The games that there were three Patriots interceptions; one interception by a Patriots Defensive Back and an interception by two Patriots Linebackers

1960 regular season

Ross O'Hanley, Harry Jacobs, and Jack Rudolph had interceptions in the 34–0 loss to the Dallas Texans at the Cotton Bowl on 12-11-60

1971 regular season

Randy Beverly, Jim Cheyunski, and Steve Kiner had interceptions in the 28–20 win over the Houston Oilers at Schaefer Stadium on 11-07-71

1980 regular season

Roland James, Steve Nelson, and Rod Shoate had interceptions in the 47–21 rout of the Baltimore Colts at Schaefer Stadium on 11-23-80

1989 regular season

Roland James, Larry McGrew, and Johnny Rembert had interceptions in the 24–10 loss to the Miami Dolphins at Sullivan Stadium on 09-17-89

The 17 games with three Patriots interceptions in the game; two by the same Patriots Defensive Back and another by a different Patriots Defensive Back

1963 regular season

2 by Ross O'Hanley and one by Chuck Shonta in the 20–14 win over the Oakland Raiders at Fenway Park on 10-11-63

2 by Bob Suci and one by Dick Felt in the 46–28 win over the Houston Oilers at Jeppesen Stadium on 12-08-63

1964 regular season
2 by Ross O'Hanley and one by Ron Hall in the 12–7 win over the Denver Broncos at Fenway Park on 11-20-64

2 by Ron Hall and one by Don Webb in the 24–14 loss to the Buffalo Bills at Fenway Park on 12-20-64

1966 regular season
2 interceptions by Tom Hennessey and one by Ron Hall in the 24–24 tie with the New York Jets at Fenway Park on 10-02-66

1973 regular season
2 interceptions by Ron Bolton and one by Ralph Anderson in the 24–23 loss to the Philadelphia Eagles at Veterans Stadium on 11-04-73

1974 regular season
2 by Ron Bolton and one by Jack Mildren in the 17–14 comeback win over the Minnesota Vikings at Metropolitan Stadium on on 10-27-74

2 interceptions by John Sanders and one by Prentice McCray in the 34–27 loss to the Miami Dolphins at the Orange Bowl on 12-15-74

Left to right: Wesley Walker (85) and Mike Haynes (40)

1978 regular season
2 by Mike Haynes and one by Raymond Clayborn in the 19–17 win over the New York Jets at Shea Stadium on 11-19-78

1984 regular season
2 interceptions by Ronnie Lippett and one by Fred Marion in the 38–10 win over the Buffalo Bills at Sullivan Stadium on 11-11-84

1985 regular season
2 interceptions by Fred Marion and one by Roland James in the 20–13 win over the Seattle Seahawks at the Kingdome on 11-17-85

1993 regular season
2 interceptions by Darryl Wren and one by Maurice Hurst in the 19–16 overtime loss to the Detroit Lions at Foxboro Stadium on 09-12-93

1997 regular season
2 interceptions by Larry Whigham and one by Jimmy Hitchcock in the 27–24 win over the Miami Dolphins at Foxboro Stadium on 11-23-97

1998 regular season
2 interceptions by Ty Law and one by Chris Canty in the 29–6 rout of the Indianapolis Colts at Foxboro Stadium on 09-13-98

2001 championship season
2 interceptions by Otis "My Man" Smith and one by Ty Law in the 38–6 rout of the Carolina Panthers at Ericsson Stadium on 01-06-02

2003 championship season
2 interceptions by Ty Law and one by Tyrone Poole in the 12–0 shutout of the Dallas Cowboys at Foxboro Stadium on 11-16-03

2007 undefeated regular season
2 interceptions by Asante Samuel and one by James Sanders in the 31–28 victory over the Philadelphia Eagles at Gillette Stadium on 11-25-07

Every game that there were three total interceptions and each was recorded by a different Patriots Defensive Back

1978 regular season
Ray Clayborn, Mike Haynes, and Dick Conn had interceptions in the 21–14 win over the Oakland Raiders at Oakland Coliseum on 09-24-78

1998 regular season

Willie Clay, Ty Law, and Larry Whigham had interceptions in the 12–9 overtime loss to the Miami Dolphins at Pro Player Park on 10-25-98

2000 regular season

Antwan Harris, Tebucky Jones, and Ty Law had interceptions in the 24–16 win over the Indianapolis Colts at Foxboro on 10-08-00

2005 regular season

Asante Samuel, Ellis Hobbs, and James Sanders had interceptions in the 35–7 rout of the Bills at Ralph Wilson Stadium on 12-11-05

2008 regular season

Brandon Meriweather, Rodney Harrison, and Deltha O'Neal had interceptions in the 30–21 win over the 49ers at Candlestick Park on 10-05-08

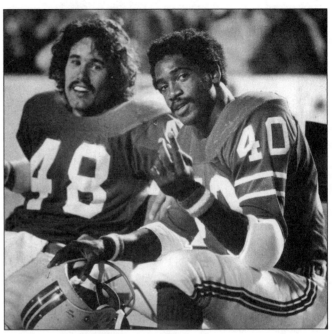

Tim Fox (48) and Mike Haynes (40)

The Patriots had four interceptions in a regular season game

Every game that three Patriots Defensive Backs and one Patriots Defensive Lineman had an interception

2002 regular season

T. Buckley, Ty Law, Tebucky Jones, and Richard Seymour had interceptions in the 27–17 win vs the Buffalo Bills at Gillette Stadium on 12-08-02

2006 regular season

E. Hobbs, J. Sanders, A. Samuel, and Richard Seymour had interceptions in the 40–7 rout of the Houston Texans at Gillette Stadium on 12-17-06

The only game that two Patriots Defensive Backs, one Patriots Linebacker, and one Patriots Defensive Lineman had an interception

Tim Fox, Mike Haynes, Mike Hawkins, Mark Buben had interceptions in the 33–17 win over the Kansas City Chiefs at Schaefer Stadium on 10-04-81

The only game that there was an interception by a Patriots Defensive Back and an interception by three Patriots Linebackers

John Sanders, Bob Geddes, Sam Hunt, and Steve King had interceptions in the 24–0 shutout of the New York Jets at Shea Stadium on 10-13-74

The only game that there was an interception by a Patriots Defensive Back and three interceptions by a Patriots Linebacker

Leroy Mitchell had one and Nick Buoniconti had three interceptions in the 23–6 win over the Buffalo Bills at Fenway Park on 10-20-68

The only game that there was an interception by a Patriots Defensive Back, one by a Linebacker, and two by another Linebacker

Ross O'Hanley and Nick Buoniconti had one and Tom Addison had two interceptions in the 24–20 win over San Diego at BU Field on 10-19-62

The three games that there were four Patriots interceptions; two by a Patriots Defensive Back, one by another Patriots Defensive Back and one by a Patriots Linebacker

1980 regular season

Ray Clayborn had two and Roland James and Steve Nelson had an interception in the 34–0 shutout of the Miami Dolphins at Schaefer Stadium on 10-12-80

1983 regular season

Rick Sanford had two and Fred Marion and Larry McGrew had an interception in the 21–7 win over the Buffalo Bills at Schaefer Stadium on 11-06-83

1986 regular season

Ronnie Lippett had two and Fred Marion and Johnny Rembert had an interception in the 23–3 rout of the Buffalo Bills on 10-26-86

Every game that there was an interception by a three Patriots Defensive Backs and one by a Patriots Linebacker

1976 regular season

Tim Fox, Mike Haynes, Prentice McCray, and Steve Nelson had interceptions in the 20–10 win over the Buffalo Bills on 11-07-76

1996 regular season

Jerome Henderson, Lawyer Milloy, Otis Smith, and Ted Johnson had interceptions in the 45–7 rout of the San Diego Chargers on 12-01-96

1997 regular season

Willie Clay, Ty Law, Lawyer Milloy, and Marty Moore had interceptions in the 33–6 rout of the Buffalo Bills on 10-12-97

Ty Law, Jimmy Hitchcock, Willie Clay, and Chris Slade had interceptions in the 31–10 rout of the Buffalo Bills on 11-09-97

2006 regular season

Rodney Harrison, Ellis Hobbs, Chad Scott, and Mike Vrabel had interceptions in the 31–7 rout of the Minnesota Vikings on 10-30-06

Every game with four total interceptions; two by a Patriots Defensive Back and one each by two other Patriots Defensive Backs

1962 regular season

Dick Felt had two and Fred Bruney and Ross O'Hanley had an interception in the 34–21 win over the Houston Oilers on 09-16-62

1977 regular season

Mike Haynes had two and Tim Fox and Prentice McCray had an interception in the 16–10 win over the Atlanta Falcons on 12-04-77

1982 regular season

Mike Haynes had two and Roland James and Rick Sanford had an interception in the 16–0 shutout of the Seattle Seahawks on 12-19-82

Jim Bowman

1987 regular season

Jim Bowman had two and Ernest Gibson and Ronnie Lippett had an interception in the 24–0 shutout of the Indianapolis Colts on 11-22-87

1990 regular season

Maurice Hurst had two and Ronnie Lippett and Fred Marion had an interception in the 16–14 win over the Colts on 09-16-90

1991 regular season

Maurice Hurst had two and Ronnie Lippett and Fred Marion had an interception in the 16–13 win over the Buffalo Bills on 11-24-91

2003 championship season

Rodney Harrison had two and Tyrone Poole and Eugene Wilson had an interception in the 17–6 win over the New York Giants on 10-12-03

The only game that there was four total interceptions by the Patriots; two each by two Patriots Defensive Backs

Mike Haynes and Bob Howard each had two interceptions in the 31–0 shutout of the Seattle Seahawks on 10-09-77

The three games with four total interceptions; one each by two Patriots Defensive Backs and one each by two Patriots Linebackers

1965 regular season

Tom Hennessey and Don Webb and linebackers Tom Addison and Mike Dukes had interceptions in the 22–6 win over San Diego on 10-31-65

1981 regular season

Tim Fox and Keith Lee and and linebackers Rod Shoate and John Zamberlin had interceptions in the 38–10 rout of Houston on 10-18-81

2004 championship season

Troy Brown and Eugene Wilson and linebackers Tedy Bruschi and Tully Banta-Cain had interceptions in the 29–6 rout of Buffalo on 11-14-04

The only game with four total interceptions; one each by two Patriots Defensive Backs and two interceptions by a Patriots Linebacker

John Charles and Larry Carwell had one and Ed Philpott had two interceptions in the 35–21 win over the Buffalo Bills on 11-23-69

The only game with four total interceptions; two by a Patriots Defensive Back and two interceptions by a Patriots Linebacker

Ronnie Lippett and Steve Nelson each had two interceptions in the 30–21 win over the Indianapolis Colts on 11-09-86

The Patriots had five interceptions in a regular season game

The only game that two Patriots Defensive Backs and three Patriots Linebackers had an interception

Ross O'Hanley, Don Webb Tom Addison, Nick Buoniconti and Mike Dukes had interceptions in the 34–17 win over Houston on 11-29-64

The only game that there were five Patriots interceptions; one by a Patriots Defensive Back, three interceptions by another Defensive Back, and one by a Defensive Lineman

1 by Bob Soltis, three by Gino Cappelletti, and one by Bob Dee in the 27–14 loss to the Oakland Raiders at Kezar Stadium on 10-16-60

The only game with five Patriots interceptions; two each by a two Patriots Defensive Backs and one by a Patriots Linebacker

2 each by Dick Felt and Ron Hall and Nick Buoniconti had an interception in the 26–10 win over the New York Jets on 09-27-64

The only game with five total interceptions; two each by a Patriots Defensive Back and a Patriots Linebacker and one by a Patriots Defensive Back

2 each by Don Webb and Nick Buoniconti and one interception by Leroy Mitchell in the 23–0 shutout of the Buffalo Bills on 09-24-67

The two games with five total interceptions; one each by three Patriots Defensive Backs and one each by a two Patriots Linebackers

1988 regular season

Jim Bowman, Fred Marion, Rod McSwain, Tim Jordan, and Johnny Rembert in the 27–21 win over the Cincinnati Bengals on 10-16-88

2003 championship season

Ty Law, Rodney Harrison, Eugene Wilson, Tedy Bruschi, and Willie McGinest in the 21–16 win over the New York Jets on 12-20-03

Games with five total interceptions, four interceptions by Patriots Defensive Backs and one interception by a Patriots Linebacker

1961 regular season

Fred Bruney had two and Clyde Washington, Don Webb, and Tom Addison had an interception in the 41–0 shutout of San Diego on 12-17-61

Eugene Wilson (26) and Asante Samuel (22)

1963 regular season

Dick Felt had two and Tom Stephens, Bob Suci, and Nick Buoniconti had an interception in the 38–14 rout of the New York Jets on 09-08-63

The only game with five Patriots interceptions; three by the same Patriots Defensive Back, one by another Patriots Defensive Back, and one by a Patriots Linebacker

Ross O'Hanley had three and Dick Felt and Tom Addison had an interception in the 21–17 loss to the Houston Oilers on 11-18-62

The two regular season games that the Patriots had six interceptions

1 by DB Ron Hall, DB Ross O'Hanley, LB Tom Addison, and DT Jim Hunt, and two by Bob Suci in the 45–3 rout of Huston at Fenway Park on 11-01-63

2 by DB Ron Hall, 2 by DB Dick Felt, 1 by LB Mike Dukes, and 1 by LB Nick Buoniconti in the 26–10 win over the New York Jets at Fenway Park on 09-27-64

The only regular season game that the Patriots had seven interceptions

The only regular season game that there were seven interceptions by the Defensive Backfield of the Patriots

3 by Mike Haynes, one by Tim Fox and Bob Howard, and Prentice McCray returned two for TDs in the 38–24 win vs the Jets on 11-21-76

The 10 greatest interceptions by the Patriots

Rodney Harrison's interception with 17 seconds left that sealed the 24–21 Super Bowl win over the Philadelphia Eagles on 02-06-05

Ty Law's 47-yard interception return for a touchdown in the 20–17 Super Bowl win over the St. Louis Rams on 02-03-02

Rodney Harrison's 87-yard interception return for a touchdown in the 41–27 playoff game win over the Pittsburgh Steelers on 01-23-05

Fred Marion's 21-yard return from Miami's 4-yard line (his third consecutive playoff game with an interception) in the 31–14 win on 01-12-86

Willie McGinest's 46-yard interception return for a TD with 41 seconds left in the 28–25 win over the Buffalo Bills on 10-27-96

Steve Nelson's interception and subsequent lateral to Clayton Weishuhn, who took it for a TD in the 28–23 win over the Pittsburgh Steelers on 09-25-83

Tedy Bruschi's five-yard return for a TD (which was his fourth consecutive return for a TD) in the 12–0 shutout of the Miami Dolphins on 12-07-03

Ronnie Lippett's 20-yard interception return for a TD for the last points scored in the 28–21 win over the Miami Dolphins on 09-13-87

Raymond Clayborn's 85-yard interception return on the last play of the 17–16 win over the Cleveland Browns on 10-07-84

Larry Izzo's interception in the end zone with 13 seconds left, which helped preserve the 31–0 shutout of the Buffalo Bills on 12-27-03

The Playoffs

The most interceptions

The progression of the most interceptions by a Patriots Defensive Back in a playoff game

2 interceptions by Ross O'Hanley in the 26–8 victory over the Buffalo Bills at War Memorial Stadium on 12-28-63

2 interceptions by Ronnie Lippett in the 27–20 win over the Los Angeles Raiders at the Los Angeles Coliseum on 01-05-86

3 interceptions by Ty Law in the 24–14 victory over the Indianapolis Colts at Gillette Stadium on 01-18-04

Every interception by a Patriots Linebacker in a playoff game

1 interception by Johnny Rembert in the 22–17 loss to the Denver Broncos at Mile High Stadium on 01-04-87

1 interception by Tedy Bruschi in the 20–6 victory over the Jacksonville Jaguars at Foxboro Stadium on 01-12-97

1 interception by Todd Collins in the 17–3 victory over the Miami Dolphins at Foxboro Stadium on 12-28-97

1 interception by Chris Slade in the 17–3 victory over the Miami Dolphins at Foxboro Stadium on 12-28-97

1 interception by Tedy Bruschi in the 24–21 victory over the Philadelphia Eagles at Alltel Stadium on 02-06-05

1 interception by Rosevelt Colvin in the 24–21 victory over the San Diego Chargers at Qualcomm Stadium on 01-14-07

The only Patriots Defensive Lineman who has intercepted two passes in a playoff game

1963 AFC Eastern Divisional playoff game

Bob Dee intercepted a pass by Daryle Lamonica in the 26–8 win over the Buffalo Bills at War Memorial Stadium on 12-28-63

Bob Dee picked off another Daryle Lamonica pass in the 26–8 victory over the Buffalo Bills at War Memorial Stadium on 12-28-63

The only Patriots Defensive Lineman who has returned an interception in a playoff game

1985 AFC Wild Card playoff game

Garin Veris returned a Pat Ryan pass 18 yards in the 26–14 victory over the New York Jets at the Meadowlands on 12-28-85

The only Patriots Defensive Back who has intercepted a pass in three consecutive playoff games

3 consecutive games that Fred Marion intercepted a pass (from 12-28-85 to 01-12-86)

Bob Dee

3 consecutive games that Rodney Harrison intercepted at least one pass (from 01-16-05 to 02-06-05)

The most career interceptions

The progression of the most career interceptions by a Patriots Linebacker in the playoffs

1 interception by Johnny Rembert in the 1986 AFC Divisional playoff game on 01-04-87

1 interception by Tedy Bruschi in the 1996 AFC Championship playoff game on 01-12-97

1 interception by Chris Slade in the 1997 AFC Wild Card playoff game on 12-28-97

1 interception by Todd Collins in the 1997 AFC Wild Card playoff game on 12-28-97

2 career interceptions by Tedy Bruschi in 22 playoff games

The progression of the most career interceptions by a Patriots Defensive Lineman in the playoffs

2 interceptions by Bob Dee in the AFL Eastern Divisional playoff game on 12-28-63

The progression of the most career interceptions by a Patriots Defensive Back in the playoffs

2 interceptions by Ross O'Hanley in the 1963 AFL Eastern Divisional playoff game on 12-28-63

3 career interceptions by Fred Marion, as he had an interception in three consecutive playoff games in the 1985 playoffs

4 career interceptions by Ty Law in 12 playoff games for the New England Patriots

7 career interceptions by Rodney Harrison in nine playoff games for the New England Patriots

The most interception return yards

The progression of the most interception return yards by a Patriots Defensive Back in a playoff game

13 interception return yards by Ross O'Hanley in the 26–8 win over the Buffalo Bills at War Memorial Stadium on 12-28-63

26 interception return yards by Fred Marion in the 26–14 victory over the New York Jets at the Meadowlands on 12-28-85

47 interception return yards by Ty Law in the 20–17 win over the St. Louis Rams at the Superdome on 02-03-02

87 interception return yards by Rodney Harrison in the 41–27 win over the Pittsburgh Steelers at Heinz Field on 01-23-05

The progression of the most interception return yards by a Patriots Linebacker in a playoff game

2 interception return yards by Johnny Rembert in the 22–17 loss to the Denver Broncos at Mile High Stadium on 01-04-87

12 interception return yards by Tedy Bruschi in the 20–6 victory over the Jacksonville Jaguars at Foxboro Stadium on 01-12-97

22 interception return yards by Chris Slade in the 17–3 victory over the Miami Dolphins at Foxboro Stadium on 12-28-97

40 interception return yards by Todd Collins in the 17–3 win over the Miami Dolphins at Foxboro Stadium on 12-28-97

Chris Slade

The progression of the most interception return yards by a Patriots Defensive Lineman in a playoff game

No return of an interception by Bob Dee in the 26–8 victory over the Buffalo Bills at War Memorial Stadium on 12-28-63

18 interception return yards by Garin Veris in the 26–14 victory over the New York Jets at the Meadowlands on 12-28-85

The most progression of the most career interception return yards by a Patriots player in the playoffs

13 career interception return yards by Ross O'Hanley in two playoff games for the Boston Patriots

69 career interception return yards by Fred Marion in six playoff games for the New England Patriots

73 career interception return yards by Ty Law in 12 playoff games for the New England Patriots

118 career interception return yards by Rodney Harrison in nine playoff games for the New England Patriots

158 career interception return yards by Asante Samuel in 14 playoff games for the New England Patriots

The progression of the longest interception return by a Patriots Defensive Back in a playoff game

13-yard return by Ross O'Hanley in the 26–8 victory over the Buffalo Bills at War Memorial Stadium on 12-28-63

26-yard return by Fred Marion in the 26–14 victory over the New York Jets at the Meadowlands on 12-28-85

47-yard return for a TD by Ty Law in the 20–17 victory over the St. Louis Rams at the Louisiana Superdome on 02-03-02

87-yard return for a TD by Rodney Harrison in the 41–27 win over the Pittsburgh Steelers at Heinz Field on 01-23-05

The progression of the longest interception return by a Patriots Linebacker in a playoff game

2-yard return by Johnny Rembert in the 22–17 loss to the Denver Broncos at Mile High Stadium on 01-04-87

12-yard return by Tedy Bruschi in the 20–6 victory over the Jacksonville Jaguars at Foxboro Stadium on 01-12-97

22-yard return by Chris Slade in the 17–3 victory over the Miami Dolphins at Foxboro Stadium on 12-28-97

40-yard return for a TD by Todd Collins in the 17–3 victory over the Miami Dolphins at Foxboro Stadium on 12-28-97

The progression of the longest interception return by a Patriots Defensive Lineman in a playoff game

No return by Bob Dee in the 26–8 victory over the Buffalo Bills at War Memorial Stadium on 12-28-63

No return on another interception by Bob Dee in the 26–8 win over the Buffalo Bills at War Memorial Stadium on 12-28-63

18-yard return by Garin Veris in the 26–14 victory over the New York Jets at the Meadowlands on 12-28-85

Every Patriots Defensive Lineman who has intercepted a pass in a playoff game

1963 AFL Eastern Divisional playoff game
Bob Dee intercepted a Daryle Lamonica pass in the 26–8 victory over the Buffalo Bills at War Memorial Stadium on 12-28-63

Bob Dee intercepted another Daryle Lamonica pass in the 26–8 win over the Buffalo Bills at War Memorial Stadium on 12-28-63

1985 AFC Wild Card playoff game
Garin Veris returned a Pat Ryan pass 18 yards in the 26–14 victory over the New York Jets at the Meadowlands on 12-28-85

Every Patriots Linebacker who has returned an interception in a playoff game

1996 AFC Championship Game
Tedy Bruschi returned a Mark Brunell pass 12 yards in the 20–6 win over the Jacksonville Jaguars at Foxboro Stadium on 01-12-97

1997 AFC Wild Card playoff game
Todd Collins returned a Dan Marino pass, 40 yards for a TD, in the 17–3 win over the Miami Dolphins at Foxboro Stadium on 12-28-97

Chris Slade returned a Dan Marino pass 22 yards in the 17–3 victory over the Miami Dolphins at Foxboro Stadium on 12-28-97

Every Patriots Linebacker who has intercepted a pass but was not able to return it during a playoff game

1986 AFC Divisional playoff game
Johnny Rembert intercepted a pass by John Elway in the 22–17 loss to the Denver Broncos at Mile High Stadium on 01-04-87

Super Bowl XXXIX
Tedy Bruschi intercepted a pass by Donovan McNabb in the 24–21 win over the Philadelphia Eagles at Alltel Stadium on 02-06-05

Every Patriots Defensive Back who has intercepted a pass late in a playoff game to seal the victory

2001 AFC Championship playoff game
Lawyer Milloy intercepted a Kordell Stewart pass with 2:11 left in the 24–17 win over the Steelers on 01-27-02

Super Bowl XXXIX
Rodney Harrison intercepted a Donovan McNabb pass with 17 seconds left in the 24–21 win over the Eagles on 02-06-05

Every Patriots Defensive Back who has returned an interception for a touchdown in a playoff game

Super Bowl XXXVI
Ty Law returned a Kurt Warner pass 47 yards for a TD in the 20–17 win over the St. Louis Rams on 02-03-02

2004 AFC Championship Game
Rodney Harrison returned a Ben Roethlisberger pass 87 yards for a TD in the 41–27 win over the Pittsburgh Steelers on 01-23-05

2005 AFC Wild Card playoff game
Asante Samuel returned a Byron Leftwich pass 73 yards for a TD in the 28–3 rout of the Jacksonville Jaguars on 01-07-06

2006 AFC Wild Card playoff game
Asante Samuel took a Chad Pennington pass 36 yards for a TD in the 37–16 rout of the New York Jets on 01-07-07

2006 AFC Championship Game
Asante Samuel took a Peyton Manning pass 39 yards for a TD in the 38–34 loss to the Indianapolis Colts on 01-21-07

The only Patriots Linebacker who has returned an interception for a touchdown in a playoff game

1997 AFC Wild Card playoff game
Todd Collins returned a Dan Marino pass 40 yards for a TD in the 17–3 win over the Miami Dolphins at Foxboro Stadium on 12-28-97

Combinations of interceptions and fumble recoveries in a Playoff Game

The only Patriots Defensive Back who has intercepted a pass and recovered a fumble in a Playoff Game

1985 AFC Divisional playoff game

Fred Marion intercepted a Marc Wilson pass and recovered a fumble in the 27–20 win over the Raiders on 01-05-86

The only Patriots Linebacker who has intercepted a pass and recovered a fumble in a playoff game

1997 AFC Wild Card playoff game

Chris Slade intercepted a Dan Marino pass and recovered a fumble in the 17–3 win over the Dolphins on 12-28-97

Fumble Recoveries

In team history, 52 offensive lineman, 22 quarterbacks, two kickers, 14 punters, 71 running backs, 43 wide receivers, 17 tight ends, 95 defensive backs, 71 linebackers, and 67 defensive linemen have recovered a fumble for the Patriots in regular season games played during the 1960–2008 seasons. This section provides numerous stats regarding offensive, defensive, and special teams fumble recoveries and returns by these players.

The first Boston Patriots lineman who recovered an offensive fumble and a defensive fumble during the regular season was Jack Davis. He recovered a fumble by the Patriots quarterback Butch Songin in the 35–0 shutout of the Los Angeles Chargers on 10-08-60, and he recovered a blocked punt in the 31–24 loss to the Denver Broncos on 10-23-60.

Some of the Boston Patriots players who recovered their share of fumbles include Jack Rudolph, Clyde Washington, Bob Dee, Larry Eisenhauer, and Jim Lee Hunt. Jack Rudolph and Clyde Washington each recovered four fumbles during the 1960 season. Did you know that Bob Dee holds the team record with five fumble recoveries in a season, and that Jim Lee Hunt holds the AFL record with 15 career fumble recoveries?

Typically, an offensive lineman will recover a fumble by the quarterback or the running back. The Patriots offensive lineman who has recovered the most fumbles in a career is John Hannah, who recovered 10 fumbles during his 13-year NFL career. Did you know that Hannah's first fumble recovery was on a fumbled punt return by Chris Farasopoulos in the 33–13 loss to the New York Jets at Shea Stadium on 11-11-73? Only two Patriots offensive lineman have recovered a fumble in the end zone for a touchdown in a regular season game. Can you name the only Patriots offensive lineman who has recovered a fumble by another Patriots offensive linemen? The answers to these questions can be found later in this section.

As you compare the information from this section and the Sacks section of this book, you will notice that many times a quarterback who was sacked also fumbled. Tebucky Jones is the only Patriots player to sack the quarterback, force the fumble, and return the fumble for a touchdown in a regular season game. Brent Williams is the only Patriots defensive lineman to return a fumble by a quarterback for a touchdown twice in a career. Willie McGinest is the only Patriots defensive player to recover a fumble in the end zone for a touchdown made by a quarterback who became the Patriots punter later in his career.

Because it is difficult to determine the exact player who caused the fumble, I have only included some of the more memorable forced fumbles that have been recovered by a Patriots player. Two of the more memorable forced fumbles by Mosi Tatupu happened during the 1980s. He caused Nesby Glasgow to fumble on a kickoff return and Rick Sanford returned it 22 yards for a touchdown in the 47–21 rout of the Baltimore Colts on 11-23-80. Tatupu also smacked Sam Seale on his kickoff return and Jim Bowman recovered the ball in the end zone for the game-winning touchdown in the 27–20 AFC Divisional playoff game win over the Los Angeles Raiders on 01-05-86.

Many of these fumbles were recovered after a poor snap to the punter, or after a blocked punt, or on a fumbled punt return or kickoff return. Rick Sanford is the only Patriots player to return a blocked punt for a touchdown and return a fumbled kickoff return for a touchdown. Perhaps you might remember the time that Andre Tippett returned a poor snap to punter Ray Guy 29 yards for a touchdown during the 1985 season. Did you know that Troy Brown is the only Patriots player to advance his teammate's fumbled kickoff return for a touchdown? Tedy Bruschi is the only Patriots linebacker to return a blocked punt for a touchdown as he returned it four yards for the score in the 46–38 victory over the Baltimore Ravens on 10-06-96.

The 10 most memorable offensive fumble recoveries by the Patriots

Randy Vataha's advance of a fumble by Mack Herron 46 yards for a touchdown in the 24–16 win on 10-07-73

Leonard Russell's 22-yard advancement of Vincent Brisby's fumble, which helped set up the overtime game-winning TD in the six-point win on 01-02-94

Logan Mankins recovered a fumble by Tom Brady in the end zone for a TD in the four-point playoff game loss on 01-21-07

John Stephens recovered a fumble by Robert Perryman in the end zone for a TD in the 27–21 win on 10-16-88

Freddie Childress recovered a fumbled snap in the end zone for a TD in the 26–23 overtime win on 10-20-91

Steve Grogan advanced a fumble by Don Calhoun six yards for a touchdown in the 41–7 victory on 10-18-76

Marc Edwards advanced a Tom Brady fumble two yards in the 29–26 come-from-behind win in overtime on 10-14-01

Fred Marion recovered a fumble by Ronnie Lippett with 38 seconds left in the 16–10 victory on 12-16-84

Damien Woody recovered a fumble by Joe Andruzzi, who had caught a pass in the 38–34 win on 11-30-03

Max Lane's advance of an airborn fumble by Troy Brown 30 yards in the five-point loss to the Kansas City Chiefs on 10-15-95

The 10 most memorable defensive fumble recoveries by the Patriots

Reche Caldwell recovered a fourth-quarter fumble that was forced by Troy Brown in the 24–21 playoff game win on 01-14-06

Tedy Bruschi ripped the ball from the hands of Dominic Rhodes in the 17-point playoff game victory on 01-16-05

Larry McGrew recovered Walton Payton's fumble on the second play of the game in the 46-point loss to the Chicago Bears on 01-26-86

Garin Veris recovered a fumble that was forced by Steve Nelson on the first play in the 17-point AFC Championship Game win on 01-12-86

Otis Smith returned a fumble by James Stewart 47 yards for a TD in the 20–6 playoff game win on 01-12-97

Terrell Buckley returned a fumble by Ricky Proehl 15 yards in the three-point Super Bowl win on 02-03-02

Richard Seymour returned a fumble by Drew Bledsoe 68 yards for a touchdown in the 31–17 win on 10-17-04

Tebucky Jones strip-sacked Vinny Testaverde and returned the loose ball 24 yards for a TD in the 37-point win on 09-15-02

Andre Tippett stole the ball out of the hands of Hall of Fame RB Eric Dickerson in the 21–7 victory on 12-11-83

Steve Nelson recorded his third defensive fumble recovery of the game in the 24–14 victory on 10-08-78

The 10 most memorable Special Teams fumble recoveries by the Patriots

Troy Brown recovered a blocked field goal and lateraled it to Antwan Harris, who took it for a TD, in the seven-point playoff game win on 01-27-02

Jim Bowman fell on a fumble by Sam Seale and scored a TD for the last points scored in the 27–20 playoff game win on 01-05-86

Johnny Rembert took Johnny Hector's fumbled kickoff return 15 yards for a TD in the 12-point playoff game win on 12-28-85

Chuck Shonta returned a fumbled snap to the punter 52 yards for a TD on the last play of the 28–24 win on 09-17-60

John Zamberlin recovered a blocked field goal and lateraled to Mike Haynes, who took it for a TD, in the 21–11 win on 10-05-80

Ron Burton advanced his own fumble on a missed field goal 91 yards for a TD in the 33–29 win on 11-11-62

Larry Izzo recovered his second of two Troy Brown fumbled punt returns in the 16–13 overtime playoff game win on 01-19-02

David Thomas recovered a fumbled punt return by Eric Parker in the three-point playoff game win over the San Diego Chargers on 01-14-07

Troy Brown advanced a fumbled kickoff return by Dave Meggett 75 yards for a TD in the 31–28 win on 12-10-95

LeRoy Moore recovered a punt that deflected off the crossbar back into the end zone for a TD in the three-point win on 11-17-61

10 of the more memorable forced fumbles by the Patriots

Mike Vrabel's strip-sack of Jake Delhomme that was recovered by Richard Seymour in the three-point Super Bowl win on 02-01-04

Mosi Tatupu's hit on Sam Seale that caused a fumble that was recovered for the final points scored in the seven-point win on 01-05-86

The strip-sack of Vinny Testaverde by Tebucky Jones, who subsequently picked up the ball and took it in for a TD in the 37-point win on 09-15-02

Tedy Bruschi forced Drew Bledsoe to fumble and Richard Seymour returned the loose ball 68 yards for a TD on 10-17-04

Lawrence McGrew's strip-sack of Jim Kelly that went out of the end zone for safety in the three-point win on 11-23-86

Garin Veris forced Dave Wilson to fumble and Brent Williams took it for a TD with two minutes left in the one-point win on 11-30-86

Todd Collins forced Richard Anderson's fumble on the 1-yard line with 15 seconds left in the half in the three-point overtime win on 09-14-97

Don Hasselbeck forced Leonard Thompson's fumble and "Houn" scored a TD on the next play in the seven-point win on 10-07-79

Ken Sims' strip-sack of Paul McDonald and Ronnie Lippett's recovery that set up the final points scored in the one-point win on 10-07-84

Rodney Harrison forced Rudi Johnson's fumble that allowed the Patriots to score first for the 18th consecutive time on 12-12-04

The first Patriots player to recover a fumble in a regular season game

Charlie Leo recovered a punt that deflected off Bob McNamara in the 13–10 loss to the Denver Broncos at BU Field on 09-09-60

The progression of the most career offensive fumble recoveries by a Patriots Offensive Lineman of a Patriots Quarterback

1 by Jack Davis; who recovered a fumble by Butch Songin on 10-08-60

2 by Billy Neighbors; who recovered a fumble by Tom Yewcic and Babe Parilli during the 1962–63 seasons

3 by Lennie St. Jean; who recovered a fumble by Don Trull, Mike Taliaferro, and Jim Plunkett during the 1967–72 seasons

3 by John Hannah; who recovered a fumble by Tom Owen and two fumbles by Steve Grogan during the 1978–83 seasons

Dan Koppen

3 by Pete Brock; who recovered a fumble by Matt Cavanaugh and two fumbles by Steve Grogan during the 1981–86 seasons

3 by Brian Holloway; who recovered a fumble by Matt Cavanaugh and two fumbles by Tony Eason during the 1981–86 seasons

4 by Bruce Armstrong; who recovered a fumble by Hugh Millen and three fumbles by Drew Bledsoe during the 1992–98 seasons

5 by Dan Koppen; who recovered five fumbles by Tom Brady during the 2003–06 regular seasons

The only Patriots Offensive Lineman who has recovered two fumbles by a Patriots Quarterback in the same regular season game

Max Lane recovered two fumbles by Drew Bledsoe in the 27–13 victory over the Indianapolis Colts at Foxboro Stadium on 11-24-96

Every Patriots Running Back who has recovered two fumbles by a Patriots Quarterback in the same regular season game

1978 regular season

Andy Johnson recovered two fumbles by Steve Grogan in the 34–27 loss to the Baltimore Colts at Schaefer Stadium on 09-18-78

2002 regular season
Antowain Smith recovered two fumbles by Tom Brady in the 24–17 victory over the Minnesota Vikings at Gillette Stadium on 11-24-02

Players who have advanced an offensive fumble recovery

The progression of the longest advancement of a fumble by a Patriots player in a regular season game

10-yard advancement of a fumble recovery by Jim Colclough in the 23–21 win over the Buffalo Bills on 09-23-61

91-yard advancement for a TD of his own fumble recovery by Ron Burton in the 33–29 win over the Denver Broncos on 11-11-62

100-yard advancement for a TD of his own fumble recovery by Jon Vaughn in the 20–10 loss to the Bengals on 12-20-92

Every Patriots Running Back who has advanced a fumble by a Patriots Quarterback in a regular season game

1971 regular season
Jack Maitland advanced a Jim Plunkett fourth down fumble three yards for a first down in the 13–6 loss to the New York Jets at Shea Stadium on 12-12-71

1988 regular season
John Stephens advanced a Doug Flutie fumble four yards in the 45–3 loss to the Green Bay Packers at County Stadium on 10-09-88

1993 regular season
Kevin Turner advanced a fumble by Scott Secules six yards in the 28–14 loss to the Houston Oilers at Foxboro Stadium on 10-17-93

2001 championship season
Marc Edwards advanced a Tom Brady fumble two yards in the 29–26 overtime win vs the San Diego Chargers at Foxboro Stadium on 10-14-01

Every Patriots Offensive Lineman who has advanced a fumble by a Patriots Quarterback in a regular season game

1975 regular season
Shelby Jordan advanced a Jim Plunkett fumble 12 yards on the last play in the 34–31 loss to the Dallas Cowboys at Schaefer Stadium on 11-16-75

Leon Gray advanced a Steve Grogan fumble four yards in the 30–28 loss to the New York Jets at Schaefer Stadium on 12-07-75

1990 regular season
Bruce Armstrong advanced a Marc Wilson fumble four yards in the 17–10 loss to the Miami Dolphins at Joe Robbie Stadium on 10-18-90

1992 regular season
Gene Chilton advanced a Hugh Millen fumble two yards in the 10–6 loss to the Seattle Seahawks at Foxboro Stadium on 09-20-92

2000 regular season
Joe Andruzzi advanced a Drew Bledsoe fumble two yards in the 10–3 loss to the Miami Dolphins at Pro Player Stadium on 09-24-00

Every Patriots Quarterback who has advanced a fumble by a Patriots Running Back in a regular season game

1961 regular season
Babe Parilli advanced a Larry Garron fumble one yard for a TD in the 28–21 win over the Dallas Texans at BU Field on 11-03-61

1976 regular season
Steve Grogan advanced a Don Calhoun fumble six yards for a TD in the 41–7 rout of the New York Jets at Schaefer Stadium on 10-18-76

1988 regular season
Tony Eason advanced a fumble by John Stephens two yards in the 10–7 overtime win vs the Buccaneers at Sullivan Stadium on 12-11-88

The Only Patriots Offensive Lineman who has advanced a fumble by a Patriots Running Back in a regular season game

Charlie Long advanced a Ron Burton fumble two yards in the 27–7 loss to the Dallas Texans at BU Field on 10-12-62

Every Patriots Wide Receiver who has advanced a fumble by a Patriots Running Back in a regular season game

1961 regular season
Jim Colclough advanced a fumble by Billy Lott 10 yards in the 23–21 win over the Buffalo Bills at War Memorial Stadium on 09-23-61

1964 regular season

Gino Cappelletti advanced a Ron Burton fumble four yards in the 12–7 win over the Denver Broncos at Fenway Park on 11-20-64

1973 regular season

Randy Vataha took a Mack Herron fumble 46 yards for a TD in the 24–16 win vs the Baltimore Colts at Schaefer Stadium on 10-07-73

1975 regular season

Darryl Stingley advanced a Sam Cunningham fumble 14 yards in the 22–14 loss to the Miami Dolphins at Schaefer Stadium on 09-28-75

1980 regular season

Stanley Morgan advanced a Don Calhoun fumble three yards in the 37–31 win over the Seattle Seahawks at the Kingdome on 09-21-80

1983 regular season

Stanley Morgan advanced a Tony Collins fumble 20 yards in the 30–0 loss to the Cleveland Browns at Sullivan Stadium on 11-20-83

1984 regular season

Stephen Starring advanced a Tony Collins fumble eight yards in the 38–23 win over the Seattle Seahawks at Sullivan Stadium on 09-16-84

The only Patriots Wide Receiver to advance a teammate's fumble on a running play from scrimmage for a touchdown

Randy Vataha took a Mack Herron fumble 46 yards for a TD in the 24–16 win over the Colts at Schaefer Stadium on 10-07-73 (Bill Lenkaitis slapped the ball upfield about 10 yards before Vataha picked it up and ran it in for the touchdown)

Every Patriots player who has advanced a fumble by a Patriots Wide Receiver in a regular season game

1993 regular season

Leonard Russell advanced Vincent Brisby's fumble 22 yards in the final quarter of the 33–27 overtime win vs the Miami Dolphins at Foxboro Stadium on 01-02-94 (Leonard's fumble advancement helped set up the overtime game-winning 36-yard TD reception by Michael Timpson)

1995 regular season

Max Lane advanced an airborne fumble by Troy Brown 30 yards in the 31–26 loss to the Chiefs at Arrowhead on 10-15-95

Every Patriots Player who has advanced a fumbled kickoff return by his teammate in a regular season game

1962 regular season

Rommie Loudd advanced Ron Burton's fumbled return three yards in the 20–0 loss to the Oakland Raiders at Frank Youell Field on 12-16-62

1963 regular season

Larry Garron advanced Bob Suci's fumbled return two yards in the 46–28 win over the Houston Oilers at Jeppesen Stadium on 12-08-63

1990 regular season

Marvin Allen advanced a fumble by Jamie Morris three yards in the 37–7 loss to the Kansas City Chiefs at Foxboro Stadium on 12-02-90

1995 regular season

Troy Brown advanced Dave Meggett's fumble 75 yards for a TD in the 31–28 win over the New York Jets at Foxboro Stadium on 12-10-95

1997 regular season

Chris Canty advanced a fumble by Derrick Cullors nine yards in the 14–12 win over the Miami Dolphins at Pro Player Stadium on 12-22-97

Every Patriots player who has advanced a fumbled punt return by his teammate in a regular season game

1966 regular season

Billy Johnson advanced Joe Bellino's fumbled punt return three yards in the 24–21 win over the Oakland Raiders at Fenway Park on 10-30-66

Joe Bellino

Troy Brown

1968 regular season

Willie Porter advanced Billy Johnson's fumbled punt return two yards in the 31–17 loss to the Kansas City Chiefs at Municipal Stadium on 11-17-68

The only Patriots Special Teams player to recover and advance a teammates kickoff return fumble for a TD

Troy Brown advanced Dave Meggett's fumbled return 75 yards for a TD in the 31–28 win over the New York Jets on 12-10-95

The only Patriots player who recovered and advanced his own return of a missed field-goal attempt for a touchdown

Ron Burton caught his own mid-air fumble on his 91-yard TD return of a missed field goal in the 33–29 win over the Denver Broncos on 11-11-62

The only Patriots player who recovered and advanced his own kickoff return fumble for a touchdown

Jon Vaughn advanced his own fumbled return 100 yards for a TD in the 20–10 loss to the Cincinnati Bengals at Riverfront Stadium on 12-20-92

Offensive fumble recoveries

The progression of the most career fumble recoveries by a Patriots Quarterback of a fumble by a Patriots Running Back

3 by Babe Parilli; who recovered fumbles by Larry Garron, JD Garrett, and Joe Bellino during the 1963–65 seasons

4 by Steve Grogan; who recovered a fumble by Don Calhoun and Tony Collins and two fumbles by Sam Cunningham

Every Patriots Running Back who has recovered a fumble by a Patriots Wide Receiver in a regular season game

1973 regular season

Josh Ashton recovered a fumble by Reggie Rucker in the 24–23 loss to the Eagles at Veterans Stadium on 11-04-73

1981 regular season

Vagas Ferguson recovered a fumble by Harold Jackson in the 27–20 loss to the St. Louis Cardinals at Schaefer Stadium on 11-29-81

Every Patriots Receiver who has recovered a fumble by another Patriots Receiver in a regular season game

1961 regular season

Tom Stephens recovered a fumble by Jim Colclough in the 20–17 victory over the Oakland Raiders at BU Field on 11-17-61

1989 regular season

Cedric Jones recovered a fumble by Hart Lee Dykes in the 22–16 win over the Indianapolis Colts at Sullivan Stadium on 12-03-89

1999 regular season

Shawn Jefferson fell on a Rod Rutledge fumble in the 27–3 rout of the Arizona Cardinals at Sun Devil Stadium on 10-31-99

The only Patriots Player who has recovered a poor lateral from a Patriots Tight End in a regular season game

John Stephens recovered a lateral by Eric Sievers on the last play of the 17–10 loss to the Miami Dolphins at Joe Robbie Stadium on 10-18-90

The only Patriots Lineman who has recovered a fumble by another Patriots Lineman who had just caught a pass

Damien Woody recovered a fumble by receiver Joe Andruzzi in the 38–34 win over the Indianapolis Colts at the RCA Dome on 11-30-03

Every Patriots Offensive Lineman who has recovered a fumble by a Patriots Tight End in a regular season game

1989 regular season

Mike Baab recovered a fumble by Eric Sievers in the 27–26 loss to the New York Jets at Sullivan Stadium on 11-05-89

1991 regular season

Danny Villa fell on a fumble by Marv Cook in the 20–0 loss to the Cleveland Browns at Foxboro Stadium on 09-08-91

Every Patriots Offensive Lineman who has recovered a fumble by a Patriots Wide Receiver in a regular season game

1967 regular season

Tom Neville recovered a fumble by Gino Cappelletti in the 26–21 loss to the Denver Broncos at Bears Stadium on 09-03-67

Matt Light

1978 regular season

John Hannah recovered a fumble by Stanley Morgan in the 35–14 win over the Baltimore Colts at Memorial Stadium on 11-26-78

1983 regular season

John Hannah recovered a fumble by Cedric Jones in the 33–13 loss to the San Francisco 49ers at Sullivan Stadium on 10-02-83

2002 regular season

Matt Light fell on a David Givens fumble in the 27–20 loss to the Oakland Raiders at Network Assoc. Coliseum on 11-17-02

Every Patriots Tight End who has recovered a fumble by a Patriots Quarterback in a regular season game

1992 regular season

Marv Cook fell on a fumble by Scott Zolak in the 27–20 loss to the Kansas City Chiefs at Arrowhead Stadium on 12-13-92

1994 regular season

Ben Coates recovered a fumble by Drew Bledsoe in the 13–6 loss to the Browns at Cleveland Stadium on 11-06-94

Every Patriots Offensive Lineman who has recovered a fumble in the end zone for a touchdown

1974 regular season

John Hannah recovered a fumbled snap in the end zone for a TD in the 34–27 loss to the Miami Dolphins on 12-15-74

1991 regular season

Freddie Childress recovered a fumbled snap in the end zone for a TD in the 26–23 overtime win vs the Minnesota Vikings on 10-20-91

The only Patriots Receiver who has recovered a teammates fumble in the end zone for a touchdown

Cedric Jones fell on Mosi Tatupu's fumble for a TD in the 27–17 loss to the Eagles at Veterans Stadium on 12-09-84 (Mosi Tatupu fumbled into the end zone after being hit at the end of his 13-yard run)

The only Patriots Running Back who has recovered a teammates fumble in the end zone for a touchdown

John Stephens recovered a fumble by Robert Perryman in the end zone of their 27–21 win over the Bengals on 10-16-88

The only Patriots Running Back who has run for a touchdown and recovered two fumbles in the same game

Andy Johnson ran one yard for a TD and recovered two fumbles in the 34–27 win over the Baltimore Colts on 09-18-78

The only Patriots Tight End who has caught a touchdown pass and returned a fumble in the same game

Tom Beer caught a 10-yard TD pass and returned a fumbled punt return five yards in the 38–33 win over the Buffalo Bills on 11-14-71

Every Patriots Special Teams player who has recovered a live ball after a Patriots field-goal attempt was blocked

1968 regular season

Doug Satcher recovered a blocked field goal that was mishandled by Jim Kearney in the 31–17 loss to the Kansas City Chiefs on 11-17-68 (Tom Sherman threw a one-yard touchdown pass to R.C. Gamble on the Patriots' next play)

1969 regular season

Ray Jacobs recovered a blocked field goal that was mishandled by a Dolphins player in the 17–16 loss to Miami on 11-09-69

The only Patriots Offensive Lineman who has recovered an opponent's fumble on a lateral after an interception

Bob Cryder recovered a fumble by Kendall Williams after receiving a lateral from Jeff Delaney, who had intercepted a pass

The only Patriots Quarterback who has recovered a fumble on an opponent's interception return

Babe Parilli fell on Dainard Paulson's fumble after his interception return in the 30–20 loss to the Jets at Fenway Park on 11-14-65

The only Patriots Receiver who has advanced a lateral from a Patriots Quarterback in a regular season game

Irving Fryar advanced a lateral from Hugh Millen eight yards in the 30–21 loss to the New York Jets at the Meadowlands on 10-04-92

Players who have scored a touchdown and advanced an offensive fumble in the same regular season game

The only Patriots Quarterback who has run for a TD and has advanced a fumble for a TD in the same game

Steve Grogan ran 41 yards for a TD and advanced a fumble six yards for a TD in the 41–7 rout of the New York Jets on 10-18-76

Every Patriots Quarterback who has thrown a TD pass and has advanced a fumble for a TD in the same game

1961 regular season

Babe Parilli threw a seven-yard TD pass and advanced a fumble one yard for a TD in the 28–21 win over Dallas on 11-03-61

1976 regular season

Steve Grogan threw a 10-yard TD pass and advanced a fumble six yards for a TD in the 41–7 rout of the New York Jets on 10-18-76

The only Patriots Player to pass for a TD, run for a TD, and advance a fumble for a TD in the same game

Steve Grogan threw a TD pass, ran 41 yards for a TD, and advanced a Don Calhoun fumble six yards for a TD on 10-18-76 in the 41–7 rout of the Jets

Every Patriots Running Back who has caught a touchdown pass and advanced a fumble in the same game

1973 regular season

Mack Herron caught a 15-yard TD pass and advanced his own fumble six yards in the 18–13 loss to the Baltimore Colts on 12-16-73

1993 regular season

Kevin Turner caught a seven-yard TD pass and advanced a fumble by Scott Secules six yards in the 28–14 loss to the Oilers on 10-17-93

The only Patriots Receiver who has recovered a lateral and then lateraled it back whereby the play resulted in a TD

Randy Moss took a lateral from Tom Brady and tossed it back to Tom in the 34–13 win over Pitts at Gillette Stadium on 12-09-07 (Tom Brady then completed a 56-yard double lateral flea flicker touchdown pass to Jabar Gaffney)

Fumble recoveries on the first play and the last play of the game

The only Patriots Defensive Player who has returned a fumble for a touchdown on the first play of the game

Tim Goad returned a Christian Okoye fumble 19 yards for a TD on the first play, in the 27–20 loss to Kansas City on 12-13-92

The only Patriots Defensive Player who has returned a fumble for a touchdown on the last play of the game

Chuck Shonta returned a fumble by the punter 52 yards for a TD on the last play of their 28–24 win over the New York Titans on 09-17-60

The progression of the longest fumble returns

The progression of the longest fumble return by a Patriots Defensive player in a regular season game

11-yard fumble return by Jim Lee Hunt in the 42–14 rout of the Dallas Texans on 11-18-60

30-yard fumble return by Bob Dee in the 52–21 rout of the Buffalo Bills on 10-22-61

51-yard fumble return by Jim Lee Hunt in the 45–17 loss to the Houston Oilers on 12-15-68

68-yard return for a touchdown by Richard Seymour in the 31–17 victory over the Buffalo Bills on 10-03-04

The progression of the longest fumble return by a Patriots Special Teams Player in a regular season game

52 yards for a TD by Chuck Shonta; who returned a mishandled snap to the punter in the 28–24 win over the New York Titans on 09-17-60

91 yards for a TD by Ron Burton; who returned his own fumbled return of a missed field-goal attempt in the 33–29 win over the Denver Broncos on 11-11-62

100 yards for a TD by Jon Vaughn; who returned his own fumbled kickoff return in the 20–10 loss to the Cincinnati Bengals on 12-20-92

Fumbles that were returned for a touchdown by a Patriots Player

Every Patriots Defensive Player who has returned a fumble for a touchdown to score the game-winning points

1960 regular season

Chuck Shonta returned a fumble 52 yards for a TD on the last play in the 28–24 win over the New York Titans on 09-17-60

1986 regular season

Brent Williams returned a Dave Wilson fumble 21 yards for a TD in the fourth quarter in the 21–20 win over the Saints on 11-30-86

Fumble returns of a blocked punt

Every Patriots Special Teams player who has returned a blocked a punt for a TD in a regular season game

1961 regular season

Don Webb returned a blocked punt 20 yards for a TD in the 41–0 shutout of the San Diego Chargers at Balboa Stadium on 12-17-61

1971 regular season

Roland Moss returned a blocked punt 10 yards for a TD in the 38–33 win over the Buffalo Bills at Schaefer Stadium on 11-14-71

1979 regular season

Rick Sanford returned a blocked punt eight yards for a TD in the 50–21 rout of the Baltimore Colts at Schaefer Stadium on 11-18-79

1986 regular season

Rod McSwain returned a blocked punt 31 yards for a TD in the 30–28 win over the Los Angeles Rams at Anaheim Stadium on 11-16-86

Mosi Tatupu returned a blocked punt 17 yards for a TD in the 21–20 win over the New Orleans Saints at the Superdome on 11-30-86

1987 regular season

Willie Scott returned a blocked punt three yards for a TD in the 24–0 shutout of the Indianapolis Colts at Sullivan Stadium on 11-22-87

1996 regular season

Tedy Bruschi returned a blocked punt four yards for a TD in the 46–38 win over the Baltimore Ravens at Memorial Stadium on 10-06-96

The only Patriots DE/Special Teams player who has recovered a blocked punt in the end zone for a touchdown

LeRoy Moore recovered a punt in the end zone that deflected off the goal post in the 20–17 win vs Oakland at BU Field on 11-17-61

The only Patriots LB/Special Teams player who has recovered a blocked punt in the end zone for a touchdown

Will Foster recovered a blocked punt in the end zone for a TD in the 9–7 loss to the New York Jets at Schaefer Stadium on 10-14-73

Fumble returns after a poor exchange to the punter

The only Patriots Defensive Back/Special Teams player who has returned a poor exchange to the punter for a TD in a regular season game

Chuck Shonta took the fumbled snap 52 yards for a TD in the 28–24 win over the New York Titans at the Polo Grounds on 09-17-60

The only Patriots Linebacker/Special Teams player who has returned a poor snap to the punter for a TD in a regular season game

Andre Tippett returned a poor snap to Ray Guy 25 yards for a TD in the 35–20 loss to the Los Angeles Raiders at Sullivan Stadium on 09-29-85

Fumble returns of a blocked field goal

Every Patriots Defensive Back/Special Teams player who has returned a fumble after a blocked field goal for a TD

1972 regular season

Larry Carwell returned a blocked field goal 45 yards for a TD in the 31–7 loss to the Cincinnati Bengals at Schaefer Stadium on 09-17-72

1987 regular season

Raymond Clayborn returned a blocked field goal 71 yards for a TD in the 21–7 win vs the Houston Oilers at the Astrodome on 10-18-87

The combination of a Patriots players who have returned a blocked field goal for a TD in a regular season game

John Zamberlin and Mike Haynes returned a fumble 65 yards for a TD in the 21–11 win vs the New York Jets at Shea Stadium on 10-05-80 (Steve Nelson blocked a field goal that John Zamberlin recovered and then lateraled to Mike Haynes, who ran it in for the TD)

Fumble recoveries and returns on mishandled kickoff returns

The only Patriots Special Teams player who has recovered a kickoff return fumble in the end zone for a TD

Johnny Rembert fell on a fumble by Clarence Weathers for a TD in the 24–20 loss to the Browns at Cleveland on 10-06-85

The only Patriots Defensive Back/Special Teams player who has returned an opponent's fumbled kickoff return for a TD

Rick Sanford returned Nesby Glasgow's fumble 22 yards for a TD in the 47–21 win over the Colts at Schaefer Stadium on 11-23-80 (Mosi Tatupu was credited with forcing the fumbled kickoff return by Nesby Glasgow)

The only Patriots Running Back/Special Teams player who has returned an opponent's fumbled kickoff return for a TD

Allan Clark returned Kim Anderson's fumbled kickoff return 15 yards for a TD in the 47-21 rout of the Colts on 11-23-80

The only Patriots Wide Receiver/Special Teams player who has returned a fumbled kickoff return for a TD in a regular season game

Cedric Jones returned Joe Carter's fumbled kickoff return 15 yards for a TD in the 30–27 loss to the Miami Dolphins at Miami Stadium on 12-16-85

A fumble return for a TD on a mishandled punt return

The only Patriots Special Teams player who has returned a fumbled punt return for a touchdown in a regular season game

Tom Stephens returned Paul Lowe's fumbled punt return 10 yards for a TD in the 38–27 loss to San Diego at BU Field on 10-07-61

Defensive fumble returns

Every Patriots Linebacker who has returned a fumble by a Running Back for a touchdown

1963 regular season

Nick Buoniconti returned a Bill Tobin fumble seven yards for a TD in the 46–28 win over the Houston Oilers on 12-08-63

1992 regular season

Vincent Brown returned a Thurman Thomas fumble 25 yards for a TD in the 16–7 loss to the Buffalo Bills on 11-01-92

2003 championship season

Matt Chatham returned a Tiki Barber fumble 38 yards for a TD in the 17–6 win over the New York Giants on 10-12-03

Every Patriots Defensive Lineman who has returned a fumble by a Running Back for a touchdown

1966 regular season

Jim Lee Hunt returned a Darrell Lester fumble five yards for a TD in the 17–10 loss to the Denver Broncos on 11-06-66

1992 regular season

Tim Goad took a Christian Okoye fumble 19 yards for a TD on the first play of the 27–20 loss to the Kansas City Chiefs on 12-13-92 (Maurice Hurst blitzed on the play, causing Christian Okoye to fumble on the Chiefs first play of the game)

Every Patriots Defensive Back who has returned a fumble by a Running Back for a touchdown

1969 regular season

Daryl Johnson returned a Hoyle Granger fumble 32 yards for a TD in the 24–0 shutout of the Houston Oilers on 11-02-69 (John Bramlett was credited with forcing the fumble by Hoyle Granger)

1994 regular season

Ricky Reynolds returned a Carwell Gardner fumble 25 yards for a TD in the 41–17 rout of the Buffalo Bills on 12-18-94 (Mike Pitts was credited with forcing the fumble by Carwell Garnder)

2004 championship season

Randall Gay returned a William Green fumble 41 yards for a TD in the 42–15 rout of the Cleveland Browns on 12-05-04 (Richard Seymour was credited with forcing the fumble by William Green)

2007 undefeated regular season

Ellis Hobbs returned an airborn Dwayne Wright fumble 35 yards for a TD in the 56–10 rout of the Buffalo Bills on 11-18-07 (James Sanders was credited with forcing the fumble by Dwayne Wright)

Every Patriots Defensive Back who has returned a fumble by a Wide Receiver for a touchdown

1961 regular season

Don Webb returned a Johnny Robinson fumble 49 yards for a TD in the 18–17 victory over the Dallas Texans on 10-29-61

1996 regular season

Corwin Brown returned a Bryan Still fumble 42 yards for a TD in the 45–7 rout of the San Diego Chargers on 12-01-96

2007 undefeated regular season

Ellis Hobbs returned a fumble by Dwayne Wright 35 yards for a TD in the 56–10 rout of the Buffalo Bills on 11-18-07

The only Patriots Defensive Back who has returned a fumble by a Tight End for a touchdown

Randall Gay returned a Kellen Winslow fumble 15 yards for a TD in the 34–17 win over the Cleveland Browns on 10-07-07

The only Patriots Defensive Back who has returned a fumble by the opposing Quarterback for a touchdown

Tebucky Jones returned a Vinny Testaverde fumble 24 yards for a TD in the 44–7 rout of the New York Jets on 09-15-02 (Jones sacked Testaverde, forced him to fumble, and then picked up the fumble and took it 24 yards for a touchdown)

Tebucky Jones (34), Vinny Testaverde is on the ground

Every Patriots Linebacker who has returned a fumble by the opposing Quarterback for a touchdown

1995 regular season

Chris Slade returned a fumble by Jim Kelly 27 yards for a TD in the 35–25 victory over the Buffalo Bills on 11-26-95 (Willie McGinest's strip-sack of Jim Kelly forced an airborn fumble that Chris Slade caught and took 27 yards for the TD)

2007 undefeated regular season

Rosevelt Colvin returned a fumble by Jason Campbell 11 yards for a TD in the 52–7 rout of the Washington Redskins on 10-28-07 (Mike Vrabel's third strip-sack of Jason Campbell was picked up by Rosevelt Colvin and returned 11 yards for a TD)

Rosevelt Colvin

The only Patriots Linebacker who has returned a lateral by the opposing Quarterback for a touchdown

Ed Philpott returned a Babe Parilli lateral 10 yards for a TD in the 47–31 loss to the New York Jets at Legion Field on 09-22-68 (Babe Parilli tossed a lateral behind running back Billy Joe and Ed Philpott scooped it up and rumbled in for the touchdown)

Every Patriots Defensive Lineman who has returned a fumble by the opposing Quarterback for a touchdown

1975 regular season

Ray Hamilton returned a fumbled snap by Jim Hart 23 yards for a TD in the 27–17 loss to the St. Louis Cardinals on 11-02-75

1986 regular season

Brent Williams returned Dave Wilson's fumble 21 yards for a TD in the 21–20 win over the New Orleans Saints on 11-30-86

1990 regular season

Brent Williams returned a Dave Krieg fumble 45 yards for a TD in the 33–20 loss to the Seattle Seahawks on 10-07-90

1999 regular season

Chad Eaton returned a Tony Banks fumble 23 yards for a TD in the 20–3 rout of the Baltimore Ravens on 01-02-00

2004 championship season

Richard Seymour returned a Drew Bledsoe fumble 68 yards for a TD in the 31–17 over the Buffalo Bills on 10-03-04

Fumble recoveries in the end zone

The only Patriots player who recovered a fumble in the end zone for the game-winning points in a regular season game

LeRoy Moore recovered a blocked punt for the last points scored in the 20–17 win over Oakland at BU Field on 11-17-61

The only Patriots Linebacker who has recovered a fumble by the Quarterback in the end zone for a touchdown

Johnny Rembert recovered a Gary Hogeboom fumble for a TD in the 33–3 rout of the Indianapolis Colts at Sullivan Stadium on 09-07-86 (Andre Tippett forced Gary Hogeboom to fumble after his two-yard run to the 12-yard line, and the ball bounced back to the end zone)

Every Patriots Defensive Lineman who has recovered a fumble by the Quarterback in the end zone for a touchdown

1996 regular season

Willie McGinest recovered a Stan Humphries fumble in the end zone in the 45–7 rout of the San Diego Chargers on 12-01-96 (Chris Slade strip-sacked Stan Humphires at the 12-yard line and the ball bounced into the end zone, where McGinest fell on it)

1999 regular season

Willie McGinest recovered a Tom Tupa fumble in the end zone in the 30–28 victory over the New York Jets on 09-12-99 (Steve Israel strip-sacked Jets QB Tom Tupa at the 11-yard line and the ball bounced into the end zone where McGinest fell on it)

2004 championship season

Jarvis Green recovered a Kyle Boller fumble in the end zone in the 24–3 rout of the Baltimore Ravens on 11-28-04 (Tedy Bruschi strip-sacked Kyle Boller at the 8-yard line and the ball bounced into the end zone where Green fell on it)

The only Patriots LB/Special Teams player who has recovered a fumbled punt return in the end zone for a touchdown

Johnny Rembert recovered a fumble by Clarence Weathers for a TD in the 24–20 loss to the Cleveland Browns at Cleveland on 10-06-85

Offensive fumble recoveries by a defensive player of the Patriots

Every Patriots Defensive Back who has recovered a fumble by a Patriots Linebacker on his interception return in a regular season game

1960 regular season

Fred Bruney recovered a fumble by Jack Rudolph in the 35–0 shutout of the Los Angeles Chargers at the L.A. Coliseum on 10-08-60

2001 championship season

Matt Stevens recovered a fumble by Tedy Bruschi in the 31–20 loss to the Denver Broncos at Invesco Field on 10-28-01

The only Patriots Defensive Back who recovered a fumble by a Patriots Defensive Lineman who had intercepted a pass

Clyde Washington fell on a Bob Dee fumble after his interception in the 27–14 loss to Oakland at Kezar Stadium on 10-16-60

The only Patriots Defensive Back who recovered a fumble by Patriots Defensive Lineman who had recovered a fumble

Otis Smith recovered a fumble by Anthony Pleasant, who fell on a fumble in the 27–16 win over the Cleveland Browns on 12-09-01

Every Patriots Defensive Back who has recovered a fumble by another Patriots Defensive Back after his interception in a regular season game

1984 regular season

Fred Marion recovered a Ronnie Lippett fumble with 38 seconds left in the 16–10 win vs the Indianapolis Colts at Sullivan Stadium on 12-16-84

1994 regular season

Ricky Reynolds fell on Larry Whigham's fumble with 14 seconds left in the 41–17 rout of the Buffalo Bills at Rich Stadium on 12-18-94

1999 regular season

Chris Carter recovered a fumble by Ty Law in the 27–3 rout of the Arizona Cardinals at Sun Devil Stadium on 10-31-99

The longest fumble and lateral return by two Patriots players after a Quarterback sack in a regular season game

20-yard lateral return by Willie McGinest in the 31–10 rout of the Philadelphia Eagles at Lincoln Financial Field on 09-14-03 (Anthony Pleasant returned the fumble six yards before he lateralled it to McGinest, who ran an additional 20 yards)

Recovery of a free ball after the other team failed to recover or return a kickoff

Every Patriots Special Teams player who has recovered a short kickoff that was not recovered by the Opposing Team

1994 regular season

Steve Hawkins recovered the free ball on Matt Bahr's kickoff on the 22-yard line in the 21–17 loss to the Los Angeles Raiders on 10-09-94

2004 championship season

Tully Banta-Cain recovered the free ball on Adam Vinatieri's kickoff on the 32-yard line in the 23–7 win over the New York Jets on 12-26-04

Advancement of a lateral from a teammate who had recovered an opponents fumble

The only Patriots Defensive Back who has advanced a lateral from a teammate after his fumble recovery in a regular season game

Jim Bowman advanced a lateral from Ed Williams four yards in the 31–20 loss to the Denver Broncos at Mile High Stadium on 12-06-87

The only Patriots Linebacker who has advanced a lateral from a teammate after his fumble recovery in a regular season game

John Bramlett took a lateral from Jim Cheyunski 17 yards in the 27–23 loss to the Houston Oilers at the Astrodome on 12-14-69

The only Patriots Defensive Back who caught a lateral from a teammate and was tackled, thereby ending the interception return

Ricky Reynolds caught a lateral from Myron Guyton, ending his 26-yard interception return in the 41–17 rout of Buffalo on 12-18-94

Every Patriots Defensive Lineman who has recovered two fumbles and returned one of them for a TD in the same game

1975 regular season

Ray Hamilton recovered two fumbles and returned one 23 yards for a TD in the 24–17 loss to the St. Louis Cardinals on 11-02-75

1986 regular season

Brent Williams recovered two fumbles and returned one 21 yards for a TD in the 21–20 win over the New Orleans Saints on 11-30-86

Every regular season game that two fumbles were recovered by a Defensive Lineman and a Linebacker of the Patriots

1976 regular season

Richard Bishop and Steve Nelson each recovered two fumbles in the 30–27 victory over the Pittsburgh Steelers on 09-26-76

1986 regular season

Brent Williams and Don Blackmon each recovered two fumbles in the 21–20 victory over the New Orleans Saints on 11-30-86

The only regular season game that two fumbles were recovered by two Defensive Backs of the Patriots

Ronnie Lippett and Fred Marion each recovered two fumbles in the 17–10 loss to the Miami Dolphins on 10-18-90

The number of games that a Patriots Linebacker has recovered at least two fumbles in a regular season game

2 games that Ed Philpott recovered at least two fumbles; as he recovered two fumbles on 10-22-67 and two fumbles on 11-17-68

2 games that Steve Nelson recovered at least two fumbles; as recovered two fumbles on 09-26-76 and three fumbles on 10-08-78

Left to right: Miami's Mark Duper and Ronnie Lippett (42)

2 games that Andre Tippett recovered at least two fumbles; as he recovered two fumbles on 09-21-87 and two fumbles on 11-07-93

The only Patriots player who has recovered three defensive fumbles in a regular season game

Steve Nelson recovered three fumbles in the 24–14 win over the Philadelphia Eagles at Schaefer Stadium on 10-08-78 ("Nellie" recovered fumbles by Wilbert Montgomery, Ron Jaworski, and Keith Krepfle in this game)

Every Patriots player who has recovered two defensive fumbles and an offensive fumble in a regular season game

1983 regular season

Roland James recovered two defensive fumbles and one offensive fumble in the 21–7 win over the Los Angeles Rams on 12-11-83 (He recovered Mike Barber's fumble, recovered Eric Dickerson's fumble, and fell on Rick Sanford's fumbled punt return)

1994 regular season

Ricky Reynolds recovered two defensive fumbles and one offensive fumble in the 41–17 rout of the Buffalo Bills on 12-18-94 (He took Carwell Gardner's fumble 25 yards for a TD, he recovered Andre Reed's fumble, and fell on Larry Whigham's fumble)

The only Patriots player who has intercepted a pass and returned a fumble for a touchdown in the same game

Ed Philpott intercepted a Babe Parilli pass and took a Babe Parilli lateral 10 yards for a TD in the 47–31 loss to the Jets on 09-22-68

The most fumble recoveries

The Patriots defensive player who has recovered the most fumbles in a regular season

Bob Dee recovered five fumbles during the 1961 season

The Patriots Defensive Player who holds the AFL record of the most career fumble recoveries

Jim Lee Hunt recovered 15 fumbles during the 1960–70 seasons

The progression of the most career regular season fumble recoveries by a Patriots Defensive/Special Teams player

1 special teams fumble recovery by Charlie Leo in the 13–10 loss to the Denver Broncos on 09-09-60

Steve Nelson

10 career fumble recoveries by Jack Rudolph during the 1960–65 seasons

15 career fumble recoveries by Jim Lee Hunt during the 1960–70 seasons

16 career fumble recoveries by Steve Nelson during the 1974–87 seasons

18 career fumble recoveries by Andre Tippett during the 1982–93 seasons

Combinations of fumble recoveries and interceptions

The progression of the most takeaways by a Patriots player in a game (fumble recoveries and/or interceptions)

2 by Jack Rudolph; who recovered two fumbles in the 35–0 shutout of the Los Angeles Chargers on 10-08-60

3 by Gino Cappelletti; who intercepted three passes in the 27–14 loss to the Oakland Raiders on 10-16-60

3 by Ross O'Hanley; who intercepted three passes in the 21–17 loss to the Houston Oilers on 11-18-62

3 by Ross O'Hanley; who intercepted two passes and returned a fumble in the 20–14 win over the Oakland Raiders on 10-11-63

3 by Ron Hall; who intercepted three passes in the 33–28 win over the San Diego Chargers on 09-20-64

3 by Nick Buoniconti; who intercepted three passes in the 23–6 victory over the Buffalo Bills on 10-20-68

3 by Ed Philpott; who recovered two fumbles and intercepted a pass in the 31–17 loss to the Kansas City Chiefs on 11-17-68

3 by Mike Haynes; who intercepted three passes in the 38–24 victory over the New York Jets on 11-21-76

3 by Prentice McCray; who intercepted two passes and recovered a fumble in the 38–24 win over the New York Jets on 11-21-76

3 by Steve Nelson; who recovered three fumbles in the 24–14 victory over the Philadelphia Eagles on 10-08-78

3 by Roland James; who intercepted three passes in the 31–0 shutout of the Buffalo Bills on 10-23-83

3 by Jim Bowman; who intercepted two passes and returned a fumble in the 24–0 shutout of the Indianapolis Colts on 11-22-87

3 by Ronnie Lippett intercepted Dan Marino twice and recovered a fumble by Sammie Smith in the 27–24 loss to the Miami Dolphins on 09-09-90

3 by Fred Marion; who recovered two fumbles and intercepted a pass in the 17-10 loss to the Miami Dolphins on 10-18-90

3 by Asante Samuel; who intercepted three passes in the 17–13 victory over the Chicago Bears on 11-26-06

The only Patriots Linebacker who has intercepted a pass and recovered two fumbles in the same regular season game

Ed Philpott intercepted a Len Dawson pass and returned two fumbles for four yards in the 31–17 loss to the Kansas City Chiefs on 11-17-68

The only Patriots Defensive Back who has intercepted a pass and recovered two fumbles in the same regular season game

Fred Marion intercepted a Dan Marino pass and recovered two fumbles in the 17–10 loss to the Miami Dolphins on 10-18-90

The only Patriots Defensive Back who has returned two interceptions for a TD and recovered a fumble in the same regular season game

Prentice McCray returned two Joe Namath passes for a TD and recovered a fumble by Louie Giammona in the 38–24 win on 11-21-76

Every Patriots Defensive Back who has intercepted two passes and returned a fumble in the same regular season game

1963 regular season

Ross O'Hanley intercepted Tom Flores twice and returned a Bo Roberson fumble six yards in the 20–14 win over Oakland on 10-11-63

1987 regular season

Jim Bowman caught two Gary Hogenboom passes and returned an Eric Dickerson fumble two yards in the 24–0 win vs the Colts on 11-22-87

The progression of the most takeaways by a Patriots player in a regular season

1 takeaway by Charlie Leo; who recovered a fumble in the 13–10 loss to the Denver Broncos on 09-09-60

4 takeaways by Chuck Shonta; who had two interceptions and two fumble recoveries in 1960

4 takeaways by Gino Cappelletti; who had four interceptions in 1960

4 takeaways by Harry Jacobs; who had four interceptions in 1960

7 takeaways by Don Webb; who had five interceptions and two fumble recoveries in 1961

7 takeaways by Ross O'Hanley; who had five interceptions and two fumble recoveries in 1962

8 takeaways by Bob Suci; who had seven interceptions and recovered a blocked field goal in 1963

13 takeaways by Ron Hall; who had 11 interceptions and recovered two fumbles in 1964

The progression of the most career regular season takeaways by a Patriots player

21 total career takeaways by Chuck Shonta; who had 15 interceptions and six fumble recoveries during the 1960–67 seasons

32 total career takeaways by Ron Hall; who had 29 interceptions and recovered three fumbles during the 1961–67 seasons

32 total career takeaways by Don Webb; who had 21 interceptions, nine fumble recoveries, and recovered two blocked field goals

35 total career takeaways by Mike Haynes; who had 28 interceptions and recovered seven fumbles over the 1976–82 seasons

46 total career takeaways by Raymond Clayborn; who had 36 interceptions, eight fumble recoveries, and recovered two blocked field goals

The Playoffs

Offensive Fumble Recoveries

Every Patriots Offensive Lineman who has recovered a fumble by a Patriots Quarterback in a playoff game
1978 AFC Divisional playoff game
Leon Gray recovered a fumble by Tom Owen in the 17-point loss to the Houston Oilers on 12-31-78

1986 AFC Divisional playoff game
Peter Brock recovered a fumble by Tony Eason in the five point loss to the Denver Broncos on 01-04-87

2006 AFC Divisional playoff game
Matt Light advanced a fumble by Tom Brady four yards in the three-point win over the San Diego Chargers on 01-14-07

2006 AFC Championship Game
Logan Mankins recovered a fumble by Tom Brady in the end zone for a TD in the four-point loss to the Indianapolis Colts on 01-21-07

The only Patriots Tight End who has recovered a fumble by a Patriots Quarterback in a playoff game
1963 AFL Championship Game
Tony Romeo recovered a fumble by Babe Parilli in the 41-point loss to the San Diego Chargers on 01-05-64

The only Patriots Running Back who has recovered a fumble by a Patriots Quarterback in a playoff game
1996 AFC Championship Game
Dave Meggett recovered a fumble by Drew Bledsoe in the 14-point win over the Jacksonville Jaguars on 01-12-97

The only Patriots Running Back who has recovered a fumble by another Patriots Running Back in a playoff game
1997 AFC Wild Card playoff game
Keith Byars recovered a fumble by Derrick Cullors in the 14-point win over the Miami Dolphins on 12-28-97

The only Patriots Receiver who has recovered a fumble by another Patriots Receiver in a playoff game
1985 AFC Divisional playoff game
Irving Fryar recovered a fumble by Stanley Morgan in the seven-point win over the Los Angeles Raiders on 01-05-86

The only Patriots Receiver who has recovered a fumble by a Patriots Tight End in a playoff game
2005 AFC Wild Card playoff game
Andre' Davis recovered a fumble by Benjamin Watson in the 25-point win over the Jacksonville Jaguars on 01-07-06

The only Patriots Linebacker who has recovered a teammate's fumble after his interception return in a playoff game
1985 AFC Wild Card playoff game
Steve Nelson recovered a fumble by Garin Veris at the end of Garin's 18-yard interception return in the 12-point win on 12-28-85

The only Patriots Defensive Back who has recovered an offensive fumble by another Patriots Defensive Back in a playoff game
2007 AFC Championship Game
James Sanders recovered a fumble by Ellis Hobbs at the end of his interception return in the nine-point win over the San Diego Chargers on 01-20-08

Special Teams Fumble Recoveries

The only Patriots player who has recovered a fumble on the opening kickoff of a playoff game
1963 AFL Eastern Divisional playoff game
Billy Lott recovered a fumble by Elbert Dubenion on the opening kickoff in the 26–8 win over the Buffalo Bills on 12-28-63

Every Patriots Special Teams player who has recovered a fumbled kickoff return in a playoff game

1963 AFL Eastern Divisional playoff game
Billy Lott recovered a fumble by Elbert Dubenion on the opening kickoff in the 18-point win over the Buffalo Bills on 12-28-63

1985 AFC Wild Card playoff game
Johnny Rembert took Johnny Hector's fumbled kickoff return 15 yards for aTD in the 12-point win over the New York Jets on 12-28-85

1985 AFC Divisional playoff game
Jim Bowman fell on Sam Seale's fumbled kickoff return in the end zone for the final points scored in the seven-point win on 01-05-86

1985 AFC Championship Game
Greg Hawthorne recovered a fumbled kickoff return by Lorenzo Hampton in the 17-point win over the Miami Dolphins on 01-12-86

Every Patriots Special Teams player who has recovered a fumbled punt return in a playoff game

1985 AFC Divisional playoff game
Jim Bowman recovered a fumbled punt return by Fulton Walker in the seven-point win over the Los Angeles Raiders on 01-05-86

1996 AFC Championship Game
Mike Bartrum recovered a fumbled punt return by Chris Hudson in the 14-point win over the Jacksonville Jaguars on 01-12-97

2006 AFC Divisional playoff game
Dave Thomas recovered a fumbled punt return by Eric Parker in the three-point victory over the San Diego Chargers on 01-14-07

The only Patriots Special Teams player who has recovered a blocked field goal in a playoff game

2001 AFC Championship Game
Troy Brown returned a blocked field goal 11 yards before lateraling it to Antwan Harris, who took it for a TD on 01-27-02

Larry Izzo

Every Patriots Special Teams player who has recovered a fumble by his teammate in a playoff game

1978 AFC Divisional playoff game
Don Westbrook recovered a fumbled punt return by Mike Haynes in the 17-point loss to the Houston Oilers on 12-31-78

2001 AFC Divisional playoff game
Larry Izzo recovered a fumbled punt return by Troy Brown in the three-point overtime win vs the Oakland Raiders on 01-19-02

Larry Izzo recovered another fumbled punt return by Troy Brown in the three-point overtime win vs the Oakland Raiders on 01-19-02

Defensive Fumble Recoveries

The only Patriots player who has recovered a fumble on the opponent's first offensive play in a playoff game

1985 AFC Championship Game

Garin Veris recovered a Tony Nathan fumble that was forced by Steve Nelson on Miami's first play in the 31–14 win on 01-12-86

Every Patriots Linebacker who has recovered a fumble by a Quarterback in a playoff game

1963 AFL Eastern Divisional playoff game

Tom Addison recovered a fumble by Jack Kemp on fourth-and-goal in the fourth quarter of the 26–8 win over the Buffalo Bills on 12-28-63

1997 AFC Wild Card playoff game

Chris Slade recovered Chris Canty's strip-sack of Dan Marino in the 14-point win over the Miami Dolphins on 12-28-97

2001 AFC Championship Game

Tedy Bruschi returned a Kordell Stewart fumble one yard in the seven-point win over the Pittsburgh Steelers on 01-27-02

2006 AFC Divisional playoff game

Tully Banta-Cain recovered Mike Vrabel's strip-sack of Philip Rivers in the three-point win over San Diego on 01-14-07

2007 AFC Divisional playoff game

Mike Vrabel recovered Ty Warren's strip-sack of David Garrard in the 11-point win over the Jaguars on 01-12-08

Every Patriots Defensive Lineman who has recovered a fumble by a Quarterback in a playoff game

1985 AFC Championship Playoff Game

Lester Williams recovered a fumble by Dan Marino in the 17-point victory over the Miami Dolphins on 01-12-86

Super Bowl XXXVIII

Richard Seymour recovered Mike Vrabel's strip-sack of Jake Delhomme in the three-point win over the Carolina Panthers on 02-01-04

2006 AFC Wild Card playoff game

Vince Wilfork returned a backward lateral by Chad Pennington 31 yards in the 21-point win over the New York Jets on 01-07-07

Every Patriots Linebacker who has recovered a fumble by a Running Back in a playoff game

Super Bowl XX

Larry McGrew recovered Walter Payton's fumble on the second play of the game in the 46-point loss to the Chicago Bears on 01-26-86

2004 AFC Divisional playoff game

Tedy Bruschi ripped the ball out of Dominic Rhodes hands in the 17-point win over the Indianapolis Colts on 01-16-05

2004 AFC Championship Game

Mike Vrabel returned a fumble by Jerome Bettis one yard in the 14-point win over the Pittsburgh Steelers on 01-23-05

Every Patriots Defensive Lineman who has recovered a fumble by a Running Back in a playoff game

1963 AFL Championship Game

Larry Eisenhauer recovered a fumble by Paul Lowe in the 41-point loss to the San Diego Chargers on 01-05-64

1976 AFC Divisional playoff game

Mel Lunsford recovered a fumble by Clarence Davis in the three-point loss to the Oakland Raiders on 12-18-76

1985 AFC Championship Game

Garin Veris recovered a fumble by Tony Nathan on the first play of the game in the 17-point win over the Miami Dolphins on 01-12-86

Julius Adams recovered a fumble by Joe Carter in the 17-point victory over the Miami Dolphins on 01-12-86

1994 AFC Wild Card playoff game

Mike Pitts recovered a fumble by Eric Metcalf in the seven-point loss to the Cleveland Browns on 01-01-95

Every Patriots Defensive Back who has recovered a fumble by a Running Back in a playoff game

1982 AFC first Round playoff game

Keith Lee recovered a fumble by Andra Franklin in the 15-point loss to the Miami Dolphins on 01-08-83

Rick Sanford recovered a fumble by Andra Franklin in the 15-point loss to the Miami Dolphins on 01-08-83

Rick Sanford recovered another fumble by Andra Franklin in the 15-point loss to the Miami Dolphins on 01-08-83

1985 Wild Card playoff game

Roland James recovered a fumble by Freeman McNeil in the 12-point win over the New York Jets on 12-28-85

1985 AFC Divisional playoff game

Fred Marion recovered a fumble by Marcus Allen in the seven-point win over the Los Angeles Raiders on 01-05-86

Super Bowl XX

Raymond Clayborn recovered a fumble by Matt Suhey in the 46-point loss to the Chicago Bears on 01-26-86

1996 AFC Championship Game

Otis Smith returned a fumble by James Stewart 47 yards for a TD in the 14-point win over the Jaguars on 01-12-97

The only Patriots Linebacker who has recovered a fumble by a Wide Receiver in a playoff game

2004 AFC Divisional playoff game

Tedy Bruschi recovered a fumble by Reggie Wayne in the 17-point victory over the Indianapolis Colts on 01-16-05

Every Patriots Defensive Back who has recovered a fumble by a Wide Receiver in a playoff game

Super Bowl XXXVI

Terrell Buckley returned a fumble by Ricky Proehl in the three-point win over the St. Louis Rams on 02-03-02

2003 AFC Championship Game

Tyrone Poole recovered a fumble by Marvin Harrison in the 10-point win over the Indianapolis Colts on 01-18-04

The only Patriots Defensive Back who has recovered a fumble by a Tight End in a playoff game

Super Bowl XXXIX

Eugene Wilson recovered a fumble by L.J. Smith in the three-point win over the Philadelphia Eagles on 02-06-05

The only Patriots Receiver who has recovered a fumble by a Defensive Back on his interception return in a playoff game

2006 AFC Divisional playoff game

Reche Caldwell recovered a fumble by Marlon McCree that was forced by Troy Brown in the three-point win over the San Diego Chargers on 01-14-07

The longest

The progression of the longest fumble return by a Patriots Player in a playoff game

21-yard fumble return by Rick Sanford in the 28–13 loss to the Miami Dolphins at the Orange Bowl on 01-08-83

47-yard fumble return for a TD by Otis Smith in the 20–6 victory over the Jacksonville Jaguars at Foxboro on 01-12-97

The longest fumble return by two Patriots players in a playoff game

60-yard return for a TD by Troy Brown and Antwan Harris in the 24–17 win over the Pittsburgh Steelers at Heinz Field on 01-27-02 (Brandon Mitchell blocked a FGA that Troy Brown returned 11 yards before lateraling it to Antwan Harris)

Every Patriots Defensive Back who has returned a fumble in a playoff game

1982 AFC first round playoff game

Rick Sanford returned a fumble by Andra Franklin 21 yards in the 28–13 loss to the Miami Dolphins at Miami on 01-08-83

1996 AFC Championship Game

Otis Smith returned a James Stewart fumble 47 yards for a TD in the 20–6 win over the Jacksonville Jaguars on 01-12-97

Super Bowl XXXVI

Terrell Buckley returned a Ricky Proehl fumble 15 yards in the 20–17 win over the St. Louis Rams on 2-03-02

Every Patriots Linebacker who has returned a fumble in a playoff game

2001 AFC Championship Game

Tedy Bruschi returned a fumble by Kordell Stewart one yard in the 24-17 win over the Pittsburgh Steelers on 01-27-02

2004 AFC Championship Game

Mike Vrabel returned a fumble by Jerome Bettis one yard in the 41–27 win over the Pittsburgh Steelers on 01-23-05

Two fumble recoveries in a game

The only Patriots Linebacker who has recovered two fumbles in a playoff game

2004 AFC Divisional playoff game

Tedy Bruschi stole the ball from Dominic Rhodes and fell on Reggie Wayne's fumble in the 20–3 rout of the Indianapolis Colts at Gillette Stadium on 01-16-05

The only Patriots Defensive Back who has recovered two fumbles in a playoff game

1982 AFC first round playoff game

Rick Sanford recovered two fumbles by Andra Franklin in the 28–13 loss to the Miami Dolphins at the Orange Bowl on 01-08-83

The only Patriots Running Back who has recovered two of his own fumbles in a playoff game

1998 AFC Wild Card playoff game

Derrick Cullors recovered two of his own fumbles in the 25–10 loss to the Jacksonville Jaguars at Alltel Stadium on 01-03-99

The only Patriots Special Teams player who has recovered two fumbles by a Patriots Punt Returner in a playoff game

2001 AFC Divisional playoff game

Larry Izzo recovered two fumbles by Troy Brown in the 16–13 overtime win vs the Oakland Raiders at Foxboro Stadium on 01-19-02

Fumble recoveries for a touchdown

The only Patriots player who recovered a fumble in the end zone for the game-winning points in a playoff game

1985 AFC Divisional playoff game

Jim Bowman fell on a Sam Seale fumble for the last points scored in the 27–20 win over the Los Angeles Raiders on 01-05-86

The only Patriots Special Teams player who has recovered a fumbled kickoff return in the end zone for a TD

1985 AFC Divisional playoff game

Jim Bowman fell on a Sam Seale fumble for a TD in the 27–20 win over the Los Angeles Raiders at the L.A. Coliseum on 01-05-86

The only Patriots Special Teams player who has returned a fumbled kickoff return for a TD in a playoff game

1985 AFC Wild Card playoff game

Johnny Rembert returned a Johnny Hector fumble 15 yards for a TD in the 26–14 win over the New York Jets on 12-28-85

The only Patriots Offensive Lineman who has recovered a fumble in the end zone for a TD in a playoff game

2006 AFC Championship Game

Logan Mankins fell on a Tom Brady fumble in the end zone for a TD in the 38–34 loss to the Colts at the RCA Dome on 01-21-07

Every combination of a Patriots Players who have returned a blocked field goal for a touchdown in a playoff game

2001 AFC Championship Game

Troy Brown and Antwan Harris returned a blocked FG 60 yards for a TD in the 24–17 win over the Pittsburgh Steelers on 01-27-02

The only Patriots Defensive Back who has returned a fumble by a Running Back for a TD in a playoff game

1996 AFC Championship Game

Otis Smith returned a fumble by James Stewart 47 yards for a TD in the 20–6 win over Jacksonville on 01-12-97 (Chris Slade was credited with forcing the fumble by James Stewart)

The progression of the most takeaways by a Patriots player in a playoff game

1 fumble recovery by Billy Lott in the 26–8 victory over the Buffalo Bills on 12-28-63

2 interceptions by Bob Dee in the 26–8 victory over the Buffalo Bills on 12-28-63

2 interceptions by Ross O'Hanley in the 26–8 victory over the Buffalo Bills on 12-28-63

2 fumble recoveries by Rick Sanford in the 28–13 loss to the Miami Dolphins on 01-08-83

2 interceptions by Ronnie Lippett in the 27–20 victory over the Los Angeles Raiders on 01-05-86

2 fumble recoveries by Jim Bowman in the 27–20 victory over the Los Angeles Raiders on 01-05-86

3 interceptions by Ty Law in the 24–14 victory over the Indianapolis Colts on 01-18-04

The progression of the most career takeaways by a Patriots player in the playoffs

1 career takeaway by Billy Lott in two playoff games for the Boston Patriots

2 career takeaways by Bob Dee in two playoff games

2 career takeaways by Ross O'Hanley in two playoff games

2 career takeaways by Rick Sanford; who recovered two fumbled kickoff returns on 01-08-83

2 career takeaways by Garin Veris; who had one interception and fumble recovery in five playoff games

3 career takeaways by Fred Marion; who intercepted three passes in six playoff games

5 career takeaways by Tedy Bruschi; who has intercepted two passes and recovered three fumbles in 22 playoff games

7 career takeaways by Rodney Harrison; who has intercepted seven passes in nine playoff games for the Patriots

Tedy Bruschi

Sacks

Although sacking a quarterback was not an official statistic in the NFL until 1982, we were able to go back to record every sack by every Patriots player. Over the course of the 1960–2008 regular seasons, 87 defensive lineman, 59 linebackers, and 39 defensive backs have shared in a sack or have sacked the opposing team's passer in a regular season game. Julius Adams is the only Patriots player who has sacked a wide receiver who was attempting to pass the ball downfield. Adams tackled wide receiver Mark Clayton for a seven-yard loss in the 17–13 win over the Miami Dolphins at Sullivan Stadium on 11-03-85.

Eighteen defensive linemen, 13 linebackers, and six defensive backs have shared in a sack or have sacked the opposing team's passer in a playoff game. Dennis Owens sacked William "The Refrigerator" Perry for a one-yard loss in the 36-point loss to the Chicago Bears in Super Bowl XX.

Linebacker Jack Rudolph led the Boston Patriots with four quarterback sacks in the inaugural 1960 season. Rommie Loudd, who had seven sacks in 1961, held the Patriots record for the most sacks by a linebacker in a regular season until 1983.

Defensive end Larry "Wildman" Eisenhauer led the team with the most sacks during the 1962, 1963, 1964, and 1965 regular seasons. Defenisve tackles Jim Lee Hunt, who had the most sacks in 1966, and Houston Antwine then led the team in sacks during the 1967–68 and 1969 regular seasons. Defensive end Ron "the Whopper" Berger led the Boston Patriots with nine sacks during the 1970 regular season.

Linebacker Steve Kiner was the third linebacker of the Patriots to lead the team in sacks when he had 6.5 during the 1971 regular season. Over the next ten seasons either Julius "the Jewel" Adams or Tony "Mac the Sack" McGee led the team in sacks each year. Adams led the team during the 1972–74 and 1980 regular seasons, and McGee had the most sacks for the team during the 1975–79 and 1981 regular seasons. Tony McGee was the first Patriots player to have three consecutive seasons with 10 or more sacks as he had 12, 12, and 10 sacks in the 1977–79 regular seasons. McGee is the only Patriots player to lead the team in sacks for five consecutive seasons.

Linebacker Don Blackmon led the team with 4.5 sacks during the strike-shortened 1982 regular season. Pro Football Hall of Fame linebacker Andre Tippett, who finished his career with a team record 100 sacks, led the team during the 1983–85, 1987–88, and 1991–92 regular seasons. Tippett was the first Patriots player to have 15 or mores sacks in consecutive seasons as he had 18.5 sacks in 1984 and 16.5 sacks in 1985. No other linebacker in the history of the NFL had more sacks in consecutive regular seasons than Andre Tippett. He is the only Patriots player to lead the team with the most sacks in consecutive seasons four different times.

Defensive End Garin Veris led the team with 11 sacks during the 1986 regular season. Defensive End Brent Williams led the Patriots in sacks during the 1989 and 1990 regular seasons. Chris Slade and Willie McGinest each had consecutive seasons leading the team in sacks during the 1993–96 regular seasons. Chris Slade and Henry Thomas had the most sacks for the Patriots in the 1997 and 1998 regular seasons, respectively. Defensive ends Willie McGinest and Greg Spires tied for the team lead with six sacks each during the 2000 regular season.

Defensive end Bobby Hamilton was the team leader with seven sacks during the Patriots first championship season in 2001. Willie McGinest and Richard Seymour shared the honors for the most sacks with 5.5 each during the 2002 regular season. Mike Vrabel, who has caught a TD pass and recorded a sack in a Super Bowl game, led the Patriots with 9.5 sacks during their second championship season in 2003. Willie "Big Mac" McGinest, who has been named to the AFC Pro Bowl as a defensive end and a linebacker, led the Patriots with 9.5 sacks during their third championship season in 2004. Rosevelt Colvin led the 2005 team with seven sacks and the 2006 team with 8.5 sacks. AFC All Pro linebacker Mike Vrabel led the Patriots with 12.5 sacks during their 2007 undefeated regular season. Richard Seymour led the Patriots with eight sacks during the 2008 regular season.

The progression of the most consecutive regular season games that a Patriots player had at least one sack

2 consecutive games that Bob Dee recorded at least one sack (from 09-09-60 to 09-17-60)

2 consecutive games that Harry Jacobs recorded at least one sack (from 10-08-60 to 10-23-60)

2 consecutive games that Bob Dee recorded at least one sack (from 11-18-60 to 11-25-60)

2 consecutive games that Rommie Loudd recorded at least one sack (from 10-22-61 to 10-29-61)

3 consecutive games that Bob Dee sacked the quarterback (from 10-29-61 to 11-12-61)

Andre Tippett sacks Ken O'Brien

7 consecutive games that Tom Addison sacked the quarterback (from 11-17-61 to 09-21-62)

8 consecutive games that Andre Tippett recorded at least one sack (from 11-04-84 to 09-08-85)

The progression of the most sacks by a Defensive End of the Patriots in a regular season game

1 sack by Bob Dee in the 13–10 loss to the Denver Broncos at BU Field on 09-09-60

1 sack by Bob Dee in the 28–24 victory over the New York Titans at the Polo Grounds on 09-17-60

2.5 sacks by Larry Eisenhauer in the 42–14 rout of the Houston Oilers at Fenway Park on 12-18-65

2.5 sacks by Larry Eisenhauer in the 27–21 victory over the Houston Oilers at Fenway Park on 11-13-66

3 sacks by Donnell Smith in the 42–3 rout of the Baltimore Colts at Schaefer Stadium on 10-06-74

3 sacks by Tony McGee in the 38–14 victory over the Denver Broncos at Schaefer Stadium on 11-28-76

4 sacks by Julius Adams in the 16–10 victory over the Atlanta Falcons at Fulton County Stadium on 12-04-77

4 sacks by Tony McGee in the 35–14 victory over the Baltimore Colts at Memorial Stadium on 11-26-78

Jim Lee Hunt (79) sacks Earl Morrall

The progression of the most sacks by a Defensive Tackle of the Patriots in a regular season game

1/2 of a sack by Art Hauser in the 42–14 rout of the Dallas Texans at BU Field on 11-18-60

1 sack by Jim Lee Hunt in the 21–20 loss to the New York Titans at BU Field on 09-16-61

1 sack by Dick Klein in the 28–21 victory over the Dallas Texans at BU Field on 11-03-61

1 sack by Jim Lee Hunt in the 28–24 victory over the Denver Broncos at Bears Stadium on 12-03-61

1 sack by Jim Lee Hunt in the 35–21 victory over the Oakland Raiders at Candlestick Park on 12-09-61

2 sacks by Jim Lee Hunt in the 31–24 victory over the Kansas City Chiefs at Municipal Stadium on 12-06-64

2.5 sacks by Jim Lee Hunt in the 24–10 victory over the Denver Broncos at Bears Stadium on 09-18-66

4 sacks by Jim Lee Hunt in the 14–3 victory over the Buffalo Bills in "The Game" at Fenway Park on 12-04-66

The progression of the most sacks by a Nose Tackle of the Patriots in a regular season game

2 sacks by Ray Hamilton in the 34–24 victory over the Miami Dolphins at Schaefer Stadium on 09-15-74

2 sacks by Ray Hamilton in the 21–10 victory over the Baltimore Colts at Schaefer Stadium on 10-19-75

2 sacks by Ray Hamilton in the 34–31 loss to the Dallas Cowboys at Schaefer Stadium on 11-16-75

3 sacks by Ray Hamilton in the 38–14 victory over the Denver Broncos at Schaefer Stadium on 11-28-76

3 sacks by Ray Hamilton in the 34–0 shutout of the Miami Dolphins at Schaefer Stadium on 10-12-80

3 sacks by Richard Bishop in the 34–21 victory over the New York Jets at Schaefer Stadium on 11-02-82

The progression of the most sacks by a Patriots Linebacker in a regular season game

3 sacks by Jack Rudolph in the 28–24 victory over the New York Titans at the Polo Grounds on 09-17-60

3 sacks by Harry Jacobs in the 31–24 loss to the Denver Broncos at Bears Stadium on 10-23-60

3 sacks by Ed Philpott in the 20–17 victory over the Denver Broncos at Bears Stadium on 09-29-68

3 sacks by Pete Barnes in the 21–14 victory over the Baltimore Colts at Memorial Stadium on 11-14-76

4 sacks by Mike Hawkins in the 56–3 rout of the New York Jets at Schaefer Stadium on 09-09-79

The progression of the most sacks by a Patriots Defensive Back in a regular season game

1 sack by Fred Bruney in the 41–16 victory over the Denver Broncos at BU Field on 09-21-62

2 sacks by Ron Hall in the 20–14 victory over the Oakland Raiders at Frank Youell Field on 09-22-63

2 sacks by Tim Fox in the 21–17 victory over the Kansas City Chiefs at Schaefer Stadium on 09-18-77

2 sacks by Larry Whigham in the 31–3 rout of the Chicago Bears at Foxboro Stadium on 09-21-97

2 sacks by Rodney Harrison in the 23–12 victory over the Arizona Cardinals at Sun Devil Stadium on 09-19-04

The only regular season game that the Patriots defensive team recorded 10 sacks

The Boston Patriots defeated the Oakland Raiders 20–14 at Frank Youell Field on 09-22-63

Defensive back Ron Hall sacked Tom Flores twice

Linebackers Nick Buoniconti and Jack Rudolph each sacked Tom Flores

Defensive linemen Larry Eisenhauer, Jim Lee Hunt, and Jesse Richardson each sacked Tom Flores

Defensive tackle Houston Antwine sacked Cotton Davidson once

Defensive end Bob Dee sacked Cotton Davidson twice

The only Patriots defensive lineman with a Quarterback sack and an interception return for a TD in a regular season game

Willie McGinest sacked Jim Kelly and returned a Jim Kelly pass 46 yards for a TD in the 28–25 win over the Buffalo Bills on 10-27-96

The only Patriots Linebacker with a Quarterback sack and an interception return for a TD in a regular season game

Tedy Bruschi sacked Donovan McNabb and returned one of his passes 18 yards for a TD in the 31–10 rout of the Philadelphia Eagles on 09-14-03

The only Patriots Linebacker to sack one Quarterback and return the pass of another Quarterback for a TD in the same game

Rod Shoate sacked Greg Landry and returned a Bert Jones pass 42 yards for a TD in the 47–21 rout of the Indianapolis Colts on 11-23-80

The only Patriots Linebacker to share a sack of a Quarterback, intercept a pass, and lateral the ball to a teammate in a game

Rod Shoate shared in a sack of Joe Ferguson, intercepted Joe Ferguson, and then lateraled it to Rick Sanford on 11-04-79

The only Patriots Linebacker with 1.5 sacks and an interception return in a regular season game

Tully Banta-Cain sacked Drew Bledsoe 1.5 times and returned a J.P. Losman pass four yards in the 29–6 win vs the Buffalo Bills on 11-14-04

Every Patriots Linebacker who recorded a Quarterback sack and had two interceptions in the same regular season game

1962 regular season
Tom Addison sacked John Hadl and intercepted two Dick Wood passes in the 24-20 win over the San Diego Chargers on 10-19-62

1963 regular season
Nick Buoniconti sacked Tom Flores and intercepted Cotton Davidson and T. Flores in the 20–14 win over the Oakland Raiders on 09-22-63

The only Patriots Linebacker with two sacks and an interception return for a touchdown in a regular season game

Andy Katzenmoyer sacked Damon Huard twice and took a Dan Marino pass 57 yards for a TD in the 31–30 loss on 10-17-99

Every Patriots Linebacker with two Quarterback sacks and an interception in the same regular season game

1961 regular season
Rommie Loudd sacked Tom Flores twice and intercepted Tom Flores in the 35–21 win over the Oakland Raiders on 10-09-61

1964 regular season
Nick Buoniconti sacked George Blanda and Don Trull and intercepted Don Trull in the 34–17 win vs the Houston Oilers on 11-29-64

1971 regular season
Steve Kiner sacked John Brodie twice and intercepted a John Brodie pass in the 27–10 loss to the San Francisco 49ers on 10-31-71

1980 regular season
Rod Shoate sacked Richard Todd twice and intercepted him once in the 21–11 win over the New York Jets on 10-05-80

Rod Shoate

1999 regular season

Andy Katzenmoyer sacked Damon Huard twice and intercepted Dan Marino in the 31–30 loss to the Miami Dolphins on 10-17-99

2007 undefeated regular season

Rosevelt Colvin sacked Philip Rivers twice and intercepted him once in the 38–14 win over the San Diego Chargers on 09-16-07

The only Patriots Linebacker with three sacks and an interception in a regular season game

Ed Philpott sacked Jim LeClair three times and intercepted a Jim LeClair pass in the 20–17 win over the Denver Broncos on 09-29-68

Every Patriots Linebacker with a Quarterback sack, an interception, and a fumble recovery in a regular season game

1980 regular season

Rod Shoate sacked Dan Manucci, intercepted a David Humm pass, and recovered a fumble in the 24–3 win on 12-14-80

1982 regular season

Don Blackmon shared in a sack of David Humm, intercepted Art Schlitcher, and fell on a fumble in the 24–13 win on 09-12-82

The only Patriots Defensive Back to sack a Quarterback, force him to fumble, recover, and return the fumble for a TD

Tebucky Jones sacked Vinny Testaverde and returned the fumble 24 yards for a TD in the 44–7 win over the Jets on 09-15-02

The only Patriots player with a Quarterback sack and a return for a TD of a fumbled kickoff in a regular season game

Rick Sanford sacked Bert Jones and took a fumbled kickoff return 22 yards for a TD in the 47–21 rout of the Colts on 11-23-80

The only Patriots Lineman with a Quarterback sack and a return of a RB's fumble for a TD in a regular season game

Jim Lee Hunt sacked Max Chobian and took a Darrell Lester fumble five yards for a TD in the 17–10 loss to the Denver Broncos on 11-06-66

The only Patriots Player with two Quarterback sacks and a return of a blocked punt for a TD in a regular season game

Tedy Bruschi sacked Vinny Testaverde twice and returned a blocked punt four yards for a TD in the 46–38 win on 10-06-96

The only Patriots Player with two Quarterback sacks and a fumble return for a TD in a regular season game

Nick Buoniconti had two quarterback sacks and he returned a Bill Tobin fumble seven yards for a TD in the 46–28 win on 12-08-63

The only Patriots player with a quarterback sack and a fumble recovery in the end zone for a TD in a regular season game

1996 regular season

Willie McGinest shared in a sack of Sean Salisbury and recovered an end zone fumble for a TD in the 45–7 rout on 12-01-96

1999 regular season

Willie McGinest sacked Vinny Testaverde and Tom Tupa and recovered a fumble for a TD in the 30–28 win on 09-12-99

Every Patriots Linebacker with three sacks and a fumble recovery in a regular season game

1960 regular season

Jack Rudolph sacked Dick Jamieson twice, Al Dorow once, and recovered a fumble in the 28–24 win over New York on 09-17-60

1993 regular season

Chris Slade sacked Rodney Peete three times and recovered a fumble in the 19–16 overtime loss to the Detroit Lions on 09-13-93

The only Patriots Defensive Lineman with four sacks and a fumble recovery in a regular season game

Jim Hunt sacked Jack Kemp twice, Daryle Lamonica twice, and recovered a fumble in the 14–3 win over the Buffalo Bills on 12-04-66

Every Patriots Defensive Lineman with a sack and a fumble return for a TD in a regular season game

1966 regular season

Jim Hunt sacked Max Chobian and returned a Darrell Lester fumble five yards for a TD in the 17–10 loss to the Denver Broncos on 11-06-66

2004 championship season

Richard Seymour sacked Drew Bledsoe and returned a fumble by Bledsoe 68 yards for a TD in the 31–17 win on 10-03-04

Every Patriots Defensive Lineman with a sack and a blocked extra point in a regular season game

1991 regular season

Garin Veris sacked Jim Kelly and blocked a Scott Norwood PAT in the 22–17 loss to the Buffalo Bills on 11-03-91

1995 regular season

Troy Barnett sacked Jim Kelly and blocked a Doug Christie PAT in the 35–25 win over the Buffalo Bills on 11-26-95

The only Patriots Linebacker with a Quarterback sack and a blocked extra point in a regular season game

Don Blackmon sacked Lynn Dickey three times and blocked an Al DelGreco PAT in the 26–20 win vs the Green Bay Packers on 09-08-85

The only Patriots player with a Quarterback sack for a safety and a blocked extra point in a regular season game

Don Blackmon sacked Lynn Dickey for a safety and blocked a PAT in the 26–20 win over the Packers on 09-08-85

The only Patriots player with two sacks and two blocked field goals in a regular season game

Chad Eaton sacked Doug Flutie twice and blocked two FGAs by Steve Christie in the 13–10 overtime win vs the Buffalo Bills on 12-17-00

The only Patriots player with a sack, fumble recovery, and a blocked field goal in a regular season game

Chad Eaton sacked Doug Flutie twice, recovered a fumble, and blocked two FGs in the 13–10 overtime win vs the Buffalo Bills on 12-17-00

The only Patriots player with three sacks and a blocked FGA in a regular season game

Andre Tippett sacked Brent Pease three times and blocked a Tony Zendejas 48-yard FGA in the 21–7 win on 10-18-87

The only Patriots player with a sack and a blocked FGA that was returned for a TD in a regular season game

Andre Tippett sacked Brent Pease and blocked a FG that was returned 71 yards for a TD by Ray Clayborn on 10-18-87

Safeties

Every Patriots Linebacker who has tackled the Quarterback in the end zone for a safety

1963 regular season

Jack Rudolph sacked Jacky Lee for a safety in the 46–28 win over the Houston Oilers at Jeppesen Stadium on 12-08-63

1964 regular season

Jack Rudolph sacked Jacky Lee for a safety in the 12–7 win over the Denver Broncos at Fenway Park on 11-20-64

1973 regular season

Steve Kiner sacked Dan Pastorini for a safety in the 32–0 shutout of the Houston Oilers at the Astrodome on 11-25-73

1985 regular season

Don Blackmon sacked Lynn Dickey for a safety in the 26–20 win over the Green Bay Packers at Sullivan Stadium on 09-08-85

Don Blackmon sacked Steve DeBerg for a safety in the 32–14 win over the Tampa Bay Buccaneers at Tampa Stadium on 10-27-85

The only Patriots Nose Tackle who has tackled the Quarterback in the end zone for a safety

Richard Bishop tackled Bob Griese for a safety in the 33–24 victory over the Miami Dolphins at Schaefer Stadium on 10-22-78

Every Patriots Defensive End who has tackled the Quarterback in the end zone for a safety

1967 regular season

Jim Lee Hunt tackled Jack Kemp for a safety in the 44–16 loss to the Buffalo Bills at Fenway Park on 12-09-67

1982 regular season

George Crump tackled Archie Manning for a safety in the 29–21 win over the Houston Oilers at Schaefer Stadium on 11-28-82

2006 regular season

Ty Warren sacked JP Losman for the game-winning two-point safety in the 19–17 win over the Buffalo Bills at Gillette Stadium on 09-10-06

The only time that two defensive players of the Patriots were credited with a sack in a regular season game

2003 championship season

Jarvis Green and Mike Vrabel sacked Jay Fiedler for a safety in the 12–0 shutout of the Miami Dolphins at Gillette Stadium on 12-07-03 (Tom Brady's pooched punt to the Dolphins 1-yard line help set up this two point safety for the Patriots)

Every game that a safety was recorded by the Patriots because of an intentional grounding penalty on the Quarterback

1996 regular season

Mike Jones forced Jim Kelly to ground the ball in the 28–25 win over the Buffalo Bills at Foxboro Stadium on 10-27-96

1997 regular season

Henry Thomas forced Neil O'Donnell to ground the ball in the 24–19 loss to the New York Jets at the Meadowlands on 10-19-97

Every Patriots Defensive Back who has tackled a Running Back in the end zone for a safety

1965 regular season

Jay Cunningham tackled Les "Speedy" Duncan for a safety in the 22–6 win over the San Diego Chargers at Balboa Stadium on 10-31-65

1969 regular season

Daryl Johnson tackled Jess Phillips for a safety in the 25–14 win over the Cincinnati Bengals at Nippert Stadium on 11-16-69 (Tom Janik's 49-yard punt, which was downed on Cincinnati's 1-yard line, helped set up this safety)

1984 regular season

Roland James tackled Frank Middleton for a safety in the 50–17 rout of the Indianapolis Colts at the Hoosier Dome on 11-18-84

Every Patriots Linebacker who has tackled a Running Back in the end zone for a safety

1967 regular season

Nick Buoniconti tackled Roy Hopkins for a safety in the 18–7 win over the Houston Oilers at Fenway Park on 11-05-67

1968 regular season

Doug Satcher tackled Paul Robinson for a safety in the 33–14 win over the Cincinnati Bengals at Fenway Park on 12-01-68

The only Patriots Special Teams player who has tackled a Punt Returner in the end zone for a safety

Ezell Jones tackled punt returner Mercury Morris for a safety in the 38–23 win over the Miami Dolphins at Tampa Stadium on 11-30-69

The only safety that was recorded by a Patriots player even though the Quarterback was tackled on the 2-yard line

George Crump tackled Archie Manning on his 2-yard line for a safety in the 29–21 win vs Houston at Schaefer on 11-28-82

Every Patriots Defensive Back who has forced the Punter to run out of the end zone for a safety

1977 regular season

Ray Clayborn forced Mike Michel out of the end zone on the last play in the 17–5 loss to the Miami Dolphins at Miami on 11-13-77

1978 regular season

Tim Fox forced Rusty Jackson out of the end zone in the 26–24 win over the Buffalo Bills at Schaefer Stadium on 12-10-78

The only game that the Patriots defensive team forced a fumble went out of the end zone for a safety

Larry McGrew sacked Jim Kelly and forced the fumble on the second play in the 22–19 win over the Buffalo Bills at Sullivan Stadium on 11-23-86 (Don Blackmon attempted to recover the fumble but was unsuccessful as the ball went out of the end zone)

The only time that the Patriots defense recorded a safety when the opposing team recovered a fumble in the end zone

Bob Laraba fumbled in the end zone on the last play, and his teammate fell on the ball and was tackled for a safety on 10-28-60 (Bob Dee fell on and protected a boy who went on the field for the ball just before everyone jumped on the fumble)

The only regular season game that the opposing center snapped the ball out of the end zone for a safety

The Houston Center snapped it out of the end zone in the 42–14 rout of the Houston Oilers at Fenway Park on 12-18-65

The only Patriots Defensive Back who has recorded a safety and intercepted a pass in a regular season game

Daryl Johnson tackled Jess Phillips for a safety and intercepted a Greg Cook pass in the 25–14 win on 11-16-69

The only Patriots Linebacker who has recorded a safety and intercepted a pass in a regular season game

Don Blackmon sacked Steve DeBerg for a safety and returned a Steve DeBerg pass 14 yards in the 32–14 win on 10-27-85

The only Patriots Player to tie the NFL record for the most safeties by one player in a regular season

Don Blackmon recorded two safeties during the 1985 regular season

Every Patriots Linebacker who was named the AFC Defensive Player of the Month

1997 regular season
Chris Slade had four sacks and forced two fumbles during the month of September 1997

2003 championship season
Mike Vrabel had four sacks, two forced fumbles, an interception, and a fumble recovery in December 2003

Every Patriots Defensive Lineman who was named the AFC Defensive Player of the Month

1986 regular season
Garin Veris had a sack in five straight games and forced a fumble for the game-winning TD in November 1986

1996 regular season
Willie McGinest had four sacks and returned a pass 46 yards for a touchdown during the month of October 1996

Patriots players who have sacked Pro Football Hall of Fame Quarterbacks

Every Patriots player who has sacked Pro Football Hall of Fame Quarterback George Blanda

Tom Addison, Houston Antwine, Nick Buoniconti, Bob Dee, Larry Eisenhauer, and George Pyne

Every Patriots player who has sacked Pro Football Hall of Fame Quarterback Terry Bradshaw

Rickie Harris, Mike Hawkins, Steve King, Mel Lunsford, Tony McGee, Dave Rowe, and Rod Shoate

Every Patriots player who has sacked or has shared in a sack of Pro Football Hall of Fame Quarterback Len Dawson

Tom Addison, Nick Buoniconti, Dennis Byrd, Bob Dee, Larry Eisenhauer, Lonnie Farmer, Ray Hamilton, Jim Lee Hunt, Dave Rowe, and Jack Rudolph

Every Patriots player who has sacked Pro Football Hall of Fame Quarterback John Elway

Don Blackmon, Marion Hobby, Brandon Mitchell, Johnny Rembert, Ben Thomas, Andre Tippett, and Brent Williams

Steve King sacks Terry Bradshaw

Every Patriots player who has sacked or shared in a sack of Pro Football Hall of Fame Quarterback Dan Fouts

Richard Bishop, Dave Browning, Ray Hamilton, Craig Hanneman, Sam Hunt, Mel Lunsford, Tony McGee, Art Moore, Dennis Owens, Rod Shoate, and Steve Zabel

Every Patriots player who has sacked Pro Football Hall of Fame Quarterback Bob Griese

Houston Antwine, Pete Barnes, Ron Berger, Richard Bishop, John Bramlett, Bob Dee, Larry Eisenhauer, Ray Hamilton, Craig Hanneman, Jim Lee Hunt, Daryl Johnson, Steve Kiner, Steve King, Ike Lassiter, Mel Lunsford, Tony McGee, Art Moore, Steve Nelson, Ed Philpott, Rod Shoate, Donnell Smith, and Steve Zabel

Every Patriots player who has sacked Pro Football Hall of Fame Quarterback Jim Kelly

Ray Agnew, Troy Barnett, Don Blackmon, Vincent Brown, Ferric Collons, Tim Edwards, Tim Goad, Marion Hobby, Gary Jeter, Willie McGinest, Larry McGrew, Steve Nelson, Johnny Rembert, Ed Reynolds, Dwayne Sabb, Chris Slade, Andre Tippett, Garin Veris, Brent Williams, and Toby Williams

Every Patriots player who has sacked or shared in a sack of Pro Football Hall of Fame Quarterback Joe Namath

Julius Adams, Houston Antwine, Pete Barnes, Richard Bishop, Nick Buoniconti, Dennis Byrd, Pete Cusick, Bob Dee, Mike Dukes, Larry Eisenhauer, Craig Hanneman, Jim Lee Hunt, Sam Hunt, Steve King,

Steve Zabel

Charley Long, Mel Lunsford, Tony McGee, Lennie St. Jean, Dave Tipton, and Steve Zabel

Every Patriots player who has sacked or shared in a sack of Pro Football Hall of Fame Quarterback Dan Marino

Julius Adams, Ray Agnew, Don Blackmon, Chris Canty, Todd Collins, Chad Eaton, Tim Goad, Marion Hobby, Ted Johnson, Mike Jones, Willie McGinest, Brandon Mitchell, Dennis Owens, Dwayne Sabb, Kenneth Sims, Chris Slade, Rod Smith, Dwayne Sabb, Henry Thomas, Andre Tippett, Garin Veris, and Brent Williams

Every Patriots player who has sacked Pro Football Hall of Fame Quarterback Joe Montana

Mike Hawkins, Larry McGrew, Dennis Owens, Johnny Rembert, and Andre Tippett

Every Patriots player who has sacked Pro Football Hall of Fame Quarterback Ken Stabler

Julius Adams, Richard Bishop, Don Blackmon, Ray Hamilton, Sam Hunt, Mel Lunsford, Tony McGee, Rod Shoate, and John Zamberlin

Every Patriots player who has sacked Pro Football Hall of Fame Quarterback Roger Staubach

Julius Adams, Ray Hamilton, Ike Lassiter, Mel Lunsford, and Tony McGee

Every Patriots player who has sacked Pro Football Hall of Fame Quarterback Fran Tarkenton

Houston Antwine, Steve King, and George Webster

Every Patriots player who has sacked Pro Football Hall of Fame Quarterback Johnny Unitas

Houston Antwine, Ron Berger, John Bramlett, Ike Lassiter, and Art May

Every Patriots player who has sacked Pro Football Hall of Fame Quarterback Steve Young

Chirs Carter, Ferric Collons, Steve Israel, Gary Jeter, Vernon Lewis, Johnny Rembert, Chris Slade, Greg Spires, Henry Thomas, and Andre Tippett

The alphabetical listing of every Defensive Back who had at least five career sacks in the regular season with the Patriots

Player	Sacks
Rodney Harrison	9.0
Roland James	5.0
Lawyer Milloy	7.0
Larry Whigham	5.0

Mike Ruth

Every defensive player who only recorded one sack in the regular season during his career with the Patriots

Ron Acks, Monty Beisel, Ron Bolton, Bill Brown, Fred Bruney, Terrell Buckley, Je'Rod Cherry, Raymond Clayborn, George Crump, Pete Cusick, Tim Edwards, Halvor Hagen, Antwan Harris, Marshall Harris, Artrell Hawkins, Karl Henke, Ellis Hobbs, Bernard Holsey, Ray Ilg, Daryl Johnson, Dion Lambert, Ronnie Lippett, Dino Mangiero, Fred Marion, Jerry McCabe, Prentice McCray, Riddick Parker, Hank Poteat, Terry Ray, Tim Roberts, Frank Robotti, Mike Ruth, James Sanders, Rick Sanford, Doug Satcher, Ben Thomas, Ed Toner, Jim White, Murray Wichard, and Devin Wyman

Every defensive player who only recorded a share of a sack in the regular season during his career with the Patriots

Jim Bowman, Edgar Chandler, Chris Gannon, Bob Geddes, Art Hauser, Charley Long, Doug McDougald, Rod Smith, and John Tanner

The only defensive lineman who has sacked the same Quarterback at least 10 times for the Patriots

Brent Williams sacked Jim Kelly 10 times over the 1986–93 seasons

The 10 Greatest Patriots Linebackers

Nick Buoniconti—inducted into the Pro Football Hall of Fame in 2001

Andre Tippett—inducted into the Pro Football Hall of Fame in 2008

Tedy Bruschi—has played in 22 playoff games and has three Super Bowl rings

Steve Nelson—inducted into the Patriots Hall of Fame in 1993

Mike Vrabel—holds the team record with three strip-sacks in a regular season game and has three Super Bowl rings

Tom Addison—was a three time AFL All-Star linebacker

Johnny Rembert—was an AFC Pro Bowl linebacker in consecutive seasons

Vincent Brown—was known as "The Undertaker"

Don Blackmon—the only Patriots linebacker with a safety and an interception return in the same game

Chris Slade—the only Patriots linebacker with a sack, an interception and a fumble recovery in a playoff game

(Honorable mention to George Webster and Junior Seau who had spectacular careers before joining the Patriots)

The 10 Greatest Patriots Defensive Linemen

Richard Seymour—has the longest fumble return by a Patriots defensive lineman in a regular season game

Houston Antwine—was a six-time AFL All-Star defensive tackle

Jim Lee Hunt—has the longest interception return by a Patriots defensive lineman in a regular season game

Willie McGinest—had 16 sacks in 16 playoff games for the Patriots

Julius Adams—played in more regular season games than any other defensive lineman of the Patriots

Bob Dee—is the only Patriots Defensive Lineman with two interceptions in a playoff game

Larry Eisenhauer—sacked and knocked 18 quarterbacks out of a game

Tony McGee—is the only player to sack five quarterbacks at least five times during his career with the Patriots

Ray "Sugar Bear" Hamilton—the first Patriots defensive lineman to record a sack that preserved a victory for the Patriots

Brent Williams—is the only Patriots defensive lineman to return two quarterback fumbles for a touchdown

(Honorable mention to Fred Smerlas and Steve McMichael who had great careers with other teams)

The alphabetical listing of every Defensive Lineman or Linebacker who had at least 1½ sacks during his career with the Patriots

Player	Regular Season Sacks	Player	Regular Season Sacks
Julius Adams	80.5	Art May	3.5
Tom Addison	15.0	Tony McGee	72.5
Ray Agnew	8.0	Willie McGinest	78.0
Houston Antwine	39.0	Larry McGrew	16.5
TullyBanta-Cain	8.5	Brandon Mitchell	6.0
Pete Barnes	12.0	Art Moore	8.0
Troy Barnett	3.0	Steve Nelson	19.5
Ron Berger	15.5	Roman Phifer	4.0
Richard Bishop	30.5	Ed Philpott	7.0
Don Blackmon	30.5	Mike Pitts	5.0
Greg Boyd	2.0	Anthony Pleasant	10.0
John Bramlett	2.0	George Pyne	2.0
Vincent Brown	16.5	Johnny Rembert	16.0
Dave Browning	2.0	Ed Reynolds	4.0
Tedy Bruschi	30.5	Jesse Richardson	6.5
Nick Buoniconti	18.0	Doug Rogers	2.5
Dennis Byrd	3.5	Dave Rowe	6.0
Matt Chatham	2.5	Jack Rudolph	16.0
Jim Cheyunski	5.0	Dwayne Sabb	6.5
Todd Collins	2.5	Pio Sagapolutele	3.0
Ferric Collons	7.5	Lennie St. Jean	7.5
Rosevelt Colvin	26.5	Tony Sardisco	2.5
Ray Costict	2.0	Richard Seymour	39.0
Bob Dee	33.0	Rod Shoate	22.5
Mike Dukes	4.0	Kenneth Sims	17.0
Chad Eaton	14.0	Chris Singleton	4.0
Rick Cash	4.0	Chris Slade	51.0
Larry Eisenhauer	45.5	Donnell Smith	4.0
Lonnie Farmer	3.0	Sean Smith	1.5
Jim Fraser	1.5	Greg Spires	9.5
Tim Goad	11.5	Chris Sullivan	3.0
Jarvis Green	27.0	Adalius Thomas	11.5
Bobby Hamilton	10.5	Henry Thomas	20.5
Ray Hamilton	54.0	Andre Tippett	100.0
Craig Hanneman	4.5	Dave Tipton	2.0
Mike Hawkins	12.0	Junior Seau	4.5
Luther Henson	3.0	Garin Veris	39.5
Marion Hobby	5.0	Mike Vrabel	35.5
Milford Hodge	3.0	Ty Warren	19.5
David Howard	2.0	Ted Washington	2.0
Jim Lee Hunt	34.5	George Webster	5.0
Sam Hunt	5.0	Ed Weisacosky	3.0
Harry Jacobs	5.5	Clayton Weishuhn	3.0
Gary Jeter	7.0	Mark Wheeler	5.0
Ted Johnson	11.5	Reggie White	1.5
Aaron Jones	8.5	Vince Wilfork	7.5
Mike Jones	15.5	Brent Williams	43.5
Tim Jordan	3.0	Ed Williams	2.0
Andy Katzenmoyer	3.5	Lester Williams	5.0
Steve Kiner	8.0	Toby Williams	15.5
Dan Klecko	2.0	Dennis Wirgowski	5.0
Dick Klein	5.5	Mike Wright	4.0
Ike Lassiter	7.0	Steve Zabel	10.0
Rommie Loudd	8.0	John Zamberlin	3.5
Mel Lunsford	20.5		

Ray Hamilton sacks Norm Snead

Some of the more memorable sacks in a regular season game

The most powerful sack by Richard Seymour

Richard Seymour bull-rushed and sacked Ben Roethlisberger in the 23–20 win over the Pittsburgh Steelers at Heinz Field on 09-25-05

Craig Hanneman (74) sacks Bert Jones

The longest lasting sack of a Quarterback in a regular season game

Adalius Thomas who flung Brett Favre around and around for a 22-yard loss in the 19–10 win over the New York Jets on 09-14-08

The most memorable sack by "Wildman" Larry Eisenhauer

Larry Eisenhauer knocked Jack Kemp out of the game in the 14–3 win over the Buffalo Bills at Fenway Park on 12-04-66

The Patriots players who have recorded a sack late in the fourth quarter to preserve the victory in a regular season game

1976 regular season
Ray Hamilton sacked Bert Jones with 29 seconds left in the 21–14 win over the Baltimore Colts on 11-14-76

1978 regular season
Tony McGee sacked James Harris on the last play in the 28–23 win over the San Diego Chargers at Schaefer on 10-01-78

1985 regular season
Garin Veris sacked Ken O'Brien on fourth down with 52 seconds left in the 20–13 win over the Jets at Sullivan Stadium on 10-20-85

1987 regular season

Dino Mangiero sacked Willie Totten on the last play in the 14–7 win over the Buffalo Bills at Sullivan Stadium on 10-11-87

1994 regular season

Willie McGinest strip-sacked Don Majkowski to preserve a 12–10 victory over the Indianapolis Colts at the RCA Dome on 11-27-94

2001 championship season

Anthony Pleasant sacked Alex Van Pelt on the last play of the fourth quarter in the 12–9 overtime win vs the Buffalo Bills on 12-16-01

2008 regular season

Brandon Meriweather strip-sacked Seneca Wallace to preserve a 24–21 win over the Seattle Seahawks at Qwest Field on 12-07-08

The most memorable sack in a regular season game by Willie McGinest

Willie McGinest sacked Peyton Manning and forced a long FGA that was missed in the 27–24 win over the Indianapois Colts on 09-09-04

The only Patriots player who sacked a Wide Receiver who was attempting to pass in a regular season game

Julius Adams sacked WR Mark Clayton in the 17–13 win over the Miami Dolphins at Sullivan Stadium on 11-03-85

Willie McGinest

Julius Adams

Two strip-sacks that led to the Patriots offensive team scoring in a close and victorious regular season game

Tony McGee forced Joe Ferguson to fumble and the Patriots scored on the next play in the 26–24 win over the Buffalo Bills on 12-10-78

Brent Williams forced Dave Krieg to fumble and the Patriots scored on their next drive in the 13–7 win vs the Seattle Seahawks on 12-04-88

The only game-winning sack by a Patriots player

Ty Warren sacked J.P. Losman for a safety and the last points scored in the 19–17 win over the Buffalo Bills on 09-10-06

Every strip-sack that was returned for a touchdown by the Patriots in a regular season game

1990 regular season

Garin Veris forced Dave Krieg to fumble and Brent Williams returned it for a TD in the 33–20 loss to the Seattle Seahawks on 10-07-90

1996 regular season

Chris Slade strip-sacked Stan Humphries and Willie McGinest fell on it for a TD in the 45–7 rout of the San Diego Chargers on 12-01-96

1999 regular season

Steve Israel strip-sacked Tom Tupa and Willie McGinest fell on it for a TD in the 30–28 win over the New York Jets on 09-12-99

Ted Johnson strip-sacked Tony Banks and Chad Eaton took it 23 yards for a TD in the 20–3 rout of the Baltimore Ravens on 01-02-00

2002 regular season
Tebucky Jones strip-sacked Vinny Testaverde and returned it 24 yards for a TD in the 44–7 rout of the New York Jets on 09-15-02

2004 championship season
Tedy Bruschi strip-sacked Kyle Boller and Jarvis Green fell on it for a TD in the 24–3 rout of the Baltimore Ravens on 11-28-04

2007 undefeated regular season
Mike Vrabel strip-sacked Jason Campbell and Rosevelt Colvin took it 11 yards for a TD in the 52–7 rout of the Washington Redskins on 10-28-07

The Patriots player who has sacked the same Quarterback the most times in the regular season during his career

Brent Williams sacked Jim Kelly 10 times during the 1986–93 regular seasons

The Playoffs

The progression of the most sacks by a Patriots Defensive Tackle in a playoff game

1 sack by Mel Lunsford in the 24–21 loss to the Oakland Raiders at the Oakland Coliseum on 12-18-76

1 sack by Mike Pitts in the 20–13 loss to the Cleveland Browns at Cleveland Browns Stadium on 01-01-95

The progression of the most sacks by a Patriots Nose Tackle in a playoff game

1.83 sacks by Richard Bishop in the 31–14 loss to the Houston Oilers at Schaefer Stadium on 12-31-78

2 sacks by Dennis Owens in the 28–13 loss to the Miami Dolphins at the Orange Bowl on 01-08-83

2 sacks by Dennis Owens in the 46–10 loss to the Chicago Bears at the Louisiana Superdome on 01-26-86

2.5 sacks by Jarvis Green in the 24–14 victory over the Indianapolis Colts at Foxboro Stadium on 01-18-02

The progression of the most sacks by a Patriots Defensive End in a playoff game

3 sacks by Julius Adams in the 24–21 loss to the Oakland Raiders at the Oakland Coliseum on 12-18-76

3 sacks by Garin Veris in the 26–14 victory over the New York Jets at the Meadowlands on 12-28-85

The progression of the most sacks by a Patriots Linebacker in a playoff game

1 sack by Jack Rudolph in the 51–10 loss to the San Diego Chargers at Balboa Stadium on 01-05-64

1 sack by Andre Tippett in the 26–14 victory over the New York Jets at the Meadowlands on 12-28-85

1 sack by Don Blackmon in the 26–14 victory over the New York Jets at the Meadowlands on 12-28-85

2 sacks by Don Blackmon in the 27–20 win over the Los Angeles Raiders at the Los Angeles Coliseum on 01-05-86

2 sacks by Tedy Bruschi in the 35–21 loss to the Green Bay Packers at the Louisiana Superdome on 01-26-97

2 sacks by Willie McGinest in the 17–14 victory over the Tennessee Titans at Gillette Stadium on 01-10-04

4.5 sacks by Willie McGinest in the 28–3 rout of the Jacksonville Jaguars at Gillette Stadium on 01-07-06

The progression of the most sacks by a Patriots Defensive Back in a playoff game

.83 sacks by Doug Beaudoin (1/2 and 1/3 of a sack) in the 31–14 loss to Houston Oilers at Schaefer Stadium on 12-31-78

1 sack by Otis Smith in the 35–21 loss to the Green Bay Packers at the Louisiana Superdome on 01-26-97

1 sack by Chris Canty in the 17–3 victory over the Miami Dolphins at Foxboro Stadium on 12-28-97

1 sack by Rodney Harrison in the 32–29 victory over the Carolina Panthers at Reliant Stadium on 02-01-04

1 sack by Rodney Harrison in the 24–21 victory over the Philadelphia Eagles at Alltel Stadium on 02-06-05

The progression of the most career sacks by a Patriots player in the playoffs

1 career sack by Jack Rudolph; who had one sack in the 1963 AFL Championship Game on 01-05-64

3 career sacks by Julius Adams; who had three sacks in the 1976 AFC Divisional playoff game on 12-18-76

3 career sacks by Garin Veris; who had three sacks in the 1985 AFC Wild Card playoff game on 12-28-85

3 career sacks by Don Blackmon in three playoff games for the Patriots

4 career sacks by Garin Veris in five playoff games for the Patriots

4 career sacks by Don Blackmon in four playoff games for the Patriots

16 career sacks by Willie McGinest in 18 playoff games for the Patriots

The only Patriots Defensive Back with a Quarterback sack and two interceptions in a playoff game
Super Bowl XXXIX
Rodney Harrison sacked Donovan McNabb and intercepted two of his passes in the 24–21 win over the Philadelphia Eagles

Every Patriots Linebacker with a Quarterback sack and an interception in a playoff game
1997 AFC Wild Card Playoff Game
Chris Slade sacked Dan Marino and intercepted a pass by Dan Marino in the 17–3 win over the Miami Dolphins on 12-28-97

Super Bowl XXXIX
Tedy Bruschi sacked and intercepted Donovan McNabb in the 24–21 victory over the Philadelphia Eagles on 02-06-05

Tedy Bruschi

The only Patriots player with a Quarterback sack, an interception, and a fumble recovery in a playoff game
1997 AFC Wild Card Playoff Game
Chris Slade sacked Dan Marino, intercepted Dan Marino, and recovered a fumble in the 17–3 win over the Miami Dolphins on 12-28-97

The only Patriots Defensive Lineman with three sacks and an interception in a playoff game
1985 AFC Wild Card Playoff Game
Garin Veris sacked Ken O'Brien, sacked Pat Ryan twice, and intercepted Pat Ryan in the 26–14 win vs the New York Jets on 12-28-85

Every sack by a Patriots Player in a Playoff Game

1963 American Football League Championship playoff game at Balboa Stadium on 01-05-64
Jack Rudolph sacked Tobin Rote in the 51–10 loss to the San Diego Chargers

1976 American Football Conference Divisional playoff game at the Oakland Coliseum on 12-18-76
Julius Adams sacked Ken Stabler three times and Mel Lunsford sacked Ken Stabler once in the 24–21 loss to the Oakland Raiders

1978 American Football Conference Divisional playoff game at Schaefer Stadium on 12-31-78
Richard Bishop and Doug Beaudoin shared in a sack of Dan Pastorini, Richard Bishop sacked Dan Pastorini, and Richard Bishop, Steve Zabel, and Doug Beaudoin shared in a three-way sack of Dan Pastorini in the 31–14 loss to the Houston Oilers

1982 American Football Conference first Round playoff game at the Orange Bowl on 01-08-83
Dennis Owens sacked David Woodley twice in the 28–13 loss to the Miami Dolphins

1985 American Football Conference Wild Card playoff game at the Meadowlands on 12-28-85
Garin Veris sacked Ken O'Brien, Andre Tippett sacked Ken O'Brien, Garin Veris sacked Pat Ryan twice, and Don Blackmon sacked Pat Ryan once in the 26–14 victory over the New York Jets

Andre Tippett

1985 American Football Conference Divisional playoff game at the Los Angeles Coliseum on 01-05-86

Don Blackmon sacked Marc Wilson twice in the 27–20 victory over the Los Angeles Raiders

1985 American Football Conference Championship playoff game at the Orange Bowl on 01-12-86

Garin Veris sacked Dan Marino in the 31–14 victory over the Miami Dolphins

Super Bowl XX at the Louisiana Superdome on 01-26-86

Dennis Owens sacked Jim McMahon, Dennis Owens sacked (RB) William Perry, and Ben Thomas sacked Steve Fuller in the 46–10 loss to the Chicago Bears

1986 American Football Conference Divisional playoff game at Mile High Stadium on 01-04-87

Don Blackmon sacked John Elway in the 22–17 loss to the Denver Broncos

1994 American Football Conference Wild Card playoff game at Cleveland Browns Stadium on 01-01-95

Willie McGinest sacked Vinny Testaverde, and Mike Pitts sacked Vinny Testaverde in the 20–13 loss to the Browns

1996 American Football Conference Divisional playoff game at Foxboro Stadium on 01-05-97

Chris Slade and Chad Eaton shared in a sack of Mike Tomczak, Chris Slade and Mike Jones shared in a sack of Mike Tomczak, and Ted Johnson sacked Kordell Stewart in the 28–3 rout of the Pittsburgh Steelers

1996 American Football Conference Championship playoff game at Foxboro Stadium on 01-12-97

Chris Slade sacked Mark Brunell in the 20–6 victory over the Jacksonville Jaguars

Super Bowl XXXI at the Louisiana Superdome on 01-26-97

Ferric Collons sacked Brett Favre, Tedy Bruschi sacked Brett Favre, Willie McGinest sacked Brett Favre, Otis Smith sacked Brett Favre, and Tedy Bruschi sacked Brett Favre again in the 35–21 loss to the Green Bay Packers

1997 American Football Conference Wild Card playoff game at Foxboro Stadium on 12-28-97

Chris Slade, Willie McGinest, Ted Johnson, and Chris Canty sacked Dan Marino in the 17–3 win over the Miami Dolphins

1997 American Football Conference Divisional playoff game at Three Rivers Stadium on 01-03-98

Willie McGinest sacked Kordell Stewart, and Willie McGinest and Chris Slade shared in a sack of Kordell Stewart in the 7–6 loss to the Pittsburgh Steelers

1998 American Football Conference Wild Card playoff game at Alltel Stadium on 01-03-99

Greg Spires sacked Mark Brunell twice in the 25–10 loss to the Jacksonville Jaguars

2001 American Football Conference Divisonal playoff game at Foxboro Stadium on 01-19-02

Tedy Bruschi sacked Rich Gannon in the 16–13 overtime win vs the Oakland Raiders

Ted Johnson (Jay Fiedler on the ground)

2001 American Football Conference Championship Game at Heinz Field on 01-27-02

Ted Johnson and Tedy Bruschi shared in a sack of Kordell Stewart, Anthony Pleasant sacked Kordell Stewart, and Willie McGinest sacked Kordell Stewart in the 24–17 victory over the Pittsburgh Steelers

Super Bowl XXXVI at the Louisiana Superdome on 02-03-02

Bobby Hamilton, Richard Seymour, and Willie McGinest sacked Kurt Warner in the 20–17 win over the St. Louis Rams

2003 American Football Conference Divisional Playoff Game at Gillette Stadium on 01-10-04

Willie McGinest sacked Steve McNair, Mike Vrabel sacked Steve McNair, and Willie McGinest sacked Steve McNair again in the 17–14 victory over the Tennessee Titans

2003 American Conference Championship Game at Gillette Stadium on 01-18-04

Jarvis Green sacked Peyton Manning, Willie McGinest sacked Peyton Manning, Jarvis Green and Roman Phifer shared in a sack of Peyton Manning and Jarvis Green sacked Peyton Manning again in the 24–14 victory over the Indianapolis Colts

Super Bowl XXXVII at Reliant Stadium on 02-01-04

Mike Vrabel sacked Jake Delhomme, Willie McGinest sacked Jake Delhomme, Mike Vrabel sacked Jake Delhomme again, and Rodney Harrison sacked Jake Delhomme in the 32–29 victory over the Carolina Panthers

2004 AFC Divisional playoff game at Gillette Stadium on 01-16-05

Mike Vrabel sacked Peyton Manning in the 20–3 rout of the Indianapolis Colts

2004 AFC Championship Game at Heinz Field on 01-23-05

Jarvis Green sacked Ben Roethlisberger in the 41–27 victory over the Pittsburgh Steelers

Jarvis Green

Super Bowl XXXIX at Alltel Stadium on 02-06-05

Tedy Bruschi sacked Donovan McNabb on the third play, Mike Vrabel, Rodney Harrison, and Richard Seymour sacked Donovan McNabb in the 24–21 victory over the Philadephia Eagles

2005 AFC Wild Card playoff game at Gillette Stadium on 01-07-06

Willie McGinest sacked Byron Leftwich on the first play of the second quarter, Rosevelt Colin sacked Byron Leftwich, Willie McGinest sacked Byron Leftwich again, and then he sacked Byron Leftwich a third time

Willie McGinest and Richard Seymour shared in a sack of David Garrard

Willie McGinest recorded another sack of David Garrard in the 28–3 rout of the Jacksonville Jaguars

2006 AFC Wild Card playoff game at Gillette Stadium on 01-07-07

Tully Banta-Cain sacked Chad Pennington on the Jets first offensive play of the game

Junior Seau

Richard Seymour

Tully Banta-Cain sacked Chad Pennington again in the fourth quarter of their 37–16 rout of the New York Jets

Richard Seymour sacked Chad Pennington on the Jets last offensive play of the game

2006 AFC Divisional playoff game at Qualcomm Stadium on 01-14-07

Mike Vrabel strip-sacked Philip Rivers and Tully Banta-Cain recovered the fumble

Artrell Hawkins sacked Philip Rivers, and James Sanders sacked Philip Rivers in the 24–21 win over the San Diego Chargers

2006 AFC Championship Game at the RCA Dome on 01-21-07

Eric Alexander, Rosevelt Colvin, and Mike Vrabel sacked Peyton Manning in the 38–34 loss to the Indianapolis Colts

2007 AFC Divisional playoff game at Gillette Stadium on 01-12-08

Ty Warren sacked David Garrard in the 31–20 victory over the Jacksonville Jaguars

2007 AFC Championship playoff game at Gillette Stadium on 01-20-08

Junior Seau sacked Philip Rivers in the 21–12 victory over the San Diego Chargers

Super Bowl XLII at the University of Phoenix Stadium on 02-03-08

Jarvis Green sacked Eli Manning and Adalius Thomas strip-sacked Eli Manning

(Jarvis Green and Richard Seymour almost sacked Eli Manning with just over one minute left in the game)

Adalius Thomas sacked Eli Manning with just under one minute left in the 17–14 loss to the New York Giants

Combinations

Offensive, Defensive, and Special Teams Contributions

This chapter presents the Patriots players who have performed the multiple tasks of advancing and/or returning the football. It includes statistics for the players who have advanced the ball from the line of scrimmage and/or returned an interception, a fumble, a punt and/or a kickoff for the Patriots. Joe Bellino, Troy Brown, Gino Cappelletti, Kevin Faulk, Irving Fryar, Carl Garrett, Larry Garron, Mack Herron, Dave Meggett, and Darryl Stingley are a few such players.

Some linemen and a few linebackers have returned a kickoff for the Patriots. "Choo-Choo" Charlie Long and Halvor Hagen are the only linemen who have played on both sides of the line of scrimmage and have returned a kickoff. Steve DeOssie is the only player who was a long snapper and short yardage linebacker who has returned a kickoff for the Patriots. Dan Klecko is the only player who played on the defensive line, was used in the backfield, returned a kickoff, blocked a field-goal attempt, caught a pass, and carried the ball for the Patriots. John Tanner and Mike Vrabel are the only players who have been used as a linebacker, tight end, and defensive end and have also returned a kickoff for the Patriots.

The three defensive backs who have appeared in more than 50 games and have returned an interception, a punt, and a kickoff for the Patriots are Gino Cappelletti, Rick Sanford, and Troy Brown. Cappelletti had four interceptions, one punt return, and four kickoff returns. Sanford intercepted 16 passes, had two punt returns, and returned 14 kickoffs. Troy Brown had three interceptions, 252 punt returns, and 87 kickoff returns.

Although Larry Garron never had an interception return, he did play as a defensive back for three regular season games and in one AFL All-Star Game representing the Boston Patriots. Garron had 759 carries, 185 receptions, 89 kickoff returns, one pass completion, and one punt return during his nine-year career with the Boston Patriots. Versatile Walter Beach played multiple positions as well. Beach had six carries, nine receptions, nine kickoff returns, returned a punt 21 yards, and returned an interception 37 yards during his two-year career with the Boston Patriots.

Tom Greene, who played quarterback, running back, and was a punter for the Patriots in 1960, is the only player to perform at these various positions and also return a kickoff in the same season. Greene had 251 yards passing, 44 yards rushing, 43 yards receiving, 2,253 yards punting, and returned a kickoff three yards for the Boston Patriots in 1960.

Gino Cappelletti is the only Patriots player who has intercepted a pass and run for a two-point conversion in the same game. Cappelletti had his career-longest interception return of 27 yards and ran for a two-point conversion in the Boston Patriots' 27–14 loss to the Oakland Raiders on 10-16-60.

David Patten is the only Patriots wide receiver to run for a touchdown and have two touchdown receptions in the same game. Patten was the AFC Offensive Player of the Week as he ran for a 29-yard touchdown, caught two touchdown passes, and even threw a 60-yard touchdown pass to Troy Brown in the Patriots' 38–17 rout of the Indianapolis Colts on 10-21-01.

Only Stanley Morgan and Irving Fryar have caught a touchdown pass and returned a punt for a touchdown in the same game. Stanley Morgan caught a 25-yard touchdown pass from Steve Grogan and returned a punt by Bucky Dilt 80 yards for a touchdown in the Patriots

50–21 rout of the Indianapolis Colts on 11-18-79. Irving Fryar caught a five-yard touchdown pass from Steve Grogan and returned a punt by Rohn Stark 77 yards for a touchdown in the Patriots' 34–15 rout of the Indianapolis Colts on 11-10-85.

Tedy Bruschi is the only Patriots linebacker who has returned two interceptions for a touchdown and returned a kickoff in the same season. Marty Schottenheimer is the only linebacker who has gone on to become a head coach in the NFL who has returned a kickoff for the Patriots. Pro Football Hall of Famer Nick Buoniconti is the only linebacker who has returned a punt for the Patriots.

Bryan Cox is the only Patriots linebacker who has caught a pass as a running back and has returned a defensive fumble recovery in the same game. He caught a seven-yard pass from Tom Brady and returned a LaDainian Tomlinson fumble nine yards in the Patriots' 29–26 overtime win vs the San Diego Chargers on 10-14-01.

Kevin Faulk is the only Patriots running back who has more than 2,500 yards rushing, 2,500 yards receiving, and 4,000 combined punt and kickoff return yards in the regular season during his career. Faulk has had 2,663 yards rushing, 2,818 yards receiving, 769 punt return yards, and a team-record 3,918 kickoff return yards during his nine-year career with the New England Patriots.

Troy Brown is the only Patriots player with a reception and an interception in the same regular season game. He is the only wide receiver with more than 6,000 yards receiving and more than 4,000 special teams return yards for the Patriots. Brown had 6,366 yards receiving, 2,625 punt return yards, and 1,862 kickoff return yards in the regular season during his 15-year career with the New England Patriots.

Some of the more noticeable names of the non-return men who excelled on special teams are Allan "Kamikazee Kid" Clark, Bob "Harpo" Gladieux, Steve "Reno" King, Larry "H to the Izzo" Izzo, Tebucky Jones, Lonie "Snow Angel" Paxton, Mosi Tatupu, and Larry "Hollywood" Whigham.

Bob Gladieux has an interesting story. He tried to go to the opening game of the 1970 regular season at Harvard Stadium without a ticket. He had been cut by the team just four days prior to this game and his friends already had their tickets. He persuaded the ticket collector to let him in by pointing out that his picture was in the game program. Just a few minutes later, he was requested to report to the Patriots dressing

Tom Brady

room over the loudspeakers. Gladieux went to the locker room and signed a contract to play for the team. He made the tackle on the opening kickoff of Jake Scott in the Patriots' 27–14 win over the Miami Dolphins at Harvard Stadium on 09-20-70.

Many different players have been used as the long snapper for the Patriots. Tight ends Jim Whalen, Mike Bartrum, and Marv Cook have been used as the long snapper. Chris Gannon was a defensive end, tight end, and long snapper. Tim Goad was a defensive lineman and a long snapper. Walt "Mike" Cudzik, who was primarily a center and long snapper and was used sometimes as a linebacker, is the only lineman who has caught a pass, attempted a field goal, and recovered an onside kick for the Patriots.

Five Patriots players have been named to the AFC Pro Bowl Team as a special teams contributor. Running back Mosi Tatupu, defensive back Larry Whigham, and linebacker Larry Izzo were recognized as AFC Pro Bowl special teams players, and wide receiver Irving Fryar and running back Dave Meggett were recognized as AFC Pro Bowl special teams return specialists.

Dave Meggett is the only Patriots player who has run, caught a pass, returned a punt and a kickoff in a playoff game. Defensive back/wide receiver Corwin Brown is the only Patriots player who has caught a pass and recovered an onside kick in the same playoff game.

In the Same Game

The only Patriots player to take a snap as the Quarterback, catch a few passes, and return some kickoffs in the same game

Quarterback Stephen Starring ran an option play, caught four passes, and returned four kickoffs in the 38–31 win over the Colts on 12-01-85

In the Same Season

The only Patriots player who has run for two points, caught and intercepted a pass, and returned a punt and a kickoff in the same season

Gino Cappelletti ran for three two-point conversions, caught a 28-yard pass, had a three-yard punt return, returned four kickoffs for 100 yards, and returned four interceptions for 68 yards in 1960

The only Patriots player who has a TD run, a TD reception, and at least one punt return for a TD in the same season

Irving Fryar ran eight yards for a TD, caught seven TD passes, and returned two punts for a TD in 1985

The only Patriots Tight End with yards rushing, receiving, and returning a kickoff in a regular season

Ben Coates lost six yards rushing, had 95 yards receiving, and returned a kickoff six yards in 1991

The only Patriots Running Back with 500+ yards rushing, 400+ yards receiving, 500+ punt return yards, and 500+ kickoff return yards in a season

Mack Herron had 824 yards rushing, 474 yards receiving, 517 punt return yards, and 629 kickoff return yards in 1974

The only Patriots with career yards rushing, receiving, returning punts, kickoffs, and interceptions, and advancing a fumble

Troy Brown had 178 yards rushing, 6,366 yards receiving, 2,625 punt return yards, 1,862 kickoff return yards, 22 interception return yards, and advanced a fumble 75 yards for a TD. He also had two two-point pass receptions during his career.

Combined Yards Rushing, Receiving, and Returning

The progression of the most yards rushing, receiving, and returning both punts and kickoffs by a Patriots player in a game

147 yards by Dick Christy, who had 93 yards rushing, 10 receiving, nine punt return yards, and 35 kickoff return yards on 09-23-60

192 yards by Bobby Leo, who had seven yards rushing, 25 receiving, 43 punt return yards, and 117 kickoff return yards on 12-09-67

215 yards by Dave Meggett, who had 52 yards rushing, 18 receiving, 13 punt return yards, and 132 kickoff return yards on 10-01-95

The progression of the most yards from scrimmage and special teams return yards by a Patriots player in a game

47 yards by Larry Garron, who had 26 yards rushing and 21 kickoff return yards in the 13–10 loss to Denver on 09-09-60

159 yards by Dick Christy, who had 19 yards rushing, 17 receiving, and 123 kickoff return yards in the 28–24 win over New York on 09-17-60

167 yards by Larry Garron, who had 26 yards rushing and 141 kickoff return yards in the 31–31 tie with Houston on 10-13-61

273 yards by Larry Garron, who had 51 yards rushing, 49 receiving, and 173 kickoff return yards in the 28–28 tie with Buffalo on 11-03-62

Every Patriots Wide Receiver who had a rushing attempt, a reception, a punt return, and a kickoff return in a regular season game

1967 regular season

Bobby Leo ran a reverse, caught a TD pass, and returned two punts and six kickoffs in the 44–16 loss to the Buffalo Bills on 12-09-67

1985 regular season

Irving Fryar ran once, caught a pass, and returned two punts and a kickoff in the 32–14 win over the Tampa Bay Buccaneers on 10-27-85

1986 regular season

Irving Fryar ran once, caught four passes, and returned two punts and a kickoff in the 34–7 rout of the Miami Dolphins on 10-05-86

1989 regular season
Sammy Martin ran once, caught a pass, and returned three punts and three kickoffs in the 28–24 loss to the New Orleans Saints on 11-12-89

2001 championship season
Troy Brown ran twice, caught three passes, and returned two punts and a kickoff in the 44–13 rout of the Indianapolis Colts on 09-30-01

Most yards Rushing, Receiving, Returning Punts and Kickoffs in a Season

The progression of the most yards rushing, receiving, and returning both punts and kickoffs by a Patriots Wide Receiver in a season

318 yards by Bobby Leo, who had seven yards rushing, 25 receiving, 54 punt return, and 232 kickoff return yards in 1967

490 yards by Hubie Bryant, who had one yard rushing, 212 receiving, 24 punt return, and 252 kickoff return yards in 1971

567 yards by Darryl Stingley, who had 64 yards rushing, 339 receiving, 21 punt return, and 143 kickoff return yards in 1973

574 yards by Darryl Stingley, who had 39 yards rushing, 378 receiving, 113 punt return, and 44 kickoff return yards in 1975

1,183 yards by Stanley Morgan, who had 11 yards rushing, 820 receiving, 335 punt return, and 17 kickoff return yards in 1978

1,342 yards by Stanley Morgan, who had 39 yards rushing, 1,002 receiving, 289 punt return, and 12 kickoff return yards in 1979

1,509 yards by Troy Brown, who had 46 yards rushing, 944 receiving, 504 punt return, and 15 kickoff return yards in 2000

1,634 yards by Wes Welker, who had 34 yards rushing, 1,175 receiving, 240 punt return, and 176 kickoff return yards in 2007

The progression of the most yards rushing, receiving, and returning both punts and kickoffs by a Patriots Running Back in a season

1,321 total yards rushing, receiving, and returning both punts and kickoffs by Dick Christy in 1960

1,369 total yards rushing, receiving, and returning both punts and kickoffs by Ron Burton in 1961

1,884 total yards rushing, receiving, and returning both punts and kickoffs by Larry Garron in 1963

1,909 total yards rushing, receiving, and returning both punts and kickoffs by Carl Garrett in 1969

2,444 total yards rushing, receiving, and returning both punts and kickoffs by Mack Herron in 1974

Most Career Yards Rushing, Receiving, and Returning Punts and Kickoffs

The progression of the most career yards rushing, receiving, and returning both punts and kickoffs by a Patriots player

1,321 career total yards rushing, receiving, and returning both punts and kickoffs by Dick Christy

4,340 career total yards rushing, receiving, returning punts and kickoffs, and a missed field goal by Ron Burton

7,805 career total yards rushing, receiving, and returning punts and kickoffs by Larry Garron

11,468 career total yards rushing, receiving, and returning punts and kickoffs by Stanley Morgan

Yards Receiving and Returning Interceptions

The only Patriots player with a pass reception and a pass interception in the same regular season game
Troy Brown caught two passes from Tom Brady and intercepted Drew Bledsoe once in the 29–6 win over Buffalo on 11-04-04

Every Patriots Wide Receiver/Defensive Back who had yards receiving and interception return yards in the same season
1960 regular season
Gino Cappelletti had 28 yards receiving and 68 interception return yards in 1960

1961 regular season
Chuck Shonta had nine yards receiving and 12 interception return yards in 1961

2004 championship season

Troy Brown had 184 yards receiving and 22 interception return yards in 2004

The only Patriots Tight End/Linebacker who had yards receiving and interception return yards in the same season

Mike Vrabel had four yards receiving and 23 interception return yards in 2005

Every player who had yards receiving and interception return yards during his career with the Patriots

Gino Cappelletti, Chuck Shonta, Tom Stephens, Troy Brown, and Mike Vrabel each had pass receptions and interception returns

The progression of the most career yards receiving and interception return yards by a Patriots player

4,657 total career yards receiving and returning interceptions by Gino Cappelletti during the 1960–69 seasons

6,388 total career yards receiving and returning interceptions by Troy Brown during the 1993–2007 seasons

Yards Passing and Returning Interceptions

The only Patriots player with career yards passing and interception return yards

88 combined career yards passing and returning interceptions by Gino Cappelletti

Yards Rushing and Returning Interceptions

The only Patriots player who has run for a two-point conversion and has intercepted a pass in the same game

Gino Cappelletti ran for a two-point conversion and intercepted three passes in the 27–14 loss to Oakland on 10-16-60

The only Patriots player who has carried the ball and intercepted a pass in the same season

Clyde Washington ran for three yards (as the punter), returned a blocked field goal seven yards, and returned three passes for 13 yards in 1960

Clyde Washington ran for a three-yard gain as a running back and returned four interceptions for 45 yards in 1961

The progression of the most career combined yards rushing and returning interceptions

33 career combined yards rushing and returning an interception by Walter Beach during the 1960–61 seasons

64 career combined yards rushing and returning interceptions by Clyde Washington over the 1960–61 seasons

200 career combined yards rushing and returning interceptions by Troy Brown over the 1997–2004 seasons

Interception Return Yards and Special Teams Return Yards

The only Patriots Defensive Back who has returned an interception and returned a kickoff for a TD in the same game

Ellis Hobbs returned a David Carr pass nine yards and took a kickoff 93 yards for a TD in the 40–7 rout of the Houston Texans on 12-17-06

The progression of the most interception return yards and special teams return yards by a Patriots player in a game

80 total yards by Bob Suci, who had 23 interception return yards, 22 punt return, and 35 kickoff return yards on 09-08-63

125 total yards by Bob Suci, who had 62 interception return yards, 46 punt return, and 17 kickoff return yards on 10-18-63

158 total yards by Mike Haynes, who had an interception return of two yards and had 156 punt return yards on 11-07-76

The progression on the most interception return yards and special teams return yards by a Patriots player in a season

164 total yards by Gino Cappelletti, who had 61 interception return yards, three punt return yards, and 100 kickoff return yards in 1960

168 total yards by Don Webb, who had 153 interception return yards and 15 kickoff return yards in 1961

870 yards by Bob Suci, who had 277 interception return yards, 233 punt return yards, and 360 kickoff return yards in 1963

911 total yards by Ellis Hobbs, who had no return on his only interception and had 911 kickoff return yards in 2007

1,281 total yards by Ellis Hobbs, who had three interception returns for a net of zero yards, and had 1,281 kickoff return yards in 2008

The progression of the most interception return yards and punt return yards by a Patriots player in a season

71 total yards by Gino Cappelletti, who had 61 interception return yards and returned a punt three yards in 1960

129 total yards by Fred Bruney, who had 20 interception return yards and 109 punt return yards in 1961

510 total yards by Bob Suci, who had 277 interception return yards and 233 punt return yards in 1963

698 total yards by Mike Haynes, who had 90 interception return yards and 608 punt return yards in 1976

The progression of the most interception return yards and kickoff return yards by a Patriots player in a season

161 total yards by Gino Cappelletti, who had 61 interception return yards and 100 kickoff return yards in 1960

168 total yards by Don Webb, who had 153 interception return yards and returned a kickoff 15 yards in 1961

637 total yards by Bob Suci, who had 277 interception return yards and 360 kickoff return yards in 1963

681 total yards by Jay Cunningham, who returned an interception 54 yards for a TD and had 627 kickoff return yards in 1967

708 total yards by Raymond Clayborn, who had 72 interception return yards and 636 kickoff return yards in 1978

911 total yards by Ellis Hobbs, who had one interception return for no gain and 911 kickoff return yards in 2007

1,281 total yards by Ellis Hobbs, who returned three passes for a net of zero yards and had 1,281 kickoff return yards in 2008

The progression of the most career interception return yards and special teams return yards by a Patriots player

164 career interception and special teams return yards by Gino Cappelletti in 1960

168 interception and special teams return yards by Don Webb in 1961

870 career interception and special teams return yards by Bob Suci in 1963

2,093 career interception and special teams return yards by Raymond Clayborn over the 1977–89 seasons

3,000 career interception return and special teams return yards by Ellis Hobbs over the 2005–08 seasons

The Top 10 Special Teams Return Men of the Patriots

Troy Brown—returned two punts for a TD in the regular season and took one punt for a TD in the playoffs

Raymond Clayborn—returned three kickoffs for a TD and averaged 31 yards per kickoff return in 1977

Irving Fryar—returned three punts for a TD and was the first AFC Pro Bowl Return Specialist for the Patriots

Mack Herron—had more than 1,000 kickoff return yards in 1973 and set the team record with 14.8 yards per punt return in '74

Mike Haynes—set the team return record with 156 punt return yards in a game including his 89-yard return for a TD

Ellis Hobbs—set the NFL record with his 108-yard kickoff return for a TD in 2007

Kevin Faulk—has the team record for the most career kickoff return yards

Carl Garrett—averaged 11.3 yards per punt return and 28.3 yards per kickoff return in his career with the Patriots

Larry Garron—is the only Patriots player to have at a kickoff return of at least 58 yards in three consecutive seasons

Dave Meggett—is the only Patriots with more than 2,500 career kickoff return yards and over 1,000 career punt return yards

Yards Passing, Rushing, Receiving, and Returning

The only Patriots Wide Receiver who had yards passing, rushing, receiving, and yards returning punts and kickoffs in the same season

Don Westbrook had 52 yards passing, eight yards rushing, 173 yards receiving, five punt return yards, and 151 kickoff return yards in 1979

Every Patriots Running Back who had yards passing, rushing, receiving, and yards returning punts and kickoffs in a season

1960 regular season

Dick Christy had 94 yards passing, 363 yards rushing, 268 yards receiving, 73 punt return yards, and 617 kickoff return yards

1997 regular season

Dave Meggett had 35 yards passing, 60 yards rushing, 203 yards receiving, 467 punt return yards, and 816 kickoff return yards

2001 championship season

Kevin Faulk had 23 yards passing, 169 yards rushing, 189 yards receiving, 27 punt return yards, and 662 kickoff return yards

Career Yards Passing, Rushing, Receiving, and Returning

The only Patriots Wide Receiver with career yards passing, rushing, receiving, and yards returning both punts and kickoffs

Don Westbrook had 52 yards passing, six yards rushing, 393 yards receiving, five punt return yards, and 290 kickoff return yards

Every Patriots Running Back who has had career yards passing, rushing, receiving, and yards returning punts and kickoffs

Dick Christy had 94 yards passing, 363 yards rushing, 268 yards receiving, 73 punt return yards, and 617 kickoff return yards

Larry Garron had 39 yards passing, 2,981 yards rushing, 2,502 yards receiving, 23 punt return yards, and 2,299 kickoff return yards

Bob Gladieux had 48 yards passing, 239 yards rushing, 252 yards receiving, minus-6 punt return yards, and 146 kickoff return yards

Andy Johnson had 194 yards passing, 2,017 yards rushing, 1,807 yards receiving, 60 punt return yards, and 544 kickoff return yards

Dave Meggett had 35 yards passing, 432 yards rushing, 829 yards receiving, 1,438 punt return yards, and 2,561 kickoff return yards

Kevin Faulk has had 21 yards passing, 3,170 yards rushing, 3,304 yards receiving, 901 punt return yards, and 3,954 kickoff return yards

Bob Gladieux

The only Patriots player with career yards passing, rushing, receiving, and returning punts, kickoffs, and interceptions

Gino Cappelletti had 27 yards passing, three runs for a two-point conversion, caught a pass for a two-point conversion, ran as a running back for a two-yard gain, 4,589 yards receiving, three punt return yards, 100 kickoff return yards, and 68 interception return yards

Combined Yards Receiving and Returning Punts

The progression of the most yards receiving and punt return yards by a Patriots player in a game

24 yards by Dick Christy, who had a 17-yard reception and a seven-yard punt return in the 28–24 win over New York on 09-17-60

31 yards by Billy Wells, who had 25 yards receiving and a six-yard punt return in the 42–14 rout of Dallas on 11-18-60

80 yards by Ron Burton, who caught an eight-yard pass and returned a punt 62 yards in the 27–15 loss to Houston on 11-12-61

94 yards by Ron Burton, who had 94 yards receiving and returned two punts for net 0 yards in the 21–17 loss to Houston on 11-18-62

145 yards by Carl Garrett, who had 97 yards receiving and 48 punt return yards in the 38–33 win over Buffalo on 11-14-71

The progression of the most yards receiving and punt return yards by a Patriots Wide Receiver in a game

68 yards by Bobby Leo, who had a 25-yard TD reception and 43 punt return yards in the 44–16 loss to Buffalo on 12-09-67

100 yards by Darryl Stingley, who had 75 yards receiving and 25 punt return yards in the 34–31 loss to Dallas on 11-16-75

147 yards by Stanley Morgan, who had 125 yards receiving and 22 punt return yards in the 34–27 loss to Baltimore on 09-18-78

207 yards by Stanley Morgan, who had 170 receiving and 37 punt return yards in the 35–14 rout of the Colts on 11-26-78

214 yards by Troy Brown, who had 89 yards receiving and 125 punt return yards in the 27–16 win over the Browns on 12-09-01

The progression of the most yards receiving and punt return yards by a Patriots Receiver in a regular season

31 total yards by Gino Cappelletti, who caught a 28-yard pass and returned a punt three yards in 1960

79 total yards by Bobby Leo, who caught a 25-yard TD pass and had 54 punt return yards in 1967

360 total yards by Darryl Stingley, who had 339 yards receiving and 21 punt return yards in 1973

491 total yards by Darryl Stingley, who had 378 yards receiving and 113 punt return yards in 1975

663 total yards by Stanley Morgan, who had 443 yards receiving and 220 punt return yards in 1977

1,155 total yards by Stanley Morgan, who had 820 yards receiving and 335 punt return yards in 1978

1,291 total yards by Stanley Morgan, who had 1,002 yards receiving and 289 punt return yards in 1979

1,448 total yards by Troy Brown, who had 944 yards receiving and 504 punt return yards in 2000

1,612 total yards by Troy Brown, who had 1,199 yards receiving and 413 punt return yards in 2001

The progression of the most career yards receiving and returning punts by a Patriots player

4,592 total career yards receiving and returning punts by Gino Cappelletti during the 1960–69 seasons

11,312 total career yards receiving and returning punts by Stanley Morgan during the 1977–89 seasons

Combined Yards Receiving and Returning Kickoffs

The progression of the most yards receiving and kickoff return yards by a Patriots player in a game

140 yards by Dick Christy, who had a 17-yard reception and 123 kickoff return yards in the 28–24 win over New York on 09-17-60

162 yards by Larry Garron, who had a 21-yard reception and 141 kickoff return yards in the 31–31 tie with Houston on 10-13-61

222 yards by Larry Garron, who had 49 yards receiving and 173 kickoff return yards in the 28–28 tie with Buffalo on 11-03-62

258 yards by Kevin Faulk, who had 38 yards receiving and 220 kickoff return yards in the 30–17 loss to the Jets on 12-22-02

The progression of the most yards receiving and kickoff return yards by a Patriots Wide Receiver in a game

142 yards by Bobby Leo, who caught a 25-yard TD and had 117 kickoff return yards in the 44–16 loss to Buffalo on 12-09-67

199 yards by Bethel Johnson, who had seven yards receiving and 192 kickoff return yards in the 38–34 win over the Colts on 11-30-03

The progression of the most yards receiving and kickoff return yards by a Patriots Tight End in a regular season game

36 total yards by Tony Romeo, who had 31 yards receiving and a five-yard kickoff return in the 33–28 win over San Diego on 09-20-64

100 total yards by Don Hasselbeck, who had 93 yards receiving and a seven-yard kickoff return in the 35–21 loss to Dallas on 9-21-81

The progression of the most yards receiving and returning kickoffs by a Patriots Receiver in a regular season

103 total yards by Gino Cappelletti, who caught a 28-yard pass and had 100 kickoff return yards in 1960

286 total yards by Jim Colclough, who had 284 yards receiving and returned a kickoff two yards in 1966

405 yards by Aaron Marsh, who had 331 yards receiving and 74 kickoff return yards in 1968

464 total yards by Hubie Bryant, who had 212 yards receiving and 252 kickoff return yards in 1971

908 total yards by Reggie Rucker, who had 681 yards receiving and 227 kickoff return yards in 1972

1,247 total yards by Stephen Starring, who had 235 yards receiving and 1,012 kickoff return yards in 1985

1,352 total yards by Deion Branch, who had 489 yards receiving and 863 kickoff return yards in 2002

The progression of the most yards receiving and returning kickoffs by a Patriots Tight End in a regular season

192 total yards by Tom Stephens, who had 186 yards receiving and a six-yard kickoff return in 1961

450 total yards by Tony Romeo, who had 445 yards receiving and a five-yard kickoff return in 1964

815 total yards by Don Hasselbeck, who had 808 yards receiving and a seven-yard kickoff return in 1981

The progression of the most career yards receiving and kickoff return yards by a Patriots player

4,689 total career yards receiving and returning kickoffs by Gino Cappelletti during the 1960–69 seasons

10,381 total career yards receiving and returning kickoffs by Stanley Morgan during the 1977–89 seasons

The Most Yards from Scrimmage

The progression of the most yards from scrimmage by a Patriots Quarterback in a regular season game

2 yards from scrimmage by Butch Songin in the 13–10 loss to the Denver Broncos at BU Field on 09-09-60

33 yards from scrimmage by Tom Greene in the 13–0 loss to the Buffalo Bills at BU Field on 09-23-60

46 yards from scrimmage by Babe Parilli in the 35–21 victory over the Oakland Raiders at Candlestick Park on 12-09-61

Steve Grogan

90 yards from scrimmage by Tom Yewcic in the 24–17 win over the New York Titans at BU Field on 11-30-62

96 yards from scrimmage by Babe Parilli in the 25–24 victory over the Houston Oilers at Fenway Park on 11-06-64

103 yards from scrimmage by Steve Grogan in the 41–7 rout of the New York Jets at Schaefer Stadium on 10-18-76

The progression of the most yards from scrimmage by a Patriots Wide Receiver in a regular season game

42 yards from scrimmage by Jim Colclough in the 13–10 loss to the Denver Broncos at BU Field on 09-09-60

84 yards from scrimmage by Jim Colclough in the 31–24 loss to the Denver Broncos at Bears Stadium on 10-23-60

85 yards from scrimmage by Jim Colclough in the 38–21 victory over the New York Titans at BU Field on 11-11-60

85 yards from scrimmage by Jim Colclough in the 42–14 rout of the Dallas Texans at BU Field on 11-18-60

123 yards from scrimmage by Jim Colclough in the 45–17 rout of the Denver Broncos at BU Field on 09-16-61

131 yards from scrimmage by Gino Cappelletti in the 31–31 tie with the Houston Oilers at BU Field on 10-13-61

142 yards from scrimmage by Jim Colclough in the 43–14 rout of the New York Titans at the Polo Grounds on 10-06-62

147 yards from scrimmage by Gino Cappelletti in the 35–14 loss to the New York Jets at Shea Stadium on 10-31-64

167 yards from scrimmage by Art Graham in the 25–24 victory over the Houston Oilers at Fenway Park on 11-06-64

170 yards from scrimmage by Stanley Morgan in the 35–14 rout of the Baltimore Colts at Memorial Stadium on 11-26-78

193 yards from scrimmage by Stanley Morgan in the 30–27 overtime loss to the Miami Dolphins at Schaefer Stadium on 11-08-81

193 yards from scrimmage by Terry Glenn in the 23–9 victory over the Steelers at Three Rivers Stadium on 12-06-98

214 yards from scrimmage by Terry Glenn in the 19–7 victory over the Browns at Cleveland Stadium on 10-03-99

The progression of the most yards from scrimmage by a Patriots Tight End in a regular season game

65 yards from scrimmage by Oscar Lofton in the 28–24 victory over the New York Titans at the Polo Grounds on 09-17-60

149 yards from scrimmage by Tony Romeo in the 24–24 tie with the Kansas City Chiefs at Fenway Park on 11-17-63

161 yards from scrimmage by Ben Coates in the 39–35 loss to the Miami Dolphins at Joe Robbie Stadium on 09-04-94

The progression of the most yards from scrimmage by a Patriots Running Back in a regular season game

69 yards from scrimmage by Jim Crawford in the 13–10 loss to the Denver Broncos at BU Field on 09-09-60

103 yards from scrimmage by Dick Christy in the 13–0 loss to the Buffalo Bills at BU Field on 09-23-60

112 yards from scrimmage by Alan Miller in the 27–14 loss to the Oakland Raiders at Kezar Stadium on 10-16-60

168 yards from scrimmage by Ron Burton in the 31–24 loss to the Denver Broncos at Bears Stadium on 10-23-60

184 yards from scrimmage by Dick Christy in the 34–28 victory over the Oakland Raiders at BU Field on 11-04-60

208 yards from scrimmage by Jim Nance in the 24–21 win over the Oakland Raiders at Fenway Park on 10-30-66

217 yards from scrimmage by Tony Collins in the 23–13 victory over the New York Jets at Sullivan Stadium on 09-18-83

The progression of the most yards from scrimmage by a Patriots player in a regular season

700 total yards from scrimmage by Alan Miller, who had 416 yards rushing and 284 yards receiving in 1960

794 total yards from scrimmage by Jim Colclough, who had 37 yards rushing and 757 yards receiving in 1961

1,009 total yards from scrimmage by Ron Burton, who had 548 yards rushing and 461 yards receiving in 1962

1,168 total yards from scrimmage by Larry Garron, who had 750 yards rushing and 418 yards receiving in 1963

1,561 total yards from scrimmage by Jim Nance, who had 1,458 yards rushing and 103 yards receiving in 1966

1,748 total yards from scrimmage by Curtis Martin, who had 1,487 yards rushing and 261 yards receiving in 1995

The progression of the most yards from scrimmage by a Patriots Quarterback in a regular season

44 yards from scrimmage by Tom Greene in 1960

183 yards from scrimmage by Babe Parilli in 1961

200 yards from scrimmage by Babe Parilli in 1965

210 yards from scrimmage by Jim Plunkett in 1971

230 yards from scrimmage by Jim Plunkett in 1972

397 yards from scrimmage by Steve Grogan in 1976

539 yards from scrimmage by Steve Grogan in 1978

Jim Plunkett talking to head coach John Mazur

The progression of the most yards from scrimmage by a Patriots Wide Receiver in a regular season

666 yards from scrimmage by Jim Colclough, who had 666 yards receiving in 1960

794 yards from scrimmage by Jim Colclough, who had 757 yards receiving and 37 yards rushing in 1961

882 yards from scrimmage by Jim Colclough, who had 868 yards receiving and 14 yards rushing in 1962

1,025 yards from scrimmage by Harold Jackson, who had 1,013 yards receiving and 12 yards rushing in 1979

1,041 yards from scrimmage by Stanley Morgan, who had 1,002 yards receiving and 39 yards rushing in 1979

1,050 yards from scrimmage by Stanley Morgan, who had 1,029 yards receiving and 21 yards rushing in 1981

1,491 yards from scrimmage by Stanley Morgan, who had 1,491 yards receiving in 1986

1,493 yards from scrimmage by Randy Moss, who had 1,493 yards receiving in 2007

The progression of the most yards from scrimmage by a Patriots Tight End in a regular season

360 yards from scrimmage by Oscar Lofton in 1960

608 yards from scrimmage by Tony Romeo in 1962

651 yards from scrimmage by Jim Whalen in 1967

Randy Moss

718 yards from scrimmage by Jim Whalen in 1968

808 yards from scrimmage by Don Hasselbeck in 1981

808 yards from scrimmage by Marv Cook in 1991

1,174 yards from scrimmage by Ben Coates in 1994

The progression of the most career yards from scrimmage by a Patriots player

5,052 career yards from scrimmage by Jim Colclough during the 1960–68 seasons

5,483 career yards from scrimmage by Larry Garron during the 1960–68 seasons

6,167 career yards from scrimmage by Jim Nance during the 1965–71 seasons

7,358 career yards from scrimmage by Sam Cunningham during the 1973–79 and 1981–82 seasons

Sam Cunningham

10,479 career yards from scrimmage by Stanley Morgan during the 1977–89 seasons

Combined Yards Rushing and Receiving

The only Patriots Quarterback with positive yards rushing and yards receiving in a regular season game

Matt Cavanaugh had 17 yards rushing and caught an eight-yard pass in the 27–21 overtime loss to Pittsburgh on 09-27-81

The progression of the most yards rushing and receiving by Patriots Running Back in a regular season game

69 total yards by Jim Crawford, who had 29 yards rushing and 40 yards receiving in the 13–10 loss to Denver on 09-09-60

103 total yards by Dick Christy, who had 93 yards rushing and 10 yards receiving in the 13–0 loss to Buffalo on 09-23-60

112 total yards by Alan Miller, who had 94 yards rushing and 18 yards receiving in the 27–14 loss to Oakland on 10-16-60

168 total yards by Ron Burton, who had 127 yards rushing and 41 yards receiving in the 31–24 loss to Denver on 10-23-60

184 total yards by Dick Christy, who had 60 yards rushing and 124 yards receiving in the 34–28 win over Oakland on 11-04-60

189 total yards by Don Calhoun, who had 177 yards rushing and 12 yards receiving in the 38–14 rout of Denver on 11-28-76

217 total yards by Tony Collins, who had 212 yards rushing and five yards receiving in the 23–13 win over the Jets on 09-18-83

The progression of the most yards rushing and receiving by a Patriots Wide Receiver in a regular season game

31 total yards by Jim Colclough, who had a 16-yard run and 15 yards receiving in the 18–17 win over Dallas on 10-29-61

88 total yards by Jim Colclough, who had a 16-yard run and 72 yards receiving in the 35–21 win over Oakland on 12-09-61

97 total yards by Gino Cappelletti, who had a two-yard run and 95 yards receiving in the 40–21 win over Denver on 10-18-63

98 total yards by Randy Vataha, who had a five-yard run and 93 yards receiving in the 41–26 loss to Oakland on 12-01-74

Randy Vataha

125 yards by Harold Jackson, who had a seven-yard run and 118 yards receiving in the 55–21 rout of the New York Jets on 10-29-78

175 yards by Stanley Morgan, who had a five-yard run and 170 yards receiving in the 35–14 rout of Baltimore on 11-26-78

193 yards by Stanley Morgan, who had an 11-yard run and 182 yards receiving in the 30–27 overtime loss to Miami on 11-08-81

The progression of the most yards rushing and receiving by a Patriots Tight End in a regular season game

54 yards by Bob Windsor, who ran for a four-yard loss and had 58 yards receiving in the 24–23 win over Washington on 10-01-72

128 yards by Ben Watson, who ran for 11 yards and had 107 yards receiving in the 34–17 win over Cleveland on 10-07-07

The Most Yards Rushing and Receiving in a Season

The progression of the most yards rushing and receiving by a Patriots Quarterback in a regular season

86 yards rushing and receiving by Steve Grogan, who had 49 yards rushing and 27 yards receiving in 1981

101 yards rushing and receiving by Matt Cavanaugh, who had 92 yards rushing and nine yards receiving in 1981

The progression of the most yards rushing and receiving by a Patriots Running Back in a regular season

700 yards rushing and receiving by Alan Miller, who had 416 yards rushing and 284 yards receiving in 1960

794 yards rushing and receiving by Billy Lott, who had 461 yards rushing and 333 yards receiving in 1961

1,009 yards rushing and receiving by Ron Burton, who had 548 yards rushing and 461 yards receiving in 1962

1,168 yards rushing and receiving by Larry Garron, who had 750 yards rushing and 418 yards receiving in 1963

1,561 yards rushing and receiving by Jim Nance, who had 1,458 yards rushing and 103 yards receiving in 1966

1,748 yards rushing and receiving by Curtis Martin, who had 1,487 yards rushing and 261 yards receiving in 1995

The progression of the most yards rushing and receiving by a Patriots Wide Receiver in a regular season

794 yards rushing and receiving by Jim Colclough, who had 37 yards rushing and 757 yards receiving in 1961

882 yards rushing and receiving by Jim Colclough, who had 14 yards rushing and 868 yards receiving in 1962

1,025 yards rushing and receiving by Harold Jackson, who had 12 yards rushing and 1,013 yards receiving in 1979

1,041 yards rushing and receiving by Stanley Morgan, who had 39 yards rushing and 1,002 yards receiving in 1979

1,050 yards rushing and receiving by Stanley Morgan, who had 21 yards rushing and 1,029 yards receiving in 1981

1,174 yards rushing and receiving by Terry Glenn, who had 42 yards rushing and 1,132 yards receiving in 1996

1,209 yards rushing and receiving by Wes Welker, who had 34 yards rushing and 1,175 yards receiving in 2007

The progression of the most yards rushing and receiving by a Patriots Tight End in a regular season

379 yards rushing and receiving by Bob Windsor, who lost four yards rushing and 383 yards receiving in 1972

379 yards rushing and receiving by Russ Francis, who had 12 yards rushing and 367 yards receiving in 1976

1,174 yards rushing and receiving by Ben Coates, who had one carry for no gain and 1,174 yards receiving in 1994

The Most Career Yards Rushing and Receiving

The progression of the most career yards rushing and receiving by a Patriots player

5,052 career yards rushing and receiving by Jim Colclough during the 1960–68 seasons

5,483 career yards rushing and receiving by Larry Garron during the 1960–68 seasons

6,167 career yards rushing and receiving by Jim Nance during the 1965–71 seasons

7,358 career yards rushing and receiving by Sam Cunningham during the 1973–79 and 1981–82 seasons

10,479 career yards rushing and receiving by Stanley Morgan during the 1977–89 seasons

The Most Yards Passing and Rushing in a Game

The progression of the most yards passing and rushing by a Patriots Quarterback in a regular season game

147 total yards passing and rushing by Butch Songin in the 13–10 loss to the Denver Broncos on 09-09-60

177 total yards passing and rushing by Butch Songin in the 35–0 shutout of the Los Angeles Chargers on 10-08-60

371 total yards passing and rushing by Butch Songin in the 37–21 loss to the Houston Oilers on 12-18-60

400 total yards passing and rushing by Babe Parilli in the 43–43 tie with the Oakland Raiders on 10-16-64

438 total yards passing and rushing by Tony Eason in the 38–31 loss to the Seattle Seahawks on 09-21-86

441 total yards passing and rushing by Drew Bledsoe in the 26–23 win over the Buffalo Bills on 11-23-98

462 total yards by Matt Cassel, who had 400 yards passing and 62 yards rushing in the 34–31 overtime loss to the New York Jets on 11-13-08

Drew Bledsoe

The progression of the most yards passing and rushing by a Patriots Running Back in a regular season game

132 total yards passing and rushing by Dick Christy in the 13–0 loss to the Buffalo Bills on 09-23-60

179 total yards by Larry Garron, who had 39 yards passing and 140 yards rushing in the 26–16 win over the Raiders on 10-26-62

The progression of the most yards passing and receiving by a Patriots player in a regular season game

49 total yards passing and receiving by Dick Christy in the 13–0 loss to the Buffalo Bills on 09-23-60

60 total yards passing and receiving by Larry Garron in the 26–16 victory over the Oakland Raiders on 10-26-62

277 total yards passing and receiving by Steve Grogan in the 29–28 loss to the Baltimore Colts on 09-06-81

334 total yards by Matt Cavanaugh, who had 328 yards passing and eight receiving in the 27–21 overtime loss to Pittsburgh on 09-27-81

The Most Yards Passing and Receiving in a Season

The progression of the most yards passing and receiving by a Patriots player in a season

362 total yards passing and receiving by Dick Christy in 1960

795 total yards passing and receiving by Gino Cappelletti in 1961

1,886 total yards passing and receiving by Steve Grogan in 1981

2,403 total yards passing and receiving by Steve Grogan in 1983

3,498 total yards passing and receiving by Drew Bledsoe in 1995

The Most Career Yards Passing and Receiving

The progression of the most career yards passing and receiving by a Patriots player

362 career yards passing and receiving by Dick Christy in 1960

4,616 career yards passing and receiving by Gino Cappelletti during the 1960–70 seasons

26,903 career yards passing and receiving by Steve Grogan during the 1975–90 seasons

29,648 career yards passing and receiving by Drew Bledsoe during the 1993–2001 seasons

The Most Career Yards (Either by Rushing or Receiving) and Special Teams Return Yards

The progression of the most career yards rushing, receiving, and returning punts and kickoffs by a Patriots Wide Receiver

318 career yards by Bobby Leo, who had seven yards rushing, 25 receiving, 54 punt return yards, and 232 kickoff return yards

490 career yards by Hubie Bryant, who had one yard rushing, 212 receiving, 24 punt return yards, and 252 kickoff return yards

2,450 career yards by Darryl Stingley, who had 244 rushing, 1,883 receiving, 136 punt return yards, and 187 kickoff return yards

11,468 career yards by Stanley Morgan, who had 127 rushing, 10,352 receiving, 960 punt return yards, and 29 kickoff return yards

The progression of the most career yards rushing, receiving, and returning punts and kickoffs by a Patriots Running Back

1,321 career yards from scrimmage and special teams return yards by Dick Christy in 1960

4,249 career yards from scrimmage and special teams return yards by Ron Burton during the 1960–65 seasons

7,805 career yards from scrimmage and special teams return yards by Larry Garron during the 1960–68 seasons

8,353 career yards from scrimmage and special teams return yards by Tony Collins during the 1981–87 seasons

11,329 career yards from scrimmage and special teams return yards by Kevin Faulk during the 1999–2008 seasons

The Most Yards Receiving and Advancing an Offensive Fumble Recovery

The most total yards receiving and yards advancing a fumble by a Patriots Wide Receiver in a regular season game

173 yards by Irving Fryar, who had 165 yards receiving and advanced a fumble eight yards in the 30–21 loss to the Jets on 10-04-92

The progression of the most yards receiving and yards advancing a fumble by a Patriots player in a season

767 total yards by Jim Colclough, who had 757 yards receiving and advanced a fumble 10 yards in 1961

869 total yards by Gino Cappelletti, who had 865 yards receiving and advanced a fumble four yards in 1964

994 total yards by Stanley Morgan, who had 991 yards receiving and advanced a fumble three yards in 1980

The progression of the most yards rushing and yards advancing a fumble by a Patriots player in a season

184 total yards by Babe Parilli, who had 183 yards rushing and advanced a fumble one yard for a TD in 1961

639 total yards by Ron Burton, who had 548 yards rushing and advanced his own fumble 91 yards for a TD in 1962

Babe Parilli

1,172 total yards by John Stephens, who had 1,168 yards rushing and advanced a fumble four yards in 1988

The progression of the most yards passing and yards advancing a fumble by a Patriots player in a season

1,315 total yards by Babe Parilli, who had 1,314 yards passing and advanced a fumble one yard for a TD in 1961

1,909 total yards by Steve Grogan, who had 1,903 yards passing and advanced a fumble six yards for a TD in 1976

The progression of the most special teams return yards and yards advancing a fumble by a Patriots player in a season

451 total yards by Ron Burton, who had 122 punt return yards, 238 kickoff return yards, and 91 fumble advancement yards in 1962

747 total yards by Troy Brown, who had 672 kickoff return yards and advanced a fumble 75 yards for a TD in 1995

The most yards passing and advancing a lateral by a Patriots player in a regular season game

14 total yards by Dick Christy, who threw a nine-yard pass and advanced a lateral five yards in the 42–14 rout of Dallas on 11-18-60

The progression of the most yards receiving and yards advancing a lateral in a regular season game

7 total yards by Dick Christy, who had two yards receiving and advanced a lateral five yards in the 42–14 rout of Dallas on 11-18-60

34 total yards by Gino Cappelletti, who had 20 yards receiving and advanced a lateral 14 yards in the 43–43 tie on 10-16-64

87 total yards by Ron Burton, who had 80 yards receiving and advanced a lateral seven yards in the 43–43 tie on 10-16-64

173 total yards by Irving Fryar, who had 165 yards receiving and advanced a lateral eight yards in 30–21 loss to the Jets on 10-04-92

The progression of the most yards rushing and yards advancing a lateral in a regular season game

28 total yards by Dick Christy, who had 23 yards rushing and advanced a lateral five yards in the 42–14 rout of Dallas on 11-18-60

39 total yards by Ron Burton, who had 32 yards rushing and advanced a lateral seven yards in the 43–43 with Oakland on 10-16-64

185 total yards by Leonard Russell, who had 116 yards rushing and advanced a lateral 69 yards in the two-point win on 10-10-93

The most special teams return yards and yards advancing a lateral in a regular season game

43 total yards by Dick Christy, who had 38 kickoff return yards and advanced a lateral five yards in the 28-point win on 11-18-60

Interception Returns—and Lateral Advancements

Every Patriots Linebacker with interception return yards and yards advancing a lateral during his career

John Bramlett had 42 interception return yards and advanced a lateral 17 yards over the 1969–70 seasons

Andre Tippett had 10 interception return yards and advanced a lateral 32 yards over the 1982–93 seasons

Willie McGinest had 90 interception return yards and advanced a lateral 20 yards over the 1994–2005 seasons

Every Defensive Back who had interception return yards and yards advancing a lateral during his career with the Patriots

Clyde Washington had 58 interception return yards and advanced a lateral one yard during the 1960–61 seasons

Gino Cappelletti had 61 interception return yards and advanced a lateral 14 yards during the 1960–64 seasons

Mike Haynes had 388 interception return yards and advanced a lateral 65 yards during the 1976–82 seasons

Rick Sanford had 198 interception return yards and advanced a lateral 27 lateral yards during the 1979–84 seasons

Jim Bowman had three interception return yards and advanced a lateral four yards during the 1985–89 seasons

Ricky Reynolds had 22 interception return yards and advanced a lateral two yards during the 1994–96 seasons

Punt Return Yards and Yards Rushing

Every Patriots player who has led the team in punt return yards and yards rushing in the same season

1962 regular season

Ron Burton had 122 punt return yards and 548 yards rushing in 1962

1971 regular season

Carl Garrett had 124 punt return yards and 784 yards rushing in 1971

1974 regular season

Mack Herron had 517 punt return yards and 824 yards rushing in 1974

Punt Return Yards and Yards From Scrimmage

Every Patriots who has led the team in punt return yards and net yards from scrimmage in the same season

1962 regular season

Ron Burton had 122 punt return yards and 1,009 net yards from scrimmage in 1962

1969 regular season

Carl Garrett had 159 punt return yards and 958 yards from scrimmage in 1969

1971 regular season

Carl Garrett had 124 punt return yards and 1,049 net yards from scrimmage in 1971

1972 regular season

Carl Garrett had 36 punt return yards and 898 net yards from scrimmage in 1972

1974 regular season

Mack Herron had 517 punt return yards and 1,298 net yards from scrimmage in 1974

2001 championship season

Troy Brown had 413 punt return yards and 1,290 net yards from scrimmage in 2001

Punt Return Yards and Yards Receiving

Every Patriots Wide Receiver who has led the team in punt return yards and yards receiving in the same season

1981 regular season

Stanley Morgan had 116 punt return yards and 1,029 yards receiving to lead the team in 1981

2001 championship season

Troy Brown had 413 punt return yards and 1,199 yards receiving to lead the team in 2001

2002 regular season

Troy Brown had 175 punt return yards and 890 yards receiving to lead the team in 2002

The only Patriots Wide Receiver to lead team in punt return yards and net yards from scrimmage in the same season

Troy Brown had 413 punt return yards and 1,290 net yards from scrimmage to lead the team in 2001

Troy Brown

Kickoff Return Yards and Yards Rushing

Every Patriots player who has led the team in kickoff return yards and yards rushing in the same season

1963 regular season

Larry Garron had 693 kickoff return yards and 750 rushing yards in 1963

1971 regular season

Carl Garrett had 538 kickoff return yards and 784 yards rushing in 1971

1974 regular season

Mack Herron had 629 kickoff return yards and 824 yards rushing in 1974

1981 regular season

Tony Collins had 773 kickoff return yards and 873 yards rushing in 1981

2000 regular season

Kevin Faulk had 816 kickoff return yards and 570 yards rushing in 2000

Patriot Players Who Have Scored an Offensive TD and a Special Teams TD

Every Patriots Receiver who has caught a TD pass and returned a punt for a TD in the same game

1979 regular season

Stanley Morgan caught a 25-yard TD pass and returned a punt 80 yards for a TD in the 50–21 rout of the Colts on 11-18-79

1985 regular season

Irving Fryar caught a five-yard TD pass and returned a punt 77 yards for a TD in the 34–15 rout of the Colts on 11-10-85

The only Patriots player with at least one TD reception and a missed field goal return for a TD in the same season

Ron Burton caught four TD passes and returned a missed field goal 91 yards for a TD during the 1962 season

The only Patriots player with at least one TD run and a missed field goal return for a TD in the same season

Ron Burton ran for two TDs and returned a missed field goal 91 yards for a TD during the 1962 season

The progression of the most offensive TDs and special teams return TDs by a Patriots player in a season

6 total TDs by Larry Garron, who had two rushing TDs, three TD receptions, and one kickoff return for a TD in 1961

7 total TDs by Ron Burton, who has two rushing TDs, four TD receptions, and one special teams return for a TD in 1962

13 total TDs by Stanley Morgan, who had 11 TD receptions and a punt return for a TD in 1979

The progression of the most career offensive TDs and special teams return TDs by a Patriots player

19 career TDs by Ron Burton, who had nine rushing TDs, eight TD receptions, and two special teams TDs over the 1960–65 seasons

42 career TDs by Larry Garron, who had 14 rushing TDs, 26 TD receptions, and two kickoff returns for a TD from 1960-1968

68 career TDs by Stanley Morgan, who had 67 TD receptions and a punt return for a TD during the 1977–89 seasons

Every Patriots Receiver Who Scored on the Ground and Through the Air in the Same Regular Season Game

Every Patriots Wide Receiver who has run for a TD and caught a TD pass in the same game

1977 regular season

Darryl Stingley ran for a 34-yard TD and caught a 21-yard TD pass in the 21–17 win over the Chiefs on 09-18-77

1985 regular season

Irving Fryar ran for an eight-yard TD and caught a 13-yard TD pass in the fourth quarter of the 20–13 win over Seattle on 11-17-85

2001 championship season

David Patten ran for a 29-yard TD and caught two TD passes in the 38–17 rout of the Indianapolis Colts on 10-21-01

The progression of the most rushing TDs and TD receptions by a Patriots player in a season

6 TDs by Dick Christy, who had four rushing TDs and two TD receptions in 1960

11 TDs by Billy Lott, who had five rushing TDs and six TD receptions in 1961

11 TDs by Sam Cunningham, who had nine rushing TDs and two TD receptions in 1974

12 TDs by Mack Herron, who had seven rushing TDs and five TD receptions in 1974

15 TDs by Curtis Martin, who had 14 rushing TDs and one TD reception in 1995

Curtis Martin

17 TDs by Curtis Martin, who had 14 rushing TDs and three TD receptions in 1996

The progression of the most career regular season rushing TDs and TD receptions by a Patriots player

17 total TDs by Ron Burton, who had nine rushing TDs and eight TD receptions over the 1960–65 seasons

40 total TDs by Larry Garron, who had 14 rushing TDs and 26 TD receptions over the 1960–68 seasons

46 total TDs by Jim Nance, who had 45 rushing TDs and one TD reception over the 1965–71 seasons

49 total TDs by Sam Cunningham, who had 43 rushing TDs and six TD receptions over his nine-year career

Patriot Players Who Have Scored a Defensive TD and a Special Teams TD

The only Patriots player who has returned a blocked punt for a TD and returned a pass for a TD in the same game

Don Webb returned an interception 31 yards for a TD and returned the punt he blocked 20 yards for a TD on 12-17-61

The most defensive TDs and special teams return TDs scored by a Patriots player in a regular season

4 TDs by Don Webb, who returned two interceptions for a TD, a fumble for a TD, and a blocked punt for a TD in 1961

The progression of the most career defensive TDs and special teams return TDs by a Patriots player

4 total TDs by Don Webb, who returned two interceptions for a TD, a fumble for a TD, and a blocked punt for a TD

5 total TDs by Tedy Bruschi, who has returned four interceptions for a TD and a blocked punt for a TD

Blocked Punts and Interceptions

Every Patriots Defensive Back who has blocked a punt and intercepted a pass in the same regular season game

Don Webb blocked a Paul Maguire punt and intercepted a Jack Kemp pass in the 41–0 shutout of the San Diego Chargers on 12-17-61

The most blocked punts and interceptions by a Patriots player in a season

6 by Don Webb, who blocked a punt and had five interceptions in 1961

The progression of the most career blocked punts and interceptions by a Patriots player

22 by Don Webb, who blocked a punt and had 21 career interceptions during the 1961–70 seasons

28 by Maurice Hurst, who blocked a punt and had 27 career interceptions during the 1989–95 seasons

Blocked Extra Points and Interceptions

The most blocked extra points and interceptions by a Patriots player in a season

5 by Nick Buoniconti, who blocked an extra-point attempt and had four interceptions in 1966

The progression of the most career blocked extra point points and interceptions by a Patriots player

17 by Tom Addison, who blocked an extra point and had 16 career interceptions over the 1960–67 seasons

25 by Nick Buoniconti, who blocked an extra point and had 24 career interceptions over the 1962–68 seasons

Blocked Field Goals and Interceptions

The most blocked field-goal attempts and interceptions by a Patriots player in a season

5 by Harry Jacobs, who blocked a field-goal attempt and had four interceptions in 1960

27 by Nick Buoniconti, who blocked three field-goal attempts and had 24 interceptions during the 1962–68 seasons

The progression of the most career blocked field-goal attempts and interceptions by a Patriots player

5 by Harry Jacobs, who blocked a field-goal attempt and had four interceptions in 1960

26 by Nick Buoniconti, who blocked two field-goal attempts and had 24 career interceptions over the 1962–68 seasons

Special Teams Returns and Quarterback Sacks

The only Patriots Defensive Back who has returned a kickoff and recorded a Quarterback sack in the same game

Raymond Clayborn had 116 kickoff return yards and sacked Steve Bartkowski in the 16–10 win over Atlanta on 12-04-77

Every Patriots Linebacker who has returned a kickoff and recorded a Quarterback sack in the same game

1965 regular season
Mike Dukes returned a kickoff nine yards and shared in a sack of Joe Namath in the 27–23 win over the Jets on 11-28-65

2003 championship season
Mike Vrabel returned a kickoff eight yards and sacked Chad Pennington in the 21–16 win over the New York Jets on 12-20-03

2006 regular season
Tully Banta-Cain returned a kickoff nine yards and sacked David Carr twice in the 40–7 rout of the Houston Texans on 12-17-06

2007 undefeated regular season
Mike Vrabel returned a kickoff three yards and had three strip sacks in the 52–7 rout of the Washington Redskins on 10-28-07

The only Patriots Defensive Lineman who has returned a kickoff and recorded a Quarterback sack in the same game

Bob Dee returned a kickoff 14 yards and sacked Johnny Green in the 24–17 win over the New York Titans on 11-30-62

The only Patriots Lineman who has recovered an onside kick and sacked the Quarterback in the same game

Bob Dee recovered an onside kick by George Blair and he sacked John Hadl in the 33–28 win over San Diego on 09-20-64

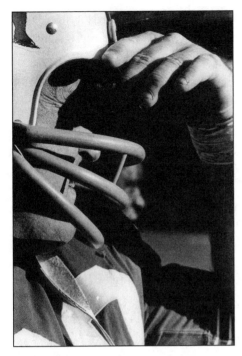

Bob Dee

The only Patriots Lineman who has recovered a squibbed kickoff and sacked the Quarterback in the same game

Bobby Hamilton recovered a squibbed kickoff and sacked Shane Matthews in the 24–17 loss to the Bears on 12-10-00

Every Patriots Defensive Back who has returned a kickoff and recorded a Quarterback sack during the regular season

Ray Clayborn and Chris Canty have returned a kickoff and recorded a sack (Chris Canty did it in consecutive seasons)

Every Patriots Defensive Lineman who has recorded a sack and returned a kickoff in the same regular season

Ron Berger, Bob Dee, Chad Eaton, Dan Klecko, and Chris Sullivan (Chris Sullivan did it twice)

Kickoff Returns, Sacks, and Interceptions

Every Patriots Linebacker who has returned a kickoff, recorded a sack, and intercepted a pass in the same season

1974 regular season
Sam Hunt returned a kickoff 21 yards, had 1.5 quarterback sacks, and returned three interceptions for 66 yards during the 1974 season

1986 regular season
Johnny Rembert returned three kickoffs for 27 yards, had four sacks, and returned an interception 37 yards during the 1986 season

2001 championship season
Tedy Bruschi returned a kickoff 10 yards, had two sacks, and returned two interceptions for seven yards during the 2001 season

2002 regular season
Tedy Bruschi returned a kickoff 11 yards, had 4.5 sacks, and returned two interceptions for 75 yards and two TDs in the 2002 season

2003 championship season
Tedy Bruschi returned a kickoff nine yards, had two sacks, and returned three interceptions for 26 yards and two TDs in the 2003 season

2004 championship season
Tully Banta-Cain returned a kickoff 21 yards, had 1.5 sacks, and returned an interception four yards during the 2004 season

The Playoffs

The only Patriots player who has run, caught a pass, and scored on a two-point conversion in a playoff game

Super Bowl XXXVIII
Kevin Faulk had six carries for 42 yards, four receptions for 19 yards, and ran for a two-point conversion in the three-point win on 02-01-04

2006 AFC Divisional playoff game
Kevin Faulk had six carries for 25 yards, two receptions for 11 yards, and ran for a two-point conversion in the three-point win on 01-14-07

Yards Rushing, Receiving and Returning

The only Patriots player who has run, caught a pass, returned a punt, and a kickoff in a playoff game

1996 AFC Championship Game
Dave Meggett had three carries, three receptions, three punt returns, and three kickoff returns yards in the 20–6 victory on 01-12-97

Super Bowl XXXI

Dave Meggett had one carry, three receptions, four punt returns, and five kickoff returns in the 14-point loss on 01-26-97

The only Patriots player who has caught a pass and returned a punt for a TD in a playoff game

Troy Brown had eight receptions for 121 yards and returned three punts for 80 yards, including one for a 55-yard TD, on 01-27-02

The only Patriots player who has caught a TD pass and returned a kickoff in a playoff game

Bethel Johnson caught a 41-yard TD pass (on the Patriots first drive) and returned a kickoff 16 yards in the three-point win on 01-10-04

The progression of the most yards rushing, receiving, and returning on special teams by a Patriots player in the playoffs

217 total yards by Larry Garron, who had 59 yards rushing, 126 yards receiving, and 32 kickoff return yards in two playoff games

325 total yards by Stanley Morgan, who had minus-2 yards rushing, 321 yards receiving, and six punt return yards in seven playoff games

397 total yards by Dave Meggett, who had 29 yards rushing, 34 yards receiving, 165 punt return yards, and 169 kickoff return yards

1,050 total yards by Troy Brown, who lost 19 yards rushing, had 694 yards receiving, and 375 special teams return yards

The most offensive TDs and special teams TDs by a Patriots player in the playoffs

3 TDs by Troy Brown, who had two TD receptions and returned a punt for a TD in 20 playoff games

The Most Yards from Scrimmage and Special Teams Return Yards

The progression of the most yards from scrimmage and special teams return yards by a Patriots player in a playoff game

56 yards by Art Graham, who had 22 yards receiving and 34 punt return yards in the 26–8 win over Buffalo on 12-28-63

77 yards by Harry Crump, who had 18 yards rushing, 28 receiving, and 31 kickoff return yards in the 51–10 loss to San Diego on 01-05-64

79 yards by Jess Phillips, who had 12 yards rushing and 67 kickoff return yards in the 24–21 loss to Oakland on 12-18-76

192 yards by Stephen Starring, who had 39 receiving and 153 kickoff return yards in the 46–10 loss to the Bears on 01-26-86

201 yards by Troy Brown, who had 121 yards receiving and 80 punt return yards in the 24–17 win over Pittsburgh on 01-27-02

The progression of the most yards from scrimmage and special teams yards by a Patriots player in the playoffs

124 total yards by Art Graham, who had 90 yards receiving and 34 punt return yards in two playoff games

217 total yards by Larry Garron, who had 59 yards rushing, 126 yards receiving, and 32 kickoff return yards in two games

325 total yards by Stanley Morgan, who had 321 yards receiving, six punt return yards, and lost two yards rushing in seven games

354 total yards by Stephen Starring, who had 39 yards receiving and 315 kickoff return yards in five playoff games

397 total yards by Dave Meggett, who had 29 yards rushing, 34 yards receiving, and 334 special teams return yards in five games

1,050 yards by Troy Brown, who had 694 yards receiving, minus-19 yards rushing, 315 kickoff return yards, and 60 punt return yards in 20 games

The Most Yards Receiving and Returning Punts

The progression of the most yards receiving and returning punts by a Patriots Wide Receiver in a playoff game

56 yards by Art Graham, who had a 22-yard reception and 34 punt return yards in the 26–8 win over Buffalo on 12-28-63

59 yards by Irving Fryar, who had 47 yards receiving and 12 punt return yards in the 26–14 win over the New York Jets on 12-28-85

73 yards by Troy Brown, who had 46 yards receiving and 27 punt return yards in the 25–10 loss to Jacksonville on 01-03-99

92 yards by Troy Brown, who had 43 yards receiving and 49 punt return yards in the 16–13 overtime win vs Oakland on 01-19-02

201 yards by Troy Brown, who had 121 yards receiving and 80 punt return yards in the 24–17 win over Pittsburgh on 01-27-02

The most yards receiving and returning punts by a Patriots Running Back in a playoff game

44 yards by Dave Meggett, who had 15 yards receiving and 29 punt return yards in the 14-point win vs the Jacksonville Jaguars on 01-12-97

The Most Yards Rushing and Returning Punts

The most yards rushing and returning punts by a Patriots player in a playoff game

90 yards by Dave Meggett, who had 18 yards rushing and 72 punt return yards in the 28–3 win over Pittsburgh on 01-05-97

The Most Yards Receiving and Returning Kickoffs

The most yards receiving and returning kickoffs by a Patriots Wide Receiver in a playoff game

192 yards by Stephen Starring, who had 39 receiving and 153 kickoff return yards in the 46–10 loss to the Bears on 01-26-86

The progression of the most yards receiving and returning kickoffs by a Patriots Running Back in a playoff game

59 yards by Harry Crump, who had 28 yards receiving and 31 kickoff return yards in the 41-point loss to San Diego on 01-05-64

67 yards by Dave Meggett, who had 15 yards receiving and 52 kickoff return yards in the 14-point win over Jacksonville on 01-12-97

125 yards by Dave Meggett, who had eight yards receiving and 117 kickoff return yards in the 14-point loss to Green Bay on 01-26-97

Defensive Fumble Recoveries and Kickoff Returns

The only Patriots player with two defensive fumble recoveries and a kickoff return in the same playoff game

Tedy Bruschi had two fumbles recoveries and returned a kickoff 15 yards in the 20–3 rout of the Colts on 01-16-05

The Most Yards Rushing and Receiving

The progression of the most yards rushing and receiving by a Patriots Running Back in a playoff game

164 total yards by Larry Garron, who had 44 yards rushing and 120 yards receiving in the 26–8 win over Buffalo on 12-28-63

175 total yards by Curtis Martin, who had 166 yards rushing and nine yards receiving in the 28–3 rout of the Steelers on 01-05-97

The progression of the most yards rushing and receiving by a Patriots Wide Receiver in a playoff game

9 yards by Irving Fryar, who lost two yards rushing and had 11 yards receiving in the 22–17 loss to Denver on 01-04-87

34 yards by Troy Brown, who lost nine yards rushing and had 43 yards receiving in the 16–13 overtime win vs Oakland on 01-19-02

66 yards by Troy Brown, who lost 10 yards rushing and had 76 yards receiving in the 32–29 win over Carolina on 02-01-04

153 yards by Deion Branch, who had 37 yards rushing and 116 yards receiving in the 41–27 win over Pittsburgh on 01-23-05

The only Patriots Wide Receiver who has run for a TD and caught a TD pass in a playoff game

Deion Branch caught a 60-yard TD pass and ran 23 yards for a TD in the 41–27 victory over the Steelers on 01-23-05

The most rushing TDs and TD receptions by a Patriots player in the playoffs

3 TDs by Larry Garron, who ran for one TD and caught two TD passes in two playoff games

3 TDs by Deion Branch, who ran for one TD and caught two TD passes in eight playoff games

The Most Yards From Scrimmage

The progression of the most yards from scrimmage by a Patriots Wide Receiver in a playoff game

109 yards from scrimmage by Gino Cappelletti in the 26–8 victory over the Buffalo Bills at War Memorial Stadium on 12-28-63

121 yards from scrimmage by Troy Brown in the 24–17 victory over the Pittsburgh Steelers at Heinz Field on 01-27-02

143 yards from scrimmage by Deion Branch in the 32–29 win over the Carolina Panthers at Reliant Stadium on 02-01-04

153 yards from scrimmage by Deion Branch in the 41–27 victory over the Pittsburgh Steelers at Heinz Field on 01-23-05

The progression of the most yards from scrimmage by a Patriots Tight End in a playoff game

96 yards from scrimmage by Russ Francis in the 24–21 loss to the Oakland Raiders at the Oakland Coliseum on 12-18-76

101 yards from scrimmage by Russ Francis in the 31–14 loss to the Houston Oilers at Schaefer Stadium on 12-31-78

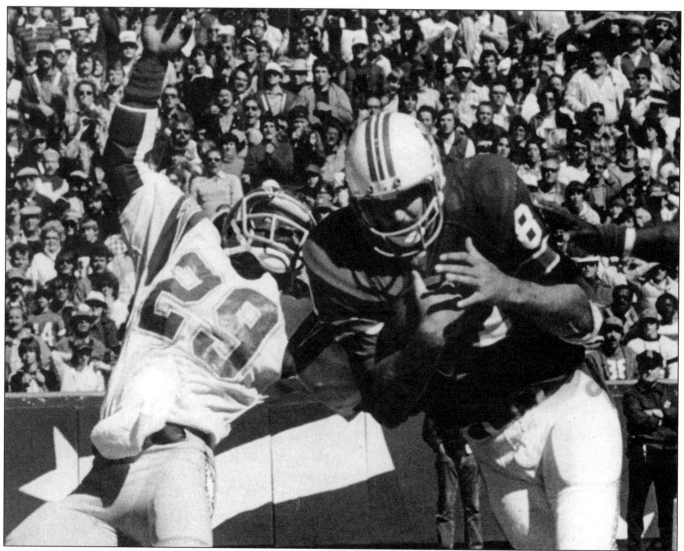

Russ Francis

The progression of the most yards from scrimmage by a Patriots Quarterback in a playoff game

10 yards from scrimmage by Babe Parilli in the 51–10 loss to the San Diego Chargers at Balboa Stadium on 01-05-64

14 yards from scrimmage by Tom Yewcic in the 51–10 loss to the San Diego Chargers at Balboa Stadium on 01-05-64

35 yards from scrimmage by Steve Grogan in the 24–21 loss to the Oakland Raiders at the Oakland Coliseum on 12-18-76

The progression of the most career yards from scrimmage by a Patriots player in the playoffs

185 career yards from scrimmage by Larry Garron, who had 59 yards rushing and 126 yards receiving in two playoff games

197 career yards from scrimmage by Russ Francis, who had 197 yards receiving in two playoff games

319 career yards from scrimmage by Stanley Morgan, who had 321 yards receiving and lost two yards rushing in seven playoff games

380 career yards from scrimmage by Craig James, who had 290 yards rushing and 90 yards receiving in five playoff games

675 career yards from scrimmage by Troy Brown, who had 694 yards receiving and lost 19 yards rushing in 20 playoff games

Interception Return Yards and Special Teams Return Yards

The only Patriots player who has returned an interception and a kickoff in a playoff game

Ellis Hobbs lost three yards returning an interception and returned two kickoffs for 39 yards in the nine-point win over San Diego on 01-20-08

The progression of the most interception return yards and special teams return yards by a Patriots player in the playoffs

27 yards by Tedy Bruschi, who returned an interception 12 yards and returned a kickoff 15 yards in 22 playoff games

Did you know that?

Mark van Eeghen is the only player to run and catch a pass for the Patriots and against the Patriots in the playoffs

Mark van Eeghen rushed for 39 yards and one TD and caught an eight-yard pass for the Oakland Raiders in the 1976 AFC Divisional playoff game against the New England Patriots at the Oakland Coliseum on 12-18-76. As a member of the New England Patriots, Mark rushed for 40 yards and caught a five-yard pass in the 1982 AFC first round playoff game against the Miami Dolphins at the Orange Bowl on 01-08-83.

491 yards by Ellis Hobbs, who returned two passes for 20 yards and 17 kickoffs for 471 yards in eight playoff games

The only Patriots player who has sacked the Quarterback and returned a kickoff in the playoffs

Tedy Bruschi has recorded 4.5 sacks and returned a kickoff 15 yards in 22 playoff games

The alphabetical listing of every former Patriots player who has won a championship on another NFL team

Bobby Abrams was a linebacker on the 1990 New York Giants team and on the 1993 Dallas Cowboys team

Matt Bahr was a kicker on the 1979 Pittsburgh Steelers team and on the 1990 New York Giants team

Rodrigo Barnes was a linebacker on the 1976 Oakland Raiders team

Morris Bradshaw was a wide receiver on the 1976 and the 1980 Oakland Raiders team

Randy Beverly was a defensive back on the 1968 New York Jets team

Eric Bjornson was a tight end on the 1995 Dallas Cowboys team

Greg Boyd was a defensive end on the 1984 San Francisco 49ers team

Marlin Briscoe was a wide receiver on the 1972 and the 1973 Miami Dolphins team

Dave Browning was a defensive end on the 1980 Oakland Raiders team

Nick Buoniconti was a linebacker on the 1972 and the 1973 Miami Dolphins team

Matt Cavanaugh was a backup quarterback on the 1984 San Francisco 49ers team and on the 1990 New York Giants team

Ben Coates was a tight end on the 2000 Baltimore Ravens team

Dick Conn was a defensive back on the 1974 Pittsburgh Steelers team

Jeff Dellenbach was an offensive center on the 1996 Green Bay Packers team

Steve DeOssie was a linebacker of the 1990 New York Giants team

Jeff Feagles was a punter for the 2007 New York Giants team

Russ Francis was a tight end on the 1984 San Francisco 49ers team

Ron Gardin was a return specialist on the 1970 Baltimore Colts team

Carl Garrett was a running back on the 1976 Oakland Raiders team

Sam Gash was a fullback on the 2000 Baltimore Ravens team

Myron Guyton was a defensive back on the 1990 New York Giants team

Don Hasselbeck was a tight end on the 1983 Los Angeles Raiders team

Greg Hawthorne was a running back on the 1979 Pittsburgh Steelers team

Mike Haynes was a cornerback on the 1983 Los Angeles Raiders team

Karl Henke was a defensive tackle on the 1968 New York Jets team

Eddie Hinton was a wide receiver on the 1970 Baltimore Colts team

Ernie Holmes was a defensive lineman on the 1974 and the 1975 Pittsburgh Steelers team

Ed Jenkins was a running back on the 1972 Miami Dolphins team

Shelby Jordan was an offensive tackle on the 1983 Los Angeles Raiders team

Dan Klecko was a lineman on the 2006 Indianapolis Colts team

Bob Kratch was an offensive lineman on the 1990 New York Giants team

Jack Maitland was a running back on the 1970 Baltimore Colts team

Tony McGee was a defensive end on the 1982 Washington Redskins team

Larry McGrew was a linebacker on the 1990 New York Giants team

Steve McMichael was a defensive lineman on the 1985 Chicago Bears team

Dave Meggett was a running back on the 1990 New York Giants team

Sean Morey was a special teams player on the 2005 Pittsburgh Steelers team

Zeke Mowatt was a tight end on the 1986 New York Giants team

Babe Parilli tossed seven TD passes for the 1968 New York Jets team

Jim Plunkett was the quarterback on the 1980 Oakland Raiders team and the Super Bowl MVP of the 1983 Los Angeles Raiders team

Bill Rademacher was a wide receiver on the 1968 New York Jets team

Tom Rehder was an offensive lineman on the 1990 New York Giants team

William Roberts was an offensive lineman on the 1986 and the 1990 New York Giants team

Dave Rowe was a defensive tackle on the 1976 Oakland Raiders team

Reggie Rucker was a wide receiver on the 1971 Dallas Cowboys team

Grey Ruegamer was an offensive lineman on the 2007 New York Giants team

Ron Sellers was a wide receiver on the 1973 Miami Dolphins team

Greg Spires was a defensive lineman on the 2002 Tampa Bay Buccaneers team

Duane Starks was a cornerback for the 2000 Baltimore Ravens team

Fred Steinfort was a kicker on the 1976 Oakland Raiders team

Renya Thompson was a defensive back on the 1990 New York Giants team

Keith Traylor was a defensive tackle for the 1997 and 1998 Denver Broncos team

Bake Turner was a wide receiver on the 1968 New York Jets team

Mark van Eeghen was a running back on the 1976 and the 1980 Oakland Raiders team

Jerrel Wilson was the punter on the 1969 Kansas City Chiefs team

Marc Wilson was a back-up quarterback on the 1980 Oakland Raiders team and on the 1983 Los Angeles Raiders team

Team Records

Throughout this book, we have documented the accomplishments of individual players. Football, however, is the ultimate sport that requires a total team effort. Offense, defense, and special teams must work in harmony with the total objective of winning the game. Certainly you have seen the footage of Patriots head coach Bill Belichik telling his players to "Just do your job." That is what we have done for you. We did our best to get you every relevant fact regarding the positive accomplishments of the Patriots offense, defense, and special teams.

When the Patriots chose to be introduced as a *team* before Super Bowl XXXVI, they made a statement. The ultimate goal of everyone in the organization is to win championships. The sacrifice of individual glory has allowed the Patriots to have a championship driven attitude. This attitude has been prelevant ever since Robert Kraft bought this team in 1994. That championship drive team attitude is established during training camp, encouraged in the locker room, and displayed on the field. Robert Kraft and the Kraft family deserve kudos for changing the culture of the New England Patriots.

The chapter includes the various team records set by the Patriots offense, defense, and special teams. Each section has information regarding various records set in a regular season game, in a playoff game, in a regular season, and in the postseason. We have listed the progression of each of these records, including the most points scored, most TDs scored, most special teams returns, most interceptions, most sacks, and the most fumble recoveries.

The most regular season wins against an opponent
The Patriots have defeated the Buffalo Bills 55 times during the regular season since 1960

The most playoff game victories against an opponent
The Patriots have beaten the Pittsburgh Steelers and the Jacksonville Jaguars three times in the playoffs

The most regular season shutouts against an opponent
The Patriots have shut out the Buffalo Bills and the Miami Dolphins three times in the regular season

The most regular season overtime victories against an opponent
The Patriots have defeated the Indianapolis Colts and the Miami Dolphins three times in overtime during the regular season

The only overtime win by the Patriots in the playoffs
The Patriots defeated the Oakland Raiders 16–13 in overtime at Foxboro Stadium on 01-19-02

Most consecutive victories

The progression of the most consecutive victories against an opponent

2 consecutive victories over the New York Titans in 1960

4 consecutive victories over the Oakland Raiders during the 1960–62 seasons

4 consecutive victories over the Denver Broncos during the 1961–62 seasons

4 consecutive victories over the Houston Oilers during the 1963–64 seasons

5 consecutive victories over the New Orleans Saints during the 1972–86 seasons

11 consecutive victories over the Buffalo Bills during the 1983–87 seasons

(They had 10 consecutive wins over the San Diego Chargers during the 1973–2001 seasons)

The progression of the most consecutive home game regular season victories for the Patriots

3 consecutive home victories in 1960

3 consecutive home victories in 1961

4 consecutive home victories in 1962

4 consecutive home victories in 1963

4 consecutive home victories in 1971

6 consecutive home victories in 1976

6 consecutive home victories in 1985

6 consecutive home victories in 1988

8 consecutive home victories in 2003

8 consecutive home victories in 2004

8 consecutive home victories in 2007

The progression of the most consecutive victories in a regular season for the Patriots

3 consecutive victories during the 1960 season (11-04-60 to 11-18-60)

3 consecutive victories during the 1961 season (10-22-61 to 11-03-61)

4 consecutive victories during the 1961 season (11-17-61 to 12-17-61)

4 consecutive victories during the 1964 season (09-13-64 to 10-04-64)

5 consecutive victories during the 1964 season (11-06-64 to 12-06-64)

5 consecutive victories during the 1974 season (09-15-74 to 10-13-74)

6 consecutive victories during the 1976 season (11-07-76 to 12-12-76)

7 consecutive victories during the 1978 season (09-24-78 to 11-26-78)

7 consecutive victories during the 1986 season (10-19-86 to 11-30-86)

7 consecutive victories during the 1994 season (11-13-94 to 12-24-94)

12 consecutive victories during the 2003 season (10-05-03 to 12-27-03)

16 consecutive regular season victories in 2007

The progression of the most consecutive regular season wins by the Patriots

3 consecutive wins in 1960

3 consecutive wins in 1961

4 consecutive wins in 1961

4 consecutive wins in 1964

5 consecutive wins in 1974

6 consecutive wins in 1976

7 consecutive wins in 1978

7 consecutive wins in 1986

7 consecutive wins in 1994

18 consecutive wins during the 2003 and 2004 regular seasons

21 consecutive wins during the 2006–08 regular seasons

The most consectuve wins by the Patriots including the playoffs

21 consecutive wins during the 2003 and 2004 regular seasons and 2003 playoff season

The most consecutive playoff game victories by the Patriots

10 consecutive playoff game victories by the Patriots

Offensive Scoring Team Records

Most points scored

The progression of the most points scored by the Patriots in a regular season game

10 points scored by the Patriots in the three-point loss to the Denver Broncos on 09-09-60

28 points were scored by the Patriots in the four-point win over the New York Titans on -09-17-60

35 points were scored by the Patriots in the 35-point shutout of the Los Angeles Chargers on 10-08-60

38 points were scored by the Patriots in the 17-point win over the New York Titans on 11-11-60

42 points were scored by the Patriots in the 28-point rout of the Dallas Texans on 11-18-60

45 points were scored by the Patriots in the 28-point rout of the Denver Broncos on 09-16-61

52 points were scored by the Patriots in the 31-point demolition of the Buffalo Bills on 10-22-61

55 points were scored by the Patriots in the 34-point rout of the New York Jets on 10-29-78

56 points were scored by the Patriots in the 53-point win over the New York Jets on 09-09-79

56 points were scored by the Patriots in the 46-point win over the Buffalo Bills on 11-18-07

The progression of the most points scored by the Patriots in a playoff game

26 points were scored by the Patriots in the 18-point win over the Buffalo Bills on 12-28-63

26 points were scored by the Patriots in the 12-point victory over the New York Jets on 12-28-85

27 points were scored by the Patriots in the seven-point win over the Los Angeles Raiders on 01-05-86

31 points were scored by the Patriots in the 17-point victory over the Miami Dolphins on 01-12-86

32 points were scored by the Patriots in the three-point win over the Carolina Panthers on 02-01-04

41 points were scored by the Patriots in the 14-point victory over the Pittsburgh Steelers on 01-23-05

The progression of the most points scored by the Patriots in a regular season

286 points in the 1960 AFL regular season (14-game season)

413 points in the 1961 AFL regular season (14-game season)

441 points in the 1980 NFL regular season (16-game season)

589 points in the 2007 NFL regular season (16-game season)

The progression of the most points scored by the Patriots in a postseason

36 points were scored by the Patriots in the two playoff games of the 1963 AFL season

94 points were scored by the Patriots in the four playoff games of the 1985 NFL season

95 points were scored by the Patriots in the three playoff games of the 2006 NFL Season

Most TDs scored

The progression of the most TDs scored by the Patriots in a regular season game

1 TD was scored by the Patriots in the 13–10 loss to the Denver Broncos at BU Field on 09-09-60

4 TDs were scored by the Patriots in the 28–24 win over the New York Titans at the Polo Grounds on 09-17-60

5 TDs were scored by the Patriots in the 35–0 shutout of the Los Angeles Chargers at the Los Angeles Coliseum on 10-08-60

6 TDs were scored by the Patriots in the 42–14 rout of the Dallas Texans at BU Field on 11-18-60

7 TDs were scored by the Patriots in the 52–21 rout of the Buffalo Bills at BU Field on 10-22-61

7 TDs were scored by the Patriots in the 48–17 rout of the Oakland Raiders at Schaefer Stadium on 10-03-76

8 TDs were scored by the Patriots in the 55–21 rout of the New York Jets at Schaefer Stadium on 10-29-78

8 TDs were scored by the Patriots in the 56–3 demolition of the New York Jets at Schaefer Stadium on 09-09-79

8 TDs were scored by the Patriots in the 56–10 blowout of the Buffalo Bills at Rich Stadium on 11-18-07

The progression of the most TDs scored by the Patriots in a playoff game

2 TDs were scored by the Patriots in the 18-point win over the Buffalo Bills on 12-28-63

3 TDs were scored by the Patriots in the three-point loss to the Oakland Raiders on 12-18-76

3 TDs were scored by the Patriots in the 7-point win over the Oakland Raiders on 01-05-86

4 TDs were scored by the Patriots in the 17-point victory over the Miami Dolphins on 01-12-86

4 TDs were scored by the Patriots in the 25-point rout of the Pittsburgh Steelers on 01-05-97

4 TDs were scored by the Patriots in the three-point win over the Carolina Panthers on 02-01-04

5 TDs were scored by the Patriots in the 14-point victory over the Pittsburgh Steelers on 01-23-05

The progression of the most TDs scored by the Patriots in a regular season

37 TDs were scored by the Boston Patriots in 1960

52 TDs were scored by the Boston Patriots in 1961

52 TDs were scored by the New England Patriots in 1980

74 TDs were scored by the New England Patriots in 2007

The progression of the most TDs scored by the Patriots in a postseason

3 TDs were scored by the Boston Patriots in the 1963 postseason

3 TDs were scored by the New England Patriots in the 1976 postseason

10 TDs were scored by the New England Patriots in the 1985 postseason

10 TDs were scored by the New England Patriots in the 2006 postseason

Most rushing TD's

The progression of the most rushing TDs by the Patriots in a regular season game

1 rushing TD was scored by the Patriots in the 28–24 win over the New York Titans on 09-17-60

3 rushing TDs were scored by the Patriots in the 35–0 shutout of the Los Angeles Chargers on 10-08-60

3 rushing TDs were scored by the Patriots in the 42–28 loss to the Dallas Texans on 09-08-62

4 rushing TDs were scored by the Patriots in the 38–14 rout of the New York Jets on 09-08-63

4 rushing TDs were sccred by the Patriots in the 48–17 rout of the Oakland Raiders on 10-03-76

4 rushing TDs were scored by the Patriots in the 41–7 rout of the New York Jets on 10-18-76

4 rushing TDs were scored by the Patriots in the 33–24 win over the Miami Dolphins on 10-22-78

4 rushing TDs were scored by the Patriots in the 55–21 rout of the New York Jets on 10-29-78

4 rushing TDs were scored by the Patriots in the 37–21 victory over the San Diego Chargers on 10-16-83

The progression of the most rushing TDs by the Patriots in a playoff game

1 rushing TD by the Patriots in the 41-point loss to the San Diego Chargers on 01-05-64

2 rushing TDs by the Patriots in the three-point loss to the Oakland Raiders on 12-18-76

3 rushing TDs by the Patriots in the 25-point rout of the Pittsburgh Steelers on 01-05-97

The progression of the most rushing TDs by the Patriots in a regular season

11 rushing TDs by the Boston Patriots in 1960

15 rushing TDs by the Boston Patriots in 1961

16 rushing TDs by the Boston Patriots in 1963

17 rushing TDs by the Boston Patriots in 1966

21 rushing TDs by the New England Patriots in 1974

24 rushing TDs by the New England Patriots in 1976

30 rushing TDs by the New England Patriots in 1978

The progression of the most rushing TDs by the Patriots in a postseason

1 rushing TD by the Boston Patriots in the 1963 postseason

2 rushing TDs by the New England Patriots in the 1976 postseason

2 rushing TDs by the New England Patriots in the 1985 postseason

5 rushing TDs by the New England Patriots in the 1996 postseason

Most TD passes

The progression of the most TD passes by the Patriots in a regular season game

1 TD pass was completed by the Patriots in the 13–10 loss to the Denver Broncos on 09-09-60

2 TD passes were completed by the Patriots in the 28–24 victory over the New York Titans on 09-17-60

3 TD passes were completed by the Patriots in the 31–24 loss to the Denver Broncos on 10-23-60

3 TD passes were completed by the Patriots in the 34–28 win over the Oakland Raiders on 11-04-60

4 TD passes were thrown by the Patriots in the 38–21 victory over the New York Titans on 11-11-60

4 TD passes were thrown by the Patriots in the 42–14 rout of the Dallas Texans on 11-18-60

5 TD passes were thrown by the Patriots in the 45–17 rout of the Denver Broncos on 09-16-61

5 TD passes were thrown by the Patriots in the 55–21 blowout of the Buffalo Bills on 10-22-61

5 TD passes were thrown by the Patriots in the 36–28 victory over the Buffalo Bills on 11-15-64

6 TD passes were thrown by the Patriots in the 56–3 demolition of the New York Jets on 09-09-79

6 TD passes were thrown by the Patriots in the 49–28 victory over the Miami Dolphins on 10-21-07

The progression of the most TD passes by the Patriots in a playoff game

2 TD passes were thrown by the Patriots in the 18-point victory over the Buffalo Bills on 12-28-63

3 TD passes were thrown by the Patriots in the 17-point victory over the Miami Dolphins on 01-12-86

3 TD passes were thrown by the Patriots in the three-point win over the Carolina Panthers on 02-01-04

3 TD passes were thrown by the Patriots in the 25-point rout of the Jacksonville Jaguars on 01-07-06

3 TD passes were thrown by the Patriots in the 11-point victory over the Jacksonville Jaguars on 01-12-08

The progression of the most TDs passes by the Patriots in a regular season

25 TD passes were thrown by the Boston Patriots in 1960

29 TD passes were thrown by the Boston Patriots in 1961

31 TD passes were thrown by the Boston Patriots in 1964

31 TD passes were thrown by the New England Patriots in 1997

50 TD passes were thrown by the New England Patriots in 2007

The progression of the most TD passes by the Patriots in a postseason

2 TD passes were thrown by the Boston Patriots in the 1963 postseason

2 TD passes were thrown by the New England Patriots in the 1978 postseason

6 TD passes were thrown by the New England Patriots in the 1985 postseason

6 TD passes were thrown by the New England Patriots in the 2007 postseason

Most interception returns for a TD

The progression of the most interception returns for a TD by the Patriots in a regular season game

1 interception was returned for a TD by the Patriots in the 55–21 rout of the Buffalo Bills on 10-22-61

1 interception was returned for a TD by the Patriots in the 41–0 shutout of the San Diego Chargers on 12-17-61

2 interceptions were returned for a TD by the Patriots in the 41–16 rout of the Denver Broncos on 09-21-62

2 interceptions were returned for a TD by the Patriots in the 45–3 destruction of the Houston Oilers on 11-01-63

2 interceptions were returned for a TD by the Patriots in the 38–24 victory over the New York Jets on 11-21-76

2 interceptions were returned for a TD by the Patriots in the 37–34 overtime win vs the Colts on 11-15-92

2 interceptions were returned for a TD by the Patriots in the 27–24 victory over the Miami Dolphins on 11-23-97

2 interceptions were returned for a TD by the Patriots in the 31–30 loss to the Miami Dolphins on 10-17-99

2 interceptions were returned for a TD by the Patriots in the 44–13 rout of the Indianapolis Colts on 09-30-01

2 interceptions were returned for a TD by the Patriots in the 38–6 rout of the Carolina Panthers on 01-06-02

Every interception return that was returned for a TD by the Patriots in a playoff game

Todd Collins returned a pass 40 yards for a TD in the 14-point win over the Miami Dolphins on 12-28-97

Ty Law returned a pass 47 yards for a TD in the three-point win over the St. Louis Rams on 02-03-02

Rodney Harrison returned a pass 87 yards for a TD in the 14-point win over the Pittsburgh Steelers on 01-23-05

Asante Samuel returned a pass 73 yards for a TD in the 25-point rout of the Jacksonville Jaguars on 01-07-06

Asante Samuel returned a pass 36 yards for a TD in the 21-point rout of the New York Jets on 01-07-07

Asante Samuel returned a pass 39 yards for a TD in the 4-point loss to the Indianapolis Colts on 01-21-07

The progression of the most interception returns for a TD by the Patriots in a regular season

2 interceptions were returned for a TD by the Boston Patriots in 1961

3 interceptions were returned for a TD by the Boston Patriots in 1962

3 interceptions were returned for a TD by the Boston Patriots in 1963

3 interceptions were returned for a TD by the New England Patriots in 1976

3 interceptions were returned for a TD by the New England Patriots in 1992

4 interceptions were returned for a TD by the New England Patriots in 1997

5 interceptions were returned for a TD by the New England Patriots in 2001

5 interceptions were returned for a TD by the New England Patriots in 2003

Most Special Teams Touchdowns

The progression of the most special teams TDs by the Patriots in a regular season game

1 TD was scored by the Patriots Special Teams in the 28–24 win over the New York Titans on 09-17-60

1 TD was scored by the Patriots Special Teams in the 38–27 loss to the San Diego Chargers on 10-07-61

1 TD was scored by the Patriots Special Teams in the 31–31 tie with the Houston Oilers on 11-03-61

2 TDs were scored by the Patriots Special Teams in the 41–0 shutout of the San Diego Chargers on 12-17-61

2 TDs were scored by the Patriots Special Teams in the 47–21 rout of the Baltimore Colts on 11-23-80

The progression of the most special teams TDs by the Patriots in a playoff game

1 TD was scored by the Patriots special teams in the 12-point win over the New York Jets on 12-28-85

1 TD was scored by the Patriots special teams in the 7-point win over the Los Angeles Raiders on 01-05-86

2 TDs were scored by the Patriots special teams in the 7-point win over the Pittsburgh Steelers on 01-27-02

The most Special Teams TDs that were scored by the Patriots in a regular season

5 special teams TDs were scored by the Boston Patriots in 1961

Most Punt Returns for a TD

The most punt returns for a TD by the Patriots in a regular season

2 punts were returned for a TD by the New England Patriots in 1976

2 punts were returned for a TD by the New England Patriots in 1985

2 punts were returned for a TD by the New England Patriots in 2001

The only punt return for a TD by the Patriots in a playoff game

Troy Brown returned a punt 55 yards for a TD by the Patriots in the seven-point win over Pittsburgh on 01-27-02

Most Kickoff Returns for a TD

The progression of the most kickoff returns for a TD by the Patriots in a regular season

2 kickoffs were returned for a TD by the Boston Patriots in 1961

3 kickoffs were returned for a TD by the New England Patriots in 1977

Most Fumble Returns for a TD

The progression of the most fumble returns for a TD by the Patriots in a regular season

1 fumble was returned 52 yards for a TD by the Boston Patriots in 1960

3 fumbles were returned for a TD by the Boston Patriots in 1961

3 fumbles were returned for a TD by the New England Patriots in 1986

3 fumbles were returned for a TD by the New England Patriots in 2007

Every fumble that was returned for a TD by the Patriots in a playoff game

Johnny Rembert returned a fumble 15 yards for a TD by the Patriots in the 12-point win over the New York Jets on 12-28-85

Otis Smith returned a fumble 47 yards for a TD by the Patriots in the 14-point win over the Jacksonville Jaguars on 01-12-97

Fumble recoveries for a TD

Every year that a fumble was recovered in the end zone for a TD by the Patriots during the regular season

1 fumble was recovered in the end zone in 1961, 1967, 1973, 1974, 1985, 1986, 1988, 1991, 1996, 1999, and 2004

Every fumble that was recovered in the end zone for a TD by the Patriots in a playoff game

Jim Bowman recovered a fumble in the end zone in the seven-point win over the Los Angeles Raiders on 01-05-86

Logan Mankins fell on a fumble in the end zone for a TD by the Patriots in the four-point loss to the Indianapolis Colts on 01-21-07

Fumble Advancements for a TD

Every offensive fumble advancement for a TD by the Patriots in a regular season

Ron Burton advanced his own fumble 91 yards for a TD in the four-pont win over the Denver Broncos on 11-11-62

Randy Vataha advanced Mack Herron's fumble 46 yards for a TD in the eight-point win over the Baltimore Ravens on 10-07-73

Steve Grogan advanced Don Calhoun's fumble six yards for a TD in the 34-point win over the New York Jets on 10-18-76

Jon Vaughn advanced his own fumbled kickoff return 100 yards for a TD in the 10-point loss on 12-20-92

Troy Brown took Dave Meggett's fumbled kickoff return 75 yds for a TD in the three-point win vs the New York Jets on 12-10-95

Lateral Advancements for a TD

Every time that a lateral was returned for a TD by the Patriots in a regular season

1 lateral was advanced 65 yards for a TD in the Patriots 10-point win over the New York Jets on 10-05-80

1 lateral was advanced 27 yards for a TD in the Patriots five-point win over the Pittsburgh Steelers on 09-25-83

Most yards rushing

The progression of the most yards rushing by the Patriots in a regular season game

70 yards rushing by the Patriots in the three-point loss to the Denver Broncos on 09-09-60

115 yards rushing by the Patriots in the four-point win over the New York Titans on 09-17-60

148 yards rushing by the Patriots in the 13-point loss to the Buffalo Bills on 09-23-60

171 yards rushing by the Patriots in the 35-point shutout of the Los Angeles Chargers on 10-08-60

211 yards rushing by the Patriots in the seven-point loss to the Denver Broncos on 10-23-60

235 yards rushing by the Patriots in the 31-point rout of the Buffalo Bills on 10-22-61

252 yards rushing by the Patriots in the 10-point win over the Oakland Raiders on 10-26-62

281 yards rushing by the Patriots in the three-point victory over the Oakland Raiders on 10-30-66

330 yards rushing by the Patriots in the 34-point rout of the New York Jets on 10-18-76

332 yards rushing by the Patriots in the 24-point victory over the Denver Broncos on 11-28-76

The progression of the most yards rushing by the Patriots in a playoff game

83 yards rushing by the Patriots in the 18-point win over the Buffalo Bills on 12-28-63

164 yards rushing by the Patriots in the three-point loss to the Oakland Raiders on 12-18-76

255 yards rushing by the Patriots in the 17-point victory over the Miami Dolphins on 01-12-86

The progression of the most yards rushing by the Patriots in a regular season

1,512 yards rushing by the 1960 team

1,675 yards rushing by the 1961 team

1,970 yards rushing by the 1962 team

2,134 yards rushing by the 1974 team

2,948 yards rushing by the 1976 team

3,165 yards rushing by the 1978 team

The progression of the most yards rushing by the Patriots in a postseason

158 yards rushing by the Boston Patriots in the 1963 postseason

164 yards rushing by the New England Patriots in the 1976 postseason

517 yards rushing by the New England Patriots in the 1985 postseason

Most yards passing

The progression of the most yards passing by the Patriots in a regular season game

149 yards passing by the Patriots in the three-point loss to the Denver Broncos on 09-09-60

197 yards passing by the Patriots in the four-point victory over the New York Titans on 09-17-60

223 yards passing by the Patriots in the seven-point loss to the Denver Broncos on 10-23-60

353 yards passing by the Patriots in the 28-point rout of the Denver Broncos on 09-16-61

366 yards passing by the Patriots in the 24-24 tie with the Kansas City Chiefs on 11-17-63

400 yards passing by the Patriots in the 43-43 tie with the Oakland Raiders on 10-16-64

414 yards passing by the Patriots in the seven-point loss to the Seattle Seahawks on 09-21-86

421 yards passing by the Patriots in the four-point loss to the Miami Dolphins on 09-04-94

426 yards passing by the Patriots in the six-point overtime win vs the Minnesota Vikings on 11-13-94

The progression of the most yards passing by the Patriots in a playoff game

300 yards passing by the Patriots in the 18-point victory over the Buffalo Bills on 12-28-63

312 yards passing by the Patriots in the three-point win in overtime vs the Oakland Raiders on 01-19-02

354 yards passing by the Patriots in the three-point victory over the Carolina Panthers on 02-01-04

The progression of the most yards passing by the Patriots in a regular season

2,865 yards passing by the 1960 team

2,930 yards passing by the 1962 team

3,467 yards passing by the 1964 team

3,600 yards passing by the 1979 team

3,904 yards passing by the 1981 team

4,321 yards passing by the 1986 team

4,583 yards passing by the 1994 team

4,806 yards passing by the 2007 team

The progression of the most yards passing by the Patriots in a postseason

528 yards passing by the Boston Patriots in the 1963 postseason

552 yards passing by the New England Patriots in the 1985 postseason

598 yards passing by the New England Patriots in the 1996 postseason

674 yards passing by the New England Patriots in the 2001 postseason

793 yards passing by the New England Patriots in the 2003 postseason

Most interception return yards

The progression of the most interception return yards by the Patriots in a regular season game

52 interception return yards by the Patriots in the three-point loss to the Denver Broncos on 09-09-60

88 interception return yards by the Patriots in the 13-point loss to the Oakland Raiders on 10-16-60

90 interception return yards by the Patriots in the four-point victory over the Denver Broncos on 12-03-61

132 interception return yards by the Patriots in the 24-point rout of the New York Jets on 09-08-63

204 interception return yards by the Patriots in the 42-point blowout of the Houston Oilers on 11-01-63

The progression of the most interception return yards by the Patriots in a playoff game

13 interception return yards by the Patriots in the 18-point victory over the Buffalo Bills on 12-28-63

44 interception return yards by the Patriots in the 12-point win over the New York Jets on 12-18-85

62 interception return yards by the Patriots in the 14-point win over the Miami Dolphins on 12-28-97

87 interception return yards by the Patriots in the 14-point win over the Pittsburgh Steelers on 01-23-05

The progression of the most interception return yards by the Patriots in a regular season

312 interception return yards by the Boston Patriots in 1960

326 interception return yards by the Boston Patriots in 1961

365 interception return yards by the Boston Patriots in 1962

645 interception return yards by the Boston Patriots in 1963

The progression of the most interception return yards by the Patriots in a postseason

13 interception return yards by the Boston Patriots in the 1963 postseason

88 interception return yards by the New England Patriots in the 1985 postseason

101 interception return yards by the New England Patriots in the 2004 postseason

Most kickoff return yards

The progression of the most kickoff return yards by the Patriots in a regular season game

30 kickoff return yards by the Patriots in the three point loss to the Denver Broncos on 09-09-60

123 kickoff return yards by the Patriots in the four-point win over the New York Titans on 09-17-60

131 kickoff return yards by the Patriots in the 29-point loss to the Los Angeles Chargers on 10-28-60

226 kickoff return yards by the Patriots in the 16-point loss to the Houston Oilers on 12-18-60

245 kickoff return yards by the Patriots in the 23-point loss to the Dallas Cowboys on 10-24-71

The progression of the most kickoff return yards by the Patriots in a playoff game

38 kickoff return yards by the Patriots in the 18-point victory over the Buffalo Bills on 12-28-63

122 kickoff return yards by the Patriots in the 41-point loss to the San Diego Chargers on 01-05-64

136 kickoff return yards by the Patriots in the 17-point loss to the Houston Oilers on 12-31-78

153 kickoff return yards by the Patriots in the 36-point loss to the Chicago Bears on 01-26-86

The progression of the most kickoff return yards by the Patriots in a regular season

1,421 kickoff return yards by the Boston Patriots in 1960

1,436 kickoff return yards by the Boston Patriots in 1967

1,442 kickoff return yards by the Boston Patriots in 1968

1,520 kickoff return yards by the New England Patriots in 1975

1,691 kickoff return yards by the New England Patriots in 1995

1,771 kickoff return yards by the New England Patriots in 2002

The progression of the most kickoff return yards by the Patriots in a postseason

160 kickoff return yards by the Boston Patriots in the 1963 postseason

304 kickoff return yards by the New England Patriots in the 1985 postseason

427 kickoff return yards by the New England Patriots in the 2006 postseason

Most Punt Return Yards

The progression of the most punt return yards by the Patriots in a regular season game

8 punt return yards by the Patriots in the three-point loss to the Denver Broncos on 09-09-60

26 punt return yards by the Patriots in the four-point win over the New York Titans on 09-17-60

30 punt return yards by the Patriots in the 13-point loss to the Buffalo Bills on 09-23-60

39 punt return yards by the Patriots in the 13-point loss to the Oakland Raiders on 10-16-60

40 punt return yards by the Patriots in the 16-point loss to the Houston Oilers on 12-18-60

66 punt return yards by the Patriots in the 12-point loss to the Houston Oilers on 11-12-61

75 punt return yards by the Patriots in the 19-point victory over the Denver Broncos on 10-18-63

137 punt return yards by the Patriots in the 11-point win over the Houston Oilers on 11-05-67

167 punt return yards by the Patriots in the 10-point victory over the Buffalo Bills on 11-07-76

The progression of the most punt return yards by the Patriots in a playoff game

34 punt return yards by the Boston Patriots in the 18-point victory over the Buffalo Bills on 12-28-63

72 punt return yards by the New England Patriots in the 25-point rout of the Pittsburgh Steelers on 01-05-97

80 punt return yards by the New England Patriots in the seven-point win over the Pittsburgh Steelers on 01-27-02

The progression of the most punt return yards by the Patriots in a regular season

194 punt return yards by the Boston Patriots in 1960

245 punt return yards by the Boston Patriots in 1961

373 punt return yards by the Boston Patriots in 1963

412 punt reurn yards by the Boston Patriots in 1967

533 punt return yards by the New England Patriots in 1974

628 punt return yards by the New England Patriots in 1976

The progression of the most punt return yards by the Patriots in a postseason

34 punt return yards by the Boston Patriots in the 1963 postseason

36 punt return yards by the New England Patriots in the 1985 postseason

131 punt return yards by the New England Patriots in the 1996 postseason

133 punt return yards by the New England Patriots in the 2001 postseason

Most Fumble Return Yards

The progression of the most fumble return yards by the Patriots in a regular season game

54 fumble return yards by the Patriots in the four-point win over the New York Titans on 09-17-60

68 fumble return yards by the Patriots in the 14-point victory over the Buffalo Bills on 10-03-04

The progression of the most fumble return yards by the Patriots in a playoff game

15 fumble return yards by the Patriots in the 12-point victory over the New York Jets on 12-28-85

47 fumble return yards by the Patriots in the 14-point win over the Jacksonville Jaguars on 01-12-97

49 fumble return yards by the Patriots in the seven-point victory over the Pittsburgh Steelers on 01-27-02

The progression of the most fumble return yards by the Patriots in a regular season

68 fumble return yards by the Boston Patriots in 1960

126 fumble return yards by the Boston Patriots in 1961

The progression of the most fumble return yards by the Patriots in a postseason

15 fumble return yards by the New England Patriots in the 1985 postseason

47 fumble return yards by the New England Patriots in the 1996 postseason

65 fumble return yards by the New England Patriots in the 2001 postseason

Most fumble advancement yards

The progression of the most fumble advancement yards by the Patriots in a regular season game

10 yards were advanced on a fumble recovery by the Patriots in the two-point win over Buffalo on 09-23-61

91 yards were advanced on a fumbled missed field goal return in the four-point win over Denver on 11-11-62

100 yards were advanced on a fumbled kickoff return recovery by the Patriots in the 10-point loss on 12-20-92

The progression of the most offensive fumble advancement yards by the Patriots in a season

11 yards were advanced on offensive fumble recoveries by the Patriots in 1961

105 yards were advanced on offensive fumble recoveries by the Patriots in 1962

105 yards were advanced on offensive fumble recoveries by the Patriots in 1995

Most lateral return yards

The progression of the most lateral return yards by the Patriots in a regular season game

5 lateral return yards by the Boston Patriots in the 28-point rout of the Dallas Texans on 11-18-60

19 lateral return yards by the Boston Patriots in the 24-point loss to the Buffalo Bills on 12-04-60

26 lateral return yards by the Boston Patriots in the 28-point rout of the Denver Broncos on 09-16-61

36 lateral return yards by the Boston Patriots in the 10-point victory over the Oakland Raiders on 10-26-62

45 lateral return yards by the Boston Patriots in the 43–43 tie with the Oakland Raiders on 10-16-64

65 lateral return yards by the New England Patriots in the 10-point win over the New York Jets on 10-05-80

69 lateral return yards by the New England Patriots in the two-point win over the Phoenix Cardinals on 10-10-93

The progression of the most lateral return yards by the Patriots in a regular season

24 lateral return yards by the Boston Patriots in 1960

26 lateral return yards by the Boston Patriots in 1961

54 lateral return yards by the Boston Patriots in 1962

80 lateral return yards by the Boston Patriots in 1970

The only lateral advancement by the Patriots in the playoffs

49 yard lateral advancement by the New England Patriots in the 2001 postseason

The Most Sacks

The progression of the most sacks by the Patriots in a regular season game

1 sack by the Boston Patriots in the three-point loss to the Denver Broncos on 09-09-60

4 sacks by the Boston Patriots in the four-point win over the New York Titans on 09-17-60

4 sacks by the Boston Patriots in the one-point win over the Dallas Texans on 10-29-61

6 sacks by the Boston Patriots in the 14-point victory over the Oakland Raiders on 12-09-61

10 sacks by the Boston Patriots in the six-point victory over the Oakland Raiders on 09-22-63

The progression of the most sacks by the Patriots in a playoff game

1 sack by the Boston Patriots in the 41-point loss to the San Diego Chargers on 01-05-64

4 sacks by the New England Patriots in the three-point loss to the Oakland Raiders on 12-18-76

5 sacks by the New England Patriots in the 12-point victory over the New York Jets on 12-28-85

5 sacks by the New England Patriots in the 14-point loss to the Green Bay Packers on 01-26-97

6 sacks by the New England Patriots in the 25-point rout of the Jacksonville Jaguars on 01-07-06

The progression of the most sacks by the Patriots in a regular season

19 sacks by the Boston Patriots in 1960

27 sacks by the Boston Patriots in 1961

28 sacks by the Boston Patriots in 1962

46 sacks by the Boston Patriots in 1963

47 sacks by the New England Patriots in 1976

58 sacks by the New England Patriots in 1977

The progression of the most sacks by the Patriots in a postseason

1 sack by the Boston Patriots in the 1963 postseason

4 sacks by the New England Patriots in the 1976 postseason

9 sacks by the New England Patriots in the 1985 postseason

9 sacks by the New England Patriots in the 1996 postseason

11 sacks by the New England Patriots in the 2003 postseason

Most offensive fumble recoveries

The progression of the most offensive fumble recoveries by the Patriots in a regular season game

3 offensive fumbles were recovered by the Patriots in the 35-point shutout of Los Angeles on 10-08-60

3 offensive fumbles were recovered by the Patriots in the 25-point victory over the Denver Broncos on 09-21-62

4 offensive fumbles were recovered by the Patriots in the 20-point loss to the Oakland Raiders on 12-16-62

4 offensive fumbles were recovered by the Patriots in the 17-point victory over the Kansas City Chiefs on 10-23-64

5 offensive fumbles were recovered by the Patriots in the eight-point victory over the Baltimore Colts on 10-07-73

5 offensive fumbles were recovered by the Patriots in the two-point loss to the Washington Redskins on 10-25-81

The progression of the most offensive fumble recoveries by the Patriots in a playoff game

1 offensive fumble recovery by the Patriots in the 41-point loss to the San Diego Chargers on 01-05-64

2 offensive fumble recoveries by the Patriots in the 17-point loss to the Houston Oilers on 12-31-78

2 offensive fumble recoveries by the Patriots in the 12-point victory over the New York Jets on 12-28-85

2 offensive fumble recoveries by the Patriots in the 14-point victory over the Miami Dolphins on 12-28-97

2 offensive fumble recoveries by the Patriots in the 15-point loss to the Jacksonville Jaguars on 01-03-99

3 offensive fumble recoveries by the Patriots in the three-point overtime win vs the Oakland Raiders on 01-19-02

3 offensive fumble recoveries by the Patriots in the 25-point rout of the Jacksonville Jaguars on 01-07-06

The progression of the most offensive fumble recoveries by the Patriots in a season

9 offensive fumble recoveries by the Boston Patriots in 1960

15 offensive fumble recoveries by the Boston Patriots in 1961

17 offensive fumble recoveries by the Boston Patriots in 1962

17 offensive fumble recoveries by the Boston Patriots in 1963

25 offensive fumble recoveries by the New England Patriots in 1973

The progression of the most offensive fumble recoveries by the Patriots in a postseason

1 offensive fumble recovery by the Boston Patriots in the 1963 postseason

2 offensive fumble recoveries by the New England Patriots in the 1978 postseason

3 offensive fumble recoveries by the New England Patriots in the 1985 postseason

3 offensive fumble recoveries by the New England Patriots in the 2001 postseason

3 offensive fumble recoveries by the New England Patriots in the 2005 postseason

Most defensive fumble recoveries

The progression of the most defensive fumble recoveries by the Patriots in a regular season game

1 defensive fumble was recovered by the Patriots in the three-point loss to Denver on 09-09-60

3 defensive fumbles were recovered by the Patriots in the four-point win over the New York Titans on 09-17-60

5 defensive fumbles were recovered by the Patriots in the seven-point loss on 10-23-60 (one was on a blocked punt)

5 defensive fumbles were recovered by the Patriots in the seven-point loss to the Denver Broncos on 11-06-66

6 defensive fumbles were recovered by the Patriots in the three-point win over the Pittsburgh Steelers on 09-26-76

6 defensive fumbles were recovered by the Patriots in the 14-point victory over the Los Angeles Rams on 12-11-83

The progression of the most defensive fumble recoveries by the Patriots in a playoff game

2 defensive fumbles were recovered by the Patriots in the 18-point victory over the Buffalo Bills on 12-28-63

3 defensive fumbles were recovered by the Patriots in the 15-point loss to the Miami Dolphins on 01-08-83

The progression of the most defensive fumble recoveries by the Patriots in a regular season

20 defensive fumbles were recovered by the Boston Patriots in 1960

20 defensive fumbles were recovered by the Boston Patriots in 1961

27 defensive fumbles were recovered by the New England Patriots in 1976

The progression of the most defensive fumble recoveries by the Patriots in a postseason

3 defensive fumbles were recovered by the Boston Patriots in the 1963 postseason

3 defensive fumbles were recovered by the New England Patriots in the 1982 postseason

11 defensive fumbles were recovered by the New England Patriots in the 1985 postseason

The most takeaways

The most takeaways by the Patriots in a regular season game

10; as the Patriots intercepted seven passes and recovered three fumbles in the 38–24 win over the New York Jets on 11-21-76

The most takeaways by the Patriots in a playoff game

6; as the Patriots intercepted three passes and recovered three fumbles in the 27–20 win over the Oakland Raiders on 01-05-86

6; as the Patriots intercepted two passes and recovered four fumbles in the 31–14 win over the Miami Dolphins on 01-12-86

The progression of the most takeaways by the Patriots in a regular season

45 takeaways by the Boston Patriots in 1960 (25 interceptions and 20 fumble recoveries)

47 takeaways by the Boston Patriots in 1964 (31 interceptions and 16 fumble recoveries)

50 takeaways by the New England Patriots in 1976 (23 interceptions and 27 fumble recoveries)

The progression of the most takeaways by the Patriots in a postseason

7 takeaways by the Boston Patriots in the 1963 postseason (4 interceptions and three fumble recoveries)

18 takeaways by the New England Patriots in the 1985 postseason (7 interceptions and 11 fumble recoveries)

Uniforms and Trivia

This chapter contains the uniform number of every Patriots player (except offensive guard Willis Perkins, who played in one game on 09-23-61)

No. 1

John Smith (K) 1974–83 (AFC Pro Bowl Kicker in 1980)
Tony Franklin (K) 1984–87 (AFC Pro Bowl Kicker in 1986)
Eric Schubert (Kicker for one game on 10-04-87)

No. 2

Pat Studstill (P) 1972
Jeff White (K) 1973
Mike Patrick (P) 1975–78
Joaquin Zendejas (K) 1983
Doug Flutie (QB) 1987–89 and 2005

No. 3

Bruce Barnes (P) 1973–74
Rich Camarillo (P) 1981–87 (AFC Pro Bowl Punter in 1983)
Matt Bahr (K) 1993–95
Stephen Gostkowski (K) 2006–08 (AFC Pro Bowl Kicker in 2008)

No. 4

Jerrel Wilson (P) 1978
Jason Staurovsky (K) 1988–91
Adam Vinatieri (K) 1996–2005 (AFC Pro Bowl Kicker in 2002 and 2004)

No. 5

Fred Steinfort (K) 1983
Joaquin Zendejas (K) 1983
Greg Davis (K) 1989
Pat O'Neill (P) 1994–95
Kevin O'Connell (QB) 2008

No. 6

Mike Hubach (P) 1980–81
Dan Miller (K) 1982
Alan Herline (P) 1987
Jeff Feagles (P) 1988–89
Rohan Davey (QB) 2002–04
Chris Hanson (P) 2007–08

No. 7

John Huarte (QB) 1966–67
Bill Murphy (WR) 1968
Charlie Gogolak (K) 1970–72
Nick Lowery (K) 1978
Ken Hartley (P) 1981
Rex Robinson (K) 1982
Teddy Garcia (K) 1988
Hugh Millen (QB) 1991–92
Mike Saxon (P) 1993
Michael Bishop (QB) 2000
Matt Gutierrez (QB) 2007–08

No. 8

Bill Bell (K) 1973
Eddie Hare (P) 1979
Bryan Wagner (P) 1991
Charlie Baumann (K) 1991–92
Brooks Barnard (P) for one game on 12-07-03
Josh Miller (P) 2004-2006

No. 9

David Posey (K) 1978
Scott Sisson (K) 1993
Bryan Wagner (P) 1995

No. 10

Harvey White (QB, RB, TE) 1960
Eric Crabtree (WR) 1971
Dave Chapple (P) 1974
Don Trull (QB) 1974
Tom Flick (QB) 1982
Bob Bleier (QB) 1987
Glenn Antrum (WR) for one game on 11-19-89
Brian Hansen (P) 1990
Scott Secules (QB) 1993
Hason Graham (WR) 1995–96
Lee Johnson (P) 1999–2001
Kevin Kasper (WR) 2004
Jabar Gaffney (WR) 2006–08

No. 11

Ed "Butch" Songin (QB) 1960–61
Joe Kapp (QB) 1970

Dick Shiner (QB) 1973–74
Charles "Tony" Eason (QB) 1983–89
Shawn McCarthy (P) 1991–92
Drew Bledsoe (QB) 1993-2001 (AFC Pro Bowl
    Quarterback in 1994, 1996, and 1997)

No. 12

Don Allard (QB) 1962
Eddie Wilson (QB) 1965
Mike Walker (K) 1972
Matt Cavanaugh (QB) 1979–82
Tom Ramsey (QB) 1986–88
Hart Lee Dykes (WR) 1989
Tom Brady (QB) 2000–08 (AFC Pro Bowl Quarterback
    in 2001, 2004, 2005, and 2007)

No. 13

RC Gamble (RB) 1968–69
Al Sykes (WR) 1971
Tommy Hodson (QB) 1990–92
Ken Walter (P) 2001–03
Bam Childress (WR/DB) for one game on 01-01-06
Bam Childress (WR) 2006

No. 14

Tom Greene (QB-P) 1960
Tom Yewcic (QB-P) 1961–66
Tom Sherman (QB) 1968–69
Brian Dowling (QB) 1972–73
Steve Grogan (QB) 1975–90
P.K. Sam (WR) 2004
Vinny Testaverde (QB) 2006

No. 15

Tom Dimitroff (QB) 1960
Vito "Babe" Parilli (QB) 1961–67 (AFL All-Star
    Quarterback in 1963, 1964, and 1966)
Jim "King" Corcoran (QB) 1968
Kim Hammond (QB) 1969
Neil Graff (QB) 1974–75
Todd Whitten (QB) for one game on 10-18-87
Marc Wilson (QB) 1989–90
Ray Lucas (Special Teams) 1996
Ken Walter (P) 2006
Kelley Washington (Special Teams/WR) 2007–08

No. 16

Jim Plunkett (QB) 1971–75
Scott Zolak (QB) 1992–98
Matt Cassel (QB) 2005–08

No. 17

Myron "Mike" Taliaferro (QB) 1968-1971 (AFL All-Star
    Quarterback in 1969)
Elmo Wright (WR) 1975
Tom Owen (QB) 1976–81
Luke Prestridge (P) 1984
Larry Linne (WR) 1987
Jeff Carlson (QB) 1992
Tony Gaiter (WR) for one game on 11-30-97
Henry Ellard (WR) 1998
John Friesz (QB) 1999–2000
Dedric Ward (WR) 2003
Chad Jackson (WR) 2006–07

No. 18

Randy Vataha (WR) 1971–76
Dietrich Jells (WR) 1996
Anthony Ladd (WR) 1998
Chris Calloway (WR) 2000
Andre' Davis (WR) 2005
Todd Sauerbrun (P) 2006
Donte' Stallworth (WR) 2007
Matthew Slater (WR) 2008

No. 19

Mike Kerrigan (QB) 1983–84
Tom Tupa (P) 1996–98
Shockmain Davis (WR) 2000
Damon Huard (QB) 2002–03
Kelvin Kight (WR) 2006

No. 20

Gino Cappelletti (DB) 1960
Gino Cappelletti (WR) 1960–69 (AFL All-Star Wide
    Receiver in 1961, 1963, 1964, 1965, and 1966)
Gino Cappelletti (K) 1960–70 (AFL All-Star Kicker in
    1963, 1964, 1965, and 1966)
(No. 20 was retired in honor of Gino Cappelletti in
    1992)

No. 21

Bob Suci (DB) 1963
Jay Cunningham (DB) 1965–67
Tom Janik (P-DB) 1969–71
Tom Reynolds (WR) 1972
Allen Carter (RB) 1975–76
Joe Blahak (DB) 1976
Sidney Brown (DB) 1978
Reggie Dupard (RB) 1986–89
Erroll Tucker (DB) 1989
Mickey Washington (DB) 1990–91
Reyna Thompson (DB) 1993

Ricky Reynolds (DB) 1994–96
Steve Israel (DB) 1997–99
J.R. Redmond (RB) 2000–02
Mike Cloud (RB) 2003
Randall Gay (DB) 2004–05
Mike Cloud (RB) 2005
Randall Gay (DB) 2006–07
Deltha O'Neal (DB) 2008

No. 22

Ron Burton (RB) 1960–65
Gene Thomas (RB) 1968
Sid Blanks (RB) 1969–70
Phil Clark (DB) 1971
Sandy Durko (DB) 1973–74
Dick Conn (DB) 1975–79
Chuck Foreman (RB) 1980
Keith Lee (DB) 1981–84
Eugene Profit (DB) 1986–88
Ricky Atkinson (DB) 1987
Eric Coleman (DB) 1989–90
Rod Smith (DB) 1992–94
Dave Meggett (RB) 1995–97 (AFC Pro Bowl Return
    Specialist in 1996)
Terrance Shaw (DB) 2001
Terrell Buckley (DB) 2002
Asante Samuel (DB) 2003–07 (AFC Pro Bowl
    Cornerback in 2007)
Terrence Wheatley (DB) 2008

No. 23

Dick Christy (RB) 1960–61
Ray Ratkowski (KR) for one game on 09-09-61
Ron Hall (DB) 1962–67 (AFL All-Star Defensive Back
    in 1963)
Daryl Johnson (DB) 1968–70
George Hoey (DB) 1972–73
Joe Wilson (RB) 1974
Horace Ivory (RB) 1977–81
Kevin Donnalley (DB) for one game on 10-25-81
Rodney McSwain (DB) 1984–90
Rod Smith (DB) 1992–94
Terry Ray (DB) 1993–96
Sedrick Shaw (RB) 1997–98
Terry Billups (DB) 1999
Antwan Harris (CB) 2000–03
Omare Lowe (DB) 2004
Duane Starks (DB) 2005
Willie Andrews (DB) 2006–07
Jason Webster (DB) 2008

No. 24

Walt Livingston (RB) 1960
Joe Johnson (TE) 1960–61
Mel West (DB) 1961
Dick Felt (DB) 1962–66 (AFL All-Star Defensive Back
　　in 1962)
Bobby Leo (WR) 1967–68
Bob Gladieux (RB) 1969–72
Bob McCall (RB) 1973
Bob Howard (DB) 1975–77
Robert Weathers (RB) 1982–86
Bruce Hansen (RB) 1987
Jamie Morris (RB) 1990
Jon Vaughn (RB) 1991–92
Ty Law (DB) 1995–2004 (AFC Pro Bowl Cornerback in
　　1998 and 2001)
Michael Stone (DB) 2005
Mel Mitchell (DB) 2007
Jonathan Wilhite (DB) 2008

No. 25

Ross O'Hanley (DB) 1960–65 (AFL All-Star Defensive
　　Back in 1960)
John Charles (DB) 1967–69
Rickie Harris (DB) 1971–72
John Sanders (DB) 1974–76
Rick Sanford (DB) 1979–84
Vencie Glenn (DB) 1986
Tony Zackery (DB) 1990–91
Darren Anderson (DB) for one game on 09-27-92
Larry Whigham (DB) 1994–2000 (AFC Pro Bowl
　　Special Teams player in 1997)
Leonard Myers (DB) 2001–02
Arturo Freeman (DB) 2005
Artrell Hawkins (DB) 2005–06

No. 26

Walter Beach (DB) 1960
Clarence Scott (DB) 1969–72
Raymond Clayborn (DB) 1977–89 (AFC Pro Bowl
　　Cornerback in 1983, 1985, and 1986)
David Key (DB) 1991
David Wilson (DB) for one game on 10-25-92
Corey Croom (RB) 1993–95
Jerome Henderson (DB) 1996
Chris Canty (DB) 1997–98
Matt Stevens (DB) 2001
Eugene Wilson (DB) 2003–07

No. 27

Joe Bellino (RB) 1965–67
Willie Porter (DB) 1968

Randy Beverly (DB) 1970–71
Ron Bolton (DB) 1972–75
Doug Beaudoin (DB) 1976–79
Ricky Smith (DB) 1982–84
Greg Hawthorne (WR-RB-TE) 1985–86
Michael LeBlanc (RB) 1987
Howard Feggins (DB) 1989
Junior Robinson (DB) 1990
David Pool (DB) 1991–92
Darryl Wren (DB) 1993–94
Mike "Scooter" McGruder (DB) 1996–97
Lamont Warren (RB) 1999
Terrell Buckley (DB) 2001
Victor Green (DB) 2002
Rabih Abdullah (RB) 2004
Ellis Hobbs III (DB) 2005–08

No. 28

Dave Cloutier (DB) 1964
Art McMahon (DB) 1968–72
Dave Mason (DB) 1973
Bill Currier (DB) 1980
Jim Bowman (DB) 1985–89
David Hendley (DB) 1987
Dion Lambert (DB) 1992–93
Curtis Martin (RB) 1995–97 (AFC Pro Bowl Running
　　Back in 1995 and 1996)
Raymont Harris (RB) for one game on 12-10-00
Corey Dillon (RB) 2004–06 (AFC Pro Bowl Running
　　Back in 2004)
Antwain Spann (Special Teams/DB) 2007–08

No. 29

Aaron Marsh (WR) 1968–69
Honor Jackson (DB) 1972–73
Greg Boyd (DB) 1973
Durwood Keeton (DB) 1975
Willie Germany (DB) 1976
Harold Jackson (WR) 1978–81
Jamie Lawson (RB) for one game on 12-30-90
Don Overton (RB) 1990
Darrell Fullington (DB) 1991
Myron Guyton (DB) 1994–95
Derrick Cullors (RB) 1997–98
Raymont Harris (RB) 2000
Hakim Akbar (DB) 2001
Chris Hayes (DB) 2002
Aric Morris (DB) 2003
Guss Scott (DB) 2005
Chidi Iwuoma (DB) 2006
Guss Scott (DB) 2006
Eddie Jackson (DB) 2007
Lewis Sanders (DB) 2008

No. 30

Jim Crawford (RB) 1960–64
Tom Hennessy (DB) 1965–66
Carl Garrett (RB) 1969–72 (AFL All-Star Running
    Back in 1969)
Ed Jenkins (RB) 1974
Mosi Tatupu (RB) 1978–90 (AFC Pro Bowl Special
    Teams player in 1986)
Frank Bianchini (RB) for one game on 10-04-87
Corwin Brown (DB) 1993–95
Tony Carter (RB) 1998–00
Je'Rod Cherry (DB) 2001–04
Chad Scott (DB) 2005–06

No. 31

Ger Schwedes (RB) 1960
Clyde Washington (DB) 1960–61
Harry Crump (RB) 1963
Vic Purvis (WR) 1966–67
Bill Murphy (WR) 1968
Josh Ashton (RB) 1972–74
Leon McQuay (RB) 1975
Fred Marion (DB) 1982–91 (AFC Pro Bowl Safety in
    1985)
Jon Sawyer (DB) 1987
Jimmy Hitchcock (DB) 1995–97
Kato Serwanga (DB) 1999–2000
Ben Kelly (DB) 2001–02
Larry Centers (FB) 2003
Hank Poteat (DB) in the three playoff games in 2004
Amos Zereoue (RB) 2005
Antwain Spann (DB) 2006
Brandon Meriweather (DB) 2007–08

No. 32

Al Miller (RB) 1960
Billy Lott (RB) 1961–63
JD Garrett (RB) 1964–67
Odell Lawson (RB) 1970–71
Andy Johnson (RB) 1974–76, 1978–81
Craig James (RB) 1984–88 (AFC Pro Bowl Running
    Back in 1985)
Chuck McSwain (RB) 1987
Leonard Russell (RB) 1991–93
Blair Thomas (RB) 1994
Willie Clay (DB) 1996–98
Antowain Smith (RB) 2001–03
Hank Poteat (DB) 2005–06
Rashad Baker (DB) 2006–07
LaMont Jordan (RB) 2008

No. 33

Fred Bruney (DB) 1960–62 (AFL All-Star Defensive
    Back in 1961 and 1962)
Bob Cappadona (RB) 1966–67
Bill Bailey (RB) 1969
Bill Rademacher (WR) 1969–70
Reggie Rucker (WR) 1971–74
Bob Anderson (RB) 1975
Tony Collins (RB) 1981–87 (AFC Pro Bowl Running
    Back in 1983)
Patrick Egu (RB) 1989
George Adams (RB) 1990–91
Sam Gash (RB) 1992–97
Kevin Faulk (RB) 1999–2008

No. 34

Joe Biscaha (End) 1960
Jake Crouthamel (RB) 1960
Bill Larsen (RB) 1960
Bobby Towns (DB) 1961
Chuck Shonta (DB) 1961–67 (AFL All-Star Defensive
    Back in 1966)
Ron Sellers (WR) 1969–71 (AFL All-Star Wide
    Receiver in 1969)
Prentice McCray (DB) 1974–80
Mark van Eeghen (RB) 1982–83
Carl Woods (RB) 1987
Robert Perryman (RB) 1987–89
Kevin Turner (RB) 1992–94
Rupert Grant (RB) 1995
Tebucky Jones (DB) 1998–2002
Chris Atkins (DB) 2003
Sammy Morris (RB) 2007–08

No. 35

Jim Nance (RB) 1965–71 (AFL All-Star Running Back
    in 1966 and 1967)
Henry Matthews (RB) 1972
Jess Philips (RB) 1976–77
Allan Clark (RB) 1979–80
George Peoples (RB) 1983
Bruce Hansen (RB) 1987
George Wonsley (RB) 1989
Anthony Landry (RB) 1990
Burnie Legette (RB) 1993–94
Marrio Grier (RB) 1996–97
Jerry Ellison (RB) 1999
Patrick Pass (RB) 2000–06
Mike Richardson (DB) 2008

No. 36

Tom Neumann (RB) 1963
Terry Swanson (P) 1967–68
Ken Herock (LB/TE) 1969
Eddie Ray (RB-TE) 1970
John Tarver (RB) 1972–74
Brian Hutson (DB) 1990
Jerome Henderson (DB) 1991–93
Leroy Thompson (RB) 1994
Lawyer Milloy (DB) 1996–2002 (AFC All-Star Safety in
    1998, 1999, 2001, and 2002)
James Sanders (DB) 2005–08

No. 37

Bill Bailey (RB) 1969
Ron Gardin (WR) 1971
Willie Osley (DB) 1974
James McAlister (RB) 1978
Maurice Hurst (DB) 1989–95
Chris Floyd (RB) 1998–2000
Jimmy Hitchcock (DB) 2002
Rodney Harrison (DB) 2003–08

No. 38

Al Snyder (WR) 1964
Ellis Johnson (RB) 1965–66
Don Martin (DB) 1973
Noe Gonzalez (RB) 1974
Ike Forte (RB) 1976–77
Roland James (DB) 1980–90
Perry Williams (DB) 1987
Adrian White (DB) 1993
David Green (RB) 1995
Steve Lofton (DB) 1997–98
Antonio Langham (DB) 2000
Tyrone Poole (DB) 2003–05
Ray Mickens (DB) 2006
Kyle Eckel (RB) 2007

No. 39

Perry Pruett (DB) 1971
Sam "Bam" Cunningham (RB) 1973–82 (AFC Pro
    Bowl Running Back in 1978)
Marvin Allen (RB) 1988–91
Rico Clark (RB) for one game on 01-02-00
Shawn Mayer (Safety) 2003–04
Laurence Maroney (RB) 2006–08

No. 40

Chuck Shonta (DB) 1960
Larry Garron (RB) 1961–68 (AFL All-Star Running
    Back in 1961, 1963, 1964, and 1967)
Bake Turner (WR) 1970
Jack Maitland (RB) 1971–72
Dave McCurry (DB) 1974
Mike Haynes (CB) 1976–82 (AFC Pro Bowl
    Cornerback in 1976, 1977, 1978, 1979, 1980, and
    1982)
Greg Hawthorne (WR-TE-RB) 1984
Elgin Davis (RB) 1987–88
Michael LeBlanc (RB) 1987 for one game on 10-04-87
Tim Hauck (DB) 1990
Harry Colon (DB) 1991
Scott Lockwood (RB) 1992–93
Carlos Yancy (DB) 1995
(No. 40 was retired in honor of Mike Haynes in 1997)

No. 41

Billy Wells (RB) 1960
Walter Beach (DB) 1961
Claude King (RB) 1962
Leroy Mitchell (DB) 1967–68 (AFL All-Star Defensive
    Back in 1968)
Larry Carwell (DB) 1969–72
Ken Pope (LB) 1974
Bo Robinson (RB) 1984
Darryl Holmes (DB) 1987–89
Tim Gordon (DB) 1991–92
Eddie Cade (DB) 1995
Keith Byars (RB) 1996–97
Tony George (DB) 1999–2000
Raymond Vetrone (Special Teams/DB) 2007–08

No. 42

Bob Soltis (DB) 1960
Don Webb (DB) 1961–71 (AFL All-Star Defensive Back
    in 1969)
Mack Herron (RB) 1973–75
Ronnie Lippett (DB) 1983–91
Ron Shegog (DB) 1987
Harlon Barnett (DB) 1993–94
Chris Carter (DB) 1997–99
Dexter Reid (DB) 2004
BenJarvus Green-Ellis (RB) 2008

No. 43

Jay Cunningham (DB) 1965–67
Irvin Mallory (DB) 1971
Claxton Welch (RB) 1973
Vagas Ferguson (RB) 1980–82
Ernest Gibson (DB) 1984–88
Duffy Cobbs (DB) 1987
Rodney Rice (DB) 1989
Vernon Lewis (DB) 1993–96

No. 44

Ger Schwedes (RB) 1961
Tom Neumann (RB) 1963
White Graves (DB) 1965–67
John Outlaw (DB) 1969–72
Don Calhoun (RB) 1975–81
Doug Dressler (RB) 1975
Larry Cowan (RB) 1982
Jon Williams (RB) 1984
Todd Frain (TE) 1987
John Stephens (RB) 1988–92 (AFC Pro Bowl
    Running Back in 1988)
Marion Butts (RB) 1994
Harold Shaw (RB) 1998–2000
Marc Edwards (FB) 2001–02
Fred McCrary (FB) 2003
Heath Evans (FB) 2005–08

No. 45

Jerry Green (RB) 1960
Tom Stephens (DB-TE) 1960–64
Ray Ilg (LB) 1967–68
Dan Kecman (LB) for one game on 09-27-70
Hubie Bryant (WR) 1971
Jack Mildren (DB) 1974
Greg Taylor (KR) for one game on 09-12-82
Joe Peterson (DB) 1987
Michael Timpson (WR) 1989–90
Ivy Joe Hunter (RB) 1991
Otis Smith (DB) 1996 and 2000–02

No. 46

Larry Garron (RB) 1960
Bob Soltis (DB) 1961
Al Romine (DB) 1961
Rommie Loudd (LB/TE) 1961–62
Bob Scarpitto (WR-Punter) 1968
Paul Gipson (DB) 1973
Mark Washington (DB) 1979
Marv Cook (TE) 1989–90
Kantroy Barber (RB) 1996
Chris Eitzmann (TE) 2000

Jeff Paulk (RB) for one game on 12-24-00
Brian Kinchen (LS) 2003
Corey Mays (LB) 2006–07

No. 47

Billy Johnson (DB) 1966–69
Jim Massey (DB) 1974–75
Darrell Wilson (DB) for one game on 11-08-81
Paul Dombroski (DB) 1981–84
Pat Coleman (KR) for one game on 11-25-90
Roger Brown (DB) 1992
Robert Edwards (RB) 1998
Maugaula Tuitele (LB) 2001
Justin Kurpeikis (LB/TE) 2004

No. 48

Don Webb (DB) 1961
Preston Johnson (RB) 1968
Tim Fox (DB) 1976-1981 (AFC Pro Bowl Safety in
    1980)
Darryal Wilson (WR) 1983
Greg Baty (TE) 1986–87
Clay Pickering (WR) for one game on 10-18-87
Dennis Gadbois (WR) 1987–88
Randy Robbins (DB) 1992
Andre President (TE) 1995
Lovett Purnell (TE) 1996–98
Rob Holmberg (LB) 2001
Tully Banta-Cain (LB) 2003–05

No. 49

Tom Richardson (WR) 1969–70
Dick Blanchard (LB) 1972
Ralph Anderson (DB) 1973
Brian Williams (TE) for one game on 11-21-82
Russ Francis (TE) for one game on 12-28-87
Kitrick Taylor (KR) 1989
Rob Holmberg (LB) 2000
Jermaine Wiggins (TE) for one game on 12-24-00
Fred Baxter (TE) for one game on 12-29-02
Sean McDermott (LS) for one game on 12-14-03
Eric Alexander (LB) 2004–05
Vince Redd (LB) 2008

No. 50

Bob Yates (OL) 1961–65
Joe Avezzano (Center) 1966
Jim Cheyunski (LB) 1968–72
Edgar Chandler (LB) 1973
Sam Hunt (LB) 1974–79
Larry McGrew (LB) 1980–89
Ilia Jarostchuk (LB) 1990

Steve DeOssie (LB) 1994
Bobby Abrams (LB) 1995
Rob Holmberg (LB) 2000
Mike Vrabel (LB) 2001–08 (AFC Pro Bowl Linebacker
 in 2007)

No. 51

Frank Robotti (LB) 1961
Don McKinnon (LB) 1963–964
Jim Fraser (LB-Punter) 1966
Mike Ballou (LB) 1970
Randy Edmunds (LB) 1971
Ron Acks (LB) 1972–73
Kent Carter (LB) 1974
Maury Damkroger (LB) 1974
Donnie Thomas (LB) 1976
Bob Golic (LB) 1979–81
Brian Ingram (LB) 1982–85
Mel Black (LB) 1987
Bruce Scholtz (LB) 1989
Eugene Lockhart (LB) 1991–92
David White (LB) 1993
Bernard Russ (LB) 1997–99
Olrick Johnson (LB) 2000
Bryan Cox (LB) 2001
Don Davis (Special Teams/LB/DB) 2003–06
Jerod Mayo (LB) 2008

No. 52

Phil Bennett (LB) 1960
Ed Meixler (LB) 1965
Ed Philpott (LB) 1967–71
Ron Kadziel (LB) 1972
Steve King (LB) 1973–81
Johnny Rembert (LB) 1983–92 (AFC Pro Bowl
 Linebacker in 1988 and 1989)
Jerry McCabe (LB) 1987
David Bavaro (LB) 1993–94
Ted Johnson (LB) 1995–2001
Ted Johnson (LB) 2001–04
Monty Beisel (LB) 2005
Eric Alexander (LB) 2006–07

No. 53

Tom Addison (LB) 1960–67 (AFL All-Star Linebacker
 1960, 1961, 1962, 1963, and 1964)
Fred Whittingham (LB) 1970
Dennis Coleman (LB) 1971
John Tanner (LB) 1973–74
Jim Romaniszyn (LB) 1976
Merv Krakau (LB) for one game on 12-10-78
Bill Matthews (LB) 1979–81

Clayton Weishuhn (LB) 1982–84, 1986
Randy Sealby (LB) for one game on 10-18-87
Tom Benson (LB) 1988
Richard Tardits (LB) 1990–92
Chris Slade (LB) 1993–2000 (AFC Pro Bowl
 Linebacker in 1997)
Larry Izzo (Special Teams/LB) 2001–08 (AFC Pro
 Bowl Special Teams in 2002 and 2004)

No. 54

Bill Brown (LB) 1960
Walt Cudzik (C) 1961–63
Mike Dukes (LB) 1964–65
Ed Koontz (LB) 1968
Marty Schottenheimer (LB) 1969–70
Ken Price (LB) for one game on 12-19-71
Gail Clark (LB) 1974
Steve Zabel (LB) 1975–78
John Zamberlin (LB) 1979–82
John Gillen (LB) 1983
Ed Williams (LB) 1984–87 and 1990
Greg Moore (LB) 1987
Todd Collins (LB) 1992–94
Alcides Catanho (LB) 1995
Tedy Bruschi (LB) 1996–08 (AFC Pro Bowl
 Linebacker in 2004)

No. 55

Lonnie Farmer (LB) 1964–66
J.R. Williamson (LB-Center) 1968–70
Ralph Cindrich (LB) 1972
Will Foster (LB) 1973–74
Rodrigo Barnes (LB) 1974–75
Kevin Reilly (LB) 1975
Ray Costict (LB) 1977–79
Don Blackmon (LB) 1981–87
Joe McHale (LB) 1987
Chris Singleton (LB) 1990–93
Willie McGinest (DE-LB) 1994–2005 (AFC Pro Bowl
 Defensive End in 1996 and AFC Pro Bowl
 Linebacker in 2003)
Junior Seau (LB) 2006–08

No. 56

Walt Cudzik (C) 1960
Jon Morris (C) 1964–74 (AFL All-Star Center from
 1964–69 and AFC Pro Bowl Center in 1970)
Rod Shoate (LB) 1975–81
Andre Tippett (LB) 1982–93 (AFC Pro Bowl
 Linebacker in 1984, 1985, 1986, 1987, and 1988)

No. 57

John Bramlett (LB) 1969–70
Steve Kiner (LB) 1971–73
Steve Nelson (LB) 1974–87 (AFC Pro Bowl Linebacker in 1980, 1984, and 1985)
(No. 57 was retired in honor of Steve Nelson in 1993)

No. 58

Doug Satcher (LB) 1966–68
Doug Dumler (Center) 1973–75
Pete Brock (Center-Guard-TE) 1976–87
Terrence Cooks (LB) 1989
Richard Harvey (LB) 1990
Rob McGovern (LB) 1992
Marty Moore (LB) 1994–99
Matt Chatham (LB) 2000–05
Pierre Woods (LB) 2006–08

No. 59

Brian Stenger (LB) 1973
Bob Geddes (LB) 1973–75
Pete Barnes (LB) 1976–77
Mike Hawkins (LB) 1978–81
Tim Golden (LB) 1982–84
Steve Doig (LB) 1986–87
Randy Sealby (LB) 1987
Vincent Brown (LB) 1988–95
Todd Collins (LB) 1996–98
Andy Katzenmoyer (LB) 1999–2000
O.J. Brigance (LB) for one game on 09-15-02
Maugaula Tuitele (LB) 2002
Rosevelt Colvin (LB) 2003–07
Gary Guyton (LB) 2008

No. 60

Bob Lee (Guard) 1960
Rommie Loudd (LB) 1961
Len St. Jean (Guard-DL) 1964–73 (AFL All-Star Offensive Guard in 1966)
Dave Tipton (DL) 1975–76
Bob Hyland (OL) 1977
Luther Henson (DL) 1982–84
Garin Veris (DL) 1985–88
Marion Hobby (DE) 1990–92
Scott Rehberg (OL) 1997–98
Garrett Johnson (DT) 2000
Wilbert Brown (G) 2003

No. 61

Bob Yates (OL) 1960
Bill Hudson (DL) 1965
Leroy Moore (DB) 1967–68

Sam Adams (OL) 1972–80
Ron Wooten (Guard) 1982–88
Greg Robinson (Tackle) 1987
Freddie Childress (OL) 1991
Bob Kratch (OL) 1994–96
Damon Denson (OL) 1997–99
Stephen Neal (OL) 2002 and 2004–08

No. 62

Abe Cohen (OL) 1960
Dick Klein (OL) 1961–62
Dave Watson (OL) 1963–64
John Cagle (DL-LB-OL) 1969
Halvor Hagen (Guard-DE) 1971–72
Kevin Hunt (T) for one game on 11-11-73
Steve Corbett (Guard) 1975
Dwight Wheeler (OL) 1978–83
Bill Bain (OL) 1986
Sean Farrell (OL) 1987–90
Dave Richards (OL) 1996

No. 63

Charlie Leo (OL) 1960–62 (AFL All-Star Offensive Guard in 1960 and 1961)
Justin Canale (Guard) 1965–68
Rick Cash (DL) 1972–73
Shelby Jordan (RT) 1975
Fred Sturt (OL) 1976–78
Ernie Holmes (DT) 1978
Mark Buben (NT) 1979 and 1981
Tom Condon (OL) for one game on 09-15-85
Adam Lingner (OL) 1986
George Colton (Guard) 1987
Gerry Feehery (OL) 1989
Gene Chilton (OL) 1990–92
Todd Jones (OL) 1993
Sylvester Stanley (DL) 1994
Heath Irwin (OL) 1996–99
Joe Andruzzi (Guard) 2000–04

No. 64

Tony Sardisco (OL) 1960–62
Jim Boudreaux (DE) 1968
Mike Montler (OL) 1969–72
Allen Gallaher (OL) 1974
Richard Bishop (DL) 1976–81
Trevor Matich (Center) 1985–88
Darren Twombly (C) for one game on 10-04-87
Jon Melander (OL) 1991
Dave Wohlabaugh (Center) 1995–98
Derrick Fletcher (Guard) 2000
Greg Robinson-Randall (Tackle) 2001–02

Gene Mruckowski (OL) 2004–06
Mark LeVoir (OL) 2008

No. 65

Jack Davis (OL) 1960
Houston Antwine (DT) 1961–71 (AFL All-Star
  Defensive Tackle from 1963-1968)
Donnell Smith (DL) 1973–974
Greg Boyd (DL) 1977–78
Steve Clark (Tackle) 1981
Doug Rogers (DL) 1984
Mike Ruth (NT) 1986–87
Tom Porrell (NT) for one game on 10-04-87
Edmund Nelson (DL) 1988
Elbert Crawford (OL) 1990–91
Mike Arthur (OL) 1993–94
Damien Woody (C/G) 1999–2003
Wesley Britt (OL) 2006–08

No. 66

Paul Feldhausen (OL) 1968–69
Barry Brown (LB/TE) 1969–70
Angelo Loukas (OL) 1970
Ed Weisacosky (LB) 1971–72
Nate Dorsey (DL) 1973
Bob McKay (OL) 1976–78
Steve McMichael (DT) 1980
John Lee (DL) 1981
Paul Fairchild (OL) 1984–90
Steve Gordon (OL) 1992–93
Jeff Dellenbach (C) 1995
Ed Ellis (Tackle) 1997–99
Lonie Paxton (LS) 2000–08

No. 67

Art Hauser (DL) 1960
Paul Lindquist (DL) 1961
Dave Watson (OL) 1963–64
Whit Canale (DL) 1968
Gary Bugenhagen (OL) 1969–70
Bill Lenkaitis (Center) 1971–81
Steve Moore (OL) 1983–87
David Douglas (OL) 1989–90
Mike Gisler (OL) 1993–97
Jason Andersen (C) 1999–2000
Grey Ruegamer (C) 2000–02
Dan Koppen (C) 2003–08 (AFC Pro Bowl Center in
  2007)

No. 68

Karl Singer (T) 1966–68
Bill DuLac (OL) 1974–75
Terry Falcon (OL) 1978–79

Darryl Haley (OL) 1982–84 and 1986
Greg Robinson (OL) 1987
Mike Baab (OL) 1988–89
Damian Johnson (OL) 1990
Calvin Stephens (OL) 1992
Doug Skene (OL) 1994
Max Lane (OL) 1994–2000
Tom Ashworth (OL) 2002–05
Ryan O'Callaghan (OL) 2006–07

No. 69

Julius Adams (DE) (for two games in 1987)
Eugene Chung (G) 1992–94
Ross Tucker (OL) for one regular season game and
  one playoff game in 2005

No. 70

Hal Smith (DL) 1960
Milt Graham (OL) 1961–63
Mel Witt (DL) 1967–68
Dennis Wirgowski (DE) 1971–72
Leon Gray (T) 1973–78 (AFC Pro Bowl Offensive
  Tackle in 1976 and 1978)
Doug McDougald (DL) 1980
Luther Henson (DL) 1982–84
Scott Virkus (DL) 1984
Art Plunkett (OL) 1985 and 1987
David Viaene (OL) 1989–90
Reggie Redding (OL) 1992
Brandon Moore (OL) 1993–95
Adrian Klemm (T) 2000, 2002, and 2004
Logan Mankins (OL) 2005–08 (AFC Pro Bowl Guard
  in 2007)

No. 71

Don Oakes (OL) 1963–68 (AFL All-Star Offensive
  Tackle in 1967)
Mel Witt (DL) 1969–70
Fred DeRiggi (DL) 1971
Art May (DL) 1971
Ray Hamilton (DL) 1973–81
Benton Reed (DL) 1987
Gregg Rakoczy (OL) 1991–92
Todd Rucci (OL) 1993–99
Russ Hochstein (OL) 2002–08

No. 72

Al Crow (DL) 1960
Bill Striegal (LB) 1960
Larry Eisenhauer (DE) 1961–69 (AFL All-Star
  Defensive End in 1962, 1963, 1964 and 1966)
Mel Lunsford (DL) 1973–80
Lester Williams (NT) 1982–85

Todd Sandham (OL) 1987
Tim Goad (NT) 1988–94
Devin Wyman (DL) 1996–97
Sale Isaia (G) 2000
Matt Light (T) 2001–08 (AFC Pro Bowl Tackle in 2006 and 2007)

No. 73

Harry Jagielski (DL) 1960–61
Billy Neighbors (OL) 1962–65 (AFL All-Star Offensive Guard in 1963)
Ed Khayat (DL) 1966
Tom Funchess (OL) 1968–70
Bill Atessis (DL) 1971
John "Hawg" Hannah (Guard) 1973–85 (AFC Pro Bowl Offensive Guard in 1976 and from 1978–85)
Danny Villa (OL) 1987–89
(No. 73 was retired in Honor of John Hannah in 1991)

No. 74

Jerry DeLucca (OL) 1960–61 and 1963–64
Bob Schmidt (OL) 1964
John Mangum (DT) 1966–67
Ezell Jones (OL) 1969–70
Bob Reynolds (OL) 1972–73
Craig Hanneman (DL) 1974–75
Shelby Jordan (OL) 1977–82
Dave Browning (DL) 1983
Bill Turner (DL) 1987
Stan Clayton (OL) 1990
Chris Gambol (OL) 1990
Rich Baldinger (OL) 1993
Doug Skene (OL) 1994
Chris Sullivan (DL) 1996–99
Reggie Grimes (DE) 2000
Kenyatta Jones (T) 2001–02
Billy Yates (OL) 2005–08

No. 75

George McGee (OL) 1960
John Simerson (OL) 1961
Jesse Richardson (DL) 1962–64
George Pyne (OL) 1965
Ed Toner (DL) 1967–70
Mike Haggerty (OL-DL) 1971
Art Moore (DL) 1973–77
Bob Cryder (OL) 1978–83
Guy Morriss (OL) 1984–87
Larry Williams (OL) 1992
Bill Lewis (OL) 1993
Pio Sagapolutele (DL) 1996
Danny Villa (OL) 1990–91 and 1997

Leonta Rheams (DL) 1998
Vince Wilfork (DL) 2004–08 (AFC Pro Bowl Defensive Lineman in 2007)

No. 76

Tony Discenzo (OL) 1960
Charley Long (T) 1961-1969 (AFL All-Star Offensive Tackle in 1962 and 1963)
Rex Mirich (DL) 1970
Dave Rowe (DL) 1971–73
Pete Cusick (DL) 1975
Greg Schaum (DL) 1978
Brian Holloway (T) 1981–86 (AFC Pro Bowl Offensive Tackle in 1983, 1984, and 1985)
Tom Rehder (OL) 1988–89
Stan Clayton (OL) 1990
Fred Smerlas (NT) 1991–92
John Washington (DL) 1993
William Roberts (OL) 1995–96
Grant Williams (T) 2000–01
Brandon Gorin (T) 2003–05

No. 77

Bob Cross (OL) 1960
Bill Danenhauer (DL) 1960
Tom Neville (Tackle) 1965–77 (AFL All-Star Offensive Tackle in 1966 and 1968)
Gary Puetz (OL) 1979–81
Ken Sims (DE) 1982–89
Pat Harlow (Tackle) 1991–95
Larry Tharpe (OL) 1996
Zefross Moss (Tackle) 1997–99
Greg Robinson-Randall (Tackle) 2000
Mike Compton (Guard) 2001–03
Nick Kaczur (OL) 2005–08

No. 78

Al Richardson (DL) 1960
Jim Boudreaux (OT) 1966–67
Dennis Byrd (DL) 1968
Willie Banks (OL) 1973
Tony McGee (DL) 1974–81
Ron Spears (DL) 1982–83
Marshall Harris (DL) 1983
Art Kuehn (OL) 1983
Eric Stokes (G) for one game on 10-04-87
Bruce Armstrong (Tackle) 1987–2000 (AFC Pro Bowl Tackle in 1990, 1991, 1994, 1995, 1996, and 1997)
(No. 78 was retired in honor of Bruce Armstrong in 2001)

No. 79

George McGee (OL) 1960
Al Richardson (DL) 1960
Jim Lee Hunt (DT) 1960–71 (AFL All-Star Defensive
    Tackle in 1961, 1966, 1967, and 1969)
(No. 79 was retired in Honor of Jim Lee Hunt in 1993)

No. 80

Jack Rudolph (LB) 1960–65
Karl Henke (OL) 1969
Bob Adams (TE) 1973–74
Don Hasselbeck (TE) 1977–83
Brooks Williams (TE) 1983
Irving Fryar (WR) 1984–92 (AFC Pro Bowl Return
    Specialist in 1985)
Larry Linne (WR) 1987
Troy Brown (WR) 1993
Steve Hawkins (WR) 1994
Troy Brown (WR) 1995–2007 (AFC Pro Bowl Wide
    Receiver in 2001)

No. 81

Jim Colclough (WR) 1960–68 (AFL All-Star Wide
    Receiver in 1962)
Charley Frazier (WR) 1969–70
Joe Sweet (WR) 1974
Russ Francis (TE) 1975–80 and 1988 (AFC Pro Bowl
    Tight End in 1976, 1977, and 1978)
Preston Brown (WR) 1980–82
Stephen Starring (WR) 1983–87
Brian Carey (WR) 1987
Zeke Mowatt (TE) 1990
Rob Carpenter (WR) 1991
Walter Stanley (WR) 1992
Ray Crittenden (WR) 1993–94
Hason Graham (WR) 1995–96
Tony Simmons (WR) 1999–00
Charles Johnson (WR) 2001
Donald Hayes (WR) 2002
Bethel Johnson (WR) 2003–05
Jonathan Smith (WR) 2006
Randy Moss (WR) 2007–08 (AFC Pro Bowl Wide
    Receiver in 2007)

No. 82

Jim Whalen (TE) 1965–69
Tom Beer (TE) 1970–72
Eddie Hinton (WR) 1974
Steve Burks (WR) 1975–77
Al Chandler (TE) 1976–79
Ken Toler (WR) 1981–82
Clarence Weathers (WR) 1983–84

Derwin Williams (WR) 1985–87
Dennis Gadbois (WR) 1987
Sammy Martin (WR) 1988–91
Gene Taylor (WR) for one game on 11-17-91
Vincent Brisby (WR) 1993–99
Chris Calloway (WR) 2000
Curtis Jackson (WR) 2000–01
Daniel Graham (TE) 2002–06
Marcellus Rivers (TE) 2007
Stephen Spach (TE) 2007–08

No. 83

Harry Jacobs (DE-LB) 1960–62
Bill Dawson (OL-DL) 1965
Tom Fussell (DL) 1967
Barry Brown (TE) 1969
Mel Baker (WR) for one game on 10-19-75
Ricky Feacher (WR) 1976
Don Westbrook (WR) 1977–81
Cedric Jones (WR) 1982–90
Wayne Coffey (WR) 1987
Michael Timpson (WR) 1991–94
Will Moore (WR) 1995
Dietrich Jells (WR) 1997
Rod Rutledge (TE) 1998–01
Deion Branch (WR) 2002–05
Wes Welker (WR) 2007–08 (AFC Pro Bowl Wide
    Receiver in 2008)

No. 84

Art Graham (WR) 1963–68
Gayle Knief (WR) 1970
Hubie Bryant (WR) 1972
Darryl Stingley (WR) 1973–77
Shawn Jefferson (WR) 1996–99
Shockmain Davis (WR) 2000
Torrance Small (WR) 2001
Fred Coleman (WR) 2001–02
Fred Baxter (TE) 2003
Benjamin Watson (TE) 2004–08

No. 85

Don McComb (DE) for one game on 09-09-60
Jack Atchason (End) for one game on 09-23-60
Nick Buoniconti (LB) 1962-1968 (AFL All-Star
    Linebacker in 1963, 1964, 1965, 1966, and 1967)
Dennis Wirgowski (DE) 1970
Julius Adams (DL) 1971–85 and 1987 (AFC Pro Bowl
    Defensive End in 1980)
Greg Baty (TE) 1987
Todd Frain (TE) 1987
Steve Johnson (TE) 1988

Eric Sievers (TE) 1989–90
Marv Cook (TE) 1991–93 (AFC Pro Bowl Tight End in
    1991 and 1992)
John Burke (TE) 1994–96
Lovett Purnell (TE) 1996–98
Sean Morey (Special Teams) 1999
Jermaine Wiggins (TE) 2000–01
Cam Cleeland (TE) 2002
JJ Stokes (WR) 2003
Jed Weaver (TE) 2004
Doug Gabriel (WR) 2006
Tyson DeVree (TE) 2008

No. 86

Oscar Lofton (End) 1960
Bill Kimber (End) 1961
Tony Romeo (TE) 1962–67
Barry Brown (TE) 1970
Roland Moss (TE) 1971
Bob Windsor (TE) 1972–75
Stanley Morgan (WR) 1977–89 (AFC Pro Bowl Wide
    Receiver in 1979, 1980, 1986, and 1987)
Greg McMurtry (WR) 1990–93
Troy Brown (WR) 1994
Kevin Lee (WR) 1994–95
Mike Bartrum (TE-LS) 1996–99
Eric Bjornson (TE) 2000
David Patten (WR) 2001–04
Tim Dwight (WR) 2005
David Thomas (TE) 2006–08

No. 87

Mike Long (End) 1960
Bobby Nichols (TE) 1967–68
Ray Jacobs (DL) 1969
Ike Lassiter (DL) 1970–71
Jim White (DL) 1972
Steve Schubert (WR) 1974
Al Chandler (TE) 1976–79
Ray Jarvis (WR) 1979
Lin Dawson (TE) 1981–90
Arnold Franklin (TE) 1987
Ben Coates (TE) 1991–99 (AFC Pro Bowl Tight End
    in 1994, 1995. 1996, 1997, and 1998)
Bert Emanuel (WR) 2001
David Givens (WR) 2002–05
Reche Caldwell (WR) 2006

No. 88

Ron Berger (DE) 1969–72
John Mosier (TE) 1973
Al Marshall (WR) 1974
Marlin Briscoe (WR) 1976

Carlos Pennywell (WR) 1978–81
Morris Bradshaw (WR) 1982
Derrick Ramsey (TE) 1983–85
Willie Scott (TE) 1986–88
Hart Lee Dykes (WR) 1989–90
Richard Griffith (TE) 1993
Andre President (TE) for one game on 09-03-95
David Frisch (TE) 1995
Terry Glenn (WR) 1996–2001 (AFC Pro Bowl Wide
    Receiver in 1996)
Christian Fauria (TE) 2002–05
Kyle Brady (TE) 2007
Sam Aiken (WR) 2008

No. 89

Bob Dee (DE) 1960–67 (AFL All-Star Defensive End in
    1961, 1963, 1964, and 1965)
(No. 89 was retired in honor of Bob Dee in 1993)

No. 90

George Webster (LB) 1974–76
Toby Williams (NT) 1983–88
Murray Wichard (DL) 1987
Peter Shorts (DT) for one game on 12-24-89
Garin Veris (DL) 1990–91
Reggie White (DL) 1995
Chad Eaton (DL) 1996–2000
Marty Moore (LB) 2001 season only
Steve Martin (DT) 2002
Dan Klecko (DT/FB) 2003–05
LeKevin Smith (DL) 2006–08

No. 91

George Crump (DL) 1982–83
Rogers Alexander (LB) 1987
Eric Napolski (LB) 1988–89
Orlando Lowry (LB) 1989
Chris Gannon (DL) 1990–93
Bruce Walker (DL) 1994–95
Jeff Kopp (LB) 1999
Bobby Hamilton (DE) 2000–03
Marquise Hill (DE) 2004–06

No. 92

Smiley Creswell (DE) for two games during the 1985
    playoffs
Emanuel McNeil (NT) for one game on 12-24-89
Ray Agnew (DL) 1990–94
Ferric Collons (DL) 1995–99
David Nugent (DE) 2000–01
Ted Washington (NT) 2003
Santonio Thomas (DL) 2007

No. 93

Rico Corsetti (Special Teams)1987
Tim Jordan (LB) 1987–89
Mike Pitts (DL) 1993–94
Monty Brown (LB) 1996
Shawn Stuckey (LB) 1998
Bob Kuberski (DT) 1999
Antico Dalton (LB) 2000
Richard Seymour (DL) 2001–08 (AFC Pro Bowl
    Defensive Lineman in 2002, 2003, 2004, 2005, and
    2006)

No. 94

Mel Black (LB) 1986
David Ward (LB) 1989
Tim Roberts (DT) 1995
Walter Scott (DE) for one game on 10-20-96
Greg Spires (DE) 1998–2000
Jace Sayler (DE) 2001
Ty Warren (DL) 2003–08

No. 95

Ed Reynolds (LB) 1983–91
Frank Sacco (LB) 1987
Dwayne Sabb (LB) 1992–96
Henry Thomas (DT) 1997–2000
Roman Phifer (LB) 2001–04
Tully Banta-Cain (LB) 2006
Rashad Moore (DL) 2007
Rosevelt Colvin (LB) 2008

No. 96

Brent Williams (DL) 1986–93
Dino Mangiero (DL) 1987
Mike Jones (DL) 1994–97
Maugaula Tuitele (LB) 2000
Brandon Mitchell (DE) 2001
Rick Lyle (DL) 2002–03
Wesly Mallard (LB) 2005
Adalius Thomas (LB) 2007–08

No. 97

Milford Hodge (DL) 1986–89
John Guzik (DL) 1987
Sean Smith (DL) 1990–91
Aaron Jones (DL) 1993–95
Mark Wheeler (DL) 1996–98
Reggie Grimes (DT) 2000
Riddick Parker (DT) 2001
Jarvis Green (DE) 2002–08

No. 98

Dennis Owens (DL) 1982–86
Tim Edwards (DL) 1992
Mario Johnson (DL) 1993
Troy Barnett (DL) 1994–95
Brandon Mitchell (DL) 1997–2000
Anthony Pleasant (DE) 2001–03
Chad Brown (LB) 2005 and 2007

No. 99

Ben Thomas (DL) 1985
Steve Wilburn (DL) 1987
Gary Jeter (DL) 1989
David Howard (LB) 1991–92
Jason Carthen (LB) 1993–94
Steve DeOssie (LB-LS) 1995
Vernon Crawford (LB) 1997–99
Marc Megna (LB) 2000
Kole Ayi (LB) for one game on 11-18-01
T.J. Turner (LB) 2001
Bernard Holsey (DL) 2002
Ethan Kelley (DT) for one game on 01-02-05
Mike Wright (DL) 2005–08

Patriot Uniform numbers that have been retired:

No. 73 was retired in honor of Offensive Guard John
Hannah in 1991

No. 20 was retired in honor of Wide Receiver and
Kicker Gino Cappelletti in 1992

No. 79 was retired in honor of Defensive Tackle Jim
Lee Hunt in 1993

No. 89 was retired in honor of Defensive End Bob Dee
in 1993

No. 57 was retired in honor of Linebacker Steve
Nelson in 1993

No. 40 was retired in honor of Cornerback Mike
Haynes in 1997

No. 78 was retired in honor of Offensive Tackle Bruce
Armstrong in 2001

Players who have worn two uniform numbers during their career with the Patriots

Offensive Linemen who have worn two uniform numbers during their career with the Patriots

Jim Boudreaux wore No. 78 and No. 64
Walt Cudzik wore No. 56 and No. 54
Steve DeOssie wore No. 50 and No. 99
Shelby Jordan wore No. 63 and No. 74
Greg Robinson-Randall wore No. 64 and No. 77
Danny Villa wore No. 73 and No. 75
Bob Yates wore No. 61 and No. 50

Running Backs who have worn two uniform numbers during their career with the Patriots

Larry Garron wore No. 46 and No. 40
Bruce Hansen wore No. 24 and No. 35
Michael LeBlanc wore No. 40 and No. 27
Ger Schwedes wore No. 31 and No. 44

Tight Ends who have worn two uniform numbers during their career with the Patriots

Greg Baty wore No. 48 and No. 85
Fred Baxter wore No. 49 and No. 84
Al Chandler wore No. 87 and No. 82
Marv Cook wore No. 46 and No. 85
Todd Frain wore No. 44 and No. 85
Russ Francis wore No. 81 and No. 49
Lovett Purnell wore No. 48 and No. 85
Jermaine Wiggins wore No. 49 and No. 85

Wide Receivers who have worn two uniforms numbers during their career with the Patriots

Troy Brown wore No. 80 and No. 86 and No. 80
Hubie Bryant wore No. 45 and No. 84
Dennis Gadbois wore No. 82 and No. 48
Deitrich Jells wore No. 18 and No. 83
Tony Simmons wore No. 15 and No. 81
Michael Timpson wore No. 45 and No. 83

The only Punter who has worn two uniform numbers during his career with the Patriots

Bryan Wagner wore No. 8 and No. 9

Defensive Linemen who have worn two uniform numbers during their career with the Patriots

Julius Adams wore No. 85 and No. 69
Le Kevin Smith wore No. 65 and No. 90
Garin Veris wore No. 60 and No. 90
Dennis Wirgowski wore No. 85 and No. 70
Mel Witt wore No. 70 and No. 71

Linebackers who have worn two uniform numbers during their career with the Patriots

Eric Alexander wore No. 49 and No. 52
Tully Banta-Cain wore No. 48 and No. 95
Mel Black wore No. 94 and No. 51
Todd Collins wore No. 54 and No. 59
Rosevelt Colvin wore No. 59 and No. 95
Steve DeOssie wore No. 50 and No. 99
Rommie Loudd wore No. 60 and No. 46
Jerry McCabe wore No. 48 and No. 52
Marty Moore wore No. 58 and No. 90
Randy Sealby wore No. 59 and No. 53
Rob Holmberg wore No. 50 and No. 47

Defensive Backs who have worn two uniform numbers during their career with the Patriots

Walter Beach wore No. 26 and No. 41
Terrell Buckley wore No. 27 and No. 22
Tim Gordon wore No. 41 and No. 28
Jerome Henderson wore No. 36 and No. 26
Jimmy Hitchcock wore No. 31 and No. 37
Hank Poteat wore No. 31 and No. 32
Chuck Shonta wore No. 40 and No. 34
Antwain Spann wore No. 31 and No. 28
Bob Soltis wore No. 42 and No. 46

Every player who has worn three uniform numbers during their career with the Patriots

Barry Brown wore No. 66, No. 83, and No. 86
Maugaula Tuitele wore No. 96, No. 47, and No. 59

Trivia

Here is the interactive section of this book. This section challenges the both casual observer and the totally obsessed fanatical follower of the Patriots. I hope that these questions are both enlightening and entertaining. Share these questions with your friends, but be aware that you might want to include some Patriots fans who are over age 40 on your team. There are a variety of categories of questions and many of the wrong answers are other Boston sports personalities. Are you ready to be challenged? Have fun.

Offense Questions

<u>Match the Patriots Offensive Lineman with his particular accomplishment</u>

1. Max Lane

a. I was the first Patriots offensive lineman to recover a fumble in the end zone for a TD

2. John Hannah

b. I advanced an airborne fumble by Troy Brown 30 yards in our 31–26 loss on 10-15-95

3. Pete Brock

c. I caught a six-yard TD pass from Steve Grogan in the 38–24 victory over the New York Jets on 11-21-76

4. Steve Moore

d. I was a blocking back on a Steve Grogan flea-flicker TD pass to Greg Hawthorne on 11-03-85

5. Bruce Armstrong

e. I was the first Patriots offensive lineman to play in more than 200 regular season games

Answers:

1. b. Max Lane advanced an airborne fumble by Troy Brown 30 yards in the 31–26 loss to the Kansas City Chiefs
2. a. John Hannah recovered a fumble in the end zone for a TD in the 34–27 loss to the Miami Dolphins on 12-15-74
3. c. Pete "Deep Throat" Brock caught a six-yard TD pass in their 38–24 win over the New York Jets on 11-21-76
4. d. Steve Moore, who was an offensive tackle, was also used as a blocking back for the Patriots during the 1985 season
5. e. Bruce Armstrong played in 212 regular seaon games and in seven playoff games for the New England Patriots

Match each Patriots Offensive Lineman with his nickname

1. Sam Adams   a. "Big Country"
2. Pete Brock   b. "Big House"
3. John Hannah   c. "Spanky"
4. Max Lane   d. "Hawg"
5. Charley Long   e. "Tree"
6. Steve Moore   f. "Boston Strong Boy"
7. Billy Neighbors   g. "Pimpin Sam"
8. Don Oakes   h. "Just Pete"
9. Len St. Jean   i. "Whimpy"
10. Dwight Wheeler   j. "Choo-Choo"

Answers:

1. g. Sam Adams had the nickname of "Pimpin Sam"
2. h. Pete Brock was "Just Pete"
3. d. John "Hawg" Hannah
4. a. Max "Big Country" Lane
5. j. "Choo-Choo" Charley Long
6. b. Steve "Big House" Moore
7. c. Billy Neighbors had the nickname of "Spanky"
8. e. Don Oakes was also known as "Tree"
9. f. Len St. Jean was the "Boston Strong Boy"
10. i. Dwight "Whimpy" Wheeler

Did you know that?

Steve Grogan ran for a TD in three consecutive regular season games twice during the 1976 season

Match each Patriots Defensive Lineman with his nickname

1. Julius Adams	a. "Earthquake"
2. Ron Berger	b. "Big Mac"
3. Rick Cash	c. "The Whopper"
4. Bob Dee	d. "Boston Strong Boy"
5. Larry Eisenhauer	e. "Bubba"
6. Jim Lee Hunt	f. "Ju Ju"
7. Willie McGinest	g. "Thumper"
8. Lennie St. Jean	h. "Wildman"
9. Kenneth Sims	i. "Game Day"
10. Mel West	j. "The Mole"

Answers:

1. f. Julius "Ju Ju" Adams
2. c. Ron "the Whopper" Berger
3. g. Rick Cash had the nickname of "Thumper"
4. e. Bob "Bubba" Dee
5. h. Larry Eisenhauer was the "Wildman"
6. a. Jim Lee Hunt was known as "Earthquake"
7. b. Willie "Big Mac" McGinest
8. d. Lennie St. Jean was the "Boston Strong Boy"
9. i. Kenneth "Game Day" Sims
10. j. Mel West was known as "the Mole"

Match the starting Patriots Offensive Linemen with their accomplishments in a game or a season

1. LT Leon Gray, LG John Hannah, C Bill Lenkaitis, RG Sam Adams, and RT Bob McKay
2. LT Leon Gray, LG John Hannah, C Bill Lenkaitis, RG Sam Adams, and RT Shelby Jordan
3. LT Brian Holloway, LG John Hannah, C Pete Brock, RB Ron Wooten, and RT Bob Cryder
4. LT Matt Light, LG Mike Compton, C Damien Woody, RG Joe Andruzzi, and RT Greg Robinson-Randall
5. LT Matt Light, G/C Russ Hochstein, C Dan Koppen, RG Joe Andruzzi, and RT Tom Ashworth

a. The Patriots set the NFL record of 3,165 yards rushing and had 30 rushing TDs during the 1978 season
b. The Patriots averaged 4.8 yards per carry and had two RBs average at least 5.5 yards per carry during the 1983 season
c. The starting lineup for the New England Patriots in the 20–17 championship victory over the St. Louis Rams
d. The Patriots averaged five yards per carry, had 2,948 yards rushing, and had 24 rushing TDs during the 1976 season
e. The starting lineup for the New England Patriots in the 32–29 Super Bowl victory over the Carolina Panthers

Answers:

1. d. Leon Gray, John Hannah, Bill Lenkaitis, Sam Adams, and Bob McKay started in all 14 games of the 1976 regular season
2. a. Leon Gray, John Hannah, Bill Lenkaitis, Sam Adams, and Shelby Jordan started in all 16 games of the 1978 regular season
3. b. Brian Holloway, John Hannah, Pete Brock, Ron Wooten, and Bob Cryder started in at least 13-of-16 games in 1983
4. c. Matt Light, Mike Compton, Damien Woody, Joe Andruzzi, and Greg Robinson-Rand all started in their first Super Bowl win
5. e. Matt Light, Russ Hochstein, Dan Koppen, Joe Andruzzi, and Tom Ashworth started in their second Super Bowl win

Did You Know?

If "death comes in threes," then the parity in Dave Meggett's stat line: three carries, three receptions, three punt returns, and three kickoff returns, was a sign of the beginning of the end for Jacksonville's season.

Match the Patriots Quarterback with his rushing accomplishment

1. Drew Bledsoe	a. I ran for a 13-yard TD in our 30–14 victory over the Miami Dolphins on 09-19-76
2. Tony Eason	b. I ran for a 13-yard TD in our 20–14 victory over the Cincinnati Bengals on 10-14-84
3. Doug Flutie	c. I ran 13 yards for the game-winning TD in our 21–17 win over the Indianapolis Colts on 10-02-88
4. Steve Grogan	d. I ran for a 13-yard TD in our 34–17 loss to the Indianapolis Colts on 10-22-00

Answers:

1. d. Drew Bledsoe scored on a 13-yard TD run in the 34–17 loss to the New York Jets 10-02-00
2. b. Tony Eason scored on a 13-yard TD run in the 20–14 win over the Cincinnati Bengals on 10-14-84
3. c. Doug Flutie scored the game-winning TD in the 21–17 victory over the Indianapolis Colts on 10-02-88
4. a. Steve Grogan ran for a 13-yard TD in the 30–14 victory over the Miami Dolphins on 09-19-76

Match the Patriots Running Back with his rushing accomplishment

1. Curtis Martin	a. I ran for a TD in five consecutive games during the 1978 season
2. Horace Ivory	b. I ran for a TD in six consecutive games during the 1998 season
3. Mosi Tatupu	c. I ran for a TD in seven consecutive games during the 1996 season
4. Robert Edwards	d. I ran for a TD in five consecutive games during the 2004 championship season
5. Kevin Faulk	e. I ran for a TD at Candlestick Park, Shea Stadium, the Hoosier Dome, and the Orange Bowl
6. Corey Dillon	f. I ran for a fourth down TD in our 30–24 Monday Night Football win over the Kansas City Chiefs on 12-04-00

Answers:

1. c. Curtis Martin scored a rushing TD in seven consecutive regular season games during the 1996 season
2. a. Horace Ivory scored a rushing TD in five consecutive regular season games during the 1978 season
3. e. Mosi scored a rushing TD in games played at Candlestick Park, Shea Stadium, the Hoosier Dome, and the Orange Bowl
4. b. Robert Edwards scored a rushing TD in his first six NFL games during the 1998 season
5. f. Kevin Faulk scored on a fourth down TD run in the 30–24 Monday Night Football win over the Kansas City Chiefs on 12-04-00
6. d. Corey Dillon ran for a TD in five consecutive regular season games during the 2004 season

Match the Patriots player with his longest run in a regular season game

1. Troy Brown	a. I ran for a 29-yard TD in our 38–17 rout of the Colts at the RCA Dome on 10-21-01
2. Irving Fryar	b. I ran 14 yards with a lateral in our 43–43 tie with Oakland at Fenway Park on 10-16-64
3. Darryl Stingley	c. I ran for a 34-yard TD in our 21–17 win over the Kansas City Chiefs at Schaefer on 09-18-77
4. Gino Cappelletti	d. I had a 35-yard gain in our 21–16 loss to the Buccaneers at Foxboro on 09-03-00
5. David Patten	e. I had a 31-yard gain in our 34–7 rout of the Miami Dolphins at Sullivan Stadium on 10-05-86

Answers:

1. d. Troy Brown led the team in rushing yards and ran for a 35-yard gain in the 21–16 loss to Tampa Bay on 09-03-00
2. e. Irving Fryar
3. c. Darryl Stingley was the first Patriots receiver to run for a TD in a regular season game
4. b. Gino Cappelletti advanced a lateral from Ron Burton 14 yards in the 43–43 tie with the Oakland Raiders on 10-16-64
5. a. David Patten dashed for a 29-yard TD on the first play in the 38–17 rout of the Indianapolis Colts on 10-21-01

Rushing Questions

15 Trivia Questions regarding the rushing statistics of Patriots players

1. Who was the Patriots player who had the last TD run in a game played at Foxboro Stadium?
a. Greg Brady   b. Tom Brady   c. Peter Brady   d. Bobby Brady

2. Who was the running back who had the last TD run by a Patriots player in the last game played at both Harvard Stadium and Boston College Alumni Stadium?
a. Carl Lewis   b. Carl Garrett   c. Garrett Morris   d. Sammy Morris

3. Who was the former AFL All-Star fullback and AFL League MVP who had the last TD run in a regular season game for the Boston Patriots in a game played at Fenway Park?
a. Jim Lampley   b. Jim Nance   c. Jim Nantz   d. Jim Donaldson

4. Who was the first Patriots receiver to run for a TD and catch a TD pass in the same game?
a. Troy Brown   b. Darryl Stingley   c. David Patten   d. Irving Fryar

5. Who is the only Patriots quarterback to rush for more than 100 yards in a regular season game?
a. Peter King   b. Steve Grogan   c. Steve Urkel   d. Steve Austin

6. Who was the first Patriots running back to run for a first down on a fourth down play in a regular season game played at Sullivan Stadium?
a. Van Earl Wright   b. Mark van Eeghen   c. Brad Van Pelt   d. Scott Van Pelt

7. Who was the first Patriots quarterback to run for a first down on a fourth down play in a regular season game played at Gillette Stadium?
a. Colin Cowherd   b. Tom Brady   c. Matt Cassel   d. Doug Flutie

8. Who is the only Patriots quarterback to rush for a TD in a playoff game?
a. Tom Joiner   b. Tom Brady   c. Tom Brokaw   d. Tully Banta-Cain

9. Who is the only Patriots player to rush for a TD in an overtime playoff game?
a. Corey Dillon   b. Tom Brady   c. Kevin Faulk   d. Greg Hill

10. Who is the only Patriots running back to run for a two-point conversion in a Super Bowl?
a. Sam Gash   b. Kevin Faulk   c. Ricky Martin   d. Ricky Ricardo

11. Who was the Patriots running back who ran for 12 touchdowns and, in every game that he ran for a TD, the Patriots were victorious?
a. Jim Craig   b. Craig James   c. Jim Lonborg   d. Jeff Fuller

12. Who was the player who scored the Patriots' first rushing TD in a game played at Fenway Park?
a. Harry Agganis   b. Harry Crump   c. Harry Truman   d. Harry Hooper

13. Who was the first Patriots quarterback to rush for two touchdowns in a regular season game?
a. Tom Ellis   b. Tom Yewcic   c. Tom Yawkey   d. Tom Jones

14. Who was the first Patriots running back to have more than 100 yards rushing in a regular season game?
a. Ron Hobson   b. Ron Burton   c. Brian Daubach   d. Bob Lobel

15. Who was the first New England Patriots running back to average more than 100 yards per game over a 16-game regular season?
a. Corey Croom   b. Corey Dillon   c. Corey Briggs   d. Chad Bradford

Answers:

1. Tom Brady ran for a six-yard TD in the 16–13 overtime playoff game win vs the Oakland Raiders on 01-19-02
2. Carl Garrett scored the last rushing TD by a Patriots player in a game played at Harvard Stadium and BC Alumni Stadium
3. Jim Nance, an All-Star running back in 1966 and 1967 and the AFL MVP in 1966, scored the Patriots last rushing TD at Fenway Park
4. Darryl Stingley ran for a 34-yard TD and caught a 21-yard TD pass in the 21–17 win over the Chiefs on 09-18-77
5. Steve Grogan rushed for 103 yards in the 41–7 rout of the New York Jets at Schaefer Stadium on Monday Night Football on 10-18-76
6. Mark van Eeghen
7. Tom Brady
8. Tom Brady
9. Tom Brady
10. Kevin Faulk
11. Craig James
12. Harry Crump
13. Tom Yewcic
14. Ron Burton
15. Corey Dillon had 1,635 yards rushing in 16 games during the 2004 regular season

Five Trivia Questions relating to memorable runs by Patriots players

1. Who are the six Patriots quarterbacks who have run for a game-winning TD in a regular season game?
a. Bill Parcells, Jimmy Piersal, Steve Spurrier, Bob Nuemeier, Dan Fouts, and Herman Moore
b. Babe Parilli, Jim Plunkett, Steve Grogan, Bob Bleier, Doug Flutie, and Hugh Millen
c. Brad Pitt, Jim Palmer, Steve Young, Bob Trumpy, Derrick Fletcher, and Howie Mandell
d. Bernie Parent, Jack Parker, Steven Wright, Bob Watson, Darren Flutie, and Harold Melvin

Answer:
b. Babe Parilli, Jim Plunkett, Steve Grogan, Bob Bleier, Doug Flutie, and Hugh Millen have run for a game-winning TD

2. Who are the three Patriots running backs who have run for a game-winning TD twice in their career with the Patriots?
a. Randall Cunningham, Todd Collins, and Curtis Rowe
b. Sam Cunningham, Tony Collins, and Curtis Martin
c. Richie Cunningham., Tom Collins, and Curtis Joseph
d. Billy Cunningham, Tom Cruise, and Curtis Strange

Answer:
b. Sam Cunningham, Tony Collins, and Curtis Martin each ran for two game-winning TDs in their careers with the Patriots

3. Who are the three Patriots wide receivers who have run for a TD in a regular season game?
a. Don Imus, Christian Fauria, and Dale Arnold
b. Darryl Stingley, Irving Fryar, and David Patten
c. Dwayne Sabb, Jack Fisher, and Dale Jarrett
d. Don Shula, Fred Funk, and Dale Ernhardt

Answer:
b. Darryl Stingley, Irving Fryar, and David Patten have run for a TD in a regular season game for the Patriots

4. Who are the four Patriots receivers who have a run from scrimmage of at least 30 yards in a regular season game?
a. Bethel Johnson, Darrell Johnson, Ted Johnson, and Dennis Johnson
b. Darryl Stingley, Irving Fryar, Terry Glenn, and Troy Brown
c. Don Banks, Fred Kirsch, Paul Perillo, and Jerry Remy
d. Sam Jones, Dalton Jones, K.C. Jones, and Cedric Jones

Answer:
b. Darryl Stingley, Irving Fryar, Terry Glenn, and Troy Brown have had a run from scrimmage of 30+ yards for the Patriots

5. Who are the four Patriots running backs who have rushed for a TD in at least 25 regular season games?
a. Craig Mustard, Tom Curran, Sean McDonough, and Jimmy Myers
b. Curtis Martin, Tony Collins, Sam Cunningham, and Jim Nance
c. Connie Mack, Ted Cox, Sandy Moger, and Jimmy Tingle
d. Cedric Maxwell, Todd Collins, John Stephens, and Joe Haggerty

Answer:
b. Curtis Martin, Tony Collins, Sam Cunningham, and Jim Nance have scored at least 25 rushing touchdowns with the Patriots

Passing Questions

10 Trivia Questions regarding the passing exploits of a Patriots player

1. Who was the first Patriots quarterback to complete a pass in a regular season game?
a. Butch Stearns   b. Butch Songin   c. Bobby Schmatz   d. Boris Spasky

2. Who caught the first pass completion by Tom Brady in a regular season game?
a. Pete Sheppard   b. Rod Rutledge   c. Rod Rust   d. Sal Palontonio

3. Who caught Scott Zolak's longest pass completion of 72 yards in a regular season game?
a. Kevin Winter   b. Vincent Brisby   c. Lovett Purnell   d. Larry Ridley

4. Who was the first Patriots player to complete two two-point conversion passes in the same game?
a. Bill Tierney   b. Drew Bledsoe   c. Tom Brady   d. Gino Cappelletti

5. Who was the first Patriots player to complete a two-point pass and catch a pass for a two-point conversion?
a. Glenn Beck   b. Gino Cappelletti   c. Sean Hannity   d. Bill O'Reilly

6. Who threw a 91-yard TD pass to David Patten in the 38–17 rout of the Indianapolis Colts on 10-21-01?
a. Troy Brown   b. Tom Brady   c. Don Criqui   d. Peyton Manning

7. Who completed a 23-yard pass to quarterback Tom Brady in the 20–13 win over the Miami Dolphins on 12-22-01?
a. JR Redmond   b. Kevin Faulk   c. Patrick Pass   d. Troy Brown

8. Who was the first Patriots quarterback to complete all 13 of his passes in the first half of a regular season game?
a. Hugh Hefner   b. Hugh Millen   c. Matt Millen   d. Mike Vallee

9. Who was the first Patriots quarterback to complete all 12 of his passes in the first half of a playoff game?
a. Bob Ryan   b. Tom Brady   c. Mac Bledsoe   d. Mac Davis

10. Who was the first Patriots quarterback to complete all eight of his passes in the overtime period of a playoff game?
a. Ken Stabler   b. Tom Brady   c. Rich Gannon   d. Dan Roche

Answers:

1. Butch Songin completed a one-yard pass to Boston Patriots wide receiver Jim Colclough on 09-09-60
2. Tom Brady completed his first NFL pass to Rod Rutledge in the 34–9 loss to the Detroit Lions on 11-23-00
3. Vincent Brisby caught a 72-yard pass from Scott Zolak in the 30–17 loss to the Altanta Falcons on 10-01-95
4. Drew Bledsoe threw a two-point pass to Sam Gash and Ben Coates in the 46–38 win over the Baltimore Ravens on 10-06-96
5. Gino Cappelletti
6. Tom Brady
7. Kevin Faulk
8. Hugh Millen was 13-of-13 in the first half in the 41–7 loss to the Buffalo Bills on 09-27-92
9. Tom Brady was 12-of-12 in the first half of their 31–20 playoff game win over the Jacksonville Jaguars on 01-12-08
10. Tom Brady was 8-of-8 in the overtime period of the 16–13 overtime playoff win vs the Oakland Raiders on 01-19-02

Match the Patriots Quarterback with his passing accomplishment

1. Babe Parilli   a. I was the first Patriots quarterback to throw four TD passes in a game played at BU Field

2. Butch Songin   b. I was the first Patriots quarterback to throw four TD passes in a game played at Fenway Park

3. Jim Plunkett   c. I was the first Patriots quarterback to throw four TD passes in a game played at Schaefer Stadium

4. Steve Grogan   d. I was the first Patriots quarterback to throw four TD passes in a game played at Sullivan Stadium

5. Tom Brady   e. I was the first Patriots quarterback to throw four TD passes in a game played at Gillette Stadium

Answers:

1. b. Babe Parilli tossed four TD passes in the 43–43 Tie with the Oakland Raiders at Fenway Park on 10-16-64
2. a. Butch Songin tossed four TD passes in the 45–17 rout of the Denver Broncos at BU Field on 09-16-61
3. c. Jim Plunkett tossed four TD passes in the 38–33 victory over the Buffalo Bills at Schaefer Stadium on 11-14-71
4. d. Steve Grogan tossed four TD passes in the 42–20 win over the New York Jets at Sullivan Stadium on 10-30-88
5. e. Tom Brady tossed four TD passes in the 41–38 overtime win vs the Kansas City Chiefs at Gillette Stadium on 09-22-02

Match the Patriots Quarterback with his passing accomplishment

6. Drew Bledsoe   a. I was the first Patriots quarterback to complete a TD pass of at least 75 yards in a game at BU Field

7. Doug Flutie   b. I was the first Patriots quarterback to complete a TD pass of at least 75 yards in game at Fenway Park

8. Jim Plunkett   c. I was the first Patriots quarterback to complete a TD pass of at least 75 yards in a game at Schaefer Stadium

9. Babe Parilli   d. I was the first Patriots quarterback to complete a TD pass of at least 75 yards in a game at Sullivan Stadium

10. Tom Yewcic   e. I was the first Patriots quarterback to complete a TD pass of more than 75 yards at Foxboro Stadium

Answers:

6. e. Drew Bledsoe threw an 84-yard TD to Ben Coates in the 42–23 win over the Miami Dolphins at Foxboro Stadium on 11-03-96
7. d. Doug Flutie threw an 80-yard TD to Irving Fryar in the 30–7 win over the Chicago Bears at Sullivan Stadium on 10-30-88
8. c. Jim Plunkett threw an 80-yard TD to Carl Garrett in the 38–33 victory over the Buffalo Bills at Schaefer Stadium on 11-14-71
9. b. Babe Parilli threw a 76-yard TD to Larry Garron in the 45–3 rout of the Houston Oilers at Fenway Park on 11-01-63
10. a. TomYewcic threw a 78-yard TD to Jim Colclough in the 24–17 win over the New York Titans at BU Field on 11-30-62

Five Trivia Questions on Passing

1. Who was the Patriots quarterback who tossed an 88-yard TD pass to Randy Vataha in the fourth quarter to help defeat the defending World Champion Baltimore Colts, 21–17, at Memorial Stadium on 12-19-71?

a. Mike Reiss   b. Jim Plunkett   c. Daryle Lamonica   d. Upton Bell

2. Who was the Patriots quarterback who tossed a two-yard TD pass to Ben Coates in the fourth quarter to defeat the Phoenix Cardinals, 23–21, at Sun Devil Stadium on 10-10-93?

a. Scott Mitchell   b. Scott Secules   c. Scott Zolak   d. Scott Cooper

3. Who was the Patriots quarterback who tossed a 13-yard TD pass to Ben Coates on fourth down to defeat the New York Giants, 23–22, at Giants Stadium on 12-21-96?

a. Gerry Callahan   b. Drew Bledsoe   c. Scott Zolak   d. Phil Simms

4. Who was the Patriots quarterback who tossed an 18-yard TD pass to David Givens with 36 seconds left in the game to defeat the Denver Broncos, 30–26, at Invesco Field on 11-03-03?

a. John Elway   b. Tom Brady   c. Jake Plummer   d. Randy Cross

5. Who has thrown a TD pass in 14 consecutive playoff games for the Patriots?

a. Rob Bradford   b. Tom Brady   c. Ron Borges   d. Chris Price

Answers:

1. Jim Plunkett threw an 88-yard TD pass to Randy Vataha to beat the Colts, 21–17, at Memorial Stadium on 12-19-71
2. Scott Secules threw a two-yard TD pass to Ben Coates to beat the Phoenix Cardinals, 23–21, at Sun Devil Stadium on 10-10-93
3. Drew Bledsoe tossed a 13-yard TD to Ben Coates on fourth down to beat the New York Giants, 23–22, at Giants Stadium on 12-21-96
4. Tom Brady threw an 18-yard TD pass to David Givens to defeat the Broncos, 30–26, at Invesco Field on 11-03-03
5. Tom Brady has thrown a TD pass in 14 consecutive playoff games

Match the Patriots Quarterback with his TD pass to a Patriots Running Back in a victorious home game vs Buffalo

1. Drew Bledsoe

2. Tom Brady

3. Matt Cavanaugh

4. Babe Parilli

5. Jim Plunkett

6. Tom Yewcic

a. I tossed a two-yard TD to Robert Edwards in our 25–21 win over Buffalo at Foxboro Stadium on 11-29-98

b. I tossed an 80-yard TD to Carl Garrett in our 38–33 win over Buffalo at Schaefer Stadium on 11-14-71

c. I tossed a 44-yard TD to Larry Garron in our 17–7 win over Buffalo at Fenway Park on 12-01-63

d. I tossed a six-yard TD to Kevin Faulk in our 21–11 victory over the Bills at Foxboro Stadium on 11-11-01

e. I tossed a five-yard TD pass to Andy Johnson in our 24–2 rout of the Bills at Schaefer Stadium on 12-14-80

f. I tossed a 69-yard TD to Ron Burton in our 21–10 victory over the Bills at BU Field on 11-23-62

Answers:

1. a. Drew Bledsoe threw a two-yard TD pass to Robert Edwards in the 25–21 victory over the Buffalo Bills on 11-29-98
2. d. Tom Brady tossed a six-yard TD pass to Kevin Faulk in the 21–11 victory over the Buffalo Bills on 11-11-01
3. e. Matt Cavanaugh threw a five-yard TD pass to Andy Johnson in the 24–2 rout of the Buffalo Bills on 12-14-80
4. c. Babe Parilli connected on a 44-yard TD pass to Larry Garron in the 17–7 victory over the Buffalo Bills on 12-01-63
5. b. Jim Plunkett completed an 80-yard TD pass to Carl Garrett in the 38–33 victory over the Buffalo Bills on 11-14-71
6. f. Tom Yewcic connected on a 69-yard TD pass to Ron Burton in the 21–10 victory over the Buffalo Bills on 11-23-62

Match the Patriots Quarterback with his TD pass to a Patriots Tight End in a victorious home game vs the Buffalo Bills

7. Steve Grogan

    a. I tossed a 10-yard TD to Tom Beer in our 38–33 victory over the Bills at Schaefer Stadium on 11-14-71

8. Tony Eason

    b. I tossed a two-yard TD to Don Hasselbeck in our 30–19 win over Buffalo at Schaefer Stadium on 01-02-83

9. Matt Cavanaugh

    c. I tossed a five-yard TD to Russ Francis in our 24–2 rout of the Bills at Schaefer Stadium on 12-14-80

10. Mike Taliaferro

    d. I tossed a one-yard TD to Daniel Graham in our 31–0 shutout of the Bills at Gillette Stadium on 12-27-03

11. Jim Plunkett

    e. I tossed two TDs to Jim Whalen in our 23–6 win over the Bills at Fenway Park on 10-20-68

12. Drew Bledsoe

    f. I tossed a fourth quarter 13-yard TD to Greg Baty in our 22–19 win vs Buffalo at Sullivan Stadium on 11-23-86

13. Tom Brady

    g. I tossed a last second one-yard TD to Ben Coates to defeat Buffalo 25–21 at Foxboro Stadium on 11-29-98

Answers:

7. b. Steve Grogan tossed a one-yard TD pass to Don Hasselbeck in the 30–19 victory over the Buffalo Bills on 01-02-83
8. f. Tony Eason threw an eight-yard TD pass to Greg Baty in the 22–19 victory over the Buffalo Bills on 11-23-86
9. c. Matt Cavanaugh tossed a five-yard TD pass to Russ Francis in the 24–2 rout of the Buffalo Bills on 12-14-80
10. e. Mike Taliaferro threw two TD passes to Jim Whalen in the 23–6 victory over the Buffalo Bills on 10-20-68
11. a. Jim Plunkett connected on a 10-yard TD pass to Tom Beer in the 38–33 win over the Buffalo Bills on 11-14-71
12. g. Drew Bledsoe tossed a one-yard TD pass to Ben Coates with no time left in the 25–21 win over the Buffalo Bills on 11-29-98
13. d. Tom Brady completed a one-yard TD pass to Daniel Graham in the 31–0 shutout of the Buffalo Bills on 12-27-03

Match the Patriots quarterback with his TD pass to a Patriots Wide Receiver in a victorious home game vs Buffalo

14. Tom Brady

    a. I tossed a five-yard TD to Gino Cappelletti in our 52–21 rout of the Buffalo Bills at BU Field on 10-22-61

15. Steve Grogan

    b. I tossed a nine-yard TD pass to Bethel Johnson in our 31–0 shutout of the Buffalo Bills at Gillette Stadium on 12-27-03

16. Jim Plunkett

    c. I tossed a 24-yard TD to Stanley Morgan in our 38–10 rout of the Buffalo Bills at Sullivan Stadium on 11-11-84

17. Tony Eason

    d. I tossed a 16-yard TD to Irving Fryar in our 14–3 victory over the Buffalo Bills at Sullivan Stadium on 10-13-85

18. Drew Bledsoe

    e. I tossed a 16-yard TD to Randy Vataha in our 38–33 win over the Buffalo Bills at Schaefer Stadium on 11-14-71

19. Tom Yewcic

    f. I tossed a five-yard TD to Vincent Brisby in our 27–14 win over the Buffalo Bills at Foxboro Stadium on 10-23-95

20. Butch Songin

    g. I tossed a 19-yard TD to Gino Cappelletti in our 21–10 win over the Buffalo Bills at BU Field on 11-23-62

Answers:

14. b. Tom Brady tossed a nine-yard TD pass to Bethel Johnson in the 31–0 shutout of the Buffalo Bills on 12-27-03
15. d. Steve Grogan connected on a 16-yard TD pass to Irving Fryar in the 14–3 victory over the Buffalo Bills on 10-13-85
16. e. Jim Plunkett tossed a 16-yard TD pas to Randy Vataha in the 38–33 win over the Buffalo Bills on 11-14-71
17. c. Tony Eason completed a 24-yard TD pass to Stanley Morgan in the 38–10 rout of the Buffalo Bills on 11-11-84
18. f. Drew Bledsoe completed a five-yard TD pass to Vincent Brisby in the 27–14 win over the Buffalo Bills on 10-23-95
19. g. Tom Yewcic completed a 19-yard TD pass to Gino Cappelletti in the 21–10 victory over the Buffalo Bills on 11-23-62
20. a. Butch Songin threw a five-yard TD pass to Gino Cappelletti in the 52–21 rout of the Buffalo Bills on 10-22-61

Did you know that?

The Neil Graff Award is awarded to the most underrated Seattle Seahawks player of the year

Match the Patriots Quarterback with his specific TD pass to a Patriots Receiver in a lopsided victory in front of the home crowd

21. Doug Flutie

a. I tossed a 15-yard TD pass to Randy Vataha in our 20–0 shutout of the Jets at Schaefer Stadium on 10-10-71

22. Steve Grogan

b. I tossed a 24-yard TD pass to Darryl Stingley in our 31–0 shutout of Seattle at Schaefer Stadium on 10-09-77

23. Drew Bledsoe

c. I tossed a 12-yard TD pass to Russ Francis in our 34–0 shutout of the Dolphins at Schaefer Stadium on 10-12-80

24. M.Cavanaugh

d. I tossed a 30-yard TD pass to Michael Timpson in our 38–0 shutout of the Colts at Foxboro Stadium on 12-26-93

25. Jim Plunkett

e. I tossed a 19-yard TD pass to Troy Brown in our 31–0 shutout of the Bills at Gillette Stadium on 12-27-03

26. Babe Parilli

f. I tossed a 14-yard TD pass to Don Westbrook in our 56–3 rout of the New York Jets at Schaefer Stadium on 09-09-79

27. Tony Eason

g. I tossed an 18-yard HB Option TD pass to Jim Colclough in our 45–17 rout of Denver at BU Field on 09-16-61

28. Tom Brady

h. I tossed a 38-yard TD pass to Irving Fryar in our 34–7 rout of the Dolphins at Sullivan Stadium on 10-05-86

29. Tom Owen

i. I tossed a 26-yard TD pass to Stanley Morgan in our 30–7 rout of the Bears at Sullivan Stadium on 10-30-88

30. Tom Yewcic

j. I tossed a seven-yard TD pass to Gino Cappelletti in our 41–16 rout of the Broncos at BU Field on 09-21-62

Answers:

21. i. Doug Flutie tossed a 26-yard TD pass to Stanley Morgan in the 30–7 rout of the Chicago Bears on 10-30-88
22. b. Steve Grogan tossed a 24-yard TD pass to Darryl Stingley in the 31–0 shutout of the Seahawks on 10-09-77
23. d. Drew Bledsoe threw a 30-yard TD pass to Michael Timpson in the 38–0 shutout of the Colts on 12-26-93
24. c. Matt Cavanaugh completed a 12-yard TD pass to Russ Francis in the 34–0 shutout of Miami on 10-12-80
25. a. Jim Plunkett tossed a 15-yard TD pass to Randy Vataha in the 20–0 shutout of the New York Jets on 10-10-71
26. j. Babe Parilli completed a seven-yard TD pass to Gino Cappelletti in the 41–16 rout of the Broncos on 09-21-62
27. h. Tony Eason tossed a 38-yard TD pass to Irving Fryar in the 34–7 rout of the Miami Dolphins on 10-05-86
28. e. Tom Brady threw a 19-yard TD pass to Troy Brown in the 31–0 shutout of the Buffalo Bills on 12-27-03
29. f. Tom Owen tossed a 14-yard TD pass to Don Westbrook in the 56–3 rout of the New York Jets on 09-09-79
30. g. Tom Yewcic threw an 18-yard halfback option TD pass to Jim Colclough in the 45–17 rout of Denver on 09-16-61

Match the Patriots player with his particular TD pass of at least 50 yards in a victorious home game

31. Tom Brady

a. I tossed an 84-yard TD to Ben Coates in our 42–23 win over Miami at Foxboro Stadium on 11-03-96

32. Tom Yewcic

b. I tossed a 76-yard TD to Larry Garron in our 45–3 rout of the Oilers at Fenway Park on 11-01-63

33. Tony Eason

c. I tossed a 58-yard TD to Troy Brown in our 38–30 win over Tennessee at Gillette Stadium on 10-05-03

34. Drew Bledsoe

d. I tossed a 78-yard TD to Jim Colclough in our 24–17 win vs the Titans at BU Field on 11-30-62

35. Jim Plunkett

e. I tossed a 67-yard TD to Stanley Morgan in our 34–17 win vs Cleveland at Schaefer Stadium on 09-07-80

36. Steve Grogan

f. I tossed a 63-yard TD to Reggie Rucker in our 33–24 win vs Green Bay at Schaefer Stadium on 11-18-73

37. Andy Johnson

g. I tossed a 66-yard TD to Stanley Morgan in our 33–17 win vs the Chiefs at Schaefer Stadium on 10-04-81

38. Babe Parilli

h. I tossed a 52-yard TD to Gino Cappelletti in our 45–17 rout of Denver at BU Field on 09-16-61

39. Butch Songin

i. I tossed a 50-yard TD to Stanley Morgan in our 34–23 win vs the Bengals at Sullivan Stadium on 12-22-85

40. Doug Flutie

j. I tossed an 80-yard TD pass to Irving Fryar in our 30–7 win vs the Chicago Bears at Sullivan Stadium on 10-30-88

Answers:

31. c. Tom Brady connected on a 58-yard TD pass to Troy Brown in the 38–30 win over the Titans on 10-05-03
32. d. Tom Yewcic connected on a 78-yard TD pass to Jim Colclough in the 24–17 win over the Titans on 11-30-62
33. i. Tony Eason connected on a 50-yard TD pass to Stanley Morgan in the 34–23 win over the Bengals on 12-22-85
34. a. Drew Bledsoe completed an 84-yard TD pass to Ben Coates in the 42–23 win over the Dolphins on 11-03-96
35. f. Jim Plunkett connected on a 63-yard TD pass to Reggie Rucker in the 33–24 win over Green Bay on 11-18-73
36. e. Steve Grogan completed a 67-yard TD pass to Stanley Morgan in the 34–17 win over the Browns on 09-07-80
37. g. Andy Johnson threw a 66-yard HB option TD pass to Stanley Morgan in the 33–17 win over the Chiefs on 10-04-81
38. b. Babe Parilli tossed a 76-yard TD pass to Larry Garron in the 45–3 rout of the Houston Oilers on 11-01-63
39. h. Butch Songin connected on a 52-yard TD pass to Gino Cappelletti in the 45–17 rout of Denver on 09-16-61
40. j. Doug Flutie connected on an 80-yard TD to Irving Fryar in the 30–7 win over the Chicago Bears on 10-30-88

Match the Patriots Quarterback with his particular accomplishment in a home game that the Patriots shut out their opponent

41. Tom Brady

a. I tossed a two TD passes in our 24–0 shutout of the Oilers at BC Alumni Stadium on 11-02-69

42. Tom Ramsey

b. I tossed two TD passes in our 20–0 shutout of the New York Jets at Schaefer Stadium on 10-10-71

43. Steve Grogan

c. I tossed three TD passes in our 31–0 shutout of the Seattle Seahawks at Schaefer Stadium on 10-09-77

44. Jim Plunkett

d. I tossed an eight-yard TD pass in our 24–0 shutout of the Indianapolis Colts at Sullivan Stadium on 11-22-87

45. Mike Taliaferro

e. I tossed four TD passes in our 31–0 shutout of the Buffalo Bills at Gillette Stadium on 12-27-03

Answers:

41. e. Tom Brady tossed four TD passes in the 31–0 shutout of the Buffalo Bills on 12-27-03
42. d. Tom Ramsey completed an eight-yard TD pass to Irving Fryar in the 24–0 shutout of the Indianapolis Colts on 11-22-87
43. c. Steve Grogan threw three TD passes in the 31–0 shutout of the Seattle Seahawks on 10-09-77
44. b. Jim Plunkett tossed two TD passes in the 20–0 shutout of the New York Jets on 10-10-71
45. a. Mike Taliaferro threw two TD passes in the 24–0 shutout of the Houston Oilers on 11-02-69

Match the Patriots Quarterback with his particular accomplishment in a game that the Patriots won by more than 33 points

46. Tom Brady

a. I tossed five TD passes in our 56–3 rout of the New York Jets on 09-09-79

47. Matt Cavanaugh

b. I tossed two TD passes in our 44–7 rout of the New York Jets on 09-15-02

48. Drew Bledsoe

c. I tossed a TD pass to Russ Francis in our 34–0 shutout of the Miami Dolphins on 10-12-80

49. Butch Songin

d. I tossed a TD pass to Jim Colclough in our 35–0 shutout of the Los Angeles Chargers on 10-08-60

50. Steve Grogan

e. I tossed two TD passes in our 38–0 shutout of the Indianapolis Colts on 12-26-93

Answers:

46. b. Tom Brady threw two TD passes in the 44–7 rout of the New York Jets on 09-15-02
47. c. Matt Cavanaugh tossed a 12-yard TD pass to Russ Francis in the 34–0 shutout of the Miami Dolphins on 10-12-80
48. e. Drew Bledsoe threw two TD passes in the 38–0 shutout of the Indianapolis Colts on 12-26-93
49. d. Butch Songin tossed a 19-yard TD pass to Jim Colclough in the 35–0 shutout of the Los Angeles Chargers on 10-08-60
50. a. Steve Grogan threw five TD passes in the 56–3 rout of the New York Jets on 09-09-79

Match the Patriots player with his dramatic accomplishment in a victorious Patriots Game

51. Adam Vinatieri	a. I tossed an 18-yard TD pass to David Givens with 30 seconds left to beat Denver, 30–26, on 11-03-03
52. Jim Plunkett	b. I tossed a 25-yard TD pass to Irving Fryar on the last play in our 30–28 win vs the Rams on 11-16-86
53. Babe Parilli	c. I tossed a four-yard TD pass to Troy Brown in our 40–22 win over the St. Louis Rams on 11-07-04
54. Tony Eason	d. I tossed two TD passes to Larry Garron in our 26–8 playoff game win over Buffalo on 12-28-63
55. Scott Secules	e. I tossed two TD passes in our 24–21 comeback win over the San Francisco 49ers on 12-20-98
56. Hugh Millen	f. I tossed a 16-yard TD pass to Don Hasselback in the fourth quarter to beat the Seahawks, 37–31, on 09-21-80
57. Drew Bledsoe	g. I tossed a two-yard TD pass to Ben Coates in the fourth quarter to beat the Cardinals 23–21 on 10-10-93
58. Scott Zolak	h. I tossed a 14-yard TD pass to Kevin Turner to defeat the Vikings 26–20 in overtime on 11-13-94
59. Steve Grogan	i. I tossed a 45-yard TD pass to Michael Timpson to beat the Colts, 23–17, in overtime on 12-08-91
60. Tom Brady	j. I tossed an 88-yard TD pass to Randy Vatahain in the fourth quarter to beat the Baltimore Colts, 21–17, on 12-19-71

Answers:

51. c. Adam Vinatieri tossed a four-yard TD pass to Troy Brown in the 40–22 win over the St. Louis Rams
52. j. Jim Plunkett tossed an 88-yard TD to Randy Vataha to defeat the former Super Bowl Champion Baltimore Colts, 21–17
53. d. Babe Parilli threw two TD passes to Larry Garron in the 1963 AFL Divisional Playoff Game win over the Buffalo Bills
54. b. Tony Eason tossed a 25-yard "Hail Mary" TD pass to Irving Fryar on the last play of the 30–28 win over the Los Angeles Rams
55. g. Scott Secules threw a two-yard TD pass to Ben Coates in the fourth quarter of the 23–21 victory over the Phoenix Cardinals
56. i. Hugh Millen tossed a 45-yard TD pass to Michael Timpson to defeat the Indianapolis Colts, 23–17, in overtime
57. h. Drew Bledsoe threw a 14-yard TD pass to Kevin Turner to defeat the Minnesota Vikings, 26–20, in overtime
58. e. Scott Zolak completed two TD passes in the 24–21 comeback win over the San Francisco 49ers
59. f. Steve Grogan tossed a 16-yard TD pass in the fourth quarter to defeat the Seattle Seahawks, 37–31
60. a. Tom Brady threw an 18-yard TD pass to David Givens with 30 seconds left in the 30–26 win over the Denver Broncos

Receiving Questions

Part One Receiving Questions

1. Who was the first Patriots player with a reception in a playoff game?

a. Rick Barry   b. Ron Burton   c. Robbie Benson   d. Roger Bannister

2. Who was the Patriots receiver who caught an 88-yard TD pass in the fourth quarter for the game-winning TD in the 21–17 win over the defending Super Bowl Champion Baltimore Colts at Memorial Stadium on 12-19-71?

a. Rabbit Maranville   b. Randy "The Rabbit" Vataha   c. Speedy Gonzalez   d. Speedy Duncan

3. Who was the Patriots receiver who caught a fourth down pass on his knees in the snow to help set up the over-time game-winning 23-yard field goal by Adam Vinatieri to beat the Oakland Raiders 16–13 in the 2001 AFC Divisional Playoff Game at Foxboro Stadium on 01-19-02?
a. Jacoby Ellsbury   b. David Patten   c. Troy Brown   d. Ed Harding

4. Who is the only Patriots tight end who has caught a TD pass from six different players? (Steve Grogan, Marc Wilson, Tommy Hodson, Jon Vaughn, Hugh Millen, and Drew Bledsoe)
a. Tom Beer   b. Marv Cook   c. Marv Albert   d. Ben Coates

5. Who is the only Patriots wide receiver who has caught a TD pass from seven Patriots quarterbacks? (Tony Eason, Steve Grogan, Tom Ramsey, Doug Flutie, Marc Wilson, Hugh Millen, and Tommy Hodson)
a. Michael Timpson   b. Irving Fryar   c. Greg McMurtry   d. Conan O'Brien

6. Who is the only Patriots player to catch a TD pass thrown by a quarterback, a running back, a wide receiver, and a kicker?
a. Mosi Tatupu   b. Troy Brown   c. Wes Welker   d. Kevin Faulk

7. Who was the first Patriots wide receiver with at least 100 yards receiving in a playoff game?
a. Terry Glenn   b. Gino Cappelletti   c. Howie Carr   d. Stanley Morgan

8. Who was the first Patriots tight end with at least 100 yards receiving in a playoff game?
a. Jermaine Wiggins   b. Russ Francis   c. Billy Costa   d. Jim Whalen

9. Who was the first Patriots receiver to have at least 100 yards receiving in consecutive Super Bowls?
a. Dana Barros   b. Deion Branch   c. Don Baylor   d. Dave Bing

10. Who was the first Patriots receiver with at least 100 yards receiving in consecutive games that the Patriots won?
a. Russel Baxter   b. Darryl Stingley   c. Randy Vataha   d. Jon Scott

Answers:
1. Ron Burton caught a nine-yard pass for the first reception in the first playoff game for the Patriots on 12-28-63
2. Randy Vataha
3. David Patten
4. Marv Cook
5. Irving Fryar
6. Troy Brown has caught a TD pass from Drew Bledsoe, Tom Brady, Dave Meggett, David Patten, and Adam Vinatieri
7. Gino Cappelletti had 109 yards receiving in the 26–8 playoff game victory over the Bills on 12-28-63
8. Russ Francis had 101 yards receiving the playoff game on 12-31-78
9. Deion Branch scored on a 60-yard TD pass in the 41–27 playoff game win over the Steelers on 01-23-05
10. Darryl Stingley had 116 yards receiving and 121 yards receiving in wins over Baltimore and New York in October 1977

Match the Receiver with his longest reception as a Patriots player

1. Greg McMurtry
a. I caught a 72-yard pass from Scott Zolak in our 30–17 loss to the Falcons on 10-01-95

2. Terry Glenn
b. I caught an 86-yard TD pass from Drew Bledsoe in our 23–9 win over the Steelers on 12-06-98

3. Vincent Brisby
c. I caught a 65-yard TD pass from Scott Zolak in our 37–34 overtime win over the Colts on 11-15-92

4. Michael Timpson
d. I caught a 60-yard TD pass from Hugh Millen in our 29–7 loss to the Bengals on 12-22-91

5. Irving Fryar
e. I caught an 80-yard TD pass from Doug Flutie in our 30–7 win over the Bears on 10-30-88

Match these receivers with his career longest reception as a Patriots player

6. Tony Simmons

a. I caught a 69-yard TD pass from Jim Plunkett in our 42–3 rout of the Colts on 10-06-74

7. Reggie Rucker

b. I caught a 68-yard pass from Steve Grogan in our 17–3 win over the Colts on 10-23-77

8. Randy Vataha

c. I caught an 88-yard TD pass from Jim Plunkett in our 21–17 win over the Colts on 12-19-71

9. Darryl Stingley

d. I caught a 63-yard TD pass from Drew Bledsoe in our 21–16 win over the Colts on 11-01-98

10. Henry Ellard

e. I caught a 19-yard pass from Drew Bledsoe in our 21–16 win over the Colts on 11-01-98

Answers:
6. d. Tony Simmons scored on a 63-yard TD pass from Drew Bledsoe in the 21–16 win over the Colts on 11-01-98
7. a. Reggie Rucker scored on a 69-yard TD pass from Jim Plunkett in the 42–3 rout of the Colts on 10-06-74
8 c. Randy Vataha scored on an 88-yard TD pass from Jim Plunkett in the 21–17 win over the Colts on 12-19-71
9. b. Darryl Stingley hauled in a 68-yard pass from Steve Grogan in the 17–3 win over the Colts on 10-23-77
10. e. Henry Ellard caught a 19-yard pass from Drew Bledsoe in the 21–16 win over the Colts on 11-01-98

Match the player with his receiving accomplishment in a victorious overtime game for the Patriots

11. Troy Brown

a. I tied a team record of four catches by a running back in a playoff game in our 16–13 overtime win on 01-19-02

12. Ben Coates

b. I had 10 receptions in our 16–13 overtime win vs the Oakland Raiders on 01-19-02

13. Leroy Thompson

c. I had 11 receptions in our 26–20 overtime win vs the Minnesota Vikings on 11-13-94

14. Jermaine Wiggins

d. I only had 10 receptions in our 26–20 overtime win vs the Minnesota Vikings on 11-13-94

15. J.R. Redmond

e. I set the team record with 16 receptions in our 41–38 overtime win vs the Kansas City Chiefs on 09-22-02

Answers:
11. e. Troy Brown had 16 receptions in the 41–38 overtime win over the Kansas City Chiefs on 09-22-02
12. d. Ben Coates had 10 receptions in the 26–20 overtime win vs the Minnesota Vikings on 11-13-94
13. c. Leroy Thompson had 11 receptions in the 26–20 overtime win vs the Minnesota Vikings on 11-13-94
14. b. Jermaine Wiggins had 10 receptions in the 16–13 overtime playoff game win vs the Raiders on 01-19-02
15. a. J.R. Redmond had four receptions in the 16–13 overtime playoff game win vs the Oakland Raiders on 01-19-02

Match the Patriots player with his particular achievement in the playoffs

16. Corey Dillon

a. I had at least four receptions in three consecutive playoff games for the Patriots

17. Keith Byars

b. My only career pass reception in a playoff game was in our 20–3 rout of the Colts on 01-16-05

18. Mark van Eeghen

c. I had a key pass reception to help set up the first Super Bowl game-winning FG on 02-03-02

19. J.R. Redmond

d. I have caught a pass both for and against the Patriots in the playoffs

20. Patrick Pass

e. I set the team record of five receptions by a Patriots running back in a playoff game

Answers:
16. e. Corey Dillon had five receptions in the 20–3 rout of the Indianapolis Colts on 01-16-05
17. a. Keith Byars had four receptions in three consecutive playoff games for the New England Patriots
18. d. Mark van Eeghen had a reception in a playoff game against the Patriots and for the Patriots
19. c. J.R. Redmond
20. b. Patrick Pass

Match the Patriots player with the specific game that he recorded his first TD reception in a regular season game

21. Tony Simmons   a. I caught a 21-yard TD pass in our 31–6 rout of the Indianapolis Colts on 09-07-97

22. Tory Brown   b. I hauled in a 63-yard TD pass in our 21–16 victory over the Indianapolis Colts on 11-01-98

23. Micheal Timpson   c. I caught a 30-yard TD pass in our 24–13 victory over the Baltimore Colts on 09-12-82

24. Ken Toler   d. I caught a two-yard TD pass on the last play to force overtime in our 23–17 overtime win on 12-08-91

25. Ben Coates   e. I caught a 45-yard TD pass to beat the Indianapolis Colts 23–17 in overtime on 12-08-91

Answers:
21. b. Tony Simmons scored on a 63-yard TD pass from Drew Bledsoe in the 21–16 win over the Indianapolis Colts on 11-01-98
22. a. Troy Brown scored on a 21-yard TD pass from Drew Bledsoe in the 31–6 victory over the Indianapolis Colts on 09-07-97
23. e. Micheal Timpson hauled in a 45-yard TD pass to the beat the Indianapolis Colts 23–17 in overtime on 12-08-91
24. c. Ken Toler scored on a 30-yard TD pass from Matt Cavanaugh in the 24–13 win over the Indianapolis Colts on 09-12-82
25. d. Ben Coates caught a two-yard TD pass from Hugh Millen in the 23–17 overtime win vs the Indianapolis Colts on 12-08-91

Match the Patriots player with the specific game that he had his only game with 100+ yards receiving in that season

26. Troy Brown   a. The Patriots beat the Kansas City Chiefs 27–19 at Arrowhead Stadium on 11-22-04

27. Deion Branch   b. The Patriots beat the Dolphins 19–13 in overtime at Pro Player Stadium on 10-19-03

28. Irving Fryar   c. The Patriots destroyed the Indianapolis Colts 38–17 at the RCA Dome on 10-21-01

29. David Patten   d. The Patriots defeated the Buffalo Bills 14–3 at Sullivan Stadium on 10-13-85
30. Reggie Rucker   e. The Patriots beat the Green Bay Packers 33–24 at Schaefer Stadium on 11-18-73

Answers:
26. b. Troy Brown had 131 yards receiving in the 19–13 overtime win vs the Miami Dolphins on 10-19-03
27. a. Deion Branch had 105 yards receiving in the 27–19 victory over the Kansas City Chiefs on 11-22-04
28. d. Irving Fryar had 132 yards receiving in the 14–3 victory over the Buffalo Bills on 10-13-85
29. c. David Patten had 117 yards receiving in the 38–17 rout of the Indianapolis Colts on 10-21-01
30. e. Reggie Rucker had 108 yards receiving in the 33–24 victory over the Green Bay Packers on 11-18-73

True or False?

1. Jerry Rice was a teammate of former Patriots linebacker Vincent Brown at Mississippi Valley State
2. Former Patriots tight end Tony Romeo was a teammate of Burt Reynolds at Florida State
3. Former Patriots receiver Hart Lee Dykes was a teammate Barry Sanders at Oklahoma State
4. Former Patriots receiver Irving Fryar was a teammate of Christian Fauria at Colorado State
5. Former Patriots tight end Pete Brock was a teammate of Tim Fox at Ohio State
6. Former Patriots receiver Clarence Weathers was a teammate of Dick Albert at Delaware State
7. Former Patriots receiver Terry Glenn was a teammate of Vencie Glenn at Indiana State

8. Former Patriots players Steve Grogan and Don Calhoun were teammates at Kansas State

9. Former Patriots tight end Lin Dawson was a teammate of Richard Dawson at North Carolina State

10. Adam Vinatieri was a teammate of Robert "Evel" Knievel at South Dakota State

11. Stanley Morgan set an NFL record for accumulating 10,000 career yards receiving in the shortest time frame

12. Harold Jackson and Stanley Morgan are the only Patriots teammates to each have 1,000 yards receiving in the same season

13. Deion Branch and Troy Brown are the only Patriots wide receivers to have at least 13 receptions in a game in the same season

14. Irving Fryar is the only Patriots player with more than 200 yards receiving in a regular season game

15. Troy Brown was the first Patriots player with 100 receptions in a regular season

Answers:
1. True
2. True
3. True
4. False. Irving Fryar played for Nebraksa and Christian Fauria played for Colorado
5. False. Pete Brock played for Colorado and Tim Fox played for Ohio State
6. False. Dick Albert did not play college football
7. False. Terry Glenn played for Ohio State and Vencie Glenn played for Indiana State
8. True
9. False. Richard Dawson did not play College Football
10. False. Adam Vinatieri and Robert "Evel" Knievel are cousins but were not teammates in college
11. True
12. False. Wes Welker and Randy Moss each had more than 1,000 yards receiving in 2007 and 2008
13. True
14. False. Terry Glenn is the only Patriots receiver with more than 200 yards receiving in a regular season game
15. True

Part Two Receiving Questions

1. Who was the first Patriots receiver to catch his first three NFL TD passes from three different Patriots quarterbacks? (Hint: These Patriots quarterbacks were Tony Eason, Marc Wilson, and Steve Grogan)
a. Tommy Lee Jones   b. Hart Lee Dykes   c. Jim Lee Hunt   d. Jamie Lee Curtis

2. Who was the first Patriots running back to catch his first four NFL TD passes from four different Patriots quarterbacks? (Hint: These Patriots quarterbacks were Hugh Millen, Jeff Carlson, Scott Secules, and Drew Bledsoe)
a. Kevin Stacom   b. Kevin Turner   c. Bake Turner   d. Bake McBride

3. Who was the first Patriots wide receiver to catch a TD pass from seven different Patriots quarterbacks? (Hint: These quarterbacks were Tony Eason, Steve Grogan, Tom Ramsey, Doug Flutie, Marc Wilson, Tommy Hodson, and Hugh Millen)
a. Stanley Morgan   b. Irving Fryar   c. Billy Mays   d. Greg McMurtry

4. Who was the only Patriots tight end who has caught a TD pass from both Drew Bledsoe and Tom Brady?
a. Harry Manion   b. Jermaine Wiggins   c. Benjamin Watson   d. David Thomas

5. Who was the Patriots wide receiver who caught three halfback option TD passes from Andy Johnson during the 1981 season?
a. EF Hutton   b. Stanley Morgan   c. Merrill Lynch   d. Jim Cramer

Answers:
1. Hart Lee Dykes caught his first three TD passes from three different Patriots quarterbacks
2. Kevin Turner caught his first four TD passes from four different Patriots quarterbacks
3. Irving Fryar caught a TD pass thrown by seven different Patriots quarterbacks
4. Jermaine Wiggins
5. Stanley Morgan

Match the Patriots player with his particular achievement

1. Stanley Morgan
2. Irving Fryar
3. Mike Vrabel
4. David Patten
5. David Givens

a. I was the first Patriots receiver with a TD reception in a victorious Super Bowl

b. I was the first Patriots player with a quarterback sack and a TD reception in a Super Bowl

c. I was the first Patriots receiver with a TD reception in seven consecutive playoff games

d. I was the first Patriots receiver with a fourth down TD reception in a playoff game

e. I was the first Patriots receiver to catch a flea flicker pass for a TD in a playoff game

Answers:
1. e. Stanley Morgan caught a 45-yard flea-flicker TD pass in the 1986 AFC Divisional Playoff Game on 01-04-87
2. d. Irving Fryar caught an eight-yard TD pass from Steve Grogan on fourth-and-goal in Super Bowl XX
3. b. Mike Vrabel
4. a. David Patten caught an eight-yard TD pass in the 20–17 Super Bowl win over the St. Louis Rams on 02-03-02
5. c. David Givens caught a TD pass in seven consecutive playoff games for the Patriots

Match the Receiver with the game that he recorded his first TD pass for the Patriots

6. Troy Brown
7. Tony Simmons
8. Michael Timpson
9. Ken Toler
10. David Patten

a. I caught my first NFL TD pass in our 21–16 victory over the Colts on 11-01-98

b. I had my first NFL TD reception in our 23–17 overtime win vs the Colts on 12-08-91

c. I caught my first NFL TD pass in our 31–6 rout of the Indianapolis Colts on 09-07-97

d. I caught my first TD pass as a receiver of the Patriots in our 38–17 rout of the Colts on 10-21-01

e. I caught my first NFL TD pass in our 24–13 victory over the Baltimore Colts on 09-12-82

Answers:
6. c. Troy Brown had his first NFL TD reception in the 31–6 victory over the Indianapolis Colts on 09-07-97
7. a. Tony Simmons had his first NFL TD reception in the 21–16 victory over the Indianapolis Colts on 11-01-98
8. b. Michael Timpson had his first NFL TD reception in the 23–17 overtime win vs the Indianapolis Colts on 12-08-91
9. e. Ken Toler had his first NFL TD reception in the 24–13 victory over the Baltimore Colts on 09-12-82
10. d. David Patten hauled in a 91-yard TD pass for his first TD reception as a Patriots player in the 38–17 rout of the Indianapolis Colts on 10-21-01

Match the Patriots Receiver with his particular reception accomplishment in a victorious game against the Raiders

11. Gino Cappelletti
12. Irving Fryar
13. Ron Sellers
14. Darryl Stingley
15. Russ Francis

a. I caught a 25-yard TD pass from Steve Grogan in our 21–14 win over the Raiders on 09-24-78

b. I caught two TD passes in our 48–17 rout of the Oakland Raiders at Schaefer Stadium on 10-03-76

c. I caught a 33-yard TD pass from Jim Plunkett in our 20–6 victory over the Raiders at Schaefer on 09-19-71

d. I caught a 24-yard TD pass in our 24–21 victory over the Oakland Raiders at Fenway Park on 10-30-66

e. I caught a 25-yard TD pass from Steve Grogan in our 26–23 win over the Raiders at Sullivan on 11-01-87

Answers:
11. d. Gino Cappelletti caught a 24-yard TD from Babe Parilli in the 24–21 win over the Raiders at Fenway Park on 10-30-66
12. e. Irving Fryar caught a 25-yard TD pass from Steve Grogan in the 26–23 win over the Raiders at Sullivan Stadium on 11-01-87
13. c. Ron Sellers caught a 33-yard TD pass from Jim Plunkett in the 20–6 win over the Raiders at Schaefer Stadium on 09-19-71
14. b Darryl Stingley caught a 21-yard TD and a 15-yard TD pass from Steve Grogan in the 48–17 rout of the Raiders on 10-03-76
15. a. Russ Francis caught a 25-yard TD pass from Steve Grogan in the 21–14 victory over the Raiders on 09-24-78

Match the Patriots Receiver with his particular reception accomplishment in a victorious game against the Cardinals

16. Ben Coates

a. I caught a TD pass from Drew Bledsoe and Scott Secules in our 23–21 win over Phoenix on 10-10-93

17. Russ Francis

b. I caught two TD passes in our 23–12 victory over the Arizona Cardinals on 09-19-04

18. Shawn Jefferson

c. I caught a 65-yard TD pass and a 35-yard TD pass in our 27–3 rout of the Arizona Cardinals on 10-31-99

19. Curtis Martin

d. I caught two TDs from Drew Bledsoe in our 31–0 shutout of the Cardinals at Foxboro on 09-16-96

20. Daniel Graham

e. I hauled in a 24-yard TD from Steve Grogan in our 16–6 win over the St. Louis Cardinals on 09-10-78

Answers:
16. a. Ben Coates caught a four-yard TD from Drew Bledsoe and a two-yard TD from Scott Secules to beat Phoenix, 23–21, on 10-10-93
17. e. Russ Francis caught a 24-yard TD pass from Steve Grogan in the 16–6 win over the St. Louis Cardinals on 09-10-78
18. c. Shawn Jefferson caught two TD passes from Drew Bledsoe in the 27–3 rout of the Arizona Cardinals on 10-31-99
19. d. Curtis Martin caught two TD passes from Drew Bledsoe in the 31–0 shutout of the Arizona Cardinals on 09-15-96
20. b. Daniel Graham caught two TD passes from Tom Brady in the 23–12 victory over the Cardinals on 09-19-04

Match the Patriots Receiver with his reception in a victorious game against the team from Los Angeles

21. Darryl Stingley

a. I caught a 19-yard TD pass from Butch Songin in our 35–0 shutout of the Los Angeles Chargers on 10-08-60

22. Jim Colclough

b. I caught a 15-yard HB option TD pass from Mosi Tatupu in our 26–23 win over the Los Angeles Raiders on 11-01-87

23. Tony Collins

c. I caught a 20-yard TD pass from Jim Plunkett in our 20–4 win over the Los Angeles Rams at Schaefer on 09-29-74

24. Irving Fryar

d. I caught a 21-yard TD, in the fourth quarter for the game-winning TD in our 20–14 win over the Los Angles Rams on 09-29-74

25. Randy Vataha

e. I caught a 25-yard TD pass on the last play to defeat the Los Angeles Rams 30–28 at Anaheim Stadium on 11-16-86

Answers:
21. c. Darryl Stingley caught a 20-yard TD from Jim Plunkett in the 20–14 win over the Los Angeles Rams at Schaefer Stadium on 09-29-74
22. a. Jim Colcough caught a 19-yard TD from Butch Songin in the 35–0 shutout of the L.A. Chargers at the L.A. Coliseum on 10-08-60
23. b. Tony Collins caught a 15-yard TD pass from Mosi Tatupu in the 26–23 win over the Los Angeles Raiders at Sullivan Stadium on 11-01-87
24. d. Irving Fryar caught a 25-yard "Hail Mary" TD pass on the last play of the 30–28 win over the Los Angeles Rams on 11-16-86
25. e. Randy Vataha caught a 21-yard TD pass in the fourth quarter to defeat the Los Angeles Rams, 20–14, at Schaefer Stadium on 09-29-74

Points Scored

Five Trivia Questions on Points Scored

1. Who scored the first points in the first regular season American Football League Game on 09-09-60?
a. Johnny Pesky   b. Gino Cappelletti   c. John Havlicek   d. Ray Bourque

2. Who was the Patriots special teams player who scored the game-winning TD in the 1985 AFC Divisional Playoff Game victory over the Los Angeles Raiders?
a. Jimmy Fallon   b. Jim Bowman   c. Bob Beamon   d. Jim Beam

3. Who was the first Patriots wide receiver with three TD receptions in a regular season game?
a. Randy Moss   b. Gino Cappelletti   c. Wes Welker   d. Stanley Morgan

4. Who was the first Patriots linebacker to score a TD in consecutive games during the regular season?
a. Vinny Pazienza   b. Vincent Brown   c. Vinnie Johnson   d. Vinnie Barbarino

5. Who is the only Patriots player to punt, kick a field goal, and run for a two point conversion in his career?
a. Wes Walker   b. Adam Vinatieri   c. Gino Cappelletti   d. Mike Lynch

Answers:
1. Gino Cappelletti kicked a 35-yard field goal for the first points scored in the AFL on 09-09-60
2. Jim Bowman recovered a fumble by Sam Seale in the end zone for a TD
3. Gino Cappelletti caught three TD passes and pass for a two-point conversion in the 36–28 win over the Buffalo Bills on 11-15-64
4. Vincent Brown returned a fumble for a TD on 11-01-92 and he returned an interception for a TD on 11-08-92
5. Adam Vinatieri

Match the Patriots player with his regular season scoring accomplishment

1. Gino Cappelletti   a. The first Patriots player to kick an extra point in a game played on Sunday night

2. Adam Vinatieri   b. The first Patriots player to kick an extra point in a game played on Monday night

3. John Smith   c. The first Patriots player to kick an extra point in a game played on Thursday night

4. Charlie Gogolak   d. The first Patriots player to kick an extra point in a game played on Friday night

5. Nick Lowery   e. The first Patriots player to kick an exrta point in a game played on Saturday afternoon

Answers:
1. d. Gino Cappelletti kicked an extra point in the 13–10 loss to Denver on Friday night 09-09-60
2. e. Adam Vinatieri kicked four extra points in the 31–0 shutout of the Bills on Saturday afternoon 12-27-03
3. c. John Smith kicked three extra points in the 39–24 loss to the Miami Dolphins on Thursday night 11-29-79
4. b. Charlie Gogolak kicked two extra points in the 24–17 loss to the Baltimore Colts on Monday night 11-06-72
5. a. Nick Lowery kicked three extra points in the 21–14 win over the Oakland Raiders on Sunday night 09-24-78

Match the Patriots player with his his particular regular season scoring accomplishment

6. Jon Vaughn   a. Returned a lateral from Steve Nelson 27 yards for a TD on 09-25-83
7. Clayton Weishuhn   b. Returned a lateral from John Zamberlin 65 yards for a TD on 10-05-80
8. Mike Haynes   c. Advanced a fumble by Dave Meggett 75 yards for a TD on 12-10-95
9. Troy Brown   d. Advanced a fumble by Mack Herron 46 yards for a TD on 10-07-73
10. Randy Vataha   e. Advanced his own fumble 100 yards for a TD on 12-20-92

Answers:
6. e. Jon Vaughn advanced his own fumbled kickoff return 100 yards for a TD in the 20–10 loss on 12-20-92
7. a. Clayton Weishuhn returned a lateral after a Steve Nelson interception 27 yards for a TD in the 28–23 win on 09-25-83
8. b. Mike Haynes returned a lateral after a blocked field goal 65 yards for a TD in the 21–11 win on 10-05-80
9. c. Troy Brown advanced a fumbled kickoff return by Dave Meggett 75 yards for a TD in the 31–28 win on 12-10-95
10. d. Randy Vataha advanced a fumble that was kicked by Bill Lenkaitis 46 yards for a TD in the 24–16 win on 10-07-73

Match the Patriots player with his particular scoring accomplishment

11. Mike Vrabel   a. The first Patriots player to suffer a knee injury while catching a game-winning TD pass

12. Bob Windsor   b. The first Patriots player with two TD receptions in a game played on Monday night

13. Russ Francis   c. I caught a 13-yard TD pass on the last play of our 23–22 win over the New York Giants on 12-12-96

14. Daniel Graham   d. The first Patriots player with a TD reception and a quarterback sack in the same playoff game

15. Ben Coates   e. The first Patriots player to score in a regular season game played on Saturday afternoon

Answers:

11. d. Mike Vrabel caught a TD pass and had two quarterback sacks in the 32–29 win over the Carolina Panthers on 02-01-04
12. a. Bob Windsor missed the rest of the season after his 10-yard TD on the last play of the 17–14 win over Minnesota on 10-27-74
13. b. Russ Francis actually caught two TD passes in two different games playing for the Patriots on Monday night
14. e. Daniel Graham caught a one yard TD pass in the 31–0 shutout of the Buffalo Bills on 12-27-03
15. c. Ben Coates caught a 13-yard TD pass on the last play of the 23–22 win over the New York Giants on 12-12-96

Match the Patriots player with his particular playoff game scoring accomplishment

16. Ty Law   a. The first Patriots player to return a punt for a TD in a playoff game

17. Troy Brown   b. The first Patriots player to return an interception for a TD in a Super Bowl

18. Mike Vrabel   c. The first Patriots player with a fourth down TD reception in a playoff game

19. Irving Fryar   d. The first Patriots player with a fourth down TD run in a playoff game

20. Antowain Smith   e. The first Patriots LB/TE with a TD reception in a playoff game

Answers:

16. b. Ty Law returned a Kurt Warner pass 47 yards for a TD in the 20–17 win over the St. Louis Rams on 02-03-02
17. a. Troy Brown returned a punt 55 yards for a TD in the 24–17 win over the Pittsburgh Steelers on 01-27-02
18. e. Mike Vrabel caught a one-yard TD pass in the 32–29 victory over the Carolina Panthers on 02-01-04
19. c. Irving Fryar caught a fourth down eight-yard TD pass from Steve Grogan in the 46–10 loss to the Chicago Bears on 01-26-86
20. d. Antowain Smith ran for a one-yard TD on fourth down in the 32–29 victory over the Carolina Panthers on 02-01-04

Kicking Questions

Five Trivia Questions on Kicking

1. Who was the long snapper for Adam Vinatieri when he kicked the overtime game-winning 23-yard field goal to beat the Oakland Raiders, 16–13, in the AFC Divisional Playoff Game at Foxboro Stadium on 01-19-02?
a. Lonnie Farmer   b. Lonie Paxton   c. Paxton Crawford   d. Jim Crawford

2. Who holds American Football League (AFL) record of kicking six field goals in a regular season game?
a. Lloyd Mumphrey   b. Gino Cappelletti   c. Claude Humphrey   d. Humphrey Bogart

3. Who is the only Patriots player to attempt to kick seven field goals in at least three regular season games?
a. Roger Twibell   b. Gino Cappelletti   c. Zip Rzepa   d. Gene Lavanchy

4. Who was the Patriots kicker/wide receiver who was inducted into the Patriots Hall of Fame in 1992?
a. John Havlicek   b. Gino Cappelletti   c. Bailey Howell   d. Jo Jo White

5. Who drove the snow brush vehicle and cleared a path for John Smith in the Patriots 3–0 victory over the Miami Dolphins at Schaefer Stadium on 12-12-82?
a. Dave Henderson   b. Mark Henderson   c. Gerald Henderson   d. Harry Henderson

Answers:

1. Lonie "The Snow Angel" Paxton was the long snapper for the New England Patriots
2. Gino Cappelletti held the record for the most field goals kicked in a game without a miss until 1999
3. Gino Cappelletti attempted seven field goals in a game three times (on 09-20-64, 09-24-67, and 11-16-69)
4. Gino Cappelletti
5. Mark Henderson

Match the Patriots player with his kicking accomplishment in a game with poor weather conditions

1. John Smith
2. Adam Vinatieri
3. Gino Cappelletti
4. Jason Staurovsky
5. Jeff White

a. I kicked a 23-yard FG to defeat the Raiders 16–13 in overtime in the snow on 01-19-02

b. I hit a 15-yard FG in our 45–3 loss to the Chiefs in 11-degree weather on 12-14-63

c. I kicked a 33-yard FG to beat the Dolphins 3–0 in the "Snow Plow" game on 12-12-82

d. I hit a 27-yard FG to beat Tampa 10–7 in overtime in cold weather at Sullivan on 12-11-88

e. I kicked two FGs during a snowstorm in our 37–13 loss to Buffalo on 12-09-73

Answers:
1. c. John Smith kicked a 33-yard field goal to beat the Miami Dolphins 3–0 at Schaefer Stadium on 12-12-82
2. a. Adam Vinatieri kicked a 23-yard field goal to beat the Oakland Raiders 16–13 in overtime in the last game played at Foxboro Stadium
3. b. Gino Cappelletti kicked a 15-yard field goal at Municipal Stadium on 12-14-63
4. d. Jason Staurovsky kicked a 27-yard field goal to beat the Tampa Bay Buccaneers 10–7 in overtime on 12-11-88
5. e. Jeff White kicked two field goals during a snow storm at Rich Stadium on 12-09-73

Match the player with his scoring accomplishment with the Patriots

6. Gino Cappelletti
7. Tony Franklin
8. John Smith
9. Matt Bahr
10. Adam Vinatieri

a. I hold the Patriots record with 32 FGs kicked during a regular season

b. I hold the Patriots record of scoring 21 points by a kicker in a regular season game

c. I hold the Patriots record of scoring 16 points by a kicker in a playoff game

d. I led the NFL in scoring in 1979 and 1980

e. I was the oldest NFL player to kick a FG of 55 yards (in the 34–17 win on 11-12-95)

Answers:
6. b. Gino Cappelletti kicked six field goals and three extra points in the 39–10 rout of the Denver Broncos
7. a. Tony Franklin kicked 32 field goals on 1986
8. d. John Smith led the NFL in scoring in 1979 and 1980
9. e. Matt Bahr kicked a 55-yard field in the 34–17 win over the Miami Dolphins on 11-12-95
10. c. Adam Vinatieri kicked five field goals and one extra point in the 24–14 playoff game win over the Colts

Six Trivia Questions on Extra Points

1. Who kicked the extra point that deflected off both goal posts in the New England Patriots 12–0 shutout of the Miami Dolphins on 12-07-03?
a. Matt Turk   b. Adam Vinatieri   c. Steve Mariucci   d. Bob Halloran

2. Who holds the Patriots record of most extra points kicked in a season without a miss with 74?
a. Fran Charles   b. Stephen Gostkowski   c. Mike Giardi   d. Chris Collins

3. Who was only the Patriots player to intercept four passes, run for three two-point conversions and kick at least 50 extra points?
a. Deion Sanders   b. Gino Cappelletti   c. Alan Segel   d. Tom Waddle

4. Who is the only Patriots player to complete a two-point conversion pass and kick a PAT in the same game?
a. Anthony Pepe   b. Gino Cappelletti   c. Doug Flutie   d. Rich Eisen

5. Who is the only Patriots kicker to run for a two-point conversion because the opponent's defensive team (the Buffalo Bills) had left the field?
a. Wade Phillips   b. Adam Vinatieri   c. Steve Sabol   d. Tom Brookshier

6. Who was the Patriots placekicker who was nicknamed "Superfoot?"
a. Wes Welker   b. Mike Walker   c. Johnny Walker   d. Walt Perkins

Answers:
1. Adam Vinatieri kicked an extra point that bounced of both sides of the goal post during a snow storm
2. Stephen Gostkowski
3. Gino Cappelletti
4. Gino Cappelletti
5. Adam Vinatieri ran for a two point conversion in the 25–21 win over the Buffalo Bills on 11-29-98
6. Mike "Superfoot" Walker

Punting Questions

10 Trivia Questions on Punting

1. Who is the only Patriots punter to punt a team record 11 times in a game *twice* during his career?
a. John Molori   b. Rich Camarillo   c. Jay Severin   d. Pete Colford

2. Who holds the Patriots record of the longest punt of 93 yards in a regular season game?
a. Shawn McKeckern   b. Shawn McCarthy   c. Sean Penn   d. Sean Connery

3. Who is the only Patriots punter to record a quarterback sack while playing as a linebacker in a game?
a. Frasier Crane   b. Jim Fraser   c. Jim Rome   d. Icabod Crane

4. Who was the former Patriots and Detroit Lions punter who appeared in the movie *Paper Lion*?
a. Pat Sajack   b. Pat Studstill   c. Pat Patriots   d. Patrick Pass

5. Who was the Patriots punter who also played as a quarterback and as a running back who caught a 46-yard pass during a game?
a. Craig James   b. Tom Yewcic   c. Stephan Ward Smith   d. Kevin Mannix

6. Who was the Patriots quarterback who pooch-punted the ball 36 yards in the 12–0 shutout of Miami on 12-07-03?
a. Tom Burgmeier   b. Tom Brady   c. Troy Brown   d. Tedy Bruschi

7. Who has the most punts (10) by a Patriots punter in a game played during the 2003 regular season?
a. Barry Burbank   b. Brooks Barnard   c. Barry Bellwood   d. Billy Buckner

8. Tom Brady's 36-yard punt to the 2-yard line helped set up a Patriots safety in a game against the?
a. Oakland Raiders   b. Miami Dolphins   c. Baltimore Ravens   d. Tennessee Titans

9. Who was the Patriots punter who completed an 18-yard pass to Eric Bjornson in the 24–16 win over the Indianapolis Colts at Foxboro Stadium on 10-08-00?
a. Lee Jansen   b. Lee Johnson   c. Lee Majors   d. Bill Lee

10. Who was the former Detroit Lions player who once led the NFL in receiving yards, punt return yards, and yards punted during a season who played his final year of pro football as the punter for Patriots in 1972?
a. David Seymour   b. Pat Studstill   c. Pat Summerall   d. Alex Karras

Answers:
1. Rich Camarillo
2. Shawn McCarthy booted a 93-yard punt in the 22–17 loss to the Buffalo Bills at Rich Stadium on 11-03-91
3. Punter Jim Fraser also played linebacker for the Boston Patriots during the 1966 season
4. Pat Studstill
5. Tom Yewcic
6. Tom Brady
7. Brooks Barnard
8. Miami Dolphins
9. Lee Johnson
10. Pat Studstill punted 75 times for 2,859 yards for the New England Patriots in 1972

Match the Patriots player with his particular achievement

1. Tom Brady

a. I threw a TD pass, had seven carries, three receptions, a kickoff return, and punted 61 times in 1960

2. Tom Janik

b. I threw seven TD passes, ran for two TDs, and punted 69 times during the 1962 season

3. Tom Yewcic

c. As the Phoenix Cardinals quarterback, I was sacked by Patriots linebacker Vincent Brown on 09-29-91

4. Tom Tupa

d. I returned an interception eight yards, returned a punt for no gain, and punted 70 times in 1969

5. Tom Greene

e. I led the team to 15 consecutive victories had a 36-yard punt during the 2003 season

Answers:

1. e. Tom Brady led the Patriots to 15 consecutive wins including three playoff game victories in 2003
2. d. Tom Janik was a defensive back and the punter for the Patriots in the 1969 season
3. b. Tom Yewcic threw six TD passes and ran for a TD while leading the team to three consecutive wins late in the 1962 season
4. c. Tom Tupa was also sacked by Steve Israel and Willie McGinest in the 30–28 win over the New York Jets in 09-12-99
5. a. Tom Greene was a quarterback, running back, and a punter for the Boston Patriots during the 1960 season

Match the Patriots player with his particular achievement

6. Mike Patrick

a. I was the first Patriots player to return a punt for TD in a regular season game

7. Mike Hubach

b. I was an AFL All-Star quarterback for the Boston Patriots in 1969

8. Mike Saxon

c. I was the AFC Special Teams Player of the Week in our 23–21 win over Phoenix on 10-10-93

9. Mike Taliaferro

d. My onside kick was recovered by Mosi Tatupu in our 38–34 loss to Houston on 11-10-80

10. Mike Haynes

e. I was the first New England Patriots player to punt in a playoff game

Answers:

6. e. Mike Patrick was the first New England Patriots player to punt in a playoff game
7. d. Mike Hubach attempted an onside kick that was recovered by Mosi Tatupu on 11-10-80
8. c. Mike Saxon had three punts inside the 20-yard line in the 23–21 win over the Phoenix Cardinals at Sun Devil Stadium
9. b. Mike Taliaferro was an AFL All-Star quarterback for the Boston Patriots in 1969
10. a. Mike Haynes was the first Patriots player to return a punt for a TD in a regular season game

Special Teams Return Questions

10 Trivia Questions on Punt Returns

1. Who returned a punt 89 yards for a TD for the longest punt return in Patriots history?
a. Ron Burton   b. Mike Haynes   c. Troy Brown   d. Roland James

2. Who is the only Patriots player to return a punt, an interception, and a blocked field goal for a TD?
a. Michael Graham   b. Mike Haynes   c. Mike Adams   d. Phil Castinetti

3. Who is the only Patriots player to return a punt for a TD in the regular season and in the playoffs?
a. Mike Haynes   b. Troy Brown   c. Irving Fryar   d. Dave Meggett

4. Who is the only former Heisman Trophy winner to return a punt for the Patriots?
a. Roger Staubach   b. Joe Bellino   c. Chuck Foreman   d. Doug Flutie

5. Who is the Patriots player who holds the team record with the most punt returns (45) during a year without signaling for a fair catch?
a. Clark Gaines   b. Mike Haynes   c. Claude Raines   d. Tim Raines

6. Who holds the Patriots Team record of the most punt return yards (156) in a game?
a. Michael Holley   b. Mike Haynes   c. Moe Howard   d. Mack Herron

7. Who was the first Patriots player to lead the team in net yards from scrimmage and punt return yards in the same year?
a. Philip Burton   b. Ron Burton   c. Ron Burton Jr.   d. Paul Burton

8. Who was the first Patriots wide receiver to lead the team in receiving yards and punt return yards in the same year?
a. Michael Madden   b. Stanley Morgan   c. Wes Welker   d. Irving Fryar

9. Who was the first Patriots player to return a punt for a TD and intercept a pass in the same game *twice* during his career?
a. Mike Tyson   b. Mike Haynes   c. Otis Smith   d. Willie Clay

10. Who is the first Patriots player to return a punt for a TD and catch a TD pass in the same game?
a. Stanley Pritchard   b. Stanley Morgan   c. Stanley Livingston   d. Walter Stanley

Answers:
1. Mike Haynes returned a punt 89 yards for a TD in the 20–10 victory over the Buffalo Bills on 11-07-76
2. Mike Haynes returned two punts for a TD, an interception for a TD, and a blocked field goal for a TD
3. Troy Brown returned two punts for a TD in the 2001 season and returned a punt for a TD in the 2001 playoffs
4. Joe Bellino
5. Mike Haynes
6. Mike Haynes
7. Ron Burton led the Patriots with 1,009 net yards from scrimmage and 122 punt return yards in 1962
8. Stanley Morgan led the Patriots with 1,029 yards receiving and 116 punt return yards in 1981
9. Mike Haynes returned a punt for a TD and intercepted a pass on 11-07-76, and he returned a punt for a TD and intercepted a pass on 11-28-76
10. Stanley Morgan returned a punt 80 yards for a TD and he caught a 25-yard TD pass on 11-02-80

Match the Patriots player with his punt return achievement

1. Mike Haynes — a. I returned at least one punt for the New England Patriots in eight consecutive seasons

2. Roland James — b. I was the first Patriots player to return a punt at least 60 yards in a game

3. Carl Garrett — c. I was the first Patriots player to return a punt at least 50 yards in consecutive seasons

4. Ron Burton — d. I returned a punt 75 yards for a TD in our 34–21 win vs the New York Jets at Schaefer Stadium on 11-02-80

5. Irving Fryar — e. I was the first Patriots player to return a punt for a TD in a regular season game

6. Troy Brown — f. I am the only Heisman Trophy winner to lead the team in punt return yards

7 Mack Herron — g. I had a 35-yard punt return and ran for a TD in our 30–24 Monday Night Football win over the Kansas City Chiefs

8. Dave Meggett — h. My longest punt return was for 66 yards in our 42–3 rout of the Baltimore Colts

9. Kevin Faulk — i. I was the first Patriots with at least three receptions, three interceptions, and three punt returns in the same season

10. Joe Bellino — j. I am the only Patriots to be the only player to return a punt for the team in three consecutive seasons

Answers:
1. e. Mike Haynes returned a punt 89 yards for a TD in the 20–10 win over the Bills at Schaefer on 11-07-76
2. d. Roland James
3. c. Carl Garrett returned a punt 62 yards on 09-27-70 and he returned a punt 50 yards on 11-28-71
4. b. Ron Burton returned a punt 62 yards on 11-12-61
5. a. Irving Fryar returned at least one punt over the 1984–91 seasons for the New England Patriots
6. i. Troy Brown had 17 receptions, three interceptions, and 12 punt returns during the 2004 regular season
7. h. Mini-Mack Herron
8. j. Dave Meggett was the only Patriots player to return a punt during the 1995, 1996, and 1997 seasons
9. g. Kevin Faulk's longest return was 35 yards in the 30–24 Monday Night Football win over the Kansas City Chiefs on 12-04-00
10. f. Joe Bellino, who won the Heisman Trophy in 1960, led the Patriots with 129 punt return yards in 1967

15 Trivia Questions regarding kickoff returns by the Patriots

1. Who is the only player to kick off (not an onside kick) for the Patriots and return a kickoff for the Patriots?
a. Dino Crocetti   b. Gino Cappelletti   c. Rocky Marciano   d. Tom Menino

2. Who is the only Patriots player to lead the team in kickoff return yards, punt return yards, yards rushing, and had the most pass receptions in the same season?
a. Phil Bissel   b. Mack Herron   c. Doug Meehan   d. Kevin Faulk

3. Who was the former Patriots and former Notre Dame running back whose name was mentioned during the bar scene in the movie *Rudy*?
a. Buddy Harrelson   b. Bob Gladieux   c. Hawk Harrelson   d. Woody Harrelson

4. Who was the first Patriots player to return the opening kickoff for a touchdown?
a. Tim Allen   b. Allen Carter   c. Carter Allen   d. Andy Gresh

5. Who is the only New England Patriots first round draft pick to recover an onside kick by the opposing team?
a. Doug Mientkiewicz   b. Darryl Stingley   c. David Ortiz   d. Doug Mirabelli

6. Who was requested to report to the locker room, even though he was in the stands and had hoped to watch the game as a spectator, who made the tackle of Jake Scott on the opening kickoff in the 27–14 victory over the Miami Dolphins at Harvard Stadium on 09-20-70?
a. Jon Meterparel   b. Bob Gladieux   c. Michael Holley   d. Michael Felger

7. Who is the only Patriots linebacker to return at least five kickoffs and intercept at least five passes?
a. Ted Sarandis   b. Tedy Bruschi   c. Ted Hendricks   d. Ted Koppel

8. In 1980, who was the Patriots player who led the AFC with the most kickoff return yards, the most kickoff returns, the longest kickoff return and best kickoff return average?
a. Horace Grant   b. Horace Ivory   c. Howard Cunningham   d. Ickey Woods

8. Who was the former BU Terrier who averaged over 28 yards per kickoff return for the Patriots in 1972?
a. Reggie Smith   b. Reggie Rucker   c. Reggie Lewis   d. Ryen Russillo

9. Who is the only former Heisman Trophy Winner to return a kickoff for the Patriots?
a. Vagas Ferguson   b. Joe Bellino   c. Keith Byars   d. Chuck Foreman

10. Who is the only Patriots player with an 80-yard run from scrimmage, an 80-yard pass reception, a 60+ yard punt return, and a 60+ yard kickoff return?
a. Mack Herron   b. Carl Garrett   c. Wally Brine   d. Tom Doyle

11. Who is the only Patriots player to return a kickoff for a TD and return a missed field-goal attempt for a TD?
a. Charlie Pierce   b. Ron Burton   c. Larry Whiteside   d. Dan Shaughnessy

12. Who is the only Patriots defensive back to intercept a pass and recover an onside kick in the same game?
a. Brian Baldinger   b. Ronnie Lippett   c. Boomer Esiason   d. Lenny Megliola

13. Who is the only Patriots player to throw a TD pass and return a kickoff for a touchdown?
a. Troy Brown   b. Jon Vaughn   c. Kevin Faulk   d. Tony Massarotti

14. Who was the Patriots player who led the AFC with longest kickoff return, best kickoff return average, and most kickoffs that were returned for a TD in 1977?
a. Ray Liota   b. Raymond Clayborn   c. Ray Goulding   d. Bob Elliott

15. Who is the only Patriots linebacker to return two kickoffs during the regular season and catch a TD pass in a Super Bowl?
a. Tedy Bruschi   b. Mike Vrabel   c. Willie McGinest   d. Mike Schlereth

Answers:
1. Gino Cappelletti was the Patriots kicker from 1960–70 and he returned four kickoffs during the 1960 season
2. Mack Herron led the Patriots with 629 kickoff return yards, 517 punt return yards, 824 yards rushing, and had 474 yards receiving for a NFL best 2,444 all-purpose yards during the 1974 season
3. Bob Gladieux, the Notre Dame running back who scored the TD in the famous 10–10 tie with Michigan State
4. Allen Carter
5. Darryl Stingley, a first-round pick in 1973, recovered a San Diego Chargers onside kick on 10-16-77
6. Bob Gladieux
7. Tedy Bruschi
8. Horace Ivory
9. Reggie Rucker
10. Carl Garrett
11. Ron Burton returned a missed field goal 91 yards for a TD and he returned a kickoff 91 yards for a TD
12. Ronnie Lippett intercepted a Jeff George pass and he recovered a Dean Biasucci onside kick on 09-16-90
13. Jon Vaughn completed a TD pass and returned two kickoffs for a TD
14. Raymond Clayborn
15. Mike Vrabel returned two kickoffs during the 2003 regular season and caught a TD pass in the Super Bowl

Match the Patriots player with his particular kickoff return accomplishment

1. Gino Cappelletti
2. Jim Nance
3. Marty Schottenheimer
4. Fred Bruney
5. Bob Dee

a. I had two kickoff returns and was named the NFL Coach of the Year in 2004
b. I had four kickoff returns and was named the 1964 AFL player of the Year
c. I had one kickoff return and was the first AFL player to have his uniform number retired
d. I had two kickoff returns and I went undefeated as the head coach of a NFL team
e. I had three kickoff returns and was the named the 1967 AFL player of the Year

Answers:
1. b. Gino Cappelletti, who returned four kickoffs for 100 yards in 1960, was the AFL player of the Year in 1964, and was the runner up for the AFL player of the Year in 1961
2. e. Jim Nance, who returned three kickoffs for 40 yards in 1965, was the AFL player of the Year in 1967
3. a. Marty Schottenheimer returned a kickoff for the Boston Patriots 13 yards on 11-09-69 and another kickoff eight yards
4. d. Fred Bruney, who returned two kickoffs for 39 yards during the 1960 season, was the head coach of the Philadelphia Eagles in the 37–35 victory over the Minnesota Vikings on 12-22-85
5. c. Bob Dee, who had a 14-yard kickoff return in 1962, had his uniform No. 89 retired on "Dee Day" October 13, 1968

Match the Patriots player with his career longest kickoff return

6. Bethel Johnson
7. Marc Edwards
8. Horace Ivory
9. Marion Hobby
10. Doug Beaudoin

a. I returned it 98 yards for a TD in our 37–21 victory over the Colts on 10-19-80
b. I returned a kickoff 23 yards in our 44–17 rout of the Colts on 09-30-01
c. I returned a kickoff 11 yards in our 37–34 Overtime win vs the Colts on 11-15-92
d. I returned a kickoff 44 yards in our 21–14 victory over the Colts on 11-14-76
e. I returned it 92 yards for a TD in our 38–34 win over the Colts on 11-30-03

Answers:
6. e. Bethel Johnson
7. b. Marc Edwards
8. a. Horace Ivory
9. c. Marion Hobby
10. d. Doug Beaudoin

Fumble Recovery Questions

Five Trivia Questions related to fumble recoveries by a Patriots player

1. Who is the only Patriots player to advance a fumble recovery for a TD, run for another TD, and throw a TD pass in the same game?
a. Scott Secules   b. Steve Grogan   c. Scott Mitchell   d. Matt Seigel

2. Who is the Patriots linebacker who holds the team record for the most career fumbles returned for a TD (2)?
a. Nick Buoniconti   b. Andre Tippett   c. Vincent Brown   d. Johnny Rembert

3. Who was the Patriots player who returned a James Stewart fumble 47 yards for a TD in the 20–6 AFC Divisional Playoff Game victory over the Jacksonville Jaguars at Foxboro Stadium on 01-12-97?
a. Otis Redding   b. Otis Smith   c. Otis Nixon   d. Otis Campbell

4. Who was the Patriots player who returned a Tiki Barber fumble 38 yards for a TD in the 17–6 victory over the New York Giants at Gillette Stadium on 10-12-03?
a. Matt Bourne   b. Matt Chatham   c. Matthew Sandwich   d. Matt Falmouth

5. Who was the Patriots player who sacked Vinny Testaverde, forced him to fumble, and then returned the fumble 24 yards for a TD in the 44–7 rout of the New York Jets on 09-15-02?
a. Ed "Too Tall" Jones   b. Tebucky Jones   c. Sam Jones   d. Casey Jones

Answers:
1. Steve Grogan scored two TDs and threw a TD pass in the 41–7 rout of the New York Jets on 10-18-76
2. Andre Tippett returned two fumbles for a touchdown
3. Otis "My Man" Smith
4. Matt Chatham
5. Tebucky Jones

Match the Patriots player with his fumble recovery or fumble return for a touchdown

1. Jon Vaughn

a. I advanced a Don Calhoun fumble six yards for a TD in our 41–7 rout of the New York Jets on 10-18-76

2. Troy Brown

b. I recovered a Robert Perryman fumble for a TD in our 27–21 win over Cincinnati on 10-16-88

3. Randy Vataha

c. I took a Mack Herron fumble 46 yards for a TD in our 24–16 win over Baltimore on 10-07-73

4. John Stephens

d. I advanced a Dave Meggett fumble 75 yards for a TD in our 31–28 win vs the New York Jets on 12-10-95

5. Steve Grogan

e. I advanced my own kickoff return 100 yards for a TD in our 20–10 loss to Cincinnati on 12-20-92

Answers:
1. e. Jon Vaughn returned his own fumbled kickoff return 100 yards for a TD in the 20–10 loss to the Bengals
2. d. Troy Brown advanced Dave Meggett's fumbled kickoff return 75 yards for a TD in the 31–28 win over the Jets
3. c. Randy Vataha advanced a fumble by Mack Herron 46 yards for a TD in the 24–16 victory over the Colts
4. b. John Stephens fell on a fumble by Robert Perryman in the end zone for a TD in the 27–21 win over the Bengals
5. a. Steve Grogan advanced a fumble by Don Calhoun six yards for a TD in the 41–7 rout of the New York Jets

Match the Patriots player with his fumble recovery accomplishment

6. Steve Nelson

7. Andre Tippett

8. Ed Philpott

9. Vincent Brown

10. Don Blackmon

a. I recovered a Walter Payton fumble to set up the fastest points scored in a Super Bowl

b. I returned a Thurman Thomas fumble 25 yards for a TD in our 16–7 loss to Buffalo on 11-01-92

c. I returned a Babe Parilli lateral 10 yards for a TD in our 47–31 loss to the New York Jets on 09-22-68

d. I returned a bad snap to Ray Guy 25 yards for a TD in our 35–20 loss to the Raiders on 09-29-85

e. I recovered three fumbles in our 24–14 victory over the Philadelphia Eagles on 10-08-78

Answers:
6. e. Steve Nelson recovered three defensive fumbles in the 24–14 victory over the Philadelphia Eagles on 10-08-78
7. d. Andre Tippett
8. c. Ed Philpott
9. b. Vincent Brown
10. a. Don Blackmon recovered a fumble that was forced when Larry McGrew tackled Walter Payton

Match the Patriots player with his particular accomplishment

11. Dan Klecko

12. Bryan Cox

13. Ty Law

14. Tim Goad

15. Chris Slade

a. I returned a Jim Kelly fumble 27 yards for a TD in our 35–25 win over Buffalo on 11-26-95

b. I returned a Christian Okoye fumble 19 yards for a TD in our 27–20 loss to Kansas City on 12-13-92

c. I recovered a Jerry Rice fumble in our 24–21 comeback win over the 49ers on 12-20-98

d. I recovered a fumble and caught a seven yard pass as a running back in our 29–26 overtime win vs San Diego on 10-14-01

e. I returned a Peyton Manning fumble four yards in our 38–34 victory over the Colts on 11-30-03

Answers:
11. e. Dan Klecko returned a Peyton Manning fumble four yards in the 38–34 win over the Colts on 11-30-03
12. d. Bryan Cox
13. c. Ty Law recovered a fumble by Jerry Rice in the 24–21 comeback win over the 49ers on 12-20-98
14. b. Tim Goad returned a fumble by Christian Okoye 19 yards for a TD in the 27–20 loss to the Kansas City Chiefs on 12-13-92
15. a. Chris Slade returned a fumble by Jim Kelly 27 yards for a TD in the 35–25 win over Buffalo on 11-26-95

Match the Patriots player with his particular accomplishment

16. Nick Buoniconti

17. Otis Smith

18. Richard Seymour

19. Jim Lee Hunt

20. Tim Goad

a. I was the first Patriots defensive lineman to return a fumble for a TD on the first play of the game

b. I was the first Patriots defensive back to return a fumble by a running back for a TD in a playoff game

c. I was the first Patriots defensive lineman to return a fumble by a running back for a TD

d. I was the first Patriots linebacker to return a fumble by a running back for a TD

e. I was the first Patriots defensive lineman to return a fumble more than 50 yards for a TD

Answers:

16. d. Nick Buoniconti returned a fumble by Bill Tobin seven yards for a TD in the 46–28 win over Houston on 12-08-63
17. b. Otis Smith returned a James Stewart fumble 47 yards for a TD in the 20–6 playoff win over Jacksonville on 01-12-97
18. e. Richard Seymour returned a Drew Bledsoe fumble 68 yards for a TD in the 31–17 win over Buffalo on 10-03-04
19. c. Jim Lee Hunt returned a fumble by Darrell Lester five yards for a TD in the 17–10 loss to Denver on 11-06-66
20. a. Tim Goad returned a fumble by Christian Okoye that was forced by Maurice Hurst on the first play of the game

Match the Patriots player with his particular accomplishment

21. Johnny Rembert
22. Willie McGinest
23. Mike Haynes
24. Tebucky Jones
25. Troy Brown

a. I returned a lateral 65 yards for a TD in our 21–11 victory over the New York Jets
b. I advanced a fumble by Dave Meggett 75 yards for a TD in our 31–28 win over the New York Jets
c. I returned a fumble by Johnny Hector 15 yards for a TD in our 26–14 win over the New York Jets
d. I recovered a Tom Tupa fumble in the endzone for a TD in our 30–28 win vs the New York Jets
e. I sacked Vinny Testaverde and returned the ball 24 yards for a TD in our 44–7 rout of the New York Jets

Answers:

21. c. Johnny Rembert returned a fumbled kickoff return by Johnny Hector 15 yards for a TD in a playoff game
22. d. Willie McGinest recovered a fumble by the New York Jets quarterback Tom Tupa in the end zone for a TD on 09-12-99
23. a. Mike Haynes returned a lateral from John Zamerlin after Steve Nelson blocked a Pat Leahy FG on 10-05-80
24. e. Tebucky Jones sacked and returned a fumble by Vinny Testaverde in the 44–7 rout of the New York Jets on 09-15-02
25. b. Troy Brown advanced a fumbled kickoff return by Dave Meggett 75 yards for a TD on 12-10-95

Match the Patriots player with his fumble recovery in a victorious game against the Baltimore Colts

26. Prentice McCray
27. Rod Shoate
28. Rick Sanford
29. John Sanders
30. Sam Hunt

a. I recovered a Lydell Mitchell fumble in our 21–14 win over the Baltimore Colts on 11-14-76
b. I recovered a Joe Washington fumble in our 50–21 rout of the Baltimore Colts on 11-18-79
c. I recovered a Don McCauley fumble in our 21–10 win over the Baltimore Colts on 10-19-75
d. I returned a Nesby Glasgow fumble for a TD in our 47–21 win over the Baltimore Colts on 11-23-80
e. I returned a Ray Chester fumble in our 42–3 rout of the Baltimore Colts on 10-06-74

Answers:

26. b. Prentice McCray returned a fumble by Raymond Chester two yards in the 42–3 rout of the Colts at Schaefer Stadium
27. e. Rod Shoate recovered a fumble by Joe Washington in the 50–21 rout of the Colts at Schaefer Stadium
28. d. Rick Sanford returned a fumble by Nesby Galsgow 22 yards for a TD in the 47–21 win at Schaefer Stadium
29. c. John Sanders recovered a fumble by Don McCauley in the 21–10 win over the Colts at Schaefer Stadium
30. a. Sam Hunt recovered a fumble by Lydell Mitchell in the 21–14 win over the Colts at Memorial Stadium

Match the Patriots player with his specific fumble recovery in a game played in the beginning of each decade

31. Ray Agnew
32. Houston Antwine
33. Pete Brock
34. Ron Burton
35. Patrick Pass

a. I recovered a fumble in our 42–14 rout of the Dallas Texans at BU Field on 11-18-60
b. I recovered a fumble in our 14–10 win over the Bills at War Memorial Stadium on 11-29-70
c. I recovered a fumble in our 23–14 victory over Denver at Schaefer Stadium on 09-29-80
d. I recovered a fumble in our 16–14 win over the Colts at the Hoosier Dome on 09-16-90
e. I recovered a fumble in our 16–13 victory over the Bengals at Foxboro Stadium on 11-19-00

Answers:
31. d. Ray Agnew recovered a fumble by Albert Bentley in the 16–14 win over the Colts on 09-16-90
32. b. Houston Antwine recovered a fumble in the 14–10 victory over the Buffalo Bills on 11-29-70
33. c. Pete Brock recovered a fumble in the 23–14 victory over the Denver Broncos on 09-29-80
34. a. Ron Burton recovered his own fumble in the 42–14 rout of the Dallas Texans on 11-18-60
35. e. Patrick Pass recovered a fumble by Drew Bledsoe in the 16–13 win over the Cincinnati Bengals on 11-19-00

Match the Patriots player with his particular accomplishment

36. Dan Klecko a. I returned a James Stewart fumble 47 yards for a TD in our 20–6 AFC playoff game victory

37. Nick Buoniconti b. I returned a William Green fumble 41 yards for a TD in our 42–15 rout of the Browns

38. Andre Tippett c. I stole the ball from Eric Dickerson in our 21–7 win over the Los Angeles Rams on 12-11-83

39. Steve Nelson d. I ripped the ball from Dominic Rhodes in our 20–3 playoff game win over the Colts

40. Tedy Bruschi e. I returned a Drew Bledsoe fumble 68 yards for a TD in our 31–17 win over the Bills

41. Ted Johnson f. I recovered a fumble by Karim Abdul Jabbar in our 42–23 win over Miami on 11-03-96

42. Ty Law g. I recovered a fumble by Jerry Rice in our 24–21 win over the 49ers on 12-20-98

43. Otis Smith h. I recovered a fumble by Terry Bradshaw in our 30–27 win over the Steelers on 09-26-76

44. Randall Gay i. I recovered a fumble by George Blanda in our 45–3 rout of the Houston Oilers on 11-01-63

45. Richard Seymour j. I returned a Peyton Manning fumble four yards in our 38–34 win over the Colts on 11-30-03

Answers:
36. j. Dan Klecko returned a fumble by Peyton Manning four yards in the 38–34 win over the Indianapolis Colts
37. i. Nick Buoniconti recovered a fumble by George Blanda in the 45–3 rout of the Houston Oilers at Fenway Park
38. c. Andre Tippett stole the ball from Eric Dickerson in the 21–7 win over the Los Angeles Rams
39. h. Steve Nelson recovered a fumble by Terry Bradshaw in the 30–27 win over the Pittsburgh Steelers
40. d. Tedy Bruschi ripped the ball from Dominic Rhodes in the 20–3 rout of the Indianapolis Colts
41. f. Ted Johnson recovered a fumble by Karim Abdul Jabbar in the 42–23 win over the Miami Dolphins
42. g. Ty Law recovered a fumble by Jerry Rice in the 24–21 win over the San Francisco 49ers at Foxboro
43. a. Otis Smith returned a fumble by James Stewart 47 yards for a TD in the 20–6 win over the Jaguars
44. b. Randall Gay returned a fumble by William Green 41 yards for a TD in the 42–15 rout of the Browns
45. e. Richard Seymour returned a fumble by Drew Bledsoe 68 yards for a TD in the 31–17 win over the Bills

Sacks Questions

Five Trivia Questions relating to Quarterback sacks by a Patriots player

1. Who is the only player to have at least 100 sacks during his career with the Patriots?
a. Julius Adams   b. Andre Tippett   c. Tony McGee   d. Willie McGinest

2. Who was the first player to record a quarterback sack and catch a TD pass in a Super Bowl?
a. Bryan Cox   b. Mike Vrabel   c. Mike Bartrum   d. Michael Barkann

3. Who was the first Patriots linebacker to sack four future Pro Football Hall of Fame quarterbacks in the same season? (Bob Griese, Joe Namath, Fran Tarkenton, and Terry Bradshaw)
a. Albert King   b. Steve "Reno" King   c. Don King   d. Larry King

4. Who was the defensive back who recorded a sack of the quarterback in consecutive Super Bowl victories for the New England Patriots?

a. Lawyer Milloy   b. Rodney Harrison   c. Ronnie Lott   d. Glen Farley

5. Who was the first linebacker of the Patriots with a sack of the quarterback and an interception return for a TD in the same regular season game?

a. Steve Nelson   b. Tedy Bruschi   c. Andre Tippett   d. Bill Burt

Answers:
1. Andre Tippett
2. Mike Vrabel
3. Steve King
4. Rodney Harrison
5. Tedy Bruschi

Match the Patriots player with his particular accomplishment

1. Julius Adams	a. I sacked Peyton Manning, Steve McNair, Donovan McNabb, Jim Miller, and Michael Vick
2. Houston Antwine	b. I sacked Joe Montana, Art Schlichter, Dan Marino, Randall Cunningham, and Vince Ferragamo
3. Vincent Brown	c. I sacked Bob Griese, Ron Jaworski, Jim Kelly, Art Schlichter, and Vince Ferragamo
4. Tedy Bruschi	d. I sacked Boomer Esiason, Troy Aikman, Tom Tupa, Brian Griese, Doug Flutie, and Drew Bledsoe
5. Ray Hamilton	e. I sacked Bob Griese, Ron Jaworski, Joe Namath, Roger Staubach, and Joe Theisman
6. Tony McGee	f. I sacked Bob Griese, Ron Jaworski, Joe Namath, Roger Staubach, and Vince Ferragamo
7. Willie McGinest	g. I sacked Brian Griese, Rich Gannon, Brett Favre, Drew Bledsoe, and Vinny Testaverde
8. Steve Nelson	h. I sacked Boomer Esiason, Rich Gannon, Jeff George, Tom Tupa, and Vinny Testeverde
9. Andre Tippett	i. I sacked Bob Griese, Jack Kemp, Len Dawson, Fran Tarkenton, and Johnny Unitas
10. Mike Vrabel	j. I sacked Bob Griese, Joe Namath, Roger Staubach, Roman Gabriel, Dan Fouts, and Terry Bradshaw

Answers:
1 .j. Julius Adams sacked Bob Griese, Joe Namath, Roger Staubach, Roman Gabriel, and Terry Bradshaw
2. i. Houston Antwine sacked Bob Griese, Jack Kemp Len Dawson, Fran Tarkenton, and Johnny Unitas
3. h. Vincent Brown sacked Boomer Esiason, Rich Gannon, Jeff George, Tom Tupa, and Vinny Testaverde
4. g. Tedy Bruschi has sacked Brian Griese, Rich Gannon, Brett Favre, Drew Bledsoe, and Vinny Testaverde
5. f. Ray Hamilton sacked Bob Griese, Joe Namath, Roger Staubach, Ron Jaworski, and Vince Ferragamo
6. e. Tony McGree sacked Bob Griese, Joe Namath, Roger Staubach, Ron Jaworski, and Joe Theisman
7. d. Willie McGinest sacked Boomer Esiason, Tom Tupa, Brian Griese, Doug Flutie, and Drew Bledsoe
8. c. Steve Nelson sacked Bob Griese, Ron Jaworski, Jim Kelly, Art Schlitcher, and Vince Ferragamo
9. b. Andre Tippett sacked Joe Montana, Art Schlitcher, Dan Marino, Randall Cunningham, and Vince Ferragamo
10. a. Mike Vrabel has sacked Peyton Manning, Steve McNair, Donovan McNabb, Jim Miller, and Michael Vick

Did you know that?

Richard Seymour blocked a FG, had a quarterback sack, and recovered a fumble in the 24–17 win vs the Minnesota Vikings on 11-24-02

Match the Patriots player with his accomplishment in a regular season game where the Patriots shut out their opponent

11. Julius Adams

12. Don Blackmon

13. Ray Hamilton

14. Rodney Harrison

15. Andre Tippett

a. I sacked Ken Stabler in our 7–0 shutout of the New Orleans Saints at Sullivan Stadium on 12-04-83

b. I sacked Don Stock in our 34–0 shutout of the Miami Dolphins at Schaefer Stadium on 10-12-80

c. I sacked Jay Fiedler in our 12–0 shutout of the Miami Dolphins at Gillette Stadium on 12-07-03

d. I sacked David Woodley three times in our 34–0 shutout of the Miami Dolphins at Schaefer Stadium on 10-12-80

e. I sacked Gary Hogenboom three times in our 24–0 shutout of the Indianapolis Colts at Sullivan Stadium on 11-22-87

Answers:

11. b. Julius Adams sacked Don Strock
12. a. Don Blackmon sacked Ken Stabler
13. d. Ray "Sugar Bear" Hamilton sacked David Woodley
14. c. Rodney Harrison sacked Jay Fiedler
15. e. Andre Tippett sacked Gary Hogenboom

Match the first and last names of these NFL Quarterbacks who were sacked by Patriots Defensive Tackle Art Moore

16. Brian   a. Demory   Hint: Here are the teams;   Cleveland Browns
17. Bobby   b. Jones   Chicago Bears
18. Bert   c. Griese   Baltimore Colts
19. Bob   d. Sipe   Miami Dolphins
20. Bill   e. Douglass   New York Jets

Answers:

16. d. Brian Sipe, who was the quarterback of the Cleveland Browns
17. e. Bobby Douglass, who was the quarterback of the Chicago Bears
18. b. Bert Jones, who was the quarterback of the Baltimore Colts
19. c. Bob Griese, who was the quarterback of the Miami Dolphins
20. a. Bill Demory, who was the quarterback of the New York Jets

Interceptions Questions

10 Trivia Questions regarding pass interceptions by the Patriots

1. Who was the Patriots rookie defensive back who intercepted a Chad Pennington pass to seal the 21–16 win over the New York Jets on 12-20-03?

a. Champ Bailey   b. Eugene Wilson   c. Dennis Wilson   d. Woodrow Wilson

2. Who was the Patriots rookie defensive back who returned a Vinny Testaverde pass 55 yards for a TD in the 23–16 victory over the New York Jets at Gillette Stadium on 09-21-03?

a. Kato Serwanga   b. Asante Samuel   c. Samuel Jackson   d. Armand Asante

3. Who was the Patriots defensive back who returned a Kurt Warner pass 47 yards for a TD in the 20–17 Super Bowl victory over the St. Louis Rams at the Louisiana Superdome on 02-03-02?

a. Ted Wayman   b. Ty Law   c. Dean Wermer   d. Curt Warner

4. Who is the only Patriots player to intercept a pass and return a punt for a TD in the same game twice during his career?

a. Mike Barnicle   b. Mike Haynes   c. Mike Greenwell   d. Mike Dowling

5. Who was the Patriots linebacker who returned a Steve Spurrier pass 68 yards for a TD in the 31–14 victory over the Tampa Bay Buccaneers on 12-12-76?

a. Sam Houston   b. Sam Hunt   c. Sam Spade   d. Marty Schottenheimer

6. Who is the only Patriots defensive lineman who has blocked an extra point in a regular season game and intercepted a pass in a playoff game?

a. Gaylord Perry   b. Garin Veris   c. Gary Tanguay   d. Gabby Hayes

7. Who was the first Patriots defensive back to intercept three passes in a regular season game?

a. Chuck Norris   b. Gino Cappelletti   c. Chuck Connors   d. Chuck Jones

8. Who is the only Patriots defensive back to return two interceptions for a TD in the same game?

a. Jimmy Hitchcock   b. Prentice McCray   c. Abner Hayes   d. Mike Haynes

9. Who is the only Patriots player to intercept a pass and then lateral to another Patriots player with his same initials?

a. Claxton Welch lateraled it to Clayton Weishuhn
b. Rod Shoate lateraled it to Rick Sanford
c. Brent Williams lateraled it to Brooks Williams
d. Tedy Bruschi lateraled it to Troy Brown

10. Who was the Boston Patriots linebacker who returned a Jack Kemp pass three yards in the 23–16 loss to the Buffalo Bills on 10-11-69?

a. Marty Feldman   b. Marty Schottenheimer c. Marty Moore   d. John Jacob Jingleheimer

Answers:
1. Eugene Wilson
2. Asante Samuel
3. Ty Law
4. Mike Haynes
5. Sam Hunt
6. Garin Veris
7. Gino Cappelletti intercepted three passes by Tom Flores on 10-16-60
8. Prentice McCray
9. Rod Shoate to Rick Sanford
10. Marty Schottenheimer

Match the Patriots Defensive Back with his career longest interception return for a touchdown

1. Prentice McCray   a. I returned a Vinny Testaverde pass 90 yards for a TD in our 44–7 rout of the New York Jets on 09-15-02

2. Otis Smith   b. I returned a Joe Namath pass 63 yards for a TD in our 38–24 win over the New York Jets on 11-21-76

3. John Outlaw   c. I took a Johnny Unitas pass 60 yards for a TD in our 21–17 win vs the Baltimore Colts on 12-19-71

4. Jimmy Hitchcock   d. I returned a Dan Marino pass 100 yards for a TD in our 27–24 win over Miami on 11-23-97

5. Victor Green   e. I returned a Peyton Manning pass 78 yards for a TD in our 44–13 rout of the Colts on 09-30-01

Answers:
1. b. Prentice McCray actually returned two passes by Joe Namath for a TD in the 38–24 win over the New York Jets on 11-21-76
2. e. Otis "My Man" Smith returned a Peyton Manning pass 78 yards for a TD in the 44–13 rout of the Colts on 09-30-01
3. c. John Outlaw returned a Johnny Unitas pass 60 yards for a TD in the 21–17 win over the Colts on 12-19-71
4. d. Jimmy Hitchcock returned a Dan Marino pass 100 yards for a TD in the 27–24 win over Miami on 11-23-97
5. a. Victor Green returned a Vinny Testaverde pass 90 yards for a TD in the 44–7 rout of the Jets on 09-15-02

Match the Patriots Defensive Back with his interception of a pass thrown by Vinny Testaverde

6. Terrell Buckley

   a. I returned a Vinny Testaverde pass 55 yards for a TD in our 23–16 win over the Jets on 09-21-03

7. Willie Clay

   b. I intercepted a Vinny Testaverde pass to seal our 17–16 victory over the New York Jets on 12-02-01

8. Maurice Hurst

   c. I intercepted a Vinny Testaverde pass in our 46–38 victory over the Ravens on 10-06-96

9. Asante Samuel

   d. I returned a Vinny Testaverde pass nine yards to seal our 20–17 win over the Browns on 12-19-93

10. Roland James

   e. I returned a Vinny Testaverde pass one yard in our 10–7 overtime win vs the Buccaneers on 12-11-88

Answers:
6. b. Terrell Buckley intercepted a Vinny Testaverde pass in the 17–16 win over the New York Jets on 12-02-01
7. c. Willie Clay intercepted a Vinny Testaverde pass in the 46–38 win over the Ravens on 10-06-96
8. d. Maurice Hurst returned a Vinny Testaverde pass nine yards in the 20–17 win over the Browns on 12-19-93
9. a. Asante Samuel returned a Vinny Testaverde pass 55 yards for a TD in the 23–16 win over the Jets on 09-21-03
10. e. Roland James returned a Vinny Testaverde pass one yard in the 10–7 Overtime win vs the Buccaneers on 12-11-88

Match the Patriots player with his interception accomplishment

11. Tedy Bruschi

   a. I returned a pass by Bobby Hebert 49 yards for a TD in our 31–14 loss to the Saints on 11-08-92

12. Vincent Brown

   b. I intercepted three passes by Dan Darragh in our 23–6 win over the Bills at Fenway Park on 10-20-68

13. Nick Buoniconti

   c. I returned a Dan Marino pass 40 yards for a TD in our AFC Wild Card Playoff Game on 12-28-97

14. Todd Collins

   d. I returned a Chad Pennington pass 15 yards for a TD in our 21–16 win over the Jets on 12-20-03

15. Willie McGinest

   e. I returned a Jay Fiedler pass five yards for a TD and then fell to my knees in the snow on 12-07-03

Answers:
11. e. Tedy Bruschi returned a Jay Fiedler pass five yards for a TD in the 12–0 shutout of Miami on 12-07-03
12. a. Vincent Brown returned a Bobby Hebert pass 49 yards for a TD on 11-08-92
13. b. Nick Buoniconti is the only Patriots Linebacker with three interceptions in a game
14. c. Todd Collins is the only Patriots Linebacker to return an interception for a TD in a playoff game
15. d. Willie McGinest returned a Chad Pennington pass 15 yards for a TD in the 21–16 win over the Jets on 12-20-03

Match the Patriots Defensive player with his interception in a victorious game against the Buffalo Bills

16. Richard Seymour

   a. I returned a pass by Drew Bledsoe 39 yards in our 27–17 win over the Bills on 12-08-02

17. Mike Vrabel

   b. I intercepted but did not return a Drew Bledsoe pass in our 27–17 win over the Bills on 12-08-02

18. Terrell Buckley

   c. I returned a pass by Drew Bledsoe 29 yards in our 38–7 win over the Bills on 11-03-02

19. Tebucky Jones   d. I returned a pass by Drew Bledsoe six yards in our 27–17 victory over the Bills on 12-08-02

20. Ty Law   e. I returned a pass by Drew Bledsoe 14 yards in our 31–0 shutout of the Bills on 12-27-03

Answers:

16. d. Richard Seymour returned a Drew Bledsoe pass six yards in the 27–17 win over the Buffalo Bills on 12-08-02
17. e. Mike Vrabel returned a Drew Bledsoe pass 14 yards in the 31–0 shutout of the Buffalo Bills on 12-27-03
18. a. Terrell Buckley returned a Drew Bledsoe pass 39 yards in the 27–17 win over the Buffalo Bills on 12-08-02
19. b. Tebucky Jones intercepted but was not able to return a Drew Bledsoe pass in the 27–17 win over Buffalo on 12-08-02
20. c. Ty Law returned a Drew Bledsoe pass 29 yards in the 38–7 rout of the Buffalo Bills on 11-03-02

Blocked Field Goal or Extra Point Questions

Five Trivia Questions on blocked field goals or extra points

1. Who was the Patriots defensive lineman who blocked the field-goal attempt that was returned for a TD in the 24–17 AFC Championship playoff game victory over the Pittsburgh Steelers at Heinz Field on 01-27-02?
a. Darrell Brandon b. Brandon Mitchell c. Brad Faxon d. Lyndon Byers

2. Who was the Patriots player recovered this blocked field goal and then lateraled it to Antwan Harris who took it 49 yards for the touchdown?
a. Tom Brunansky b. Troy Brown c. Troy O'Leary d. Terry O'Reilly

3. Who blocked a 49-yard field-goal attempt by Pat Leahy on 10-05-80 that was run back for a touchdown?
a. Willie Nelson b. Steve Nelson c. Nelson Riddle d. Neal Biron

4. Who returned Larry Whigham's block of a punt by Greg Montgomery four yards for a TD on 10-06-96?
a. Teddy Ballgame b. Tedy Bruschi c. Teddy Roosevelt d. Teddy Bear

5. Who was the first Patriots linebacker to block two extra-point attempts in the same season?
a. Chris Singleton b. Steve Nelson c. Vincent Brown d. Lenny Clarke

Answers:

1. Brandon Mitchell
2. Troy Brown ran 11 yards with the football before lateralling it to Antwan Harris on 01-27-02
3. Steve Nelson
4. Tedy Bruschi returned a blocked punt four yards for a TD in the 46–38 win over the Baltimore Ravens
5. Steve Nelson blocked two extra-point attempts during the 1984 season

Combinations Questions

Five Questions relating to the combination of special teams, offensive, and defensive contributions of Patriots players

1. Who was the first Patriots wide receiver with rushing, receiving, punt return, and kickoff return yards in the same year?
a. Dave Henderson b. Darryl Stingley c. Gerald Henderson d. Jerome Henderson

2. Who is the only Patriots wide receiver with more than 1,000 kickoff yards in a season?
a. Steve Sweeney b. Stephen Starring c. Stephen Stills d. Steve Doocy

3. Who was the first former Patriots linebacker, who had returned an interception and a kickoff, to become the head coach of three NFL teams?

a. Steve Nelson   b. Marty Schottenheimer   c. Mike Dikta   d. Bum Phillips

4. Who was the first former Patriots defensive back who returned an interception, a punt, and a kickoff in the same season to become a head coach in the NFL? (Hint: He is the only undefeated head coach in the NFL)

a. Jerry Glanville   b. Fred Bruney   c. Ron Meyer   d. Phil Bengston

5. Who was only Patriots quarterback to rush for more than 100 hundred yards and catch a pass in the same season?

a. Steve McQueen   b. Steve Grogan   c. Steven Tyler   d. Matt Cavanaugh

Answers:
1. Darryl Stingley
2. Stephen Starring
3. Marty Schottenheimer
4. Fred Bruney
5. Steve Grogan

Ten Questions relating to the combination of special teams, offensive, and defensive contributions of Patriots players

6. Who are the three Patriots receivers who have returned a punt for a TD and caught at least one TD pass in a season?

a. Tom Dewey, Howie Cheatham, and Andy Howe
b. Stanley Morgan, Irving Fryar, and Troy Brown
c. Larry Bird, Kevin McHale, and Robert Parish
d. Phil Esposito, Ken Hodge, and Wayne Cashman

7. Who are the three Patriots receivers who have run for a TD and caught a TD pass in the same game?

a. Darryl Sittler, Stanley Morgan, and Bethel Johnson
b. Darryl Stingley, Irving Fryar, and David Patten
c. Dave Shea, Troy Brown, and David Givens
d. Dale Sveum, Gino Cappelletti, and Deion Branch

8. Who are the five Patriots running backs who have at least 1,000 yards rushing, 1,000 yards receiving, and 1,000 yards returning?

a. Dave Meggett, Curtis Martin, Mosi Tatupu, Marc Edwards, and Mack Herron
b. Ron Burton, Tony Collins, Kevin Faulk, Carl Garrett, and Larry Garron
c. Robert Edwards, John Stephens, Sam Cunningham, Dave Gavitt, and Chris Heron
d. Jon Vaughn, Andy Johnson, Don Calhoun, Mike Garrett, and Jay Croxton

9. Who are the three Patriots wide receivers who have caught a pass and returned a kickoff in same playoff game?

a. Cedric Jones, Stanley Morgan, Deion Branch
b. Stephen Starring, Troy Brown, and Bethel Johnson
c. David Patten, Irving Fryar, and David Givens
d. Darryl Stingley, Gino Cappelletti, and P.K. Sam

10. Who are the six running backs who have completed a pass, returned a punt, and returned a kickoff for the Patriots?

a. Jon Vaughn, John Stephens, Johnny Pesky, Johnny Damon, Curtis Martin, and Corey Dillon
b. Dick Christy, Larry Garron, Bob Gladieux, Andy Johnson, Dave Meggett, and Kevin Faulk
c. Eddie Yost, Eddie Popowski, Eddie Shore, Robert Edwards, Marc Edwards, and Mosi Tatupu
d. Mack Herron, Don Calhoun, Larry Centers, Jim Nance, Corey Croom, and Patrick Pass

11. Who are the five defensive lineman who have returned a kickoff and recorded a sack in the same season for the Patriots?
a. Rob Deer, Tom Beer, Billy Sullivan, Ernie DiGregorio, and Mark Gastineau
b. Bob Dee, Ron Berger, Chris Sullivan, Chad Eaton, and Dan Klecko
c. Tony McGee, Carl Eller, John L. Sullivan, Tim Nearing, and Chad Eaton
d. John Doe, Marv Cook, Patrick Sullivan, Julius Erving, and Joe Klecko

12. Who are the three former Patriots players who have won a National Punt, Pass and Kick competition as a young man?
a. Dave McCarty, Howie Long, and A.J. Doggart
b. Shawn McCarthy, Tom Tupa, and Hart Lee Dykes
c. Craig MacTavish, Pat McNally, and Eric McHugh
d. Ed McMahon, Jack Lemmon, and Hank Goldberg

13. Who are the three players who have completed at least 10 TD passes and have punted for the Patriots?
a. Dan Marino, Joe Montana, and Doug V.B. Goudie
b. Tom Yewcic, Babe Parilli, and Tom Brady
c. Tom Tupa, Shawn McCarthy, and Hart Lee Dykes
d. Eddie Hare, Eddie Wilson, and Eddie Andleman

14. Who are the three Patriots wide receivers who have run for a TD and caught a TD pass in the same game?
a. Ben Stiller, Jim Dwyer, and Dale Arnold
b. Darryl Stingley, Irving Fryar, and David Patten
c. Jerry Stiller, Ron Meyer, and Dan Patrick
d. Jerry Springer, Chris Speier, and Don Orsillo

15. Who are the three Patriots wide receivers who had a carry, a reception, a punt return, and a kickoff return in the same game?
a. Hart Lee Dykes, Steve Martin, and John Salley
b. Irving Fryar, Sammy Martin, and Troy Brown
c. Chris Rose, Dean Martin, and Terrell Buckley
d. Ty Law, Don Martin, and Tedy Bruschi

Answers:
6. Stanley Morgan did it in 1979, Irving Fryar did it in 1985 and 1986, and Troy Brown did it during the 2001 season
7. Darryl Stingley, Irving Fryar, and Troy Brown
8. Ron Burton, Tony Collins, Kevin Faulk Carl Garrett, and Larry Garron
9. Stephen Starring, Troy Brown, and Bethel Johnson
10. Dick Christy, Larry Garron, Bob Gladieux, Andy Johnson, Dave Meggett, and Kevin Faulk
11. Bob Dee, Ron Berger, Chris Sullivan, Chad Eaton, and Dan Klecko
12. Hart Lee Dykes, Shawn McCarthy, Tom Tupa
13. Tom Brady, Babe Parilli, and Tom Yewcic
14. Darryl Stingley did it in 1977, Irving Fryar did it in 1985, and David Patten did it during the 2001 season
15. Irving Fryar did it in 1985, Sammy Martin did it in 1989, and Troy Brown did it during the 2001 season

Uniform Numbers Questions

10 Trivia Questions pertaining to the uniform number of a Patriots player

1. Who is the only player wearing uniform No. 2 who has drop-kicked an extra point for the Patriots?
a. Lou Merloni   b. Doug Flutie   c. Mike Cataldo   d. Paul D'Angelo

2. Who was the Pro Football Hall of Fame player who had his uniform No. 40 retired by the Patriots in 1997?
a. John Hannah   b. Mike Haynes   c. Nick Buoniconti   d. David DiLorenzo

3. Who was the Pro Football Hall of Fame player who had his uniform No. 73 retired by the Patriots in 1991?
a. Fred Smerlas   b. John Hannah   c. Billy Sullivan   d. Dick Radatz

4. Who was the only Boston Patriots AFL All-Star and AFL MVP to wear No. 35?
a. Jim Corsi   b. Jim Nance   c. Jim Rice   d. Joe Scarborough

5. Only three Patriots Players have worn No. 57; John Bramlett, Steve Kiner, and?
a. Steve DeOssie   b. Steve Nelson   c. Glen Ordway   d. Pete Brock

6. Who is the only Patriots player to wear the No. 20?
a. Bruce Allen   b. Gino Cappelletti   c. Kyle Psaty   d. David Scott

7. In 1993, the Patriots retired uniform No. 79 and uniform No. 89 in the honor of?
a. Steve Colbert and Jon Stewart
b. Jim Lee Hunt and Bob Dee
c. Bill Lee and Stan Papi
d. Mike Greenburg and Mike Golic

8. Who is the only Patriots AFC Pro Bowl player who has worn No. 4?
a. Bobby Orr   b. Adam Vinatieri   c. Bobby Doerr   d. Adam Oates

9. Which number did Jermaine Wiggins wear for the Patriots in the AFC playoff game victory on 01-19-02?
a. No. 49   b. No. 85   c. No. 87   d. No. 99

10. Who are the three quarterbacks who have worn No. 16 for the New England Patriots?
a. Steve Burton, Steve Buckley, and Sean McAdam
b. Jim Plunkett, Scott Zolak, and Matt Cassel
c. Huey Lewis, Dewey Evans, and Louie Prima
d. Rick Reilly, Bill Simmons, and Warner Wolf

Answers:
1. Doug Flutie drop kicked an extra point in the 28–26 loss to the Miami Dolphins at Gillette Stadium on 01-01-06
2. Mike Haynes wore No. 40 for the New England Patriots
3. John Hannah wore No. 73 for the New England Patriots
4. No. 35 Jim Nance was an AFL All-Star running back in 1966 and 1967 and was the AFL MVP in 1966
5. No. 57 was worn by and was retired in honor of Steve Nelson
6. No. 20 was only worn by Gino Cappelletti
7. No. 79 was retired in honor of defensive tackle Jim Lee Hunt, and No. 89 was retired in honor of defensive end Bob Dee
8. No. 4 was worn by two-time AFC Pro Bowl kicker Adam Vinatieri
9. No. 85 was worn by Jermaine Wiggins in the 16–13 overtime win vs the Oakland Raiders on 01-19-02
10. Jim Plunkett, Scott Zolak, and Matt Cassel

The Appendix

Individual Rushing

The Most Rushing Attempts by a Patriots player in a regular season game

#	Running Back	Score, Outcome, Opponent, and Date
40	Curtis Martin	27–24 overtime win vs the New York Jets on 09-14-97
38	Jim Nance	24–21 victory over the Oakland Raiders on 10-30-66
36	Curtis Martin	27–14 win over the Buffalo Bills on 10-23-95
35	Curtis Martin	27–13 victory over the Indianapolis Colts on 11-24-96
35	Curtis Martin	20–7 win over the New York Jets on 11-05-95
35	Michael LeBlanc	14–7 victory over the Buffalo Bills on 10-11-87
35	John Stephens	30–7 rout of the Chicago Bears on 10-30-88
34	Jim Nance	23–0 shutout of the Buffalo Bills on 09-24-67
32	Tony Collins	29–21 victory over the Houston Oilers on 11-28-82
32	Tony Collins	16–0 shutout of the Seattle Seahawks on 12-19-82
32	Corey Dillon	23–12 victory over the Arizona Cardinals on 09-19-04

The Most Rushing Attempts by a Patriots player in a playoff game

#	Running Back	Score, Outcome, Opponent, and Date
26	Antowain Smith	32–29 victory over the Carolina Panthers on 02-01-04
25	Laurence Maroney	21–12 win over the San Diego Chargers on 01-20-08
24	Corey Dillon	41–27 victory over the Pittsburgh Steelers on 01-23-05
23	Craig James	27–20 win over the Los Angeles Raiders on 01-05-86
23	Corey Dillon	20–3 rout of the Indianapolis Colts on 01-16-05
22	Craig James	26–14 win over the New York Jets on 12-28-85
22	Craig James	31–14 victory over the Miami Dolphins on 01-12-86
22	Derrick Cullors	17–3 win over the Miami Dolphins on 12-28-97
22	Antowain Smith	24–14 victory over the Indianapolis Colts on 01-18-04
22	Laurence Maroney	31–20 win over the Jacksonville Jaguars on 01-12-08

The Most Yards Rushing by a Patriots player in a regular season game

Yds	Running Back	Score, Outcome, Opponent, and Date
212	Tony Collins	23–13 victory over the New York Jets on 09-18-83
208	Jim Nance	24–21 win over the Oakland Raiders on 10-30-66
199	Curtis Martin	27–24 overtime win vs the New York Jets on 09-14-97
196	Robert Edwards	32–18 loss to the St. Louis Rams on 12-13-98
185	Jim Nance	23–0 shutout of the Buffalo Bills on 09-24-67
177	Don Calhoun	38–14 rout of the Denver Broncos on 11-28-76
177	Don Calhoun	27–6 rout of the New Orleans Saints on 12-05-76
166	Curtis Martin	20–7 victory over the New York Jets on 11-05-95
164	Jim Nance	41–32 loss to the Miami Dolphins on 12-17-67
161	Tony Collins	29–21 victory over the Houston Oilers on 11-28-82

The Most Yards Rushing by a Patriots player in a playoff game

Yds	Running Back	Score, Outcome, Opponent, and Date
166	Curtis Martin	28–3 rout of the Pittsburgh Steelers on 01-05-97
144	Corey Dillon	20–3 rout of the Indianapolis Colts on 01-16-05
122	Laurence Maroney	31–20 win over the Jacksonville Jaguars on 01-12-08
122	Laurence Maroney	21–12 win over the San Diego Chargers on 01-20-08
105	Craig James	31–14 victory over the Miami Dolphins on 01-12-86
104	Craig James	27–20 win over the Los Angeles Raiders on 01-05-86
100	Antowain Smith	24–14 victory over the Indianapolis Colts on 01-18-04
92	Antowain Smith	20–17 win over the St. Louis Rams on 02-03-02
86	Derrick Cullors	17–3 victory over the Miami Dolphins on 12-28-97
83	Antowain Smith	32–29 victory over the Carolina Panthers on 02-01-04

The 10 Longest Runs by a Patriots player in a regular season game

85-yard TD run by Larry Garron in the 31-point demolition of the Buffalo Bills on 10-22-61

80-yard TD run by Carl Garrett in the one-point loss to the Miami Dolphins on 11-09-69

77-yard run by Robert Weathers in the six-point overtime loss to the Baltimore Colts on 09-04-83

77-yard run by Ron Burton in the seven-point loss to the Denver Broncos on 10-23-60

75-yard TD run by Sam Cunningham on the first play in the two-point loss to the Buffalo Bills on 10-20-74

74-yard run by Don Calhoun in the 10-point win over the St. Louis Cardinals on 09-10-78

73-yard run by Craig James in the 23-point loss to the St. Louis Cardinals 12-02-84

71-yard TD run by Claude King in the 25-point rout of the Denver Broncos on 09-21-62

71-yard run by Sedrick Shaw in the 21-point loss to the New York Jets on 12-27-98

70-yard TD run by Curtis Martin in the 28-point rout of the Chicago Bears on 09-21-97

The 10 Longest Runs by a Patriots player in a playoff game

78-yard TD run by Curtis Martin in the 25-point rout of the Pittsburgh Steelers on 01-05-97

45-yard run by Robert Weathers in the 17-point victory over the Miami Dolphins on 01-12-86

42-yard run by Corey Dillon in the 17-point victory over the Indianapolis Colts on 01-16-05

35-yard run by Corey Dillon in the four-point loss to the Indianapolis Colts on 01-21-07

35-yard run by Antowain Smith in the 10-point victory over the Indianapolis Colts on 01-18-04

29-yard run by Laurence Maroney in the 11-point win over the Jacksonville Jaguars on 01-12-08

27-yard run by Corey Dillon in the 17-point victory over the Indianapolis Colts on 01-16-05

25-yard TD run by Corey Dillon in the 14-point win over the Pittsburgh Steelers on 01-23-05

25-yard run by Corey Dillon in the three-point victory over the Philadelphia Eagles on 02-06-05

23-yard run by Tony Collins in the five-point loss to the Denver Broncos on 01-04-87

The Most Yards Rushing in a regular season

Yards	Player	Year
1,635	Corey Dillon	2004
1,487	Curtis Martin	1995
1,458	Jim Nance	1966
1,227	Craig James	1985
1,216	Jim Nance	1967
1,168	John Stephens	1988
1,160	Curtis Martin	1997
1,157	Antowain Smith	2001
1,152	Curtis Martin	1996
1,115	Robert Edwards	1998

The Most Career Yards Rushing

Yards	Player	Seasons
5,453	Sam Cunningham	1973–82
5,323	Jim Nance	1965–71
4,647	Tony Collins	1981–87
3,799	Curtis Martin	1995–97
3,391	Don Calhoun	1975–81
3,249	John Stephens	1988–92
3,180	Corey Dillon	2004–06
3,179	Kevin Faulk	1999–2008
2,981	Larry Garron	1960–68
2,781	Antowain Smith	2001–03

The Most Career Yards Rushing in the playoffs

Yards	Player
508	Corey Dillon
456	Antowain Smith
373	Kevin Faulk
367	Laurence Maroney
290	Craig James
267	Curtis Martin
200	Tony Collins
110	Sam Cunningham
105	Robert Weathers
104	Derrick Cullors

The Most Rushing TDs in a Regular Season

TDs	Player	Year
14	Curtis Martin	1995
14	Curtis Martin	1996
13	Corey Dillon	2006
12	Steve Grogan	1976
12	Antowain Smith	2001
12	Corey Dillon	2004
12	Corey Dillon	2005
11	Jim Nance	1966
11	Horace Ivory	1978
10	Tony Collins	1983

The Most Career Regular Season Rushing TDs

TDs	Player	Seasons
45	Jim Nance	1965–71
43	Sam Cunningham	1973–82
37	Corey Dillon	2004–06
35	Steve Grogan	1975–90
32	Tony Collins	1981–87
32	Curtis Martin	1995–97
23	Don Calhoun	1975–81
21	Antowain Smith	2001–03
18	Mosi Tatupu	1978–90
17	John Stephens	1988–92

The Most Career Playoff Rushing TDs (Through 2008)

TDs	Player
5	Curtis Martin
4	Corey Dillon
3	Laurence Maroney
2	Antowain Smith
2	Tom Brady

Team Rushing Records

The Most Rushing Attempts in a regular season game

#	Score, Outcome, Opponent, and Date
62	38–14 rout of the Denver Broncos on 11-28-76
60	16–0 shutout of the Seattle Seahawks on 12-19-82
58	38–0 shutout of the Indianapolis Colts on 12-26-93
55	24–21 victory over the Oakland Raiders on 10-30-66
55	31–0 shutout of the Seattle Seahawks on 10-09-77
55	14–7 victory over the Buffalo Bills on 10-11-87
55	13–7 win over the Seattle Seahawks on 12-04-88
54	20–7 victory over the Buffalo Bills on 11-20-77
54	30–7 rout of the Chicago Bears on 10-30-88
52	48–17 destruction of the Oakland Raiders on 10-03-76

The Most Rushing Attempts in a playoff game

#	Score, Outcome, Opponent, and Date
59	31–14 win over the Miami Dolphins on 01-12-86
49	24–21 loss to the Oakland Raiders on 12-18-76
49	27–20 win over the Los Angeles Raiders on 01-05-86
39	20–3 rout of the Indianapolis Colts on 01-16-05
39	26–14 win over the New York Jets on 12-28-85
38	37–16 demolition of the New York Jets on 01-07-07
36	26–8 victory over the Buffalo Bills on 12-28-63
35	32–29 win over the Carolina Panthers on 02-01-04
32	24–14 victory over the Indianpolis Colts on 01-18-04
32	28–3 rout of the Pittsburgh Steelers on 01-05-97
32	41–27 win over the Pittsburgh Steelers on 01-23-05

The Most Yards Rushing in a regular season game

Yds	Score Outcome, Opponent, and Date
332	38–14 rout of the Denver Broncos on 11-28-76
330	41–7 demolition of the New York Jets on 10-18-76
328	23–13 victory over the New York Jets on 09-18-83
296	48–17 destruction of the Oakland Raiders 10-03-76
281	24–21 victory over the Oakland Raiders on 10-30-66
281	34–23 AFC title-clinching win over the Cincinnati Bengals on 12-22-85
279	14–10 victory over the Buffalo Bills on 11-05-78
269	16–6 win over the St. Louis Cardinals on 09-10-78
257	38–0 shutout of the Indianapolis Colts on 12-26-93
256	20–7 victory over the Buffalo Bills on 11-20-77

The Most Yards Rushing in a playoff game

Yds	Outcome, Opponent, and Date
255	17-point victory over the Miami Dolphins on 01-12-86
210	17-point rout of the Indianapolis Colts on 01-16-05
194	25-point rout of the Pittsburgh Steelers on 01-05-97
164	3-point loss to the Oakland Raiders on 12-18-76
158	21-point romp over the New York Jets on 01-07-07
156	7-point win over the Los Angeles Raiders on 01-05-86
149	9-point victory over the San Diego Chargers on 01-20-08
145	11-point win over the Jacksonville Jaguars on 01-12-08
126	14-point victory over the Pittsburgh Steelers on 01-23-05
112	3-point win over the Philadelphia Eagles on 02-06-05

The Best Yards Per Rushing Attempt in a regular season game

Avg	Score, outcome, opponent, and date
7.84	28–7 rout of the Miami Dolphins on 12-23-07
7.39	41–16 rout of the Denver Broncos on 09-21-62
7.29	49–26 rout of the Oakland Raiders on 12-14-08
7.12	52–21 rout of the Buffalo Bills on 10-22-61
7.02	41–17 rout of the New York Jets on 10-18-76
6.97	23–13 victory over the New York Jets on 09-18-83
6.83	26–16 victory over the Oakland Raiders on 10-26-62
6.76	41–7 rout of the Denver Broncos on 10-20-008
6.75	30–28 loss to the Buffalo Bills on 10-20-74
6.67	31–14 win over the Tampa Bay Buccaneers on 12-12-76

The Best Yards Per Rushing Attempt in a playoff game

Avg	Score, outcome, opponent, and date
6.1	28–3 rout of the Pittsburgh Steelers on 01-05-97
5.4	20–3 rout of the Indianapolis Colts on 01-16-05
5.3	20–17 victory over the St. Louis Rams on 02-03-02
5.0	22–17 loss to the Denver Broncos on 01-04-87
5.0	31–20 win over the Jacksonville Jaguars on 01-12-08
4.8	21–12 victory over the San Diego Chargers on 01-20-08
4.7	51–10 loss to the San Diego Chargers on 01-05-64
4.3	31–14 victory over the Miami Dolphins on 01-12-86
4.2	28–13 loss to the Miami Dolphins on 01-08-83
4.2	28–3 rout of the Jacksonville Jaguars on 01-07-06

The Best Average Yards Per Carry in a regular season

Avg	Year
4.98	1976
4.84	1983
4.71	1978
4.56	1962
4.44	2008
4.30	1961
4.21	1984
4.16	1966
4.15	1982
4.12	1985

The Most Yards Rushing in a season

Yards	Year
3,165	1978 (NFL record)
2,948	1976
2,605	1983
2,331	1985
2,303	1977
2,278	2008
2,252	1979
2,240	1980
2,134	1974
2,134	2004

The Most Rushing TDs in a season

TDs	Year
30	1978
24	1976
23	1981
21	1974
21	2008
20	2006
19	1980
19	1983
17	1966
17	1988
17	2007

Passing

Individual Passing

The Most Passing Attempts in a regular season game

#	Quarterback	Outcome, opponent, and date
70	Drew Bledsoe	6-point overtime win vs the Minnesota Vikings on 11-13-94
60	Drew Bledsoe	14-point loss to the Pittsburgh Steelers on 12-16-95
59	Steve Grogan	4-point loss to the New Orleans Saints on 11-12-89
56	Drew Bledsoe	34-point loss to the Denver Broncos on 10-08-95
56	Marc Wilson	18-point loss to the Pittsburgh Steelers on 12-17-89
55	Tom Brady	3-point comeback win over the Chicago Bears on 11-10-02
55	Drew Bledsoe	4-point loss to the Los Angeles Raiders on 10-09-94
55	Tom Brady	10-point loss to the Denver Broncos on 09-24-06
54	Drew Bledsoe	3-point victory over the Miami Dolphins on 11-23-98
54	Tom Brady	3-point victory over the Philadelphia Eagles on 11-25-07
54	Tom Brady	3-point overtime win vs the Kansas City Chiefs on 09-22-02
54	Tom Brady	3-point overtime win vs the San Diego Chargers on 10-14-01

The Most Passing Attempts in a playoff game

#	Quarterback	Outcome, opponent, and date
52	Tom Brady	3-point overtime win vs the Oakland Raiders on 01-19-02
51	Tom Brady	3-point victory over the San Diego Chargers on 01-14-07
50	Drew Bledsoe	7-point loss to the Cleveland Browns on 01-01-95
48	Tom Brady	3-point loss to the New York Giants on 02-03-08
48	Tom Brady	3-point victory over the Carolina Panthers on 02-01-04
48	Drew Bledsoe	14-point win over the Jacksonville Jaguars on 01-26-97
44	Scott Zolak	15-point loss to the Jacksonville Jaguars on 01-03-99
44	Drew Bledsoe	1-point loss to the Pittsburgh Steelers on 01-03-98
41	Tom Brady	3-point victory over the Tennessee Titans on 01-10-04
37	Tom Brady	10-point win over the Indianapolis Colts on 01-18-04

The Most Completions in a regular season game

#	Quarterback	Outcome, opponent, and date
45	Drew Bledsoe	6-point overtime win vs the Minnesota Vikings on 11-13-94
39	Drew Bledsoe	14-point loss to the Pittsburgh Steelers on 12-16-95
39	Tom Brady	3-point overtime win vs the Kansas City Chiefs on 09-22-02
36	Tony Eason	2-point win over the Los Angeles Rams on 11-16-86
36	Tom Brady	7-point loss to the San Diego Chargers on 09-29-02
36	Tom Brady	3-point victory over the Chicago Bears on 11-10-02
34	Tom Ramsey	3-point overtime loss to the Philadelphia Eagles on 11-29-87
34	Tom Brady	3-point victory over the Philadelphia Eagles on 11-25-07
33	Tom Brady	3-point overtime win vs the San Diego Chargers on 10-14-01
32	Drew Bledsoe	4-point loss to the Miami Dolphins on 09-04-94
32	Drew Bledsoe	3-point win over the Buffalo Bills on 10-27-96
32	Tom Brady	3-point victory over the New York Giants on 12-29-07

The Most Completions in a playoff game

#	Quarterback	Outcome, opponent, and date
32	Tom Brady	3-point victory over the Carolina Panthers on 02-01-04
32	Tom Brady	3-point overtime win vs the Oakland Raiders on 01-19-02
29	Tom Brady	3-point loss to the New York Giants on 02-03-08
27	Tom Brady	3-point victory over the San Diego Chargers on 01-14-07
26	Tom Brady	11-point win over the Jacksonville Jaguars on 01-12-08
23	Drew Bledsoe	1-point loss to the Pittsburgh Steelers on 01-13-98
23	Tom Brady	3-point win over the Philadelphia Eagles on 02-06-05
22	Tom Brady	21-point rout of the New York Jets on 01-07-07
22	Tom Brady	10-point victory over the Indianapolis Colts on 01-18-04

The Best Completion percentage in a regular season game (10+ attempts)

%	Quarterback	Score, outcome, opponent, and date
84.6	Tom Brady	38–7 destruction of the Buffalo Bills on 11-03-02
84.0	Tom Brady	49–28 blowout of the Miami Dolphins on 10-21-07
81.8	Steve Grogan	23–13 victory over the New York Jets on 09-18-83
81.8	Drew Bledsoe	38–0 shutout of the Indianapolis Colts on 12-26-93
81.5	Tom Brady	31–28 victory over the Atlanta Falcons on 10-09-05
80.6	Tom Brady	38–14 rout of the San Diego Chargers on 09-16-07
80.0	Tom Brady	38–17 victory over the Indianapolis Colts on 10-21-01
80.0	Babe Parilli	41–10 blowout of the Miami Dolphins on 10-15-67
79.5	Tom Brady	56–10 pulverizing of the Buffalo Bills on 11-18-07
79.3	Tom Brady	38–7 rout of the Buffalo Bills on 09-23-07

The Best Completion percentage in a playoff game

%	Quarterback	Score, outcome, opponent, and date
92.9	Tom Brady	31–20 win over the Jacksonville Jaguars on 01-12-08 (NFL record)
83.3	Tony Eason	31–14 victory over the Miami Dolphins on 01-12-86
75	Tony Eason	26–14 win over the New York Jets on 12-28-85
69.7	Tom Brady	24–21 win over the Philadelphia Eagles on 02-06-05
66.7	Tom Brady	24–17 victory over the Pittsburgh Steelers on 01-27-02
66.7	Tom Brady	32–29 win over the Carolina Panthers on 02-01-04
66.7	Tom Brady	20–3 rout of the Indianapolis Colts on 01-16-05
66.7	Tom Brady	41–27 victory over the Pittsburgh Steelers on 01-23-05
60.6	Drew Bledsoe	20–6 win over the Jacksonville Jaguars on 01-12-97
59.5	Tom Brady	24–14 victory over the Indianapolis Colts on 01-18-04

The Best Pass Completion percentage in a regular season

%	Quarterback	Year
68.9	Tom Brady	2007
65.1	Tony Eason	1988
63.9	Tom Brady	2001
63.4	Matt Cassel	2008
63.0	Tom Brady	2005
62.1	Tom Brady	2002
61.8	Tom Brady	2006
61.6	Tony Eason	1986
61.1	Hugh Millen	1992
60.78	Steve Grogan	1986

The Best Career Pass Completion percentage

%	Quarterback	Seasons
63.0	Tom Brady	2000–08
62.9	Matt Cassel	2005–08
60.5	Hugh Millen	1991–92
58.4	Tony Eason	1983–89
56.3	Drew Bledsoe	1993–2001
54.3	Tommy Hodson	1990–92
53.5	Matt Cavanaugh	1978–82
52.3	Steve Grogan	1975–90
51.6	Marc Wilson	1989–90
50.8	Scott Zolak	1992–98

The Most Yards Passing in a regular season game

Yds	Quarterback	Score, outcome, opponent, and date
426	Drew Bledsoe	26–20 overtime win vs the Minnesota Vikings on 11-13-94
423	Drew Bledsoe	26–23 victory over the Miami Dolphins on 11-23-98
421	Drew Bledsoe	39–35 loss to the Miami Dolphins on 09-04-94
419	Drew Bledsoe	42–23 victory over the Miami Dolphins on 11-03-96
415	Matt Cassel	48–28 rout of the Miami Dolphins on 11-23-08
414	Tony Eason	38–31 loss to the Seattle Seahawks on 09-21-86
410	Tom Brady	41–38 overtime win vs the Kansas City Chiefs on 09-22-02
402	Tom Ramsey	34–31 overtime loss to the Philadelphia Eagles on 11-29-87
401	Steve Grogan	31–24 loss to the New York Jets on 10-12-86
400	Babe Parilli	43–43 tie with the Oakland Raiders on 10-16-64
400	Matt Cassel	34–31 overtime loss to the New York Jets on 11-13-08

The Most Yards Passing in a playoff game

Yds	Quarterback	Score, outcome, opponent, and date
354	Tom Brady	32–29 win over the Carolina Panthers on 02-01-04
341	Tom Brady	27–13 loss to the Denver Broncos on 01-14-06
312	Tom Brady	16–13 overtime win vs the Oakland Raiders on 01-19-02
300	Babe Parilli	26–8 victory over the Buffalo Bills on 12-28-63
280	Tom Brady	24–21 victory over the San Diego Chargers on 01-14-07
266	Tom Brady	17–14 loss to the New York Giants on 02-03-08
264	Drew Bledsoe	7–6 loss to the Pittsburgh Steelers on 01-03-98
262	Tom Brady	31–20 win over the Jacksonville Jaguars on 01-12-08
253	Drew Bledsoe	35–21 loss to the Green Bay Packers on 01-26-97
237	Tom Brady	24–14 victory over the Indianapolis Colts on 01-18-04

The 10 Longest Completions in a regular season game

91-yard TD by Tom Brady to David Patten in the 21-point rout of the Indianapolis Colts on 10-21-01

90-yard TD by Tony Eason to Craig James in the 13-point loss to the Chicago Bears on 09-15-85

88-yard TD by Jim Plunkett to Randy Vataha in the four-point win over the Baltimore Colts on 12-19-71

87-yard TD by Tom Sherman to Jim Whalen in the 34-point loss to the New York Jets on 10-27-68

86-yard TD by Drew Bledsoe to Terry Glenn in the 14-point win over the Pittsburgh Steelers on 12-06-98

85-yard TD by Tom Brady to Troy Brown for the game-winning TD in the six-point overtime win vs the Mami Dolphins on 10-19-03

84-yard TD by Drew Bledsoe to Ben Coates in the 19-point victory over the Miami Dolphins on 11-03-96

80-yard TD by Babe Parilli to Art Graham in the 17-point win over the Houston Oilers on 11-29-64

80-yard TD by Jim Plunkett to Carl Garrett in the five-point victory over the Buffalo Bills on 11-14-71

80-yard TD by Doug Flutie to Irving Fryar on the first play in the 23-point win over the Chicago Bears on 10-30-88

The 10 Longest Completions in a playoff game

73-yard pass by Tom Brady to Deion Branch in the 14-point loss to the Denver Broncos on 01-14-06
63-yard TD by Tom Brady to Benjamin Watson in the 25-point rout of the Jacksonville Jaguars on 01-07-06
60-yard TD by Tom Brady to Deion Branch in the 14-point victory over the Pittsburgh Steelers on 01-23-05
59-yard TD by Babe Parilli to Larry Garron in the 18-point victory over the Buffalo Bills on 12-28-63
53-yard pass by Drew Bledsoe to Terry Glenn in the 25-point rout of the Pittsburgh Steelers on 01-05-97
52-yard pass by Tom Brady to Deion Branch in the three-point victory over the Carolina Panthers on 02-01-04
51-yard pass by Babe Parilli to Gino Cappelletti in the 18-point win over the Buffalo Bills on 12-28-63
49-yard pass by Babe Parilli to Gino Cappelletti in the 41-point loss to the San Diego Chargers on 01-05-64
45-yard TD by Tony Eason to Stanley Morgan in the five-point loss to the Denver Broncos on 01-04-87
44-yard pass by Drew Bledsoe to Terry Glenn in the 14-point loss to the Green Bay Packers on 01-26-97

The Most Passing Attempts in a season

#	Quarterback	Year
691	Drew Bledsoe	1994
636	Drew Bledsoe	1995
623	Drew Bledsoe	1996
601	Tom Brady	2002
578	Tom Brady	2007
539	Drew Bledsoe	1999
531	Drew Bledsoe	2000
530	Tom Brady	2005
527	Tom Brady	2003
522	Drew Bledsoe	1997

The Most Pass Completions in a season

#	Quarterback	Year
400	Drew Bledsoe	1994
398	Tom Brady	2007
373	Drew Bledsoe	1996
373	Tom Brady	2002
334	Tom Brady	2005
327	Matt Cassel	2008
323	Drew Bledsoe	1995
319	Tom Brady	2006
317	Tom Brady	2003
314	Drew Bledsoe	1997

The Most Yards Passing in a season

Yards	Quarterback	Year
4,806	Tom Brady	2007
4,555	Drew Bledsoe	1994
4,110	Tom Brady	2005
4,086	Drew Bledsoe	1996
3,985	Drew Bledsoe	1999
3,764	Tom Brady	2002
3,706	Drew Bledsoe	1997
3,693	Matt Cassel	2008
3,692	Tom Brady	2004
3,633	Drew Bledsoe	1998

The Most Career Regular Season Pass Attempts

#	Quarterback	Seasons
4,518	Drew Bledsoe	1993–2001
3,653	Tom Brady	2000–08
3,593	Steve Grogan	1975–90
2,413	Babe Parilli	1961–67
1,503	Jim Plunkett	1971–75
1,500	Tony Eason	1983–89
680	Mike Taliaferro	1968–70
612	Hugh Millen	1991–92
604	Butch Songin	1960–61
555	Matt Cassel	2005–08

The Most Career Regular Season Completions

#	Quarterback	Seasons
2,544	Drew Bledsoe	1993–01
2,301	Tom Brady	2000–08
1,879	Steve Grogan	1975–90
1,140	Babe Parilli	1961–67
876	Tony Eason	1983–89
729	Jim Plunkett	1971–75
370	Hugh Millen	1991–92
349	Matt Cassel	2005–08
305	Mike Taliaferro	1968–70
285	Butch Songin	1960–61

Touchdown Passes

The Most TD Passes in a regular season game

#	Quarterback	Score, outcome, opponent, and date
6	Tom Brady	49–28 rout of the Miami Dolphins on 10-21-07
5	Tom Brady	56–10 pulverizing of the Buffalo Bills on 11-18-07
5	Babe Parilli	36–28 victory over the Buffalo Bills on 11-15-64
5	Babe Parlli	41–10 demolition of the Miami Dolphins on 10-15-67
5	Steve Grogan	56–3 pummelling of the New York Jets on 09-09-79

The Most TD Passes in a playoff game

#	Quarterback	Score, outcome, opponent, and date
3	Tom Brady	31–20 victory over the Jacksonville Jaguars on 01-12-08
3	Tom Brady	28–3 rout of the Jacksonville Jaguars on 01-07-06
3	Tom Brady	32–29 win over the Carolina Panthers on 02-01-04
3	Tony Eason	31–14 victory over the Miami Dolphins on 01-12-86

The Most Touchdown Passes in a season

TDs	Quarterback	Year
50	Tom Brady	2007
31	Babe Parilli	1964
28	Steve Grogan	1979
28	Drew Bledsoe	1997
28	Tom Brady	2002
28	Tom Brady	2004
27	Drew Bledsoe	1996
26	Tom Brady	2005
25	Drew Bledsoe	1994
24	Tom Brady	2006

The Most Career Regular Season TD Passes

TDs	Quarterback	Seasons
197	Tom Brady	2000–08
182	Steve Grogan	1975–90
166	Drew Bledsoe	1993–2001
132	Babe Parilli	1961–67
62	Jim Plunkett	1971–75
60	Tony Eason	1983–89
36	Butch Songin	1960–61
27	Mike Taliaferro	1968–70
23	Matt Cassel	2005–08
19	Matt Cavanaugh	1978–82

The Most Career TD passes in the playoffs (through 2008)

TDs	Quarterback
26	Tom Brady
7	Tony Eason
6	Drew Bledsoe
3	Steve Grogan
2	Babe Parilli

Team Records

The Most Passing Attempts in a season

#	Year
699	1994
686	1995
628	1996
610	1989
605	2002
586	2007
566	1993
565	2000
564	2005
557	1986

The Most Pass Completions in a season

#	Year
405	1994
403	2007
374	1996
374	2002
352	2005
351	1995
340	1986
339	2008
328	2000
326	2006

The Most Yards Passing in a season

Yards	Year
4,859	2007
4,583	1994
4,322	2005
4,321	1986
4,091	1996
4,004	1998
3,985	1999
3,972	1989
3,904	1981
3,808	1997

Receiving
Individual Receiving

The Most Yards Receiving in a regular season game

Yds	Receiver	Outcome, opponent, and date
214	Terry Glenn	12-point victory over the Cleveland Browns on 10-03-99
193	Terry Glenn	14-point victory over the Pittsburgh Steelers 12-06-98
183	Randy Moss	24-point rout of the New York Jets on 09-09-07
182	Stanley Morgan	3-point overtime loss to the Miami Dolphins on 11-08-81
176	Troy Brown	3-point overtime win vs the Kansas City Chiefs on 09-22-02
170	Stanley Morgan	21-point rout of the Baltimore Colts on 11-26-78
167	Art Graham	1-point win over the Houston Oilers on 11-06-64
165	Irving Fryar	9-point loss to the New York Jets on 10-04-92
163	Terry Glenn	18-point loss to the Green Bay Packers on 10-27-97
162	Stanley Morgan	7-point loss to the New York Jets on 10-12-86

The Most Yards Receiving in a playoff game

Yds	Receiver	Outcome, opponent, and date
153	Deion Branch	14-point loss to the Denver Broncos on 01-14-06
143	Deion Branch	3-point victory over the Carolina Panthers on 02-01-04
133	Deion Branch	3-point victory over the Philadelphia Eagles on 02-06-05
121	Troy Brown	7-point victory over the Pittsburgh Steelers on 01-27-02
120	Larry Garron	18-point win over the Buffalo Bills on 12-28-63
116	Deion Branch	14-point win over the Pittsburgh Steelers on 01-23-05
109	Gino Cappelletti	18-point win over the Buffalo Bills on 12-28-63
104	Shawn Jefferson	1-point loss to the Pittsburgh Steelers on 01-03-98
104	Jabar Gaffney	21-point rout of the New York Jets on 01-07-07
103	Jabar Gaffney	3-point win over the San Diego Chargers on 01-14-07
103	Wes Welker	3-point loss to the New York Giants on 02-03-08

The 10 Longest Receptions in a regular season game

91-yard TD by David Patten in the 21-point rout of the Indianapolis Colts on 10-21-01

90-yard TD by Craig James in the 13-point loss to the Chicago Bears on 09-15-85

88-yard TD by Randy Vataha in the four-point win over the Baltimore Colts on 12-19-71

87-yard TD by Jim Whalen in the 34-point loss to the New York Jets on 10-27-68

86-yard TD by Terry Glenn in the 14-point victory over the Pittsburgh Steelers on 12-06-98

85-yard TD by Troy Brown for the game winning score in the six-point overtime win vs the Miami Dolphins on 10-19-03

84-yard TD by Ben Coates in the 19-point win over the Miami Dolphins on 11-03-96

80-yard TD by Art Graham in the 17-point win over the Houston Oilers on 11-29-64

80-yard TD by Carl Garrett in the five-point victory over the Buffalo Bills on 11-14-71

80-yard TD by Irving Fryar on the first play in the 23-point rout of the Chicago Bears 10-30-88

The 10 Longest Receptions in a playoff game

73-yard reception by Deion Branch in the 14-point loss to the Denver Broncos on 01-14-06

63-yard TD by Benjamin Watson in the 25-point rout of the Jacksonville Jaguars on 01-07-06

60-yard TD by Deion Branch in the 14-point victory over the Pittsburgh Steelers on 01-23-05

59-yard TD by Larry Garron in the 18-point victory over the Buffalo Bills on 12-28-63

53-yard reception by Terry Glenn in the 25-point rout of the Pittsburgh Steelers on 01-05-97

52-yard reception by Deion Branch in the three-point victory over the Carolina Panthers on 02-01-04

51-yard reception by Gino Cappelletti in the 18-point victory over the Buffalo Bills on 12-28-63

49-yard reception by Gino Cappelletti in the 41-point loss to the San Diego Chargers on 01-05-64

45-yard TD by Stanley Morgan in the 5-point loss to the Denver Broncos on 01-04-87

44-yard reception by Terry Glenn in the 14-point loss to the Green Bay Packers on 01-26-97

The Most Receptions in a regular season game

#	Receiver	Outcome, opponent, and date
16	Troy Brown	3-point overtime win vs the Kansas City Chiefs on 09-22-02
13	Wes Welker	3-point victory over the Philadelphia Eagles on 11-25-07
13	Deion Branch	7-point loss to the San Diego Chargers on 09-29-02
13	Terry Glenn	12-point win over the Cleveland Browns on 10-03-99
12	Ben Coates	2-point victory over the Indianapolis Colts on 11-27-94
12	Troy Brown	6-point win over the Kansas City Chiefs on 12-04-00
12	Wes Welker	3-point victory over the Seattle Seahawks on 12-07-08

The Most Receptions in a playoff game

#	Receiver	Outcome, opponent, and date
11	Wes Welker	3-point loss to the New York Giants on 02-03-08
11	Deion Branch	3-point win over the Philadelphia Eagles on 02-06-05
10	Deion Branch	3-point victory over the Carolina Panthers on 02-01-04
10	Jermaine Wiggins	3-point overtime win vs the Oakland Raiders on 01-19-02
9	Shawn Jefferson	1-point loss to the Pittsburgh Steelers on 01-03-98
9	Wes Welker	11-point win over the Jacksonville Jaguars on 01-12-08

The Most Career Regular Season Receptions

#	Receiver	Seasons
557	Troy Brown	1993–2007
534	Stanley Morgan	1977–89
490	Ben Coates	1991–99
381	Kevin Faulk	1999–2008
363	Irving Fryar	1984–92
329	Terry Glenn	1996–2001
292	Gino Cappelletti	1960–70
283	Jim Colclough	1960–68
261	Tony Collins	1981–87
223	Wes Welker	2007–08

The Most Career Receptions in the playoffs (through 2008)

#	Receiver
58	Troy Brown
45	Kevin Faulk
41	Deion Branch
35	David Givens
27	Wes Welker
24	Shawn Jefferson
22	Ben Coates
19	Stanley Morgan
18	Terry Glenn
18	Benjamin Watson

The Most Career Regular Season Yards Receiving

Yards	Receiver	Seasons
10,352	Stanley Morgan	1977–89
6,366	Troy Brown	1993–2007
5,726	Irving Fryar	1984–92
5,471	Ben Coates	1991–99
5,001	Jim Colclough	1960–68
4,669	Terry Glenn	1996–2001
4,589	Gino Cappelletti	1960–70
3,304	Kevin Faulk	1999–2008
3,162	Harold Jackson	1978–81
3,157	Russ Francis	1975–80 and 1987–88

The Most Career Yards Receiving in the playoffs (through 2008)

Yards	Receiver
694	Troy Brown
629	Deion Branch
375	Kevin Faulk
324	David Givens
321	Stanley Morgan
317	Terry Glenn
284	Shawn Jefferson
213	Wes Welker
204	Ben Coates
197	Russ Francis

The Most TD Receptions in a regular season game

TDs	Receiver	Outcome, opponent, and date
4	Randy Moss	56–10 pulverizing of the Buffalo Bills on 11-18-07
3	Billy Lott	52–21 rout of the Buffalo Bills on 10-22-61
3	Gino Cappelletti	36–28 victory over the Buffalo Bills on 11-15-64
3	Jim Whalen	41–10 blowout of the Miami Dolphins on 10-15-67
3	Harold Jackson	56–3 pummelling of the New York Jets on 09-09-79
3	Derrick Ramsey	50–17 blowout of the Indianapolis Colts on 11-18-84
3	Stanley Morgan	38–31 loss to the Seattle Seahawks on 09-21-86
3	Ben Coates	35–25 victory over the Buffalo Bills on 11-26-95

The Most TD Receptions in a playoff game

#	Receiver	Outcome, opponent, and date
2	Larry Garron	26–8 victory over the Buffalo Bills on 12-28-63
2	Stanley Morgan	22–17 loss to the Denver Broncos on 01-04-87
2	Ben Watson	31–20 win over the Jacksonville Jaguars on 01-12-08

The Most TD Receptions in a season

TDs	Receiver	Year
23	Randy Moss	2007
12	Stanley Morgan	1979
11	Randy Moss	2008
10	Jim Colclough	1962
10	Stanley Morgan	1986
9	Jim Colclough	1960
9	Jim Colclough	1961
9	Gino Cappelletti	1965
9	Randy Vataha	1971
9	Ben Coates	1996

The Most TD Receptions in the playoffs (through 2008)

TDs	Receiver
7	David Givens
3	Stanley Morgan
3	Jabar Gaffney
3	Benjamin Watson

The Most Career TD Receptions

TDs	Receiver	Seasons
67	Stanley Morgan	1977–89
50	Ben Coates	1991–99
42	Gino Cappelletti	1960–70
39	Jim Colclough	1960–68
38	Irving Fryar	1984–92
34	Randy Moss	2007–08
31	Troy Brown	1993–2007
28	Russ Francis	1975–80
26	Larry Garron	1960–68
23	Randy Vataha	1971–76

Points Scored
Individual Scoring

The Most Points Scored in a regular season game

Pts	Player	Outcome, opponent, and date
28	Gino Cappelletti	28-point rout of the Houston Oilers on 12-18-65
24	Gino Cappelletti	8-point win over the Buffalo Bills on 11-15-64
24	Randy Moss	46-point pulverizing of the Buffalo Bills on 11-18-07
22	Gino Cappelletti	19-point rout of the Denver Broncos on 10-18-63
21	Gino Cappelletti	5-point win over the San Diego Chargers on 09-20-64
21	Gino Cappelletti	29-point blowout of the Denver Broncos on 10-04-64
21	Gino Cappelletti	6-point victory over the Houston Oilers on 11-13-66
20	Gino Cappelletti	10-point win over the Oakland Raiders on 10-26-62
20	Gino Cappelletti	16-point win over the San Diego Chargers on 10-31-65
20	Curtis Martin	31-0 shutout of the Arizona Cardinals on 09-15-96

The Most Points Scored in a playoff game

Pts	Player	Outcome, opponent, and date
18	Curtis Martin	25-point rout of the Pittsburgh Steelers on 01-05-97
16	Adam Vinatieri	10-point win over the Indianapolis Colts on 01-18-04
14	Gino Cappelletti	18-point victory over the Buffalo Bills on 12-28-63
14	Tony Franklin	12-point win over the New York Jets on 12-28-85
13	Stephen Gostkowski	21-point romp over the New York Jets on 01-07-07
12	Larry Garron	18-point victory over the Buffalo Bills on 12-28-63
12	Stanley Morgan	5-point loss to the Denver Broncos on 01-04-87
12	Deion Branch	14-point victory over the Pittsburgh Steelers on 01-23-05
12	Benjamin Watson	11-point win over the Jacksonville Jaguars on 01-12-08
11	Adam Vinatieri	14-point victory over the Pittsburgh Steelers on 01-23-05

The Most Points Scored in a season

Pts	Player	Year
155	Gino Cappelletti	1964
148	Stephen Gostkowski	2008
147	Gino Cappelletti	1961
141	Adam Vinatieri	2004
140	Tony Franklin	1986
138	Randy Moss	2007
137	Stephen Gostkowski	2007
132	Gino Cappelletti	1965
129	John Smith	1980
128	Gino Cappelletti	1962

The Most Career regular season Points Scored

Points	Player	Seasons
1,158	Adam Vinatieri	1996–2005
1,130	Gino Cappelletti	1960–70
692	John Smith	1974–83
442	Tony Franklin	1984–87
408	Stanley Morgan	1977–89
388	Stephen Gostkowski	2006–08
302	Ben Coates	1991–99
294	Sam Cunningham	1973–82
276	Jim Nance	1965–71
264	Tony Collins	1981–87

The Most Career Playoff Points Scored (through 2008)

Pts	Player
117	Adam Vinatieri
45	Stephen Gostkowski
42	David Givens
39	Tony Franklin
30	Curtis Martin

The Most Career Regular Season TDs

TDs	Player
68	Stanley Morgan
50	Ben Coates
49	Sam Cunningham
46	Jim Nance
44	Tony Collins

The Most Career TDs Scored in the playoffs

TDs	Player
7	David Givens
5	Curtis Martin
4	Corey Dillon

Team Records

The Most Points Scored in a regular season game

56–3 pummelling of the New York Jets on 09-09-79
56–10 pulverizing of the Buffalo Bills on 11-18-07
55–21 rout of the New York Jets on 10-29-78
52–21 blowout of the Buffalo Bills on 10-22-61
50–21 rout of the Baltimore Colts on 11-18-79
50–17 rout of the Indianapolis Colts on 11-18-84
49–28 blowout of the Miami Dolphins on 10-21-07
49–26 demolition of the Oakland Raiders on 12-14-08
48–17 demolition of the Oakland Raiders on 10-03-76
48–27 victory over the Dallas Cowboys on 10-14-07
48–28 victory over the Miami Dolphins on 11-23-08

The Most Points Scored in a playoff game

41–27 win over the Pittsburgh Steelers on 01-23-05
38–34 loss to the Indianapolis Colts on 01-21-07
37–16 rout of the New York Jets on 01-07-07
32–29 win over the Carolina Panthers on 02-01-04
31–14 victory over the Miami Dolphins on 01-12-86
31–20 win over the Jacksonville Jaguars on 01-21-08
28–3 rout of the Pittsburgh Steelers on 01-05-97
27–20 victory over the Los Angeles Raiders on 01-05-86
26–8 win over the Buffalo Bills on 12-28-63
26–14 victory over the New York Jets on 12-28-85

The Most Points Scored in a season

Pts	Year
589	2007
441	1980
437	2004
418	1996
413	1961
412	1986
411	1979
410	2008
385	2006
381	2002

Kicking

The Most Successful Field Goals in a regular season game

FG's	Kicker	Score, outcome, opponent, and date
6	Gino Cappelletti	39–10 rout of the Denver Broncos on 10-64-64
5	Jason Staurovsky	22–16 win over the Indianapolis Colts on 12-03-89
5	Adam Vinatieri	28–25 overtime win vs the Jacksonville Jaguars on 09-22-96
5	Adam Vinatieri	29–6 victory over the Buffalo Bills on 11-14-04

The Most Successful Field Goals in a playoff game

#	Kicker	Score, outcome, opponent, and date
5	Adam Vinatieri	24–14 win over the Indianapolis Colts on 01-18-04
4	Tony Franklin	26–14 win over the New York Jets on 12-28-85
4	Gino Cappelletti	26–8 win over the Buffalo Bills on 12-28-63
3	Adam Vinatieri	16–13 overtime win vs the Oakland Raiders on 01-19-02
3	Stephen Gostkowski	37–16 rout of the New York Jets on 01-07-07
3	Stephen Gostkowski	24–21 win over San Diego on 01-14-07

The 10 Longest Field Goals in a regular season game

57-yard field goal by Adam Vinatieri in the three-point comeback win over the Chicago Bears on 11-10-02

55-yard field goal by Matt Bahr in the 17-point victory over the Miami Dolphins on 11-12-95

55-yard field goal by Adam Vinatieri in the 14-point loss to the St. Louis Rams on 12-13-98

54-yard field goal by Adam Vinatieri in the 11-point victory over the Cleveland Browns on 12-09-01

53-yard field goal by Gino Cappelletti in the four-point victory over the New York Jets on 11-28-65

53-yard field goal by Jason Staurvosky in the 13-point loss to the Seattle Seahawks on 10-07-90

53-yard fiedl goal by Adam Vinatieri in the 30–24 win over the Kansas City Chiefs on 12-04-00

52-yard field goal by Adam Vinatieri in the 27-point rout of the Buffalo Bills on 10-12-97

52-yard field goal by Stephen Gostkowski in the four-point victory over the Chicago Bears on 11-26-06

51-yard field goal by Gino Cappelletti in the five-point victory over the Denver Broncos on 11-20-64

The 10 Longest Field Goals in a playoff game

50-yard field goal by Stephen Gostkowski in the three-point win over the San Diego Chargers on 01-14-07

48-yard field goal by Adam Vinatieri on the last play to beat the St. Louis Rams by three points on 02-03-02

48-yard field goal by Adam Vinatieri in the 14-point victory over the Pittsburgh Steelers on 01-23-05

46-yard filed goal by Adam Vinatieri for the last points scored in the three-point win over the Tennessee Titans on 01-10-04

46-yard field goal by Adam Vinatieri in the one-point loss to the Pittsburgh Steelers on 01-03-98

45-yard field goal by Tony Franklin in the seven-point victory over the Los Angeles Raiders on 01-05-86

45-yard field goal by Adam Vinatieri with 32 seconds left to force overtime in the three-point win on 01-19-02

44-yard field goal by Adam Vinatieri in the seven-point victory over the Pittsburgh Steelers on 01-27-02

42-yard field goal by John Smith in the 15-point loss to the Miami Dolphins on 01-08-83

41-yard field goal by Adam Vinatieri for the last points scored in the three-point win over the Carolina Panthers on 02-01-04

The Most Successful Field Goals in a season

FG's	Kicker	Year(s)
36	Stephen Gostkowski	2008
32	Tony Franklin	1986
31	Adam Vinatieri	1998 and 2004
27	Matt Bahr	1994
27	Adam Vinatieri	1996, 2000, and 2002
26	John Smith	1980
26	Adam Vinatieri	1999

The Most Successful Field Goals in the playoffs (thru 2008)

FG's	Kicker
26	Adam Vinatieri
9	Tony Franklin
9	Stephen Gostkowski
5	Gino Cappelletti
2	John Smith and Matt Bahr

Special Team Returns
Kickoff Returns

The Longest Kickoff Returns in a regular season game
108-yard return for a TD by Ellis Hobbs in the 38–14 blowout of the New York Jets on 09-09-07
101-yard return for a TD by Raymond Clayborn in the 30–24 loss to the Baltimore Colts on 12-18-77
100-yard return for a TD by Raymond Clayborn in the 30–27 loss to the New York Jets on 10-02-77
100-yard return for a TD by Jon Vaughn in the 20–10 loss to the Cincinnati Bengals on 12-20-92
99-yard TD by Allen Carter on the opening kickoff in the 34–21 loss to the Baltimore Colts on 12-21-75
99-yard return for a TD by Jon Vaughn in the 24–10 loss to the Phoenix Cardinals on 09-29-91
98-yard return for a TD by Horace Ivory in the 37–21 victory over the Baltimore Colts on 10-19-80
98-yard return for a TD by Ricky Smith in the 31–7 loss to the New York Jets on 09-19-82
95-yard return for a TD by Larry Garron in the 28–28 tie with the Buffalo Bills on 11-03-62
95-yard TD by Sammy Martin on the opening kickoff in the 24–21 loss to the Indianapolis Colts on 11-27-88
95-yard return by Kevin Faulk in the 24–17 loss to the New York Jets on 11-15-99
95-yard return for a TD by Ellis Hobbs in the 49–26 rout of the Oakland Raiders on 12-14-08

The Longest Kickoff Returns in a playoff game
80-yard kickoff return by Ellis Hobbs in the four-point loss to the Indianapolis Colts on 01-21-07
47-yard kickoff return by Raymond Clayborn in the 17-point loss to the Houston Oilers on 12-31-78
43-yard kickoff return by Laurence Maroney in the three-point loss to the New York Giants on 02-03-08
41-yard kickoff return by Ellis Hobbs in the four-point loss to the Indianapolis Colts on 01-21-07
37-yard kickoff return by Stephen Starring in the 17-point victory over the Miami Dolphins on 01-12-86
36-yard kickoff return by Stephen Starrring in the 36-point loss to the Chicago Bears on 01-26-86
35-yard kickoff return by Patrick Pass in the seven-point victory over the Pittsburgh Steelers on 01-27-02
35-yard kickoff return by Patrick Pass in the three-point victory over the St. Louis Rams on 02-03-02
32-yard kickoff return by Ellis Hobbs in the 14-point loss to the Denver Broncos on 01-14-06

The Most Kickoff Returns in a regular season game
#	Returman	Score, outcome, opponent, and date
8	Willie Porter	47–31 loss to the New York Jets on 09-22-68
7	Deion Branch	41–38 overtime win vs the Kansas City Chiefs on 09-22-02
7	Deion Branch	33–30 comeback win over the Chicago Bears on 11-10-02
7	Kevin Faulk	30–17 loss to the New York Jets on 12-22-02
7	Bethel Johnson	40–21 loss to the Indianapolis Colts on 11-07-05

The Most Kickoff Returns in a playoff game
#	Returnman	Score, outcome, opponent, and date
7	Stephen Starring	46–10 loss to the Chicago Bears on 01-26-86
6	Derrick Cullors	25–10 loss to the Jacksonville Jaguars on 01-03-99
6	Ellis Hobbs	38–34 loss to the Indianapolis Colts on 01-21-07
5	Patrick Pass	16–13 overtime win vs the Oakland Raiders on 01-19-02
5	Dave Meggett	35–21 loss to the Green Bay Packers on 01-26-97

The Most Kickoff Return Yards in a regular season game
Yds	Returnman	Score, outcome, opponent, and date
237	Ellis Hobbs	38–13 loss to the Miami Dolphins on 09-21-08
220	Kevin Faulk	30–17 loss to the New York Jets on 12-22-02
206	Allen Carter	34–21 loss to the Baltimore Colts on 12-21-75
201	Deion Branch	41–38 overtime win vs the Kansas City Chiefs on 09-22-02
192	Bethel Johnson	38–34 win over the Indianapolis Colts on 11-30-03

The Most Kickoff Return Yards in a playoff game

Yds	Returnman	Score, outcome, opponent, and date
220	Ellis Hobbs	38–34 loss to the Indianapolis Colts on 01-21-07
153	Stephen Starring	46–10 loss to the Chicago Bears on 01-26-86
117	Dave Meggett	35–21 loss to the Green Bay Packers on 01-26-97
95	Patrick Pass	16–13 overtime win vs the Oakland Raiders on 01-19-02
94	Laurence Maroney	17–14 loss to the New York Giants on 02-03-08

The Most Kickoff Returns in a season

#	Returnman	Year
48	Stephen Starring	1985
45	Derrick Cullors	1998
45	Ellis Hobbs	2008
42	Ricky Smith	1983
41	Mack Herron	1973
41	Bethel Johnson	2004
39	Tony Collins	1981
39	Kevin Faulk	1999
38	Kevin Faulk	2000
38	Dave Meggett	1995

The Most Kickoff Return Yards in a season

Yds	Returnman	Year
1,281	Ellis Hobbs	2008
1,092	Mack Herron	1973
1,085	Derrick Cullors	1998
1,016	Bethel Johnson	2004
1,012	Stephen Starring	1985
992	Horace Ivory	1980
964	Dave Meggett	1995
943	Kevin Faulk	1999
916	Ricky Smith	1983
911	Ellis Hobbs	2007

The Most Career regular season Kickoff Returns

#	Returnman	Seasons
175	Kevin Faulk	1999–2008
107	Stephen Starring	1983–87
105	Dave Meggett	1995–97
105	Ellis Hobbs	2005–08
102	Bethel Johnson	2003–05
92	Carl Garrett	1969–72
89	Larry Garron	1960–68
88	Sammy Martin	1988–91
87	Troy Brown	1993–2007
71	Mack Herron	1973–75

The Most Career regular season Kickoff Return Yards

Yards	Returnman	Seasons
3,954	Kevin Faulk	1999–2008
2,913	Ellis Hobbs	2005–08
2,561	Dave Meggett	1995–97
2,557	Bethel Johnson	2003–05
2,299	Larry Garron	1960–68
2,259	Stephen Starring	1983–87
2,251	Carl Garrett	1969–72
2,102	Sammy Martin	1988–91
1,862	Troy Brown	1993–2007
1,796	Mack Herron	1973–75

The Most Kickoff Returns in the playoffs

#	Returnman
17	Ellis Hobbs
15	Stephen Starring
15	Patrick Pass
12	Laurence Maroney
11	Bethel Johnson

The Most Kickoff Return Yards in the playoffs

Yds	Returnman
471	Ellis Hobbs
336	Patrick Pass
315	Stephen Starring
257	Laurence Maroney
228	Bethel Johnson

Team Records

The Most Kickoff Return Yards in a regular season game

Yds	Score, outcome, opponent, and date
248	38–13 loss to the Miami Dolphins on 09-21-08
245	44–21 loss to the Dallas Cowboys on 10-24-71
230	34–21 loss to the Baltimore Colts on 12-21-75
229	38–34 win over the Indianapolis Colts on 11-30-03
220	30–17 loss to the New York Jets on 12-22-02
220	38–30 win over the Tennessee Titans on 10-05-03

The Most Kickoff Returns in a season

#	Year
77	1990
75	1995
75	2002
73	1967
71	1968

The Most Kickoff Return Yards in a season

Yds	Year
1,771	2002
1,691	1995
1,562	2008
1,553	2006
1,520	1975

Punt Returns
Individual Records

The 10 Longest Punt Returns in a regular season game

89-yard return for a TD by Mike Haynes in the 20–10 win over the Buffalo Bills on 11-07-76
85-yard return for a TD by Troy Brown in the 27–16 win over the Cleveland Browns on 12-09-01
85-yard return for a TD by Irving Fryar in the 17–14 win over the Buffalo Bills on 09-22-85
80-yard return for a TD by Stanley Morgan in the 50–21 rout of the Baltimore Colts on 11-18-79
77-yard return for a TD by Irving Fryar in the 34–15 rout of the Indianapolis Colts on 11-10-85
75-yard return for a TD by Roland James in the 34–21 win over the New York Jets on 11-02-80
68-yard return for a TD by Troy Brown in the 38–6 rout of the Carolina Panthers on 01-06-02
66-yard return for a TD by Troy Brown in the 21–16 loss to the Tampa Bay Buccaneers on 09-03-00
66-yard return by Mack Herron in the 42–3 rout of the Baltimore Colts on 10-06-74
62-yard return by Ron Burton in the 27–15 loss to the Houston Oilers on 11-12-61
62-yard return by Carl Garrett in the 31–21 loss to the New York Jets on 09-27-70

The 10 Longest Punt Returns in a playoff game

55-yard TD by Troy Brown in the seven-point victory over the Pittsburgh Steelers on 01-27-02
28-yard return by Troy Brown in the three-point victory over the Carolina Panthers on 02-01-04
28-yard return by Art Graham in the 18-point win over the Buffalo Bills on 12-28-63
27-yard return by Tim Dwight in the 21-point rout of the New York Jets on 01-07-06
27-yard return by Troy Brown in the three-point overtime win vs the Oakland Raiders on 01-19-02
25-yard return by Troy Brown in the seven-point victory over the Pittsburgh Steelers on 01-27-02
20-yard return by Dave Meggett in the 14-point loss to the Green Bay Packers on 01-26-97
20-yard return by Troy Brown in the 17-point victory over the Indianapolis Colts on 01-16-05
17-yard return by Troy Brown in the 15-point loss to the Jacksonville Jaguars on 01-03-99
16-yard return by Troy Brown in the 10-point victory over the Indianapolis Colts on 01-18-04

The Most Punt Returns in a regular season game

#	Returnman	Score, outcome, opponent, and date
10	Ronnie Harris	17–14 loss to the Pittsburgh Steelers on 12-05-93
7	Ray Crittenden	17–16 win over the Green Bay Packers on 10-02-94
7	Irving Fryar	20–17 loss to the Dallas Cowboys on 11-22-84
7	Dave Meggett	31–28 victory over the New York Jets on 12-10-95

The Most Punt Returns in a playoff game

#	Returnman	Score, outcome, opponent, and date
7	Dave Meggett	28–3 rout of the Pittsburgh Steelers on 01-05-97
5	Troy Brown	16–13 overtime win vs the Oakland Raiders on 01-19-02

The Most Punt Returns in a season

#	Returnman	Year
52	Dave Meggett	1996
45	Dave Meggett	1997
45	Dave Meggett	1995
45	Mike Haynes	1976
39	Troy Brown	2000

The Most Punt Return Yards in a season

Yds	Returnman	Year
608	Mike Haynes	1976
588	Dave Meggett	1996
520	Irving Fryar	1985
517	Mack Herron	1974
504	Troy Brown	2000

The Most Career Punt Returns

#	Returnman	Seasons
252	Troy Brown	1993–2007
206	Irving Fryar	1984–91
142	Dave Meggett	1995–97
111	Mike Haynes	1976–80
94	Kevin Faulk	1999–2008
92	Stanley Morgan	1977–89
74	Mack Herron	1973–75
56	Ron Burton	1960–65
54	Ricky Smith	1982–84
49	Wes Welker	2007–08

The Most Career Punt Return Yards

Yards	Returnman	Seasons
2,625	Troy Brown	1993–2007
2,055	Irving Fryar	1984–92
1,438	Dave Meggett	1995–97
1,159	Mike Haynes	1976–82
960	Stanley Morgan	1977–89
901	Kevin Faulk	1999–2008
888	Mack Herron	1973–75
537	Ricky Smith	1982–84
487	Carl Garrett	1969–72
486	Wes Welker	2007–08

The Best Career Punt Return Average (at least 10 returns)

Avg	Returnman
12.0	Mack Herron
11.3	Carl Garrett
10.6	Chris Canty
10.4	Mike Haynes
10.4	Stanley Morgan
10.4	Troy Brown
10.1	Dave Meggett
10.0	Irving Fryar
9.9	Ricky Smith
9.9	Wes Welker

Team Records

The Most Punt Return Yards in a regular season game

Yds	Score, outcome, opponent, and date
167	20–10 win over the Buffalo Bills on 11-07-76
139	20–7 victory over the Buffalo Bills on 11-20-77
137	18–7 win over the Houston Oilers on 11-05-67
133	17–14 victory over the Buffalo Bills on 09-22-85
133	27–16 win over the Cleveland Browns on 12-09-01

The Most Punt Returns in a season

#	Year
60	1980
52	1996
51	1993
48	1976, 1984, and 1999

The Most Punt Return Yards in a season

Yds	Year
628	1976
588	1996
562	2000
533	1974
530	1985

Punting

The Longest Punts in a regular season game

Yds	Punter	Score, outcome, opponent, and date
93	Shawn McCarthy	22–17 loss to the Buffalo Bills on 11-03-91
89	Like Prestridge	44–24 loss to the Miami Dolphins on 10-21-84
87	Bob Scarpitto	20–17 win over the Denver Broncos on 09-29-68
82	Like Prestridge	30–20 win over the New York Jets on 10-28-84
76	Rich Camarillo	31–7 loss to the New York Jets on 09-18-82
76	Lee Johnson	23–17 loss to the Cincinnati Bengals on 09-09-01

The Longest Punt in a playoff game

Yds	Punter	Score, outcome, opponent, and date
68	Tom Yewcic	51–10 loss to the San Diego Chargers on 101-05-64
62	Rich Camarillo	46–10 loss to the Chicago Bears on 01-26-86
60	Rich Camarillo	22–17 loss to the Denver Broncos on 01-04-87
59	Todd Sauerbrun	38–34 loss to the Indianapolis Colts on 01-21-07
58	Tom Tupa	25–10 loss to the Jacksonville Jaguars on 01-03-99
58	Rich Camarillo	28–13 loss to the Miami Dolphins on 01-08-83

The Most Punts in a regular season game

#	Punter	Score, outcome, opponent, and date
11	Jim Fraser	24–24 tie with the New York Jets on 10-02-66
11	Rich Camarillo	20–17 loss to the Dallas Cowboys on 11-22-84
11	Rich Camarillo	20–7 loss to the Chicago Bears on 09-15-85
11	Shawn McCarthy	31–14 loss to the New Orleans Saints on 11-08-92

The Most Punts in a playoff game

#	Punter	Score, outcome, opponent, and date
9	Rich Camarillo	22–17 loss to the Denver Broncos on 01-04-87
8	Ken Walter	20–17 win over the St. Louis Rams on 02-03-02
8	Ken Walter	16–13 overtime win vs the Oakland Raiders on 01-19-02
8	Tom Tupa	25–10 loss to the Jacksonville Jaguars on 01-03-99
8	Tom Tupa	35–21 loss to the Green Bay Packers on 01-26-97

The Most Yards Punted in a regular season game

Yds	Punter	Score, outcome, opponent, and date
514	Rich Camarillo	20–7 loss to the Chicago Bears on 09-15-85
479	Rich Camarillo	20–17 loss to the Dallas Cowboys on 11-22-84
436	Bob Scarpitto	41–10 loss to the Oakland Raiders on 10-06-68
426	Rich Camarillo	27–17 loss to the Oakland Raiders on 11-01-81
417	Tom Yewcic	36–28 win over the Buffalo Bills on 11-15-64

The Most Yards Punted in a playoff game

Yds	Punter	Score, outcome, opponent, and date
452	Rich Camarillo	22–17 loss to the Denver Broncos on 01-04-87
378	Tom Tupa	25–10 loss to the Jacksonville Jaguars on 01-03-99
361	Tom Tupa	35–21 loss to the Green Bay Packers on 01-26-97
345	Ken Walter	20–17 win over the St. Louis Rams on 02-03-02
329	Tom Yewcic	51–10 loss to the San Diego Chargers on 01-05-64

The Most Career Punts

#	Punter	Seasons
468	Rich Camarillo	1981–87
377	Tom Yewcic	1961–66
243	Tom Janik	1969–71
225	Mike Patrick	1975–78
215	Tom Tupa	1996–98

The Most Career Punts in the playoffs

#	Punter
43	Tom Tupa
36	Rich Camarillo
34	Ken Walter
23	Josh Miller
14	Todd Sauerbrun

The Most Career Yards Punted

#	Punter	Seasons
19,922	Rich Camarillo	1981–87
14,553	Tom Yewcic	1961–66
9,602	Tom Tupa	1996–98
9,516	Tom Janik	1969–71
8,578	Lee Johnson	1999–2001

The Most Career Yards Punting in the playoffs

1,833	Tom Tupa
1,559	Rich Camarillo
1,254	Ken Walter
990	Josh Miller
640	Todd Sauerbrun

The Best Regular Season Punting Average

Avg	Punter
44.7	Tom Tupa
43.6	Josh Miller
42.6	Rich Camarillo
42.3	Lee Johnson
40.6	Shawn McCarthy

The Best Punting Average in the playoffs

Avg	Punter
45.7	Todd Sauerbrun
44.0	Mike Patrick
43.3	Rich Camarillo
43.3	Jerel Wilson
43.0	Josh Miller

Punting and Kicking

The Most Punts and Kickoffs by the same Patriots player in a regular season game

#	Punter/Kicker	Score, outcome, opponent, and date
13	Mike Hubach	34–21 win over the New York Jets on 11-02-80
13	Pat O'Neill	31–26 loss to the Kansas City Chiefs on 10-05-95
13	Bryan Wagner	31–28 win over the New York Jets on 12-10-95

Team Records

The Most Punts in a season

#	Year
103	1992
96	1968
92	1984, 1985, 1986, and 1990

The Most Yards Punted in a season

Yds	Year
4,212	1992
3,953	1985
3,904	1984
3,831	1968
3,798	2000

Interceptions
Individual Records

The 10 Longest Interception Returns in a regular season game
100-yard TD return by Jimmy Hitchcock in the 27–24 win over the Miami Dolphins on 11-23-97
99-yard TD return by Rick Sanford in the 26–13 loss to the Chicago Bears on 12-05-82
98-yard TD return by Bob Suci in the 45–3 rout of the Houston Oilers on 11-01-63
90-yard TD return by Victor Green in the 44–7 pummelling of the New York Jets on 09-15-02
87-yard return by Ron Hall in the 24–10 victory over the Denver Broncos on 09-18-66
85-yard return by Raymond Clayborn on the last play in the 17–16 win over the Cleveland Browns on 10-07-84
83-yard return by Fred Marion in the 20–13 win over the Seattle Seahawks on 11-17-85
82-yard TD return by Chris Singleton in the 37–34 overtime win over the Indianapolis Colts on 11-15-92
78-yard TD return by Jim Lee Hunt in the 45–3 rout of the Houston Oilers on 11-01-63
76-yard TD return by Otis Smith in the 38–7 rout of the Carolina Panthers on -1-06-02

The 10 Longest Interception Returns in a playoff game
87-yard TD return by Rodney Harrison in the 41–27 win over the Pittsburgh Steelers on 01-23-05
73-yard TD return by Asante Samuel in the 28–3 rout of the Jacksonville Jaguars on 01-07-06
47-yard TD return by Ty Law in the 20–17 win over the St. Louis Rams on 02-03-02
40-yard TD return by Todd Collins in the 17–3 victory over the Miami Dolphins on 12-28-97
39-yard TD return by Asante Samuel in the 38–34 loss to the Indianapolis Colts on 01-21-07
36-yard TD return by Asante Samuel in the 37–16 rout of the New York Jets on 01-07-07
30-yard return by Otis Smith in the 20–17 win over the St. Louis Rams on 02-03-02
26-yard return by Fred Marion in the 26–14 victory over the New York Jets on 12-28-85
23-yard return by Ellis Hobbs in the 17–14 loss to the New York Giants on 02-03-08
22-yard return by Fred Marion in the 27–20 win over the Los Angeles Raiders on 01-05-86
22-yard return by Chris Slade in the 17–3 victory over the Miami Dolphins on 12-28-97

The Most Interception Return Yards in a regular season game

Yds	Defender	Score, outcome, opponent, and date
118	Prentice McCray	38–24 win over the New York Jets on 11-21-76
115	Fred Marion	20–13 victory over the Seattle Seahawks on 11-17-85
110	Bob Suci	45–3 rout of the Houston Oilers on 11-01-63
100	Jimmy Hitchcock	27–24 win over the Miami Dolphins on 11-23-97
99	Rick Sanford	26–13 loss to the Chicago Bears on 12-05-82
90	Victor Green	44–7 pummelling of the New York Jets on 09-15-02
87	Ron Hall	24–10 victory over the Denver Broncos on 09-18-66
85	Raymond Clayborn	17–16 win over the Cleveland Browns on 10-07-84
85	Otis Smith	38–6 blowout of the Carolina Panthers on 01-06-02
82	Chris Singleton	37–34 overtime win vs the Indianapolis Colts on 11-15-92

The Most Interception Return Yards in a playoff game

Yds	Defender	Score, outcome, opponent, and date
87	Rodney Harrison	41–27 win over the Pittsburgh Steelers on 01-23-05
73	Asante Samuel	28–3 rout of the Jacksonville Jaguars on 01-07-06
47	Ty Law	20–17 win over the St. Louis Rams on 02-03-02
40	Todd Collins	17–3 victory over the Miami Dolphins on 12-28-97
39	Asante Samuel	38–34 loss to the Indianapolis Colts on 01-21-07
36	Asante Samuel	37–16 rout of the New York Jets on 01-07-07
30	Otis Smith	20–17 win over the St. Louis Rams on 02-03-02
26	Fred Marion	26–14 victory over the New York Jets on 12-28-85
26	Ty Law	24–14 win over the Indianapolis Colts on 01-19-04
23	Ellis Hobbs	17–14 loss to the New York Giants on 02-03-08

The Most Interceptions in a regular season game

#	Defender	Score, outcome, opponent, and date
3	Gino Cappelletti	27–14 loss to the Oakland Raiders on 10-16-60
3	Ross O'Hanley	21–17 loss to the Houston Oilers on 11-18-62
3	Ron Hall	33–28 win over the San Diego Chargers on 09-20-64
3	Nick Buoniconti	23–6 victory over the Buffalo Bills on 10-20-68
3	Mike Haynes	38–24 win over the New York Jets on 11-21-76
3	Roland James	31–0 shutout of the Buffalo Bills on 10-23-83
3	Asante Samuel	17–13 win over the Chicago Bears on 11-26-06

The Most Interceptions in a playoff game

#	Defender	Score, outcome, opponent, and date
3	Ty Law	24–14 victory over the Indianapolis Colts on 01-18-04
2	Bob Dee	26–8 win over the Buffalo Bills on 12-28-63
2	Ross O'Hanley	26–8 win over the Buffalo Bills on12-28-63
2	Ronnie Lippett	27–20 victory over the Los Angeles Raiders on 01-05-86
2	Eugene Wilson	41–27 victory over the Pittsburgh Steelers on 01-23-05
2	Rodney Harrison	24–21 win over the Philadelphia Eagles on 02-06-05

The Most Interceptions in a regular season

#	Defender	Year
11	Ron Hall	1964
10	Asante Samuel	2006
9	Ty Law	1998
8	Bob Suci	1963
8	Mike Haynes	1976
8	Ronnie Lippett	1986

The Most Career Regular Season Interceptions

#	Defender	Seasons
36	Raymond Clayborn	1977–89
36	Ty Law	1995–2004
29	Ron Hall	1961–67
29	Fred Marion	1980–90
29	Roland James	1982–91
28	Mike Haynes	1976–82
27	Maurice Hurst	1989–95
24	Nick Buoniconti	1962–68
24	Ronnie Lippett	1984–91
22	Asante Samuel	2003–07

The Most Career Playoff Interceptions

#	Defender
7	Rodney Harrison
5	Asante Samuel
4	Ty Law
3	Fred Marion

The Most Regular Season Career Interception Return Yards

Yds	Defender	Seasons
583	Ty Law	1995–2004
555	Raymond Clayborn	1977–89
476	Ron Hall	1961–67
457	Fred Marion	1980–90
420	Ronnie Lippett	1984–91
383	Roland James	1982–91
366	Don Webb	1961–70
352	Prentice McCray	1974–80
313	Asante Samuel	2003–07
288	Ross O'Hanley	1960–65

The Most Regular Season Interception Returns for a TD

TDs	Defender
6	Ty Law
4	Tedy Bruschi
3	Asante Samuel

The Most Interception Returns for a TD in the playoffs

TDs	Defender
3	Asante Samuel
1	Todd Collins
1	Ty Law
1	Rodney Harrison

Team Records

The Most Interceptions in a regular season game

#	Score, outcome, opponent, and date
7	38–24 win over the New York Jets on 11-21-76
6	26–19 victory over the New York Jets on 09-27-64
6	45–3 rout of the Houston Oilers on 11-01-63

The Most Interceptions in a playoff game

#	Score, outcome, opponent, and date
4	24–14 win over the Indianapolis Colts on 01-18-04
4	26–8 victory over the Buffalo Bills on 12-28-63
3	27–20 win over the Los Angeles Raiders on 01-05-86
3	24–17 victory over the Pittsburgh Steelers on 01-27-02
3	41–27 win over the Pittsburgh Steelers on 01-23-05
3	24–21 victory over the Philadelphia Eagles on 02-06-05

The Most Interceptions in a season

#	Year
31	1964
29	2003 and 1963
25	1962 and 1960

The Most Interception Return Yards in a season

Yds	Year
645	1963
505	1976
427	1964 and 1985
422	2001

Fumbles
Individual Records

The 10 Longest Fumble Returns in a regular season game

71-yard TD by Raymond Clayborn on a blocked FG in the 21–7 win over the Houston Oilers on 10-18-87

68-yard TD by Richard Seymour of a fumble by Drew Bledsoe in the 31–17 win over the Buffalo Bills on 10-03-04

52-yard TD by Chuck Shonta on the last play in the 28–24 win over the New York Titans on 09-17-60

51-yard return by Jim Lee Hunt of a fumble by Don Trull in the 45–17 rout of the Houston Oilers on 12-15-68

49-yard TD by Don Webb of a Johnny Robinson fumble in the 18–17 win over the Dallas Texans on 10-29-61

45-yard TD by Larry Carwell on a blocked FG in the 31–7 loss to the Cincinnati Bengals on 08-17-72

45-yard TD by Brent Williams of a strip sack of Dave Krieg in the 33–20 loss to Seattle on 10-07-90

42-yard TD by Corwin Brown of a Bryan Still fumble in the 45–7 rout of the San Diego Chargers on 12-01-96

41-yard TD by Randall Gay of a William Green fumble in the 42–15 win over Cleveland on 12-05-04

38-yard TD by Matt Chatham of a Tiki Barber fumble in the 17–6 win over the New York Giants on 10-20-03

The longest fumble returns in a playoff game

47-yard TD by Otis Smith of a fumble by James Stewart in the 14-point win over the Jacksonville Jaguars on 01-12-97

31-yard return by Vince Wilfork of a backwards lateral by Chad Pennington in the 21-point win over the New York Jets on 01-07-07

21-yard return by Rick Sanford of a fumble by Andra Franklin in the 15-point loss to the Miami Dolphins on 01-08-83

15-yard TD by Johnny Rembert of a fumble by Johnny Hector in the 12-point win over the New York Jets on 12-28-85

15-yard return by Terrell Buckley of Ricky Proehl's fumble in the three-point win over the St. Louis Rams on 02-03-02

11-yard return by Troy Brown of a blocked FG in the seven-point victory over the Pittsburgh Steelers on 01-27-02

The 10 Longest Fumble Advancements in a regular season game

100-yard TD by Jon Vaughn of his own fumble in the 10-point loss on 12-20-92

91-yard TD by Ron Burton of his own fumble for a TD in the four-point win on 11-11-62

75-yard TD by Troy Brown of a fumble by Dave Meggett in the three-point win on 12-10-95

46-yard TD by Randy Vataha of a fumble by Mack Herron in the eight-point win on 10-07-73

30-yard advancement by Max Lane of a fumble by Troy Brown in the five-point loss on 10-15-95

22-yard advancement by Leonard Russell of a fumble by Vincent Brisby in the six-point overtime win on 01-02-94

20-yard advancement by Stanley Morgan of a fumble by Tony Collins in the 30-point loss on 11-20-83

14-yard advancement by Darryl Stingley of a fumble by Sam Cunningham in the eight-point loss on 09-28-75

12-yard advancement by Shelby Jordan of a fumble by Jim Plunkett in the three-point loss on 11-16-75

10-yard advancement by Jim Colclough of a fumble by Billy Lott in the two-point win on 09-23-61

The only fumble advancement by a Patriots player in a playoff game
4-yard fumble advancement by Matt Light of a fumble by Tom Brady in the three-point win on 01-14-07

The longest lateral advancements in a regular season game
69-yard advancement by Leonard Russell of a lateral from Kevin Turner in the two-point win on 10-10-93
65-yard TD by Mike Haynes of a lateral from John Zamberlin after a blocked FG in the 10-point win on 10-05-80
32-yard advancement by Andre Tippett of a lateral from Johnny Rembert in the 20-point win on 10-26-86
27-yard TD by Clayton Weishuhn of a lateral from Steve Nelson in the five-point win on 09-25-83
20-yard advancement by Willie McGinest of a lateral from Anthony Pleasant in the 21-point win on 09-14-03

The only lateral advancement by a Patriots player in a playoff game
49-yard advancement by Antwan Harris of a lateral from Troy Brown in the 7-point win on 01-27-02

The Most Defensive Fumble Recoveries in a regular season

#	Player	Season
5	Bob Dee	1961
4	Jack Rudolph	1960
4	Larry Eisenhauer	1964
4	John Sanders	1975
4	Steve Nelson	1978
4	Brent Williams	1986
4	Andre Tippett	1993

The Most Career Defensive Fumble Recoveries

#	Player	Seasons
18	Andre Tippett	1982–93
16	Steve Nelson	1974–87
15	Jim Lee Hunt	1960–70
15	Willie McGinest	1994–2005
14	Raymond Hamilton	1973–80

The Most Fumble Recoveries in the playoffs

#	Player
3	Tedy Bruschi
2	Rick Sanford
2	Jim Bowman

Team Records

The Most Opponent's Fumble Recoveries in a regular season game

#	Score, outcome, opponent, and date
6	21–7 victory over the Los Angeles Rams on 12-11-83
6	30–27 win over the Pittsburgh Steelers on 09-26-76
5	21–20 victory over the New Orleans Saints on 11-30-86
5	17–10 loss to the Denver Broncos on 11-06-66

The Most Opponent's Fumble Recoveries by the Patriots in a season

#	Season
27	1976
24	1985
21	1978 and 1987

Takeaways
Individual Records

The Most Takeaways by a Patriots player in a regular season game

#	Player	How	Score, outcome, opponent, and date
3	Gino Cappelletti	3 Ints	27–14 loss to the Oakland Raiders on 10-16-60
3	Ross O'Hanley	3 Ints	21–17 loss to the Houston Oilers on 11-18-62
3	Ross O'Hanley	2 Ints and 1 FR	20–14 victory over the Oakland Raiders on 10-11-63
3	Ron Hall	3 Ints	33–28 win over the San Diego Chargers on 09-20-64
3	Nick Buoniconti	3 Ints	23–6 victory over the Buffalo Bills on 10-20-68
3	Ed Philpott	2 FRs and 1 Int	31–17 loss to the Kansas City Chiefs on 11-17-68
3	Mike Haynes	3 Ints	38–24 victory over the New York Jets on 11-21-76
3	Prentice McCray	2 Ints and 1 FR	38–24 win over the New York Jets on 11-21-76
3	Steve Nelson	3 FRs	24–14 victory over the Philadelphia Eagles on 10-08-78
3	Roland James	3 Ints	31–0 shutout of the Buffalo Bills on 10-23-83
3	Jim Bowman	2 Ints and 1 FR	24–0 shutout of the Indianapolis Colts on 11-22-87
3	Ronnie Lippett	2 Ints and 1 FR	27–24 loss to the Miami Dolphins on 09-09-90
3	Fred Marion	2 FRs and 1 Int	17–10 loss to the Miami Dolphins on 10-18-90
3	Asante Samuel	3 Ints	17–13 victory over the Chicago Bears on 11-26-06

The Most Takeaways by a Patriots player in a playoff game

#	Player	How	Score, Outcome, opponent, and date
3	Ty Law	3 Ints	24–14 victory over the Indianapolis Colts on 01-18-04
2	Bob Dee	2 Ints	26–8 victory over the Buffalo Bills on 12-28-63
2	Ross O'Hanley	2 Ints	26–8 victory over the Buffalo Bills on 12-28-63
2	Rick Sanford	2 FRs	28–13 loss to the Miami Dolphins on 01-08-83
2	Ronnie Lippett	2 Ints	27–20 victory over the Los Angeles Raiders on 01-05-86
2	Jim Bowman	2 FRs	27–20 victory over the Los Angeles Raiders on 01-05-86

The Most Takeaways by a Patriots player in a regular season

#	Player	Year	Accomplishment
13	Ron Hall	1964	11 interceptions and 2 fumble recoveries
10	Mike Haynes	1976	8 interceptions and 2 fumble recoveries
10	Fred Marion	1985	7 interceptions and 3 fumble recoveries
10	Ty Law	1998	9 interceptions and 1 fumble recovery
10	Asante Samuel	2006	10 interceptions

The Most Takeaways in the playoffs

#	Player	Accomplishment
7	Rodney Harrison	7 interceptions
5	Tedy Bruschi	2 interceptions and 3 fumble recoveries
3	Fred Marion	3 interceptions
3	Ty Law	3 interceptions

The Most Career Regular Season Takeaways by a Patriots player

#	Player	Accomplishment
46	Raymond Clayborn	36 Ints, eight FRs, and recovered two blocked field goals
42	Fred Marion	29 Ints and 13 FRs
40	Ty Law	36 Ints and 4 FRs
39	Roland James	29 Ints and 10 FRs
38	Mike Haynes	28 Ints and 10 FRs
33	Steve Nelson	17 Ints and 16 FRs
33	Ronnie Lippett	24 Ints and 9 FRs
32	Don Webb	21 Ints, 9 FRs, and recovered 2 blocked field goals
32	Ron Hall	29 Ints and 3 FRs
30	Nick Buoniconti	24 Ints and 6 FRs

Sacks

The Most Sacks by a Patriots player in a regular season game

#	Defender	Score, outcome, opponent, and date
4.0	Jim Lee Hunt	14–3 win over the Buffalo Bills on 12-04-66
4.0	Julius Adams	16–10 victory over the Atlanta Falcons on 12-04-77
4.0	Tony McGeee	35–14 rout of the Baltimore Colts on 11-26-78
4.0	Mike Hawkins	56–3 demolition of the New York Jets on 09-09-79

The Most Sacks by a Patriots player in a playoff game

#	Defender	Score, outcome, opponent, and date
4.5	Willie McGinest	28–3 rout of the Jacksonville Jaguars on 01-07-06
3.0	Willie McGinest	17–14 win over the Tennessee Titans on 01-10-04
3.0	Julius Adams	24–21 loss to the Oakland Raiders on 12-18-76
3.0	Garin Veris	26–14 victory over the New York Jets on 12-28-85

The Most Sacks by a Patriots player in a season

#	Defender	Year
18.5	Andre Tippett	1984
16.5	Andre Tippett	1985
12.5	Andre Tippett	1987
12.5	Mike Vrabel	2007
12.0	Tony McGee	1977
12.0	Tony McGee	1978
11.0	Garin Veris	1986
11.0	Willie McGinest	1995
10.5	Tony McGee	1979

The Most Career Regular Season Sacks

#	Defender
100	Andre Tippett
79.5	Julius Adams
78	Willie McGinest
72.5	Tony McGee
54	Ray Hamilton
50.5	Chris Slade
48	Mike Vrabel
45.5	Larry Eisenhauer
43.5	Brent Williams
39	Houston Antwine

The Most Career Playoff Sacks

#	Defender
16	Willie McGinest
7	Mike Vrabel
5	Jarvis Green
4.5	Tedy Bruschi
4.5	Richard Seymour

Team Records

The Most Sacks by the Patriots in a season

#	Year
58	1977
57	1979
56	1963
55	1984
51	1985

The Most Games

The Most regular season games

212	Bruce Armstrong
206	Julius Adams
194	Mosi Tatupu
192	Troy Brown
191	Raymond Clayborn
189	Tedy Bruschi
183	John Hannah
180	Stanley Morgan
174	Steve Nelson
171	Willie McGinest

The Most playoff games

22	Tedy Bruschi
20	Troy Brown
18	Willie McGinest
17	Adam Vinatieri
17	Larry Izzo
17	Mike Vrabel
17	Tom Brady
17	Kevin Faulk
15	Matt Light
15	Richard Seymour

The Most Seasons

16	Steve Grogan
15	Julius Adams
15	Troy Brown
14	Steve Nelson
14	Bruce Armstrong
13	Tom Neville
13	John Hannah
13	Raymond Clayborn
13	Stanley Morgan
13	Mosi Tatupu